The

DOCTRINE & COVENANTS
STUDY GUIDE

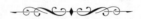

The
DOCTRINE &
COVENANTS
STUDY GUIDE

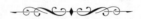

START TO FINISH

GENERAL EDITOR
THOMAS R. VALLETTA

ASSOCIATE EDITORS

BRUCE L. ANDREASON   RYAN C. JENKINS
RANDALL C. BIRD   ROBERT E. LUND
LEE L. DONALDSON   GEORGE R. SIMS
JOHN L. FOWLES   BRUCE G. STEWART
NORMAN W. GARDNER   DIANE C. THOMAS

DESERET
BOOK

SALT LAKE CITY, UTAH

Excerpts from addresses given by General Authorities and General Officers of The Church of Jesus Christ of Latter-day Saints are © Intellectual Reserve, Inc., and used by permission.

Book design © Deseret Book Company

Library of Congress Cataloging-in-Publication Data

(CIP data on file)
ISBN 978-1-63993-337-2

Printed in China
RR Donnelley, Dongguan, China

10 9 8 7 6 5 4 3 2 1

CONTENTS

INTRODUCTION TO
THE DOCTRINE AND COVENANTS STUDY GUIDE

In a worldwide broadcast for young adults, President Russell M. Nelson offered the following challenge: "Study [the Lord's] words as recorded in the Doctrine and Covenants, for He continues to teach His people in this dispensation" ("Prophets, Leadership, and Divine Law"). The revelations recorded in the Doctrine and Covenants "are for the benefit of all mankind and contain an invitation to all people everywhere to hear the voice of the Lord Jesus Christ, speaking to them for their temporal well-being and their everlasting salvation" (Introduction to the Doctrine and Covenants, paragraph 1).

"The Doctrine and Covenants is a collection of modern revelations from God received mainly through the Prophet Joseph Smith. Many of these revelations were given in answer to questions that Joseph and other early members of the Church asked of God" (Gardiner, "Doctrine and Covenants: An Overview," *For the Strength of Youth*, Jan. 2021, 14).

The Doctrine and Covenants Study Guide: Start to Finish was developed to help guide Latter-day Saints in their study of this sacred volume of scripture. It is an innovative approach that can empower both beginning and experienced students of the scriptures to grow in their understanding and application of latter-day revelation. *Through faithful and purposeful study of the Doctrine and Covenants, members of the Church can come to testify, as did the original Twelve Apostles in Joseph Smith's day,* "that the Lord has borne record to our souls, through the Holy Ghost shed forth upon us, that these commandments [or revelations] were given by inspiration of God, and are profitable for all men and are verily true" (in "Testimony of the Twelve Apostles to the Truth of the Book of Doctrine and Covenants," Introduction to the Doctrine and Covenants, paragraph 13).

What will I find in this book?

"The book of Doctrine and Covenants is a witness of [an] outpouring of continuing revelation. Each section answers pressing questions, reveals important truths, or gives practical guidance. These revelations are the fruit of an ongoing dialogue between the Lord and His people. But in many cases, the Doctrine and Covenants contains only half of the dialogue—the Lord's revealed responses. In this way, it is unique among Latter-day Saint books of scripture. In the Bible, Book of Mormon, and Pearl of Great Price, gospel teaching is often couched in narrative. The narrative gives us clues that help us interpret the teachings and see how they influenced the lives of men and women of the scriptures. But the Doctrine and Covenants does not contain the stories behind the revelations" (*Revelations in Context*, vii).

As a companion to your study of the Doctrine and Covenants, this *Study Guide* can help you unlock the meaning of Doctrine and Covenants scripture passages and deepen your understanding of doctrine, Church history, and other aspects of the revelations received by the Prophet Joseph Smith and other latter-day prophets. The *Study Guide* is a collection of inspired prophetic insights and helpful historical commentary to unlock this sacred volume of scripture. To help you get the most out of your study of the Doctrine and Covenants, this book will:

- Provide an introduction for each section. Great effort has been made to ensure that descriptions of historical context for each section found in the *Study Guide* draw from the latest research from historical studies, including the Joseph Smith Papers.

- Pose thoughtful questions rising from the scripture verses that prepare the mind and heart to better understand the scriptures, receive spiritual promptings, and apply gospel truths the scriptures are teaching. Such questions can also be used to improve personal and family scripture study, as well as enhance classroom discussions.

- Provide some of the best insights and commentary from living and recent prophets, Church leaders, and faithful gospel writers. This *Study Guide* places priority on grounding its doctrinal commentary on the teachings of latter-day prophets.

The questions and insightful notes described above are presented in columns alongside the 2013 edition of the scriptures. The 2013 edition of the English-language scriptures includes revisions to the study aids and adjustments to chapter and section headings. This edition of the scriptures also includes some corrections to spelling, minor typographical errors, and punctuation. Arranging the scripture text side by side with the study guide allows readers to study the Doctrine and Covenants without having to turn to other books or open multiple screens.

Other beneficial features of the *Study Guide* include:

- Commentary that clarifies the meaning of difficult terms or phrases, explains essential doctrine, helps clear up historical issues, and gives possible interpretations for symbolic passages.

- Subheadings in the scriptural text to help break up lengthy passages of text into smaller, more manageable chunks. These subheadings are taken from the Church's official edition of the Doctrine and Covenants. The subheadings play a valuable role in enhancing the readability, organization, and comprehension of each section of the Doctrine and Covenants. They serve as a valuable tool for both casual and in-depth study, enabling you and your family to engage with the scriptures more effectively and gain a deeper understanding of their sacred message.

- Often, commentary will help one ponder or apply truths taught in particular passages. As President Dallin H. Oaks taught, "In contrast to the institutions of the world, which teach us to *know* something, the gospel of Jesus Christ challenges us to *become* something" (*With Full Purpose of Heart*, 37). A study of the Doctrine and Covenants will help people draw nearer to Heavenly Father and Jesus Christ and become more like Them.

- The eBook edition of *The Doctrine and Covenants Study Guide* contains hyperlinks to hundreds of pages of additional quotations from authoritative sources to enrich your Doctrine and Covenants study. An icon in the printed book (⊙) indicates where additional information may be accessed from within the eBook. Also, this unique eBook format takes you to additional resources that will deepen your understanding of the Doctrine and Covenants.

How can studying the Doctrine and Covenants benefit me?

President Ezra Taft Benson testified that "the Doctrine and Covenants is a glorious book of scripture given directly to our generation. It contains the will of the Lord for us in these last days that precede the second coming of Christ. It contains many truths and doctrines not fully revealed in other scripture. . . . It will strengthen those who carefully and prayerfully study from its pages" (*Ezra Taft Benson* [manual], 133).

As President Jeffrey R. Holland once explained in detail: "The book of Doctrine and Covenants is a revelatory document, revelations abounding, a promise of prophetic utterance. These communications are delivered through the Urim and Thummim, by open vision, through the still, small voice, by audible voice, through translated scripture, by angels, through dedicatory prayers, by letters, by items of instruction, by declarations of belief through historical items, by priesthood ordinations, by answers to scriptural questions, by prophecies, in minutes of meetings, and on, and on, and on to impress in bold relief that undergirding and inevitable and absolutely essential principle of revelation to the gospel of Jesus Christ in its fullest dispensation. And why are these revelations given? To tear down the graven images of our time, to reenthrone God as Father to His children, to reestablish those covenants linking heaven and earth which the prince of darkness beneath the earth would have us mutilate. In the language of the Doctrine and Covenants itself, the revelations are given so 'that you may understand and know how to worship, and know what you worship, that you may come unto the Father in my name, and in due time receive of his fulness' (D&C 93:19), *to know how to worship and what we worship so that we might come unto Him and receive of His fulness.* To that end the dispensation and its doctrines and these compilations are dedicated" ("Lord's Preface (D&C 1)," 33–34).

We hope that as you study, the questions and commentary in this *Study Guide* will provoke a deeper inquiry into the Doctrine and Covenants and inspire you to follow President Russell M. Nelson's counsel to "ponder sincere questions about the gospel in an environment of revelation" ("Embrace the Future with Faith," *Ensign*, Nov. 2020, 75).

INTRODUCTION

The Prophet Joseph Smith said that the revelations contained in the Doctrine and Covenants are "the foundation of the Church in these last days, and a benefit to the world, showing that the keys of the mysteries of the kingdom of our Savior are again entrusted to man" (Joseph Smith Papers, "History, 1838–1856, volume A-1," 173). President Gordon B. Hinckley also testified: "The grand objective of this cause and kingdom comes from an understanding of the remarkable revelations found in the Doctrine and Covenants" (*Teachings*, 164).

Therefore, as you begin a study of the Doctrine and Covenants, it is helpful to understand that when the Church published a new edition of the scriptures in 2013, adjustments were made to the Introduction to the Doctrine and Covenants as well as to many of the section headings. These changes were based on the most recent historical research, including findings from the Joseph Smith Papers project.

The Doctrine and Covenants is a collection of divine revelations and inspired declarations given for the establishment and regulation of the kingdom of God on the earth in the last days. Although most of the sections are directed to members of The Church of Jesus Christ of Latter-day Saints, the messages, warnings, and exhortations are for the benefit of all mankind and contain an invitation to all people everywhere to hear the voice of the Lord Jesus Christ, speaking to them for their temporal well-being and their everlasting salvation.

Most of the revelations in this compilation were received through Joseph Smith Jr., the first prophet and president of The Church of Jesus Christ of Latter-day Saints. Others were issued through some of his successors in the Presidency (see headings to D&C 135, 136, and 138, and Official Declarations 1 and 2).

The book of Doctrine and Covenants is one of the standard works of the Church

What is the Doctrine and Covenants? (See Introduction to the Doctrine and Covenants, paragraphs 1–3) "The Doctrine and Covenants is made up of several types of documents, including dictated revelations, epistles, visions, minutes, a dedicatory prayer, and even a translation. The most common component of the volume is dictated revelations—that is, documents in the voice of the Lord dictated by the Prophet Joseph Smith and others and recorded by scribes" (Turley and Slaughter, *How We Got the Doctrine and Covenants*, 1).

President Gordon B. Hinckley testified: "The Doctrine and Covenants is unique among our books of scripture. It is the constitution of the Church. While the Doctrine and Covenants includes writings and statements of various origins, it is primarily a book of revelation given through the Prophet of this dispensation.

"These revelations open with a thundering declaration of the encompassing purposes of God in the restoration of His great latter-day work [see D&C 1:1–2]. . . .

"From that majestic opening there unfolds a wonderous doctrinal panorama that comes from the fountain of eternal truth. Some is direct revelation, with the Lord dictating to His prophet. Some is the language of Joseph Smith, written or spoken as he was moved upon by the Holy Ghost. Also included is his narrative of events that occurred in various circumstances. All brought together, they constitute in very substantial measure the doctrine and practices of The Church of Jesus Christ of Latter-day Saints" (*Teachings*, 163).

How were the revelations included in the Doctrine and Covenants received? (See Introduction to the Doctrine and Covenants, paragraphs 4–7) "These revelations were given by the spirit of prophecy and revelation through visions (see D&C 76; 137; 138), heavenly visitations (see D&C 2; 13; 27; 110), the Urim and Thummim (see D&C 3; 6–7; 11; 14–17), and the inspiration of the Holy Ghost. Several revelations came as a result of questions the Prophet asked as he worked on an inspired translation of the Bible (see D&C 35; 73; 76–77; 86; 91; 132). Other revelations came during the translation of the Book of Mormon and because of questions about Church structure and the building up of Zion" (*Doctrine and Covenants Student Manual* [2018], 3).

in company with the Holy Bible, the Book of Mormon, and the Pearl of Great Price. However, the Doctrine and Covenants is unique because it is not a translation of an ancient document, but is of modern origin and was given of God through His chosen prophets for the restoration of His holy work and the establishment of the kingdom of God on the earth in these days. In the revelations, one hears the tender but firm voice of the Lord Jesus Christ, speaking anew in the dispensation of the fulness of times; and the work that is initiated herein is preparatory to His Second Coming, in fulfillment of and in concert with the words of all the holy prophets since the world began.

Joseph Smith Jr. was born December 23, 1805, in Sharon, Windsor County, Vermont. During his early life, he moved with his family to present-day Manchester, in western New York. It was while he was living there in the spring of 1820, when he was fourteen years of age, that he experienced his first vision, in which he was visited in person by God, the Eternal Father, and His Son Jesus Christ. He was told in this vision that the true Church of Jesus Christ that had been established in New Testament times, and which had administered the fulness of the gospel, was no longer on the earth. Other divine manifestations followed in which he was taught by many angels; it was shown to him that God had a special work for him to do on the earth and that through him the Church of Jesus Christ would be restored to the earth.

In the course of time, Joseph Smith was enabled by divine assistance to translate and publish the Book of Mormon. In the meantime he and Oliver Cowdery were ordained to the Aaronic Priesthood by John the Baptist in May 1829 (see D&C 13), and soon thereafter they were also ordained to the Melchizedek Priesthood by the ancient Apostles Peter, James, and John (see D&C 27:12). Other ordinations followed in which priesthood keys were conferred by Moses, Elijah, Elias, and many ancient prophets (see D&C 110; 128:18, 21). These ordinations were, in fact, a restoration of divine authority to man on the earth. On April 6, 1830, under heavenly direction, the Prophet Joseph Smith organized the Church, and thus the true Church of Jesus Christ is once again operative as an institution among men, with authority to teach the gospel and administer the ordinances of salvation. (See D&C 20 and the Pearl of Great Price, Joseph Smith—History 1.)

These sacred revelations were received in answer to prayer, in times of need, and came out of real-life situations involving real people. The Prophet and his associates sought for divine guidance, and these revelations certify that they received it. In the revelations, one sees the restoration and unfolding of the gospel of Jesus Christ and the ushering in of the dispensation of the fulness of times. The westward movement of the Church from New York and Pennsylvania to Ohio, to Missouri, to Illinois, and finally to the Great Basin of western America and the mighty struggles of the Saints in attempting to build Zion on the earth in modern times are also shown forth in these revelations.

Several of the earlier sections involve matters regarding the translation and publication of the Book of Mormon (see sections 3, 5, 10, 17, and 19). Some later sections reflect the work of the Prophet Joseph Smith in making an inspired translation of the Bible, during which many of the great doctrinal sections were received (see, for example, sections 37, 45, 73, 76, 77, 86, 91, and 132, each of which has some direct relationship to the Bible translation).

Why is the Doctrine and Covenants valuable to readers today? (See Introduction to the Doctrine and Covenants, paragraph 8) President Joseph Fielding Smith emphasized the value of the Doctrine and Covenants this way:

"*In my judgment there is no book on earth yet come to man as important as the book known as the Doctrine and Covenants,* with all due respect to the *Book of Mormon,* and the *Bible,* and the *Pearl of Great Price,* which we say are our *standards in doctrine.* The book of *Doctrine and Covenants* to us stands in a peculiar position above them all.

"I am going to tell you why....

" ... this *Doctrine and Covenants* contains the word of God to those who dwell here *now. It is our book.* It belongs to the Latter-day Saints. More precious than gold, the Prophet says we should treasure it more than the riches of the whole earth. I wonder if we do? If we value it, understand it, and know what it contains, we will value it more than wealth; it is worth more to us than the riches of the earth" (*Doctrines of Salvation,* 3:198, 199).

Elder David A. Bednar had this to say about the value of the Doctrine and Covenants: "A number of years ago, President Ezra Taft Benson [see "Book of Mormon and the Doctrine and Covenants," *Ensign,* May 1987, 83] highlighted the fact that the Book of Mormon is the keystone of our religion. If you have an arch, then the keystone is the stone at the very top of the arch that holds both of the sides together. So the Book of Mormon is the keystone. President Benson taught that the Doctrine and Covenants is the capstone. It's the crowning piece of masonry that you would put onto that wall. And the Book of Mormon and the Doctrine and Covenants are the keystone and the capstone of our religion.

"The Book of Mormon invites all to come unto Christ. The Doctrine and Covenants invites all to come unto Christ's kingdom on the earth, The Church of Jesus Christ of Latter-day Saints. So those two volumes of scriptures testify of each other and they complete and complement each other. And so we learn more about the Book of Mormon as we study the Doctrine and Covenants. As we study the Book of Mormon it prepares us for the latter-day revelations that we find in the Doctrine and Covenants" ("Welcome to Seminary" [video], 3:25–4:25).

In the revelations, the doctrines of the gospel are set forth with explanations about such fundamental matters as the nature of the Godhead, the origin of man, the reality of Satan, the purpose of mortality, the necessity for obedience, the need for repentance, the workings of the Holy Spirit, the ordinances and performances that pertain to salvation, the destiny of the earth, the future conditions of man after the Resurrection and the Judgment, the eternity of the marriage relationship, and the eternal nature of the family. Likewise, the gradual unfolding of the administrative structure of the Church is shown with the calling of bishops, the First Presidency, the Council of the Twelve, and the Seventy and the establishment of other presiding offices and quorums. Finally, the testimony that is given of Jesus Christ—His divinity, His majesty, His perfection, His love, and His redeeming power—makes this book of great value to the human family and "worth to the Church the riches of the whole Earth" (see heading to D&C 70).

The revelations were originally recorded by Joseph Smith's scribes, and Church members enthusiastically shared handwritten copies with each other. To create a more permanent record, scribes soon copied these revelations into manuscript record books, which Church leaders used in preparing the revelations to be printed. Joseph and the early Saints viewed the revelations as they did the Church: living, dynamic, and subject to refinement with additional revelation. They also recognized that unintentional errors had likely occurred through the process of copying the revelations and preparing them for publication. Thus, a Church conference asked Joseph Smith in 1831 to "correct those errors or mistakes which he may discover by the Holy Spirit."

After the revelations had been reviewed and corrected, Church members in Missouri began printing a book titled *A Book of Commandments for the Government of the Church of Christ,* which contained many of the Prophet's early revelations. This first attempt to publish the revelations ended, however, when a mob destroyed the Saints' printing office in Jackson County on July 20, 1833.

Upon hearing of the destruction of the Missouri printing office, Joseph Smith and other Church leaders began preparations to publish the revelations in Kirtland, Ohio. To again correct errors, clarify wording, and recognize developments in Church doctrine and organization, Joseph Smith oversaw the editing of the text of some revelations to prepare them for publication in 1835 as the *Doctrine and Covenants of the Church of the Latter Day Saints.* Joseph Smith authorized another edition of the Doctrine and Covenants, which was published only months after the Prophet's martyrdom in 1844.

The early Latter-day Saints prized the revelations and viewed them as messages from God. On one occasion in late 1831, several elders of the Church gave solemn

What led to the publication of the Doctrine and Covenants? (See Introduction to the Doctrine and Covenants, paragraphs 9–12) "The Doctrine and Covenants is a book of answers. . . .

"The Saints in the early days of this dispensation asked many questions about specific issues and situations. The answers to their questions came as revelations that they recorded in the Doctrine and Covenants. The Lord encouraged his Saints to develop humility balanced with initiative and independence, and he tutored them as they engaged in the active process of inviting revelation" (Hartshorn, Wright, and Ostler, *Doctrine and Covenants: A Book of Answers,* vii).

Richard O. Cowan explained that "these revelations were copied by hand for the use of the early Saints, but there was a growing demand for them to be more widely available" ("How Our Doctrine and Covenants Came to Be," 3). Such enthusiasm led Joseph Smith and others to publish the Book of Commandments in 1833 (which was ultimately disrupted by a mob attack before it could be completed). The addition of other revelations led to the publication of the Doctrine and Covenants in 1835 followed by other editions in 1844, 1845, 1876, 1879, 1921, and 1981 (see Turley and Slaughter, *How We Got the Doctrine and Covenants*). The most recent edition of the Doctrine and Covenants was published under the direction of the First Presidency in 2013.

testimony that the Lord had borne record to their souls of the truth of the revelations. This testimony was published in the 1835 edition of the Doctrine and Covenants as the written testimony of the Twelve Apostles:

TESTIMONY OF THE TWELVE APOSTLES TO THE TRUTH OF THE BOOK OF DOCTRINE AND COVENANTS

The Testimony of the Witnesses to the Book of the Lord's Commandments, which commandments He gave to His Church through Joseph Smith, Jun., who was appointed by the voice of the Church for this purpose:

We, therefore, feel willing to bear testimony to all the world of mankind, to every creature upon the face of the earth, that the Lord has borne record to our souls, through the Holy Ghost shed forth upon us, that these commandments were given by inspiration of God, and are profitable for all men and are verily true.

We give this testimony unto the world, the Lord being our helper; and it is through the grace of God the Father, and His Son, Jesus Christ, that we are permitted to have this privilege of bearing this testimony unto the world, in the which we rejoice exceedingly, praying the Lord always that the children of men may be profited thereby.

The names of the Twelve were:

Thomas B. Marsh	Parley P. Pratt
David W. Patten	Luke S. Johnson
Brigham Young	William Smith
Heber C. Kimball	Orson Pratt
Orson Hyde	John F. Boynton
William E. McLellin	Lyman E. Johnson

How did the Testimony of the Twelve Apostles become part of the Introduction to the Doctrine and Covenants? (See Introduction to the Doctrine and Covenants, paragraphs 13–14) "When Church leaders decided at the November 1831 conference to compile the revelations and organize them for publication, the Prophet Joseph Smith prepared a statement of testimony regarding the divine origin of the revelations (see [Joseph Smith Papers, *Documents, Volume 2*], 110–14). Those who were present indicated their willingness to bear testimony of the truthfulness of the revelations. It may be that this testimony was going to be published in the back of the Book of Commandments much like the testimonies of the Three and the Eight Witnesses were included at the end of the 1830 edition of the Book of Mormon. However, the statement of testimony does not appear in the existing copies of the Book of Commandments. This may be because the publication was cut short when the print shop was destroyed. The testimony of the Twelve Apostles was included in the 1835 edition of the Doctrine and Covenants" (*Doctrine and Covenants Student Manual* [2018], 6–7).

Other prophets and apostles have borne witness of the Doctrine and Covenants. For example, President Wilford Woodruff testified:

"[The Doctrine and Covenants] contains some of the most glorious and sublime revelations God ever gave to man. It shows unto us what lies before us, what awaits this nation and the nations of the earth, and what is at the door of the inhabitants of the earth. These things are clear, they are pointed, they are strong, and they are the revelations of God, and they will be fulfilled, whether men believe it or not" (*Wilford Woodruff* [manual], 120).

President Joseph F. Smith stated: "By the testimony of the Holy Spirit of God to me, I know that this book, the Book of Doctrine and Covenants, which I hold in my hand, is the word of God through Joseph Smith to the world, and especially to the members of the Church of Jesus Christ of Latter-day Saints throughout the world" (*Joseph F. Smith* [manual], 42).

President Gordon B. Hinckley declared: "The Doctrine and Covenants is a conduit for the expressions of the Lord to His people.

"The variety of matters the book deals with is amazing. They include principles and procedures concerning the governance of the Church. Unique and remarkable rules of health, with promises both physical and spiritual, are set forth. The covenant of the eternal priesthood is described in a manner not found elsewhere in scripture. The privileges and blessings—and the limitations and opportunities—of the three degrees of glory are announced. ... Repentance is proclaimed in language clear and compelling. The correct mode of baptism is given. The nature of the Godhead, which has troubled theologians for centuries, is described in language understandable to all. The Lord's law of finance is pronounced, mandating how funds for the operation of the Church are to be acquired and disbursed. Work for the dead is revealed to bless the sons and daughters of God of all generations. . . .

"I love the language of the book. I love the tone of its words. I marvel at the clarity and strength of its statements, of its doctrinal expositions and prophetic promises" ("Order and Will of God," *Ensign*, Jan. 1989, 4).

What are some changes that have occurred in subsequent editions of the Doctrine and Covenants? (See Introduction to the Doctrine and Covenants, paragraphs 15–17) "Since the first version of the Doctrine and Covenants, several editions have been published, each including additional sections of revelations and official declarations. By 1876 the Doctrine and Covenants contained 136 sections. The 1921 edition included the same 136 sections. The *Lectures on Faith*, however, being judged as important teachings but not revelations, were removed from the publication. This edition also contained the 'Official Declaration,' or 'Manifesto,' which announced the cessation of plural marriage. The 1921 edition also featured new headings and footnotes. This edition remained in place until 1981, when two additional sections, 137 and 138, were added, along with a second Official Declaration, a report of the revelation giving the priesthood to all worthy male members. New and improved headings and footnotes replaced those found in the 1921 edition" (Garrett, "Doctrine and Covenants," 301).

In successive editions of the Doctrine and Covenants, additional revelations or other matters of record have been added, as received and as accepted by competent assemblies or conferences of the Church. The 1876 edition, prepared by Elder Orson Pratt under Brigham Young's direction, arranged the revelations chronologically and supplied new headings with historical introductions.

Beginning with the 1835 edition, a series of seven theological lessons was also included; these were titled the *Lectures on Faith*. These had been prepared for use in the School of the Prophets in Kirtland, Ohio, from 1834 to 1835. Although profitable for doctrine and instruction, these lectures have been omitted from the Doctrine and Covenants since the 1921 edition because they were not given or presented as revelations to the whole Church.

In the 1981 edition of the Doctrine and

Covenants, three documents were included for the first time. These are sections 137 and 138, setting forth the fundamentals of salvation for the dead; and Official Declaration 2, announcing that all worthy male members of the Church may be ordained to the priesthood without regard for race or color.

Each new edition of the Doctrine and Covenants has corrected past errors and added new information, particularly in the historical portions of the section headings. The present edition further refines dates and place-names and makes other corrections. These changes have been made to bring the material into conformity with the most accurate historical information. Other special features of this latest edition include revised maps showing the major geographical locations in which the revelations were received, plus improved photographs of Church historical sites, cross-references, section headings, and subject-matter summaries, all of which are designed to help readers to understand and rejoice in the message of the Lord as given in the Doctrine and Covenants. Information for the section headings has been taken from the Manuscript History of the Church and the published *History of the Church* (collectively referred to in the headings as Joseph Smith's history) and the *Joseph Smith Papers*.

How has recent research influenced the 2013 edition of the Doctrine and Covenants? (See Introduction to the Doctrine and Covenants, paragraph 18) In 2013, the First Presidency announced that an updated edition of the standard works would be published by the Church, replacing the previous 1981 edition. Revisions included adjustments to study aids, new photos, updated maps, and new printing plates. A formal announcement clarified that "the Church has taken the opportunity to make adjustments and updates and to implement new historical findings from the *Joseph Smith Papers*" ("Summary of Approved Adjustments," 1).

"The 2013 edition of the scriptures includes revised section headings for some sections of the Doctrine and Covenants. Changes to the section headings have been made to reflect recent research and historical findings and to provide additional or clearer context for the scriptures. In some cases, dates or locations have been adjusted in the section headings to reflect newly available research" (*Doctrine and Covenants Student Manual* [2018], vii).

CHRONOLOGICAL ORDER
OF CONTENTS

* At or near place specified

* At or near place specified

* At or near place specified

THE
DOCTRINE AND
COVENANTS

"Though this revelation now appears as the first section of our Doctrine and Covenants, many revelations had previously been given. The Doctrine and Covenants is the only book to have a preface directly dictated by Jesus Christ ... giving the revelations divine endorsement. Designated by the Lord as His preface to the [earlier] Book of Commandments, section 1 gives an introduction to revelations, doctrines, covenants, commandments, and warnings contained in the present-day Doctrine and Covenants" (Woodger, *Essential Doctrine and Covenants Companion*, viii).

The Lord's preface, found today in Doctrine and Covenants 1, was revealed at a special conference held at the John and Elsa Johnson home in Hiram, Ohio, on November 1–2, 1831. By this time, more than 60 revelations had been given through the Prophet Joseph Smith. Church leaders determined to make these revelations more available to Church members by printing them in a volume that would be called the Book of Commandments. During the conference, a committee attempted to write a preface for this volume (see Joseph Smith Papers, Historical Introduction to "Minutes, 1–2 November 1831"). Subsequently, Joseph Smith received the revelation recorded in Doctrine and Covenants 1 by speaking the "words slowly as Sidney Rigdon wrote them down, but they are in the voice of Jesus Christ, who gave them to be what he called '*my* preface unto the book of *my* commandments' (v. 6; emphasis added)" (Harper, *Making Sense of the Doctrine & Covenants*, 18).

SECTION 1

Revelation given through Joseph Smith the Prophet, on November 1, 1831, during a special conference of elders of the Church, held at Hiram, Ohio. Many revelations had been received from the Lord prior to this time, and the compilation of these for publication in book form was one of the principal subjects passed upon at the conference. This section constitutes the Lord's preface to the doctrines, covenants, and commandments given in this dispensation.

1 Hearken, O ye people of my church, saith the voice of him who dwells on high, and whose eyes are upon all men; yea, verily I say: Hearken ye people from afar; and ye that are upon the islands of the sea, listen together.

Doctrine and Covenants 1:1–7. The Voice of Warning Is to All People

Why is it vital to "hearken" to the Lord? (1:1)

"Our Father knows that when we are surrounded by uncertainty and fear, what will help us the very most is to hear His Son.

"Because when we seek to hear—truly hear—His Son, we will be guided to know what to do in any circumstance.

"The very first word in the Doctrine and Covenants is *hearken*. It means 'to listen with the intent to obey.' To hearken means to 'hear Him'—to *hear* what the Savior says and then to *heed* His counsel. In those two words—'Hear Him'—God gives us the pattern for success, happiness, and joy in this life. We are to *hear* the words of the Lord, *hearken* to them, and *heed* what He has told us!" (Nelson, "Hear Him," *Ensign*, May 2020, 89). ⊕

What is each member's charge in helping all hear His voice? (1:2) "As viewed through a clear lens, members of The Church of Jesus Christ of Latter-day Saints have the great privilege of loving, sharing, inviting, and helping gather Israel to receive the fulness of the Lord's covenant blessings. This includes Africans and Europeans, South and North Americans, Asians, Australians, and those upon the isles of the sea. 'For verily the voice of the Lord is unto all men' [D&C 1:2]. 'This gathering shall continue until the righteous are assembled in the congregations of the Saints in the nations of the world' [*Teachings of Spencer W. Kimball*, 438]" (Quentin L. Cook, "Safely Gathered Home," *Liahona*, May 2023, 22).

2 For verily the voice of the Lord is unto all men, and there is none to escape; and there is no eye that shall not see, neither ear that shall not hear, neither heart that shall not be penetrated.

3 And the rebellious shall be pierced with much sorrow; for their iniquities shall be spoken upon the housetops, and their secret acts shall be revealed.

How We Got the Doctrine and Covenants (Doctrine and Covenants 1)

In the years that followed Joseph Smith's First Vision, the young prophet received a number of revelations from the Lord. By the organization of the Church in April 1830, the Prophet had received and recorded more than twenty revelations. As the number of revelations increased, many were being "copied by hand for the use of the early Saints, but there was a growing demand for them to be more widely available" (Cowan, "How Our Doctrine and Covenants Came to Be," 3).

"During the summer of 1830, the Prophet Joseph Smith began to prepare for publication the revelations received to that point. A conference of elders held in Hiram, Ohio, during the first week of November 1831 decided to publish the revelations in what would be called the Book of Commandments. Because of mob activities against members of the Church in Jackson County, Missouri, the publication of the Book of Commandments was thwarted. Efforts continued, and an expanded compilation

Joseph Smith, Jr.

was completed in Kirtland, Ohio, in August 1835. The book contained 102 sections of revelations, along with the *Lectures on Faith*, warranting a change of name. The new title was 'Doctrine and Covenants'—representing the doctrine, as reflected in the *Lectures on Faith*, and the revelations, referred to as the covenants. The compilation was presented to the membership of the Church, and it was accepted as one of the standard works.

"Since the first version of the Doctrine and Covenants, several editions have been published, each including additional sections of revelations and official declarations. . . .

"This book stands as evidence of the power of revelation that is active in the Church today, testifying that the heavens are open and that God reveals his will in this time and age. While Joseph Smith referred to the Book of Mormon as the 'keystone' of our religion, President Ezra Taft Benson identified the Doctrine and Covenants as the 'capstone'" (Garrett, "Doctrine and Covenants," 301, 302).

4 And the voice of warning shall be unto all people, by the mouths of my disciples, whom I have chosen in these last days.

5 And they shall go forth and none shall stay them, for I the Lord have commanded them.

6 Behold, this is mine authority, and the authority of my servants, and my preface unto the book of my commandments, which I have given them to publish unto you, O inhabitants of the earth.

7 Wherefore, fear and tremble, O ye people, for what I the Lord have decreed in them shall be fulfilled.

8 And verily I say unto you, that they who go forth, bearing these tidings unto the inhabitants of the earth, to them is power given to seal both on earth and in heaven, the unbelieving and rebellious;

9 Yea, verily, to seal them up unto the day when the wrath of God shall be poured out upon the wicked without measure—

10 Unto the day when the Lord shall come to recompense unto every man according to his work, and measure to every man according to the measure which he has measured to his fellow man.

How will the Lord's warning voice reach "unto all people"? (1:4) "The voice of warning is to go to 'all people' through the Lord's chosen ministers—including his prophets and the missionaries. The warning is that the day of the Lord is near, and all must prepare by repenting of their sins and adhering to the commandments of God.

" . . . Though some may attempt to hinder the Lord's missionaries in their work, they will not be able to do so, for the Lord's power and blessing are with his disciples (Dan. 4:35; Morm. 8:26). Further, the Lord has commanded his disciples to go forth with the warning voice, and no one—whether on earth, in heaven, or in hell—has power to countermand that which the Lord has decreed (D&C 1:38)" (Parry and Parry, *Understanding the Signs of the Times*, 70). ☉

Doctrine and Covenants 1:8–16. Apostasy and Wickedness Precede the Second Coming

In what sense will the wicked be sealed up? (1:8–10) "The servants of the Lord have been given 'power to seal.' . . . The power to seal conferred upon the servants of the Lord in this, the last dispensation, extends to the 'unbelieving' and 'rebellious.' . . . They have power to put the seal of deapprobation [disapproval] upon the children of men who persist in unbelief and rebellion, and those who are thus 'sealed' and remain in that condition, will suffer the wrath of God" (Smith and Sjodahl, *Doctrine and Covenants Commentary*, 6).

"Notice that those who are sealed by this power are those who reject the gospel, and also those who rebel against the servants of the Lord after having accepted his message ([Doctrine and Covenants] 1:8–9)" (Roy W. Doxey, *Doctrine and Covenants Speaks*, 1:23).

"And None Shall Stay Them" (Doctrine and Covenants 1:5)

President M. Russell Ballard declared: "Even Joseph's closest associates in those early years did not fully understand the trials that the Latter-day Saints would endure as the Church rolled forth from its small beginnings in the early 1800s. But Joseph Smith knew that no enemy then present or in the future would have sufficient power to frustrate or stop the purposes of God. We are all familiar with his prophetic words: 'The Standard of Truth has been erected; no unhallowed hand can stop the work from progressing; persecutions may rage, mobs may combine, armies may assemble, calumny may defame, but the truth of God will go forth boldly, nobly, and independent, till it has penetrated every continent, visited every clime, swept every country, and sounded in every ear, till the purposes of God shall be accomplished, and the Great Jehovah shall say the work is done' [Joseph Smith Papers, "History, 1838–1856, volume C-1," 1285]" ("Truth of God Shall Go Forth," *Ensign*, Nov. 2008, 81).

What is the meaning of the Lord's sword being "bathed in heaven"? (1:12–13) "A *sword bathed in heaven* may be symbolic of a sword in striking position, unsheathed and raised, or it may be a representation of the ancient practice of bathing a sword in oil before a battle. Either way, it is ready at a moment's notice to pierce the wicked and those who love creation more than the Creator (see Rom. 1:25)" (Black, *400 Questions and Answers*, 21).

Clearly, "God is infinitely patient and long-suffering, but the world has now exceeded the limits of justice, and even in love God can no longer forbear.

" . . . The sword is a metaphor that symbolizes powerful judgments and destruction upon the wicked (see Isa. 34:5–6)" (Horton, "Knowing the Calamity," 42–43).

What does it mean to be "cut off from among the people"? (1:14) "This language comes from Moses' prophecy to the children of Israel describing what would become of those who failed to accept Christ (Deuteronomy 18:18–19). 'The people' to whom reference is made are the rightful heirs of Abraham, Isaac, and Jacob. To be cut off is to be left without family ties in the worlds to come" (McConkie and Ostler, *Revelations of the Restoration*, 47). ⊕

11 Wherefore the voice of the Lord is unto the ends of the earth, that all that will hear may hear:

12 Prepare ye, prepare ye for that which is to come, for the Lord is nigh;

13 And the anger of the Lord is kindled, and his sword is bathed in heaven, and it shall fall upon the inhabitants of the earth.

14 And the arm of the Lord shall be revealed; and the day cometh that they who will not hear the voice of the Lord, neither the voice of his servants, neither give heed to the words of the prophets and apostles, shall be cut off from among the people;

15 For they have strayed from mine ordinances, and have broken mine everlasting covenant;

Hearing the Voice of the Lord and His Servants (Doctrine and Covenants 1:14)

Elder Neil L. Andersen taught: "Anchoring our souls to the Lord Jesus Christ requires listening to those He sends. Following the prophet in a world of commotion is like being wrapped in a soothing, warm blanket on a freezing cold day.

"We live in a world of reason, debate, argument, logic, and explanation. Questioning, 'Why?' is positive in so many aspects of our lives, allowing the power of our intellect to guide a multitude of choices and decisions we face each day.

"But the Lord's voice often comes without explanation. . . .

"The prophet's voice, while spoken kindly, will often be a voice asking us to change, to repent, and to return to the Lord. When correction is needed, let's not delay. And don't be alarmed when the prophet's warning voice counters popular opinions of the day. The mocking fireballs of annoyed disbelievers are always hurled the moment the prophet begins to speak. As you are humble in following the counsel of the Lord's prophet, I promise you an added blessing of safety and peace.

"Don't be surprised if at times your personal views are not initially in harmony with the teachings of the Lord's prophet. These are moments of learning, of humility, when we go to our knees in prayer. We walk forward in faith, trusting in God, knowing that with time we will receive more spiritual clarity from our Heavenly Father" ("Prophet of God," *Ensign*, May 2018, 26).

16 They seek not the Lord to establish his righteousness, but every man walketh in his own way, and after the image of his own god, whose image is in the likeness of the world, and whose substance is that of an idol, which waxeth old and shall perish in Babylon, even Babylon the great, which shall fall.

Why is it wrong for people to walk in their own way? (1:16) "Sadly, . . . we find that to be shown the way is not necessarily to walk in it. . . . [Many] have submitted themselves in one degree or another to the enticings of Satan and his servants and joined with those of 'the world' in lives of ever-deepening idolatry. . . .

"Carnal man has tended to transfer his trust in God to material things. Therefore, in all ages men have fallen under the power of Satan and lost the faith. . . . Whatever thing a man sets his heart and his trust in most is his god; and if his god doesn't also happen to be the true and living God of Israel, that man is laboring in idolatry" (Kimball, "False Gods We Worship," *Ensign*, Jun. 1976, 4).

Doctrine and Covenants 1:17–23. Joseph Smith Is Called to Restore to Earth the Lord's Truths and Powers

How does the Lord prepare His children for the "calamity" He knows is coming? (1:17–18) " . . . The warning voice is one of hope and reassurance—a reminder that the Lord has never allowed a major calamity of judgment to come without forewarning. . . .

"The Lord knows what is coming. Through his servants and these revelations he has forewarned all men in order that they might gain strength, exercise faith, enter into covenants, and be prepared for whatever comes. Thus, 'knowing the calamity which should come upon the inhabitants of the earth,' the Lord has called upon his servant Joseph Smith and others and has opened the heavens to them, revealing to the Saints and to the world the things of eternity. Thereby the people of God can prepare for the day of judgment and blessing. The Doctrine and Covenants contains many of those revelations" (Horton, "Knowing the Calamity," 44, 47).

17 Wherefore, I the Lord, knowing the calamity which should come upon the inhabitants of the earth, called upon my servant Joseph Smith, Jun., and spake unto him from heaven, and gave him commandments;

18 And also gave commandments to others, that they should proclaim these things unto the world; and all this that it might be fulfilled, which was written by the prophets—

19 The weak things of the world shall come forth and break down the mighty and strong ones, that man should not counsel his fellow man, neither trust in the arm of flesh—

Why does the Lord refer to His servants as "the weak things of the world"? (1:19) "Perhaps you might think that you are not needed, that you are overlooked or unwanted, that you are nobody. . . .

"Do you not know that 'God hath chosen the foolish things of the world to [put to shame] the wise; and God hath chosen the weak things of the world to [put to shame] the things which are mighty'? [1 Cor. 1:27].

"Perhaps it is true that we are weak. Perhaps we are not wise or mighty. But when God works through us, no one and nothing can stand against us" (Uchtdorf, "Four Titles," *Ensign*, May 2013, 60–61).

What can happen when the Saints speak and testify in the Lord's name? (1:20–23) Speaking to a general priesthood session of conference, President Russell M. Nelson stated, "[Heavenly Father] wants *all* of His ordained sons to represent Him, to speak for Him, to act for Him, and to bless the lives of God's children throughout the world, to the end 'that faith also might increase in [all] the earth' (Doctrine and Covenants 1:21)" (*Teachings*, 291).

President Nelson testified concerning women in the Church: "The kingdom of God is not and cannot be complete without women who make sacred covenants and then keep them, women who can speak with the power and authority of God!" (*Teachings*, 397).

Doctrine and Covenants 1:24–33. The Book of Mormon Is Brought Forth and the True Church Is Established

Why does the Lord speak to us after the manner of our language? (1:24) "In the Lord's Preface to the Doctrine and Covenants, he points out that the revelations 'are of me, and were given unto my servants in their weakness, *after the manner of their language, that they might come to understanding*' (Doctrine and Covenants 1:24; emphasis added). Our Lord is a perfect communicator who yearns for his children to seek after him, to strive to know his mind and will, and, most importantly, to understand the message he delivers" (Millet, *Holy Spirit*, 159).

What blessings come from being humble? (1:27–28) "All of us face times in our lives when we need heavenly help in a special and urgent way. We all have moments when we are overwhelmed by circumstances or confused by the counsel we get from others, and we feel a great need to receive spiritual guidance, a great need to find the right path and do the right things. In the scriptural preface to this latter-day dispensation, the Lord promised that if we would be humble in such times of need and turn to him for aid, we would 'be made strong, and [be] blessed from on high, and receive knowledge from time to time' (D&C 1:28)" (*Howard W. Hunter* [manual], 76).

Why did the Lord describe His Church as "the only true and living church"? (1:30) President Dallin H. Oaks explained: "We refer to this, His Church—our Church—as the 'only true Church.' Sometimes we do this in a way that gives great offense to people who belong to other churches or who subscribe to other

20 But that every man might speak in the name of God the Lord, even the Savior of the world;

21 That faith also might increase in the earth;

22 That mine everlasting covenant might be established;

23 That the fulness of my gospel might be proclaimed by the weak and the simple unto the ends of the world, and before kings and rulers.

24 Behold, I am God and have spoken it; these commandments are of me, and were given unto my servants in their weakness, after the manner of their language, that they might come to understanding.

25 And inasmuch as they erred it might be made known;

26 And inasmuch as they sought wisdom they might be instructed;

27 And inasmuch as they sinned they might be chastened, that they might repent;

28 And inasmuch as they were humble they might be made strong, and blessed from on high, and receive knowledge from time to time.

29 And after having received the record of the Nephites, yea, even my servant Joseph Smith, Jun., might have power to translate through the mercy of God, by the power of God, the Book of Mormon.

30 And also those to whom these commandments were given, might have power to lay the foundation of this church, and to bring it forth out of obscurity and out of darkness, the only true and living church upon the face of the whole earth, with which I, the Lord, am well pleased, speaking unto the church collectively and not individually—

31 For I the Lord cannot look upon sin with the least degree of allowance;

32 Nevertheless, he that repents and does the commandments of the Lord shall be forgiven;

33 And he that repents not, from him shall be taken even the light which he has received; for my Spirit shall not always strive with man, saith the Lord of Hosts.

34 And again, verily I say unto you, O inhabitants of the earth: I the Lord am willing to make these things known unto all flesh;

35 For I am no respecter of persons, and will that all men shall know that the day speedily cometh; the hour is not yet, but is nigh at hand, when peace shall be taken from the earth, and the devil shall have power over his own dominion.

philosophies. But God has not taught us anything that should cause us to feel superior to other people. . . .

"So what does it mean that The Church of Jesus Christ of Latter-day Saints is the only true Church?

"Three features—(1) fulness of doctrine, (2) power of the priesthood, and (3) testimony of Jesus Christ—explain why God has declared and why we as His servants maintain that this is the only true and living Church upon the face of the whole earth" ("Only True and Living Church," *New Era*, Aug. 2011, 3).

What hope do God's children have when we are all in need of repentance? (1:31–32) "God made it clear that we cannot violate His standards without suffering the consequences, but because He is loving and compassionate beyond measure, He gives us this glorious hope: [D&C 1:31–32].

"To all honest souls who change their hearts and forsake their sins, He has promised, 'Though your sins be as scarlet, they shall be as white as snow' (Isaiah 1:18).

"However, it is always better to remain clean than to sin and repent afterward. . . . Our goal in life is not just to be clean but also to be perfect. The quest for perfection is accelerated when we are clean, but it is stymied when we are not" (Callister, "Lord's Standard of Morality," *Ensign*, Mar. 2014, 48–49).

What light is taken away from those who refuse to repent? (1:33) President Harold B. Lee once warned that "one of the most tragic experiences that can come to individuals [is] to have the Lord withdraw His Spirit from us" (*Teachings*, 101).

President Spencer W. Kimball also testified: "God's Spirit continues with the honest in heart to strengthen, to help, and to save, but invariably the Spirit of God ceases to strive with the man who excuses himself in his wrong doing" (*Spencer W. Kimball* [manual], 128).

Doctrine and Covenants 1:34–36. Peace Will Be Taken from the Earth

What should our attitude be when peace is taken from the earth? (1:35–36) "As the showdown between good and evil approaches with its accompanying trials and tribulations, Satan is increasingly striving to overcome the Saints with despair, despondency, and depression.

"Yet, of all people, we as Latter-day Saints should be the most optimistic and the least pessimistic. For while we know that 'peace shall be taken from the earth, and the devil shall have power over his own dominion,' we are also assured that 'the Lord shall have power over his saints, and shall reign in their midst' (D&C 1:35–36)" (Benson, "Do Not Despair," *Ensign*, Nov. 1974, 65; see also 1 Nephi 14:14).

What is Idumea? (1:36) "'Idumea is equivalent to Edom, the nation so despised by the prophets of the Old Testament. Edomites were descendants of Esau and their actions made them a symbol of crass materialism and wickedness towards the servants of God' ([Smith and Sjodahl, *Doctrine and Covenants Commentary*], 15). Therefore, Idumea, or the world . . . is representative of everything that is in contrast to the Lord's revealed ways" (Brewster, *Doctrine & Covenants Encyclopedia* [2012], 268–69).

Doctrine and Covenants 1:37–39. Search These Commandments

Which "commandments" are we to search ? (1:37) The "commandments" were the latter-day revelations given through the Prophet Joseph Smith to be published in the Book of Commandments but that are now contained in the Doctrine and Covenants. In the August 1832 edition of the Church's first newspaper, *The Evening and the Morning Star*, an editorial published under the direction of Joseph Smith stated: "Search the revelations which we publish, and ask your Heavenly Father, in the name of His Son Jesus Christ, to manifest the truth unto you, and if you do it with an eye single to His glory, he will answer you by the power of his Holy Spirit; you will then know for yourselves, and not for another" (Joseph Smith Papers, "History, 1838–1856, volume A-1," 227).

Why can we have confidence in prophetic counsel from the Lord's servants? (1:38) "The Church of Jesus Christ has always been led by living prophets and apostles. Though mortal and subject to human imperfection, the Lord's servants are inspired to help us avoid obstacles that are spiritually life threatening and to help us pass safely through mortality to our final, ultimate, heavenly destination. . . .

"Make no mistake about it: the Lord directs His Church through living prophets and apostles. This is the way He has always done His work. Indeed, the Savior taught, 'Verily, verily, I say unto you, He that receiveth whomsoever I send receiveth me' [John 13:20]. We cannot separate Christ from His servants" (Ballard, "God Is at the Helm," *Ensign*, Nov. 2015, 24).

36 And also the Lord shall have power over his saints, and shall reign in their midst, and shall come down in judgment upon Idumea, or the world.

37 Search these commandments, for they are true and faithful, and the prophecies and promises which are in them shall all be fulfilled.

38 What I the Lord have spoken, I have spoken, and I excuse not myself; and though the heavens and the earth pass away, my word shall not pass away, but shall all be fulfilled, whether by mine own voice or by the voice of my servants, it is the same.

39 For behold, and lo, the Lord is God, and the Spirit beareth record, and the record is true, and the truth abideth forever and ever. Amen.

"The earliest dated section in the Doctrine and Covenants [section 2] consists of words spoken to Joseph Smith by the angel Moroni [during the night of September 21–22,] 1823, when the Smith family lived near Palmyra, New York. During that visit, Moroni shared several important prophecies from the Old and New Testaments, including one from Malachi about the promised mission of the prophet Elijah in the latter days. . . .

"The importance of this prophecy is evident by how often it appears in the standard works (see Malachi 4:4–6; Luke 1:17; 3 Nephi 25:5–6; D&C 2; Joseph Smith—History 1:38–39)" (*Doctrine and Covenants Student Manual* [2018], 1, 7).

"The coming of Elijah was so important that the ancient prophet Malachi had prophesied of it centuries earlier, and the Savior had repeated the prophecy to the Nephites (see Malachi 4:5–6; 3 Nephi 25:5–6; 26:1–2). Elijah came to commit to Joseph and Oliver the keys of sealing—the power to bind and validate in the heavens all ordinances performed on the earth [see D&C 110:13–16]. The restoration of the sealing power was necessary to prepare the world for the Savior's Second Coming, for without it, 'the whole earth would be utterly wasted at his coming' (Joseph Smith—History 1:39)" (*Joseph Smith* [manual], 308).

"The differences in the text, as quoted by Moroni [in Doctrine and Covenants 2], should not be thought of as the original words of Malachi [see Malachi 4:5–6], but more correctly as a plainer translation to fit our own language and understanding. It is an example of the differences in languages, as spoken of in D&C 1:24. . . . This explanation is supported by . . . the Prophet Joseph quoting the biblical text of Malachi 4:5–6 in a letter to the members of the Church, and then stating: 'I might have rendered a plainer translation to this, but it is sufficiently plain to suit my purpose as it stands' (D&C 128:18)" (Nyman, *Doctrine and Covenants Commentary*, 1:42).

SECTION 2

An extract from Joseph Smith's history relating the words of the angel Moroni to Joseph Smith the Prophet, while in the house of the Prophet's father at Manchester, New York, on the evening of September 21, 1823. Moroni was the last of a long line of historians who had made the record that is now before the world as the Book of Mormon. (Compare Malachi 4:5–6; also sections 27:9; 110:13–16; and 128:18.)

1 Behold, I will reveal unto you the Priesthood, by the hand of Elijah the prophet, before the coming of the great and dreadful day of the Lord.

Doctrine and Covenants 2:1. Elijah Is to Reveal the Priesthood

Why was it necessary for the Lord to send Elijah in the latter days? (2:1) Elder David A. Bednar stated: "Elijah was an Old Testament prophet through whom mighty miracles were performed. . . .

"'We learn from latter-day revelation that Elijah held the sealing power of the Melchizedek Priesthood and was the last prophet to do so before the time of Jesus Christ' (Bible Dictionary, 'Elijah'). . . . This sacred sealing authority is essential for priesthood ordinances to be valid and binding both on earth and in heaven.

"Elijah appeared with Moses on the Mount of Transfiguration (see Matthew 17:3) and conferred this authority upon Peter, James, and John. Elijah appeared again with Moses and others on April 3, 1836, in the Kirtland Temple and conferred the same keys upon Joseph Smith and Oliver Cowdery" ("Hearts of the Children Shall Turn," *Ensign*, Nov. 2011, 24). See also commentary in this volume on Doctrine and Covenants 110:13–16.

What is the "great and dreadful day of the Lord"? (2:1) "This 'great and dreadful day' has reference to Christ's second coming and is referred to by the following terms in the Doctrine and Covenants: 'day when the Lord shall come' ([D&C] 1:10); 'day of my coming' ([D&C] 29:12); 'great day' ([D&C] 34:7–9); . . . 'day of vengeance' ([D&C] 133:51); and 'day . . . that shall burn as an oven' ([D&C] 133:64). . . .

"Elder Orson Pratt defined 'the great and dreadful day of the Lord' as 'the day in which wickedness should be entirely swept from the earth, and no remnants of the wicked left, when every branch of them and every root of them should become as stubble, and be consumed from the face of the earth' ([in *Journal of Discourses*], 7:76–77)" (Brewster, *Doctrine & Covenants Encyclopedia* [2012], 228). ●

The Return of Elijah the Prophet (Doctrine and Covenants 2:1–3)

"The prophecy about Elijah's coming and the resulting turning of the hearts of fathers and children is one of the few that is found in all the standard works: the Bible (see Malachi 4:5–6), the Book of Mormon (see 3 Nephi 25:5–6), the Doctrine and Covenants (see D&C 2:1–3; 110:13–16; 128:17–18), and the Pearl of Great Price (see Joseph Smith—History 1:38–39). Prophecies of Elijah's return to the earth appear to be prevalent in the scriptures and in traditional folklore. For example, a custom is still observed during the Jewish Passover where a cup of wine is placed on the table but is not drunk, and the door is opened in the expectation that Elijah will return to unify the people and bring deliverance from oppression.

"Although many people expect Elijah to return, they do not understand why or what he will do when he comes. Without the Restoration and the further understanding that Joseph Smith provided in this dispensation, the purpose and fulfillment of Elijah's return would not be accessible to us. . . .

"Some of the 'variation' that is found between Moroni's quotation and Malachi's original found in the Bible helps Latter-day Saints understand Elijah's mission in the latter days more fully. . . .

"Malachi's prophecy states that Elijah will come back at some time before the Second Coming of the Lord Jesus Christ, with the purpose of turning the hearts of fathers and children to each other. If this scripture were all that we had to go on, however, we might wonder what Elijah would be doing when he returned. Would he just come to visit people and bring love to families? Why would the earth be cursed if he did not come? . . .

"We learn from Moroni's words that Elijah is not just coming for a visit at the Passover meal; he actually will reveal the priesthood or confer priesthood authority having to do with uniting families for eternity" (Cynthia Doxey, "Elijah's Mission, Message, and Milestones," 158, 159).

2 And he shall plant in the hearts of the children the promises made to the fathers, and the hearts of the children shall turn to their fathers.

Doctrine and Covenants 2:2–3. The Promises of the Fathers Are Planted in the Hearts of the Children

What are the "promises" and who are the "fathers"? (2:2) "Through the coming of Elijah and his prophetic colleagues in Kirtland [see D&C 110:11–16], the promises made to the fathers—the promises of the gospel, the priesthood, and the possibility of eternal life granted to Abraham, Isaac, and Jacob—are planted in our hearts, the hearts of the children (see D&C 2). More specifically, because of what took place through Joseph Smith in Kirtland in 1836, the desire of our hearts to have all the blessings enjoyed by the ancients can be realized. And because of the spirit of Elijah, which moves upon the faithful, there comes also a desire to make those same blessings available for our more immediate fathers [ancestors] through family history and vicarious temple ordinances" (Millet, *Selected Writings*, 267). ⊕

3 If it were not so, the whole earth would be utterly wasted at his coming.

Why would the earth be wasted if Elijah did not return and restore priesthood keys? (2:3) President Russell M. Nelson explained: "The Creation required the Fall. The Fall required the Atonement. The Atonement enabled the purpose of the Creation to be accomplished. Eternal life, made possible by the Atonement, is the supreme purpose of the Creation. To phrase that statement in its negative form, if families were not sealed in holy temples, the whole earth would be utterly wasted" ("The Atonement," *Ensign*, Nov. 1996, 35; see also D&C 138:48). ⊕

"In [Harmony,] Pennsylvania, Joseph and Martin [Harris] labored together on the translation [of the Book of Mormon] until 14 June 1828. By that time the translation filled 116 foolscap pages (roughly legal-size)" (*Church History in the Fulness of Times* [manual], 47).

"In the summer of 1828, Martin Harris left Harmony, Pennsylvania, with 116 pages of the Book of Mormon manuscript to show to members of his family living in Palmyra, New York. When Martin did not return to Harmony at the appointed time, Joseph Smith traveled to his parents' home in Manchester, New York, where he learned that Martin had lost the manuscript pages. Joseph was distraught and left the next day for his home in Harmony. . . .

"After returning to his home in Harmony, Pennsylvania, without the manuscript pages, Joseph Smith poured out his soul to God for forgiveness. The heavenly messenger Moroni appeared to Joseph and gave him the interpreters, or Urim and Thummim, that Joseph had used while translating. The Urim and Thummim had been taken from Joseph because he had 'wearied the Lord in asking for the privilege of letting Martin Harris take the writings' (in [Joseph Smith Papers, "History, 1838–1856, volume A-1,"] 10). After Moroni appeared and returned the Urim and Thummim, Joseph received the revelation recorded in Doctrine and Covenants 3" (*Doctrine and Covenants Student Manual* [2018], 27, 30).

For more on Martin Harris, see commentary in this volume on Doctrine and Covenants 10:5–7.

SECTION 3

Revelation given to Joseph Smith the Prophet, at Harmony, Pennsylvania, July 1828, relating to the loss of 116 pages of manuscript translated from the first part of the Book of Mormon, which was called the book of Lehi. The Prophet had reluctantly allowed these pages to pass from his custody to that of Martin Harris, who had served for a brief period as scribe in the translation of the Book of Mormon. The revelation was given through the Urim and Thummim. (See section 10.)

Doctrine and Covenants 3:1–4. The Lord's Course Is One Eternal Round

Why did the loss of the Book of Mormon manuscript fail to frustrate God's work? (3:1) "God cannot be caught unaware, unprepared, surprised, or deceived. He governs by law and has ordained that identical results always flow from the same causes. The work of men is frustrated but not the work of God. His eternal purposes are always worked out" (Woodger, *Essential Doctrine and Covenants Companion*, 4). ◉

1 The works, and the designs, and the purposes of God cannot be frustrated, neither can they come to naught.

How does knowing that God does "not walk in crooked paths" increase your faith in Him? (3:2) Alma taught the people of Gideon that God "cannot walk in crooked paths; neither doth he vary from that which he hath said; neither hath he a shadow of turning from the right to the left, or from that which

2 For God doth not walk in crooked paths, neither doth he turn to the right hand nor to the left, neither doth he vary from that which he hath said, therefore his paths are straight, and his course is one eternal round.

is right to that which is wrong" (Alma 7:20). Elder Gerrit W. Gong testified, "We can always trust God. The Lord knows us better and loves us more than we know or love ourselves. His infinite love and perfect knowledge of past, present, and future make His covenants and promises constant and sure" ("Trust Again," *Liahona*, Nov. 2021, 98). How can these truths give you confidence in His words?

What is meant by God's course being "one eternal round"? (3:2) "The description of the Lord's course as being 'one eternal round' is found twice in the Doctrine and Covenants ([D&C] 3:2; 35:1) and three times in the Book of Mormon (1 Ne. 10:19; Alma 7:20; 37:12). God's work—'to bring to pass the immortality and eternal life of man'—is a fixed, constant course from which he does not deviate (Moses 1:39). God follows 'one [singular or unified] eternal [recurring] round [course], the same today as yesterday, and forever,' of providing the means whereby His children might receive a fulness of His glory (D&C 35:1; 93:20).

"Just as a ring has no beginning or ending, and as His priesthood has neither 'beginning of days or end of years' (Alma 13:7), so is the course of God one eternal round" (Brewster, *Doctrine & Covenants Encyclopedia* [2012], 399).

The Loss of 116 Pages of Book of Mormon Translation

Joseph Smith recorded: "Mr. Harris had begun to write for me, he began to importune me to give him liberty to carry the writings home and show them; and desired of me that I would inquire of the Lord, through the Urim and Thummim, if he might not do so. I did inquire, and the answer was that he must not. However, he was not satisfied with this answer, and desired that I should inquire again. I did so, and the answer was as before. Still he could not be contented, but insisted that I should inquire once more. After much solicitation I again inquired of the Lord, and permission was granted him to have the writings on certain conditions; which were, that he show them only to his brother, Preserved Harris, his own wife, his father and his mother, and a Mrs. Cobb, a sister to his wife. In accordance with this last answer, I required of him that he should bind himself in a covenant to me in a most solemn manner that he would not do otherwise than had been directed. He did so. He bound himself as I required of him, took the writings, and went his way.

"Notwithstanding, however, the great restrictions which he had been laid under, and the solemnity of the covenant which he had made with me, he did show them to others, and by stratagem they got them away from him, and they never have been recovered unto this day.

"In the meantime, while Martin Harris was gone with the writings, I went to visit my father's family at Manchester. I continued there for a short season, and then returned to my place in Pennsylvania. Immediately after my return home, I was walking out a little distance, when behold, the former heavenly messenger appeared and handed to me the Urim and Thummim again (for it had been taken from me in consequence of my having wearied the Lord in asking for the privilege of letting Martin Harris take the writings which he lost by transgression) and I inquired of the Lord through them and obtained the [following] revelation [in July 1828]" (Joseph Smith Papers, "History, 1838–1856, volume A-1," 9–10).

What can we learn from Joseph Smith's experience with disregarding the counsels of God? (3:4) "More anxious to be heard than to hear, Joseph disregarded the Lord's counsel that he not entrust the 116 pages to Martin Harris. Having been twice refused by the Lord, he asked yet a third time and received the answer he sought. The stage was set for him to learn a lesson as important as it was painful.

"No office or calling can excuse either man or woman from the responsibility of following the Lord's counsel and direction. For this reason, the life of Christ becomes such a perfect example for us. In all things he sought only to do the will of his Father (Mosiah 15:7)" (McConkie and Ostler, *Revelations of the Restoration*, 60). See also commentary in this volume on Doctrine and Covenants 10:1.

Doctrine and Covenants 3:5–15. Joseph Smith Must Repent or Lose the Gift to Translate

How often did the Prophet Joseph Smith transgress God's commandments? (3:6) "The Lord's rebuke that Joseph had 'oft ... transgressed the commandments and the laws of God' (verse 6) should not be interpreted to mean that the Prophet was guilty of a grave moral sin. The Prophet later wrote: 'No one need suppose me guilty of any great or malignant sins. A disposition to commit such was never in my nature' [Joseph Smith—History 1:28].

"The Prophet had, however, submitted to the importunings of Martin Harris, even after the Lord had informed him that the 116 pages of manuscript should not be given to Mr. Harris. It is for this indiscretion (following after 'the persuasions of men') that the Prophet is being reprimanded here" (Daniel H. Ludlow, *Companion to Your Study*, 1:61).

Why did Joseph Smith give in to the "persuasions of men"? (3:6–7) "Perhaps Joseph wanted to show gratitude to Martin [Harris] for his support. We know that Joseph was extremely anxious for other eyewitnesses to stand with him against the distressing falsehoods and lies being spread about him.

3 Remember, remember that it is not the work of God that is frustrated, but the work of men;

4 For although a man may have many revelations, and have power to do many mighty works, yet if he boasts in his own strength, and sets at naught the counsels of God, and follows after the dictates of his own will and carnal desires, he must fall and incur the vengeance of a just God upon him.

5 Behold, you have been entrusted with these things, but how strict were your commandments; and remember also the promises which were made to you, if you did not transgress them.

6 And behold, how oft you have transgressed the commandments and the laws of God, and have gone on in the persuasions of men.

7 For, behold, you should not have feared man more than God. Although men set at naught the counsels of God, and despise his words—

"Whatever Joseph's reasons were, or as justified as they may appear, the Lord did not excuse them and sharply rebuked him . . . (D&C 3:6–7). This poignant experience helped Joseph remember, forever after, which way he faced.

"When people try to *save face* with men, they can unwittingly *lose face* with God. Thinking one can please God and at the same time condone the disobedience of men isn't neutrality but duplicity, or being *two-faced* or trying to 'serve two masters' (Matthew 6:24; 3 Nephi 13:24)" (Robbins, "Which Way Do You Face?" *Ensign*, Nov. 2014, 9–10).

What can we do to show that we value God's counsel? (3:7) "When a person learns what the Lord's counsel is and follows it, he irresistibly draws close to the Spirit. From its very beginning, the history of God's dealings with his children on the earth testifies to the fact that those who disregard his counsel fail and come to grief. . . .

"When we do not keep ourselves advised as to what the counsel of the Lord is, we are prone to substitute our own counsel for His. As a matter of fact, there is nothing else we can do but follow our own counsel when we do not know the Lord's instructions" (Romney, "Seek Not to Counsel the Lord," *Ensign*, Aug. 1985, 2, 5).

8 Yet you should have been faithful; and he would have extended his arm and supported you against all the fiery darts of the adversary; and he would have been with you in every time of trouble.

What does this passage teach us about Heavenly Father's constant support? (3:8) "The Prophet Joseph Smith learned from firsthand experience that the Lord expects us to avoid misery by living His gospel and wants us to understand that we can repent. When he lost the 116 pages of the manuscript of the Book of Mormon translation by giving in to the persuasions of men, Joseph was miserable. The Lord told him: 'You should have been faithful; and [God] would have extended his arm and supported you against all the fiery darts of the adversary; and he would have been with you in every time of trouble' (D&C 3:8). Such is the case for each of you . . . : be faithful, and you will be supported by the hand of God. The Prophet was then reminded that—as with each of us—he would be forgiven if he repented. Imagine what joy he felt" (Marcus B. Nash, "Great Plan of Happiness," *Ensign*, Nov. 2006, 50).

9 Behold, thou art Joseph, and thou wast chosen to do the work of the Lord, but because of transgression, if thou art not aware thou wilt fall.

Why would Joseph Smith allow this personal chastisement from the Lord to be published? (3:9) Neither the Lord nor Joseph Smith tried to hide the young Prophet's weaknesses.

"[Joseph] made known this rebuke to his friends and to the world in allowing the revelation to become known and printed. At times people have questioned the integrity of the Prophet, but this revelation stands as a monument to the basic honesty of Joseph Smith" (Roy W. Doxey, *Doctrine and Covenants Speaks*, 1:38).

"Joseph's candor about his shortcomings is evident in the fact that one of the first revelations he recorded in writing and published to the world was a crushing rebuke he received from the Lord. . . . The Lord told Joseph to repent or he would be stripped of his prophetic role" (Oaks, "Joseph, the Man and the Prophet," *Ensign*, May 1996, 71–72). ⊕

What did the Lord mean by saying Joseph Smith was "still chosen"? (3:9–11) "Had Joseph not measured up, the Lord would have made a change in the cast by appointing another to take his place. But he did measure up, as attested by further revelations from God which commended him for his faithfulness.

"The Lord said that this kingdom, which would be established in the latter days, 'shall never be destroyed.' We needn't question whether this church that God has set up is going to fail. It will not! For God has so decreed!" (Derrick, "Valiance in the Drama of Life," *Ensign*, May 1983, 24).

Why did the Lord call Martin Harris a "wicked man"? (3:12) See commentary in this volume on Doctrine and Covenants 10:5–7.

How long were the Prophet's privileges revoked? (3:14) After Joseph Smith received the revelation recorded in Doctrine and Covenants 3, "Moroni took back the interpreters and the plates while Joseph acted on the revelation's command to repent. Then in September 1828, one year after Joseph first received them, the plates were again entrusted to him. By choosing to obey the revelation, Joseph was still chosen and was again called to the work" (Harper, *Making Sense of the Doctrine & Covenants*, 28).

10 But remember, God is merciful; therefore, repent of that which thou hast done which is contrary to the commandment which I gave you, and thou art still chosen, and art again called to the work;

11 Except thou do this, thou shalt be delivered up and become as other men, and have no more gift.

12 And when thou deliveredst up that which God had given thee sight and power to translate, thou deliveredst up that which was sacred into the hands of a wicked man,

13 Who has set at naught the counsels of God, and has broken the most sacred promises which were made before God, and has depended upon his own judgment and boasted in his own wisdom.

14 And this is the reason that thou hast lost thy privileges for a season—

15 For thou hast suffered the counsel of thy director to be trampled upon from the beginning.

16 Nevertheless, my work shall go forth, for inasmuch as the knowledge of a Savior has come unto the world, through the testimony of the Jews, even so shall the knowledge of a Savior come unto my people—

17 And to the Nephites, and the Jacobites, and the Josephites, and the Zoramites, through the testimony of their fathers—

18 And this testimony shall come to the knowledge of the Lamanites, and the Lemuelites, and the Ishmaelites, who dwindled in unbelief because of the iniquity of their fathers, whom the Lord has suffered to destroy their brethren the Nephites, because of their iniquities and their abominations.

19 And for this very purpose are these plates preserved, which contain these records—that the promises of the Lord might be fulfilled, which he made to his people;

20 And that the Lamanites might come to the knowledge of their fathers, and that they might know the promises of the Lord, and that they may believe the gospel and rely upon the merits of Jesus Christ, and be glorified through faith in his name, and that through their repentance they might be saved. Amen.

What is meant by trampling upon the "counsel of thy director"? (3:15) "This term likely refers to the Lord and perhaps also to Moroni, the angel who appeared to Joseph at least twenty-two times in his career and instructed him along the way. Hyrum M. Smith and Janne M. Sjodahl suggest that 'thy director' is the Urim and Thummim [Smith and Sjodahl, *Doctrine and Covenants Commentary*, 20], but elsewhere in scripture (see D&C 17:1; Mosiah 1:16; Alma 37:38, 45) and in early LDS usage, 'director' or 'directors' always referred to the Liahona rather than the Urim and Thummim. Because there is no evidence that Joseph had possession of the Liahona 'from the beginning' of his work, this reference is more likely to the One who ultimately directed Joseph, who is Jesus Christ, or to Moroni, the Lord's messenger" (Robinson and Garrett, *Commentary on the Doctrine and Covenants*, 1:39).

Doctrine and Covenants 3:16–20. The Book of Mormon Comes Forth to Save the Seed of Lehi

How does the Doctrine and Covenants testify of the Book of Mormon? (3:16–20) President Ezra Taft Benson declared: "Excluding the witnesses to the Book of Mormon, the Doctrine and Covenants is by far the greatest external witness and evidence which we have from the Lord that the Book of Mormon is true. At least thirteen sections in the Doctrine and Covenants give us confirming knowledge and divine witness that the Book of Mormon is the word of God [see D&C 1, 3, 5, 8, 10–11, 17–18, 20, 27, 42, 84, 135].

"The Doctrine and Covenants is the binding link between the Book of Mormon and the continuing work of the Restoration through the Prophet Joseph Smith and his successors" ("Book of Mormon and the Doctrine and Covenants," *Ensign*, May 1987, 83).

"In early 1829, Joseph Smith Sr. visited his son Joseph in Harmony, Pennsylvania. While there, Joseph Smith Sr. desired to know what he could do to assist in the Lord's work. The Prophet inquired of the Lord and received the revelation recorded in Doctrine and Covenants 4. In this revelation, the Lord identified attributes that qualify a person to assist in His work" (*Doctrine and Covenants Student Manual* [2018], 87).

"Dictated shortly before the translation work resumed, this revelation spoke of a 'marvelous work' about to come forth and added that the 'field is white already to harvest.' These phrases, also used in several [Joseph Smith] revelations in the spring of 1829, invoked a sense of urgency and an impending spiritual harvest. Though addressed to Joseph Smith Sr., this revelation was written as if it could apply to all who read it.

"The degree to which Joseph Smith Sr. acted upon this revelation is unknown, but his call 'to the work' may have had a significant immediate impact when he returned to Palmyra, New York, where Oliver Cowdery was boarding at his house. Joseph Sr. and Lucy Mack Smith had met Cowdery when he began teaching school in the Manchester, New York, district late in the fall of 1828. Lucy wrote that although Cowdery had questioned Joseph Sr. about the gold plates, he 'did not succeed in eliciting any information' for 'a long time.' This revelation may have prompted Joseph Sr. to share a 'sketch of the facts which related to the plates' with Cowdery, who became convinced that he had been called by God to assist [Joseph Smith] as his scribe" (Joseph Smith Papers, Historical Introduction to "Revelation, February 1829 [D&C 4]," 1).

Doctrine and Covenants 4:1–4. Valiant Service Saves the Lord's Ministers

What is the "marvelous work" often spoken of in the Doctrine and Covenants? (4:1) The Lord said to the Nephites, "For in that day, for my sake shall the Father work a work, which shall be a great and a marvelous work among them; and there shall be among them those who will not believe it, although a man shall declare it unto them" (3 Nephi 21:9). In Joseph Smith's time, according to the Webster's 1828 dictionary, *marvelous* meant, "wonderful; strange; exciting; . . . that which exceeds natural power" (Webster, *American Dictionary* [1828], s.v. "marvelous"). "The 'marvelous work' [exceeding natural power] refers to the Latter-day restoration including the publication of the Book of Mormon, organization of the Church, and proclamation of the gospel in its fullness" (Cowan, *Doctrine & Covenants: Our Modern Scripture*, 21). See also commentary in this volume on Doctrine and Covenants 11:1; 14:1.

What are the requirements for those called to serve God? (4:2) "We learn from this command [in D&C 4:2] that it is not enough to serve God with all of our *might and strength*. He who looks into our hearts and knows our minds demands more than this. In order to stand blameless before God at the last day, we must also serve him with all our *heart and mind*.

SECTION 4

Revelation given through Joseph Smith the Prophet to his father, Joseph Smith Sr., at Harmony, Pennsylvania, February 1829.

1 Now behold, a marvelous work is about to come forth among the children of men.

2 Therefore, O ye that embark in the service of God, see that ye serve him with all your heart, might, mind and strength, that ye may stand blameless before God at the last day.

"Service with all of our heart and mind is a high challenge for all of us. Such service must be free of selfish ambition. It must be motivated only by the pure love of Christ" (Oaks, "Why Do We Serve?" *Ensign*, Nov. 1984, 15). See also commentary in this volume on Doctrine and Covenants 59:5. ☉

3 Therefore, if ye have desires to serve God ye are called to the work;

Why is having a desire to serve God so vital? (4:3) "Actually, everything depends—initially and finally—on our desires. These shape our thought patterns. Our desires thus precede our deeds and lie at the very cores of our souls, tilting us toward or away from God (see D&C 4:3). . . . Others seek to manipulate our desires. But it is we who form the desires, the 'thoughts and intents of [our] hearts' (Mosiah 5:13)."

"The end rule is 'according to [our] desires . . . shall it be done unto [us]' (D&C 11:17) 'for I, the Lord, will judge all men according to their works, according to the desire of their hearts' (D&C 137:9). One's individual will thus remains uniquely his. God will not override it nor overwhelm it. Hence we'd better want the consequences of what we want!" (Maxwell, "Swallowed Up in the Will of the Father," *Ensign*, November 1995, 23). ☉

4 For behold the field is white already to harvest; and lo, he that thrusteth in his sickle with his might, the same layeth up in store that he perisheth not, but bringeth salvation to his soul;

What blessings come to those who "thrusteth in their sickle" in God's service? (4:4) "One of the first revelations given in our dispensation announced that those who go forth in the name of the Lord must serve with all their heart, might, mind, and strength that they might stand blameless before him at the

Joseph Smith Sr.

Joseph Smith Sr., who was a faithful and noble man, was born 12 July 1771 in Topsfield, Essex County, Massachusetts. He was the son of Asael Smith and Mary Duty. He died on 14 September 1840 at Nauvoo, Hancock County, Illinois.

"At age twenty-four Joseph Smith Sr. married Lucy Mack and settled on a farm in Tunbridge, Vermont. . . .

"Where many fathers might have lacked the humility to follow their sons, Joseph Smith Sr. never sought prominence over young Joseph. He was supportive of his son's prophetic calling and even suffered persecution for his beliefs. He was privileged to be one of the Eight Witnesses of the Book of Mormon who saw the plates and the engravings on them. . . .

"At age sixty-four Father Smith served a mission with his brother John. They traveled nearly twenty-four hundred miles throughout the East, strengthening the Saints, pronouncing patriarchal blessings, and sharing the gospel with relatives. . . .

"In Nauvoo Father Smith was physically weak and suffered from continual coughing. Before he died he invited family members to receive a blessing at his hands. 'To Joseph he said: . . . "You shall even live to finish your work." At this Joseph cried out, weeping, "Oh! My father, shall I?" "Yes," said his father, "you shall live to lay out the plan of all the work which God has given you to do. This is my dying blessing upon your head in the name of Jesus."' . . .

"Where is this noble man who so faithfully fulfilled his role in the latter days? The Lord through his anointed Prophet revealed that Father Smith is in a celestial realm and sits 'with Abraham at his right hand, and blessed and holy is he, for he is mine' (D&C 124:19)" (Black, *Who's Who*, 289, 290, 291).

day of judgment. The revelation promised those so laboring that through such service they may lay 'up in store' that they perish not, but bring salvation to their own souls (D&C 4:2–4). That is simply to say that we serve to work out our own salvation" (McConkie and Millet, *Doctrinal Commentary on the Book of Mormon*, 2:312). See also commentary in this volume on Doctrine and Covenants 11:3–4. ◉

Why does the Lord frequently compare His work to a harvest? (4:4) "The Lord's observation that 'the field is white already to harvest' is found frequently in early sections of the Doctrine and Covenants (4:4; 6:3; 11:3; 14:3; 31:4; 33:3, 7). Jesus used the same symbolic language in a discussion with his disciples in Samaria. He reminded them that though the time for the harvest of wheat was yet four months distant, the harvest of souls was imminent (John 4:31–42).

"One knows when wheat is ripe because of the white appearance of the fields. The Lord has declared that this same condition now prevails where the human harvest of souls is concerned" (Brewster, *Doctrine & Covenants Encyclopedia* [2012], 185).

Doctrine and Covenants 4:5–6. Godly Attributes Qualify Them for the Ministry

Why does this revelation mention both charity and love? (4:5) The Lord mentioned that both charity and love are essential qualities of His work. "The *and* here indicates that charity is not used merely as a synonym for love as in the King James Version. The 1828 edition of Webster's dictionary defines *charity* specifically as a 'brotherly predisposition,' whereas the New Testament generally uses *charity* to mean 'love' in a more general sense (see 1 Corinthians 13:1–13; Moroni 7:47)" (Robinson and Garrett, *Commentary on the Doctrine and Covenants*, 1:43).

Why does the Lord ask His servants to develop these divine characteristics? (4:5–6) "The attributes of the Savior, as we perceive them, are not a script to be followed or list to be checked off. They are interwoven characteristics, added one to another, which develop in us in interactive ways. In other words, we cannot obtain one Christlike characteristic without also obtaining and influencing others. As one characteristic becomes strong, so do many more....

"As we earnestly strive to be true disciples of Jesus Christ, these characteristics will be interwoven, added upon, and interactively strengthened in us.... We will be as honest when no one is looking as when

5 And faith, hope, charity and love, with an eye single to the glory of God, qualify him for the work.

6 Remember faith, virtue, knowledge, temperance, patience, brotherly kindness, godliness, charity, humility, diligence.

others are watching. We will be as devoted to God in the public square as we are in our private closet" (Hales, "Becoming a Disciple of Our Lord Jesus Christ," *Ensign*, May 2017, 46, 48).

Doctrine and Covenants 4:7. The Things of God Must Be Sought After

How can we prepare ourselves to "ask" and "knock"? (4:7) "For each of you to receive revelation unique to your own needs and responsibilities, certain guidelines prevail. The Lord asks you to develop 'faith, hope, charity and love, with an eye single to the glory of God.' Then with your firm 'faith, virtue, knowledge, temperance, patience, brotherly kindness, godliness, charity, humility, [and] diligence,' you may *ask*, and you will receive; you may *knock*, and it will be opened unto you [see D&C 4:5–7].

7 Ask, and ye shall receive; knock, and it shall be opened unto you. Amen.

"Revelation from God is always compatible with His eternal law. It never contradicts His doctrine. It is facilitated by proper reverence for Deity. . . .

"Every Latter-day Saint may merit personal revelation" (Nelson, "Ask, Seek, Knock," *Ensign*, Nov. 2009, 83, 84). See also commentary in this volume on Doctrine and Covenants 12:5–6.

"For months Martin Harris remained at his Palmyra home, haunted by the loss of the manuscript. He was also distressed to discover that his wife and others sought to discredit Joseph Smith and make him out to be a fraud who was simply after Martin's money. Longing for reconciliation and bearing news of these disturbing efforts, he visited Joseph Smith in Harmony in March 1829" (McBride, "Contributions of Martin Harris," 6).

"It had been eight months since Martin Harris had lost the 116 pages of translation. Martin knew full well the magnitude of his error and that he had lost his privilege to serve as scribe, but apparently he also still felt an obligation to the work and to assist financially with the printing of the Book of Mormon. Therefore, . . . a somewhat humbled Martin Harris traveled to Harmony from his home in Palmyra to determine whether Joseph Smith still had the plates and the power to translate them (see [D&C 5:1]). To settle the question to his satisfaction, he wanted to see the plates, and in response to his request Joseph Smith received Doctrine and Covenants 5" (Robinson and Garrett, *Commentary on the Doctrine and Covenants*, 1:45).

"Doctrine and Covenants 5 reorients Martin Harris. 'Show me, and I'll believe,' Martin essentially says. 'Believe, and I'll show you,' the Lord, in effect, replies, and in doing so exposes the mistaken idea that seeing is believing. The Lord instructs Joseph to tell Martin to seek humility and faith as prerequisites to receiving the witness he desires.

"Martin received the greater witness he sought *after* he met the Lord's conditions of humility and faith. As the translation neared completion, Joseph gathered one morning with his family and friends for singing and prayer. Martin was there, having traveled from Palmyra to Fayette to see how the translation progressed. Joseph had recently read in the translated manuscript that the Lord would call three eyewitnesses of the plates and their translation. David Whitmer, Oliver Cowdery, and Martin Harris volunteered, hoping to be chosen. 'They teased me so much,' Joseph said, 'almost without intermission for some time,' that he finally asked the Lord for approval and received an exciting answer. Joseph rose from his knees and said to Martin, 'You have got to humble yourself before God this day and obtain, if possible, a forgiveness of your sins. If you will do this, it is God's will that you and Oliver Cowdery and David Whitmer should look upon the plates'" (Harper, *Making Sense of the Doctrine & Covenants*, 33–34).

Doctrine and Covenants 5:1–10. This Generation Will Receive the Lord's Word through Joseph Smith

What was the witness that Martin Harris desired? (5:1) "When he arrived again in Harmony, Pennsylvania, in March 1829, Martin confided to Emma's father, Isaac Hale, that he desired a 'greater witness' of the plates (see Joseph Smith Papers, "Revelation, March 1829 [D&C 5]," 1)" (*Doctrine and Covenants Student Manual* [2018], 45).

"Martin Harris had already received a remarkable proof of the truth of the claims made by the Prophet Joseph regarding the Book of Mormon, when he carried a facsimile of the engravings to New York scientists. Professor Anthon had told him, as he himself states, that the 'hieroglyphics were true characters.' He had also, through the Prophet received revelations ([D&C] 3:12). But he was not yet satisfied" (Smith and Sjodahl, *Doctrine and Covenants Commentary*, 25). ⊕

SECTION 5

Revelation given through Joseph Smith the Prophet, at Harmony, Pennsylvania, March 1829, at the request of Martin Harris.

1 Behold, I say unto you, that as my servant Martin Harris has desired a witness at my hand, that you, my servant Joseph Smith, Jun., have got the plates of which you have testified and borne record that you have received of me;

2 And now, behold, this shall you say unto him—he who spake unto you, said unto you: I, the Lord, am God, and have given these things unto you, my servant Joseph Smith, Jun., and have commanded you that you should stand as a witness of these things;

3 And I have caused you that you should enter into a covenant with me, that you should not show them except to those persons to whom I commanded you; and you have no power over them except I grant it unto you.

4 And you have a gift to translate the plates; and this is the first gift that I bestowed upon you; and I have commanded that you should pretend to no other gift until my purpose is fulfilled in this; for I will grant unto you no other gift until it is finished.

5 Verily, I say unto you, that woe shall come unto the inhabitants of the earth if they will not hearken unto my words;

6 For hereafter you shall be ordained and go forth and deliver my words unto the children of men.

7 Behold, if they will not believe my words, they would not believe you, my servant Joseph, if it were possible that you should show them all these things which I have committed unto you.

8 Oh, this unbelieving and stiffnecked generation—mine anger is kindled against them.

9 Behold, verily I say unto you, I have reserved those things which I have entrusted

How did the Prophet Joseph fulfill the command to "stand as a witness" to the Book of Mormon? (5:2–3) "The Lord told the Prophet Joseph Smith that his role was to bear witness of the Book of Mormon and his sacred calling by testifying to the world, rather than by making the plates available for all to see. Because Joseph Smith was the prophet and seer chosen to translate the plates by the gift and power of God, his testimony of the divinity of the Book of Mormon stands as a preeminent witness of the reality of the Restoration of the gospel.

"The Prophet fulfilled this commandment of the Lord even to the last hours of his mortal life. [President] Jeffrey R. Holland of the Quorum of the Twelve Apostles recounted: 'Tell me whether in this hour of death [Carthage] these two men would enter the presence of their Eternal Judge quoting from and finding solace in a book which, if *not* the very word of God, would brand them as imposters and charlatans until the end of time? *They would not do that!* They were willing to die rather than deny the divine origin and the eternal truthfulness of the Book of Mormon' (["Safety for the Soul," *Ensign*, Nov. 2009, 89])" (*Doctrine and Covenants Student Manual* [2018], 45–46).

How did Joseph Smith translate the Book of Mormon plates? (5:4) "In the preface to the 1830 edition of the Book of Mormon, Joseph Smith wrote: 'I would inform you that I translated [the book], by the gift and power of God.' When pressed for specifics about the process of translation, Joseph repeated on several occasions that it had been done 'by the gift and power of God' and once added, 'It was not intended to tell the world all the particulars of the coming forth of the book of Mormon'" ("Book of Mormon Translation").

Why did the Lord prohibit Joseph from displaying the plates to the world? (5:7) President Ezra Taft Benson said, "We do not have to prove the Book of Mormon is true. The book is its own proof. All we need to do is read it and declare it! The Book of Mormon is not on trial—the people of the world, including the members of the Church, are on trial as to what they will do with this second witness for Christ" ("New Witness for Christ," *Ensign*, Nov. 1984, 8). ☉

What is the meaning of "this generation shall have my word through you"? (5:10) "What this means is that if we are going to receive the knowledge of God, the knowledge of truth, the knowledge of salvation, and know the things that we must do to work out our salvation with fear and trembling before the Lord, this must come in and through Joseph Smith and in no other way. He is the agent, the representative, the instrumentality that the Lord has appointed to give the truth about himself and his laws to all men in all the world in this age" (Bruce R. McConkie, *Doctrines of the Restoration*, 19). ⊕

Doctrine and Covenants 5:11–18. Three Witnesses Will Testify of the Book of Mormon

By what "power" will the three servants become witnesses of "these things"? (5:11–13) "The true Church of Jesus Christ is not man-made. Thus, God provides and gives his own witness by His power. The strength of the testimony of these three men did not come from any mortal man, including Joseph Smith. Therefore, the knowledge of the truthfulness of the Lord's work is not an issue between the world and Joseph Smith (see D&C 17:4). Rather it is a matter between each individual and the Savior Himself. Each person must accept the responsibility to accept or reject the Lord's witness as declared by these three men" (Otten and Caldwell, *Sacred Truths*, 1:39). ⊕

Why is the Church described using the imagery of the moon, the sun, and an army with banners? (5:14) The description of the Church being "clear as the moon, and fair as the sun, and terrible as an army with banners" is found in three passages in the Doctrine and Covenants (D&C 5:14; D&C 105:31; D&C 109:73).

"According to one commentary, the phrase means that the Church is 'indescribably beautiful, but at the same time inaccessible to flatterers, unconquerable, as an army under banners' [Smith and Sjodahl, *Doctrine and Covenants Commentary*, 27–28]. . . .

"In our day, a veritable army of missionaries goes forth throughout the earth seeking to rally people to the cause of Christ under the banner of his priesthood and Church" (Brewster, *Doctrine & Covenants Encyclopedia* [2012], 27).

unto you, my servant Joseph, for a wise purpose in me, and it shall be made known unto future generations;

10 But this generation shall have my word through you;

11 And in addition to your testimony, the testimony of three of my servants, whom I shall call and ordain, unto whom I will show these things, and they shall go forth with my words that are given through you.

12 Yea, they shall know of a surety that these things are true, for from heaven will I declare it unto them.

13 I will give them power that they may behold and view these things as they are;

14 And to none else will I grant this power, to receive this same testimony among this generation, in this the beginning of the rising up and the coming forth of my church out of the wilderness—clear as the moon, and fair as the sun, and terrible as an army with banners.

15 And the testimony of three witnesses will I send forth of my word.

16 And behold, whosoever believeth on my words, them will I visit with the manifestation of my Spirit; and they shall be born of me, even of water and of the Spirit—

17 And you must wait yet a little while, for ye are not yet ordained—

18 And their testimony shall also go forth unto the condemnation of this generation if they harden their hearts against them;

19 For a desolating scourge shall go forth among the inhabitants of the earth, and shall continue to be poured out from time to time, if they repent not, until the earth is empty, and the inhabitants thereof are consumed away and utterly destroyed by the brightness of my coming.

20 Behold, I tell you these things, even as I also told the people of the destruction of Jerusalem; and my word shall be verified at this time as it hath hitherto been verified.

21 And now I command you, my servant Joseph, to repent and walk more uprightly before me, and to yield to the persuasions of men no more;

What blessing is promised to those who obtain a testimony of the Book of Mormon? (5:16) "The promise here is that those who believe in the Book of Mormon will also experience other manifestations of the Spirit of the Lord. The knowledge obtained from the Book of Mormon brings with it greater faith in the God of heaven, which faith in turn brings a greater yield in the blessings of the Spirit" (McConkie and Ostler, *Revelations of the Restoration*, 73). ☉

Doctrine and Covenants 5:19–20. The Word of the Lord Will Be Verified as in Previous Times

What is a "desolating scourge"? (5:19) "One definition of a *scourge* is a whip used to flog and inflict great pain upon individuals. From time to time the Lord uses a scourge (meaning, the Lord punishes or afflicts) to whip earth's inhabitants on account of their wickedness....

"The Lord has decreed one or more great scourges for the last days, scourges that will cleanse the world. Four separate passages from the Doctrine and Covenants speak of such latter-day scourges (D&C 5:19; 45:30–32; 84:96–98; 97:23–24)....

"Zion's inhabitants, those who 'stand in holy places,' should be consoled in knowing that they will not fall on account of the scourge of the Lord" (Parry and Parry, *Understanding the Signs of the Times*, 347, 348).

Doctrine and Covenants 5:21–35. Martin Harris May Repent and Be One of the Witnesses

Why would the Lord command Joseph Smith to repent? (5:21) It appears from this verse that Joseph Smith had yielded to "the persuasions of men." President Gordon B. Hinckley stated: "We recognize that our forebears were human. They doubtless made mistakes....

"There was only one perfect man who ever walked the earth. The Lord has used imperfect people in the process of building his perfect society. If some of them occasionally stumbled, or if their characters may have been slightly flawed in one way or another, the wonder is the greater that they accomplished so much" ("Continuing Pursuit of Truth," *Ensign*, Apr. 1986, 5).

What do we understand about the promise made to Joseph Smith in this verse? (5:22) "This is the first hint in the revelations given to Joseph Smith that a martyr's death awaited him. While incarcerated in Liberty Jail, he was told that 'there is a time appointed for every man, according as his works shall be' (D&C 121:25), and that 'bounds' had been set beyond which his enemies could not go. 'Thy days are known, and thy years shall not be numbered less; therefore, fear not what man can do, for God shall be with you forever and ever' (D&C 122:9)" (McConkie and Ostler, *Revelations of the Restoration*, 74).

How would gaining humility prepare Martin Harris to become a witness of the Book of Mormon plates? (5:23–28) "God will have a humble people. Either we can choose to be humble or we can be compelled to be humble. . . .

"We can choose to humble ourselves by conquering enmity toward our brothers and sisters, esteeming them as ourselves, and lifting them as high or higher than we are. . . .

"We can choose to humble ourselves by receiving counsel and chastisement. . . .

"We can choose to humble ourselves by forgiving those who have offended us. . . .

"We can choose to humble ourselves by confessing and forsaking our sins and being born of God. . . .

"We can choose to humble ourselves by loving God, submitting our will to His, and putting Him first in our lives" (Benson, "Beware of Pride," *Ensign*, May 1989, 6–7). ☉

22 And that you be firm in keeping the commandments wherewith I have commanded you; and if you do this, behold I grant unto you eternal life, even if you should be slain.

23 And now, again, I speak unto you, my servant Joseph, concerning the man that desires the witness—

24 Behold, I say unto him, he exalts himself and does not humble himself sufficiently before me; but if he will bow down before me, and humble himself in mighty prayer and faith, in the sincerity of his heart, then will I grant unto him a view of the things which he desires to see.

25 And then he shall say unto the people of this generation: Behold, I have seen the things which the Lord hath shown unto Joseph Smith, Jun., and I know of a surety that they are true, for I have seen them, for they have been shown unto me by the power of God and not of man.

26 And I the Lord command him, my servant Martin Harris, that he shall say no more unto them concerning these things, except he shall say: I have seen them, and they have been shown unto me by the power of God; and these are the words which he shall say.

27 But if he deny this he will break the covenant which he has before covenanted with me, and behold, he is condemned.

28 And now, except he humble himself and acknowledge unto me the things that he has done which are wrong, and covenant with me that he will keep my commandments, and exercise faith in me, behold, I say unto him, he shall have no such views, for I will grant unto him no views of the things of which I have spoken.

29 And if this be the case, I command you, my servant Joseph, that you shall say unto him, that he shall do no more, nor trouble me any more concerning this matter.

30 And if this be the case, behold, I say unto thee Joseph, when thou hast translated a few more pages thou shalt stop for a season, even until I command thee again; then thou mayest translate again.

31 And except thou do this, behold, thou shalt have no more gift, and I will take away the things which I have entrusted with thee.

32 And now, because I foresee the lying in wait to destroy thee, yea, I foresee that if my servant Martin Harris humbleth not himself and receive a witness from my hand, that he will fall into transgression;

33 And there are many that lie in wait to destroy thee from off the face of the earth; and for this cause, that thy days may be prolonged, I have given unto thee these commandments.

34 Yea, for this cause I have said: Stop, and stand still until I command thee, and I will provide means whereby thou mayest accomplish the thing which I have commanded thee.

35 And if thou art faithful in keeping my commandments, thou shalt be lifted up at the last day. Amen.

How did the Lord provide means for Joseph Smith to continue translating the Book of Mormon? (5:30–34) "When Martin Harris broke his covenant and subsequently lost the 116-page manuscript, he no longer served as a scribe. Emma, Joseph's wife, stated that she and her brother, Reuben Hale, both aided as scribes for part of the translation (*Saints' Herald*, 26:289). The Lord did not intend for either Emma or Reuben to be the primary scribe for the Book of Mormon translation. Within a few weeks, Oliver Cowdery would be led by the hand of the Lord to Harmony, where he would offer his help to the Prophet" (McConkie and Ostler, *Revelations of the Restoration*, 75). Oliver Cowdery ended up serving as "the Prophet's scribe throughout almost the entire translation project" (Cowan, *Doctrine & Covenants: Our Modern Scripture*, 23).

Introduction to Doctrine and Covenants 6

When this revelation was received in April 1829, the Prophet Joseph Smith was living with his wife in Harmony, Pennsylvania. "Translation of the plates had stopped for a time after Joseph's scribe Martin Harris lost the manuscript the previous summer. Despite this setback, Joseph had reassured his mother, telling her that an angel told him the Lord would send him a scribe. 'And I trust his promise will be verified,' Joseph said" (Jeffrey G. Cannon, "Oliver Cowdery's Gift," 15–16).

In Manchester, New York, "A young man named Oliver Cowdery was staying with Joseph's parents. Oliver was a year younger than Joseph, and in the fall of 1828 he had begun teaching school about a mile south of the Smiths' farm." After some time, "Joseph's parents opened up to him about their son's divine calling.

"What they said captivated Oliver, and he longed to help with the translation. . . . Oliver told the family he wanted to go to Harmony to help Joseph when the school term was over. Lucy and Joseph Sr. urged him to ask the Lord if his desires were right. . . . Oliver prayed privately to know if what he had heard about the gold plates was true. The Lord showed him a vision of the gold plates and Joseph's efforts to translate them. A peaceful feeling rested over him, and he knew then that he should volunteer to be Joseph's scribe" (*Saints*, 1:59–60).

"Oliver came to Harmony believing he had been called to write for Joseph; now he was there and wanted to know what else the Lord had in store for him" (Jeffrey G. Cannon, "Oliver Cowdery's Gift," 16). The Prophet Joseph Smith described what followed: "Two days after the arrival of Mr. Cowdery (being the seventh of April) I commenced to translate the book of Mormon and he commenced to write for me, which having continued for some time I enquired of the Lord through the Urim and Thummin and obtained the following revelation [D&C 6]" (Joseph Smith Papers, "History, 1838–1856, volume A-1," 13); orthography modernized.

SECTION 6

Revelation given to Joseph Smith the Prophet and Oliver Cowdery, at Harmony, Pennsylvania, April 1829. Oliver Cowdery began his labors as scribe in the translation of the Book of Mormon, April 7, 1829. He had already received a divine manifestation of the truth of the Prophet's testimony respecting the plates on which was engraved the Book of Mormon record. The Prophet inquired of the Lord through the Urim and Thummim and received this response.

1 A great and marvelous work is about to come forth unto the children of men.

2 Behold, I am God; give heed unto my word, which is quick and powerful, sharper than a two-edged sword, to the dividing asunder of both joints and marrow; therefore give heed unto my words.

Doctrine and Covenants 6:1–6. Laborers in the Lord's Field Gain Salvation

Why is God's word described as "quick" and "sharper than a two-edged sword"? (6:2) "The word *quick* in the King James Version of the Bible does not mean swift but rather 'living, alive' ([Bible Dictionary, s.v. 'quick,' 756]). To be quickened by the Spirit means to be given spiritual life. The word of the Lord is quick and powerful because it is a source of life, energy, and power" (*Doctrine and Covenants Student Manual* [2001], 15).

"A two-edged sword is one which has been sharpened on both sides to make it twice as effective.

God's word and the still small voice of the Spirit are even sharper than this, for they are capable of piercing the most pernicious armament and of penetrating to the inner most depths of one's soul (D&C 85:6)" (Brewster, *Doctrine & Covenants Encyclopedia* [2012], 516). See also commentary in this volume on Doctrine and Covenants 11:2. ⊕

3 Behold, the field is white already to harvest; therefore, whoso desireth to reap, let him thrust in his sickle with his might, and reap while the day lasts, that he may treasure up for his soul everlasting salvation in the kingdom of God.

4 Yea, whosoever will thrust in his sickle and reap, the same is called of God.

What does the Lord promise to those who thrust in their sickle to reap during the harvest? (6:3–4) "We can reach out to others in missionary service in response to the Savior's injunction to 'go . . . into all the world, and preach the gospel to every creature' [Mark 16:15]. The Lord used a harvest analogy when he instructed the early Saints to proclaim the gospel. . . .

"Missionaries labor diligently to teach and baptize those who accept the gospel. In the process their own testimonies become deeply rooted. Missionary service provides the finest foundation possible for young people as they move into adulthood. The deep roots they sink into the gospel will sustain them for a lifetime and for all eternity" (Wirthlin, "Deep Roots," *Ensign*, Nov. 1994, 77). See also commentary in this volume on Doctrine and Covenants 4:4.

5 Therefore, if you will ask of me you shall receive; if you will knock it shall be opened unto you.

Why are we counseled by the Lord to "ask" and "knock"? (6:5) Milton Camargo explained: "Asking seems simple, and yet it is powerful because it reveals our desires and our faith. However, it takes time and patience to learn to understand the voice of the Lord. We pay attention to thoughts and feelings that come to our minds and hearts, and we write them down, as our prophet has counseled us to do. Recording our impressions is an important part of receiving. It helps

Oliver Cowdery: Scribe for the Prophet Joseph Smith (Doctrine and Covenants 6:1)

"Born October 3, 1806, in Wells, Rutland County, Vermont, Oliver Cowdery was the son of William Cowdery Jr. and Rebecca Fuller. No man except the Prophet Joseph Smith had a more responsible position in the early days of the fledgling Church than did Oliver. Coparticipant in receiving keys of authority from heavenly messengers, Oliver felt divine hands laid upon his head from the following angelic beings: John the Baptist (D&C 13; 27:7–8; JS—H 1:66–75); Peter, James, and John (D&C 27:12; 128:20); Moses, Elijah, and Elias (D&C 110). . . .

Oliver Cowdery

"Oliver came into the Prophet's life on April 5, 1829, when he arrived in Harmony, Pennsylvania, to inquire personally after Joseph's work on the Book of Mormon. The effect of that visit had eternal ramifications, for within two days he was serving as the scribe for Joseph Smith. He personally penned almost the entire first copy of the translation.

"His first month with the Prophet brought to Oliver at least four revelations (D&C 6, 7, 8, 9). Among these was the reminder from the Lord that Oliver had been brought to Joseph's aid through the manifestations of the Spirit (D&C 6:14–24). Evidently Oliver desired to participate in the translating process but learned that great things do not come without great effort (D&C 9)" (Brewster, *Doctrine & Covenants Encyclopedia* [2012], 110).

us recall, review, and refeel what the Lord is teaching us....

"Seeking implies mental and spiritual effort— pondering, testing, trying, and studying. We seek because we trust the Lord's promises ...

"To knock is to act in faith. When we actively follow Him, the Lord opens the way before us" ("Ask, Seek, and Knock," *Ensign*, Nov. 2020, 107). See also commentary in this volume on Doctrine and Covenants 4:7.

What does it mean to "bring forth and establish the cause of Zion"? (6:6) "This is the first mention of Zion in the Doctrine and Covenants. To 'bring forth and establish the cause of Zion' could be understood as the work of restoring the gospel of Jesus Christ, organizing the Church of Jesus Christ anew in our day, and preaching the gospel in order to gather others to Zion" (*Doctrine and Covenants Student Manual* [2018], 58–59). See also commentary in this volume on Doctrine and Covenants 21:7–8.

Doctrine and Covenants 6:7–13. There Is No Gift Greater Than the Gift of Salvation

How might the mysteries of God be unfolded to us? (6:7) The "mysteries of God are spiritual truths known only by revelation" (Guide to the Scriptures, "Mysteries of God"). Elder David A. Bednar taught that sometimes revelation happens "quickly, completely, and all at once [like turning on a light in a dark room]. ... [But] most frequently, revelation comes in small increments over time....

"Sometimes the sun rises on a morning that is cloudy or foggy. Because of the overcast conditions, perceiving the light is more difficult, and identifying the precise moment when the sun rises over the horizon is not possible....

"In a similar way, we many times receive revelation without recognizing precisely how or when we are receiving revelation" ("Spirit of Revelation," *Ensign*, May 2011, 88, 89). See also commentary in this volume on Doctrine and Covenants 11:17.

Why are we to "say nothing but repentance"? (6:9) "How important is repentance? Alma taught that we should 'preach nothing save it were repentance and faith on the Lord.' Repentance is required of every accountable person who desires eternal glory. There are no exceptions. In a revelation to the Prophet Joseph Smith, the Lord chastised early Church leaders for not

6 Now, as you have asked, behold, I say unto you, keep my commandments, and seek to bring forth and establish the cause of Zion;

7 Seek not for riches but for wisdom, and behold, the mysteries of God shall be unfolded unto you, and then shall you be made rich. Behold, he that hath eternal life is rich.

8 Verily, verily, I say unto you, even as you desire of me so it shall be unto you; and if you desire, you shall be the means of doing much good in this generation.

9 Say nothing but repentance unto this generation; keep my commandments, and assist to bring forth my work, according to my commandments, and you shall be blessed.

teaching the gospel to their children. Repenting is the *key* to progress. . . .

"Please do not fear or delay repenting. Satan delights in your misery. Cut it short. Cast his influence out of your life! Start today to experience the joy of putting off the natural man. The Savior loves us always but *especially* when we repent" (Nelson, "Power of Spiritual Momentum," *Liahona*, May 2022, 98). See also commentary in this volume on Doctrine and Covenants 11:9.

What gift did the Lord give Oliver Cowdery? (6:10) "Oliver Cowdery had been given two gifts. The first was the gift of revelation by which he could obtain a knowledge of the mysteries of the kingdom [D&C 6:10–12], and the second was the gift to translate (D&C 6:25–28). In the realm of spiritual things, few men have been so richly favored" (McConkie and Ostler, *Revelations of the Restoration*, 79). See also commentary in this volume on Doctrine and Covenants 8:6–9.

What does it mean to "trifle not with sacred things"? (6:12) An American dictionary used in the Prophet Joseph Smith's day defines the word *trifle* as, "To act or talk without seriousness, gravity, weight or dignity" (Webster, *American Dictionary* [1828], s.v. "trifle").

Elder Richard G. Scott taught us to recognize that revelation from the Lord is a sacred trust and should be recorded. He said, "Inspiration carefully recorded shows God that His communications are sacred to us. Recording will also enhance our ability to recall

10 Behold thou hast a gift, and blessed art thou because of thy gift. Remember it is sacred and cometh from above—

11 And if thou wilt inquire, thou shalt know mysteries which are great and marvelous; therefore thou shalt exercise thy gift, that thou mayest find out mysteries, that thou mayest bring many to the knowledge of the truth, yea, convince them of the error of their ways.

12 Make not thy gift known unto any save it be those who are of thy faith. Trifle not with sacred things.

13 If thou wilt do good, yea, and hold out faithful to the end, thou shalt be saved in the kingdom of God, which is the greatest of all the gifts of God; for there is no gift greater than the gift of salvation.

Why Is Repentance Important? (Doctrine and Covenants 6:9)

President Russell M. Nelson taught: "The word for *repentance* in the Greek New Testament is *metanoeo*. The prefix *meta-* means 'change.' The suffix *-noeo* is related to Greek words that mean 'mind,' 'knowledge,' 'spirit,' and 'breath.'

"Thus, when Jesus asks you and me to 'repent,' He is inviting us to change our mind, our knowledge, our spirit—even the way we breathe. He is asking us to change the way we love, think, serve, spend our time, treat our wives, teach our children, and even care for our bodies.

"Nothing is more liberating, more ennobling, or more crucial to our individual progression than is a regular, daily focus on repentance. Repentance is not an event; it is a process. It is the key to happiness and peace of mind. When coupled with faith, repentance opens our access to the power of the Atonement of Jesus Christ.

"Whether you are diligently moving along the covenant path, have slipped or stepped from the covenant path, or can't even see the path from where you are now, I plead with you to repent. Experience the strengthening power of daily repentance—of doing and being a little better each day.

"When we choose to repent, we choose to change! We allow the Savior to transform us into the best version of ourselves. We choose to grow spiritually and receive joy—the joy of redemption in Him. When we choose to repent, we choose to become more like Jesus Christ!" ("We Can Do Better and Be Better," *Ensign*, May 2019, 67).

revelation. Such recording of direction of the Spirit should be protected from loss or intrusion by others" ("How to Obtain Revelation," *Ensign*, May 2012, 46). ⊕

Doctrine and Covenants 6:14–27. "Thou Hast Been Enlightened by the Spirit of Truth"

What was the Lord teaching Oliver Cowdery about revelation? (6:14–15) "The Savior . . . revealed to Oliver that as often as he had prayed for guidance, he had received direction from the Spirit of the Lord. . . . Thus, Oliver received a revelation through the Prophet Joseph Smith informing him that he had been receiving revelation. Apparently, Oliver had not recognized how and when he had been receiving direction from God and needed this instruction to increase his understanding about the spirit of revelation.

"When we are exercising our faith and doing the simple things we know we should do, we gradually begin to recognize and come to know that we are being guided" (Bednar, *Spirit of Revelation*, 28–29). ⊕

How does the Lord enlighten our minds? (6:15) "Revelation shows us that God 'speaketh, not spake.' [President] Jeffrey R. Holland declared, 'The fundamental fact of the Restoration [is the] spirit of revelation.' It can take many forms: personal divine communication, mysteries understood, commandments from God, or collective instruction to the Church. It likewise covers many themes—from the practical to the transcendent. One *Woman's Exponent* author explained, divine revelation is 'learning of a better quality.' As many Americans searched for new revelation and prophetic authority, Latter-day Saints heard God speaking in their lives. Revelation had the power to combat calamity on an individual level as well as collectively for the Saints as a whole" (Johnson and Reeder, *Witness of Women*, 37). ⊕

In what way was this revelation evidence to Oliver Cowdery that God knew his thoughts and intents? (6:16) Joseph Smith related, "After we had received this revelation [currently Doctrine and Covenants 6] he (Oliver Cowdery) stated to me that after he had gone to my father's to board, and after the family communicated to him concerning my having got the plates, that one night after he had retired to bed, he called upon the Lord to know if these things were so, and that the Lord had manifested to him that they were true, but that he had kept the circumstance entirely secret, and had mentioned it to no being, so

14 Verily, verily, I say unto thee, blessed art thou for what thou hast done; for thou hast inquired of me, and behold, as often as thou hast inquired thou hast received instruction of my Spirit. If it had not been so, thou wouldst not have come to the place where thou art at this time.

15 Behold, thou knowest that thou hast inquired of me and I did enlighten thy mind; and now I tell thee these things that thou mayest know that thou hast been enlightened by the Spirit of truth;

16 Yea, I tell thee, that thou mayest know that there is none else save God that knowest thy thoughts and the intents of thy heart.

17 I tell thee these things as a witness unto thee—that the words or the work which thou hast been writing are true.

18 Therefore be diligent; stand by my servant Joseph, faithfully, in whatsoever difficult circumstances he may be for the word's sake.

19 Admonish him in his faults, and also receive admonition of him. Be patient; be sober; be temperate; have patience, faith, hope and charity.

20 Behold, thou art Oliver, and I have spoken unto thee because of thy desires; therefore treasure up these words in thy heart. Be faithful and diligent in keeping the commandments of God, and I will encircle thee in the arms of my love.

21 Behold, I am Jesus Christ, the Son of God. I am the same that came unto mine own, and mine own received me not. I am the light which shineth in darkness, and the darkness comprehendeth it not.

that after this revelation having been given, he knew that the work was true, because that no mortal being living knew of the thing alluded <to> in the revelation but God and himself" (Joseph Smith Papers, "History, 1838–1856, volume A-1," 15).

What was Oliver Cowdery counseled to do regarding his relationship with the Prophet Joseph Smith? (6:18–19) "Oliver learned that he had a duty to 'stand by,' or be loyal to and supportive of, the Lord's servant (D&C 6:18) and to patiently receive 'admonition,' or correction, from him (D&C 6:19). . . . Oliver was also counseled by the Lord to 'admonish' Joseph when needed (D&C 6:19). The Prophet had human frailties and never claimed to be infallible. . . . Joseph Smith declared, 'I never told you I was perfect; but there is no error in the revelations which I have taught' ([*Joseph Smith* (manual)], 522). However, when describing the frailties of his youth, the Prophet [explained]: 'No one need suppose me guilty of any great or malignant sins. A disposition to commit such was never in my nature' (Joseph Smith—History 1:28)" (*Doctrine and Covenants Student Manual* [2018], 60).

What can we learn from the imagery of being encircled in the arms of the Savior's love? (6:20) "Reconciliation between God and man is figuratively and literally symbolized by an embrace [see 2 Nephi 1:15]. . . . What a beautiful metaphor. What child does not feel safety in the arms of his kind and loving father? . . .

"Who among us will be safely encircled in those arms of love? Are there a chosen few reserved for this honor? Alma lets it be known there is no exclusionary policy [see Alma 5:33; see also 2 Nephi 26:25–33; 28:32; 3 Nephi 9:14; 10:6]. . . . Even in God's moments of anger, his arms are stretched out still, anxiously enticing the repentant soul" (Callister, *Infinite Atonement*, 27, 28). ●

What does it mean that darkness cannot comprehend light? (6:21) "Jesus said, 'I am the light [that] shineth in darkness, and the darkness comprehendeth it not' (D&C 6:21). That means no matter how hard it tries, the darkness cannot put out that light. Ever. You can trust that His light will be there for you" (Eubank, "Christ: The Light That Shines in Darkness," *Ensign*, May 2019, 75). See also commentary in this volume on Doctrine and Covenants 34:1–2.

How is the feeling of peace related to revelation?
(6:22–23) "There are certain distinct feelings of the
Spirit which Satan cannot counterfeit. . . . There are
certain feelings of the heart and impressions of the
mind that come only from heaven. Even Satan, the
great counterfeiter cannot duplicate them. . . . One
is peace. The Savior said, 'My peace I give unto you.'
Oliver Cowdery had been in Joseph Smith Senior's
home and prayed to know the truth of the Book of
Mormon. There he received a convincing assurance of
peace, but he never told Joseph Smith of this experience. . . . There was no way Joseph Smith could have
known of Oliver's earlier experience except through
revelation. This was the Lord's confirmation that
peace comes only from Him" (Callister, "Receiving and
Recognizing Revelation"). ✦

What might "those parts of my scriptures" refer
to in these verses? (6:26–27) Robert J. Matthews
explained that these verses "have a direct relationship to the Joseph Smith Translation. . . . The brethren
had already commenced the translation of the Book
of Mormon. In Doctrine and Covenants 6:26 and 27
the Lord speaks of records containing much of the
gospel that have been kept back because of iniquity.
Oliver Cowdery is promised that he can assist Joseph
Smith to bring this hidden knowledge to light. At
first it might seem that this passage is speaking only
of the Book of Mormon, but subsequent revelations
indicate that other records are also included [see also
Doctrine and Covenants 8:11 and 9:1–2]" ("Doctrinal
Connections," 29). ✦

Doctrine and Covenants 6:28–37. Look unto Christ, and Do Good Continually

How did Oliver Cowdery serve as a witness of
God's work alongside Joseph Smith? (6:28) The
Prophet Joseph Smith and Oliver became "two witnesses who could testify that [the Lord's] words had
been brought to light. It is significant that Joseph had
Oliver at his side as a witness when other important
events of the Restoration occurred. For example . . .

"1. The translation of the Book of Mormon and its
publication (see Joseph Smith—History 1:71, note).

"2. The restoration of the Aaronic Priesthood
through John the Baptist (see D&C 13).

22 Verily, verily, I say unto you, if you desire
a further witness, cast your mind upon the
night that you cried unto me in your heart,
that you might know concerning the truth of
these things.

23 Did I not speak peace to your mind concerning the matter? What greater witness can
you have than from God?

24 And now, behold, you have received a
witness; for if I have told you things which
no man knoweth have you not received a
witness?

25 And, behold, I grant unto you a gift, if
you desire of me, to translate, even as my servant Joseph.

26 Verily, verily, I say unto you, that there are
records which contain much of my gospel,
which have been kept back because of the
wickedness of the people;

27 And now I command you, that if you
have good desires—a desire to lay up treasures for yourself in heaven—then shall you
assist in bringing to light, with your gift,
those parts of my scriptures which have been
hidden because of iniquity.

28 And now, behold, I give unto you, and
also unto my servant Joseph, the keys of this
gift, which shall bring to light this ministry;
and in the mouth of two or three witnesses
shall every word be established.

"3. The restoration of the Melchizedek Priesthood through Peter, James, and John (see Joseph Smith—History 1:72).

"4. The organization of the Church with two elders to lead it (see D&C 20:2–3).

"5. The restoration of priesthood keys through Moses, Elias, and Elijah (see D&C 110)" (*Doctrine and Covenants Student Manual* [2018], 61–62).

How did the Lord ease Joseph Smith's and Oliver Cowdery's concerns regarding the work? (6:29–31) "In these verses both Joseph and Oliver are admonished to be faithful in the labors to which they have been called. The Lord, who knows the unspoken thoughts of our hearts, understood Joseph and Oliver's anxiety about the translation and its acceptance in an unbelieving world. The Lord assures them that if men reject his message, Joseph and Oliver will still be blessed. He also reminds them of his own rejection and suffering at the hands of men. They are told that should men accept the Book of Mormon there will be great cause to rejoice and though they are only two in number, he will be with them. Joseph and Oliver need but do that which is good, and in so doing they will reap that which is good" (McConkie and Ostler, *Revelations of the Restoration*, 81–82).

In what way will the Lord be in the midst of His disciples? (6:32) President Henry B. Eyring explained, "More important than our gathering together is in whose name we do so. The Lord promised that even with the great number of His disciples on the earth today, He would be close to each of us. . . .

"A multitude of His disciples are gathered in this conference, and as promised, the Lord is in our midst. Because He is a resurrected and glorified being, He is not physically everyplace where Saints gather. But, by the power of the Spirit, we can feel that He is here with us today" ("Where Two or Three Are Gathered," *Ensign*, May 2016, 19).

29 Verily, verily, I say unto you, if they reject my words, and this part of my gospel and ministry, blessed are ye, for they can do no more unto you than unto me.

30 And even if they do unto you even as they have done unto me, blessed are ye, for you shall dwell with me in glory.

31 But if they reject not my words, which shall be established by the testimony which shall be given, blessed are they, and then shall ye have joy in the fruit of your labors.

32 Verily, verily, I say unto you, as I said unto my disciples, where two or three are gathered together in my name, as touching one thing, behold, there will I be in the midst of them—even so am I in the midst of you.

33 Fear not to do good, my sons, for whatsoever ye sow, that shall ye also reap; therefore, if ye sow good ye shall also reap good for your reward.

34 Therefore, fear not, little flock; do good; let earth and hell combine against you, for if ye are built upon my rock, they cannot prevail.

35 Behold, I do not condemn you; go your ways and sin no more; perform with soberness the work which I have commanded you.

How can we look unto the Savior in every thought? (6:36) Sister Joy D. Jones explained: "The Lord counseled, 'Look unto me in every thought.' And each week we covenant to do just that—to 'always remember him.' Can such a godly focus apply in everything we do? Can performing even a menial task become an opportunity to demonstrate our love and devotion to Him? I believe it can and will.

"We can make each item on our to-do list become a way to glorify Him. We can see each task as a privilege and opportunity to serve Him, even when we are in the midst of deadlines, duties, or dirty diapers. . . .

"When serving our God becomes our main priority in life, we lose ourselves, and in due course, we find ourselves" ("For Him," *Ensign*, Nov. 2018, 51). ☉

What is the Lord inviting us to do in this passage? (6:36–37) "When the Lord calls the elders in Israel to 'look unto me in every thought' and 'behold the wounds' in His resurrected body, it is a call to turn away from sin and the world and to turn to Him and love and obey Him. It is a call to teach His doctrine and do His work in His way. It is, therefore, a call to trust Him completely, surrender our will and yield our hearts to Him, and through His redeeming power become like Him" (Kim B. Clark, "Look unto Jesus Christ," *Ensign*, May 2019, 54–55).

Did Oliver Cowdery see the Savior at this time? (6:37) In this passage, the Lord gave Oliver "promises or premonitions of [his] opportunities. . . . [Whether] Oliver Cowdery actually saw what he was here invited to see is not known. However, to behold such would certainly qualify him as a special witness of Christ and would also prepare him for other miraculous manifestations" (Nyman, "Witnesses of the Book of Mormon," 67).

36 Look unto me in every thought; doubt not, fear not.

37 Behold the wounds which pierced my side, and also the prints of the nails in my hands and feet; be faithful, keep my commandments, and ye shall inherit the kingdom of heaven. Amen.

"Ancient writings besides the Book of Mormon began to interest [Joseph Smith] and Oliver Cowdery not long after they started their translation of the gold plates. The Book of Mormon manuscript itself mentioned several ancient texts, and additionally, [the Prophet] had dictated a revelation promising Cowdery the privilege, if he so desired, of translating 'records which contain much of my gospel, which have been kept back because of the wickedness of the people' [D&C 6:26]" (Joseph Smith Papers, Historical Introduction to "Account of John, April 1829–C [D&C 7]," 13).

In April 1829 [at Harmony, Pennsylvania] Joseph Smith and Oliver Cowdery "[discussed] the fate of the Apostle John.... Joseph's history records they differed in their opinions and 'mutually agreed to settle [it] by the Urim and Thummim' [Joseph Smith Papers, "History, 1838–1856, volume A-1," 15]. The answer came in a vision of a parchment that Joseph translated, which is now Doctrine and Covenants 7" (Cannon, "Oliver Cowdery's Gift," 16). "The parchment John wrote and hid is apparently the original source for his New Testament Gospel. The revelation of the parchment to Joseph and Oliver restores much that was lost from the final few verses of John 21" (Harper, *Making Sense of the Doctrine & Covenants*, 41).

SECTION 7

Revelation given to Joseph Smith the Prophet and Oliver Cowdery, at Harmony, Pennsylvania, April 1829, when they inquired through the Urim and Thummim as to whether John, the beloved disciple, tarried in the flesh or had died. The revelation is a translated version of the record made on parchment by John and hidden up by himself.

1 And the Lord said unto me: John, my beloved, what desirest thou? For if you shall ask what you will, it shall be granted unto you.

2 And I said unto him: Lord, give unto me power over death, that I may live and bring souls unto thee.

Doctrine and Covenants 7:1–3. John the Beloved Will Live until the Lord Comes

What had qualified John to be granted anything he righteously desired? (7:1) "Joseph Smith received a revelation confirming that John's mission will continue as a translated being until the Savior's return (see Doctrine and Covenants 7:1–6). In other words, he not only prophesied of the end times, but his mission includes helping fulfill these prophecies as well as witnessing the fulfillment of the things that were revealed to him.

"Although our own missions may not be as grand, John's example teaches us that our love for Jesus Christ leads us to accept our own calls and challenges in life, no matter how bittersweet they at times may seem" (Huntsman, "John, the Disciple Whom Jesus Loved," *Ensign*, Jan. 2019, 22).

Why did John request power over death? (7:2) President Jeffrey R. Holland explained, "The Apostle John asked the Lord if he, John, might remain on the earth beyond the normal span of life for no other purpose than to bring more souls unto God. In granting that wish, the Savior said that this was 'a greater work' and a nobler 'desire' even than that of desiring to come into the presence of the Lord 'speedily.'

"Like all prophets and apostles, the Prophet Joseph Smith understood the deep meaning of John's request when he said, 'After all that has been said, [our] greatest and most important duty is to preach the Gospel' [Joseph Smith Papers, "History, 1838–1856, volume B-1," 757]. I bear witness of that gospel and of Jesus Christ, who embodied it. I testify that 'the worth of souls is great in the sight of God' [D&C 18:10]" ("Witnesses unto Me," *Ensign*, May 2001, 16).

What does this verse clarify about John's ministry? (7:3) "The original edition [in the 1833 Book of Commandments] declares that John would 'tarry until I come in my glory' while the current version [following the 1835 Doctrine and Covenants] adds 'and shalt prophesy before nations, kindreds, tongues and people' (D&C 7:3)" (Judd and Szink, "John the Beloved in Latter-day Scripture (D&C 7)," 97).

"An angel that appeared to John on the Isle of Patmos said unto him, 'Thou must prophesy again before many peoples, and nations, and tongues and kings' (Revelation 10:11). . . . John had the same desire as the three transfigured Nephite disciples [3 Nephi 28:4–16], to bring souls unto Christ [D&C 7:4]" (Nyman, *Doctrine and Covenants Commentary*, 1:47–48). ⊕

Doctrine and Covenants 7:4–8. Peter, James, and John Hold Gospel Keys

3 And the Lord said unto me: Verily, verily, I say unto thee, because thou desirest this thou shalt tarry until I come in my glory, and shalt prophesy before nations, kindreds, tongues and people.

4 And for this cause the Lord said unto Peter: If I will that he tarry till I come, what is that to thee? For he desired of me that he might bring souls unto me, but thou desiredst that thou mightest speedily come unto me in my kingdom.

What Do Peter and John's Differing Desires Teach Us? (Doctrine and Covenants 7:5, 8)

"This section adds important detail to the account in John 21 and retells how John expressed his heartfelt wish to have 'power over death, that [he could] live and bring souls unto [Christ]' until Jesus comes again. We learn in section 7 of the Doctrine and Covenants that Peter, on the other hand, had desired that he might 'speedily come unto [the Lord] in [His] kingdom.'

"Here is how I have imagined this scenario playing out. This is my mental screenplay of the scriptural story. Peter approaches the Savior a bit hesitantly and quietly asks, 'What was John's heartfelt wish?' Peter learns that John desired to stay on the earth until the Second Coming to preach the gospel. I can see Peter keeping a forced smile and saying, 'Wow. That is wonderful.' But in his mind he is really thinking, 'Ahhh! I am so dumb! Why didn't I ask for that? Why didn't I even *think* of that? John is so much more righteous than I am! Not to mention he is a faster runner than I am! Why do I always have to be so impetuous and jump in first on everything?'

"In this reading, one might assume that Doctrine and Covenants 7:5 would read like this: 'I say unto thee, Peter, [your desire to come speedily into my kingdom] was a good desire; but my beloved [John] has desired that he might do more, or a greater work yet among men than what [you have done, *thou slacker*].' I can still remember where I was, however, when I realized that of course the verse did not read that way. Here is how it really reads: 'I say unto thee, Peter, this was a good desire; but my beloved has desired that he might do more, or a greater work yet among men than what *he* has before done' [D&C 7:5, emphasis added].

5 I say unto thee, Peter, this was a good desire; but my beloved has desired that he might do more, or a greater work yet among men than what he has before done.

6 Yea, he has undertaken a greater work; therefore I will make him as flaming fire and a ministering angel; he shall minister for those who shall be heirs of salvation who dwell on the earth.

7 And I will make thee to minister for him and for thy brother James; and unto you three I will give this power and the keys of this ministry until I come.

8 Verily I say unto you, ye shall both have according to your desires, for ye both joy in that which ye have desired.

How can a translated being also be a ministering angel? (7:6–7) "Attention is drawn to the phrase 'I will make him . . . a ministering angel.' In partial fulfillment of this statement, this same John, in concert with Peter and James, was a ministering angel to Joseph Smith 'in the wilderness between Harmony, Susquehanna county, and Colesville, Broome county, on the Susquehanna river, declaring [himself] as possessing the keys of the kingdom' (D&C 128:20). This is a further illustration of a translated being used as an angel" (Oscar W. McConkie, *Angels*, 18–19).

What can we learn from God blessing different righteous desires? (7:8) "Men with righteous desires are not necessarily clones of one another. We are all on the road to salvation and exaltation, each with various talents and gifts. The righteous desires of one's heart derive from our pre-mortal experiences coupled with our experiences upon the earth. We are all headed toward the same goal, but our beginnings are various. Thus, Peter and John could both express righteousness in their service to God, even though they might be called upon to serve in different venues. We should all take consolation in that" (Paul Nolan Hyde, *Comprehensive Commentary* [1–72], 57).

"In this reading, one might assume that Doctrine and Covenants 7:5 would read like this: 'I say unto thee, Peter, [your desire to come speedily into my kingdom] was a good desire; but my beloved [John] has desired that he might do more, or a greater work yet among men than what [you have done, *thou slacker*].' I can still remember where I was, however, when I realized that of course the verse did not read that way. Here is how it really reads: 'I say unto thee, Peter, this was a good desire; but my beloved has desired that he might do more, or a greater work yet among men than what *he* has before done' [D&C 7:5, emphasis added].

"I feel this with the force of truth: our perfect, loving God makes no horizontal comparisons. In this verse Jesus only compared John with John's former self—John with old John. He only compared Peter with old Peter, with former Peter. And He only compares me with old me" (Haws, "Wrestling with Comparisons").

President Jeffrey R. Holland declared: "No one of us is less treasured or cherished of God than another. I testify that He loves each of us—insecurities, anxieties, self-image, and all. He doesn't measure our talents or our looks; He doesn't measure our professions or our possessions. He cheers on *every* runner, calling out that the race is against sin, *not* against each other" ("Other Prodigal," *Ensign*, May 2002, 64).

Introduction to Doctrine and Covenants 8

"Shortly before [D&C 8] was received, Oliver Cowdery had been promised the gift of translating the Book of Mormon plates if he so desired (see Doctrine and Covenants 6:25). Soon thereafter, Oliver informed Joseph that he did desire it and that he was now ready to make the attempt. Consequently, Joseph inquired of the Lord through the Urim and Thummim about how they should proceed and received this revelation in Oliver's behalf sometime in the latter half of April 1829 [in Harmony, Pennsylvania]" (Robinson and Garrett, *Commentary on the Doctrine and Covenants*, 1:62).

"After permission to proceed was granted and the Lord had given instructions as to how divine help could be obtained, Oliver made the attempt to translate. As a result of his failure in that endeavor, the Lord kindly explained the cause of his failure and revoked Oliver's privilege to translate as recorded in section 9 of the Doctrine and Covenants. . . .

"These two revelations combined, describe a process for seeking and receiving divine revelation. The process was revealed to Oliver but the principles are applicable to all mankind. In fact, the entire work of the restoration of the Lord's kingdom is a process of the Lord communicating with man. It is not man's initiative to organize—but only to inquire. In order that man might properly seek revelation and know how to obtain divine direction, the Lord gave these two revelations as instructions to Oliver and to all His children who would seek His mind and will" (Otten and Caldwell, *Sacred Truths*, 1:45–46).

Doctrine and Covenants 8:1–5. Revelation Comes by the Power of the Holy Ghost

What did the Lord teach Oliver about receiving revelation? (8:1–5) "In these verses Oliver Cowdery is told that he has been given the gift of revelation. If he asks in faith, doing so with an honest heart, he is promised that he will be able to translate ancient records. From the Book of Mormon we learn that there are many records which are yet to come forth. These records will also contain a witness of Christ and the assurance of the promises made to the posterity of Abraham. And like the Book of Mormon, these sacred records can be translated only by the gift and power of God (2 Nephi 29:10–14; 3 Nephi 26:6–11; Ether 3:22–28; 4:5–7)" (McConkie and Ostler, *Revelations of the Restoration*, 85).

How can we prepare ourselves to hear the Lord's voice? (8:2) "Asking in faith, fasting and praying, repenting regularly, forgiving and seeking forgiveness, worshiping in the temple where we may 'receive

SECTION 8

Revelation given through Joseph Smith the Prophet to Oliver Cowdery, at Harmony, Pennsylvania, April 1829. In the course of the translation of the Book of Mormon, Oliver, who continued to serve as scribe, writing at the Prophet's dictation, desired to be endowed with the gift of translation. The Lord responded to his supplication by granting this revelation.

1 Oliver Cowdery, verily, verily, I say unto you, that assuredly as the Lord liveth, who is your God and your Redeemer, even so surely shall you receive a knowledge of whatsoever things you shall ask in faith, with an honest heart, believing that you shall receive a knowledge concerning the engravings of old records, which are ancient, which contain those parts of my scripture of which has been spoken by the manifestation of my Spirit.

2 Yea, behold, I will tell you in your mind and in your heart, by the Holy Ghost, which shall come upon you and which shall dwell in your heart.

a fulness of the Holy Ghost,' and being obedient—all help us better hear the voice of the Lord in our minds and hearts. Conversely, there are things we cannot do—movies we cannot watch, clothes we cannot wear, gossip we cannot spread, Internet sites we cannot visit, thoughts we cannot entertain, books we cannot read, and dishonesty we cannot tolerate—if we want the Spirit to be with us" (Dew, "Knowing Who You Are," 271–72).

Why does the Lord speak to both our mind and our heart? (8:2) "The spirit of revelation as defined (D&C 8:2–3) has two parts, the mind and the heart. The mind is an intellectual experience. The heart is a spiritual witness. One without the other may be false. If it is only in the mind, it may be the reasoning of man and not agree with the reasoning of God. If it is only an internal feeling, it may be caused by emotion or excitement. The combination of the two—reasoning with God and edification of the Spirit is verification of it being a revelation from God (see D&C 50:10–12, 22–23). The experience will help us grow in the principle of revelation" (Nyman, *Doctrine and Covenants Commentary*, 1:123). See also commentary in this volume on Doctrine and Covenants 11:12–13.

3 Now, behold, this is the spirit of revelation; behold, this is the spirit by which Moses brought the children of Israel through the Red Sea on dry ground.

What does it mean to have the spirit of revelation? (8:3) "The spirit of revelation is available to every person who receives by proper priesthood authority the saving ordinances of baptism by immersion for the remission of sins and the laying on of hands for

---

The Lord's Promise of Revelation (Doctrine and Covenants 8 and 9)

Speaking of how the Lord gives revelation, President Russell M. Nelson explained: "One of the things the Spirit has repeatedly impressed upon my mind since my new calling as President of the Church is how willing the Lord is to reveal His mind and will. The privilege of receiving revelation is one of the greatest gifts of God to His children. . . .

"If we will truly receive the Holy Ghost and learn to discern and understand His promptings, we will be guided in matters large and small. . . .

"The Prophet Joseph Smith set a pattern for us to follow in resolving our questions. Drawn to the promise of James that if we lack wisdom we may ask of God, the boy Joseph took his question directly to Heavenly Father. He sought personal revelation, and his seeking opened this last dispensation.

"In like manner, what will your seeking open for you? What wisdom do you lack? What do you feel an urgent need to know or understand? Follow the example of the Prophet Joseph. Find a quiet place where you can regularly go. Humble yourself before God. Pour out your heart to your Heavenly Father. Turn to Him for answers and for comfort.

"Pray in the name of Jesus Christ about your concerns, your fears, your weaknesses—yes, the very longings of your heart. And then listen! Write the thoughts that come to your mind. Record your feelings and follow through with actions that you are prompted to take. As you repeat this process day after day, month after month, year after year, you will 'grow into the principle of revelation'" ("Revelation for the Church, Revelation for Our Lives," *Ensign*, May 2018, 94, 95).

the gift of the Holy Ghost—and who is acting in faith to fulfill the priesthood injunction to 'receive the Holy Ghost.' . . . Sincere desire and worthiness invite the spirit of revelation into our lives.

"Joseph Smith and Oliver Cowdery gained valuable experience with the spirit of revelation as they translated the Book of Mormon. These brethren learned they could receive whatever knowledge was necessary to complete their work if they asked in faith, with an honest heart, believing they would receive" (Bednar, "Spirit of Revelation," *Ensign*, May 2011, 87–88). ⊕

What can we learn about the spirit of revelation from the example of Moses at the Red Sea? (8:3) "Revelation almost always comes in response to a question, usually an urgent question—not always, but usually. In that sense it does provide information, but it is urgently needed information, special information. Moses' challenge was how to get himself and the children of Israel out of [the] horrible predicament they were in. . . . He needed information [to know] what to do, but it wasn't a casual thing he was asking. In this case it was literally a matter of life and death. . . .

"The Red Sea will open to the honest seeker of revelation" (Holland, "Cast Not Away Therefore Your Confidence," 4, 5).

Doctrine and Covenants 8:6–12. Knowledge of the Mysteries of God and the Power to Translate Ancient Records Come by Faith

What was the gift of Aaron? (8:6–9) The "spirit of revelation . . . is now Oliver's gift. 'Apply unto it,' the Lord commands him (v. 4). . . . And he reminds Oliver of his other gift: the gift possessed by Moses' brother, Aaron—the gift of working with a divining rod. It has already told Oliver many things (D&C 6). Only God can cause it to bless Oliver. He should not doubt it. It is God's gift to him. He can hold it in his hands. He can do marvelous works with it. . . .

"Gifts such as Oliver's rod, Lehi's 'miraculous directors,' the brother of Jared's Urim and Thummim, and Joseph Smith's interpreters may have been used more commonly in ancient times and in Joseph's Day than in ours (D&C 17:1)" (Harper, *Making Sense of the Doctrine & Covenants*, 42–43; see also Church History Topics, "Divining Rods"). See also commentary in this volume on Doctrine and Covenants 6:10. ⊕

4 Therefore this is thy gift; apply unto it, and blessed art thou, for it shall deliver you out of the hands of your enemies, when, if it were not so, they would slay you and bring your soul to destruction.

5 Oh, remember these words, and keep my commandments. Remember, this is your gift.

6 Now this is not all thy gift; for you have another gift, which is the gift of Aaron; behold, it has told you many things;

7 Behold, there is no other power, save the power of God, that can cause this gift of Aaron to be with you.

8 Therefore, doubt not, for it is the gift of God; and you shall hold it in your hands, and do marvelous works; and no power shall be able to take it away out of your hands, for it is the work of God.

9 And, therefore, whatsoever you shall ask me to tell you by that means, that will I grant unto you, and you shall have knowledge concerning it.

10 Remember that without faith you can do nothing; therefore ask in faith. Trifle not with these things; do not ask for that which you ought not.

11 Ask that you may know the mysteries of God, and that you may translate and receive knowledge from all those ancient records which have been hid up, that are sacred; and according to your faith shall it be done unto you.

12 Behold, it is I that have spoken it; and I am the same that spake unto you from the beginning. Amen.

What did Oliver learn about prayer and faith while translating the Book of Mormon? (8:10) "The translation of the Book of Mormon was a miracle. The scriptures teach that miracles are wrought by faith (e.g., Moroni 7:37; Matthew 17:19–20; Mormon 9:21; Moroni 10:12, 19, 23–24). When Peter walked on water, he did not focus on technique; he walked by faith, and for the lack of faith, he began to sink. To move a mountain, the brother of Jared needed only to have faith and say, 'remove,' and 'it was removed' (Ether 12:30). While God performed the miracle, the actuation of his divine power was dependent on the faith of his servant. The translation of the Book of Mormon was also dependent on faith" (Spencer, "Faith to See," 18:230).

What are these ancient records that have been hid up? (8:11) "From the Book of Mormon we learn that there are many records which are yet to come forth. These records will also contain a witness of Christ and the assurance of the promises made to the posterity of Abraham. And like the Book of Mormon, these sacred records can be translated only by the gift and power of God (2 Nephi 29:10–14; 3 Nephi 26:6–11; Ether 3:22–28; 4:5–7)" (McConkie and Ostler, *Revelations of the Restoration*, 85).

Introduction to Doctrine and Covenants 9

"During April of 1829, the work of translating the Book of Mormon continued on Joseph's farm in Harmony, Pennsylvania. The Lord had granted permission for Oliver Cowdery to translate the plates if he so desired (see D&C 6:25). Oliver had responded by affirming his desire and had been given instructions on how to proceed with the translation (see D&C 8). But when Oliver actually made an attempt to translate from the plates, though he began well enough, he was not able to continue with the same success. Doctrine and Covenants 9 was given to Oliver through the Prophet Joseph after Oliver's largely unsuccessful attempt to translate" (Robinson and Garrett, *Commentary on the Doctrine and Covenants*, 1:66).

"Oliver learned a lesson about revelation that is best understood through experience. Revelation is an active, not a passive, process requiring a combination of spiritual sensitivity and intellectual exertion.... As a result of Oliver's failure to 'continue as you commenced, when you began to translate' and the Lord's explanation 'that I have taken away this privilege from you' (v. 5), Oliver gained a respect for Joseph's gift he would never lose and a knowledge about the process of revelation he would never forget" (Harper, *Making Sense of the Doctrine & Covenants*, 45).

Doctrine and Covenants 9:1–6. Other Ancient Records Are Yet to Be Translated

What other records did Oliver Cowdery help translate? (9:2) "This forthright declaration leaves no doubt that it was the Lord's desire that after the Book of Mormon was translated there were 'other records' he wanted the Prophet Joseph and Oliver Cowdery to translate. The footnote in current editions of the Doctrine and Covenants 9:2 states that this passage refers to the Joseph Smith Translation of the Bible and also to the book of Abraham, in both of which Oliver Cowdery assisted the Prophet" (Matthews, "Doctrinal Connections," 30).

Why did Oliver lose his ability to translate? (9:5) "In the process of revelation and in making important decisions, fear almost always plays a destructive, sometimes paralyzing role. To Oliver Cowdery,

SECTION 9

Revelation given through Joseph Smith the Prophet to Oliver Cowdery, at Harmony, Pennsylvania, April 1829. Oliver is admonished to be patient and is urged to be content to write, for the time being, at the dictation of the translator, rather than to attempt to translate.

1 Behold, I say unto you, my son, that because you did not translate according to that which you desired of me, and did commence again to write for my servant, Joseph Smith, Jun., even so I would that ye should continue until you have finished this record, which I have entrusted unto him.

2 And then, behold, other records have I, that I will give unto you power that you may assist to translate.

3 Be patient, my son, for it is wisdom in me, and it is not expedient that you should translate at this present time.

4 Behold, the work which you are called to do is to write for my servant Joseph.

5 And, behold, it is because that you did not continue as you commenced, when you began to translate, that I have taken away this privilege from you.

who missed the opportunity of a lifetime because he didn't seize it in the lifetime of the opportunity, the Lord said, 'You did not continue as you commenced.' Does that sound familiar to those who have been illuminated and then knuckled under to second thoughts and returning doubts? 'It is not expedient that you should translate now,' the Lord said in language that must have been very hard for Oliver to hear. 'Behold, it was expedient when you commenced; *but you feared,* and the time is past, and it is not expedient now' (D&C 9:5, 10–11; emphasis added)" (Holland, "Cast Not Away Therefore Your Confidence," 5). ●

6 Do not murmur, my son, for it is wisdom in me that I have dealt with you after this manner.

What does it mean to murmur? (9:6) "A scriptural survey of murmuring indicates it is equated with complaining. (See 1 Nephi 17:22.) It has occurred in an individual's heart or in groups out in the open. . . . Common causes are: resentment at personal chastisement, as with Oliver Cowdery (D&C 9:6); pique at things withheld by the Lord, as with Emma Smith (D&C 25:4); lack of perspective or because of incomplete information (1 Nephi 2:12; 1 Nephi 16:3; Alma 58); reactions to persecution and fears (Mosiah 27:1; Numbers 14:2; Deuteronomy 1:27); failure to accept central doctrines and hard sayings (John 6:41, 61; 1 Nephi 16:1–2); and inability to sustain prophetic leaders, such as Moses and Nephi, which is really rebellion against the Lord (Exodus 16:8–9; 2 Nephi 5:3)" (Maxwell, *Notwithstanding My Weakness*, 51–52). ●

Doctrine and Covenants 9:7–14. The Book of Mormon Is Translated by Study and by Spiritual Confirmation

Why is it important to both study and pray when seeking a divine answer? (9:7–9) "The correct relationship between study and faith in the receipt of sacred knowledge is illustrated in Oliver Cowdery's attempt to translate ancient records. He failed because he 'took no thought,' but only asked God (D&C 9:7). The Lord told him he should have 'stud[ied] it out in [his] mind' and then asked if it was right (D&C 9:8). Only then would the Lord reveal whether the translation was correct or not. And only on receiving that revelation could the text be written, because 'you cannot write that which is sacred save it be given you from me' (D&C 9:9). In the acquisition of sacred knowledge, scholarship and reason are not alternatives to revelation. They are a means to an end, and the end is revelation from God" (Oaks, "Alternate Voices," *Ensign*, May 1989, 30). ●

7 Behold, you have not understood; you have supposed that I would give it unto you, when you took no thought save it was to ask me.

8 But, behold, I say unto you, that you must study it out in your mind; then you must ask me if it be right, and if it is right I will cause that your bosom shall burn within you; therefore, you shall feel that it is right.

9 But if it be not right you shall have no such feelings, but you shall have a stupor of thought that shall cause you to forget the thing which is wrong; therefore, you cannot write that which is sacred save it be given you from me.

What is a burning in the bosom? (9:8) "I have met persons who told me they have never had a witness from the Holy Ghost because they have never felt their bosom 'burn within' them.

"What does a 'burning in the bosom' mean? Does it need to be a feeling of caloric heat, like the burning produced by combustion? If that is the meaning, I have never had a burning in the bosom. Surely, the word 'burning' in this scripture signifies a feeling of comfort and serenity. That is the witness many receive. That is the way revelation works" (Oaks, "Teaching and Learning by the Spirit," *Ensign*, Mar. 1997, 13).

What does it mean that "you shall feel that it is right"? (9:8) "Feelings are the language of the Spirit. All true religion is a feeling. 'Ye were past feeling, that ye could not feel his [the Lord's] words,' Nephi said to his brothers Laman and Lemuel, who were given up to wickedness (1 Nephi 17:45). Having taught truth, Joseph Smith said: 'This is good doctrine. It tastes good. I can taste the principles of eternal life, and so can you. They are given to me by the revelations of Jesus Christ; and I know that when I tell you these words of eternal life as they are given to me, you taste them' [Joseph Smith Papers, "History, 1838–1856, volume E-1," 1974]" (McConkie and Ostler, *Revelations of the Restoration*, 99). ⊕

What could a stupor of thought feel like? (9:9) LaNae Valentine observed: "I looked up the word *stupor* in the dictionary and found these descriptions: a 'dazed state, a . . . lack of mental alertness' (*Encarta World English Dictionary*, s.v. "stupor"). Other descriptors are *sluggish, numbness, absence of the ability to move or feel, apathy, languidness, dullness,* or *not feeling inspired to go forward.* I was struck by the depressive mood created by all of these words. There is nothing inspiring, exciting, or comforting about any of them.

"Contrast the stupor descriptors with words describing the Spirit: *enlightens, enlivens, quickens, enlarges, expands, purifies, inspires, fills the soul with light, peace, love, clarity,* and *joy* (see [Pratt, *Key to the Science of Theology*], 101)" ("Discerning the Will of the Lord for Me," 3).

What does the word "expedient" mean? (9:10) Expedient (or a variation) appears forty-four times in the Doctrine and Covenants. Webster's 1828 *American Dictionary* defines expedient as: "suitable for the purpose; proper under the circumstances. . . . Useful; profitable" (*American Dictionary* [1828], s.v. "expedient").

10 Now, if you had known this you could have translated; nevertheless, it is not expedient that you should translate now.

11 Behold, it was expedient when you commenced; but you feared, and the time is past, and it is not expedient now;

12 For, do you not behold that I have given unto my servant Joseph sufficient strength, whereby it is made up? And neither of you have I condemned.

13 Do this thing which I have commanded you, and you shall prosper. Be faithful, and yield to no temptation.

14 Stand fast in the work wherewith I have called you, and a hair of your head shall not be lost, and you shall be lifted up at the last day. Amen.

In this verse, the Lord told Oliver that it was not needful or proper for Oliver to translate at that time, although he would continue as Joseph's scribe.

How can we overcome fear and continue doing what the Lord has commanded us? (9:11) Another "lesson from the Lord's spirit of revelation . . . is that, *along with the illuminating revelation that points us toward a righteous purpose or duty, God will also provide the means and power to achieve that purpose.* Trust in that eternal truth. If God has told you something is right, if something is indeed true for you, *he will provide the way for you to accomplish it.* That is true of joining the Church. It is true of getting an education, of going on a mission or of getting married or of any of a hundred worthy tasks. . . . God's grace is sufficient!" (Holland, "Cast Not Away Therefore Your Confidence," 6).

How had the Lord given Joseph "sufficient strength" to complete his work? (9:12) "As the prophet Nephi observed many centuries before, 'the Lord giveth no commandment unto the children of men, save he shall prepare a way for them that they may accomplish the things which he commandeth them' (1 Ne. 3:7). . . . Although the Prophet was relatively unlearned by worldly standards and had not formally studied ancient languages, yet he succeeded in translating the Book of Mormon by the gift and power of God and through the use of the Urim and Thummim. . . .

"When Oliver failed in his attempts [to translate], the Lord gave unto his 'servant Joseph sufficient strength, whereby it is made up.' Thus, the total responsibility for translation was left with Joseph" (Daniel H. Ludlow, *Companion to Your Study*, 1:96).

Why might Joseph and Oliver be cautioned to "stand fast in the work"? (9:13–14) "Joseph and Oliver experienced a decided increase in opposition to their work of translation and other activities in the area of Harmony. Mother Lucy Mack Smith mentions that the situation became so bad that 'evil-designing people were seeking to take away his (Joseph's) life, in order to prevent the work of God from going forth to the world'" (Larry C. Porter, "Historical Background of the Fifteen Harmony Revelations," 180).

Introduction to Doctrine and Covenants 10

"The Prophet Joseph Smith received the revelation recorded in Doctrine and Covenants 10 in Harmony, Pennsylvania, but it is not known exactly when. The Prophet may have received portions of this revelation as early as July 1828, after the revelation recorded in Doctrine and Covenants 3 was received. However, the revelation seems to have been recorded the following spring, in April 1829 (see section heading, Doctrine and Covenants 10).

"Some time following the loss of the 116 manuscript pages, the golden plates and the Urim and Thummim were returned to the Prophet, along with the Lord's assurance that the gift to translate was 'now restored unto [him] again' (D&C 10:3). By March 1829, the Prophet resumed the Book of Mormon translation, with his wife, Emma, assisting at times as his scribe, but the translation proceeded slowly until Oliver Cowdery arrived on April 5 and began serving as Joseph's scribe the next day" (*Doctrine and Covenants Student Manual* [2018], 36). For the circumstances regarding the loss of the 116 pages of manuscript, see the introduction to Doctrine and Covenants 3 in this volume.

"Joseph did not begin translating the Book of Mormon where the book begins today. Martin Harris lost what he translated first, which included Mormon's abridgment of the Lehi's writings. When Joseph resumed translating, he picked up where he left off and continued on through the book of Moroni. At some point, Joseph asked the Lord if he could retranslate what had been lost. In the spring of 1829, the Lord answered this question with the revelation recorded in Doctrine and Covenants 10, which led Joseph to translate the small plates of Nephi, beginning with 1 Nephi" (Harper, *Making Sense of the Doctrine & Covenants*, 46).

Doctrine and Covenants 10:1–26. Satan Stirs Up Wicked Men to Oppose the Lord's Work

What was Joseph's mistake that resulted in losing the 116 pages? (10:1) Bruce A. Carlson explained: "The Prophet Joseph Smith petitioned the Lord on two occasions, asking if a prominent friend, Martin Harris, could take the first 116 handwritten pages of translated material from the book of Lehi from Harmony, Pennsylvania, back to Palmyra. Each time, the Lord counseled Joseph to avoid entrusting the manuscript to Mr. Harris.

"Martin was seeking to use the translated material as evidence to stop his associates from spreading rumors about his friendship with Joseph Smith. On the third request the Lord granted Joseph's appeal.

"Martin lost the manuscript, and as a result the plates were taken from the Prophet Joseph Smith for an extended period. This was a painful lesson for the Prophet Joseph, who said, 'I made this my rule: *When the Lord commands, do it*' (Joseph Smith [manual], 160)" ("When the Lord Commands," *Ensign*, May 2010, 39).

SECTION 10

Revelation given to Joseph Smith the Prophet, at Harmony, Pennsylvania, likely around April 1829, though portions may have been received as early as the summer of 1828. Herein the Lord informs Joseph of alterations made by wicked men in the 116 manuscript pages from the translation of the book of Lehi, in the Book of Mormon. These manuscript pages had been lost from the possession of Martin Harris, to whom the sheets had been temporarily entrusted. (See the heading to section 3.) The evil design was to await the expected retranslation of the matter covered by the stolen pages and then to discredit the translator by showing discrepancies created by the alterations. That this wicked purpose had been conceived by the evil one and was known to the Lord even while Mormon, the ancient Nephite historian, was making his abridgment of the accumulated plates, is shown in the Book of Mormon (see Words of Mormon 1:3–7).

1 Now, behold, I say unto you, that because you delivered up those writings which you had power given unto you to translate by the means of the Urim and Thummim, into the hands of a wicked man, you have lost them.

2 And you also lost your gift at the same time, and your mind became darkened.

3 Nevertheless, it is now restored unto you again; therefore see that you are faithful and continue on unto the finishing of the remainder of the work of translation as you have begun.

4 Do not run faster or labor more than you have strength and means provided to enable you to translate; but be diligent unto the end.

5 Pray always, that you may come off conqueror; yea, that you may conquer Satan, and that you may escape the hands of the servants of Satan that do uphold his work.

6 Behold, they have sought to destroy you; yea, even the man in whom you have trusted has sought to destroy you.

7 And for this cause I said that he is a wicked man, for he has sought to take away the things wherewith you have been entrusted; and he has also sought to destroy your gift.

8 And because you have delivered the writings into his hands, behold, wicked men have taken them from you.

9 Therefore, you have delivered them up, yea, that which was sacred, unto wickedness.

What were the consequences of Joseph's failure to obey? (10:2) "When the Prophet Joseph lost the 116 pages of manuscript known as the book of Lehi, the Lord took away his translating privileges" (Brewster, *Doctrine & Covenants Encyclopedia* [2012], 363). "[He lost] the seeric gift of translating the ancient Nephite records by the power of inspiration (D&C 10:2). His 'mind became darkened' because he had lost the divine light which had previously illuminated his understanding. This came about as the natural consequence of his disobedience and willful neglect which led to the loss of 116 pages of translated manuscript" (Brewster, *Doctrine & Covenants Encyclopedia* [2012], 215–16).

Why was Joseph cautioned to not run faster than he had strength? (10:4) "Human tendency would cause Joseph to accelerate his efforts, making up for the time lost due to the loss of the manuscript. . . . This tendency would be more likely because of the chastisement Joseph had received from the Lord. However, the admonition to not run faster than one has strength is a general principle applicable to most situations. King Benjamin, the beloved Nephite leader, gave the same principle and admonition to his subjects when instructing them before turning over the reign to his son (see Mosiah 4:27). The Lord was apparently more concerned with accuracy in the Book of Mormon translation than He was with the time element" (Nyman, *Doctrine and Covenants Commentary*, 1:63). ⊕

Why has the Lord exhorted us to "pray always"? (10:5) "[The Lord] warns you to 'pray always.' You may have wondered, as have I, why He used the word *always*. . . . You know from experience how hard it is to think of anything consciously all the time. Even in service to God, you will not be consciously praying always. So why does the Master exhort us to 'pray always'? . . .

"He knows the mistake we can so easily make: to underestimate the forces working for us and to rely too much on our human powers. And so He offers us the covenant to 'always remember Him' and the warning to 'pray always' so that we will place our reliance on Him, our only safety" (Eyring, "Always," *Ensign*, Oct. 1999, 8, 9). See also commentary in this volume on Doctrine and Covenants 19:38–39.

How can we escape the wiles of Satan and his servants? (10:5–7) Elder Ulisses Soares testified: "The adversary's purpose is to make all people as miserable as he is. Satan and his angels will try to shroud our thoughts and assert control by tempting us to sin. If they can, they will corrupt all that is good.

Nevertheless, it is essential to understand that they will have power over us only if we allow it. . . .

"We cannot allow ourselves to be confused by popular messages that are easily accepted by the world and that contradict the doctrine and true principles of the gospel of Jesus Christ. . . . As we encounter these worldly messages, great courage and a solid knowledge of the plan of our Heavenly Father will be required to choose the right" (Soares, "Yes, We Can and Will Win!" *Ensign*, May 2015, 75). ☻

How does section 10 help us understand Satan's designs and strategies to thwart the Lord's work? (10:10–11) "Nowhere in scripture do we learn more about the evil designs and purposes of Satan than in section 10. We learn that Satan is cunning and enlists those who love darkness rather than light (v. 21), and that he stirreth up their hearts to commit iniquity against that which is good, that they may get glory of the world (v. 19, 20). Satan uses deception and flattery and encourages his people to lie and deceive (v. 25, 26). A major tactic of Satan is to stir up contention regarding Christ's doctrine (v. 63–69). Ultimately, the adversary wants to destroy the souls of men and drag them down to hell (v. 22, 26), and to destroy the work of God (v. 15, 23; see 2 Ne. 28:20–22)" (Cowan and Manscill, *A to Z of the Doctrine and Covenants*, 28).

What was the devil's cunning plan? (10:12–13) "The Lord, who knows all things, including thoughts and the intents of the heart (D&C 6:16), here explains the evil designs of those who have stolen the 116 pages of manuscript. They intend to withhold their purloined [stolen] copy of the translation until Joseph Smith has retranslated the same pages. Then they intend to alter the words of the earlier translation and try to convince others that Joseph Smith is a liar

10 And, behold, Satan hath put it into their hearts to alter the words which you have caused to be written, or which you have translated, which have gone out of your hands.

11 And behold, I say unto you, that because they have altered the words, they read contrary from that which you translated and caused to be written;

12 And, on this wise, the devil has sought to lay a cunning plan, that he may destroy this work;

13 For he hath put into their hearts to do this, that by lying they may say they have caught you in the words which you have pretended to translate.

What Were Martin Harris's Contributions to the Church? (Doctrine and Covenants 10:5–7)

President Dallin H. Oaks pleaded for understanding on behalf of Martin Harris: "Having a special interest in Martin Harris, I have been saddened at how he is remembered by most Church members. He deserves better than to be remembered solely as the man who unrighteously obtained and then lost the initial manuscript pages of the Book of Mormon. . . .

"I will review some of the high points of Martin Harris's life following the devastating episode of the stolen and lost manuscript. . . .

"Martin Harris was selected as one of the Three Witnesses. . . .

"One of Martin Harris's greatest contributions to the Church, for which he should be honored for all time, was his financing the publication of the Book of Mormon. . . .

Martin Harris

"In Missouri [1831,] he was commanded to 'be an example unto the church, in laying his moneys before the bishop of the church' (D&C 58:35), thus becoming the first man the Lord called by name to consecrate his property in Zion. . . .

14 Verily, I say unto you, that I will not suffer that Satan shall accomplish his evil design in this thing.

15 For behold, he has put it into their hearts to get thee to tempt the Lord thy God, in asking to translate it over again.

16 And then, behold, they say and think in their hearts—We will see if God has given him power to translate; if so, he will also give him power again;

17 And if God giveth him power again, or if he translates again, or, in other words, if he bringeth forth the same words, behold, we have the same with us, and we have altered them;

18 Therefore they will not agree, and we will say that he has lied in his words, and that he has no gift, and that he has no power;

19 Therefore we will destroy him, and also the work; and we will do this that we may not be ashamed in the end, and that we may get glory of the world.

when he pretends to translate, for they would claim he cannot translate the same way twice. Thus, the plan of Satan was to 'overpower' the testimony of the Prophet so 'that the work may not come forth in this generation' (D&C 10:33)" (Daniel H. Ludlow, *Companion to Your Study*, 1:99).

How did the Lord's instructions thwart the designs of Satan and his servants? (10:14–19) Joseph declared the Lord's instruction and warnings regarding the manuscript in the preface to the first edition of the Book of Mormon (see Joseph Smith Papers, "Book of Mormon, 1830, Page i," [iii]). "By publishing this information, it became futile for the men who had the pages of translation and had altered them to carry out their plans. Indeed, if the men revealed that they had the pages, they would also reveal that not only were they thieves but also that they were the designing men identified in the preface of the Book of Mormon" (McConkie and Ostler, *Revelations of the Restoration*, 106).

"In 1832 Martin [and his] older brother, Emer, . . . spent a year preaching the gospel near his former home in northeastern Pennsylvania. . . . The Harris brothers baptized about 100 persons. . . .

"After his mission, in February 1834 Martin Harris was chosen by revelation to serve on the first high council in the Church. Less than three months later, he left Kirtland with the men of Zion's Camp, marching 900 miles to Missouri to relieve the oppressed Saints there. . . .

"The Three Witnesses, including Martin Harris, were appointed to 'search out the Twelve' (D&C 18:37), to select them and, under authority granted by the Prophet and his counselors, to ordain them. . . .

"When he reiterated his testimony of the Book of Mormon in the closing days of his life, Martin Harris declared, 'I tell you of these things that you may tell others that what I have said is true, and I dare not deny it; I heard the voice of God commanding me to testify to the same'" ("Witness," *Ensign*, May 1999, 36, 37).

**What do these verses tell us about the individu-
als who fell under Satan's scheme? (10:20–23)**
"'Their hearts are corrupt, and full of wickedness
and abominations' (D&C 10:21), which tells us that
these men were not amateurs in wickedness. . . . In
stirring these wicked men up against this great work,
[Satan] needed men whose hearts were already
turned to iniquity. He was endeavoring to lead them
to destruction. As Lehi had learned from the plates
of brass, 'he sought also the misery of all mankind'
(2 Nephi 2:17–18). Misery loves company. Those who
become Satan's co-workers will be accountable and
condemned at the day of judgment (v. 23)" (Nyman,
Doctrine and Covenants Commentary, 1:65).

**What can we do when the devil stirs up anger
against God's work? (10:24)** "This is God's work,
and God's work will not be frustrated. But there is
still much to be done before the Great Jehovah can
announce that the work is done. . . .

"Instead of angry mobs, we face those who
constantly try to defame. Instead of extreme
exposure and hardship, we face alcohol and drug
abuse, pornography, all kinds of filth, sleaze, greed,
dishonesty, and spiritual apathy. Instead of families
being uprooted and torn from their homes, we see
the institution of the family, including the divine
institution of marriage, under attack. . . .

"Our testimonies must run deep, with spiritual
roots firmly embedded in the rock of revelation. And
we must continue to move the work forward as a
covenanted, consecrated people, with faith in every
footstep" (Ballard, "Truth of God Shall Go Forth,"
Ensign, Nov. 2008, 83–84).

**What are some of Satan's traps and snares and
how can we avoid them? (10:25–29)** "Like the fly
fisherman who knows that trout are driven by hunger,
Lucifer knows our 'hunger,' or weaknesses, and
tempts us with counterfeit lures which, if taken, can
cause us to be yanked from the stream of life into his
unmerciful influence. . . .

"One of the main methods he uses against us is
his ability to lie and deceive to convince us that evil is
good and good is evil. . . .

"Satan knows how to exploit and ensnare us
with artificial substances and behaviors of temporary
pleasure. . . .

20 Verily, verily, I say unto you, that Satan has
great hold upon their hearts; he stirreth them
up to iniquity against that which is good;

21 And their hearts are corrupt, and full of
wickedness and abominations; and they love
darkness rather than light, because their deeds
are evil; therefore they will not ask of me.

22 Satan stirreth them up, that he may lead
their souls to destruction.

23 And thus he has laid a cunning plan,
thinking to destroy the work of God; but I
will require this at their hands, and it shall
turn to their shame and condemnation in the
day of judgment.

24 Yea, he stirreth up their hearts to anger
against this work.

25 Yea, he saith unto them: Deceive and lie
in wait to catch, that ye may destroy; behold,
this is no harm. And thus he flattereth them,
and telleth them that it is no sin to lie that
they may catch a man in a lie, that they may
destroy him.

26 And thus he flattereth them, and leadeth them along until he draggeth their souls
down to hell; and thus he causeth them to
catch themselves in their own snare.

"Our love for our Father in Heaven and the Lord Jesus Christ needs to be reflected in our daily choices and actions. They have promised peace, joy, and happiness to those who keep Their commandments" (Ballard, "O That Cunning Plan," *Ensign*, Nov. 2010, 108, 110).

27 And thus he goeth up and down, to and fro in the earth, seeking to destroy the souls of men.

28 Verily, verily, I say unto you, wo be unto him that lieth to deceive because he supposeth that another lieth to deceive, for such are not exempt from the justice of God.

29 Now, behold, they have altered these words, because Satan saith unto them: He hath deceived you—and thus he flattereth them away to do iniquity, to get thee to tempt the Lord thy God.

30 Behold, I say unto you, that you shall not translate again those words which have gone forth out of your hands;

31 For, behold, they shall not accomplish their evil designs in lying against those words. For, behold, if you should bring forth the same words they will say that you have lied and that you have pretended to translate, but that you have contradicted yourself.

32 And, behold, they will publish this, and Satan will harden the hearts of the people to stir them up to anger against you, that they will not believe my words.

Doctrine and Covenants 10:27–33. Satan Seeks to Destroy the Souls of Men

How can Satan harden our hearts so we don't believe? (10:32) "Doubt is an enemy of faith and joy. . . . Satan seeks to lead us to the breeding ground of doubt. He seeks to harden our hearts so that we will not believe. The breeding ground of doubt can appear inviting because its seemingly peaceful, warm waters do not require us to 'live by every word that proceedeth forth from the mouth of God' [D&C 84:44]. In such waters Satan tempts us to relax our spiritual vigilance. That inattention can induce a lack of spiritual conviction, where we are 'neither cold nor hot' [Rev. 3:15–16]. If we are not anchored on Christ, doubt and its allures will lead us away to apathy, where we shall find neither miracles, lasting happiness, nor 'rest unto [our] souls' [see Moses 6:27–29]" (Douglas, "Facing Our Spiritual Hurricanes," *Liahona*, Nov. 2021, 109, 110).

Why must we constantly work on strengthening our testimonies of the gospel of Jesus Christ? (10:33) "We live in a very difficult era in the history of the world, when Satan is going to and fro on the earth among the children of God, doing all manner of evil to thwart the desires of a righteous God. The scriptures teach us that Satan's evil designs upon the peoples of the earth will intensify as the Second Coming of our Lord and Savior Jesus Christ draws near at hand" (Hales, "Fulfilling Our Duty to God," *Ensign*, Nov. 2001, 39).

Sister Bonnie H. Cordon explained: "The adversary creates so much noise that it can be difficult to hear the Lord's voice. Our world, our challenges, our circumstances will not get quieter, but we can and must hunger and thirst after the things of Christ to 'hear Him' with clarity. We want to create muscle memory of discipleship and testimony that will bring into focus our reliance on our Savior each day" ("Never Give Up an Opportunity," *Liahona*, May 2023, 12). ◉

Doctrine and Covenants 10:34–52. The Gospel Is to Go to the Lamanites and All Nations through the Book of Mormon

Why was Joseph told to not show the translation until it was completed? (10:34–35) "Joseph had probably considered that Martin was righteous and could be trusted since he had financed the project. However, through the efforts of his wife, Martin had allowed the manuscript to be shared with the world. Therefore, the Lord would now make the decision of when and to whom the contents of the plates would be shown to others, and to the world (v. 37). The Lord knows the hearts of all men, and man may be deceived. This course of action was to preserve the life of Joseph Smith. His life had been in danger since he had obtained the plates, and would continue to be until his mission was completed" (Nyman, *Doctrine and Covenants Commentary*, 1:67–68).

Why wasn't Joseph always able to judge between the wicked and the righteous? (10:37) President Dallin H. Oaks remarked: "In order to perform their personal ministries, Church leaders cannot be suspicious and questioning of each of the hundreds of people they meet each year. Ministers of the gospel function best in an atmosphere of trust and love. In that kind of atmosphere, they fail to detect a few deceivers, but that is the price they pay to increase their effectiveness in counseling, comforting, and blessing the hundreds of honest and sincere people they see.

33 Thus Satan thinketh to overpower your testimony in this generation, that the work may not come forth in this generation.

Rev. 12:11

34 But behold, here is wisdom, and because I show unto you wisdom, and give you commandments concerning these things, what you shall do, show it not unto the world until you have accomplished the work of translation.

35 Marvel not that I said unto you: Here is wisdom, show it not unto the world—for I said, show it not unto the world, that you may be preserved.

36 Behold, I do not say that you shall not show it unto the righteous;

37 But as you cannot always judge the righteous, or as you cannot always tell the wicked from the righteous, therefore I say unto you, hold your peace until I shall see fit to make all things known unto the world concerning the matter.

38 And now, verily I say unto you, that an account of those things that you have written, which have gone out of your hands, is engraven upon the plates of Nephi;

39 Yea, and you remember it was said in those writings that a more particular account was given of these things upon the plates of Nephi.

40 And now, because the account which is engraven upon the plates of Nephi is more particular concerning the things which, in my wisdom, I would bring to the knowledge of the people in this account—

41 Therefore, you shall translate the engravings which are on the plates of Nephi, down even till you come to the reign of king Benjamin, or until you come to that which you have translated, which you have retained;

42 And behold, you shall publish it as the record of Nephi; and thus I will confound those who have altered my words.

43 I will not suffer that they shall destroy my work; yea, I will show unto them that my wisdom is greater than the cunning of the devil.

44 Behold, they have only got a part, or an abridgment of the account of Nephi.

45 Behold, there are many things engraven upon the plates of Nephi which do throw greater views upon my gospel; therefore, it is wisdom in me that you should translate this first part of the engravings of Nephi, and send forth in this work.

46 And, behold, all the remainder of this work does contain all those parts of my gospel which my holy prophets, yea, and also my disciples, desired in their prayers should come forth unto this people.

It is better for a church leader to be occasionally disappointed than to be constantly suspicious" ("Recent Events Involving Church History," *Ensign*, Oct. 1987, 65–66).

What were the "greater views" the Lord desired to bring forth from the plates of Nephi? (10:38–40, 45) "We do not know exactly what we have missed in the lost 116 pages, but we do know that what we received on the small plates was the personal declarations of three great witnesses, three of the great doctrinal voices [Nephi, Jacob, and Isaiah] of the Book of Mormon, testifying that Jesus is the Christ" (Holland, "For a Wise Purpose," *Ensign*, Jan. 1996, 14). ◉

When the ability to translate was restored, how was Joseph instructed to proceed? (10:41–42) "[Joseph] had already translated the abridgment made by Mormon up to the book of Mosiah. This means that he had translated the accounts from the time of Lehi leaving Jerusalem through the time of King Benjamin. The renewed efforts of translation began with Mosiah chapter one. After finishing the translation of the plates through the book of Moroni, Joseph then continued as instructed in this revelation to translate the small plates of Nephi, or what we know as First and Second Nephi, Jacob, Enos, Jarom, Omni, and the Words of Mormon" (McConkie and Ostler, *Revelations of the Restoration*, 104).

How have all men and women been blessed by the prophetic prayers that brought forth the Book of Mormon? (10:46–49) "The Book of Mormon provides the fullest and most authoritative understanding of the Atonement of Jesus Christ to be found anywhere. It teaches what it really means to be born again. From the Book of Mormon we learn about the gathering of scattered Israel. We know why we are here on earth. These and other truths are more powerfully and persuasively taught in the Book of Mormon than in any other book. The full power of the gospel of Jesus Christ is contained in the Book of Mormon. Period" (Nelson, "Book of Mormon: What Would Your Life Be Like without It?" *Ensign*, Nov. 2017, 62).

How has the Nephite prophets' blessing on the promised land been fulfilled? (10:50–51) "The Nephite prophets also left a blessing upon future generations, that those who lived here might believe the gospel and have eternal life. God has honored those prayers and that blessing by giving us in the latter days political freedom, the fulness of the gospel, and the true Church" (Robinson and Garrett, *Commentary on the Doctrine and Covenants*, 1:75).

Father Lehi, in the earliest days of the Book of Mormon, declared this land to be a "choice" land, a "consecrated" land, a land that "shall never be brought down into captivity," and that if its people "shall keep [the Lord's] commandments they shall be blessed upon the face of the land, and there shall be none to molest them" (2 Nephi 1:5–9).

47 And I said unto them, that it should be granted unto them according to their faith in their prayers;

48 Yea, and this was their faith—that my gospel, which I gave unto them that they might preach in their days, might come unto their brethren the Lamanites, and also all that had become Lamanites because of their dissensions.

49 Now, this is not all—their faith in their prayers was that this gospel should be made known also, if it were possible that other nations should possess this land;

50 And thus they did leave a blessing upon this land in their prayers, that whosoever should believe in this gospel in this land might have eternal life;

51 Yea, that it might be free unto all of whatsoever nation, kindred, tongue, or people they may be.

52 And now, behold, according to their faith in their prayers will I bring this part of my gospel to the knowledge of my people. Behold, I do not bring it to destroy that which they have received, but to build it up.

God's Wisdom Is Greater Than the Cunning of the Devil (Doctrine and Covenants 10:43)

"God is both omniscient and benevolent. Where Satan uses his influence to blind, to enslave, and to deceive, the Lord uses his power to bless, to save, and to preserve our agency. Theologians have long wrestled with the assumption that if God is all-knowing, there can be no such thing as individual agency. The whole script of human action must have been predetermined, this assumption goes, and therefore we have no power to stray from it. One alternative is to believe in a less than omniscient God. Section 10 presents a refreshing, completely different alternative. It reveals an omniscient Lord who uses his foreknowledge to preserve and protect individual agency" (Harper, *Making Sense of the Doctrine & Covenants*, 49).

The following statement was included in the preface to the 1830 edition of the Book of Mormon: "I will not suffer that Satan shall accomplish his evil design in this thing; therefore thou shalt translate from the plates of Nephi, until ye come to that which ye have translated, which ye have retained; and behold ye shall publish it as the record of Nephi; and thus I will confound those who have altered my words. I will not suffer that they shall destroy my work;

53 And for this cause have I said: If this generation harden not their hearts, I will establish my church among them.

54 Now I do not say this to destroy my church, but I say this to build up my church;

55 Therefore, whosoever belongeth to my church need not fear, for such shall inherit the kingdom of heaven.

56 But it is they who do not fear me, neither keep my commandments but build up churches unto themselves to get gain, yea, and all those that do wickedly and build up the kingdom of the devil—yea, verily, verily, I say unto you, that it is they that I will disturb, and cause to tremble and shake to the center.

57 Behold, I am Jesus Christ, the Son of God. I came unto mine own, and mine own received me not.

58 I am the light which shineth in darkness, and the darkness comprehendeth it not.

Doctrine and Covenants 10:53–63. The Lord Will Establish His Church and His Gospel among Men

What does it mean that the Lord will establish His church? (10:53–55) "There are many references which confirm this is the time for His Church to be established in preparation for His Second Coming. . . .

"Establishing His Church is a unique assignment. We must take the gospel of Jesus Christ to all people in their own language without defiling the purity of the message. The Church must help develop leaders of integrity, leaders from whom honest people everywhere can receive inspired guidance. The Church has an equal obligation for all who have lived, who now live, and for those who will yet live on this earth. The Church must teach correct laws and ordinances, in the Lord's way, which qualify the obedient believer for eternal life. . . . [It is an] assignment from the Lord" (Earl M. Monson, "Establishing the Church," *Ensign*, Nov. 1998, 80).

How can Jesus Christ be the light of the world? (10:57–58) Sister Sharon Eubank testified: "Jesus said, 'I am the light [that] shineth in darkness, and the darkness comprehendeth it not' [D&C 6:21]. That means no matter how hard it tries, the darkness cannot put out that light. Ever. You can trust that His light will be there for you" ("Christ: The Light That Shines in Darkness," *Ensign*, May 2019, 75). See also commentary in this volume on Doctrine and Covenants 11:28.

yea, I will show unto them that my wisdom is greater than the cunning of the devil" (Joseph Smith Papers, "Printer's Manuscript of the Book of Mormon, circa August 1829–circa January 1830," [iii]).

"Nephi was commanded to keep both the large plates (a record of the more secular matters, such as the reigns of the kings, the wars, the journeyings of the people, etc.) and the small plates (a record of the spiritual experiences of the people and of God's dealings with them). He stated that he had been commanded to keep the small plates for 'a wise purpose' in the Lord. That purpose would not be fully realized until the year 1828, when Joseph Smith would be involved (with Martin Harris) in the loss of the first 116 manuscript pages of the Book of Mormon, pages translated from the large plates. At that point the Lord commanded Joseph Smith to turn to the small plates and undertake a translation of material which would cover approximately the same time period as that which had been lost (see 1 Nephi 6; Words of Mormon 1:5–7; D&C 10). Indeed, the Lord knows all things from the beginning" (McConkie and Millet, *Doctrinal Commentary on the Book of Mormon*, 1:62).

Who are the Lord's "other sheep"? (10:59–61)
"Joseph Smith knew that after Jesus Christ was resurrected from the dead, he would not only appear to representatives of the Jews in the land of Israel but also to other branches of the house of Israel, including those in the Americas and even to the lost tribes of Israel. The resurrected Jesus Christ spoke to the righteous Lehites in the Americas who survived the destruction associated with his crucifixion [see 3 Nephi 15:21, 24; 16:1–3; 17:4]" (Daniel H. Ludlow, *Selected Writings*, 550).

How can establishing the gospel help reduce contention in the world? (10:62–63) "Contention violates everything the Savior stood for and taught. I love the Lord Jesus Christ and testify that His gospel is the *only* enduring solution for peace. His gospel is a gospel of peace.

"His gospel is the *only* answer when many in the world are stunned with fear. This underscores the urgent need for us to follow the Lord's instruction to His disciples to 'go . . . into *all* the world, and preach the gospel to *every* creature' [Mark 16:15; emphasis added]. We have the sacred responsibility to share the power and peace of Jesus Christ with all who will listen and who will let God prevail in their lives" (Nelson, "Preaching the Gospel of Peace," *Liahona*, May 2022, 6).

Why does the Lord want us to know the true points of His doctrine? (10:62) "The Lord wants us to know the doctrine and to know it well. One purpose of the coming forth of the Book of Mormon is so that we can learn—mark what it says—'the very points of his doctrine' (1 Nephi 15:14). And in D&C 10:62, the Lord says he wants 'the true points of my doctrine' to be brought forth so as to lessen contention. The Lord also says that those who have only the Bible in its imperfect, altered condition are in 'that awful state of blindness' because they lack the greater knowledge they ought to have about the gospel (1 Nephi 13:32)" (Matthews, *Selected Writings*, 131).

Doctrine and Covenants 10:64–70.
He Will Gather the Repentant into His Church and Will Save the Obedient

What is this "great mystery" that the Lord will unfold? (10:64–66) "Even with repeated efforts to teach [his] truths and reaffirm [his] promises, God has not always seen his children turn to the gospel of his Son. . . .

59 I am he who said—Other sheep have I which are not of this fold—unto my disciples, and many there were that understood me not.

60 And I will show unto this people that I had other sheep, and that they were a branch of the house of Jacob;

61 And I will bring to light their marvelous works, which they did in my name;

62 Yea, and I will also bring to light my gospel which was ministered unto them, and, behold, they shall not deny that which you have received, but they shall build it up, and shall bring to light the true points of my doctrine, yea, and the only doctrine which is in me.

63 And this I do that I may establish my gospel, that there may not be so much contention; yea, Satan doth stir up the hearts of the people to contention concerning the points of my doctrine; and in these things they do err, for they do wrest the scriptures and do not understand them.

64 Therefore, I will unfold unto them this great mystery;

"So he has offered us one last covenant, given us one last testament, as part of his final outreach to fallen man. He has offered us one last written witness of his love and his mercy extended for the final time, speaking dispensationally. As one Book of Mormon prophet foresaw it, God is sending laborers into the vineyard one final time, and 'then cometh the season and the end' [Jacob 5:77]. That testament and culminating witness, that 'new covenant' offered to the children of men but once more, is the message of the Book of Mormon" (Holland, *Christ and the New Covenant*, 8–9). ✪

65 For, behold, I will gather them as a hen gathereth her chickens under her wings, if they will not harden their hearts;

66 Yea, if they will come, they may, and partake of the waters of life freely.

67 Behold, this is my doctrine—whosoever repenteth and cometh unto me, the same is my church.

How has the Lord begun to gather Israel? (10:65) President Russell M. Nelson declared: "This doctrine of the gathering is one of the important teachings of The Church of Jesus Christ of Latter-day Saints. . . . The coming forth of the Book of Mormon is a sign to the entire world that the Lord has commenced to gather Israel and fulfill covenants He made to Abraham, Isaac, and Jacob. . . .

"The Book of Mormon is central to this work. It declares the doctrine of the gathering. It causes people to learn about Jesus Christ, to believe His gospel, and to join His Church. In fact, if there were no Book of Mormon, the promised gathering of Israel would not occur" ("Gathering of Scattered Israel," *Ensign*, Nov. 2006, 80). ✪

68 Whosoever declareth more or less than this, the same is not of me, but is against me; therefore he is not of my church.

69 And now, behold, whosoever is of my church, and endureth of my church to the end, him will I establish upon my rock, and the gates of hell shall not prevail against them.

70 And now, remember the words of him who is the life and light of the world, your Redeemer, your Lord and your God. Amen.

What does it mean to declare "more or less than this"? (10:68) "When anyone strays very far from preaching the pure gospel of faith, repentance, baptism, and receiving the gift of the Holy Ghost, he or she ceases to be representative of the Church and becomes instead a potential obstacle to the faithful. All the standard works reveal the same basic and pure doctrine. To say either more or less than the Lord has said or commanded us to say—either to put words in the Lord's mouth or take them out—both distort the message the Lord wants delivered (see also D&C 93:25; 3 Nephi 11:40; 18:13). We are not justified in preaching as doctrine that which we have added to the Lord's word, neither are we justified in ignoring or failing to preach and practice what the Lord has clearly revealed" (Robinson and Garrett, *Commentary on the Doctrine and Covenants*, 1:77–78).

Introduction to Doctrine and Covenants 11

Shortly after the restoration of the Aaronic Priesthood in May 1829, the Prophet Joseph Smith's brother Samuel traveled to Harmony, Pennsylvania. Joseph and Oliver shared truths about the Book of Mormon with Samuel. Joseph recorded, "About this time my brother, Samuel H. Smith came to visit us. We informed him of what the Lord was about to do for the children of men; and to reason with him out of the Bible: We also showed him that part of the work which we had translated, and labored to persuade him concerning the Gospel of Jesus Christ which was now about to be revealed in its fulness.

"[Samuel] was not however very easily persuaded of these things, but after much enquiry and explanation, he retired to the woods, in order that by secret and fervent prayer he might obtain of a merciful God, wisdom to enable him to judge for himself: The result was that he obtained revelation for himself sufficient to convince him of the truth of our assertions to him . . . Oliver Cowdery baptized him, And [Samuel] returned to his father's house greatly glorifying and praising God, being filled with the Holy Spirit.

"Not many days afterwards, my brother Hyrum Smith came to us to enquire concerning these things, when at his earnest request, I enquired of the Lord through the Urim and Thummin, and received for him [D&C 11]" (Joseph Smith Papers, "History, circa June 1839–circa 1841 [Draft 2]," 18–19).

"Doctrine and Covenants 11 channels Hyrum's zeal. Here the Lord bridles him, careful not to break his spirit but to train him. This revelation gives Hyrum and so many others the formula for becoming successful preachers of the gospel. Promised power to convince by the Spirit if he will first learn the gospel, Hyrum spends a year searching the scriptures and helping with the publication of the Book of Mormon. When the Lord speaks to him in April 1830, the Book of Mormon is printed, the Church is organized, the marvelous work has come forth, and Hyrum has the knowledge to match his desire to declare it" (Harper, *Making Sense of the Doctrine & Covenants*, 52–53).

Doctrine and Covenants 11:1–6. Laborers in the Vineyard Will Gain Salvation

Why are the words *great* and *marvelous* used to describe the Lord's work? (11:1) These two words perfectly describe the coming forth of the Book of Mormon. It was "great" as far as the amount of scripture given to the prophet by the gift and power of God. It was "marvelous" in the sense of the overall experience being "that which exceeds natural power" (Webster, *American Dictionary* [1828], s.v. "marvelous"). This definition might also be why Joseph Smith referred to Satan's power during his first vision experience as a "power of some actual being from the unseen world, who had such marvelous [exceeding in natural] power as I had never before felt" (Joseph Smith—History 1:16).

SECTION 11

Revelation given through Joseph Smith the Prophet to his brother Hyrum Smith, at Harmony, Pennsylvania, May 1829. This revelation was received through the Urim and Thummim in answer to Joseph's supplication and inquiry. Joseph Smith's history suggests that this revelation was received after the restoration of the Aaronic Priesthood.

1 A great and marvelous work is about to come forth among the children of men.

2 Behold, I am God; give heed to my word, which is quick and powerful, sharper than a two-edged sword, to the dividing asunder of both joints and marrow; therefore give heed unto my word.

3 Behold, the field is white already to harvest; therefore, whoso desireth to reap let him thrust in his sickle with his might, and reap while the day lasts, that he may treasure up for his soul everlasting salvation in the kingdom of God.

4 Yea, whosoever will thrust in his sickle and reap, the same is called of God.

5 Therefore, if you will ask of me you shall receive; if you will knock it shall be opened unto you.

6 Now, as you have asked, behold, I say unto you, keep my commandments, and seek to bring forth and establish the cause of Zion.

How is the word of God like a two-edged sword? **(11:2)** Susan Easton Black stated: "The phrase 'sharper than a two-edged sword' descriptively illustrates the power of God to penetrate the thoughts and intents of the heart (see D&C 6:2; 11:2; 12:2; 14:2; 33:1; 85:6; Heb. 4:12; Isa. 49:2; Eph. 6:17; Rev. 2:16; 3 Ne. 11:3). The Lord can reach the repentant and rebellious alike (see D&C 85:6). With His power the Lord defends the repentant. With His strength He pierces the rebellious for embracing false ideas and carnal thoughts" (see D&C 136:33; Hel. 3:29)" (*400 Questions and Answers*, 44). See also commentary in this volume on Doctrine and Covenants 6:2.

What might the "sickle" represent in the harvest? **(11:3–4)** A sickle is a curved blade used in the harvesting of grain. The imagery of harvesting reminds us of the work of the gathering of Israel. Elder D. Todd Christofferson provided the following insight to new mission presidents: "The Book of Mormon carries out the Lord's purposes in this gospel dispensation by being the Lord's 'tool of the harvest' of the gathering of Israel, by being an instrument of conversion for this dispensation, and in drawing people closer to God....

"Given, then, the power of the Book of Mormon comes as we allow the book to speak for itself, the question for you is, how will [you] get people to read the Book of Mormon and also to pray with real intent about its truthfulness?"(Lloyd, "Elder Christofferson Says"). See also commentary in this volume on Doctrine and Covenants 4:4.

What Is the "Great and Marvelous Work" Prophesied? (Doctrine and Covenants 11:1)

"This marvelous work and wonder, to which the Lord referred, was heralded by the coming forth of the Book of Mormon. The Lord, in speaking to Nephi, foretold the time when he would remember his covenants to the house of Israel and recover them a second time (2 Ne. 29:1). When the Savior visited among the Nephites, following his resurrection in Jerusalem, he referred to the coming forth of the Book of Mormon and the great and marvelous work which was to come among the Gentiles (3 Ne. 21:9). . . . The Book of Mormon serves as a 'standard' of another kind as well, since it is closely associated with 'the ensign,' as translated in the KJV [King James Version], which the prophet Isaiah foretold would be lifted up to the nations in the last days (Isa. 11:12; 18:3). This concept is used throughout the KJV book of Isaiah but is sometimes translated 'banner' (Isa. 13:2), or 'standard' (Isa. 49:22; 62:10)" (Nyman, "Great and Marvelous Work," 74).

"In February of 1829 the Lord told Joseph Smith, Sr. through his son, the Prophet Joseph Smith: 'A marvelous work is about to come forth among the children of men' (D&C 4:1). In April, May, and June of that same year, Oliver Cowdery, Hyrum Smith, Joseph Knight, and David Whitmer were also informed of this same event through the same medium, Joseph Smith the Prophet, but with added emphasis—calling it 'a great and marvelous work' (D&C 6:1; 11:1; 12:1; 14:1). . . .

"While the Book of Mormon is an essential part of the marvelous work to which the Lord referred in these revelations, the subsequent events which led to the establishment of the Church and restoration of the fulness of the gospel are also a continuation of that great work and may collectively be referred to as the great and marvelous work" (Nyman, "Great and Marvelous Work," 73, 78).

Doctrine and Covenants 11:7–14. Seek Wisdom, Cry Repentance, Trust in the Spirit

What are the "mysteries of God"? (11:7) "Mysteries of God are spiritual truths known only by revelation. God reveals His mysteries to those who are obedient to the gospel. Some of God's mysteries are yet to be revealed" (Guide to the Scriptures, "Mysteries of God"). See also commentary in this volume on Doctrine and Covenants 6:7.

Why did the Lord counsel Hyrum Smith to "say nothing but repentance unto this generation"? (11:9) President Russell M. Nelson taught, "The gospel of Jesus Christ is a gospel of repentance [see D&C 13:1]. Because of the Savior's Atonement, His gospel provides an invitation to keep changing, growing, and becoming more pure. It is a gospel of hope, of healing, and of progress. Thus, the gospel is a message of *joy*! Our spirits rejoice with every small step forward we take" ("Welcome Message," *Liahona*, May 2021, 7).

Elder D. Todd Christofferson has taught: "Only repentance leads to the sunlit uplands of a better life. And, of course, only through repentance do we gain access to the atoning grace of Jesus Christ and salvation" ("Divine Gift of Repentance," *Ensign*, Nov. 2011, 38). See also commentary in this volume on Doctrine and Covenants 6:9.

What was Hyrum Smith's promised gift? (11:10–14) The Lord promised Hyrum "a spiritual gift to know whatever he righteously desires by faith and the power of the Holy Ghost. The Lord tells him to trust the Spirit and promises to enlighten his mind and fill

7 Seek not for riches but for wisdom; and, behold, the mysteries of God shall be unfolded unto you, and then shall you be made rich. Behold, he that hath eternal life is rich.

8 Verily, verily, I say unto you, even as you desire of me so it shall be done unto you; and, if you desire, you shall be the means of doing much good in this generation.

9 Say nothing but repentance unto this generation. Keep my commandments, and assist to bring forth my work, according to my commandments, and you shall be blessed.

10 Behold, thou hast a gift, or thou shalt have a gift if thou wilt desire of me in faith, with an honest heart, believing in the power of Jesus Christ, or in my power which speaketh unto thee;

Hyrum Smith, a Devoted Brother to the Prophet Joseph Smith

President M. Russell Ballard, a descendant of Hyrum Smith, has commented frequently about the contributions and legacy of Hyrum and his relationship to his brother Joseph. He wrote: "There is much in this noble man's character that is worthy of emulation. I would like to be as loyal to my family and friends as Hyrum was to his younger brother Joseph. One historian noted that Hyrum 'guarded his younger and more favored brother as tenderly as if the Prophet had been his son instead of his younger brother' [Brewster, *Doctrine & Covenants Encyclopedia* (2012), 529]. When the boy Joseph was stricken with a serious leg infection, it was his teenage brother Hyrum who tenderly applied pressure to the afflicted limb night and day for more than a week.

Hyrum Smith

"President Joseph Fielding Smith observed, 'It seems almost, from the tender solicitude Hyrum displayed for Joseph that he felt in some way that there had been placed upon him a guardianship for his younger brother' [*Life*

11 For, behold, it is I that speak; behold, I am the light which shineth in darkness, and by my power I give these words unto thee.

12 And now, verily, verily, I say unto thee, put your trust in that Spirit which leadeth to do good—yea, to do justly, to walk humbly, to judge righteously; and this is my Spirit.

13 Verily, verily, I say unto you, I will impart unto you of my Spirit, which shall enlighten your mind, which shall fill your soul with joy;

14 And then shall ye know, or by this shall you know, all things whatsoever you desire of me, which are pertaining unto things of righteousness, in faith believing in me that you shall receive.

him with joy" (Harper, *Making Sense of the Doctrine & Covenants*, 52). See also commentary in this volume on Doctrine and Covenants 11:22; 124:15.

How can trusting in the Spirit help you do good and become more like Jesus Christ? (11:12) Just like Hyrum Smith, "There are many ways [for us] to build the kingdom of God as covenant-making, covenant-keeping disciples of Jesus Christ. As His faithful disciple, you can receive personal inspiration and revelation, consistent with His commandments, that is tailored to you. You have unique missions and roles to perform in life and will be given unique guidance to fulfill them. . . .

"Each one of us, regardless of age or circumstance, can strive to *seek, receive, and act*. As you follow this eternal pattern ordained for our day, you will draw nearer to Jesus Christ—His love, His light, His direction, His peace, and His healing and enabling power. And you will increase your spiritual capacity to become an everyday instrument of His hands in accomplishing His great work (Craig, "Spiritual Capacity," *Ensign*, Nov. 2019, 21).

What are some ways the Holy Ghost enlightens our minds? (11:12–13) Elder Quentin L. Cook explained: "Although [the Holy Ghost's] impact can be incredibly powerful, it most often comes quietly as a still, small voice [see Helaman 5:30; D&C 85:6]. The scriptures include many examples of how the Spirit influences our minds, including speaking peace to our minds [see D&C 6:23], occupying our minds [see D&C 128:1], enlightening our minds [see D&C 11:13], and even sending a voice to our minds [see Enos 1:10]" ("Blessing of Continuing Revelation," *Ensign*, May 2020, 99). See also commentary in this volume on Doctrine and Covenants 8:2. ⊕

of Joseph F. Smith, 39]. Such loyalty is rare. Remember how the elder sons of Jacob treated their younger brother, Joseph? They were so jealous of his favored position that they sold him into slavery and convinced their grief-stricken father that he had been killed by wild beasts. . . .

"But you'll find none of that in the recorded history of Hyrum's relationship with Joseph. Rather, you'll find a lifetime of loving devotion, service, kindness, and constancy" ("Legacy of Hyrum," *Ensign*, Sep. 1994, 57).

The Prophet Joseph said of his brother Hyrum, "I could pray in my heart that all my brethren were like unto my beloved brother Hyrum, who possesses the mildness of a lamb, and the integrity of a Job, and in short, the meekness and humility of Christ; and I love him with that love that is stronger than death, for I never had occasion to rebuke him, nor he me" (Joseph Smith Papers, "Journal, 1835–1836," 76).

Doctrine and Covenants 11:15–22. Keep the Commandments, and Study the Lord's Word

Why did the Lord need to explain to Hyrum that he was not yet called to preach? (11:15–17) "One cannot be self-appointed to preach in God's kingdom. In the early stages of the Restoration, while the Book of Mormon was still being translated, Hyrum Smith wanted to go forth immediately and issue the warning voice. He was told by the Lord: 'You need not suppose that you are called to preach until you are called' (D&C 11:15). In giving his law to the Church, the Lord declared: 'It shall not be given to anyone to go forth to preach my gospel, or to build up my church, except he be ordained by someone who has authority' (D&C 42:11)" (Garrett, "Missionary Work," 131).

Where do we find the Lord's doctrine? (11:16) Sister Ardeth G. Kapp taught: "'True points,' like stars in the heavens to guide us, are readily available for anyone earnestly seeking direction. These true points of doctrine are found in the true church. Conversion to the truth comes by accepting true doctrine, and the truth of doctrine can be known only by revelation gained as a result of obedience. The Savior taught: 'My doctrine is not mine, but his that sent me. If any man will do his will, he shall know of the doctrine, whether it be of God, or whether I speak of myself'" ("Drifting, Dreaming, Directing," 198).

What does it mean to "cleave"? (11:19) "This verb [*cleave*] has two almost contradictory meanings: 'to split or separate,' as in cleaving firewood, and 'to bond or stick to,' as in spouses cleaving to one another. The usage here might be understood colloquially as a command to 'stick like glue'" (Robinson and Garrett, *Commentary on the Doctrine and Covenants*, 1:82–83).

What is the work that all people are called to fulfill? (11:20) Elder David A. Bednar clarified: "One of the most well-known and frequently cited passages of scripture is found in Moses 1:39. This verse clearly and concisely describes the work of the Eternal Father: 'For behold, this is *my work* and my glory—to bring to pass the immortality and eternal life of man' (emphasis added).

"A companion scripture found in the Doctrine and Covenants describes with equal clarity and conciseness our primary work as the sons and daughters of the Eternal Father. Interestingly, this verse does not seem to be as well-known and is not quoted with

15 Behold, I command you that you need not suppose that you are called to preach until you are called.

16 Wait a little longer, until you shall have my word, my rock, my church, and my gospel, that you may know of a surety my doctrine.

17 And then, behold, according to your desires, yea, even according to your faith shall it be done unto you.

18 Keep my commandments; hold your peace; appeal unto my Spirit;

19 Yea, cleave unto me with all your heart, that you may assist in bringing to light those things of which has been spoken—yea, the translation of my work; be patient until you shall accomplish it.

20 Behold, this is your work, to keep my commandments, yea, with all your might, mind and strength.

great frequency. 'Behold, this is *your work*, to keep my commandments, yea, with all your might, mind and strength' (D&C 11:20; emphasis added)" ("Tender Mercies of the Lord," *Ensign*, May 2005, 101). ☉

21 Seek not to declare my word, but first seek to obtain my word, and then shall your tongue be loosed; then, if you desire, you shall have my Spirit and my word, yea, the power of God unto the convincing of men.

What can we learn from Hyrum's obedience to the Lord's command to seek His word? (11:21) President M. Russell Ballard noted: "Hyrum's life is a witness to his obedience to this instruction. To the very last day of his life, he devoted himself to obtaining the word through study of the scriptures. In Carthage Jail, he read and commented on extracts from the Book of Mormon. The scriptures were obviously part of Hyrum's being, and he turned to them during times when he needed comfort and strength the most.

"Just think of the spiritual strength we could gain in our lives and how much more effective we would be as teachers, missionaries, and friends if we studied the scriptures regularly. I am sure we, like Hyrum, will be able to endure our greatest trials if we search the word of God as he did" ("Hyrum Smith," 79). ☉

22 But now hold your peace; study my word which hath gone forth among the children of men, and also study my word which shall come forth among the children of men, or that which is now translating, yea, until you have obtained all which I shall grant unto the children of men in this generation, and then shall all things be added thereto.

Why was Hyrum Smith commanded to hold his peace for now? (11:22) "The special gift given Hyrum would center in his ability to declare with great power the message of the Restoration. Given that we cannot teach that which we do not know, it was required that he prepare himself that he might be a suitable companion of the Holy Spirit. The scriptures were to constitute the foundation of his understanding. Hyrum was to become a student of the Bible ('my word which hath gone forth among the children of men') and the Book of Mormon ('my word which shall come forth among the children of men'). Building upon the foundation of these books, he would enjoy the Spirit

How Can We Prepare to Effectively Teach the Gospel? (Doctrine and Covenants 11:21)

President Jeffrey R. Holland taught, "No eternal learning can take place without the quickening of the Spirit from heaven. So, parents, teachers, and leaders, we must face our tasks the way Moses faced the promised land. Knowing he could not succeed any other way, Moses said to Jehovah, 'If thy presence go not with me, carry us not up hence' [Ex. 33:15].

"That is what our members really want when they gather in a meeting or come into a classroom anyway. Most people don't come to church looking merely for a few new gospel facts or to see old friends, though all of that is important. They come seeking a spiritual experience. They want peace. They want their faith fortified and their hope renewed. They want, in short, to be nourished by the good word of God, to be strengthened by the powers of heaven. Those of us who are called upon to speak or teach or lead have an obligation to help provide that, as best we possibly can. We can only do that if we ourselves are striving to know God, if we ourselves are continually seeking the light of His Only Begotten Son. Then, if our hearts are right, if we are as clean as we can be, if we have prayed and wept and prepared and worried until we don't know what more we can do, God can say to us as He did to Alma and the sons of Mosiah: 'Lift up thy head and rejoice. . . . I will give unto you success' [Alma 8:15; 26:27]" ("Teacher Come from God," *Ensign*, May 1998, 26).

of revelation" (McConkie and Ostler, *Revelations of the Restoration*, 114). See also commentary in this volume on Doctrine and Covenants 11:10.

Doctrine and Covenants 11:23–27. Deny Not the Spirit of Revelation and of Prophecy

Why is it vital for us to build upon the rock of the gospel? (11:24) President Russell M. Nelson testified: "These *are* the latter days. If you and I are to withstand the forthcoming perils and pressures, it is imperative that we each have a *firm* spiritual foundation built upon the rock of our Redeemer, Jesus Christ.

"So I ask each of you, how firm is *your* foundation? And what reinforcements to your testimony and understanding of the gospel are needed?

"The temple lies at the center of strengthening our faith and spiritual fortitude because the Savior and His doctrine are the very heart of the temple. . . .

"Please believe me when I say that when your spiritual foundation is built solidly upon Jesus Christ, you have *no need to fear*" ("Temple and Your Spiritual Foundation," *Liahona*, Nov. 2021, 93, 96).

Why can it be spiritually dangerous to deny the spirit of revelation and prophecy? (11:25) "To deny the Spirit of revelation is not only to close the windows of heaven to further light and knowledge but also to lose the understanding of the divine word already given. 'I will give unto the children of men line upon line, precept upon precept, here a little and there a little; and blessed are those who hearken unto my precepts, and lend an ear unto my counsel, for they shall learn wisdom; for unto him that receiveth I will give more; and from them that shall say, We have enough, from them shall be taken away even that which they have' (2 Nephi 28:30)" (McConkie and Ostler, *Revelations of the Restoration*, 115).

Doctrine and Covenants 11:28–30. Those Who Receive Christ Become the Sons of God

How is Jesus Christ "the life and the light of the world"? (11:28) President Dallin H. Oaks once explained: "Jesus Christ is the light and life of the world because all things were made by him. Under the direction and according to the plan of God the Father, Jesus Christ is the Creator, the source of the light and life of all things. Through modern revelation we have

23 Behold thou art Hyrum, my son; seek the kingdom of God, and all things shall be added according to that which is just.

24 Build upon my rock, which is my gospel;

25 Deny not the spirit of revelation, nor the spirit of prophecy, for wo unto him that denieth these things;

26 Therefore, treasure up in your heart until the time which is in my wisdom that you shall go forth.

27 Behold, I speak unto all who have good desires, and have thrust in their sickle to reap.

28 Behold, I am Jesus Christ, the Son of God. I am the life and the light of the world.

29 I am the same who came unto mine own and mine own received me not;

the testimony of John, who bore record that Jesus Christ is 'the light and the Redeemer of the world, the Spirit of truth, who came into the world, because the world was made by him, and in him was the life of men and the light of men.

"'The worlds were made by him, men were made by him; all things were made by him, and through him, and of him' (D&C 93:9–10)" ("Light and Life of the World," *Ensign*, Nov. 1987, 63). See also commentary in this volume on Doctrine and Covenants 10:57–58.

30 But verily, verily, I say unto you, that as many as receive me, to them will I give power to become the sons of God, even to them that believe on my name. Amen.

How is this invitation to become a son or daughter of God different from our divine identity as God's children? (11:30) Elder D. Todd Christofferson clarified: "The scriptures use these terms in two ways. In one sense, we are all literal spirit children of our Heavenly Father. In another sense, God's sons and daughters are those who have been born again through the Atonement of Christ" (Guide to the Scriptures, "Sons and Daughters of God").

"It was Jesus who stated that entry into the kingdom of God requires that one be born again—born of water and of the Spirit (see John 3:3–5). His teaching about a physical and a spiritual baptism helps us understand that both our own action and the intervention of divine power are needed for this transformative rebirth—for the change from natural man to saint (see Mosiah 3:19)" ("Born Again," *Ensign*, May 2008, 77). See also commentary in this volume on Doctrine and Covenants 34:1–2.

Introduction to Doctrine and Covenants 12

In May of 1829, the Prophet Joseph Smith related that while he and Oliver Cowdery were translating the Book of Mormon, in Harmony, Pennsylvania, "an old Gentleman [came] to visit us, of whose name I wish to make honorable mention; Mr Joseph Knight [Sr.] of Colesville, Broom County, Penn [New York]; who having heard of the manner in which we were occupying our time, very kindly and considerately brought us, a quantity of provisions, in order that we might not be interrupted in the work of translation, by the want of such necessaries of life: and I would just mention here (as in duty bound) that he several times brought us supplies (a distance of at least thirty miles) which enabled us to continue the work when otherwise we must have relinquished it for a season.

"Being very anxious to know his duty as to this work, I enquired of the Lord for [Joseph Knight, Sr.], and obtained as follows [D&C 12]" (Joseph Smith Papers, "History, 1838–1856, volume A-1," 20–21).

Among the great truths we learn from Doctrine and Covenants 12 are what qualifies us for God's work. "Wealth, intelligence, or education do not qualify us for service in the kingdom of God. Instead, characteristics of humility, love, faith, hope, charity, and temperance qualify us for the kingdom of God and the companionship of the Holy Ghost" (Woodger, *Essential Doctrine and Covenants Companion*, 22).

Doctrine and Covenants 12:1–6. Laborers in the Vineyard Are to Gain Salvation

What might be the distinction between the "marvelous work and a wonder" and the "great and marvelous work"? (12:1) "In February of 1829 the Lord told Joseph Smith Sr. through his son, the Prophet Joseph Smith: 'A marvelous work is about to come forth among the children of men' (D&C 4:1). In April, May, and June of that same year [other brethren] were also informed of this same event ... but with added emphasis—calling it 'a great and marvelous work' (D&C 6:1; 11:1; 12:1; 14:1). . . . [The] marvelous work and wonder, to which the Lord referred, was heralded by the coming forth of the Book of Mormon" (Nyman, "Great and Marvelous Work," 73, 74). ◉

What is the symbolic significance of the two-edged sword? (12:2) See commentary in this volume on Doctrine and Covenants 6:2 and 11:2.

SECTION 12

Revelation given through Joseph Smith the Prophet to Joseph Knight Sr., at Harmony, Pennsylvania, May 1829. Joseph Knight believed the declarations of Joseph Smith concerning his possession of the Book of Mormon plates and the work of translation then in progress and several times had given material assistance to Joseph Smith and his scribe, which enabled them to continue translating. At Joseph Knight's request, the Prophet inquired of the Lord and received the revelation.

1 A great and marvelous work is about to come forth among the children of men.

2 Behold, I am God; give heed to my word, which is quick and powerful, sharper than a two-edged sword, to the dividing asunder of both joints and marrow; therefore, give heed unto my word.

3 Behold, the field is white already to harvest; therefore, whoso desireth to reap let him thrust in his sickle with his might, and reap while the day lasts, that he may treasure up for his soul everlasting salvation in the kingdom of God.

4 Yea, whosoever will thrust in his sickle and reap, the same is called of God.

5 Therefore, if you will ask of me you shall receive; if you will knock it shall be opened unto you.

6 Now, as you have asked, behold, I say unto you, keep my commandments, and seek to bring forth and establish the cause of Zion.

How does bringing salvation to others treasure up salvation for our own soul? (12:3–4) President Henry B. Eyring explained: "When you give your heart to inviting people to come unto Christ, your heart will be changed. You will be doing His work for Him. You will find that He keeps His promise to be one with you in your service. You will come to know Him. And in time you will come to be like Him and 'be perfected in him' (Moroni 10:32). By helping others come unto Him, you will find that you have come unto Him yourself" ("Come unto Christ," *Ensign*, Mar. 2008, 52). ⊕

Why is it important to know how to "ask" and "knock"? (12:5–6) Elder Richard G. Scott clarified: "Life in today's world can be at times so complicated and the challenges so overwhelming as to be beyond our individual capacity to resolve them. We all need help from the Lord. Yet there are many individuals who don't know how to receive that help. They feel their urgent pleas for help have often gone unattended. . . . [God] has said, 'Ask, and ye shall receive; knock, and it shall be opened unto you.' . . .

"Now, to summarize, blessings come when we—

"Ask the Father in the name of Christ

"Diligently keep His commandments

"Ask with faith in Christ

"Ask for that which is right

"Harden not our hearts

"Express gratitude" ("Obtaining Help from the Lord," *Ensign*, Nov. 1991, 84). See also commentary in this volume on Doctrine and Covenants 4:7.

Joseph Knight Sr.

Joseph Smith had many friends whom he loved. One such was Joseph Knight Sr. On August 23, 1842, the Prophet wrote a tribute to him: "'For fifteen years [Joseph Knight, Sr.] has been faithful and true, and even-handed and exemplary, and virtuous and kind, never deviating to the right hand or to the left. Behold he is a righteous man, may God Almighty lengthen out the old man's days; and may his trembling, tortured, and broken body be renewed, and in the vigor of health turn upon him, if it be Thy will, consistently, O God; and it shall be said of him, by the sons of Zion, while there is one of them remaining, that this man was a faithful man in Israel; therefore his name shall never be forgotten.'

"Joseph Knight, Sr., was born 3 November 1772 at Oakham, Worcester, Massachusetts. In 1809 he moved to Bainbridge, Chenango County, New York and two years later to Colesville, Broome County, New York where he remained for nineteen years. He owned a farm, a gristmill and carding machine, and according to his son Newel, 'was not rich, yet possessed enough of this world's goods to secure to himself and family the necessaries and comforts of life.' His family consisted of three sons and four daughters. . . .

"Although not numbered among those present at the organization of the church in April 1930, Joseph Knight was baptized in June of that year. His family formed the nucleus of a small branch of the Church in Colesville, New York. In 1831 he moved with the Colesville Saints to Kirtland, Ohio, and a few months later continued with them to Independence, Missouri, where he helped pioneer the Latter-day Saint settlement of that state. Joseph Knight died on 3 February 1847 at Mt. Pisgah, Iowa, during the Mormon exodus from Illinois" (Jessee, "Joseph Knight's Recollection," 29, 30).

Doctrine and Covenants 12:7–9. All Who Desire and Are Qualified May Assist in the Lord's Work

How can we best serve those "entrusted to [our] care"? (12:8) Elder Dieter F. Uchtdorf said: "It is [Christ's] work, in which we are privileged to assist. 'And no one can assist in this work except he shall be humble and full of love' [D&C 12:8]. . . .

"We do not act for personal gain, but rather we seek to serve and to lift up others. We lead not by force but through 'persuasion, . . . long-suffering, . . . gentleness and meekness, and by love unfeigned' [D&C 121:41]" ("Joy of the Priesthood," *Ensign*, Nov. 2012, 59).

Sister Barbara Thompson pointed out: "[Those we minister to] have been entrusted to our care. Let us have love and compassion and thus make a difference in the lives of those who have been entrusted to our care" ("And of Some Have Compassion," *Ensign*, Nov. 2010, 121).

How could being temperate relate to being humble and full of love? (12:8) Elder Kent D. Watson explained: "In a spiritual sense, temperance is a divine attribute of Jesus Christ. . . .

"Being temperate means to carefully examine our expectations and desires, to be diligent and patient in seeking righteous goals. . . .

"Tempered glass, like tempered steel, undergoes a well-controlled heating process which increases strength. Thus, when tempered glass is under stress, it will not easily break into jagged shards that can injure.

"Likewise, a temperate soul—one who is humble and full of love—is also a person of increased spiritual strength. With increased spiritual strength, we are able to develop self-mastery and to live with moderation. We learn to control, or temper, our anger, vanity, and pride" (Watson, "Being Temperate in All Things," *Ensign*, Nov. 2009, 38).

7 Behold, I speak unto you, and also to all those who have desires to bring forth and establish this work;

8 And no one can assist in this work except he shall be humble and full of love, having faith, hope, and charity, being temperate in all things, whatsoever shall be entrusted to his care.

9 Behold, I am the light and the life of the world, that speak these words, therefore give heed with your might, and then you are called. Amen.

"As Joseph and Oliver were translating from the plates, they read the Savior's instructions to the Nephites regarding baptism for the remission of sins. On May 15 [1829], they went to a wooded area near the Prophet's home [in Harmony Township, Pennsylvania] to ask the Lord for more understanding about this important ordinance. 'Our souls were drawn out in mighty prayer,' Oliver Cowdery recalled, 'to know how we might obtain the blessings of baptism and of the Holy Spirit, according to the order of God, and we diligently sought for the right of the fathers and the authority of the holy priesthood, and the power to administer in the same'" (*Joseph Smith* [manual], 79–80).

In his 1838 history, the Prophet Joseph Smith recorded, "We still continued the work of translation, when, in the ensuing month (May, 1829), we on a certain day went into the woods to pray and inquire of the Lord respecting baptism for the remission of sins, that we found mentioned in the translation of the plates. While we were thus employed, praying and calling upon the Lord, a messenger from heaven [John the Baptist] descended in a cloud of light, and having laid his hands upon us, he ordained us" (Joseph Smith—History 1:68).

In October 1834, Oliver Cowdery provided additional detail about this sacred event: "'On a sudden, as from the midst of eternity, the voice of the Redeemer spake peace to us, while the veil was parted and the angel of God came down clothed with glory, and delivered the anxiously looked for message, and the keys of the Gospel of repentance. . . .

"'The assurance that we were in the presence of an angel, the certainty that we heard the voice of Jesus, and the truth unsullied as it flowed from a pure personage, dictated by the will of God, is to me past description, and I shall ever look upon this expression of the Savior's goodness with wonder and thanksgiving while I am permitted to tarry'" (Joseph Smith—History 1:71, note).

"The priesthood was both essential and central to the Restoration. Women recognized the priesthood as the eternal power and authority of God, used to bless, redeem, and exalt His daughters and sons. They recognized Joseph Smith as one given authority to restore the priesthood as it had been organized in the ancient Church. They studied the Bible and searched for truth in regard to the administration of the Church of God and to the blessings afforded to them as daughters of God.

"The restoration of the priesthood through Joseph Smith was indeed a marvelous series of events. Women testified of being both participants in and recipients of the priesthood in the latter days" (Johnson and Reeder, *Witness of Women*, 59).

SECTION 13

An extract from Joseph Smith's history recounting the ordination of the Prophet and Oliver Cowdery to the Aaronic Priesthood near Harmony, Pennsylvania, May 15, 1829. The ordination was done by the hands of an angel who announced himself as John, the same that is called John the Baptist in the New Testament. The angel explained that he was acting under the direction of Peter, James, and John, the ancient Apostles, who held the keys of the higher priesthood, which was called the Priesthood of Melchizedek. The promise was given to Joseph and Oliver that in due time this higher priesthood would be conferred upon them. (See section 27:7–8, 12.)

Doctrine and Covenants 13. The Keys and Powers of the Aaronic Priesthood Are Set Forth

Why was John the Baptist sent to restore the Aaronic Priesthood? (13:1) "The last man to hold the keys of the Aaronic Priesthood anciently was John the Baptist. Because the major function of the Aaronic Priesthood is to prepare Israel for receiving the Melchizedek Priesthood, it is entirely fitting that John should prepare the way for Christ, who holds the keys of the Melchizedek Priesthood. Thus, John goes before the Savior and prepares the way for him, the preparatory priesthood preceding the higher priesthood. John prepared the way for the Savior in his mortal ministry, in his ministry to the spirits in the postmortal spirit world, and in the restoration of the gospel in the latter days before Jesus' second coming (see Matthew 17:11–13)" (Robinson and Garrett, *Commentary on the Doctrine and Covenants*, 1:89–90).

Who are the sons of Levi? (13:1) "In a broad sense, a son of Levi is one who is of the posterity of Levi, the son of Jacob and the father of that tribe of Israel charged with the responsibility of ministering the priesthood to the other tribes (Gen. 29:34; Num. 3:12; 8:14–26). More specifically, however, sons of Levi are those brethren who hold the priesthood in our day [*Doctrines of Salvation*, 3:93; *Doctrine and Covenants Compendium*, 81]. At some future day, these 'sons' will be called upon to reinstate the law of sacrifice in order that the 'restoration of all things' may be accomplished [Acts 3:19–21]" (Brewster, *Doctrine & Covenants Encyclopedia* [2012], 545).

1 Upon you my fellow servants, in the name of Messiah I confer the Priesthood of Aaron, which holds the keys of the ministering of angels, and of the gospel of repentance, and of baptism by immersion for the remission of sins; and this shall never be taken again from the earth, until the sons of Levi do offer again an offering unto the Lord in righteousness.

What Are the "Keys of the Ministering of Angels"? (Doctrine and Covenants 13:1)

President Gordon B. Hinckley taught: "[John] conferred the Priesthood of Aaron—Aaron who held this marvelous power and authority. John went on to say that this priesthood 'holds the keys of the ministering of angels.' What are keys? They represent the authority to unlock and make available certain specific and wonderful blessings including the 'ministering of angels.' Every boy who holds the Aaronic Priesthood is entitled to the ministering of angels if he lives worthy of it. That means that he may call upon divine power for protection, for guidance, for comfort, for strength. I believe that John was not using idle words when he spoke of ministering angels. I think he was conferring a resource of priceless worth to be made available to those holding the priesthood provided they sought it and lived for it" ("Upon You My Fellow Servants," *Liahona*, May 1989, 6).

President Dallin H. Oaks explained: "Through the Aaronic Priesthood ordinances of baptism and the sacrament, we are cleansed of our sins and promised that if we keep our covenants we will always have His Spirit to be with us. I believe that promise not only refers to the Holy Ghost but also to the ministering of angels, for 'angels speak by the power of the Holy Ghost; wherefore, they speak the words of Christ' (2 Ne. 32:3). So it is that those who hold the Aaronic Priesthood open the door for all Church members who worthily partake of the sacrament to enjoy the companionship of the Spirit of the Lord and the ministering of angels" ("Aaronic Priesthood and the Sacrament," *Ensign*, Nov. 1998, 39).

What is the offering that will be made in righteousness? (13:1) "*All things* are to be restored since the beginning. . . . The law of sacrifice will have to be restored, or *all things* which were decreed by the Lord would not be restored. It will be necessary, therefore, for the sons of Levi, who offered the blood sacrifices anciently in Israel, to offer such a sacrifice again to round out and complete this ordinance in this dispensation. . . .

"The sacrifice of animals will be done to complete the restoration when the temple spoken of is built; at the beginning of the millennium, or in the restoration, blood sacrifices will be performed long enough to complete the fulness of the restoration in this dispensation. Afterwards sacrifice will be of some other character" (Joseph Fielding Smith, *Doctrines of Salvation*, 3:94). ⊕

Introduction to Doctrine and Covenants 14

Joseph Smith received this revelation sometime in June 1829 after arriving in Fayette, New York, from Harmony, Pennsylvania. (For a map showing the locations of Fayette and Harmony, see Map 3 in the Appendix.)

"[The Prophet Joseph Smith] dictated this revelation for David Whitmer after Whitmer traveled to Harmony, Pennsylvania, and helped [Joseph] and Oliver Cowdery move to Peter Whitmer Sr.'s house in Fayette. . . . The move was undertaken to facilitate completion of the Book of Mormon translation, which had caused [Joseph] trouble with both Isaac Hale and other residents in Harmony. David Whitmer had heard about [Joseph Smith] in the fall of 1828 when rumors about [his] retrieval of the plates circulated widely in the Palmyra, New York, region. While in Palmyra, Whitmer discussed the story of [Joseph] and the plates with Cowdery and others but initially supposed it was a rumor. Cowdery, who was acquainted with the [Smith family], told Whitmer that 'there must be some truth in the story of the plates, and that he intended to investigate the matter.' Several months later, Cowdery informed Whitmer that he intended to go to Harmony to see [Joseph] about the plates. On his journey, Cowdery stopped in Fayette to visit Whitmer and promised to write to him regarding what he learned. Cowdery sent at least three letters to Whitmer from Harmony, the last of which directed Whitmer to bring his wagon to Harmony and move [Joseph] and Cowdery to Fayette" (Joseph Smith Papers, Historical Introduction to "Revelation, June 1829–A [D&C 14]," 32).

SECTION 14

Revelation given through Joseph Smith the Prophet to David Whitmer, at Fayette, New York, June 1829. The Whitmer family had become greatly interested in the translating of the Book of Mormon. The Prophet established his residence at the home of Peter Whitmer Sr., where he dwelt until the work of translation was carried to completion and the copyright on the forthcoming book was secured. Three of the Whitmer sons, each having received a testimony as to the genuineness of the work, became deeply concerned over the matter of their individual

Doctrine and Covenants 14:1–6. Laborers in the Vineyard Will Gain Salvation

What is the "great and marvelous work"? (14:1)
"What is the work of our Father in Heaven? And how do we *serve* Him? 'For behold, this is my *work* . . . to bring to pass the immortality and eternal life of man' [Moses 1:39; emphasis added]. . . .

"Simply and respectfully said, Father's employment is to save the souls of His children. His efforts are to assist and help them become like Him. Are we aware and do we realize that when we are called to His work we are actually being invited to labor with Him for the souls of men? With such an understanding, how could any of us refuse to work with Him and say 'No' to His authorized servants who extend His calls?" (Otten and Caldwell, *Sacred Truths*, 1:31). See also commentary in this volume on Doctrine and Covenants 4:1 and 11:1.

What is the significance of the two-edged sword? (14:2) See commentary in this volume on Doctrine and Covenants 6:2 and 11:2.

How can we participate in the great latter-day harvest of souls? (14:3) "I invite you to consider ways you can love, share, and invite. As you do so, you will feel a measure of joy knowing that you are heeding the words of our beloved Savior.

"What I am urging you to do is not a new program. You have heard these principles before. This is not the 'next big thing' the Church is asking you to do. These three things are merely an extension of who we already are as disciples of Jesus Christ.

"No name badge or letter is required.

"No formal calling is needed.

"As these three things become a natural part of who we are and how we live, they will become an automatic, unforced expression of genuine love" (Stevenson, "Love, Share, Invite," *Liahona*, May 2022, 87). ✪

duty. *This revelation and the two following (sections 15 and 16) were given in answer to an inquiry through the Urim and Thummim. David Whitmer later became one of the Three Witnesses to the Book of Mormon.*

1 A great and marvelous work is about to come forth unto the children of men.

2 Behold, I am God; give heed to my word, which is quick and powerful, sharper than a two-edged sword, to the dividing asunder of both joints and marrow; therefore give heed unto my word.

3 Behold, the field is white already to harvest; therefore, whoso desireth to reap let him thrust in his sickle with his might, and reap while the day lasts, that he may treasure up for his soul everlasting salvation in the kingdom of God.

4 Yea, whosoever will thrust in his sickle and reap, the same is called of God.

5 Therefore, if you will ask of me you shall receive; if you will knock it shall be opened unto you.

6 Seek to bring forth and establish my Zion. Keep my commandments in all things.

Doctrine and Covenants 14:7–8. Eternal Life Is the Greatest of God's Gifts

7 And, if you keep my commandments and endure to the end you shall have eternal life, which gift is the greatest of all the gifts of God.

What is one connection between the concept of enduring to the end and becoming like Jesus Christ? (14:7) "Some think of enduring to the end as simply suffering through challenges. It is so much more than that—it is the process of coming unto Christ and being perfected in Him. . . .

"Enduring to the end means that we have planted our lives firmly on gospel soil, staying in the mainstream of the Church, humbly serving our fellow men, living Christlike lives, and keeping our covenants. Those who endure are balanced, consistent, humble, constantly improving, and without guile. Their testimony is not based on worldly reasons—it is based on truth, knowledge, experience, and the Spirit" (Wirthlin, "Press On," *Ensign*, Nov. 2004, 101).

How might enduring to the end be a warning to David Whitmer? (14:7) "The Lord seems to be warning David Whitmer of the need to endure to the end. This admonition seems appropriate in view of his being a special witness to The Book of Mormon and his subsequent excommunication from the Church on April 13, 1838" (Roy W. Doxey, *Doctrine and Covenants Speaks*, 1:79).

"Although [David Whitmer] never denied his testimony of the Book of Mormon, he was a constant critic of Joseph Smith and died outside the Church. We note with particular interest that when Moroni showed the Three Witnesses the plates, he turned directly to David Whitmer and said, 'David, blessed is he that endureth to the end' (Roberts, [in] Conference Report, Oct. 1926, 126)" (McConkie and Ostler, *Revelations of the Restoration*, 124).

8 And it shall come to pass, that if you shall ask the Father in my name, in faith believing, you shall receive the Holy Ghost, which giveth utterance, that you may stand as a witness of the things of which you shall both hear and see, and also that you may declare repentance unto this generation.

How was David Whitmer to be a witness? (14:8) "David Whitmer is specifically promised that he will be a witness in a special way 'of the things of which you shall both hear and see' (14:8.) As will be shown in connection with section 17, David Whitmer was called by the Lord as one of the three special witnesses of the Book of Mormon; on that occasion he *heard* the voice of the Lord and *saw* the angel and the plates of Mormon, exactly as this blessing promised" (Daniel H. Ludlow, *Companion to Your Study*, 1:121).

Doctrine and Covenants 14:9–11. Christ Created the Heavens and the Earth

In what way is Jesus Christ "a light which cannot be hid"? (14:9) "In the Bible, we read His teaching: 'I am the light of the world: he that followeth me shall not walk in darkness, but shall have the light of life' (John 8:12). And in modern revelation, we read, 'Behold, I am Jesus Christ . . . a light which cannot be hid in darkness' (Doctrine and Covenants 14:9). If we follow His teachings, He lights our path in this life and assures our destiny in the next" (Oaks, "What Has Our Savior Done for Us?" *Liahona*, May 2021, 76).

What experience showed David Whitmer that he had been blessed spiritually and temporally? (14:11) Prior to this revelation, in the latter part of May 1829, the Lord richly blessed David Whitmer. Lucy Smith, the mother of Joseph Smith, recounted the following: "David went to the field, and found that he had two heavy days' work before him. . . . He then fastened his horses to the harrow; and instead of dividing the field into what is usually termed lands by farmers, drove around the whole of it: and continued harrowing in this way till noon; when, on stopping for dinner, he looked around, and discovered to his surprise, that he had harrowed in full half the wheat. After dinner he went on as before; and by evening, he finished the whole two days work" (Joseph Smith Papers, "Lucy Mack Smith, History, 1845," [chapter 30]). ⊕

9 Behold, I am Jesus Christ, the Son of the living God, who created the heavens and the earth, a light which cannot be hid in darkness;

10 Wherefore, I must bring forth the fulness of my gospel from the Gentiles unto the house of Israel.

11 And behold, thou art David, and thou art called to assist; which thing if ye do, and are faithful, ye shall be blessed both spiritually and temporally, and great shall be your reward. Amen.

Why Do Doctrine and Covenants 15 and 16 Contain the Same Words?

"At times, the Lord reveals the same message to different individuals because they may have similar desires or circumstances. For example, mission calls that are extended today by the President of the Church have nearly identical wording. Nevertheless, those who receive the calls recognize the personal application of the direction given as it guides them in their missionary service. As recorded in Doctrine and Covenants 15–16, the Lord called John Whitmer and Peter Whitmer by name and revealed His will to them one at a time" (*Doctrine and Covenants Student Manual* [2018], 100).

"David [Whitmer] transported Joseph and Oliver to Fayette, New York, arriving in the early part of June 1829. Joseph Smith later wrote that 'David, John, and Peter Whitmer Jr became our zealous friends and assistants in the work" (in [Joseph Smith Papers, *Histories, Volume 1*], 308). These three brothers, 'each having received a testimony as to the genuineness of the work, became deeply concerned over the matter of their individual duty' (D&C 14, section heading). In response to their inquiry, the Prophet Joseph Smith received a revelation for each of the brothers (see D&C 14–16)" (*Doctrine and Covenants Student Manual* [2018], 99).

"[John Whitmer] learned the value of religious worship in his youth by attending the German Reformed Church. His religious life dramatically changed in June 1829 when Joseph Smith accepted the hospitality of the Whitmers. John readily received the prophetic calling of Joseph and his message of the Restoration. He assisted the young Prophet as a scribe for the translation of the Book of Mormon before being baptized by Oliver Cowdery.

"Sacred events in holy writ witness of his devotion and the Lord's love for him (see D&C 15). He remembered with gratitude his privilege to be one of the Eight Witnesses to the Book of Mormon" (Black, *Who's Who*, 331).

SECTION 15

Revelation given through Joseph Smith the Prophet to John Whitmer, at Fayette, New York, June 1829 (see the heading to section 14). The message is intimately and impressively personal in that the Lord tells of what was known only to John Whitmer and Himself. John Whitmer later became one of the Eight Witnesses to the Book of Mormon.

1 Hearken, my servant John, and listen to the words of Jesus Christ, your Lord and your Redeemer.

2 For behold, I speak unto you with sharpness and with power, for mine arm is over all the earth.

3 And I will tell you that which no man knoweth save me and thee alone—

4 For many times you have desired of me to know that which would be of the most worth unto you.

Doctrine and Covenants 15:1–2.
The Lord's Arm Is over All the Earth

Why was this revelation to John Whitmer preserved for our day? (15:1) "The publication of these three sections (D&C 14–16) illustrates the importance that Joseph Smith and those who assisted in the Restoration attached to the Lord's words. Elder John A. Widtsoe explained: . . . 'This simple revelation is directed to the individual and at first sight has no permanent value for the Church. Yet as a revelation from God it was preserved and published. An insincere man could have eliminated this and other similar revelations as of little consequence. Not so with Joseph. The Lord had spoken. The words were part of the building of the kingdom of God, and the same advice would be useful to many men then and now'" (McConkie and Ostler, *Revelations of the Restoration*, 126).

Doctrine and Covenants 15:3–6.
To Preach the Gospel and Save Souls Is the Thing of Most Worth

What would be of most worth to John Whitmer, and to us? (15:4–6) "I testify that the Lord expects us to bring souls unto Him by inviting all men to come unto Christ, and by so doing, find Him ourselves. It truly is 'the thing . . . of the most worth unto you' (D&C 15:6). In fact, your very ordination is 'to preach faith and repentance and remission of sins, according to [his] word' (D&C 53:3), 'that you may bring souls unto [him].' It is the greatest offering that man can give to God (D&C 15:6; see D&C 29:7; Alma 17:11; Alma 29:9; Alma 31:34–35)" (Gene R. Cook, "Inviting Others to 'Come unto Christ,'" *Ensign*, Nov. 1988, 37).

How can we fulfill the Lord's charge to declare repentance to all the world in our day? (15:6) As President M. Russell Ballard has said, for many years "the Lord's expectation [to serve a full-time mission] . . . has not changed. I am grateful that President Russell M. Nelson also reaffirmed the Lord's expectation this morning [April 2, 2022]. . . .

"As an Apostle of the Lord Jesus Christ, I now call upon you young men—and those young women who desire to serve a mission—to begin right now to talk with your parents about serving a mission. I also invite you to talk with your friends about serving a mission, and if one of your friends is not sure about serving, encourage them to talk with their bishop" ("Missionary Service Blessed My Life Forever," *Liahona*, May 2022, 9). ✪

Why is teaching repentance such an important message to take to the world? (15:6) President Russell M. Nelson taught: "What does it mean to repent? We begin with a dictionary's definition that to repent is 'to turn from sin . . . to feel sorrow [and] regret'

5 Behold, blessed are you for this thing, and for speaking my words which I have given you according to my commandments.

6 And now, behold, I say unto you, that the thing which will be of the most worth unto you will be to declare repentance unto this people, that you may bring souls unto me, that you may rest with them in the kingdom of my Father. Amen.

Who Was John Whitmer? (Doctrine and Covenants 15:1)

"'Next to his brother David, John was the most prominent and able man among the Whitmers, and rendered efficient service to the Church in various ways, as long as he remained faithful,' said Andrew Jenson. He was the recipient of four revelations in the Doctrine and Covenants (D&C 15; 26; 30; 47) and is the major benefactor of instructions in another (D&C 69:2–8). His name also appears among a select group of men in Doctrine and Covenants 70:1.

"John was affiliated with the Church in its beginning stages, being baptized by Oliver Cowdery within a month after the latter received this authority from a heavenly messenger. He accompanied the Prophet Joseph on his first missionary trips to Colesville, New York, and became the first regularly appointed Church Historian. He became one of the presiding officers of the Church in Missouri and served on the high council in Kirtland, where he also attended the temple dedication. In November 1837, some objections were raised as to his leadership in Missouri; and in February 1838, he and several others were rejected by the assembled Saints.

"On March 10, 1838, he was excommunicated by action of the high council at Far West, Missouri, 'for persisting in un-christianlike conduct.' After his spiritual severance, Whitmer refused to deliver up the Church records and documents that were in his possession. He remained in Far West, but in spite of his bitterness and antagonism against the Saints, he never denied the reality of the experience which would make his name known to generations thereafter. He, as one of the Eight Witnesses to the Book of Mormon, had seen the plates from which that sacred book was translated. Even among the worst enemies of the Church, John Whitmer would continue to affirm the truthfulness of America's second witness for Christ ([Jenson], 1:251–52)" (Brewster, *Doctrine & Covenants Encyclopedia* [2012], 632–33).

[Webster's Ninth New Collegiate Dictionary, s.v. "repent"]. To repent from sin is not easy. But the prize is worth the price. Repentance needs to be done one step at a time. Humble prayer will facilitate each essential step. As prerequisites to forgiveness, there must first be recognition, remorse, then confession" ("Repentance and Conversion," *Ensign*, May 2007, 102). ☉

Introduction to Doctrine and Covenants 16

This revelation was directed to Peter Whitmer Jr. at Fayette, New York, June 1829. "[Peter Whitmer Jr.] was reared by a hard-working, God-fearing father who valued strict discipline. He and his family worshiped with the German Reformed congregation of Zion's Church, just south of the Whitmer farm, until 1829. In the summer of 1829 young Peter became acquainted with Joseph Smith. Their friendship grew as the Prophet resided in the family home in Fayette. Peter was privileged to assist him sometimes as scribe in the translation of the Book of Mormon and to be one of Eight Witnesses who saw and handled the Book of Mormon plates" (Black, *Who's Who*, 334).

SECTION 16

Revelation given through Joseph Smith the Prophet to Peter Whitmer Jr., at Fayette, New York, June 1829 (see the heading to section 14). Peter Whitmer Jr. later became one of the Eight Witnesses to the Book of Mormon.

1 Hearken, my servant Peter, and listen to the words of Jesus Christ, your Lord and your Redeemer.

2 For behold, I speak unto you with sharpness and with power, for mine arm is over all the earth.

3 And I will tell you that which no man knoweth save me and thee alone—

4 For many times you have desired of me to know that which would be of the most worth unto you.

Doctrine and Covenants 16:1–2. The Lord's Arm Is over All the Earth

What can you do to better hearken to the Lord in your life? (16:1) The word *hearken* means to listen attentively and obey. See also commentary in this volume on Doctrine and Covenants 1:1.

Doctrine and Covenants 16:3–6. To Preach the Gospel and Save Souls Is the Thing of Most Worth

What Do We Know about Peter Whitmer Jr.? (Doctrine and Covenants 16:1)

- Given a revelation in June 1829 through Joseph Smith of what would "be of the most worth" to him (see D&C 16).
- One of first seven elders ordained as part of the restoration.
- Was called to preach the gospel with Oliver Cowdery (see D&C 30, 32).
- In 1833, suffered at the hands of mobs and "religious persecution before fleeing to Clay County."
- "Extended hospitality to the sick of Zion's Camp."
- "On 22 September 1836, Peter died near Liberty, Clay County," Missouri (adapted and modified from Black, *Who's Who*, 334–36).

Why is sharing the gospel an important work?
(16:6) "Many of those who came in contact with the Prophet Joseph, even prior to the organization of the Church, became convinced and received testimonies of the genuineness of his message. It was not an uncommon thing for them to approach the Prophet and ask him to inquire of the Lord as to their responsibilities and obligations. You recall the important part played by the Whitmer family.... The Prophet made inquiry and we have three sections of the Doctrine and Covenants devoted to the answer to these inquiries. They are very similar....

"And so, my brethren of the priesthood, our message is a world message, the obligation is ours. The Lord expects us to carry his message to the inhabitants of the earth" (Benson, in Conference Report, Apr. 1945, 106, 110). ●

5 Behold, blessed are you for this thing, and for speaking my words which I have given unto you according to my commandments.

6 And now, behold, I say unto you, that the thing which will be of the most worth unto you will be to declare repentance unto this people, that you may bring souls unto me, that you may rest with them in the kingdom of my Father. Amen.

Introduction to Doctrine and Covenants 17

Joseph Smith received this revelation given to Oliver Cowdery, David Whitmer, and Martin Harris at Fayette, New York, in June 1829. Writing about this revelation, the Prophet recorded: "In the course of the work of translation [at Fayette], we ascertained that three special witnesses were to be provided by the Lord, to whom he would grant, that they should see the plates from which this work (the Book of Mormon) should be translated, and that these witnesses should bear record of the same....

"Almost immediately after we had made this discovery, it occurred to Oliver Cowdery, David Whitmer, and ... Martin Harris ... that they would have me enquire of the Lord, to know if they might not obtain of him to be these three special witnesses; ... and through the Urim and [Thummim], I obtained of the Lord for them the following Revelation [Section 17]" (Joseph Smith Papers, "History, 1838–1856, volume A-1," 23).

SECTION 17

Revelation given through Joseph Smith the Prophet to Oliver Cowdery, David Whitmer, and Martin Harris, at Fayette, New York, June 1829, prior to their viewing the engraved plates that contained the Book of Mormon record. Joseph and his scribe, Oliver Cowdery, had learned from the translation of the Book of Mormon plates that three special witnesses would be designated (see Ether 5:2–4; 2 Nephi 11:3; 27:12). Oliver Cowdery, David Whitmer, and Martin Harris were moved upon by an inspired desire to be the three special witnesses. The Prophet inquired of the Lord, and this revelation was given in answer through the Urim and Thummim.

Doctrine and Covenants 17:1–4. By Faith the Three Witnesses Will See the Plates and Other Sacred Items

1 Behold, I say unto you, that you must rely upon my word, which if you do with full purpose of heart, you shall have a view of the plates, and also of the breastplate, the sword of Laban, the Urim and Thummim, which were given to the brother of Jared upon the mount, when he talked with the Lord face to face, and the miraculous directors which were given to Lehi while in the wilderness, on the borders of the Red Sea.

Why might it have been important for the Three Witnesses to see sacred and ancient items in addition to the plates? (17:1) "The Lord covenants . . . [to] show them the Book of Mormon plates, the breastplate, Laban's sword, the seer stones the Lord gave to the brother of Jared, and the Liahona. . . . The witnesses will view these artifacts by faith like that of the brother of Jared or Lehi. Such evidence proves more than the fact that Joseph had plates. Witnesses of Lehi's miraculous compass, Laban's sword, and the brother of Jared's seer stones know that the plates are inscribed with ancient writing about actual people who received revelations, knew the Lord, were directed to a promised land, and committed their testimonies of Christ to writing that has been translated by Joseph Smith" (Harper, *Making Sense of the Doctrine & Covenants*, 62–63).

2 And it is by your faith that you shall obtain a view of them, even by that faith which was had by the prophets of old.

3 And after that you have obtained faith, and have seen them with your eyes, you shall testify of them, by the power of God;

How did the Lord fulfill His promise to provide the Three Witnesses with a view of the plates? (17:2) "The four men entered the nearby woods. They had agreed to take turns praying, first Joseph, then the other three. The first attempt brought nothing, and they tried again. Again nothing. Before they made a third attempt, [Martin] Harris offered to leave, saying he was the obstacle. The remaining three knelt again and before many minutes, according to their account, saw a light in the air over their heads. An angel appeared with the plates in his hands. . . .

"After the appearance to Cowdery and Whitmer, Joseph went searching for Harris. . . . Harris asked

The Consistent Testimony of The Three Witnesses (Doctrine and Covenants 17:3)

"The testimony of the Three Witnesses to the Book of Mormon stands forth in great strength. Each of the three had ample reason and opportunity to renounce his testimony if it had been false, or to equivocate on details if any had been inaccurate. As is well known, because of disagreements or jealousies involving other leaders of the Church, each one of these three witnesses was excommunicated from The Church of Jesus Christ of Latter-day Saints by about eight years after the publication of their testimony. All three went their separate ways, with no common interest to support a collusive effort. Yet to the end of their lives—periods ranging from 12 to 50 years after their [loss of Church membership]—not one of these witnesses deviated from his published testimony or said anything that cast any shadow on its truthfulness.

"Furthermore, their testimony stands uncontradicted by any other witnesses. Reject it one may, but how does one explain three men of good character uniting and persisting in this published testimony to the end of their lives in the face of great ridicule and other personal disadvantage? Like the Book of Mormon itself, there is no better explanation than is given in the testimony itself, the solemn statement of good and honest men who told what they saw" (Oaks, "Witness," *Ensign*, May 1999, 36).

Joseph to pray with him, and . . . their desires were fulfilled. . . . Harris cried out . . . ''Tis enough; mine eyes have beheld'" (Bushman, *Rough Stone Rolling*, 78). See also Book of Mormon, "Testimony of Three Witnesses." ⊕

In what way did the testimony of the Three Witnesses prevent Joseph Smith from being destroyed? (17:4) Lucy Mack Smith testified: "When Joseph came in he threw himself down beside me. 'Father!—Mother!—' said he, 'you do not know how happy I am. The Lord has caused the plates to be shown to 3 more besides me who have also seen an angel and will have to testify to the truth of what I have said, for they know for themselves that I do not go about to deceive the people. And I do feel as though I was relieved of a dreadful burden, which was almost too much for me to endure, but they will now have to bear a part, and it does rejoice my soul, that I am not any longer to be entirely alone in the world'" (Joseph Smith Papers, "Lucy Mack Smith, History, 1844–1845," [chapter 31]).

Doctrine and Covenants 17:5–9. Christ Bears Testimony of the Divinity of the Book of Mormon

Why is the Lord's declaration about the Book of Mormon so significant? (17:6) "One of the most solemn oaths ever given to man is found in these words of the Lord relative to Joseph Smith and the Book of Mormon. 'He [meaning Joseph Smith] has translated the book, even that part which I have commanded him,' saith the Lord, 'and as your Lord and your God liveth it is true' (D&C 17:6).

"This is God's testimony of the Book of Mormon. In it Deity himself has laid his godhood on the line. Either the book is true or God ceases to be God. There neither is nor can be any more formal or powerful language known to men or gods" (Bruce R. McConkie, "Doctrine of the Priesthood," *Ensign*, May 1982, 33).

What promises did the Lord make to the Three Witnesses? (17:8) The Three Witnesses faced great opposition as a result of the Lord's commandment to declare their testimony. The Lord promised that if they kept "these last commandments" the "gates of hell shall not prevail against you; for my grace is sufficient for you, and you shall be lifted up at the last day" (D&C 17:8). The Three Witnesses testified: "Wherefore, to be obedient unto the commandments

4 And this you shall do that my servant Joseph Smith, Jun., may not be destroyed, that I may bring about my righteous purposes unto the children of men in this work.

5 And ye shall testify that you have seen them, even as my servant Joseph Smith, Jun., has seen them; for it is by my power that he has seen them, and it is because he had faith.

6 And he has translated the book, even that part which I have commanded him, and as your Lord and your God liveth it is true.

7 Wherefore, you have received the same power, and the same faith, and the same gift like unto him;

8 And if you do these last commandments of mine, which I have given you, the gates of hell shall not prevail against you; for my grace is sufficient for you, and you shall be lifted up at the last day.

9 And I, Jesus Christ, your Lord and your God, have spoken it unto you, that I might bring about my righteous purposes unto the children of men. Amen.

of God, we bear testimony of these things. And we know that if we are faithful in Christ, we shall rid our garments of the blood of all men, and be found spotless before the judgment-seat of Christ, and shall dwell with him eternally in the heavens" (Book of Mormon, "Testimony of Three Witnesses").

Introduction to Doctrine and Covenants 18

"In June 1829, Joseph Smith and Oliver Cowdery continued the translation of the Book of Mormon in the home of Peter Whitmer Sr. in Fayette, New York. During this time, Joseph and Oliver also sought to know how to exercise the keys of the Melchizedek Priesthood that had been recently conferred upon them by heavenly messengers. While praying in a room of the Whitmer home, the word of the Lord came to them and directed them to exercise the priesthood to ordain elders, administer the sacrament, and bestow the gift of the Holy Ghost by the laying on of hands. However, the Lord instructed them to wait to perform these ordinances until a group of believers could be assembled (see [Joseph Smith Papers, *Histories: Volume 1*], 326, 328).

"Meanwhile, as they awaited the Lord's command to organize the Church, the Prophet and Oliver Cowdery were nearing completion of the translation of the Book of Mormon, which included translating the books of 3 Nephi and Moroni. Both of these books contain instructions on priesthood ordinances and Church procedure, which likely inspired and guided them as they contemplated the time when the Lord would direct them to organize His Church anew upon the earth.

"It was in the context of these events that the Prophet received the revelation recorded in Doctrine and Covenants 18. This revelation was addressed to Joseph Smith, Oliver Cowdery, and David Whitmer, giving direction about building up the Church. It also contains instructions to those who would be called as the Twelve Apostles" (*Doctrine and Covenants Student Manual* [2018], 80).]

SECTION 18

Revelation to Joseph Smith the Prophet, Oliver Cowdery, and David Whitmer, given at Fayette, New York, June 1829. According to the Prophet, this revelation made known "the calling of twelve apostles in these last days, and also instructions relative to building up the Church."

1 Now, behold, because of the thing which you, my servant Oliver Cowdery, have desired to know of me, I give unto you these words:

2 Behold, I have manifested unto you, by my Spirit in many instances, that the things which you have written are true; wherefore you know that they are true.

Doctrine and Covenants 18:1–5. Scriptures Show How to Build Up the Church

What did Oliver Cowdery desire to know from the Lord? (18:1–2) "It is apparent from the language of verse 1 that Oliver Cowdery had asked a question to which the Lord was responding with this revelation. . . . Oliver's actual question, however, was not recorded" (Robinson and Garrett, *Commentary on the Doctrine and Covenants*, 1:104–5).

How does the Lord manifest truth to us through His Spirit? (18:2) There are many ways the Spirit is manifested. Elder Robert D. Hales explained: "Personal revelation is essential, but it is only one part of the work of the Holy Ghost. As the scriptures attest, the Holy Ghost also testifies of the Savior and God the

Father [see John 15:26]. He teaches us 'the peaceable things of the kingdom' [D&C 39:6] and causes us to 'abound in hope' [Romans 15:13]. He 'leadeth [us] to do good . . . [and] to judge righteously' [D&C 11:12]. He gives 'to [everyone] . . . a [spiritual] gift . . . that all may be profited thereby' [D&C 46:11–12]. He 'giveth [us] knowledge' [Alma 18:35] and 'bring[s] all things to [our] remembrance' [John 14:26]" ("Holy Ghost," *Ensign*, May 2016, 105).

What were the "written" things and how do they relate to the foundation of the Lord's Church? (18:3–4) The phrase "the things which are written" refers to the Book of Mormon translation, which Oliver himself had recorded as Joseph's scribe. President Russell M. Nelson stated, "The Book of Mormon provides the fullest and most authoritative understanding of the Atonement of Jesus Christ to be found anywhere. It teaches what it really means to be born again. From the Book of Mormon we learn about the gathering of scattered Israel. We know why we are here on earth. These and other truths are more powerfully and persuasively taught in the Book of Mormon than in any other book. The full power of the gospel of Jesus Christ is contained in the Book of Mormon. Period" ("Book of Mormon: What Would Your Life Be Like without It?" *Ensign*, Nov. 2017, 62).

What might the words "my rock" refer to in these verses? (18:4–5) "The Doctrine and Covenants refers to Christ as the 'stone of Israel' (50:44), and the writings of Moses describe the Lord as the 'Rock of Heaven,' which is an appropriate title for one from whom revelation proceeds (Moses 7:53). Thus, in order to maintain 'a sure foundation' (Hel. 5:12), one builds upon the rock of revealed truth emanating from the 'Rock of Heaven'" (Brewster, *Doctrine & Covenants Encyclopedia* [2012], 479). ✛

Doctrine and Covenants 18:6–8. The World Is Ripening in Iniquity

Why would the Lord warn that the world is "ripening" in iniquity? (18:6) When food crops ripen and are left unharvested, they quickly deteriorate and rot, having no value. "It has been nearly [200] years since the Lord said the world was ripening in iniquity (v. 6). When a people or the world is ripe in iniquity, or their iniquity is full, the Lord destroys them (see Genesis 15:16; 1 Nephi 17:35; Ether 2:9, 9:20). The world seems to be close to that ripened stage. The Second Coming is nigh at hand. We should follow the example of

3 And if you know that they are true, behold, I give unto you a commandment, that you rely upon the things which are written;

4 For in them are all things written concerning the foundation of my church, my gospel, and my rock.

5 Wherefore, if you shall build up my church, upon the foundation of my gospel and my rock, the gates of hell shall not prevail against you.

6 Behold, the world is ripening in iniquity; and it must needs be that the children of men are stirred up unto repentance, both the Gentiles and also the house of Israel.

7 Wherefore, as thou hast been baptized by the hands of my servant Joseph Smith, Jun., according to that which I have commanded him, he hath fulfilled the thing which I commanded him.

Joseph and do the things the Lord commands us, as did he (D&C 11:7–8), that we might escape the coming destruction of the wicked (see D&C 61:31; 101:11)" (Nyman, *Doctrine and Covenants Commentary*, 1:146).

8 And now, marvel not that I have called him unto mine own purpose, which purpose is known in me; wherefore, if he shall be diligent in keeping my commandments he shall be blessed unto eternal life; and his name is Joseph.

Why might the Lord have counseled Oliver to "marvel not" at Joseph's calling? (18:8) "Although we may not know exactly what was troubling Oliver regarding the nature of Joseph's role in the opening of this dispensation, the Lord assures Oliver that He knows what He is doing. Oliver had been a teacher by profession, a somewhat educated man. Joseph on the other hand was a young man who had not enjoyed a great deal of formal education. It may have been that Oliver considered himself more qualified to serve in the great leadership responsibilities that had been placed upon his friend's shoulders. In the eyes of the world that may have been true, but prophecy and foreordination reflected the Lord's perspective as to the innate talents and spirituality of His choice" (Paul Nolan Hyde, *Comprehensive Commentary* [1–72], 100). ✛

Doctrine and Covenants 18:9–16. The Worth of Souls Is Great

9 And now, Oliver Cowdery, I speak unto you, and also unto David Whitmer, by the way of commandment; for, behold, I command all men everywhere to repent, and I speak unto you, even as unto Paul mine apostle, for you are called even with that same calling with which he was called.

What might the Lord have meant by comparing Oliver Cowdery and David Whitmer with the Apostle Paul? (18:9) "The Apostle Paul did anciently what Oliver and David were about to do—take the gospel to the Gentiles. Theirs is the same calling as was Paul's in the meridian of time. This verse further reflects the fact that apostolic authority had already been given to Joseph, Oliver, and David at this time, June 1829. According to Brigham Young, 'Joseph Smith, Oliver Cowdery, and David Whitmer were the first Apostles of this dispensation, though in the early days of the Church David Whitmer lost his standing, and another took his place' [Brigham Young, (in *Journal of Discourses*), 6:320]" (Robinson and Garrett, *Commentary on the Doctrine and Covenants*, 1:105–6). ✛

10 Remember the worth of souls is great in the sight of God;

11 For, behold, the Lord your Redeemer suffered death in the flesh; wherefore he suffered the pain of all men, that all men might repent and come unto him.

12 And he hath risen again from the dead, that he might bring all men unto him, on conditions of repentance.

What do these verses teach us about God's love for His children? (18:10–11) "I believe that if we could truly understand the Atonement of the Lord Jesus Christ, we would realize how precious is *one* son or daughter of God. . . . At the heart of the English word *atonement* is the word *one*. If all mankind understood this, there would never be anyone with whom we would not be concerned, regardless of age, race, gender, religion, or social or economic standing. We would strive to emulate the Savior and would never be unkind, indifferent, disrespectful, or insensitive to others" (Ballard, "Atonement and the Value of One Soul," *Ensign*, May 2004, 86). ⊕

What is the significance of the title *Redeemer*? (18:11) "Among the most significant of Jesus Christ's descriptive titles is Redeemer. . . . The word *redeem* means to pay off an obligation or a debt. *Redeem* can also mean to rescue or set free as by paying a ransom. If someone commits a mistake and then corrects it or makes amends, we say he has redeemed himself. Each of these meanings suggests different facets of the great Redemption accomplished by Jesus Christ through His Atonement, which includes, in the words of the dictionary, 'to deliver from sin and its penalties, as by a sacrifice made for the sinner' [*Webster's New World College Dictionary*, 3rd ed. (1988), s.v. 'redeem']" (Christofferson, "Redemption," *Ensign*, May 2013, 109).

How can joy become an element of repentance? (18:13) "The fact that we can repent is the good news of the gospel! Guilt can be 'swept away' [Enos 1:6]. We can be filled with joy, receive a remission of our sins, and have 'peace of conscience' [Mosiah 4:3]. We can be freed from feelings of despair and the bondage of sin. We can be filled with the marvelous light of God and be 'pained no more' [Mosiah 27:29]. Repentance is not only possible but also joyful because of our Savior. . . .

"I invite you to feel . . . joy in the Savior's ability, willingness, and desire to forgive; and joy in choosing to repent. Let us follow the instruction to 'with joy . . . draw water out of the wells of salvation' [Isaiah 12:3]" (Renlund, "Repentance," *Ensign*, Nov. 2016, 124).

What are some ways we can labor all our days sharing the gospel? (18:15–16) Sister Cristina B. Franco observed, "Can we invite a friend who is not of our faith to come to church with us on Sunday? Or can we perhaps share a copy of the Book of Mormon with a relative or a friend? Can we help others find their

13 And how great is his joy in the soul that repenteth!

14 Wherefore, you are called to cry repentance unto this people.

15 And if it so be that you should labor all your days in crying repentance unto this people, and bring, save it be one soul unto me, how great shall be your joy with him in the kingdom of my Father!

What Is the Worth of Souls? (Doctrine and Covenants 18:10)

"The magnificent and incomprehensible effect of the Atonement of Jesus Christ is based on God's love for each of us. It affirms His declaration that 'the worth of souls'—every one—'is great in the sight of God' (Doctrine and Covenants 18:10). In the Bible, Jesus Christ explained this in terms of our Heavenly Father's love: 'For God so loved the world, that he gave his only begotten Son, that whosoever believeth in him should not perish, but have everlasting life' (John 3:16). In modern revelation, our Redeemer, Jesus Christ, declared that *He* 'so loved the world that he gave his own life, that as many as would believe might become the sons of God' (Doctrine and Covenants 34:3).

"Is it any wonder, then, that the Book of Mormon: Another Testament of Jesus Christ concludes with the teaching that to become 'perfect' and 'sanctified in Christ,' *we* must 'love God with all [our] might, mind and strength'? (Moroni 10:32–33). His plan motivated by love must be received with love" (Oaks, "What Has Our Savior Done for Us?" *Liahona*, May 2021, 76).

16 And now, if your joy will be great with one soul that you have brought unto me into the kingdom of my Father, how great will be your joy if you should bring many souls unto me!

17 Behold, you have my gospel before you, and my rock, and my salvation.

18 Ask the Father in my name in faith, believing that you shall receive, and you shall have the Holy Ghost, which manifesteth all things which are expedient unto the children of men.

19 And if you have not faith, hope, and charity, you can do nothing.

20 Contend against no church, save it be the church of the devil.

21 Take upon you the name of Christ, and speak the truth in soberness.

22 And as many as repent and are baptized in my name, which is Jesus Christ, and endure to the end, the same shall be saved.

ancestors on FamilySearch or share with others what we have learned during the week as we have been studying *Come, Follow Me*? Can we be more like our Savior, Jesus Christ, and share with others what brings us joy to our lives? The answer to all of these questions is yes! We can do it!" ("Finding Joy in Sharing the Gospel," *Ensign*, Nov. 2019, 85).

Doctrine and Covenants 18:17–25. To Gain Salvation, Men Must Take upon Themselves the Name of Christ

What could it mean to contend with "the church of the devil"? (18:20) To *contend* is to strive or struggle against. "President Joseph Fielding Smith gave the following explanation of this exhortation: 'We must understand that this is instruction to us to *contend against all evil, that which is opposed to righteousness and truth*' ([*Church History and Modern Revelation*] 1:83; [emphasis] added). The Book of Mormon proclaims 'that which is evil cometh from the devil' (Omni 1:25). Therefore, as we contend against evil we wage war against the 'author of evil,' the devil (Hel. 8:28). Smith and Sjodahl state that the devil's church 'consists of those who adopt his plan and seek to destroy the . . . agency of man by brute force' ([Smith and Sjodahl, *Doctrine and Covenants Commentary*], 86)" (Brewster, *Doctrine & Covenants Encyclopedia* [2012], 85–86). ✪

What does it mean to endure to the end? (18:22) "Enduring to the end requires faithfulness to the end. . . . Obviously, this is not an easy task. It is intended to be difficult, challenging, and, ultimately, refining as we prepare to return to live with our Father in Heaven and receive eternal blessings.

"Enduring to the end is definitely not a do-it-yourself project. First, it requires the Savior's redemptive power. We cannot return to our Heavenly Father's presence unless we are clean, and so we must continue to repent. . . . We must always maintain faith and hope in Christ to endure to the end, [by] praying, fasting, and reading the scriptures. These practices will fortify us against the subtle schemes and fiery darts of the adversary" (Perry, "Gospel of Jesus Christ," *Ensign*, May 2008, 46).

How is it that the name of Jesus Christ can save us? (18:23) "Just as there is but one true God, so is there but one true name endowed by him with saving power: Jesus Christ. . . . The restoration of the gospel of necessity involved the restoration of the saving name of Jesus Christ. Not, of course, the literal name familiar to all Christians, but the correct understanding of the personality behind that name, together with that authority and those doctrines and ordinances encompassed by it. For just as there are false gods, so are there false Christs or, rather, false concepts associated with him" (Turner, "Jesus Christ and the Command to Repent," 101). See also 2 Nephi 25:20; Mosiah 3:17; Acts 4:10–12. ⊕

What are some ways we take upon ourselves the Savior's name? (18:24) "We take the name of Christ upon us in the waters of baptism. We renew the effect of that baptism each week as we partake of the sacrament, signifying our willingness to take His name upon us and promising always to remember Him (see D&C 20:77, 79). . . .

"This means that we must be willing to let others know whom we follow and to whose Church we belong: the Church of Jesus Christ. We certainly want to do this in the spirit of love and testimony. We want to follow the Savior by simply and clearly, yet humbly, declaring that we are members of His Church" (Ballard, "Importance of a Name," *Ensign*, Nov. 2011, 79, 80). ⊕

Doctrine and Covenants 18:26–36. The Calling and Mission of the Twelve Are Revealed

How would the Twelve show they had taken the name of Jesus Christ upon themselves? (18:27) Speaking to the newly called Twelve, Oliver Cowdery instructed: "Remember the souls of men are committed to your charge, and if you mind your calling you shall always prosper. . . . It is necessary that you receive a testimony from heaven, for yourselves, so that you can bear testimony to the truth of the Book of Mormon. . . . Strengthen your faith[,] cast off your doubts, your sins and all your unbelief, and nothing can prevent you from coming to God. . . . You are called to preach the gospel of the Son of God to the nations of the earth. It is the will of your Heavenly Father that you proclaim his gospel to the ends of the earth, and the Islands of the sea. Be zealous to save souls" (Joseph Smith Papers, "History, 1838–1856, volume B-1," 572).

23 Behold, Jesus Christ is the name which is given of the Father, and there is none other name given whereby man can be saved;

24 Wherefore, all men must take upon them the name which is given of the Father, for in that name shall they be called at the last day;

25 Wherefore, if they know not the name by which they are called, they cannot have place in the kingdom of my Father.

26 And now, behold, there are others who are called to declare my gospel, both unto Gentile and unto Jew;

27 Yea, even twelve; and the Twelve shall be my disciples, and they shall take upon them my name; and the Twelve are they who shall desire to take upon them my name with full purpose of heart.

28 And if they desire to take upon them my name with full purpose of heart, they are called to go into all the world to preach my gospel unto every creature.

29 And they are they who are ordained of me to baptize in my name, according to that which is written;

30 And you have that which is written before you; wherefore, you must perform it according to the words which are written.

31 And now I speak unto you, the Twelve—Behold, my grace is sufficient for you; you must walk uprightly before me and sin not.

32 And, behold, you are they who are ordained of me to ordain priests and teachers; to declare my gospel, according to the power of the Holy Ghost which is in you, and according to the callings and gifts of God unto men;

33 And I, Jesus Christ, your Lord and your God, have spoken it.

34 These words are not of men nor of man, but of me; wherefore, you shall testify they are of me and not of man;

35 For it is my voice which speaketh them unto you; for they are given by my Spirit unto you, and by my power you can read them one to another; and save it were by my power you could not have them;

36 Wherefore, you can testify that you have heard my voice, and know my words.

What could it mean to serve with full purpose of heart? (18:28) "When the Lord measures an individual, . . . He measures the heart as an indicator of the person's capacity and potential to bless others.

"Why the heart? Because the heart is a synonym for one's entire makeup. We often use phrases about the heart to describe the total person. Thus, we describe people as being 'big-hearted' or 'goodhearted' or having a 'heart of gold.' Or we speak of people with faint hearts, wise hearts, pure hearts, willing hearts, deceitful hearts, conniving hearts, courageous hearts, cold hearts, hearts of stone, or selfish hearts. . . .

"As used by the Lord, the 'heart' of a person describes his effort to better self, or others, or the conditions he confronts. A question I suggest to you is this: How do you measure up?" (Ashton, "Measure of Our Hearts," *Ensign*, Nov. 1988, 15).

What other instructions clarified the role of the Twelve Apostles? (18:28–33) Oliver Cowdery testified: "The greatness of your commission consists in this; you are to hold the keys of this ministry. You are to go to the nations afar off, nations that sit in darkness. The day is coming when the work of God must be done. Israel shall be gathered. The seed of Jacob shall be gathered from their long dispersion. There will be a feast to Israel the Elect of God. . . . You will be stewards over this ministry. You have a work to do that no other men can do. You must proclaim the gospel in its Simplicity and purity, and we commend you to God and the word of his grace" (Joseph Smith Papers, "History, 1838–1856, volume B-1," 574).

Why is it important to understand that prophets speak the Lord's words? (18:34) "Prophets speak by the power of the Holy Spirit. They testify of Christ and His divine mission on earth. They represent the mind and heart of the Lord and are called to represent Him and teach us what we must do to return to live in the presence of God and His Son, Jesus Christ. We are blessed as we exercise our faith and follow their teachings. By following them, our lives are happier and less complicated, our difficulties and problems are easier to bear, and we create a spiritual armor around us that will protect us from the attacks of the enemy in our day" (Soares, "Prophets Speak by the Power of the Holy Spirit," *Ensign*, May 2018, 99). ☉

How can we come to hear the Lord's voice and know His words? (18:36) Elder Bruce R. McConkie testified of his own experience: "[In speaking] I shall use my own words, though you may think they are the words of scripture, words spoken by other Apostles and prophets.

"True it is they were first proclaimed by others, but they are now mine, for the Holy Spirit of God has borne witness to me that they are true, and it is now as though the Lord had revealed them to me in the first instance. I have thereby heard his voice and know his word" ("Purifying Power of Gethsemane," *Ensign*, May 1985, 9). ●

Doctrine and Covenants 18:37–39. Oliver Cowdery and David Whitmer Are to Search Out the Twelve

Why were Oliver Cowdery and David Whitmer appointed to identify the Twelve Apostles? (18:37–39) "The Twelve are to be special witness to all the world in much the same way that Oliver, David, and Martin Harris, the Three Witnesses to the Book of Mormon, were special witnesses to all the world. Thus, it is fitting that the first three 'special witnesses' should search out the other twelve. Only Oliver and David are specified here . . . but in 1835 Joseph Smith directed that Martin should also assist in choosing the Twelve" (Robinson and Garrett, *Commentary on the Doctrine and Covenants*, 1:108). The first members of the Quorum of the Twelve Apostles in the latter days were called on February 14, 1835. ●

Doctrine and Covenants 18:40–47. To Gain Salvation, Men Must Repent, Be Baptized, and Keep the Commandments

Why are we commanded to worship the Father in the name of Jesus Christ? (18:40) "God the Eternal Father is the ultimate object of our worship [see D&C 20:17–19]. . . .

"Indeed, from the beginning men have been commanded to call upon the Father in the name of the Son (see Moses 5:8) [see also Jacob 4:3–5]. . . .

"God the Eternal Father is our God and he is Christ's God. . . . Christ glorified the Father (see John 17:1, 4), and so must we. The Lord Jesus worshiped the Father and gained salvation, and so must we. He kept the commandments of the Father, prayed to the Father, and sought the guidance of the Father's Spirit in all he did; so must we" (Millet and McConkie, *In His Holy Name*, 50, 51).

37 And now, behold, I give unto you, Oliver Cowdery, and also unto David Whitmer, that you shall search out the Twelve, who shall have the desires of which I have spoken;

38 And by their desires and their works you shall know them.

39 And when you have found them you shall show these things unto them.

40 And you shall fall down and worship the Father in my name.

41 And you must preach unto the world, saying: You must repent and be baptized, in the name of Jesus Christ;

42 For all men must repent and be baptized, and not only men, but women, and children who have arrived at the years of accountability.

43 And now, after that you have received this, you must keep my commandments in all things;

44 And by your hands I will work a marvelous work among the children of men, unto the convincing of many of their sins, that they may come unto repentance, and that they may come unto the kingdom of my Father.

In what ways does the Lord use us to accomplish His marvelous work? (18:44) "As we emulate [the Savior's] perfect example, our hands can become His hands; our eyes, His eyes; our heart, His heart. . . .

"Let our hearts and hands be stretched out in compassion toward others, for everyone is walking his or her own difficult path. As disciples of Jesus Christ, our Master, we are called to support and heal rather than condemn. . . .

"Let us commit to become His hands, that others through us may feel His loving embrace" (Uchtdorf, "You Are My Hands," *Ensign*, May 2010, 68, 69, 75).

45 Wherefore, the blessings which I give unto you are above all things.

46 And after that you have received this, if you keep not my commandments you cannot be saved in the kingdom of my Father.

47 Behold, I, Jesus Christ, your Lord and your God, and your Redeemer, by the power of my Spirit have spoken it. Amen.

To which blessings could the Lord be referring in this verse? (18:45) God the Father "offers to all His children something unimaginable: to become 'heirs of God, and joint-heirs with Christ' [Romans 8:17; see also Doctrine and Covenants 84:38].

"What does this mean?

"That we will live forever, receive a fulness of joy [see 3 Nephi 28:10], and have the potential to 'inherit thrones, kingdoms, principalities, and powers' [D&C 132:19].

"It is so humbling to know that this magnificent and supernal future is possible—not because of who we are but because of who God is" (Uchtdorf, "God among Us," *Liahona*, May 2021, 8).

How Do Sections 18 and 19 Reveal the Mercy and Righteous Judgment of the Redeemer?

"[Doctrine and Covenants] 18 stresses the Lord's gentle but firm command to all mankind to repent by taking upon them his name so that they might inherit 'the kingdom of my Father' (D&C 18:25, 46). [Doctrine and Covenants] 19 underscores this commandment by vividly describing the fate of those who ignore it. Thus, the first revelation is essentially positive in its approach while that of the second is somewhat negative. It reveals the dual mission of the Redeemer with great clarity. On the one hand he is a merciful Savior who has assumed the moral burden of every soul. On the other hand he is a just but demanding Judge whose wrath will be poured out without measure upon those who reject his sacrifice and refuse to repent. Nowhere in all scripture is the [Atonement of Jesus Christ] so graphically described, nor the need for repentance emphasized with more power and directness" (Turner, "Jesus Christ and the Command to Repent," 100).

Introduction to Doctrine and Covenants 19

Soon after the Book of Mormon translation was completed sometime in June 1829, Joseph Smith and Martin Harris earnestly sought a publisher among several printers from the surrounding area. E. B. Grandin of Palmyra, New York, finally agreed to print the Book of Mormon. Harris "initiated the negotiations and planned to pay for the printing" and they settled on a price of $3,000 for 5,000 copies. However, Grandin refused to begin work until "Harris had promised to insure the payment for the printing." The commitment was steep, Martin would have to impart essentially all the property to which he had legal right (see Joseph Smith Papers, "Revelation, circa Summer 1829 [D&C 19]," 39–42).

"This moment of decision would sound the depth of Martin Harris's trust in Joseph Smith and his faith in the Book of Mormon. Seeking guidance [sometime during the summer of 1829], he spoke with Joseph, who received yet another revelation [in Manchester, New York]. Known today as Doctrine and Covenants 19, the revelation admonished Martin, 'Thou shalt not covet thine own property, but impart it freely to the printing of the book of Mormon' [D&C 19:26]. On August 25, 1829, he mortgaged his property to Grandin as payment for the publication. . . .

"Martin eventually sold enough of his property to pay the debt. By so doing, he secured his place as the most significant financial supporter of the Book of Mormon and thus the early Church. None among Joseph Smith's younger and poorer friends could have provided this critical contribution" (McBride, "Contributions of Martin Harris," 8).

"Doctrine and Covenants 19 restores doctrine related to the Atonement, emphasizing that there is no repentance without suffering, especially the exquisite suffering of Christ. It unfolds the mystery of divine punishment. It confirms a literal reading of the account in the Gospel of Luke of Christ sweating blood as he suffered in Gethsemane, adding that the Atonement caused Christ to 'bleed at every pore' (v. 18). Thus, where other Christians cite the crucifixion, Latter-day Saints consider Christ's suffering in the garden as commencing the crucible of his Atonement. . . .

"Section 19 is unique in the standard works; it is the only text in which Christ describes his atonement so vividly. It is an extremely compelling revelation on the nature of the Atonement and the related doctrines of repentance or punishment. While it may sound harsh, this is a merciful text. Christ has already suffered for the sins of all mankind, but his unfathomably exquisite vicarious suffering does not negate the free will of those who choose not to repent" (Harper, *Making Sense of the Doctrine & Covenants*, 70–71).

Doctrine and Covenants 19:1–3. Christ Has All Power

What does "Alpha and Omega" symbolize? (19:1)
"These are the first and last letters of the Greek alphabet. Their meaning is synonymous with 'the first and the last' and 'the beginning and the end,' suggesting the permanent, everlasting, never-failing presence of Jesus Christ in the great plan of redemption, in His triumph of life over death, in salvation from sin. He is omnipresent, immovable, and victorious from start to finish in the cause of eternal life. He is with us through it all, always reliable and always nearby" (Holland, *Witness for His Names*, 20). In Elder Gerrit W. Gong's words, the Savior is "with us in the beginning, He is with us to the end" ("Christ the Lord Is Risen Today," *Ensign*, May 2018, 98). See also commentary in this volume on Doctrine and Covenants 35:1 and 38:1.

SECTION 19

Revelation given through Joseph Smith, at Manchester, New York, likely in the summer of 1829. In his history, the Prophet introduces it as "a commandment of God and not of man, to Martin Harris, given by him who is Eternal."

1 I am Alpha and Omega, Christ the Lord; yea, even I am he, the beginning and the end, the Redeemer of the world.

2 I, having accomplished and finished the will of him whose I am, even the Father, concerning me—having done this that I might subdue all things unto myself—

3 Retaining all power, even to the destroying of Satan and his works at the end of the world, and the last great day of judgment, which I shall pass upon the inhabitants thereof, judging every man according to his works and the deeds which he hath done.

4 And surely every man must repent or suffer, for I, God, am endless.

5 Wherefore, I revoke not the judgments which I shall pass, but woes shall go forth, weeping, wailing and gnashing of teeth, yea, to those who are found on my left hand.

How did Jesus Christ subdue all things? (19:2–3) President Dallin H. Oaks testified: "I witness with the prophets of the Book of Mormon that the Messiah, the Holy One of Israel, suffered 'according to the flesh' (Alma 7:13), the pains, the infirmities, and the griefs and sorrows of every living creature in the family of Adam. (See 2 Ne. 9:21; Alma 7:12–13; Mosiah 14:4; D&C 18:11.)

"I testify that when the Savior suffered and died for all men, all men became subject unto him (see 2 Ne. 9:5) and to his commandment that all must repent and be baptized in his name, having faith in him, 'or they cannot be saved in the kingdom of God' (2 Ne. 9:23; see also Alma 11:40; John 3:5; John 8:24)" ("What Think Ye of Christ?" *Ensign*, Nov. 1988, 68).

When will Satan's works be destroyed? (19:3) "Christ's power to destroy Satan and His works at the end of the world (D&C 19:3) is the binding of him at the beginning of the millennium, which is the end of the telestial world (D&C 45:55). Christ will bind him by destroying the wicked and bringing about the righteousness of the people who will not be destroyed, leaving Satan with no power (1 Nephi 22:26)" (Nyman, *Doctrine and Covenants Commentary*, 1:161).

Doctrine and Covenants 19:4–5. All Men Must Repent or Suffer

What is the relationship between repenting or suffering in this context? (19:4) President Dallin H. Oaks explained, "Our Savior has redeemed us from the sin of Adam, but what about the effects of our own sins? Since 'all have sinned' (Rom. 3:23), we are all spiritually dead. Again, our only hope for life is our Savior, who, the prophet Lehi taught, 'offereth himself a sacrifice for sin, to answer the ends of the law' (2 Ne. 2:7).

"In order to lay claim upon our Savior's life-giving triumph over the spiritual death we suffer because of our own sins, we must follow the conditions he has prescribed. As he has told us in modern revelation, 'I, God, have suffered these things for all, that they might not suffer if they would repent;

"'But if they would not repent they must suffer even as I' (D&C 19:16–17)" ("Light and Life of the World," *Ensign*, Nov. 1987, 65). ❂

Doctrine and Covenants 19:6–12. Eternal Punishment Is God's Punishment

What does it mean to "enter into [the Lord's] rest"? (19:9) President Russell M. Nelson prophetically promised: "Dear brothers and sisters, I grieve for those who leave the Church because they feel membership requires too much of them. They have not yet discovered that making and keeping covenants actually makes life easier! Each person who makes covenants in baptismal fonts and in temples—and keeps them—has increased access to the power of Jesus Christ. Please ponder that stunning truth!

"The reward for keeping covenants with God is heavenly power—power that strengthens us to withstand our trials, temptations, and heartaches better. This power eases our way. Those who live the higher laws of Jesus Christ have access to His higher power. Thus, covenant keepers are entitled to a special kind of *rest* that comes to them through their covenantal relationship with God" ("Overcome the World and Find Rest," *Liahona*, Nov. 2022, 96). See also commentary in this volume on Doctrine and Covenants 84:24. ◉

6 Nevertheless, it is not written that there shall be no end to this torment, but it is written *endless torment.*

7 Again, it is written *eternal damnation;* wherefore it is more express than other scriptures, that it might work upon the hearts of the children of men, altogether for my name's glory.

8 Wherefore, I will explain unto you this mystery, for it is meet unto you to know even as mine apostles.

9 I speak unto you that are chosen in this thing, even as one, that you may enter into my rest.

What Is "Endless Torment" and "Eternal Damnation"? (Doctrine and Covenants 19:6–7)

Elder James E. Talmage has written: "As to the duration of punishment, we may take assurance that it will be graded according to the sin; and that the conception of every sentence for misdeeds being interminable [never ending] is false.... Yet the scriptures speak of eternal and endless punishment. Any punishment ordained of God is eternal, for He is eternal. His is a system of endless punishment, for it will always exist as a place or condition prepared for disobedient spirits; yet the infliction of the penalty will have an end in every case of acceptable repentance and reparation.... However, as seen, there are some sins so great that their consequent punishments are not made known to man; these extreme penalties are reserved for the sons of Perdition.

"The false doctrine that the punishment to be visited upon erring souls is endless, that every sentence for sin is of interminable [never ending] duration, must be regarded as one of the most pernicious results of misapprehension of scripture.... True, the scriptures speak of everlasting burnings, eternal damnation, and the vengeance of eternal fire, as characteristics of the judgment provided for the wicked; yet in no instance is there justification for the inference that the individual sinner will have to suffer the wrath of offended justice forever and ever. The punishment in any case is sufficiently severe without the added and supreme horror of unending continuation. Justice must have her due; but when 'the uttermost farthing' is paid, the prison doors shall open and the captive be free. But the prison remains, and the law prescribing punishment for offenses is not to be repealed" (*Articles of Faith*, 60–61).

10 For, behold, the mystery of godliness, how great is it! For, behold, I am endless, and the punishment which is given from my hand is endless punishment, for Endless is my name. Wherefore—

11 Eternal punishment is God's punishment.

12 Endless punishment is God's punishment.

13 Wherefore, I command you to repent, and keep the commandments which you have received by the hand of my servant Joseph Smith, Jun., in my name;

14 And it is by my almighty power that you have received them;

15 Therefore I command you to repent—repent, lest I smite you by the rod of my mouth, and by my wrath, and by my anger, and your sufferings be sore—how sore you know not, how exquisite you know not, yea, how hard to bear you know not.

Why does the Lord use "Endless" as a name? (19:10) "The significance of this title is that the word is traditionally used in scripture as an adjective modifying a noun, whereas in modern revelation the word is appropriately used as a noun itself. Thus, in traditional usage a phrase like 'endless punishment' (with *endless* as an adjective) would have meant punishment that never ended. However, with *endless* as a noun—a name for Deity—*endless* punishment means it is God's punishment, thus taking on a qualitative rather than quantitative meaning" (Holland, *Witness for His Names*, 47; see also Moses 1:3; 7:35).

What is "eternal punishment" and "endless punishment"? (19:11–12) "In referring to the judgment that comes upon those who choose not to repent of their sins, the terms 'endless punishment' and 'eternal punishment' (see D&C 19:11–12) do not refer to the length of time that the wicked will suffer. The Savior said, 'I am endless, and the punishment which is given from my hand is endless punishment, for Endless is my name' (D&C 19:10). Because the Savior is Endless and Eternal, the terms 'endless punishment' and 'eternal punishment' refer to the source of punishment rather than the duration" (*Doctrine and Covenants Student Manual* [2018], 106).

Doctrine and Covenants 19:13–20. Christ Suffered for All, That They Might Not Suffer if They Would Repent

How did Martin Harris respond to the Lord's commandments? (19:13–14) In Section 19 the Lord issued several commands to Martin (see verses 13, 15, 20, 21, 25, 26, and 28). Clearly the Lord had important expectations for this good man. Months later, in March 1830, "Martin hoped to redeem his mortgaged farm by selling copies of the Book of Mormon.... According to Joseph Knight, Martin was carrying several copies of the Book of Mormon. He said, 'The Books will not sell for no Body wants them,' and told Joseph [Smith], 'I Want a Commandment.' Joseph's reply referred Martin to the previous revelation [D&C 19]: 'Fulfill what you have got.' 'But I must have a commandment,' repeated Martin. He received no further commandment" (McBride, "Contributions of Martin Harris," 8).

How do we avoid the suffering described by Jesus Christ? (19:15–17) Matthew S. Holland explained: "From direct, personal experience the Savior thus warns us, in modern scripture, that we have no idea how 'exquisite' our 'sufferings' will be if we do not repent," but "Thanks to [the Savior's] 'immediate goodness' (Mosiah 25:10), the *instant* we come unto [Him]—demonstrating faith in Him and a true change of heart—the crushing weight of our sins starts to shift from our backs to His" ("Exquisite Gift of the Son," *Ensign*, Nov. 2020, 46).

"Elder Neal A. Maxwell summarized it well: 'We will end up either choosing Christ's manner of living or His manner of suffering!' As we choose his manner of living we overcome spiritual death through the miraculous cleansing powers of the Atonement" (Callister, *Infinite Atonement*, 194–95).

What frees us from eternal suffering? (19:16) "A loving and wise Father sent us Jesus Christ to redeem us from the effects of sin, ensuring that we would not be left in a perpetual state of estrangement from God. Instead, through our Savior's gift of divine mercy, we are all unconditionally granted immortality and a return to the presence of God to be judged. In the Garden of Gethsemane and at Calvary, He used His power, given to Him by the Father, to suffer 'for all, that [we] might not suffer if [we] would repent.' Then He hung upon that tree and laid down His life—for us" (Browning, "Preserving Our Relationship with Heavenly Father and Jesus Christ," 4).

Why did the Savior's suffering cause Him to "bleed at every pore"? (19:18–19) "Luke substantiates the reality of his suffering: 'And being in an agony he prayed more earnestly' (Luke 22:44). Were not all his prayers earnest? Can we comprehend the intensity of suffering, the depth of pain that caused him now to pray even *more* earnestly? What overwhelming burden must he have been shouldering to have elicited from a God the admission that he was 'exceedingly sorrowful' (Matthew 26:38)? What torment pressed upon him so deeply that he 'fell on his face' in prayerful pleading (Matthew 26:39)? This was a crisis moment in the galaxy.

"As his agony accelerated, and eventually raced towards its climax without restraint and without release, his physical body finally revolted, and he sweat great drops of blood" (Callister, *Infinite Atonement*, 120). ⊕

When did the Lord withdraw the Holy Spirit from Martin Harris? (19:20) The phrase "at the time I withdrew my Spirit" may have had reference to the experience Martin Harris went through after losing the 116 pages of the Book of Mormon manuscript (see the section heading for Doctrine and Covenants 3). Both Joseph and Martin suffered serious chastisement from the Lord. It was as if the Lord were saying: "'Don't you remember, Martin, that a few months ago

16 For behold, I, God, have suffered these things for all, that they might not suffer if they would repent;

17 But if they would not repent they must suffer even as I;

18 Which suffering caused myself, even God, the greatest of all, to tremble because of pain, and to bleed at every pore, and to suffer both body and spirit—and would that I might not drink the bitter cup, and shrink—

19 Nevertheless, glory be to the Father, and I partook and finished my preparations unto the children of men.

20 Wherefore, I command you again to repent, lest I humble you with my almighty power; and that you confess your sins, lest you suffer these punishments of which I have spoken, of which in the smallest, yea, even in the least degree you have tasted at the time I withdrew my Spirit.

you disobeyed me? Do you recall how you suffered inwardly? That is just a foretaste of the suffering that comes to the man who will not be tempered to repentance'" (Widtsoe, *Message of the Doctrine and Covenants*, 36).

Doctrine and Covenants 19:21–28. Preach the Gospel of Repentance

Why was Martin Harris commanded to not share everything he knew? (19:21–22) "Martin Harris was instructed to 'preach naught but repentance,' and not to divulge to the 'world' things he had recently learned until it was wisdom in God to do so. The reason given was that 'they cannot bear meat now, but milk.' . . .

"The milk/meat metaphor, often employed in the scriptures, communicates the principle effectively because of our common experience in feeding children. Children thrive on milk, but would choke on meat. . . . When we are first introduced to the gospel, we are as children needing doctrinal milk. As we mature in learning and living the gospel, however, it is expected that gradually our spiritual digestive system will be able to handle more meaty doctrines" (Dahl, "Doctrinal Teachings in Nauvoo," 129).

How do we walk in the meekness of the Spirit? (19:23–24) "Please notice the characteristic the Lord used to describe Himself in the following scripture: 'Take my yoke upon you, and learn of me; for I am *meek and lowly in heart*' [Matthew 11:29; emphasis added]. . . .

"Instructively, the Savior chose to emphasize meekness from among all the attributes and virtues He potentially could have selected.

"A similar pattern is evident in a revelation received by the Prophet Joseph Smith in 1829 [see D&C 19:23]. . . .

"Meekness is a defining attribute of the Redeemer and is distinguished by righteous responsiveness, willing submissiveness, and strong self-restraint" (Bednar, "Meek and Lowly of Heart," *Ensign*, May 2018, 31–32).

Why was Martin warned about coveting his neighbor's wife? (19:25) "It is not known why Martin Harris would receive this particular warning. Martin's marriage was unhappy, due in part to his wife's decided opposition to his involvement in the translation and publication of the Book of Mormon. It may be that problems in his marriage were opening the door to temptation" (McConkie and Ostler, *Revelations of the Restoration*, 152).

21 And I command you that you preach naught but repentance, and show not these things unto the world until it is wisdom in me.

22 For they cannot bear meat now, but milk they must receive; wherefore, they must not know these things, lest they perish.

23 Learn of me, and listen to my words; walk in the meekness of my Spirit, and you shall have peace in me.

24 I am Jesus Christ; I came by the will of the Father, and I do his will.

25 And again, I command thee that thou shalt not covet thy neighbor's wife; nor seek thy neighbor's life.

Was Martin Harris obedient to the Lord's commandment to pay for the printing of the Book of Mormon? (19:26) President Dallin H. Oaks explained: "One of Martin Harris's greatest contributions to the Church, for which he should be honored for all time, was his financing the publication of the Book of Mormon. In August 1829 he mortgaged his home and farm to Egbert B. Grandin to secure payment on the printer's contract. Seven months later, the 5,000 copies of the first printing of the Book of Mormon were completed. Later, when the mortgage note fell due, the home and a portion of the farm were sold for $3,000. In this way, Martin Harris was obedient to the Lord's revelation [D&C 19:26, 35]" ("Witness," *Ensign*, May 1999, 36).

What does the word *Gentile* refer to in this context? (19:27) See commentary in this volume on Doctrine and Covenants 35:7.

Doctrine and Covenants 19:29–41. Declare Glad Tidings

Why was Martin counseled against discussing "tenets" while declaring the gospel? (19:30–31) "Tenets are the dogmas or principles generally accepted by a majority as true, whether those principles are factual or not. Thus we should not dispute with others about such matters, nor pursue discussions among ourselves about such matters that can cause feelings to be hurt or cause disputations to arise.

"We should rather preach the first principles of the gospel, which are so necessary for our full growth and development. When we understand the basics or true fundamental principles of the gospel, we will not be buffeted by the doctrines and beliefs of men that so often lead to quarrels and misunderstandings" (Theodore M. Burton, in Conference Report, Oct. 1969, 35).

What led Martin to meet his financial obligation to the Lord? (19:34–35) "Martin did not make payment within the prescribed time period. Instead he

26 And again, I command thee that thou shalt not covet thine own property, but impart it freely to the printing of the Book of Mormon, which contains the truth and the word of God—

27 Which is my word to the Gentile, that soon it may go to the Jew, of whom the Lamanites are a remnant, that they may believe the gospel, and look not for a Messiah to come who has already come.

28 And again, I command thee that thou shalt pray vocally as well as in thy heart; yea, before the world as well as in secret, in public as well as in private.

29 And thou shalt declare glad tidings, yea, publish it upon the mountains, and upon every high place, and among every people that thou shalt be permitted to see.

30 And thou shalt do it with all humility, trusting in me, reviling not against revilers.

31 And of tenets thou shalt not talk, but thou shalt declare repentance and faith on the Savior, and remission of sins by baptism, and by fire, yea, even the Holy Ghost.

32 Behold, this is a great and the last commandment which I shall give unto you concerning this matter; for this shall suffice for thy daily walk, even unto the end of thy life.

33 And misery thou shalt receive if thou wilt slight these counsels, yea, even the destruction of thyself and property.

34 Impart a portion of thy property, yea, even part of thy lands, and all save the support of thy family.

35 Pay the debt thou hast contracted with the printer. Release thyself from bondage.

36 Leave thy house and home, except when thou shalt desire to see thy family;

37 And speak freely to all; yea, preach, exhort, declare the truth, even with a loud voice, with a sound of rejoicing, crying—Hosanna, hosanna, blessed be the name of the Lord God!

38 Pray always, and I will pour out my Spirit upon you, and great shall be your blessing—yea, even more than if you should obtain treasures of earth and corruptibleness to the extent thereof.

39 Behold, canst thou read this without rejoicing and lifting up thy heart for gladness?

40 Or canst thou run about longer as a blind guide?

41 Or canst thou be humble and meek, and conduct thyself wisely before me? Yea, come unto me thy Savior. Amen.

dickered, bargained, and handled the transaction in his own way, seemingly unmindful of the Lord's directive to 'not covet thine own property . . . ' (D&C 19:26). . . . Then, in no uncertain terms, the Lord said, 'Pay the debt . . . ' (D&C 19:35). Belatedly but with determination, Martin did as the Lord commanded. The contractual arrangement, however, was not fully satisfied until January 12, 1832, as certified by Truman Hemingway, the commissioner of deeds for Wayne County" (Black, *400 Questions and Answers*, 72).

What can we learn from the Lord's counsel to Martin Harris about debt? (19:35) "Avoid the philosophy that yesterday's luxuries have become today's necessities. They aren't necessities unless we make them so. Many enter into long-term debt only to find that changes occur: people become ill or incapacitated, companies fail or downsize, jobs are lost, natural disasters befall us. . . .

"I urge you to live within your means. One cannot spend more than one earns and remain solvent. I promise you that you will then be happier than you would be if you were constantly worrying about how to make the next payment on nonessential debt. In the Doctrine and Covenants we read: 'Pay the debt thou hast contracted. . . . Release thyself from bondage' (D&C 19:35)" (Thomas S. Monson, *Teachings*, 83).

What are some things for which we should "pray always"? (19:38–39) President M. Russell Ballard testified: "I invite you to pray always. Pray for your family. Pray for the leaders of nations. Pray for the courageous people who are on the front lines in the current battles against social, environmental, political, and biological plagues that impact all people throughout the world: the rich and the poor, the young and the old" ("Watch Thee Therefore, and Pray Always," *Ensign*, Nov. 2020, 78). See also commentary in this volume on Doctrine and Covenants 10:5. ⊕

How did Martin Harris finally accept the Savior's invitation to "come unto me"? (19:40–41) "During 1837 there were intense financial and spiritual conflicts in Kirtland, Ohio. Martin Harris later said that he 'lost confidence in Joseph Smith' and 'his mind became darkened' (quoted in [Richard Lloyd] Anderson, *Investigating the Book of Mormon Witnesses*, 110). He was released from the high council in September 1837 and three months later was excommunicated. . . .

"Finally, in 1870, Martin's desire to be reunited with his family in Utah resulted in a warm invitation from Brigham Young, a ticket for his passage, and an official escort from one of the Presidents of Seventy.

A Utah interviewer of the 87-year-old man described him as 'remarkably vigorous for one of his years, . . . his memory being very good' (*Deseret News*, 31 Aug. 1870). He was rebaptized" (Oaks, "Witness," *Ensign*, May 1999, 37). ⊕

Introduction to Doctrine and Covenants 20

"The Lord began revealing parts of Doctrine and Covenants 20 in the summer of 1829. The complete revelation was probably recorded shortly after the Church was organized (April 6, 1830)" (see section heading, Doctrine and Covenants 20).

"In June 1829, the Lord gave Oliver Cowdery instructions to write a document that would serve as the Articles and Covenants of the Church. Oliver sought further information from the Lord as to what should be included in that document [see D&C 18:2–4]. . . . The manuscript of the soon-to-be-published Book of Mormon served as a primary source for the Articles and Covenants of the Church. In addition, through the Holy Ghost, the voice of the Lord guided Oliver Cowdery and later the Prophet Joseph Smith in writing this revelation" (Ostler, "Articles and Covenants," 84–85).

Joseph Smith's history describes how the Articles and Covenants came to be: "'In this manner did the Lord continue to give us instructions from time to time, concerning the duties which now devolved upon us, and among many other things of the kind, we obtained of him the following [that is, Articles and Covenants], by the Spirit of Prophecy and revelation; which not only gave us much information, but also pointed out to us the precise day upon which, according to his will and commandment, we should proceed to organize his Church once again, here upon the earth'" (Joseph Smith Papers, Historical Introduction to "Articles and Covenants, circa April 1830 [D&C 20]," [4]).

"The role Oliver's 'Articles of the Church of Christ' played in the organization [of the Church] is unclear. Some time after Oliver had completed the articles, Joseph told him there was more. Joseph's superseding revelation, now part of Doctrine and Covenants 20, seems to have been completed after the organizational meeting in April but before the Church's first conference, held in June. At the June conference, this revealed document was accepted as a statement of polity [organization] for the new church. Its importance was highlighted by the fact that it was the first revelatory text published in the Church's newspaper, and it was later printed as section 2 of the 1835 edition of the Doctrine and Covenants, after the preface dictated as a revelation in 1835" (Jeffrey G. Cannon, "Build Up My Church," 31).

"[D&C 20] proclaims the role of God's Church in restoring the gospel. It establishes basic doctrines such as the Godhead, the creation, the fall, the atonement, faith, repentance, baptism, sanctification and justification. It establishes the qualifications for and covenant of baptism. And it outlines the duties and organization of the priesthood leadership and of the general Church membership" (Elieson, *Historical Context*, 1:136).

SECTION 20

Revelation on Church organization and government, given through Joseph Smith the Prophet, at or near Fayette, New York. Portions of this revelation may have been given as early as summer 1829. The complete revelation, known at the time as the Articles and Covenants, was likely recorded soon after April 6, 1830 (the day the Church was organized). The Prophet wrote, "We obtained of Him [Jesus Christ] the following, by the spirit of prophecy and revelation; which not only gave us much information, but also pointed out to us the precise day upon which, according to His will and commandment, we should proceed to organize His Church once more here upon the earth."

1 The rise of the Church of Christ in these last days, being one thousand eight hundred and thirty years since the coming of our Lord and Savior Jesus Christ in the flesh, it being regularly organized and established agreeable to the laws of our country, by the will and commandments of God, in the fourth month, and on the sixth day of the month which is called April—

2 Which commandments were given to Joseph Smith, Jun., who was called of God, and ordained an apostle of Jesus Christ, to be the first elder of this church;

3 And to Oliver Cowdery, who was also called of God, an apostle of Jesus Christ, to be the second elder of this church, and ordained under his hand;

4 And this according to the grace of our Lord and Savior Jesus Christ, to whom be all glory, both now and forever. Amen.

Doctrine and Covenants 20:1–16. The Book of Mormon Proves the Divinity of the Latter-Day Work

Why is the Church's name listed differently than we know it today? (20:1) "The Church's name was specified by revelation and is a statement of its true identity. The Savior instructed the Nephites that his Church should bear his name (3 Ne. 27:8). Hence, following the 1830 organization of the Church, it was commonly known as 'The Church of Christ.' . . . In the mid-1830s, the title 'Church of the Latter-day Saints' was frequently used. A revelation in 1838, however, specified that the Church's proper name should be 'The Church of Jesus Christ of Latter-day Saints' (D&C 115:4)" (Cowan, "Church, Names of," 206).

Does this verse give the exact date of the Lord's birth? (20:1) If this was an exact date, it would place the Lord's birth as April 1, 1 B.C. (see Talmage, *Jesus the Christ*, 97). However, Richard Lloyd Anderson stated, "Does this give the exact year of Christ's birth? That calculation places too much weight on what may have been an elaborate phrase of dating or an incidental statement. The first edition of the Doctrine and Covenants Commentary (Hyrum M. Smith) cautioned against using this to prove that Christ was born at the exact beginning of the Christian Era; so have [President] J. Reuben Clark and [Elder] Bruce R. McConkie. Part of the problem is that Christ was alive at the death of Herod the Great, an event of 4 B.C. in careful chronologies" ("Organization Revelations," 114–15).

Who were the "first elder" and the "second elder" of the Church? (20:2–3) "Oliver was the 'second elder' of the Church (D&C 20:1–3). Thus, in the beginning, he stood by Joseph Smith's side as his successor, holding the same keys that the Prophet held, but he was subservient to the 'first elder' of the Church. ([Note] that the terms 'first elder' and 'second elder' were added to the original revelation in 1835 when it was published as part of the Doctrine and Covenants. Prior to this time the wording was simply 'elder.' However, from the onset Oliver's position was clearly secondary to Joseph's)" (Brewster, *Prophets, Priesthood Keys, and Succession*, 31). See also commentary in this volume on Doctrine and Covenants 28:2–3.

What were the "vanities of the world" that led Joseph Smith to seek forgiveness? (20:5–6) For the Prophet's comments regarding this period of his life, see Joseph Smith—History 1:28–29. "Joseph and his friends were young and lighthearted. Sometimes they made foolish mistakes, and Joseph found that being forgiven once did not mean he would never need to repent again. . . .

"Joseph was still unsure if God was pleased with him. He could no longer feel the forgiveness and peace he had felt after his vision of the Father and Son. Instead, he often felt condemned for his weakness and imperfections.

"On September 21, 1823, seventeen-year-old Joseph . . . began to pray, pleading fervently that God would forgive his sins" (*Saints*, 1:20, 21).

In what way does the Book of Mormon contain the fulness of the gospel? (20:9) "The Lord Himself has stated that the Book of Mormon contains the 'fulness of the gospel of Jesus Christ' (D&C 20:9). That does not mean it contains every teaching, every doctrine ever revealed. Rather, it means that in the Book of Mormon we will find the fulness of those doctrines required for our salvation. And they are taught plainly and simply so that even children can learn the ways of salvation and exaltation. The Book of Mormon offers so much that broadens our understandings of the doctrines of salvation. Without it, much of what is taught in other scriptures would not be nearly so plain and precious" (*Ezra Taft Benson* [manual], 131).

5 After it was truly manifested unto this first elder that he had received a remission of his sins, he was entangled again in the vanities of the world;

6 But after repenting, and humbling himself sincerely, through faith, God ministered unto him by an holy angel, whose countenance was as lightning, and whose garments were pure and white above all other whiteness;

7 And gave unto him commandments which inspired him;

8 And gave him power from on high, by the means which were before prepared, to translate the Book of Mormon;

9 Which contains a record of a fallen people, and the fulness of the gospel of Jesus Christ to the Gentiles and to the Jews also;

10 Which was given by inspiration, and is confirmed to others by the ministering of angels, and is declared unto the world by them—

Where Was the Church of Christ Organized on April 6, 1830? (Doctrine and Covenants 20:1)

"The Church of Christ was officially established at a meeting at Peter Whitmer, Sr.'s home in Fayette Township, New York" (Joseph Smith Papers, Documents: Volume 1, "Part 3 Introduction April–September 1830").

"On Tuesday, April 6, 1830, Joseph Smith, Oliver Cowdery, and others convened to organize the Church of Christ. They had anticipated this meeting since the summer of 1829, when revelations directed Joseph and Oliver to establish a church as soon as the Book of Mormon could be published and believers could be gathered. No minutes of the meeting have survived, but a few sources, including a revelation received on the occasion, indicate some of what transpired. The meeting opened with prayer, and the assembly sustained Joseph and Oliver as elders and teachers in the Church. Joseph

Restored Peter Whitmer Family Home, Fayette, New York.

and Oliver then ordained each other as Church elders, the participants in the meeting partook of the sacrament of the Lord's Supper, Joseph and Oliver laid hands on the heads of those who had previously been baptized to give

11 Proving to the world that the holy scriptures are true, and that God does inspire men and call them to his holy work in this age and generation, as well as in generations of old;

12 Thereby showing that he is the same God yesterday, today, and forever. Amen.

How does the Book of Mormon prove that the Bible is true? (20:11) "The Bible is the word of God. It is always identified first in our canon, our 'standard works.'...

"One of the great purposes of continuing revelation through living prophets is to declare to the world through additional witnesses that the Bible is true. '*This* is written,' an ancient prophet said, speaking of the Book of Mormon, 'for the intent that ye may believe *that*,' speaking of the Bible [Mormon 7:9]. In one of the earliest revelations received by Joseph Smith, the Lord said, 'Behold, I do not bring [the Book of Mormon forth] to destroy [the Bible] but to build it up' [D&C 10:52]" (Holland, "My Words . . . Never Cease," *Ensign*, May 2008, 92).

13 Therefore, having so great witnesses, by them shall the world be judged, even as many as shall hereafter come to a knowledge of this work.

How will the world be judged by the Book of Mormon? (20:13) President Jeffrey R. Holland testified of the importance of receiving the Book of Mormon in the last days: "My witness echoes that of Nephi, who wrote part of the book in his 'last days':

"'Hearken unto these words and believe in Christ; and if ye believe not in these words believe in Christ. *And if ye shall believe in Christ ye will believe in these words, for they are the words of Christ*, . . . and they teach all men that they should do good.

"'And if they are not the words of Christ, judge ye—for Christ will show unto you, with power and great glory, that they are his words, *at the last day*' [2 Nephi 33:10–11; emphasis added]" ("Safety for the Soul," *Ensign*, Nov. 2009, 90). ✛

14 And those who receive it in faith, and work righteousness, shall receive a crown of eternal life;

What blessings can come to those who receive the Book of Mormon? (20:14–15) "Each individual who prayerfully studies the Book of Mormon can also receive a testimony of its divinity. In addition, this book

them the gift of the Holy Ghost and confirm them members of the Church, and Joseph received the revelation now found in Doctrine and Covenants 21.

"Between April 6 and June 9, when the first Church conference was held, Joseph and Oliver organized branches in Fayette, Manchester, and Colesville, New York. A few early accounts confused the locations of these meetings, suggesting the April 6 organizational meeting took place in Manchester rather than in Fayette. An early manuscript copy of Doctrine and Covenants 21 includes a notation suggesting the revelation was given in Manchester. William W. Phelps used this notation when he prepared the revelation for publication in the 1833 Book of Commandments. Other records linked to Phelps and Orson Pratt—neither of whom was present at the organizational meeting—also name Manchester as the location of the April 6 meeting. However, several early documents produced by Joseph and Oliver, together with later printings of the Doctrine and Covenants, either state that the meeting occurred at Fayette or omit references to Manchester. Accordingly, most historians concur with the principal observers and locate the founding meeting in Fayette" (Church History Topics, "Founding Meeting of the Church of Christ").

can help with personal problems in a very real way. Do you want to get rid of a bad habit? Do you want to improve relationships in your family? Do you want to increase your spiritual capacity? Read the Book of Mormon! It will bring you closer to the Lord and His loving power. He who fed a multitude with five loaves and two fishes—He who helped the blind to see and the lame to walk—can also bless you! He has promised that those who live by the precepts of this book 'shall receive a crown of eternal life'" (Nelson, "Testimony of the Book of Mormon," *Ensign*, Nov. 1999, 71).

Doctrine and Covenants 20:17–28. The Doctrines of Creation, Fall, Atonement, and Baptism Are Affirmed

What are the doctrinal truths made clear by the Book of Mormon? (20:17) "In Doctrine and Covenants 20:17, the phrase 'by these things' refers to the truths we know through the Book of Mormon (see D&C 20:8–10). Through the Book of Mormon and the Restoration of the fulness of the gospel, Latter-day Saints have been given a clearer understanding of the doctrines related to our personal salvation, especially the central role of Jesus Christ as our Lord and Savior" (*Doctrine and Covenants Student Manual* [2018], 124).

15 But those who harden their hearts in unbelief, and reject it, it shall turn to their own condemnation—

16 For the Lord God has spoken it; and we, the elders of the church, have heard and bear witness to the words of the glorious Majesty on high, to whom be glory forever and ever. Amen.

17 By these things we know that there is a God in heaven, who is infinite and eternal, from everlasting to everlasting the same unchangeable God, the framer of heaven and earth, and all things which are in them;

18 And that he created man, male and female, after his own image and in his own likeness, created he them;

19 And gave unto them commandments that they should love and serve him, the only living and true God, and that he should be the only being whom they should worship.

The Doctrine and Covenants Highlights Doctrinal Truths Taught in the Book of Mormon

"In the twentieth section of the Doctrine and Covenants, the Lord devotes several verses to summarizing the vital truths which the Book of Mormon teaches (see D&C 20:17–36). It speaks of God, the creation of man, the Fall, the Atonement, the ascension of Christ into heaven, prophets, faith, repentance, baptism, the Holy Ghost, endurance, prayer, justification and sanctification through grace, and loving and serving God.

"We must know these essential truths. Aaron and Ammon and their brethren in the Book of Mormon taught these same kinds of truths to the Lamanite people (see Alma 18:22–39), who were 'in the darkest abyss' (Alma 26:3). After accepting these eternal truths, the Book of Mormon states, those converted Lamanites never did fall away (see Alma 23:6).

"If our children and grandchildren are taught and heed these same truths, will they fall away? We best instruct them in the Book of Mormon at our dinner table, by our firesides, at their bedsides, and in our letters and phone calls—in all of our goings and comings. . . .

"'The elders, priests and teachers of this church shall teach the principles of my gospel, which are in . . . the Book of Mormon,' says the Lord in the 42nd section of the Doctrine and Covenants ([D&C 42:12])" (Benson, "New Witness for Christ," *Ensign*, Nov. 1984, 7).

20 But by the transgression of these holy laws man became sensual and devilish, and became fallen man.

21 Wherefore, the Almighty God gave his Only Begotten Son, as it is written in those scriptures which have been given of him.

22 He suffered temptations but gave no heed unto them.

23 He was crucified, died, and rose again the third day;

24 And ascended into heaven, to sit down on the right hand of the Father, to reign with almighty power according to the will of the Father;

25 That as many as would believe and be baptized in his holy name, and endure in faith to the end, should be saved—

26 Not only those who believed after he came in the meridian of time, in the flesh, but all those from the beginning, even as many as were before he came, who believed in the words of the holy prophets, who spake as they were inspired by the gift of the Holy Ghost, who truly testified of him in all things, should have eternal life,

27 As well as those who should come after, who should believe in the gifts and callings of God by the Holy Ghost, which beareth record of the Father and of the Son;

28 Which Father, Son, and Holy Ghost are one God, infinite and eternal, without end. Amen.

What temptations did Jesus face? (20:22) "The Savior's temptations were not limited to direct confrontations with the Evil One [see Matthew 4:1–11]. . . . Alma knew that he would suffer 'temptations of every kind' (Alma 7:11). This would include temptations relating to 'pain of body, hunger, thirst, and fatigue' (Mosiah 3:7). No doubt he would face temptations of greed, power, and fame. Every temptation of the flesh would face him. As Paul said, he 'was in *all points* tempted like as we are' (Hebrews 4:15; emphasis added). Abinadi made it clear, however, that while he 'suffereth temptation,' he 'yieldeth not to the temptation' (Mosiah 15:5). The Doctrine and Covenants confirms this same truth: 'He suffered temptations but gave no heed unto them' (D&C 20:22). There were choices, confrontations, and encounters, but never internalization, rationalization, or indulgence" (Callister, *Infinite Atonement*, 107).

In what ways are the Father, Son, and Holy Ghost one God? (20:28) "They are distinct beings, but they are one in purpose and effort. They are united as one in bringing to pass the grand, divine plan for the salvation and exaltation of the children of God. . . .

"Christ pleaded with His Father concerning the Apostles, whom He loved, saying:

"'Neither pray I for these alone, but for them also which shall believe on me through their word;

"'That they all may be one; as thou, Father, art in me, and I in thee, that they also may be one in us' (John 17:20–21).

"It is that perfect unity between the Father, the Son, and the Holy Ghost that binds these three into the oneness of the divine Godhead" (Hinckley, "Father, Son, and Holy Ghost," *Ensign*, Nov. 1986, 51). See also commentary in this volume on Doctrine and Covenants 35:2.

Doctrine and Covenants 20:29–37. Laws Governing Repentance, Justification, Sanctification, and Baptism Are Set Forth

What happens when we are sanctified and justified through Jesus Christ? (20:30–31) "Because of 'the infinite virtue of His great atoning sacrifice,' Jesus Christ can satisfy or 'answer the ends of the law' on our behalf. Pardon comes by the grace of Him who has satisfied the demands of justice by His own suffering. . . . He removes our condemnation without removing the law. We are pardoned and placed in a condition of righteousness with Him. We become, like Him, without sin. We are sustained and protected by the law, by justice. We are, in a word, *justified*. . . .

"To be sanctified through the blood of Christ is to become clean, pure, and holy. If justification removes the punishment for past sin, then sanctification removes the stain or effects of sin" (Christofferson, "Justification and Sanctification," *Ensign*, Jun. 2001, 20, 22). ✪

How can we avoid a "fall from grace"? (20:32–33) "To be Christlike, a person chooses God, walks humbly with Him, seeks to please Him, and keeps covenants with Him. Individuals who walk humbly with God remember what Heavenly Father and Jesus Christ have done for them.

"'Am I doing enough? What else should I be doing?' The action we take in response to these questions is central to our happiness in this life and in the eternities. The Savior does not want us to take salvation for granted. Even after we have made sacred covenants, there is a possibility that we may 'fall from grace and depart from the living God.' So we should 'take heed and pray always' to avoid falling 'into temptation'" (Renlund, "Do Justly, Love Mercy, and Walk Humbly with God," *Ensign*, Nov. 2020, 111).

How is it that the restored gospel does not add to nor diminish from truths revealed previously? (20:35) "The revelations received through the Prophet Joseph Smith and other latter-day prophets reflect all the truths that have been revealed by God since the time of Adam, neither adding to it nor diminishing

29 And we know that all men must repent and believe on the name of Jesus Christ, and worship the Father in his name, and endure in faith on his name to the end, or they cannot be saved in the kingdom of God.

30 And we know that justification through the grace of our Lord and Savior Jesus Christ is just and true;

31 And we know also, that sanctification through the grace of our Lord and Savior Jesus Christ is just and true, to all those who love and serve God with all their mights, minds, and strength.

32 But there is a possibility that man may fall from grace and depart from the living God;

33 Therefore let the church take heed and pray always, lest they fall into temptation;

34 Yea, and even let those who are sanctified take heed also.

35 And we know that these things are true and according to the revelations of John, neither adding to, nor diminishing from the prophecy of his book, the holy scriptures, or the revelations of God which shall come hereafter by the gift and power of the Holy Ghost, the voice of God, or the ministering of angels.

36 And the Lord God has spoken it; and honor, power and glory be rendered to his holy name, both now and ever. Amen.

37 *And again, by way of commandment to the church concerning the manner of baptism—* All those who humble themselves before God, and desire to be baptized, and come forth with broken hearts and contrite spirits, and witness before the church that they have truly repented of all their sins, and are willing to take upon them the name of Jesus Christ, having a determination to serve him to the end, and truly manifest by their works that they have received of the Spirit of Christ unto the remission of their sins, shall be received by baptism into his church.

38 *The duty of the elders, priests, teachers, deacons, and members of the church of Christ—* An apostle is an elder, and it is his calling to baptize;

39 And to ordain other elders, priests, teachers, and deacons;

40 And to administer bread and wine—the emblems of the flesh and blood of Christ—

41 And to confirm those who are baptized into the church, by the laying on of hands for the baptism of fire and the Holy Ghost, according to the scriptures;

42 And to teach, expound, exhort, baptize, and watch over the church;

from it. In nothing does the restored gospel contradict, add to, or diminish from the fulness of the gospel (in the narrow and scriptural sense explained ... in v. 9) as revealed to other prophets, including John, the last prophet of the former dispensation (see Revelation 22:18–19)" (Robinson and Garrett, *Commentary on the Doctrine and Covenants,* 1:138).

Why is baptism essential for a person to be received into the Church? (20:37) "Baptism stands out in modern revelation as the foundation covenant for salvation. And to bring about this eternal result, the following conditions must be met: full repentance as measured by a worthy life before baptism (D&C 20:37). . . .

"Theologians have resisted baptism as an essential element of salvation because a ceremony would thus be valued higher than inner faith or righteousness. But since Latter-day Saints view baptism as a covenant expressing faith and a means to virtue, ritual and reality are designed to blend. This covenant is a profound causal factor, a personal and social commitment, the specific obligations of which continue in the covenant of the Lord's Supper (D&C 20:37 and 20:77)" (Richard Lloyd Anderson, "Organization Revelations," 117). ◉

Doctrine and Covenants 20:38–67. Duties of Elders, Priests, Teachers, and Deacons Are Summarized

In what way is an *apostle* also an *elder*? (20:38) Elder D. Todd Christofferson explained: "Years ago, President Boyd K. Packer observed that 'the priesthood is greater than any of its offices. . . . The priesthood is not divisible. An elder holds as much priesthood as an Apostle (see D&C 20:38). When a man [has the priesthood conferred upon him], he receives all of it. However, there are offices within the priesthood— divisions of authority and responsibility. . . . Sometimes one office is spoken of as being "higher than" or "lower than" another office. Rather than "higher" or "lower," offices in the Melchizedek Priesthood represent different areas of service.' Brethren, I devoutly hope that we will no longer speak in terms of being 'advanced' to another office in the Melchizedek Priesthood" ("Elders Quorum," *Ensign,* May 2018, 56).

What does it mean to conduct Church meetings as "led by the Holy Ghost"? (20:45) "Leaders should prayerfully seek the guidance of the Lord in planning meetings, in selecting speakers and the topics to be addressed, and in the choosing of the sacred hymns of praise. Meetings should be conducted in a reverential manner that will be conducive to the spirit of true worship. This scriptural injunction . . . is not reserved or directed solely to presiding officers. Speakers and teachers should likewise prayerfully seek inspiration that their part will be 'led by the Spirit.' Congregation members, too, have a sacred obligation to spiritually prepare for meetings and attend them in the proper frame of mind so as to be touched by the power of the Holy Ghost" (McConkie, Millet, and Top, *Doctrinal Commentary on the Book of Mormon*, 4:332).

What do we understand about the different offices in the Aaronic Priesthood? (20:46–59) "The Lord Himself held those of the lesser priesthood with a regard that honors their potential and their value to Him. Listen to these words, spoken by John the Baptist when the Aaronic Priesthood was restored [see D&C 13:1]. . . .

"Quorums of deacons, teachers, and priests counsel regularly to draw every member of the quorum to the Lord. Presidencies assign members to reach out in faith and love. Deacons pass the sacrament with reverence and with faith that members will feel the effect of the Atonement and resolve to keep commandments as they partake of those sacred emblems.

"Teachers and priests pray with their companions to fulfill the charge to watch over the Church, person by person. And those companionships pray together as they learn the needs and the hopes of heads of families. As they do, they are being prepared for the great day when they will preside as a father, in faith, in a family of their own" (Eyring, "Preparatory Priesthood," *Ensign*, Nov. 2014, 62).

Like the Young Men, "Young Women class presidencies function under priesthood authority when the presidencies are set apart (see Doctrine and Covenants 42:11; 107:5; Articles of Faith 1:5; *General Handbook*, 3.4.1)" ("Aaronic Priesthood Quorum and Young Women Class Presidency Orientation," 2). They

43 And to confirm the church by the laying on of the hands, and the giving of the Holy Ghost;

44 And to take the lead of all meetings.

45 The elders are to conduct the meetings as they are led by the Holy Ghost, according to the commandments and revelations of God.

46 The priest's duty is to preach, teach, expound, exhort, and baptize, and administer the sacrament,

47 And visit the house of each member, and exhort them to pray vocally and in secret and attend to all family duties.

48 And he may also ordain other priests, teachers, and deacons.

49 And he is to take the lead of meetings when there is no elder present;

50 But when there is an elder present, he is only to preach, teach, expound, exhort, and baptize,

51 And visit the house of each member, exhorting them to pray vocally and in secret and attend to all family duties.

52 In all these duties the priest is to assist the elder if occasion requires.

53 The teacher's duty is to watch over the church always, and be with and strengthen them;

54 And see that there is no iniquity in the church, neither hardness with each other, neither lying, backbiting, nor evil speaking;

55 And see that the church meet together often, and also see that all the members do their duty.

56 And he is to take the lead of meetings in the absence of the elder or priest—

57 And is to be assisted always, in all his duties in the church, by the deacons, if occasion requires.

58 But neither teachers nor deacons have authority to baptize, administer the sacrament, or lay on hands;

59 They are, however, to warn, expound, exhort, and teach, and invite all to come unto Christ.

60 Every elder, priest, teacher, or deacon is to be ordained according to the gifts and callings of God unto him; and he is to be ordained by the power of the Holy Ghost, which is in the one who ordains him.

61 The several elders composing this church of Christ are to meet in conference once in three months, or from time to time as said conferences shall direct or appoint;

62 And said conferences are to do whatever church business is necessary to be done at the time.

63 The elders are to receive their licenses from other elders, by vote of the church to which they belong, or from the conferences.

are "are called and set apart to plan and implement the Young Women program. . . . This is a sacred invitation to participate in temple and family history work, serve in leadership positions, minister to your fellow sisters, and share your testimony with your family and friends" (Cordon, "150th Anniversary," *Liahona*, Jun. 2020, 56, 57).

How does this instruction apply to all members of the Church today? (20:53) Speaking to Church members, President Jeffrey R. Holland taught: "[Jesus] summarized [our] task in one fundamental commandment: 'Love one another; as I have loved you.' . . .

"We have a heaven-sent opportunity as an entire Church to demonstrate 'pure religion . . . undefiled before God'—'to bear one another's burdens, that they may be light' and to 'comfort those that stand in need of comfort,' to minister to the widows and the fatherless, the married and the single, the strong and the distraught, the downtrodden and the robust, the happy and the sad—in short, all of us, every one of us, because we all need to feel the warm hand of friendship and hear the firm declaration of faith" ("Be With and Strengthen Them," *Ensign*, May 2018, 101–2).

Why isn't general conference held every three months today? (20:61–62) "About two months after being organized on April 6, 1830, The Church of Jesus Christ of Latter-day Saints held its first general conference at the Peter Whitmer home in Fayette, Seneca County, New York. At that June 9 meeting about thirty members were in attendance and other people who were anxious to learn. This commenced a vital and enduring tradition. . . .

"The conferences from 1830 to 1837 were called as needed by the Prophet Joseph Smith, the first President of the Church. . . .

"From 1838 to 1844 the concept of a regular general conference for the Church was set firmly in place and the precedents were established for the annual and semiannual conferences in April and October" (Burnett, "General Conference," 1:307).

What was the purpose of a priesthood holder having a certificate or license? (20:63–67) From the Joseph Smith Papers we learn that a certificate or license was: "A document certifying an individual's office in the church and authorizing him 'to perform the duty of his calling.' The 'Articles and Covenants' of the church implied that only elders could issue licenses; individuals ordained by a priest to an office in the lesser priesthood had to take a certificate to an elder before receiving a license. Licenses were routinely issued to those holding church offices to certify their standing and authority in the church and could be revoked as a measure of church discipline. Licenses were also provided to those sent out to proselytize or build up the church in order to signify that they had been appointed and ordained according to church procedures" (Joseph Smith Papers, Joseph Smith Papers Glossary, s.v. "License").

Doctrine and Covenants 20:68–74. Duties of Members, Blessing of Children, and the Mode of Baptism Are Revealed

What is the current Church policy for confirming recent converts? (20:68–69) "After a person is baptized, he or she is confirmed a member of the Church and receives the Holy Ghost by the laying on of hands (see Doctrine and Covenants 20:41; Acts 19:1–6). The person becomes a member of the Church after both of these ordinances are completed and properly recorded (see John 3:5; Doctrine and Covenants 33:11; 3 Nephi 27:20). . . .

"The bishop oversees the performance of confirmations. Eight-year-old children are typically confirmed on the day they are baptized. Converts are typically confirmed in any sacrament meeting in the ward where they live, preferably on the Sunday after their baptism. However, the bishop can allow the confirmation to take place at the baptismal service as an exception" (*General Handbook* [2021], 18.8). ☉

What is meant by a "godly walk"? (20:69) "[The Apostle] Paul taught, those who have put on Christ enjoy the 'fruit of the Spirit' (Galatians 5:22), the sweet manifestations of righteousness that follow naturally from a changed heart. Paul concluded, 'If we live in the Spirit, let us also walk in the Spirit' (Galatians 5:25). In today's parlance, if we talk the talk we really ought to walk the walk. There's something different about

64 Each priest, teacher, or deacon, who is ordained by a priest, may take a certificate from him at the time, which certificate, when presented to an elder, shall entitle him to a license, which shall authorize him to perform the duties of his calling, or he may receive it from a conference.

65 No person is to be ordained to any office in this church, where there is a regularly organized branch of the same, without the vote of that church;

66 But the presiding elders, traveling bishops, high councilors, high priests, and elders, may have the privilege of ordaining, where there is no branch of the church that a vote may be called.

67 Every president of the high priesthood (or presiding elder), bishop, high councilor, and high priest, is to be ordained by the direction of a high council or general conference.

68 *The duty of the members after they are received by baptism*—The elders or priests are to have a sufficient time to expound all things concerning the church of Christ to their understanding, previous to their partaking of the sacrament and being confirmed by the laying on of the hands of the elders, so that all things may be done in order.

69 And the members shall manifest before the church, and also before the elders, by a godly walk and conversation, that they are worthy of it, that there may be works and faith agreeable to the holy scriptures—walking in holiness before the Lord.

70 Every member of the church of Christ having children is to bring them unto the elders before the church, who are to lay their hands upon them in the name of Jesus Christ, and bless them in his name.

71 No one can be received into the church of Christ unless he has arrived unto the years of accountability before God, and is capable of repentance.

72 Baptism is to be administered in the following manner unto all those who repent—

73 The person who is called of God and has authority from Jesus Christ to baptize, shall go down into the water with the person who has presented himself or herself for baptism, and shall say, calling him or her by name: Having been commissioned of Jesus Christ, I baptize you in the name of the Father, and of the Son, and of the Holy Ghost. Amen.

74 Then shall he immerse him or her in the water, and come forth again out of the water.

75 It is expedient that the church meet together often to partake of bread and wine in the remembrance of the Lord Jesus;

76 And the elder or priest shall administer it; and after this manner shall he administer it—he shall kneel with the church and call upon the Father in solemn prayer, saying:

individuals who have been born again, who have given themselves to the Lord and his work and whose highest aspiration is to learn the will of God and do it. They evidence that they are worthy of membership in the Lord's Church, and their walk and talk are uplifting to everyone they meet" (Millet and Newell, *Draw Near unto Me*, 70).

Why does baptism need to be performed in this manner? (20:72–74) "Baptism by immersion in water by one having authority is the first saving ordinance of the gospel and is necessary for an individual to become a member of The Church of Jesus Christ of Latter-day Saints and to receive eternal salvation. . . .

"The Savior revealed the true method of baptism to the Prophet Joseph Smith, making clear that the ordinance must be performed by one having priesthood authority and that it must be done by immersion. . . .

"Immersion is symbolic of the death of a person's sinful life and the rebirth into a spiritual life, dedicated to the service of God and His children. It is also symbolic of death and resurrection (see Romans 6:3–6)" (Topics and Questions, s.v. "Baptism"). ⊕

Doctrine and Covenants 20:75–84. Sacramental Prayers and Regulations Governing Church Membership Are Given

Why do we use water instead of wine with the sacrament today? (20:75) "The sacrament gives us the sacred opportunity to remember Jesus Christ and to renew our baptismal covenants. Although the Savior gave His disciples wine when He first introduced this ordinance (see Matthew 26:23–24), the Prophet Joseph Smith received the following revelation in August 1830:

"'It mattereth not what ye shall eat or what ye shall drink when ye partake of the sacrament, if it so be that ye do it with an eye single to my glory' (D&C 27:2–3).

"Today, of course, we also follow the Word of Wisdom. And since 'it mattereth not' what we drink for the sacrament, Church leaders have asked us to use water, which is inexpensive and universally available" ("Why do we use water instead of wine?" *New Era*, Nov. 2008, 22). See also commentary in this volume on Doctrine and Covenants 27:3.

How can worthily partaking of the sacrament prepare us to receive the Holy Ghost? (20:77–79) "By participating weekly and appropriately in the ordinance of the sacrament we qualify for the promise that we will 'always have his Spirit to be with [us]' (D&C 20:77). That Spirit is the foundation of our testimony. It testifies of the Father and the Son, brings all things to our remembrance, and leads us into truth. It is the compass to guide us on our path. This gift of the Holy Ghost, President Wilford Woodruff taught, 'is the greatest gift that can be bestowed upon man' (*Deseret Weekly*, Apr. 6, 1889, 451)" (Oaks, "Sacrament Meeting and the Sacrament," *Ensign*, Nov. 2008, 17). ✛

What do the scriptures teach about repentance? (20:80) "Repentance requires that sins be confessed to Heavenly Father. Jesus Christ said, 'By this ye may know if a man repenteth of his sins—behold, he will confess them and forsake them' (Doctrine and Covenants 58:43; see also Mosiah 26:29).

"When Church members commit serious sins, their repentance also includes confession to their bishop or stake president. He is then able to exercise the keys of the gospel of repentance on their behalf (see Doctrine and Covenants 13:1; 84:26–27; 107:18, 20). This helps them heal and return to the gospel path through the power of the Savior's Atonement" (*General Handbook* [2021], 32.4.1).

What is the purpose of maintaining Church membership records? (20:82–84) God has always commanded His people to take the names of those who have been gathered to Him (see Moroni 6:4). "In this dispensation, the Lord gave . . . record-keeping instructions to Joseph Smith. . . . The spirit of those guidelines is evident today as member-information systems in the Church continue to evolve and accomplish their twofold purpose of recording ordinances

77 O God, the Eternal Father, we ask thee in the name of thy Son, Jesus Christ, to bless and sanctify this bread to the souls of all those who partake of it, that they may eat in remembrance of the body of thy Son, and witness unto thee, O God, the Eternal Father, that they are willing to take upon them the name of thy Son, and always remember him and keep his commandments which he has given them; that they may always have his Spirit to be with them. Amen.

78 The manner of administering the wine—he shall take the cup also, and say:

79 O God, the Eternal Father, we ask thee in the name of thy Son, Jesus Christ, to bless and sanctify this wine to the souls of all those who drink of it, that they may do it in remembrance of the blood of thy Son, which was shed for them; that they may witness unto thee, O God, the Eternal Father, that they do always remember him, that they may have his Spirit to be with them. Amen.

80 Any member of the church of Christ transgressing, or being overtaken in a fault, shall be dealt with as the scriptures direct.

81 It shall be the duty of the several churches, composing the church of Christ, to send one or more of their teachers to attend the several conferences held by the elders of the church,

82 With a list of the names of the several members uniting themselves with the church since the last conference; or send by the hand of some priest; so that a regular list of all the names of the whole church may be kept in a book by one of the elders, whomsoever the other elders shall appoint from time to time;

83 And also, if any have been expelled from the church, so that their names may be blotted out of the general church record of names.

84 All members removing from the church where they reside, if going to a church where they are not known, may take a letter certifying that they are regular members and in good standing, which certificate may be signed by any elder or priest if the member receiving the letter is personally acquainted with the elder or priest, or it may be signed by the teachers or deacons of the church.

and providing useful information to local priesthood leaders....

"Membership records and reports are useful tools, aiding Church leaders as they seek inspiration to help members progress toward exaltation. The more accurate, complete, and readily accessible those records are, the more likely it is that Church members will be better served" (Heber M. Thompson, "What is the purpose and history of Church membership records?" *Ensign*, Jun. 1994, 59, 60).

Introduction to Doctrine and Covenants 21

"Following the Lord's instructions to organize His Church, the Prophet Joseph Smith gathered approximately 60 believers together at the home of Peter Whitmer Sr. in Fayette, New York, on Tuesday, April 6, 1830. Joseph Smith and Oliver Cowdery organized the Church according to the will of God and according to the laws of the state of New York. The meeting consisted of prayer, sustainings, ordinations, the administration of the sacrament, and confirmations of those previously baptized. At this meeting, the Prophet received the revelation recorded in Doctrine and Covenants 21" (*Doctrine and Covenants Student Manual* [2018], 128).

"This revelation seems to point out very clearly the special role of the prophet and the responsibility of Church members to look to that prophet; this, however, was a difficult lesson for Church members to learn and a test of their faith. The Lord warned in a later revelation that enemies would prevail against the Church as long as the members did not give heed unto his commandments through his prophet (D&C 103:4–8)" (A. Gary Anderson, "Being Valiant by Following the Lord's Anointed," 37).

SECTION 21

Revelation given to Joseph Smith the Prophet, at Fayette, New York, April 6, 1830. This revelation was given at the organization of the Church, on the date named, in the home of Peter Whitmer Sr. Six men, who had previously been baptized, participated. By unanimous vote these persons expressed their desire and determination to organize, according to the commandment of God (see section 20). They also voted to accept and sustain Joseph Smith Jr. and Oliver Cowdery as the presiding officers of the Church. With the laying on of hands, Joseph then ordained Oliver an elder of the Church, and Oliver similarly ordained Joseph. After

Doctrine and Covenants 21:1–3. Joseph Smith Is Called to Be a Seer, Translator, Prophet, Apostle, and Elder

What is the record that the Lord commanded the Church to keep? (21:1) "The history of the Church of Jesus Christ and its people deserves our remembrance. The scriptures give the Church's history high priority. In fact, much of scripture is Church history. On the very day the Church was organized, God commanded Joseph Smith, 'Behold, there shall be a record kept among you.' Joseph acted on this command by appointing Oliver Cowdery, the second elder in the Church and his chief assistant, as the first Church historian. We keep records to help us remember, and a record of the Church's rise and progress has been kept from Oliver Cowdery's time to the present day. This extraordinary historical record reminds us that God has again opened the heavens and revealed truths that call our generation to action" (Marlin K. Jensen, "Remember and Perish Not," *Ensign*, May 2007, 37). ◉

What blessings come to Church members who are willing to be guided by prophets, seers, and revelators? (21:1–2) "The apostolic and prophetic foundation of the Church was to bless in all times, but *especially* in times of adversity or danger.... Against such times as come in our modern day, the First Presidency and Quorum of the Twelve are commissioned by God and sustained by you as prophets, seers, and revelators, with the President of the Church sustained as *the* prophet, seer, and revelator, the

administration of the sacrament, Joseph and Oliver laid hands upon the participants individually for the bestowal of the Holy Ghost and for the confirmation of each as a member of the Church.

1 Behold, there shall be a record kept among you; and in it thou shalt be called a seer, a translator, a prophet, an apostle of Jesus Christ, an elder of the church through the will of God the Father, and the grace of your Lord Jesus Christ,

2 Being inspired of the Holy Ghost to lay the foundation thereof, and to build it up unto the most holy faith.

3 Which church was organized and established in the year of your Lord eighteen hundred and thirty, in the fourth month, and on the sixth day of the month which is called April.

Giving Heed to the Living Prophet with Patience and Faith (Doctrine and Covenants 21:4–5)

"Why should we listen to and follow prophets? Because prophets receive revelation for us *today*—revelation that contemplates the unique circumstances in the world *now*. Their counsel is unencumbered by the opinions, philosophies, and personal biases of even the smartest, brightest, and most accomplished experts. Their words help guide us through the mists of darkness Lehi and Nephi saw and help us hold tightly to the rod of iron (See 1 Nephi 8:24; 11:25). Sometimes their words are meant for a global audience, and at other times their counsel is for a specific individual....

"The question for us today is the same question the children of men have faced whenever prophets have been on the earth: Will we heed their words?

"Remember when the Lord warned Nephi to take all who would go with him and flee into the wilderness? Nephi recorded that '*all those who would go with me*' were those who believed in the warnings and the revelations of God; wherefore they did hearken unto my words' [2 Nephi 5:6; emphasis added].

"Of the eight billion people on the earth, the Lord has entrusted just fifteen men with His restored priesthood keys. Wouldn't we want to listen to them first? And wouldn't we want to listen to them most?

"Simply put, will we go with the prophet today, meaning the living prophets? Will we hear their words and act upon them?" (Dew, *Prophets See around Corners*, 97, 99).

senior Apostle. . . . These officers form the foundation stones of the true Church, positioned around and gaining their strength from the chief cornerstone, 'the rock of our Redeemer, who is [Jesus] Christ, the Son of God' [Helaman 5:12], He who is the great 'Apostle and High Priest of our profession' [Hebrews 3:1]" (Holland, "Prophets, Seers, and Revelators," *Ensign*, Nov. 2004, 7). ⊕

Doctrine and Covenants 21:4–8. His Word Will Guide the Cause of Zion

Why is it essential for Church members today to give heed to the words of the prophet? (21:4–5)
"Now the only safety we have as members of this church is to do exactly what the Lord said to the Church in that day when the Church was organized. We must learn to give heed to the words and commandments that the Lord shall give through His prophet. . . . There will be some things that take patience and faith. You may not like what comes from the authority of the Church. It may contradict your political views. It may contradict your social views. It may interfere with some of your social life. But if you listen to these things, as if from the mouth of the Lord Himself, with patience and faith, the promise is that 'the gates of hell shall not prevail against you; yea, and the Lord God will disperse the powers of darkness from before you, and cause the heavens to shake for your good, and his name's glory' (D&C 21:6). . . .

"Look to the President of the Church for your instructions. If ever there is a conflict, you keep your eyes on the President if you want to walk in the light" (*Harold B. Lee* [manual], 84–85). ⊕

4 Wherefore, meaning the church, thou shalt give heed unto all his words and commandments which he shall give unto you as he receiveth them, walking in all holiness before me;

5 For his word ye shall receive, as if from mine own mouth, in all patience and faith.

6 For by doing these things the gates of hell shall not prevail against you; yea, and the Lord God will disperse the powers of darkness from before you, and cause the heavens to shake for your good, and his name's glory.

President Henry B. Eyring also cautioned: "Looking for the path to safety in the counsel of prophets makes sense to those with strong faith. When a prophet speaks, those with little faith may think that they hear only a wise man giving good advice. Then if his counsel seems comfortable and reasonable, squaring with what they want to do, they take it. If it does not, they consider it either faulty advice or they see their circumstances as justifying their being an exception to the counsel. Those without faith may think that they hear only men seeking to exert influence for some selfish motive. . . .

"[It is a fallacy] to believe that the choice to accept or not accept the counsel of prophets is no more than deciding whether to accept good advice and gain its benefits or to stay where we are. But the choice not to take prophetic counsel changes the very ground upon which we stand. It becomes more dangerous. The failure to take prophetic counsel lessens our power to take inspired counsel in the future. The best time to have decided to help Noah build the ark was the first time he asked. Each time he asked after that, each failure to respond would have lessened sensitivity to the Spirit. And so each time his request would have seemed more foolish, until the rain came. And then it was too late" ("Finding Safety in Counsel," *Ensign*, May 1997, 25).

What is the "cause of Zion"? (21:7–8) "One of the great purposes of God's servants throughout the ages has been to 'bring forth and establish the cause of Zion' (D&C 6:6; 11:6; 12:6; 21:7; [Joseph Smith Papers, "History, 1838–1856, volume C-1," 1327]). Speaking of this cause, President Joseph Fielding Smith said: 'That is our work, to establish Zion, to build up the kingdom of God, to preach the gospel to every creature in the world, that not one soul may be overlooked where there is the possibility for us to present unto him the truth' (in [Conference Report], Apr. 1951, 152–53). Zion is 'THE PURE IN HEART' (D&C 97:21), and the society of Zion is one in which the people live in such a state of purity and love that the Lord dwells in the midst of them" (Brewster, *Doctrine & Covenants Encyclopedia* [2012], 75). See also commentary in this volume on Doctrine and Covenants 6:6.

Doctrine and Covenants 21:9–12. The Saints Will Believe His Words as He Speaks by the Comforter

Why does the Lord invite all to believe in the words of Joseph Smith? (21:9) "In every age when the Lord has a people on earth, the great question confronting all mankind is whether they will believe and obey the prophet who presides over their dispensation....

"For our day and dispensation the issue facing all men is clearly set. It is this: *Is Jesus Christ the Son of the living God, and was Joseph Smith called of God? ...*

"Joseph Smith is the one through whom the fulness of the everlasting gospel—the gospel of the Lord Jesus Christ, not of any man—has been restored for the last and final time on earth.... He is the one who was called of God and endowed with power from on high" (Bruce R. McConkie, *New Witness*, 11, 12). ❂

Why was Oliver Cowdery considered the first preacher of the Church? (21:11–12) "In Nauvoo Joseph Smith was a confident and powerful speaker; in Fayette he was not. As with all men he had to grow up into the office that was his. Oliver Cowdery was called on to deliver the first public discourse in this dispensation. That took place five days later, on Sunday [April 11, 1830], at the home of Peter Whitmer Sr., where this revelation was received on the day the Church was organized" (McConkie and Ostler, *Revelations of the Restoration*, 178).

7 For thus saith the Lord God: Him have I inspired to move the cause of Zion in mighty power for good, and his diligence I know, and his prayers I have heard.

8 Yea, his weeping for Zion I have seen, and I will cause that he shall mourn for her no longer; for his days of rejoicing are come unto the remission of his sins, and the manifestations of my blessings upon his works.

9 For, behold, I will bless all those who labor in my vineyard with a mighty blessing, and they shall believe on his words, which are given him through me by the Comforter, which manifesteth that Jesus was crucified by sinful men for the sins of the world, yea, for the remission of sins unto the contrite heart.

10 Wherefore it behooveth me that he should be ordained by you, Oliver Cowdery mine apostle;

11 This being an ordinance unto you, that you are an elder under his hand, he being the first unto you, that you might be an elder unto this church of Christ, bearing my name—

12 And the first preacher of this church unto the church, and before the world, yea, before the Gentiles; yea, and thus saith the Lord God, lo, lo! to the Jews also. Amen.

Introduction to Doctrine and Covenants 22

Elder Orson Pratt once shared the background to Doctrine and Covenants 22: "In the early days of this Church there were certain persons, belonging to the Baptist denomination, very moral and no doubt as good people as you could find anywhere, who came, saying they believed the Book of Mormon, and that they had been baptized into the Baptist Church, and they wished to come into our Church. The Prophet had not, at that time, particularly inquired in relation to this matter, but he did inquire, and received a revelation from the Lord [see D&C 22]" (in *Journal of Discourses*, 16:293).

The Prophet received Doctrine and Covenants 22 on April 16, 1830, in Manchester, New York. In it the Lord "proclaims the indispensability of baptism in the proper manner and with the proper authority and clearly defines that baptism is the gate by which we enter into the Lord's kingdom" (Woodger, *Essential Doctrine and Covenants Companion*, 40).

"The new Church of Christ was more than simply another Christian denomination. After years of keeping a distance from the churches he saw around him, Joseph Smith Sr. saw in the restored Church something different: a legitimate successor to the apostolic church with prophets, apostles, revelations, and authority" (Jeffrey G. Cannon, "Build Up My Church," 32).

SECTION 22

Revelation given through Joseph Smith the Prophet, at Manchester, New York, April 16, 1830. This revelation was given to the Church in consequence of some who had previously been baptized desiring to unite with the Church without rebaptism.

1 Behold, I say unto you that all old covenants have I caused to be done away in this thing; and this is a new and an everlasting covenant, even that which was from the beginning.

Doctrine and Covenants 22:1. Baptism Is a New and Everlasting Covenant

What is the "new and everlasting covenant"? (22:1)
President Russell M. Nelson taught: "I have spoken frequently about the importance of the Abrahamic covenant and the gathering of Israel. When we embrace the gospel and are baptized, we take upon ourselves the sacred name of Jesus Christ. Baptism is the gate that leads to becoming joint heirs to all the promises given anciently by the Lord to Abraham, Isaac, Jacob, and their posterity.

"'The new and everlasting covenant' (Doctrine and Covenants 132:6) and the Abrahamic covenant are essentially the same—two ways of phrasing the covenant God made with mortal men and women at different times." [In footnote 2 of this article, President Nelson explains: "The new and everlasting covenant is the fulness of the gospel of Jesus Christ. It includes all ordinances and covenants necessary for our salvation (see Doctrine and Covenants 66:2). It is 'new' whenever the Lord renews or restores it, and it is 'everlasting' because it does not change."] ("Everlasting Covenant," *Liahona*, Oct. 2022, 4, 11n2). ⊕

Doctrine and Covenants 22:2–4.
Authoritative Baptism Is Required

In what way were some baptisms considered "dead"? (22:2–3) "An ordinance performed without the Lord's true authority is invalid; no covenant is established; no sealing by the Spirit takes place. Dead works are just that—dead, without power or efficacy. Every ordinance depends upon the presence of the Spirit for life. The Holy Ghost must ratify, or seal, an ordinance for it to be a valid, living covenant (D&C 132:7). For that to be possible, both proper priesthood authority to transact the ordinance and worthiness on the part of the covenant maker are necessary (Articles of Faith 1:5)" (Millet and Newell, *Draw Near unto Me*, 72).

What might dead works be today? (22:3) "Contextually, the term *dead works* in this revelation refers to baptisms performed in other churches which had not the authority from God to perform them. By extension, dead works could mean labors not grounded in faith, deeds and actions and covenants not performed in righteousness. . . . Dead works may also consist of works void of the motivation and staying power found in and through the Holy Ghost" (Millet, *Life in Christ*, 100).

What are some ways in which we seek to counsel God? (22:4) "It truly is folly for us with our mortal myopia to presume to judge God, to think, for example, 'I'm not happy, so God must be doing something wrong.' To us, His mortal children in a fallen world, who know so little of past, present, and future, He declares, 'All things are present with me, for I know them all' [Moses 1:6]. Jacob wisely cautions: 'Seek not to counsel the Lord, but to take counsel from his hand. For behold, ye yourselves know that he counseleth in wisdom, and in justice, and in great mercy, over all his works' [Jacob 4:10]" (Christofferson, "Our Relationship with God," *Liahona*, May 2022, 78).

2 Wherefore, although a man should be baptized an hundred times it availeth him nothing, for you cannot enter in at the strait gate by the law of Moses, neither by your dead works.

3 For it is because of your dead works that I have caused this last covenant and this church to be built up unto me, even as in days of old.

4 Wherefore, enter ye in at the gate, as I have commanded, and seek not to counsel your God. Amen.

Introduction to Doctrine and Covenants 23

There are five separate revelations contained in Doctrine and Covenants 23. "Each of the . . . five revelations, which were dictated [at Manchester, New York] soon after the organization of the Church of Christ on 6 April 1830, addressed one of [Joseph Smith's] family members or a close associate who desired to know the Lord's will concerning himself. All five texts include similar content and phrasing, and [the Prophet] likely dictated them one after the other. John Whitmer recorded them separately in Revelation Book 1 and assigned the date 'AD 1830' to each one. Though the editors of the Book of Commandments printed the revelations separately and gave each the date of 6 April 1830, that date appears to be in error and was dropped two years later, in 1835, when the Doctrine and Covenants combined the texts into a single document with a general 'April, 1830' date. [Joseph Smith's] history and other sources suggest that the revelations date between the 6 April organization and an 11 April meeting, both of which took place in Fayette Township, New York" (Joseph Smith Papers, Historical Introduction to "Revelation, April 1830–A [D&C 23:1–2]," 29).

The content of section 23 includes the Lord's directions to the following five individuals: Oliver Cowdery, Hyrum Smith, Samuel H. Smith, Joseph Smith Sr., and Joseph Knight Sr. "All of these brethren, except Joseph Knight, Sr., had been baptized and were in a covenant relationship with the Savior. Each of the four church members were told by the Lord they were 'under no condemnation' at that time (see D&C 23:1, 3–5). This statement does not suggest that they were without responsibility to maintain that status in the future. They had done all that the Lord required of them up to that time" (Otten and Caldwell, *Sacred Truths*, 1:100).

SECTION 23

A series of five revelations given through Joseph Smith the Prophet, at Manchester, New York, April 1830, to Oliver Cowdery, Hyrum Smith, Samuel H. Smith, Joseph Smith Sr., and Joseph Knight Sr. As the result of earnest desire on the part of the five persons named to know of their respective duties, the Prophet inquired of the Lord and received a revelation for each person.

1 Behold, I speak unto you, Oliver, a few words. Behold, thou art blessed, and art under no condemnation. But beware of pride, lest thou shouldst enter into temptation.

2 Make known thy calling unto the church, and also before the world, and thy heart shall be opened to preach the truth from henceforth and forever. Amen.

Doctrine and Covenants 23:1–7. These Early Disciples Are Called to Preach, Exhort, and Strengthen the Church

Why might Oliver Cowdery have been cautioned about pride? (23:1) President Dieter F. Uchtdorf noted that pride "has many faces. It leads some to revel in their own perceived self-worth, accomplishments, talents, wealth, or position. They count these blessings as evidence of being 'chosen,' 'superior,' or 'more righteous' than others. . . . At its core is the desire to be admired or envied. It is the sin of self-glorification" ("Pride and the Priesthood," *Ensign*, Nov. 2010, 56).

This warning from the Lord proved timely. Only a few months later, Oliver exhibited prideful inclinations as he made several challenges to Joseph's prophetic authority, and he fell. See also commentary in this volume on Doctrine and Covenants 28, Introduction. ⊕

How was Hyrum's calling to serve the Church connected with his family? (23:3) "Like many things in patriarchal blessings this promise could not have been fully understood at the time it was given. It would be three years before the office of church patriarch would be restored and Joseph Smith Sr. identified as the man through whom this lineal office would descend. At his death in September of 1840, that office fell to Hyrum, his oldest living son. Thus Hyrum was destined because of his family to serve in the Church. At the time of his death he was serving both as church patriarch and as an associate president of the Church with his brother the Prophet (D&C 124:94–96)" (McConkie and Ostler, *Revelations of the Restoration*, 181).

When was Samuel Smith called to preach the gospel? (23:4) "Samuel Smith, a younger brother of the Prophet, was the third person baptized after the restoration of the Aaronic Priesthood in May 1829. . . . After he was ordained an elder on June 9, 1830, Samuel was called as the first missionary in the Church and began to visit neighboring towns around Palmyra to sell copies of the Book of Mormon and preach the gospel. On one such trip he sold a copy of the Book of Mormon that eventually led to the conversion of Brigham Young and Heber C. Kimball and many of their family members" (*Doctrine and Covenants Student Manual* [2018], 136).

In what ways did Joseph Smith Sr. fulfill his duty throughout his life? (23:5) "[Joseph Smith Sr.] was supportive of his son's prophetic calling and even suffered persecution for his beliefs. He was privileged to be one of the Eight Witnesses of the Book of Mormon. . . . On the day the Church was organized, Father Smith was baptized. . . . On 18 December 1833. . . . he was ordained the first Patriarch in this dispensation. . . . At age sixty-four, Father Smith served a mission with his brother John. They traveled nearly twenty-four hundred miles throughout the East, strengthening the Saints, pronouncing patriarchal blessings, and sharing the gospel with relatives" (Black, *Who's Who*, 290).

Why was Joseph Knight counseled to "take up his cross"? (23:6–7) "Though Joseph Knight had been associated with Joseph Smith and worked closely with him, still it remained for him to seek a personal witness from the Lord [in prayer]. . . .

"[The Lord] defined Joseph Knight's duty ' . . . to unite with the true church, and give your language to

3 Behold, I speak unto you, Hyrum, a few words; for thou also art under no condemnation, and thy heart is opened, and thy tongue loosed; and thy calling is to exhortation, and to strengthen the church continually. Wherefore thy duty is unto the church forever, and this because of thy family. Amen.

4 Behold, I speak a few words unto you, Samuel; for thou also art under no condemnation, and thy calling is to exhortation, and to strengthen the church; and thou art not as yet called to preach before the world. Amen.

5 Behold, I speak a few words unto you, Joseph; for thou also art under no condemnation, and thy calling also is to exhortation, and to strengthen the church; and this is thy duty from henceforth and forever. Amen.

6 Behold, I manifest unto you, Joseph Knight, by these words, that you must take up your cross, in the which you must pray vocally before the world as well as in secret, and in your family, and among your friends, and in all places.

7 And, behold, it is your duty to unite with the true church, and give your language to exhortation continually, that you may receive the reward of the laborer. Amen.

exhortation continually, that you may receive the reward of the laborer' (D&C 23:7). The Lord made plain to a non-member that there is a 'true church.' Well might we follow this pattern of the Lord and likewise bear testimony and invite others to unite with the Lord's true church. Only through our affiliation with and labor within the Lord's church can there be a reward for us, as laborers" (Otten and Caldwell, *Sacred Truth*, 1:103).

What is the reward of the laborer? (23:7) In Matthew 20:1–16, a householder hired temporary laborers at different times throughout the day, paying them an agreed-upon wage. At the end of the day, some laborers were upset that those hired at the end of the day received the same wage as those hired at dawn.

"Whether people become disciples of Christ in their youth, in their young adulthood, in the later stages of life, or in some instances in the spirit world (see D&C 137:7–8), eternal life is the reward for all people who make and keep sacred covenants with the Lord (see D&C 76:95; 84:38; 88:107)" (*New Testament Student Manual* [2018], 63). Two months after this revelation, Joseph Knight Sr. was baptized and remained faithful to the end of his life in February 1847.

Introduction to Doctrine and Covenants 24

"During the two months after the Church of Christ was organized, [Joseph Smith] met with believers in three New York locations: the areas of Manchester, Fayette, and Colesville. Several people were baptized and the first church conference was convened before [the Prophet] returned home to his wife Emma in Harmony, Pennsylvania, around mid-June. About 26 June, [Joseph], Emma, Oliver Cowdery, David Whitmer, and John Whitmer traveled to Colesville, where Emma and a number of others were baptized, even though several Colesville residents destroyed a previously constructed dam in the stream in an attempt to prevent the baptisms. Before these believers could be confirmed, however, [Joseph] was twice arrested and charged, as his history recounted, with 'being a disorderly person; of setting the country in an uproar by preaching the Book of Mormon' [Joseph Smith History, vol. A-1, 44]. He was released in both instances, but he needed the help of a constable to escape from his antagonists and make his way to the house of Emma's sister, Elizabeth Hale Wasson, in Harpursville, where he and Emma were reunited. They returned to Harmony the next day, quite likely 3 July, and a few days later [Joseph and Oliver] came back to Colesville to confirm the recently baptized converts. Before they could do so, a mob assembled, and [they] quickly left again. Sometime between their return to Harmony and Cowdery's departure for Fayette around mid-July [1830], [Joseph] dictated [D&C 24]....

"The revelation specifically commanded [the Prophet] to continue confirming baptized believers, dictating revelations, and expounding the scriptures, and commanded Cowdery (and perhaps [Joseph] with him) to go forth and preach" (Joseph Smith Papers, Historical Introduction to "Revelation, July 1830-A [D&C 24]," 34).

In Doctrine and Covenants 24, "the Lord combines encouragement and reproof while giving individual commandments to Joseph and Oliver. The Prophet was told his gifts were of a spiritual nature, not a financial or temporal nature. The Lord promised Joseph that if he magnified his calling, he would always have what he needed, but the kingdom of God was his first and chief concern" (Woodger, *Essential Doctrine and Covenants Companion*, 44).

Doctrine and Covenants 24:1–9. Joseph Smith Is Called to Translate, Preach, and Expound Scriptures

How was Joseph delivered from his enemies in Colesville? (24:1) When Joseph was harassed and arrested in South Bainbridge for "being a disorderly person," the constable protected him from the gathering mob. Upon Joseph's second arrest, the second constable "'took me to a tavern, and gathered a number of men, who used every means to abuse, ridicule, and insult me.' They spat on Joseph and demanded that he prophesy to them.... Following a second trial the next day, Joseph was again acquitted. The constable, ... now 'asked my forgiveness.' Learning of plans by the mob to tar and feather Joseph, the constable helped him escape. Joseph arrived safely at the nearby house of Elizabeth Hale Wasson, Emma's sister" (Grow, "Thou Art an Elect Lady," 35).

SECTION 24

Revelation given to Joseph Smith the Prophet and Oliver Cowdery, at Harmony, Pennsylvania, July 1830. Though less than four months had elapsed since the Church was organized, persecution had become intense, and the leaders had to seek safety in partial seclusion. The following three revelations were given at this time to strengthen, encourage, and instruct them.

1 Behold, thou wast called and chosen to write the Book of Mormon, and to my ministry; and I have lifted thee up out of thine afflictions, and have counseled thee, that thou hast been delivered from all thine enemies, and thou hast been delivered from the powers of Satan and from darkness!

2 Nevertheless, thou art not excusable in thy transgressions; nevertheless, go thy way and sin no more.

Why would Joseph include the Lord's censure for his own failings? (24:2) "Chosen to be a prophet and leader of God's people, [Joseph] was conscious that he was only human, subject to human temptations and human frailties. Having the honesty and courage inspired by the Spirit of the Lord, he dared to confess this openly; and under the same inspiration, acknowledge his transgression and make his contrition known. He was not above any law which applied to his fellow-man. Of his responsibility to God and his brethren of the Church, he was required by the law revealed through himself to the Church, to give as strict an account as any other member. They who participated with him in authority owed not to him as an individual, but to the eternal power to which they were alike responsible" (Cannon, *Life of Joseph Smith the Prophet*, 67).

3 Magnify thine office; and after thou hast sowed thy fields and secured them, go speedily unto the church which is in Colesville, Fayette, and Manchester, and they shall support thee; and I will bless them both spiritually and temporally;

Why might the Lord have commanded Joseph to plant his crops before preaching to the Colesville Saints? (24:3) "This revelation was given in July, which is not a good time to plant in Harmony, Pennsylvania, but the Prophet had been too busy planting and nurturing the Church and the Saints to plant his own fields at the appropriate time. The Lord's advice is to go ahead and plant his crops late, and then rely on the Saints for additional help if he

"Magnify Thine Office" (Doctrine and Covenants 24:3)

"The divine instructions given in Doctrine and Covenants 24 served to remind Joseph that his time and attention were now to be devoted to his office as the Lord's prophet rather than to temporal concerns. The Lord explained that the Church members would support Joseph Smith temporally, for which they would be blessed (see also D&C 41:7; 43:12–14). In the face of the persecution that Joseph and early Church members were experiencing, the natural desire for many may have been to minimize their efforts to build the Church to avoid further persecution. However, the Lord counseled the Prophet to magnify his office, meaning to enlarge his time and devotion to his calling" (*Doctrine and Covenants Student Manual* [2018], 139).

Addressing priesthood holders, President Gordon B. Hinckley taught, "That word *magnify* is interesting. As I interpret it, it means to enlarge, to make more clear, to bring closer, and to strengthen. . . .

"All of you, of course, are familiar with binoculars. When you put the lenses to your eyes and focus them, you magnify and in effect bring closer all within your field of vision. But if you turn them around and look through the other end, you diminish and make more distant that which you see. . . .

"If we are to magnify our callings, we cannot live only unto ourselves. As we serve with diligence, as we teach with faith and testimony, as we lift and strengthen and build convictions of righteousness in those whose lives we touch, we magnify our priesthood. To live only unto ourselves, on the other hand, to serve grudgingly, to give less than our best effort to our duty, diminishes our priesthood just as looking through the wrong lenses of binoculars reduces the image and makes more distant the object. . . .

"To each of us the Lord has said, 'Magnify your calling.' It is not always easy. But it is always rewarding. It blesses him who holds this divine authority. On the other hand, looking through the wrong lens shrinks and shrivels our power and diminishes our contribution. In working from the opposite perspective, the true and the natural and the godly perspective, we enlarge and lift, we grow in strength and gladness, we bless the lives of others now and forever" ("Magnify Your Calling," *Ensign*, May 1989, 46, 47, 49).

should need it" (Robinson and Garrett, *Commentary on the Doctrine and Covenants*, 1:164).

How was Joseph Smith able to know what to say or do "in the very moment"? (24:5–7) "By the power of the Holy Ghost one can speak or write spontaneously. Joseph Smith did both. He commonly received revelations in meetings with others present. Indeed, we would be within the mark to say that most of his revelations were received in this manner. Initially, he did not record revelations as he received them; he had, however, the ability to recall them at will. . . . This revelation directed him to prepare the revelations he had received so that copies could be made of them" (McConkie and Ostler, *Revelations of the Restoration*, 189). ◉

Why might the Lord counsel Joseph Smith to be patient in afflictions? (24:8) "Let us not presume that because the way is at times difficult and challenging, our Heavenly Father is not mindful of us. He is rubbing off our rough edges and sensitizing us for our great responsibilities ahead. May His blessings be upon us spiritually, that we may have a sweet companionship with the Holy Ghost, and that our footsteps might be guided along paths of truth and righteousness. And may each of us follow the Lord's comforting counsel: 'Be patient in afflictions, for thou shalt have many; but endure them, for, lo, I am with thee, even unto the end of thy days' (D&C 24:8)" (Faust, "Blessings of Adversity," *Ensign*, Feb. 1998, 7).

Why might Joseph's strength be limited in temporal things? (24:9) President Dallin H. Oaks explained: "[Joseph Smith] was almost continually on the edge of financial distress. In the midst of trying to fulfill the staggering responsibilities of his sacred calling, he had to labor as a farmer or merchant to provide a living for his family. He did this without the remarkable spiritual gifts that sustained him in his prophetic calling. The Lord had advised him that 'in temporal labors thou shalt not have strength, for this is not thy calling' (D&C 24:9)" ("Joseph, the Man and the Prophet," *Ensign*, May 1996, 71).

Doctrine and Covenants 24:10–12. Oliver Cowdery Is Called to Preach the Gospel

How can we, like Oliver, declare the gospel "day and night"? (24:10) "Always look for opportunities to bring up your faith in natural and normal ways with people—both in person as well as online. I am asking

4 But if they receive thee not, I will send upon them a cursing instead of a blessing.

5 And thou shalt continue in calling upon God in my name, and writing the things which shall be given thee by the Comforter, and expounding all scriptures unto the church.

6 And it shall be given thee in the very moment what thou shalt speak and write, and they shall hear it, or I will send unto them a cursing instead of a blessing.

7 For thou shalt devote all thy service in Zion; and in this thou shalt have strength.

8 Be patient in afflictions, for thou shalt have many; but endure them, for, lo, I am with thee, even unto the end of thy days.

9 And in temporal labors thou shalt not have strength, for this is not thy calling. Attend to thy calling and thou shalt have wherewith to magnify thine office, and to expound all scriptures, and continue in laying on of the hands and confirming the churches.

10 And thy brother Oliver shall continue in bearing my name before the world, and also to the church. And he shall not suppose that he can say enough in my cause; and lo, I am with him to the end.

11 In me he shall have glory, and not of himself, whether in weakness or in strength, whether in bonds or free;

12 And at all times, and in all places, he shall open his mouth and declare my gospel as with the voice of a trump, both day and night. And I will give unto him strength such as is not known among men.

13 Require not miracles, except I shall command you, except casting out devils, healing the sick, and against poisonous serpents, and against deadly poisons;

14 And these things ye shall not do, except it be required of you by them who desire it, that the scriptures might be fulfilled; for ye shall do according to that which is written.

15 And in whatsoever place ye shall enter, and they receive you not in my name, ye shall leave a cursing instead of a blessing, by casting off the dust of your feet against them as a testimony, and cleansing your feet by the wayside.

16 And it shall come to pass that whosoever shall lay their hands upon you by violence, ye shall command to be smitten in my name; and, behold, I will smite them according to your words, in mine own due time.

17 And whosoever shall go to law with thee shall be cursed by the law.

that you 'stand as witnesses' [Mosiah 18:9] of the power of the gospel at all times—and when necessary, use words.

"Because 'the gospel of Christ . . . is the power of God unto salvation' [Romans 1:16], you can be confident, courageous, and humble as you share it. Confidence, courage, and humility may seem like contradictory attributes, but they are not. They reflect the Savior's invitation not to hide gospel values and principles under a bushel but to let your light shine, that your good works may glorify your Father in Heaven" (Uchtdorf, "Missionary Work," *Ensign*, May 2019, 17).

Doctrine and Covenants 24:13–19. The Law Is Revealed Relative to Miracles, Cursings, Casting Off the Dust of One's Feet, and Going without Purse or Scrip

Why should blessings and miracles require a sincere desire or request? (24:13–14) Miracles and signs of themselves do not lead to conversion. "Miracles are an important element in the work of Jesus Christ. They include healings, restoring the dead to life, and resurrection. Miracles are a part of the gospel of Jesus Christ. Faith is necessary in order for miracles to be manifested (Mark 6:5–6; Morm. 9:10–20; Ether 12:12)" (Guide to the Scriptures, "Miracle"). A sign is "an event or experience that people understand to be evidence or proof of something. A sign is usually a miraculous manifestation from God. . . . [Saints] should not seek for signs to satisfy curiosity or sustain faith" (Guide to the Scriptures, "Sign"). ☉

What did casting off the dust of their feet symbolize? (24:15) "To ceremonially shake the dust from one's feet as a testimony against another was understood by the Jews to symbolize a cessation of fellowship and a renunciation of all responsibility for consequences that might follow. It became an ordinance of accusation and testimony by the Lord's instructions to His apostles. . . . In the current dispensation, the Lord has similarly directed His authorized servants to so testify against those who willfully and maliciously oppose the truth when authoritatively presented [see D&C 24:15; 60:15; 75:20; 84:92; 99:4]. The responsibility of testifying before the Lord by this accusing symbol is so great that the means may be employed only . . . as the Spirit of the Lord may direct" (Talmage, *Jesus the Christ*, 345). See also commentary in this volume on Doctrine and Covenants 99:4.

Why would Church members be expected to provide money, clothing, and other necessities to Joseph and Oliver? (24:18–19) "When the Lord called the prophet to full-time service, He directed the church members to provide him with his temporal necessities of life, and promised the Church blessings both temporally and spiritually for so doing. If they failed to heed this instruction, they could expect a cursing instead of a blessing....

"When the Lord calls certain people to fulltime service in His kingdom, He provides for their physical needs while so engaged in His work. This principle is of the Lord and makes it possible for His servants to accomplish what the Lord calls them to do" (Otten and Caldwell, *Sacred Truths*, 1:106, 107).

18 And thou shalt take no purse nor scrip, neither staves, neither two coats, for the church shall give unto thee in the very hour what thou needest for food and for raiment, and for shoes and for money, and for scrip.

19 For thou art called to prune my vineyard with a mighty pruning, yea, even for the last time; yea, and also all those whom thou hast ordained, and they shall do even according to this pattern. Amen.

Introduction to Doctrine and Covenants 25

"Numbered among the revelations contained in the Doctrine and Covenants are those given to people collectively and individually. This, however, is the only revelation given specifically to a woman. What is of greatest significance here is that this revelation given to the Prophet's wife, Emma Smith, is intended in principle and purpose for the instruction and blessing of faithful women everywhere" (McConkie and Ostler, *Revelations of the Restoration*, 193).

Doctrine and Covenants 25 was received by the Prophet Joseph Smith in July 1830, while he and Emma were living in Harmony, Pennsylvania. "Section 25 shows that the Lord knew his daughter Emma. He encourages her to be meek and warns her against pride. He counseled her not to murmur because she had not seen the marvelous things her husband had seen. He invited her to sacrifice the things of this world for infinitely better things. He knew before she knew that she was capable of scribing for Joseph, of learning much, and of teaching the Saints by the power of the Holy Ghost. Perhaps because these callings could cause Emma anxiety, the Lord assured her that Joseph would support her. She needed Joseph and Joseph needed her, and he called her to comfort and sustain her husband" (Harper, *Making Sense of the Doctrine & Covenants*, 88).

Doctrine and Covenants 25:1–6. Emma Smith, an Elect Lady, Is Called to Aid and Comfort Her Husband

What can we learn from the Lord referring to Emma as His daughter? (25:1–2) Sister Julie B. Beck testified: "Our Heavenly Father knows His daughters. He loves them, He has given them specific responsibilities, and He has spoken to and guided them during their mortal missions....

"From the beginning of the restored Church, the sisters have been there first, last, and always in responding to the happenings of everyday life. ... Sisters have been at the forefront in sharing the gospel, and they continue this effort as they serve

SECTION 25

Revelation given through Joseph Smith the Prophet, at Harmony, Pennsylvania, July 1830 (see the heading to section 24). This revelation manifests the will of the Lord to Emma Smith, the Prophet's wife.

1 Hearken unto the voice of the Lord your God, while I speak unto you, Emma Smith, my daughter; for verily I say unto you, all those who receive my gospel are sons and daughters in my kingdom.

2 A revelation I give unto you concerning my will; and if thou art faithful and walk in the paths of virtue before me, I will preserve thy life, and thou shalt receive an inheritance in Zion.

missions, prepare young men and women to serve missions, and invite their friends, neighbors, and family members to share in the blessings of the gospel" ("Daughters in My Kingdom," *Ensign*, Nov. 2010, 114). ⊕

3 Behold, thy sins are forgiven thee, and thou art an elect lady, whom I have called.

What is noteworthy about the Lord naming Emma an "elect lady"? (25:3) Mary Jane Woodger wrote: "*Elect* does not mean 'special' or 'superior' but rather 'chosen,' which refers to those who are chosen because of their faithfulness to bear the burden of God's work" (*Essential Doctrine and Covenants Companion*, 46).

Carol Cornwall Madsen noted: "Being of the elect also carried responsibilities, foreordained missions that varied with each individual according to God's purposes. A passage in Joseph Smith's private journal for March 17, 1842 [the date the Relief Society was organized], affirms that definition: '*Elect* means to be

Emma Smith—An Elect Lady

Speaking of her daughter-in-law Emma Hale Smith, Lucy Mack Smith stated: "I have never seen a woman in my life, who would endure every species of fatigue and hardship, from month to month, and from year to year, with that unflinching courage, zeal and patience, which she has always done; for I know that which she has had to endure; that she has been tossed upon the ocean of uncertainty; that she has breasted the storm of persecution, and buffeted the rage of men and devils, until she has been swallowed up in a sea of trouble which [would] have borne down almost any other woman" (Joseph Smith Papers, "Lucy Mack Smith, History, 1845," 190).

Emma Hale Smith

"Emma Hale Smith, daughter of Isaac and Elizabeth Hale, was born July 10, 1804, in Harmony, Pennsylvania. A year and a half older than her husband, she met Joseph while he was working for Josiah Stowell in the Harmony area. Despite her father's disapproval, Emma and Joseph were married on January 18, 1827, in South Bainbridge, New York. . . .

"A literate and competent woman, Emma served at times as scribe of the Book of Mormon translation as well as the translation of the Bible. Emma believed in her prophet-husband and chose to be baptized a member of the church on June 28, 1830. From that time on, her life consisted of persecution and transitory living" (Woodger, *Essential Doctrine and Covenants Companion*, 48).

"As the 'elect lady,' [Emma] presided over the Female Relief Society of Nauvoo from its founding in 1842 until 1844, providing relief to new immigrants and destitute families. Her service in the Relief Society, however, achieved much more than benevolent work. As president, Emma taught the women doctrine, managed membership, and publicly defended principles of moral purity. Emma was the first woman to receive temple ordinances; she then initiated other women in these sacred rituals. As the first lady of Nauvoo, she hosted diplomats in her home, made public appearances with Joseph at civic and community events, and presented political petitions in support of the Church and her husband. . . .

"Joseph Smith's death on June 27, 1844, created tremendous upheaval for Emma. In addition to grieving the loss of her husband, she was expecting their final child. . . . When most of the Saints left for the Great Basin in 1846, Emma remained in Nauvoo. . . . She maintained her belief in Joseph Smith's prophetic role and in the divine truth of the Book of Mormon. 'My belief is that the Book of Mormon is of divine authenticity—I have not the slightest doubt of it,' she testified in an interview she gave late in life [Joseph Smith III, "Last Testimony of Sister Emma," 290]. Emma . . . passed away in Nauvoo on April 30, 1879, and is buried next to Joseph. Her name and character have been both revered and misunderstood in Latter-day Saint memory, but her actions and influence cannot be erased" (Church History Topics, "Emma Hale Smith").

Elected to a *certain work*,' a broad definition of the term. The Prophet then noted that Emma fulfilled this part of the 1830 revelation when she was elected president of the Relief Society, the specific work to which she had been 'previously ordained' [Joseph Smith Papers, "Journal, December 1841–December 1842," 91]" ("'Elect Lady' Revelation," 127). ⊕

What had Emma not seen that caused her to murmur? (25:4) Sister Carol Cornwall Madsen proposed: "[The Lord] may have been referring only to Emma's regret at not having seen the gold plates, though she had held them, protected them, and acted as scribe in their translation, but He may also have been alluding to the tumultuous experiences Emma had endured since her marriage to Joseph. . . . The attempts by gold seekers to wrest the plates from Joseph, the harassment during their translation, the mobs who interfered with Emma's baptism, the unwarranted arrest of Joseph the same night, as well as the alienation of her parents, the loss of home and roots, and the death of her first child. . . . Only patience and trust in God's wisdom . . . would sustain her through the difficult times" ("'Elect Lady' Revelation," 120). ⊕

How did Emma's call to assist Joseph in the work help establish roles of women in the Church? (25:5–6) Sister Julie B. Beck affirmed: "As the Lord began restoring His Church through the Prophet Joseph Smith, He again included women in a pattern of discipleship. A few months after the Church was formally organized, the Lord revealed that Emma Smith was to be set apart as a leader and teacher in the Church and as an official helper to her husband, the Prophet. In her calling to help the Lord build His kingdom, she was given instructions about how to increase her faith and personal righteousness, how to strengthen her family and her home, and how to serve others. . . .

"From the day the gospel began to be restored in this dispensation, the Lord has needed faithful women to participate as His disciples" ("What I Hope My Granddaughters . . . Will Understand," *Ensign*, Nov. 2011, 110).

How can spouses support and comfort each other in a spirit of meekness? (25:5–6) "If every husband and every wife would constantly do whatever might be possible to ensure the comfort and happiness of his or her companion, there would be very little, if any, divorce. Argument would never be heard. Accusations would never be leveled. Angry explosions would not

4 Murmur not because of the things which thou hast not seen, for they are withheld from thee and from the world, which is wisdom in me in a time to come.

5 And the office of thy calling shall be for a comfort unto my servant, Joseph Smith, Jun., thy husband, in his afflictions, with consoling words, in the spirit of meekness.

6 And thou shalt go with him at the time of his going, and be unto him for a scribe, while there is no one to be a scribe for him, that I may send my servant, Oliver Cowdery, whithersoever I will.

occur. Rather, love and concern would replace abuse and meanness. . . . We can look for and recognize the divine nature in one another, which comes to us as children of our Father in Heaven. We can live together in the God-given pattern of marriage in accomplishing that of which we are capable if we will exercise discipline of self and refrain from trying to discipline our companion" (Hinckley, "Women in Our Lives," *Ensign*, Nov. 2004, 84).

Doctrine and Covenants 25:7–11. Emma Smith Is Also Called to Write, to Expound Scriptures, and to Select Hymns

7 And thou shalt be ordained under his hand to expound scriptures, and to exhort the church, according as it shall be given thee by my Spirit.

What might the word *ordained* likely mean in this verse? (25:7) Note that footnote 7a indicates that *ordain* can be understood as "set apart." The *General Handbook* states: "To set apart a member to a calling means to give him or her the authority to act in that calling (see 3.4.3.1). A setting apart also includes a blessing and promises guided by the Spirit" (*General Handbook* [2023], 30.4).

Susan Easton Black pointed out: "In the early days of the Church, the word *ordain* was used in conjunction with priesthood ordinations and the setting apart of women to specific callings. Through the passage of time, a distinction has developed between being 'ordained' and being 'set apart.' Brethren are ordained to priesthood offices and set apart to preside over administrative assignments, such as stakes, wards, branches, and missions. Sisters are no longer ordained to a specific calling but are set apart for their callings" (*400 Questions and Answers*, 82).

Why was the command for Emma to expound scriptures significant? (25:7) Carol Cornwall Madsen recorded: "With only a few exceptions, no religious denominations at that time gave public platforms in mixed congregations to women. Tradition and contemporary ideals of feminine propriety were powerful agents in defining a woman's appropriate public behavior, and preaching in public was not a feminine occupation in the nineteenth century. . . . In Nauvoo, women regularly addressed the mixed Church gatherings in one another's homes for a Sunday or weeknight prayer, blessing, or cottage meeting. Along with the men, they bore testimony, expounded doctrine, and read scriptures to the assembled members. They prophesied, spoke in tongues, and blessed one another. Emma often accompanied Joseph to such meetings. Few could have been more conversant with Mormon doctrine than Emma Smith or had more incentive to expound its truths" ("'Elect Lady' Revelation," 124).

What were the circumstances under which Emma received the Holy Ghost? (25:8) Along with twelve other Saints, Emma Smith was baptized by Oliver Cowdery in Colesville, New York, on June 28, 1830. When a mob gathered and the Prophet was arrested on false charges, the planned confirmation meeting was delayed.

"In early August . . . Newel and Sally Knight traveled from Colesville, New York, to visit Joseph and Emma Smith in Harmony, Pennsylvania. Sally Knight had been baptized on the same day as Emma, but neither had been confirmed. . . . Joseph Smith's history records, 'We partook together of the sacrament, after which we confirmed these two sisters into the church. . . . The Spirit of the Lord was poured out upon us, we praised the Lord God, and rejoiced exceedingly' [Joseph Smith, "History, 1838–1856, volume A-1," 51–52]" (Grow, "Thou Art an Elect Lady," 37–38).

Why might Emma have been concerned about receiving support? (25:9) "At the time of the revelation Emma had just turned twenty-six and Joseph was not yet twenty-five. They were relatively inexperienced and unsophisticated young people who had been given momentous responsibilities. A supportive and trusting relationship would be crucial to the fulfillment of their respective callings. . . . The import of this counsel became clear as circumstances challenged Joseph and Emma's efforts to fulfill their obligations to each other. While Joseph's support gave legitimacy and significance to Emma's assignments in the Church, her support of Joseph eased the burden of his calling. But the merging of their marital and ecclesiastical relationships often created an emotional kaleidoscope alternating joy with sorrow, peace with anxiety, trust with suspicion, and unity with doubt" (Madsen, "'Elect Lady' Revelation," 121). ⊕

How can we effectively lay aside the things of this world? (25:10) Sister Joy D. Jones observed: "The Lord instructed Emma Smith to 'receive the Holy Ghost,' learn much, 'lay aside the things of this world, and seek for the things of a better' [see D&C 25:8, 10]. Learning is integral to progression, especially as the constant companionship of the Holy Ghost teaches us what is needful for each of us to lay aside—meaning that which could *distract* us or *delay* our progression" ("Especially Noble Calling," *Ensign*, May 2020, 16).

8 For he shall lay his hands upon thee, and thou shalt receive the Holy Ghost, and thy time shall be given to writing, and to learning much.

9 And thou needest not fear, for thy husband shall support thee in the church; for unto them is his calling, that all things might be revealed unto them, whatsoever I will, according to their faith.

10 And verily I say unto thee that thou shalt lay aside the things of this world, and seek for the things of a better.

President Russell M. Nelson has said: "Sometimes we speak almost casually about walking away from the world with its contention, pervasive temptations, and false philosophies. But *truly* doing so requires you to examine your life meticulously and regularly. As you do so, the Holy Ghost will prompt you about what is no longer needful, what is no longer worthy of your time and energy" ("Spiritual Treasures," *Ensign*, Nov. 2019, 77). ⊕

11 And it shall be given thee, also, to make a selection of sacred hymns, as it shall be given thee, which is pleasing unto me, to be had in my church.

Why would the Lord direct Emma "to make a selection of sacred hymns"? (25:11) "Inspirational music is an essential part of our church meetings. The hymns invite the Spirit of the Lord, create a feeling of reverence, unify us as members, and provide a way for us to offer praises to the Lord.

"Some of the greatest sermons are preached by the singing of hymns. Hymns move us to repentance and good works, build testimony and faith, comfort the weary, console the mourning, and inspire us to endure to the end.... Hymns can lift our spirits, give us courage, and move us to righteous action. They can fill our souls with heavenly thoughts and bring us a spirit of peace" ("First Presidency Preface," *Hymns* [1985], ix, x). ⊕

Doctrine and Covenants 25:12–14. The Song of the Righteous Is a Prayer unto the Lord

12 For my soul delighteth in the song of the heart; yea, the song of the righteous is a prayer unto me, and it shall be answered with a blessing upon their heads.

How can hymns communicate the "song of the heart" and why is it delightful to the Lord? (25:12) President Russell M. Nelson taught, "Through music we raise our voices in powerful praise and prayer.

"Make a Selection of Sacred Hymns" (Doctrine and Covenants 25:11)

"Just a few months after the Church was organized, a revelation was received by the Prophet Joseph Smith for his wife Emma. The Lord directed her 'to make a selection of sacred hymns, as it shall be given thee, which is pleasing unto me, to be had in my church' [D&C 25:11].

"Emma Smith assembled a collection of hymns which first appeared in [the] Kirtland hymnal in 1836. There were only 90 songs included in [the] thin little booklet. Many of them were hymns from Protestant faiths. At least 26 of them were written by William W. Phelps, who later prepared and assisted in the printing of the hymnal. Only the lyrics were written; no musical notes accompanied the texts. This humble little hymnal proved to be a great blessing to early

The First Latter-day Saint Hymnal, 1835

members of the Church.... Many of the selections which Emma chose so many years earlier are still included in our hymnbook, such as 'I Know That My Redeemer Lives' and 'How Firm a Foundation'" (Steven E. Snow, "Be Thou Humble," *Ensign*, May 2016, 36).

Hymns provide a pattern of worship that is pleasing to God. He taught us through the Prophet Joseph Smith to 'praise the Lord with singing, with music, ... and with a prayer of praise and thanksgiving' (D&C 136:28). . . .

"Music has power to provide spiritual nourishment. It has healing power. It has the power to facilitate worship, allowing us to contemplate the Atonement and the Restoration of the gospel, with its saving principles and exalting ordinances. It provides power for us to express prayerful thoughts and bear testimony of sacred truths" ("Power and Protection of Worthy Music," *Ensign*, Dec. 2009, 13, 16).

Why should we cleave unto our covenants? (25:13)
"In July 1830, the Lord told Emma Smith: 'Cleave unto the covenants which thou hast made.' Emma was baptized into the Church of Christ on June 28, 1830, and this revelation, which came a short time after her baptism, provided a pattern by which Latter-day Saint women made and received covenants and ordinances with the Lord. A key part of the Restoration was the authority by which to seal on earth what could be sealed in heaven—both individuals to Jesus Christ and the Church, and families to each other. . . . David E. Sorensen taught, 'Each ordinance is calculated to reveal to us something about Christ and our relationship to God.' . . . The ordinances both connect us to God and teach us about becoming like God" (Johnson and Reeder, *Witness of Women*, 175).

13 Wherefore, lift up thy heart and rejoice, and cleave unto the covenants which thou hast made.

14 Continue in the spirit of meekness, and beware of pride. Let thy soul delight in thy husband, and the glory which shall come upon him.

Keeping Covenants Accesses the Power of God (Doctrine and Covenants 25:13)

Speaking to women of the Church, President Russell M. Nelson testified: "Every woman and every man who makes covenants with God and keeps those covenants, and who participates worthily in priesthood ordinances, has direct access to the power of God. Those who are endowed in the house of the Lord receive a gift of God's priesthood power by virtue of their covenant, along with a gift of knowledge to know how to draw upon that power.

"The heavens are just as open to *women* who are endowed with God's power flowing from their priesthood covenants as they are to men who bear the priesthood. I pray that truth will register upon each of your hearts because I believe it will change your life. Sisters, you have the right to draw liberally upon the Savior's power to help your family and others you love.

"Now, you might be saying to yourself, 'This sounds wonderful, but how do I do it? How do I draw the Savior's power into my life?'

"You won't find this process spelled out in any manual. The Holy Ghost will be your personal tutor as you seek to understand what the Lord would have you know and do. This process is neither quick nor easy, but it *is* spiritually invigorating. What could possibly be more exciting than to labor with the Spirit to understand God's power—priesthood power?

"What I *can* tell you is that accessing the power of God in your life requires the same things that the Lord instructed Emma and each of you to do.

"So, I invite you to study prayerfully section 25 of the Doctrine and Covenants and discover what the Holy Ghost will teach *you*. Your personal spiritual endeavor will bring you joy as you gain, understand, and use the power with which you have been endowed" ("Spiritual Treasures," *Ensign*, Nov. 2019, 77).

Shortly before receiving this revelation, Emma had been baptized and covenanted to follow the Lord. Emma's dedicated and often selfless service to the Church and its members may suggest that she did "cleave" to the opportunities and obligations of her baptismal covenant (see Doctrine and Covenants 20:37; Mosiah 18:8–10). ⊕

15 Keep my commandments continually, and a crown of righteousness thou shalt receive. And except thou do this, where I am you cannot come.

16 And verily, verily, I say unto you, that this is my voice unto all. Amen.

Doctrine and Covenants 25:15–16. Principles of Obedience in This Revelation Are Applicable to All

What messages can we apply to our lives from Doctrine and Covenants 25? (25:16) Carol Cornwall Madsen noted: "Unlike personal revelations, patriarchal blessings, or even some of the other personally directed revelations in the Doctrine and Covenants, [this revelation] concludes with these significant words, which Joseph Smith repeated years later to the Relief Society in reference to the revelation: 'And this is my word unto all.' Thus, in significant ways, it transcends the merely personal, fitting the parameters of scripture and thereby acquiring permanence, authority, and universality. While its specifics are addressed to Emma, its principles are applicable to all.

"And what was God's message to Emma and, by implication, to the Church? The revelation's sixteen verses address four essential aspects of Emma's life: her actions and desires, her relationship to her prophet-husband, her responsibilities to the Church, and her relationship with the Lord" ("'Elect Lady' Revelation," 120).

"After the publication of the Book of Mormon in March 1830, [Joseph] spent much of his time building up the church and ministering to its members. He traveled back and forth between Harmony, Pennsylvania, and the three branches of the church in New York, leaving him less time to work on his farm and care for his material needs. Around mid-July 1830, a revelation addressed these matters, instructing him to 'magnify thy office & after that thou hast sowed thy fields & Secured them then go speedily unto the Church which is in Colesville Fayette & Manchester & they shall support thee.' Shortly thereafter, this revelation called [Joseph], Oliver Cowdery, and John Whitmer to study the scriptures, preach, confirm the Colesville believers, and work on [Joseph's] farm until the next conference" (Joseph Smith Papers, Historical Introduction to "Revelation, July 1830–B [D&C 26]," 34).

In conjunction with the revelations contained in Doctrine and Covenants 20 and this revelation received in July 1830 at Harmony, Pennsylvania, Joseph Smith and Oliver Cowdery learned line upon line that "common consent was a vital part of the operations and functions of the Lord's kingdom" (Otten and Caldwell, *Sacred Truths*, 1:119).

Several months earlier, before the Church was officially organized on April 6, 1830, they had been commanded to ordain each other to the office of elder. But, they were to "defer [their] ordination until such times as it should be practicable to have our brethren, who had been and who should be baptized, assembled together, *when we must have their sanction* to our thus proceeding to ordain each other, and have them decide by vote whether they were willing to accept us as spiritual teachers, or not" (Joseph Smith Papers, "History, circa June 1839–circa 1841 [Draft 2]," 27; emphasis added).

During the organization of the Church, those present sanctioned the action and "consented by a unanimous vote" that Joseph Smith and Oliver Cowdery be ordained elders and be recognized as presiding elders of the Church (see Otten and Caldwell, *Sacred Truths*, 1:120). Doctrine and Covenants 26 solidified the practice of common consent in the Church.

Doctrine and Covenants 26:1. They Are Instructed to Study the Scriptures and to Preach

Why was devoting time to studying the scriptures essential to the Prophet Joseph's ministry? (26:1) "During the translation of the Book of Mormon, the Prophet Joseph Smith learned that 'many plain and precious things" (1 Nephi 13:28) had been lost from the Bible and that those truths would someday be restored (see 1 Nephi 13:28, 32)....

"In October 1829, Joseph Smith and Oliver Cowdery purchased a Bible from E. B. Grandin in Palmyra, New York, that was used during the inspired translation of the Bible....

"It is possible that the Lord's direction to 'let your time be devoted to the studying of the scriptures' (D&C 26:1) was an instruction for Joseph to continue with his inspired translation of the Bible that is known today as the Joseph Smith Translation of the Bible" (*Doctrine and Covenants Student Manual* [2018], 152).

What is *preaching*? (26:1) "Preaching is teaching and teaching, in many respects, is a perfected form

SECTION 26

Revelation given to Joseph Smith the Prophet, Oliver Cowdery, and John Whitmer, at Harmony, Pennsylvania, July 1830 (see the heading to section 24).

1 Behold, I say unto you that you shall let your time be devoted to the studying of the scriptures, and to preaching, and to confirming the church at Colesville, and to performing your labors on the land, such as is required, until after you shall go to the west to hold the next conference; and then it shall be made known what you shall do.

of preaching. . . . There is worldly teaching and there is gospel teaching. There is teaching by the power of the intellect alone, and there is teaching by the power of the intellect when quickened and enlightened by the power of the Holy Spirit" (Bruce R. McConkie, *Doctrines of the Restoration*, 321, 322). Preaching must be done according to truth, prophecy and revelation, and after the holy order of God by which one is called (see Alma 43:2). "As to 'preaching the word,' the Lord commands his servants to go forth 'saying none other things than that which the prophets and apostles have written, and that which is taught them by the Comforter through the prayer of faith' (D&C 52:9)" (Bruce R. McConkie, *Promised Messiah*, 516).

Doctrine and Covenants 26:2. The Law of Common Consent Is Affirmed

2 And all things shall be done by common consent in the church, by much prayer and faith, for all things you shall receive by faith. Amen.

How was common consent established in early Church gatherings? (26:2) "Early Church leaders adopted procedures used in other organizations— such as raising hands to vote—in their attempts to fulfill the Lord's command that business be conducted by common consent. Formalities like calling meetings to order, sustaining officers and decisions by vote, keeping minutes, and announcing agenda items had become commonplace in many different organizations during the previous century. Churches, government bodies, and private clubs alike employed similar procedures" (Church History Topics, "Common Consent"). Of its significance, Elder Robert D. Hales taught that "when we [raise] our hands to the square, it [is] not just a vote in that we [give] of ourselves a private and personal commitment, even a covenant, to sustain and to uphold the laws, ordinances, commandments, and the prophet of God" ("Gaining a Testimony," *Ensign*, May 2008, 29). ☉

Introduction to Doctrine and Covenants 27

Doctrine and Covenants 27 is unique because a portion of it was given by angelic visitation. "The first four verses were written down in August of 1830 [in Harmony, Pennsylvania], shortly after the recorded words were spoken by an angel. The rest was written down the following month, late September 1830, while Joseph was in Fayette, New York, in connection with a Church conference being held there" (Robinson and Garrett, *Commentary on the Doctrine and Covenants*, 1:177).

"We might correctly suppose that by September they were reviewing the revelation that they had received the month before and the additional text was generated to more fully expand the ideas and principles that had been hinted at in the original instructions given by the angel. There is also a distinct possibility that Joseph had not written down everything that the angel had told him in early August because of time constraints and was then prompted a month later to include the entire conversation as he reviewed what had been preserved" (Paul Nolan Hyde, *Comprehensive Commentary* [1–72], 154–55).

At Harmony, Pennsylvania, in 1830, Joseph Smith recalled: "Early in the month of August, Newel Knight and his wife paid us a visit, at my place at Harmony, Penn; and as neither his wife nor mine had been as yet confirmed, it was proposed that we should confirm them, and partake together of the sacrament, before he and his wife should leave us. In order to prepare for this; I set out to go to procure some wine for the occasion, but had gone but had gone only a short distance when I was met by a heavenly messenger" (Joseph Smith Papers, "History, circa June 1839–circa 1841 [Draft 2]," 51).

"The angel warned Joseph Smith not to 'Purchase Wine neither strong drink of your enemies.' Joseph then returned home and 'prepared some wine of our own make' for the confirmation meeting, which consisted of the Smiths, the Knights, and John Whitmer. Joseph Smith's history records, 'We partook together of the sacrament, after which we confirmed these two sisters into the church, and spent the evening in a glorious manner. The Spirit of the Lord was poured out upon us, we praised the Lord God, and rejoiced exceedingly'" (Grow, "Thou Art an Elect Lady," 37–38).

SECTION 27

Revelation given to Joseph Smith the Prophet, at Harmony, Pennsylvania, August 1830. In preparation for a religious service at which the sacrament of bread and wine was to be administered, Joseph set out to procure wine. He was met by a heavenly messenger and received this revelation, a portion of which was written at the time and the remainder in the September following. Water is now used instead of wine in the sacramental services of the Church.

1 Listen to the voice of Jesus Christ, your Lord, your God, and your Redeemer, whose word is quick and powerful.

2 For, behold, I say unto you, that it mattereth not what ye shall eat or what ye shall drink when ye partake of the sacrament, if it so be that ye do it with an eye single to my glory—remembering unto the Father my

Doctrine and Covenants 27:1–4. The Emblems to Be Used in Partaking of the Sacrament Are Set Forth

What do we learn regarding the sacrament from this verse? (27:2) "Doctrine and Covenants 27 penetrates to the heart of the sacrament. If one's eye is not single to God's glory in that ordinance, tradition can transcend substance. It does not matter what the Saints eat or what they drink in that ordinance.

body which was laid down for you, and my blood which was shed for the remission of your sins.

3 Wherefore, a commandment I give unto you, that you shall not purchase wine neither strong drink of your enemies;

4 Wherefore, you shall partake of none except it is made new among you; yea, in this my Father's kingdom which shall be built up on the earth.

5 Behold, this is wisdom in me; wherefore, marvel not, for the hour cometh that I will drink of the fruit of the vine with you on the earth, and with Moroni, whom I have sent unto you to reveal the Book of Mormon, containing the fulness of my everlasting gospel, to whom I have committed the keys of the record of the stick of Ephraim;

What matters is what the emblems signify, namely, Jesus' body laid down for us and his blood shed to remit our sins" (Harper, *Making Sense of the Doctrine & Covenants*, 93). ✪

Why do we no longer use wine in the sacrament? (27:3) "At the time the Church was organized, wine was commonly used. Only a few months later, however, the Lord instructed that 'it mattereth not' what emblems we use for the sacrament as long as we remember the Savior's body and blood. He specifically instructed Joseph Smith not to buy wine from those who might be the Saints' enemies (see D&C 27:2–4). [Over time] water became the most commonly used emblem. Though the red color of wine may remind us of the Savior's blood, water is also an appropriate symbol because it is essential to life and because its clearness reminds us of the Savior's cleansing power" (Cowan, *Answers to Your Questions*, 30). See also commentary in this volume on Doctrine and Covenants 20:75.

Doctrine and Covenants 27:5–14. Christ and His Servants from All Dispensations Are to Partake of the Sacrament

When will the Savior drink of the fruit of the vine? (27:5–14) "Jesus is going to partake of the sacrament again with his mortal disciples on earth. But it will not be with mortals only. He names others who will be present and who will participate in the sacred ordinance [see D&C 27:5–14]. . . . The sacrament is to be administered in a future day, on this earth, when the Lord Jesus is present, and when all the righteous of all ages are present. This, of course, will be a part of the grand council at Adam-ondi-Ahman" (Bruce R. McConkie, *Millennial Messiah*, 587).

"Every faithful person in the whole history of the world, every person who has so lived as to merit eternal life in the kingdom of the Father will be in attendance and will partake, with the Lord, of the sacrament" (Bruce R. McConkie, *Promised Messiah* [1978], 595).

What is the stick of Ephraim? (27:5) "A record of one group from the tribe of Ephraim that was led from Jerusalem to America about 600 B.C. This group's record is called the stick of Ephraim or Joseph, or the Book of Mormon. It and the stick of Judah (the Bible) form a unified testimony of the Lord Jesus Christ, His Resurrection, and His divine work among these two segments of the house of Israel" (Guide to the Scriptures, "Ephraim").

"Moroni is correctly said here to hold 'the keys of *the record* of the stick of Ephraim,' that is, the record of the house of Ephraim, which is the Book of Mormon. . . . Moroni holds the keys for all of God's work that involves the Book of Mormon, the record of the stick of Ephraim" (Robinson and Garrett, *Commentary on the Doctrine and Covenants*, 1:181).

Who is this Elias? (27:6–7) "In this sense the name *Elias* is a title, which properly belongs to all the ancient prophets who came to aid in the restoration of all things. No single messenger from the presence of God restored all things; rather the composite of all messengers is properly referred to as Elias. Each of the individual messengers is also referred to as such. 'Who is Elias?' the Savior asked. He then responded to his own question, saying, 'Behold, this is Elias, whom I send to prepare the way before me' (JST, Matthew 17:13).

"The specific messenger mentioned in this verse is identified in the verse that follows. The Elias who appeared to Zacharias was Gabriel, who in turn was identified by the Prophet Joseph Smith as Noah" (McConkie and Ostler, *Revelations of the Restoration*, 202).

What important role does Adam, "the father of all," have? (27:11) "Adam holds the keys of the dispensation of the fulness of times, i.e. the dispensation of all the times, have been and will be revealed through him from the beginning to Christ and from Christ to the end of all the dispensations that are to be revealed. . . . [God] set the ordinances to be the same for ever and ever, and set Adam to watch over them, to reveal them from heaven to man or to send Angels to reveal them. . . . These Angels are under the direction of Michael or Adam, who acts under the direction of the Lord" (Joseph Smith Papers, "History, 1838–1856, volume C-1 [addenda]," 16 [addenda]).

6 And also with Elias, to whom I have committed the keys of bringing to pass the restoration of all things spoken by the mouth of all the holy prophets since the world began, concerning the last days;

7 And also John the son of Zacharias, which Zacharias he (Elias) visited and gave promise that he should have a son, and his name should be John, and he should be filled with the spirit of Elias;

8 Which John I have sent unto you, my servants, Joseph Smith, Jun., and Oliver Cowdery, to ordain you unto the first priesthood which you have received, that you might be called and ordained even as Aaron;

9 And also Elijah, unto whom I have committed the keys of the power of turning the hearts of the fathers to the children, and the hearts of the children to the fathers, that the whole earth may not be smitten with a curse;

10 And also with Joseph and Jacob, and Isaac, and Abraham, your fathers, by whom the promises remain;

11 And also with Michael, or Adam, the father of all, the prince of all, the ancient of days;

12 And also with Peter, and James, and John, whom I have sent unto you, by whom I have ordained you and confirmed you to be apostles, and especial witnesses of my name, and bear the keys of your ministry and of the same things which I revealed unto them;

13 Unto whom I have committed the keys of my kingdom, and a dispensation of the gospel for the last times; and for the fulness of times, in the which I will gather together in one all things, both which are in heaven, and which are on earth;

14 And also with all those whom my Father hath given me out of the world.

What is the fulness of times? (27:13) We live in the dispensation of the fulness of times. "We have had in the different ages various dispensations; for instance what may be called the Adamic dispensation, the dispensation of Noah, the dispensation of Abraham, the dispensation of Moses and of the prophets who were associated with that dispensation; the dispensation of Jesus Christ, when he came to take away the sins of the world by the sacrifice of himself, and in and through those various dispensations, certain principles, powers, privileges and priesthoods have been developed. But in the dispensation of the fulness of times a combination or a fulness, a completeness of all those dispensations was to be introduced among the human family" (Taylor, *Gospel Kingdom*, 101). See also commentary in this volume on Doctrine and Covenants 128:18. ⦿

Who else, according to verse 14, will be invited to this great event? (27:14) Latter-day revelation identifies several more individuals who would join the Savior at this hour, including "'All those whom my Father hath given me out of the world,' which is to say that the righteous saints of all ages, from Adam down to that hour, will all assemble with the Lord Jesus in that great congregation" (Bruce R. McConkie, *Mortal Messiah*, 4:66; see also 3 Nephi 15:24). At the last supper in an upper room with His apostles Jesus Chris stated: "But I say unto you, I will not drink

A Dispensation of the Gospel for the Last Times

Elder David A. Bednar explained our dispensation thus: "We live in a truly distinctive dispensation.

"A gospel dispensation is a period of time in which the necessary priesthood authority, ordinances, and doctrinal knowledge are found on the earth to implement the Father's plan of salvation for His children. Essential to the establishment of a dispensation is an authorized servant of God, a dispensation head, who holds and exercises the authority and keys of the holy priesthood.

"Gospel dispensations were established through Adam, Enoch, Noah, Abraham, Moses, Jesus Christ, Joseph Smith, and others. In every dispensation gospel truths are revealed anew—or dispensed—so the people of that period are not entirely dependent upon past dispensations for knowledge of Heavenly Father's plan.

"Apostasy from the truth occurred in each previous dispensation. However, the work of salvation that was commenced but not completed in those earlier eras continues into the final dispensation. The Prophet Joseph Smith explained that for this reason, the rolling forward of the latter-day glory, even the dispensation of the fulness of times, 'is a cause that has interested the people of God in every age; it is a theme upon which prophets, priests and kings have dwelt with peculiar delight; they have looked forward with joyful anticipation to the day in which we live; and fired with heavenly and joyful anticipations they have sung and written and prophesied of this our day' (*Joseph Smith* [manual], 186).

"In this greatest and last of all gospel dispensations, 'a whole and complete and perfect union, and welding together of dispensations, and keys, and powers, and glories should take place, and be revealed from the days of Adam even to the present time. And not only this, but those things which have never been revealed from the foundation of the world, but have been kept hid from the wise and the prudent, shall be revealed . . . in this, the dispensation of the fulness of times' (D&C 128:18)" ("Flood the Earth through Social Media," *Liahona*, Aug. 2015, 49).

henceforth of this fruit of the vine, until that day when I drink it new with you in my Father's kingdom" (Matthew 26:29). "Were it not for latter-day revelation, no one would know the significance of this promise" (Bruce R. McConkie, *Mortal Messiah*, 4:65).

Doctrine and Covenants 27:15–18. Put on the Whole Armor of God

How can we acquire the whole armor of God? (27:15–18) "The heavy armor worn by soldiers of a former day, including helmets, shields, and breast-plates, determined the outcome of some battles. However, the real battles of life in our modern day will be won by those who are clad in a spiritual armor—an armor consisting of faith in God, faith in self, faith in one's cause, and faith in one's leaders. The piece of armor called the temple garment not only provides the comfort and warmth of a cloth covering, it also strengthens the wearer to resist temptation, fend off evil influences, and stand firmly for the right" (Asay, "Temple Garment," *Ensign*, Aug. 1997, 21).

How do we put on this armor? (27:15) In his letter to the Ephesians, Paul set forth the imagery of "the whole armor of God" (see Ephesians 6:11–17). In Doctrine and Covenants 27:15 it reads "my whole armor," reflecting a personal tone in modern revelation. The Lord wishes to extend His armor.

"I like to think of this spiritual armor not as a solid piece of metal molded to fit the body but more like chain mail. Chain mail consists of dozens of tiny pieces of steel fastened together to allow the user greater flexibility without losing protection. I say that because it has been my experience that there is not one great and grand thing we can do to arm ourselves spiritually. True spiritual power lies in numerous smaller acts woven together in a fabric of spiritual fortification that protects and shields from all evil" (Ballard, "Be Strong in the Lord," *Ensign*, Jul. 2004, 8). See also commentary in this volume on Doctrine and Covenants 35:14 and 61:38.

How can we "stand" in truth and righteousness? (27:16) "When we are involved in watching, reading, or experiencing anything that is below our Heavenly Father's standards, it weakens us. Regardless of our age, if what we look at, read, listen to, or choose to do does not meet the Lord's standards . . . turn it off, rip it up, throw it out, and slam the door" (Reeves, "Worthy of Our Promised Blessings," *Ensign*, Nov. 2015, 10). "To be righteous is to seek intently to be obedient to the

15 Wherefore, lift up your hearts and rejoice, and gird up your loins, and take upon you my whole armor, that ye may be able to withstand the evil day, having done all, that ye may be able to stand.

16 Stand, therefore, having your loins girt about with truth, having on the breastplate of righteousness, and your feet shod with the preparation of the gospel of peace, which I have sent mine angels to commit unto you;

commandments of God. It is to be clean in thought and act. It is to be honest and just. Righteousness is shown more in acts than in words. A righteous life requires discipline" (Scott, "Power of Righteousness," *Ensign*, Nov. 1998, 69).

17 Taking the shield of faith wherewith ye shall be able to quench all the fiery darts of the wicked;

What kind of faith helps us "quench all the fiery darts of the wicked"? (27:17) "The Lord does not require *perfect* faith for us to have access to His *perfect* power. But He does ask us to believe. . . . Through your faith, Jesus Christ will increase your ability. . . . Increasing your faith and trust in Him takes effort" (Nelson, "Christ Is Risen," *Liahona*, May 2021, 102, 103). "The Latter-day Saint who would ward off Satan's fiery darts (flaming arrows) takes the shield of faith. When persecution, heartbreak, temptation, disappointment, illness, etc., come into the life of a Latter-day Saint, the first thing he should do is get behind the shield of faith. He must let the Lord help him; if he does not, then Satan's fiery darts may wound him spiritually. Some have sustained so many wounds that their recovery is lengthy, and there are some who have never recovered" (Hartshorn, "Where I Am Ye Shall Be Also," 129). ☉

18 And take the helmet of salvation, and the sword of my Spirit, which I will pour out upon you, and my word which I reveal unto you, and be agreed as touching all things whatsoever ye ask of me, and be faithful until I come, and ye shall be caught up, that where I am ye shall be also. Amen.

How do we put on the "helmet of salvation"? (27:18) "Our head or our intellect is the controlling member of our body. It must be well protected against the enemy. . . . Salvation means the attainment of the eternal right to live in the presence of God the Father and the Son as a reward for a good life in mortality.

"With the goal of salvation ever in our mind's eye as the ultimate to be achieved, our thinking and our decisions which determine action will always challenge all that would jeopardize that glorious future state. Lost indeed is that soul who is intellectually without the 'helmet of salvation' which tells him that death is the end and that the grave is a victory over life, and brings to defeat the hopes, the aspirations, and the accomplishments of life" (Lee, *Stand Ye in Holy Places*, 334–35).

Introduction to Doctrine and Covenants 28

The summer of 1830 were anxious months for the young Prophet Joseph Smith. "This revelation [given at Fayette, New York, in September 1830] was a response to actions by Oliver Cowdery and Hiram Page that raised the question of whether [Joseph Smith] was the only one authorized to deliver revelation to the church. The question first arose in summer 1830 when Oliver Cowdery 'commanded' [Joseph] to change a passage in 'Articles and Covenants.' . . . [Oliver] objected to the requirement that candidates for baptism 'truly manifest by their works that they have received the gift of Christ unto the remission of their sins.' . . . In response, [Joseph] traveled from Harmony, Pennsylvania, to Fayette, New York, to persuade Cowdery and the Whitmers that they were mistaken. . . . [With] support from Christian Whitmer, [Joseph] convinced Cowdery and the Whitmer family 'that they had been in error, and that the sentence in dispute was in accordance of the rest of the commandment'" (Joseph Smith Papers, Historical Introduction to "Revelation, September 1830–B [D&C 28]," 41).

"Within months, Joseph again needed to assert his authority as the mouthpiece of revelation. Persecution around his home in Harmony, Pennsylvania, had forced Joseph and his wife, Emma, to take up residence with the Whitmers in August 1830. Upon arriving, Joseph found that Hiram Page, the husband of one of the Whitmers' daughters, had used a stone to receive two revelations concerning the Church.

"Perhaps remembering his success persuading Oliver Cowdery and the Whitmers of their error concerning the 'Articles and Covenants,' Joseph intended to reason with them until a conference that was to be convened in September. He soon discovered, however, that belief in Hiram Page's supposed revelations was more widespread than he had thought, so he sought a revelation on the matter" (Jeffrey G. Cannon, "All Things Must Be Done in Order," 51).

"In the revelation recorded in Doctrine and Covenants 28 [September 1830], given through the Prophet Joseph Smith to Oliver Cowdery, the Lord gave the proper order of revelation in the Church. Although Oliver was ordained as the second elder of the Church, his role was not to receive revelations or write commandments for the Church. Rather, Oliver was to follow the pattern found in the example of Aaron, 'to declare faithfully the commandments and the revelations' (D&C 28:3) that had been given to the Lord's prophet. Like Moses, Joseph Smith was the prophet who had received the keys of the kingdom in his day. Nevertheless, Oliver was promised that he would be led by the Comforter and would be blessed with power and authority as he taught the things revealed to the Prophet Joseph Smith" (*Doctrine and Covenants Student Manual* [2018], 161).

Doctrine and Covenants 28:1–7. Joseph Smith Holds the Keys of the Mysteries, and Only He Receives Revelations for the Church

SECTION 28

Revelation given through Joseph Smith the Prophet to Oliver Cowdery, at Fayette, New York, September 1830. Hiram Page, a member of the Church, had a certain stone and professed to be receiving revelations by its aid concerning the upbuilding of Zion and the order of the Church. Several members had been deceived by these claims, and even Oliver Cowdery was wrongly influenced thereby. Just prior to an appointed conference, the Prophet inquired earnestly of the Lord concerning the matter, and this revelation followed.

1 Behold, I say unto thee, Oliver, that it shall be given unto thee that thou shalt be heard by the church in all things whatsoever thou

shalt teach them by the Comforter, concerning the revelations and commandments which I have given.

2 But, behold, verily, verily, I say unto thee, no one shall be appointed to receive commandments and revelations in this church excepting my servant Joseph Smith, Jun., for he receiveth them even as Moses.

3 And thou shalt be obedient unto the things which I shall give unto him, even as Aaron, to declare faithfully the commandments and the revelations, with power and authority unto the church.

Why wasn't Oliver Cowdery permitted to receive and declare revelation for the Church? (28:2–3) The Prophet Joseph noted: "I will inform you that it is contrary to the economy of God for any member of the Church, or any one, to receive instructions for those in authority higher than themselves; therefore you will see the impropriety of giving heed to them; but if any person have a vision or a visitation from a heavenly messenger, it must be for his own benefit and instruction, for the fundamental principles, government and doctrine of the Church [are] invested in the keys of the kingdom" (Joseph Smith Papers, "Letter to John S. Carter, 13 April 1833," 30). See also commentary in this volume on Doctrine and Covenants 20:2–3. ●

4 And if thou art led at any time by the Comforter to speak or teach, or at all times by the way of commandment unto the church, thou mayest do it.

How do we receive revelation and teach by the spirit? (28:4) President Dallin H. Oaks taught: "The best way to have the spirit of revelation is to listen to and study words spoken under the influence of the Holy Ghost. In other words, we obtain the Spirit by reading the scriptures or reading or listening to the talks of inspired leaders....

"Teaching by the Spirit is the Lord's way. How do we do this? First, we must keep the commandments,

Hiram Page

Hiram Page was born in 1800 in Westminster, Windham County, Vermont. His father apparently died shortly before he was born, and his mother apprenticed Hiram to a country doctor at the early age of ten. Page learned of the Book of Mormon from the Peter and Mary Whitmer family and subsequently married Catherine Whitmer. He was baptized five days after the organization of the Church, 11 April 1830. Hiram became one of the Eight Witnesses of the Book of Mormon.

Page remained faithful until 1838 when his brothers-in-law, Oliver Cowdery, David Whitmer, and John Whitmer, were excommunicated, and the majority of the Whitmer family withdrew from the Church. How much Hiram shared their discontent is unclear. However, evidence shows that Hiram was not excommunicated (see Joseph F. Smith, in *Contributor*, Vol. 8, No. 4 (February 1887): 158), and his affiliation with the Church was more likely influenced by family ties.

Hiram Page died at the relatively young age of fifty-two. Five years before his death he left a stirring testimony as a Book of Mormon witness. In 1847, William E. McLellin wrote to him, asking if he had retained his faith in the Book of Mormon. Page responded: "It would be doing injustice to myself, and to the work of God of the last days, to say that I could know a thing to be true in 1830, and know that same thing to be false in 1847. To say my mind was so treacherous that I had forgotten what I saw.... And to say that those holy Angels who came and showed themselves to me as I was walking through the field, to confirm me in the work of the Lord of the last days—three of whom came to me afterwards and sang an hymn in their own pure language; yea, it would be treating the God of heaven with contempt, to deny these testimonies, with too many others to mention here" ("Letter to William E. McLellan, Ray Co., Missouri, 30 May 1847," in *Ensign of Liberty*, Vol. 1, No. 4: 63).

especially the commandment to keep our thoughts and actions clean. Second, we must prepare. Third, we must desire to be led and be willing to be led by the Spirit. The Lord will speak to us in his own time and in his own way" ("Teaching and Learning by the Spirit," *Ensign*, Mar. 1997, 9, 14).

Who is authorized to receive revelations for the Church? (28:5–7) "In the Lord's Church, the First Presidency and the Quorum of the Twelve Apostles are prophets, seers, and revelators to the Church and to the world. The President of the Church is the only one whom the Lord has authorized to receive revelation for the Church (D&C 28:2–7). Every person may receive personal revelation for his own benefit" (Guide to the Scriptures, "Revelation"). ☉

Doctrine and Covenants 28:8–10. Oliver Cowdery Is to Preach to the Lamanites

Why was it so important to take the gospel to Indigenous communities? (28:8) "When the Lord brought forth the record of the Book of Mormon to Joseph Smith in this dispensation, he committed to his Church with that important record the responsibility of taking to the [Indigenous peoples] the knowledge of their forefathers and the fulness of the gospel, which record also includes the Lord's promises to them as a branch of the house of Israel [D&C 3:16–20].

"Very shortly after this revelation was given, the Lord gave another revelation [D&C 28:8–9] that instructed the Prophet to open the work among the [Indigenous nations] . . . , wherein Oliver Cowdery was called as the first missionary to the [native peoples] from the newly restored Church" (Stapley,

5 But thou shalt not write by way of commandment, but by wisdom;

6 And thou shalt not command him who is at thy head, and at the head of the church;

7 For I have given him the keys of the mysteries, and the revelations which are sealed, until I shall appoint unto them another in his stead.

8 And now, behold, I say unto you that you shall go unto the Lamanites and preach my gospel unto them; and inasmuch as they receive thy teachings thou shalt cause my church to be established among them; and thou shalt have revelations, but write them not by way of commandment.

Oliver Cowdery's Mission to the "Lamanites" (Indigenous Nations)

Oliver Cowdery and three other men were called to preach the gospel to the Indigenous nations (see D&C 28:8; 30:5; 32:1–5). This mission was closely tied to identifying the location of the city of Zion. Oliver wrote the following prior to his departure:

"I, Oliver [Cowdery], being commanded of the Lord God, to go forth unto the Lamanites, to proclaim glad tidings of great joy unto them, by presenting unto them the fulness of the Gospel, of the only begotten son of God; and also, to rear up a pillar as a witness where the Temple of God shall be built, in the glorious New-Jerusalem; and having certain brothers with me, who are called of God to assist me, whose names are Parley [P. Pratt], Peter [Whitmer Jr.] and Ziba [Peterson], do therefore most solemnly covenant before God, that I will walk humbly before him, and do this business, and this glorious work according as he shall direct me by the Holy Ghost; ever praying for mine and their prosperity, and deliverance from bonds, and from imprisonments, and whatsoever may [befall] us, with all patience and faith.—Amen. [signed] OLIVER COWDERY" (Joseph Smith Papers, "Covenant of Oliver Cowdery and Others, 17 October 1830," [1]). For a map of the first missionary journey to the Lamanites, see Map 6 in the Appendix.

"Responsibility to the Lamanites," *Improvement Era*, Jun. 1956, 416). ⊕

9 And now, behold, I say unto you that it is not revealed, and no man knoweth where the city Zion shall be built, but it shall be given hereafter. Behold, I say unto you that it shall be on the borders by the Lamanites.

10 Thou shalt not leave this place until after the conference; and my servant Joseph shall be appointed to preside over the conference by the voice of it, and what he saith to thee thou shalt tell.

11 And again, thou shalt take thy brother, Hiram Page, between him and thee alone, and tell him that those things which he hath written from that stone are not of me and that Satan deceiveth him;

12 For, behold, these things have not been appointed unto him, neither shall anything be appointed unto any of this church contrary to the church covenants.

13 For all things must be done in order, and by common consent in the church, by the prayer of faith.

14 And thou shalt assist to settle all these things, according to the covenants of the church, before thou shalt take thy journey among the Lamanites.

Why does verse 9 mention "the city Zion" in conjunction with the Page revelations? (28:9) "Apparently, one of the topics addressed in Hiram Page's false revelations had been the location and development of Zion. Interest in this subject may have intensified at this time as a result of the revelation of Moses 7 to Joseph Smith, for this material in the Joseph Smith Translation seems to have led many in the Church to assume Zion was going to be established immediately. The Lord clarified in this verse that no one even knew at that time where the city of Zion would be built. This information would come later in Doctrine and Covenants 57:2–3" (Robinson and Garrett, *Commentary on the Doctrine and Covenants*, 1:192). See also commentary in this volume on Doctrine and Covenants 42:9 and 57:2–3.

Doctrine and Covenants 28:11–16. Satan Deceived Hiram Page and Gave Him False Revelations

Why was Oliver directed to counsel with Hiram Page over the error of his revelations? (28:11) "This is the correct procedure for reconciling a brother or sister who has offended. First Hiram Page was spoken to privately; then, since his error affected the Church, the details of his error were discussed openly at the conference, and his 'seer-stone' and its revelations were renounced publicly by all present, including Hiram himself. Notice that Hiram Page was not evil, but he was mistaken and deceived, and it is the duty of the Brethren to correct those who would teach, preach, write, or otherwise spread false doctrine to the Church, even when those persons believe themselves to be in the right" (Robinson and Garrett, *Commentary on the Doctrine and Covenants*, 1:193).

What was the outcome of the conference at which Hiram Page's stone was rejected? (28:11–12) When the Lord and the conference rejected the Page stone and revelations, Hiram humbled himself and submitted to Joseph and the Lord and the will of the conference. Emer Harris (brother of Martin), who was at the conference, noted specifically that Hiram "broke [his stone] to powder" and "burnt [the writings]" ("Emer Harris Statement, 6 April 1856"). Newell Knight remembered: "During this time we have much of the power of God manifested and it was wonderful to witness the wisdom that Joseph displayed on this occasion, for truly God gave unto him great wisdom and power, and it seems to me, even now, that none who saw him administer righteousness under such strange circumstances, could doubt that the Lord was with him" (Newel Knight's Journal, *Classic Experiences and Adventures*, 65).

What is the role of revelation in individual lives of the Saints? (28:15) "Pray in the name of Jesus Christ about your concerns, your fears, your weaknesses—yes, the very longings of your heart. And then listen! Write the thoughts that come to your mind. Record your feelings and follow through with actions that you are prompted to take. As you repeat this process day after day, month after month, year after year, you will 'grow into the principle of revelation.' . . .

"I urge you to stretch beyond your current spiritual ability to receive personal revelation. . . .

"I promise that as you continue to be obedient, expressing gratitude for every blessing the Lord gives you, and as you patiently honor the Lord's timetable, you will be given the knowledge and understanding you seek" (Nelson, "Revelation for the Church, Revelation for Our Lives," *Ensign*, May 2018, 95–96).

15 And it shall be given thee from the time thou shalt go, until the time thou shalt return, what thou shalt do.

16 And thou must open thy mouth at all times, declaring my gospel with the sound of rejoicing. Amen.

Introduction to Doctrine and Covenants 29

"This revelation [received in September 1830 in Fayette, New York,] addressed the interest of some early church members in a Book of Mormon prophecy [3 Nephi 20:10–22:17] that described the physical gathering of God's chosen people in America. The Book of Mormon explained that during Christ's ministry in the Americas he prophesied that his chosen people would establish a sacred city, the New Jerusalem. According to the prophecies, 'the remnant of Jacob,' which early church members identified as the [Indigenous communities already inhabiting the land], 'and also, as many of the house of Israel as shall come' were to build this sacred city and gather to it, assisted by Gentiles who embraced the book's message. Christ further prophesied that when the progeny of the people described in the Book of Mormon were taught 'this gospel' again [see 3 Nephi 21:23–26], Zion would be established among them.

"The setting for this revelation was a gathering of 'Six Elders of the Church & three members' who 'understood from Holy Writ that the time had come that the People of God should see eye to eye.' The book of Isaiah declared that God's people would 'see eye to eye, when the Lord shall bring again Zion'; the Book of Mormon expressed the same sentiment and located Zion in the Americas. . . . This small group, believing that the Book of Mormon prophecy about Zion would soon be fulfilled, therefore 'enquired of the Lord & thus came the word of the Lord through Joseph the seer.'

"The revelation affirmed the imminent advent of the Millennium and declared that members of the Church of Christ were called to help gather God's people before the great event" (Joseph Smith Papers, Historical Introduction to "Revelation, September 1830–A [D&C 29]," 36).

"The truths taught in Doctrine and Covenants 29 added to the Saints' understanding about the need for Zion in the last days and may have corrected some of the doctrinal confusion caused by Hiram Page's writings. . . . Furthermore, Doctrine and Covenants 29 provided important truths about the gathering of Israel and the plan of salvation before Oliver Cowdery and his companions left on a mission to preach the gospel" (*Doctrine and Covenants Student Manual* [2018], 166–67).

SECTION 29

Revelation given through Joseph Smith the Prophet, in the presence of six elders, at Fayette, New York, September 1830. This revelation was given some days prior to the conference, beginning September 26, 1830.

1 Listen to the voice of Jesus Christ, your Redeemer, the Great I Am, whose arm of mercy hath atoned for your sins;

2 Who will gather his people even as a hen gathereth her chickens under her wings, even as many as will hearken to my voice and humble themselves before me, and call upon me in mighty prayer.

3 Behold, verily, verily, I say unto you, that at this time your sins are forgiven you, therefore ye receive these things; but remember to sin no more, lest perils shall come upon you.

4 Verily, I say unto you that ye are chosen out of the world to declare my gospel with the sound of rejoicing, as with the voice of a trump.

5 Lift up your hearts and be glad, for I am in your midst, and am your advocate with the Father; and it is his good will to give you the kingdom.

6 And, as it is written—Whatsoever ye shall ask in faith, being united in prayer according to my command, ye shall receive.

Doctrine and Covenants 29:1–8. Christ Gathers His Elect

Who is "the Great I AM"? (29:1) "I AM is a divine descriptive title that refers to the pre-earthly Jehovah, who was known on the earth as Jesus Christ. This name-title emphasizes the eternal nature of the power, authority, might, mission, and calling of Jesus Christ" (Daniel H. Ludlow, *Companion to Your Study*, 2:136).

"Christ revealed Himself in the Old Testament as 'I am,'—Hebrew, *'Ehyeh 'asher 'Ehyeh* (Ex. 3:14), which implies that, while He *is*, or exists, and is therefore different from all non-existing deities of merely human imagination, He is not an abstract existence without form or substance, but He is a real Being, manifesting Himself in history ever anew; He is always with His people, active for their welfare" (Smith and Sjodahl, *Doctrine and Covenants Commentary*, 86).

What did these six elders learn about the Lord's forgiving nature? (29:3) "In [the Lord's] forgiveness we see the enabling *and* the redeeming power of the Atonement harmoniously and graciously applied. If we exercise faith in the Lord Jesus Christ, the enabling power of His Atonement *strengthens* us in our moment of need, and His redeeming power *sanctifies* us. . . . This brings hope to all, especially to those who feel that recurring human weakness is beyond the Savior's willingness to help and to save. . . . The Lord loves us and wants us to understand His willingness to forgive. On more than 20 occasions in the Doctrine and Covenants, the Lord told those to whom He was speaking, 'Thy sins are forgiven thee,' or similar words" (Cardon, "Savior Wants to Forgive," *Ensign*, May 2013, 15,16). ☉

How can we become united in prayer? (29:6) Jedediah M. Grant testified: "We talk about being one; now if our faith is right, let our works correspond. If you have faith to pray, and prayer is offered up in the stand, pray too; and if you cannot confine your thoughts in any other way, mentally repeat the prayer of the one who is praying aloud, word for word, and let every Saint of God pray when the hour of prayer comes. When prayer is offered up in this manner to the God of high heaven for the sick and afflicted, you will find that the sick will be healed, for the prayers of the people of God ascend as incense before Him, and He has decreed that He will answer their prayers because they are united" (in *Journal of Discourses*, 2:277–78).

How can we find the Lord's elect? (29:7) President Spencer W. Kimball explained: "Our goal should be to identify as soon as possible which of our Father's children are spiritually prepared to proceed all the way to baptism into the kingdom. . . . What you need to do is find out if they are the elect. '[My] elect hear my voice and harden not their hearts' (D&C 29:7). If they hear and have hearts open to the gospel, it will be evident immediately. If they won't listen and their hearts are hardened with skepticism or negative comments, they are not ready" (*Spencer W. Kimball* [manual], 263–64).

How will Israel know when and where to gather in the last days? (29:8) "The Lord has placed the responsibility for directing the work of gathering in the hands of the leaders of the Church to whom he will reveal his will where and when such gatherings would take place in the future. It would be well, before the frightening events concerning the fulfillment of all God's promises and predictions are upon us, that the Saints in every land prepare themselves and look forward to the instruction that shall come

7 And ye are called to bring to pass the gathering of mine elect; for mine elect hear my voice and harden not their hearts;

8 Wherefore the decree hath gone forth from the Father that they shall be gathered in unto one place upon the face of this land, to prepare their hearts and be prepared in all things against the day when tribulation and desolation are sent forth upon the wicked.

What Signs Foreshadow the Savior's Second Coming?

1. Social and political conflict
   • "Wars and rumors of wars" (D&C 45:26; see also 87:1–6)
   • Whole earth in commotion (see D&C 88:91)
   • Sword of Zion (see D&C 45:68–69)
   • "The wicked shall slay the wicked" (D&C 63:33)
2. Fear and despair
   • "Weeping and wailing among the hosts of men" (D&C 29:15)
   • "Among the wicked, men shall lift up their voices and curse God and die" (D&C 45:32)
   • "Men's hearts shall fail them; for fear shall come upon all people" (D&C 88:91; see also D&C 63:33)
3. Great wickedness
   • All flesh will be corrupt before God (see D&C 112:23)
   • Love will wax cold, and iniquity shall abound (see D&C 45:27)
   • The wicked will have turned their hearts from God because of the precepts of men (see D&C 45:29)
4. Famines, pestilences, and sickness
   • A great hailstorm will destroy the crops of the earth (see D&C 29:16)
   • "An overflowing scourge"; "a desolating sickness" (D&C 45:31)
   • Flies and maggots; flesh will fall from bones and eyes from sockets (see D&C 29:18–20)
   • "Many desolations . . . yet men will harden their hearts" (D&C 45:33)
5. Extensive natural calamities
   • Earthquakes, thunderings, lightnings, and tempests as the Lord's testimony, to follow the testimony of his earthly servants (D&C 43:25; 87:6)

9 For the hour is nigh and the day soon at hand when the earth is ripe; and all the proud and they that do wickedly shall be as stubble; and I will burn them up, saith the Lord of Hosts, that wickedness shall not be upon the earth;

10 For the hour is nigh, and that which was spoken by mine apostles must be fulfilled; for as they spoke so shall it come to pass;

11 For I will reveal myself from heaven with power and great glory, with all the hosts thereof, and dwell in righteousness with men on earth a thousand years, and the wicked shall not stand.

to them from the First Presidency of this Church as to where they shall be gathered. They should not be disturbed in their feelings until such instruction is given to them as it is revealed by the Lord to the proper authority" (Lee, *Teachings*, 410). See also commentary in this volume on D&C 45:66–73.

Doctrine and Covenants 29:9–11. Christ's Coming Ushers in the Millennium

Why will the Lord use fire to destroy the wicked at His coming? (29:9) "This physical earth shall be literally cleansed of all wickedness by being burned with fire in the brightness of the Lord's coming, so that the terrestrial Millennium may begin. 'It is not a figure of speech that is meaningless, or one not to be taken literally when the Lord speaks of the burning. All through the scriptures we have the word of the Lord that at his coming the wicked and the rebellious will be as stubble and will be consumed.' Many have confused the description of this literal burning at the last day with the figurative fires of hell, to create a false picture of the ultimate fate of the wicked" (Robinson and Garrett, *Commentary on the Doctrine and Covenants*, 1:198).

- Waves heaving themselves beyond their bounds (D&C 88:90)
- Earth to reel to and fro as a drunken man (D&C 88:87)
6. The gospel preached to every nation (see D&C 133:37–38)
7. Gathering of both the righteous and the wicked
  - "Disciples shall stand in holy places, and shall not be moved" (D&C 45:32; see also D&C 101:16–23)
  - "Zion shall flourish upon the hills . . . *and* shall be assembled together unto *the place* which I have appointed" (D&C 49:25; emphasis added)
  - A remnant of believing Jews will be gathered at Jerusalem (see D&C 45:43–44)
  - "The tares are bound in bundles" [the wicked are prepared for destruction] (D&C 86:7; see also D&C 88:94; 101:66)
  - Some of the wicked will "curse God and die" (D&C 45:32); others will wish to curse God, but "their tongues shall be stayed" (D&C 29:19)
8. "Jacob shall flourish in the wilderness, and the Lamanites shall blossom as the rose" (D&C 49:24)
9. Signs in the heavens and the earth
  - Sun, moon, and stars phenomena; blood, fire, and vapors of smoke (see D&C 29:14; 45:39–42)
  - The sign of the Son of Man (D&C 88:93; Joseph Smith—Matthew 1:36)
10. Deception and hypocrisy among members of the Church (see D&C 41:1; 45:56–57; 50:4–9; 52:14–19; 64:34–39; 76:28–29; 112:23–26)

(Revised from handout by Dahl, "Doctrine and Covenants and the Second Coming.")

Doctrine and Covenants 29:12–13. The Twelve Will Judge All Israel

What do the robes of righteousness represent? (29:12) "Robes of righteousness are those white robes given celestial Saints, whose names are to be found in the book of life (Rev. 3:5), symbolizing their purity before God. They are 'cleansed every whit from [their] iniquity' (3 Ne. 8:1). The whiteness of these robes testifies to the complete sanctification and purification of the Saints wearing them" (Brewster, *Doctrine & Covenants Encyclopedia* [2012], 478–79).

What is the trump described in this verse? (29:13) "The trumpet is a musical instrument that can be made to produce a loud, blaring sound that can be heard for a considerable distance. Sometimes the expression 'sound of a trumpet' is used in the scriptures in a literal sense—an actual trumpet will be blown and the actual sound of the trumpet will be heard. On other occasions, however, the expression is used only in the figurative sense that the message will be loud and clear, just as the sound of the trumpet can be loud and clear" (Daniel H. Ludlow, *Companion to Your Study*, 2:310).

Anciently, this trump was "the *shofar,* the ram's horn, [and was] sounded repeatedly to call the people to repentance" (Frankel and Teutsch, *Encyclopedia of Jewish Symbols*, 136).

Doctrine and Covenants 29:14–21. Signs, Plagues, and Desolations Will Precede the Second Coming

How can we know when the signs in the heavens at the Lord's coming will occur? (29:14) "This does not imply that these heavenly bodies will be destroyed, only that their light is diminished here on earth. This could be caused by several things happening on the earth such as widespread fires, massive dust storms, volcanic eruptions, nuclear explosions, or even severe air pollution" (Lund, *Second Coming of the Lord*, 164).

For example, President Gordon B. Hinckley taught: "The vision of Joel has been fulfilled wherein [the Lord] declared: 'And it shall come to pass afterward, that I will pour out my spirit upon all flesh. . . . And I will shew wonders in the heavens and in the

12 And again, verily, verily, I say unto you, and it hath gone forth in a firm decree, by the will of the Father, that mine apostles, the Twelve which were with me in my ministry at Jerusalem, shall stand at my right hand at the day of my coming in a pillar of fire, being clothed with robes of righteousness, with crowns upon their heads, in glory even as I am, to judge the whole house of Israel, even as many as have loved me and kept my commandments, and none else.

13 For a trump shall sound both long and loud, even as upon Mount Sinai, and all the earth shall quake, and they shall come forth—yea, even the dead which died in me, to receive a crown of righteousness, and to be clothed upon, even as I am, to be with me, that we may be one.

14 But, behold, I say unto you that before this great day shall come the sun shall be darkened, and the moon shall be turned into blood, and the stars shall fall from heaven, and there shall be greater signs in heaven above and in the earth beneath;

15 And there shall be weeping and wailing among the hosts of men;

16 And there shall be a great hailstorm sent forth to destroy the crops of the earth.

17 And it shall come to pass, because of the wickedness of the world, that I will take vengeance upon the wicked, for they will not repent; for the cup of mine indignation is full; for behold, my blood shall not cleanse them if they hear me not.

18 Wherefore, I the Lord God will send forth flies upon the face of the earth, which shall take hold of the inhabitants thereof, and shall eat their flesh, and shall cause maggots to come in upon them;

19 And their tongues shall be stayed that they shall not utter against me; and their flesh shall fall from off their bones, and their eyes from their sockets;

20 And it shall come to pass that the beasts of the forest and the fowls of the air shall devour them up.

21 And the great and abominable church, which is the whore of all the earth, shall be cast down by devouring fire, according as it is spoken by the mouth of Ezekiel the prophet, who spoke of these things, which have not come to pass but surely must, as I live, for abominations shall not reign.

earth, blood, and fire, and pillars of smoke. The sun shall be turned into darkness, and the moon into blood, before the great and the terrible day of the Lord come. . . . (Joel 2:28–32)" ("Living in the Fulness of Times," *Ensign*, Nov. 2001, 4). ◐

What do we know about the great hailstorm in this prophecy? (29:16) "John the Revelator saw 'a great hail out of heaven, every stone about the weight of a talent' (Revelation 16:21). The immensity of this destruction is evident in the fact that a talent is 75.6 pounds. There are yet other references in the Old and New Testaments that add another dimension to the plague of hail. This could yet be another disaster, for it is spoken of in the context of the final battle of Armageddon. Speaking of Gog, the enemy of God, the prophet Ezekiel proclaims: 'And I will plead against him with pestilence and with blood; and I will rain upon him, and upon his bands, and upon the many people that are with him, an overflowing rain, and great hailstones, fire, and brimstone (Ezekiel 38:22)'" (Brewster, *Behold, I Come Quickly*, 33). ◐

How might these plagues be fulfilled in the last days? (29:18–20) It "seems descriptive of nuclear and chemical warfare. . . . One who has read a description of the deplorable physical condition of a person who has been exposed to nuclear, chemical, or bacteriological weaponry can surely envision a fulfillment of this prophecy" (Brewster, *Doctrine & Covenants Encyclopedia* [2012], 195).

Wilford Woodruff stated: "No man can contemplate the truth concerning the nations of the earth without sorrow, when he sees the wailing, the mourning, and death, that will come in consequence of judgments, plagues, and war. It has already begun, and it will continue to multiply and increase until the scene is ended, and wound up" (in *Journal of Discourses*, 2:201).

What is the great and abominable church? (29:21) "This is the only occurrence of this phrase in the Doctrine and Covenants, though it is probably to be identified with the churches built up 'to get gain' in Doctrine and Covenants 10:56 and 'the church of the devil' in Doctrine and Covenants 18:20. 'The great and abominable church' does *not* refer to any particular denomination, neither Roman Catholics, nor Jews, nor Baptists, nor any other individual church. In its broadest definition, the great and abominable church is the collective term for all who oppose or fight against Zion (see 2 Nephi 10:16)" (Robinson and Garrett, *Commentary on the Doctrine and Covenants*, 202). ◐

Doctrine and Covenants 29:22–28. The Last Resurrection and Final Judgment Follow the Millennium

What is meant by all things becoming new? (29:23–24) "Eventually, 'the earth will be renewed and receive its paradisiacal glory' [Articles of Faith 1:10]. At the Second Coming of the Lord, the earth will be changed once again. It will be returned to its paradisiacal state and be made new. There will be a new heaven and a new earth" (Nelson, "Creation," *Ensign*, May 2000, 85).

What is the significance that not one hair of the head be lost? (29:25) "The minute nature of human hair is also symbolic. For example, our many hairs show that God is omnipotent and omniscient, because he will not allow a hair of our heads to be lost (see Alma 11:44; 40:23; D&C 29:25), for every hair of our head is numbered to him (see Matthew 10:30; D&C 84:116). Indeed, as a sign of his omnipotence, God is frequently said to protect every head of those who fight for Israel (see 1 Samuel 14:45; 2 Samuel 14:11; 1 Kings 1:52; Acts 27:34; D&C 9:14). God's protection of the hair implies an eternal protection of our spiritual life" (Gaskill, *Lost Language of Symbolism*, 42).

Who is Michael, the archangel? (29:26) "Michael is Adam, the first man (D&C 27:11). He is chief among God's sons and has been given 'the keys of salvation under the counsel and direction of the Holy One' (D&C 78:16), who is Jesus Christ. The sounding of Michael's trump is to announce the resurrection of the dead....

"The prophet Daniel associated Adam with the time of the resurrection of his people (Daniel 12:1–2). Thus, it appears that the trump with which Adam announces the resurrection from the dead also signifies keys that Adam possesses in directing the resurrection. It is altogether appropriate that Adam, who imposed death upon all of his posterity, be the one to call them forth from their graves" (McConkie and Ostler, *Revelations of the Restoration*, 237, 238).

22 And again, verily, verily, I say unto you that when the thousand years are ended, and men again begin to deny their God, then will I spare the earth but for a little season;

23 And the end shall come, and the heaven and the earth shall be consumed and pass away, and there shall be a new heaven and a new earth.

24 For all old things shall pass away, and all things shall become new, even the heaven and the earth, and all the fulness thereof, both men and beasts, the fowls of the air, and the fishes of the sea;

25 And not one hair, neither mote, shall be lost, for it is the workmanship of mine hand.

26 But, behold, verily I say unto you, before the earth shall pass away, Michael, mine archangel, shall sound his trump, and then shall all the dead awake, for their graves shall be opened, and they shall come forth—yea, even all.

27 And the righteous shall be gathered on my right hand unto eternal life; and the wicked on my left hand will I be ashamed to own before the Father;

28 Wherefore I will say unto them—Depart from me, ye cursed, into everlasting fire, prepared for the devil and his angels.

29 And now, behold, I say unto you, never at any time have I declared from mine own mouth that they should return, for where I am they cannot come, for they have no power.

30 But remember that all my judgments are not given unto men; and as the words have gone forth out of my mouth even so shall they be fulfilled, that the first shall be last, and that the last shall be first in all things whatsoever I have created by the word of my power, which is the power of my Spirit.

31 For by the power of my Spirit created I them; yea, all things both spiritual and temporal—

32 First spiritual, secondly temporal, which is the beginning of my work; and again, first temporal, and secondly spiritual, which is the last of my work—

33 Speaking unto you that you may naturally understand; but unto myself my works have no end, neither beginning; but it is given unto you that ye may understand, because ye have asked it of me and are agreed.

34 Wherefore, verily I say unto you that all things unto me are spiritual, and not at any time have I given unto you a law which was temporal; neither any man, nor the children of men; neither Adam, your father, whom I created.

35 Behold, I gave unto him that he should be an agent unto himself; and I gave unto him commandment, but no temporal commandment gave I unto him, for my commandments are spiritual; they are not natural nor temporal, neither carnal nor sensual.

Doctrine and Covenants 29:29–35. All Things Are Spiritual unto the Lord

What does it mean that God's work is first spiritual and secondly temporal? (29:31–32) "Some Christians at the time of Joseph Smith believed that God spoke and created the earth and all things thereon *ex nihilo*, or out of nothing. They also did not believe that a spiritual creation preceded the physical creation. . . .

"According to the restored gospel of Jesus Christ, God created all things spiritually before they were created temporally. And the earth was organized from existing elements, which are eternal" (Bednar, "That Ye May Believe, Part 1").

What difference does it make to understand that all things are spiritual to the Lord? (29:34) Our perspective changes when we understand the spiritual meaning behind acts and events. "The Latter-day Saint men and women who settled these valleys of the mountains acted upon that principle. Judged in terms of the values and aspirations of the world, some pioneer enterprises were failures. . . .

"But, when measured against the eternal values of loyalty, cooperation, and consecration, some of the most conspicuous worldly failures are seen as the pioneer enterprisers' greatest triumphs. Whatever their financial outcome, these enterprises called forth the sacrifices that molded pioneers into Saints and prepared Saints for exaltation. Unto God, 'all things . . . are spiritual' (D&C 29:34)" (Oaks, "Spirituality," *Ensign*, Nov. 1985, 62). ●

Doctrine and Covenants 29:36–39. The Devil and His Hosts Were Cast out of Heaven to Tempt Man

What are some reasons for the devil's rebellion against God? (29:36) "In the pre-earthly council, Lucifer placed his proposal in competition with the Father's plan as advocated by Jesus Christ (see Moses 4:1–3). He wished to be honored above all others (see 2 Nephi 24:13). In short, his prideful desire was to dethrone God (see D&C 29:36; 76:28)" (Benson, "Beware of Pride," *Ensign*, May 1989, 4–5).

"Satan's purpose was to gain for himself the Father's honor and power" (Oaks, "Opposition in All Things," *Ensign*, May 2016, 115). ☉

Who became the devil's angels? (29:37–38) "Demons, devils, and evil spirits are the beings who followed Lucifer in his war of rebellion in the premortal world. They comprise one-third of those spirit children of the Father who were to come to this earth as a mortal probation (see D&C 29:36–41; Revelation 12:3–9). In New Testament terminology they are 'the angels which kept not their first estate' (Jude 1:6), or, as Peter puts it, 'God spared not the angels that sinned, but cast them down to hell' (2 Peter 2:4). They are fallen angels and are angels of the devil (see D&C 29:36–38; 2 Nephi 9:9)" (Oscar W. McConkie, *Angels*, 84).

How can experiencing the bitter increase our appreciation for the sweet in life? (29:39) "[Our] Father's plan subjects us to temptation and misery in this fallen world as the price to comprehend authentic joy. Without tasting the bitter, we actually *cannot* understand the sweet. We require mortality's discipline and refinement as the 'next step in [our] development' toward becoming like our Father. But growth means growing pains. It also means learning from our mistakes in a continual process made possible by the Savior's grace, which He extends both during and *after all we can do*' [2 Nephi 25:23; emphasis added]" (Hafen, "Atonement," *Ensign*, May 2004, 97). ☉

Doctrine and Covenants 29:40–45. The Fall and Atonement Bring Salvation

How might we become subject to "the will of the devil" as Adam was? (29:40) "We are all like Adam in that when we partake of 'forbidden fruits' or do the things we are commanded not to do, we are ashamed, and we draw away from the Church and from God and hide ourselves, and if we continue in sin, the Spirit of

36 And it came to pass that Adam, being tempted of the devil—for, behold, the devil was before Adam, for he rebelled against me, saying, Give me thine honor, which is my power; and also a third part of the hosts of heaven turned he away from me because of their agency;

37 And they were thrust down, and thus came the devil and his angels;

38 And, behold, there is a place prepared for them from the beginning, which place is hell.

39 And it must needs be that the devil should tempt the children of men, or they could not be agents unto themselves; for if they never should have bitter they could not know the sweet—

40 Wherefore, it came to pass that the devil tempted Adam, and he partook of the forbidden fruit and transgressed the commandment, wherein he became subject to the will of the devil, because he yielded unto temptation.

God withdraws from us. There is no happiness in disobedience or sin. We have all learned from our childhood that we are happier when we are doing right.

"Sometimes we do not understand why it is necessary for us to keep the commandments and do certain things to receive certain blessings, except that the Lord commanded it. . . . But if by faith we obey his commandments, we will receive the promised blessings" (N. Eldon Tanner, "Where Art Thou?" *Ensign*, Dec. 1971, 33).

What does it mean that Adam became spiritually dead? (29:41) "By yielding to temptation, Adam and Eve were 'cut off from the presence of the Lord' (Helaman 14:16). In the scriptures this separation is called spiritual death (see Helaman 14:16; D&C 29:41).

"The atonement of our Savior overcame this spiritual death. . . .

"In order to lay claim upon our Savior's life-giving triumph over the spiritual death we suffer because of our own sins, we must follow the conditions he has prescribed. As he has told us in modern revelation, 'I, God, have suffered these things for all, that they might not suffer if they would repent;

"'But if they would not repent they must suffer even as I' (D&C 19:16–17)" (Oaks, "Light and Life of the World," *Ensign*, Nov. 1987, 64–65).

Why is our natural death such an important part of God's plan? (29:43) "Physical death is the separation of the spirit from the mortal body. . . . Death is an essential part of Heavenly Father's plan of salvation (see 2 Nephi 9:6). In order to become like our Eternal Father, we must experience death and later receive perfect, resurrected bodies" (Topics and Questions, s.v. "Death, Physical").

Doctrine and Covenants 29:46–50. Little Children Are Redeemed through the Atonement

Are all little children saved in the celestial kingdom? (29:46) "To this question the answer is a thunderous *yes*, which echoes and re-echoes from one end of heaven to the other. Jesus taught it to his disciples. Mormon said it over and over again. Many of the prophets have spoken about it, and it is implicit in the whole plan of salvation. If it were not so the redemption would not be infinite in its application. And

41 Wherefore, I, the Lord God, caused that he should be cast out from the Garden of Eden, from my presence, because of his transgression, wherein he became spiritually dead, which is the first death, even that same death which is the last death, which is spiritual, which shall be pronounced upon the wicked when I shall say: Depart, ye cursed.

42 But, behold, I say unto you that I, the Lord God, gave unto Adam and unto his seed, that they should not die as to the temporal death, until I, the Lord God, should send forth angels to declare unto them repentance and redemption, through faith on the name of mine Only Begotten Son.

43 And thus did I, the Lord God, appoint unto man the days of his probation—that by his natural death he might be raised in immortality unto eternal life, even as many as would believe;

44 And they that believe not unto eternal damnation; for they cannot be redeemed from their spiritual fall, because they repent not;

45 For they love darkness rather than light, and their deeds are evil, and they receive their wages of whom they list to obey.

46 But behold, I say unto you, that little children are redeemed from the foundation of the world through mine Only Begotten;

so, as we would expect, Joseph Smith's Vision of the Celestial Kingdom contains this statement: 'And I also beheld that all children who die before they arrive at the years of accountability are saved in the celestial kingdom of heaven' [D&C 137:10]" (Bruce R. McConkie, "Salvation of Little Children," *Ensign*, Apr. 1977, 4).

What should parents do while children are young? (29:46–47) Sister Joy D. Jones taught: "There is a uniquely special time in children's lives when they are protected from Satan's influence. It is a time when they are innocent and sin free. It is a sacred time for parent and child. Children are to be taught, by word and example, before and after they have 'arrived unto the years of accountability before God'" ("Essential Conversations," *Liahona*, May 2021, 12).

When do little children begin to become accountable? (29:47) "Accountability does not burst full-bloom upon a child at any given moment in his life. Children become accountable gradually, over a number of years. Becoming accountable is a process, not a goal to be attained when a specified number of years, days, and hours have elapsed. In our revelation the Lord says, 'They cannot sin, for power is not given unto Satan to tempt little children, until they begin to become accountable before me' (D&C 29:47)" (Bruce R. McConkie, "Salvation of Little Children," *Ensign*, Apr. 1977, 6).

"The Lord extends special protection to children and shares jurisdiction with earthly parents, even as we enjoy their presence. They cannot sin until they reach the age of accountability, which the Lord has declared to be eight years (see D&C 18:42; D&C 29:47). In fact, the power to even tempt them to commit sin has been taken from Satan. The prophet Mormon taught that 'little children are whole, for they are not capable of committing sin. . . .

"'Little children are alive in Christ, even from the foundation of the world; if not so, God is a partial God, and also a changeable God, and a respecter to persons; for how many little children have died without baptism!' (Moro. 8:8, 12.)" (Lybbert, "Special Status of Children," *Ensign*, May 1994, 31).

47 Wherefore, they cannot sin, for power is not given unto Satan to tempt little children, until they begin to become accountable before me;

48 For it is given unto them even as I will, according to mine own pleasure, that great things may be required at the hand of their fathers.

49 And, again, I say unto you, that whoso having knowledge, have I not commanded to repent?

50 And he that hath no understanding, it remaineth in me to do according as it is written. And now I declare no more unto you at this time. Amen.

Introduction to Doctrine and Covenants 30

"Immediately after the second Church conference, held in late September 1830 in Fayette, New York, the Prophet Joseph Smith received revelations for David Whitmer, Peter Whitmer Jr., and John Whitmer. These revelations are recorded in Doctrine and Covenants 30.... These revelations were originally published separately in the Book of Commandments, but Joseph Smith combined them into one section in the 1835 edition of the Doctrine and Covenants" (*Doctrine and Covenants Student Manual* [2018], 178, 179).

At the Church conference held in September 1830, the Hiram Page matter was resolved. Joseph Smith wrote: "At length, our conference assembled; the subject of the stone ... was discussed, and after considerable investigation, Brother Page, as well as the whole Church who were present, renounced the said stone, and all things connected therewith, much to our mutual satisfaction and happiness. We now partook of the sacrament, confirmed and ordained many, and attended to a great variety of Church business on that and the following day; during which time we had much of the power of God manifested amongst us; the Holy Ghost came upon us, and filled us with joy unspeakable; and peace, and faith, and hope, and charity abounded in our midst. Before we separated we received [D&C 30]" (Joseph Smith Papers, "History, circa June 1839–circa 1841 [Draft 2]," 58).

"According to Newel Knight, Joseph's behavior at that conference was 'wonderful to witness ... for truly God gave unto him great wisdom and power, and ... none who saw him administer righteousness under such trying circumstance could doubt that the Lord was with him.' [Newel Knight, "Journal," 65]" (Hill, *Joseph Smith*, 118).

SECTION 30

Revelation given through Joseph Smith the Prophet to David Whitmer, Peter Whitmer Jr., and John Whitmer, at Fayette, New York, September 1830, following the three-day conference at Fayette, but before the elders of the Church had separated. Originally this material was published as three revelations; it was combined into one section by the Prophet for the 1835 edition of the Doctrine and Covenants.

1 Behold, I say unto you, David, that you have feared man and have not relied on me for strength as you ought.

2 But your mind has been on the things of the earth more than on the things of me, your Maker, and the ministry whereunto you have been called; and you have not given heed unto my Spirit, and to those who were set over you, but have been persuaded by those whom I have not commanded.

3 Wherefore, you are left to inquire for yourself at my hand, and ponder upon the things which you have received.

Doctrine and Covenants 30:1–4. David Whitmer Is Chastened for Failure to Serve Diligently

Why was David Whitmer chastened by the Lord? (30:1–2) "The Lord chastens David Whitmer in Doctrine and Covenants 30 for fearing man and failing to serve faithfully in the ministry to which the Lord has called him. David has allowed his mind to dwell more on the things of the earth than on his Creator or his callings. He has refused to listen to the Spirit and to Joseph, relying instead on Hiram Page for direction (D&C 28), resulting in his temporary separation from the Spirit. Left to reconsider his recent actions, David is instructed to remain home, serve in the Church, and proselyte locally until the Lord commands him otherwise" (Harper, *Making Sense of the Doctrine & Covenants*, 101–2).

How might David have avoided challenges to his membership in the Church? (30:2) The Prophet Joseph Smith warned: "It is contrary to the economy of God for any member of the Church, or any one, to receive instruction for those in authority, higher than themselves; therefore you will see the impropriety of giving heed to them; but if any person have a vision or a visitation from a heavenly messenger, it must be for his own benefit and instruction; for the fundamental principles, government, and doctrine of the Church are vested in the keys of the kingdom" (*Joseph Smith* [manual], 197–98).

Doctrine and Covenants 30:5–8. Peter Whitmer Jr. Is to Accompany Oliver Cowdery on a Mission to the Lamanites

Why was Peter Whitmer Jr. commanded to follow the direction of Oliver Cowdery? (30:5–7) "An 1830 revelation named Oliver Cowdery next only to Joseph Smith in priesthood leadership (D&C 20:2–3), a status formalized in December 1834, when he was ranked above Sidney Rigdon, who had long served as Joseph's first counselor. Each would 'officiate in the absence of the President, according to his rank and appointment, viz. [namely]: President Cowdery first; President Rigdon second, and President Williams third.' . . . His office next to the Prophet—sometimes called 'associate president'—was given to Hyrum Smith in 1841 (D&C 124: 194–196), after Cowdery's ex-communication" (Richard Lloyd Anderson, "Cowdery, Oliver," 1:337, 338).

Doctrine and Covenants 30:9–11. John Whitmer Is Called to Preach the Gospel

Why do members of the Church have a duty to proclaim the gospel? (30:9–11) "When we were baptized, each of us entered into a perpetual covenant with God to 'serve him and keep his commandments,' which includes 'to stand as witnesses of [Him] at all times and in all things, and in all places.' . . .

"The gathering of Israel—the greatest cause on this earth—is *our* covenant responsibility. And this is *our* time! My invitation today is simple: share

4 And your home shall be at your father's house, until I give unto you further commandments. And you shall attend to the ministry in the church, and before the world, and in the regions round about. Amen.

5 Behold, I say unto you, Peter, that you shall take your journey with your brother Oliver; for the time has come that it is expedient in me that you shall open your mouth to declare my gospel; therefore, fear not, but give heed unto the words and advice of your brother, which he shall give you.

6 And be you afflicted in all his afflictions, ever lifting up your heart unto me in prayer and faith, for his and your deliverance; for I have given unto him power to build up my church among the Lamanites;

7 And none have I appointed to be his counselor over him in the church, concerning church matters, except it is his brother, Joseph Smith, Jun.

8 Wherefore, give heed unto these things and be diligent in keeping my commandments, and you shall be blessed unto eternal life. Amen.

9 Behold, I say unto you, my servant John, that thou shalt commence from this time forth to proclaim my gospel, as with the voice of a trump.

The First Missionary Journey to the Indigenous Nations

"The Book of Mormon was published the same year the Indian Removal Act passed. It gave Church members a different perspective on the past history and future destiny of [Indigenous nations]. The early Saints believed that all American [Indigenous peoples] were the descendants of Book of Mormon peoples, and that they shared a covenant heritage connecting them to ancient Israel. They often held the same prejudices toward [native peoples] shared by other European Americans, but Latter-day Saints believed [native peoples] were heirs to God's promises. . . . This belief instilled in the early Saints a deeply felt obligation to bring the message of the Book of Mormon to [Indigenous nations].

"Within months of the founding of the Church in 1830, Latter-day Saint missionaries journeyed to Indian Territory,

the gospel. Be you and hold up the light. Pray for heaven's help and follow spiritual promptings. Share your life normally and naturally; invite another person to come and see, to come and help, and to come and belong. And then rejoice as you and those you love receive the promised blessings" (Marcus B. Nash, "Hold Up Your Light," *Liahona*, Nov. 2021, 72).

10 And your labor shall be at your brother Philip Burroughs', and in that region round about, yea, wherever you can be heard, until I command you to go from hence.

Who was Philip Burroughs? (30:10) "Before becoming a gentry farmer in Fayette, Seneca County, New York, Philip Burroughs fought in the War of 1812 with the New York militia and was elected 'overseer of the highways and fence viewer' for Junius, Seneca County, New York, in April 1819.

"In September 1830 his neighbor, twenty-eight-year-old John Whitmer, was directed by the Lord to 'proclaim my gospel, as with the voice of a trump. And your labor shall be at your brother Philip Burroughs,' and in that region round about' (D&C 30:9–10). A Church meeting was held at the Burroughs's home on 5 September 1830. Parley P. Pratt, ordained an elder only a few days before, addressed a large audience at the home.... Whether Philip Burroughs was converted remains a mystery" (Black, *Who's Who*, 41).

11 And your whole labor shall be in Zion, with all your soul, from henceforth; yea, you shall ever open your mouth in my cause, not fearing what man can do, for I am with you. Amen.

What blessings come by opening our mouths despite how others receive our testimonies? (30:11) An early Latter-day Saint, Elizabeth Anderson Howard, testified: "I felt assured I had found the truth, and I was desirous my friends and relations should also come to a knowledge of it. For this purpose, I took every opportunity of presenting to them the principles I had embraced by my books and by correspondence, but failed to make any impression upon them. They were so wrapped up in theories and traditions of their forefathers to accept or even investigate the glorious truths, which had been once more revealed to mankind, but this did not influence me from following on in the path I had commenced to travel. I felt the assurance day by day that God, my Heavenly Father, had accepted of my obedience" (Johnson and Reeder, *Witness of Women*, 74–75).

on the borders of the United States. Parley P. Pratt reported that William Anderson (Kik-Tha-We-Nund), the leader of a group of Delaware (Lenape) who had relocated [after forcible removal] to the area near Independence, Missouri, warmly received the missionaries, and an interpreter told Oliver Cowdery that the 'chief says he believes every word' of the Book of Mormon. However, a government agent soon barred them from further evangelizing among [native peoples] in the area because they had not secured proper authorization. Latter-day Saint interactions with [Indigenous peoples] remained sparse for the next few years, though Pratt and others still spoke of a day when [Indigenous peoples] would embrace the Book of Mormon" (Church History Topics, "American Indians").

Introduction to Doctrine and Covenants 31

"This revelation was received at the conference of the Church September 26, 1830, at Fayette, New York. . . . It was addressed to Thomas B. Marsh nearly five years before he would be called as the President of the first Quorum of Twelve Apostles in this dispensation" (Otten and Caldwell, *Sacred Truths*, 1:149).

"[This section] calls Thomas to the ministry. It answers his questions, including how he should provide for his family and how he could best serve the Lord. . . .

"Doctrine and Covenants 31 marked a turning point for Thomas Marsh. His years of seeking the gospel were over. His years of declaring it were about to begin. The revelation's rich metaphors spoke to him. He served Saints who were sick, but at least as important was his work of prescribing the gospel of repentance. He was also to be a harvester of souls, to cut and bundle wheat all day long before it grew too late" (Harper, *Making Sense of the Doctrine & Covenants*, 105).

SECTION 31

Revelation given through Joseph Smith the Prophet to Thomas B. Marsh, September 1830. The occasion was immediately following a conference of the Church (see the heading to section 30). Thomas B. Marsh had been baptized earlier in the month and had been ordained an elder in the Church before this revelation was given.

Doctrine and Covenants 31:1–6. Thomas B. Marsh Is Called to Preach the Gospel and Is Assured of His Family's Well-Being

How did the Lord bless Thomas B. Marsh because of his faith? (31:1) "In the revelation recorded in Doctrine and Covenants 31, he was promised that through his faith and service to the Lord, his family would one day believe and be with him in the Church. At that time, Thomas and his wife, Elizabeth, had three sons, ages nine, seven, and three. Elizabeth was later converted in 1831 (see [*Joseph Smith Papers, Documents: Volume 1*, 194n412]). The Lord's promise to bless the Marsh family would have strengthened Thomas as he was called to assist in God's work" (*Doctrine and Covenants Student Manual* [2018], 182).

1 Thomas, my son, blessed are you because of your faith in my work.

2 Behold, you have had many afflictions because of your family; nevertheless, I will bless you and your family, yea, your little ones; and the day cometh that they will believe and know the truth and be one with you in my church.

Who Was Thomas B. Marsh? (Doctrine and Covenants 31:1)

"Born in Massachusetts in 1799, Thomas B. Marsh left home at age 14 and engaged in a series of short-lived professions in Vermont and New York. . . . Dissatisfied with existing religions, he withdrew from all churches, anticipating the day when a new church would arise with 'the truth in its purity.' In 1830, he learned of the restored gospel and journeyed to Palmyra, New York, where he met Martin Harris and was given 16 pages of the Book of Mormon, just off the press. Marsh returned to Massachusetts and showed the pages to his wife, Elizabeth Godkin Marsh, who believed the translation to be the work of God.

"The Marshes moved with their three children to Palmyra in September 1830 and were baptized into the Church shortly thereafter. . . .

Thomas B. Marsh

"Marsh filled important callings during those years. Soon after joining the Church, he was called by revelation to be a 'Physician unto the Church.' It is unclear whether Marsh, who had no formal medical training, was to serve as a medical doctor or rather as a spiritual healer. . . . In April 1835, he was ordained a member of the newly created Quorum of the Twelve Apostles. At age 36, he was the oldest member of that body and was therefore sustained as the first president of the quorum in the Church's history. . . .

3 Lift up your heart and rejoice, for the hour of your mission is come; and your tongue shall be loosed, and you shall declare glad tidings of great joy unto this generation.

4 You shall declare the things which have been revealed to my servant, Joseph Smith, Jun. You shall begin to preach from this time forth, yea, to reap in the field which is white already to be burned.

5 Therefore, thrust in your sickle with all your soul, and your sins are forgiven you, and you shall be laden with sheaves upon your back, for the laborer is worthy of his hire. Wherefore, your family shall live.

6 Behold, verily I say unto you, go from them only for a little time, and declare my word, and I will prepare a place for them.

What evidence shows that Thomas's tongue was loosed? (31:3) In addition to preaching the glad tidings of the Restoration, we find that "as long as Thomas B. Marsh was faithful he was an eloquent speaker. At the time of the troubles in Clay County, Mo., he was elected a member of a committee to lay the grievances of the Saints before the authorities of the State. On that occasion he spoke so impressively that General Atchison, who was present, shed tears, and the meeting passed resolutions to assist the Saints in finding a new location" (Smith and Sjodahl, *Doctrine and Covenants Commentary*, 165).

Why does the Lord command missionaries to declare the things that were given to the Prophet Joseph Smith? (31:4) "There has been some hesitation in the past to utilize the Book of Mormon as the supreme missionary tool it was intended to be. Some have worried that they would give offense to those of other faiths by suggesting the need for another book of scripture. Some have sought to 'prove' the Restoration from the Bible alone, trying to stay with what they perceive to be 'common ground' between themselves and the rest of the Judaeo-Christian world. The Lord's plan for effective proselyting is set forth plainly in modern revelation. . . .

"'*You shall declare the things which have been revealed to my servant, Joseph Smith, Jr.*' (D&C 31:3–4; emphasis added)" (Millet, *Selected Writings*, 104, 105).

Why is the word *burned* used in place of *harvested* as found in other similar passages? (31:4) "As the Savior called these individuals to the ministry, he clearly communicated to them a sense of urgency in their assignment. To Thomas B. Marsh he did not

"In 1837, during a time of economic crisis and dissension in Kirtland, some of the Twelve questioned Joseph Smith's leadership, and Marsh struggled to unify the quorum. Although four of the Twelve were excommunicated from the Church, Marsh was instrumental in helping others in the quorum, including Parley P. Pratt, to overcome their concerns and remain faithful. . . .

"Yet, after moving to Far West, Missouri, in 1838, Marsh grew critical of Joseph Smith and opposed Latter-day Saints using violence to fight mobs in Missouri. He and Orson Hyde signed an affidavit detailing their concerns about Mormon violence, which became one piece of evidence used against the Saints by Missouri officials. 'I got a beam in my eye and thought I could discover a mote in Joseph's,' he recounted years later, 'though it was nothing but a beam in my eye.' He withdrew from the Church in October 1838. In 1857 he sought readmittance and was baptized in Florence, Nebraska, where he was assisting Church emigration. Eventually settling in Utah, Marsh married Hannah Adams, taught school in Spanish Fork, and later moved to Ogden, where he died in 1862" (Church History Topics, "Thomas B. Marsh").

describe the field as being 'white already to harvest,' but rather he suggested a much more advanced state of affairs with his surprising declaration that the field was now ready to be burned (contrast D&C 31:4 with 4:4). The Lord described Ezra [Thayer's] and Northrop Sweet's calls as coming during the 'eleventh hour' (the twelfth hour being the end), and hence 'the last time' he would be calling servants into his vineyard (D&C 33:3). He reminded Sidney Rigdon of the parable of the fig-tree and affirmed that 'even now already summer [the time of his coming] is nigh' (D&C 35:16)" (Cowan, "Calls to Preach the Gospel," 163).

Doctrine and Covenants 31:7–13. Thomas B. Marsh Is Counseled to Be Patient, Pray Always, and Follow the Comforter

Why was this divine counsel needed by Thomas B. Marsh? (31:9–13) "While Thomas B. Marsh was commended for his faith (see D&C 31:1) and promised great blessings, the Lord also gave him important cautions and counsel. In 1835, Thomas was called to serve in the first Quorum of the Twelve Apostles in this dispensation. He was later called to be the President of that Quorum. Yet, within a few years—in March 1839—he was excommunicated for apostasy. The Lord's instructions in Doctrine and Covenants 31 would have blessed him with spiritual protection if he had heeded them. Thomas B. Marsh was rebaptized July 16, 1857, at Florence, Nebraska, and he came to Utah that same year" (*Doctrine and Covenants Student Manual* [2018], 185).

Why was Thomas B. Marsh referred to as a "physician"? (31:10) "Though Thomas was not a medical doctor, he was on occasion sought out to attend the sick. His greater calling was, however, as a spiritual physician, for he solved problems, resolved conflicts, and answered many questions for the members of the Church until he became disaffected. When Thomas Marsh was faithful, he had a reputation for receiving frequent and specific revelations in answer to his prayers. His calling as 'physician unto the Church' was primarily to help heal the hearts, minds, and spirits of the members rather than their bodies" (Robinson and Garrett, *Commentary on the Doctrine and Covenants*, 1:217).

7 Yea, I will open the hearts of the people, and they will receive you. And I will establish a church by your hand;

8 And you shall strengthen them and prepare them against the time when they shall be gathered.

9 Be patient in afflictions, revile not against those that revile. Govern your house in meekness, and be steadfast.

10 Behold, I say unto you that you shall be a physician unto the church, but not unto the world, for they will not receive you.

11 Go your way whithersoever I will, and it shall be given you by the Comforter what you shall do and whither you shall go.

12 Pray always, lest you enter into temptation and lose your reward.

13 Be faithful unto the end, and lo, I am with you. These words are not of man nor of men, but of me, even Jesus Christ, your Redeemer, by the will of the Father. Amen.

"[In September 1830], Oliver Cowdery and Peter Whitmer Jr. had been called to go on a mission to the [Indigenous peoples] (see D&C 28:8; 30:5). Their mission created considerable excitement in the Church because of the many prophecies concerning the Lamanites in the Book of [Mormon, whom they understood to be Indigenous peoples]. The Prophet Joseph said, 'At this time a great desire was manifest by several of the Elders respecting the remnants of the house of Joseph—the Lamanites residing in the west, knowing that the purposes of God were great to that people and hoping that the time had come when the promises of the Almighty in regard to that people were about to be accomplished, and that they would receive the gospel and enjoy its blessings. The desire being so great that it was agreed upon we should enquire of the Lord respecting the propriety of sending some of the Elders among them, which we accordingly did and received the following revelation [Section 32]'" (Joseph Smith Papers, "History, circa June 1839–circa 1841 [Draft 2]," 60).

"The destination of the missionaries was 'the border by the Lamanites' (D&C 28:9). This phrase was understood to refer to the line between Missouri and the Indian territory to the west . . ."

"When the elders arrived in northeastern Ohio, they reached an area popularly known as the Western Reserve. . . . Parley P. Pratt was familiar with this country, having lived at Amherst, fifty miles west of Kirtland, for about four years before his conversion to the Church. Parley had studied under Sidney Rigdon, a prominent minister in the area who presided over a group of *seekers* (people seeking a return to New Testament Christianity). . . .

"Within three weeks of the missionaries' arrival, 127 persons were baptized" (*Church History in the Fulness of Times* [manual], 79, 80, 81).

SECTION 32

Revelation given through Joseph Smith the Prophet to Parley P. Pratt and Ziba Peterson, in Manchester, New York, early October 1830. Great interest and desires were felt by the elders respecting the Lamanites, of whose predicted blessings the Church had learned from the Book of Mormon. In consequence, supplication was made that the Lord would indicate His will as to whether elders should be sent at that time to the Indian tribes in the West. The revelation followed.

1 And now concerning my servant Parley P. Pratt, behold, I say unto him that as I live I will that he shall declare my gospel and learn of me, and be meek and lowly of heart.

Doctrine and Covenants 32:1–3. Parley P. Pratt and Ziba Peterson Are Called to Preach to the Lamanites and to Accompany Oliver Cowdery and Peter Whitmer Jr.

Why is it important for missionaries to "be meek and lowly of heart"? (32:1) Missionaries represent the Savior, therefore: "Please notice the characteristic the Lord used to describe Himself in the following scripture: 'Take my yoke upon you, and learn of me; for I am *meek and lowly in heart:* and ye shall find rest unto your souls.' . . .

"Meekness is a defining attribute of the Redeemer and is distinguished by righteous responsiveness, willing submissiveness, and strong self-restraint. . . .

"The Christlike quality of meekness often is misunderstood in our contemporary world. Meekness is strong, not weak; active, not passive; courageous, not timid; restrained, not excessive; modest, not self-aggrandizing; and gracious, not brash. A meek person is not easily provoked, pretentious, or overbearing and readily acknowledges the accomplishments of others" (Bednar, "Meek and Lowly of Heart," *Ensign*, May 2018, 31, 32).

Who were the Lamanites referred to in this revelation? (32:2) "The Book of Mormon recounts the history of two peoples, the Nephites and the Lamanites, who lived in almost constant religious and political conflict for centuries. These groups began as the descendants of two Israelite brothers. Over time, the group known as Lamanites grew to include others, such as some who 'had become Lamanites because of their dissensions' from the Nephites. Thus, the terms *Nephite* and *Lamanite* came to describe cultural and religious distinctions. . . . While some early Latter-day Saints speculated about which specific groups were the descendants of Book of Mormon peoples, most considered the Native Americans broadly as heirs to Book of Mormon promises" (Church History Topics, "Lamanite Identity"). ●

How is the Lord in our midst as we fulfill His commandments? (32:3) "God magnifies those He calls, even in what may seem to you a small or inconspicuous service. You will have the gift of seeing your service magnified. Give thanks while that gift is yours. . . .

"The Lord will not only magnify the power of your efforts. He will work with you Himself. . . .

"The Father and His Beloved Son will send the Holy Ghost as your companion to guide you. . . . And when you look back on what may now seem trying times of service and sacrifice, the sacrifice will have become a blessing, and you will know that you have seen the arm of God lifting those you served for Him, and lifting you" (Eyring, "Rise to Your Call," *Ensign*, Nov. 2002, 77, 78).

2 And that which I have appointed unto him is that he shall go with my servants, Oliver Cowdery and Peter Whitmer, Jun., into the wilderness among the Lamanites.

3 And Ziba Peterson also shall go with them; and I myself will go with them and be in their midst; and I am their advocate with the Father, and nothing shall prevail against them.

Who Was Parley P. Pratt? (Doctrine and Covenants 32:1)

"In 1830, then 23, Parley felt a call to abandon his farm and preach the gospel, believing that God would provide financially for him and Thankful [his wife]. After selling their property at 'great sacrifice,' the young couple, with $10 in their pockets, took a boat from Cleveland, Ohio, to Buffalo, New York [Pratt, *Autobiography*, 18]. At Buffalo they took passage on the Erie Canal, headed for Albany. But Parley followed a prompting to disembark prematurely at Newark, while Thankful traveled on to their final destination.

Parley P. Pratt

"As a result, Parley was introduced to the Book of Mormon, an experience that forever changed his life. He later recalled: 'I read all day; eating was a burden, I had no desire for food; sleep was a burden when the night came, for I preferred reading to sleep.' Feeling the confirmation of the Holy Ghost, Parley wrote: 'I knew and comprehended that the book was true. . . . My joy was now full.' [Pratt, *Autobiography*, 20]. Determined to meet Joseph Smith, Parley traveled to Palmyra, where he instead found Hyrum Smith, who instructed him about the Restoration. In the Church of Jesus Christ, Parley recognized the authority, simplicity, and purity he had long sought. On September 1, 1830, he was baptized by Oliver Cowdery. . . .

"In October 1830 Joseph Smith received a revelation directing Parley and three other missionaries (including Oliver Cowdery) to take the gospel to [Indigenous communities] on the western frontier in Missouri (see D&C 32:1–2)" (Grow, "Extraordinary Life of Parley P. Pratt," *Ensign*, Apr. 2007, 57, 58).

Doctrine and Covenants 32:4–5. Parley P. Pratt and Ziba Peterson Are to Pray for an Understanding of the Scriptures

4 And they shall give heed to that which is written, and pretend to no other revelation; and they shall pray always that I may unfold the same to their understanding.

5 And they shall give heed unto these words and trifle not, and I will bless them. Amen.

What does the phrase "pretend to no other revelation" mean? (32:4) "Only the Lord's prophet is authorized by Him to speak as His mouthpiece (see D&C 21:4–5). Prior to the conference of the Church in September 1830, the Lord proclaimed His prophet to be the only channel through which the Lord would speak to the entire membership of the Church. No one else is authorized by the Lord to so speak (see D&C 28:2). While the conference was assembled, the Lord gave three revelations and in each one of them, He stressed the need to follow His instructions as given to the Church through His prophet and rely upon no other source of information (see D&C 30:2; 31:4; 32:4)" (Otten and Caldwell, *Sacred Truths*, 1:156–57).

Introduction to Doctrine and Covenants 33

"The Prophet Joseph Smith introduced Doctrine and Covenants 33 saying, 'The Lord, who is ever ready to instruct such as diligently seek in faith, gave the following revelation [D&C 33] at Fayette New York' (Joseph Smith Papers, "History, 1838–1856, volume A-1," 76).

This revelation was received in October 1830 in behalf of Ezra Thayer and Northrop Sweet. "Ezra Thayer was living near Palmyra, New York, when he learned about the Restoration of the gospel of Jesus Christ. He had previously hired members of the Smith family to help him on construction projects. He was finally convinced to attend a meeting where Hyrum Smith preached the gospel. He later wrote about his reaction to what Hyrum taught: 'Every word touched me to the inmost soul. I thought every word was pointed to me. . . . The tears rolled down my cheeks, I was very proud and stubborn. There were many there who knew me. . . . I sat until I recovered myself before I dare look up' ([McBride, "Ezra Thayer," 62]). . . .

"Northrop Sweet was baptized a member of the Church by Parley P. Pratt in October 1830, in Palmyra, New York. He was married to Martin Harris's niece. Shortly after his baptism, he was appointed to serve a mission. Northrop had moved to Kirtland, Ohio, by June 1831, where he was ordained an elder; however, he left the Church shortly thereafter and attempted, with others, to form another church, claiming that Joseph Smith was a false prophet" (*Doctrine and Covenants Student Manual* [2018], 188).

SECTION 33

Revelation given through Joseph Smith the Prophet to Ezra Thayre and Northrop Sweet, at Fayette, New York, October 1830. In introducing this revelation, Joseph Smith's history affirms that "the Lord . . . is ever ready to instruct such as diligently seek in faith."

1 Behold, I say unto you, my servants Ezra and Northrop, open ye your ears and hearken to the voice of the Lord your God, whose

Doctrine and Covenants 33:1–4. Laborers Are Called to Declare the Gospel in the Eleventh Hour

word is quick and powerful, sharper than a two-edged sword, to the dividing asunder of the joints and marrow, soul and spirit; and is a discerner of the thoughts and intents of the heart.

2 For verily, verily, I say unto you that ye are called to lift up your voices as with the sound of a trump, to declare my gospel unto a crooked and perverse generation.

3 For behold, the field is white already to harvest; and it is the eleventh hour, and the last time that I shall call laborers into my vineyard.

What is expected of those called to labor during the "last time"? (33:3) Sheri Dew observed: "We who are here now, in the last wave of laborers in the Lord's vineyard (see D&C 33:3), have been born now for very specific reasons. Yes, we're here to receive bodies and ordinances and to be tested. But the doctrine seems to be clear about the fact that, for us, it goes even further. We know that our Father has held us in reserve until the latter part of the latter-days—that, in fact, as President George Q. Cannon expressed it, he held those in reserve who would have the courage and the determination to face the world and all the powers of the evil one and to yet be fearless in building Zion (see *Gospel Truth*, 18)" (*No One Can Take Your Place*, 11–12). ✚

What had corrupted the Lord's vineyard? (33:4) "The world of the 1830s had become corrupt 'every whit' with false teachings, theories, and practices about the nature of God. The Lord revealed in this section that the prophesied corruption was complete, for apostasy or a falling away from understanding the true nature of God had penetrated the entire world. The Lord expressed an urgent need for elders to carry the message of the Restoration at this last, even the eleventh hour. Elders who willingly accepted and acted upon the call to missionary service were promised the same reward or blessing given to faithful laborers of former dispensations, that of joy in the eternal realms (see Matt. 20:6)" (Black, *400 Questions and Answers*, 90).

4 And my vineyard has become corrupted every whit; and there is none which doeth good save it be a few; and they err in many instances because of priestcrafts, all having corrupt minds.

Doctrine and Covenants 33:5–6. The Church Is Established, and the Elect Are to Be Gathered

How has the Church come out of the wilderness? (33:5–6) "In the book of Revelation, Chap. 12, we have a very vivid symbolical description of the Church being driven into the wilderness by the great dragon. 'And to the woman (Church) were given two wings of

5 And verily, verily, I say unto you, that this church have I established and called forth out of the wilderness.

6 And even so will I gather mine elect from the four quarters of the earth, even as many as will believe in me, and hearken unto my voice.

7 Yea, verily, verily, I say unto you, that the field is white already to harvest; wherefore, thrust in your sickles, and reap with all your might, mind, and strength.

8 Open your mouths and they shall be filled, and you shall become even as Nephi of old, who journeyed from Jerusalem in the wilderness.

9 Yea, open your mouths and spare not, and you shall be laden with sheaves upon your backs, for lo, I am with you.

10 Yea, open your mouths and they shall be filled, saying: Repent, repent, and prepare ye the way of the Lord, and make his paths straight; for the kingdom of heaven is at hand;

11 Yea, repent and be baptized, every one of you, for a remission of your sins; yea, be baptized even by water, and then cometh the baptism of fire and of the Holy Ghost.

12 Behold, verily, verily, I say unto you, this is my gospel; and remember that they shall have faith in me or they can in nowise be saved;

13 And upon this rock I will build my church; yea, upon this rock ye are built, and if ye continue, the gates of hell shall not prevail against you.

a great eagle, that she might fly into the wilderness, into her place, where she is nourished for a time, and times, and half a time, from the face of the serpent.' ... Now in the Dispensation of the Fulness of Times, the Church is again called forth from the wilderness, and her man-child (the Priesthood) is restored to her again" (Joseph Fielding Smith, *Church History and Modern Revelation*, 1:153–54).

Doctrine and Covenants 33:7–10. Repent, for the Kingdom of Heaven Is at Hand

Why is heeding the Lord's charge to open our mouths so important? (33:8–10) "At some moment in the world to come, everyone you will ever meet will know what you know now. They will know that the only way to live forever in association with our families ... was to choose to enter into the gate by baptism at the hands of those with authority from God. They will know that the only way families can be together forever is to accept and keep sacred covenants offered in the temples of God on this earth. And they will know that you knew. And they will remember whether you offered them what someone had offered you" (Eyring, "Voice of Warning," *Ensign*, Nov. 1998, 33). ☯

What could it mean to be "laden with sheaves upon [our] backs"? (33:9) "The scriptures refer to the sheaves of harvested wheat representing the fruits of missionary labors, including converted souls" (*Doctrine and Covenants Student Manual* [2018], 184).

Doctrine and Covenants 33:11–15. The Church Is Built upon the Gospel Rock

Why is the reception of the Holy Ghost called the "baptism of fire"? (33:11) "Sins are remitted not in the waters of baptism, as we say in speaking figuratively, but when we receive the Holy Ghost. It is the Holy Spirit of God that erases carnality and brings us into a state of righteousness. We become clean when we actually receive the fellowship and companionship of the Holy Ghost. It is then that sin and dross and evil are burned out of our souls as though by fire. The baptism of the Holy Ghost is the baptism of fire. There have been miraculous occasions when visible flames enveloped penitent persons, but ordinarily the cleansing power of the Spirit simply dwells, unseen and unheralded, in the hearts of those who have made the Lord their friend. And the Spirit will not dwell in an unclean tabernacle" (Bruce R. McConkie, *New Witness*, 290).

What were the "articles and covenants"? (33:14)
"The Articles and Covenants [see D&C 20] of the
Church outlined Church history, doctrine, and procedures and served as a handbook for early Church
members. Its importance is demonstrated by the
fact that it was presented for approval at the first
conference of the newly organized Church in June
1830. Priesthood holders at that conference received
licenses certifying that they had been 'baptized and
received into the Church according to the Articles
& Covenants of the Church.' This document laid the
foundation for the Church of Jesus Christ" ("Articles
and Covenants of the Church"). ◉

Doctrine and Covenants 33:16–18. Prepare for the Coming of the Bridegroom

**How can we prepare for the coming of the
Bridegroom? (33:17–18)** "As the wise virgins emphasized properly, each of us must 'buy for ourselves.' These inspired women were not describing a
business transaction; rather, they were emphasizing
our individual responsibility to keep our lamp of
testimony burning and to obtain an ample supply of
the oil of conversion. This precious oil is acquired one
drop at a time—'line upon line [and] precept upon
precept' (2 Nephi 28:30) patiently and persistently. No
shortcut is available; no last-minute flurry of preparation is possible" (Bednar, "Converted unto the Lord,"
Ensign, Nov. 2012, 109). ◉

**What is meant by the Lord's declaration, "I come
quickly"? (33:18)** "When the Savior says, 'I come
quickly,' which he does many times, both in the Bible
(Revelation 22:20) and especially in modern revelation (D&C 33:18; 34:12; 35:27; 39:24; 41:4; 49:28; 51:20;
54:10; 68:35; 88:126; 99:5; 112:34), he does not mean
he is coming at any moment; rather, the Savior will
come suddenly, unannounced. It is the Lord's call to
spiritual vigilance" (Millet, *Living in the Eleventh Hour*,
105).

14 And ye shall remember the church articles
and covenants to keep them.

15 And whoso having faith you shall confirm
in my church, by the laying on of the hands,
and I will bestow the gift of the Holy Ghost
upon them.

16 And the Book of Mormon and the holy
scriptures are given of me for your instruction; and the power of my Spirit quickeneth
all things.

17 Wherefore, be faithful, praying always,
having your lamps trimmed and burning,
and oil with you, that you may be ready at
the coming of the Bridegroom—

18 For behold, verily, verily, I say unto you,
that I come quickly. Even so. Amen.

On November 4, 1830, Orson Pratt "came from his home in Canaan, New York, to Fayette, [New York,] to ask of the Lord for light and help concerning his individual duty. The Prophet [Joseph Smith] complied with the youth's desire and inquired of the Lord for him; and in response a revelation [see D&C 34] was given in Orson's behalf, which . . . had a wondrous fulfilment in his life" (George Q. Cannon, *Life of Joseph Smith the Prophet*, 85).

SECTION 34

Revelation given through Joseph Smith the Prophet to Orson Pratt, at Fayette, New York, November 4, 1830. Brother Pratt was nineteen years old at the time. He had been converted and baptized when he first heard the preaching of the restored gospel by his older brother, Parley P. Pratt, six weeks before. This revelation was received in the Peter Whitmer Sr. home.

1 My son Orson, hearken and hear and behold what I, the Lord God, shall say unto you, even Jesus Christ your Redeemer;

2 The light and the life of the world, a light which shineth in darkness and the darkness comprehendeth it not;

Doctrine and Covenants 34:1–4. The Faithful Become the Sons of God through the Atonement

Why do some people fail to comprehend the light and life of Jesus Christ? (34:1–2) Jesus identified Himself as "the light and the life of the world" (v. 2; see also John 8:12). Speaking to Nicodemus, Jesus explained, "he that believeth not is condemned already, because he hath not believed in the name of the only begotten Son of God. And this is the condemnation, that light is come into the world, and *men loved darkness rather than light, because their deeds were evil*"

Orson Pratt was born in Harford, New York. He was the younger brother of Parley P. Pratt. As "a youth of eighteen years, [Orson] fervently importuned the Lord night and day to reveal to him whether true Christianity was to be found on the earth. This young man went out at night into the solitude of the fields and wooded spots near his home to 'plead with the Lord, hour after hour, that he would show [him] what to do—that he would teach [him] the way of life and inform and instruct [his] understanding.' . . . When his brother Parley and another elder came to him with the message of Mormonism, he knew 'that if the Bible was true, their doctrine was true' [*Deseret News*, 20 Jul. 1859]. . . .

Orson Pratt

"Orson [wrote]: 'Being convinced of the divine authenticity of the doctrine they taught, I was baptized September 19, 1830. This was my birthday, being nineteen years old. . . . ' [*Orson Pratt's Works*, xii]" (Barrett, *Joseph Smith and the Restoration*, 16, 150).

"[In] December [1830] he was ordained an elder and appointed to serve a mission to Colesville, New York. In 1831, he moved to Kirtland, Ohio. After being called by revelation (Doctrine and Covenants 52:26; 75:13; 103:40), he subsequently served missions to Missouri, to the eastern United States (twice), to Upper Canada, and to Great Britain. . . . [In 1835] he was ordained a member of the Quorum of the Twelve Apostles" (Doctrine and Covenants Historical Resources, "Orson Pratt").

Orson Pratt "was one of the most energetic missionaries in the history of the Church. Thousands have been converted through his preaching in many lands, and thousands more by his writings" (Barrett, *Joseph Smith and the Restoration*, 150).

(John 3:18–19; emphasis added; see also Doctrine and Covenants 93:39).

President Jeffrey R. Holland taught, "Light is not the absence of darkness; rather, darkness is the absence of light. Light and truth exist independently. . . . We must also fill our hearts and minds with truth and light, with love and the Spirit of God" (*Broken Things to Mend*, 133). See also commentary in this volume on Doctrine and Covenants 6:21.

In what ways has the Savior's love been made evident? (34:3) "The Atonement of Jesus Christ is the grandest demonstration of love this world has ever known. The compelling, driving force behind his sacrifice was love, not duty or glory or honor or any other temporal reward. It was love in its purest, deepest, most enduring sense. . . .

"Of all the acts of love, the atoning sacrifice far exceeds and transcends them all. No one has ever given so much to so many so willingly" (Callister, *Infinite Atonement*, 157, 158). ◉

What does it mean to become a son or daughter of God? (34:3) "God is our Father in Heaven, the Father of the spirits of all humankind (Numbers 16:22; 27:16; Hebrews 12:9). We are his spirit children. Because of the Fall, however, we come forth into a world of sin, a fallen world in which we are alienated from things of righteousness, including the royal family of God. Through faith in the Lord Jesus Christ—which brings forth repentance, baptism, and the reception of the Spirit—we are forgiven of our sins and become innocent before God. In addition, through the Atonement we are reinstated into the family of God. That is, we become 'children of God' in this sense by rebirth, by adoption, by regeneration" (Millet, "Children of God," 107). See also commentary in this volume on Doctrine and Covenants 11:30. ◉

What blessings came to Orson Pratt for believing? (34:4) Orson Pratt explained in his own words, "I called upon the Lord with more faith than before, for I had then received the first principles of the Gospel. The gift of the Holy Ghost was given to me; and when it was shed forth upon me, it gave me a testimony concerning the truth of this work that no man can ever take from me. It is impossible for me, so long as I have my reasoning faculties and powers of mind, to doubt the testimony I then received as among the first evidences that were given, and that, too, by the gift and power of the Holy Ghost" (in *Journal of Discourses*, 7:178).

3 Who so loved the world that he gave his own life, that as many as would believe might become the sons of God. Wherefore you are my son;

4 And blessed are you because you have believed;

5 And more blessed are you because you are called of me to preach my gospel—

6 To lift up your voice as with the sound of a trump, both long and loud, and cry repentance unto a crooked and perverse generation, preparing the way of the Lord for his second coming.

7 For behold, verily, verily, I say unto you, the time is soon at hand that I shall come in a cloud with power and great glory.

8 And it shall be a great day at the time of my coming, for all nations shall tremble.

9 But before that great day shall come, the sun shall be darkened, and the moon be turned into blood; and the stars shall refuse their shining, and some shall fall, and great destructions await the wicked.

Doctrine and Covenants 34:5–9. The Preaching of the Gospel Prepares the Way for the Second Coming

How might repentance help us prepare the world for the Savior's Second Coming? (34:6) President Russell M. Nelson testified, "I promise that if we will do our best to exercise faith in Jesus Christ and access the power of His Atonement through repentance, we will have the knowledge and power of God to help us take the blessings of the restored gospel of Jesus Christ to every nation, kindred, tongue, and people and to prepare the world for the Second Coming of the Lord" ("Future of the Church," *Ensign*, Apr. 2020, 16).

What do we know about the time of the Savior's Second Coming? (34:7) "In response to the question of when he will come, the Lord told his disciples, 'Of that day, and hour, no one knoweth; no, not the angels of God in heaven, but my Father only' (Joseph Smith—Matthew 1:40 [see also v. 48]). . . . Paul wrote that his coming will be 'as a thief in the night' (1 Thessalonians 5:2). It seems obvious that the precise time of his coming has been left deliberately and purposefully obscure (Matthew 24:42–51). Joseph Smith said: 'Jesus Christ never did reveal to any man the precise time that He would come. Go and read the Scriptures, and you cannot find anything that specifies the exact hour He would come; and all that say so are false teachers' [*Joseph Smith* [manual], 253]" (Dahl, "Second Comings of the Lord," 162). ❂

Why will there be destruction upon the earth prior to and at the Lord's Second Coming? (34:8–9) "The disasters of earth—controlled as they are in the infinite wisdom of that Lord who knoweth all things—are used by him to temper and train us. He uses natural disasters to bring to us the conscious realization that we are dependent upon a Supreme Being for all things. He uses them as a means of judgment to punish us for evil deeds done in the flesh. He uses them to humble us so that perchance we will repent and live as he would have us live [see Helaman 12:3]. . . . And all of this has particular application in this day of wickedness when the world is being prepared to receive its rightful King" (Bruce R. McConkie, *Millennial Messiah*, 374, 375).

Doctrine and Covenants 34:10–12. Prophecy Comes by the Power of the Holy Ghost

What does it mean to prophesy? (34:10) "Among the gifts of the Spirit is the ability to prophesy (D&C 46:22). One possessing this gift speaks under the influence of divine inspiration and proclaims some future event that God has decreed shall come to pass....

"Note that the word *prophesy* is a verb (the action) whereas the word *prophecy* is a noun (the subject)" (Brewster, *Doctrine & Covenants Encyclopedia* [2012], 448, 449).

How might we respond to the Lord's declaration "I come quickly"? (34:12) See also commentary in this volume on Doctrine and Covenants 33:18.

10 Wherefore, lift up your voice and spare not, for the Lord God hath spoken; therefore prophesy, and it shall be given by the power of the Holy Ghost.

11 And if you are faithful, behold, I am with you until I come—

12 And verily, verily, I say unto you, I come quickly. I am your Lord and your Redeemer. Even so. Amen.

Introduction to Doctrine and Covenants 35

The revelation recorded in Doctrine and Covenants 35 directed to Sidney Rigdon was received by the Prophet Joseph on December 7, 1830 near Fayette, New York. "While living in Mentor, [Ohio,] Sidney [Rigdon] and [his wife] Phebe were introduced to the LDS Church by Parley P. Pratt. Parley had been an earlier associate of Sidney's and was traveling through Ohio on his way to preach the gospel to the [Kickapoo and Shawnee tribes] in Missouri. Initially Sidney was quite skeptical of the new religious ideas preached to him. When he read the Book of Mormon, however, he saw the truth" (Manscill, "Rigdon, Sidney," 1031).

"Rigdon had become convinced that the missionaries did, indeed, have authority previously not found on the earth. He desired to be baptized and discussed the matter with his wife, Phebe, warning her of how their lives might change if they obeyed the gospel:

"'"My dear, you have once followed me into poverty; are you again willing to do the same?" She answered, "I have weighed the matter; I have contemplated . . . the circumstances in which we may be placed; I have counted the cost, and I am perfectly satisfied to follow you. Yea, it is my desire to do the will of God, come life or come death"' [Joseph Smith Papers, 'History, 1838–1856, volume A-1,' 75; punctuation and capitalization modernized]....

"Sidney and Phebe Rigdon were baptized in November 1830. Rigdon gave up preaching and . . . soon left for New York with 'much anxiety to see Joseph Smith Jr. the Seer whom the Lord had raised up in these last days.' . . .

[Sidney Rigdon] "met Joseph in New York in early December 1830, and . . . was soon 'desirous to have the Seer enquire of the Lord, to know what the will of the Lord was concerning him.' In response, Joseph dictated the revelation now known as Doctrine and Covenants 35. Rigdon was praised for his work in his ministry in Ohio and charged to be Joseph's companion and scribe for the ongoing translation of the Bible. He was told that as he did so, 'the scriptures shall be given, even as they are in mine own bosom, to the salvation of mine own elect' [D&C 35:20]. Accordingly, Rigdon stayed in Fayette with Joseph and began his service as scribe" (Maki, "Go to the Ohio," 71–72).

SECTION 35

Revelation given to Joseph Smith the Prophet and Sidney Rigdon, at or near Fayette, New York, December 7, 1830. At this time, the Prophet was engaged almost daily in making a translation of the Bible. The translation was begun as early as June 1830, and both Oliver Cowdery and John Whitmer had served as scribes. Since they had now been called to other duties, Sidney Rigdon was called by divine appointment to serve as the Prophet's scribe in this work (see verse 20). As a preface to the record of this revelation, Joseph Smith's history states: "In December Sidney Rigdon came [from Ohio] to inquire of the Lord, and with him came Edward Partridge. . . . Shortly after the arrival of these two brethren, thus spake the Lord."

1 Listen to the voice of the Lord your God, even Alpha and Omega, the beginning and the end, whose course is one eternal round, the same today as yesterday, and forever.

2 I am Jesus Christ, the Son of God, who was crucified for the sins of the world, even as many as will believe on my name, that they may become the sons of God, even one in me as I am one in the Father, as the Father is one in me, that we may be one.

Doctrine and Covenants 35:1–2. How Men May Become the Sons of God

Why is Jesus Christ referred to as Alpha and Omega? (35:1) "Alpha is the first letter in the Greek alphabet; Omega is the last. They are also names given to Jesus Christ and are used as symbols to show that Christ is both the beginning and the end (Rev. 1:8; D&C 19:1)" (Guide to the Scriptures, "Alpha and Omega"). See also commentary in this volume on Doctrine and Covenants 19:1 and 38:1.

Sheri Dew observed, "Jesus Christ is Alpha and Omega, literally the beginning and the end, which means He'll stick with us from start to finish" (*Amazed by Grace*, 56). ☉

What can an understanding of the oneness of the Father and the Son teach us about our own potential? (35:2) "The Father and the Son are united for their common purposes and virtually synonymous in their interchangeable roles and functions. Indeed, their unity is the primary fact of their relationship. . . .

"Christ . . . claimed a major portion of [his] divine, fatherly power through the fundamental gospel principle of obedience. By his obedience Christ showed the way to godhood. . . .

Sidney Rigdon (1793–1876), Spokesman for Joseph Smith and Defender of the Faith

Sidney Rigdon

"Sidney Rigdon, who became noted in Church history, was born in Saint Claire, Pa., Feb. 19th, 1793. At the age of 25 years he joined a Baptist church. In 1819 he obtained a license as a minister, and a couple of years later he received a call to take charge of a church at Pittsburg, Pa. . . . While engaged in this ministry, he became convinced that some of the doctrines [his church taught] were not Scriptural, and he resigned his position and joined his brother-in-law in the tanning business. At this time he became acquainted with Alexander Campbell, the reputed founder of the church known as 'Disciples,' or 'Campbellites,' and with one Mr. Walter Scott, and these three started that religious movement. Rigdon left Pittsburg and went to Bainbridge, and later to Mentor, preaching faith, repentance, baptism by immersion for the remission of sins, and righteous conduct. He had many adherents.

"In the fall of 1830, Parley P. Pratt, Ziba Peterson, Oliver Cowdery, and Peter Whitmer, Jr., who were on their mission to the [local tribes], called at the house of Sidney Rigdon, and Parley P. Pratt, who knew him, presented him a copy of the Book of Mormon and related its story" (Smith and Sjodahl, *Doctrine and Covenants Commentary*, 181).

Sidney Rigdon "began an intense study of [the Book of Mormon]. His son later remarked that Sidney became so engaged in reading the Book of Mormon that 'he could hardly lay it aside long enough to eat his meals. He continued to read it night and day until he had read it through and then he thought about and pondered over it' (John W. Rigdon, "Lecture on the Early History of the Mormon Church" [1906], 18, Church History Library, Salt Lake City; capitalization and punctuation modernized)" (*Doctrine and Covenants Student Manual* [2018], 195).

"From the time of his baptism, Sidney held important positions in the Church. He was asked to dedicate Independence, Missouri, as the land of Zion. . . . He scribed much of the translation of the Old and New Testament as dictated by the Prophet Joseph Smith. He was named or shared in many revelations received by the Prophet, including the visions of glory (D&C 76). He became a spokesman for Joseph Smith and a strong defender of the faith" (Black, "Sidney Rigdon").

"Christ teaches us as mortal men and women that we can be one with the Father in a crucial, fundamental, eternally significant way: We can obey him. We can subject the flesh to the spirit. We can yield our will as children to the will of our Heavenly Father" (Holland, *Christ and the New Covenant*, 180, 192). See also commentary in this volume on Doctrine and Covenants 20:28. ◉

Doctrine and Covenants 35:3–7. Sidney Rigdon Is Called to Baptize and to Confer the Holy Ghost

How had the Lord prepared Sidney Rigdon for a "greater work"? (35:3–4) "All of his life Sidney was a dedicated student of the Bible. He read it not only by the dim light of the hickory fire because his father refused to give him a candle but also when he apprenticed to become a minister in 1819. In pursuing his self-taught course of learning the Bible, he read and memorized extensive portions of the scriptures.

"Sidney truly loved and immersed himself in the Bible....

"Sidney's grounding in the Bible played a larger role later, not only in preparing people to receive the restored gospel but also in his critical mission as scribe for Joseph's translation of the Bible" (Karl Ricks Anderson, *Savior in Kirtland*, 13).

Who are the Gentiles? (35:7) "The word *Gentiles* means 'the nations' and eventually came to be used to mean all those not of the house of Israel.... As used throughout the scriptures it has a dual meaning, sometimes to designate peoples of non-Israelite lineage and other times to designate nations that are without the gospel, even though there may be some Israelite blood therein. This latter usage is especially characteristic of the word as used in the Book of Mormon" (Bible Dictionary, "Gentile").

Doctrine and Covenants 35:8–12. Signs and Miracles Are Wrought by Faith

What does it mean that God's "arm is not shortened"? (35:8) "The outstretched arm is always a symbol of God's power being exercised" (Gaskill, *Lost Language of Symbolism*, 28).

In Isaiah, the Lord asks, "Is my hand shortened at all, that it cannot redeem? or have I no power to

3 Behold, verily, verily, I say unto my servant Sidney, I have looked upon thee and thy works. I have heard thy prayers, and prepared thee for a greater work.

4 Thou art blessed, for thou shalt do great things. Behold thou wast sent forth, even as John, to prepare the way before me, and before Elijah which should come, and thou knewest it not.

5 Thou didst baptize by water unto repentance, but they received not the Holy Ghost;

6 But now I give unto thee a commandment, that thou shalt baptize by water, and they shall receive the Holy Ghost by the laying on of the hands, even as the apostles of old.

7 And it shall come to pass that there shall be a great work in the land, even among the Gentiles, for their folly and their abominations shall be made manifest in the eyes of all people.

8 For I am God, and mine arm is not shortened; and I will show miracles, signs, and wonders, unto all those who believe on my name.

9 And whoso shall ask it in my name in faith, they shall cast out devils; they shall heal the sick; they shall cause the blind to receive their sight, and the deaf to hear, and the dumb to speak, and the lame to walk.

10 And the time speedily cometh that great things are to be shown forth unto the children of men;

11 But without faith shall not anything be shown forth except desolations upon Babylon, the same which has made all nations drink of the wine of the wrath of her fornication.

12 And there are none that doeth good except those who are ready to receive the fulness of my gospel, which I have sent forth unto this generation.

13 Wherefore, I call upon the weak things of the world, those who are unlearned and despised, to thresh the nations by the power of my Spirit;

deliver?" (Isaiah 50:2). "The Doctrine and Covenants uses the word 'arm' in place of 'hand.' The Lord's ability to extend His saving hands or arms is not limited. He can reach out and encompass all, without restriction. 'His grasp is galactic,' noted Elder Neal A. Maxwell ["Jesus of Nazareth, Savior and King," *Ensign*, May 1976, 26]" (Brewster, *Isaiah Plain and Simple*, 208).

What kind of miracles, signs, and wonders are available today for those with faith in Jesus Christ? (35:8–9) "Just as undaunted faith has stopped the mouths of lions, made ineffective fiery flames, . . . and brought heavenly manifestations at the instance of prophets, so in each of our lives faith can heal the sick, bring comfort to those who mourn, strengthen resolve against temptation, relieve from the bondage of harmful habits, lend the strength to repent and change our lives, and lead to a sure knowledge of the divinity of Jesus Christ. Indomitable faith can help us live the commandments with a willing heart and thereby bring blessings unnumbered, with peace, perfection, and exaltation in the kingdom of God" (*Spencer W. Kimball* [manual], 143). ❂

What are the desolations to come upon Babylon? (35:11) "Babylon—the ultimate image of the world's almost infinite love of wickedness—shall finally reap the consequences of her choices. . . . No one is going to stop that from happening. The harvest is finally at hand. . . . It boggles the mind to think that however it may happen, in one great swoop the wickedness of the world comes to an end. But the scriptures and the prophets have testified to us over and over that this is what is coming. . . .

"The wicked and evil of the world will be bound—i.e., they will no longer be free to work their havoc on the world—and will await the fires of the Great Judgment" (Lund, *Second Coming of the Lord*, 338, 367).

Doctrine and Covenants 35:13–16. The Lord's Servants Will Thresh the Nations by the Power of the Spirit

Why does the Lord call upon the "weak things of the world"? (35:13) "This principle—that the Lord uses the weak and simple [v.13] to accomplish a great work—was demonstrated in [Joseph Smith's] life again and again. He didn't come from a prominent family or leading city. . . . Joseph was but fourteen when he saw the Father and the Son, just seventeen when Moroni visited him, only twenty-one when he was entrusted with the gold plates and their translation, and just twenty-four when he organized the Church. In other words, a young adult was the first President of the Church in this dispensation....

"As President Thomas S. Monson has often said, 'The Lord qualifies those whom He calls to His service'" (Dew, *God Wants a Powerful People*, 128, 129). ⊕

How are we to "thresh the nations"? (35:13) "The word *thresh* ... refers to the practice of threshing grain. Threshing is the process by which grain, such as wheat, is separated from its stalk and husk. The grain is kept, and the stalk and husk are discarded. Therefore, 'to thresh the nations' refers to the work of preaching the gospel so that converts can be gathered in as grain. (*Note:* In previous English editions of the Doctrine and Covenants, D&C 35:13 used the word *thrash* instead of *thresh*. In the 2013 edition the word was changed to *thresh* to reflect the wording of the original revelation)" (*Doctrine and Covenants Student Manual* [2018], 200).

In what way is the Lord a shield for His servants? (35:14) "Our missionaries also seem weak and defenseless, powerless against the armaments of the adversary and those who serve him. But the Lord has promised them that he 'will be their shield' (D&C 35:14), and that promise is fulfilled every day in many places around the world.

"The shield the Lord gives to the faithful also protects us against our own harmful impulses. The revelation that commands modern Saints to refrain from alcohol, tobacco, hot drinks, and other harmful things promises the faithful that 'the destroying angel shall pass by them, as the children of Israel, and not slay them' (D&C 89:21)" (Oaks, "Bible Stories and Personal Protection," *Ensign*, Nov. 1992, 38).

How does one "gird up their loins" and "fight manfully" for the Lord? (35:14) "Enoch said that one purpose for the establishment of Zion would be that the Lord's people 'may gird up their loins.' This figurative expression from the Old Testament means to belt the garment that is worn ungirded in the house or in times of relaxation. The reasons for girding one's garment are to prepare for work, travel, or battle. This phrase is found 11 times in the Doctrine and Covenants and is consistently used to motivate recipients of the revelations to be prepared" (Woodford, "Remarkable Doctrine and Covenants," *Ensign*, Jan. 1997, 46–47).

The word *manfully* (v. 14) means "boldly; courageously; honorably" (Webster, *American Dictionary* [1828], s.v. "manfully").

14 And their arm shall be my arm, and I will be their shield and their buckler; and I will gird up their loins, and they shall fight manfully for me; and their enemies shall be under their feet; and I will let fall the sword in their behalf, and by the fire of mine indignation will I preserve them.

15 And the poor and the meek shall have the gospel preached unto them, and they shall be looking forth for the time of my coming, for it is nigh at hand—

Why are the poor and meek identified as a group who "shall have the gospel preached unto them"? (35:15) "Typically, when the gospel message goes to a nation or city the first willing to hear and accept it are those of the lower social classes. Humility of circumstances and humility of spirit are often found in company together. . . . [This] has been echoed by thousands of missionaries who have been the first to open various cities and regions to the teaching of the gospel; in so doing, they have found that the well-to-do, those resting comfortably in their own self-sufficiency, have little or no interest in their message, while those whose conditions are appreciably more humble are often more willing to listen" (McConkie and Millet, *Doctrinal Commentary on the Book of Mormon*, 3:222, 223).

Brigham Young wrote to Joseph Smith: "Almost without exception it is the poor that receive the Gospel" (Joseph Smith Papers, "Letter from Brigham Young, 7 May 1840," 151).

16 And they shall learn the parable of the fig tree, for even now already summer is nigh.

What might the Lord have been teaching through the parable of the fig tree? (35:16) "Rigdon had devoted his life to studying scriptures and the life of Christ; consequently, Rigdon was undoubtedly well aware of the parable of the fig tree and its reference to the signs of the Second Coming. Thus in referencing a parable, the Lord quickly conveys much to Rigdon. First, the parable effectively sums up the much-anticipated Second Coming of the Lord and possibly strokes Rigdon's desire to be a part of the work, since he learns the signs are soon to become apparent. Second, the repetition of a parable from the New Testament reinforces that the Lord who speaks to Joseph Smith, and now Rigdon, is not a new Lord, but the same Lord who lived on the earth" (Easton-Flake, "Revealing Parables," 152). ◉

Doctrine and Covenants 35:17–19. Joseph Smith Holds the Keys of the Mysteries

17 And I have sent forth the fulness of my gospel by the hand of my servant Joseph; and in weakness have I blessed him;

How did the Lord bless Joseph Smith in his weakness? (35:17) "To the human mind it is amazing that such rich revelations and translations should come through an untrained individual such as Joseph was. The reason, of course, is that, though Joseph did not spell perfectly, he came to know the grammar of the gospel, because he was God's apt pupil. . . .

"Joseph's 'weaknesses' included what the world would call inadequacies—in literary and grammatical skills, for example. But the Book of Mormon itself propounds the encouraging doctrine that for those who humble themselves before God, he will make their weaknesses strengths (see 2 Nephi 3:13; Ether 12:27, 37). Nowhere is this transformation better exemplified than in the translation of the Book of Mormon, in which, because of Joseph's 'weakness,' both the process and the substance were directed of the Savior" (Maxwell, *But for a Small Moment*, 44, 45). ⊕

What are "the keys of the mystery of those things which have been sealed" that were given to Joseph Smith? (35:18) "Joseph Smith holds with these priesthood keys control over what God has hidden from the world. He can at his discretion and as allowed by the Spirit make any of these things known to individuals, to the Saints, or to the world in the latter days. Joseph Smith, as head of the dispensation of the fulness of times, holds the responsibility and authority to direct the revealing of all the knowledge and light that is to come to the world in this dispensation. One exercise of these keys was the translation of the Book of Mormon, of the Joseph Smith Translation, and of the book of Abraham. Another was the revelation of the ordinances of the temple, and a third was the revelations now found in the Doctrine and Covenants—'the things which shall come from this time until the time of my coming'" (Robinson and Garrett, *Commentary on the Doctrine and Covenants*, 1:242).

Doctrine and Covenants 35:20–21. The Elect Will Abide the Day of the Lord's Coming

What are the "scriptures" that the Lord refers to in this verse? (35:20) Sidney Rigdon was called to be a scribe as the Prophet worked on inspired corrections and additions to the Bible [now known as the Joseph Smith Translation (JST)]. In the Doctrine and Covenants, the Lord refers to the JST "as 'my scriptures' (35:20; 42:56; 93:53), 'the fulness of my scriptures' (42:15; 104:58), 'the work of translation'

18 And I have given unto him the keys of the mystery of those things which have been sealed, even things which were from the foundation of the world, and the things which shall come from this time until the time of my coming, if he abide in me, and if not, another will I plant in his stead.

19 Wherefore, watch over him that his faith fail not, and it shall be given by the Comforter, the Holy Ghost, that knoweth all things.

20 And a commandment I give unto thee—that thou shalt write for him; and the scriptures shall be given, even as they are in mine own bosom, to the salvation of mine own elect;

The Doctrine and Covenants and the Joseph Smith Translation (JST)

The Joseph Smith Translation is a "revision or translation of the King James Version of the Bible begun by the Prophet Joseph Smith in June 1830. He was divinely commissioned to make the translation and regarded it as 'a branch of his calling' as a prophet. Although the major portion of the work was completed by July 1833, he continued to make modifications while preparing a manuscript for the press until his death in 1844, and it is possible that some additional modifications would have been made had he lived to publish the entire work. Some parts of the translation were published during his lifetime" (Bible Dictionary, s.v. "Joseph Smith Translation (JST)").

Elder Bruce R. McConkie described the Joseph Smith Translation as "a thousand times over the best Bible now existing on earth. It contains all that the King James Version does, plus pages of additions and corrections and an

(73:4; 76:15), 'translation of the prophets,' referring to the Old Testament (90:13), and 'the new translation of my holy word' (124:89). Hence it appears that it is appropriate to call it a 'translation,' even though the Prophet Joseph was not, at least at this early date, acquainted with the ancient languages used in writing the original Bible manuscripts and did not have those manuscripts at his disposal" (Dahl, "Joseph Smith Translation and the Doctrine and Covenants," 105). ⊕

21 For they will hear my voice, and shall see me, and shall not be asleep, and shall abide the day of my coming; for they shall be purified, even as I am pure.

How may we hear the Lord's voice? (35:21) "If you have not heard His voice speaking to you lately, return with new eyes and new ears to the scriptures. They are our spiritual lifeline. Behind the darkness of the Iron Curtain, the Saints survived because they heard His voice through the scriptures. In other parts of the world, when members couldn't attend Church for a time, they continued to worship God because they heard His voice through the scriptures. Throughout all the wars of the past century and the conflicts that rage today, Latter-day Saints survive because they hear His voice through the scriptures" (Hales, "Holy Scriptures," *Ensign*, Nov. 2006, 27).

Doctrine and Covenants 35:22–27. Israel Will Be Saved

What responsibilities did the Lord give Sidney Rigdon? (35:22–23) "Sidney Rigdon was called to assist Joseph Smith in at least two ways. He was to serve as a scribe, the Lord promising that 'the scriptures shall be given, even as they are in mine own bosom' (D&C 35:20). Rigdon would provide substantial help in the Prophet's recently commenced inspired revision or 'new translation' of the Bible. He also was called to draw on his background as a minister to 'preach [the] gospel and call on the holy prophets to prove [Joseph Smith's] words as they shall be given him' (D&C 35:23). A later revelation would explain that while Rigdon would be a spokesman for the Prophet, the latter would be a revelator to him (D&C 35:22 and 100:9–11)" (Cowan, "Calls to Preach the Gospel," 161).

22 And now I say unto you, tarry with him, and he shall journey with you; forsake him not, and surely these things shall be fulfilled.

23 And inasmuch as ye do not write, behold, it shall be given unto him to prophesy; and thou shalt preach my gospel and call on the holy prophets to prove his words, as they shall be given him.

occasional deletion. It was made by the spirit of revelation, and the changes and additions are the equivalent of the revealed word in the Book of Mormon and the Doctrine and Covenants" (*Doctrines of the Restoration*, 289).

"Many of the revelations that comprise the Doctrine and Covenants have a direct relationship to the translation of the Bible which the Prophet Joseph was making at the time the revelations were received. They consist of two kinds: (1) directions or instructions to the Prophet about the Bible translation [such as when to start the translation, the appointment of scribes, and several reminders to publish the translation and use it in teaching] and (2) doctrinal revelations given to the Prophet while he was engaged in the translation process [including sections 76, 77, and 86]" (Matthews, *"Plainer Translation,"* 255).

What does the Lord promise to those who keep all of His commandments and covenants? (35:24) When we keep our sacred covenants and the Lord's commandments, God sends abundant blessings. "Obedience allows God's blessings to flow without constraint. He will bless His obedient children with freedom from bondage and misery. And He will bless them with more light" (Nelson, *Teachings*, 231).

"By following the Prophet Joseph Smith and his rightful successors, Latter-day Saints [will] allow the 'heavens to shake' and rain down revelation upon their heads 'for your good' (D&C 21:6)" (Brewster, *Doctrine & Covenants Encyclopedia* [2012], 75).

How will Israel be saved and led in God's own due time? (35:25) "Every person who has made covenants with God has promised to care about others and serve those in need. . . . Each of us has a role to play in the gathering of Israel" (Nelson, "Preaching the Gospel of Peace," *Liahona*, May 2022, 6).

This saving of Israel, according to this verse, will occur under the direction of priesthood keys. According to Elder Dale G. and Sister Ruth L. Renlund: "Priesthood leaders receive . . . priesthood keys, the right to preside over an organizational division of the Church or a quorum. In this regard, priesthood keys are the authority and power to direct, lead, and govern in the Church. Other priesthood holders administer saving ordinances and serve in the priesthood within the limits outlined by those who hold the priesthood keys. Leaders receive priesthood keys from those in authority over them" (*Melchizedek Priesthood*, 26).

24 Keep all the commandments and covenants by which ye are bound; and I will cause the heavens to shake for your good, and Satan shall tremble and Zion shall rejoice upon the hills and flourish;

25 And Israel shall be saved in mine own due time; and by the keys which I have given shall they be led, and no more be confounded at all.

26 Lift up your hearts and be glad, your redemption draweth nigh.

27 Fear not, little flock, the kingdom is yours until I come. Behold, I come quickly. Even so. Amen.

Joseph Smith received this revelation for Edward Partridge near Fayette, New York, on December 9, 1830. "Edward Partridge [was] an Ohioan who had come to New York to meet [Joseph Smith]. Partridge, a hatter living in Painesville, Ohio, and his wife, Lydia, were members of Sidney Rigdon's reformed Baptist congregation. In early November 1830 they became interested in the Church of Christ when Oliver Cowdery, Parley P. Pratt, Ziba Peterson, and Peter Whitmer Jr. began preaching to and baptizing many individuals from Rigdon's congregation. Lydia soon converted, but her husband [Edward] remained skeptical and insisted on visiting [Joseph Smith] in New York before becoming a member. Partridge and Rigdon traveled to the Palmyra area and then went on to Waterloo in Seneca County. They arrived at the home of Joseph Smith Sr. while [Joseph Smith] was giving a sermon. When [Joseph Smith] finished speaking, 'a request was made that any who felt to speak should,' and Partridge stood and stated that he and Rigdon had visited the Smith family's Manchester farm and had spoken with their neighbors about the character of the Smith family. Based on those conversations, Partridge declared that the Smiths 'had [sacrificed] for the truth's sake' and that he was ready to be baptized. . . . Soon thereafter, [Joseph Smith] dictated this revelation [D&C 36] for Partridge. Two days later, on 11 December, [Joseph Smith] baptized Partridge, and on 15 December, Sidney Rigdon ordained him an elder" (Joseph Smith Papers, Historical Introduction to "Revelation, 9 December 1830 [D&C 36]," 48).

SECTION 36

Revelation given through Joseph Smith the Prophet to Edward Partridge, near Fayette, New York, December 9, 1830 (see the heading to section 35). Joseph Smith's history states that Edward Partridge "was a pattern of piety, and one of the Lord's great men."

1 Thus saith the Lord God, the Mighty One of Israel: Behold, I say unto you, my servant Edward, that you are blessed, and your sins are forgiven you, and you are called to preach my gospel as with the voice of a trump;

2 And I will lay my hand upon you by the hand of my servant Sidney Rigdon, and you shall receive my Spirit, the Holy Ghost, even the Comforter, which shall teach you the peaceable things of the kingdom;

3 And you shall declare it with a loud voice, saying: Hosanna, blessed be the name of the most high God.

Doctrine and Covenants 36:1–3. The Lord Lays His Hand upon Edward Partridge by the Hand of Sidney Rigdon

What is inferred by the Savior's title "the Mighty One of Israel"? (36:1) "[The] Lord announces Himself as 'the Mighty One of Israel.' This name also occurs in Isaiah (1:24; 30:29). It means Jehovah, the Lord of Hosts, who led His people out of Egypt, with a strong arm. While the 'mighty one' of Assyria was a winged bull, and while earthly kingdoms adopt images of eagles, lions, etc., as emblems of strength, the 'Mighty One' of the Kingdom of God is Jehovah" (Smith and Sjodahl, *Doctrine and Covenants Commentary*, 191).

In what way might Sidney Rigdon's hands become as the Lord's hands? (36:2) "The Lord said He would 'lay [His] hand upon' Edward Partridge through His 'servant Sidney Rigdon' and give him the gift of the Holy Ghost. President Harold B. Lee . . . [explained how the] Lord manifests His power through His servants: 'The Lord here [in D&C 36:2] is saying that when one of his authorized servants puts his hands by authority upon the head of one to be blessed, it is as though he himself was putting his hand on . . . them to perform that ordinance. So we begin to see how he manifests his power among men through his servants to whom

He has committed the keys of authority' (['Be Secure in the Gospel,' BYU devotional, February 11, 1958])" (*Doctrine and Covenants Student Manual* [2018], 204).

How does the Holy Ghost teach us the peaceable things of the kingdom? (36:2) "When we come to understand the whisperings of the Spirit, we will be able to hear Him teach us 'the peaceable things of the kingdom' [D&C 36:2] and 'all things what [we] should do' [2 Nephi 32:1–5]. We will recognize answers to our prayers and know how to live the gospel more fully each day. We will be guided and protected. And we can cultivate this gift in our lives as we follow those spiritual promptings. Most importantly, we will feel Him witness to us of the Father and of the Son [see 2 Nephi 31:18]" (Matsumori, "Helping Others Recognize the Whisperings of the Spirit," *Ensign*, Nov. 2009, 11–12). ☉

Doctrine and Covenants 36:4–8. Every Man Who Receives the Gospel and the Priesthood Is to Be Called to Go Forth and Preach

Why does the Lord expect His followers to go forth and preach the gospel? (36:4–8) "Today I reaffirm strongly that the Lord has asked *every* worthy, able young man to prepare for and serve a mission. For Latter-day Saint young men, missionary service is a priesthood responsibility. You young men have been reserved for this time when the promised gathering of Israel is taking place. As you serve missions, you play a pivotal role in this unprecedented event!

"For you young and able sisters, a mission is also a powerful, but *optional,* opportunity. We *love* sister

4 And now this calling and commandment give I unto you concerning all men—

5 That as many as shall come before my servants Sidney Rigdon and Joseph Smith, Jun., embracing this calling and commandment, shall be ordained and sent forth to preach the everlasting gospel among the nations—

Who Was Edward Partridge? (Doctrine and Covenants 36:1)

"This faithful man was born on August 27, 1793, in Pittsfield, Berkshire County, Massachusetts, to William Partridge and Jemima Bidwell. . . . He served as the first bishop of the Church, being called by revelation to that position on February 4, 1831 (D&C 41:9). As a young boy 'he remembers that the Spirit of the Lord strove with him a number of times, insomuch that his heart was made tender and he went and wept; and that sometimes he went silently and poured the effusions of his soul to God in prayer.'

"Bishop Partridge was one of the early converts from the Campbellite movement, being baptized on December 11, 1830. Joseph Smith described this new convert as 'a pattern of piety, and one of the Lord's great men, known by his steadfastness and patient endurance to the end.' The Lord himself issued this compliment of Bishop Partridge: 'His heart is pure before me, for he is like unto Nathanael of old, in whom there is no guile' (D&C 41:11).

Edward Partridge

"He was present at the dedication of the site for the yet-to-be-built temple at Independence, Missouri, and was also in attendance at the dedication of the Kirtland Temple. During the persecutions in Missouri, he was taken from

missionaries and welcome them wholeheartedly. What you contribute to this work is magnificent! Pray to know if the Lord would have you serve a mission, and the Holy Ghost will respond to your heart and mind" (Nelson, "Preaching the Gospel of Peace," *Liahona*, May 2022, 6). ☉

6 Crying repentance, saying: Save yourselves from this untoward generation, and come forth out of the fire, hating even the garments spotted with the flesh.

7 And this commandment shall be given unto the elders of my church, that every man which will embrace it with singleness of heart may be ordained and sent forth, even as I have spoken.

8 I am Jesus Christ, the Son of God; wherefore, gird up your loins and I will suddenly come to my temple. Even so. Amen.

What do the phrases "this untoward generation" and "hating even the garments spotted with the flesh" mean? (36:6) "The Greek word *skolia* translates as 'untoward' and means 'crooked' or 'perverse.' An untoward generation carelessly or willfully casts aside the word of God. 'Garments spotted with flesh' symbolically represents garments defiled by carnal desires and disobedience to the Lord's commands" (Black, *400 Questions and Answers*, 93).

his home and publicly tarred and feathered, having rejected their offer of clemency if he would renounce his faith. To this request he replied: 'I told them that the Saints had suffered persecution in all ages of the world; that I had done nothing which ought to offend anyone; that if they abused me they would abuse an innocent person; that I was willing to suffer for the sake of Christ. . . .

"'I bore my abuse with so much resignation and meekness, that it appeared to astound the multitude, who permitted me to retire in silence, many looking very solemn, their sympathies having been touched as I thought; and as to myself, I was so filled with the Spirit and love of God, that I had no hatred toward my persecutors or anyone else' ([Joseph Smith Papers, "History, 1838–1856, volume A-1," 328]).

"As a result of the many persecutions he endured, his health was broken and he died on May 27, 1840, at the age of forty-seven. Of his demise, the Prophet wrote: 'He lost his life in consequence of the Missouri persecutions, and he is one of that number whose blood will be required at their hands.' This was not to be his final epitaph, however, for the Lord pronounced in a revelation in January 1841 that Edward Partridge 'is with me at this time' (D&C 124:19; [*Latter-day Saint Biographical Encyclopedia*], 1:218–22)" (Brewster, *Doctrine & Covenants Encyclopedia* [2012], 415).

Introduction to Doctrine and Covenants 37

The Prophet Joseph Smith and Sidney Rigdon received this revelation near Fayette, New York, on December 30, 1830. "By the time of this revelation, such notable leaders as Parley P. Pratt, Orson Pratt, Sidney Rigdon, Edward Partridge, and Thomas B. Marsh had joined the Church. Revelations had poured down from heaven as the Prophet Joseph Smith received guidance for individual Saints, direction in revising the Bible [the Joseph Smith Translation], and the records of Moses and Enoch. But Satan's efforts were unrelenting. Persecution raged, and the Prophet was arrested a number of times on false charges. Now, in December 1830, the voice of the Lord was heard again. But this time the Lord's will was that Joseph cease revising the Bible and move to Ohio. Section 37 is the first revelation directing the Saints to gather to a central place" (*Doctrine and Covenants Student Manual* [2001], 74).

"Through the efforts of the missionaries to the [Indigenous tribes], there was already a growing center of Church membership in and around Kirtland, Ohio, near the shores of Lake Erie. . . . This was the beginning of the westward movement which was to be so important a theme in Church history for several decades to come. . . .

"Section 37 was the last recorded revelation received in 1830, and section 38 was the first received in 1831—the year during which more recorded revelations were received than during any other" (Cowan, *Doctrine & Covenants: Our Modern Scripture*, 69).

SECTION 37

Revelation given to Joseph Smith the Prophet and Sidney Rigdon, near Fayette, New York, December 1830. Herein is given the first commandment concerning a gathering in this dispensation.

1 Behold, I say unto you that it is not expedient in me that ye should translate any more until ye shall go to the Ohio, and this because of the enemy and for your sakes.

Doctrine and Covenants 37:1–4. The Saints Are Called to Gather at the Ohio

Why did the Lord command Joseph to stop translating the Bible? (37:1) "The Prophet Joseph Smith began work on the Bible in June 1830. . . . In December 1830 he was living near Fayette, and the translation had reached KJV Genesis 5:22, only a few verses after Enoch is first mentioned. . . . If placed chronologically, the portion of the JST that deals with Enoch would occur just after Doctrine and Covenants section 35 was received and before section 37. . . .

"Shortly after giving this information about Enoch's Zion, the Lord instructed the brethren to cease translating the Bible for a time and to move the Church from New York into Ohio, where they would receive the law of the Lord and a special blessing (see D&C 37:1–3; D&C 38:32; D&C 39:15)" (Matthews, "Plain and Precious Things Restored," *Ensign*, Jul. 1982, 17–18).

Why were the Saints commanded to go to Ohio? (37:1–3) The Lord simply declared that "ye shall go to the Ohio, and this because of the enemy and for your sakes" (D&C 37:1).

Elizabeth Maki added context to the command to move: "[Sidney] Rigdon and [Edward] Partridge's arrival in New York brought with it word of how deeply the restored gospel had taken root in Ohio. And even as the number of converts in Ohio rapidly grew, the Church in New York faced increasing opposition. A few months previously, Joseph Smith had received a revelation declaring that the Church should be gathered in one place, though that location had not yet been revealed (see D&C 29:7–8).

"Joseph's mother, Lucy, later remembered that Joseph had received word that the fledgling congregations in Ohio were badly in need of direction, as the number of converts had ballooned to 300" ("Go to the Ohio," 72). ✚

How does one pray with "much" faith? (37:2)

"Mormon taught his son, Moroni, that we should pray 'with all the energy of heart' (Moro. 7:48). Nephi exclaimed, 'I pray continually for [my people] by day, and mine eyes water my pillow by night, . . . and I cry unto my God in faith, and I know that he will hear my cry' (2 Ne. 33:3; see also Jacob 3:1; Alma 31:38; D&C 37:2).

"The sweet power of prayer can be intensified by fasting, on occasion, when appropriate to a particular need.

"Prayers can be offered even in silence. One can *think* a prayer, especially when words would interfere. We often kneel to pray; we may stand or be seated. Physical position is less important than is spiritual submission to God" (Nelson, "Sweet Power of Prayer," *Ensign*, May 2003, 7).

2 And again, I say unto you that ye shall not go until ye have preached my gospel in those parts, and have strengthened up the church whithersoever it is found, and more especially in Colesville; for, behold, they pray unto me in much faith.

3 And again, a commandment I give unto the church, that it is expedient in me that they should assemble together at the Ohio, against the time that my servant Oliver Cowdery shall return unto them.

4 Behold, here is wisdom, and let every man choose for himself until I come. Even so. Amen.

Introduction to Doctrine and Covenants 38

At a conference of the Church at Fayette, New York, January 2, 1831, the Prophet Joseph Smith received this revelation.

"The year [1831] opened with a prospect, great and glorious, for the welfare of the kingdom; for, on the 2nd of January, 1831, a conference was held in the town of Fayette, New York, at which was received, besides the ordinary business transacted for the Church, the following revelation [D&C 38]" (Joseph Smith Papers, "History, 1838–1856, volume A-1," 88).

"At [this] conference, held at the Whitmers' home soon after the new year, many of the Saints were troubled, their minds full of questions about the commandment [to gather to the Ohio]. Ohio was sparsely settled and hundreds of miles away. Most church members knew little about it.

"Many of them had also worked hard to improve their property and cultivate prosperous farms in New York. If they moved as a group to Ohio, they would have to sell their property quickly and would probably lose money. Some might even be ruined financially, especially if the land in Ohio proved less rich and fertile than their land in New York.

"Hoping to ease concerns about the gathering, Joseph met with the Saints and received a revelation. 'I hold forth and deign to give unto you greater riches, even a land of promise,' the Lord declared, 'and I will give it unto you for the land of your inheritance, if you seek it with all your hearts' [D&C 38:18–19]. By gathering together, the Saints could flourish as a righteous people and be protected from the wicked. . . .

"The revelation calmed the minds of most of the Saints in the room, although a few people refused to believe it came from God. Joseph's family, the Whitmers, and the Knights were among those who believed and chose to follow it" (*Saints*, 1:109–10).

Doctrine and Covenants 38:1–6. Christ Created All Things

Why does the Savior use these names to introduce Himself? (38:1) The commandment to move to Ohio would have created "feelings of hesitancy about [leaving established homes and leaving] friends and family . . . [however,] the Lord gave the Saints sufficient reason to dispel doubt and place their confidence and trust in him. . . .

"He is the Great I AM, the Jehovah of the Old Testament (vv. 1, 4) . . .

"He knows all things (v. 2) . . .

"The words 'I AM' constitute a title that was another name for Jehovah, the God of the Old Testament people (see Exod. 3:14). The beautiful truth given in this revelation is that Jesus Christ is the same God that has directed the affairs of his Father's Kingdom since the world began. He is the Great Jehovah, the Great I AM" (Otten, "Heeding the Lord's Call (D&C 37–41)," 164, 165; formatting altered). See also commentary in this volume on Doctrine and Covenants 19:1, 35:1, and 38:1. ◉

SECTION 38

Revelation given through Joseph Smith the Prophet, at Fayette, New York, January 2, 1831. The occasion was a conference of the Church.

1 Thus saith the Lord your God, even Jesus Christ, the Great I Am, Alpha and Omega, the beginning and the end, the same which looked upon the wide expanse of eternity, and all the seraphic hosts of heaven, before the world was made;

2 The same which knoweth all things, for all things are present before mine eyes;

3 I am the same which spake, and the world was made, and all things came by me.

4 I am the same which have taken the Zion of Enoch into mine own bosom; and verily, I say, even as many as have believed in my name, for I am Christ, and in mine own name, by the virtue of the blood which I have spilt, have I pleaded before the Father for them.

5 But behold, the residue of the wicked have I kept in chains of darkness until the judgment of the great day, which shall come at the end of the earth;

6 And even so will I cause the wicked to be kept, that will not hear my voice but harden their hearts, and wo, wo, wo, is their doom.

7 But behold, verily, verily, I say unto you that mine eyes are upon you. I am in your midst and ye cannot see me;

8 But the day soon cometh that ye shall see me, and know that I am; for the veil of darkness shall soon be rent, and he that is not purified shall not abide the day.

Why was it vital for these early members to believe God knows all things? (38:2) "Because He knows all things, we can exercise faith in Him. The *Lectures on Faith* . . . [explain] the relationship between God's perfect knowledge and our ability to exercise complete faith in Him: 'Without the knowledge of all things God would not be able to save any portion of his creatures; for it is by reason of the knowledge which he has of all things, from the beginning to the end, that enables him to give that understanding to his creatures by which they are made partakers of eternal life; and if it were not for the idea existing in the minds of men that God had all knowledge it would be impossible for them to exercise faith in him' (*Lectures on Faith* [1985], 51–52)" (*Doctrine and Covenants Student Manual* [2018], 214).

What is the "Zion of Enoch"? (38:4) Zion was the name "given to the city of Saints who attained great spiritual stature under the inspired leadership of the Prophet Enoch. . . . Enoch's Zion was unique, and so were the people who occupied it. They stand out in recorded history as a people who successfully lived the principles of celestial law that is required of a Zion people (see D&C 105:5)" (Caldwell, "Quest for Zion," 131). ➊

Doctrine and Covenants 38:7–8. Christ Is in the Midst of His Saints, Who Will Soon See Him

How might the Savior be unseen "in our midst"? (38:7) "The Savior knows each of us in a personal way. He has assured us of His personal acquaintance, His awareness of our needs, and His presence in our times of need. He counseled, 'I say unto you that mine eyes are upon you. I am in your midst and ye cannot see me' (D&C 38:7). [President Dallin H. Oaks] explained, 'The Savior is in our midst, sometimes personally, frequently through his servants, and always by his Spirit' ([*Lord's Way*], 14). . . .

"He also knows our thoughts and the intents of our hearts. . . .

"He knows the temptations we face" (Kendrick, "Strength during Struggles," *Ensign*, Oct. 2001, 26). ➊

Doctrine and Covenants 38:9–12. All Flesh Is Corrupted before Christ

In what ways is the enemy combined? (38:11–12)
"Years ago, I wondered over the scriptural imagery of angels waiting 'day and night' for 'the great command' to come down and reap the tares in a wicked and suffering world; it seemed rather eager to me (see D&C 38:12; 86:5). . . .

"'Evils and designs' really do operate through 'conspiring [individuals] in the last days' (D&C 89:4). The Lord has even announced, 'Behold, the enemy is combined.' . . .

"One of the most subtle forms of intimidation is the gradual normalization of aberration. Alexander Pope so cautioned:

"'Vice is a monster of so frightful mien,

"'As, to be hated, needs but to be seen;

"'Yet seen too oft, familiar with her face,

"'We first endure, then pity, then embrace' ([*Essay on Man*, i.1.217])" (Maxwell, "Behold, the Enemy Is Combined," *Ensign*, May 1993, 76). ⊕

Doctrine and Covenants 38:13–22. Christ Has Reserved a Land of Promise for His Saints in Time and in Eternity

What is the "thing which is had in secret chambers"? (38:13) "The enemies of the Church had joined together in secret to plan the destruction of Joseph and the Saints (see also vv. 28–29). It appears from the historical record that the center of this activity was the area around Colesville, New York. Sidney Rigdon had preached a strong sermon there just prior to the date of this revelation, and it had greatly increased the intensity of both pro- and anti-Mormon feelings. The existence and intent of the secret combinations, however, were still unknown to the Saints" (Robinson and Garrett, *Commentary on the Doctrine and Covenants*, 1:261).

What is the Lord teaching about the poor and the rich? (38:16) When this revelation "was given, the Lord was talking about the poor and the rich. . . .

"In light of these teachings it seems to me that every Church member, and particularly every

9 Wherefore, gird up your loins and be prepared. Behold, the kingdom is yours, and the enemy shall not overcome.

10 Verily I say unto you, ye are clean, but not all; and there is none else with whom I am well pleased;

11 For all flesh is corrupted before me; and the powers of darkness prevail upon the earth, among the children of men, in the presence of all the hosts of heaven—

12 Which causeth silence to reign, and all eternity is pained, and the angels are waiting the great command to reap down the earth, to gather the tares that they may be burned; and, behold, the enemy is combined.

13 And now I show unto you a mystery, a thing which is had in secret chambers, to bring to pass even your destruction in process of time, and ye knew it not;

14 But now I tell it unto you, and ye are blessed, not because of your iniquity, neither your hearts of unbelief; for verily some of you are guilty before me, but I will be merciful unto your weakness.

15 Therefore, be ye strong from henceforth; fear not, for the kingdom is yours.

16 And for your salvation I give unto you a commandment, for I have heard your prayers, and the poor have complained before me, and the rich have I made, and all

flesh is mine, and I am no respecter of persons.

17 And I have made the earth rich, and behold it is my footstool, wherefore, again I will stand upon it.

18 And I hold forth and deign to give unto you greater riches, even a land of promise, a land flowing with milk and honey, upon which there shall be no curse when the Lord cometh;

19 And I will give it unto you for the land of your inheritance, if you seek it with all your hearts.

20 And this shall be my covenant with you, ye shall have it for the land of your inheritance, and for the inheritance of your children forever, while the earth shall stand, and ye shall possess it again in eternity, no more to pass away.

21 But, verily I say unto you that in time ye shall have no king nor ruler, for I will be your king and watch over you.

22 Wherefore, hear my voice and follow me, and you shall be a free people, and ye shall have no laws but my laws when I come, for I am your lawgiver, and what can stay my hand?

priesthood bearer who wishes peace and joy here and eternal life hereafter, would give bounteously of his sustenance to the poor" (Romney, "Church Welfare," *Ensign*, Jan. 1974, 91).

"We are all equal before God. . . .

"Anyone who claims superiority under the Father's plan because of characteristics like race, sex, nationality, language, or economic circumstances is morally wrong and does not understand the Lord's true purpose for all of our Father's children" (Quentin L. Cook, "Eternal Everyday," *Ensign*, Nov. 2017, 51). ⊕

What must the Saints do to receive the Lord's promise? (38:18–20) "One of the first hints to the Latter-day Saints that they would be granted valued inheritances from the Lord and that they must abide a certain law to receive these blessings came in the form of a revelation to Joseph Smith . . . , 2 January 1831. 'I . . . deign to give unto you greater riches,' the revelation promised, 'even a land of promise, . . . the land of your inheritance, if you seek it with all your hearts.' This inheritance from the Lord would be received by covenant and a 'law' pertaining to the same would be received when the Saints reached Ohio (D&C 38:18–19, 32)" (Van Orden, "Law of Consecration," 83).

How will Jesus Christ rule and reign as our king? (38:21–22) "The prophetic word declares that with the return of Christ there will be 'a full end of all nations' (D&C 87:6), meaning all man-made governments will surrender their authority to the Lord of lords and King of kings, who 'will reign personally upon the earth' ([Articles of Faith 1:10]). Joseph Smith explained that 'Christ and the resurrected Saints will reign over the earth, during the 1000 years, but will not dwell on the Earth. They will visit it when they please, or when it is necessary to govern it' ([Joseph Smith Papers, "History Draft (1 July–31 December 1942)," 22]). . . .

"'When the Lord reigns, how will he do it? . . . Christ reigneth in and through and by means of the gospel. There is no other way' (Bruce R. McConkie, *Millennial Messiah*, 590)" (McConkie and Ostler, *Revelations of the Restoration*, 284–85). ⊕

Doctrine and Covenants 38:23–27. The Saints Are Commanded to Be One and Esteem Each Other as Brethren

How can we acquire holiness? (38:24) "Although the Lord has commanded us to 'practice virtue and holiness before [him]' (D&C 38:24), he knows that we will not become perfect overnight. The key is *practice*. As we practice remembering Christ each week during the sacrament, it becomes easier to follow his example. As we follow him, we become more like him, receiving 'grace for grace,' going from 'grace to grace' until we are glorified in Christ and receive a fulness of the glory of God (See D&C 93:11–20)" (Woolley, "I Have a Question," *Ensign*, Dec. 1987, 27).

What can we learn from the Lord about esteeming others? (38:24–25) "While one portion of the human race is judging and condemning the other without mercy, the Great Parent of the universe looks upon the whole human family with a fatherly care and paternal regard; He views them as His offspring, and without any of those contracted feelings that influence the children of men, causes 'His sun to rise on the evil and on the good, and sendeth rain on the just and on the unjust' [Matthew 5:45]" (*Joseph Smith* [manual], 404).

How do we become one with others? (38:27) "Joy comes when we are blessed with unity. . . . His desire is to grant us that sacred wish for unity out of His love for us.

"He cannot grant it to us as individuals. The joy of unity He wants so much to give us is not solitary. We must seek it and qualify for it with others. It is not surprising then that God urges us to gather so that He can bless us. He wants us to gather into families. He has established classes, wards, and branches and commanded us to meet together often. In those gatherings, which God has designed for us, lies our great opportunity. We can pray and work for the unity that will bring us joy and multiply our power to serve" (Eyring, "Our Hearts Knit as One," *Ensign*, Nov. 2008, 69). ◉

Doctrine and Covenants 38:28–29. Wars Are Predicted

What was in the hearts of men that the Saints could not discern? (38:29) "The Saints could read newspapers and discern what was going on in Europe or in other places around the world, but they did not know that the people across town, or around the

23 But, verily I say unto you, teach one another according to the office wherewith I have appointed you;

24 And let every man esteem his brother as himself, and practice virtue and holiness before me.

25 And again I say unto you, let every man esteem his brother as himself.

26 For what man among you having twelve sons, and is no respecter of them, and they serve him obediently, and he saith unto the one: Be thou clothed in robes and sit thou here; and to the other: Be thou clothed in rags and sit thou there—and looketh upon his sons and saith I am just?

27 Behold, this I have given unto you as a parable, and it is even as I am. I say unto you, be one; and if ye are not one ye are not mine.

28 And again, I say unto you that the enemy in the secret chambers seeketh your lives.

29 Ye hear of wars in far countries, and you say that there will soon be great wars in far countries, but ye know not the hearts of men in your own land.

corner, or down their own street, were conspiring together to put them to death. . . .

"Many . . . felt they were immune from the civil disturbances that plagued other countries. But even then, there were evil men hatching evil plans for the country generally and for the Saints in particular. The Civil War was one result of this hidden evil for the nation as a whole, while the expulsion from Missouri and Illinois out into the wilderness was one result for the Saints in particular" (Robinson and Garrett, *Commentary on the Doctrine and Covenants*, 1:264–65).

Doctrine and Covenants 38:30–33. The Saints Are to Be Given Power from on High and to Go Forth among All Nations

30 I tell you these things because of your prayers; wherefore, treasure up wisdom in your bosoms, lest the wickedness of men reveal these things unto you by their wickedness, in a manner which shall speak in your ears with a voice louder than that which shall shake the earth; but if ye are prepared ye shall not fear.

31 And that ye might escape the power of the enemy, and be gathered unto me a righteous people, without spot and blameless—

How can we prepare in such a way that we "shall not fear"? (38:30) "We live in troubled times—very troubled times. We hope, we pray, for better days. But that is not to be. The prophecies tell us that. We will not as a people, as families, or as individuals be exempt from the trials to come. No one will be spared the trials common to home and family, work, disappointment, grief, health, aging, ultimately death.

"'What then shall we do?' That question was asked of the Twelve on the day of Pentecost. Peter answered, 'Repent, and be baptized every one of you in the name of Jesus Christ for the remission of sins, and ye shall receive the gift of the Holy Ghost.' . . .

"We need not live in fear of the future. We have every reason to rejoice and little reason to fear. If we follow the promptings of the Spirit, we will be safe, whatever the future holds. We will be shown what to do" (Packer, "Cloven Tongues of Fire," *Ensign*, May 2000, 8). ◉

32 Wherefore, for this cause I gave unto you the commandment that ye should go to the Ohio; and there I will give unto you my law; and there you shall be endowed with power from on high;

33 And from thence, whosoever I will shall go forth among all nations, and it shall be told them what they shall do; for I have a great work laid up in store, for Israel shall be saved, and I will lead them whithersoever I will, and no power shall stay my hand.

What was the promised endowment of power? (38:32) "President Joseph Fielding Smith taught that 'the Lord commanded the Saints to build a temple . . . in which he could reveal the keys of authority and where the apostles could be endowed and prepared to prune his vineyard for the last time' [*Doctrines of Salvation*, 2:234]. Although the temple endowment as we know it today wasn't administered in the Kirtland Temple, in fulfillment of prophecy, preparatory temple ordinances began to be introduced there, along with an outpouring of spiritual manifestations which armed those called on missions with the promised endowment of 'power from on high' [D&C 38:32] that led to a great gathering through missionary service" (Eyring, "He Goes before Us," *Ensign*, May 2020, 67–68). ◉

When did the Lord deliver His law? (38:32–33)
"The law of the Lord was revealed to Joseph Smith on February 9, 1831, about eight days after he arrived in Kirtland, Ohio (see D&C 42). The promise given to those who obey the law is to be 'endowed with power from on high' (D&C 38:32). The Greek word for endow is *enduo*, meaning 'to be clothed.' Therefore, to be endowed means to be clothed with power or priesthood from on high" (Black, *400 Questions and Answers*, 97).

Doctrine and Covenants 38:34–42. The Church Is Commanded to Care for the Poor and Needy and to Seek the Riches of Eternity

Who were the "certain men" appointed? (38:34–36)
"It is the duty and an obligation of the Church to care for the poor. It is not a self-imposed obligation. It is divinely imposed [see D&C 38:34–36]. . . .
    "This has reference to the bishops of the Church. No bishop in this Church is a good bishop who is not watchful of the poor. He must be a father to them, and feel toward the poor as a father in the flesh feels toward his suffering boys and girls. . . .
    "One who does not love the poor and care for them has not the Spirit of the Lord" (Widtsoe, *Message of the Doctrine and Covenants*, 93, 94).

Why did the Lord wait to send missionaries? (38:38)
"It seems that the Kirtland Temple was important to the Lord's step-by-step plan for at least two reasons: First, Moses waited until the temple was completed to restore the keys of the gathering of Israel. And second, President Joseph Fielding Smith taught that 'the Lord commanded the Saints to build a temple [the Kirtland Temple] in which he could reveal the keys of authority and where the apostles could be endowed and prepared to prune his vineyard for the last time.' Although the temple endowment as we know it today wasn't administered in the Kirtland Temple, in fulfillment of prophecy, preparatory temple ordinances began to be introduced there, along with an outpouring of spiritual manifestations which armed those called on missions with the promised endowment of 'power from on high' that led to a great gathering through missionary service" (Eyring, "He Goes before Us," *Ensign*, May 2020, 67–68). ●

34 And now, I give unto the church in these parts a commandment, that certain men among them shall be appointed, and they shall be appointed by the voice of the church;

35 And they shall look to the poor and the needy, and administer to their relief that they shall not suffer; and send them forth to the place which I have commanded them;

36 And this shall be their work, to govern the affairs of the property of this church.

37 And they that have farms that cannot be sold, let them be left or rented as seemeth them good.

38 See that all things are preserved; and when men are endowed with power from on high and sent forth, all these things shall be gathered unto the bosom of the church.

39 And if ye seek the riches which it is the will of the Father to give unto you, ye shall be the richest of all people, for ye shall have the riches of eternity; and it must needs be that the riches of the earth are mine to give; but beware of pride, lest ye become as the Nephites of old.

40 And again, I say unto you, I give unto you a commandment, that every man, both elder, priest, teacher, and also member, go to with his might, with the labor of his hands,

to prepare and accomplish the things which I have commanded.

41 And let your preaching be the warning voice, every man to his neighbor, in mildness and in meekness.

42 And go ye out from among the wicked. Save yourselves. Be ye clean that bear the vessels of the Lord. Even so. Amen.

What does the phrase "be ye clean that bear the vessels of the Lord" mean? (38:42) President Jeffrey R. Holland explained that one of the meanings of this phrase "refers to the recovery and return to Jerusalem of various temple implements that had been carried into Babylon by King Nebuchadnezzar. In physically handling the return of these items, the Lord reminded those early brethren of the sanctity of anything related to the temple. Therefore as they carried back to their homeland these various bowls, basins, cups, and other vessels, they themselves were to be as clean as the ceremonial instruments they bore [see 2 Kings 25:14–15; Ezra 1:5–11]" ("Sanctify Yourselves," *Ensign*, Nov. 2000, 39). ●

Introduction to Doctrine and Covenants 39

On January 5, 1831, in Fayette, New York, Joseph Smith stated, "there was a man by the name of James Covel who covenanted with the Lord that he would obey any commandment that the Lord would give through his [servant] Joseph & accordingly he [inquired] of the Lord & he received [D&C 39] given at Fayette Seneca County state New York" (Joseph Smith Papers, "Revelation, 5 January 1831 [D&C 39]," 58).

"Covel was preaching in the Richmond circuit, 45 miles east of Fayette, New York, when he attended a conference of Latter-day Saints at Fayette in early January 1831. The Church was on its way out of New York then, the call to settle in Ohio having already come through revelation (see D&C 37:3). . . .

"[Evidently, Covel] seemed poised to convert. He lingered a few days, talking with Church leaders, and covenanted with God to obey the call to repent and be baptized" (Woodworth, "James Covel and the 'Cares of the World,'" 75).

SECTION 39

Revelation given through Joseph Smith the Prophet to James Covel, at Fayette, New York, January 5, 1831. James Covel, who had been a Methodist minister for about forty years, covenanted with the Lord that he would obey any command that the Lord would give to him through Joseph the Prophet.

1 Hearken and listen to the voice of him who is from all eternity to all eternity, the Great I Am, even Jesus Christ—

Doctrine and Covenants 39:1–4. The Saints Have Power to Become the Sons of God

What can we learn from the divine declaration that Jesus Christ is "from all eternity to all eternity"? (39:1) "As we view things from our mortal perspective, it is natural to speak of things that are part of eternity past and of other things that will take place in the eternity of the future. Those past ages when all men dwelt in the presence of their Eternal Father were one eternity, and those future ages in which we hope to obtain an exaltation and to give birth to spirit children of our own and begin again the cycle of creation, redemption, and salvation constitute eternity future. Thus it will yet be said of those who obtain that exalted status, as it is of God and Christ, that they are from eternity to eternity or that they are from everlasting to everlasting (D&C 132:20)" (McConkie and Millet, *Doctrinal Commentary on the Book of Mormon*, 2:146–47). ●

Why is Jesus Christ called "the light and the life of the world"? (39:2) [Jesus Christ] has repeated this declaration in many modern revelations (see D&C 12:9, D&C 39:2, D&C 45:7). In harmony with his words, we solemnly affirm that Jesus Christ, the Only Begotten Son of God the Eternal Father, is the light and life of the world.

"Jesus Christ is the light and life of the world because all things were made by him. Under the direction and according to the plan of God the Father, Jesus Christ is the Creator, the source of the light and life of all things. Through modern revelation we have the testimony of John, who bore record that Jesus Christ is 'the light and the Redeemer of the world, the Spirit of truth, who came into the world, because the world was made by him, and in him was the life of men and the light of men" (Oaks, "Light and Life of the World," *Ensign*, Nov. 1987, 63).

What does the "meridian of time" mean? (39:3) "The word [*meridian*] suggests the middle....

"The meridian of time may also be seen as the high point of mortal time. Latter-day revelation shows that all of the ancient prophets looked forward to the Messiah's coming (Jacob 4:4; Mosiah 13:33–35; 15:11). His coming fulfilled their prophecies, and he was prefigured in the Law of Moses (Mosiah 13:29–32) and in ancient ceremonial ordinances (Moses 5:5–8). The meridian of time is the apex of all dispensations because of the birth, ministry, and Atonement of Christ. Without him all prophetic writings and utterances would have had no efficacy, and the hopes of mankind today and forever would be but futile desires and yearnings without possibility of fulfillment" (Marshall T. Burton, "Meridian of Time," 2:892).

What does it mean to become the sons and daughters of God? (39:4) "Men may become children of Jesus Christ by being born anew—born of God, as the inspired word states [see 1 John 3:8–10].

"Those who have been born unto God through obedience to the Gospel may by valiant devotion to righteousness obtain exaltation and even reach the status of Godhood [see D&C 76:58; 132:17, 20, 37]....

"By the new birth—that of water and the Spirit—mankind may become children of Jesus Christ, being through the means by Him provided 'begotten sons and daughters unto God' [D&C 76:24; see also 1 Corinthians 4:15; D&C 84:33–34; 93:21–22]" (*Joseph F. Smith* [manual], 358). See also commentary in this volume on Doctrine and Covenants 11:30; 25:1–2. ✚

2 The light and the life of the world; a light which shineth in darkness and the darkness comprehendeth it not;

3 The same which came in the meridian of time unto mine own, and mine own received me not;

4 But to as many as received me, gave I power to become my sons; and even so will I give unto as many as will receive me, power to become my sons.

5 And verily, verily, I say unto you, he that receiveth my gospel receiveth me; and he that receiveth not my gospel receiveth not me.

6 And this is my gospel—repentance and baptism by water, and then cometh the baptism of fire and the Holy Ghost, even the Comforter, which showeth all things, and teacheth the peaceable things of the kingdom.

7 And now, behold, I say unto you, my servant James, I have looked upon thy works and I know thee.

8 And verily I say unto thee, thine heart is now right before me at this time; and, behold, I have bestowed great blessings upon thy head;

9 Nevertheless, thou hast seen great sorrow, for thou hast rejected me many times because of pride and the cares of the world.

10 But, behold, the days of thy deliverance are come, if thou wilt hearken to my voice, which saith unto thee: Arise and be baptized, and wash away your sins, calling on my name, and you shall receive my Spirit, and a blessing so great as you never have known.

Doctrine and Covenants 39:5–6. To Receive the Gospel Is to Receive Christ

What must a person do to receive the gospel of Jesus Christ? (39:5–6) Jesus Christ revealed, "Behold I have given unto you my gospel, and this is the gospel which I have given unto you—that I came into the world to do the will of my Father" (3 Nephi 27:13). To receive the gospel one "must be willing to be baptized 'as a witness before him that ye have entered into a covenant with him, that ye will serve him and keep his commandments' (Mosiah 18:10). Those who confess that the Restoration is the work of God but are unwilling to covenant in the waters of baptism will not receive the blessings of the gift of the Holy Ghost or enter the gate to eternal life" (McConkie and Ostler, *Revelations of the Restoration*, 291–92). ☉

Doctrine and Covenants 39:7–14. James Covel Is Commanded to Be Baptized and Labor in the Lord's Vineyard

How can pride slow our spiritual progress? (39:8–9) Pride is "a lack or absence of humility or teachableness. Pride sets people in opposition to each other and to God. A proud person sets himself above those around him and follows his own will rather than God's will. Conceit, envy, hardheartedness, and haughtiness are also typical of a proud person" (Guide to the Scriptures, "Pride"). See also commentary in this volume on Doctrine and Covenants 121:34–40.

What was the blessing the Lord had in store for James Covel? (39:10) "It would seem from the circumstances which brought this clergyman to the Prophet, that he was not at peace. There were unanswered questions and difficulties which had not been resolved in his mind.

"In applying this idea to us who are members of the kingdom, how may we receive peace of mind? A function of the Holy Ghost is to give to the son or daughter of Jesus Christ a sense of security, peace, and joy. This satisfaction comes by having the influence of the Holy Spirit through living the laws of the gospel, just as James [Covel] was promised 'a blessing so great as you never have known' [v. 10] by his adherence to the same laws" (Roy W. Doxey, *Doctrine and Covenants Speaks*, 1:209).

What may have been the work the Lord prepared for James Covel? (39:11–13) James Covel's introduction to the restored gospel was similar to Sidney Rigdon, who was a Campbellite preacher before joining the church. The Lord told Sidney, "Behold, verily, verily, I say unto my servant Sidney, I have looked upon thee and thy works. I have heard thy prayers, and prepared thee for a greater work" (Doctrine and Covenants 35:3).

"[James Covel] was now commanded to be baptized by priesthood authority. . . . Like Sidney Rigdon, he was prepared, for a 'greater work'—to preach the *fulness* of the gospel" (Cowan, *Doctrine & Covenants: Our Modern Scripture*, 69).

How are missionaries called to labor today? (39:14) Elder Ronald A. Rasband related an experience with President Henry B. Eyring when missionaries were assigned their fields of labor in our day: "[President Eyring] then referred to another [computer] screen which displayed areas and missions across the world. Finally, as he was prompted by the Spirit, he would assign the missionary to his or her field of labor.

"From others of the Twelve, I have learned that this general method is typical each week as Apostles of the Lord assign scores of missionaries to serve throughout the world. . . .

"Every missionary called in this Church, and assigned or reassigned to a particular mission, is called by revelation from the Lord God Almighty through one of these, His servants" ("Divine Call of a Missionary," *Ensign*, May 2010, 52, 53). ◉

Doctrine and Covenants 39:15–21. The Lord's Servants Are to Preach the Gospel before the Second Coming

What great blessing had the Lord prepared for the Saints to receive in Ohio? (39:15) "In terms of its enormous significance to mankind, [the Kirtland Temple] was *eternity-shaping*. Ancient prophets restored priesthood keys for the eternal saving ordinances of the gospel of Jesus Christ. . . .

"These keys provide the 'power from on high' [D&C 38:38] for divinely appointed responsibilities that constitute the primary purpose of the Church . . . defined as gathering Israel, sealing them as families, and preparing the world for the Lord's Second Coming" (Quentin L. Cook, "Prepare to Meet God," *Ensign*, May 2018, 114).

11 And if thou do this, I have prepared thee for a greater work. Thou shalt preach the fulness of my gospel, which I have sent forth in these last days, the covenant which I have sent forth to recover my people, which are of the house of Israel.

12 And it shall come to pass that power shall rest upon thee; thou shalt have great faith, and I will be with thee and go before thy face.

13 Thou art called to labor in my vineyard, and to build up my church, and to bring forth Zion, that it may rejoice upon the hills and flourish.

14 Behold, verily, verily, I say unto thee, thou art not called to go into the eastern countries, but thou art called to go to the Ohio.

15 And inasmuch as my people shall assemble themselves at the Ohio, I have kept in store a blessing such as is not known among the children of men, and it shall be poured forth upon their heads. And from thence men shall go forth into all nations.

16 Behold, verily, verily, I say unto you, that the people in Ohio call upon me in much faith, thinking I will stay my hand in judgment upon the nations, but I cannot deny my word.

17 Wherefore lay to with your might and call faithful laborers into my vineyard, that it may be pruned for the last time.

18 And inasmuch as they do repent and receive the fulness of my gospel, and become sanctified, I will stay mine hand in judgment.

19 Wherefore, go forth, crying with a loud voice, saying: The kingdom of heaven is at hand; crying: Hosanna! blessed be the name of the Most High God.

20 Go forth baptizing with water, preparing the way before my face for the time of my coming;

21 For the time is at hand; the day or the hour no man knoweth; but it surely shall come.

22 And he that receiveth these things receiveth me; and they shall be gathered unto me in time and in eternity.

23 And again, it shall come to pass that on as many as ye shall baptize with water, ye shall lay your hands, and they shall receive the gift of the Holy Ghost, and shall be looking forth for the signs of my coming, and shall know me.

24 Behold, I come quickly. Even so. Amen.

Who are the laborers called to help in the Lord's vineyard? (39:17) "We should pause to remember that it is the Lord's work and He is doing it. He is the Lord of the vineyard, and we are His servants. He bids us labor in the vineyard with our might this 'last time,' and He labors with us [see Jacob 5:71–72]. It would probably be more accurate to say He permits us to labor with Him. . . . It is He who is hastening His work in its time. Employing our admittedly imperfect efforts—our 'small means'—the Lord brings about great things [see 1 Nephi 16:29]" (Christofferson, "Preparing for the Lord's Return," *Ensign*, May 2019, 83–84).

"This is going to be the last time the Lord will prune the vineyard. In the Doctrine and Covenants the Lord talks approximately thirty times of pruning and laboring in the vineyard" (Fowles, "Zenos' Prophetic Allegory of Israel," 35). ◉

Doctrine and Covenants 39:22–24.
Those Who Receive the Gospel Will Be Gathered in Time and in Eternity

What does it mean to receive the Holy Ghost? (39:23) "These four words—'Receive the Holy Ghost'—are not a passive pronouncement; rather, they constitute a priesthood injunction—an authoritative admonition to act and not simply to be acted upon (see 2 Nephi 2:26). . . .

"What should we do to make this authorized admonition to seek for the companionship of the third member of the Godhead an ongoing reality? Let me suggest that we need to (1) sincerely desire to receive the Holy Ghost, (2) appropriately invite the

---

No Man Knows the Day or Hour of the Second Coming (Doctrine and Covenants 39:21)

Throughout the scriptures the Lord has consistently reminded us regarding His Second Coming:

"But of that day and hour knoweth no man, no, not the angels of heaven, but my Father only" (Matthew 24:36).

"Watch therefore, for ye know neither the day nor the hour wherein the Son of man cometh" (Matthew 25:13).

"For the time is at hand; the day or the hour no man knoweth; but it surely shall come" (Doctrine and Covenants 39:21).

"I, the Lord God, have spoken it; but the hour and the day no man knoweth, neither the angels in heaven, nor shall they know until he comes" (Doctrine and Covenants 49:7).

"And the hour and the day is not given unto them, wherefore let them act upon this land as for years, and this shall turn unto them for their good" (Doctrine and Covenants 51:17).

"Watch, therefore, for ye know neither the day nor the hour" (Doctrine and Covenants 133:11).

"But of that day, and hour, no one knoweth; no, not the angels of God in heaven, but my Father only" (Joseph Smith—Matthew 1:40).

Holy Ghost into our lives, and (3) faithfully obey God's commandments" (Bednar, "Receive the Holy Ghost," *Ensign*, Nov. 2010, 95).

What are the signs of the Savior's Second Coming? (39:23) President Harold B. Lee instructed: "Let me give you the sure word of prophecy on which you should rely for your guide. . . .

"Read the 24th chapter of Matthew—particularly that inspired version as contained in the Pearl of Great Price [Joseph Smith–Matthew 1].

"Then read the 45th section of the Doctrine and Covenants where the Lord, not man, has documented the signs of the times.

"Now turn to section 101 and section 133 of the Doctrine and Covenants and hear the step-by-step recounting of events leading up to the coming of the Savior.

"Finally, turn to the promises the Lord makes to those who keep the commandments when these judgments descend upon the wicked, as set forth in the Doctrine and Covenants, section 38" ("Admonitions for the Priesthood of God," *Ensign*, Jan. 1973, 106).

"Behold, I Come Quickly" (Doctrine and Covenants 39:24)

President Dallin H. Oaks counseled: "What if the day of His coming were tomorrow? If we knew that we would meet the Lord tomorrow—through our premature death or through His unexpected coming—what would we do today? What confessions would we make? What practices would we discontinue? What accounts would we settle? What forgivenesses would we extend? What testimonies would we bear?

"If we would do those things then, why not now? Why not seek peace while peace can be obtained? If our lamps of preparation are drawn down, let us start immediately to replenish them.

"We need to make both temporal and spiritual preparation for the events prophesied at the time of the Second Coming. And the preparation most likely to be neglected is the one less visible and more difficult—the spiritual. A 72-hour kit of temporal supplies may prove valuable for earthly challenges, but, as the foolish virgins learned to their sorrow, a 24-hour kit of spiritual preparation is of greater and more enduring value" ("Preparation for the Second Coming," *Ensign*, May 2004, 9).

"By 6 January 1831, the day after a revelation called him to preach the gospel, Methodist preacher James Covel had departed Fayette, New York, leaving [Joseph Smith] and Sidney Rigdon searching for an explanation. As [Joseph Smith] later recalled, after Covel 'rejected the word of the Lord, and returned to his former principles and people,' the Lord gave [Joseph Smith] and Sidney Rigdon this 6 January 1831 revelation, 'explaining why he obeyed not the word'" (Joseph Smith Papers, Historical Introduction to "Revelation, 6 January 1831 [D&C 40]," 60).

"At the time James Covel heard the restored gospel of Jesus Christ, he was about 60 years old. He was a prominent leader of the Methodist reform movement and had built extensive associations over his 40-year career as a traveling preacher. Furthermore, two of his sons were Methodist preachers. To become a member of the Church and move west to Ohio to fulfill the Lord's call to preach the gospel would have required leaving his home in New York and cutting ties with his former associates. The sacrifice required by the Lord was apparently too much for him to accept. The adversary tempted him, and the fear of persecution and personal loss caused him to reject God's word" (*Doctrine and Covenants Student Manual* [2018], 208).

SECTION 40

Revelation given to Joseph Smith the Prophet and Sidney Rigdon, at Fayette, New York, January 6, 1831. Preceding the record of this revelation, the Prophet's history states, "As James [Covel] rejected the word of the Lord, and returned to his former principles and people, the Lord gave unto me and Sidney Rigdon the following revelation" (see section 39).

1 Behold, verily I say unto you, that the heart of my servant James Covel was right before me, for he covenanted with me that he would obey my word.

2 And he received the word with gladness, but straightway Satan tempted him; and the fear of persecution and the cares of the world caused him to reject the word.

Doctrine and Covenants 40:1–3. Fear of Persecution and Cares of the World Cause Rejection of the Gospel

What does it mean to covenant to obey the Lord's word? (40:1) "To receive Jesus Christ, a person must be willing to believe and obey His gospel, which includes repenting, being baptized, and receiving the gift of the Holy Ghost. Because he had been a Methodist preacher for about 40 years, James Covel may have felt that he had already received the Savior and His gospel. Nevertheless, the Lord's message to James Covel was to repent of his sins and be baptized into His restored Church. The Lord's message is the same today. Regardless of a person's professed beliefs or previous baptism into another Christian denomination, the Lord commands people everywhere to receive Him by accepting the restored gospel, repenting of their sins, and receiving baptism from His authorized servants" (*Doctrine and Covenants Student Manual* [2018], 205). See also commentary in this volume on Doctrine and Covenants 22, Introduction.

Why did James Covel turn away so quickly from the Church? (40:2) "James [Covel] received a most wonderful revelation and blessing, provided he would turn to the Lord and in humility and faith seek to bring forth and establish Zion...

"[He] was convinced of the truth, for it is clear that the Lord revealed to him things which he and the Lord alone knew to be the truth. However, when he withdrew from the influence of the Spirit of the Lord and had time to consider the fact that he would lose the fellowship of the world, and his place and position among his associates, he failed and rejected the promises and blessings which the Lord offered him" (Joseph Fielding Smith, *Church History and Modern Revelation*, 1:174).

What is meant by the Lord's statement "it remaineth with me to do with him as seemeth me good"? (40:3) The Lord has all power and His plans do not fail. "The works, and the designs, and the purposes of God cannot be frustrated, neither can they come to naught" (Doctrine and Covenants 3:1).

On another occasion, the Lord said, "Verily, thus saith the Lord unto you, my friends Sidney and Joseph, your families are well; they are in mine hands, and I will do with them as seemeth me good; for in me there is all power" (Doctrine and Covenants 100:1). "Jesus honored the agency of James [Covel], but would undoubtedly still do whatever He could for Him 'as seemeth me good' (v. 3). It was probably another time that Jesus wept" (Nyman, *Doctrine and Covenants Commentary*, 1:342).

3 Wherefore he broke my covenant, and it remaineth with me to do with him as seemeth me good. Amen.

Introduction to Doctrine and Covenants 41

Doctrine and Covenants 41 was received on February 4, 1831, at Kirtland, Ohio. The Lord prepared the early converts in the Kirtland, Ohio, area to receive Joseph Smith and his family. Prior to the visit from the prophet, Elizabeth Ann Whitney, the wife of Newel K. Whitney, recalled, "'It was midnight—as my husband and I, in our house at Kirtland, were praying to the Father to be shown the way, the Spirit rested upon us and a cloud overshadowed the house. . . . The house passed away from our vision. We were not conscious of anything but the presence of the Spirit and the cloud that was over us. . . . A solemn awe pervaded us. We saw the cloud and felt the Spirit of the Lord. Then we heard a voice out of the cloud, saying, "Prepare to receive the word of the Lord, for it is coming." At this we marveled greatly, but from that moment we knew that the word of the Lord was coming to Kirtland' [Orson F. Whitney, "Newel K. Whitney," *Contributor*, Jan. 1885, 125]" (Staker, "Thou Art the Man," *Ensign*, Apr. 2005, 36).

When Joseph Smith and his group arrived in Kirtland they stopped at the Whitneys' store. Joseph entered and offered his hand across the counter and said, "Newel K. Whitney, thou art the man." When Newel expressed that he was at a disadvantage because he did not know to whom he was speaking, the Prophet "'answered, "I am Joseph the Prophet; you have prayed me here, now what do you want of me?"'" (Staker, "Thou Art the Man," *Ensign*, Apr. 2005, 37).

This revelation directed these early Saints in the way the Lord's law was to operate more perfectly as well, designating Edward Partridge to be the first bishop. Joseph Smith said, "The branch of the church in this part of the Lord's vineyard, which had increased to nearly one hundred members, were striving to do the will of God, so far as they knew it; though some strange notions and false spirits had crept in among them. With a little caution, and some wisdom, I soon assisted the brethren and sisters to overcome them. The plan of 'common stock,' which had existed in what was called 'the family,' whose members generally had embraced the everlasting gospel, . . . was readily abandoned for the more perfect law of the Lord: and the false spirits were easily discerned and rejected by the light of revelation" (Joseph Smith Papers, "History, 1838–1856, volume A-1," 93)

SECTION 41

Revelation given through Joseph Smith the Prophet to the Church, at Kirtland, Ohio, February 4, 1831. This revelation instructs the Prophet and Church elders to pray to receive God's "law" (see section 42). Joseph Smith had just arrived in Kirtland from New York, and Leman Copley, a Church member in nearby Thompson, Ohio, "requested Brother Joseph and Sidney [Rigdon] . . . live with him and he would furnish them houses and provisions." The following revelation clarifies where Joseph and Sidney should live and also calls Edward Partridge to be the Church's first bishop.

1 Hearken and hear, O ye my people, saith the Lord and your God, ye whom I delight to bless with the greatest of all blessings, ye that hear me; and ye that hear me not will I curse, that have professed my name, with the heaviest of all cursings.

2 Hearken, O ye elders of my church whom I have called, behold I give unto you a commandment, that ye shall assemble yourselves together to agree upon my word;

3 And by the prayer of your faith ye shall receive my law, that ye may know how to govern my church and have all things right before me.

Doctrine and Covenants 41:1–3. The Elders Will Govern the Church by the Spirit of Revelation

Who is the Lord warning in this passage? (41:1) "By keeping the commandments of the gospel, members are candidates for the greatest of all blessings—exaltation in the celestial kingdom. By disobedience to the commandments of the gospel, however, we might conceivably become candidates for the greatest of God's cursings. . . . There is no blessing higher than that received by faithful Saints, and no cursing harsher than that received by willful apostates. Certainly those Saints who profess the name of Christ but who will not obey his commandments should reexamine their future in light of this verse" (Robinson and Garrett, *Commentary on the Doctrine and Covenants*, 2:3). See also 1 Nephi 14:7.

How is the Lord's Church governed? (41:2–3) "The Church of Jesus Christ of Latter-day Saints is the Lord's Church, and His Church is governed by and through priesthood authority and priesthood keys. 'Priesthood keys are the authority God has given to priesthood leaders to direct, control, and govern the use of His priesthood on earth.' . . .

"It takes both men who respect women and their distinctive spiritual gifts and women who respect the priesthood keys held by men to invite the full blessings of heaven in any endeavor in the Church" (Ballard, "Men and Women in the Work of the Lord," *New Era*, April 2014, 3–4).

Newel K. Whitney Store (Doctrine and Covenants 41)

"The Newel K. Whitney store played a major role in the history of the Church in Kirtland. Joseph and Emma Smith lived here for a short while. Several significant revelations were received here. The School of the Prophets was held in the store from January 24, 1833, until sometime in April 1833" ("Newel K. Whitney and Company Store," ChurchofJesusChrist.org).

Restored Newel K. Whitney Store, Kirtland, Ohio

Doctrine and Covenants 41:4–6. True Disciples Will Receive and Keep the Lord's Law

How will Jesus Christ be our ruler when He comes? (41:4) The First Presidency and the Quorum of the Twelve Apostles declared: "We testify that He [Christ] will someday return to earth. 'And the glory of the Lord shall be revealed, and all flesh shall see it together' (Isaiah 40:5). He will rule as King of Kings and reign as Lord of Lords, and every knee shall bend and every tongue shall speak in worship before Him. Each of us stand to be judged of Him according to our works and the desires of our hearts" ("Living Christ," *Ensign*, Apr. 2000, 3).

What does it mean to be a disciple of the Lord Jesus Christ? (41:5) "A disciple is one who has been baptized and is willing to take upon him or her the name of the Savior and follow Him. A disciple strives to become as He is by keeping His commandments in mortality, much the same as an apprentice seeks to become like his or her master.

"Many people hear the word *disciple* and think it means only 'follower.' But genuine discipleship is a state of being. This suggests more than studying and applying a list of individual attributes. Disciples live so that the characteristics of Christ are woven into the fiber of their beings, as into a spiritual tapestry" (Hales, "Becoming a Disciple of Our Lord Jesus Christ," *Ensign*, May 2017, 46). ⊕

What does the phrase "pearls to be cast before swine" mean? (41:6) "Always remember, as holiness grows within and you are entrusted with greater knowledge and understanding, you must treat these things with care. The Lord said, 'That which cometh from above is sacred, and must be spoken with care, and by constraint of the Spirit' (D&C 63:64). He also commanded that we must not cast pearls before swine or give that which is holy to dogs (see 3 Ne. 14:6; D&C 41:6), meaning sacred things should not be discussed with those who are not prepared to appreciate their value.

"Be wise with what the Lord gives you. It is a trust. . . . We hold an almost incomprehensible store of sacred things in our hands. We cannot neglect or let them slip away" (Christofferson, "Sense of the Sacred," *New Era*, Jun. 2006, 31).

4 And I will be your ruler when I come; and behold, I come quickly, and ye shall see that my law is kept.

5 He that receiveth my law and doeth it, the same is my disciple; and he that saith he receiveth it and doeth it not, the same is not my disciple, and shall be cast out from among you;

6 For it is not meet that the things which belong to the children of the kingdom should be given to them that are not worthy, or to dogs, or the pearls to be cast before swine.

7 And again, it is meet that my servant Joseph Smith, Jun., should have a house built, in which to live and translate.

8 And again, it is meet that my servant Sidney Rigdon should live as seemeth him good, inasmuch as he keepeth my commandments.

9 And again, I have called my servant Edward Partridge; and I give a commandment, that he should be appointed by the voice of the church, and ordained a bishop unto the church, to leave his merchandise and to spend all his time in the labors of the church;

10 To see to all things as it shall be appointed unto him in my laws in the day that I shall give them.

11 And this because his heart is pure before me, for he is like unto Nathanael of old, in whom there is no guile.

12 These words are given unto you, and they are pure before me; wherefore, beware how you hold them, for they are to be answered upon your souls in the day of judgment. Even so. Amen.

Doctrine and Covenants 41:7–12. Edward Partridge Is Named as a Bishop unto the Church

How was Edward Partridge called as a bishop? (41:9) "The calling of a bishop was essential to the operation of the new law. Note how Edward Partridge's appointment as the first bishop in the Church included three essential steps: (1) a call by the Lord; (2) sustaining by the 'voice of the Church'; and (3) ordination by proper authority" (Cowan, *Doctrine & Covenants: Our Modern Scripture*, 70).

What does it mean to have "no guile"? (41:11) Elder Joseph B. Wirthlin explained, "If we are without guile, we are honest, true, and righteous. All of these are attributes of Deity and are required of the Saints. Those who are honest are fair and truthful in their speech, straightforward in their dealings, free of deceit, and above stealing, misrepresentation, or any other fraudulent action. Honesty is of God and dishonesty of the devil; the devil was a liar from the beginning. Righteousness is living a life that is in harmony with the laws, principles, and ordinances of the gospel" ("Without Guile," *Ensign*, May 1988, 80–81). ⊕

Edward Partridge Was Called as the First Bishop of the Church (Doctrine and Covenants 41:9)

"The office of bishop was one of the first priesthood offices restored in this dispensation, and, like other offices, an understanding of the duties of a bishop came line upon line. Unlike bishops today, [Edward] Partridge was instructed to not only be 'ordained a bishop unto the Church' but also to 'leave his merchandise and to spend all his time in the labors of the Church' [D&C 41:9]" (Farnes, "Bishop unto the Church," 78).

"What kind of a person was Edward Partridge? Early revelations refer to him as a man without guile 'like Nathanael of old,' and commend him for the 'integrity' of his heart ([D&C 41:11]). Local townsmen trusted Edward's inquiry at the New York scene of Mormon beginnings because of his reputation as 'a man who would not lie.' [Philo Dibble, "Philo Dibble's Narrative," *Early Scenes in Church History*, 77]. And Joseph Smith described him as 'a pattern of piety, and one of the Lord's great men known by his steadfastness and patient endurance to the end' (["History of Joseph Smith," *Times and Seasons*, vol. 4 (15 Sep. 1843): 320])" (Jessee, "Steadfastness and Patient Endurance," *Ensign*, Jun. 1979, 41).

"Bishop Edward Partridge was called to the bishopric February 4, 1831. . . . Before this, he was a member of the Campbellites and joined the Church in December 1830. During the severe persecution of the saints in Missouri (due partly to their failure to keep the commandments [of] the Lord), he 'acted a most noble, and self-sacrificing part, and bore many indignities with the greatest patience.' Partly stripped of his clothing, the bishop was taken to the public square in Independence, Missouri, because he would not denounce the Book of Mormon, and he was tarred and feathered as the mob jeered. Later, he, with five others, offered themselves as ransom for the Church, even to be scourged and put to death, if that would stop the inhuman cruelties heaped upon the saints by the Missourians. Later, he assisted the saints in their flight from Missouri and assisted in their location in Illinois. On May 27, 1840, Bishop Partridge died in Nauvoo, accepted of the Lord" (Roy W. Doxey, *Doctrine and Covenants Speaks*, 2:80).

"On February 9, 1831, just days after Joseph and Emma Smith arrived in Ohio, twelve elders 'were called together, and united in mighty prayer, and were agreed, as touching the reception of the law [see D&C 38:32].' On that occasion, Joseph received the 'Laws of the Church of Christ,' or simply 'the Law' as it was commonly known among the Saints. . . . On February 23, the Prophet and seven elders met to determine 'how the Elders of the church of Christ are to act upon the points of the Law.' As a result, several additional paragraphs of instruction, comprising what is now Doctrine and Covenants 42:74–93, were recorded. The revelations of these two days constitute what is now section 42" (Underwood, "Laws of the Church of Christ," 108–9; see also Staker, *Hearken O Ye People*, 102–3).

"The revelation answered many questions of importance to the Church at that time. Joseph and the elders . . . first asked if the Church should 'come to gether into one place or continue in separate establishments.' The Lord answered with what are now essentially the first 10 verses of Doctrine and Covenants 42. . . .

"The Lord then answered a question that had troubled Christianity for centuries: was Christ's Church an orderly, authoritative institution or an unfettered outpouring of the Spirit and its gifts? Some people made extreme claims to spiritual gifts, and others responded with an equal and opposite reaction, stripping away the spontaneity of the Spirit, completely in favor of rigid rules. [Answered in verses 11–69]. . . .

"'How,' the elders wondered, should they care for 'their families while they are proclaiming repentance or are otherwise engaged in the Service of the Church?' The Lord answered with what has become verses 70–73. . . .

"Early versions of the law also include short answers to two additional questions: Should the Church have business dealings—especially get into debt—with people outside the Church, and what should the Saints do to accommodate those gathering from the East? The answers have been left out of later versions of the text, perhaps because Doctrine and Covenants 64:27–30 answers the first question, while the answer to the second is so specific to a past place and time that it may have been considered unimportant for future generations" (Harper, "Law," 95, 96).

Doctrine and Covenants 42:1–10. The Elders Are Called to Preach the Gospel, Baptize Converts, and Build up the Church

Why did the Lord instruct His Church to hear and obey His law? (42:1–2) "Since the beginning of creation . . . family happiness has been central to our Heavenly Father's plan. Having been cast out of the Garden of Eden, Adam and Eve began to multiply and replenish the earth. As their family increased, they called upon the Lord for help. He gave them commandments and told them to teach them to their children. These eternal laws were reiterated to Moses on Sinai, summed up by the Savior in the two great commandments, and repeated to Joseph Smith in a revelation known as the 'law of the Church.' We also must teach these commandments to our children. Our happiness in this life and joy in the future as eternal families depend on how well we *live* them" (Mickelson, "Eternal Laws of Happiness," *Ensign*, Nov. 1995, 79).

SECTION 42

Revelation given in two parts through Joseph Smith the Prophet, at Kirtland, Ohio, February 9 and 23, 1831. The first part, consisting of verses 1 through 72, was received in the presence of twelve elders and in fulfillment of the Lord's promise previously made that the "law" would be given in Ohio (see section 38:32). The second portion consists of verses 73 through 93. The Prophet specifies this revelation as "embracing the law of the Church."

1 Hearken, O ye elders of my church, who have assembled yourselves together in my name, even Jesus Christ the Son of the living God, the Savior of the world; inasmuch as ye believe on my name and keep my commandments.

2 Again I say unto you, hearken and hear and obey the law which I shall give unto you.

3 For verily I say, as ye have assembled yourselves together according to the commandment wherewith I commanded you, and are agreed as touching this one thing, and have asked the Father in my name, even so ye shall receive.

4 Behold, verily I say unto you, I give unto you this first commandment, that ye shall go forth in my name, every one of you, excepting my servants Joseph Smith, Jun., and Sidney Rigdon.

5 And I give unto them a commandment that they shall go forth for a little season, and it shall be given by the power of the Spirit when they shall return.

6 And ye shall go forth in the power of my Spirit, preaching my gospel, two by two, in my name, lifting up your voices as with the sound of a trump, declaring my word like unto angels of God.

7 And ye shall go forth baptizing with water, saying: Repent ye, repent ye, for the kingdom of heaven is at hand.

8 And from this place ye shall go forth into the regions westward; and inasmuch as ye shall find them that will receive you ye shall build up my church in every region—

Why was it important for the Saints to assemble? (42:3–4) "One has protection from being deceived when he is assembled with the saints under authorized leadership. Part of the reason for such protection is that instructions are given in company with the spirit that edifies and is a sanctifying influence in one's life. It is apparent that anyone who has received the Lord's authority to direct the saints when assembled, is under strict command from the Lord to teach the law and commandments so that the saints are edified and sanctified. Failure to be obedient to this divine commandment results in the loss of spiritual truths and powers. On the other hand, obedience brings glory to the Lord's kingdom (see D&C 43:10)" (Otten and Caldwell, *Sacred Truths*, 1:211).

What is the "first commandment" designated by the Lord in this revelation? (42:4–8) "This is the law concerning the preaching of the gospel. It was given for the instruction of the Elders present when the Revelation came, but the principles it embodies are of general interest and application. . . .

"Those who go out to preach the gospel must go in the name of Jesus Christ; that is, on his behalf, in his stead. They are His ambassadors. . . .

"[Repentance] is the gospel message. A true messenger of the Lord may be put to this test. He preaches repentance. . . . A pretender may preach philosophical or ethical discourses. He may read essays on civic or political problems, but he does not deliver *the* all-important message of the gospel" (Smith and Sjodahl, *Doctrine and Covenants Commentary*, 219, 220).

How are those who preach the gospel like God's angels? (42:6) "The commission of missionaries and of angels is one and the same. Both have been called by God to teach the same gospel. Referring to angels and, by implication, to missionaries, Mormon taught: 'The office of their ministry is to call men unto repentance, and to fulfil and to do the work of the covenants of the Father, which he hath made unto the children of men, to prepare the way among the children of men, by declaring the word of Christ unto the chosen vessels of the Lord, that they may bear testimony of him. And by so doing, the Lord God prepareth the way that the residue of men may have faith in Christ, that the Holy Ghost may have place in their hearts, according to the power thereof; and after this manner bringeth to pass the Father, the covenants which he hath made unto the children of men' (Moroni 7:31–32)" (McConkie and Ostler, *Revelations of the Restoration*, 301–2).

What is the city of the New Jerusalem? (42:9)
"[The] terms, Zion and Jerusalem, are used frequently interchangeably.... However, there are many references which point clearly to the fact that Zion and Jerusalem are two separate and distinct places.... There are to be two great capitals. One Jerusalem of old and the other the City of Zion, or New Jerusalem. The latter is to be on this continent. The one will be the Lord's headquarters for the people of Judah and Israel his companions; the other for Joseph and his companions on the Western Hemisphere, which was given to Joseph and his seed after him as an everlasting inheritance" (Joseph Fielding Smith, *Church History and Modern Revelation*, 2:171–72). See also commentary in this volume on Doctrine and Covenants 28:9 and 57:2–3. ❂

To what office did the Lord appoint Edward Partridge? (42:10) The Lord appointed Edward Partridge to be the first bishop of the Church in this dispensation. See also commentary in this volume on Doctrine and Covenants 41:9.

Doctrine and Covenants 42:11–12. Elders Must Be Called and Ordained and Are to Teach the Principles of the Gospel Found in the Scriptures

Why was it important that an elder be known to the church and that he be regularly ordained by the heads of the church? (42:11) "There is purpose in members of the Church everywhere in the world being able to identify the general and local authorities. In that way they can know from whom they learn" (Packer, "From Such Turn Away," *Ensign*, May 1985, 34).

"We always know who is called to lead or to teach and have the opportunity to sustain or to oppose the action. It did not come as an invention of man but was set out in the revelations [D&C 42:11].... In this way, the Church is protected from any imposter who would take over a quorum, a ward, a stake, or the Church" (Packer, "Weak and the Simple of the Church," *Ensign*, Nov. 2007, 6).

What does the Lord expect missionaries and teachers to use as their sources from which to teach? (42:11–12) "Our charge is to teach the principles of the gospel using the scriptures as our primary text. At the time this revelation was given, the Doctrine and Covenants and the Pearl of Great Price had not yet been compiled or they would have been included with the Bible and the Book of

9 Until the time shall come when it shall be revealed unto you from on high, when the city of the New Jerusalem shall be prepared, that ye may be gathered in one, that ye may be my people and I will be your God.

10 And again, I say unto you, that my servant Edward Partridge shall stand in the office whereunto I have appointed him. And it shall come to pass, that if he transgress another shall be appointed in his stead. Even so. Amen.

11 Again I say unto you, that it shall not be given to any one to go forth to preach my gospel, or to build up my church, except he be ordained by some one who has authority, and it is known to the church that he has authority and has been regularly ordained by the heads of the church.

12 And again, the elders, priests and teachers of this church shall teach the principles of my gospel, which are in the Bible and the Book of Mormon, in the which is the fulness of the gospel.

Mormon. There is a spirit and power in teaching from the scriptures that cannot be found in other sources. In the Church today we have a great dependency on dramatic stories to illustrate principles we design to teach. As popular and helpful as such teaching devices are, they do not have the power to expand the mind and bring additional revelation that is found in the scriptures" (McConkie and Ostler, *Revelations of the Restoration*, 303).

Doctrine and Covenants 42:13–17. Church Leaders Are to Teach and Prophesy by the Power of the Spirit

13 And they shall observe the covenants and church articles to do them, and these shall be their teachings, as they shall be directed by the Spirit.

14 And the Spirit shall be given unto you by the prayer of faith; and if ye receive not the Spirit ye shall not teach.

Why must the Spirit of the Lord accompany gospel teaching? (42:14) "The scriptures say, 'The Spirit shall be given unto you by the prayer of faith; and if ye receive not the Spirit ye shall not teach' (D&C 42:14). This teaches not just that you won't teach or that you can't teach or that it will be pretty shoddy teaching. No, it is stronger than that. It is the imperative form of the verb. 'Ye *shall not* teach.' Put a *thou* in there for *ye* and you have Mount Sinai language. This is a commandment. These are God's students, not yours, just like it is Christ's Church, not Peter's or Paul's or Joseph's or Brigham's" (Holland, "Teaching, Preaching, Healing," *Ensign*, Jan. 2003, 41). ☉

15 And all this ye shall observe to do as I have commanded concerning your teaching, until the fulness of my scriptures is given.

16 And as ye shall lift up your voices by the Comforter, ye shall speak and prophesy as seemeth me good;

17 For, behold, the Comforter knoweth all things, and beareth record of the Father and of the Son.

What did the Lord mean by "until the fulness of my scriptures is given"? (42:15) "This phrase [the fulness of my scriptures] refers to future revelations now recorded in the Doctrine and Covenants, the Pearl of Great Price, and the Joseph Smith Translation, and others yet to come—for example, the sealed portions of the Book of Mormon" (Robinson and Garrett, *Commentary on the Doctrine and Covenants*, 2:15).

Doctrine and Covenants 42:18–29. The Saints Are Commanded Not to Kill, Steal, Lie, Lust, Commit Adultery, or Speak Evil against Others

18 And now, behold, I speak unto the church. Thou shalt not kill; and he that kills shall not have forgiveness in this world, nor in the world to come.

What does it mean that the murderer will not be forgiven in this world or the next? (42:18) "In this dispensation, the Lord gave further insight on the eternal condition of those members of the Church who commit murder. In giving the law of the Church, the Lord declared: [D&C 42:18]. This appears to contradict Alma 34:6, but it is important to note the Doctrine and Covenants section 42 is the Law of the

Church, and in verse 18 the Lord specifically stated that he was speaking to the Church. Elder [Bruce R.] McConkie wrote: 'We do know that there are murders committed by Gentiles for which they at least can repent, be baptized, and receive a remission of their sins' (*New Witness*, 231; see also 3 Nephi 30:12). The light and knowledge that the murderer possesses will be a factor in determining his or her eternal condition" (Garrett, "Three Most Abominable Sins," 161–62).

Why is it important that a portion of the Ten Commandments was emphasized by the Lord in this dispensation? (42:18–29) "Modern prophets . . . have often referred to the eternal nature of the Ten Commandments, declaring they were given for 'the salvation and . . . happiness of the children of Israel and for *all of the generations* which were to come after them' (Hinckley, ['Our Solemn Responsibilities,'] *Ensign*, Nov. 1991, 51; emphasis added]. Another reason the Ten Commandments are easily identifiable as eternal laws is that they have all been emphasized by the Lord in the Doctrine and Covenants. A brief analysis of the Ten Commandments reveals they were not unique to the Mosaic dispensation only, but they are eternal laws and the expected conduct for Saints in any age" (Lund, "Teaching Old Testament Laws," 53–54). ⊕

What is the Church's position on capital punishment? (42:19) "The Church of Jesus Christ of Latter-day Saints regards the question of whether and in what circumstances the state should impose capital punishment as a matter to be decided solely by the prescribed processes of civil law. We neither promote nor oppose capital punishment" (Newsroom, Topics, "Capital Punishment").

What does it mean for spouses to cleave to each other? (42:22) "God has commanded husbands and wives to cleave to each other (see Genesis 2:24; Doctrine and Covenants 42:22). In this context, the word *cleave* means to be completely devoted and faithful to someone. Married couples cleave together by loving and serving each other.

"Cleaving also includes total fidelity between husband and wife. Physical intimacy between husband and wife is intended to be beautiful and sacred. It is ordained of God for the creation of children and for the expression of love between husband and wife. Tenderness and respect—not selfishness—should guide their intimate relationship" (*General Handbook* [2023], 2.1.2.).

19 And again, I say, thou shalt not kill; but he that killeth shall die.

20 Thou shalt not steal; and he that stealeth and will not repent shall be cast out.

21 Thou shalt not lie; he that lieth and will not repent shall be cast out.

22 Thou shalt love thy wife with all thy heart, and shalt cleave unto her and none else.

23 And he that looketh upon a woman to lust after her shall deny the faith, and shall not have the Spirit; and if he repents not he shall be cast out.

Why is this warning to not look upon a woman "to lust" so relevant today? (42:23) "Pornography is any depiction, in pictures or writing, that is intended to inappropriately arouse sexual feelings. Pornography is more prevalent in today's world than ever before. It may be found in written material (including romance novels), photographs, movies, electronic images, video games, social media posts, phone apps, erotic telephone conversations, music, or any other medium.

"Physical intimacy is a sacred part of Heavenly Father's plan of happiness. However, the adversary tries to thwart the Lord's plan of happiness by suggesting that physical intimacy is only for personal gratification. Pornography is a tool of the adversary and its use causes the Spirit of the Lord to withdraw from us" (Topics and Questions, "Pornography"). ⊕

24 Thou shalt not commit adultery; and he that committeth adultery, and repenteth not, shall be cast out.

25 But he that has committed adultery and repents with all his heart, and forsaketh it, and doeth it no more, thou shalt forgive;

26 But if he doeth it again, he shall not be forgiven, but shall be cast out.

27 Thou shalt not speak evil of thy neighbor, nor do him any harm.

28 Thou knowest my laws concerning these things are given in my scriptures; he that sinneth and repenteth not shall be cast out.

Why does the Lord consider the sin of adultery to be so serious? (42:24–26) President Gordon B. Hinckley stated: "Was there ever adultery without dishonesty? In the vernacular, the evil is described as 'cheating.' And cheating it is, for it robs virtue, it robs loyalty, it robs sacred promises, it robs self-respect, it robs truth. It involves deception. It is personal dishonesty of the worst kind, for it becomes a betrayal of the most sacred of human relationships, and a denial of covenants and promises entered into before God and man. It is the sordid violation of a trust. It is a selfish casting aside of the law of God, and like other forms of dishonesty its fruits are sorrow, bitterness, heartbroken companions, and betrayed children" ("Honest Man," *Ensign*, May 1976, 61). ⊕

29 If thou lovest me thou shalt serve me and keep all my commandments.

How do we show our love for the Savior? (42:29) Sister Jean B. Bingham noted: "What better way to prepare to meet Him than to strive to become *like* Him through lovingly ministering to one another! As Jesus Christ taught His followers at the beginning of this dispensation, 'If thou lovest me thou shalt serve me.' Our service to others is a demonstration of discipleship and our gratitude and love for God and His Son, Jesus Christ" ("Ministering as the Savior Does," *Liahona*, May 2018, 104).

Doctrine and Covenants 42:30–39. Laws Governing the Consecration of Properties Are Set Forth

What does the Lord require of His Saints relative to the poor? (42:30) The Prophet Joseph Smith counseled the Church: "Consider the state of the afflicted and try to alleviate their sufferings; let your bread feed the hungry, and your clothing cover the naked; let your liberality dry up the tear of the orphan, and cheer the disconsolate widow; let your prayers, and presence, and kindness, alleviate the pains of the distressed, and your liberality contribute to their necessities; do good unto all men, especially unto the household of faith, that you may be harmless and blameless, the sons of God without rebuke. Keep the commandments of God—all that he has given, does give, or will give, and an halo of glory will shine around your path; the poor will rise up and call you blessed" (Joseph Smith Papers, "Times and Seasons, 15 October 1842," 952).

What was the bishop's role in the law of consecration? (42:31–33) "Upon the basic principle that the earth and everything on it belongs to the Lord, every person who was a member of the church at the time the system was introduced or became a member thereafter was asked to 'consecrate' or deed all his property, both real and personal, to the bishop of the church. The bishop would then grant an 'inheritance' or 'stewardship' to every family out of the property so received, the amount depending on the wants and needs of the family, as determined jointly by the

30 And behold, thou wilt remember the poor, and consecrate of thy properties for their support that which thou hast to impart unto them, with a covenant and a deed which cannot be broken.

31 And inasmuch as ye impart of your substance unto the poor, ye will do it unto me; and they shall be laid before the bishop of my church and his counselors, two of the elders, or high priests, such as he shall appoint or has appointed and set apart for that purpose.

32 And it shall come to pass, that after they are laid before the bishop of my church, and after that he has received these testimonies

The Law of Consecration and Stewardship (Doctrine and Covenants 42:30–34)

"In the centuries since the dawn of the Christian era, many groups have tried to emulate the New Testament Christians mentioned in the book of Acts who 'had all things common.' Joseph Smith learned through revelation that this way of living had much earlier roots. While working on his inspired Bible translation during the summer of 1830, Joseph dictated a revelation about the ancient city of Enoch, whose people were 'of one heart and of one mind' and had 'no poor among them.'

"The following January, Joseph Smith received a revelation in New York directing the Latter-day Saints there to relocate to Ohio, where the Lord would 'give unto you my law.' . . .

"Sometimes called the 'law of consecration and stewardship,' this revelation taught the Saints how to pursue economic equality without neglecting voluntary choice and responsibility. It accomplished this not through communal ownership, but by requiring the Saints to consecrate their property, or make it sacred by using it to further the Lord's work. In acknowledgment that all their earthly goods really belonged to God, Latter-day Saints signed over their property to the Lord through the bishop but retained stewardship for—and de facto ownership of—the land and goods they needed for themselves. Whatever they considered surplus they donated to the Church to alleviate poverty and build Zion. The primary role of the office of bishop in the early Church was to administer the law of consecration.

concerning the consecration of the properties of my church, that they cannot be taken from the church, agreeable to my commandments, every man shall be made accountable unto me, a steward over his own property, or that which he has received by consecration, as much as is sufficient for himself and family.

33 And again, if there shall be properties in the hands of the church, or any individuals of it, more than is necessary for their support after this first consecration, which is a residue to be consecrated unto the bishop, it shall be kept to administer to those who have not, from time to time, that every man who has need may be amply supplied and receive according to his wants.

34 Therefore, the residue shall be kept in my storehouse, to administer to the poor and the needy, as shall be appointed by the high council of the church, and the bishop and his council;

bishop and the prospective steward. . . . Out of the surplus thus made possible the bishop would grant stewardships to the poorer and younger members of the church who had no property to consecrate" (Arrington, Fox, and May, *Building the City of God*, 15). ⊕

What was the Lord's storehouse? (42:34) "Anciently, the Lord declared, 'Bring ye all the tithes into the storehouse, that there may be meat in mine house' (Malachi 3:10). The keeping of the Lord's storehouse to provide for the poor was restored with this revelation. One of the most sacred trusts that is placed in the bishop's hands is that of providing for the poor and needy. In this law the bishop uses the property or goods that are surplus to provide for the needs of the members. Although sometimes referred to as a 'bishop's storehouse' the bishop is but a servant of the Lord in distributing goods from the Lord's storehouse. These storehouses containing food and wares are part of the Church welfare program. In addition, much of the burden of providing for the poor rests with the fast offering monies collected as a free-will offering from the Saints each fast day" (McConkie and Ostler, *Revelations of the Restoration*, 308).

"Implementation of the law of consecration proved difficult, as needs always seemed to exceed resources. Many Saints arrived in Ohio and Missouri in an impoverished state, the Church needed to purchase land in Zion and construct buildings, and the Saints also faced hostility from their neighbors. The members of the United Firm—the council tasked in 1832 with managing the Church's finances—disagreed on how to prioritize expenditures. Some Saints were generous in what they considered surplus and donated to the bishop; others clung to spare land and property.

"Two revelations in 1838 introduced the law of tithing as a component of the law of consecration. These revelations taught that after consecrating their surplus property, Saints should donate 'one tenth of all their interest annually.' Subsequent prophets reemphasized that tithing is one means by which Church members live the law of consecration.

"While the principles underlying the law of consecration have remained consistent, the ways the Saints have implemented the law have changed under prophetic direction and in response to changing circumstances" (Church History Topics, "Consecration and Stewardship").

How does living the law of consecration prepare God's people for the Second Coming? (42:35–36) "The law of consecration and stewardship is the highest manifestation of gospel living. Many view this law as only a temporal economic program, but it is a spiritual command as well (see D&C 29:35). . . . It is the basis upon which Zion, the New Jerusalem, is to be built and the preparations completed for the glorious Messianic reign. . . . Early attempts to build Zion in this dispensation failed because . . . the Saints were 'not united according to the union required by the law of the celestial kingdom; and Zion cannot be built up unless it is by the principles of the law of the celestial kingdom' (D&C 105:4–5). These principles are a part of the law of Christ to prepare the sanctified for celestial glory (see D&C 88:20–21)" (*Doctrine and Covenants Student Manual* [2001], 421).

What important clarification did Joseph Smith make concerning this verse? (42:39) Originally, verse 39 stated: "'For it shall come to pass that which I spake by the mouths of my prophets shall be fulfilled for I will consecrate the riches of the Gentiles unto my people which are of the house of Israel [1833].' This alludes to the prophecy of Isaiah that Israel would one day 'eat the riches of the gentiles, and in their glory shall ye boast yourselves' (Isaiah 61:6). . . . In the face of [misreadings by the Saints], the Prophet was impressed to make a crucial clarification when he published this passage in the Doctrine and Covenants [1835]: 'For I will consecrate of the riches *of those who embrace my gospel among* the Gentiles, unto *the poor of* my people *who* are of the House of Israel' (D&C 42:39; emphasis added)" (Underwood, "Laws of the Church of Christ," 121).

Doctrine and Covenants 42:40–42. Pride and Idleness Are Condemned

What does "idle" mean in this verse? (42:42) "Now, some may ask, 'What about those who are poor because they are idle and unwilling to work?' They should heed these words of warning: [D&C 42:42, 56:17]

"Judgment of worthiness is made by the bishop, and ultimately by the Lord, as taught by Nephi: 'With righteousness shall the Lord God judge the poor, and reprove with equity for the meek of the earth' (2 Ne. 30:9).

35 And for the purpose of purchasing lands for the public benefit of the church, and building houses of worship, and building up of the New Jerusalem which is hereafter to be revealed—

36 That my covenant people may be gathered in one in that day when I shall come to my temple. And this I do for the salvation of my people.

37 And it shall come to pass, that he that sinneth and repenteth not shall be cast out of the church, and shall not receive again that which he has consecrated unto the poor and the needy of my church, or in other words, unto me—

38 For inasmuch as ye do it unto the least of these, ye do it unto me.

39 For it shall come to pass, that which I spake by the mouths of my prophets shall be fulfilled; for I will consecrate of the riches of those who embrace my gospel among the Gentiles unto the poor of my people who are of the house of Israel.

40 And again, thou shalt not be proud in thy heart; let all thy garments be plain, and their beauty the beauty of the work of thine own hands;

41 And let all things be done in cleanliness before me.

42 Thou shalt not be idle; for he that is idle shall not eat the bread nor wear the garments of the laborer.

"Ours is not to judge; ours is a covenantal obligation to care for the poor and the needy, to prepare for their rejoicing when the Messiah shall come again" (see D&C 56:18–19)" (Nelson, "In the Lord's Own Way," *Ensign*, May 1986, 27).

Doctrine and Covenants 42:43–52. The Sick Are to Be Healed through Administrations and by Faith

43 And whosoever among you are sick, and have not faith to be healed, but believe, shall be nourished with all tenderness, with herbs and mild food, and that not by the hand of an enemy.

44 And the elders of the church, two or more, shall be called, and shall pray for and lay their hands upon them in my name; and if they die they shall die unto me, and if they live they shall live unto me.

What is the counsel of the Church to those seeking help during times of illness? (42:43–44) "Latter-day Saints believe in applying the best available scientific knowledge and techniques.... The use of medical science is not at odds with our prayers of faith and our reliance on priesthood blessings. When a person requested a priesthood blessing, Brigham Young would ask, 'Have you used any remedies?' To those who said no because 'we wish the Elders to lay hands upon us, and we have faith that we shall be healed,' President Young replied: 'That is very inconsistent according to my faith.... It appears consistent to me to apply every remedy that comes within the range of my knowledge, and [then] to ask my Father in Heaven ... to sanctify that application to the healing of my body' ([*Discourses of Brigham Young*], 163)" (Oaks, "Healing the Sick," *Ensign*, May 2010, 47).

45 Thou shalt live together in love, insomuch that thou shalt weep for the loss of them that die, and more especially for those that have not hope of a glorious resurrection.

What purpose does the tearful separation of loved ones serve? (42:45) "Moreover, we can't fully appreciate joyful reunions later without tearful separations now. The only way to take sorrow out of death is to take love out of life" (Nelson, "Doors of Death," *Ensign*, May 1992, 72).

46 And it shall come to pass that those that die in me shall not taste of death, for it shall be sweet unto them;

47 And they that die not in me, wo unto them, for their death is bitter.

What does it mean to "not taste of death"? (42:46–47) "To some members of the church the saying that those who die in the Lord shall not taste of death has been a hard saying. They have seen good faithful men and women suffer days and at times for months before they were taken. But here the Lord does not say they shall not suffer pain of body, but that they shall be free from the anguish and torment of soul which will be partaken of by the wicked, and although they may suffer in body, yet death to them will be sweet in that they will realize that they are worthy before the Lord" (Joseph Fielding Smith, *Church History and Modern Revelation*, 1:186).

What does "appointed unto death" mean? (42:48)
"We are assured by the Lord that the sick will be healed if the ordinance is performed, if there is sufficient faith, and if the ill one is 'not appointed unto death. . . .'

"God controls our lives, guides and blesses us, but gives us our agency. We may live our lives in accordance with his plan for us or we may foolishly shorten or terminate them.

"I am positive in my mind that the Lord has planned our destiny. Sometime we'll understand fully, and when we see back from the vantage point of the future, we shall be satisfied with many of the happenings of this life that are so difficult for us to comprehend" (*Spencer W. Kimball* [manual], 19, 20). ⊕

What role does faith play in seeking the blessings of healing? (42:49–52) "Priesthood leaders [cannot] provide all of the help. They are agents of the Lord, and His law requires that you do your part. They will show you the way. They can provide priesthood blessings. Your faith, purity, and obedience and that of the priesthood holder have great effect on the pronouncement and realization of the blessing. Healing can occur in the act, yet more often it occurs over a period of time determined by the faith and obedience of the individual and the will of the Lord. I feel that the pace is generally set by the individual, not by the Lord. He expects you to use other resources available, including competent professional help when indicated; then He provides the balance needed according to His will" (Scott, "To Be Healed," *Ensign*, May 1994, 8).

Doctrine and Covenants 42:53–60. The Scriptures Govern the Church and Are to Be Proclaimed to the World

Why should we give our excess to the Lord's storehouse? (42:53–55) One of the "governing principle[s] of the law of consecration was that the members of the society were to earn their own living from working their stewardship (v. 53). If items were needed for their living comfort, they could be purchased from another person's stewardship, but were not to be taken without purchase (v. 54). If items were produced beyond their needs, the surplus was to be given to the storehouse for the bishop's use (v. 55)" (Nyman, *Doctrine and Covenants Commentary*, 1:378).

What were the "scriptures" referred to by the Lord in these verses? (42:56–59) "This statement is clearly a reference to the Joseph Smith Translation, which was being worked on at the time this revelation was

48 And again, it shall come to pass that he that hath faith in me to be healed, and is not appointed unto death, shall be healed.

49 He who hath faith to see shall see.

50 He who hath faith to hear shall hear.

51 The lame who hath faith to leap shall leap.

52 And they who have not faith to do these things, but believe in me, have power to become my sons; and inasmuch as they break not my laws thou shalt bear their infirmities.

53 Thou shalt stand in the place of thy stewardship.

54 Thou shalt not take thy brother's garment; thou shalt pay for that which thou shalt receive of thy brother.

55 And if thou obtainest more than that which would be for thy support, thou shalt give it into my storehouse, that all things may be done according to that which I have said.

56 Thou shalt ask, and my scriptures shall be given as I have appointed, and they shall be preserved in safety;

57 And it is expedient that thou shouldst hold thy peace concerning them, and not teach them until ye have received them in full.

58 And I give unto you a commandment that then ye shall teach them unto all men; for they shall be taught unto all nations, kindreds, tongues and people.

59 Thou shalt take the things which thou hast received, which have been given unto thee in my scriptures for a law, to be my law to govern my church;

60 And he that doeth according to these things shall be saved, and he that doeth them not shall be damned if he so continue.

61 If thou shalt ask, thou shalt receive revelation upon revelation, knowledge upon knowledge, that thou mayest know the mysteries and peaceable things—that which bringeth joy, that which bringeth life eternal.

62 Thou shalt ask, and it shall be revealed unto you in mine own due time where the New Jerusalem shall be built.

63 And behold, it shall come to pass that my servants shall be sent forth to the east and to the west, to the north and to the south.

received. The scriptures here, however, probably also refer to the revelations in the Doctrine and Covenants, since verse 59, 'my law to govern my church,' likely refers to section 42 itself. . . . The Church was not to use the Joseph Smith Translation and the other new scriptures in preaching publicly until they had been given 'in full,' or completed. This is perhaps because the Latter-day Saint belief in continuing revelation and in additional scripture may have an inflammatory effect upon non–Latter-day Saints" (Robinson and Garrett, *Commentary on the Doctrine and Covenants*, 2:28).

Doctrine and Covenants 42:61–69. The Site of the New Jerusalem and the Mysteries of the Kingdom Will Be Revealed

How can a person receive "revelation upon revelation"? (42:61) "Some principles that prepare us to receive revelation include:

"Praying for spiritual guidance. Reverently and humbly we need to seek and ask and be patient and submissive.

"Preparing for inspiration. This requires that we be in harmony with the Lord's teachings and in compliance with His commandments.

"Partaking of the sacrament worthily. When we do this, we witness and covenant with God that we take upon ourselves the name of His holy Son and that we remember Him and keep His commandments.

"These principles prepare us to receive, recognize, and follow the prompting and guidance of the Holy Ghost. This includes the 'peaceable things . . . which bringeth joy [and] . . . life eternal' (D&C 42:61)" (Quentin L. Cook, "Blessing of Continuing Revelation," *Ensign*, May 2020, 99; paragraphing altered).

Where will the New Jerusalem be built? (42:62) "The land for the city of Zion, or the New Jerusalem, was set apart from the time of the creation of the earth. The land near Independence, Missouri, encompasses the area of the garden planted eastward in Eden, in which Adam and Eve were placed. We learn from Brigham Young that 'our God will finish his work where he commenced it, where the center [place] of Zion is, and where the garden of Eden was' ([in] *Journal of Discourses*, 8:72)" (McConkie and Ostler, *Revelations of the Restoration*, 411). See also commentary in this volume on Doctrine and Covenants 57:1–2.

What do we know about secret combinations in the last days? (42:64) President Ezra Taft Benson took special note of dangers posed by organized evil in the last days: "I testify that wickedness is rapidly expanding in every segment of our society (see D&C 1:14–16; D&C 84:49–53). It is more highly organized, more cleverly disguised, and more powerfully promoted than ever before. Secret combinations lusting for power, gain, and glory are flourishing. A secret combination that seeks to overthrow the freedom of all lands, nations, and countries is increasing its evil influence and control over America and the entire world (see Ether 8:18–25)" ("I Testify," *Ensign*, Nov. 1988, 87).

What are the Church covenants that prepare the Saints to establish the New Jerusalem? (42:67–69) "Much of the work to be done in establishing Zion consists in our individual efforts to become 'the pure in heart' (D&C 97:21). 'Zion cannot be built up unless it is by the principles of the law of the celestial kingdom,' said the Lord; 'otherwise I cannot receive her unto myself' (D&C 105:5). The law of the celestial kingdom is, of course, the gospel law and covenants, which include our constant remembrance of the Savior and our pledge of obedience, sacrifice, consecration, and fidelity" (Christofferson, "Come to Zion," *Ensign*, Nov. 2008, 38).

Doctrine and Covenants 42:70–73. Consecrated Properties Are to Be Used to Support Church Officers

Why did families of Church officers receive support from the consecrated properties? (42:71–73) "At this time, the bishop and his counselors served full time in their callings, so they were entitled to receive remuneration, or support, from the Church" (Cowan and Mancill, *A to Z of the Doctrine and Covenants*, 66).

Mary Jane Woodger added: "Those who administer in temporal affairs and give all their time to the Church should receive a just remuneration" (*Essential Doctrine and Covenants Companion*, 83).

Today, "General Authorities leave their careers when they are called into full time Church service. When they do so, they are given a living allowance which enables them to focus all of their time on serving in the Church. This practice allows for far more church members on a worldwide basis to be considered for a calling to serve as a General Authority, rather than limiting considerations to only those who

64 And even now, let him that goeth to the east teach them that shall be converted to flee to the west, and this in consequence of that which is coming on the earth, and of secret combinations.

65 Behold, thou shalt observe all these things, and great shall be thy reward; for unto you it is given to know the mysteries of the kingdom, but unto the world it is not given to know them.

66 Ye shall observe the laws which ye have received and be faithful.

67 And ye shall hereafter receive church covenants, such as shall be sufficient to establish you, both here and in the New Jerusalem.

68 Therefore, he that lacketh wisdom, let him ask of me, and I will give him liberally and upbraid him not.

69 Lift up your hearts and rejoice, for unto you the kingdom, or in other words, the keys of the church have been given. Even so. Amen.

70 The priests and teachers shall have their stewardships, even as the members.

71 And the elders or high priests who are appointed to assist the bishop as counselors in all things, are to have their families supported out of the property which is consecrated to the bishop, for the good of the poor, and for other purposes, as before mentioned;

72 Or they are to receive a just remuneration for all their services, either a stewardship or otherwise, as may be thought best or decided by the counselors and bishop.

73 And the bishop, also, shall receive his support, or a just remuneration for all his services in the church.

may be financially independent. The living allowance is uniform for all General Authorities. None of the funds for this living allowance come from the tithing of Church members, but instead from proceeds of the Church's financial investments" ("Do General Authorities Get Paid?"). ⊕

Doctrine and Covenants 42:74–93. Laws Governing Fornication, Adultery, Killing, Stealing, and Confession of Sins Are Set Forth

What is the difference between fornication and adultery? (42:74) "The First Presidency has declared: 'The Lord has drawn no essential distinctions between fornication, adultery, and harlotry or prostitution' ([in Conference Report], Oct. 1942, 11). Therefore, the distinction made in verses 74 and 75 is not between fornication and adultery but rather between those who are personally guilty or innocent of the offense. Verses 76 and 77 suggest that sexual immorality is a more serious transgression for married [adultery] than for single individuals [fornication]; a married person is not only committing the immoral act, but is also breaking the covenant of marriage" (Cowan and Mancill, *A to Z of the Doctrine and Covenants*, 66).

Why would those guilty of adultery need to be cast out? (42:75–77) "Reference [in these verses] is to individuals who leave their husbands or wives because they themselves are committing adultery and wish to live with the adulterous companion....

"Adulterers who abandon their wives for an adulterous alliance are not dealt with in the same manner as those who remain with their wives and family, repenting and seeking forgiveness as previously explained in this revelation. 'He that has committed adultery and repents with all his heart, and forsaketh it, and doeth it no more, thou shalt forgive' (D&C 42:25). In contrast, the man or woman who leaves a spouse to live with the companion in sin has placed himself or herself in a more serious situation—complicating the ability to repent 'with all his heart' and to forsake adultery. In such cases the Lord indicates that such individuals are to ... [lose] their membership in the Church of Jesus Christ" (McConkie and Ostler, *Revelations of the Restoration*, 321).

74 Behold, verily I say unto you, that whatever persons among you, having put away their companions for the cause of fornication, or in other words, if they shall testify before you in all lowliness of heart that this is the case, ye shall not cast them out from among you;

75 But if ye shall find that any persons have left their companions for the sake of adultery, and they themselves are the offenders, and their companions are living, they shall be cast out from among you.

76 And again, I say unto you, that ye shall be watchful and careful, with all inquiry, that ye receive none such among you if they are married;

77 And if they are not married, they shall repent of all their sins or ye shall not receive them.

78 And again, every person who belongeth to this church of Christ, shall observe to keep all the commandments and covenants of the church.

79 And it shall come to pass, that if any persons among you shall kill they shall be delivered up and dealt with according to the laws of the land; for remember that he hath no forgiveness; and it shall be proved according to the laws of the land.

What is the procedure for determining the membership status of adulterers? (42:80–83) "Adulterous men and women are to be tried by two or more elders of the Church, and the charges against them established by at least two credible witnesses who are not antagonistic toward the accused. After hearing the witnesses, the elders are to present the case to the Church to ensure any action taken is in accordance with the law set forth in section 42. Adulterous spouses are to be excommunicated. The Lord commands the elders to carefully interview candidates for baptism to prevent [unrepentant] adulterous men and women from being baptized. Fornicators who completely repent can join the Church" (Harper, *Making Sense of the Doctrine & Covenants*, 143).

How are grievances and offenses to be handled in the Church? (42:88–89) Following the precedent established in Matthew 18:15–18: "The first responsibility for correct moral behavior rests upon the individual members. They should privately attempt to settle their grievances (v. 88). The next step is to seek the help of the Church. Once more the Lord tells them to do so in privacy, before the elders, or leadership of the Church (v. 89)" (Nyman, *Doctrine and Covenants Commentary*, 1:365).

How should the Church treat those guilty of serious sin? (42:90–93) "Confession of sin does not imply unnecessary humiliation of him who confesses. The good name, reputation and feelings of our brethren and sisters, whether in fault or not, should be

80 And if any man or woman shall commit adultery, he or she shall be tried before two elders of the church, or more, and every word shall be established against him or her by two witnesses of the church, and not of the enemy; but if there are more than two witnesses it is better.

81 But he or she shall be condemned by the mouth of two witnesses; and the elders shall lay the case before the church, and the church shall lift up their hands against him or her, that they may be dealt with according to the law of God.

82 And if it can be, it is necessary that the bishop be present also.

83 And thus ye shall do in all cases which shall come before you.

84 And if a man or woman shall rob, he or she shall be delivered up unto the law of the land.

85 And if he or she shall steal, he or she shall be delivered up unto the law of the land.

86 And if he or she shall lie, he or she shall be delivered up unto the law of the land.

87 And if he or she do any manner of iniquity, he or she shall be delivered up unto the law, even that of God.

88 And if thy brother or sister offend thee, thou shalt take him or her between him or her and thee alone; and if he or she confess thou shalt be reconciled.

89 And if he or she confess not thou shalt deliver him or her up unto the church, not to the members, but to the elders. And it shall be done in a meeting, and that not before the world.

90 And if thy brother or sister offend many, he or she shall be chastened before many.

91 And if any one offend openly, he or she shall be rebuked openly, that he or she may be ashamed. And if he or she confess not, he or she shall be delivered up unto the law of God.

92 If any shall offend in secret, he or she shall be rebuked in secret, that he or she may have opportunity to confess in secret to him or her whom he or she has offended, and to God, that the church may not speak reproachfully of him or her.

93 And thus shall ye conduct in all things.

carefully protected. If the fault has been of a public nature the confession must be made publicly; if it be a secret or personal offense, there should be only a secret or personal confession. It is against the spirit of the Church to spread news of a brother's faults. Modern revelation is very pointed on this matter" (Widtsoe, *Program of the Church*, 171). ⊕

Introduction to Doctrine and Covenants 43

In February 1831, the Prophet Joseph Smith "dictated this revelation following his arrival in Kirtland, Ohio. It clarified [his] position as the only person authorized to 'receive commandments & Revelations' for the Church of Christ.

"Before [the Prophet's] arrival in Kirtland, the converts in the area were left for several months without any experienced leadership. . . . Concerned about the lack of leadership, [Joseph] sent John Whitmer to Ohio with copies of the revelations 'to comfort and strengthen my brethren in that land.' When [John] Whitmer arrived in mid-January, the conduct of the Ohio members surprised and concerned him. He wrote, 'The enemy of all righteous had . . . made them think that an angel of God appeared to them, and showed them writings on the outside cover of the Bible, . . . and many such foolish and vain things, others lost their strength, and some slid on the floor, and such like maneuvers, which proved greatly to th[e] injury of the cause.' . . .

"In February 1831, the same month that [Joseph Smith] and other members arrived from New York, a woman referred to as Mrs. 'Hubble' claimed to receive revelations, which she shared publicly with other members. As John Whitmer explained . . . : [she] 'professed to be a prophetess of the Lord and professed to have many revelations, and knew that the Book of Mormon was true; and that she should become a teacher in the Church of Christ'" (Joseph Smith Papers, Historical Introduction to "Revelation, February 1831–A [D&C 43]," 67).

"The issues surrounding [Hubble's] receipt of revelations were clearly much more significant than merely the need to clarify Joseph's role as prophet, something that previous revelation had already addressed (D&C 28:2). . . . The principal issue connected with [her] proposal was whether individuals could receive a revelation directing them to be ordained as teachers and granting them responsibility for revelations that would confer authority on them to provide direction in Church administration. . . .

"This revelation [clarifies that] ordinations or appointments to Church office (later characterized as 'setting apart') would not come through personal revelation but only through an ordained priesthood leader" (Staker, *Hearken, O Ye People*, 113).

SECTION 43

Revelation given through Joseph Smith the Prophet, at Kirtland, Ohio, in February 1831. At this time some members of the Church were disturbed by people making false claims as revelators. The Prophet inquired of the Lord and received this communication addressed to the elders of the Church. The first part deals with matters of Church polity; the latter part contains a warning that the elders are to give to the nations of the earth.

Doctrine and Covenants 43:1–7. Revelations and Commandments Come Only through the One Appointed

What do we understand about the order of prophetic succession as described in this passage? (43:3–4) "While at first thought this may seem strange—giving a fallen prophet the power to appoint (ordain) his successor—it really was a safeguard against false prophets. Under these guidelines, if a man claimed that Joseph Smith was a fallen prophet and that the Lord had selected him to take the Prophet's place, one would merely have to ask the claimant if he had been ordained to this calling by Joseph Smith. If he had not, then the claim could be quickly dismissed. Because the Lord knows the end from the beginning, this procedure was not likely ever intended to be used. But it did provide a stopgap to any pretenders to authority" (Brewster, *Prophets, Priesthood Keys, and Succession*, 32). ●

How can this revelation help us avoid being deceived? (43:6) President Joseph F. Smith declared: "We can accept nothing as authoritative but that which comes directly through the appointed channel, the constituted organizations of the priesthood, which is the channel that God has appointed through which to make known his mind and will to the world. . . . The moment that individuals look to any other source . . . they lose sight of the true order through

1 O hearken, ye elders of my church, and give ear to the words which I shall speak unto you.

2 For behold, verily, verily, I say unto you, that ye have received a commandment for a law unto my church, through him whom I have appointed unto you to receive commandments and revelations from my hand.

3 And this ye shall know assuredly—that there is none other appointed unto you to receive commandments and revelations until he be taken, if he abide in me.

4 But verily, verily, I say unto you, that none else shall be appointed unto this gift except it be through him; for if it be taken from him he shall not have power except to appoint another in his stead.

5 And this shall be a law unto you, that ye receive not the teachings of any that shall come before you as revelations or commandments;

6 And this I give unto you that you may not be deceived, that you may know they are not of me.

7 For verily I say unto you, that he that is ordained of me shall come in at the gate and be ordained as I have told you before, to teach those revelations which you have received and shall receive through him whom I have appointed.

Beware of Those Who Claim Special Authority or Gifts (Doctrine and Covenants 43:2–7)

President James E. Faust cautioned the Saints: "From the beginning some from both inside and outside of the Church have sought to persuade members of the Church against following the inspired declarations of those who hold the keys of the kingdom of God on earth. Some of those seeking to mislead have done so claiming special endowments of intelligence or inspiration beyond the established order of the Church. As a warning against those so claiming special authority, the Lord made it clear 'that it shall not be given to any one to preach my gospel, or to build up my church, except he be ordained by some one who has authority, and it is known to the church that he has authority and has been regularly ordained by the heads of the church' [D&C 42:11] . . .

"To validate those who have authority, the Lord also said, 'All things shall be done by common consent in the church, by much prayer and faith' [D&C 26:2]. Yet he also said 'that every man might speak in the name of God' [D&C 1:20]. How can this be? . . . Members, men and women, may receive inspiration by the gift of the Holy Ghost for their personal lives and for their areas of responsibility.

"Only the prophet and President, and no one else, can use *all* of the keys of the kingdom of God on earth. . . . [The President] and his counselors and the Quorum of the Twelve Apostles have delegated specific authority and

which the blessings of the Priesthood are to be enjoyed; they step outside of the pale of the kingdom of God, and are on dangerous ground. Whenever you see a man rise up claiming to have received direct revelation from the Lord to the Church, independent of the order and channel of the priesthood, you may set him down as an imposter" (*Gospel Doctrine*, 42).

How can the Saints recognize someone who has "come in at the gate"? (43:6–7) "Any question about who the Lord has chosen to lead His people has been clearly answered in scripture. The Savior taught:

"'He that entereth not by the door into the sheepfold, but climbeth up some other way, the same is a thief and a robber.

"'But he that entereth in by the door is the shepherd of the sheep' (John 10:1–2).

"Church members can be confident that no leader will rise up through unusual circumstances or by secret ordination, for the Lord promised that priesthood leaders will 'be ordained by someone who has authority, and it is known to the church that he has authority and has been regularly ordained by the heads of the church' (D&C 42:11)" (*Doctrine and Covenants Student Manual* [2018], 245).

Doctrine and Covenants 43:8–14. The Saints Are Sanctified by Acting in All Holiness before the Lord

Why is it important to teach and to be taught about the Lord's law? (43:8) "By study of the principles of the Gospel, and by teaching each other, we learn how to act and how the Church should be governed. Every member of the Church should so live that by study, reflection, faith and prayer, and

8 And now, behold, I give unto you a commandment, that when ye are assembled together ye shall instruct and edify each other, that ye may know how to act and direct my church, how to act upon the points of my law and commandments, which I have given.

responsibility to other General Authorities and to local authorities and auxiliary leaders to direct the work in their own areas of responsibility. . . .

"The Prophet Joseph Smith stated that 'it is contrary to the economy of God for any member of the Church . . . to receive instruction for those in authority, higher than themselves' [Joseph Smith Papers, "Letter to John S. Carter, 13 April 1833," 30].

"In addition, some have claimed higher spiritual gifts or authority outside the established priesthood authority of the Church. They say that they believe in the principles and ordinances of the gospel and accept the President of the Church as the legal administrator thereof, but claim they have a higher order which the President does not have. This is often done to justify an activity which is not in accordance with the doctrines of the Church. There can be no higher order, however, because the President of the Church both holds and exercises all of the keys of the kingdom of God on earth. The Lord has said of the President of the Church 'that none else shall be appointed [to receive commandments and revelations] except it be through him' [D&C 43:4]" ("Prophetic Voice," *Ensign*, May 1996, 5, 6–7).

association with his fellow members in study, he may understand the order of the Church and how it is governed. Then, if we will be faithful to the principles of truth that have been given us for our guidance, we will be sanctified and will act in all holiness before the Lord.... We are informed if we follow an unrighteous course, the knowledge which we have shall be taken away" (Joseph Fielding Smith, *Church History and Modern Revelation*, 1:190). See also commentary in this volume on Doctrine and Covenants 11:21. ☉

Why do we bind ourselves to act in holiness? (43:9) Paul V. Johnson suggested one way we might bind ourselves to act in holiness: "In order for the messages of general conference to change our lives, we need to be willing to follow the counsel we hear. The Lord explained in a revelation to the Prophet Joseph Smith 'that when ye are assembled together ye shall instruct and edify each other, that ye may know ... how to act upon the points of my law and commandment' [D&C 43:8]. But knowing 'how to act' isn't enough. The Lord in the next verse said, 'Ye shall bind yourselves to act in all holiness before me' [D&C 43:9]. This willingness to take action on what we have learned opens the doors for marvelous blessings" ("Blessings of General Conference," *Ensign*, Nov. 2005, 52). ☉

Why were the Saints commanded to "uphold" Joseph Smith? (43:12–14) "As recorded in Doctrine and Covenants 43:12–14, the Lord told the Saints that they could sustain the Prophet Joseph Smith through faith and prayer and also by providing for the temporal needs of his family. The Prophet was devoting his full attention to the administrative and spiritual affairs of the Church. Providing material support to him would result in blessings for Church members, including doctrinal understanding gained from the inspired translation of the Bible" (*Doctrine and Covenants Student Manual* [2018], 247).

Doctrine and Covenants 43:15–22. Elders Are Sent Forth to Cry Repentance and Prepare Men for the Great Day of the Lord

What are some reasons the Lord commands His missionaries to teach and not be taught? (43:15–16) "We are the Restored Church of Jesus Christ, therefore, we are to teach the principles of the Restoration, not the learning of the world (v. 15). The Lord will teach us as we teach those to whom we are assigned, or sent. The degree to which we are taught

9 And thus ye shall become instructed in the law of my church, and be sanctified by that which ye have received, and ye shall bind yourselves to act in all holiness before me—

10 That inasmuch as ye do this, glory shall be added to the kingdom which ye have received. Inasmuch as ye do it not, it shall be taken, even that which ye have received.

11 Purge ye out the iniquity which is among you; sanctify yourselves before me;

12 And if ye desire the glories of the kingdom, appoint ye my servant Joseph Smith, Jun., and uphold him before me by the prayer of faith.

13 And again, I say unto you, that if ye desire the mysteries of the kingdom, provide for him food and raiment, and whatsoever thing he needeth to accomplish the work wherewith I have commanded him;

14 And if ye do it not he shall remain unto them that have received him, that I may reserve unto myself a pure people before me.

15 Again I say, hearken ye elders of my church, whom I have appointed: Ye are not sent forth to be taught, but to teach the children of men the things which I have put into your hands by the power of my Spirit;

16 And ye are to be taught from on high. Sanctify yourselves and ye shall be endowed with power, that ye may give even as I have spoken.

17 Hearken ye, for, behold, the great day of the Lord is nigh at hand.

18 For the day cometh that the Lord shall utter his voice out of heaven; the heavens shall shake and the earth shall tremble, and the trump of God shall sound both long and loud, and shall say to the sleeping nations: Ye saints arise and live; ye sinners stay and sleep until I shall call again.

19 Wherefore gird up your loins lest ye be found among the wicked.

20 Lift up your voices and spare not. Call upon the nations to repent, both old and young, both bond and free, saying: Prepare yourselves for the great day of the Lord;

21 For if I, who am a man, do lift up my voice and call upon you to repent, and ye hate me, what will ye say when the day cometh when the thunders shall utter their voices from the ends of the earth, speaking to the ears of all that live, saying—Repent, and prepare for the great day of the Lord?

is dependent upon our own spiritual preparation. If we make ourselves worthy, or sanctify ourselves, we will learn to recognize the Spirit and follow it. Wherefore, we can give what the Lord speaks to us (v. 16)" (Nyman, *Doctrine and Covenants Commentary*, 1:271). ⊕

What might be the challenge to sanctifying ourselves? (43:16) "Once we set our foot on the path to godliness and purity, we can't turn back without consequences. As we steadily, within the limits of our moral capacity, work here a little, there a little toward ever-increasing purity, what was once acceptable and appropriate to do may no longer feel or be acceptable and appropriate. We can't hit the 'pause' button and say, 'I want to indulge in what I used to indulge in,' and go on, business as usual. It doesn't work that way....

"If we're serious about sanctification, if we're serious about learning to draw upon the power of God, purity is key" (Dew, *God Wants a Powerful People*, 45, 46).

Why will saints arise but sinners stay asleep when the Lord calls? (43:18) "A certain order of resurrection will be followed where the righteous and just individuals will be resurrected prior to the wicked and selfish people on the earth.

"When the Lord himself was resurrected on earth, he ushered in what is called the 'morning' of the first resurrection as a part of the resurrection of the just [see Matt. 27:52–53]....

"The 'afternoon' or 'evening' of the first resurrection will ensue, bringing forth for the first time the dead who lived an honorable earthly or terrestrial law....

"At the end of the Millennium, the Lord will finally call forth the wicked in the second and last resurrection, or 'the resurrection of the unjust'" (Victor L. Ludlow, *Principles and Practices*, 236, 237).

Who is the "man" speaking in this passage? (43:20–21) "Although Christ, like his Father, is an exalted Man, the colon after the word *saying* in verse 20 indicates that the missionaries of the Church are the speakers here. In essence, missionaries say to the world: 'If you hate and reject me, a mere mortal, for saying these things, what will you do when God himself says them to you with the voice of overwhelming natural disasters until you either repent or die?'" (Robinson and Garrett, *Commentary of the Doctrine and Covenants*, 2:40–41).

Doctrine and Covenants 43:23–28. The Lord Calls upon Men by His Own Voice and through the Forces of Nature

How might the forces of nature communicate God's message to His children? (43:25) In describing the last days, President Marion G. Romney said, "The Lord said that the conduct of the inhabitants of the earth, unless reformed, would bring disaster. . . .

"Calamities will come as a matter of cause and effect. They follow naturally 'and inevitably the sins of mankind . . .' ([Talmage, *Improvement Era,* Jun. 1921, 739]).

"And let it not be supposed, now, that the Lord takes pleasure in these calamities. He does not. He graphically foretells the inevitable consequences of men's sins for the purpose of inducing them to repent and thereby avoid the calamities. . . .

"As the Lord has repeatedly warned that breaking His commandments would bring on calamity, so has He promised that observance of His commandments would avert calamity and bring blessings" ("Silver Lining," *Ensign,* May 1977, 51, 53). See also commentary in this volume on Doctrine and Covenants 88:87–91. ●

What is the cup of the Lord's wrath? (43:26) The cup may symbolize God's judgment and punishment of the wicked (see Psalm 75:8; Isaiah 51:17; Mosiah 3:24–26). Joseph Fielding McConkie and Donald Parry note: "Every man chooses whether to drink from the 'cup of the Lord' or from the 'cup of devils' [see 1 Corinthians 10:21]. . . .

"However, 'when the cup of their iniquity is full' (D&C 101:11) with their transgressions (D&C 103:3), then the Lord will share of his cup, which is the cup of 'fury' (2 Ne. 8:17, 22), 'wrath' (Mosiah 3:26), and divine 'indignation' (D&C 29:17; Rev. 14:10). These are they who have 'drunk damnation to their own souls'

22 Yea, and again, when the lightnings shall streak forth from the east unto the west, and shall utter forth their voices unto all that live, and make the ears of all tingle that hear, saying these words—Repent ye, for the great day of the Lord is come?

23 And again, the Lord shall utter his voice out of heaven, saying: Hearken, O ye nations of the earth, and hear the words of that God who made you.

24 O, ye nations of the earth, how often would I have gathered you together as a hen gathereth her chickens under her wings, but ye would not!

25 How oft have I called upon you by the mouth of my servants, and by the ministering of angels, and by mine own voice, and by the voice of thunderings, and by the voice of lightnings, and by the voice of tempests, and by the voice of earthquakes, and great hailstorms, and by the voice of famines and pestilences of every kind, and by the great sound of a trump, and by the voice of judgment, and by the voice of mercy all the day long, and by the voice of glory and honor and the riches of eternal life, and would have saved you with an everlasting salvation, but ye would not!

26 Behold, the day has come, when the cup of the wrath of mine indignation is full.

27 Behold, verily I say unto you, that these are the words of the Lord your God.

28 Wherefore, labor ye, labor ye in my vineyard for the last time—for the last time call upon the inhabitants of the earth.

29 For in mine own due time will I come upon the earth in judgment, and my people shall be redeemed and shall reign with me on earth.

30 For the great Millennium, of which I have spoken by the mouth of my servants, shall come.

31 For Satan shall be bound, and when he is loosed again he shall only reign for a little season, and then cometh the end of the earth.

(Mosiah 3:25), and 'the portion of their cup' will be 'snares, fire and brimstone, and an horrible tempest,' and the sword (Ps. 11:6; Jer. 25:15–28)" (*Guide to Scriptural Symbols*, 35).

Doctrine and Covenants 43:29–35. The Millennium and the Binding of Satan Will Come

What is the great Millennium? (43:30) "The thousand-year Millennium begins when Jesus Christ . . . returns to earth in power and glory. When the Lord of Hosts—literally, the Lord of armies—returns in glory, every corruptible thing will be destroyed (D&C 133:41, 49). Those who are of a celestial or a terrestrial state will abide the day; all else will be cleansed from the surface of the earth. . . .

"At the beginning of the Millennium, the earth and all things upon it will be quickened, made alive, and transfigured—lifted spiritually to a higher plane for a season. The earth will be transformed from a telestial to a terrestrial glory, to that paradisiacal condition of which the scriptures and the prophets speak, that glorious condition that prevailed in Eden before the Fall ([see] Articles of Faith 1:10)" (Millet, "Millennium," 425–26).

In what ways will Satan be bound during the Millennium? (43:31) After quoting D&C 43:31 and 88:110, Gerald N. Lund exclaimed: "This has to be one of the most profound of all the promises. Satan bound! The numberless minions who followed after him, bodied and unembodied, will no longer be able to go about doing what they have done for a thousand years. Think of the effect that will have on the whole world!

"Will this be a literal binding of Satan and his followers, as with chains? Nephi spoke of this and gave us a clear understanding that they will be bound in another way. After speaking of the time when the Lord's people would be blessed by the Holy One of Israel, Nephi goes on to say, 'And he [the Lord] gathereth his children from the four quarters of the earth; and he numbereth his sheep, and they know him; . . . and *because of the righteousness of his people, Satan has no power; wherefore, he cannot be loosed for the space of many years; for he hath no power over the hearts of the people*, for they dwell in righteousness, and the Holy One of Israel reigneth' (1 Nephi 22:25–26)" (*Second Coming of the Lord*, 378–79). See also commentary in this volume on Doctrine and Covenants 45:55.

What does "changed in the twinkling of an eye" mean? (43:32) "[This phrase] appears three times in the Doctrine and Covenants and has reference to the instantaneous change from life to death to resurrection that will occur to those who are righteous at the Lord's coming and to those who will live during the millennial period of earth's history ([D&C] 43:32; 63:51; 101:31). There will be no funerals and burials for these people, for their change to immortality will occur in no more time than it takes one to blink an eye. This phrase was used by the resurrected Lord when He spoke to the three Nephites who will remain on earth until His coming (3 Ne. 28:8), and Paul referred to it in his epistle to the Corinthians (1 Cor. 15:52)" (Brewster, *Doctrine & Covenants Encyclopedia* [2012], 606).

What are the "solemnities of eternity"? (43:34) "The word *solemnity* means something very serious or sublimely important. The Lord tells the members of the Church to let the serious things of eternity—their covenants and the great blessings that will be given the faithful—rest upon their minds. What changes could come into the lives of mortal men and women if they continually let the eternal perspective guide them!" (*Doctrine and Covenants Student Manual* [2001], 90).

32 And he that liveth in righteousness shall be changed in the twinkling of an eye, and the earth shall pass away so as by fire.

33 And the wicked shall go away into unquenchable fire, and their end no man knoweth on earth, nor ever shall know, until they come before me in judgment.

34 Hearken ye to these words. Behold, I am Jesus Christ, the Savior of the world. Treasure these things up in your hearts, and let the solemnities of eternity rest upon your minds.

35 Be sober. Keep all my commandments. Even so. Amen.

Introduction to Doctrine and Covenants 44

"Shortly after [Joseph] and Emma Smith relocated to Kirtland, Ohio, in early February 1831, . . . [Joseph] dictated the revelation . . . which commanded the elders to assemble together so that the Lord could 'pour out' his Spirit in preparation for more missionary work. . . . [The Prophet] wrote to his brother Hyrum shortly after the revelation was written and told him that 'the work is [breaking] forth on the right hand and on the left and there is a great call for Elders in this place.'

"The June conference [June 3–6, 1831] . . . [is] likely the meeting to which the elders were called to gather" (Joseph Smith Papers, Historical Introduction to "Revelation, February 1831–B [D&C 44]," 70).

The revelation recorded in Doctrine and Covenants 44 was "received at the Whitney home in Kirtland, Ohio. . . .

"Just days earlier, section 42, which was on the law of consecration, had been received. Implementing the plan would prove difficult because there were not enough Ohio Saints to consecrate sufficient land to support all of the new converts in addition to the members of the Church coming from the East to settle in the Kirtland area. . . . Section 44 commanded missionaries to 'go forth into the regions round about and preach' the gospel ([see v. 3]). Many converts were promised ([see v. 4]). Until there were enough members to implement the law of consecration, the Saints must not lose track of the poor and needy ([see vv. 4–6 and D&C 42:30])" (James W. McConkie, *Looking at the Doctrine and Covenants Again*, 254).

SECTION 44

Revelation given to Joseph Smith the Prophet and Sidney Rigdon, at Kirtland, Ohio, in the latter part of February 1831. In compliance with the requirement herein set forth, the Church appointed a conference to be held early in the month of June following.

1 Behold, thus saith the Lord unto you my servants, it is expedient in me that the elders of my church should be called together, from the east and from the west, and from the north and from the south, by letter or some other way.

2 And it shall come to pass, that inasmuch as they are faithful, and exercise faith in me, I will pour out my Spirit upon them in the day that they assemble themselves together.

3 And it shall come to pass that they shall go forth into the regions round about, and preach repentance unto the people.

Doctrine and Covenants 44:1–3. Elders Are to Assemble in Conference

How has the Lord's commandment to "assemble themselves together" continued to bless Church members today? (44:1–2) "Conferences have always been part of the true Church of Jesus Christ. . . .

"In conferences we can receive the word of the Lord meant just for us. . . .

"This is possible because the Holy Ghost carries the word of the Lord unto our hearts in terms we can understand. . . .

"What is *said* is not as important as what we *hear* and what we *feel*. That is why we make an effort to experience conference in a setting where the still, small voice of the Spirit can be clearly heard, felt, and understood. . . .

"Through conferences our faith is fortified and our testimonies deepened" (Hales, "General Conference," *Ensign*, Nov. 2013, 6).

How is the effort to "preach repentance" the same as sharing the gospel? (44:3) "The Lord has commanded His servants to cry repentance unto all people. The Master has restored His gospel to bring joy to His children, and repentance is a crucial component of that gospel. . . .

"To repent fully is to convert completely to the Lord Jesus Christ and His holy work. . . .

"Repentant converts find that the truths of the restored gospel govern their thoughts and deeds, shape their habits, and forge their character. They are more resilient and able to deny themselves of all ungodliness. . . .

"Repentance is the Lord's regimen for spiritual growth. . . . Brothers and sisters, that means conversion! Repentance is conversion! A repentant soul is a converted soul, and a converted soul is a repentant soul" (Nelson, "Repentance and Conversion," *Ensign*, May 2007, 102, 103–4).

Doctrine and Covenants 44:4–6. The Church Is to Organize according to the Laws of the Land and to Care for the Poor

Why was there a need to organize the Church according to the laws of man? (44:4–5) "When large numbers of Latter-day Saints gather, there is more protection for the Church from lawsuits and other kinds of legal persecution. President Joseph F. Smith indicated the reason for this concern: . . . 'The Lord commanded the people . . . that they should be organized under the laws of the land, so that they might not be helpless and dependent and without influence or power; but that by means of united effort and faith they should become a power for the accomplishment of righteousness in the earth' ([in Conference Report], Apr. 1900, 47). . . .

"When the Church goes into any land, country, or state, members obey the laws of the land and organize themselves as a recognized, legal entity" (Woodger, *Essential Doctrine and Covenants Companion*, 86–87). ⊕

Why are the Saints commanded to care for the poor and needy? (44:6) "The poor and the needy have nearly always been present. Regardless of cause, our Heavenly Father is concerned for them. They are all his children. He loves and cares for them. . . .

"Few, if any, of the Lord's instructions are stated more often, or given greater emphasis, than the commandment to care for the poor and the needy. Our dispensation is no exception" (Nelson, "In the Lord's Own Way," *Ensign*, May 1986, 25, 26).

"Members of the Church covenant to 'bear one another's burdens, . . . mourn with those that mourn . . . , and comfort those that stand in need of comfort' (Mosiah 18:8–9). Caring for those who have temporal needs is part of the work of salvation and exaltation. This responsibility applies to all members of the Church as they minister to one another" (*General Handbook* [2023], 22.0).

4 And many shall be converted, insomuch that ye shall obtain power to organize yourselves according to the laws of man;

5 That your enemies may not have power over you; that you may be preserved in all things; that you may be enabled to keep my laws; that every bond may be broken wherewith the enemy seeketh to destroy my people.

6 Behold, I say unto you, that ye must visit the poor and the needy and administer to their relief, that they may be kept until all things may be done according to my law which ye have received. Amen.

Joseph Smith "dictated this revelation . . . [as] a 'prophecy,' sometime around 7 March 1831 [at Kirtland, Ohio], during a period when, according to [Joseph Smith's] history, 'many false reports, lies, and foolish stories were published in the newspapers, and circulated in every direction, to prevent people from investigating the work, or embracing the faith.' [Joseph Smith's] history reported that the revelation was the 'joy of the saints who had to struggle against every thing that prejudice and wickedness could invent'" (Joseph Smith Papers, Historical Introduction to "Revelation, circa 7 March 1831 [D&C 45]," 71).

"In 1831, as now, the exact circumstances and details of the second coming of Christ generated a lot of specula-tion among the Saints—the type of speculation that is not particularly healthy. In Kirtland during this period, counterfeit spiritual phenomena and false spirits accompanied extreme doctrinal speculations about the Second Coming and were greatly troubling to the Church. Section 45 may have been given in part to answer some of the questions of the members and to quiet down the extreme speculations and doctrinal hysteria that some were indulging in" (Robinson and Garrett, *Commentary on the Doctrine and Covenants*, 2:48–49).

"Section 45 is an unusual revelation. It is a commentary on one of the most complicated and even contested passages of the Bible. That's not remarkable. There is no shortage of interpreters of Jesus's Olivet discourse. The remarkable thing is that the interpreter in section 45 is the Savior himself. This is the finest text in the world for understanding Matthew 24, Mark 13, and Luke 21. One could go to any number of commentaries on Matthew 24 and find all kinds of analysis. These would be helpful, perhaps, but section 45 is the only source on earth in which the Savior of the world interprets and applies his own Olivet discourse" (Harper, "Historical Context and Background of D&C 45").

"If we are to 'prepare for that which is to come' (D&C 1:12), we need to understand what is ahead of us. Perhaps no other scripture gives a more comprehensive outline of the latter days than does Doctrine and Covenants 45" (Cowan, *Answers to Your Questions*, 62).

SECTION 45

Revelation given through Joseph Smith the Prophet to the Church, at Kirtland, Ohio, March 7, 1831. Prefacing the record of this revelation, Joseph Smith's history states that "at this age of the Church . . . many false reports . . . and foolish stories, were published . . . and cir-culated, . . . to prevent people from investigating the work, or embracing the faith. . . . But to the joy of the Saints, . . . I received the following."

1 Hearken, O ye people of my church, to whom the kingdom has been given; hearken ye and give ear to him who laid the founda-tion of the earth, who made the heavens and all the hosts thereof, and by whom all things were made which live, and move, and have a being.

Doctrine and Covenants 45:1–5. Christ Is Our Advocate with the Father

Why might we be warned not to let death "overtake" us? (45:2) "In our contemporary success and sophistication we too may walk away from the vitally crucial bread of eternal life; we may actually *choose* to be spiritually malnourished, willfully indulging in a kind of spiritual anorexia. Like those childish Galileans of old, we may turn up our noses when divine sustenance is placed before us. Of course the tragedy then as now is that one day, as the Lord Himself has said, 'In an hour when ye think not the summer shall be past, and the harvest ended,' and we will find that our 'souls [are] not saved' (D&C 45:2)" (Holland, "He Hath Filled the Hungry with Good Things," *Ensign*, Nov. 1997, 65).

Why is Christ called our advocate with the Father? (45:3–5) "In Jesus Christ, 'we have an advocate with the Father.' After completing His atoning sacrifice, Jesus 'ascended into heaven . . . to claim of the Father his rights of mercy which he hath upon the children of men.' And, having claimed the rights of mercy, 'he advocateth the cause of the children of men' [Moroni 7:27, 28]. . . .

"Christ's advocacy is, at least in part, to remind us that He has paid for our sins and that no one is excluded from the reach of God's mercy. For those who believe in Jesus Christ, repent, are baptized, and endure to the end—a process that leads to reconciliation—the Savior forgives, heals, and advocates. He is our helper, consoler, and intercessor—attesting to and vouching for our reconciliation with God [see 1 John 2:1]" (Renlund, "Choose You This Day," *Ensign*, Nov. 2018, 104, 105). ⊕

Doctrine and Covenants 45:6–10. The Gospel Is a Messenger to Prepare the Way before the Lord

What is called "today" in this verse? (45:6) "The word *today*, when used in connection to the second coming of Jesus Christ, refers to the period between the present time and the second coming" (Daniel H. Ludlow, *Companion to Your Study*, 2:308).

What is significant about the title "Alpha and Omega"? (45:7) See commentary in this volume on Doctrine and Covenants 19:1 and 35:1.

2 And again I say, hearken unto my voice, lest death shall overtake you; in an hour when ye think not the summer shall be past, and the harvest ended, and your souls not saved.

3 Listen to him who is the advocate with the Father, who is pleading your cause before him—

4 Saying: Father, behold the sufferings and death of him who did no sin, in whom thou wast well pleased; behold the blood of thy Son which was shed, the blood of him whom thou gavest that thyself might be glorified;

5 Wherefore, Father, spare these my brethren that believe on my name, that they may come unto me and have everlasting life.

6 Hearken, O ye people of my church, and ye elders listen together, and hear my voice while it is called today, and harden not your hearts;

7 For verily I say unto you that I am Alpha and Omega, the beginning and the end, the light and the life of the world—a light that shineth in darkness and the darkness comprehendeth it not.

8 I came unto mine own, and mine own received me not; but unto as many as received me gave I power to do many miracles, and to become the sons of God; and even unto them that believed on my name gave I power to obtain eternal life.

9 And even so I have sent mine everlasting covenant into the world, to be a light to the world, and to be a standard for my people, and for the Gentiles to seek to it, and to be a messenger before my face to prepare the way before me.

10 Wherefore, come ye unto it, and with him that cometh I will reason as with men in days of old, and I will show unto you my strong reasoning.

11 Wherefore, hearken ye together and let me show unto you even my wisdom—the wisdom of him whom ye say is the God of Enoch, and his brethren,

12 Who were separated from the earth, and were received unto myself—a city reserved until a day of righteousness shall come—a day which was sought for by all holy men, and they found it not because of wickedness and abominations;

13 And confessed they were strangers and pilgrims on the earth;

14 But obtained a promise that they should find it and see it in their flesh.

15 Wherefore, hearken and I will reason with you, and I will speak unto you and prophesy, as unto men in days of old.

What is meant by "mine everlasting covenant"? (45:9) Marcus B. Nash, referring to the phrase "mine everlasting covenant," wrote: "This covenant, often referred to by the Lord as the 'new and everlasting covenant,' encompasses the fulness of the gospel of Jesus Christ, including all ordinances and covenants necessary for the salvation of mankind" ("New and Everlasting Covenant," *Ensign*, Dec. 2015, 42).

How are we to understand the word *standard* in this verse? (45:9) "A *standard* is a flag or ensign that serves as a rallying point around which people may gather. The scriptures define the *standard* as God's words (specifically, the Book of Mormon; 2 Ne. 29:2), the everlasting covenant (D&C 45:9), the great Zion of the last days (D&C 64:41–43), and the light of the righteous or the Church and its faithful members (D&C 115:3–5). Overall, the *standard* is the true gospel and church of Jesus Christ (Isa. 5:26; 11:10; 62:10; Zech. 9:16)" (Parry and Parry, *Understanding the Signs of the Times*, 64).

Doctrine and Covenants 45:11–15. Enoch and His Brethren Were Received by the Lord unto Himself

Why were Enoch's people "separated from the earth" or lifted up? (45:11–13) "These people had raised themselves to a higher order of living that was incompatible with the other residents of this world. In the words of President Joseph Fielding Smith, they 'were as pilgrims and strangers on the earth . . . due to the fact that they were living the celestial law in a telestial world.' ([*Church History and Modern Revelation*], 1:195)" (Brewster, *Behold, I Come Quickly*, 165–66).

What were these ancient Saints promised to find and see? (45:14) "God promised many ancient Saints, including Abraham, Isaac, and Jacob, that they and their children, if they were faithful, would inherit the millennial kingdom and that they would see it in their resurrected flesh at the second coming of Christ. All who have received the fulness of the gospel and its ordinances have received this same promise made to the patriarchs" (Robinson and Garrett, *Commentary on the Doctrine and Covenants*, 2:54).

Doctrine and Covenants 45:16–23. Christ Revealed Signs of His Coming as Given on the Mount of Olives

How does this section clarify the teachings of the Savior found in Matthew 24? (45:16) Doctrine and Covenants 45 "makes a clear division between those events that transpired in the days of the apostles and those that are still to take place in the future. Doctrine and Covenants 45:16–25 deals with events pertaining to the destruction of Jerusalem in A.D. 70 while verses 26–59 deal with events connected with the present and the future—from the 'times of the Gentiles' (the restoration of the gospel) until the glorious return of the Son of God, when he will declare to all the world, 'I am he who was lifted up. I am Jesus that was crucified' (D&C 45:52)" (Seely, "Olivet Discourse," 394).

Why might the separation of the body and the spirit be considered a "bondage"? (45:17) "Through His Resurrection, the Savior showed us that a physical, embodied existence is an integral part of the eternal being of God and His children. As the Lord revealed to Joseph Smith, 'The elements are eternal, and spirit and element, inseparably connected, receive a fulness of joy' (D&C 93:33). This inseparable connection fuses spirit and physical matter together so that they are one immortal, incorruptible, glorious, and perfect body—the only kind of body capable of receiving the fulness of joy that God possesses.

"By contrast, after having a physical body and then being separated from it to enter the spirit world, 'the dead [look] upon the . . . absence of their spirits from their bodies as a bondage' (D&C 138:50; see also D&C 45:17)" (Edwards, "Resurrection of Jesus Christ," *Ensign*, Apr. 2017, 29). See also commentary in this volume on Doctrine and Covenants 138:15–16, 18. ☉

What desolation or destruction came upon the Jews during the Savior's generation? (45:19) Wilford Woodruff detailed the fulfillment of Jesus's prophecies concerning the destruction of Jerusalem: "The city was soon surrounded by the Roman army . . . and a scene of calamity, judgement, and woe immediately overspread the inhabitants of that city, . . . such a calamity as never before rested upon the nation of Israel. Blood flowed through the streets; tens of thousands fell by the edge of the sword, and thousands by famine. . . . The Jews were crucified in such numbers . . . that they could find no more wood for crosses, or room for their bodies; and while despair was in every face, and every heart sinking while

16 And I will show it plainly as I showed it unto my disciples as I stood before them in the flesh, and spake unto them, saying: As ye have asked of me concerning the signs of my coming, in the day when I shall come in my glory in the clouds of heaven, to fulfil the promises that I have made unto your fathers,

17 For as ye have looked upon the long absence of your spirits from your bodies to be a bondage, I will show unto you how the day of redemption shall come, and also the restoration of the scattered Israel.

18 And now ye behold this temple which is in Jerusalem, which ye call the house of God, and your enemies say that this house shall never fall.

19 But, verily I say unto you, that desolation shall come upon this generation as a thief in the night, and this people shall be destroyed and scattered among all nations.

20 And this temple which ye now see shall be thrown down that there shall not be left one stone upon another.

21 And it shall come to pass, that this generation of Jews shall not pass away until every desolation which I have told you concerning them shall come to pass.

22 Ye say that ye know that the end of the world cometh; ye say also that ye know that the heavens and the earth shall pass away;

23 And in this ye say truly, for so it is; but these things which I have told you shall not pass away until all shall be fulfilled.

24 And this I have told you concerning Jerusalem; and when that day shall come, shall a remnant be scattered among all nations;

25 But they shall be gathered again; but they shall remain until the times of the Gentiles be fulfilled.

suffering under the chastening hand of God" (Wilford Woodruff Papers, Journal, Sep. 10, 1843).

How was this prophecy pertaining to the stones of the temple fulfilled? (45:20) "In literal fulfillment of the Lord's prophecy, Roman soldiers under the command of Titus dismantled the buildings associated with the temple, stone by stone, following the siege of Jerusalem in A.D. 70. The temple was left a heap of rubble. During the late twentieth century archaeologists uncovered the ancient road that ran at the base of the retaining wall built by Herod when he extended the original platform of the temples built under the direction of Solomon and Zerubbabel. They discovered that the massive stones of the temple had been pushed over the precipice of the temple mount down onto the road below. Huge ashlars, or hand-dressed stones, were broken on the road and revealed in the excavations. Today an archaeological garden stands as a witness to the Savior's words" (McConkie and Ostler, *Revelations of the Restoration*, 342–43).

How is the phrase "end of the world" to be understood in this verse? (45:22) "The 'end of the world' (D&C 19:3; 45:22; 132:49) is defined in Joseph Smith's inspired rendition of the twenty-fourth chapter of Matthew. . . . The Savior's disciples asked, 'What is the sign of thy coming, and of the end of the world, or *the destruction of the wicked,* which is the end of the world?' (JS—M 1:4; [emphasis] added). The 'end of the world' (or the end of the wicked) will actually occur in two phases: the first phase will be prior to the Second Coming as the earth is cleansed of all but celestial and terrestrial beings; and the second and final phase will be at the end of the Millennium, when Satan's hosts of hell will be defeated and banished to outer darkness" (Brewster, *Doctrine & Covenants Encyclopedia* [2012], 155).

Doctrine and Covenants 45:24–38. The Gospel Will Be Restored, the Times of the Gentiles Will Be Fulfilled, and a Desolating Sickness Will Cover the Land

What is meant by the phrase "the times of the Gentiles"? (45:25–30) "The times of the Gentiles is that time or era, that expanse of time or years, during which the gospel goes to the Gentiles on a preferential basis. In Jesus' day the gospel was offered first to his Jewish kinsmen; only later was it preached in Gentile ears. In our day it has been restored to the

Gentiles, meaning to non-Jewish people—people, however, who are of the house of Israel. It is now being taught on a preferential basis to Gentiles....

"The restoration of the gospel foreshadows the end of the Gentile era.... That the Jews, a few of them, are now beginning to believe the restored gospel and are returning to their true Messiah is well known. The times of the Gentiles shall soon be fulfilled" (Bruce R. McConkie, *Mortal Messiah*, 1:97). ✚

What are some signs that will appear in the last days? (45:26–27) "Admittedly, the Lord has spoken of our day in sobering terms. He warned that in our day 'men's hearts [would fail] them' [Luke 21:26] and that even the very elect would be at risk of being deceived [see Matthew 24:24; Joseph Smith—Matthew 1:22]. He told the Prophet Joseph Smith that 'peace [would] be taken from the earth' [D&C 1:35] and calamities would befall mankind [see D&C 1:17]" (Nelson, "Embrace the Future with Faith," *Ensign*, Nov. 2020, 73–74). See commentary in this volume on Doctrine and Covenants 29:14–21.

What can cause love to diminish or "wax cold"? (45:27) "As we hear of wars and rumors of war, as natural disasters increase, as old and new diseases spread, as iniquity abounds, even Saints are prone to give into the inclinations of the natural man and hunker down and avoid the battle against evil that we came to this earth to fight. As long as one's relatives, friends, and neighbors are safe and sound, it's tempting to write off 'the world' and sit back and hope that the Lord comes soon.... If our bowels are not filled with charity for the whole world, we have

26 And in that day shall be heard of wars and rumors of wars, and the whole earth shall be in commotion, and men's hearts shall fail them, and they shall say that Christ delayeth his coming until the end of the earth.

27 And the love of men shall wax cold, and iniquity shall abound.

"Men's Hearts Shall Fail Them" (Doctrine and Covenants 45:26)

President Jeffrey R. Holland declared: "Prophecies regarding the last days often refer to large-scale calamities such as earthquakes or famines or floods. These in turn may be linked to widespread economic or political upheavals of one kind or another.

"But there is one kind of latter-day destruction that has always sounded to me more personal than public, more individual than collective—a warning, perhaps more applicable inside the Church than outside it. The Savior warned that in the last days even those of the covenant, the very elect, could be deceived by the enemy of truth. If we think of this as a form of spiritual destruction, it may cast light on another latter-day prophecy. Think of the heart as the figurative center of our faith, the poetic location of our loyalties and our values; then consider Jesus's declaration that in the last days 'men's hearts [shall fail] them' [Luke 21:26].

"The encouraging thing, of course, is that our Father in Heaven knows all of these latter-day dangers, these troubles of the heart and soul, and has given counsel and protections regarding them....

"God always provides safety for the soul, and with the Book of Mormon, He has again done that in our time. Remember this declaration by Jesus Himself: 'Whoso treasureth up my word, shall not be deceived' [Joseph Smith—Matthew 1:37]—and in the last days neither your heart nor your faith will fail you" ("Safety for the Soul," *Ensign*, Nov. 2009, 88, 90).

not understood the parable of the good Samaritan. If we shun the fight, our lamps are likely to run out of oil, and before we know it, we may find the door shut before us and hear the Lord say to our request to enter, 'I know you not' (Matthew 25:12).

"No one can be faulted for hoping that the coming of the Lord is nigh. What we must guard against is the tendency to assume that it is too late for us to make a difference. We must pray for love to replace fear, for 'there is no fear in love; but perfect love casteth out fear' (1 John 4:18)" (Belnap, "Wars, Rumors of Wars, and Wise and Faithful Servants," 2).

When did this prophesied light break forth? (45:28–29) President Russell M. Nelson testified: "Wisdom is to be found in pure intelligence, in that divine light which can guide people in all countries, all climes, and all continents. The Lord promised that 'a light shall break forth among them that sit in darkness, and it shall be the fulness of my gospel' (D&C 45:28). . . . In bright contrast to such bitter chaos [as will be seen in the last days], the light of the gospel of Jesus Christ beams as the hope of the world. Missionaries and members courageously proclaim its brilliance" ("Where Is Wisdom?" *Ensign*, Nov. 1992, 8). ⊕

28 And when the times of the Gentiles is come in, a light shall break forth among them that sit in darkness, and it shall be the fulness of my gospel;

29 But they receive it not; for they perceive not the light, and they turn their hearts from me because of the precepts of men.

30 And in that generation shall the times of the Gentiles be fulfilled.

31 And there shall be men standing in that generation, that shall not pass until they shall see an overflowing scourge; for a desolating sickness shall cover the land.

32 But my disciples shall stand in holy places, and shall not be moved; but among the wicked, men shall lift up their voices and curse God and die.

33 And there shall be earthquakes also in divers places, and many desolations; yet men will harden their hearts against me, and they will take up the sword, one against another, and they will kill one another.

34 And now, when I the Lord had spoken these words unto my disciples, they were troubled.

How can disciples of Christ stand in holy places? (45:32) "Let me suggest that holding fast to the word of God entails (1) remembering, honoring, and strengthening the personal connection we have with the Savior and His Father through the covenants and ordinances of the restored gospel and (2) prayerfully, earnestly, and consistently using the holy scriptures and the teachings of living prophets and apostles as sure sources of revealed truth. As we are bound and 'hold fast' to the Lord and are transformed by living His doctrine [see 2 Corinthians 5:17; Mosiah 3:19; 5:2; 27:25–26; Alma 5:49; Moroni 10:32], I promise that individually and collectively we will be blessed to 'stand in holy places, and shall not be moved' [D&C 45:32]" (Bednar, "But We Heeded Them Not," *Liahona*, May 2022, 16). See also commentary in this volume on Doctrine and Covenants 115:7–8. ⊕

How can we not be troubled with all the commotion around us? (45:35) President Dallin H. Oaks noted: "We give thanks for the revealed truths that provide a standard against which to measure all things. . . . Those who view every calamity and measure every new assertion or discovery against the standard of revealed truth need not be 'tossed to and fro' but can be steady and at peace. God is in His heavens, and His promises are sure. 'Be not troubled,' He has said to us concerning the destructions that will precede the end of the world, 'for, when all these things shall come to pass, ye may know that the promises which have been made unto you shall be fulfilled' (D&C 45:35). What an anchor to the soul in these troubled times!" ("Give Thanks in All Things," *Ensign*, May 2003, 95). ●

Why does the Lord use summer as a sign of the times? (45:37–38) "Summer has been given as a symbol in the parable of the fig tree for the time of the second coming of Jesus Christ: When the fig tree puts forth its leaves, then you know that summer is nigh. In this sense, the term *summer is nigh* refers to the closeness of the second coming of Jesus Christ. The word *summer* is also used as a symbol of the time of harvest, a time when work can be done, or as a symbol of this mortal earthly probation. The Lord warns us to work while we can; otherwise 'the summer shall be past, and the harvest ended, and your souls not saved' ([D&C] 45:2)" (Daniel H. Ludlow, *Companion to Your Study*, 2:286–87).

Doctrine and Covenants 45:39–47. Signs, Wonders, and the Resurrection Are to Attend the Second Coming

Why is it important to look for the signs of the Lord's coming? (45:39–42) The Prophet Joseph Smith cautioned: "I will prophesy that the signs of the coming of the Son of Man are already commenced. One pestilence will desolate after another. We shall soon have war and bloodshed, the moon will be turned to blood. I testify of these things, and that the coming of the Son of Man is nigh, even at your very doors. If our souls and our bodies are not looking forth for the coming of the Son of Man, and after we are dead if we are not looking forth, we shall be among those who are calling for the rocks to fall upon us" (Joseph Smith Papers, "Discourse, between circa 26 June and circa 4 August 1839–A, as Reported by William Clayton," 19).

35 And I said unto them: Be not troubled, for, when all these things shall come to pass, ye may know that the promises which have been made unto you shall be fulfilled.

36 And when the light shall begin to break forth, it shall be with them like unto a parable which I will show you—

37 Ye look and behold the fig trees, and ye see them with your eyes, and ye say when they begin to shoot forth, and their leaves are yet tender, that summer is now nigh at hand;

38 Even so it shall be in that day when they shall see all these things, then shall they know that the hour is nigh.

39 And it shall come to pass that he that feareth me shall be looking forth for the great day of the Lord to come, even for the signs of the coming of the Son of Man.

40 And they shall see signs and wonders, for they shall be shown forth in the heavens above, and in the earth beneath.

41 And they shall behold blood, and fire, and vapors of smoke.

42 And before the day of the Lord shall come, the sun shall be darkened, and the moon be turned into blood, and the stars fall from heaven.

43 And the remnant shall be gathered unto this place;

44 And then they shall look for me, and, behold, I will come; and they shall see me in the clouds of heaven, clothed with power and great glory; with all the holy angels; and he that watches not for me shall be cut off.

45 But before the arm of the Lord shall fall, an angel shall sound his trump, and the saints that have slept shall come forth to meet me in the cloud.

46 Wherefore, if ye have slept in peace blessed are you; for as you now behold me and know that I am, even so shall ye come unto me and your souls shall live, and your redemption shall be perfected; and the saints shall come forth from the four quarters of the earth.

47 Then shall the arm of the Lord fall upon the nations.

What is the "day of the Lord" that will come? (45:42) See commentary in this volume on Doctrine and Covenants 29:14.

Where is "this place" to which the remnant is to gather? (45:43) "Part of Doctrine and Covenants 45 is a review of the prophecy Christ made to his disciples on the Mount of Olives (compare the latter part of verse 16 with Matthew 24:1–3). Hence, 'this place' refers to the Holy Land in the Eastern Hemisphere" (Cowan, *Answers to Your Questions*, 62).

The Savior's Appearances at His Second Coming (Doctrine and Covenants 45:44–75)

"We learn from this revelation that the Savior's second coming includes at least three general appearances:

"1. *To the saints* (see D&C 45:45–46, 56–57) . . .

"Referring to the saints receiving the Savior, it should be noted that these are people who have made and kept covenants with the Lord. They are referred to as 'children of light' (D&C 106:5). These are they who have heeded the counsel of the Lord to:

"'Gird up your loins and be watchful and be sober, looking forth for the coming of the Son of Man, for he cometh in an hour you think not' (D&C 61:38).

"These saints received the truth, received the Holy Ghost, and were not deceived, thus fulfilling the parable concerning the five wise virgins (see D&C 45:56–57).

"2. *To the Jews at Jerusalem* (see D&C 45:47–53)

"The Lord's appearance to the Jews will take place at a time when they will be engaged in a battle for their survival. When the Savior intervenes in their behalf, He will be recognized and acknowledged as the Messiah and Savior of the world.

"3. *To the world* (see D&C 45:74–75)

"The Lord's appearance to the world will not be to a select group of people. This appearance will be of such magnitude that the wicked will be destroyed and the remaining righteous will see, know, and dwell with Him upon the earth for a millennial period" (Otten and Caldwell, *Sacred Truths*, 1:219–20).

Doctrine and Covenants 45:48–53. Christ Will Stand on the Mount of Olives, and the Jews Will See the Wounds in His Hands and Feet

What is the mount the Lord will set His foot upon? (45:48) "Eventually the Lord will return to the land which He made holy. In triumph, He will come again to Jerusalem. In flaming royal robes of red, to symbolize His blood, which oozed from every pore, He shall return to the holy city. . . .

"When Christ comes again, the Mount of Olives to which He will return 'shall cleave in twain' (Doctrine and Covenants 45:48). Then He will utter these words: 'I was wounded in the house of my friends. I am he who was lifted up. I am Jesus that was crucified. I am the Son of God' (Doctrine and Covenants 45:52).

"Our sacred charge is to help prepare the world for that Second Coming of the Lord" (Nelson, *Teachings*, 350).

What does it mean to "watch for iniquity"? (45:50) "This description refers to those who pursue evil and to those who find fault with others, whether justified or unjustified" (Parry, Parry, and Peterson, *Understanding Isaiah*, 273).

Why will the Savior appear to the Jews and show the wounds in His hands? (45:51–53) "The second coming of the Son of Man will be a day of Jewish glory and triumph. As they were singled out to see his face and hear his voice when he came to atone for the sins of the world, so—after long centuries of being cursed and scourged and slain—they will be chosen again to see the wounds in his flesh, to accept the salvation of the cross, and to find at long last their Promised Messiah. They will yet play the role assigned them for that glorious day when he comes to complete the salvation of man and to crown his work before delivering the kingdom spotless to his Father" (Bruce R. McConkie, *Millennial Messiah*, 220–21). ●

How will the Jews be affected when they come to recognize their Messiah? (45:53) "With words that can only evoke sorrow and compassion in the hearts of readers, the Lord foretold the reaction of those of Judah who would witness their Master's return: 'And then . . . shall they lament because they persecuted their king' (D&C 45:53). With this event the great millennial day of Jewish conversion and gathering will begin. Truly, those who had been first to hear their Savior speak in mortality—but rejected his

48 And then shall the Lord set his foot upon this mount, and it shall cleave in twain, and the earth shall tremble, and reel to and fro, and the heavens also shall shake.

49 And the Lord shall utter his voice, and all the ends of the earth shall hear it; and the nations of the earth shall mourn, and they that have laughed shall see their folly.

50 And calamity shall cover the mocker, and the scorner shall be consumed; and they that have watched for iniquity shall be hewn down and cast into the fire.

51 And then shall the Jews look upon me and say: What are these wounds in thine hands and in thy feet?

52 Then shall they know that I am the Lord; for I will say unto them: These wounds are the wounds with which I was wounded in the house of my friends. I am he who was lifted up. I am Jesus that was crucified. I am the Son of God.

53 And then shall they weep because of their iniquities; then shall they lament because they persecuted their king.

pleas—will be the last to accept his words in the final dispensation. But the end of the day of the Gentile will herald the dawn of a different day—the day of the Jew" (Jackson, "Signs of the Times," 196).

Doctrine and Covenants 45:54–59. The Lord Will Reign during the Millennium

54 And then shall the heathen nations be redeemed, and they that knew no law shall have part in the first resurrection; and it shall be tolerable for them.

Who are the heathen nations and when will they be redeemed? (45:54) "In the scriptures the phrase 'heathen nations' generally refers to those nations or peoples who do not believe in the God of Israel and are not part of the gospel covenant. . . . In modern revelation the term is used for those, regardless of lineage or religious tradition, who have not had the opportunity to hear and embrace the gospel of Jesus Christ (D&C 45:54; 75:22; 90:7–11). Many passages of scripture declare that the heathens will eventually be given a full opportunity to repent of their ways, turn to the true God, accept the gospel covenant, and be saved in the kingdom of God (Ezekiel 39:21; Zechariah 9:10; Malachi 1:11; Galatians 3:8; 2 Nephi 26:33; D&C 45:54)" (Top, "Heathen Nations," 299).

55 And Satan shall be bound, that he shall have no place in the hearts of the children of men.

How will Satan be bound? (45:55) "How, then, will Satan be bound during the Millennium? It will be by the righteousness of the people. Thus Nephi says: 'The time cometh speedily that Satan shall have no more power over the hearts of the children of men; for the day soon cometh that all the proud and they who do wickedly shall be as stubble; and the day cometh that they must be burned.' The destruction of the wicked sets the stage for millennial righteousness. . . .

"It is, then, in this blessed millennial setting that the great proclamation about the binding of Satan is made. 'And because of the righteousness of his people, Satan has no power; wherefore, he cannot be loosed for the space of many years; for he hath no power over the hearts of the people, for they dwell in righteousness, and the Holy One of Israel reigneth' (1 Ne. 22:15, 24–26). Thus Satan is bound because he 'shall have power over the hearts of the children of men no more, for a long time' (2 Ne. 30:18). Thus the probationary nature of man's second estate is preserved even during the Millennium. It is not that men cannot sin, for the power is in them to do so—they have their agency—but it is that they do not sin because Satan is subject to them, and they are not enticed by his evil whisperings" (Bruce R. McConkie, *Millennial Messiah*, 668, 669). See also commentary in this volume on Doctrine and Covenants 43:31.

What can we learn in our day from the parable of the ten virgins? (45:56–59) President Dallin H. Oaks taught: "All ten were invited to the wedding feast, but only half of them were prepared with oil in their lamps when the bridegroom came. The five who were prepared went into the marriage feast, and the door was shut. The five who had delayed their preparations came late. The door had been closed, and the Lord denied them entrance....

"The arithmetic of this parable is chilling. The ten virgins obviously represent members of Christ's Church, for all were invited to the wedding feast and all knew what was required to be admitted when the bridegroom came. But only half were ready when he came" ("Preparation for the Second Coming," *Ensign*, May 2004, 8). ○

What blessings will come to children who grow up during the Millennium? (45:58–59) "During this glorious time [the Millennium], the earth will be given to the righteous 'for an inheritance; and they shall multiply and wax strong, and their children shall grow up without sin unto salvation' (D&C 45:58).

"Some may ask, Won't the devil be loosed at the end of the Millennium? Could not those who left mortality without trial be tested during that 'little season'? No, for these children will already have come forth from the grave as resurrected and immortal beings" (Millet, *Precept upon Precept*, 264–65).

Doctrine and Covenants 45:60–62. The Prophet Is Instructed to Begin the Translation of the New Testament, through Which Important Information Will Be Made Known

To which chapter of scripture is the Lord referring? (45:60–61) "The Savior's review of his Mount of Olives prophecy concluded with verse 59 of Doctrine and Covenants 45. Hence 'this chapter' likely refers to Matthew 24. The manuscript of the Joseph Smith Translation indicates that the Prophet began working on the book of Matthew beginning with chapter 1 the day after Doctrine and Covenants 45 was received in March 1831. He probably completed his work on Matthew 24 before leaving for Missouri in mid-June the same year" (Cowan, *Answers to Your Questions*, 62). ○

56 And at that day, when I shall come in my glory, shall the parable be fulfilled which I spake concerning the ten virgins.

57 For they that are wise and have received the truth, and have taken the Holy Spirit for their guide, and have not been deceived—verily I say unto you, they shall not be hewn down and cast into the fire, but shall abide the day.

58 And the earth shall be given unto them for an inheritance; and they shall multiply and wax strong, and their children shall grow up without sin unto salvation.

59 For the Lord shall be in their midst, and his glory shall be upon them, and he will be their king and their lawgiver.

60 And now, behold, I say unto you, it shall not be given unto you to know any further concerning this chapter, until the New Testament be translated, and in it all these things shall be made known;

61 Wherefore I give unto you that ye may now translate it, that ye may be prepared for the things to come.

62 For verily I say unto you, that great things await you;

Why might the Prophet have been commanded to translate the New Testament at this time? (45:60–61) David R. Seely has suggested: "On 7 March 1831, when the Saints were facing many trials and much persecution, the Lord gave to Joseph Smith the revelation that is now section 45 in the Doctrine and Covenants. In this section, he said to the Prophet that he would 'speak unto you and prophesy' as he had to his disciples in days of old when they 'asked of me concerning the signs of my coming . . . ' (D&C 45:15, 16). In verses 16 to 59, the Lord cites and elaborates on many passages from Matthew 24. Then toward the end of the revelation, he says, . . . 'I give unto you that ye may now translate it, that ye may be prepared for the things to come' ([D&C 45:61])" ("Joseph Smith Translation," *Ensign*, Aug. 1997, 15).

Doctrine and Covenants 45:63–75. The Saints Are Commanded to Gather and Build the New Jerusalem, to Which People from All Nations Will Come

What could have been the war in "your own lands"? (45:63) "The Lord knows the hearts of men and knew beforehand the eventual carnage that would result due to the Civil War. Two years following this revelation, the Prophet Joseph Smith stated, 'I am prepared to say by the authority of Jesus Christ, that not many years shall pass away before the United States shall present such a scene of bloodshed as has not a parallel in the history of our nation' [Joseph Smith Papers, "History, 1838–1856, volume A-1," 262]" (McConkie and Ostler, *Revelations of the Restoration*, 357). The Prophet also received a revelation in 1832 that "the commencement of the difficulties which will cause much bloodshed previous to the coming of the Son of Man will be in South Carolina. It may probably arise through the slave question" (D&C 130:12–13).

How are the City of Zion and the New Jerusalem similar? (45:65–67) "According to President Joseph Fielding Smith, the terms *City of Zion* and *New Jerusalem* 'have reference to the same sanctified place' ([*Doctrines of Salvation*], 3:67). This will be a millennial city 'from whence the law and the word of the Lord shall go forth to all people' ([*Doctrines of Salvation*], 3:68–69). It will be one of two world capitals, the other being the old Jerusalem (Isa. 2:2–5; Micah 4:1–7; 2 Ne. 12:2–5). The inhabitants of these holy cities will be 'they whose garments are white through the blood of the Lamb' (Ether 13:10–11)" (Brewster, *Doctrine & Covenants Encyclopedia* [2012], 388).

63 Ye hear of wars in foreign lands; but, behold, I say unto you, they are nigh, even at your doors, and not many years hence ye shall hear of wars in your own lands.

64 Wherefore I, the Lord, have said, gather ye out from the eastern lands, assemble ye yourselves together ye elders of my church; go ye forth into the western countries, call upon the inhabitants to repent, and inasmuch as they do repent, build up churches unto me.

65 And with one heart and with one mind, gather up your riches that ye may purchase an inheritance which shall hereafter be appointed unto you.

66 And it shall be called the New Jerusalem, a land of peace, a city of refuge, a place of safety for the saints of the Most High God;

67 And the glory of the Lord shall be there, and the terror of the Lord also shall be there, insomuch that the wicked will not come unto it, and it shall be called Zion.

Why is Zion called a place of safety? (45:68–71)
The Prophet Joseph Smith declared: "The building up of Zion is a cause that has interested the people of God in every age . . .

"Anyplace where the Saints gather is Zion, which every righteous man will build up for a place of safety for his children.

"There will be here and there a Stake [of Zion] for the gathering of the Saints. . . . There your children shall be blessed, and you in the midst of friends where you may be blessed.

" . . . We ought to have the building up of Zion as our greatest object. . . . The time is soon coming, when no man will have any peace but in Zion and her stakes" (*Joseph Smith* [manual], 186). ☉

What can the rejoicing of the Saints in Zion communicate to the world? (45:71) "As members of the Church, each of us needs to model what it truly means to be a believing and behaving Latter-day Saint. Our example will have a powerful effect on others, making the restored gospel become much more relevant, meaningful, convincing, and desirable to them. Let us, each one, radiate to others the joy, confidence, love, and warmth of being part of the true Church of Christ. Our discipleship is not something to be endured with long face and heavy heart. Nor is it something to be jealously clutched to our bosoms and not shared with others. As we come to understand the love of the Father and the Son for us, our spirits will soar, and we will 'come to Zion, singing with songs of everlasting joy' (D&C 45:71)" (Ballard, "Beware of False Prophets and False Teachers," *Ensign*, Nov. 1999, 64).

Why will the Lord be terrible to the wicked? (45:74–75) "There will be some time between the resurrection of the righteous and the final destruction of the wicked. Apparently, this will be ample time for the wicked to realize what is happening and to wish the mountains would fall on them instead (see also v. 75)" (Robinson and Garrett, *Commentary on the Doctrine and Covenants*, 2:70).

68 And it shall come to pass among the wicked, that every man that will not take his sword against his neighbor must needs flee unto Zion for safety.

69 And there shall be gathered unto it out of every nation under heaven; and it shall be the only people that shall not be at war one with another.

70 And it shall be said among the wicked: Let us not go up to battle against Zion, for the inhabitants of Zion are terrible; wherefore we cannot stand.

71 And it shall come to pass that the righteous shall be gathered out from among all nations, and shall come to Zion, singing with songs of everlasting joy.

72 And now I say unto you, keep these things from going abroad unto the world until it is expedient in me, that ye may accomplish this work in the eyes of the people, and in the eyes of your enemies, that they may not know your works until ye have accomplished the thing which I have commanded you;

73 That when they shall know it, that they may consider these things.

74 For when the Lord shall appear he shall be terrible unto them, that fear may seize upon them, and they shall stand afar off and tremble.

75 And all nations shall be afraid because of the terror of the Lord, and the power of his might. Even so. Amen.

Introduction to Doctrine and Covenants 46

Joseph Smith received Doctrine and Covenants section 46 in Kirtland on 8 March 1831. "The Prophet wrote only one line in the [record]: 'The next day after [D&C 45] was received, I also received the following revelation, relative to the gifts of the Holy Ghost' [Joseph Smith Papers, "History, 1838–1856, volume A-1," 109]—D&C 46.

"John Whitmer, who . . . was appointed Church historian, recorded some additional background to Doctrine and Covenants 46: 'In the beginning of the church, while yet in her infancy, the disciples used to exclude unbelievers, which caused some to marvel, and converse of this matter because of the things that were written in the Book of Mormon [see 3 Nephi 18:22–33]. Therefore the Lord deigned to speak on this subject [D&C 46], that his people might come to understanding and said that he had always given to his Elders to conduct all meetings as they were led by the Spirit.' Thus, verses 1–7 were likely given to correct what had become the practice of the Church at that time in excluding nonmembers from its services" (Robinson and Garrett, *Commentary on the Doctrine and Covenants*, 2:71).

"Besides clarifying matters related to church meetings, this revelation also addressed spiritual gifts, which were described in both the New Testament and the Book of Mormon. After [Joseph Smith's] arrival in Ohio, he encountered spiritual expressions that he deemed unacceptable. . . . This revelation lists some acceptable spiritual gifts and warns that others are of the devil" (Joseph Smith Papers, Historical Introduction to "Revelation, circa 8 March 1831–A [D&C 46]," 76).

"After the departure of the missionaries, the [Ohio] converts had little experience. . . . Flush with zeal, some of them began to introduce elements of enthusiastic worship—or 'spiritual operations' as they sometimes called them—into their meetings. However, it was not always clear which manifestations were inspired and which were spurious. . . .

"Still in New York, Joseph Smith became concerned about the lack of leadership among the new Ohio converts and sent John Whitmer to Kirtland. . . . When [he] arrived in mid-January 1831, he was surprised by the variety of spiritual operations he witnessed.

"Shortly after his own arrival in Kirtland in February, Joseph Smith set about to check these displays of enthusiasm. He wrote to his brother Hyrum (then in Colesville, New York) on March 3 reporting, 'I have been engaged in regulating the Churches here as the disciples are numerous and the devil had made many attempts to over throw them' [Joseph Smith Papers, "Letter to Hyrum Smith, 3–4 March 1831," (1)]" (McBride, "Religious Enthusiasm," 107, 108).

SECTION 46

Revelation given through Joseph Smith the Prophet to the Church, at Kirtland, Ohio, March 8, 1831. In this early time of the Church, a unified pattern for the conducting of Church services had not yet developed. However, a custom of admitting only members and earnest investigators to the sacrament meetings and other assemblies of the Church had become somewhat general. This revelation expresses the will of the Lord relative to governing and conducting meetings and His direction on seeking and discerning the gifts of the Spirit.

1 Hearken, O ye people of my church; for verily I say unto you that these things were spoken unto you for your profit and learning.

Doctrine and Covenants 46:1–2. Elders Are to Conduct Meetings as Guided by the Holy Spirit

What does it mean to have Church meetings directed by the Spirit? (46:2) "The planning and conducting of meetings must not become too controlled by habit, tradition, agendas, or set procedures. The Church is, after all, a 'living church' (D&C 1:30), one that receives and responds to the direct revelations of God granted through the Spirit, and the Spirit must then have the final say in how to conduct our meetings, just as it must have the final say in how to conduct our lives" (Robinson and Garrett, *Commentary on the Doctrine and Covenants*, 2:72).

President Russell M. Nelson instructed that members also have a responsibility in our meetings: "Our meetings are always to be conducted as directed by the Spirit (see D&C 46:2). . . . Each member of the Church bears responsibility for the spiritual enrichment that can come from a sacrament meeting" ("Worshiping at Sacrament Meeting," *Ensign*, Aug. 2004, 28). ✪

Doctrine and Covenants 46:3–6. Truth Seekers Should Not Be Excluded from Sacramental Services

What did the Lord reveal concerning excluding others from our church meetings? (46:3) "The practice had arisen among some to exclude unbelievers from sacrament meetings. Other members of the Church regarded this custom as wrong in light of the Lord's instructions in the Book of Mormon (3 Nephi 18:22–34) to the effect that those in need of repentance should not be forbidden but should be welcomed in sacrament meetings, since this might be a means of bringing them to repentance. The Lord settled this matter in the first seven verses of section 46 by reemphasizing the fact that no one is to be excluded from any public meetings such as the sacrament meeting" (Cowan, *Doctrine & Covenants: Our Modern Scripture*, 82–83).

What reconciliation should one make before partaking of the sacrament? (46:4) "Before partaking of the sacrament, we are to prepare ourselves spiritually. The Lord emphasizes that no one should partake of the sacrament unworthily. That means we must repent of our sins before taking the sacrament. . . .

"We should examine our lives and look for ways to improve. We should also renew our determination to keep the commandments.

"We do not need to be perfect before partaking of the sacrament, but we must have the spirit of repentance in our hearts. The attitude with which we

2 But notwithstanding those things which are written, it always has been given to the elders of my church from the beginning, and ever shall be, to conduct all meetings as they are directed and guided by the Holy Spirit.

3 Nevertheless ye are commanded never to cast any one out from your public meetings, which are held before the world.

4 Ye are also commanded not to cast any one who belongeth to the church out of your sacrament meetings; nevertheless, if any have trespassed, let him not partake until he makes reconciliation.

5 And again I say unto you, ye shall not cast any out of your sacrament meetings who are earnestly seeking the kingdom—I speak this concerning those who are not of the church.

partake of the sacrament influences our experience with it" (*Gospel Principles*, 137). ☉

6 And again I say unto you, concerning your confirmation meetings, that if there be any that are not of the church, that are earnestly seeking after the kingdom, ye shall not cast them out.

7 But ye are commanded in all things to ask of God, who giveth liberally; and that which the Spirit testifies unto you even so I would that ye should do in all holiness of heart, walking uprightly before me, considering the end of your salvation, doing all things with prayer and thanksgiving, that ye may not be seduced by evil spirits, or doctrines of devils, or the commandments of men; for some are of men, and others of devils.

What were "confirmation meetings"? (46:6) "By 'confirmation meetings' is apparently meant meetings at which baptized persons are to be confirmed members of the Church" (Sperry, *Doctrine and Covenants Compendium,* 195).

"In the early days of the Church, special meetings were conducted for the specific purpose of confirming members of the Church. These did not always follow immediately after the baptism of water. Emma Smith, for example, was baptized in June 1830, yet she was not confirmed until August ([see Joseph Smith Papers, "History, 1838–1856, volume A-1, 43, 52])" (Brewster, *Doctrine & Covenants Encyclopedia* [2012], 97).

Doctrine and Covenants 46:7–12. Ask of God and Seek the Gifts of the Spirit

How do we act in holiness? (46:7) "The Lord has called us to do all that we do with 'holiness of heart.' And holiness is a product of covenant living. . . . May our individual covenants that bind us to our loving Heavenly Father guide us, protect us, sanctify us, and allow us to do likewise for all his children" (Bonnie D. Parkin, "With Holiness of Heart," 281–82).

Why is it so vital to be able to discern between spirits? (46:7) The Prophet Joseph Smith said: "A man must have the discerning of spirits before he can drag into daylight this hellish influence and unfold it unto the world in all its soul-destroying, diabolical, and horrid colors; for nothing is a greater injury to the children of men than to be under the influence of a false spirit

---

Partaking of the Sacrament (Doctrine and Covenants 46:4)

John H. Groberg spoke about personal worthiness before partaking of the sacrament: "If we desire to improve (which is to repent) and are not under priesthood restriction, then, in my opinion, we are worthy. If, however, we have no desire to improve, if we have no intention of following the guidance of the Spirit, we must ask: Are we worthy to partake, or are we making a mockery of the very purpose of the sacrament, which is to act as a catalyst for personal repentance and improvement? . . .

"The sacrament is an intensely personal experience, and we are the ones who knowingly are worthy or otherwise" ("Beauty and Importance of the Sacrament," *Ensign,* May 1989, 38).

One church article observed: "If [non-members] ask whether they should take the sacrament, simply tell them that they may choose to do so but that it is intended for Church members, who are renewing their baptismal covenants. . . . We should help nonmembers understand this important ordinance, ensuring that they also feel comfortable at our meetings" ("Can nonmembers take the sacrament?" *Liahona,* Mar. 2012, 47).

President Joseph Fielding Smith taught: "If non-members are present and partake of the sacrament, we would not do anything to prevent it, for evidently they would take it in good faith, notwithstanding the nature of the covenant" (*Doctrines of Salvation,* 2:350).

when they think they have the spirit of God" (Joseph Smith Papers, "History, 1838–1856, volume C-1," 1305).

What are some important blessings that come to those who seek the gifts of the Spirit? (46:8–11) "The gifts of the Spirit can guide and enrich our lives. They can strengthen us spiritually and temporally. They can help us bless the lives of others. Most important, they can bring us comfort in times of trial. They can help us magnify our callings. They can help guide us in our relationships. They can help us avoid being deceived" (Hales, "Gifts of the Spirit," *Ensign*, Feb. 2002, 20). ☉

How can we appropriately seek "the best gifts"? (46:8) President Boyd K. Packer taught, "I must emphasize that the word *gift* is of great significance, for a gift may not be demanded or it ceases to be a gift....

"Inasmuch as spiritual gifts are gifts, the conditions under which we may receive them are established by Him who offers them to us. Spiritual gifts cannot be forced.... They cannot be ... earned in the sense that we make some gesture in payment and expect them to automatically be delivered on our own terms.

"There are those who seek such gifts with such persistence that each act moves them farther from them. And in that persistence and determination they place themselves in spiritual danger. Rather, we are to live to be worthy of the gifts, and they will come according to the will of the Lord" (*Shield of Faith*, 98).

Who can claim the gifts of the Spirit? (46:9) "The Lord teaches us that it is those who love him and keep all of his commandments. The difficulty here is that none of us keep all of the commandments; at least we do not keep them perfectly. Attesting to the mercy and grace of heaven comes this phrase, which extends hope to all: 'And him [or her] that seeketh so to do.' Each of heaven's gifts is within our grasp, if we will but reach" (McConkie and Ostler, *Revelations of the Restoration*, 364). ☉

How can we know what our spiritual gifts are? (46:10–11) "Access to the gifts of the Holy Ghost is guaranteed only when we live our lives in harmony with the principles of the gospel....

"A prerequisite for seeking after the gifts may require that we find out which gifts we have been given....

"To find the gifts we have been given, we must pray and fast. Often patriarchal blessings tell us the gifts we have received and declare the promise of

8 Wherefore, beware lest ye are deceived; and that ye may not be deceived seek ye earnestly the best gifts, always remembering for what they are given;

9 For verily I say unto you, they are given for the benefit of those who love me and keep all my commandments, and him that seeketh so to do; that all may be benefited that seek or that ask of me, that ask and not for a sign that they may consume it upon their lusts.

10 And again, verily I say unto you, I would that ye should always remember, and always retain in your minds what those gifts are, that are given unto the church.

11 For all have not every gift given unto them; for there are many gifts, and to every man is given a gift by the Spirit of God.

12 To some is given one, and to some is given another, that all may be profited thereby.

gifts we can receive if we seek after them. I urge you each to discover your gifts and to seek after those that will bring direction to your life's work and that will further the work of heaven" (Hales, "Gifts of the Spirit," *Ensign*, Feb. 2002, 15, 16). ◉

Doctrine and Covenants 46:13–26. An Enumeration of Some of These Gifts Is Given

What is a responsibility of those who are given the gift "to know that Jesus Christ is the Son of God"? (46:13–14) "One of these [spiritual] gifts is 'to know that Jesus Christ is the Son of God, and that he was crucified for the sins of the world' (D&C 46:13). Those who receive that gift have the duty to testify of it. We know this because immediately after describing the gift of knowing that Jesus Christ is the Son of God, the Lord says: 'To others it is given to believe on their words, that they also might have eternal life if they continue faithful' (D&C 46:14; see also 3 Ne. 19:28). Those who have the gift to know must give their witness so that those who have the gift to believe on their words can enjoy the benefit of that gift" (Oaks, "Witnesses of Christ," *Ensign*, Nov. 1990, 30). ◉

13 To some it is given by the Holy Ghost to know that Jesus Christ is the Son of God, and that he was crucified for the sins of the world.

14 To others it is given to believe on their words, that they also might have eternal life if they continue faithful.

How are we influenced by others in meetings? (46:14) Sister Elicia A. Grist testified: "We have each a mission to perform. . . . But can we not, dear sisters, carry with us a pure sentiment of kindly feeling, and assist to create a lively spirit and devoted earnestness to the cause; and I need not name one great privilege we have, when there is ample opportunity afforded us for testifying and exercising the gifts of the Spirit. How many times have we been forcibly struck by the manifest power of God in our meetings! In many instances, when we have participated in these holy inspirations, our testimony may have caused some who have been present to reflect more deeply and closely upon what has been said" ("We Have Each a Mission to Perform," 35).

15 And again, to some it is given by the Holy Ghost to know the differences of administration, as it will be pleasing unto the same Lord, according as the Lord will, suiting his mercies according to the conditions of the children of men.

16 And again, it is given by the Holy Ghost to some to know the diversities of operations,

What distinguishes "the differences of administration" from "diversities of operations"? (46:15–16) "The significance of these terms may be clarified by referring to the meaning of the Greek words which Paul used and which have been translated into English as 'administration' and 'operations.' *Administration* describes the various courses or duties of the priesthood. The Lord directs his authorized servants by revelation through the Holy Ghost. Knowing the *diversities of operations* means being able to discern whether or not a given form of spiritual manifestation is of the Lord" (Cowan, *Doctrine & Covenants: Our Modern Scripture*, 83–84).

What manner of wisdom and knowledge is referred to in these verses? (46:17–18) "Worldly wisdom and knowledge gained by intellectual talents are available to all men. But the knowledge of God and his eternal laws—gospel knowledge, saving knowledge, the hidden wisdom that comes from on high, the wisdom of those to whom the wonders of eternity are an open book, divine wisdom—all these are gifts of the Spirit. 'The things of God knoweth no man but the Spirit of God' (1 Corinthians 2:11). . . .

"'We have received, not the spirit of the world, but the spirit which is of God; that we might know the things that are freely given to us of God. Which things also we speak, not in the words which man's wisdom teacheth, but which the Holy Ghost teacheth' (1 Corinthians 2:12–13)" (Bruce R. McConkie, *New Witness*, 372, 373).

Why is faith a prerequisite to being healed? (46:19–20) "Faith is essential for healing by the powers of heaven. The Book of Mormon even teaches that 'if there be no faith among the children of men God can do no miracle among them' (Ether 12:12). . . . President Spencer W. Kimball said: 'The need of faith is often underestimated. The ill one and the family often seem to depend wholly on the power of the priesthood and the gift of healing that they hope the administering brethren may have, whereas the greater responsibility is with him who is blessed. . . . The major element is the faith of the individual when that person is conscious and accountable'" (Oaks, "Healing the Sick," *Ensign*, May 2010, 49). ◉

What is necessary for a person to perform miracles? (46:21) "It is an eternal principle that the powers of heaven are inseparably connected with righteousness (D&C 121:36). The working of miracles in the name of Jesus is an evidence that one is 'cleansed every whit from his iniquity' and thus worthy of the companionship of the Holy Ghost and the powers of God. The wonders of God—the signs and the miracles which always attend a dispensation of the gospel—require righteousness in the human instrument (see D&C 50:27–30)" (McConkie, Millet, and Top, *Doctrinal Commentary on the Book of Mormon*, 4:35).

whether they be of God, that the manifestations of the Spirit may be given to every man to profit withal.

17 And again, verily I say unto you, to some is given, by the Spirit of God, the word of wisdom.

18 To another is given the word of knowledge, that all may be taught to be wise and to have knowledge.

19 And again, to some it is given to have faith to be healed;

20 And to others it is given to have faith to heal.

21 And again, to some is given the working of miracles;

22 And to others it is given to prophesy;

What does it mean to prophesy? (46:22) John defined the spirit of prophecy as receiving the testimony of Jesus Christ (see Rev. 19:10).

Elder Robert D. Hales explained, "Of the sacred gifts of the Spirit, one that I believe has impact on each of our lives is the gift of prophecy or revelation. This gift is different from the priesthood office of prophet. The gift of prophecy is the testimony of Jesus.

"The Apostle Paul taught that Christians should 'desire spiritual gifts, but rather that ye may prophesy [meaning to testify of the Savior]' (1 Cor. 14:1).

"President Joseph Fielding Smith . . . taught, 'All members of the Church should seek for the gift of prophecy, for their own guidance' [*Church History and Modern Revelation*, 1:201].

"Every Church member, if faithful, has the right to receive revelation for his or her personal blessing" ("Gifts of the Spirit," *Ensign*, Feb. 2002, 15).

23 And to others the discerning of spirits.

How can having the gift of "discerning of spirits" help us personally? (46:23) "The gift of discernment operates basically in four major ways.

"First, as we 'read under the surface,' discernment helps us detect hidden error and evil in others.

"Second, and more important, it helps us detect hidden errors and evil in ourselves. Thus the spiritual gift of discernment is not exclusively about discerning other people and situations, but . . . also about discerning things as they really are within us.

"Third, it helps us find and bring forth the good that may be concealed in others.

"And fourth, it helps us find and bring forth the good that may be concealed in us. Oh, what a blessing and a source of protection and direction is the spiritual gift of discernment!" (Bednar, "Quick to Observe," *Ensign*, Dec. 2006, 35). ❂

24 And again, it is given to some to speak with tongues;

25 And to another is given the interpretation of tongues.

How is the gift of tongues manifested in this dispensation? (46:24–25) Elder Robert D. Hales explained: "Many of you who have gone to foreign lands have been given the gift to speak with tongues and to translate, or have the interpretation of tongues. . . .

"We are told by prophets in this dispensation that revelation for the direction of the Church will not be given through the gift of tongues. The reason for this is that it is very easy for Lucifer to falsely duplicate the gift of tongues and confuse the members of the Church.

"Satan has the power to trick us as it pertains to some of the gifts of the Spirit. . . . Joseph Smith and Brigham Young [both] explained the need to be cautious when considering the gift of tongues" ("Gifts of the Spirit," *Ensign*, Feb. 2002, 14). ❂

What should we remember and appreciate about God's gifts? (46:26) Elder Dale G. Renlund testified, "I invite you to remember each day the greatness of Heavenly Father and Jesus Christ and what They have done for you. Let your consideration of Their goodness more firmly bind your wandering heart to Them [see "Come, Thou Fount of Every Blessing"]. Ponder Their compassion, and you will be blessed with added spiritual sensitivity and become more Christlike....

"As I have reflected on gifts from our Heavenly Father and from Jesus Christ, I have come to know of Their infinite love and Their incomprehensible compassion for all Heavenly Father's children" ("Consider the Goodness and Greatness of God," *Ensign*, May 2020, 44).

Doctrine and Covenants 46:27–33. Church Leaders Are Given Power to Discern the Gifts of the Spirit

Why is it essential for the bishop or presiding officer to have the gift of discernment for all gifts? (46:27) "Bishops and other presiding authorities cultivate the gift to discern and judge these gifts in those over whom they preside, guarding against those who testify and yet are not of God" (Harper, *Making Sense of the Doctrine & Covenants*, 161).

President Boyd K. Packer taught: "Occasionally we will find someone who claims to receive spiritual revelations.... They seem to think somehow that the inspiration they receive supersedes that which the bishops or stake presidents might receive and comes from some higher source than these brethren are privileged to have....

26 And all these gifts come from God, for the benefit of the children of God.

27 And unto the bishop of the church, and unto such as God shall appoint and ordain to watch over the church and to be elders unto the church, are to have it given unto them to discern all those gifts lest there shall be any among you professing and yet be not of God.

28 And it shall come to pass that he that asketh in Spirit shall receive in Spirit;

29 That unto some it may be given to have all those gifts, that there may be a head, in order that every member may be profited thereby.

Spiritual Gifts Are Found in the Church Today (Doctrine and Covenants 46:29)

"It is characteristic of the ways of God that He manifests His power by the bestowal of a variety of ennobling graces, which are properly called gifts of the Spirit.... Whenever the power of the Priesthood has operated through an organized Church on the earth, the members have been strengthened in their faith and otherwise blessed in numerous related ways, by the possession of these gifts....

"The Latter-day Saints claim to possess within the Church all the sign-gifts promised as the heritage of the believer. They point to the unimpeached testimonies of thousands who have been blessed with direct and personal manifestations, of heavenly power; to the once blind, deaf, dumb, halt, and weak in body, who have been freed from their infirmities through their faith and by the ministrations of the Holy Priesthood; to a multitude who have voiced their testimony in tongues with which they were naturally unfamiliar, or who have demonstrated their possession of the gift by a phenomenal mastery of foreign languages when such was necessary to the discharge of their duties as preachers of the word of God; to many who have enjoyed personal communion with heavenly beings; to others who have prophesied in words that have found speedy vindication in literal fulfilment; and to the Church itself, whose growth has been guided by the voice of God, made known through the gift of revelation" (Talmage, *Articles of Faith*, 217, 233).

30 He that asketh in the Spirit asketh according to the will of God; wherefore it is done even as he asketh.

31 And again, I say unto you, all things must be done in the name of Christ, whatsoever you do in the Spirit;

32 And ye must give thanks unto God in the Spirit for whatsoever blessing ye are blessed with.

33 And ye must practice virtue and holiness before me continually. Even so. Amen.

"The key is to follow the counsel of your bishop and those elders who are ordained to watch over the Church. Then you will be safe" (*Shield of Faith*, 103, 104).

What could it mean to practice virtue in our lives? (46:33) "Virtue 'is a pattern of thought and behavior based on high moral standards' [*Preach My Gospel* (2004), 118]. It encompasses chastity and moral purity. Virtue begins in the heart and in the mind. It is nurtured in the home. It is the accumulation of thousands of small decisions and actions. *Virtue* is a word we don't hear often in today's society, but the Latin root word *virtus* means strength. Virtuous women and men possess a quiet dignity and inner strength. They are confident because they are worthy to receive and be guided by the Holy Ghost" (Dalton, "Return to Virtue," *Ensign*, Nov. 2008, 79).

Introduction to Doctrine and Covenants 47

This section of the Doctrine and Covenants was received by the Prophet Joseph Smith on March 8, 1831, at Kirtland, Ohio. "The revelation that organized the Church commanded the Saints to keep a written record of its activities (see D&C 21:1). Oliver Cowdery assumed the responsibility to do so, and then the Lord called him on a mission. John Whitmer, meanwhile, returned from a mission and 'was appointed by the voice of the Elders to keep the Church record.' Joseph asked him also to write and preserve a history of the Church. 'I would rather not do it,' John explained, 'but observed that the will of the Lord be done, and if he desires it, I desire that he would manifest it through Joseph the Seer' [Joseph Smith Papers, *Histories, Volume 2*, 36]. Joseph asked, and the Lord answered with the revelation recorded in Doctrine and Covenants 47.

"[John Whitmer] is called to assist Joseph in transcribing revelation until such time as the Lord assigns him more responsibilities. John is also given authority to preach to the Saints whenever necessary. The Lord repeats his will for a second time, saying that John should succeed Oliver Cowdery as the Church historian and recorder; the Lord needs Oliver elsewhere. The Lord promises that for as long as John is faithful, he will have the guidance of the Holy Ghost to direct him in fulfilling his calling" (Harper, *Making Sense of the Doctrine & Covenants*, 162).

SECTION 47

Revelation given through Joseph Smith the Prophet, at Kirtland, Ohio, March 8, 1831. John Whitmer, who had already served as a clerk to the Prophet, initially hesitated when he was asked to serve as the Church historian and recorder, replacing Oliver Cowdery. He wrote, "I would rather not do it but observed that the will of the Lord be done, and if he desires it, I desire that he would manifest it through Joseph the Seer." After Joseph Smith received this revelation, John Whitmer accepted and served in his appointed office.

Doctrine and Covenants 47:1–4. John Whitmer Is Designated to Keep the History of the Church and to Write for the Prophet

How would keeping a "regular history" benefit the Church? (47:1) Joseph Smith sorrowfully stated: "It is a fact if I now had in my possession every decision which has been had, upon important items of doctrine and duties, since the commencement of this work, I would not part with them for any sum of money; but we have neglected to take minutes of such things, thinking, perhaps, that they would never benefit us afterwards, which, had we now, would decide almost any point of doctrine, which might be agitated. But this has been neglected, and now we cannot bear record to the church and to the world of the great and glorious manifestations, which have been made to us, with that degree of power and authority we otherwise could, if we now had these things to publish abroad" (Joseph Smith Papers, "History, 1838–1856, volume B-1," 575). ⊕

Why is keeping a "history continually" important for the Church and its members? (47:3) "Joseph's history says that John Whitmer was set apart 'as a historian inasmuch as he was faithful.' He was sustained by the Church at a special conference in April 1831, a month after the revelation was received, and he began writing in June. 'I shall proceed to continue this record,' his first sentence says, 'being commanded of the Lord and Savior Jesus Christ, to write the things that transpire in this church.' John was not nearly as good a historian as Oliver [Cowdery] had been. His

1 Behold, it is expedient in me that my servant John should write and keep a regular history, and assist you, my servant Joseph, in transcribing all things which shall be given you, until he is called to further duties.

2 Again, verily I say unto you that he can also lift up his voice in meetings, whenever it shall be expedient.

3 And again, I say unto you that it shall be appointed unto him to keep the church record and history continually; for Oliver Cowdery I have appointed to another office.

John Whitmer, Church Historian (Doctrine and Covenants 47:1)

"John Whitmer was born in Pennsylvania. He was baptized in Seneca County, New York, in June 1829. Whitmer served as one of Joseph Smith's scribes during the translation of the Book of Mormon and for the Bible revision, and he was one of the Eight Witnesses of the Book of Mormon. Several early revelations were directed wholly or in part to Whitmer (Doctrine and Covenants 15; 26; 30). . . . In 1831 he was appointed Church Historian (Doctrine and Covenants 47) and began writing a history of The Church of Jesus Christ of Latter-day Saints (Doctrine and Covenants 69)" (Doctrine and Covenants Historical Resources, "John Whitmer").

"Prior to the dictation of this revelation, record keeping in the Church was often sporadic and incomplete. After Whitmer was appointed church historian and recorder, the number of documents recording Church history increased substantially. Minutes of church conferences generally contained more detail than they had previously, and Whitmer's creation of Revelation Book I preserved most of [Joseph Smith's] early revelations. Whitmer also wrote a ninety-six-page narrative history that primarily described events from fall 1830 through the mid-1830s" (Joseph Smith Papers, Historical Introduction to "Revelation, circa 8 March 1831–B [D&C 47]," 79).

John Whitmer

4 Wherefore, it shall be given him, inasmuch as he is faithful, by the Comforter, to write these things. Even so. Amen.

history is an important but sketchy source of early Church history that becomes quite cynical about the Church as John apostatized in 1838. John also transcribed revelations as Doctrine and Covenants 47 commanded. Many of the earliest existing revelation and Bible manuscripts are in his handwriting" (Harper, *Making Sense of the Doctrine & Covenants*, 163). ⊕

How did John Whitmer respond to his calling?
(47:4) "The Lord promised John Whitmer that if he was faithful he could write that which was given him by the Holy Ghost (verse 4); thus his work could be a truly unusual history and have a unique claim to certain truth. The Lord gave Elder Whitmer further instructions in section 69 concerning the history he was compiling 'for the benefit of the Church and for the rising generations' [D&C 69:8].

"John Whitmer, unfortunately, accepted his calling reluctantly, and only after section 47 had been received. He kept a sketchy history, eighty-five manuscript pages in length. Upon his apostasy, he refused to turn his history over to the Church; only years later did it become available" (Cowan, *Doctrine & Covenants: Our Modern Scripture*, 84–85).

Introduction to Doctrine and Covenants 48

"In former Revelations (Secs. 37:3; 38:32; 39:15) our Lord had commanded the Saints in the East to gather in Ohio, where they would be 'endowed with power from on high.' The spirit of gathering was poured out upon them, and in the spring of 1831, shortly after the arrival of the Prophet Joseph in Kirtland, many Saints began the westward move from the State of New York. The Saints in Kirtland then began to make inquiries as to how the newcomers could obtain land to settle upon, and where they should make a permanent location" (Smith and Sjodahl, *Doctrine and Covenants Commentary*, 280). The Prophet asked the Lord regarding this issue and received what is now known as Doctrine and Covenants 48 on March 10, 1831, at Kirtland, Ohio.

"The revelation logically divides into two parts. The first part deals with the problems then current ([vv. 1–3]), that is to say, what should be done about providing suitable places for the migrant Saints to dwell in, whether in or near Kirtland. The second part has to do with the question of locating and purchasing lands for a permanent inheritance of the Saints ([vv. 4–6]), including the building of a city" (Sperry, *Doctrine and Covenants Compendium*, 203).

"[John] Whitmer added that some Easterners believed that Kirtland was the 'place of gathering, even the place of the New Jerusalem spoken of in the Book of Mormon.' . . . Members were told that the place of the New Jerusalem had not yet been revealed and the Ohio Saints were to share their surplus property with the 'eastern brethren.' If needed, the immigrants were to purchase additional property (see D&C 48:2–5)" (Backman and Perkins, "United under the Laws," 175).

SECTION 48

Revelation given through Joseph Smith the Prophet, at Kirtland, Ohio, March 10, 1831. The Prophet had inquired of the Lord as to the mode of procedure in procuring lands for the

Doctrine and Covenants 48:1–3. The Saints in Ohio Are to Share Their Lands with Their Brethren

What is significant about the phrase "for the present time" in these verses? (48:1–3) "This phrase ['for the present time'], used three times in the first three verses, clearly implies that the stay in Ohio would not be permanent. Yet in Doctrine and Covenants 51:17 the Lord advised the Saints to act as though they would be in Ohio for years (and many were), and in Doctrine and Covenants 64:21 they were told to maintain a strong presence in Kirtland for at least five more years—until the Kirtland Temple could be dedicated" (Robinson and Garrett, *Commentary on the Doctrine and Covenants*, 2:87).

Doctrine and Covenants 48:4–6. The Saints Are to Purchase Lands, Build a City, and Follow the Counsel of Their Presiding Officers

What city or area was eventually designated as a land for the Saints' future inheritance? (48:4–5) "The city is the New Jerusalem, which is to be built through the sacrifice and consecration of the Saints. The Church had first learned about the city from Ether 13:3–8 and two previous revelations to Joseph Smith (see D&C 28:9; 42:6–9). The exact location of this city had not been revealed at this point in the history of the Church (see D&C 48:5). Three months after section 48 was given, however, the Lord indicated that Missouri was the place for the gathering (see D&C 52:2–3), but he did not reveal the specific location as being Jackson County until July 1831 (see D&C 57:1–3)" (*Doctrine and Covenants Student Manual* [2001], 104).

settlement of the Saints. This was an important matter in view of the migration of members of the Church from the eastern United States, in obedience to the Lord's command that they should assemble in Ohio (see sections 37:1–3; 45:64).

1 It is necessary that ye should remain for the present time in your places of abode, as it shall be suitable to your circumstances.

2 And inasmuch as ye have lands, ye shall impart to the eastern brethren;

3 And inasmuch as ye have not lands, let them buy for the present time in those regions round about, as seemeth them good, for it must needs be necessary that they have places to live for the present time.

4 It must needs be necessary that ye save all the money that ye can, and that ye obtain all that ye can in righteousness, that in time ye may be enabled to purchase land for an inheritance, even the city.

5 The place is not yet to be revealed; but after your brethren come from the east there are to be certain men appointed, and to them it shall be given to know the place, or to them it shall be revealed.

6 And they shall be appointed to purchase the lands, and to make a commencement to lay the foundation of the city; and then shall ye begin to be gathered with your families, every man according to his family, according to his circumstances, and as is appointed to him by the presidency and the bishop of the church, according to the laws and commandments which ye have received, and which ye shall hereafter receive. Even so. Amen.

"In this revelation, given 7 [May] 1831, [Leman Copley] along with Sidney Rigdon and Parley P. Pratt were directed to take the message of the Restoration to the Shakers. Some months previously, Elder Pratt had spent two days with them and left them seven copies of the Book of Mormon. This revelation, which Sidney Rigdon read in its entirety to the Shakers, was given so that the missionaries might respond by the spirit of revelation to the matters of particular interest to the Shakers" (McConkie and Ostler, *Revelations of the Restoration*, 374).

"Before joining the Church, Leman Copley associated with the North Union Shakers, perhaps attending their meetings, though he did not immerse himself fully in their austere communal life. The fact that he lived 35 miles from the community and remained married gives some indication of his level of commitment to Shaker principles. While clearly attracted to some of their teachings and perhaps their mode of worship, he was not a full participant. In fact, [Ashbel] Kitchell [the Shakers leader] chided Copley for rejecting a life of celibacy and for having 'taken up with Mormonism as the easier plan.' . . .

"Copley decided to visit Joseph Smith—who was then living at the home of his friend Isaac Morley near Kirtland—on Saturday, May 7, 1831. Though we have no record of their conversation, Copley likely hoped for clarification about certain Shaker beliefs and perhaps suggested the idea of a mission to North Union. As a result of this meeting, Joseph received the revelation now canonized as Doctrine and Covenants 49. This revelation authoritatively addressed the doctrinal differences between the two faiths" (McBride, "Leman Copley and the Shakers," 118, 119).

SECTION 49

Revelation given through Joseph Smith the Prophet to Sidney Rigdon, Parley P. Pratt, and Leman Copley, at Kirtland, Ohio, May 7, 1831. Leman Copley had embraced the gospel but still held to some of the teachings of the Shakers (United Society of Believers in Christ's Second Appearing), to which he had formerly belonged. Some of the beliefs of the Shakers were that Christ's Second Coming had already occurred and that He had appeared in the form of a woman, Ann Lee. They did not consider baptism by water essential. They rejected marriage and believed in a life of total celibacy. Some Shakers also forbade the eating of meat. In prefacing this revelation, Joseph Smith's history states, "In order to have [a] more perfect understanding on the subject, I inquired of the Lord, and received the following." The revelation refutes some of the basic concepts of the Shaker group. The aforementioned brethren took a copy of the revelation to the Shaker community (near Cleveland, Ohio) and read it to them in its entirety, but it was rejected.

Doctrine and Covenants 49:1–7. The Day and Hour of Christ's Coming Will Remain Unknown until He Comes

Who were the Shakers? (49:1) "The Shakers, or United Society of Believers in Christ's Second Appearing, had their beginning in England during the 1700s. The main group soon came to America under the leadership of Ann Lee and flourished in the revivalist climate of the early 1800s. A large community was established in the vicinity of Kirtland, Ohio. Leman Copley was a recent convert from the Shakers, and with Sidney Rigdon and Parley P. Pratt he was called to carry the restored gospel to his former coreligionists. This mission was not very successful, at least in terms of converts baptized" (Cowan, *Doctrine & Covenants: Our Modern Scripture*, 85). ✚

What are some sacred truths the Shakers rejected? (49:2) "The missionaries were going to the Shakers to teach them and to call them to repentance. Though the Shakers have become thoroughly romanticized in modern thought, there was something distinctly 'not right' about their beliefs and practices at the time of Joseph Smith. The Shaker rejection of the sacred nature of marriage, sexuality, and the family would alone account for the Lord's statement here. John Whitmer recorded later that the Shakers had been 'bound up in tradition and priestcraft, and thus they are led away with foolish and vain imaginations' [*Early Latter-day Saint History*, 61]" (Robinson and Garrett, *Commentary on the Doctrine and Covenants*, 2:93).

1 Hearken unto my word, my servants Sidney, and Parley, and Leman; for behold, verily I say unto you, that I give unto you a commandment that you shall go and preach my gospel which ye have received, even as ye have received it, unto the Shakers.

2 Behold, I say unto you, that they desire to know the truth in part, but not all, for they are not right before me and must needs repent.

3 Wherefore, I send you, my servants Sidney and Parley, to preach the gospel unto them.

Significant Beliefs of the Shakers (Doctrine and Covenants 49:1–4)

"Some of the leading practices and beliefs of this unique group were:

"1. The leading authority of the Shakers was vested in a committee, usually four persons, two females and two males.

"2. Private ownership of property was eliminated and several communal groups were established throughout the United States.

"3. God was both male and female.

"4. God first made his appearance in the form of a male, Jesus Christ. In Ann Lee the female principle of God was manifested, and in her the promise of the Second Coming was fulfilled.

"5. Confession was all that was necessary for forgiveness of sins, and, therefore, outward ordinances (baptism and laying on of hands) were unnecessary.

"6. It was possible for people to live without sin.

"7. Although the Shakers did not forbid marriage, they believed that those who lived a celibate life abided a higher law; they called this 'the cross,' probably having reference to the cross they had to bear.

"8. Pork was forbidden in their diet and many ate no meat.

"9. The resurrection consisted of the resurrection of the spirit but not the physical body" (Perkins, "Ministry to the Shakers," 212).

4 And my servant Leman shall be ordained unto this work, that he may reason with them, not according to that which he has received of them, but according to that which shall be taught him by you my servants; and by so doing I will bless him, otherwise he shall not prosper.

5 Thus saith the Lord; for I am God, and have sent mine Only Begotten Son into the world for the redemption of the world, and have decreed that he that receiveth him shall be saved, and he that receiveth him not shall be damned—

6 And they have done unto the Son of Man even as they listed; and he has taken his power on the right hand of his glory, and now reigneth in the heavens, and will reign till he descends on the earth to put all enemies under his feet, which time is nigh at hand—

7 I, the Lord God, have spoken it; but the hour and the day no man knoweth, neither the angels in heaven, nor shall they know until he comes.

8 Wherefore, I will that all men shall repent, for all are under sin, except those which I have reserved unto myself, holy men that ye know not of.

9 Wherefore, I say unto you that I have sent unto you mine everlasting covenant, even that which was from the beginning.

How was Leman Copley directed to preach the gospel? (49:4) "Leman Copley, a recent convert from the Shakers, is cautioned not to reason with his former colleagues on their ground. His commission now is to declare the message of the Restoration. . . . The principle is applicable to all missionary work. Our commission is to declare the message of the Restoration from the revelations of the Restoration. Such a course is consistently rewarded with a marvelous outpouring of the Spirit and a rich harvest of souls. Those insisting on giving credence to the restored gospel by 'proving' it, as it were, from Old and New Testament texts or arguing for its credibility in some other way do not enjoy the same outpouring of the Spirit or the same power of conversion" (McConkie and Ostler, *Revelations of the Restoration*, 375).

What does it mean to "put all enemies under his feet"? (49:6) "When the Son of Man comes he will 'put all enemies under his feet' (D&C 49:6; see also 76:61; Ps. 66:3). This simply means that the wicked will no longer have free reign in their pursuit of evil but will instead be in subjection to Christ and his Father" (Brewster, *Doctrine & Covenants Encyclopedia* [2012], 607).

What do we know about the timing of the Lord's return? (49:7) "No man knows or shall know the day or the hour of our Lord's return; that knowledge is retained in the bosom of heaven, for good and sufficient reasons. But all men may read the signs of the times, and those whose souls are attuned to the things of the Spirit know that the great and dreadful day of the Lord is near, even at the door. But they also know there are many things yet to be done before earth's rightful King comes to change the kingdoms of this world into the kingdom of our God and of his Christ" (Bruce R. McConkie, *New Witness*, 591). See also commentary in this volume on Doctrine and Covenants 39:21.

Doctrine and Covenants 49:8–14. Men Must Repent, Believe the Gospel, and Obey the Ordinances to Gain Salvation

Who might these "holy men" be? (49:8) "There are men who have been made 'perfect in Christ' (Moroni 10:32–33), who have been taken by God for his own purposes and whose carnal natures have been erased or otherwise overcome. Perhaps these are translated beings, about whom we know nothing, who have been given missions and assignments upon the earth or elsewhere" (Robinson and Garrett, *Commentary on the Doctrine and Covenants*, 2:94–95).

10 And that which I have promised I have so fulfilled, and the nations of the earth shall bow to it; and, if not of themselves, they shall come down, for that which is now exalted of itself shall be laid low of power.

11 Wherefore, I give unto you a commandment that ye go among this people, and say unto them, like unto mine apostle of old, whose name was Peter:

12 Believe on the name of the Lord Jesus, who was on the earth, and is to come, the beginning and the end;

13 Repent and be baptized in the name of Jesus Christ, according to the holy commandment, for the remission of sins;

14 And whoso doeth this shall receive the gift of the Holy Ghost, by the laying on of the hands of the elders of the church.

15 And again, verily I say unto you, that whoso forbiddeth to marry is not ordained of God, for marriage is ordained of God unto man.

16 Wherefore, it is lawful that he should have one wife, and they twain shall be one

Doctrine and Covenants 49:15–16. Marriage Is Ordained of God

Why is the doctrine of marriage essential to understanding the fulness of the gospel? (49:15–16) The Lord revealed to Joseph Smith that marriage is ordained of God, contrary to the Shaker's doctrine that celibacy was more holy. President Dallin H. Oaks emphasized, "Fundamental to us is God's revelation that exaltation can be attained only through faithfulness to the covenants of an eternal marriage between a man

The Shakers Reject the Message of the Restored Gospel (Doctrine and Covenants 49:11–13)

Sidney Rigdon, Leman Copley and Parley P. Pratt's missionary meeting with the Shakers did not go well. "At the conclusion of his reading of the revelation [D&C 49], Elder Rigdon asked the Shakers if they were willing to be baptized for the remission of their sins and receive the laying on of hands for the gift of the Holy Ghost. Ashbel Kitchell, the leader of the group of Shakers, responded: 'The Christ that dictated that, I was well acquainted with, and had been from a boy, that I had been much troubled to get rid of his influence, and I wished to have nothing more to do with him; and as for any gift he had authorized them to exercise among us, I would release them [and] their Christ from any further burden about us, and take all the responsibility on myself' [Kitchell Journal, 12]." ...

The Shaker membership agreed with their leader. "Young Parley P. Pratt, however would not let the meeting come to a close without a further witness against the Shakers [see D&C 24:15]. He arose and shook his coattails: 'He shook the dust from his garments as a testimony against us, that we had rejected the word of the Lord Jesus' [Kitchell Journal, 13].

"This greatly angered Kitchell, a much larger man than Elder Pratt, and he severely rebuked him: 'You filthy Beast, dare you presume to come in here, and try to imitate a man of God by shaking your filthy tail ...' [Kitchell Journal, 15]. It is clear why the Lord found it necessary later to clarify to those early missionaries that any physical witness performed against those who reject the gospel should not be done 'in their presence, lest thou provoke them, but in secret' (D&C 60:15). We can also discern why the Brethren today instruct us that such actions not be undertaken at all" (Perkins, "Ministry to the Shakers," 215–16).

flesh, and all this that the earth might answer the end of its creation;

17 And that it might be filled with the measure of man, according to his creation before the world was made.

18 And whoso forbiddeth to abstain from meats, that man should not eat the same, is not ordained of God;

19 For, behold, the beasts of the field and the fowls of the air, and that which cometh of the earth, is ordained for the use of man for food and for raiment, and that he might have in abundance.

20 But it is not given that one man should possess that which is above another, wherefore the world lieth in sin.

21 And wo be unto man that sheddeth blood or that wasteth flesh and hath no need.

and a woman [see D&C 131:1–3; "The Family]" ("Divine Love in the Father's Plan," *Liahona*, May 2022, 103).

Sister Julie B. Beck added: "We know that in the great premortal conflict we sided with our Savior, Jesus Christ, to preserve our potential to belong to eternal families. We know we are daughters of God, and we know what we are to do. Women find true happiness when they understand and delight in their unique role within the plan of salvation. The things women can and should do very best are championed and taught without apology here. We believe in the formation of eternal families. That means we believe in getting married" ("What Latter-day Saint Women Do Best," *Ensign*, Nov. 2007, 110).

Doctrine and Covenants 49:17–21. The Eating of Meat Is Approved

What does the Doctrine and Covenants reveal about abstaining from meat? (49:18–19) "Some, if not all, of the Shakers abstained from eating meat. This revelation is the first of three in the Doctrine and Covenants that teach that meat from animals and fowls were ordained for the use of food and raiment for man [D&C 49:19]. Section 59 mentions beasts, fowls, and that which climbs trees or walks on the earth were made for the benefit and use of man [D&C 59:16–19]. Section 89 states that the beasts and fowls are to be used with thanksgiving, but sparingly, and in times of cold and famine [D&C 89:12–13]" (Nyman, *Doctrine and Covenants Commentary*, 1:443).

Why would the Lord direct that one person should not possess more than another? (49:20) "The Lord claims ownership of 'the earth' and 'all things therein.' . . . Thus the revelations do not apologize for such radical notions as one of the [Law of Consecration's] stated purposes: 'I will consecrate of the riches of those who embrace my gospel among the Gentiles unto the poor of my people who are of the house of Israel' (D&C 42:39), or the Lord's decree 'that the poor shall be exalted, in that the rich are made low' (D&C 104:16; see also 58:8–12). Indeed, the revelations give stewards no right to keep or use the Lord's things for any other purposes than His" (Harper, "All Things Are the Lord's," 221).

What have the prophets taught about wasting flesh by needlessly killing animals? (49:21) President Joseph F. Smith firmly taught, "I do not believe any man should kill animals or birds unless he needs them for food, and then he should not kill innocent little birds that are not intended for food for man. I think it is wicked for men to thirst in their souls to kill almost everything which possesses animal life. It is wrong" (*Gospel Doctrine*, 266).

Doctrine and Covenants 49:22–28. Zion Will Flourish and the Lamanites Blossom as the Rose before the Second Coming

Why did the Lord need to clarify that He would not come as a woman? (49:22) One of the Shakers' beliefs was that: "The Deity is dual in nature. God is both male and female. The male principle of Christ came to earth as Jesus, the son of a Jewish carpenter. The female is represented as 'Mother Ann [Lee],' and in her the promise of our Lords' Second Advent was fulfilled" (Sperry, *Doctrine and Covenants Compendium*, 205).

"The Lord corrects this strange doctrine, and adds that He will not be a man traveling on the earth, or another human being [D&C 49:22]. He then repeats the signs of Christ's coming as He had given in [D&C 45:45–48], and adds what Isaiah had prophesied about the valleys and mountains (D&C 49:23; see Isaiah 40:4)" (Nyman, *Doctrine and Covenants Commentary*, 1:444).

What did the Lord provide to avoid deception? (49:23) "As time passed and Church membership grew through avid missionary work and conversion, there were consistently those who fell 'out by the way side.' Some decided the restored gospel required too much. Some believed that things had changed too much from the time of their baptism. Others had difficulties with Church structure or choices made by Church leadership. There was no single reason for separating oneself from the body of the Church. In the year following the temple dedication, Kirtland became an early center of divergence....

"Disaffiliation and declension became a significant part of the Saints' experience. The new revelations warned the Saints to 'be not deceived' and offered them patterns and gifts of the Spirit to help" (Johnson and Reeder, *Witness of Women*, 143).

What will happen before the Lord comes? (49:24) President Wilford Woodruff looked forward to "the fulfillment of all things that the Lord has spoken, and they will come to pass as the Lord God lives. Zion is bound to rise and flourish. The [Indigenous tribes of the Americas] will blossom as the rose on the

22 And again, verily I say unto you, that the Son of Man cometh not in the form of a woman, neither of a man traveling on the earth.

23 Wherefore, be not deceived, but continue in steadfastness, looking forth for the heavens to be shaken, and the earth to tremble and to reel to and fro as a drunken man, and for the valleys to be exalted, and for the mountains to be made low, and for the rough places to become smooth—and all this when the angel shall sound his trumpet.

24 But before the great day of the Lord shall come, Jacob shall flourish in the wilderness, and the Lamanites shall blossom as the rose.

mountains. . . . Every word that God has ever said of them will have its fulfillment, and they, by and by, will receive the Gospel. It will be a day of God's power among them, and a nation will be born in a day" (in *Journal of Discourses*, 15:282).

25 Zion shall flourish upon the hills and rejoice upon the mountains, and shall be assembled together unto the place which I have appointed.

26 Behold, I say unto you, go forth as I have commanded you; repent of all your sins; ask and ye shall receive; knock and it shall be opened unto you.

27 Behold, I will go before you and be your rearward; and I will be in your midst, and you shall not be confounded.

28 Behold, I am Jesus Christ, and I come quickly. Even so. Amen.

How has this prophecy to "flourish upon the hills and rejoice upon the mountains" been partially fulfilled? (49:25) "In the beginning of this dispensation, the Lord said 'Zion shall flourish upon the hills and rejoice upon the mountains, and shall be assembled together unto the place which I have appointed' (D&C 49:25). Our assemblage today in these mountains beneath the shadow of the [Salt Lake Temple], hewn from the stone of these mountains, stands as a fulfillment of these prophecies" (Benson, *Teachings*, 247).

Why does it appear that Heavenly Father is speaking in verse five and Jesus Christ is speaking in verse twenty-eight? (49:28) "Why would the person speaking change in the same revelation? We answer: what better way is there to establish firmly in the minds of the Saints that the words of Jehovah are the very same words as those of Elohim; that these two glorious beings have the same mind and thus the same thoughts? . . . In this way the Savior establishes that he acts in the full authority of his Father. In like manner, the Holy Ghost, being one with Christ, is empowered to speak the words of Christ and the Father (see Moses 5:9). And as we have seen, angels similarly speak in behalf of their Master (see 2 Nephi 32:3; Revelation 22:8–13)" (Millet and McConkie, *In His Holy Name*, 41). See also Doctrine and Covenants 29:1, 42. ●

"In late fall 1830, Oliver Cowdery and his missionary companions left Kirtland, Ohio, on their way to preach to the [Indigenous nations] in the territory just west of Missouri after having baptized more than one hundred persons into the church [in Kirtland]. In addition, several leaders among the Ohio converts departed as well. Frederick G. Williams, who accompanied Cowdery on the mission to the [Indigenous peoples], departed in November, and Edward Partridge and Sidney Rigdon traveled to New York soon afterward to meet with [the Prophet]. The new church members in Ohio were left without an experienced leader until John Whitmer arrived in January 1831. Upon his arrival, Whitmer noted with dismay that 'the enemy of all righteous had got hold of some of those who [professed] to be his followers, because they had not [sufficient] knowledge to detect him in all his devices.'..."

"After [the Prophet] arrived in Ohio in February 1831, he worked to curtail what he perceived to be excessive and ostentatious spiritual behaviors among the believers" (Joseph Smith Papers, Historical Introduction to "Revelation, 9 May 1831 [D&C 50]," 82). See also commentary in this volume on Doctrine and Covenants 46.

"When Parley P. Pratt returned from Missouri in March, he too noted the continued displays of enthusiasm as he visited the congregations scattered about the Kirtland area. He later wrote, 'Feeling our weakness and inexperience, and lest we should err in judgment concerning spiritual phenomena, myself, John Murdock, and several other Elders, went to Joseph Smith, and asked him to inquire of the Lord concerning these spirits or manifestations.'

"They met on May 9, [1831], and after they prayed together, Joseph Smith received the revelation now found in Doctrine and Covenants 50" (McBride, "Religious Enthusiasm," 109).

Steven C. Harper observed, "Doctrine and Covenants 50 is a masterpiece, perhaps the finest example of teaching anywhere. Christ speaks on the elders' intellectual level in order to be understood. He reaches them where they are and enlightens them. This kind of teaching has results beyond mastery of facts. As a result of it, the weak become strong, and the deceived become discerning. Though Satan had power over the deceived elders, those who 'attend to the words' (v. 1) of this revelation are promised power over him. Christ assures them, 'The spirits shall be subject unto you' (v. 30), on condition that they act on his instructions precisely" (*Making Sense of the Doctrine & Covenants*, 178–79).

Doctrine and Covenants 50:1–5. Many False Spirits Are Abroad in the Earth

What "words of wisdom" has the Lord given concerning false spirits? (50:1–2) "The adversary seeks to trick you. He disguises the destructive consequences of illicit drugs or drinking and instead suggests that it will bring pleasure. He immerses us in the various negative elements that can exist in social media, including debilitating comparisons and idealized reality. In addition, he camouflages other dark, harmful content found online—such as pornography, blatant attacks on others through cyberbullying, and misinformation to cause doubt and fear in our hearts and minds.

"May we recognize Satan's deceptions for what they are. We must continue to be faithful and vigilant,

SECTION 50

Revelation given through Joseph Smith the Prophet, at Kirtland, Ohio, May 9, 1831. Joseph Smith's history states that some of the elders did not understand the manifestations of different spirits abroad in the earth and that this revelation was given in response to his special inquiry on the matter. So-called spiritual phenomena were not uncommon among the members, some of whom claimed to be receiving visions and revelations.

1 Hearken, O ye elders of my church, and give ear to the voice of the living God; and attend to the words of wisdom which shall be given unto you, according as ye have asked and are agreed as touching the church, and the spirits which have gone abroad in the earth.

2 Behold, verily I say unto you, that there are many spirits which are false spirits, which have gone forth in the earth, deceiving the world.

3 And also Satan hath sought to deceive you, that he might overthrow you.

4 Behold, I, the Lord, have looked upon you, and have seen abominations in the church that profess my name.

for so is the only way to discern truth and to hear the voice of the Lord through His servants. As we obey the Lord's commandments, we will always be led in the right way and will not be deceived" (Stevenson, "How to Avoid Deception," *New Era*, Aug. 2020, 48). See also commentary in this volume on Doctrine and Covenants 43:6 and 46:7. ◉

How might Satan's deceptions attempt to "overthrow" us in our day? (50:3) "One kind of deception seeks to mislead us about whom we should follow. In speaking of the last days, the Savior taught: 'Take heed that no man deceive you. For many shall come in my name, saying, I am Christ; and shall deceive many' [Matt. 24:4–5]. In other words, many will seek to deceive us by saying that they or their teachings will save us, so there is no need for a Savior or His gospel. . . .

"Satan also seeks to deceive us about right and wrong and persuade us that there is no such thing as sin. This detour typically starts off with what seems to be only a small departure: 'Just try it once.' . . . If we choose the wrong road, we choose the wrong destination" (Oaks, "Be Not Deceived," *Ensign*, Nov. 2004, 43–44). ◉

A Warning against False Manifestations and Teachings (Doctrine and Covenants 50:1–2)

In all dispensations when the gospel has been on the earth, Satan has sought to counterfeit revelation. The Prophet Joseph Smith observed:

"Soon after the Gospel was established in Kirtland, and during the absence of the authorities of the Church, many false spirits were introduced, many strange visions were seen, and wild, enthusiastic notions were entertained; men ran out of doors under the influence of this spirit, and some of them got upon the stumps of trees and shouted, and all kinds of extravagances were entered into by them; one man pursued a ball that he said he saw flying in the air, until he came to a precipice, when he jumped into the top of a tree, which saved his life; and many ridiculous things were entered into, calculated to bring disgrace upon the church of God, to cause the spirit of God to be withdrawn, and to uproot and destroy those glorious principles which had been developed for the salvation of the human family" (Joseph Smith Papers, "History, 1838–1856, volume C-1," 1311).

John Whitmer recorded that several acted as though they had the sword of Laban, imitated a serpent, "and many other vain and foolish maneuvers that are unseeming and unprofitable to mention. Thus the devil blinded the eyes of some good and honest disciples. I write these things to show how ignorant and undiscerning children are, and how easy mankind is led astray, notwithstanding the things of God that are written concerning his kingdom" (Joseph Smith Papers, "John Whitmer, History, 1831–circa 1847," 26–27).

In our day, false and deceiving spirits may be manifested differently. President M. Russell Ballard has warned: "As Apostles of the Lord Jesus Christ, it is our duty to be watchmen on the tower, warning Church members to beware of false prophets and false teachers who lie in wait to ensnare and destroy faith and testimony. . . . When we think of false prophets and false teachers, we tend to think of those who espouse an obviously false doctrine or presume to have authority to teach the true gospel of Christ according to their own interpretation. We often assume that such individuals are associated with small radical groups on the fringes of society. However, I reiterate: there are false prophets and false teachers who have or at least claim to have membership in the Church. There are those who, without authority, claim Church endorsement to their products and practices. Beware of such" ("Beware of False Prophets and False Teachers," *Ensign*, Nov. 1999, 62).

How does one faithfully endure to the end? (50:5)
Elder L. Tom Perry declared: "Enduring to the end requires faithfulness to the end. . . . Obviously, this is not an easy task. It is intended to be difficult, challenging, and, ultimately, refining as we prepare to return to live with our Father in Heaven and receive eternal blessings.

"Enduring to the end is definitely not a do-it-yourself project.

"1. It requires the Savior's redemptive power. . . .

"2. Enduring to the end requires the Holy Ghost, who will both guide and sanctify us.

"3. We must be an integral part of a community of Saints, serving and receiving service from our brothers and sisters in the gospel. . . .

"4. We must share the gospel with others. . . .

"5. We must always maintain faith and hope in Christ to endure to the end, and among the many ways we do this are praying, fasting, and reading the scriptures. These practices will fortify us against the subtle schemes and fiery darts of the adversary" ("How to Endure to the End," *New Era*, Jun. 2012, 48). ☉

Doctrine and Covenants 50:6–9. Wo unto the Hypocrites and Those Who Are Cut Off from the Church

What influence could hypocrites have on Church members? (50:6–8) Elder D. Todd Christofferson observed, "The Savior's sternest rebukes were to hypocrites. Hypocrisy is terribly destructive, not only to the hypocrite but also to those who observe or know of his or her conduct, especially children. It is faith destroying" ("Reflections on a Consecrated Life," *Ensign*, Nov. 2010, 19).

5 But blessed are they who are faithful and endure, whether in life or in death, for they shall inherit eternal life.

6 But wo unto them that are deceivers and hypocrites, for, thus saith the Lord, I will bring them to judgment.

7 Behold, verily I say unto you, there are hypocrites among you, who have deceived some, which has given the adversary power; but behold such shall be reclaimed;

8 But the hypocrites shall be detected and shall be cut off, either in life or in death, even as I will; and wo unto them who are cut off from my church, for the same are overcome of the world.

9 Wherefore, let every man beware lest he do that which is not in truth and righteousness before me.

10 And now come, saith the Lord, by the Spirit, unto the elders of his church, and let us reason together, that ye may understand;

11 Let us reason even as a man reasoneth one with another face to face.

12 Now, when a man reasoneth he is understood of man, because he reasoneth as a man; even so will I, the Lord, reason with you that you may understand.

13 Wherefore, I the Lord ask you this question—unto what were ye ordained?

14 To preach my gospel by the Spirit, even the Comforter which was sent forth to teach the truth.

15 And then received ye spirits which ye could not understand, and received them to be of God; and in this are ye justified?

16 Behold ye shall answer this question yourselves; nevertheless, I will be merciful unto you; he that is weak among you hereafter shall be made strong.

17 Verily I say unto you, he that is ordained of me and sent forth to preach the word of truth by the Comforter, in the Spirit of truth, doth he preach it by the Spirit of truth or some other way?

Doctrine and Covenants 50:10–14. Elders Are to Preach the Gospel by the Spirit

For what purpose were the elders of the Church instructed to "reason together"? (50:10–12) The Lord's counsel "suggested to the brethren a simple procedure for knowing if a thing be of God or of some other source. The basis for judging was their own growing certitude as they had been taught the gospel and had gained testimonies and, as teachers, had born witness of its truthfulness. On those occasions they were first given and then themselves gave of the Spirit of Truth. Whereas, that which is of God gives light and continues to enlighten . . . that which is of the evil one is a devourer of light and neither edifies nor magnifies the mind of the individual (D&C 50:13–25).

"Thus, sound reasoning based on personal spiritual awareness was their key to discernment" (Christianson, "And Now Come . . . Let Us Reason Together," 207).

Why is it essential that we preach the gospel by the Spirit? (50:13–14) "We must fully realize that it is the Holy Ghost who is the *real* teacher and witness of all truth. Those who do not fully understand this either try to take over for the Holy Ghost and do everything themselves, politely invite the Spirit to be with them but only in a supporting role, or believe they are turning all their teaching over to the Spirit when, in truth, they are actually just 'winging it.' All parents, leaders, and teachers have the responsibility to teach 'by the Spirit' [D&C 50:14]. They should not teach 'in front of the Spirit' or 'behind the Spirit' but 'by the Spirit' so the Spirit can teach the truth unrestrained" (Richardson, "Teachings after the Manner of the Spirit," *Ensign*, Nov. 2011, 94).

Doctrine and Covenants 50:15–22. Both Preachers and Hearers Need to Be Enlightened by the Spirit

What does preaching or receiving truth in "some other way" denote? (50:17–20) After quoting Doctrine and Covenants 50:17–18 to religious educators, Elder Bruce R. McConkie explained: "It said, 'If it be by some other way it is *not* of God' (D&C 50:18).

"What is the antecedent of *it*? It is *the word of truth*. That is to say, if you teach the word of truth—now note, you are saying what is true, everything you say is accurate and right—by some other way than the Spirit, it is not of God. Now what is the other way to teach than by the Spirit? Well, obviously, it is by the power of the intellect" (*Sermons and Writings*, 332). ☉

What does it mean to be edified? (50:22) "The verb *edify* comes from the Latin *aedificare* (pronounced ee-de-fe-CAHR-ee), which means 'to build, erect, or construct.' But what that definition does not specify is that the first part of the word comes from the Latin *aedis,* which means 'a temple, shrine, or tomb,' that is, a sacred building. Thus, directly related to the word *edify* is the word *edifice,* which is a building that is particularly impressive, splendid, or beautiful.

"What a wonderful metaphor! When someone is edified, it is as if a spiritual temple, an edifice, is being constructed in the person's heart. This is why edification is the end goal of all our teaching and preaching. . . . This is *why* we are called to teach and preach the gospel" (Lund, *In Tune*, 23–24). ☉

Doctrine and Covenants 50:23–25. That Which Doth Not Edify Is Not of God

What is the relationship between truth, light, and darkness? (50:24–25) "God our Heavenly Father has given us the right to know the truth. He has shown that the way to receive that truth is simple, so simple that a child can follow it. Once it is followed, more light comes from God to enlighten the understanding of His faithful spirit child. That light will become brighter even as the world darkens. The light that comes to us with truth will be brighter than the darkness that comes from sin and error around us. A foundation built on truth and illuminated by the light of God will free us from the fear that we might be overcome" (Eyring, "Life Founded in Light and Truth," *Ensign,* Jul. 2001, 13). ☉

18 And if it be by some other way it is not of God.

19 And again, he that receiveth the word of truth, doth he receive it by the Spirit of truth or some other way?

20 If it be some other way it is not of God.

21 Therefore, why is it that ye cannot understand and know, that he that receiveth the word by the Spirit of truth receiveth it as it is preached by the Spirit of truth?

22 Wherefore, he that preacheth and he that receiveth, understand one another, and both are edified and rejoice together.

23 And that which doth not edify is not of God, and is darkness.

24 That which is of God is light; and he that receiveth light, and continueth in God, receiveth more light; and that light groweth brighter and brighter until the perfect day.

25 And again, verily I say unto you, and I say it that you may know the truth, that you may chase darkness from among you;

26 He that is ordained of God and sent forth, the same is appointed to be the greatest, notwithstanding he is the least and the servant of all.

27 Wherefore, he is possessor of all things; for all things are subject unto him, both in heaven and on the earth, the life and the light, the Spirit and the power, sent forth by the will of the Father through Jesus Christ, his Son.

28 But no man is possessor of all things except he be purified and cleansed from all sin.

29 And if ye are purified and cleansed from all sin, ye shall ask whatsoever you will in the name of Jesus and it shall be done.

30 But know this, it shall be given you what you shall ask; and as ye are appointed to the head, the spirits shall be subject unto you.

Doctrine and Covenants 50:26–28. The Faithful Are Possessors of All Things

In what way are those who are sent forth appointed to be the greatest? (50:26–27) "An ordination of God gives one the potential to become the greatest of all missionaries, bishops; or whatever calling it may be. However, to do so one must put himself last in priority of concerns, serving all others ahead of him (v. 26). The Gospel of Mark teaches the same concept in slightly different words. 'If any man desire to be first, the same shall be last of all, and servant of all' (Mark 9:35; see also 10:44)" (Nyman, *Doctrine and Covenants Commentary*, 1:451–52).

How does one qualify to become a "possessor of all things"? (50:28) "No unclean thing can enter the presence of God, nor can any unclean thing receive the fulness of the Father. To possess all things, one must 'be purified and cleansed from all sin.' Hence the command to all who would be servants of God: 'Prepare yourselves, and sanctify yourselves; yea, purify your hearts, and cleanse your hands and your feet before me, that I may make you clean; that I may testify unto your Father, and your God, and my God, that you are clean from the blood of this wicked generation' (D&C 88:74–75). Christ alone can make us clean. In the full and proper sense, according to the order he has established, those of our day are invited to go to the temple where the ritual here described is performed" (McConkie and Ostler, *Revelations of the Restoration*, 384–85).

Doctrine and Covenants 50:29–36. The Prayers of the Purified Are Answered

How will the righteous know what to pray for? (50:29–30) "For prayers to be efficacious, they must be in harmony with the plan of heaven. The prayer of faith bears fruit when such harmony exists, and this harmony exists when prayers are inspired by the Holy Spirit. The Spirit manifests what our petitions should be. Absent this inspired guidance, we are inclined to 'ask amiss,' to seek only our will and not 'Thy will.' It is as important to be guided by the Holy Spirit while praying as it is to be enlightened by that same Spirit while receiving an answer to prayer. Such prayer brings forth the blessings of heaven because our Father 'knoweth what things [we] have need of, before [we] ask him,' and He answers every sincere prayer" (McMullin, "Our Path of Duty," *Ensign*, May 2010, 15).

How were the elders of the Church to exercise power over false spirits? (50:31–34) "Because faithful leaders may call upon all the powers of heaven, and because even the spirits are subject to them in the righteous pursuit of their duties, such leaders may ask the Lord to reveal the nature and purpose of any spirit who manifests itself within their stewardship, and the Lord will cause them to receive it. If, however, knowledge and understanding are not forthcoming, if a leader receives 'not that spirit,' that is, if he still cannot understand it after praying about it, then he may know that the spirit or influence in question is not from God (see [D&C 50:32])" (Robinson and Garrett, *Commentary on the Doctrine and Covenants*, 2:106–7). ☉

What is a "railing accusation"? (50:33) "To rail is to revile or scold in harsh or abusive language.... In latter days, the Lord counseled against using railing accusations (D&C 50:33)" (Brewster, *Doctrine & Covenants Encyclopedia* [2012], 455).

Why is it important to "give heed" and "do" those things the Lord counsels? (50:35) "Spiritual truth cannot be ignored—especially divine commandments. Keeping divine commandments brings blessings, every time! Breaking divine commandments brings a loss of blessings, every time!" (Nelson, "Let Your Faith Show," *Ensign*, May 2014, 30).

President Dallin H. Oaks has taught: "Commandments are a blessing, my brothers and sisters, because our Father in heaven has given them to us in order to help us grow and develop the qualities we must have if we are to obtain eternal life and dwell with him" ("Blessing of Commandments," 2).

Doctrine and Covenants 50:37–46. Christ Is the Good Shepherd and the Stone of Israel

Why did the Lord refer to the Saints as "little children"? (50:40–42) "This term of endearment indicates to those Saints that honor their covenants, though they may be immature and childlike, that they

31 Wherefore, it shall come to pass, that if you behold a spirit manifested that you cannot understand, and you receive not that spirit, ye shall ask of the Father in the name of Jesus; and if he give not unto you that spirit, then you may know that it is not of God.

32 And it shall be given unto you, power over that spirit; and you shall proclaim against that spirit with a loud voice that it is not of God—

33 Not with railing accusation, that ye be not overcome, neither with boasting nor rejoicing, lest you be seized therewith.

34 He that receiveth of God, let him account it of God; and let him rejoice that he is accounted of God worthy to receive.

35 And by giving heed and doing these things which ye have received, and which ye shall hereafter receive—and the kingdom is given you of the Father, and power to overcome all things which are not ordained of him—

36 And behold, verily I say unto you, blessed are you who are now hearing these words of mine from the mouth of my servant, for your sins are forgiven you.

37 Let my servant Joseph Wakefield, in whom I am well pleased, and my servant Parley P. Pratt go forth among the churches and strengthen them by the word of exhortation;

38 And also my servant John Corrill, or as many of my servants as are ordained unto this office, and let them labor in the vineyard; and let no man hinder them doing that which I have appointed unto them—

39 Wherefore, in this thing my servant Edward Partridge is not justified; nevertheless let him repent and he shall be forgiven.

40 Behold, ye are little children and ye cannot bear all things now; ye must grow in grace and in the knowledge of the truth.

41 Fear not, little children, for you are mine, and I have overcome the world, and you are of them that my Father hath given me;

42 And none of them that my Father hath given me shall be lost.

43 And the Father and I are one. I am in the Father and the Father in me; and inasmuch as ye have received me, ye are in me and I in you.

44 Wherefore, I am in your midst, and I am the good shepherd, and the stone of Israel. He that buildeth upon this rock shall never fall.

45 And the day cometh that you shall hear my voice and see me, and know that I am.

46 Watch, therefore, that ye may be ready. Even so. Amen.

may take heart in being *Christ's* children through the second birth of the gospel. Faithful Saints then and now should be comforted in knowing that they belong to Christ and that Christ has overcome all things. He will not lose any of them, and nothing can take them out of his hand (see [D&C 50:42]). Further, if the Father and the Son are one, and the faithful Saints are one with the Son, then they are one with the Father (see [D&C 50:43]). There is nothing the faithful Saints need fear in this life or the next—so long as they remain faithful" (Robinson and Garrett, *Commentary on the Doctrine and Covenants*, 2:108).

What can we learn from the Lord's title of "Good Shepherd"? (50:44) "Pastoral symbolism is found in several revelations contained in the Doctrine and Covenants: 'I am the good shepherd' (D&C 50:44), 'the Lamb, who was slain' (D&C 76:39; 135:4), 'feed my sheep' (D&C 112:14), and 'take care of your flocks' (D&C 88:72).... This suggests a biblical influence on modern-day scriptures and shows that pastoral imagery is timeless" (Black, *400 Questions and Answers*, 113).

"The Savior foretold that He would 'feed his flock like a shepherd' [Isaiah 40:11], 'seek [out] that which [is] lost, . . . bring again that which [is] driven away, . . . bind up that which [is] broken, and . . . strengthen that which [is] sick' [Ezekiel 34:16].... Our Good Shepherd is unchanging and feels the same way today about sin and sinners as He did when He walked the earth" (Renlund, "Our Good Shepherd," *Ensign*, May 2017, 30, 32).

How does faithfully watching for the Lord lead to seeing and hearing Him? (50:45–46) "Spiritual complacency and casualness make us vulnerable to the advances of the adversary.... Constant vigilance is required to counteract complacency and casualness. To be vigilant is the state or action of *keeping careful watch* for possible danger or difficulties. And keeping watch denotes the act of *staying awake* to guard and protect....

"Focusing our lives in and on the Savior and His gospel enables us to overcome the tendency of the natural man to be spiritually snoozy and lazy. As we are blessed with eyes to see and ears to hear [see Matthew 13:16], the Holy Ghost can increase our capacity to look and listen when we may not typically think we need to look or listen or when we may not think anything can be seen or heard" (Bednar, "Watchful unto Prayer Continually," *Ensign*, Nov. 2019, 33).

Joseph Smith received the revelation recorded in Doctrine and Covenants 51 while visiting the Colesville Saints on May 20, 1831, at Thompson, Ohio. "The group of sixty or more members residing in and around Colesville in Broome and Chenango counties, New York, constituted one of three groups that emigrated from New York to Ohio." After a month-long journey that included delays due to inclement weather, they arrived in Ohio about mid-May 1831. According to Newel Knight, when they arrived "'it was advised that the Colesville Branch remain together and go to [a] neighboring town called Thompson, as a man by the name [Leman] Copley owned a considerable tract of land there which he offered to let the Brethren occupy'" (Joseph Smith Papers, Historical Introduction to "Revelation, 20 May 1831 [D&C 51]," 86). Bishop Partridge sought instruction from the Prophet on how to provide for the newly arrived Saints, and Joseph enquired of the Lord.

"The revelation presented here gave specific directions to Partridge about how he should implement the consecration of properties and money in Thompson among the newly arrived Colesville members. Although Copley apparently offered to allow church members to live on his land in exchange for making improvements upon it, he may have lacked clear title, a possibility suggested by the language in this revelation that instructed Partridge to 'go & obtain a deed or Article of this land.' Joseph Knight Sr.'s later history affirmed that one of [Joseph Smith's] revelations gave instruction 'to purchase a thousand acres of Land which was Claimed By [sic] Leman Copley and not paid for.'

"There was little opportunity to do as this revelation directed because Copley soon rescinded his agreement to permit the Colesville group to live and work on his land" (Joseph Smith Papers, Historical Introduction to "Revelation, 20 May 1831 [D&C 51]," 86).

Doctrine and Covenants 51:1–8. Edward Partridge Is Appointed to Regulate Stewardships and Properties

What laws were to be used by Bishop Partridge in organizing the Saints? (51:1–2) "When the Lord refers to 'my laws'..., He has reference to His Law of Consecration as first recorded in Doctrine and Covenants 42:30–42. In Section 51, the Lord gave additional insights pertaining to that law and gave commandment for the Colesville Saints. They were to organize themselves under the provisions of the law [at the Copley farm in Thompson, Ohio] and thus become the first people of this dispensation to live under the Law of Consecration. This experience served somewhat as a pilot program and provided Bishop Partridge the opportunity to learn and gain experience with the law (see D&C 51:15, 18)" (Otten and Caldwell, *Sacred Truths*, 1:250).

What does *equal* imply in this verse? (51:3) "Bishop Partridge had chosen Isaac Morley and John Corrill to serve as his counselors. [They discovered that no] two families have exactly the same needs. In the division of properties, the number of children in a family, as well as the ages and abilities of the children, are

SECTION 51

Revelation given through Joseph Smith the Prophet, at Thompson, Ohio, May 20, 1831. At this time the Saints migrating from the eastern states began to arrive in Ohio, and it became necessary to make definite arrangements for their settlement. As this undertaking belonged particularly to the bishop's office, Bishop Edward Partridge sought instruction on the matter, and the Prophet inquired of the Lord.

1 Hearken unto me, saith the Lord your God, and I will speak unto my servant Edward Partridge, and give unto him directions; for it must needs be that he receive directions how to organize this people.

2 For it must needs be that they be organized according to my laws; if otherwise, they will be cut off.

3 Wherefore, let my servant Edward Partridge, and those whom he has chosen, in whom I am well pleased, appoint unto this people their portions, every man equal according to his family, according to his circumstances and his wants and needs.

4 And let my servant Edward Partridge, when he shall appoint a man his portion, give unto him a writing that shall secure unto him his portion, that he shall hold it, even this right and this inheritance in the church, until he transgresses and is not accounted worthy by the voice of the church, according to the laws and covenants of the church, to belong to the church.

5 And if he shall transgress and is not accounted worthy to belong to the church, he shall not have power to claim that portion which he has consecrated unto the bishop for the poor and needy of my church; therefore, he shall not retain the gift, but shall only have claim on that portion that is deeded unto him.

6 And thus all things shall be made sure, according to the laws of the land.

7 And let that which belongs to this people be appointed unto this people.

8 And the money which is left unto this people—let there be an agent appointed unto this people, to take the money to provide food and raiment, according to the wants of this people.

9 And let every man deal honestly, and be alike among this people, and receive alike, that ye may be one, even as I have commanded you.

taken into consideration. A farmer would receive farm land as his stewardship; a printer, a printing office; a tanner, a tannery; and a businessman, a mercantile establishment (D&C 57:8, 11; 104:19–42). . . . In this manner the needs of the poor were provided for and individuals were placed in a position in which they could supply their own wants and aid others in doing the same thing" (McConkie and Ostler, *Revelations of the Restoration*, 389). ⊕

What was the "writing" Bishop Partridge was to give? (51:4–6) "When section 51 was first published in 1835, much of verse 5 was amended then to prevent people from suing the bishop or . . . having 'power to disinherit the poor by obtaining again that which they have consecrated'" (Harper, *Let's Talk about the Law of Consecration*, 33).

In a letter to Bishop Partridge, Joseph clarified: "You are bound by the law of the Lord, to give a deed, securing to him who receives inheritances, his inheritance, for an everlasting inheritance, or in other words, to be his individual property, his private stewardship, and if he is found a transgressor & should be cut off, out of the church, his inheritance is his still. . . . But the property which he consecrated to the poor, for their benefit, & inheritance, & stewardship, he cannot obtain again by the law of the Lord" (Harper, *Let's Talk about the Law of Consecration*, 32–33; spelling modernized).

Why did the Colesville Saints need an agent? (51:7–8) "The community [Colesville branch] was to be represented by an Agent, whose special duty it would be to handle the money required for food and clothing by the people. There is great wisdom manifested in the distribution of responsibilities. The Bishopric would receive the property, distribute it in 'stewardships,' and receive the earnings of each stewardship; the Agent would see to it that property was not unduly accumulated, but that the needs of all were supplied" (Smith and Sjodahl, *Doctrine and Covenants Commentary*, 298).

Doctrine and Covenants 51:9–12. The Saints Are to Deal Honestly and Receive Alike

What were the churches mentioned in this passage? (51:10–11) "This phrase refers to another *branch* of the Church, such as the Church in Missouri as opposed to the Church in Thompson. Contemporary terms might be other stakes, districts, or missions. At this time, apparently, the Lord wished the different areas of the Church to remain financially separate from each other, and the consecration of properties within the different units were to be handled separately" (Robinson and Garrett, *Commentary on the Doctrine and Covenants*, 2:114).

Doctrine and Covenants 51:13–15. They Are to Have a Bishop's Storehouse and to Organize Properties according to the Lord's Law

What is the storehouse described in this verse? (51:13) See commentary in this volume on Doctrine and Covenants 42:34; 42:53–55.

Doctrine and Covenants 51:16–20. Ohio Is to Be a Temporary Gathering Place

What is meant by the Colesville Saints acting upon the land in Ohio "as for years"? (51:16–17) "Because Leman Copley's faith [wavered] and he broke his covenant to consecrate his land, the Colesville Saints occupied his farm in Thompson, Ohio, for only a few weeks. Doctrine and Covenants 51:16 indicates that the Lord was aware that their stay would be just 'for a little season.' Nevertheless, He counseled the Saints to work and live as though they would be there for years. The majority of the Colesville Saints followed these instructions. During their short stay they cleared land, planted crops, and began to build homes, all of which they left behind when Leman Copley demanded that they leave. The Lord later instructed the Colesville Branch to move to Missouri to help lay the foundation of Zion (see D&C 54; 58:6–7)" (*Doctrine and Covenants Student Manual* [2018], 289–90).

How could being a wise steward lead to an inheritance in the joy of the Lord? (51:19) President Dieter F. Uchtdorf observed, "If Jesus Christ were to sit down with us and ask for an accounting of our stewardship, I am not sure He would focus much

10 And let that which belongeth to this people not be taken and given unto that of another church.

11 Wherefore, if another church would receive money of this church, let them pay unto this church again according as they shall agree;

12 And this shall be done through the bishop or the agent, which shall be appointed by the voice of the church.

13 And again, let the bishop appoint a storehouse unto this church; and let all things both in money and in meat, which are more than is needful for the wants of this people, be kept in the hands of the bishop.

14 And let him also reserve unto himself for his own wants, and for the wants of his family, as he shall be employed in doing this business.

15 And thus I grant unto this people a privilege of organizing themselves according to my laws.

16 And I consecrate unto them this land for a little season, until I, the Lord, shall provide for them otherwise, and command them to go hence;

17 And the hour and the day is not given unto them, wherefore let them act upon this land as for years, and this shall turn unto them for their good.

18 Behold, this shall be an example unto my servant Edward Partridge, in other places, in all churches.

19 And whoso is found a faithful, a just, and a wise steward shall enter into the joy of his Lord, and shall inherit eternal life.

20 Verily, I say unto you, I am Jesus Christ, who cometh quickly, in an hour you think not. Even so. Amen.

on programs and statistics. What the Savior would want to know is the condition of our heart. He would want to know how we love and minister to those in our care, how we show our love to our spouse and family, and how we lighten their daily load. And the Savior would want to know how you and I grow closer to Him and to our Heavenly Father" ("On Being Genuine," *Ensign*, May 2015, 82).

Introduction to Doctrine and Covenants 52

The revelation recorded in Doctrine and Covenants 52 was received "by an heavenly vision" to Joseph Smith on June 6, 1831. This was the last day of a conference in Kirtland, Ohio, "which all of the elders of the church had been directed to attend by a February revelation" (Joseph Smith Papers, Historical Introduction to "Revelation, 6 June 1831 [D&C 52]," 87).

"On 3 June 1831 the elders of Israel, then scattered throughout the country to declare the gospel, assembled in Kirtland for a priesthood conference. They came with the promise that the Lord would pour out his Spirit upon them (D&C 44:2). The minutes of the first day of the conference list sixty-two present and tell us that their time was spent in ordaining and giving exhortation. . . . The conference lasted for three days" (McConkie and Ostler, *Revelations of the Restoration*, 394).

"During the conference 'the Lord displayed his power to the most perfect satisfaction of the saints' ([Joseph Smith Papers, 'History, 1838–1856, volume A-1'], 118). Several testified that they saw God in vision during the meeting (see ['Life of Levi Hancock,' quoted in Karl Ricks Anderson, *Joseph Smith's Kirtland*, 107–8]). Lyman Wight said that he witnessed 'the visible manifestations of the power of God as plain as could have been on the day of pentecost,' which included 'the healing of the sick, casting out devils, speaking in unknown tongues, discerning of spirits, and prophesying with mighty power' (in [*Joseph Smith Papers, Documents, Volume 1*, 322; spelling modernized)]. Church historian John Whitmer wrote: 'The Spirit of the Lord fell upon Joseph in an unusual manner. And [Joseph] prophesied that John the Revelator was then among the ten tribes of Israel . . . to prepare them for their return from their long dispersion' (in [*Joseph Smith Papers, Histories, Volume 2*, 39; spelling and capitalization modernized)]).

"Also during the conference, the Prophet Joseph Smith ordained some of the elders to the office of high priest. These were the first ordinations to the office of high priest in the restored Church. The Prophet declared, 'It was clearly evident that the Lord gave us power in proportion to the work to be done, and strength according to the race set before us, and grace and help as our needs required' [*Joseph Smith* (manual)], 352.

"Although Church members at the conference had joyful spiritual experiences, John Whitmer recorded that the adversary was also present: 'While the Lord poured out his spirit upon his servants, the Devil took occasion to make known his power, [and] he bound Harvey Whitlock . . . so that he could not speak.' The Lord revealed the design of the adversary to the Prophet, and Joseph 'commanded the devil in the name of Christ and he departed to our Joy and comfort' (in [*Joseph Smith Papers, Histories, Volume 2*, 40–41; spelling and punctuation modernized)]" (*Doctrine and Covenants Student Manual* [2018], 291–92).

SECTION 52

Revelation given through Joseph Smith the Prophet to the elders of the Church, at Kirtland, Ohio, June 6, 1831. A conference had been held at Kirtland, beginning on the 3rd and closing on the 6th of June. At this conference the first distinctive ordinations to the office of high priest

Doctrine and Covenants 52:1–2. The Next Conference Is Designated to Be Held in Missouri

What did the early revelations indicate relative to Zion's location? (52:1–2) "When the revelation recorded in Doctrine and Covenants 52 was given, the Saints eagerly anticipated the building of the city of Zion, which had been prophesied in the scriptures (see Ether 13:3–6; D&C 28:9; Moses 7:62). In a revelation given in March 1831, the Lord promised that He would reveal the location of the land that the Saints were to purchase for an inheritance (see D&C 48:4–6). They were to gather on this land and build the city of Zion, or New Jerusalem. This city was to be a place of refuge and safety for the Saints (see D&C 45:64–71). In June 1831 the Lord instructed the Prophet Joseph Smith and Sidney Rigdon to go to Missouri and to hold the next conference of the Church there" (*Doctrine and Covenants Student Manual* [2018], 292). See also commentary in this volume on Doctrine and Covenants 42:9, 62.

Doctrine and Covenants 52:3–8. Appointments of Certain Elders to Travel Together Are Made

What preparations and sacrifices faced Joseph and others as they prepared for their journey to Missouri? (52:3) "This was a special hardship for Joseph and his wife Emma. Emma had arrived in Kirtland six months pregnant. The Smiths had first boarded with the Whitneys, and had been in their own quarters on the Morley farm less than three months. Barely a month before this call was received, Emma had given birth to twins who both died within a few hours—her second and third babies to die at birth. Soon afterward the Smiths had adopted the Murdock twins, and now Joseph was called to leave Emma in Kirtland to the care of friends and travel to Missouri for the sake of Zion. The sacrifices required by the Lord in these early days were no less difficult for Joseph and Emma than they were for the other Saints" (Robinson and Garrett, *Commentary on the Doctrine and Covenants*, 2:119).

were made, and certain manifestations of false and deceiving spirits were discerned and rebuked.

1 Behold, thus saith the Lord unto the elders whom he hath called and chosen in these last days, by the voice of his Spirit—

2 Saying: I, the Lord, will make known unto you what I will that ye shall do from this time until the next conference, which shall be held in Missouri, upon the land which I will consecrate unto my people, which are a remnant of Jacob, and those who are heirs according to the covenant.

3 Wherefore, verily I say unto you, let my servants Joseph Smith, Jun., and Sidney Rigdon take their journey as soon as preparations can be made to leave their homes, and journey to the land of Missouri.

4 And inasmuch as they are faithful unto me, it shall be made known unto them what they shall do;

5 And it shall also, inasmuch as they are faithful, be made known unto them the land of your inheritance.

6 And inasmuch as they are not faithful, they shall be cut off, even as I will, as seemeth me good.

7 And again, verily I say unto you, let my servant Lyman Wight and my servant John Corrill take their journey speedily;

8 And also my servant John Murdock, and my servant Hyrum Smith, take their journey unto the same place by the way of Detroit.

9 And let them journey from thence preaching the word by the way, saying none other things than that which the prophets and apostles have written, and that which is taught them by the Comforter through the prayer of faith.

10 Let them go two by two, and thus let them preach by the way in every congregation, baptizing by water, and the laying on of the hands by the water's side.

11 For thus saith the Lord, I will cut my work short in righteousness, for the days come that I will send forth judgment unto victory.

12 And let my servant Lyman Wight beware, for Satan desireth to sift him as chaff.

13 And behold, he that is faithful shall be made ruler over many things.

14 And again, I will give unto you a pattern in all things, that ye may not be deceived; for Satan is abroad in the land, and he goeth forth deceiving the nations—

Doctrine and Covenants 52:9–11. The Elders Are to Teach What the Apostles and Prophets Have Written

What are the Lord's servants sent forth to teach? (52:9) "Those who preach by the power of the Holy Ghost use the scriptures as their basic source of knowledge and doctrine. They begin with what the Lord has before revealed to other inspired men. But it is the practice of the Lord to give added knowledge to those upon whose hearts the true meanings and intents of the scriptures have been impressed. Many great doctrinal revelations come to those who preach from the scriptures. . . . In a living, growing, divine church, new truths will come from time to time and old truths will be applied with new vigor to new situations, all under the guidance of the Holy Spirit of God" (Bruce R. McConkie, *Promised Messiah*, 515–16).

How might the Lord "cut his work short in righteousness"? (52:11) "The Lord will make 'short work' of the world when he moves suddenly and in total righteousness to end it and to establish his millennial kingdom of righteousness. Missionaries, like these called to Missouri, are sent out to warn and prepare the world for the sudden and righteous judgments of God that are soon to come" (Robinson and Garrett, *Commentary on the Doctrine and Covenants*, 2:119–20).

Doctrine and Covenants 52:12–21. Those Enlightened by the Spirit Bring Forth Fruits of Praise and Wisdom

Why are those failing to obey God compared to "chaff"? (52:12–13) "In 1831 Lyman Wight is warned that Satan desired to sift him as chaff . . . Chaff is the non-nutritious waste product of wheat and is separated from the grain by the wind when it is tossed into the air. This process is called sifting. Chaff is like a rudderless vessel that is driven at will by the wind. Satan desires to sift the Saints like chaff, to separate them from the soul-saving, nutritious grain of the gospel and carry them away in the winds of wickedness" (Brewster, *Doctrine & Covenants Encyclopedia* [2012], 521). But those who remain faithful "shall be made ruler over many things" (Doctrine and Covenants 52:13).

What is the Lord's pattern for discerning those who intend to deceive? (52:14–21) Elder David A. Bednar taught: "A pattern is a guide or a model. Vital spiritual patterns are evident in the life of the Savior, in the scriptures, and in the teachings of living prophets and apostles. These spiritual patterns are sources of direction and protection for us and are essential in avoiding the deception that is so pervasive in our world today" ("Pattern in All Things").

One who follows the Lord's pattern may be described as follows (see Doctrine and Covenants 52:14–21):

"1. He is one who prays

"2. He is one whose spirit is contrite, or humble

"3. He is one who receives the Lord's ordinances and obeys the requirements thereof

"4. He is one whose language is meek and uplifting

"5. He is one who receives and recognizes the Lord's power

"6. He is one whose works and teachings will reflect truths given by revelation from the Lord" (Otten and Caldwell, *Sacred Truths*, 1:258). ⊕

Doctrine and Covenants 52:22–44. Various Elders Are Appointed to Go Forth Preaching the Gospel While Traveling to Missouri for the Conference

What can we learn from the Lord mentioning missionaries by name? (52:22–38) Sister Sydney S. Reynolds said, "I believe the Lord knows my name and your name as well . . . The Lord not only knows who we are, He knows where we are, and He leads us to do good" ("He Knows Us; He Loves Us," *Ensign*, Nov. 2003, 76).

15 Wherefore he that prayeth, whose spirit is contrite, the same is accepted of me if he obey mine ordinances.

16 He that speaketh, whose spirit is contrite, whose language is meek and edifieth, the same is of God if he obey mine ordinances.

17 And again, he that trembleth under my power shall be made strong, and shall bring forth fruits of praise and wisdom, according to the revelations and truths which I have given you.

18 And again, he that is overcome and bringeth not forth fruits, even according to this pattern, is not of me.

19 Wherefore, by this pattern ye shall know the spirits in all cases under the whole heavens.

20 And the days have come; according to men's faith it shall be done unto them.

21 Behold, this commandment is given unto all the elders whom I have chosen.

22 And again, verily I say unto you, let my servant Thomas B. Marsh and my servant Ezra Thayre take their journey also, preaching the word by the way unto this same land.

23 And again, let my servant Isaac Morley and my servant Ezra Booth take their journey,

Ezra Booth: One of the First Apostates (Doctrine and Covenants 52:23)

"Ezra Booth was a gifted Methodist preacher from Mantua, Ohio, who joined the Church in the Hiram, Ohio, vicinity around May 1831. He witnessed Joseph Smith's miraculous healing of Elsa Johnson's rheumatic arm, which influenced him to join the Church. Lyman Wight ordained Ezra Booth a high priest 3 June 1831.

"Booth accompanied Isaac Morley on a trip from Ohio to Jackson County, Missouri, in the summer of 1831" (Marrott, "Booth, Ezra," 123).

"On the mission [with Isaac Morley,] Ezra lost his faith in the prophetic calling of Joseph Smith. . . . When Ezra returned to Ohio in September 1831, he was an apostate. Fellowship was withdrawn from him on 6 September 1831: 'I, the Lord, was angry with him who was my servant Ezra Booth, . . . for [he] kept not the law, neither the commandment' (D&C 64:15). Ezra officially denounced Mormonism on 12 September 1831 and published a series of nine letters in the *Ohio Star*, a paper printed in Ravenna, Ohio, explaining [what he called] the 'Mormon delusion.' . . .

"The letters, with what Joseph Smith described as their 'vain calculations to overthrow the work of the Lord,' exposed the 'weakness, wickedness and folly [of Ezra Booth], and left him a monument of his own shame, for the world to wonder at'" (Black, *Who's Who*, 30–31).

also preaching the word by the way unto this same land.

24 And again, let my servants Edward Partridge and Martin Harris take their journey with my servants Sidney Rigdon and Joseph Smith, Jun.

25 Let my servants David Whitmer and Harvey Whitlock also take their journey, and preach by the way unto this same land.

26 And let my servants Parley P. Pratt and Orson Pratt take their journey, and preach by the way, even unto this same land.

27 And let my servants Solomon Hancock and Simeon Carter also take their journey unto this same land, and preach by the way.

28 Let my servants Edson Fuller and Jacob Scott also take their journey.

29 Let my servants Levi W. Hancock and Zebedee Coltrin also take their journey.

30 Let my servants Reynolds Cahoon and Samuel H. Smith also take their journey.

31 Let my servants Wheeler Baldwin and William Carter also take their journey.

32 And let my servants Newel Knight and Selah J. Griffin both be ordained, and also take their journey.

33 Yea, verily I say, let all these take their journey unto one place, in their several courses, and one man shall not build upon another's foundation, neither journey in another's track.

34 He that is faithful, the same shall be kept and blessed with much fruit.

35 And again, I say unto you, let my servants Joseph Wakefield and Solomon Humphrey take their journey into the eastern lands;

36 Let them labor with their families, declaring none other things than the prophets and apostles, that which they have seen and heard

What instructions were given to early missionaries regarding building "upon another's foundation"? (52:33) "During a Church conference held at Kirtland in June of 1831, a number of elders were called to travel to Missouri, preaching the gospel along the way. 'Though the western frontier of Missouri was their destination, they were commanded to take different routes and not build on each other's foundation or travel in each other's track' ([George Q. Cannon, *Life of Joseph Smith the Prophet*], 116; D&C 52:33). These early missionaries were to spend their time breaking new ground for the gospel message. Indeed, their instructions were consistent with the philosophy of the Apostle Paul, who declared, 'Yea, so have I strived to preach the gospel, not where Christ was named, lest I should build upon another man's foundation' (Rom. 15:20)" (Brewster, *Doctrine & Covenants Encyclopedia* [2012], 18–19).

and most assuredly believe, that the prophecies may be fulfilled.

37 In consequence of transgression, let that which was bestowed upon Heman Basset be taken from him, and placed upon the head of Simonds Ryder.

38 And again, verily I say unto you, let Jared Carter be ordained a priest, and also George James be ordained a priest.

39 Let the residue of the elders watch over the churches, and declare the word in the regions round about them; and let them labor with their own hands that there be no idolatry nor wickedness practiced.

40 And remember in all things the poor and the needy, the sick and the afflicted, for he that doeth not these things, the same is not my disciple.

41 And again, let my servants Joseph Smith, Jun., and Sidney Rigdon and Edward Partridge take with them a recommend from the church. And let there be one obtained for my servant Oliver Cowdery also.

42 And thus, even as I have said, if ye are faithful ye shall assemble yourselves together to rejoice upon the land of Missouri, which is the land of your inheritance, which is now the land of your enemies.

43 But, behold, I, the Lord, will hasten the city in its time, and will crown the faithful with joy and with rejoicing.

44 Behold, I am Jesus Christ, the Son of God, and I will lift them up at the last day. Even so. Amen.

Why is laboring with our own hands important to the law of consecration? (52:39–40) "This phrase is a reminder that the law of consecration as practiced in Kirtland was not going to mean a free ride for anyone but was an opportunity and an obligation to work as faithful stewards for the benefit of all. Those who were more interested in what they could get from the labor of others than they were in what they could contribute to the building of Zion valued material possessions above their covenant obligations and therefore could be accused of 'idolatry' as well as wickedness. Practicing even the true religion for purposes of financial benefit rather than to serve and worship God is a form of idolatry—worshiping the blessings more than the Lord who gives them" (Robinson and Garrett, *Commentary on the Doctrine and Covenants*, 2:121–22). ⊕

What can we learn from the Lord's mandate to care for those in need? (52:40) "As Saints of the Most High God, we are to 'remember in all things the poor and the needy, the sick and the afflicted, for he that doeth not these things, the same is not my disciple' (D&C 52:40). Opportunities to go about doing good and to serve others are limitless. We can find them in our communities, in our wards and branches, and certainly in our homes" (Uchtdorf, "Greatest among You," *Ensign*, May 2017, 80).

What did the phrase "the land of your inheritance" mean to the Saints in Missouri? (52:42–43) "Section 52 is exciting. This is the first revelation to identify Missouri as the location of Zion, the Saint's inheritance. . . . The Saints received section 52 with great anticipation, and many went to great lengths to obey its commands" (Harper, *Making Sense of the Doctrine & Covenants*, 188–89).

"Lands of inheritance were located in Jackson County, Missouri, and were given to specific Latter-day Saints as part of the united firm, or united order, for this life and the next" (Black, *400 Questions and Answers*, 114).

This revelation was given to Algernon Sidney Gilbert through the Prophet Joseph Smith at Kirtland, Ohio, in June of 1831. "Sidney Gilbert . . . was a partner to Newel K. Whitney in his general merchandise store in Kirtland during 1830. He approached Joseph Smith after the June 1831 conference and asked what the Lord would have him do. Joseph received this revelation in answer to Gilbert's inquiry. . . .

"This revelation, received in response to [his] request, instructed him to forsake the world, preach the gospel, and be ordained an elder. Gilbert obeyed this commandment and traveled with Joseph Smith and others to Independence, Missouri, where he eventually opened a store and was appointed to serve as the Church's agent" (Woodger, *Essential Doctrine and Covenants Companion*, 104).

SECTION 53

Revelation given through Joseph Smith the Prophet to Algernon Sidney Gilbert, at Kirtland, Ohio, June 8, 1831. At Sidney Gilbert's request, the Prophet inquired of the Lord as to Brother Gilbert's work and appointment in the Church.

1 Behold, I say unto you, my servant Sidney Gilbert, that I have heard your prayers; and you have called upon me that it should be made known unto you, of the Lord your God, concerning your calling and election in the church, which I, the Lord, have raised up in these last days.

2 Behold, I, the Lord, who was crucified for the sins of the world, give unto you a commandment that you shall forsake the world.

3 Take upon you mine ordination, even that of an elder, to preach faith and repentance and remission of sins, according to my word, and the reception of the Holy Spirit by the laying on of hands;

Doctrine and Covenants 53:1–3. Sidney Gilbert's Calling and Election in the Church Is to Be Ordained an Elder

Why would the Lord give such a powerful revelation to Sidney Gilbert? (53:1) Susan Easton Black explained: "[Sidney Gilbert] lived only four years after his baptism. During these years he established a mercantile store for the blessing of 'the affairs of the poor' in Independence, Missouri (D&C 82:12). He was persecuted when mob action erupted in Independence. On 23 July 1833 he was one of six men who offered to give their lives as a ransom for the rest of the Saints in Jackson County" (Black, "Gilbert, A. Sidney," 429).

What does the term "calling and election" refer to in this verse? (53:1) "For some time [Sidney Gilbert] had been concerned with his 'calling and election in the Church' (D&C 53:1). This term, as used here, seems to mean his duty or responsibility in the Church. He was told that his talents would be used for the kingdom but that he must forsake the world and that salvation came only by enduring in righteousness (vv. 2, 4, 7)" (Draper, "To Do the Will of the Lord," 1:229).

Why was Sidney Gilbert told to forsake the world? (53:2) "To forsake the world is to abandon it and its secular concerns and values. For Sidney Gilbert this meant leaving his business in Kirtland to attend to the Lord's business in Missouri. Sidney was to become an elder, preach the gospel, and labor as an agent for the Church and as an assistant to Bishop Partridge" (Robinson and Garrett, *Commentary on the Doctrine and Covenants*, 1:125).

Doctrine and Covenants 53:4–7. Sidney Gilbert Is Also to Serve as a Bishop's Agent

What was an agent in the Church in Sidney Gilbert's time? (53:4) See commentary in this volume on Doctrine and Covenants 51:7–8.

Why would the Lord counsel Sidney Gilbert that to be saved he must "endure to the end"? (53:6–7) "To endure to the end is to remain faithful to one's covenants until death—as did A. Sidney Gilbert. No amount of righteous living early in their lives will save those who abandon their commitments to God later on. To receive all our promised blessings, we must still be faithful and obedient at the end of our lives. One cannot 'retire' from gospel covenants, nor can any amount of youthful righteousness justify disobedience as we grow older. Time and circumstance may reduce our abilities, but they must not reduce our commitment" (Robinson and Garrett, *Commentary on the Doctrine and Covenants*, 1:126).

4 And also to be an agent unto this church in the place which shall be appointed by the bishop, according to commandments which shall be given hereafter.

5 And again, verily I say unto you, you shall take your journey with my servants Joseph Smith, Jun., and Sidney Rigdon.

6 Behold, these are the first ordinances which you shall receive; and the residue shall be made known in a time to come, according to your labor in my vineyard.

7 And again, I would that ye should learn that he only is saved who endureth unto the end. Even so. Amen.

Introduction to Doctrine and Covenants 54

This revelation to Newel Knight was received at Kirtland, Ohio, in June of 1831. The "New York Saints began arriving [at Kirtland] in May [1831], and it was necessary to get them settled. The responsibility rested with Bishop Partridge, so he sought direction from the Prophet. The bishop was instructed to begin apportioning stewardships to the immigrants....

"Joseph Smith directed the Colesville immigrants to settle in Thompson, Ohio, a few miles east of Kirtland, on property owned by Leman Copley. The Saints in Seneca County were assigned to live on the Isaac Morley farm, where they erected log cabins and planted crops. Although Bishop Partridge tried to inaugurate the law of consecration in Thompson, conflicts prevented its full implementation. Because of the failure of his mission to the Shakers, Leman Copley broke his contract that allowed Latter-day Saints to occupy his farmland and ordered them off his property. When informed of the difficulties, the Prophet sought and obtained a revelation instructing Newel Knight, president of the Colesville branch, and others living on the Copley farm to 'repent of all their sins, and ... journey into the regions westward, unto the land of Missouri, unto the borders of the Lamanites' (D&C 54:3, 8). Shortly thereafter, at least fourteen families under Newel Knight's direction left for the Missouri frontier" (*Church History in the Fulness of Times* [2003], 99).

SECTION 54

Revelation given through Joseph Smith the Prophet to Newel Knight, at Kirtland, Ohio, June 10, 1831. Members of the Church living in Thompson, Ohio, were divided on questions having to do with the consecration of properties. Selfishness and greed were manifest. Following his mission to the Shakers (see the heading to section 49), Leman Copley had broken his covenant to consecrate his large farm as a place of inheritance for the Saints arriving from Colesville, New York. As a consequence, Newel Knight (leader of the members living in Thompson) and other elders had come to the Prophet asking how to proceed. The Prophet inquired of the Lord and received this revelation, which commands the members in Thompson to leave Leman Copley's farm and journey to Missouri.

1 Behold, thus saith the Lord, even Alpha and Omega, the beginning and the end, even he who was crucified for the sins of the world—

2 Behold, verily, verily, I say unto you, my servant Newel Knight, you shall stand fast in the office whereunto I have appointed you.

3 And if your brethren desire to escape their enemies, let them repent of all their sins, and become truly humble before me and contrite.

4 And as the covenant which they made unto me has been broken, even so it has become void and of none effect.

5 And wo to him by whom this offense cometh, for it had been better for him that he had been drowned in the depth of the sea.

Doctrine and Covenants 54:1–6. The Saints Must Keep the Gospel Covenant to Gain Mercy

What does Alpha and Omega mean? (54:1) See commentary in this volume on Doctrine and Covenants 19:1.

What were the consequences of Leman Copley breaking the covenant with the Colesville Saints? (54:3–6) "Leman Copley's decision to evict the members of the Colesville Branch from his land was also a decision to break the sacred covenant that he had made to consecrate his property to the Lord. The Saints from New York had also made a covenant to consecrate all that they had (see D&C 51). Unfortunately, Leman's refusal to keep his covenant made it impossible for the Colesville Saints to fulfill their covenant; therefore, the Lord declared that the covenant had 'become void and of none effect' (D&C 54:4). The Lord also alluded to severe consequences for those who broke their covenants and promised mercy to those who kept their covenants (see D&C 54:5–6)" (*Doctrine and Covenants Student Manual* [2018], 297).

In what ways were these Saints seeking to obtain mercy? (54:6) "From these circumstances the Lord, in answering the prayer of his prophet for guidance, recognized the faithfulness of those who, in good faith, endeavored to live by the covenants which they had made" (Roy W. Doxey, Doctrine and Covenants Speaks, 1:376). ⊕

Doctrine and Covenants 54:7–10. They Must Be Patient in Tribulation

Where were the Colesville Saints to resettle? (54:7) "Having left their homes in New York just a month earlier, the members of the Colesville Branch were again without a place to live. In answer to this concern, the Lord provided another commandment for them to move—this time to Missouri, almost 900 miles (1,448 kilometers) away. Although this commandment was difficult for this group of more than 60 faithful Church members, the Lord asked the Saints to 'be patient in tribulation until I come.' . . . In obedience to the Lord's commandment, the Colesville Saints, led by Newel Knight, left Ohio and arrived in Independence, Missouri, at the end of July 1831. They were among the first Latter-day Saints who gathered to the land of Zion" (Doctrine and Covenants Student Manual [2018], 298).

What does the phrase "rest to their souls" mean? (54:10) President Joseph F. Smith taught, "The ancient prophets speak of 'entering into God's rest' [see Alma 12:34; D&C 84:23–24]; what does it mean? To my mind, it means entering into the knowledge and love of God, having faith in his purpose and in his plan, to such an extent that we know we are right, and that we are not hunting for something else, we are not disturbed by every wind of doctrine, or by the cunning and craftiness of men who lie in wait to deceive. . . . The man who has reached that degree of faith in God that all doubt and fear have been cast from him, he has entered into 'God's rest'" (Joseph F. Smith [manual], 56). ⊕

6 But blessed are they who have kept the covenant and observed the commandment, for they shall obtain mercy.

7 Wherefore, go to now and flee the land, lest your enemies come upon you; and take your journey, and appoint whom you will to be your leader, and to pay moneys for you.

8 And thus you shall take your journey into the regions westward, unto the land of Missouri, unto the borders of the Lamanites.

9 And after you have done journeying, behold, I say unto you, seek ye a living like unto men, until I prepare a place for you.

10 And again, be patient in tribulation until I come; and, behold, I come quickly, and my reward is with me, and they who have sought me early shall find rest to their souls. Even so. Amen.

This revelation was given through the Prophet Joseph Smith to William W. Phelps at Kirtland, Ohio, in June of 1831. "William W. Phelps edited the *Ontario Phoenix* newspaper in Canandaigua, New York. He . . . became convinced of the truth of the Book of Mormon and bore a beautiful testimony of its truthfulness. In that spirit he went to Ohio to find Joseph just as the Prophet was leaving for Missouri. William told the Prophet that he had come 'to do the will of the Lord.' Joseph asked the Lord what that was, and the Lord answered with the revelation recorded in Doctrine and Covenants 55, calling both William Phelps and Joseph Coe to the work" (Harper, *Making Sense of the Doctrine & Covenants*, 194).

SECTION 55

Revelation given through Joseph Smith the Prophet to William W. Phelps, at Kirtland, Ohio, June 14, 1831. William W. Phelps, a printer, and his family had just arrived at Kirtland, and the Prophet sought the Lord for information concerning him.

1 Behold, thus saith the Lord unto you, my servant William, yea, even the Lord of the whole earth, thou art called and chosen; and after thou hast been baptized by water, which if you do with an eye single to my glory, you shall have a remission of your sins and a reception of the Holy Spirit by the laying on of hands;

2 And then thou shalt be ordained by the hand of my servant Joseph Smith, Jun., to be an elder unto this church, to preach repentance and remission of sins by way of baptism in the name of Jesus Christ, the Son of the living God.

3 And on whomsoever you shall lay your hands, if they are contrite before me, you shall have power to give the Holy Spirit.

4 And again, you shall be ordained to assist my servant Oliver Cowdery to do the work of printing, and of selecting and writing books for schools in this church, that little children also may receive instruction before me as is pleasing unto me.

Doctrine and Covenants 55:1–3. William W. Phelps Is Called and Chosen to Be Baptized, to Be Ordained an Elder, and to Preach the Gospel

What does it mean to have an "eye single to [God's] glory"? (55:1) "Imagine, if you will, a pair of powerful binoculars. Two separate optical systems are joined together with a gear to focus two independent images into one three-dimensional view. To apply this analogy, let the scene on the left side of your binoculars represent *your perception* of your task. Let the picture on the right side represent the *Lord's* perspective of your task—the portion of His plan He has entrusted to you. Now, connect your system to His. By mental adjustment, fuse your focus. Something wonderful happens. Your vision and His are now the same. You have developed an 'eye single to the glory of God' ([D&C 4:5; see also Morm. 8:15])" (Nelson, *Teachings*, 253). See also commentary in this volume on Doctrine and Covenants 59:1. ☉

Doctrine and Covenants 55:4. William W. Phelps Is Also to Write Books for Children in Church Schools

To what important responsibility was W. W. Phelps called? (55:4) In June 1831, at the end of a Church conference, "Phelps presented himself to the Prophet 'to do the will of the Lord.' In response, section 55 was received. Phelps was commanded to be baptized, be ordained an elder, become Church printer, and move to Independence, Missouri, there to assist Oliver Cowdery. . . .

"Phelps was well prepared for his new Church assignment to be the printer. He was an experienced writer, editor, and publisher. . . . He became known as the 'printer unto the church' and would later become the publisher of the Church's first newspaper, *The Evening and Morning Star*" (James W. McConkie, *Looking at the Doctrine and Covenants Again*, 297).

Doctrine and Covenants 55:5–6. W. W. Phelps Is to Travel to Missouri, Which Will Be the Area of His Labors

Why was W. W. Phelps appointed to his work in Zion? (55:5) "W. W. Phelps was informed that his work would be in the soon-to-be designated site of latter-day Zion. His journey to Kirtland, Ohio, to be baptized was only the beginning of his travels. Once he put his hand to the plow there was to be no turning back. His talents were needed in Independence, Missouri, where he would become editor for the Church newspaper, *The Evening and the Morning Star*, and where he would be called to supervise the printing of the revelations to be published as the Book of Commandments (D&C 57:11)" (McConkie and Ostler, *Revelations of the Restoration*, 405).

Who is Joseph Coe? (55:6) The name of Joseph Coe "appears three times in the Doctrine and Covenants: once in connection with his call to accompany the Prophet Joseph to Missouri (55:6), and twice in regards to his call as a member of the high council at Kirtland (102:3, 34). 'He was one of eight men present

5 And again, verily I say unto you, for this cause you shall take your journey with my servants Joseph Smith, Jun., and Sidney Rigdon, that you may be planted in the land of your inheritance to do this work.

6 And again, let my servant Joseph Coe also take his journey with them. The residue shall be made known hereafter, even as I will. Amen.

Who Was William Wines Phelps? (Doctrine and Covenants 55:1)

"William W. Phelps was first introduced to the Church when he purchased a Book of Mormon on 9 April 1830 from Parley P. Pratt. He 'sat up all night to compare the Book of Mormon with the Bible.' The following morning William exclaimed, 'I am going to join that church; I am convinced that it is true.' In a letter to Oliver Cowdery that was printed in the *Messenger and Advocate* he wrote, 'From the first time I read this volume of volumes, even till now, I have been struck with a kind of sacred joy at its title page. . . . What a wonderful volume! . . .'

"He was baptized on 10 June 1831 and ordained an elder by Joseph Smith" (Black, *Who's Who*, 223–24).

William W. Phelps

"William was appointed as printer for the Church and printed the Book of Commandments as well as the first newspaper of the Church, *The Evening and the Morning Star*. During the early persecution in Missouri, he offered himself as ransom if the mob would stop their destruction. William helped prepare the first Church hymnbook and is the author of a number of well-known hymns, including 'The Spirit of God,' 'Praise to the Man,' 'Now Let Us Rejoice,' and 'Redeemer of Israel.' He also served as scribe for Joseph Smith for the writings of the book of Abraham. In 1838 William became embittered against the Church and testified against its leaders. He was excommunicated in 1839 but later repented and was received back into full fellowship in 1841. He moved west with the Saints and helped draft the constitution for the State of Deseret [now Utah]. He served as an ordinance worker in the Endowment House and died March 6, 1872, at the age of eighty (see [Black, *Who's Who*], 224–26)" (Leavitt and Christensen, *Scripture Study for Latter-day Saint Families: Doctrine and Covenants*, 115).

when the Temple site, west of Independence, was dedicated, August 3rd, 1831. Unfortunately ... he did not remain in the Church. In the year 1837 he cast his lot with John F. Boynton, Luke S. Johnson, Warren Parrish, and others. ... They alleged that Joseph Smith was a "fallen prophet." ... For some time these dissenters took a leading part in the persecution of the Saints at Kirtland' [Smith and Sjodahl, *Doctrine and Covenants Commentary*, 319–20]" (Brewster, *Doctrine & Covenants Encyclopedia* [2012], 90).

Introduction to Doctrine and Covenants 56

"Ezra [Thayer] was an early convert to the restored gospel. After moving from New York to Kirtland, Ohio, [Thayer] was instructed to live and work with Joseph Smith Sr. on the farm of Frederick G. Williams, who was serving a mission in Missouri. On June 6, 1831, the Lord called Thomas B. Marsh and Ezra [Thayer] to travel to Missouri and preach the gospel along the way (see D&C 52:22). Nine days later, Thomas was ready to depart with other elders traveling to Missouri. Ezra, however, was not ready, leaving Thomas without a companion. Thomas approached the Prophet Joseph Smith, desiring to know what to do. The Prophet inquired of the Lord on June 15, 1831, and received the revelation recorded in Doctrine and Covenants 56. It is not clear what prevented Ezra [Thayer] from fulfilling his mission. However, in the revelation to Joseph Smith, the Lord commanded Ezra to 'repent of his pride, and of his selfishness and obey the former commandment' ([D&C 56:8; see also *Joseph Smith Papers, Documents, Volume 1*], 309–14, 339–40)" (*Doctrine and Covenants Student Manual* [2018], 299).

After addressing individuals, including Ezra Thayer, the Lord speaks to the Colesville Saints gathered at the Copley farm in Thompson, and to all Saints generally. As summarized by Steven C. Harper, "They have much to accomplish and many sins to confess and forsake. He knows their sins and has not pardoned them because they seek their own will, not his. ... The Lord curses the rich among them who will not share with the poor. ... The Lord curses the poor who refuse to be humble and content, who lust and covet greedily and refuse to work with their own hands. The Lord blesses the humble and repentant poor. They will be delivered from sorrow and suffering at the Lord's second coming" (Harper, *Making Sense of the Doctrine & Covenants*, 197).

SECTION 56

Revelation given through Joseph Smith the Prophet, at Kirtland, Ohio, June 15, 1831. This revelation chastises Ezra Thayre for not obeying a former revelation (the "commandment" referred to in verse 8), which Joseph Smith had received for him, instructing Thayre concerning his duties on Frederick G. Williams' farm, where he lived. The following revelation also revokes Thayre's call to travel to Missouri with Thomas B. Marsh (see section 52:22).

1 Hearken, O ye people who profess my name, saith the Lord your God; for behold, mine anger is kindled against the rebellious, and they shall know mine arm and mine

Doctrine and Covenants 56:1–2. The Saints Must Take Up Their Cross and Follow the Lord to Gain Salvation

Why is the Lord's anger "kindled against the rebellious"? (56:1) "We have those in the Church these days, as there were in Nauvoo [or even Kirtland], who profess membership but spend much of their time in criticizing, in finding fault, and in looking for defects in the Church, in its leaders, in its programs. They contribute nothing to the building of the kingdom. They rationalize their efforts, trying to justify with pretenses of doing good for the cause, but the result of those efforts is largely only a fragmentation of faith, their own and that of others" (Hinckley, *Teachings*, 121–22).

Joseph Smith once warned of such: "That man who rises up to condemn others, finding fault with the Church, saying that they are out of the way, while he himself is righteous, then know assuredly, that that man is in the high road to apostasy" (*Joseph Smith* [manual], 318).

What might it mean to take up our cross? (56:2)
"We take up our cross as we seek to put down our sins and thereby enter the realm of divine experience. Thus Jesus instructed those who desired discipleship: 'If any man will come after me, let him deny himself, and take up his cross and follow me. And now *for a man to take up his cross, is to deny himself all ungodliness, and every worldly lust, and keep my commandments*' (JST, Matt. 16:25–26; emphasis added)" (Millet, *Eye Single to the Glory of God*, 38). ☉

Doctrine and Covenants 56:3–13. The Lord Commands and Revokes, and the Disobedient Are Cast Off

Why does the Lord sometimes revoke His commandments? (56:3–10) "The Lord speaks of revoking his own commandments. Because he and his purposes are unchanging, and man is constantly changing, he modifies his instructions so as to accomplish his eternal goals in a variety of situations" (Cowan, *Doctrine & Covenants: Our Modern Scripture*, 91). Otten and Caldwell state: "It is important to know that there may be many reasons why the Lord revokes a commandment. But the one He mentions in Section 56 is rebellion (see D&C 56:1–4). This same reason is echoed again as discussed by the Lord in a later revelation: . . . 'I command and men obey not; I revoke and they receive not the blessing' [D&C 58:32]" (*Sacred Truths*, 1:270).

Why did the Lord revoke Newel Knight's commandment? (56:6–7) Once the Colesville Saints learned that their inheritance in Ohio had been dissolved and they were to move to Missouri, they "prepared for their journey [D&C 54]. They selected Newel Knight to continue to preside over them despite his

indignation, in the day of visitation and of wrath upon the nations.

2 And he that will not take up his cross and follow me, and keep my commandments, the same shall not be saved.

3 Behold, I, the Lord, command; and he that will not obey shall be cut off in mine own due time, after I have commanded and the commandment is broken.

4 Wherefore I, the Lord, command and revoke, as it seemeth me good; and all this to be answered upon the heads of the rebellious, saith the Lord.

5 Wherefore, I revoke the commandment which was given unto my servants Thomas B. Marsh and Ezra Thayre, and give a new commandment unto my servant Thomas, that he shall take up his journey speedily to the land of Missouri, and my servant Selah J. Griffin shall also go with him.

6 For behold, I revoke the commandment which was given unto my servants Selah J. Griffin and Newel Knight, in consequence of the stiffneckedness of my people which are in Thompson, and their rebellions.

7 Wherefore, let my servant Newel Knight remain with them; and as many as will go may go, that are contrite before me, and be led by him to the land which I have appointed.

8 And again, verily I say unto you, that my servant Ezra Thayre must repent of his pride, and of his selfishness, and obey the former commandment which I have given him concerning the place upon which he lives.

9 And if he will do this, as there shall be no divisions made upon the land, he shall be appointed still to go to the land of Missouri;

10 Otherwise he shall receive the money which he has paid, and shall leave the place, and shall be cut off out of my church, saith the Lord God of hosts;

11 And though the heaven and the earth pass away, these words shall not pass away, but shall be fulfilled.

12 And if my servant Joseph Smith, Jun., must needs pay the money, behold, I, the Lord, will pay it unto him again in the land of Missouri, that those of whom he shall receive may be rewarded again according to that which they do;

13 For according to that which they do they shall receive, even in lands for their inheritance.

14 Behold, thus saith the Lord unto my people—you have many things to do and to repent of; for behold, your sins have come up unto me, and are not pardoned, because you seek to counsel in your own ways.

15 And your hearts are not satisfied. And ye obey not the truth, but have pleasure in unrighteousness.

previous call, by revelation, to serve a proselyting mission (see Doctrine and Covenants 52). In a revelation now canonized as Doctrine and Covenants 56, Knight was authorized to set aside his mission call and instead travel to Missouri as the head of the Colesville Branch" (Joseph F. Darowski, "Journey of the Colesville Branch," 43).

What might have kept Ezra Thayer (Thayre) from leaving immediately on a mission to Missouri? (56:8–11) "It is uncertain what prevented Thayer from accompanying Marsh, but this revelation refers to the 'former commandment which I have given him [Thayer] concerning the place upon which he lives' and the money Thayer had apparently paid for it. It is likely that he paid some of the balance Williams owed Isaac Moore on the farm where he and the Joseph Smith Sr. family lived and worked. Because the revelation asserts that 'there shall no divisions be made upon the land,' Thayer may have previously requested that before his departure for Missouri, a title be assigned to him for the portion of land he had paid for. The revelation also suggests that he might have requested that the money he had paid toward the debt be returned to him if he was not assigned title" (Joseph Smith Papers, Historical Introduction to "Revelation, 15 June 1831 [D&C 56]," 91).

Doctrine and Covenants 56:14–17. Wo unto the Rich Who Will Not Help the Poor, and Wo unto the Poor Whose Hearts Are Not Broken

How were some Saints seeking "to counsel in [their] own ways"? (56:14) "[These Saints] sought to explain to God why he must do things the way they think he should. Seeking to correct God—to lead, guide, counsel, advise, or instruct him—continues to be a major stumbling block for some people in the Church today. Many who disagree with the Lord's commandments seek to explain why his ways are wrong while their own ways are correct" (Robinson and Garrett, Commentary on the Doctrine and Covenants, 2:138).

Why is it important to examine how we share with the poor? (56:16) "We control the disposition of our means and resources, but we account to God for this stewardship over earthly things. . . . As we pursue the cause of Zion, each of us should prayerfully consider whether we are doing what we should and all that we should in the Lord's eyes with respect to the poor and the needy.

"We might ask ourselves, living as many of us do in societies that worship possessions and pleasures, whether we are remaining aloof from covetousness and the lust to acquire more and more of this world's goods. Materialism is just one more manifestation of the idolatry and pride that characterize Babylon. Perhaps we can learn to be content with what is sufficient for our needs" (Christofferson, "Come to Zion," *Ensign*, Nov. 2008, 39).

What is the Lord's caution for "the poor men, whose hearts are not broken"? (56:17) "This phrase refers to those who would get more back temporally from living the law of consecration than they would put in. Those poor who receive increased assets through the law of consecration must do it with a spirit of humility and gratitude rather than with a 'welfare rights' mentality, demanding the assets of working people. Greed is a sin that plagues both the rich and the poor! Just as the unredeemed and greedy rich often despise the poor and withhold from them what is necessary to live, so the unredeemed and greedy poor often hate the rich and lust after their wealth. Those poor who seek to live the law of consecration out of greed or out of the desire to avoid working for a living can neither establish Zion nor inherit the celestial kingdom" (Robinson and Garrett, *Commentary on the Doctrine and Covenants*, 2:139).

Doctrine and Covenants 56:18–20. Blessed Are the Poor Who Are Pure in Heart, for They Will Inherit the Earth

How will the poor "who are pure in heart" be blessed with the "fatness of the earth"? (56:18) "*Fatness* in this context means abundance, having more than is needed. The poor who are pure and contrite in heart will have all they need, all they can use, of the bounties of this earth—and more besides. When the law of consecration is implemented to its fullest extent by a Zion people, all those who live under it will have enough and to spare—not just of their needs, but of their wants as well (see D&C 51:3;

16 Wo unto you rich men, that will not give your substance to the poor, for your riches will canker your souls; and this shall be your lamentation in the day of visitation, and of judgment, and of indignation: The harvest is past, the summer is ended, and my soul is not saved!

17 Wo unto you poor men, whose hearts are not broken, whose spirits are not contrite, and whose bellies are not satisfied, and whose hands are not stayed from laying hold upon other men's goods, whose eyes are full of greediness, and who will not labor with your own hands!

18 But blessed are the poor who are pure in heart, whose hearts are broken, and whose spirits are contrite, for they shall see the kingdom of God coming in power and great glory unto their deliverance; for the fatness of the earth shall be theirs.

19 For behold, the Lord shall come, and his recompense shall be with him, and he shall reward every man, and the poor shall rejoice;

20 And their generations shall inherit the earth from generation to generation, forever and ever. And now I make an end of speaking unto you. Even so. Amen.

82:17)" (Robinson and Garrett, *Commentary on the Doctrine and Covenants*, 2:140).

What are ways the poor can be delivered in preparation for the coming of the Lord? (56:18–20)
President Russell M. Nelson explained: "Few, if any, of the Lord's instructions are stated more often, or given greater emphasis, than the commandment to care for the poor and the needy. Our dispensation is no exception. . . .

"Ours is not to judge; ours is a covenantal obligation to care for the poor and the needy, to prepare for their rejoicing when the Messiah shall come again (see Doctrine and Covenants 56:18–19).

"The Lord's 'own way' includes, first, reliance on self, then on the family. . . .

"If one's family can't help, the Lord's 'own way' includes the Church organization" (*Teachings*, 263, 264).

Introduction to Doctrine and Covenants 57

"In obedience to the Lord's command to convene a Church conference in Missouri (see D&C 52:2–5), the Prophet Joseph Smith and several others traveled approximately 900 miles from Ohio to Missouri. On July 20, 1831, a few days after arriving in Jackson County, Missouri, Joseph Smith received the revelation recorded in Doctrine and Covenants 57. In this revelation the Lord declared that Independence, Missouri, was to be the center place of the city of Zion and its temple, and He instructed several individuals regarding their roles in building Zion" (*Doctrine and Covenants Student Manual* [2018], 301).

"[Until Doctrine and Covenants 57 was received] no one, including the Prophet, knew exactly where Zion was to be built. Previous revelations had suggested that it would be [near the borders of territories still occupied by several Indigenous tribes] (see D&C 28:9), 'into the western countries' (see D&C 45:64), and 'into the regions westward, unto the land of Missouri' (see D&C 54:8). Oliver Cowdery and the missionaries to the [Indigenous nations], however, still faithful to their call (see D&C 28:8), were laboring in the vicinity of Independence in Jackson County, Missouri, so it was there that the Prophet and his company first headed. The Prophet and his companions . . . [arrived] in Independence by 17 July 1831" (Robinson and Garrett, *Commentary on the Doctrine and Covenants*, 2:141–42).

"According to the history [Joseph Smith] initiated in 1838, [Joseph] spent time upon his arrival in Independence ruminating on the situation of the [Indigenous tribes] living . . . across the border. Perhaps because an earlier revelation explained that the city of Zion was to be built 'among [them],' these meditations prompted him to ask questions about when and where the city would be built" (Joseph Smith Papers, Historical Introduction to "Revelation, 20 July 1831 [D&C 57]," 93).

SECTION 57

Revelation given through Joseph Smith the Prophet, in Zion, Jackson County, Missouri, July 20, 1831. In compliance with the Lord's command to travel to Missouri, where He would reveal "the land of your inheritance" (section 52), the elders had journeyed from

Doctrine and Covenants 57:1–3. Independence, Missouri, Is the Place for the City of Zion and the Temple

How was Joseph able to identify the place for the city of Zion? (57:1–2) The Prophet wrote: "Having received, by an heavenly vision, a commandment . . . to take my journey to the western boundaries of the State of Missouri, and there designate the very spot, which was to be the central spot, for the commencement of the gathering together of those who embrace the fulness of the everlasting gospel—I accordingly undertook the journey with certain ones of my brethren. . . . I arrived in Jackson county Missouri; and, after viewing the country, seeking diligently at the hand of God, He manifested himself unto me, and designated to me and others, the very spot upon which he designed to commence the work of the gathering, and the upbuilding of an holy city, which should be called Zion" (Joseph Smith Papers, "Letter to the Elders of the Church, 2 October 1835," 179).

Why would this revelation have been important to the early members of the Church? (57:2–3) Through the Prophet Joseph Smith, the Lord revealed "that eventually the center place [of Zion] was to be in Independence, Jackson County, Missouri (D&C 57:1–3; 101:17–21). It was to this center place that the King of kings would come to his temple and to the priesthood

Ohio to Missouri's western border. Joseph Smith contemplated the state of the Lamanites and wondered: "When will the wilderness blossom as the rose? When will Zion be built up in her glory, and where will Thy temple stand, unto which all nations shall come in the last days?" Subsequently he received this revelation.

1 Hearken, O ye elders of my church, saith the Lord your God, who have assembled yourselves together, according to my commandments, in this land, which is the land of Missouri, which is the land which I have appointed and consecrated for the gathering of the saints.

2 Wherefore, this is the land of promise, and the place for the city of Zion.

3 And thus saith the Lord your God, if you will receive wisdom here is wisdom. Behold, the place which is now called Independence is the center place; and a spot for the temple is lying westward, upon a lot which is not far from the courthouse.

Zion and the Temple (Doctrine and Covenants 57:1–3)

Elder Bruce R. McConkie wrote: "In July 1831, in Jackson County, Missouri, 'the Prophet exclaimed in yearning prayer: "When will the wilderness blossom as the rose? When will Zion be built up in her glory, and where will thy Temple stand, unto which all nations shall come in the last days?"' [see Heading to D&C 57].

"In the true sense, the wilderness shall blossom as the rose when the earth is renewed and receives its paradisiacal glory. In the full sense, Zion shall regain her ancient glory, and attain that grandeur and might promised in the prophetic word, only during the Millennium, though the work of establishing Zion and building the New Jerusalem must precede our Lord's return. And as to the temple unto which all nations shall come in the last days, it shall be built in the New Jerusalem before the Second Coming, all as a part of the preparatory processes that will make ready a people for their Lord's return.

"And so the Lord, giving line upon line, as his purposes mandate, revealed to the Prophet a partial answer to his yearning plea. He named the heaven-selected site of the temple and also what the little flock should then do relative to the building of that holy house. 'The land of Missouri . . . is the land which I have appointed and consecrated for the gathering of the saints. Wherefore, this is the land of promise, and the place for the city of Zion. And thus saith the Lord your God, if you will receive wisdom here is wisdom. Behold, the place which is now called Independence is the center place; and a spot for the temple is lying westward, upon a lot which is not far from the courthouse' (D&C 57:1–3)" (*New Witness*, 594–95).

council at Adam-ondi-Ahman (Malachi 3:1; D&C 84:2–5; 116). The Saints rejoiced in the knowledge that their trials and vicissitudes were temporary and that the millennial Messiah would one day cleanse the earth of all wickedness and dwell in peace for a thousand years on a paradisiacal earth with his covenant people" (Millet, *Precept upon Precept*, 296–97).

What is the significance of Independence being divinely declared as the "center place"? (57:3)
"The center place! Let Israel gather to the stakes of Zion in all nations.... But still there is a center place, a place where the chief temple shall stand, a place to which the Lord shall come, a place whence the law shall go forth to govern all the earth in that day when the Second David reigns personally upon the earth. And that center place is what men now call Independence in Jackson County, Missouri, but which in a day to come will be the Zion of our God and the City of Holiness of his people. The site is selected; the place is known; the decree has gone forth; and the promised destiny is assured" (Bruce R. McConkie, *New Witness*, 595).

The Temple Lot in Independence, Missouri (Doctrine and Covenants 57:3)

"Where is the temple lot?

"The temple lot is in the western portion of the city of Independence.... People who visit the Independence Visitors' Center can see the lot when they exit through the front doors. It lies immediately to the northwest....

"When was the land dedicated as a temple lot? Who pronounced the dedication?

"John Whitmer wrote that on August 3, 1831, eight elders 'assembled together where the temple [was] to be erected.' Those eight elders were the Prophet Joseph Smith, Oliver Cowdery, Sidney Rigdon, Peter Whitmer Jr., Frederick G. Williams, William W. Phelps, Martin Harris, and Joseph Coe. John Whitmer recorded: 'Sidney Rigdon dedicated the ground where the city is to stand, and Joseph Smith Jr. laid a stone at the northeast corner of the contemplated temple in the name of the Lord Jesus of Nazareth. After all present had rendered thanks to the great ruler of the universe, Sidney Rigdon pronounced this spot of ground wholly dedicated unto the Lord forever.' ...

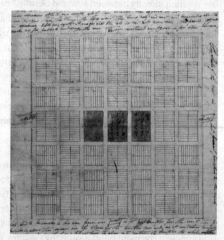

Temple Lot Plat Map, Independence, Missouri

"When did the Saints acquire the temple lot?

"On December 19, 1831, Bishop Edward Partridge purchased 63.27 acres from the Flournoys. That land included the area that had been dedicated for a temple....

"Who owns the temple lot today?

"Community of Christ owns most of the 63.27 acres purchased by Bishop Partridge. The Church of Jesus Christ of Latter-day Saints owns the next-largest portion.

"The smallest portion of the land—including the spot dedicated for a temple—is owned by the Church of Christ, once known as the Church of Christ (Temple Lot)" (West, "Questions and Answers about the Temple Lot").

Doctrine and Covenants 57:4–7. The Saints Are to Purchase Lands and Receive Inheritances in That Area

What is "the line running ... between Jew and Gentile"? (57:4) "For generations, a small number of Europeans—mainly Spanish and French traders—lived among the [native peoples] along the Missouri River, intermarried, and entered into commerce with them. But as white families pushed westward, settling in lands then occupied by [Indigenous peoples], they overwhelmingly rejected these cultural exchanges. Whites demanded that all [Indigenous nations] be removed from the state. Between 1824 and 1830, [Indigenous nations] who had lived within Missouri's borders for centuries ceded virtually all of their territory. The mighty Osage sold their lands in 1825 and migrated further west to Kansas and Oklahoma. By the time the Latter-day Saints arrived in Jackson County in 1831, [Indigenous peoples] had vacated their settlements and evacuated beyond a newly established line dividing [Indigenous nations] and white territories.

"Doctrine and Covenants 57 observed the existence of this settlement line without endorsing it. The revelation noted that Zion should be built along "the line running directly between Jew and Gentile," or the line separating the state of Missouri from Indian Territory to the west. The revelation resisted the usual categories, however, primarily through its curious use of the terms *Jew* and *Gentile*. The standard terms then used by [white] Americans—*white* and *Indian* or *white* and *red*—suggested a racial and cultural divide. The two groups were worlds apart, and white people often deployed the terminology to emphasize this incompatibility.

"The categories of Jew and Gentile, however, indicated a distinction between groups but not an incompatibility between them. According to the Book of Mormon, both Jew and Gentile had a vital role in God's unfolding plan. God invited them to work together. The gospel in ancient times would go from the Jews, God's ancient covenant people, unto the Gentiles, who would be grafted into the covenant. In the latter days the relationship would be reversed—the gospel would proceed from the Gentiles unto the Jews, who would come to recognize Jesus as the Messiah. Doctrine and Covenants 57 echoes this covenantal structure by designating [Indigenous peoples] as Jews, in this way recognizing the group as part of God's covenant people. The [Indigenous nations] were of the house of Israel, chosen, beloved, and remembered by God.

4 Wherefore, it is wisdom that the land should be purchased by the saints, and also every tract lying westward, even unto the line running directly between Jew and Gentile;

5 And also every tract bordering by the prairies, inasmuch as my disciples are enabled to buy lands. Behold, this is wisdom, that they may obtain it for an everlasting inheritance.

6 And let my servant Sidney Gilbert stand in the office to which I have appointed him, to receive moneys, to be an agent unto the church, to buy land in all the regions round about, inasmuch as can be done in righteousness, and as wisdom shall direct.

"At the time when Indian removal—the separation of one race from another—had become a national policy of the U.S. government, Joseph Smith's revelations moved in another direction. Rather than marginalizing [Indigenous nations], pushing them to the outskirts of civilization, the revelations brought Zion to them, putting God's holy city in their midst. Zion was to be found between Jew and Gentile, between the races. In this arrangement, people of multiple races could play an essential role in God's work. People on every compass point of the center, if they were willing, could become 'the pure in heart' and dwell in Zion in safety and peace" (Woodworth, "Center Place," 125–26).

When did the Saints begin to fulfill the commandment to purchase land in Missouri? (57:4–5)
Preparation for the purchasing of lands began "on August 2, 1831 [when] Sidney Rigdon pronounced the land 'consecrated and dedicated to the Lord for a possession and inheritance for the Saints.' The next day, Rigdon dedicated a site half a mile west of the center of Independence for the building of a temple, and Joseph Smith laid the first cornerstone.

"Under the direction of Bishop Edward Partridge, the first Saints who settled in the area began purchasing property and preparing for other Saints to gather to build Zion. Between 1831 and 1833, the Church purchased 180 acres in Independence and 1,200 acres in surrounding areas of Jackson County, and some 1,200 Saints gathered to the county and organized five branches" (Church History Topics, "Independence, Missouri").

What were the Lord's instructions to Edward Partridge? (57:7) "Bishop Partridge was to continue in his calling (see D&C 41:9; 42:10), receiving consecrations and assigning stewardships to the Saints just as he had been instructed in Doctrine and Covenants 51" (Robinson and Garrett, *Commentary on the Doctrine and Covenants*, 2:144). See also commentary in this volume on Doctrine and Covenants 41:9.

7 And let my servant Edward Partridge stand in the office to which I have appointed him, and divide unto the saints their inheritance, even as I have commanded; and also those whom he has appointed to assist him.

Doctrine and Covenants 57:8–16.
Sidney Gilbert Is to Establish a Store, William W. Phelps Is to Be a Printer, and Oliver Cowdery Is to Edit Material for Publication

Why was Sidney Gilbert charged to establish a store in Independence? (57:8–10) "The Lord appoints Sidney Gilbert as the bishop's real estate agent, directing him to establish a store and use the revenue to buy land. Gilbert is also to obtain a license from the [federal] agents that would permit him to sell supplies to the [Indigenous nations]. The idea is that he would receive government subsidies for that purpose, providing employment and resources for the Saints and opening opportunities for preaching the gospel to the [Indigenous peoples]" (Harper, *Making Sense of the Doctrine & Covenants*, 200).

How did W. W. Phelps and Oliver Cowdery respond to the Lord's instructions in this revelation? (57:11–13) "Brother Phelps was instructed to carry on his assignment of printing, selecting, and writing (see D&C 55:4) in Independence, Missouri. His stewardship was to be a printer and to make whatever money he could at that trade . . . while also meeting the printing needs of the Church. . . .

"Oliver Cowdery was a literate man, and it may be that some of his literary skills would be needed to help W. W. Phelps complete his assignment. Oliver was not being demoted, however, to a printer's helper. Rather, as Oliver presided over the Church in Zion, he was to see that W. W. Phelps had whatever he needed—including Oliver's personal help" (Robinson and Garrett, *Commentary on the Doctrine and Covenants*, 2:145). See also commentary in this volume on Doctrine and Covenants 55:4. ☉

How did Edward Partridge respond to the Lord's invitation to "be planted" with his family in the land of Zion? (57:14) "In a letter to Lydia written a few days later, [Edward] Partridge broke the news that he wouldn't be returning to Ohio that summer and instead asked that she and their five daughters join him on the Missouri frontier. . . . [Edward] also warned that once she joined him in Missouri, 'We have to suffer & shall for some time many privations here which you & I have not been much used to for year[s].' . . . Lydia

8 And again, verily I say unto you, let my servant Sidney Gilbert plant himself in this place, and establish a store, that he may sell goods without fraud, that he may obtain money to buy lands for the good of the saints, and that he may obtain whatsoever things the disciples may need to plant them in their inheritance.

9 And also let my servant Sidney Gilbert obtain a license—behold here is wisdom, and whoso readeth let him understand—that he may send goods also unto the people, even by whom he will as clerks employed in his service;

10 And thus provide for my saints, that my gospel may be preached unto those who sit in darkness and in the region and shadow of death.

11 And again, verily I say unto you, let my servant William W. Phelps be planted in this place, and be established as a printer unto the church.

12 And lo, if the world receive his writings—behold here is wisdom—let him obtain whatsoever he can obtain in righteousness, for the good of the saints.

13 And let my servant Oliver Cowdery assist him, even as I have commanded, in whatsoever place I shall appoint unto him, to copy, and to correct, and select, that all things may be right before me, as it shall be proved by the Spirit through him.

14 And thus let those of whom I have spoken be planted in the land of Zion, as speedily as can be, with their families, to do those things even as I have spoken.

willingly obeyed the revelation to move, packing her home and gathering her five daughters to travel west to a place she had never seen before" (Farnes, "Bishop unto the Church," 79–80).

15 And now concerning the gathering—Let the bishop and the agent make preparations for those families which have been commanded to come to this land, as soon as possible, and plant them in their inheritance.

16 And unto the residue of both elders and members further directions shall be given hereafter. Even so. Amen.

What families were specifically "commanded to come" to the land of Zion? (57:15) "Reference here is particularly to members of the Colesville Branch, who traveled under the direction of Newel Knight. Obedient to the Lord's command that they relocate in Missouri (D&C 54:8), this group of Saints arrived in Independence 25 July 1831. Arrangements were made for them to settle near the Big Blue River in Jackson County, approximately twelve miles west of Independence" (McConkie and Ostler, *Revelations of the Restoration*, 416).

Introduction to Doctrine and Covenants 58

"On 1 August 1831, [Joseph Smith] dictated this revelation to the elders of the church who had joined him in western Missouri. Just a few days earlier, a revelation had designated Jackson County, Missouri, as the location at which to build the 'City of Zion.' Upon arriving in Jackson County, however, some of the elders expressed disappointment with what they found. Oliver Cowdery, Ziba Peterson, Peter Whitmer Jr., and Frederick G. Williams had been preaching to white settlers in Independence and the vicinity since they were ejected from Indian Territory west of Missouri by February 1831. Despite their efforts, those arriving in Missouri in July found fewer than ten converts, whereas some had expected a burgeoning community of believers and perhaps a settlement that would soon be able to accommodate the migration of church members" (Joseph Smith Papers, Historical Introduction to "Revelation, 1 August 1831 [D&C 58]," 94).

"In spite of disappointment and the enormity of the city building project, Joseph was determined to make a start. Together with Sidney Rigdon and others, he set to work. They consecrated the land near Independence for a place of gathering, laid the first log for a house in Zion, and set the northeast cornerstone for a temple" (McBride, "Ezra Booth and Isaac Morley," 132).

"The first Sabbath after our arrival in Jackson county, Brother W. W. Phelps preached to a western audience over the boundary of the United States, wherein were present [people] of all the families of the earth; Shem, Ham and Japheth . . . [including] citizens of the surrounding country, and fully represented themselves as pioneers of the West. At this meeting two were baptized, who had previously believed in the fulness of the Gospel" (Joseph Smith Papers, "History, 1838–1856, volume A-1," 129).

SECTION 58

Revelation given through Joseph Smith the Prophet, in Zion, Jackson County, Missouri, August 1, 1831. Earlier, on the first Sabbath after the arrival of the Prophet and his party in Jackson County, Missouri, a religious service had been held, and two members had been received by baptism. During that week, some of the Colesville Saints from the Thompson Branch

Doctrine and Covenants 58:1–5.
Those Who Endure Tribulation Will Be
Crowned with Glory

What were the early Saints to expect when laying the foundation of Zion? (58:1–4) "'The revelation implied that the enjoyment of Zion lay in the future.' Three times in its first four verses Doctrine and Covenants 58 warns of 'tribulation' or 'much tribulation' before the establishment of Zion. The revelation tempers the Saints' zeal even as it points to the promised land.

"Indeed, the revelation launches into a grand vision of Zion's preparing a feast to which all nations should be invited.... These first few Saints called to Zion have the privilege of laying its foundation and testifying of its potential. Their calling is to pioneer" (Harper, *Making Sense of the Doctrine & Covenants*, 202, 203).

What are the Saints to learn concerning this land of Zion? (58:2–5) "Here we learn several interesting things. Verse 2 speaks of death and urges the Saints to faithfulness even in the face of it. Why mention death at this point? Well, the fact is that Polly Knight, wife of Joseph Knight, Sr., has just died. She had made a great effort to live until she could place her feet upon the land of Zion. In addition, others were yet to lose their lives in sacrifice for the kingdom. Hence the Lord speaks of those things to 'come hereafter, and the glory which shall follow after much tribulation' [v. 3]. Now—a second question: Why mention tribulation at this point? There hasn't been any—not in Missouri at least. But there is going to be, the Lord knows and so warns the Saints" (Gentry, "Design of God in Latter-day Saint Church History," 126).

What blessings come from remaining faithful during trials and tribulations? (58:2) "Day by day we move forward, undeterred by the refining challenges of mortality....

"We develop patience and trust in the Lord. We are able to rely on His design for our lives, even though we cannot see it with our own natural eyes [see D&C 58:3].... When faced with the storms of tribulation, we ask, 'What wouldst Thou have me learn from this experience?' With His plan and purposes in our hearts, we move forward not only enduring all things but also enduring them patiently and well" (Hales, "Becoming a Disciple of Our Lord Jesus Christ," *Ensign*, May 2017, 47–48). ◉

and others arrived (see section 54). Many were eager to learn the will of the Lord concerning them in the new place of gathering.

1 Hearken, O ye elders of my church, and give ear to my word, and learn of me what I will concerning you, and also concerning this land unto which I have sent you.

2 For verily I say unto you, blessed is he that keepeth my commandments, whether in life or in death; and he that is faithful in tribulation, the reward of the same is greater in the kingdom of heaven.

3 Ye cannot behold with your natural eyes, for the present time, the design of your God concerning those things which shall come hereafter, and the glory which shall follow after much tribulation.

4 For after much tribulation come the blessings. Wherefore the day cometh that ye shall be crowned with much glory; the hour is not yet, but is nigh at hand.

5 Remember this, which I tell you before, that you may lay it to heart, and receive that which is to follow.

6 Behold, verily I say unto you, for this cause I have sent you—that you might be obedient, and that your hearts might be prepared to bear testimony of the things which are to come;

7 And also that you might be honored in laying the foundation, and in bearing record of the land upon which the Zion of God shall stand;

8 And also that a feast of fat things might be prepared for the poor; yea, a feast of fat things, of wine on the lees well refined, that the earth may know that the mouths of the prophets shall not fail;

9 Yea, a supper of the house of the Lord, well prepared, unto which all nations shall be invited.

10 First, the rich and the learned, the wise and the noble;

How did the perceptions of the early Saints differ from the Lord's vision for Zion? (58:4) The Saints were anxious to build the city of Zion and anticipated its fulfillment. But the Prophet Joseph Smith warned: "I would remind you of a certain clause in one [revelation] which says, that after *much* tribulation cometh the blessing [see D&C 58:4]. By this . . . I know that Zion, in the due time of the lord, will be redeemed; but how many will be the days of purification, tribulation, and affliction, the Lord has kept hid from my eyes; and when I inquire concerning this subject, the voice of the Lord is: Be still, and know that I am God!" (*Joseph Smith* [manual], 185–86).

Doctrine and Covenants 58:6–12. The Saints Are to Prepare for the Marriage of the Lamb and the Supper of the Lord

Why did the Lord have the Saints go to Missouri (Zion) at this time? (58:6–7) "There are four basic purposes outlined by the Lord [for having the Saints come to Missouri]. The first was a test of obedience for those Saints. . . . [The second purpose was to] prepare their hearts so that they could bear testimony of what was to come—the building of Zion. . . . The third purpose . . . was to lay the foundation for the city of the Zion of God. This was an honor that the Lord gave them, but it also enhanced their ability to bear testimony of the land. Their last purpose . . . was not understood by the Saints then nor by many today. It was to prepare a feast for the poor" (Nyman, "Redemption of Zion (D&C 57–62)," 235, 236).

How might the poor be blessed by the establishment of Zion? (58:8–12) "A central part of the latter-day mission of the Church is to eradicate the poverty that exists in our communities and in our hearts; establish a unified Zion; and prepare the people for the return of Jesus Christ, the Son of God. . . .

"If we are serious about our covenants, we will each strive to be of one heart and one mind, to live in righteousness, and to have no poor among us. This will knit our hearts together and help to reduce the inequities in the world. But there is an even greater power when people of the covenant combine their efforts: families, quorums, Relief Society, Young Women classes, and stakes can organize to address specific needs in their communities to tremendous effect" (Eubank, "Lord Called His People Zion," *Liahona*, Mar. 2020, 27, 29).

What is the meaning of the marriage of the Lamb and the supper of the Lord? (58:11) "Israel's covenant relationship with God is symbolically portrayed in the scriptures as a marriage covenant [see Hosea 2; Matthew 23]. Marriage is the relationship that requires the most fidelity, sacrifice, commitment, and long-suffering of all relationships. The 'marriage supper of the Lamb' is a symbolic reference to the Second Coming of Jesus Christ.... Elder Bruce R. McConkie ... explained: 'In this dispensation the Bridegroom, who is the Lamb of God, shall come to claim his bride, which is the Church composed of the faithful saints who have watched for his return. As he taught in the parable of the marriage of the king's son, the great marriage supper of the Lamb shall then be celebrated. (Matt. 22:1–14.)' ([*Doctrinal New Testament Commentary*, 3:563])" (*New Testament Student Manual* [2018], 562).

Doctrine and Covenants 58:13–18. Bishops Are Judges in Israel

How might the phrase "that the testimony might go forth from Zion" be understood? (58:13) "The testimony is that of future events associated with the end of the world and the second coming of Christ and the changes these events will bring to the earth and its people (see vv. 7–11)" (Robinson and Garrett, *Commentary on the Doctrine and Covenants*, 2:152).

Why did the Lord rebuke Edward Partridge at this time? (58:14–15) "Tension arose between Bishop Edward Partridge and [Joseph Smith].... According to one observer, Partridge argued with [Joseph] about the quality of the land selected for purchase. The disagreement apparently generated hard feelings on both sides" (Joseph Smith Papers, Historical Introduction to "Revelation, 1 August 1831 [D&C 58]," 94). Minutes of a meeting in Zion that considered the argument between the Prophet Joseph and Bishop Partridge say that Partridge said that "he is & has always been sorry" for the disagreement (Joseph Smith Papers, "Minute Book 2, [Mar. 10, 1832]," 23).

What is "blindness of heart"? (58:15) "'Blindness of heart' means affections not guided by the light of the Spirit. Those who place their affection upon wrong objects, such as belong to the world, in preference to those that pertain to the Kingdom of God, are blind at heart, no matter how clear the physical or mental vision may be...."

11 And after that cometh the day of my power; then shall the poor, the lame, and the blind, and the deaf, come in unto the marriage of the Lamb, and partake of the supper of the Lord, prepared for the great day to come.

12 Behold, I, the Lord, have spoken it.

13 And that the testimony might go forth from Zion, yea, from the mouth of the city of the heritage of God—

14 Yea, for this cause I have sent you hither, and have selected my servant Edward Partridge, and have appointed unto him his mission in this land.

15 But if he repent not of his sins, which are unbelief and blindness of heart, let him take heed lest he fall.

16 Behold his mission is given unto him, and it shall not be given again.

"Unbelief and blindness are sins. . . . If we are weak in faith and blind in affections, we need to go to [the] Great Physician, who can heal us, and if we neglect to do this, we are guilty" (Smith and Sjodahl, *Doctrine and Covenants Commentary*, 338, 339).

What does it mean to be "a judge in Israel"? (58:17–18) "Reference is to judges and officers that sat in the gates of the cities of ancient Israel. To them were brought the disputes and legal matters of the community, which they were to settle. Judges also taught the law of God to the Lord's people and instructed them in the ways of righteousness. . . . In this revelation the Lord restored the principle of receiving a land inheritance that was integral to the Abrahamic covenant. Bishop Edward Partridge filled a similar role to the ancient judges when Saints received inheritances at his hand. This land assignment also prefigured the day when the Saints will literally inherit the earth" (McConkie and Ostler, *Revelations of the Restoration*, 421).

Doctrine and Covenants 58:19–23. The Saints Are to Obey the Laws of the Land

Why was the law of obedience an essential principle for these Saints in Missouri? (58:19) This revelation "continues by outlining obedience to law as a second principle upon which Zion must be built. 'My law shall be kept on this land,' the Lord declared (v. 19). Using Martin Harris as 'an example unto the church, in laying his moneys before the bishop of the church,' the Lord linked consecration specifically to the establishment of Zion, declaring that consecration is 'a law unto every man that cometh unto this land [Zion] to receive an inheritance.' To be a part of Zion, each man must do 'with his moneys according as the law directs' (vv. 35–36).

"Obedience to God is connected to the proactive use of agency" (Scott C. Esplin, "Let Zion in Her Beauty Rise," 137).

How might bishops today benefit from the counsel to Edward Partridge? (58:20) "In other words, a Bishop is here reminded that he ought not to rely on his own wisdom but should always be sure that his judgment is compatible with the will of the Lord who is truly the ruler.

"Knowing that the Lord rules through His Bishops, Latter-day Saints can and should have confidence in the counsel and judgment given by one who occupies that sacred position by appointment of the

17 And whoso standeth in this mission is appointed to be a judge in Israel, like as it was in ancient days, to divide the lands of the heritage of God unto his children;

18 And to judge his people by the testimony of the just, and by the assistance of his counselors, according to the laws of the kingdom which are given by the prophets of God.

19 For verily I say unto you, my law shall be kept on this land.

20 Let no man think he is ruler; but let God rule him that judgeth, according to the counsel of his own will, or, in other words, him that counseleth or sitteth upon the judgment seat.

Lord. The Saints should be humbly grateful to have such an intimate relationship with the Lord through His equally-humble servant, the Bishop. In Zion, such is the relationship among the Saints, the Bishops, and the Lord" (Otten and Caldwell, *Sacred Truths*, 1:283).

How are obeying God's law and the laws of the land related? (58:21) "The Saints are directed to be 'subject to the powers that be' and to keep what are called 'the laws of the land' in addition to what are called 'the laws of God' or 'the laws of the Church' (D&C 58:21–23). The official 'declaration of belief' of The Church of Jesus Christ of Latter-day Saints, adopted in 1835 and published in the first edition of the Doctrine and Covenants, declares that 'human laws [are] instituted for the express purpose of regulating our interests as individuals and nations, between man and man,' and that 'divine laws [are] given of heaven' to prescribe 'rules on spiritual concerns, for faith and worship.' Significantly, the scripture adds that 'both [are] to be answered by man to his Maker' (D&C 134:6)" (Oaks, *Lord's Way*, 210).

Why must the Saints be subject to "the powers that be"? (58:21–22) "Because all things are spiritual unto God (D&C 29:34), it is impossible to fully separate heavenly law from the laws of the land. Stated more bluntly, in striving for spirituality, we cannot seek to obey all the commandments of God and at the same time ignore or spurn the laws of the land. In the United States, we have a system of government that can maintain decency and morality in society only as its citizens observe the laws. Because we do not now live in a theocracy does not mean that we do not have a spiritual obligation to be good citizens and thereby uphold 'that law of the land which is constitutional' (D&C 98:5)" (Millet and Newell, *Draw Near unto Me*, 151).

Doctrine and Covenants 58:24–29. Men Should Use Their Agency to Do Good

In what way does the Lord honor our agency as we move forward in faith? (58:25–26) "Some may think we shouldn't expect daily guidance from the Spirit because 'it is not meet that [God] should command in all things,' lest we become slothful servants

21 Let no man break the laws of the land, for he that keepeth the laws of God hath no need to break the laws of the land.

22 Wherefore, be subject to the powers that be, until he reigns whose right it is to reign, and subdues all enemies under his feet.

23 Behold, the laws which ye have received from my hand are the laws of the church, and in this light ye shall hold them forth. Behold, here is wisdom.

24 And now, as I spake concerning my servant Edward Partridge, this land is the land of his residence, and those whom he has appointed for his counselors; and also the land of the residence of him whom I have appointed to keep my storehouse;

25 Wherefore, let them bring their families to this land, as they shall counsel between themselves and me.

26 For behold, it is not meet that I should command in all things; for he that is compelled in all things, the same is a slothful and not a wise servant; wherefore he receiveth no reward.

27 Verily I say, men should be anxiously engaged in a good cause, and do many things of their own free will, and bring to pass much righteousness;

28 For the power is in them, wherein they are agents unto themselves. And inasmuch as men do good they shall in nowise lose their reward.

29 But he that doeth not anything until he is commanded, and receiveth a commandment with doubtful heart, and keepeth it with slothfulness, the same is damned.

[D&C 58:26]. This scripture, however, was given to some early missionaries who asked Joseph Smith to obtain revelation they should have received for themselves. . . .

"These missionaries wanted a specific revelation about their travel plans. They hadn't yet learned to seek their own direction in personal matters. The Lord called this attitude what it is: slothful. Early Church members may have been so happy to have a true prophet that they were in danger of failing to learn how to receive revelation themselves. Being spiritually self-reliant is hearing the Lord's voice through His Spirit for one's own life" (Wilson, "Take the Holy Spirit as Your Guide," *Ensign*, May 2018, 76–77).

How are we blessed when we seek to be anxiously engaged in doing good? (58:27–28) Sister Joy D. Jones observed: "The Lord loves effort, and effort brings rewards. We keep practicing. We are always progressing as long as we are striving to follow the Lord [see D&C 58:26–28]. He doesn't expect perfection today. We keep climbing our personal Mount Sinai. As in times past, our journey does indeed take effort, hard work, and study, but our commitment to progress brings eternal rewards [see D&C 6:33]" ("Especially Noble Calling," *Ensign*, May 2020, 16). ◉

How important is agency in Heavenly Father's plan? (58:28) Elder Dieter F. Uchtdorf spoke of the vital gift of agency in God's plan: "There must have been parts of the mortal adventure that worried and even terrified God's children, since a large number of our spiritual brothers and sisters decided against it.

"By the gift and power of moral agency, we determined that the potential of what we could learn and eternally become was worth the risk. . . .

"The Prophet Joseph Smith described agency as 'that free independence of mind which heaven has so graciously bestowed upon the human family as one of its choicest gifts' [Joseph Smith Papers, "Letter to the Church, circa February 1834," 135]. This 'free independence of mind,' or agency, is the power that allows individuals to be 'agents unto themselves' (D&C 58:28)" ("Your Great Adventure," *Liahona*, Nov. 2019, 87, 90n5). ◉

Why should we not wait to be commanded in all things? (58:29) "While wholesome pleasure results from much we do that is good, it is not our prime purpose for being on earth. Seek to know and do the will of the Lord, not just what is convenient or what makes life easy. You have His plan of happiness. You know what to do, or can find out through study and prayer. Do it willingly.

"The Lord declared: . . .

"'But he that doeth not anything until he is commanded, and receiveth a commandment with doubtful heart, and keepeth it with slothfulness, the same is damned' [D&C 58:29]—meaning stopped in progress and development" (Scott, "First Things First," *Ensign*, May 2001, 8).

Doctrine and Covenants 58:30–33. The Lord Commands and Revokes

How would the Saints know if God ever revokes a commandment? (58:32) The Lord has repeatedly affirmed that "He [would] reveal His will to His authorized servants: 'For him to whom these keys are given there is no difficulty in obtaining a knowledge of facts in relation to the salvation of the children of men' (D&C 128:11).

"That principle of revelation has been with the Church ever since. Those who hold the keys have obtained knowledge on what to do. When changes have come, they have come through that process. The Lord does as He said He would do: 'I, the Lord, command and revoke, as it seemeth me good' (D&C 56:4). 'I command and men obey not; I revoke and they receive not the blessing' (D&C 58:32)" (Packer, "Revelation in a Changing World," *Ensign*, Nov. 1989, 16).

What could the Saints learn from this warning? (58:33) "The Lord told the Saints that if they did not obey His command, He would revoke it and take away the blessing they would have received if they had been obedient (see D&C 58:32). This truth served as a warning to the early Saints who were commanded to establish Zion. If they did not obey His commandments, the Lord would revoke the command to establish Zion and the Saints would lose the blessings they might have received.

"The Lord also prophesied that if He revoked the command to establish Zion and withheld blessings because of the Saints' disobedience, some would claim that it was 'not the work of the Lord' (D&C 58:33). The Lord warned those who would make this claim that their reward would come from 'beneath, and not from above' (D&C 58:33)" (*Doctrine and Covenants Student Manual* [2018], 312).

30 Who am I that made man, saith the Lord, that will hold him guiltless that obeys not my commandments?

31 Who am I, saith the Lord, that have promised and have not fulfilled?

32 I command and men obey not; I revoke and they receive not the blessing.

33 Then they say in their hearts: This is not the work of the Lord, for his promises are not fulfilled. But wo unto such, for their reward lurketh beneath, and not from above.

34 And now I give unto you further directions concerning this land.

35 It is wisdom in me that my servant Martin Harris should be an example unto the church, in laying his moneys before the bishop of the church.

36 And also, this is a law unto every man that cometh unto this land to receive an inheritance; and he shall do with his moneys according as the law directs.

37 And it is wisdom also that there should be lands purchased in Independence, for the place of the storehouse, and also for the house of the printing.

38 And other directions concerning my servant Martin Harris shall be given him of the Spirit, that he may receive his inheritance as seemeth him good;

39 And let him repent of his sins, for he seeketh the praise of the world.

40 And also let my servant William W. Phelps stand in the office to which I have appointed him, and receive his inheritance in the land;

41 And also he hath need to repent, for I, the Lord, am not well pleased with him, for he seeketh to excel, and he is not sufficiently meek before me.

42 Behold, he who has repented of his sins, the same is forgiven, and I, the Lord, remember them no more.

43 By this ye may know if a man repenteth of his sins—behold, he will confess them and forsake them.

Doctrine and Covenants 58:34–43. To Repent, Men Must Confess and Forsake Their Sins

What did it mean that W. W. Phelps had sought to excel? (58:40–42) "W. W. Phelps's attitude toward other Saints was *competitive* rather than *cooperative*. He wanted to get ahead of them rather than become one with them. It is not evil to pursue excellence; indeed, Jesus was the most excellent of all men. But Jesus also sought to share his merits with us to make us as he is, rather than simply wanting to outperform us. The pursuit of personal excellence for the glory of God and the benefit of our fellows is a positive virtue, but the competitive urge that simply compels us to win for our ego's sake is not. Evidently, it is in this latter sense that Brother Phelps '[sought] to excel' and was condemned for it" (Robinson and Garrett, *Commentary on the Doctrine and Covenants*, 2:156–57).

What is the Lord's promise to those who repent? (58:42) Sister Sharon Eubank taught: "The scarlet dye of the Old Testament was not only colorful but also colorfast, meaning that its vivid color stuck to the wool and would not fade no matter how many times it was washed. Satan wields this reasoning like a club: white wool stained scarlet can never go back to being white. But Jesus Christ declares, 'My ways [are] higher than your ways,' and the miracle of His grace is that when we repent of our sins, His scarlet blood returns us to purity. It isn't logical, but it is nevertheless true.

"'Though your sins be as scarlet, they shall be as white as snow; though they be red like crimson, they shall be as wool.' The Lord says emphatically: he or she 'who has repented of . . . sins, the same is forgiven, and I, the Lord, remember them no more'" ("Christ: The Light That Shines in Darkness," *Liahona*, May 2019, 75).

Why is confession an essential part of repentance? (58:42–43) "Repentance requires that sins be confessed to Heavenly Father. . . . (Doctrine and Covenants 58:43; see also Mosiah 26:29).

"When Church members commit serious sins, their repentance also includes confession to their bishop or stake president. He is then able to exercise the keys of the gospel of repentance on their behalf (see Doctrine and Covenants 13:1; 84:26–27; 107:18, 20). This helps them heal and return to the gospel path through the power of the Savior's Atonement.

"The purpose of confession is to encourage members to unburden themselves so they can fully seek the Lord's help in changing and healing. Developing a 'broken heart and a contrite spirit' is aided by confession (2 Nephi 2:7). Voluntary confession shows that a person desires to repent" (*General Handbook* [2023], 32.4.1). See also commentary in this volume on Doctrine and Covenants 61:2. ✪

Doctrine and Covenants 58:44–58. The Saints Are to Purchase Their Inheritance and Gather in Missouri

Why did the Lord caution that Church members were only to move to Missouri when directed? (58:44) "The Lord was not willing for most members of the Church to go to Zion yet, nor for many years to come (compare D&C 51:17, 'as for years'; D&C 64:21, 'space of five years'). It would actually not be until seven years later, in 1838, that most of the Ohio Saints were called to Missouri. The Lord desired that Zion be built up slowly (see v. 56), that the land be purchased by contributions from the Ohio Saints (see v. 49), that missionary work be done in Missouri (see v. 48) and in all the world (see v. 64), that the Prophet remain in Kirtland (see v. 58), and that other preparations be made over a period of years" (Robinson and Garrett, *Commentary on the Doctrine and Covenants*, 2:158).

44 And now, verily, I say concerning the residue of the elders of my church, the time has not yet come, for many years, for them to receive their inheritance in this land, except they desire it through the prayer of faith, only as it shall be appointed unto them of the Lord.

45 For, behold, they shall push the people together from the ends of the earth.

46 Wherefore, assemble yourselves together; and they who are not appointed to stay in this land, let them preach the gospel in the regions round about; and after that let them return to their homes.

47 Let them preach by the way, and bear testimony of the truth in all places, and call upon the rich, the high and the low, and the poor to repent.

48 And let them build up churches, inasmuch as the inhabitants of the earth will repent.

49 And let there be an agent appointed by the voice of the church, unto the church in Ohio, to receive moneys to purchase lands in Zion.

50 And I give unto my servant Sidney Rigdon a commandment, that he shall write a description of the land of Zion, and a statement of the will of God, as it shall be made known by the Spirit unto him;

51 And an epistle and subscription, to be presented unto all the churches to obtain moneys, to be put into the hands of the bishop, of himself or the agent, as seemeth him good or as he shall direct, to purchase lands for an inheritance for the children of God.

52 For, behold, verily I say unto you, the Lord willeth that the disciples and the children of men should open their hearts, even to purchase this whole region of country, as soon as time will permit.

53 Behold, here is wisdom. Let them do this lest they receive none inheritance, save it be by the shedding of blood.

54 And again, inasmuch as there is land obtained, let there be workmen sent forth of all kinds unto this land, to labor for the saints of God.

55 Let all these things be done in order; and let the privileges of the lands be made known from time to time, by the bishop or the agent of the church.

56 And let the work of the gathering be not in haste, nor by flight; but let it be done as it shall be counseled by the elders of the church at the conferences, according to the

What description of Zion did Sidney Rigdon write? (58:50–51) The country was "unlike the timbered states of the East. . . . As far as the eye can glance the beautiful rolling prairies lay spread around like a sea of meadows. . . . The shrubbery was beautiful, and consisted in part of plums, grapes, crabapples and persimmons. . . .

"The soil is rich and fertile; from three to ten feet deep, and generally composed of a rich black mould, intermingled with clay and sand. It yields in abundance, wheat, corn, and many other common agricultural products" (Joseph Smith Papers, "History, 1838–1856, volume A-1," 138). ⊕

Why did the Lord caution that the gathering be done in order? (58:55–56) "*Let the work of the gathering be not in haste, nor by flight.* These words were first given by the Lord to the prophet Isaiah (Isaiah 52:12) and later taught to the Nephites by the Savior (3 Nephi 21:29). Sad experience taught the Saints the wisdom of the Lord's counsel. Those members that gathered to Zion before they had consecrated their property and, in turn, received an inheritance from the bishop, created confusion and lacked the Spirit of the Lord necessary to build up Zion. Today, unwise zeal should not influence Saints to gather to Jackson County, Missouri. The proper course is to follow counsel from the president of the Church in gathering" (McConkie and Ostler, *Revelations of the Restoration*, 426).

Doctrine and Covenants 58:59–65. The Gospel Must Be Preached unto Every Creature

Why did the Lord revoke Ziba Peterson's calling? (58:60) "[Ziba] Peterson is publicly chastised in a revelation received in August 1831 for not confessing his sins and for attempting to hide them (D&C 58:60). He was subsequently mentioned in a letter signed by the First Presidency of the Church in June 1833, wherein they said: 'We deliver Brother Ziba Peterson over to the buffetings of Satan, in the name of the Lord, that he may learn not to transgress the commandments of God' ([Joseph Smith Papers, "History, 1838–1856, volume A-1," 314]). He did not return to fellowship in the faith that could have brought him the blessings of eternal life. He died in Placerville, Eldorado County, California" (Brewster, *Doctrine & Covenants Encyclopedia* [2012], 425).

What blessings can we experience for not hiding our sins? (58:60) "Hiding sins from God never elicits true repentance (see Alma 39:8). It can't. Repentance is only possible through your Redeemer (see 2 Nephi 10:24; Mosiah 16:13; Alma 13:5). You must come unto Him to be made whole and receive complete forgiveness. When shame convinces you to hide your sins from God, repentance can't occur. Satan wants this. If you don't repent, if you don't call on the power of Jesus Christ and the blessings of His Atonement, Satan wins (see Alma 12:35). Christ pleads for you to come unto Him and become better through His grace (see Matthew 11:28; John 7:37). Messing up, learning from your mistakes, and moving forward through repentance is an ongoing cycle on your journey to become like Him" (Jorgensen, "Shame versus Guilt," *Ensign*, Jan. 2020).

knowledge which they receive from time to time.

57 And let my servant Sidney Rigdon consecrate and dedicate this land, and the spot for the temple, unto the Lord.

58 And let a conference meeting be called; and after that let my servants Sidney Rigdon and Joseph Smith, Jun., return, and also Oliver Cowdery with them, to accomplish the residue of the work which I have appointed unto them in their own land, and the residue as shall be ruled by the conferences.

59 And let no man return from this land except he bear record by the way, of that which he knows and most assuredly believes.

60 Let that which has been bestowed upon Ziba Peterson be taken from him; and let him stand as a member in the church, and labor with his own hands, with the brethren, until he is sufficiently chastened for all his sins; for he confesseth them not, and he thinketh to hide them.

61 Let the residue of the elders of this church, who are coming to this land, some of whom are exceedingly blessed even above measure, also hold a conference upon this land.

62 And let my servant Edward Partridge direct the conference which shall be held by them.

63 And let them also return, preaching the gospel by the way, bearing record of the things which are revealed unto them.

64 For, verily, the sound must go forth from this place into all the world, and unto the uttermost parts of the earth—the gospel must be preached unto every creature, with signs following them that believe.

65 And behold the Son of Man cometh. Amen.

In what ways does this command to the early Saints to go forth preaching the Gospel reflect the universal mandate for missionary work? (58:63) Consider how this commandment to preach the gospel was like that given by the Resurrected Lord to His disciples in Galilee (see Matthew 28:19). Elder Gary E. Stevenson taught: "Imagine with me, for a moment, standing on a mountain in Galilee, witnessing the wonder and glory of the resurrected Savior visiting His disciples. How awe-inspiring to consider personally hearing these words, which He shared with them, His solemn charge to 'go ye therefore, and teach all nations, baptizing them in the name of the Father, and of the Son, and of the Holy Ghost' [Matthew 28:19]. Surely these words would empower, inspire, and move each of us, as they did His Apostles. Indeed, they devoted the rest of their lives to doing just that" ("Love, Share, Invite," *Liahona*, May 2022, 84). ❂

Why will the gospel continue to go forth to fill the entire world? (58:64) "As the Church of Jesus Christ was restored to the earth 183 years ago, the Lord's charge to His small band of disciples echoed His words spoken centuries before: 'The voice of warning shall be unto all people' [D&C 1:4]. 'For, verily, the sound must go forth . . . into all the world, and unto the uttermost parts of the earth' [D&C 58:64].

"'All people'? 'All the world'? 'The uttermost parts of the earth'? Was it possible?

"The Savior reassured His Latter-day Saints [see D&C 1:5], but could they foresee the reach and destiny of this marvelous work? They must have wondered if miracles really would accompany them in spreading the gospel. . . .

" . . . We are few in number, just as Nephi foretold [see 1 Nephi 14:12]. But at the same time, you and I are eyewitnesses of Daniel's prophetic words: the 'stone . . . cut . . . without hands . . . [is filling] the whole earth' [Daniel 2:34–35]" (Andersen, "It's a Miracle," *Ensign*, May 2013, 77, 78).

Introduction to Doctrine and Covenants 59

Joseph Smith received the revelation recorded in Doctrine and Covenants 59 on Sunday, August 7, 1831, in Jackson County, Missouri. The occasion was the funeral of Polly Knight. Polly "had traveled with her husband, Joseph Knight Sr., and the rest of the Colesville Branch at the Lord's direction to settle in Zion (see D&C 54:8). So ill on her journey that her son Newel 'bought lumber to make a coffin in case she should die before we arrived at our place of destination,' Polly Knight had her 'greatest desire' fulfilled to 'set her feet upon the land of Zion, and to have her body interred in that land.' . . . Of Polly Knight, Joseph Smith later wrote, 'a worthy member sleeps in Jesus till the resurrection' [Joseph Smith Papers, "History, 1838–1856, volume A-1," 139].

"In addition to expounding the role of tribulation in becoming like Zion, the Lord praised obedience in section 59. . . . This revelation, however, went further than its predecessor in explaining the role of obedience in shaping Zion. . . . Saints serious about becoming Zion are to live a higher standard of obedience. Furthermore, not needing to be commanded in all things, they go beyond merely not committing sin to avoiding even its very appearance" (Scott C. Esplin, "Let Zion in Her Beauty Rise," 139, 140).

"During the summer of 1831, as Church members settled in Jackson County, Missouri, they encountered a frontier community whose conduct sharply contrasted with the laws and standards of the gospel. Gambling, drinking, and violence were prevalent among the residents, some of whom had come to the Missouri frontier to avoid the justice of the law. These residents also had a blatant disregard for the Sabbath day that was noticed not only by the Saints but by other travelers who came to Missouri. One Protestant missionary observed: 'Christian Sabbath observance here appears to be unknown. It is a day for merchandising, jollity, drinking, gambling, and general anti-Christian conduct' (in [Lyon, "Independence, Missouri, and the Mormons, 1827–1833]," 16). . . . In this environment the Lord outlined standards of conduct for those Saints gathering to Zion" (*Doctrine and Covenants Student Manual* [2018], 317).

SECTION 59

Revelation given through Joseph Smith the Prophet, in Zion, Jackson County, Missouri, August 7, 1831. Preceding this revelation, the land was consecrated, as the Lord had directed, and the site for the future temple was dedicated. On the day this revelation was received, Polly Knight, the wife of Joseph Knight Sr., died, the first Church member to die in Zion. Early members characterized this revelation as "instructing the Saints how to keep the sabbath and how to fast and pray."

1 Behold, blessed, saith the Lord, are they who have come up unto this land with an eye single to my glory, according to my commandments.

2 For those that live shall inherit the earth, and those that die shall rest from all their labors, and their works shall follow them; and they shall receive a crown in the mansions of my Father, which I have prepared for them.

Doctrine and Covenants 59:1–4. The Faithful Saints in Zion Will Be Blessed

How does one obey the Lord "with an eye single" to God's glory? (59:1) "Latter-day Saints whose eyes are single to God's glory see life from a vastly different perspective than those whose attention is directed elsewhere. Such members, for instance, care little about receiving credit or recognition for their good deeds. They are more interested in feeding the Lord's sheep than in counting them. In fact, they frequently find their greatest happiness in serving anonymously, thereby leaving the beneficiaries of their kindness with no one to thank or praise except the Lord" (Marlin K. Jensen, "Eye Single to the Glory of God," *Ensign*, Nov. 1989, 27). See also commentary in this volume on Doctrine and Covenants 55:1. ☉

3 Yea, blessed are they whose feet stand upon the land of Zion, who have obeyed my gospel; for they shall receive for their reward the good things of the earth, and it shall bring forth in its strength.

4 And they shall also be crowned with blessings from above, yea, and with commandments not a few, and with revelations in their time—they that are faithful and diligent before me.

5 Wherefore, I give unto them a commandment, saying thus: Thou shalt love the Lord thy God with all thy heart, with all thy might, mind, and strength; and in the name of Jesus Christ thou shalt serve him.

6 Thou shalt love thy neighbor as thyself. Thou shalt not steal; neither commit adultery, nor kill, nor do anything like unto it.

In what way are we blessed when we receive more commandments? (59:4) "At times, some people get confused, thinking that the commandments are restrictions or limitations that complicate life, that take away opportunities or happiness or the pleasures of life. In reality, the commandments protect us and guide us to happiness. They are not to restrict but rather to make possible—to allow us to achieve in this life and in the next—what we truly desire and what our Heavenly Father, who loves us, wants for us.

"They are like a flight of stairs. Each step may represent one commandment, and with each commandment that we obey, we can move upward. Then, if we understand the essence of the commandments, we want more. We don't feel resentment regarding the commandments; we want more in order to be able to progress more. And a Heavenly Father who loves us gives unto us according to our desires. If we desire it, He is going to give us more commandments in order to facilitate our progress" (Christofferson, "Steps to Happiness," *Liahona*, Sep. 2013, 47). ◉

Doctrine and Covenants 59:5–8. They Are to Love and Serve the Lord and Keep His Commandments

How does one love the Lord with all their heart, might, mind, and strength? (59:5) "To love God with all your heart, soul, mind, and strength is all-consuming and all-encompassing. It is no lukewarm endeavor. . . .

"The breadth, depth, and height of this love of God extend into every facet of one's life. Our desires, be they spiritual or temporal, should be rooted in a love of the Lord. Our thoughts and affections should be centered on the Lord. . . .

"When we put God first, all other things fall into their proper place or drop out of our lives. Our love of the Lord will govern the claims for our affection, the demands on our time, the interests we pursue, and the order of our priorities" (Ezra Taft Benson [manual], 39, 40). See also commentary in this volume on Doctrine and Covenants 4:2.

How can we love our neighbor and also love God with all our hearts? (59:5–6) "We are commanded to love everyone, since Jesus's parable of the good

Samaritan teaches that everyone is our neighbor. But our zeal to keep this second commandment must not cause us to forget the first, to love God with all our heart, soul, and mind. We show that love by 'keep[ing] [His] commandments' [John 14:15]. God requires us to obey His commandments because only through that obedience, including repentance, can we return to live in His presence and become perfect as He is. . . .

"Our walk demands that we not compromise on commandments but show forth a full measure of understanding and love" (Oaks, "Two Great Commandments," Ensign, Nov. 2019, 73–74, 75).

Why would God command us to thank Him in all things? (59:7) "The grateful man sees so much in the world to be thankful for, and with him the good outweighs the evil. Love overpowers jealousy, and light drives darkness out of his life. Pride destroys our gratitude and sets up selfishness in its place. How much happier we are in the presence of a grateful and loving soul, and how careful we should be to cultivate, through the medium of a prayerful life, a thankful attitude toward God and man!" (Joseph F. Smith, Gospel Doctrine, 263).

How does one offer a sacrifice of a broken heart and a contrite spirit? (59:8) "Those who have a broken heart and a contrite spirit are willing to do anything and everything that God asks of them, without resistance or resentment. We cease doing things our way and learn to do them God's way instead. In such a condition of submissiveness, the Atonement can take effect and true repentance can occur. . . .

"There is yet another dimension of a broken heart—namely, our deep gratitude for Christ's suffering on our behalf. . . . His great heart literally broke with an all-encompassing love for the children of God. When we remember the Savior and His suffering, our hearts too will break in gratitude for the Anointed One" (Bruce D. Porter, "Broken Heart and a Contrite Spirit," Ensign, Nov. 2007, 32).

Doctrine and Covenants 59:9–19. By Keeping the Lord's Day Holy, the Saints Are Blessed Temporally and Spiritually

How does worshipping on the Sabbath keep us "unspotted from the world"? (59:9) "We remain 'unspotted from the world' not just by . . . our resting from temporal labors on the Sabbath day but also by worthily partaking of the sacrament of the Lord's Supper. The Sabbath as a holy day is inextricably

7 Thou shalt thank the Lord thy God in all things.

8 Thou shalt offer a sacrifice unto the Lord thy God in righteousness, even that of a broken heart and a contrite spirit.

9 And that thou mayest more fully keep thyself unspotted from the world, thou shalt go to the house of prayer and offer up thy sacraments upon my holy day;

linked to the sacrament. A remission of our sins and the companionship of the Holy Ghost are part of the 'rest' promised by the Lord. Thus, the sacrament should be the very essence of our Sabbath worship. When honoring the Sabbath as a day of delight rather than viewing it merely as a day of don'ts, as did the Pharisees of old, we receive spiritual strength, 'rest,' and temporal blessings ([see] Leviticus 26:2–13). The Sabbath is an oasis in the spiritual deserts of life" (Top, "Sabbath," 547).

10 For verily this is a day appointed unto you to rest from your labors, and to pay thy devotions unto the Most High;

11 Nevertheless thy vows shall be offered up in righteousness on all days and at all times;

What important practices help us rest from our labors and pay devotions to God? (59:10) "In harmony with this revelation, Church members seek to keep the Sabbath day holy at church and at home. At church, members participate in the sacred ordinance of the sacrament, which Jesus Christ instituted at the Last Supper and when He visited the Nephites (see Matthew 26:26–28; Luke 22:19–20; 3 Nephi 18:1–12). At home, members participate in uplifting activities that help them learn the gospel, strengthen faith in Jesus Christ, build family relations, and provide service.

"By participating in these activities at church and at home, members can establish family traditions that will help nurture multigenerational families who are faithful to the Lord and who call the Sabbath a delight (see Isaiah 58:13–14)" (Topics and Questions, "Sabbath Day").

12 But remember that on this, the Lord's day, thou shalt offer thine oblations and thy sacraments unto the Most High, confessing thy sins unto thy brethren, and before the Lord.

What are *oblations*? (59:12) Footnote *b* in Doctrine and Covenants 59:12 indicates that *oblations* are "offerings, whether of time, talents, or means, in service of God and fellowman." Hyrum M. Smith and Janne M. Sjodahl wrote that "on the Lord's day, the Saints will devote themselves especially to the

A Prophet's Counsel on Keeping the Sabbath Day Holy (Doctrine and Covenants 59:10)

President Russell M. Nelson reflected: "In my much younger years, I studied the work of others who had compiled lists of things to do and things *not* to do on the Sabbath. It wasn't until later that I learned from the scriptures that my conduct and my attitude on the Sabbath constituted a *sign* between me and my Heavenly Father. [See Exodus 31:13; Ezekiel 20:12, 20.] With that understanding, I no longer needed lists of dos and don'ts. When I had to make a decision whether or not an activity was appropriate for the Sabbath, I simply asked myself, 'What *sign* do I want to give to God?' That question made my choices about the Sabbath day crystal clear. . . .

"Isaiah . . . taught us how to make [the Sabbath] delightful. He said:

"'If thou turn away . . . from doing thy pleasure on my holy day; and call the sabbath a delight, . . . and shalt honour [the Lord], not doing thine own ways, nor finding thine own pleasure, nor speaking thine own words:

"'Then shalt thou delight thyself *in the Lord*' [Isaiah 58:13–14; emphasis added].

"Not pursuing your 'own pleasure' on the Sabbath requires self-discipline. You may have to deny yourself of something you might like. If you choose to delight yourself in the Lord, you will not permit yourself to treat it as any other day. Routine and recreational activities can be done some other time" ("Sabbath Is a Delight," *Ensign*, May 2015, 130, 131–32).

service of the Lord in spiritual things" and "the Lord graciously accepts tithes and offerings, donations and gifts; and the Lord's day is a very proper day upon which to remember such oblations" (*Doctrine and Covenants Commentary*, 351, 352).

In what way is *fasting* related to *joy* and *rejoicing*? (59:13–14) "In D&C 59:13, footnote 13a provides insight into the meaning of the word *fasting* in that verse: 'hungering and thirsting after righteousness.' It is interesting that part of earnestly seeking righteousness is to suppress our physical hunger and thirst and to replace that desire with a fervent spiritual desire. To the Nephites, Jesus said, 'Blessed are all they who do hunger and thirst after righteousness, for they shall be filled with the Holy Ghost' (3 Ne. 12:6).

"It is being thus filled that causes the soul to rejoice. . . . When we approach the Lord in fasting and prayer, we can be of glad countenance because we know that whatever the outcome, we will be blessed with the joy of the Spirit" (Robertson, "How can we feel the joy and rejoicing the scriptures equate with fasting?" *Ensign*, Oct. 1993, 62).

What should we be thankful for on the Sabbath? (59:15) "For Latter-day Saints, the Sabbath is . . . a day, of gratitude and love. The Lord instructed the Saints in Jackson County, Missouri, in 1831 that their prayers and thanks should be directed heavenward. The early Saints were given a revelation about how to keep the Sabbath day and how to fast and pray [see D&C 59].

"They, and we, were told by the Lord how to worship and give thanks on the Sabbath. . . .

"Of all the blessings we can count, the greatest by far is the feeling of forgiveness that comes as we partake of the sacrament. We will feel greater love and appreciation for the Savior, whose infinite sacrifice made possible our being cleansed from sin. As we partake of the bread and water, we remember that He suffered for us. And when we feel gratitude for what He has done for us, we will feel His love for us and our love for Him" (Eyring, "Gratitude on the Sabbath Day," *Ensign*, Nov. 2016, 99, 100).

What blessings are promised to those who keep the Sabbath day holy? (59:15–19) "If we follow the commandment concerning the Sabbath day and are faithful in keeping the other commandments, our harvest will be rich. . . .

"In keeping the Sabbath day holy, joy is received, and rich blessings are promised (D&C 59:15–19). Keeping the commandments brings the favor of

13 And on this day thou shalt do none other thing, only let thy food be prepared with singleness of heart that thy fasting may be perfect, or, in other words, that thy joy may be full.

14 Verily, this is fasting and prayer, or in other words, rejoicing and prayer.

15 And inasmuch as ye do these things with thanksgiving, with cheerful hearts and countenances, not with much laughter, for this is sin, but with a glad heart and a cheerful countenance—

16 Verily I say, that inasmuch as ye do this, the fulness of the earth is yours, the beasts of the field and the fowls of the air, and that which climbeth upon the trees and walketh upon the earth;

17 Yea, and the herb, and the good things which come of the earth, whether for food or for raiment, or for houses, or for barns, or for orchards, or for gardens, or for vineyards;

18 Yea, all things which come of the earth, in the season thereof, are made for the benefit and the use of man, both to please the eye and to gladden the heart;

19 Yea, for food and for raiment, for taste and for smell, to strengthen the body and to enliven the soul.

heaven. In [these] verses there is stated the purpose for which the things of the earth—food, clothing, and shelter—are provided, to strengthen one physically and spiritually. Implicit in these verses is the same thought expressed in an earlier revelation [see D&C 29:34–35]" (Roy W. Doxey, *Doctrine and Covenants Speaks*, 1:454).

Elder Bruce R. McConkie promised: "If we would keep the Sabbath, the Lord would bless and prosper us beyond anything we have ever known" (*New Witness*, 301).

Doctrine and Covenants 59:20–24. The Righteous Are Promised Peace in This World and Eternal Life in the World to Come

20 And it pleaseth God that he hath given all these things unto man; for unto this end were they made to be used, with judgment, not to excess, neither by extortion.

21 And in nothing doth man offend God, or against none is his wrath kindled, save those who confess not his hand in all things, and obey not his commandments.

22 Behold, this is according to the law and the prophets; wherefore, trouble me no more concerning this matter.

How do we avoid offending God? (59:21) "It is clear to me from [D&C 59:21] that to 'thank the Lord thy God in all things' (D&C 59:7) is more than a social courtesy; it is a binding commandment. . . . A grateful heart is a beginning of greatness. It is an expression of humility. It is a foundation for the development of such virtues as prayer, faith, courage, contentment, happiness, love, and well-being" (Faust, "Gratitude as a Saving Principle," *Ensign*, May 1990, 85, 86).

"As we strive to make our prayers more meaningful, we should remember [D&C 59:21]. Let me recommend that periodically you and I offer a prayer in which we only give thanks and express gratitude. Ask for nothing; simply let our souls rejoice and strive to communicate appreciation with all the energy of our hearts" (Bednar, "Pray Always," *Ensign*, Nov. 2008, 43). ☉

23 But learn that he who doeth the works of righteousness shall receive his reward, even peace in this world, and eternal life in the world to come.

24 I, the Lord, have spoken it, and the Spirit beareth record. Amen.

How do we prepare ourselves to have "peace in this world, and eternal life in the world to come"? (59:23) Adeyinka A. Ojediran declared: "We need the Spirit to help us navigate through mortality as we faithfully keep covenants, and we need the sacrament to energize our spiritual being. Renewing our baptismal covenant and partaking of the sacrament drive faithfulness to all other covenants. A happy ending is assured as we prayerfully study and honor the Savior's invitation and enjoy His promised blessings. He said, 'And that thou mayest more fully keep thyself unspotted from the world, thou shalt go to the house of prayer and offer up thy sacraments upon my holy day' (Doctrine and Covenants 59:9).

"I testify that covenant keepers are promised 'peace in this world, and eternal life in the world to come' (Doctrine and Covenants 59:23). I bear witness that as you regularly partake of the Savior's emblems through the sacrament, you will have His Spirit to guide you on the covenant path and stay faithful to your covenants" ("Covenant Path," *Liahona*, May 2022, 106). ⊕

Introduction to Doctrine and Covenants 60

"On 8 August 1831, [Joseph Smith] dictated a revelation instructing 'some of the Elders' who had traveled to Missouri to return to Ohio, preaching along the way. These elders had reached Missouri in mid- to late July and participated in the dedication of the land for the building of the city of Zion, the dedication of a temple site, and a conference with [Joseph Smith] and other leaders. 'Finding but little or no business for us to accomplish' once this 'work' was done, Ezra Booth wrote, 'most of us became anxious to return home.' A later [Joseph Smith] history recounts that the elders inquired of [Joseph Smith] 'what they were to do,' and this revelation was the response" (Joseph Smith Papers, Historical Introduction to "Revelation, 8 August 1831 [D&C 60]," 101).

The returning missionaries were "to travel on the Missouri River east to St. Louis. [The group likely consisted of Joseph Smith, Sidney Rigdon, Oliver Cowdery, Sidney Gilbert, W. W. Phelps, Reynolds Cahoon, Samuel Smith, Ezra Booth, Frederick G. Williams, Peter Whitmer Jr., and Joseph Coe.] There Joseph and Sidney Rigdon would travel speedily to Cincinnati, Ohio, to preach, while the others were to travel 'two by two & preach the word not in haste among the congregations of the wicked' [Joseph Smith Papers, 'Revelation, 8 August 1831 (D&C 60)']" (McBride, "Ezra Booth and Isaac Morley," 133).

SECTION 60

Revelation given through Joseph Smith the Prophet, in Independence, Jackson County, Missouri, August 8, 1831. On this occasion the elders who had traveled to Jackson County and participated in the dedication of the land and the temple site desired to know what they were to do.

Doctrine and Covenants 60:1–9. The Elders Are to Preach the Gospel in the Congregations of the Wicked

What talent did the missionaries hide? (60:2–3)
Recall the Savior's parable of the talents: "Three servants were given talents (pieces of money) to improve upon. Two were faithful in doubling the amount they received from their master. The third 'went and digged in the earth, and hid his lord's money' (Matthew 25:18). The first two were blessed for their wisdom while the third was cursed for being a 'wicked and slothful servant' (Matthew 25:26). The message to the elders in Missouri was that they must share the gospel and its saving ordinances with others or they would lose the blessings the gospel offers" (McConkie and Ostler, *Revelations of the Restoration*, 436). ⊕

1 Behold, thus saith the Lord unto the elders of his church, who are to return speedily to the land from whence they came: Behold, it pleaseth me, that you have come up hither;

2 But with some I am not well pleased, for they will not open their mouths, but they hide the talent which I have given unto them, because of the fear of man. Wo unto such, for mine anger is kindled against them.

3 And it shall come to pass, if they are not more faithful unto me, it shall be taken away, even that which they have.

4 For I, the Lord, rule in the heavens above, and among the armies of the earth; and in the day when I shall make up my jewels, all men shall know what it is that bespeaketh the power of God.

5 But, verily, I will speak unto you concerning your journey unto the land from whence you came. Let there be a craft made, or bought, as seemeth you good, it mattereth not unto me, and take your journey speedily for the place which is called St. Louis.

6 And from thence let my servants, Sidney Rigdon, Joseph Smith, Jun., and Oliver Cowdery, take their journey for Cincinnati;

7 And in this place let them lift up their voice and declare my word with loud voices, without wrath or doubting, lifting up holy hands upon them. For I am able to make you holy, and your sins are forgiven you.

8 And let the residue take their journey from St. Louis, two by two, and preach the word, not in haste, among the congregations of the wicked, until they return to the churches from whence they came.

9 And all this for the good of the churches; for this intent have I sent them.

Why didn't the Lord care whether the missionaries made or purchased a boat? (60:5). See commentary in this volume on Doctrine and Covenants 62:5.

What does it mean to lift up holy hands? (60:7) "When both hands are lifted, the action is a manifestation of 'supplication to God, and of dependence on God (Exodus 17:12; 1 Timothy 2:8)'" (Gaskill, *Lost Language of Symbolism*, 44).

Who are the "congregations of the wicked"? (60:8) "The phrase 'congregations of the wicked' as used in Doctrine and Covenants 60:8 and other revelations (see also D&C 61:33; 62:5) does not necessarily mean that all people in these places were guilty of gross wickedness. Rather, the phrase likely refers to people who did not have a knowledge or understanding of the restored gospel of Jesus Christ. Without a knowledge of gospel principles and saving ordinances, they were living outside God's covenant. For this reason the Lord called missionaries to preach the gospel to the congregations or communities of people and invite them to repent and receive the ordinances of salvation" (*Doctrine and Covenants Student Manual* [2018], 325).

What were the "churches" in this passage? (60:8–9) "The churches 'from whence they came' [D&C 60:8] are the branches of the [Lord's] churches around the Kirtland area. How their missionary work will be for the good of those churches (v. 9) is probably the experiences they will have and report to their fellow members. These reports will bolster and build the members' testimonies. When the missionaries, in our day, report their missionary experiences, it has the same effect" (Nyman, *Doctrine and Covenants Commentary*, 1:510).

Doctrine and Covenants 60:10-14. The Elders Should Not Idle Away Their Time, Nor Bury Their Talents

Why does the Lord counsel His missionaries to not idle away their time? (60:13) The missionary guide *Preach My Gospel* instructs missionaries: "The principle of accountability is fundamental in God's eternal plan (see Alma 5:15–19; Doctrine and Covenants 104:13; 137:9). This principle influences how you think and feel about the sacred responsibility the Lord has given you. Accountability also influences how you approach your work" (*Preach My Gospel* [2023], 154).

Doctrine and Covenants 60:15-17. The Elders May Wash Their Feet as a Testimony against Those Who Reject the Gospel

What does it mean to "shake off the dust of thy feet"? (60:15) See commentary in this volume on Doctrine and Covenants 24:15 and 99:4.

10 And let my servant Edward Partridge impart of the money which I have given him, a portion unto mine elders who are commanded to return;

11 And he that is able, let him return it by the way of the agent; and he that is not, of him it is not required.

12 And now I speak of the residue who are to come unto this land.

13 Behold, they have been sent to preach my gospel among the congregations of the wicked; wherefore, I give unto them a commandment, thus: Thou shalt not idle away thy time, neither shalt thou bury thy talent that it may not be known.

14 And after thou hast come up unto the land of Zion, and hast proclaimed my word, thou shalt speedily return, proclaiming my word among the congregations of the wicked, not in haste, neither in wrath nor with strife.

15 And shake off the dust of thy feet against those who receive thee not, not in their presence, lest thou provoke them, but in secret; and wash thy feet, as a testimony against them in the day of judgment.

16 Behold, this is sufficient for you, and the will of him who hath sent you.

17 And by the mouth of my servant Joseph Smith, Jun., it shall be made known concerning Sidney Rigdon and Oliver Cowdery. The residue hereafter. Even so. Amen.

Introduction to Doctrine and Covenants 61

The Prophet Joseph Smith received this revelation on August 12, 1831, while at McIlwaine's Bend on the bank of the Missouri River.

"Having overseen the dedication of the land for the establishment of Zion, [the Prophet] departed Independence, Jackson County, Missouri, for Ohio on 9 August 1831 in the company of ten elders. On 12 August, at a location on the Missouri River that a later [Joseph Smith] history calls 'McIlwaine's Bend,' [Joseph] dictated a revelation explaining the many dangers that existed on the river and instructing most of those returning to Ohio to leave the water and travel by land. The content of the revelation reflected experiences [the Prophet] and his group had gone through as they made their way to St. Louis, Missouri. Although nothing eventful occurred in the first day or two of their journey, discord apparently arose within the group when Oliver Cowdery chastised some of the elders for inappropriate conduct and warned them that misfortune would befall them if they did not repent. Soon after, a sawyer—a submerged tree anchored to the bottom of the river—nearly capsized the canoe carrying [Joseph Smith] and Sidney Rigdon. Unnerved by this encounter, [the Prophet] instructed the group to exit the water and camp for the night. According to a later [Joseph Smith] history, William W. Phelps then experienced 'an open vision, by daylight,' of 'the Destroyer, in his most horrible power, rid[ing] upon the face of the waters.' The contention within the group was resolved later that night, and [the Prophet] dictated the revelation the next morning" (Joseph Smith Papers, Historical Introduction to "Revelation, 12 August 1831 [D&C 61]," 101).

"The elders had been instructed to 'preach by the way' as they traveled home (D&C 58:46–48). The Lord now reminded them that it was not necessary for the whole group to be sailing swiftly down the river while people on either side were 'perishing in unbelief' (v. 3). Nevertheless, He had allowed them to have this experience so they could warn others about the dangers on the waters (vv. 4, 18). While in the beginning the waters were blessed (Gen. 1:20) and the land cursed (Moses 4:23), in the latter days this will be reversed (vv. 13–17; Rev. 8:8–10). Still, a person with sufficient faith not only can command the waters, but will know by the Spirit what to do (vv. 27–28). Therefore, the Lord declared that it mattered not to Him whether the elders went by land or by water, 'if it so be that they fill[ed] their mission' (v. 22). In conclusion, the Savior gave this assurance: 'Be of good cheer, little children; for I am in your midst, and I have not forsaken you.' He then urged the Saints to be humble, to watch for His Coming, and to pray always (vv. 36–39)" (Cowan and Manscill, *A to Z of the Doctrine and Covenants*, 90).

SECTION 61

Revelation given through Joseph Smith the Prophet, on the bank of the Missouri River, McIlwaine's Bend, August 12, 1831. On their return trip to Kirtland, the Prophet and ten elders had traveled down the Missouri River in canoes. On the third day of the journey, many dangers were experienced. Elder William W. Phelps, in a daylight vision, saw the destroyer riding in power upon the face of the waters.

1 Behold, and hearken unto the voice of him who has all power, who is from everlasting to everlasting, even Alpha and Omega, the beginning and the end.

Doctrine and Covenants 61:1–12. The Lord Has Decreed Many Destructions upon the Waters

Why does the Lord emphasize humility and confession as necessary for forgiveness of sins? (61:2) "In a powerful teaching to our generation, the Lord said, 'By this ye may know if a man repenteth of his sins—behold, he will confess them and forsake them' [D&C 58:43]. The Lord is not saying that this is all that is required in repenting, but that these vital steps are an outward demonstration that repentance has begun. Humbly confessing to God is required for all sin. Serious sin needs to be confessed to the proper priesthood authority. Confessing our sins to those we have hurt is also essential if it is possible" (Andersen, *Divine Gift of Forgiveness*, 202). See commentary in this volume on Doctrine and Covenants 58:42.

What was wrong with traveling swiftly on the river? (61:3) "When the elders traveled 'swiftly upon the waters' of the Missouri River, they weren't able to preach the gospel to the people living on both sides of the river who were 'perishing in unbelief' (D&C 61:3). Similarly, at times we might neglect the needs of those around us because we are so busy 'moving swiftly' along in our lives" (*Doctrine and Covenants Student Manual* [2018], 327).

To what might the Lord be referring when speaking of dangers "more especially hereafter . . . and especially upon these waters"? (61:4–5) "Whatever dangers were inherent in traveling upon the waters of the Missouri River would be more readily apparent in the future than in Joseph's day. It is likely that the destructive power of the waters described here will be part of the woes and destructions prophesied for the very last days (compare Moses 7:66, where Enoch described the sea in the last days as becoming 'troubled'). While there was some danger in river travel in Joseph's day, especially to those whose faith was weak, the real evidence of a curse upon the waters and of their destructive power will be seen in a future time, immediately preceding the second coming of Christ" (Robinson and Garrett, *Commentary on the Doctrine and Covenants*, 2:176–77).

Why was the Lord angry? (61:5) "Joseph and the elders launched their canoes at the Missouri River landing just north of Independence, Missouri, to return home to Ohio. . . . By the second day 'a spirit of animosity and discord' had infected the group. . . . Contention continued the next day. Joseph was frustrated. . . . Joseph urged the frightened group to get off the river. Some of the men called him a coward. They landed on the north side of the river at McIlwaine's Bend (now

2 Behold, verily thus saith the Lord unto you, O ye elders of my church, who are assembled upon this spot, whose sins are now forgiven you, for I, the Lord, forgive sins, and am merciful unto those who confess their sins with humble hearts;

3 But verily I say unto you, that it is not needful for this whole company of mine elders to be moving swiftly upon the waters, whilst the inhabitants on either side are perishing in unbelief.

4 Nevertheless, I suffered it that ye might bear record; behold, there are many dangers upon the waters, and more especially hereafter;

5 For I, the Lord, have decreed in mine anger many destructions upon the waters; yea, and especially upon these waters.

Miami), Missouri, set up camp as best they could, and convened a council to address the contention.... The council went on for some hours until, early in the morning, everyone reconciled" (Harper, *Making Sense of the Doctrine & Covenants*, 212).

6 Nevertheless, all flesh is in mine hand, and he that is faithful among you shall not perish by the waters.

Who is the Lord teaching should fear the power of Satan over the waters? (61:6) "Despite some popular belief to the contrary, Doctrine and Covenants 61 does *not* prohibit travel by water, or even swimming, for missionaries, for God is more powerful than Satan [see D&C 61:1], and those who are faithful need not fear to ride even upon the wild Missouri.... It is the unfaithful and the rebellious, like the rebellious elders on the previous day, who need to fear the power of Satan over the waters, for by their unfaithfulness, they render themselves susceptible to that power. Notice that when the elders at McIlwaine's Bend repented, they were allowed to continue their journey even *upon the waters* of the Missouri river (see v. 22)" (Robinson and Garrett, *Commentary on the Doctrine and Covenants*, 2:177).

7 Wherefore, it is expedient that my servant Sidney Gilbert and my servant William W. Phelps be in haste upon their errand and mission.

8 Nevertheless, I would not suffer that ye should part until you were chastened for all your sins, that you might be one, that you might not perish in wickedness;

9 But now, verily I say, it behooveth me that ye should part. Wherefore let my servants Sidney Gilbert and William W. Phelps take their former company, and let them take their journey in haste that they may fill their mission, and through faith they shall overcome;

10 And inasmuch as they are faithful they shall be preserved, and I, the Lord, will be with them.

11 And let the residue take that which is needful for clothing.

12 Let my servant Sidney Gilbert take that which is not needful with him, as you shall agree.

What errand was given to Sidney Gilbert and W. W. Phelps? (61:7) "These men were to purchase a printing press and transport it to Missouri. William W. Phelps was to be the printer for the Church (see D&C 55:4; 57:11), and Sidney Gilbert had been appointed purchasing agent (see D&C 57:6)" (*Doctrine and Covenants Student Manual* [2001], 132).

Doctrine and Covenants 61:13–22. The Waters Were Cursed by John, and the Destroyer Rides upon Their Face

Where in John's record did the Lord curse the waters in the last days? (61:14–18) "In describing the curse on the waters in the last days, the Lord may have been referring to passages in the book of Revelation in which the Apostle John described destruction that will occur in the waters before the Second Coming of Jesus Christ (see Revelation 8:8–11; 16:2–6). In Doctrine and Covenants 61, the Lord refers specifically to the danger of 'these waters,' meaning the Missouri River (see D&C 61:5, 18). At the time of this revelation, the dangers of the Missouri River included accidents due to difficulties in navigating the waters and contracting cholera, a disease most commonly spread by contaminated water" (*Doctrine and Covenants Student Manual* [2018], 328).

How was the land cursed in the beginning, but blessed in the last days? (61:17) The cursing of the land "refers to the Lord's words to Adam after he partook of the forbidden fruit [see Genesis 3:17–19]. . . . [The blessing in the last days] has come a little at a time. The Prophet Joseph Smith and the Saints turned a virtual, mosquito-infested swamp along the Mississippi River into Nauvoo, the City Beautiful. Later, those pioneers who settled the barren regions of the western United States saw the desert 'rejoice, and blossom as the rose' (Isaiah 35:1). In both instances the faith and determination of the Saints was blessed from on high. A future millennial day will see greater

13 And now, behold, for your good I gave unto you a commandment concerning these things; and I, the Lord, will reason with you as with men in days of old.

14 Behold, I, the Lord, in the beginning blessed the waters; but in the last days, by the mouth of my servant John, I cursed the waters.

15 Wherefore, the days will come that no flesh shall be safe upon the waters.

16 And it shall be said in days to come that none is able to go up to the land of Zion upon the waters, but he that is upright in heart.

17 And, as I, the Lord, in the beginning cursed the land, even so in the last days have I blessed it, in its time, for the use of my saints, that they may partake the fatness thereof.

18 And now I give unto you a commandment that what I say unto one I say unto all, that you shall forewarn your brethren concerning these waters, that they come not in journeying upon them, lest their faith fail and they are caught in snares;

What Were the Dangers in Traveling on Water for the Early Saints? (D&C 61:4–6, 14–19)

The Joseph Smith Papers historical introduction to the revelation in Doctrine and Covenants 61 describes the concern for safety many had when traveling on the Missouri River: "The revelation stated that God had permitted the elders to travel via the Missouri River to St. Louis, as instructed in an 8 August revelation [D&C 60], so that they could testify of the dangers on the water and warn church members not to travel to Zion on the river. At the time, the Missouri River was considered navigable only approximately three months out of the year. An 1837 Missouri gazetteer referred to the 'mad water' of the river and noted that 'freights and ensurance and pilot-wages' were higher for Missouri River navigation than for other waterways because of 'the dangers of the ever-varying channel of the river.' . . . After speaking to some of the elders who journeyed to Missouri, Elizabeth Godkin Marsh relayed that the river 'is always rily and bubly and looks mad as if it had been cursed'" (Joseph Smith Papers, Historical Introduction to "Revelation, 12 August 1831 [D&C 61]," 101).

The Prophet Joseph Smith recorded that on the third day of their journey from Independence, Missouri to Kirtland, Ohio, "many of the dangers, so common upon the western waters, manifested themselves; and after we had encamped upon the bank of the river, at McIlwaine's bend, brother William W. Phelps, in an open vision, by daylight, saw the Destroyer, in his most horrible power, ride upon the face of the waters. Others heard the noise, but saw not the vision" (Joseph Smith Papers, "History, 1838–1856, volume A-1," 142).

changes [see Isaiah 35:6–7]" (McConkie and Ostler, *Revelations of the Restoration*, 441).

Who might the destroyer be? (61:19) "A thorough textual analysis of section 61 demonstrates that the destroyer in the context of this section is linked to the destroying angels in Doctrine and Covenants 86:5; 89:21; and 105:15—angels who are agents of God carrying out divine judgments on the wicked. While Satan is represented as a destroyer elsewhere in scripture (such as Doctrine and Covenants 101:51), his destructive power is limited in the physical realm and most often comes in his influence over mortals to carry out the destruction. The message of any discussion about destroyers, divine or devilish, is that God's power supersedes that of the adversary and that the faithful will prevail....

"Phelps and company experienced the destroyer so they could be examples and admonish the Saints to be faithful" (Hord, "Beings Divine or Devilish," 111).

19 I, the Lord, have decreed, and the destroyer rideth upon the face thereof, and I revoke not the decree.

20 I, the Lord, was angry with you yesterday, but today mine anger is turned away.

21 Wherefore, let those concerning whom I have spoken, that should take their journey in haste—again I say unto you, let them take their journey in haste.

22 And it mattereth not unto me, after a little, if it so be that they fill their mission, whether they go by water or by land; let this be as it is made known unto them according to their judgments hereafter.

23 And now, concerning my servants, Sidney Rigdon, Joseph Smith, Jun., and Oliver Cowdery, let them come not again upon the waters, save it be upon the canal, while journeying unto their homes; or in other words they shall not come upon the waters to journey, save upon the canal.

24 Behold, I, the Lord, have appointed a way for the journeying of my saints; and behold, this is the way—that after they leave the canal they shall journey by land, inasmuch as they are commanded to journey and go up unto the land of Zion;

25 And they shall do like unto the children of Israel, pitching their tents by the way.

26 And, behold, this commandment you shall give unto all your brethren.

27 Nevertheless, unto whom is given power to command the waters, unto him it is given by the Spirit to know all his ways;

28 Wherefore, let him do as the Spirit of the living God commandeth him, whether upon the land or upon the waters, as it remaineth with me to do hereafter.

Doctrine and Covenants 61:23–29. Some Have Power to Command the Waters

Why was the Prophet Joseph Smith instructed to travel by canal? (61:23) "Travel on the waterways was a common mode of transportation in the 1830s. 'The canal' refers to man-made waterways in the state of Ohio. Canal barges were towed by teams of mules or horses moving at fewer than five miles an hour. The Prophet Joseph Smith and other Saints used the canal system to travel to Missouri" (McConkie and Ostler, *Revelations of the Restoration*, 442).

Who was given power to command the waters? (61:27–29) Verse 27 "implies that only a select few will have [power to command the waters]. While it is a priesthood power, all will not have the faith, or the gift of the Spirit developed to use it. Those few will know when to travel the waters, or when to go by land, because the Lord will tell him what to do through the Spirit (v. 28). Once more the Lord designates Joseph as the one who will give directions to the church as a whole (v. 29)" (Nyman, *Doctrine and Covenants Commentary*, 1:518). ◉

29 And unto you is given the course for the saints, or the way for the saints of the camp of the Lord, to journey.

Doctrine and Covenants 61:30–35. Elders Are to Journey Two by Two and Preach the Gospel

30 And again, verily I say unto you, my servants, Sidney Rigdon, Joseph Smith, Jun., and Oliver Cowdery, shall not open their mouths in the congregations of the wicked until they arrive at Cincinnati;

31 And in that place they shall lift up their voices unto God against that people, yea, unto him whose anger is kindled against their wickedness, a people who are well-nigh ripened for destruction.

32 And from thence let them journey for the congregations of their brethren, for their labors even now are wanted more abundantly among them than among the congregations of the wicked.

Who are "the congregations of their brethren"? (61:32) The Lord was speaking of "the Saints in Kirtland, where the leadership of Joseph and Sydney was both missed and needed. John Whitmer recorded that while Joseph and the other leaders were in Missouri, a number of the Saints had apostatized in Kirtland, though of these many were reclaimed when their leaders returned" (Robinson and Garrett, *Commentary on the Doctrine and Covenants*, 2:181).

What does it mean for missionaries to "rid their garments"? (61:33–34) "The Lord promises that missionaries who 'declare the word among the congregations of the wicked ... shall rid their garments, and they shall be spotless before me' (D&C 61:33–34). Those who have fulfilled the charge to 'declare the word' and have raised their voice of warning and witness to the world will stand 'blameless before God at the last day' (D&C 4:2). They will have rid their garments of the blood and sins of the wicked (see Ezek. 33, 34). ...

"The righteous are those who have rid their garments of the stain of sin, having washed them in the atoning blood of the Lamb who is without blemish, and are prepared to stand spotless in the presence of Deity" (Brewster, *Doctrine & Covenants Encyclopedia* [2012], 474). ⊕

33 And now, concerning the residue, let them journey and declare the word among the congregations of the wicked, inasmuch as it is given;

34 And inasmuch as they do this they shall rid their garments, and they shall be spotless before me.

35 And let them journey together, or two by two, as seemeth them good, only let my servant Reynolds Cahoon, and my servant Samuel H. Smith, with whom I am well pleased, be not separated until they return to their homes, and this for a wise purpose in me.

36 And now, verily I say unto you, and what I say unto one I say unto all, be of good cheer, little children; for I am in your midst, and I have not forsaken you;

37 And inasmuch as you have humbled yourselves before me, the blessings of the kingdom are yours.

38 Gird up your loins and be watchful and be sober, looking forth for the coming of the Son of Man, for he cometh in an hour you think not.

39 Pray always that you enter not into temptation, that you may abide the day of his coming, whether in life or in death. Even so. Amen.

Doctrine and Covenants 61:36–39. The Elders Are to Prepare for the Coming of the Son of Man

How does humility bring the "blessings of the kingdom"? (61:36–37) "Humility opens the way for us to *receive* our Heavenly Father's gifts through the enabling power of His Son, Jesus Christ. . . .

"The Savior has said, 'Behold, I stand at the door, and knock: if any man hear my voice, and open the door, I will come in to him, and will sup with him, and he with me' [Rev. 3:20].

"The Savior waits at the door of our hearts but will not override our agency. Softening our hearts invites Him in.

"The Savior's gifts are worth every effort it takes to receive them; they have the power to change our souls and enable us to do God's holy work" (Susan Porter, "Receiving the Gifts of God," 3).

Why does the Lord command us to be "looking forth" for His Second Coming, but withholds telling us when He will come? (61:38) "The primary purpose of the signs and prophecies concerning the last days—inspired writings in the scriptures and teachings uttered by prophets and apostles—is more about preparation than identification, more about conversion than chronology. . . . It is clear that we are to look to the signs and prophecies not in an effort to identify with precision when the Second Coming will occur but to be spiritually and temporally vigilant—ever prepared and worthy. . . . The parable of the ten virgins (Matthew 25:1–13) teaches that spiritual preparation cannot be done hastily or at the last minute. It requires consistent, continual, conscientious effort" (Top, "Second Coming of Christ, Signs of," 571, 572, 573). ❂

How are we to abide the day of Christ's coming? (61:39) "'Abide' is not a word we use much anymore. . . . The sense of [the word *abide*] is 'stay—but stay *forever*.' That is the call of the gospel message. . . . Come with conviction and endurance. Come permanently, for your sake and the sake of all the generations who must follow you, and we will help each other be strong to the very end. . . . Christ is everything to us and we are to 'abide' in Him permanently, unyieldingly, steadfastly, forever" (Holland, "Abide in Me," *Ensign*, May 2004, 32). ❂

Introduction to Doctrine and Covenants 62

"On August 13, 1831, the Prophet Joseph Smith and the elders traveling with him to Kirtland, Ohio, met Hyrum Smith, John Murdock, Harvey Whitlock, and David Whitmer at Chariton, Missouri. These elders had not yet reached Independence, Missouri, partly because they had been preaching the gospel along the way and partly because John Murdock's illness delayed travel. Joseph Smith later recounted that 'after the joyful salutations with which brethren meet each other' he received the revelation recorded in Doctrine and Covenants 62 (in [Joseph Smith Papers, "History, 1838–1856, volume A-1," 145])" (*Doctrine and Covenants Student Manual* [2018], 328).

"A lot had happened since [Joseph and Hyrum's] last visit. Joseph had arrived in Jackson County, Missouri, in mid-July and received a revelation identifying Independence as the 'center place' of Zion and designating a location for the temple there (D&C 57:3). On August 2, he had assisted the Saints in laying the first log of a house as a foundation of Zion, while Sidney Rigdon had dedicated the land of Zion for the gathering of the Saints. The following day, Joseph had dedicated the temple site.

"Some time during Hyrum's brief reunion with his brother in Chariton, the Prophet received [D&C 62,] a revelation of encouragement and direction" (O'Driscoll, *Hyrum Smith*, 49).

Doctrine and Covenants 62:1–3. Testimonies Are Recorded in Heaven

How can Jesus Christ succor us when we are tempted? (62:1) "The Savior was a participant, a player, who not only understood our plight intellectually, but who felt our wounds because they became his wounds. He had firsthand, 'in the trenches,' experience. He knew 'according to the flesh how to succor [which means to give relief or aid to] his people according to their infirmities' (Alma 7:12). He could comfort with empathy, not just sympathy. . . .

"'Man's needs . . . will never outdistance God's succoring powers. . . . He is always there. He never tells us not to come back home. He is never found in short supply of anxious concern. He never wants for a remedy. The Savior's love and compassion will always circumscribe every real and imaginable need of man'" (Callister, *Infinite Atonement*, 208, 209–10). ⊕

Whom was the Lord blessing "for the testimony which ye have borne"? (62:3) "Unlike the earlier group of missionaries who were traveling with the Prophet and were chastened for not preaching along the way as they had been commanded (see D&C 60:2–3), this later group of missionaries had, by and

SECTION 62

Revelation given through Joseph Smith the Prophet, on the bank of the Missouri River at Chariton, Missouri, August 13, 1831. On this day the Prophet and his group, who were on their way from Independence to Kirtland, met several elders who were on their way to the land of Zion, and, after joyful salutations, received this revelation.

1 Behold, and hearken, O ye elders of my church, saith the Lord your God, even Jesus Christ, your advocate, who knoweth the weakness of man and how to succor them who are tempted.

2 And verily mine eyes are upon those who have not as yet gone up unto the land of Zion; wherefore your mission is not yet full.

3 Nevertheless, ye are blessed, for the testimony which ye have borne is recorded in heaven for the angels to look upon; and they rejoice over you, and your sins are forgiven you.

large, successfully preached the gospel along the way and had built up the Church as they did so. Levi Hancock, Zebedee Coltrin, Solomon Hancock and Simeon Carter, for example, baptized over 120 persons between them on the way to Zion, and Parley P. Pratt recorded having established branches of the Church in Ohio, Illinois, and Indiana" (Robinson and Garrett, *Commentary on the Doctrine and Covenants*, 2:184–85).

Doctrine and Covenants 62:4–9. The Elders Are to Travel and Preach according to Judgment and as Directed by the Spirit

What was the meeting that the missionaries were commanded to hold? (62:4–5) Shortly after arriving in Jackson County, Missouri, "Hyrum and the other elders attended a missionary conference on August 24 to 'offer a sacrament to the Most High to fill the commandment which they received at [Chariton]' [see D&C 62:4] . . .

"In accordance with the revelation received in Chariton (D&C 62:5), Hyrum commenced the next leg of his missionary assignment and left for Kirtland the following day, accompanied by David Whitmer, Martin Harris, Harvey Whitlock, Simeon Carter, and William McLellin. Whitlock abandoned the party and returned to Zion just two days later, and Carter followed him the next day. The other four continued toward Kirtland undeterred, holding meetings on the way" (O'Driscoll, *Hyrum Smith*, 50).

Why do some of our choices not matter to the Lord? (62:5) "The Lord's statement that such things 'mattereth not unto me' initially may seem surprising. Clearly, the Savior was not saying to these missionaries that He did not care about what they were doing. Rather, He was emphasizing the importance of putting first things first and focusing upon the right things— which, in these instances, were getting to the assigned field of labor and initiating the work. They were to exercise faith, use good judgment, act in accordance with the direction of the Spirit, and determine the best way to travel to their assignments. The essential thing was the work they had been called to perform; how they got there was important but was not essential" (Bednar, "Reservoir of Living Water," 5). ✚

4 And now continue your journey. Assemble yourselves upon the land of Zion; and hold a meeting and rejoice together, and offer a sacrament unto the Most High.

5 And then you may return to bear record, yea, even altogether, or two by two, as seemeth you good, it mattereth not unto me; only be faithful, and declare glad tidings unto the inhabitants of the earth, or among the congregations of the wicked.

6 Behold, I, the Lord, have brought you together that the promise might be fulfilled, that the faithful among you should be preserved and rejoice together in the land of Missouri. I, the Lord, promise the faithful and cannot lie.

Why did the Lord comment about the means of travel for the missionaries? (62:7–9) "The most demanding judgments we ever make are seldom between good or bad or between attractive and unattractive alternatives. Usually, our toughest choices are between good and good. In this scriptural episode [D&C 62:7–9], horses, mules, and chariots may have been equally effective options for missionary travel. In a similar way, you and I also might identify at various times in our lives more than one acceptable opportunity or option that we could choose to pursue. We should remember this pattern from the scriptures as we approach such important decisions. If we put essential things first in our lives—things such as dedicated discipleship, honoring covenants, and keeping the commandments—then we will be blessed with inspiration and strong judgment as we pursue the path that leads us back to our heavenly home. If we put essential things first, we 'cannot go amiss' (D&C 80:3)" (Bednar, "Reservoir of Living Water," 6).

7 I, the Lord, am willing, if any among you desire to ride upon horses, or upon mules, or in chariots, he shall receive this blessing, if he receive it from the hand of the Lord, with a thankful heart in all things.

8 These things remain with you to do according to judgment and the directions of the Spirit.

9 Behold, the kingdom is yours. And behold, and lo, I am with the faithful always. Even so. Amen.

Introduction to Doctrine and Covenants 63

"Joseph Smith, Oliver Cowdery, and Sidney Rigdon returned to Kirtland from their mission to Missouri on 27 August 1831. . . . Since the revelations contained in Doctrine and Covenants 57–62 had been received by the Prophet while he was in Missouri, the Kirtland Saints were not yet aware of them. Consequently, Joseph and Sidney's report . . . caused great excitement among the Ohio Saints, who rejoiced to know that the center place of Zion had been located, that a temple site had been designated there, and that the land of Zion had been dedicated for their future inheritance. Understandably, the homecoming of the missionaries greatly increased the Saints' interest in Zion, and on 30 August 1831, . . . Joseph received this additional revelation, Doctrine and Covenants 63, on the subject of Zion and how it was to be established" (Robinson and Garrett, *Commentary on the Doctrine and Covenants*, 2:187).

This revelation "addressed many of the issues [Joseph Smith] faced on his return to Kirtland, providing instruction on how those who were to move to Zion would be selected, how quickly the Saints should gather to Zion, and how to prepare for Christ's return to the earth. It condemned the wicked both in and out of the church, especially sign seekers and adulterers, and appointed Newel K. Whitney and [Oliver] Cowdery to raise money for Zion. As [Sidney] Rigdon wrote the next day, the revelation gave instruction on how to 'escape . . . the day of tribulation which is coming on the earth'" (Joseph Smith Papers, Historical Introduction to "Revelation, 30 August 1831 [D&C 63]").

SECTION 63

Revelation given through Joseph Smith the Prophet, at Kirtland, Ohio, August 30, 1831. The Prophet, Sidney Rigdon, and Oliver Cowdery had arrived in Kirtland on August 27 from their visit to Missouri. Joseph Smith's history describes this revelation: "In these infant days of the Church, there was a great anxiety to obtain the word of the Lord upon every subject that in any way concerned our salvation; and as the land of Zion was now the most important temporal object in view, I enquired of the Lord for further information upon the gathering of the Saints, and the purchase of the land, and other matters."

1 Hearken, O ye people, and open your hearts and give ear from afar; and listen, you that call yourselves the people of the Lord, and hear the word of the Lord and his will concerning you.

2 Yea, verily, I say, hear the word of him whose anger is kindled against the wicked and rebellious;

3 Who willeth to take even them whom he will take, and preserveth in life them whom he will preserve;

4 Who buildeth up at his own will and pleasure; and destroyeth when he pleases, and is able to cast the soul down to hell.

5 Behold, I, the Lord, utter my voice, and it shall be obeyed.

6 Wherefore, verily I say, let the wicked take heed, and let the rebellious fear and tremble; and let the unbelieving hold their lips, for the day of wrath shall come upon them as a whirlwind, and all flesh shall know that I am God.

Doctrine and Covenants 63:1–6. A Day of Wrath Will Come upon the Wicked

What is the Lord saying when he asks us to "hearken," "give ear," and "listen"? (63:1) "To 'hearken' is to hear, as a judge hears a case on which he must give a decision. To 'open' one's 'heart' is to listen to the Word of God with love and affection, and with an eager desire to understand." it and to do the will of God. To 'give ear' is to devote the sense of hearing to the search for truth, and to 'listen' is to give attention, lest any word escape" (Smith and Sjodahl, *Doctrine and Covenants Commentary*, 373). See also commentary in this volume on Doctrine and Covenants 1:1.

Why does the Lord, though angry with the wicked, allow some to live and others to die? (63:2–4) "The power of life and death rests with God alone. No one dies contrary to the will of the Lord. This does not mean, however, that God arbitrarily 'kills' people. Though he takes or leaves whom he will, we must remember that his work and his glory is 'to bring to pass the immortality and eternal life' of his children (Moses 1:39). This is God's ruling motive in *all* that he does. Thus, God's purpose in taking or leaving this or that individual is always to maximize eternal prospects" (Robinson and Garrett, *Commentary on the Doctrine and Covenants*, 2:189).

Who might be among the wicked in the last days who must take heed? (63:6) The Book of Mormon prophet Nephi declared: "For the time speedily shall come that all churches which are built up to get gain, and all those who are built up to get power over the flesh, and those who are built up to become popular in the eyes of the world, and those who seek the lusts of the flesh and the things of the world, and to do all manner of iniquity; yea, in fine, all those who belong to the kingdom of the devil are they who need fear, and tremble, and quake; they are those who must be brought low in the dust; they are those who must be consumed as stubble" (1 Nephi 22:23).

Doctrine and Covenants 63:7–12. Signs Come by Faith

Why does seeking a sign impede a person's salvation? (63:7–9) President Dallin H. Oaks taught: "The viewing of signs or miracles is not a secure foundation for conversion. Scriptural history attests that people converted by signs and wonders soon forget them and again become susceptible to the lies and distortions of Satan and his servants (Hel. 16:23; 3 Ne. 1:22, 2:1, 8:4). . . .

"In contrast to the witness of the Spirit, which can be renewed from time to time as needed by a worthy recipient, the viewing of a sign or the experiencing of a miracle is a one-time event that will fade in the memory of its witness and can dim in its impact upon him or her" (*Lord's Way*, 87). ◉

7 And he that seeketh signs shall see signs, but not unto salvation.

8 Verily, I say unto you, there are those among you who seek signs, and there have been such even from the beginning;

9 But, behold, faith cometh not by signs, but signs follow those that believe.

10 Yea, signs come by faith, not by the will of men, nor as they please, but by the will of God.

11 Yea, signs come by faith, unto mighty works, for without faith no man pleaseth God; and with whom God is angry he is not well pleased; wherefore, unto such he showeth no signs, only in wrath unto their condemnation.

12 Wherefore, I, the Lord, am not pleased with those among you who have sought after signs and wonders for faith, and not for the good of men unto my glory.

What Is an Example of Signs Coming by Faith? (Doctrine and Covenants 63:10–12)

Elizabeth Ann Whitney is an example of "signs follow those that believe." She wrote: "We had been praying to know from the Lord how we could obtain the gift of the Holy Ghost. My husband, Newel K. Whitney, and myself, were Campbellites. We had been baptized for the remission of our sins, and believed in the laying on of hands and the gifts of the spirit. But there was no one with authority to confer the Holy Ghost upon us. We were seeking to know how to obtain the spirit and the gifts bestowed upon the ancient saints. . . .

"One night—it was midnight—as my husband and I, in our house at Kirtland, were praying to the father to be shown the way, the spirit rested upon us and a cloud overshadowed the house.

"It was as though we were out of doors. The house passed away from our vision. We were not conscious of anything but the presence of the spirit and the cloud that was over us.

Elizabeth Ann Whitney

"We were wrapped in the cloud. A solemn awe pervaded us. We saw the cloud and we felt the spirit of the Lord.

"Then we heard a voice out of the cloud saying:

"Prepare to receive the word of the Lord, for it is coming!

"At this we marveled greatly; but from that moment we knew that the word of the Lord was coming to Kirtland" (Johnson and Reeder, *Witness of Women*, 8)

13 Nevertheless, I give commandments, and many have turned away from my commandments and have not kept them.

14 There were among you adulterers and adulteresses; some of whom have turned away from you, and others remain with you that hereafter shall be revealed.

15 Let such beware and repent speedily, lest judgment shall come upon them as a snare, and their folly shall be made manifest, and their works shall follow them in the eyes of the people.

16 And verily I say unto you, as I have said before, he that looketh on a woman to lust after her, or if any shall commit adultery in their hearts, they shall not have the Spirit, but shall deny the faith and shall fear.

17 Wherefore, I, the Lord, have said that the fearful, and the unbelieving, and all liars, and whosoever loveth and maketh a lie, and the whoremonger, and the sorcerer, shall have their part in that lake which burneth with fire and brimstone, which is the second death.

18 Verily I say, that they shall not have part in the first resurrection.

19 And now behold, I, the Lord, say unto you that ye are not justified, because these things are among you.

Doctrine and Covenants 63:13–19. The Adulterous in Heart Will Deny the Faith and Be Cast into the Lake of Fire

To whom was the Lord referring in this passage? (63:14–19) "As recorded in Doctrine and Covenants 63:14–19, the Lord warned that some of the Saints were guilty of the sin of adultery. The term *adultery* refers to a person having sexual relations with someone other than his or her spouse (see D&C 42:22–26; 59:6; 66:10). Those who are guilty 'shall not have the Spirit, but shall deny the faith' (D&C 63:16), meaning that if adulterers do not repent, they will eventually find themselves turning in opposition to God's work. Because immorality and adultery are among the most serious of sins, those who choose to persist in wickedness rather than repent will suffer searing emotional pain—'that lake which burneth with fire and brimstone'—and spiritual death, also known as the 'second death' (D&C 63:17; see also Alma 12:16; Helaman 14:16–19; D&C 29:27–29; 76:36–38)" (*Doctrine and Covenants Student Manual* [2018], 334–35).

What are some consequences of lustfulness? (63:16) "Be faithful in your marriage covenants in thought, word, and deed. Pornography, flirtations, and unwholesome fantasies erode one's character and strike at the foundation of a happy marriage. Unity and trust within marriage are thereby destroyed. One who does not control his thoughts and thus commits adultery in his heart, if he does not repent, shall not have the Spirit, but shall deny the faith and shall fear (see D&C 42:23; 63:16)" (*Howard W. Hunter* [manual], 215).

What makes fire and brimstone such effective imagery? (63:17) "One of the most excruciating physical pains known to man is the burning of the flesh. Brimstone is a very flammable sulfur compound that burns with blue flame and emits a strong odor. The mental pain of the sinner in anguish has been compared to the severity of the physical pain caused by the burning of brimstone on the flesh; hence, the mental and spiritual pain of the sinner is 'as a lake of fire and brimstone' (2 Nephi 9:16; Alma 12:17)" (Daniel H. Ludlow, *Companion to Your Study*, 1:333).

Doctrine and Covenants 63:20. The Faithful Will Receive an Inheritance upon the Transfigured Earth

What is the "day of transfiguration" that is to come? (63:20) "This earth is passing through four grand degrees or stages: 1. The *creation* and the condition antedating [before] the fall. 2. The *telestial condition* which has prevailed since the fall of Adam. 3. The *terrestrial condition* that will prevail when the Savior comes and ushers in the millennial era. 4. The *celestial* or *final* state of the earth when it has obtained its exaltation" (Joseph Fielding Smith, *Doctrines of Salvation*, 1:82). See also commentary in this volume on Doctrine and Covenants 43:30.

Doctrine and Covenants 63:21. A Full Account of the Events on the Mount of Transfiguration Has Not Yet Been Revealed

What were Peter, James, and John shown about the earth while on the Mount of Transfiguration? (63:21) "Peter, James, and John saw in vision the transfiguration of the earth, that is, they saw it renewed and returned to its paradisiacal state—an event that is to take place at the Second Coming when the millennial era is ushered in" (Bruce R. McConkie, *Doctrinal New Testament Commentary*, 1:400). ⊕

Doctrine and Covenants 63:22–23. The Obedient Receive the Mysteries of the Kingdom

What blessings are promised to the obedient in this passage? (63:23) Elder Joseph B. Wirthlin testified: "By living the gospel of Jesus Christ, we develop within ourselves a living spring that will quench eternally our thirst for happiness, peace, and everlasting life. The Lord explains clearly in the Doctrine and Covenants that only faithful obedience can tap the well of living water that refreshes and enlivens our souls: 'But unto him that *keepeth my commandments* I will give the mysteries of my kingdom, and the same shall be in him a well of living water, springing up unto everlasting life' [D&C 63:23; emphasis added]" ("Living Water," *Ensign*, May 1995, 18). ⊕

20 Nevertheless, he that endureth in faith and doeth my will, the same shall overcome, and shall receive an inheritance upon the earth when the day of transfiguration shall come;

21 When the earth shall be transfigured, even according to the pattern which was shown unto mine apostles upon the mount; of which account the fulness ye have not yet received.

22 And now, verily I say unto you, that as I said that I would make known my will unto you, behold I will make it known unto you, not by the way of commandment, for there are many who observe not to keep my commandments.

23 But unto him that keepeth my commandments I will give the mysteries of my kingdom, and the same shall be in him a well of living water, springing up unto everlasting life.

Doctrine and Covenants 63:24–31. Inheritances in Zion Are to Be Purchased

24 And now, behold, this is the will of the Lord your God concerning his saints, that they should assemble themselves together unto the land of Zion, not in haste, lest there should be confusion, which bringeth pestilence.

25 Behold, the land of Zion—I, the Lord, hold it in mine own hands;

26 Nevertheless, I, the Lord, render unto Cæsar the things which are Cæsar's.

What do we learn in these verses about the Saints assembling together in Zion? (63:24–25) "In August 1831, the Lord renewed the commands to purchase lands in Zion and to gather to that sacred spot. . . .

"An everlasting principle underlies this command. The Lord's newly converted saints must flee from Babylon lest they be swallowed up by the world and, walking with the world, partake again of the ways of the world. Always and in all ages the Lord's people must gather—gather to those places where true worship prevails; gather into congregations where they can strengthen and perfect each other; gather to holy temples where the ordinances of salvation and exaltation are performed; and, particularly in our day, gather to the holy houses wherein their dead may be redeemed. The law of the gospel includes the law of gathering. But the Lord's house is a house of order; his saints must be organized; the gathering is not a hasty, unprepared foray to a new locale. It is a wisely planned and prearranged assembling; provision must be made for food, clothing, shelter, travel, and even a future livelihood, if possible" (Bruce R. McConkie, *New Witness*, 598). See also commentary in this volume on Doctrine and Covenants 117:9. ⊕

27 Wherefore, I the Lord will that you should purchase the lands, that you may have advantage of the world, that you may have claim on the world, that they may not be stirred up unto anger.

28 For Satan putteth it into their hearts to anger against you, and to the shedding of blood.

29 Wherefore, the land of Zion shall not be obtained but by purchase or by blood, otherwise there is none inheritance for you.

30 And if by purchase, behold you are blessed;

31 And if by blood, as you are forbidden to shed blood, lo, your enemies are upon you, and ye shall be scourged from city to city, and from synagogue to synagogue, and but few shall stand to receive an inheritance.

Why were the Saints told to "purchase" lands in Zion? (63:27–31) "The only way Zion will be built up is by purchase or by blood, and the Lord forbade the shedding of blood (D&C 63:27–31). Therefore, the Lord instructed the Saints in other areas to send money to the land of Zion to make purchases. The faithful would receive an inheritance in Zion (D&C 63:37–41, 47–48). Just as David was forbidden to build the temple because he was a man of war (1 Chronicles 28:2–3), it seems that we, as a people, will also be forbidden to enter Zion if we attempt to obtain the land by force. The land of Zion will be purchased, not conquered (D&C 105:28–29)" (Nyman, "When Will Zion Be Redeemed?" 151).

What might the word *synagogue* refer to in this passage? (63:31) "Though scholars generally contend that the synagogue as an institution did not originate until the Babylonian exile, the word *synagogue* is used throughout the Book of Mormon. It is 'quite probable that at its inception the synagogue did not refer to an actual building but to a group or community of individuals who met together for worship and religious purposes' [Meyers, "Synagogue," in *Anchor Bible Dictionary*, 6:251]. The word may have been used to connote simply a 'congregation' or 'assembly' of believers" (Millet, *Power of the Word*, 283).

Doctrine and Covenants 63:32–35. The Lord Decrees Wars, and the Wicked Slay the Wicked

How can we survive a day when fear comes upon everyone? (63:33) "And as we may live in the day when the terrors and trials and struggles, all foretold by prophets, come to pass, when 'fear shall come upon every man' (D&C 63:33), and when it shall seem that there is no place safe upon the earth, may the Latter-day Saints who are living the commandments of God be comforted again by those words with which the Master has comforted those who have lived before us in similar times: Be humble, and the Lord will take you by the hand, as it were, and give you answer to your prayers (see D&C 112:10)" (Lee, *Teachings*, 405). ◉

What does it mean that the Saints shall "hardly escape" during the destruction of the wicked? (63:34) The Prophet Joseph Smith related: "[I] explained concerning the coming of the Son of Man . . . that it is a false idea that the Saints will escape all the judgments whilst the wicked will suffer; for all flesh is subject to suffer, and 'the righteous shall hardly escape' [see D&C 63:34]; still many of the Saints will escape, for the just shall live by faith [see Habakkuk 2:4]; yet many of the righteous shall fall a prey to disease, to pestilence, etc., by reason of the weakness of the flesh, and yet be saved in the Kingdom of God" (*Joseph Smith* [manual], 253). In the end, the Lord "will preserve the righteous by his power, . . . even unto the destruction of their enemies by fire" (1 Nephi 22:17). See commentary in this volume on Doctrine and Covenants 112:23–24. ◉

Doctrine and Covenants 63:36–48. The Saints Are to Gather to Zion and Provide Moneys to Build It Up

What is noteworthy about the word *wherefore* in this passage? (63:36–38) "Many times in the revelations, after information is given about the Second Coming, the word *wherefore* or *therefore* introduces what the Lord wants the Saints to do to prepare. (For examples of this see D&C 27:15; 33:17; 45:64; 63:36; and 87:8.) Three major themes that repeatedly surface are gathering [D&C 63:36], living righteously

32 I, the Lord, am angry with the wicked; I am holding my Spirit from the inhabitants of the earth.

33 I have sworn in my wrath, and decreed wars upon the face of the earth, and the wicked shall slay the wicked, and fear shall come upon every man;

34 And the saints also shall hardly escape; nevertheless, I, the Lord, am with them, and will come down in heaven from the presence of my Father and consume the wicked with unquenchable fire.

35 And behold, this is not yet, but by and by.

36 Wherefore, seeing that I, the Lord, have decreed all these things upon the face of the earth, I will that my saints should be assembled upon the land of Zion;

37 And that every man should take righteousness in his hands and faithfulness upon

his loins, and lift a warning voice unto the inhabitants of the earth; and declare both by word and by flight that desolation shall come upon the wicked.

38 Wherefore, let my disciples in Kirtland arrange their temporal concerns, who dwell upon this farm.

39 Let my servant Titus Billings, who has the care thereof, dispose of the land, that he may be prepared in the coming spring to take his journey up unto the land of Zion, with those that dwell upon the face thereof, excepting those whom I shall reserve unto myself, that shall not go until I shall command them.

40 And let all the moneys which can be spared, it mattereth not unto me whether it be little or much, be sent up unto the land of Zion, unto them whom I have appointed to receive.

41 Behold, I, the Lord, will give unto my servant Joseph Smith, Jun., power that he shall be enabled to discern by the Spirit those who shall go up unto the land of Zion, and those of my disciples who shall tarry.

42 Let my servant Newel K. Whitney retain his store, or in other words, the store, yet for a little season.

43 Nevertheless, let him impart all the money which he can impart, to be sent up unto the land of Zion.

44 Behold, these things are in his own hands, let him do according to wisdom.

[D&C 63:37], and crying repentance to the inhabitants of the earth [D&C 63:37]" (Dahl, "Second Coming of Jesus Christ," 108).

Who can rightfully "lift a warning voice"? (63:37)
Latter-day Saints "have an especial and particular obligation to stand as witnesses of the truth to the world in this day. We live in the great era of darkness, spiritual darkness and apostasy, that is to precede the second coming of the Son of Man. He has called us and appointed us to stand as lights to the world. We are expected to be witnesses of the truth; to bear record of the divine sonship; to stand valiantly and courageously on the Lord's side of the line in defense of truth and righteousness and in proclaiming the gospel to his other children in the world" (Bruce R. McConkie, *Doctrines of the Restoration*, 45).

Why did the Lord require Titus Billings to dispose of Isaac Morley's land in Kirtland? (63:39–40)
When Isaac Morley departed for his mission to Missouri in 1831, his brother-in-law, Titus Billings, was given the authority over his property. Later, "The Lord instructed [Isaac] Morley's brother-in-law Titus Billings to 'dispose of' Morley's farm. In the revelation given on September 11, the Lord explained that he commanded the farm be sold, 'that my servant Isaac [Morley] may not be tempted above that which he is able to bear' [D&C 64:20].

"Isaac and Lucy Morley willingly made the sacrifice. In October 1831, Titus Billings sold much of Morley's farm. Morley took his family back to Independence, as he was commanded, and set to work once again to establish a foundation for the temple city" (McBride, "Ezra Booth and Isaac Morley," 135).

What would Newel K. Whitney's role be as an agent? (63:45) See commentary in this volume on Doctrine and Covenants 51:7–8.

What might it mean to "overcome the world"? (63:47) "It means overcoming the temptation to care more about the things of this world than the things of God. It means trusting the doctrine of Christ more than the philosophies of men. It means delighting in truth, denouncing deception, and becoming 'humble followers of Christ' [2 Nephi 28:14]. It means choosing to refrain from anything that drives the Spirit away. It means being willing to 'give away' [Alma 22:18] even our favorite sins.

"Now, overcoming the world certainly does not mean becoming perfect in this life, nor does it mean that your problems will magically evaporate—because they won't. . . . Overcoming the world means growing to love God and His Beloved Son more than you love anyone or anything else" (Nelson, "Overcome the World and Find Rest," *Liahona*, Nov. 2022, 96–97). ◉

What inheritance will the faithful receive for sending "treasures" to Zion? (63:48) "Those who send money to Zion will inherit part of the earth and a reward in the one that will replace it. Their good

45 Verily I say, let him be ordained as an agent unto the disciples that shall tarry, and let him be ordained unto this power;

46 And now speedily visit the churches, expounding these things unto them, with my servant Oliver Cowdery. Behold, this is my will, obtaining moneys even as I have directed.

47 He that is faithful and endureth shall overcome the world.

48 He that sendeth up treasures unto the land of Zion shall receive an inheritance in this world, and his works shall follow him, and also a reward in the world to come.

Who Was Newel K. Whitney? (Doctrine and Covenants 63:42)

"Newel Kimball Whitney, a presiding bishop of the Church, was born 5 February 1795 in Marlborough, Vermont. By the age of 19 he was a merchant living in Plattsburg, New York.

"Newel moved to Painesville, Ohio, where he became a business partner with Algernon Sydney Gilbert. They later established a business in Kirtland. While living in Kirtland, Newel married Elizabeth Ann Smith 20 October 1822. In November they were converted to the gospel and baptized by Sidney Rigdon.

Newel K. Whitney

"On 4 December 1831 Whitney was called as a bishop over the Ohio area (D&C 72). Unable to see himself in this position, Whitney 'shrank from the responsibility.' The Prophet answered: 'Go and ask the Lord about it.' Newel did so and heard a voice from heaven say: 'Thy strength is in me' (Whitney, [in Conference Report], 47–48). With this comforting confirmation, he accepted the call. Whitney also participated in the School of the Prophets held in his Kirtland store.

"Whitney left Kirtland in the fall of 1838, eventually settling at Quincy, Illinois, and then Nauvoo. In May 1842 he was one of a select few to receive the endowment from Joseph Smith. When the Nauvoo Stake was organized 5 October 1839, Whitney served as bishop of the Middle Ward. . . . At Winter Quarters 6 April 1847 he was sustained as presiding bishop of the Church, which position he held until his death in Salt Lake City 23 September 1850" (*Encyclopedia of Latter-day Saint History*, 1340).

works will be consecrated for their gain. The faithful dead will be resurrected when the Lord comes and renews the earth, and the Lord will give them an inheritance in New Jerusalem, the holy city" (Harper, *Making Sense of the Doctrine & Covenants*, 220).

Doctrine and Covenants 63:49–54. Blessings Are Assured the Faithful at the Second Coming, in the Resurrection, and during the Millennium

In what way is it a blessing to "die in the Lord"? (63:49) "For the one who dies, life goes on and his . . . agency continues, and death, which seems to us such a calamity, could be a blessing in disguise. . . .

"If we say that early death is a calamity, disaster, or tragedy, would it not be saying that mortality is preferable to earlier entrance into the spirit world and to eventual salvation and exaltation? If mortality be the perfect state, then death would be a frustration, but the gospel teaches us there is no tragedy in death, but only in sin. '. . . blessed are the dead that die in the Lord. . . .' (see D&C 63:49)" (*Spencer W. Kimball* [manual], 18).

What does it mean to die at "the age of man" after the Lord's coming? (63:50–51) "The Saints will live to 'the age of man'—in the words of Isaiah, the age of one hundred (Isaiah 65:20)—and will then pass through death and be changed instantly from mortality to resurrected immortality (D&C 63:49–51; see also JST, Isaiah 65:20). Speaking of those who remain on earth when the Lord comes in glory, President Joseph Fielding Smith pointed out that 'the inhabitants of the earth will have a sort of translation. They will be transferred to a condition of the terrestrial order, and so they will have power over disease and they will have power to live until they get to a certain age and then they will die' [Joseph Fielding Smith, *Signs of the Times*, 39]" (Millet, *Precept upon Precept*, 375).

How does the parable of the Ten Virgins apply to the Second Coming of Jesus Christ? (63:53–54) "From God's perspective of time, the events of the Second Coming are 'nigh at hand' (D&C 63:53). While we do not know the hour of the Second Coming, the Lord's parable of the foolish and wise virgins reminds us to prepare now for that day (see Matthew 25:1–13). It is essential that we view the Second Coming as imminent so that we will prepare ourselves. The clarification in Doctrine and Covenants 63:54 that 'until that hour there will be foolish virgins among the wise'

49 Yea, and blessed are the dead that die in the Lord, from henceforth, when the Lord shall come, and old things shall pass away, and all things become new, they shall rise from the dead and shall not die after, and shall receive an inheritance before the Lord, in the holy city.

50 And he that liveth when the Lord shall come, and hath kept the faith, blessed is he; nevertheless, it is appointed to him to die at the age of man.

51 Wherefore, children shall grow up until they become old; old men shall die; but they shall not sleep in the dust, but they shall be changed in the twinkling of an eye.

52 Wherefore, for this cause preached the apostles unto the world the resurrection of the dead.

53 These things are the things that ye must look for; and, speaking after the manner of the Lord, they are now nigh at hand, and in a time to come, even in the day of the coming of the Son of Man.

54 And until that hour there will be foolish virgins among the wise; and at that hour cometh an entire separation of the righteous and the wicked; and in that day will I send mine angels to pluck out the wicked and cast them into unquenchable fire.

means that even among the Latter-day Saints there are those who will be found wicked and who will be separated and cast out from among the righteous. . . . Therefore, the Lord commanded the Saints to repent and prepare for His coming" (*Doctrine and Covenants Student Manual* [2018], 341). See also commentary in this volume on Doctrine and Covenants 61:38.

Why will there be an "entire separation" between the righteous and the wicked? (63:54) "The time will come, just as sure as we live, that there will be a separation between the righteous and the unrighteous" (Joseph Fielding Smith, *Doctrines of Salvation*, 3:16). "The Church will have members numbered among both. . . . The day of separation is a work directed by the Master and his angels and not left to mortal man. Thus, there is no guarantee of salvation for those who claim membership in the Lord's church. The foolish members of the kingdom who fail to live the laws revealed by God will be cut off with the rest of the wicked. This revelation, directed to the members of the Church, identifies two sins that the Saints are commanded to repent of or be cast down to hell—adultery and lying (vv. 14–19)" (McConkie and Ostler, *Revelations of the Restoration*, 455). ◉

Doctrine and Covenants 63:55–58. This Is a Day of Warning

What do we learn about Sidney Rigdon in this passage? (63:55) "In an early revelation of August 1831 the Lord warned Sidney Rigdon that he had 'exalted himself in his heart, and received not counsel, but grieved the Spirit' (D&C 63:55). Sidney Rigdon's ego was not fully tamed. The Lord counseled him to 'remain with my people' (D&C 124:104), but he did not.

"[Years later] Sidney Rigdon complained bitterly over his difficulties in Liberty Jail. These sufferings were real, but so was his stubborn self-pity. It elbowed out earlier and extraordinary spiritual experiences. . . .

"Only six years after being lifted up by the Lord in the glorious theophany in Hiram, Ohio (see D&C 76), Sidney, though truly tried, felt put upon by the Lord! He first lost his heart and then his way" (Maxwell, *Men and Women of Christ*, 105).

What writings of Sidney Rigdon were unacceptable to the Lord? (63:56) "Sidney Rigdon had been given the go ahead to 'write a description of the land of Zion, and a statement of the will of God, as it [was] made known by the Spirit unto him,' which was to be used to encourage the Saints to give money to the project (see D&C 58:50–52). . . .

55 And now behold, verily I say unto you, I, the Lord, am not pleased with my servant Sidney Rigdon; he exalted himself in his heart, and received not counsel, but grieved the Spirit;

56 Wherefore his writing is not acceptable unto the Lord, and he shall make another; and if the Lord receive it not, behold he standeth no longer in the office to which I have appointed him.

"Rigdon failed on his first attempt to write his description of the land of Zion. He had included in his statement a rather long 'apocalyptical essay calling sinners to repentance' [Van Wagoner, *Sidney Rigdon: Portrait of Religious Excess*, 103]. Having gone beyond the mark, he was reprimanded and had to start over again" (James W. McConkie, *Looking at the Doctrine and Covenants Again*, 301, 301n3).

What does the Lord ask of those who seek to bring others to repentance? (63:57–58) "Let the elders be exceedingly careful about *unnecessarily* disturbing and harrowing up the feelings of the people. Remember that your business is, to preach the gospel in all humility and meekness, and warn sinners to repent and come to Christ. Avoid contentions and vain disputes with men of corrupt minds, who do not desire to know the truth. Remember that '*it is a day of warning, and not a day of many words.*' If they receive not your testimony in one place, flee to another, remembering to cast no reflections, nor throw out any bitter sayings. If you do your duty, it will be just as well with you, as though all men embraced the gospel" (Joseph Smith Papers, "Letter to the Church, not after 18 December 1833," 120).

57 And again, verily I say unto you, those who desire in their hearts, in meekness, to warn sinners to repentance, let them be ordained unto this power.

58 For this is a day of warning, and not a day of many words. For I, the Lord, am not to be mocked in the last days.

Doctrine and Covenants 63:59–66. The Lord's Name Is Taken in Vain by Those Who Use It without Authority

What does it mean that the day will come when all things will be subject to the Lord? (63:59) Modern day apostles have declared: "We testify that He will someday return to earth. 'And the glory of the Lord shall be revealed, and all flesh shall see it together' (Isaiah 40:5). He will rule as King of Kings and reign as Lord of Lords, and every knee shall bend and every tongue shall speak in worship before Him. Each of us will stand to be judged of Him according to our works and the desires of our hearts" ("Living Christ," *Ensign*, Apr. 2000, 2).

59 Behold, I am from above, and my power lieth beneath. I am over all, and in all, and through all, and search all things, and the day cometh that all things shall be subject unto me.

What is meant by Alpha and Omega? (63:60) See commentary in this volume on Doctrine and Covenants 19:1, 35:1, and 38:1.

60 Behold, I am Alpha and Omega, even Jesus Christ.

61 Wherefore, let all men beware how they take my name in their lips—

In what ways do people use the Lord's name in vain? (63:60–62) "This scripture [D&C 63:61–62] shows that we take the name of the Lord in vain when we use his name without authority. This obviously occurs when the sacred names of God the Father and his Son, Jesus Christ, are used in what is called

62 For behold, verily I say, that many there be who are under this condemnation, who use the name of the Lord, and use it in vain, having not authority.

profanity: in hateful cursings, in angry denunciations, or as marks of punctuation in common discourse.

"The names of the Father and the Son are used with authority when we reverently teach and testify of them, when we pray, and when we perform the sacred ordinances of the priesthood.

"There are no more sacred or significant words in all of our language than the names of God the Father and his Son, Jesus Christ" (Oaks, "Reverent and Clean," *Ensign*, May 1986, 49–50).

Why must we be careful with sacred things?
(63:64) "Light and knowledge from heaven is sacred. It is sacred because heaven is its source.

"*Sacred* means worthy of veneration and respect. By designating something as sacred, the Lord signals that it is of higher value and priority than other things. Sacred things are to be treated with more care, given greater deference, and regarded with deeper reverence. Sacred ranks high in the hierarchy of heavenly values.

"That which is sacred to God becomes sacred to us only through the exercise of agency; each must choose to accept and hold sacred that which God has defined as sacred. He sends light and knowledge from heaven. He invites us to receive and treat it as sacred" (Pieper, "To Hold Sacred," *Ensign*, May 2012, 109). ✛

63 Wherefore, let the church repent of their sins, and I, the Lord, will own them; otherwise they shall be cut off.

64 Remember that that which cometh from above is sacred, and must be spoken with care, and by constraint of the Spirit; and in this there is no condemnation, and ye receive the Spirit through prayer; wherefore, without this there remaineth condemnation.

65 Let my servants, Joseph Smith, Jun., and Sidney Rigdon, seek them a home, as they are taught through prayer by the Spirit.

66 These things remain to overcome through patience, that such may receive a more exceeding and eternal weight of glory, otherwise, a greater condemnation. Amen.

The Prophet Joseph Smith "dictated [D&C 64] in Kirtland, Ohio, on 11 September 1831, just a few days after arriving back from Independence, Jackson County, Missouri. Although the Missouri trip involved the identification of the site for the city of Zion and the dedication of land for the construction of a temple, it generated disappointment and disillusionment for some.... Ezra Booth, one of the elders called to travel to Missouri in the summer of 1831, also expressed disillusionment with [Joseph Smith] himself. Booth complained that he and his companion, Isaac Morley, had to walk to Missouri while [Joseph Smith] and, Sidney [Rigdon], and other church leaders traveled by way of stagecoach and canal. Apparently, Booth witnessed a confrontation between Edward Partridge and [the Prophet] over the quality of Missouri land selected for purchase. Booth believed that [Joseph]'s conduct in these disagreements was unbecoming a Christian. [Sidney] Rigdon, likely referring to the same incident, placed the blame on Partridge, stating he had 'insulted the Lord's prophet in particular & assumed authority over him in open violation of the Laws of God.' Partridge was later penitent: the same minutes that contain Rigdon's accusation record Partridge saying that 'if Br. Joseph has not forgiven him he hopes he will, as he is & has always been sorry.' Booth, on the other hand, apparently became more resentful, and a conference barred him from preaching as an elder in the church on 6 September 1831.

"A week later, this 11 September revelation expounded on the necessity of forgiveness and specifically referred to problems involving Booth, Morley, and Partridge, indicating that the latter two were forgiven for their sins. It also discussed preparations for the gathering to Missouri. The revelation clarified the relationship between Kirtland and Missouri: a previous revelation had established Independence as the 'centre place' at which to build the city of Zion, and this revelation declared that Kirtland, where the Saints had previously gathered, would remain 'a strong hold' for five years. It also identified what property should be retained in Kirtland. Portraying a bright future for the land of Zion, the revelation offered encouragement to those who remained committed to the mission and leadership of [the Prophet]" (Joseph Smith Papers, Historical Introduction to "Revelation, 11 September 1831 [D&C 64]").

Doctrine and Covenants 64 emphasizes the righteous exercise of one's agency and the Lord's willingness to forgive the repentant. "While Ezra Booth's experiences in traveling to Missouri turned him away from the Church, Isaac Morley's ultimately drew him closer.... Unlike Ezra Booth, Isaac Morley had ceased his criticisms and changed his outlook. The revelation continued in the Lord's own voice: 'I have forgiven my servant Isaac' [Morley; see D&C 64:16]" (McBride, "Ezra Booth and Isaac Morley," 135; spelling modernized).

"This revelation contains information, counsel, and warnings for Church members. Instructions and teachings are included that would assist Latter-day Saints to better understand how to become a Zion people" (Woodger, *Essential Doctrine and Covenants Companion*, 126).

SECTION 64

Revelation given through Joseph Smith the Prophet to the elders of the Church, at Kirtland, Ohio, September 11, 1831. The Prophet was preparing to move to Hiram, Ohio, to renew his work on the translation of the Bible, which had been laid aside while he had been in Missouri. A company of brethren who had been commanded to journey to Zion (Missouri) was earnestly engaged in making preparations to leave in October. At this busy time, the revelation was received.

Doctrine and Covenants 64:1–11. The Saints Are Commanded to Forgive One Another, Lest There Remain in Them the Greater Sin

How does Christ's compassion help us overcome the world? (64:2) "Before the Savior submitted Himself to the agony of Gethsemane and Calvary, He declared to His Apostles, 'In the world ye shall have tribulation: but be of good cheer; I have *overcome the world*' [John 16:33]. Subsequently, Jesus entreated each of us to do the same when He said, 'I *will* that *ye* should *overcome* the world' [D&C 64:2]. . . .

"Because Jesus Christ overcame this fallen world, and because He atoned for each of us, you too can overcome this sin-saturated, self-centered, and often exhausting world.

"Because the Savior, through His infinite Atonement, redeemed each of us from weakness, mistakes, and sin, and because He experienced every pain, worry, and burden you have ever had, then as you truly repent and seek His help, you can rise above this present precarious world" (Nelson, "Overcome the World and Find Rest," *Liahona*, Nov. 2022, 96).

What are we to understand about the Lord forgiving these elders? (64:3) "In a remarkable display of mercy and compassion, the Lord unilaterally declared an amnesty for the elders of the Church. As of 11 September 1831, their slates were wiped clean. In doing this, the Lord provided for the Saints an example of mercy and forgiveness that set the stage for the sweeping commandment that follows in verses 9–10. First the Lord forgave his servants, freely and apparently without exception. Then he commanded the Saints to forgive one another in the same manner, following his example" (Robinson and Garrett, *Commentary on the Doctrine and Covenants*, 2:210). ◉

What were "the keys of the mysteries" that Joseph would retain? (64:5) "The 'keys of the mysteries' (D&C 28:7), or the 'keys of the mysteries of the kingdom' (D&C 64:5), are the right to receive the mind and will of the Lord in behalf of the kingdom (Church) here on the earth. . . . Only the senior Apostle on earth—the President of The Church of Jesus Christ of Latter-day Saints—may reveal the mysteries to the Church and the world" (Brewster, *Doctrine & Covenants Encyclopedia* [2012], 301).

1 Behold, thus saith the Lord your God unto you, O ye elders of my church, hearken ye and hear, and receive my will concerning you.

2 For verily I say unto you, I will that ye should overcome the world; wherefore I will have compassion upon you.

3 There are those among you who have sinned; but verily I say, for this once, for mine own glory, and for the salvation of souls, I have forgiven you your sins.

4 I will be merciful unto you, for I have given unto you the kingdom.

5 And the keys of the mysteries of the kingdom shall not be taken from my servant Joseph Smith, Jun., through the means I have appointed, while he liveth, inasmuch as he obeyeth mine ordinances.

6 There are those who have sought occasion against him without cause;

7 Nevertheless, he has sinned; but verily I say unto you, I, the Lord, forgive sins unto those who confess their sins before me and ask forgiveness, who have not sinned unto death.

8 My disciples, in days of old, sought occasion against one another and forgave not one another in their hearts; and for this evil they were afflicted and sorely chastened.

9 Wherefore, I say unto you, that ye ought to forgive one another; for he that forgiveth not his brother his trespasses standeth condemned before the Lord; for there remaineth in him the greater sin.

Why would someone seek occasion against the Prophet without cause? (64:6) See commentary in this volume on Doctrine and Covenants 56:1.

What could it mean to sin unto death? (64:7) Elder Bruce R. McConkie explained: "There are sins unto death, meaning spiritual death. There are sins for which there is no forgiveness, neither in this world and in the world to come. There are sins which utterly and completely preclude the sinner from gaining eternal life. . . .

"Our knowledge about sins unto death is limited, but providentially there are relatively few who cannot be redeemed from spiritual death through repentance. . . .

"The unpardonable sin consists in denying Christ, in fighting the truth, in joining hands with those who crucified him, knowing full well, and with a perfect knowledge, that he is the Son of God; it means pursuing this course after gaining a perfect knowledge, given of the Holy Ghost, that he is Lord of all" (*New Witness*, 231, 233). ⊕

Why is refusing to forgive others a "greater sin"? (64:9) "When we take the position of withholding forgiveness from our fellow men, we are attempting to block his progress toward salvation. This position is satanical and our motive is not Christlike. We are endeavoring to impede the progress of a living soul and deny him the forgiving blessings of the [Savior's] atonement. This philosophy is saturated with impure motives that are designed to destroy the soul. What

Forgiving and Forgiveness (Doctrine and Covenants 64:8–11)

The elders who had mercifully received the Lord's forgiveness (see D&C 64:3) were in a unique position to respond to the Lord's instruction to forgive others. Ann M. Madsen observed, "Those who have responded to the need for repentance understand the sweetness of forgiveness. . . . First, as one who has tasted the sweetness of having been forgiven and then as one who has the godly privilege to extend personal forgiveness to others. . . .

"We must be willing to encircle one another in the kind of love the Lord has offered each of us. . . . There are no qualifiers. Though our brother's sin be terrible or tiny, we will not be measured against its enormity, but we will be judged on our forgiveness or hardheartedness. We should have no problem deciding which of all those who have sinned against us to forgive. No formula is to be applied. It is required (not requested) that we forgive ALL" ("Lord Requires Our Hearts," 248–49).

President Jeffrey R. Holland provided significant counsel about our journey of forgiveness: "'Forgive, and ye shall be forgiven,' Christ taught in New Testament times [see Luke 6:37]. . . . It is, however, important for some of you living in real anguish to note what He did *not* say. He did *not* say, 'You are not allowed to feel true pain or real sorrow from the shattering experiences you have had at the hand of another.' *Nor* did He say, 'In order to forgive fully, you have to reenter a toxic relationship or return to an abusive, destructive circumstance.' But notwithstanding even the most terrible offenses that might come to us, we can rise above our pain only when we put our feet onto the path of true healing. That path is the forgiving one walked by Jesus of Nazareth, who calls out to each of us, 'Come, follow me'" ("Ministry of Reconciliation," *Ensign*, Nov. 2018, 78, 79).

greater sin is there than this? Perhaps many Latter-day Saints have failed to realize the seriousness of refusing to forgive others. But the Lord called it evil and for such we do stand condemned before Him and the greater sin remaineth" (Otten and Caldwell, *Sacred Truths*, 1:314). ⊕

Who will receive forgiveness from the Lord? (64:10) The Lord has consistently taught that He will forgive those who repent (for example, see Mosiah 26:30–32; D&C 1:31–33; 58:42–43). We can also trust that His divine justice will be imposed on unrepentant offenders. Speaking of innocent victims who had been seriously wronged, Elder Richard G. Scott taught, "Don't burden your own life with thoughts of retribution. The Lord's mill of justice grinds slowly, but it grinds exceedingly well. In the Lord's economy, no one will escape the consequences of unresolved violation of His laws. In His time and in His way full payment will be required for unrepented evil acts" ("Peace of Conscience and Peace of Mind," *Ensign*, Nov. 2004, 17).

Why are we required to forgive everyone? (64:10) "Each of us is under a divinely spoken obligation to reach out with pardon and mercy and to forgive one another. There is a great need for this Christlike attribute in our families, in our marriages, in our wards and stakes, in our communities, and in our nations.

"We will receive the joy of forgiveness in our own lives when we are willing to extend that joy freely to others. Lip service is not enough. We need to purge our hearts and minds of feelings and thoughts of bitterness and let the light and the love of Christ enter in. As a result, the Spirit of the Lord will fill our souls with the joy accompanying divine peace of conscience (see Mosiah 4:2–3)" (Uchtdorf, "Point of Safe Return," *Ensign*, May 2007, 101). ⊕

Why should we trust God when others offend us? (64:11) The Prophet Joseph Smith observed: "While one portion of the human race are judging and condemning the other without mercy, the great parent of the universe looks upon the whole of the human family with a fatherly care, and paternal regard; he views them as his offspring; and without any of those contracted feelings that influence the children of men. . . . He holds the [reins] of judgment in his hands; he is a wise lawgiver, . . . those who have lived without the law, will be judged without law, and those who have a law, will be judged by that law; we need not doubt the wisdom and intelligence of the great Jehovah" (Joseph Smith Papers, "History, 1838–1856, volume C-1," 1321). See also Matthew 7:2; 3 Nephi 14:2.

10 I, the Lord, will forgive whom I will forgive, but of you it is required to forgive all men.

11 And ye ought to say in your hearts—let God judge between me and thee, and reward thee according to thy deeds.

12 And him that repenteth not of his sins, and confesseth them not, ye shall bring before the church, and do with him as the scripture saith unto you, either by commandment or by revelation.

13 And this ye shall do that God may be glorified—not because ye forgive not, having not compassion, but that ye may be justified in the eyes of the law, that ye may not offend him who is your lawgiver—

14 Verily I say, for this cause ye shall do these things.

15 Behold, I, the Lord, was angry with him who was my servant Ezra Booth, and also my servant Isaac Morley, for they kept not the law, neither the commandment;

16 They sought evil in their hearts, and I, the Lord, withheld my Spirit. They condemned for evil that thing in which there was no evil; nevertheless I have forgiven my servant Isaac Morley.

17 And also my servant Edward Partridge, behold, he hath sinned, and Satan seeketh to destroy his soul; but when these things are made known unto them, and they repent of the evil, they shall be forgiven.

18 And now, verily I say that it is expedient in me that my servant Sidney Gilbert, after a few weeks, shall return upon his business, and to his agency in the land of Zion;

Doctrine and Covenants 64:12–22. The Unrepentant Are to Be Brought before the Church

What instruction were the elders given regarding unrepentant sinners? (64:12) See commentary in this volume on Doctrine and Covenants 42:74–77, 80–83, 88–93.

How can membership councils for the unrepentant glorify God? (64:12–14) President Dallin H. Oaks stated: "In contrast to the punishment that is the intended result of the judgment of a criminal court, the primary purpose of Church [membership councils] is to facilitate repentance—to qualify a transgressor for the mercy of God and the salvation made possible through the atonement of Jesus Christ. . . .

"The object of God's laws is to save the sinner, not simply to punish him. Consequently, there is no exemption from the conditions a transgressor must meet to qualify for the mercy necessary for salvation. The repentant transgressor must be changed, and the conditions of repentance, including confession and personal suffering, are essential to accomplish that change. To exempt a transgressor from those conditions would deprive him of the change necessary for his salvation. That would be neither just nor merciful" ("Sins, Crimes, and Atonement," 5).

What were the circumstances surrounding the Lord's displeasure with Ezra Booth and Isaac Morley? (64:15–16) "Ezra Booth and Isaac Morley were called to serve as missionary companions in traveling to Independence, Missouri (D&C 52:23). They had angered the Lord in that they had 'kept not the law, neither the commandment.' A specific knowledge of what they did or did not do has not been preserved for us. It appears that they imbibed a selfish and critical spirit relative to what they had been asked to do. Isaac Morley repented of that spirit and became a valiant servant of the Lord. Ezra Booth, on the other hand, nurtured his association with the spirit of darkness until he became its servant. Six months later he joined the mob that tarred and feathered Joseph Smith" (McConkie and Ostler, *Revelations of the Restoration*, 464). See also commentary in this volume on the Introduction to Doctrine and Covenants 64.

19 And that which he hath seen and heard may be made known unto my disciples, that they perish not. And for this cause have I spoken these things.

20 And again, I say unto you, that my servant Isaac Morley may not be tempted above that which he is able to bear, and counsel wrongfully to your hurt, I gave commandment that his farm should be sold.

21 I will not that my servant Frederick G. Williams should sell his farm, for I, the Lord, will to retain a strong hold in the land of Kirtland, for the space of five years, in the which I will not overthrow the wicked, that thereby I may save some.

22 And after that day, I, the Lord, will not hold any guilty that shall go with an open heart up to the land of Zion; for I, the Lord, require the hearts of the children of men.

Why would the Lord want the Saints to remain in Kirtland for five years? (64:21–22) "Although some of the Saints were commanded to move to Missouri, others, like Frederick G. Williams, were to remain in Kirtland, Ohio. The Lord promised that Kirtland would be 'a strong hold' of the Church for at least five more years (D&C 64:21). This promise was fulfilled, and during that period the Kirtland Temple was constructed and dedicated, priesthood keys were restored by heavenly messengers to the Prophet Joseph Smith and Oliver Cowdery, and a great outpouring of spiritual blessings was given to the Saints" (*Doctrine and Covenants Student Manual* (2018), 348–49).

What does it mean that the Lord requires "the hearts of the children of men"? (64:22) President Dallin H. Oaks explained: "In describing the state of the inner man, the scriptures commonly use the word *heart*. This word occurs over a thousand times in the standard works, almost always as a figurative expression.

"*Heart* is often used to identify the extent to which one is receptive to the message of the gospel [for example, see 1 Nephi 2:16 and Helaman 10:13]. . . .

"In the language of the scriptures, the word *heart* is a powerful figurative expression, rich in meaning. . . . In terms of God's commandments the hidden thoughts of our minds are just as important as the observed actions of our bodies" (*Pure in Heart*, vii, viii). See commentary in this volume on Doctrine and Covenants 64:34. ☉

Doctrine and Covenants 64:23–25. He That Is Tithed Will Not Be Burned at the Lord's Coming

What is important about the word *today* in these verses? (64:23–25) "The word *today*, when used in connection to the second coming of Jesus Christ, refers to the period between the present time and

23 Behold, now it is called today until the coming of the Son of Man, and verily it is a day of sacrifice, and a day for the tithing of my people; for he that is tithed shall not be burned at his coming.

24 For after today cometh the burning—this is speaking after the manner of the Lord—for verily I say, tomorrow all the proud and they that do wickedly shall be as stubble; and I will burn them up, for I am the Lord of Hosts; and I will not spare any that remain in Babylon.

25 Wherefore, if ye believe me, ye will labor while it is called today.

the second coming" (Daniel H. Ludlow, *Companion to Your Study*, 2:308).

President Howard W. Hunter declared, "This is a day for action. This is the time for decision, not tomorrow, not next week. This is the time to make our covenant with the Lord. Now is the time for those who have been noncommittal or who have had a half-hearted interest to come out boldly and declare belief in Christ and be willing to demonstrate faith by works" (*Teachings*, 46). ⊕

How is the word *tithing* to be understood in this context? (64:23) "The law of tithing was not formally instituted in the Church until July 1838 (see Section 119). At this early phase of the Restoration the word *tithing* in Section 64 seems to imply offerings in general—based on the principle of sacrifice and generous giving in support of the building up of the kingdom of God and the establishment of Zion" (Pinegar and Allen, *Unlocking the Doctrine and Covenants*, 120).

The section heading for Doctrine and Covenants 119 states that prior to 1838, tithing included "all free-will offerings, or contributions, to the Church funds" (section heading, Doctrine and Covenants 119). ⊕

How does paying tithing prepare us for the Savior's Second Coming? (64:23–24) "Some years ago one of our brethren spoke of the payment of tithing as 'fire insurance'; that statement evoked laughter. Nonetheless, the word of the Lord is clear that those who do not keep the commandments and observe the laws of God shall be burned at the time of his coming. For that shall be a day of judgment and a day of sifting, a day of separating the good from the evil. I would venture a personal opinion that no event has occurred in all the history of the earth as dreadful as will be the day of the Second Coming—no event as fraught with the destructive forces of nature, as consequential for the nations of the earth, as terrible for the wicked, or as wonderful for the righteous" (Hinckley, "We Need Not Fear His Coming," 4).

Doctrine and Covenants 64:26–32. The Saints Are Warned against Debt

Why were Newel K. Whitney and Sidney Gilbert warned not to get in debt to the Church's enemies? (64:27) "Being in debt to an enemy gives him power to prevent one's attaining his goals. This is especially vital when a servant is 'on the Lord's errand' (v. 29). Since the servant is doing the Lord's business, He will provide the way for the servant to accomplish his task" (Nyman, *Doctrine and Covenants Commentary*, 1:551).

Who are the agents of the Lord in this passage? (64:29) This passage specifically refers to Newel K. Whitney and Sidney Gilbert (see verse 26). However, it should be noted that Elder Bruce R. McConkie explained: "All of us are agents of the Lord. We are servants of the Lord. In the law there is a branch called the law of agency. And in the law of agency there are principals and there are servants. These are something akin to master and servant. An agent represents a principal and the acts of the agent bind the principal, provided they are performed within the proper scope and authorization, within the authority delegated to the agent" (*Doctrines of the Restoration*, 320).

26 And it is not meet that my servants, Newel K. Whitney and Sidney Gilbert, should sell their store and their possessions here; for this is not wisdom until the residue of the church, which remaineth in this place, shall go up unto the land of Zion.

27 Behold, it is said in my laws, or forbidden, to get in debt to thine enemies;

28 But behold, it is not said at any time that the Lord should not take when he please, and pay as seemeth him good.

29 Wherefore, as ye are agents, ye are on the Lord's errand; and whatever ye do according to the will of the Lord is the Lord's business.

30 And he hath set you to provide for his saints in these last days, that they may obtain an inheritance in the land of Zion.

31 And behold, I, the Lord, declare unto you, and my words are sure and shall not fail, that they shall obtain it.

32 But all things must come to pass in their time.

Newel K. Whitney Store (Doctrine and Covenants 64:26–32)

"Church life in Kirtland, Ohio, from 1831 to 1834 revolved around the Newel K. Whitney and Co. store. For eighteen months, this store served as the headquarters of the Church, and it was here that the First Presidency was given the keys of the kingdom. (See D&C 90:6). Joseph Smith and his family also lived here for eighteen months, and during that time, the Prophet finished his work on the texts of the Joseph Smith Translation of the Bible.

"In addition, some of the most sacred events of early Church history took place in an upstairs room at a conference held 23 January 1833. Further, the ordinance of the washing of feet was given here for the first time in this dispensation. (See D&C 88:138–41.) Several of those present experienced 'divine manifestations of the Holy Spirit,' including a vision of God the Father and his Son Jesus Christ. . . .

"Zebedee Coltrin shared the following sacred experience: 'At one of these meetings after the organization of the school, (the school being organized on the 23rd of January, 1833), when we were all together, Joseph having given instructions, and while engaged in silent prayer, kneeling, with our hands uplifted each one praying in silence, no one whispered above his breath, a personage walked through the room from east to west, and Joseph asked if we saw him. I saw him and suppose the others did and Joseph answered that is Jesus, the Son of God, our elder brother. Afterward Joseph told us to resume our former position in prayer, which we did. Another person came through; he was surrounded as with a flame of fire. . . . The Prophet Joseph said this was the Father of our Lord Jesus Christ. I saw Him' (Minutes, Salt Lake City School of Prophets, 3 Oct. 1883, 56–57)" ("House of Revelation," *Ensign*, Jan. 1993, 31, 37). For a map of Kirtland, see Map 7 in the Appendix.

33 Wherefore, be not weary in well-doing, for ye are laying the foundation of a great work. And out of small things proceedeth that which is great.

34 Behold, the Lord requireth the heart and a willing mind; and the willing and obedient shall eat the good of the land of Zion in these last days.

35 And the rebellious shall be cut off out of the land of Zion, and shall be sent away, and shall not inherit the land.

36 For, verily I say that the rebellious are not of the blood of Ephraim, wherefore they shall be plucked out.

Doctrine and Covenants 64:33–36. The Rebellious Will Be Cut Off out of Zion

Why did the Lord encourage Newel K. Whitney and Sidney Gilbert to "be not weary" in their labors? (64:33) "Even under the best of circumstances, the responsibilities that devolved upon Newel and Sidney were taxing in the extreme. They could wear out their lives attending to the needs of the saints in Missouri and caring for the assets of the Church that remained in Ohio. Yet, one day, the entire earth would become the Lord's Zion, the prosperity and unity of the citizens thereof complete. There would come a time when the meager labors which they had provided would bear fruit far beyond anything that they could have imagined" (Paul Nolan Hyde, *Comprehensive Commentary* [1–72], 390). ⊕

What could "the heart and a willing mind" mean? (64:34) "The heart is symbolic of love and commitment. We make sacrifices and bear burdens for those we love that we would not endure for any other reason. . . .

"Having 'a willing mind' connotes giving our best effort and finest thinking and seeking God's wisdom. It suggests that our most devoted lifetime study should be of things that are eternal in nature. It means that there must be an inextricable relationship between hearing the word of God and obeying it. . . .

"Those who give their heart and mind to the Lord, whether the burden is light or heavy makes no difference. We demonstrate a consecrated heart and mind by consistently following God's commandments no matter how difficult the circumstances" (Hallstrom, "Heart and a Willing Mind," *Ensign*, Jun. 2011, 31, 32). See also commentary in this volume on Doctrine and Covenants 64:22.

What is the blood of Ephraim? (64:35–36) "Ephraim was a grandson of the Old Testament prophet Jacob, whose name was changed to Israel. Ephraim was given the birthright blessing (see Genesis 48:20). The phrase 'blood of Ephraim' (D&C 64:36) refers to those who (1) are literal descendants of Ephraim, as well as (2) those who are not of the house of Israel but who, through baptism into the restored Church, are adopted into the tribe of Ephraim. Only those who are believing and obedient members of the Church are considered to be of the blood of Ephraim. The rebellious, though they may be literal descendants of Ephraim, will not receive an inheritance in Zion" (*Doctrine and Covenants Student Manual* [2018], 352). ⊕

Doctrine and Covenants 64:37–40. The Church Will Judge the Nations

How will the Church sit in judgment over the nations in the last days? (64:37–40) "To be a judge, the Church and its members must be a Zion people who have overcome the world (v. 38). They shall be the Lord's standard of measurement against other nations and their inhabitants. Those who do not measure up to these standards, such as liars and hypocrites shall be detected. Those who have pretended to be Apostles and Prophets, or have usurped authority and led the Church member astray shall be made known (v. 39). Even a bishop, who is a judge in Israel, and his counselors may be removed (v. 40)" (Nyman, *Doctrine and Covenants Commentary*, 1:554).

Doctrine and Covenants 64:41–43. Zion Will Flourish

How are people from every nation gathered to Zion? (64:41–42) "In the early years of this last dispensation, a gathering to Zion involved various locations in the United States: to Kirtland, to Missouri, to Nauvoo, and to the tops of the mountains.... With the creation of stakes and the construction of temples in most nations with sizeable populations of the faithful, the current commandment is not to gather to one place but to gather in stakes in our own homelands. There the faithful can enjoy the full blessings of eternity in a house of the Lord. There, in their own homelands, they can obey the Lord's command to enlarge the borders of His people and strengthen her stakes (see D&C 101:21; D&C 133:9, 14)" (Oaks, "Preparation for the Second Coming," *Ensign*, May 2004, 8). ⊕

What is an ensign and how will Zion be one to others? (64:42) "An ensign is a flag or standard around which people gather in a unity of purpose or identity; it also served anciently as a rallying point for soldiers in battle. In effect, the Church is an ensign to all nations of the earth in the battle for truth and righteousness.... We are ensigns to others when we exemplify virtue and goodness. Zion will prosper and spread as the pure in heart gather within her walls and seek to live and share the gospel" (Millet and Newell, *Draw Near unto Me*, 183).

37 Behold, I, the Lord, have made my church in these last days like unto a judge sitting on a hill, or in a high place, to judge the nations.

38 For it shall come to pass that the inhabitants of Zion shall judge all things pertaining to Zion.

39 And liars and hypocrites shall be proved by them, and they who are not apostles and prophets shall be known.

40 And even the bishop, who is a judge, and his counselors, if they are not faithful in their stewardships shall be condemned, and others shall be planted in their stead.

41 For, behold, I say unto you that Zion shall flourish, and the glory of the Lord shall be upon her;

42 And she shall be an ensign unto the people, and there shall come unto her out of every nation under heaven.

43 And the day shall come when the nations of the earth shall tremble because of her, and shall fear because of her terrible ones. The Lord hath spoken it. Amen.

Who are the "terrible ones" of Zion that the nations shall fear? (64:43) "This prophecy is most remarkable, since it came in a day when the enemies of the Church inflicted pain and suffering upon the Saints with impunity. Yet, the promise was that sometime in the future all the nations of the earth would find reason to fear the power held by the elders of Israel. 'Their arm shall be my arm,' the Lord promised, 'and I will be their shield and their buckler; and I will gird up their loins, and they shall fight manfully for me; and their enemies shall be under their feet; and I will let fall the sword in their behalf, and by the fire of mine indignation will I preserve them' (D&C 35:14)" (McConkie and Ostler, *Revelations of the Restoration*, 471).

Introduction to Doctrine and Covenants 65

On 30 October 1831, "[William E.] McLellin attended a Church meeting at John Johnson's home [in Hiram, Ohio], where Joseph was living, and spoke to those in attendance for an hour and a half. 'And it was not I but the Spirit and power of God which was in me,' he explained. At the same meeting, Joseph received ... [a] revelation, now canonized as Doctrine and Covenants 65. The revelation proclaimed that 'the keys of the kingdom of God' were again 'committed unto man on the Earth' and that the gospel would 'roll forth unto the ends of the Earth ... until it had filled the whole Earth' [D&C 65:2]" (Godfrey, "William McLellin's Five Questions," 138).

"The beauty, organization and literary quality of this divine declaration and its responsive prayer are easy to overlook. ... The balance and symmetry of the three double elements—two exhortations to prepare, two exhortations to pray, and two destinies of the Church—each divided neatly between the world that was and the world that is to come, deserve the appreciation of the reader. Moreover, the power of the declarations ought to call forth from us, as it did from Joseph Smith, the twin responses that the kingdom of God may go forth in this world so that the kingdom of heaven may bring with it the world to come" (Robinson and Garrett, *Commentary on the Doctrine and Covenants*, 2:222).

SECTION 65

Revelation on prayer given through Joseph Smith the Prophet, at Hiram, Ohio, October 30, 1831.

1 Hearken, and lo, a voice as of one sent down from on high, who is mighty and powerful, whose going forth is unto the ends of the earth, yea, whose voice is unto men— Prepare ye the way of the Lord, make his paths straight.

Doctrine and Covenants 65:1–2. The Keys of the Kingdom of God Are Committed to Man on Earth, and the Gospel Cause Will Triumph

What does making the Lord's paths straight mean? (65:1) "[Eastern] monarchs in ancient times seldom built permanent roads as did the Romans. So whenever the monarch intended to travel, it was customary to send out a force of workmen at various places to prepare the road for him. The laborers would remove the large stones from the road, fill in those places washed out by winter storms, straighten the way where it went too far afield, level off the high places, and generally make the road more fit for travel. ... The people of the earth are warned to prepare the Lord's 'way' or road; they are also to be ready and prepared themselves [see Alma 7:9, 19–20]"

(Sperry, *Doctrine and Covenants Compendium*, 274).
See also commentary in this volume on Doctrine and
Covenants 133:17.

How might this revelation be fulfilled? (65:2)
Wilford Woodruff recalled meeting with the Prophet
and elders of the Church in Kirtland, Ohio, in April
1834. "'When we got together the Prophet called
upon the Elders of Israel with him to bear testimony
of this work. . . . When they got through the Prophet
said, "Brethren, I have been very much edified and instructed in your testimonies here tonight, but I want
to say to you before the Lord, that you know no more
concerning the destinies of this Church and kingdom
than a babe upon its mother's lap. You don't comprehend it." I was rather surprised. He said, "It is only a
little handful of Priesthood you see here tonight, but
this Church will fill North and South America—it will
fill the world"'" (*Joseph Smith* [manual], 137).

Doctrine and Covenants 65:3–6. The Millennial Kingdom of Heaven Will Come and Join the Kingdom of God on Earth

**How are the events described in this verse to be
understood? (65:3)** "Jesus Christ is the Lamb of God
and the Bridegroom, and the Church is His bride (see
Revelation 19:7–9). At the time of His Second Coming,
the righteous Saints will rejoice. The joyful reunion
between the Lord and His people is symbolized in the
celebratory marriage feast. In fulfillment of the Lord's
invitation to prepare and make ready for the coming
of the Bridegroom and the marriage supper of the
Lamb, the Saints are to search out the righteous from
the four corners of the earth and invite them to repent and be baptized. Those who heed the invitation
and make and keep their covenants with the Lord . . .

2 The keys of the kingdom of God are committed unto man on the earth, and from
thence shall the gospel roll forth unto the
ends of the earth, as the stone which is cut
out of the mountain without hands shall roll
forth, until it has filled the whole earth.

3 Yea, a voice crying—Prepare ye the way of
the Lord, prepare ye the supper of the Lamb,
make ready for the Bridegroom.

The Gospel Shall Roll Forth to the Ends of the Earth (Doctrine and Covenants 65:1–2)

"The book of Daniel records that Nebuchadnezzar, the king of Babylon, had a dream in which he saw a large
statue in the shape of a man, constructed of various substances. . . . As the dream unfolded, Nebuchadnezzar saw
'that a stone was cut out without hands, which smote the image upon his feet that were of iron and clay, and brake
them into pieces. . . . And the stone that smote the image became a great mountain, and filled the whole earth'
(Dan 2:34–35)" (Jackson, "May the Kingdom of God Go Forth," 1:251).

President Gordon B. Hinckley testified, "The sun never sets on this work of the Lord as it is touching the lives of
people across the earth.

"And this is only the beginning. We have scarcely scratched the surface. We are engaged in a work for the souls
of men and women everywhere. Our work knows no boundaries. Under the providence of the Lord it will continue.
. . . The little stone which was cut out of the mountain without hands is rolling forth to fill the earth (see Dan.
2:31–45; D&C 65:2)" ("State of the Church," *Ensign*, Nov. 2003, 7).

4 Pray unto the Lord, call upon his holy name, make known his wonderful works among the people.

5 Call upon the Lord, that his kingdom may go forth upon the earth, that the inhabitants thereof may receive it, and be prepared for the days to come, in the which the Son of Man shall come down in heaven, clothed in the brightness of his glory, to meet the kingdom of God which is set up on the earth.

6 Wherefore, may the kingdom of God go forth, that the kingdom of heaven may come, that thou, O God, mayest be glorified in heaven so on earth, that thine enemies may be subdued; for thine is the honor, power and glory, forever and ever. Amen.

will have the joy of welcoming the Lord and rejoicing with Him at His coming" (*Doctrine and Covenants Student Manual* [2018], 355).

What wonderful works might the Saints make known today? (65:4) Describing God's marvelous latter-day works, President Gordon B. Hinckley proclaimed, "We declare without equivocation that God the Father and His Son, the Lord Jesus Christ, appeared in person to the boy Joseph Smith. . . .

"This is the restored Church of Jesus Christ. . . . We testify that the heavens have been opened, that the curtains have been parted, that God has spoken, and that Jesus Christ has manifested Himself, followed by a bestowal of divine authority.

"Jesus Christ is the cornerstone of this work, and it is built upon a 'foundation of . . . apostles and prophets' (Ephesians 2:20). . . .

"God be thanked for His marvelous bestowal of testimony, authority, and doctrine associated with this, the restored Church of Jesus Christ" ("Marvelous Foundation of Our Faith," *Ensign*, Nov. 2002, 80, 81). ⊕

How is the kingdom of God different from the kingdom of heaven? (65:5–6) "The kingdom of God on earth is The Church of Jesus Christ of Latter-day Saints (D&C 65). The purpose of the Church is to prepare its members to live forever in the celestial kingdom or kingdom of heaven. However, the scriptures sometimes call the Church the kingdom of heaven, meaning that the Church is the kingdom of heaven on earth.

"The Church of Jesus Christ of Latter-day Saints is the kingdom of God on the earth, but it is at present limited to an ecclesiastical kingdom. During the Millennium, the kingdom of God will be both political and ecclesiastical" (Guide to the Scriptures, "Kingdom of God or Kingdom of Heaven"). ⊕

Introduction to Doctrine and Covenants 66

The Lord gave the Prophet Joseph Smith this revelation for William E. McLellin on October 29, 1831, at the John Johnson home in Hiram, Ohio. "Within two months of his baptism on August 20, 1831, William E. McLellin, a former schoolteacher, became deeply involved in the restoration story.... At the conference [held in Orange, Ohio, in late October], McLellin was ordained a high priest and heard Joseph teach about the powers and duties of that office" (Godfrey, "William McLellin's Five Questions," 137).

"At the conclusion of the conference [in Orange, Ohio], [William McLellin] accompanied [Joseph Smith] to Hiram, Ohio, arriving there on 29 October" (Joseph Smith Papers, Historical Introduction to "Revelation, 29 October 1831 [D&C 66]"). While staying in the John Johnson home with Joseph Smith, "McLellin 'went before the Lord in secret, and on my knees asked him to reveal the answer to five questions through his Prophet.' Without letting Joseph know what these five questions were, McLellin asked Joseph to provide to him God's will. The resulting revelation—now known as Doctrine and Covenants 66—answered McLellin's five questions to his 'full and entire satisfaction.' Even after he later fell away from the Church, McLellin stated that he still considered this revelation an evidence of Joseph's prophetic calling, 'which,' he said, 'I cannot refute'" (Godfrey, "William McLellin's Five Questions," 138).

"Although McLellin never explained what his five [questions] were, the revelation's contents indicate that he was probably concerned about his standing before God and about what the Lord desired him to do....

"McLellin recounted that he wrote the words of this revelation as [Joseph Smith] spoke them" (Joseph Smith Papers, Documents, Volume 2, 87–92; see also Joseph Smith Papers, Historical Introduction to "Revelation, 29 October 1831 [D&C 66]").

SECTION 66

Revelation given through Joseph Smith the Prophet, at Hiram, Ohio, October 29, 1831. William E. McLellin had petitioned the Lord in secret to make known through the Prophet the answer to five questions, which were unknown to Joseph Smith. At McLellin's request, the Prophet inquired of the Lord and received this revelation.

Doctrine and Covenants 66:1–4. The Everlasting Covenant Is the Fulness of the Gospel

What is the everlasting covenant? (66:2) "The new and everlasting covenant is the gospel of Jesus Christ. In other words, the doctrines and commandments of the gospel constitute the substance of an everlasting covenant between God and man that is newly restored in each dispensation. If we were to state the new and everlasting covenant in one sentence it would be this: 'For God so loved the world, that he

1 Behold, thus saith the Lord unto my servant William E. McLellin—Blessed are you, inasmuch as you have turned away from your iniquities, and have received my truths, saith the Lord your Redeemer, the Savior of the world, even of as many as believe on my name.

2 Verily I say unto you, blessed are you for receiving mine everlasting covenant, even the fulness of my gospel, sent forth unto the children of men, that they might have life and be made partakers of the glories which are to be revealed in the last days, as it was written by the prophets and apostles in days of old.

gave his only begotten Son, that whosoever believeth in him should not perish, but have everlasting life' (John 3:16)" (Christofferson, "Power of Covenants," *Ensign*, May 2009, 20).

3 Verily I say unto you, my servant William, that you are clean, but not all; repent, therefore, of those things which are not pleasing in my sight, saith the Lord, for the Lord will show them unto you.

4 And now, verily, I, the Lord, will show unto you what I will concerning you, or what is my will concerning you.

Why is this divine counsel to repent important for everyone? (66:3) "Repentance is the key to avoiding misery inflicted by traps of the adversary. The Lord does not expect perfection from us at this point in our eternal progression. But He does expect us to become increasingly pure. Daily repentance is the pathway to purity, and purity brings power. Personal purity can make us powerful tools in the hands of God. Our repentance—our purity—will empower us to help in the gathering of Israel" (Nelson, "We Can Do Better and Be Better," *Liahona*, May 2019, 68).

Doctrine and Covenants 66:5–8. Elders Are to Preach, Testify, and Reason with the People

5 Behold, verily I say unto you, that it is my will that you should proclaim my gospel from land to land, and from city to city, yea, in those regions round about where it has not been proclaimed.

6 Tarry not many days in this place; go not up unto the land of Zion as yet; but inasmuch as you can send, send; otherwise, think not of thy property.

7 Go unto the eastern lands, bear testimony in every place, unto every people and in their synagogues, reasoning with the people.

8 Let my servant Samuel H. Smith go with you, and forsake him not, and give him thine instructions; and he that is faithful shall be made strong in every place; and I, the Lord, will go with you.

How did William McLellin fulfill the Lord's call to proclaim the gospel? (66:5) "Elder McLellin had obviously wanted to know the Lord's will concerning him. Should he go forth as a missionary? Should he go to Zion to seek an inheritance there? Or should he remain in Kirtland? The Lord responds, calling him to go back east, declaring the gospel from city to city, particularly in those places where it had not as yet been declared. He is to take Samuel Smith as his companion and be a mentor to him" (McConkie and Ostler, *Revelations of the Restoration*, 479). Of one meeting, William recorded: "The house was full of people. I opened the meeting by prayer. Samuel then spoke a while on the 12th chapter of 1 Corinthians. I then arose and made some general observations—I had preached so much to the people before and several there believed that we had declared the truth to them and I exhorted them to obedience" (*Journals of William E. McLellin*, 47, 65; spelling modernized).

Doctrine and Covenants 66:9–13. Faithful Ministerial Service Ensures an Inheritance of Eternal Life

9 Lay your hands upon the sick, and they shall recover. Return not till I, the Lord, shall send you. Be patient in affliction. Ask, and ye shall receive; knock, and it shall be opened unto you.

When was William McLellin able to minister to the sick? (66:9) "In the short time he had been a member of the Church, Elder McLellin had been raised from affliction in a healing blessing administered to him by Hyrum Smith, he had assisted Hyrum in giving a blessing in which a sick child was instantly healed, and he had been healed of a severely sprained ankle by the

Prophet. It would appear that among the blessings he had prayerfully sought from the Lord was that of the gift of healing, which is here promised him" (McConkie and Ostler, *Revelations of the Restoration*, 479).

What does "cumbered" mean? (66:10) "To be cumbered is to be troubled or burdened down with many concerns (see Luke 10:40). The parable of the wild and tame olive tree in the Book of Mormon speaks of the tree being cumbered (weighed down) with fruit; the Lord of the vineyard also expresses concern that the branches of the trees not cumber (clutter) the ground of the vineyard (Jacob 5:9, 30)" (Brewster, *Doctrine & Covenants Encyclopedia* [2012], 116).

Why did the Lord warn William McLellin regarding adultery? (66:10) "McLellin's promises for ministerial success were not absolute guarantees. The Lord instructed him concerning his personal life.... He was warned of adultery, a temptation that had troubled him in the past. There is no evidence that McLellin had been an adulterer. President Joseph Fielding Smith has written, 'He was not accused of committing such a sin, but the dangers, because of his failings, which lay in this direction.' [*Church History and Modern Revelation*, 1:245.] ... McLellin was troubled with adulterous thoughts, which the Lord warned him needed to be eliminated [see D&C 66:3]" (Peterson, "Revelations Resulting from Important Church Conferences," 1:259). When William McLellin was excommunicated from the Church in May 1838, he admitted he had "quit praying, and keeping the commandments, and indulged himself in his lustful desires" (Joseph Smith Papers, "History, 1838–1856, volume B-1," 796).

What are some of the reasons the Lord suggests that we push people to Zion today? (66:11) "Is the establishment of Zion only a golden dream, forever unobtainable, ever receding before us like an illusion? To the Latter-day Saints, who believe in the eventual perfectibility of [humankind], there *can* be a Zion on earth.... We are thus under sacred obligation to awake, arise, and get to work; to make its attainment 'our greatest object.'... There must be no sense of undue haste; the order of the kingdom must be maintained and the work done 'in the Lord's way.' But delay is inexcusable. As always, the greatest and most difficult task will be *to change ourselves*.... Our greatest task, as a people and as individual Saints, is to purify ourselves, to give away all of our sins to know Christ (see Alma 22:18), to live all of Christ's commandments" (Alexander B. Morrison, *Visions of Zion*, 17–18).

10 Seek not to be cumbered. Forsake all unrighteousness. Commit not adultery—a temptation with which thou hast been troubled.

11 Keep these sayings, for they are true and faithful; and thou shalt magnify thine office, and push many people to Zion with songs of everlasting joy upon their heads.

12 Continue in these things even unto the end, and you shall have a crown of eternal life at the right hand of my Father, who is full of grace and truth.

13 Verily, thus saith the Lord your God, your Redeemer, even Jesus Christ. Amen.

Introduction to Doctrine and Covenants 67

This revelation was received early in November 1831, during a conference held at Hiram, Ohio.

"By the fall of 1831, the Prophet Joseph Smith had received more than 60 revelations from the Lord. Preparations were made to compile and publish the revelations to make them more accessible to Church members. On November 1–2, 1831, a group of priesthood leaders convened at a conference in the home of John and Alice (Elsa) Johnson in Hiram, Ohio, to discuss the publication of the revelations in a single volume that would be titled the Book of Commandments. These priesthood leaders decided to print 10,000 copies (later the number was reduced to 3,000 copies).

"The Prophet intended to include in the Book of Commandments a written testimony from the elders declaring the truthfulness of the revelations in the same manner the Three Witnesses and the Eight Witnesses had testified of the truthfulness of the Book of Mormon. At one point in the conference, Joseph asked the elders 'what testimony they were willing to attach to these commandants [revelations] which should shortly be sent to the world' ([in *Joseph Smith Papers, Documents, Volume 2*, 97]). Several of the brethren 'arose and said that they were willing to testify to the world that they knew that [the revelations] were of the Lord' ([in *Joseph Smith Papers, Documents, Volume 2*, 97]). However, some of the elders had not received such a spiritual conviction, and they hesitated to testify that the revelations were given by inspiration from God. Some of the elders also voiced concerns regarding the language used in the revelations. In response to these concerns, the Prophet Joseph Smith received the revelation recorded in Doctrine and Covenants 67" (*Doctrine and Covenants Student Manual* [2018], 360–61).

SECTION 67

Revelation given through Joseph Smith the Prophet, at Hiram, Ohio, early November 1831. The occasion was that of a special conference, and the publication of the revelations already received from the Lord through the Prophet was considered and acted upon (see the heading to section 1). William W. Phelps had recently established the Church printing press in Independence, Missouri. The conference decided to publish the revelations in the Book of Commandments and to print 10,000 copies (which because of unforeseen difficulties was later reduced to 3,000 copies). Many of the brethren bore solemn testimony that the revelations then compiled for publication were verily true, as was witnessed by the Holy Ghost shed forth upon them. Joseph Smith's history records that after the revelation known as section 1 had been received, some conversation was had concerning the language used in the revelations. The present revelation followed.

Doctrine and Covenants 67:1–3. The Lord Hears the Prayers of and Watches over His Elders

How does God hold us responsible for our thoughts and desires? (67:1–2) "God's law can assign consequences solely on the basis of our innermost thoughts and desires. There is no uncertainty in the administration of this law. As Ammon taught King Lamoni, God 'looketh down upon all the children of men; and he knows all the thoughts and intents of the heart; for by his hand were they all created from the beginning' (Alma 18:32). . . .

"In other words, God judges us not only for our acts, but also for the desires of our hearts. He has said so again and again. This is a challenging reality, but it is not surprising. Agency and accountability are eternal principles. We exercise our . . . agency not only by what we *do*, but also by what we *decide*, or *will*, or *desire*" (Oaks, "Desires of Our Hearts," *Ensign*, Jun. 1986, 64). ◉

What was a consequence of the fears in these elders' hearts? (67:3) "Section 67 was given after Oliver Cowdery and John Whitmer had been chosen to take the Book of Commandments manuscript to W. W. Phelps in Independence, Missouri, for publication. Because 'some negative conversation was had concerning the language used in the revelations' (see the section heading), the Lord told the assembled 'elders of my church' that He had heard their prayers and knew their hearts and desires (v. 1). These elders had 'endeavored to believe' the blessings of 'the riches of eternity,' which was the promise of eternal life (D&C 66:12), but the fears in their hearts was 'the reason that ye did not receive' the blessings (vv. 2–3). For the new and inexperienced elders this is understandable, but also a great lesson to all people that the Lord is willing and capable to fulfill any promise that he makes" (Nyman, *Doctrine and Covenants Commentary*, 1:12).

Doctrine and Covenants 67:4–9. The Lord Challenges the Wisest Person to Duplicate the Least of His Revelations

What was it that some of the elders sought in their hearts? (67:5) "Joseph had much less education than several of the elders present, and these others apparently were privately embarrassed at the unpolished, frontier quality of Joseph's spelling, punctuation, diction, and such. . . .

1 Behold and hearken, O ye elders of my church, who have assembled yourselves together, whose prayers I have heard, and whose hearts I know, and whose desires have come up before me.

2 Behold and lo, mine eyes are upon you, and the heavens and the earth are in mine hands, and the riches of eternity are mine to give.

3 Ye endeavored to believe that ye should receive the blessing which was offered unto you; but behold, verily I say unto you there were fears in your hearts, and verily this is the reason that ye did not receive.

4 And now I, the Lord, give unto you a testimony of the truth of these commandments which are lying before you.

5 Your eyes have been upon my servant Joseph Smith, Jun., and his language you have known, and his imperfections you have known; and you have sought in your hearts knowledge that you might express beyond his language; this you also know.

"The more educated elders wanted to rewrite or 'improve' the revelations to make them sound more impressive to an educated audience.... These elders thought the unlearned language of the Prophet argued against the divine origins of his revelations. They also wanted to say more than Joseph had said—to 'express beyond his language.' ...

"Prophets are not, however, merely scribes taking down divine dictation in a single, pure, perfect, and timeless form. Rather, the precise wording of a revelation can be influenced by the mind, education, and verbal or literary skills of the prophet himself (see D&C 1:24)" (Robinson and Garrett, *Commentary on the Doctrine and Covenants*, 2:235).

6 Now, seek ye out of the Book of Commandments, even the least that is among them, and appoint him that is the most wise among you;

7 Or, if there be any among you that shall make one like unto it, then ye are justified in saying that ye do not know that they are true;

8 But if ye cannot make one like unto it, ye are under condemnation if ye do not bear record that they are true.

Who was selected to undertake this challenge to write a revelation? (67:6–8) The Prophet Joseph Smith described how this unfolded in his day: "William E. McLellin, as the wisest man in his own estimation, having more learning than sense, endeavored to write a commandment like unto one of the least of the Lord's, but failed; it was an awful responsibility to write in the name of the Lord. The elders, and all present, that witnessed this vain attempt of a man to imitate the language of Jesus Christ, renewed their faith in the fulness of the gospel and in the truth of the commandments and revelations which the Lord had given to the church through my instrumentality; and the elders signified a willingness to bear testimony of their truth to all the world" (Joseph Smith Papers, "History, 1838–1856, volume A-1," 162; spelling modernized). ⊕

9 For ye know that there is no unrighteousness in them, and that which is righteous cometh down from above, from the Father of lights.

What does the title "Father of lights" mean? (67:9) "The title 'Father of lights' is found in both ancient and modern scripture (D&C 67:9; James 1:17). The Apostle John wrote, 'God is light, and in him is no darkness at all' (1 Jn. 1:5). President Joseph Fielding Smith taught we should bow our 'heads in humble supplication to the Father of Lights for the blessings [we] have received through the sufferings of his beloved Son' ([*Restoration of All Things*], 278). Because our Holy Father has bestowed upon His Son His own attributes and powers (D&C 93:17; Mosiah 15:3), and because Christ is the 'light of the world' (D&C 10:70), it would not seem unreasonable to appropriately refer to Him with that same exalted title" (Brewster, *Doctrine & Covenants Encyclopedia* [2012], 181).

Doctrine and Covenants 67:10–14.
Faithful Elders Will Be Quickened by the
Spirit and See the Face of God

What does the Lord promise all those who are ordained to the ministry? (67:10) "The Lord wants all his children to gain light and truth and knowledge from on high. It is his will that we pierce the veil and rend the heavens and see the visions of eternity.

"By his own mouth he has given us this promise: [D&C 93:1]. . . .

"Such is his promise to us here and now while we yet dwell as mortals in a world of sorrow and sin. It is our privilege even now—the privilege of all who hold the holy priesthood—if we will strip ourselves from jealousies and fears and humble ourselves before him, as he has said, to have the veil rent and see him and know that he is" (Bruce R. McConkie, "Thou Shalt Receive Revelation," *Ensign*, Nov. 1978, 61).

What does it mean to be "quickened by the Spirit of God"? (67:11–12)

It is the "condition of persons who are temporarily changed in appearance and nature . . . so that they can endure the presence and glory of heavenly beings" (Guide to the Scriptures, "Transfiguration").

"After Moses had seen 'the world and the ends thereof,' . . . he said: 'Now mine eyes have beheld God; but not my natural, but my spiritual eyes, for my natural eyes could not have beheld; for I should have withered and died in his presence; but his glory was upon me; and I beheld his face, for I was transfigured before him' (Moses 1:1–11). Moses' experience accords with the reality revealed to Joseph Smith that 'no man has seen God,' and that 'neither can any natural man abide the presence of God' (D&C 67:11–12)" (Bruce R. McConkie, *Promised Messiah*, 601–2).

How were the early elders to prepare themselves to abide the presence of God and angels? (67:13–14) "It was not intended that the opening of the heavens be only upon the head of Joseph Smith. As the glory of the sunrise is for all who will get up to see it, so the glories of God's kingdom are there to bless all who will receive them. . . .

"All who ask with an honest heart will receive. All who serve in faith will be rewarded with greater faith" (McConkie and Ostler, *Revelations of the Restoration*, 484).

10 And again, verily I say unto you that it is your privilege, and a promise I give unto you that have been ordained unto this ministry, that inasmuch as you strip yourselves from jealousies and fears, and humble yourselves before me, for ye are not sufficiently humble, the veil shall be rent and you shall see me and know that I am—not with the carnal neither natural mind, but with the spiritual.

11 For no man has seen God at any time in the flesh, except quickened by the Spirit of God.

12 Neither can any natural man abide the presence of God, neither after the carnal mind.

13 Ye are not able to abide the presence of God now, neither the ministering of angels; wherefore, continue in patience until ye are perfected.

14 Let not your minds turn back; and when ye are worthy, in mine own due time, ye shall see and know that which was conferred upon you by the hands of my servant Joseph Smith, Jun. Amen.

Introduction to Doctrine and Covenants 68

"On 1–2 November 1831, ten elders convened a conference in Hiram, Ohio, to discuss the publication of the Book of Commandments, a compilation of [Joseph Smith's] revelations. According to a later [Joseph Smith] history, four of the conference attendees—Orson Hyde, Luke Johnson, Lyman Johnson, and William E. McLellin—approached [Joseph] during the conference and requested to know the Lord's will concerning them. This revelation came in response to their inquiry....

"After closing the portion of the revelation addressed specifically to the four men with an 'Amen,' [see v. 12] the document shifts its audience to the church in general and gives additional information about the office of bishop, as well as counsel to members of the church 'in Zion' about teaching and baptizing their children and avoiding idleness and greed. The text may originally have been dictated as two discrete revelations, which, like some other revelations closely related in time or content, were then copied together and presented as a single, unified text" (Joseph Smith Papers, Historical Introduction to "Revelation, 1 November 1831–A [D&C 68]").

SECTION 68

Revelation given through Joseph Smith the Prophet, at Hiram, Ohio, November 1, 1831, in response to prayer that the mind of the Lord be made known concerning Orson Hyde, Luke S. Johnson, Lyman E. Johnson, and William E. McLellin. Although part of this revelation was directed toward these four men, much of the content pertains to the whole Church. This revelation was expanded under Joseph Smith's direction when it was published in the 1835 edition of the Doctrine and Covenants.

1 My servant, Orson Hyde, was called by his ordination to proclaim the everlasting gospel, by the Spirit of the living God, from people to people, and from land to land, in the congregations of the wicked, in their synagogues, reasoning with and expounding all scriptures unto them.

2 And, behold, and lo, this is an ensample unto all those who were ordained unto this priesthood, whose mission is appointed unto them to go forth—

3 And this is the ensample unto them, that they shall speak as they are moved upon by the Holy Ghost.

4 And whatsoever they shall speak when moved upon by the Holy Ghost shall be scripture, shall be the will of the Lord, shall

Doctrine and Covenants 68:1–5. The Words of the Elders When Moved upon by the Holy Ghost Are Scripture

How can we know when the Lord's servants are moved upon by the Holy Ghost? (68:2–4) President J. Reuben Clark said: "How shall we know when the things [prophets] have spoken were said as they were 'moved upon by the Holy Ghost?'

"I have given some thought to this question, and the answer thereto so far as I can determine, is: We can tell when the speakers are 'moved upon by the Holy Ghost' only when we, ourselves, are 'moved upon by the Holy Ghost.'

"In a way, this completely shifts the responsibility from them to us to determine when they so speak" ("When Are the Writings . . . Entitled to the Claim of Scripture?" 7). ❂

be the mind of the Lord, shall be the word of the Lord, shall be the voice of the Lord, and the power of God unto salvation.

5 Behold, this is the promise of the Lord unto you, O ye my servants.

6 Wherefore, be of good cheer, and do not fear, for I the Lord am with you, and will stand by you; and ye shall bear record of me, even Jesus Christ, that I am the Son of the living God, that I was, that I am, and that I am to come.

7 This is the word of the Lord unto you, my servant Orson Hyde, and also unto my servant Luke Johnson, and unto my servant Lyman Johnson, and unto my servant William E. McLellin, and unto all the faithful elders of my church—

8 Go ye into all the world, preach the gospel to every creature, acting in the authority which I have given you, baptizing in the name of the Father, and of the Son, and of the Holy Ghost.

9 And he that believeth and is baptized shall be saved, and he that believeth not shall be damned.

Doctrine and Covenants 68:6–12. Elders Are to Preach and Baptize, and Signs Will Follow True Believers

Why did the Lord command the elders to "go ye into all the world"? (68:8) "Before His final Ascension, [the Lord] commissioned [His disciples] to 'go . . . and teach all nations, baptizing them in the name of the Father, and of the Son, and of the Holy Ghost' (Matthew 28:19). The Apostles heeded that instruction. . . .

"Today, under the direction of modern apostles and prophets, that same charge has been extended to missionaries of The Church of Jesus Christ of Latter-day Saints. These missionaries serve in more than 150 nations. As representatives of the Lord Jesus Christ, they strive to fulfill that divine command—renewed in our day by the Lord Himself—to take the fulness of the gospel abroad and bless the lives of people everywhere" (Nelson, "Ask the Missionaries!" *Ensign*, Nov. 2012, 18–19).

"The Voice of the Lord" (Doctrine and Covenants 68:4)

President Jeffrey R. Holland taught in general conference: "I ask you to reflect in the days ahead not only on the messages you have heard but also on the unique phenomenon that general conference itself is—what we as Latter-day Saints believe such conferences to be and what we invite the world to hear and observe about them. We testify to every nation, kindred, tongue, and people that God not only lives but also that He speaks, that for our time and in our day the counsel you have heard is, under the direction of the Holy Spirit, 'the will of the Lord, . . . the word of the Lord, . . . the voice of the Lord, and the power of God unto salvation' (D&C 68:4). . . .

"If we teach by the Spirit and you listen by the Spirit, some one of us will touch on your circumstance, sending a personal prophetic epistle just to you. . . .

"In general conference we offer our testimonies in conjunction with other testimonies that will come, because one way or another God *will* have His voice heard" ("Ensign to the Nations," *Ensign*, May 2011, 111, 113).

10 And he that believeth shall be blest with signs following, even as it is written.

11 And unto you it shall be given to know the signs of the times, and the signs of the coming of the Son of Man;

12 And of as many as the Father shall bear record, to you shall be given power to seal them up unto eternal life. Amen.

13 And now, concerning the items in addition to the covenants and commandments, they are these—

14 There remain hereafter, in the due time of the Lord, other bishops to be set apart unto the church, to minister even according to the first;

15 Wherefore they shall be high priests who are worthy, and they shall be appointed by the First Presidency of the Melchizedek Priesthood, except they be literal descendants of Aaron.

16 And if they be literal descendants of Aaron they have a legal right to the bishopric, if they are the firstborn among the sons of Aaron;

What signs follow those who believe? (68:10) "And these signs shall follow them that believe—in my name shall they cast out devils; they shall speak with new tongues; they shall take up serpents; and if they drink any deadly thing it shall not hurt them; they shall lay hands on the sick and they shall recover" (Mormon 9:24; see also Mark 16:17–18).

How does a servant of the Lord seal someone up unto eternal life? (68:12) "The gospel brings blessings or curses. Both are administered to men by the Lord's agents. Those whom they bless are blessed, and those whom they curse are cursed (D&C 124:93). The Lord's servants go forth 'to bind up the law and seal up the testimony, and to prepare the saints for the hour of judgment which is to come' (D&C 88:84). The crowning blessing bestowed is: 'And of as many as the Father shall bear record, to you shall be given power to seal them up unto eternal life' (D&C 68:12)" (Bruce R. McConkie, *Promised Messiah*, 174).

Doctrine and Covenants 68:13–24. The Firstborn among the Sons of Aaron May Serve as the Presiding Bishop (That Is, Hold the Keys of Presidency as a Bishop) under the Direction of the First Presidency

Why are bishops ordained and then set apart? (68:14) Since the beginning of the Church in the 1830s, many individuals have been ordained as a bishop. The distinction of being set apart is aptly explained by President Boyd K. Packer: "A man is *ordained* a bishop, an office in the priesthood; then he is *set apart* and given the keys to preside over a ward. He with his two counselors form a bishopric—a type of presidency.

"Once ordained, he is a bishop for the rest of his life. When he is released from presiding over a ward, his ordination becomes dormant. If called again to preside over a ward, his previous ordination is reactivated [set apart]. When he is released, it becomes dormant again" ("Bishop and His Counselors," *Ensign*, May 1999, 57–58).

What bishopric is being described here? (68:16–21) In these verses, the Lord was speaking of the Presiding Bishop of the Church. These verses have *"no reference whatever to bishops of wards.* Further, [a Presiding Bishop] must be designated by the First Presidency of the Church and receive his anointing and ordination under their hands. The revelation comes from the Presidency . . . to establish a claim to the right to preside in this office. In the absence of knowledge concerning such a descendant, any high priest, chosen by the Presidency, may hold the office of Presiding Bishop and serve with counselors" (Joseph Fielding Smith, *Doctrines of Salvation*, 3:92–93). See also commentary in this volume on Doctrine and Covenants 107:68–76. ✪

How would a literal descendant of Aaron be called as the Presiding Bishop? (68:18–22) "Anciently, the bishops (judges) were 'literal descendants of Aaron.' Their office had its beginning with Aaron, who was the presiding bishop of the church. Even in our dispensation, 'the firstborn among the sons of Aaron' has 'a legal right to the bishopric, . . . for the firstborn holds the right of the presidency over this priesthood, and the keys or authority of the same.' That is, it is his right to be the Presiding Bishop of the Church, if he is selected and approved by the First Presidency. So far in our day the lineage through which the office of Presiding Bishop will descend 'from father to son' has not been revealed. Until then, high priests of the Melchizedek Priesthood are chosen to officiate in this office and also as ward bishops (D&C 68:16–21)" (Bruce R. McConkie, *New Witness*, 352). See also commentary in this volume on Doctrine and Covenants 107:13–15, 16–17, 69–70.

17 For the firstborn holds the right of the presidency over this priesthood, and the keys or authority of the same.

18 No man has a legal right to this office, to hold the keys of this priesthood, except he be a literal descendant and the firstborn of Aaron.

19 But, as a high priest of the Melchizedek Priesthood has authority to officiate in all the lesser offices he may officiate in the office of bishop when no literal descendant of Aaron can be found, provided he is called and set apart and ordained unto this power, under the hands of the First Presidency of the Melchizedek Priesthood.

20 And a literal descendant of Aaron, also, must be designated by this Presidency, and found worthy, and anointed, and ordained under the hands of this Presidency, otherwise they are not legally authorized to officiate in their priesthood.

21 But, by virtue of the decree concerning their right of the priesthood descending from father to son, they may claim their anointing if at any time they can prove their lineage, or

"Inasmuch as Parents Have Children in Zion" (Doctrine and Covenants 68:25–28)

"No child in this Church should be left with uncertainty about his or her parents' devotion to the Lord Jesus Christ, the Restoration of His Church, and the reality of living prophets and apostles. . . .

"Parents simply cannot flirt with skepticism or cynicism, then be surprised when their children expand that flirtation into full-blown romance. If in matters of faith and belief children are at risk of being swept downstream by this intellectual current or that cultural rapid, we as their parents must be more certain than ever to hold to anchored, unmistakable moorings clearly recognizable to those of our own household. It won't help anyone if we go over the edge with them, explaining through the roar of the falls all the way down that we really did know the Church was true and that the keys of the priesthood really were lodged there but we just didn't want to stifle anyone's freedom to think otherwise. No, we can hardly expect the children to get to shore safely if the parents don't seem to know where to anchor their own boat. . . .

"Might we ask ourselves what our children know? From us? Personally? Do our children know that we love the scriptures? Do they see us reading them and marking them and clinging to them in daily life? Have our children ever unexpectedly opened a closed door and found us on our knees in prayer? Have they heard us not only pray

do ascertain it by revelation from the Lord under the hands of the above named Presidency.

22 And again, no bishop or high priest who shall be set apart for this ministry shall be tried or condemned for any crime, save it be before the First Presidency of the church;

23 And inasmuch as he is found guilty before this Presidency, by testimony that cannot be impeached, he shall be condemned;

24 And if he repent he shall be forgiven, according to the covenants and commandments of the church.

25 And again, inasmuch as parents have children in Zion, or in any of her stakes which are organized, that teach them not to understand the doctrine of repentance, faith in Christ the Son of the living God, and of baptism and the gift of the Holy Ghost by the laying on of the hands, when eight years old, the sin be upon the heads of the parents.

26 For this shall be a law unto the inhabitants of Zion, or in any of her stakes which are organized.

27 And their children shall be baptized for the remission of their sins when eight years old, and receive the laying on of the hands.

Doctrine and Covenants 68:25–28. Parents Are Commanded to Teach the Gospel to Their Children

What "sin be upon the heads of the parents"? (68:25) "It is important to remember that the word *sin* (singular) is used in Doctrine and Covenants 68:25, not the word *sins*. It does not refer to the sins children may commit but to the sin of the parents in not teaching their children the doctrine of the kingdom. Misreading this verse may cause some parents to mistakenly feel they are responsible for the sins of their children. Consequently, some parents blame themselves for their children's poor choices despite having diligently taught them correct principles" (*Doctrine and Covenants Student Manual* [2018], 367–68). ⊕

Why do we baptize children at eight years old? (68:27) "Children become accountable gradually, over a number of years. Becoming accountable is a process. . . . In our revelation the Lord says, 'They cannot sin, for power is not given unto Satan to tempt little children, until they begin to become

with them but also pray *for* them out of nothing more than sheer parental love? Do our children know we believe in fasting as something more than an obligatory first-Sunday-of-the-month hardship? Do they know that we have fasted for them and for their future on days about which they knew nothing? Do they know we love being in the temple, not least because it provides a bond to them that neither death nor the legions of hell can break? Do they know we love and sustain local and general leaders, imperfect as they are, for their willingness to accept callings they did not seek in order to preserve a standard of righteousness they did not create? Do those children know that we love God with all our heart and that we long to see the face—and fall at the feet—of His Only Begotten Son? I pray that they know this. . . .

"Our children take their flight into the future with our thrust and with our aim. And even as we anxiously watch that arrow in flight and know all the evils that can deflect its course after it has left our hand, nevertheless we take courage in remembering that the most important mortal factor in determining that arrow's destination will be the stability, strength, and unwavering certainty of the holder of the bow" (Holland, "Prayer for the Children," *Ensign*, May 2003, 85–86, 87).

accountable before me' (D&C 29:47). There comes a time, however, when accountability is real and actual and sin is attributed in the lives of those who develop normally. It is eight years of age, the age of baptism' (Bruce R. McConkie, "Salvation of Little Children," *Ensign*, Apr. 1977, 6).

"In other words, accountability develops within children all along, but at eight years old they are sufficiently accountable to be baptized and are therefore sufficiently accountable for their own sins" (Mathews, "Salvation of Little Children," *Liahona*, Jul. 2021, 13).

Doctrine and Covenants 68:29–35. The Saints Are to Observe the Sabbath, Labor Diligently, and Pray

Why is an idler held in remembrance before the Lord? (68:30) The "idler," the Lord says, "shall not have place in the church, except he repent and mend his ways" (D&C 75:29).

"Leisure is not idleness. The Lord condemns idleness. He said, 'Thou shalt not idle away thy time, neither shalt thou bury thy talent' (D&C 60:13.) Idleness in any form produces boredom, conflict, and unhappiness. It creates a vacancy of worth, a seedbed for mischief and evil. It is the enemy of progress and salvation" (Clarke, "Value of Work," *Ensign*, May 1982, 78).

"The poor use of time is a close cousin of idleness. As we follow the command to 'cease to be idle' (D&C 88:124), we must be sure that being busy also equates to being productive" (Ardern, "Time to Prepare," *Ensign*, Nov. 2011, 32).

Why was the Lord displeased with these inhabitants of Zion? (68:31–32) "The displeasure of the Lord with the inhabitants of Zion for not keeping these principles (v. 31) is another declaration that they have not overcome the world, or become a people that are pure in heart. To overcome the world they must learn the Lord's will, mind, word, and voice, which is scripture. Oliver [Cowdery] is to carry this message and commandment to Zion (v. 32). These commandments are true and faithful, and must be followed with exactness, or they will not achieve their Zion status" (Nyman, *Doctrine and Covenants Commentary*, 1:571).

What is the season of prayer? (68:33) "The season of prayer is in the morning before the family separates. A good time for prayer is when you assemble at the table before you partake of the morning meal, and let the members of the family take turn in the praying. That is the season of prayer. The season of prayer for the merchant is in the morning when he

28 And they shall also teach their children to pray, and to walk uprightly before the Lord.

29 And the inhabitants of Zion shall also observe the Sabbath day to keep it holy.

30 And the inhabitants of Zion also shall remember their labors, inasmuch as they are appointed to labor, in all faithfulness; for the idler shall be had in remembrance before the Lord.

31 Now, I, the Lord, am not well pleased with the inhabitants of Zion, for there are idlers among them; and their children are also growing up in wickedness; they also seek not earnestly the riches of eternity, but their eyes are full of greediness.

32 These things ought not to be, and must be done away from among them; wherefore, let my servant Oliver Cowdery carry these sayings unto the land of Zion.

33 And a commandment I give unto them— that he that observeth not his prayers before the Lord in the season thereof, let him be had in remembrance before the judge of my people.

34 These sayings are true and faithful; wherefore, transgress them not, neither take therefrom.

35 Behold, I am Alpha and Omega, and I come quickly. Amen.

goes to his place of business and before he begins his day's work, over his merchandise. The time of prayer for the shepherd, is when he is out with his flocks watching over them. The time for the farmer to pray is when he goes with his plow into the field, when he goes to sow his grain, and when he goes to gather his harvest. And if a man will pray as he is commanded to do in this passage of scripture [see Alma 34:18–28], then he more than likely will be found in all things righteously keeping the commandments of the Lord" (*Joseph Fielding Smith* [manual], 281).

Introduction to Doctrine and Covenants 69

Doctrine and Covenants 69 was received in Hiram, Ohio, at the home of John and Elsa Johnson on 11 November 1831. "[Joseph Smith] dictated this revelation assigning 'John [Whitmer]' to accompany 'Oliver [Cowdery]' on an upcoming trip to Missouri. . . . [They were] to carry [Joseph Smith's] revelations to Missouri so they could be published at the printing office William W. Phelps was establishing there. John Whitmer later wrote that he was appointed by revelation to accompany Cowdery. This 11 November directive for Whitmer—who, according to a March 1831 revelation, was responsible for keeping 'the Church Record & History continually'—to go to Missouri indicates that the records necessary to maintain a history of the church were to be kept there" (Joseph Smith Papers, Historical Introduction to "Revelation, 11 November 1831–A [D&C 69]").

The day after this revelation was given, another conference convened at the Johnson home. "This conference culminated nearly two weeks of early November meetings. . . . [Joseph Smith] and other elders spent much time during those two weeks 'reviewing the commandments' and discussing the planned publication of the Book of Commandments. . . . [Joseph Smith], Oliver Cowdery, and Sidney Rigdon spent hours reading through the revelations and making corrections. During this period, Cowdery and John Whitmer also apparently spent considerable time copying revelations into Revelation Book 1, which they later took with them to Missouri. With all the work that these individuals and others at the conferences put into preparing the revelations for publication, it was perhaps fitting that participants at this final conference voted [Joseph Smith's] revelations to be not only of significant value to the church but even its foundation and the source of 'the riches of Eternity'" (Joseph Smith Papers, Historical Introduction to "Minutes, 12 November 1831").

SECTION 69

Revelation given through Joseph Smith the Prophet, at Hiram, Ohio, November 11, 1831. The compilation of revelations intended for early publication had been passed upon at the special conference of November 1–2. On November 3, the revelation herein appearing as section 133, later called the Appendix, was added. Oliver Cowdery had previously been appointed to carry the manuscript of the compiled revelations and commandments to Independence, Missouri, for printing. He was also to take with him money that had been contributed for the building up of the Church in Missouri. This revelation

Doctrine and Covenants 69:1–2. John Whitmer Is to Accompany Oliver Cowdery to Missouri

Why was John Whitmer appointed to accompany Oliver Cowdery to Missouri? (69:1–2) "In this commandment the Lord declared that it was not wisdom that Oliver Cowdery should make the journey alone. The journey was about one thousand miles and through a sparsely settled country. There were many dangers on the way. The revelations were considered to be priceless and then, besides, Oliver carried with him sums of money to assist in the work in Missouri. John Whitmer was therefore appointed to accompany Oliver" (Joseph Fielding Smith, *Church History and Modern Revelation*, 1:249).

Doctrine and Covenants 69:3–8. John Whitmer Is Also to Preach and to Collect, Record, and Write Historical Data

Why does the Church emphasize recording and preserving its history? (69:3) "Doctrine and Covenants 69, in combination with sections 21 and 47, records the Lord's commandments to document the history of the Church. In the restored Church of Jesus Christ, history functions much as theology does in other Christian traditions. Latter-day Saints know the nature of God and Christ not from the philosophical creeds of traditional Christianity but through records of historical experiences in which Joseph Smith saw and spoke with Them. We know, for example, that the priesthood needed to be restored because ministering angels brought it to Joseph Smith. We know of these experiences because they are described in documents. Thus, revelations such as section 69 are perhaps more important than they might at first seem" (Harper, *Making Sense of the Doctrine & Covenants*, 242). See also commentary in this volume on Doctrine and Covenants 21:1 and 47:1, 3–4.

Why were the Saints to send an accounting of their stewardship to Missouri? (69:6) "The Lord here affirms once again that the land of Zion will eventually become the geographical center of the Church. This thread is carefully woven throughout the Doctrine and Covenants. In commanding that the revelations be printed in Missouri, the Lord is emphasizing the importance of Zion and its development for the work of the Church in the latter days" (Griffiths, "Historical Context . . . of D&C 69").

instructs John Whitmer to accompany Oliver Cowdery and also directs Whitmer to travel and collect historical material in his calling as Church historian and recorder.

1 Hearken unto me, saith the Lord your God, for my servant Oliver Cowdery's sake. It is not wisdom in me that he should be entrusted with the commandments and the moneys which he shall carry unto the land of Zion, except one go with him who will be true and faithful.

2 Wherefore, I, the Lord, will that my servant, John Whitmer, should go with my servant Oliver Cowdery;

3 And also that he shall continue in writing and making a history of all the important things which he shall observe and know concerning my church;

4 And also that he receive counsel and assistance from my servant Oliver Cowdery and others.

5 And also, my servants who are abroad in the earth should send forth the accounts of their stewardships to the land of Zion;

6 For the land of Zion shall be a seat and a place to receive and do all these things.

7 Nevertheless, let my servant John Whitmer travel many times from place to place, and from church to church, that he may the more easily obtain knowledge—

8 Preaching and expounding, writing, copying, selecting, and obtaining all things which shall be for the good of the church, and for the rising generations that shall grow up on the land of Zion, to possess it from generation to generation, forever and ever. Amen.

How would a history of the Church benefit the rising generations? (69:7–8) The Prophet Joseph Smith observed: "I have for myself learned—a fact by experience which on reflection gives me deep sorrow. It is a truth that if I now had in my possession every decision which has been given upon important items of doctrine and duties since the rise of this church, they would be of incalculable worth to the saints, but we have neglected to keep records of such things, thinking that perhaps that they would never benefit us afterwards, which had we now, would decide almost any point that might be agitated; and now we cannot bear record to the church nor unto the world of the great and glorious manifestations that have been made to us with that degree of power and authority which we otherwise could" (Joseph Smith Papers, "Record of the Twelve, 14 February–28 August 1835"; spelling modernized). ◉

Introduction to Doctrine and Covenants 70

Joseph Smith received Doctrine and Covenants 70 on November 12, 1831, at the home of John and Elsa Johnson in Hiram, Ohio—the last day of a series of conferences that began 1 November 1831. In the conference minutes, Joseph described receiving this revelation: "My time was occupied closely in reviewing the commandments [collected for the Book of Commandments] and sitting in conference for nearly two weeks; . . . After deliberate consideration, in consequence of the book of Revelations, now to be printed, being the foundation of the church in these last days; and a benefit to the world, showing that the keys of the mysteries of the Kingdom of our Savior, are again entrusted to man. . . . In answer to an enquiry, I received the following" (Joseph Smith Papers, "History, 1838–1856, volume A-1," 172).

At one of these conferences, "Joseph recognized the brethren who had contributed to the sacred writings of the Church: 'Br. Oliver has labored with me from the beginning in writing &c Br. Martin has labored with me from the beginning, brs. John [Whitmer] and Sidney also for a considerable time.' Due to the diligence of those named 'in bringing to light by the grace of God these sacred things,' they were appointed to manage like undertakings according to the laws of the Church and the commandments of the Lord. These brethren became the nucleus or original members of the Literary Firm. As such, they were to consecrate, manage, print, and distribute revelations so 'that the revelations may be published, and go forth unto the ends of the earth' (D&C 72:21). They were to be 'stewards' of the sacred writings and were promised proceeds from the sale of these writings for their temporal use" (Black, *400 Questions and Answers*, 132–33).

"The brethren mentioned in Section 70 were told that their obligation in caring for the revelations, as given above, referred to as a stewardship. As stewards, these elders were to discharge their responsibilities to the letter. The importance of caring for their stewardship in this manner is thus indicated:

"'And an account of this stewardship will I require of them in the day of judgment.' (D&C 70:4). . . .

"All of us are stewards over the things of this earth which are ours legally, but, in fact, they are the Lord's. (Mosiah 2:20–26.) An accounting of what we do with these blessings, including offices in the Church, will be required of us in the day of judgment" (Roy W. Doxey, *Doctrine and Covenants Speaks*, 1:553–54).

SECTION 70

Revelation given through Joseph Smith the Prophet, at Hiram, Ohio, November 12, 1831. The Prophet's history states that four special

Doctrine and Covenants 70:1–5. Stewards Are Appointed to Publish the Revelations

What were the responsibilities of those called to oversee the revelations and commandments? (70:1–3) "Doctrine and Covenants 70 creates what is often called the Literary Firm, a corporation assigned by the Lord to receive, write, revise, print, bind, and sell the revelations according to the law of consecration. . . . Joseph received the revelations. He also edited and amended them as he saw fit. One of Joseph's stewardships in the Literary Firm was to 'correct those errors or mistakes which he may discover by the holy Spirit.' Joseph believed in his revelations, but he never believed that any scripture was pristine. He edited his own revelations because he regarded them as his best efforts to represent the voice of the Lord condescending to speak in what Joseph called 'a crooked, broken, scattered, and imperfect Language'" (Harper, *Making Sense of the Doctrine & Covenants*, 244–45). See also commentary in this volume on Doctrine and Covenants 78: introduction and 1–3, 4; 72:20–21; and 82:11–13, 15–18.

Why were members of the Literary Firm called "stewards"? (70:3) "Joseph modeled and taught his brethren the law of consecration as section 70 explained it. When William Phelps began acting like the owner of the Lord's press rather than a steward over the revelations (D&C 70:3), Joseph gently but directly sent him the following postscript. It penetrates to the heart of consecration and section 70: 'Bro. William— you say "my press, my types, &c." Where, our brethren ask, did you get them, & and how came they to be "*yours*"? No hardness, but a caution; For you know, that it is, *We*, not *I*, and all things are the Lord's, and he opened the hearts of his Church to furnish these things, or *we* should not have been privileged with using them'" (Harper, *Let's Talk about the Law of Consecration*, 37).

conferences were held from the 1st to the 12th of November, inclusive. In the last of these assemblies, the great importance of the revelations that would later be published as the Book of Commandments and then the Doctrine and Covenants was considered. This revelation was given after the conference voted that the revelations were "worth to the Church the riches of the whole Earth." Joseph Smith's history refers to the revelations as "the foundation of the Church in these last days, and a benefit to the world, showing that the keys of the mysteries of the kingdom of our Savior are again entrusted to man."

1 Behold, and hearken, O ye inhabitants of Zion, and all ye people of my church who are afar off, and hear the word of the Lord which I give unto my servant Joseph Smith, Jun., and also unto my servant Martin Harris, and also unto my servant Oliver Cowdery, and also unto my servant John Whitmer, and also unto my servant Sidney Rigdon, and also unto my servant William W. Phelps, by the way of commandment unto them.

2 For I give unto them a commandment; wherefore hearken and hear, for thus saith the Lord unto them—

3 I, the Lord, have appointed them, and ordained them to be stewards over the revelations and commandments which I have given unto them, and which I shall hereafter give unto them;

4 And an account of this stewardship will I require of them in the day of judgment.

5 Wherefore, I have appointed unto them, and this is their business in the church of God, to manage them and the concerns thereof, yea, the benefits thereof.

6 Wherefore, a commandment I give unto them, that they shall not give these things unto the church, neither unto the world;

7 Nevertheless, inasmuch as they receive more than is needful for their necessities and their wants, it shall be given into my storehouse;

8 And the benefits shall be consecrated unto the inhabitants of Zion, and unto their generations, inasmuch as they become heirs according to the laws of the kingdom.

Will we be required to account for our efforts at Judgment Day? (70:4) "Once we have accepted the gospel, we are given additional stewardships and opportunities to serve. At the Judgment we will be expected to account for how we responded to those opportunities and will be rewarded or punished accordingly: 'Wherefore, now let every man learn his duty, and to act in the office in which he is appointed, in all diligence. He that is slothful shall not be counted worthy to stand, and he that learns not his duty and shows himself not approved shall not be counted worthy to stand' (D&C 107:99–100; see also D&C 70:3–4; 104:13; Matthew 25:14–30)" (Ball, "Day of Judgment," 199–200).

Doctrine and Covenants 70:6–13. Those Who Labor in Spiritual Things Are Worthy of Their Hire

Why were members of the Literary Firm instructed to sell the published scriptures rather than give them away? (70:6–7) "The business of the conference on 12 November had included a proposal to provide compensation to the Prophet Joseph Smith and to his scribes Oliver Cowdery, Martin Harris, John Whitmer, and Sidney Rigdon for their labors and sacrifices in receiving, writing, copying, and preparing the revelations of God for the Church in the latter days. This compensation would come out of any proceeds from the sale of the revelations."

In verse 6, "'These things' refers to the elements of their stewardship, both the responsibilities and the benefits of managing and publishing the scriptures" (Robinson and Garrett, *Commentary on the Doctrine and Covenants*, 2:255–56, 257).

What was to be done with the profits from the sale of Church publications? (70:7–8) "The Lord did not intend those individuals whom he named to become rich out of the avails of the sale of the Book of Mormon and the Book of Doctrine and Covenants, and other revelations and the literary concerns of his Church, he never intended that they should become rich while others were poor, ... but inasmuch as they received more than was needful for their support ... they were to give all the surplus, over and above what was really necessary to support them, into the Lord's storehouse, and it was to be for the benefit of all the people of Zion, not only the living but for their generations after them, inasmuch as they became heirs according to the laws of the kingdom of God" (Orson Pratt, in *Journal of Discourses*, 17:105–6). ☉

What did it mean that no one in the Church was exempt from the responsibilities of stewardship? (70:9–11) "We learn from this and other revelations that all who went up, or who contemplated going up, to Zion, were bound by the law of consecration by which Zion was to be built. They were commanded to be equal in temporal things, and not enter into the covenants grudgingly" (Joseph Fielding Smith, *Church History and Modern Revelation*, 1:268).

What does it mean that those called to administer spiritual things are worthy of their hire? (70:12) "The Lord herein indicated that all those who were required to spend full time in the service of the Church, whether in administering spiritual things or temporal things, were worthy to receive their support from the funds of the Church. This would indicate that other service in the Church would be on an unpaid or 'Church-service' basis" (Daniel H. Ludlow, *Companion to Your Study*, 1:370). ✛

Doctrine and Covenants 70:14–18. The Saints Should Be Equal in Temporal Things

Why does the Lord want us to share temporal blessings willingly? (70:14) "It is of fundamental importance to remember that there are temporal aspects to each spiritual calling and spiritual aspects to every temporal calling. . . .

"The Lord tells us in section 70 of the Doctrine and Covenants that an abundance of the manifestation of the Spirit among us depends upon our willingness to share temporal blessings (see D&C 70:12–14).

"Therefore, we must sacrifice our narrow traditions, local interests, and selfish pride to achieve the love and unity indispensable in a Zion society. The principles of love, service, work, self-reliance, consecration, and stewardship must relate to a specific plan. . . .

"The abstract becomes concrete when we identify welfare services principles with people, places, and things we know. Temporal application of spiritual laws transforms theology into religion" (Poelman, "Priesthood Councils," *Ensign*, May 1980, 91–92).

9 Behold, this is what the Lord requires of every man in his stewardship, even as I, the Lord, have appointed or shall hereafter appoint unto any man.

10 And behold, none are exempt from this law who belong to the church of the living God;

11 Yea, neither the bishop, neither the agent who keepeth the Lord's storehouse, neither he who is appointed in a stewardship over temporal things.

12 He who is appointed to administer spiritual things, the same is worthy of his hire, even as those who are appointed to a stewardship to administer in temporal things;

13 Yea, even more abundantly, which abundance is multiplied unto them through the manifestations of the Spirit.

14 Nevertheless, in your temporal things you shall be equal, and this not grudgingly, otherwise the abundance of the manifestations of the Spirit shall be withheld.

15 Now, this commandment I give unto my servants for their benefit while they remain, for a manifestation of my blessings upon their heads, and for a reward of their diligence and for their security;

16 For food and for raiment; for an inheritance; for houses and for lands, in whatsoever circumstances I, the Lord, shall place them, and whithersoever I, the Lord, shall send them.

17 For they have been faithful over many things, and have done well inasmuch as they have not sinned.

18 Behold, I, the Lord, am merciful and will bless them, and they shall enter into the joy of these things. Even so. Amen.

How does the Lord care for His full-time servants? (70:15–16) "The ministers of salvation must eat and drink; they must be clothed, marry, raise families, and live as other men do. When all of their time and strength is expended in building up the kingdom, others—happily, those blessed by their ministrations—must supply the just needs and wants of the laborers in the vineyard, for 'the laborer is worthy of his hire' (D&C 84:79). 'But the laborer in Zion shall labor for Zion; for if they labor for money they shall perish' (2 Ne. 26:31)" (Bruce R. McConkie, *Doctrinal New Testament Commentary*, 2:351).

How does faithfully carrying out our stewardships bring us the Lord's blessings? (70:17–18) "The word *stewardship* calls to mind the Lord's law of consecration (see, for example, D&C 42:32, 53), which has an economic role but, more than that, is an application of celestial law to life here and now (see D&C 105:5). To consecrate is to set apart or dedicate something as sacred, devoted to holy purposes. True success in this life comes in consecrating our lives—that is, our time and choices—to God's purposes (see John 17:1, 4; D&C 19:19). In so doing, we permit Him to raise us to our highest destiny" (Christofferson, "Reflections on a Consecrated Life," *Ensign*, Nov. 2010, 16).

Joseph Smith noted in his history that "After Oliver Cowdery and John Whitmer had departed for Jackson County, Missouri [20 Nov. 1831], I resumed the translation of the Scriptures [Joseph Smith Translation] and continued to labor in this branch of my calling with Elder Sidney Rigdon as my scribe (Joseph Smith Papers, "History, 1838–1856, volume A-1," 174; spelling modernized).

On December 1, 1831, while working at Hiram, Ohio, the Lord interrupted Joseph and Sidney's work by revealing the instructions contained in Doctrine and Covenants 71. "This revelation directs Joseph Smith and Sidney Rigdon to set aside the labor of translation on the Bible for a time while they went forth in defense of the restored gospel. This was required by the deluge of falsehoods that had been spread by Ezra Booth, who has the dubious distinction of being the first apostate from the youthful Church to take up the pen against it" (McConkie and Ostler, *Revelations of the Restoration*, 497). See also commentary in this volume on Doctrine and Covenants 52:23.

Joseph and Sydney also responded to attacks by Symonds Ryder. "Ryder . . . became a member of the Church after witnessing what he considered to be a miracle. Shortly after his baptism he was ordained an elder of the Church. Later accounts suggest that when he received an official commission to preach the gospel, he found that his name was misspelled on the certificate. Supposing that a revealed call would have been free from even small errors, Symonds began to question the extent of Joseph Smith's prophetic inspiration. . . . (see [Hayden, *Early History of the Disciples*], 220–21, 251–52). After separating himself from the Church in the fall of 1831, Symonds Ryder gave copies of one of the Prophet Joseph Smith's unpublished revelations to the *Western Courier* newspaper in an attempt to dissuade people from joining the Church. Ryder later claimed that new converts could learn from these revelations that 'a plot was laid to take their property from them and place it under the control of Joseph Smith the prophet' (in [*Joseph Smith Papers, Documents, Volume 2*], 144–45; see also Hayden, *Early History of the Disciples*, 221)" (*Doctrine and Covenants Student Manual* [2018], 372).

Doctrine and Covenants 71:1–4. Joseph Smith and Sidney Rigdon Are Sent Forth to Proclaim the Gospel

How did Joseph Smith respond to the Lord's call to proclaim the gospel? (71:1) Two days after receiving Doctrine and Covenants 71, Joseph remembered: "Knowing now the mind of the Lord, that the time had come that the gospel should be proclaimed in power and demonstration to the world, from the scriptures, reasoning with men as in days of old, I took a journey to Kirtland, in company with Elder Sidney Rigdon, on the 3rd day of December to fulfill the above Revelation" (Joseph Smith Papers, "History, 1838–1856, volume A-1," 176; spelling modernized).

Why were Joseph and Sidney commanded to expound the mysteries of the kingdom out of the scriptures? (71:1) "As these two men were called by the Lord to perform a special service in the ministry, they were instructed that they would have power in their ministry provided that they did the following: 1. *Proclaim the gospel.* . . . 2. *Proclaim the gospel out of the scriptures.* . . . In order to teach the gospel out of the scriptures, one must first know the gospel out of the scriptures. . . . Note that the time had come that it was

SECTION 71

Revelation given to Joseph Smith the Prophet and Sidney Rigdon, at Hiram, Ohio, December 1, 1831. The Prophet had continued to translate the Bible with Sidney Rigdon as his scribe until this revelation was received, at which time it was temporarily laid aside so as to enable them to fulfill the instruction given herein. The brethren were to go forth to preach in order to allay the unfriendly feelings that had developed against the Church as a result of the publication of letters written by Ezra Booth, who had apostatized.

1 Behold, thus saith the Lord unto you my servants Joseph Smith, Jun., and Sidney Rigdon, that the time has verily come that it is necessary and expedient in me that you should open your mouths in proclaiming my gospel, the things of the kingdom, expounding the mysteries thereof out of the scriptures, according to that portion of Spirit and power which shall be given unto you, even as I will.

necessary and expedient to teach from the scriptures. ... It is one thing to know the gospel is true—it is quite another to know the gospel. [And] 3. *Proclaim the gospel by the power of the Spirit*" (Otten and Caldwell, *Sacred Truths*, 2:2–3). ☉

2 Verily I say unto you, proclaim unto the world in the regions round about, and in the church also, for the space of a season, even until it shall be made known unto you.

3 Verily this is a mission for a season, which I give unto you.

Where were the "regions round about"? (71:2–3)
The Prophet Joseph Smith wrote: "From this time [1 Dec. 1831] until the 8th or 10th of January 1832 myself and Elder [Sidney] Rigdon continued to preach in Shalersville, Ravenna, and other places [in northeastern Ohio], setting forth the truth; vindicating the cause of our Redeemer; shewing that the day of vengeance was coming upon this generation like a thief in the night: that prejudice, blindness, and darkness, filled the minds of many, and caused them to persecute the true church, and reject the true light: by which means we did much towards allaying the excited feelings which were growing out of the scandalous letters then being published in the 'Ohio Star,' at Ravenna, by the before mentioned apostate Ezra Booth" (Joseph Smith Papers, "History, 1838–1856, volume A-1," 179; spelling modernized). These locations are in northeast Ohio within a thirty-mile radius from Hiram, Ohio. For a map of this area, see Map 5 in the Appendix.

4 Wherefore, labor ye in my vineyard. Call upon the inhabitants of the earth, and bear record, and prepare the way for the commandments and revelations which are to come.

How does sharing the gospel with others prepare them to receive the Lord's revelations? (71:4) "The Savior [commanded] Joseph and Sidney to preach the gospel to the Saints and their neighbors in the surrounding areas until he tells them otherwise.... Their mission will prepare people to receive the Lord's wisdom in the revelations soon to be published as the Book of Commandments. Those who read it must choose whether to understand and receive the gospel it declares. To those who choose to receive, Christ gives more abundantly. He endows them with power" (Harper, *Making Sense of the Doctrine & Covenants*, 248–49).

5 Now, behold this is wisdom; whoso readeth, let him understand and receive also;

6 For unto him that receiveth it shall be given more abundantly, even power.

7 Wherefore, confound your enemies; call upon them to meet you both in public and in private; and inasmuch as ye are faithful their shame shall be made manifest.

Doctrine and Covenants 71:5–11. Enemies of the Saints Will Be Confounded

Why were Joseph Smith and Sidney Rigdon instructed to "confound [their] enemies"? (71:7–8) "Attacks upon the servants of the Lord are really directed against *Him*.

"Ezra Booth had just published a series of anti-'Mormon' letters, in an Ohio paper. These letters, the Prophet says, 'by their coloring, falsity, and vain calculations to overthrow the work of the Lord, exposed his weakness, wickedness, and folly, and left him a monument of his own shame for the world to wonder at.' It was to meet the situation that had been created by this hostile agitation, that Joseph and Sidney were called to take this mission. Sometimes it is wise to ignore the attacks of the wicked; at other times it is necessary to meet them, fearlessly and with ability" (Smith and Sjodhal, *Doctrine and Covenants Commentary*, 423). ⊕

Why will enemies fail in their attacks against the Lord's Church? (71:8–9) President Harold B. Lee remarked: "I always remember the word of the Lord when I hear these things said by those who are trying to tear down his work [see D&C 71:7–11].

"What he is trying to have us understand is that he will take care of our enemies if we continue to keep the commandments. So, you Saints of the Most High God, when these things come, and they will come—this has been prophesied—you just say,

"'No weapon formed against the work of the Lord will ever prosper, but all glory and majesty of this work that the Lord gave will long be remembered after those who have tried to befoul their names and the name of the Church will be forgotten, and their works will follow after them'" ("Closing Remarks," *Ensign*, Jan. 1974, 126). ⊕

8 Wherefore, let them bring forth their strong reasons against the Lord.

9 Verily, thus saith the Lord unto you—there is no weapon that is formed against you shall prosper;

10 And if any man lift his voice against you he shall be confounded in mine own due time.

11 Wherefore, keep my commandments; they are true and faithful. Even so. Amen.

Introduction to Doctrine and Covenants 72

"On 3 December 1831, [Joseph Smith] and Sidney Rigdon traveled to Kirtland from Hiram, Ohio, to fulfill a commandment given in a 1 December revelation [D&C 71] to preach 'unto the world in the regions round about and in the church.' According to a later [Joseph Smith] history, 'on the 4th several of the Elders and members assembled together to learn their duty and for edification'" (Joseph Smith Papers, Historical Introduction to "Revelation, 4 December 1831–A").

Doctrine and Covenants 72 "is a series of three related revelations given to answer the questions Joseph and his brethren were asking. Verses 1–8 address whether the time is right for the appointment of a new bishop. And, if so, who should it be? One imagines that the new bishop wanted to know his duties. Verses 9–23 outline them. Joseph and his brethren were concerned about maintaining order in the process of gathering the Saints to Zion in Missouri. They could not wisely arrive faster than Bishop Partridge could have land available for them to inherit. Verses 24–26 are an amendment to earlier revelations, given to regulate the migration of Saints gathering to Zion. Section 72 can be summed up as the appointment of a bishop and a description of his duties in the early 1830s" (Harper, *Making Sense of the Doctrine & Covenants*, 250).

"When the three 4 December revelations were published, they were presented as a single combined text, but manuscript copies indicate they were originally three separately dictated texts" (Joseph Smith Papers, Historical Introduction to "Revelation, 4 December 1831–A").

SECTION 72

Revelation given through Joseph Smith the Prophet, at Kirtland, Ohio, December 4, 1831. Several elders and members had assembled to learn their duty and to be further edified in the teachings of the Church. This section is a compilation of three revelations received on the same day. Verses 1 through 8 make known the calling of Newel K. Whitney as a bishop. He was then called and ordained, after which verses 9 through 23 were received, giving additional information as to a bishop's duties. Thereafter, verses 24 through 26 were given, providing instructions concerning the gathering to Zion.

1 Hearken, and listen to the voice of the Lord, O ye who have assembled yourselves together, who are the high priests of my church, to whom the kingdom and power have been given.

2 For verily thus saith the Lord, it is expedient in me for a bishop to be appointed unto you, or of you, unto the church in this part of the Lord's vineyard.

Doctrine and Covenants 72:1–8. Elders Are to Render an Account of Their Stewardship unto the Bishop

Why was there a gathering of high priests in Kirtland? (72:1) The office of high priest was first instituted and men ordained to that office several months earlier in the June 1831 conference at the Morley Farm in Kirtland (see Joseph Smith Papers, "High Priest Office Instituted"). This is the first time the Doctrine and Covenants refers to a meeting of newly ordained high priests. Joseph Smith taught: "The duty of a high priest is to administer in spiritual and holy things, and to hold communion with God. . . . It is the high priests' duty to be better qualified to teach principles and doctrines, than the elders, for the office of elder is an appendage to the high priesthood, and it concentrates and centers in one" (Joseph Smith Papers, "History, 1838–1856, volume A-1," 285–86).

Why did they need a second bishop in the Church? (72:2) "As the Savior's Church grew larger and more complicated to manage, Saints in Ohio gathered on December 4, 1831, worried about their 'temporal and Spiritual welfare' and wanting to learn their duty. Many of the ablest among them, including Bishop Edward Partridge, had moved to Missouri to obey earlier revelations, leaving a large number of Saints in Ohio without a bishop. In a revelation a month earlier, the Lord had promised to call other bishops as needed (see D&C 68:14). After Bishop Partridge was called to Missouri, the Lord called Newel K. Whitney to assist him by looking after the Saints who were still in Ohio. The Lord had also commanded Newel to keep his store in Kirtland, Ohio, and to use it to earn money to send to Zion" (Harper, *Let's Talk about the Law of Consecration*, 40).

Why do we render an accounting both in time and in eternity? (72:3–4) "Each of the Lord's servants is required to account for what he or she has done with his or her stewardship (see Matthew 25:14–30). It is the bishop who receives the accounting, the evaluating and settling up for our stewardship in time or while we live upon the earth. The Lord himself will receive the accounting for our stewardship in eternity . . . (see D&C 70:4)" (Robinson and Garrett, *Commentary on the Doctrine and Covenants*, 2:265).

Elder Joseph B. Wirthlin testified: "This most important stewardship is the glorious responsibility your Father in Heaven has given you to watch over and care for your own soul.

"At some future day, you and I will each hear the voice of the Lord calling us forward to render an account of our mortal stewardship. This accounting will occur when we are called up to 'stand before [the Lord] at the great and judgment day' [2 Nephi 9:22]" ("True to the Truth," *Ensign*, May 1997, 16).

Why would the bishop in Kirtland need to deliver records to the bishop in Missouri? (72:5–6) "[Bishop] Whitney was to operate the storehouse in Ohio to provide for the needs of the elders preaching the gospel and of the stewards over the revelations. Any debts these individuals incurred for obtaining goods from the storehouse but could not repay would be covered by funds or assets held by [Bishop] Partridge in Missouri. [Bishop] Whitney was also to receive accounts—apparently both temporal and spiritual—from the elders of their stewardships. He was then to recommend the faithful to [Bishop] Partridge as worthy to receive an inheritance in Zion. Since other revelations declared that [Joseph Smith] and conferences of elders would decide who should relocate to Missouri, [Bishop] Whitney likely was not tasked with actually sending individuals to Zion— only with providing recommends when such individuals were designated to go" (Joseph Smith Papers, Historical Introduction to "Revelation, 4 December 1831–B [D&C 72:9–23]").

How did Newel K. Whitney respond to his call as a bishop? (72:8) "Newel K. Whitney [was] the second man called to the Bishopric in this dispensation. . . . The law of consecration had been revealed and was about to be put into operation. . . . Whitney, stagger-ing under the weight of the responsibility that was about to be placed upon him, said to the Prophet: 'Brother Joseph, I can't see a Bishop in myself.' . . . The Prophet answered: 'Go and ask the Lord about it.' And

3 And verily in this thing ye have done wisely, for it is required of the Lord, at the hand of every steward, to render an account of his stewardship, both in time and in eternity.

4 For he who is faithful and wise in time is accounted worthy to inherit the mansions prepared for him of my Father.

5 Verily I say unto you, the elders of the church in this part of my vineyard shall ren-der an account of their stewardship unto the bishop, who shall be appointed of me in this part of my vineyard.

6 These things shall be had on record, to be handed over unto the bishop in Zion.

7 And the duty of the bishop shall be made known by the commandments which have been given, and the voice of the conference.

8 And now, verily I say unto you, my ser-vant Newel K. Whitney is the man who shall be appointed and ordained unto this power. This is the will of the Lord your God, your Redeemer. Even so. Amen.

Newel did ask the Lord, and he heard a voice from heaven say: '*Thy strength is in me.*' That was enough. He accepted the office, and served in it faithfully to the end of his days" (Whitney, in Conference Report, Jun. 1919, 47–48). See also commentary in this volume on Doctrine and Covenants 63:42.

Doctrine and Covenants 72:9–15. The Bishop Keeps the Storehouse and Cares for the Poor and Needy

9 The word of the Lord, in addition to the law which has been given, making known the duty of the bishop who has been ordained unto the church in this part of the vineyard, which is verily this—

10 To keep the Lord's storehouse; to receive the funds of the church in this part of the vineyard;

11 To take an account of the elders as before has been commanded; and to administer to their wants, who shall pay for that which they receive, inasmuch as they have wherewith to pay;

12 That this also may be consecrated to the good of the church, to the poor and needy.

13 And he who hath not wherewith to pay, an account shall be taken and handed over to the bishop of Zion, who shall pay the debt out of that which the Lord shall put into his hands.

14 And the labors of the faithful who labor in spiritual things, in administering the gospel and the things of the kingdom unto the church, and unto the world, shall answer the debt unto the bishop in Zion;

15 Thus it cometh out of the church, for according to the law every man that cometh up to Zion must lay all things before the bishop in Zion.

16 And now, verily I say unto you, that as every elder in this part of the vineyard must give an account of his stewardship unto the bishop in this part of the vineyard—

17 A certificate from the judge or bishop in this part of the vineyard, unto the bishop in Zion, rendereth every man acceptable,

What is the Lord's storehouse? (72:10–12) "The concept of the storehouse and the Church Welfare Services emerged from scriptural principles, elucidated by a series of revelations given to the Prophet Joseph Smith beginning in 1831.... In one revelation, Church members were directed to 'remember the poor, and consecrate [their] properties for [the poor's] support' (D&C 42:30). The goods and money thus contributed were to be 'kept in [the Lord's] storehouse'" (R. Quinn Gardner, "Bishop's Storehouse," 1124).

"The Lord's storehouse includes the time, talents, skills, compassion, consecrated materials, and financial means of faithful Church members. These may be made available to the bishop in assisting the poor and needy everywhere. Using such resources makes possible the blessing of both givers and receivers as the needy are cared for in the Lord's own way (see D&C 104:16)" (*Caring for the Needy* [1986]). See also commentary in this volume on Doctrine and Covenants 42:34.

Doctrine and Covenants 72:16–26. Bishops Are to Certify the Worthiness of Elders

and answereth all things, for an inheritance, and to be received as a wise steward and as a faithful laborer;

18 Otherwise he shall not be accepted of the bishop of Zion.

19 And now, verily I say unto you, let every elder who shall give an account unto the bishop of the church in this part of the vineyard be recommended by the church or churches, in which he labors, that he may render himself and his accounts approved in all things.

20 And again, let my servants who are appointed as stewards over the literary concerns of my church have claim for assistance upon the bishop or bishops in all things—

21 That the revelations may be published, and go forth unto the ends of the earth; that they also may obtain funds which shall benefit the church in all things;

22 That they also may render themselves approved in all things, and be accounted as wise stewards.

23 And now, behold, this shall be an ensample for all the extensive branches of my church, in whatsoever land they shall be established. And now I make an end of my sayings. Amen.

24 A few words in addition to the laws of the kingdom, respecting the members of the church—they that are appointed by the Holy Spirit to go up unto Zion, and they who are privileged to go up unto Zion—

25 Let them carry up unto the bishop a certificate from three elders of the church, or a certificate from the bishop;

26 Otherwise he who shall go up unto the land of Zion shall not be accounted as a wise steward. This is also an ensample. Amen.

What were the "literary concerns" of the Church? (72:20–21) "At a conference held the previous month (see head note to D&C 1) the Lord revealed his will that the Church publish the revelations that Joseph Smith had received in the form of the Book of Commandments. It was also determined that the Literary Firm (D&C 70) would be responsible for publishing Joseph Smith's New Translation of the Bible, when it was finished, along with a Church hymnal, children's literature, a Church almanac, and a newspaper" (McConkie and Ostler, *Revelations of the Restoration*, 503). See also commentary in this volume on Doctrine and Covenants 70:1–3.

What certificate was needed by those moving to Missouri? (72:24–26) "Members of the Church going to Zion were to carry a Bishop's certificate, or recommend, to show their standing in the Church. 'Otherwise he . . . shall not be accounted as a wise steward' (v. 26). Wisdom was required in those who went to Zion. They would show their wisdom in the management of their temporal affairs" (Smith and Sjodahl, *Doctrine and Covenants Commentary*, 428).

"It was intended that only those who consecrated all their possessions to the Lord would be called to Zion. . . . All the Saints in Zion were expected to consecrate all they had to the kingdom, thus providing the resources needed to answer the debts of the Church and to provide the resources needed for the continued growth of Zion" (Robinson and Garrett, *Commentary on the Doctrine and Covenants*, 2:268–69).

After preaching for a few weeks to combat criticism of the Prophet and the Church published by Ezra Booth, "[Joseph Smith and Sidney Rigdon] returned to Hiram, Ohio, around 8 January 1832, and on 10 January [the Prophet] dictated [the revelation recorded as Doctrine and Covenants 73], 'making known the will of the Lord' regarding what they and the elders should do until the next conference, which was held two weeks later [on January 25, 1832]. In addition to instructing [Joseph and Sidney] and the other elders to continue preaching, the revelation directed [them] to renew their work on the Bible revision after the conclusion of the upcoming conference.

"[Joseph Smith] probably dictated this revelation to Rigdon in an upstairs bedroom of the John and Alice (Elsa) Jacobs Johnson home where they worked on the Bible revision" (Joseph Smith Papers, Historical Introduction to "Revelation, 10 January 1832 [D&C 73]").

SECTION 73

Revelation given to Joseph Smith the Prophet and Sidney Rigdon, at Hiram, Ohio, January 10, 1832. Since the early part of the preceding December, the Prophet and Sidney had been engaged in preaching, and by this means much was accomplished in diminishing the unfavorable feelings that had arisen against the Church (see the heading to section 71).

1 For verily, thus saith the Lord, it is expedient in me that they should continue preaching the gospel, and in exhortation to the churches in the regions round about, until conference;

2 And then, behold, it shall be made known unto them, by the voice of the conference, their several missions.

3 Now, verily I say unto you my servants, Joseph Smith, Jun., and Sidney Rigdon, saith the Lord, it is expedient to translate again;

4 And, inasmuch as it is practicable, to preach in the regions round about until conference; and after that it is expedient to continue the work of translation until it be finished.

Doctrine and Covenants 73:1–2. Elders Are to Continue to Preach

What can we learn from the Lord's instruction to continue preaching the gospel until the conference? (73:1–2) "The elders of the Church in 1832 desired to know what the Lord wanted them to do while they were waiting to learn his will through his prophet at conference. He told them they should be anxiously engaged in productive labor and to continue doing their duty. That is good counsel for us all: while waiting, do something constructive. President Joseph F. Smith admonished 'the Latter-day Saints everywhere to cease loitering away their precious time, to cease from all idleness.... there is far too much precious time wasted by the youth of Zion, and perhaps by some that are older and more experienced and who ought to know better ...' (*Gospel Doctrine*, 235). Let us use moments of waiting productively" (Millet and Newell, *Draw Near unto Me*, 202).

Doctrine and Covenants 73:3–6. Joseph Smith and Sidney Rigdon Are to Continue to Translate the Bible until It Is Finished

Why had Joseph Smith stopped translating the Bible? (73:3–4) "Though the Prophet and Sidney Rigdon had worked diligently at the translation since the previous spring [in 1831], there had been several interruptions—conferences, a missionary journey to Missouri in July and August, Joseph and Emma's move from the Morley farm to Hiram, Ohio, in September, and most recently an assignment from the Lord in early December to 'proclaim unto the world in the regions round about [Kirtland], and in the church also, for the space of a season' to 'confound your enemies' (D&C 71:2, 7). . . .

"After this five-week hiatus it was time to translate again. The Prophet and Sidney Rigdon were instructed of the Lord to continue with the translation 'until it be finished'" (Dahl, "Joseph Smith Translation and the Doctrine and Covenants," 113, 114).

What pattern did the Lord want the elders to learn? (73:5) Joseph Smith and Sidney Rigdon had been preaching the gospel to counter the impact of harsh criticism from Ezra Booth and Symonds Rider. "When Ezra Booth fled from Sidney Rigdon's challenge to meet him in public debate, the *Ohio Star* ceased publication of his scurrilous letters. At the same time the Prophet and Sidney befriended many through their public preaching. The best way to defend the gospel is simply to teach it, as Joseph and Sidney demonstrated in this instance. Such a course is here referred to as a 'pattern unto the elders'" (McConkie and Ostler, *Revelations of the Restoration*, 504). ⊕

5 And let this be a pattern unto the elders until further knowledge, even as it is written.

When Did Joseph Smith Finish His Translation of the Bible? (Doctrine and Covenants 73:4)

Kent P. Jackson explained: "It is often heard in the Church that Joseph Smith's Bible translation [JST] was never finished, an assumption that stems from the nineteenth century when we had no access to the manuscripts and virtually no institutional memory about the translation. But careful study of the manuscripts and early historical sources teaches us otherwise. Although in one sense the JST was not finished, in the most important ways it was. It was not finished in the sense that things still needed to be done to get it ready for printing. The spelling on the manuscripts reflects the idiosyncrasies of the individual scribes, the grammar sometimes reflects the frontier English of Joseph Smith, the punctuation is inconsistent, and not all of the text was divided systematically into chapters and verses. The Prophet had assigned assistants to take care of most of those needs, but by the time of his death there was yet much technical work to be done. The Joseph Smith Translation was still in need of editors.

John and Elsa Johnson home; Hiram, Ohio. Significant work on the Joseph Smith Translation of the Bible occurred here. This is also where the Prophet Joseph Smith and Sidney Rigdon received the vision of the three degrees of glory recorded in section 76.

"But the translation itself was finished as far as was intended. We know that because the Prophet said so on more than one occasion. At the conclusion of the Old Testament, where the translation ends, the following words are written: 'Finished on the 2d day of July 1833' [Old Testament Manuscript 2, page 119, line 5]. That same day, the Prophet and his counselors, JST scribes Sidney Rigdon and Frederick G. Williams, wrote to Church members in Missouri and told them, 'We this day finished the translating of the Scriptures for which we returned gratitude to our heavenly father' [Joseph Smith Papers, 'History, 1838–1856, volume A-1,' 316]. Could more have been done with the translation? Yes, but it was not designed to be. The Lord could have revealed other things in the JST, but He did not. Instead, beginning in July 1833, Joseph Smith no longer spoke of translating the Bible but of publishing it, which he wanted and intended to do 'as soon as possible.' As Robert Matthews pointed out years ago, the Prophet's own words show that from then on, his efforts were to have it printed as a book, and he repeatedly encouraged Church members to donate money for its publication. But other priorities and a lack of funds caused that it was not printed in his lifetime" ("New Discoveries," 156).

6 Now I give no more unto you at this time. Gird up your loins and be sober. Even so. Amen.

What does "gird up your loins" mean? (73:6) "The admonition 'gird up your loins' means to be prepared for a journey, or for a certain work. In this sense it is found in the hymn 'Come, Come Ye Saints.' In this scripture, we are informed that it is to be understood as used by Peter, 'Gird up the loins of your minds' (1 Peter 1:13). In other words, the mind should be free from those things which deter one from the work at hand. To be sober means to be of a serious mind" (Roy W. Doxey, *Doctrine and Covenants Speaks*, 2:4). ❂

Introduction to Doctrine and Covenants 74

This revelation was received by Joseph Smith sometime in early 1830 at Wayne County, New York. Doctrine and Covenants 74 "clarifies a New Testament verse, 1 Corinthians 7:14, which historically had been an important passage for justifying infant baptism. Like the Book of Mormon, this document rejects the need for infant baptism by explaining that little children are made clean through the atonement of Jesus Christ, without baptism" (Joseph Smith Papers, Historical Introduction to "Explanation of Scripture, 1830 [D&C 74]"). To see the location of Wayne County, New York, see Map 4 in the Appendix.

Doctrine and Covenants 74 "provides an interpretive revelation that helps us understand a difficult passage in 1 Cor. 7:12–16. It concerns Paul's answers to a question put to him by the Corinthian Saints. . . .

"Paul gave personal counsel that a believer in Christ ought not to marry a Jew 'except the law of Moses be done away among them' . . . [D&C 74:5]. The counsel [Paul provided] is not unlike what modern Saints would receive regarding . . . marrying outside the Covenant" (Meservy, "New Testament Items," 268, 269).

SECTION 74

Revelation given to Joseph Smith the Prophet, at Wayne County, New York, in 1830. Even before the organization of the Church, questions had arisen about the proper mode of baptism, leading the Prophet to seek answers on the subject. Joseph Smith's history states that this revelation is an explanation of 1 Corinthians 7:14, a scripture that had often been used to justify infant baptism.

1 For the unbelieving husband is sanctified by the wife, and the unbelieving wife is sanctified by the husband; else were your children unclean, but now are they holy.

Doctrine and Covenants 74:1–5. Paul Counsels the Church of His Day Not to Keep the Law of Moses

What did the Apostle Paul mean when he said that the unbelieving husband is sanctified by the believing wife? (74:1) "[A] question that Paul apparently dealt with on a frequent basis had to do with the issue of interfaith marriage and whether or not a member so involved should seek a divorce, particularly in cases where the influence of the unbelieving spouse was perceived by the member to be negative or detrimental to gospel living. . . .

"Paul's counsel . . . was that if married to an unbeliever, one who would permit the spouse's continued activity in the Church rather than divorce; the member should seek to be an influence for good and to have the best marriage possible while maintaining hope that one day the unbelieving spouse would desire to unite with the Church" (Kent R. Brooks, "Paul's Inspired Teachings on Marriage," 84).

Why did the law of circumcision cause contention? (74:3–4) "Some Jews believed children were unholy and, therefore, were banned from Jehovah's presence unless they were circumcised. This belief caused tension in part-member families since the Christian, believing the law of Moses was fulfilled, did not want the child operated on. So to keep the marriage solvent, the belief that little children were unholy had to be done away by the nonmember as evidenced by not having the child circumcised (D&C 74:1–7)" (Draper and Rhodes, *Paul's First Epistle to the Corinthians*, 353).

The Joseph Smith Translation clarified: "And I will establish *a covenant of circumcision with thee, and it shall be* my covenant between me and thee, and thy seed after thee, in their generations; *that thou mayest know forever that children are not accountable before me until they are eight years old*" (JST, Genesis 17:11; italics mark changes).

Why did Paul suggest that the Corinthian Saints not unite with an unbelieving spouse? (74:5) "Paul pointed out in verses 12–14 of 1 Corinthians 7 how a church member could, through his influence and example, convert his nonmember spouse and thereby bring the sanctifying blessings of the gospel into their family and save not only themselves but also their children from being subject to false traditions. Note that Paul did not advocate marrying an unbeliever; to the contrary, he recognized the inadvisability of contracting such relationships. (See 2 Corinthians 6:14.)

2 Now, in the days of the apostles the law of circumcision was had among all the Jews who believed not the gospel of Jesus Christ.

3 And it came to pass that there arose a great contention among the people concerning the law of circumcision, for the unbelieving husband was desirous that his children should be circumcised and become subject to the law of Moses, which law was fulfilled.

4 And it came to pass that the children, being brought up in subjection to the law of Moses, gave heed to the traditions of their fathers and believed not the gospel of Christ, wherein they became unholy.

5 Wherefore, for this cause the apostle wrote unto the church, giving unto them a commandment, not of the Lord, but of himself, that a believer should not be united to an unbeliever; except the law of Moses should be done away among them,

What Was the Law of Circumcision? (Doctrine and Covenants 74:2)

"The custom of circumcision in the Old Testament is traced to Genesis 17, where Jehovah commanded Abraham to circumcise himself and all the males in his house: 'And ye shall circumcise the flesh of your foreskin; and it shall be a token of the covenant betwixt me and you' (Gen 17:11). Males were to be circumcised eight days after birth (Gen 17:12; Lev 12:3), though the JST Genesis account mentions 'that children are not accountable before me until they are eight years old' (JST Gen 17:11). Circumcision was considered a 'sign of the covenant,' and may have been connected with the covenantal promise of a great posterity. The exact symbolic relationship between circumcision and the covenant is not specified in the Bible, but the Old Testament recognized that the circumcision of the flesh was an external sign of a necessary internal conversion, expressed as a 'circumcised heart.' Deuteronomy 10:16 reads, 'Circumcise therefore the foreskin of your heart,' and Jeremiah condemned those who were circumcised only in the flesh (Jer 9:24–25). Christians believe that the law of circumcision was fulfilled in Christ (Acts 15; Moro 8:6) and place emphasis on the circumcision of the heart rather than the flesh (Col 2:11–12)" (Holzapfel, Pike, and Seely, *Jehovah and the World of the Old Testament*, 56).

"In section 74, after quoting 1 Corinthians 7:14 (in verse 1), the Lord proceeded to point out a pitfall in mixed marriages: an 'unbelieving' or non-Christian father, for example, could influence his children to follow the old Mosaic law rather than the gospel of Christ, and thus deprive them of its sanctifying blessings" (Cowan, *Doctrine and Covenants: Our Modern Scripture*, 111–12). ⊕

Doctrine and Covenants 74:6–7. Little Children Are Holy and Are Sanctified through the Atonement

6 That their children might remain without circumcision; and that the tradition might be done away, which saith that little children are unholy; for it was had among the Jews;

7 But little children are holy, being sanctified through the atonement of Jesus Christ; and this is what the scriptures mean.

Why was there a tradition that little children were unholy? (74:6–7) "The controversy among the Jewish people, at the time of the New Testament Apostles (D&C 74:3–4), is further evidence of the apostate condition they were in. The tradition that little children were unholy (v. 6) was a part of the infant baptism doctrine that later crept into the Christian apostasy that followed and is still prevalent today. . . . The same false doctrine led Mormon to write his missionary son, Moroni, concerning the mockery of baptizing little children because little children were alive in Christ (see Moroni 8). The revelation to Joseph [D&C 74] validates Mormon's epistle" (Nyman, *Doctrine and Covenants Commentary*, 2:22, 23). ⊕

Introduction to Doctrine and Covenants 75

Doctrine and Covenants 75 was given at the January 25, 1832, conference held in Amherst, Ohio.

"The Prophet Joseph Smith's history states that during the conference 'the Elders seemed anxious for me to enquire of the Lord, that they might know his will, or learn what would be most pleasing to him, for them to do, in order to bring men to a sense of their condition' (in [Joseph Smith Papers, "History, 1838–1856, volume A-1,"180]). Orson Pratt, who was appointed president of the elders at the conference, later recounted, 'At this Conference the Prophet Joseph was acknowledged President of the High Priesthood, and hands laid on him by Elder Sidney Rigdon who sealed upon his head the blessings which he had formerly received.' Elder Pratt also noted that 'by the request of the Priesthood, the Prophet inquired of the Lord, and a revelation was given and written in the presence of the whole assembly, appointing many of the Elders to missions' (["History of Orson Pratt," *Millennial Star*, vol. 27 (Jan. 28, 1865): 56]). The Prophet dictated two revelations at the conference, which were later combined and are recorded in Doctrine and Covenants 75. The first revelation (D&C 75:1–22) was given to a group of elders who had submitted their names for missionary service. The second revelation (D&C 75:23–36) was given to a group of elders desiring to know the Lord's will concerning them" (*Doctrine and Covenants Student Manual* [2018], 382).

"Two important developments occurred at [this conference]. The previous November, Joseph had received a revelation, now part of section 107 of the Doctrine and Covenants, wherein the Lord told him there should be a president for the high priesthood (see vv. 64–66). At the conference, Joseph was sustained by common consent of the members and was then ordained president of the high priesthood by Sidney Rigdon. The other important development was the reception of section 75 of the Doctrine and Covenants, which called numerous men to serve missions, principally in the eastern part of the United States. These men, who were mostly farmers, served with great sacrifice. They left just before the planting season and were gone during the entire growing season" (Woodford, "Joseph Smith and 'The Vision,' 1832," 101–2).

SECTION 75

Revelation given through Joseph Smith the Prophet, at Amherst, Ohio, January 25, 1832. This section comprises two separate revelations (the first in verses 1 through 22 and the second in verses 23 through 36) given on the same day. The occasion was a conference at which Joseph Smith was sustained and ordained President of the High Priesthood. Certain elders desired to learn more about their immediate duties. These revelations followed.

1 Verily, verily, I say unto you, I who speak even by the voice of my Spirit, even Alpha and Omega, your Lord and your God—

2 Hearken, O ye who have given your names to go forth to proclaim my gospel, and to prune my vineyard.

3 Behold, I say unto you that it is my will that you should go forth and not tarry, neither be idle but labor with your might—

Doctrine and Covenants 75:1–5. Faithful Elders Who Preach the Gospel Will Gain Eternal Life

Why would the Lord command His elders to go forth immediately to proclaim the gospel and not tarry? (75:2–3) "His gospel is the *only* answer when many in the world are stunned with fear [see Luke 21:26]. This underscores the urgent need for us to follow the Lord's instruction to His disciples to 'go . . . into *all* the world, and preach the gospel to *every* creature' [Mark 16:15, emphasis added; see also Matthew 28:19]. We have the sacred responsibility to share the power and peace of Jesus Christ with all who will listen and who will let God prevail in their lives" (Nelson, "Preaching the Gospel of Peace," *Liahona*, May 2022, 6).

4 Lifting up your voices as with the sound of a trump, proclaiming the truth according to the revelations and commandments which I have given you.

5 And thus, if ye are faithful ye shall be laden with many sheaves, and crowned with honor, and glory, and immortality, and eternal life.

6 Therefore, verily I say unto my servant William E. McLellin, I revoke the commission which I gave unto him to go unto the eastern countries;

7 And I give unto him a new commission and a new commandment, in the which I, the Lord, chasten him for the murmurings of his heart;

What "revelations and commandments" were the missionaries to use in proclaiming the truth? (75:4) "At that [January 1832] conference a revelation was given to counsel the elders who had been laboring as missionaries. Not unexpectedly, they had encountered considerable difficulty in their effort to declare the message of the Restoration. They were instructed by the Lord not to tarry or to be idle but rather to labor with their might—lifting up their voices 'as with the sound of a trump, proclaiming the truth according to the revelations and commandments which,' the Lord said, 'I have given you.' That which the Lord had given them was the Book of Mormon....

"Such is the message that we have been commissioned to take to all the earth" (Joseph Fielding McConkie, *Here We Stand*, 72, 73).

What does it mean to be "laden with many sheaves"? (75:5) "Those who go forth in the ministry, faithfully proclaiming the gospel with all their souls, shall be 'laden with sheaves,' or, in other words, reap a harvest of souls....

"*Sheaves* is plural for *sheaf,* to which Webster gives as one definition, 'any collection of things bound together.' In the gospel sense, sheaves are collections of Saints bound together by their faith in the Lord Jesus Christ, the principles and ordinances of His everlasting gospel, the power and authority of the priesthood which makes those saving ordinances possible, and the Church which He established. 'And I will gather my people together as a man gathereth his sheaves,' said the resurrected Lord (3 Ne. 20:18)" (Brewster, *Doctrine & Covenants Encyclopedia* [2012], 516). See also commentary in this volume on Doctrine and Covenants 33:9 and 79:3.

Doctrine and Covenants 75:6–12. Pray to Receive the Comforter, Who Teaches All Things

Why was William E. McLellin's previous calling revoked? (75:6–8) "[William E. McLellin] and Samuel Smith had been called on October 29, 1831, to perform a mission to the 'eastern lands.' That same revelation contained a strong admonition and caution to McLellin: 'Forsake all unrighteousness. Commit not adultery—a temptation with which thou has been troubled' (D&C 66:7–8, 10)....

"Commenting on their minimal term in the field, Elder Smith stated, 'We went a short distance, but because of disobedience, our way was hedged up before us.' Samuel does not elucidate on the nature of that disobedience. . . . Nevertheless, the Lord forgave [William] his errors and called him anew to undertake a proselyting mission to the 'south countries' with Luke Johnson (D&C 75:7–9)" (*Journals of William E. McLellin*, 300, 301).

Why are we to seek the Holy Spirit as we proclaim the gospel? (75:10–11) "When the Savior commanded Joseph Smith and Sidney Rigdon to preach His gospel, He promised them, 'The Holy Ghost shall be shed forth in bearing record unto all things whatsoever ye shall say' (Doctrine and Covenants 100:8; see also Doctrine and Covenants 42:15–17; 50:17–22). The same promise applies to all those who teach the gospel, including you. As you teach the gospel of Jesus Christ, you can have the Holy Ghost with you to guide you and to testify of the truth to the minds and hearts of those you teach (see Doctrine and Covenants 8:2). You are not alone when you teach, for 'it is not ye that speak, but the Holy Ghost' (Mark 13:11)" (*Teaching in the Savior's Way* [2022], 16).

Doctrine and Covenants 75:13–22. Elders Will Sit in Judgment on Those Who Reject Their Message

8 And he sinned; nevertheless, I forgive him and say unto him again, Go ye into the south countries.

9 And let my servant Luke Johnson go with him, and proclaim the things which I have commanded them—

10 Calling on the name of the Lord for the Comforter, which shall teach them all things that are expedient for them—

11 Praying always that they faint not; and inasmuch as they do this, I will be with them even unto the end.

12 Behold, this is the will of the Lord your God concerning you. Even so. Amen.

13 And again, verily thus saith the Lord, let my servant Orson Hyde and my servant Samuel H. Smith take their journey into the eastern countries, and proclaim the things which I have commanded them; and inasmuch as they are faithful, lo, I will be with them even unto the end.

14 And again, verily I say unto my servant Lyman Johnson, and unto my servant Orson Pratt, they shall also take their journey into the eastern countries; and behold, and lo, I am with them also, even unto the end.

15 And again, I say unto my servant Asa Dodds, and unto my servant Calves Wilson, that they also shall take their journey unto the western countries, and proclaim my gospel, even as I have commanded them.

16 And he who is faithful shall overcome all things, and shall be lifted up at the last day.

17 And again, I say unto my servant Major N. Ashley, and my servant Burr Riggs, let them take their journey also into the south country.

18 Yea, let all those take their journey, as I have commanded them, going from house to house, and from village to village, and from city to city.

19 And in whatsoever house ye enter, and they receive you, leave your blessing upon that house.

20 And in whatsoever house ye enter, and they receive you not, ye shall depart speedily from that house, and shake off the dust of your feet as a testimony against them.

21 And you shall be filled with joy and gladness; and know this, that in the day of judgment you shall be judges of that house, and condemn them;

22 And it shall be more tolerable for the heathen in the day of judgment, than for that house; therefore, gird up your loins and be faithful, and ye shall overcome all things, and be lifted up at the last day. Even so. Amen.

23 And again, thus saith the Lord unto you, O ye elders of my church, who have given your names that you might know his will concerning you—

24 Behold, I say unto you, that it is the duty of the church to assist in supporting the families of those, and also to support the families of those who are called and must needs be sent unto the world to proclaim the gospel unto the world.

Why would missionaries shake the dust off their feet? (75:20–22) "The custom of having missionaries cleanse their feet, either by washing or wiping off the dust, as a testimony against the wicked who refused to accept the gospel, was practiced in New Testament times and was reinstituted by the Lord in this dispensation. Because of the serious obligation associated with this act, Church leaders have counseled that it should only be done under the direction of the Spirit. The act appears to be associated with the commandment that the missionaries (and members) are to make certain they are clean from the sins of the wicked" (Daniel H. Ludlow, *Companion to Your Study*, 2:91). See also commentary in this volume on Doctrine and Covenants 24:15 and 99:4.

In what way could missionaries be considered as judges? (75:21) "The missionaries being judges of [a particular] house should not be interpreted to mean they will give a [verdict and ruling], but will stand as witnesses that they did give that house an opportunity to receive the gospel (D&C 75:21). The Lord 'employeth no servant' at the judgment bar, but will have his witnesses to confirm his sentence to a glory (see 2 Nephi 9:41; Mormon 3:18–21; D&C 29:12). Those who are faithful witnesses, or missionaries, will be judged with the same degree of righteousness as they have judged (see JST, Matthew 7:2)" (Nyman, *Doctrine and Covenants Commentary*, 2:16–17).

Doctrine and Covenants 75:23–36. Families of Missionaries Are to Receive Help from the Church

Why was the Church directed to support the families of missionaries? (75:24–26) "In the early years of the Church, many men who were called to serve missions had wives and children who depended on them for support. Accepting the call to serve was a great sacrifice for the whole family. A natural concern for many elders would have been what would happen to their families if they accepted a call to preach the gospel far from home. . . .

"In these verses the Lord said that the Church should help the family when a father or husband accepts the call to leave to serve a mission. Notice in verse 26 what the Lord directed the elders to do if they were able to find a place where their families would be supported" (*Doctrine and Covenants and Church History Study Guide for Home-Study Seminary Students*, 281).

What does it mean to be "diligent in all things"? (75:29) "The Lord's commandment to 'be diligent in all things' (D&C 75:29) included His commandment to those called on missions to arrange for the support of their families while they served. If such arrangements could not be made, those men were obligated to remain at home, care for their families, and labor in the Church locally (see D&C 75:24–28). To be diligent in all things is to give persistent, careful, and energetic effort, especially in serving the Lord and obeying His commandments. The scriptures contain many examples and admonitions regarding diligence. President Dieter F. Uchtdorf of the First Presidency taught, 'Diligently doing the things that matter most will lead us to the Savior of the world' (["Of Things That Matter Most," *Ensign*, Nov. 2010, 21])" (*Doctrine and Covenants Student Manual* [2018], 384).

In what way were these companionships to be "united in the ministry"? (75:30–36) "In one of the most sublime prayers ever offered among men, Jesus makes unity pre-eminent among his followers [see John 17:11, 20–21].

"Unity and its synonyms—harmony, goodwill, peace, concord, mutual understanding—express a condition for which the human heart constantly yearns. Its opposites are discord, contention, strife, confusion. . . .

25 Wherefore, I, the Lord, give unto you this commandment, that ye obtain places for your families, inasmuch as your brethren are willing to open their hearts.

26 And let all such as can obtain places for their families, and support of the church for them, not fail to go into the world, whether to the east or to the west, or to the north, or to the south.

27 Let them ask and they shall receive, knock and it shall be opened unto them, and be made known from on high, even by the Comforter, whither they shall go.

28 And again, verily I say unto you, that every man who is obliged to provide for his own family, let him provide, and he shall in nowise lose his crown; and let him labor in the church.

29 Let every man be diligent in all things. And the idler shall not have place in the church, except he repent and mend his ways.

30 Wherefore, let my servant Simeon Carter and my servant Emer Harris be united in the ministry;

31 And also my servant Ezra Thayre and my servant Thomas B. Marsh;

32 Also my servant Hyrum Smith and my servant Reynolds Cahoon;

33 And also my servant Daniel Stanton and my servant Seymour Brunson;

34 And also my servant Sylvester Smith and my servant Gideon Carter;

35 And also my servant Ruggles Eames and my servant Stephen Burnett;

36 And also my servant Micah B. Welton and also my servant Eden Smith. Even so. Amen.

"May the appeal of our Lord in his intercessory prayer for unity be realized in our homes, our wards and stakes. . . .

"Unity of purpose, with all working in harmony, is needed to accomplish God's work" (*David O. McKay* [manual], 41).

Introduction to Doctrine and Covenants 76

"On 16 February 1832, [Joseph Smith] and Sidney Rigdon saw a vision 'concerning the economy of God and his vast creation throughout all eternity,' likely while in the upstairs bedroom of the John and Alice (Elsa) Jacobs Johnson home in Hiram, Ohio. This vision came after [the Prophet] returned from the January conference in Amherst, Ohio, and after he resumed his work of revising the New Testament at the Johnson home, with Rigdon working as scribe. According to a later [Joseph Smith] history, revelations [Joseph] had dictated up to February 1832 showed 'that many important points, touching the salvation of man, had been taken from the Bible, or lost before it was compiled.' Included in these 'important points' was information on what happens after death. This information led [Joseph] to think 'that if God rewarded every one according to the deeds done in the body, the term "heaven," . . . must include more kingdoms than one' [Joseph Smith Papers, "History, 1838–1856, volume A-1," 183]. According to the description of the vision, on 16 February 1832, [the prophet] and [Sidney] reviewed John 5:29, wherein Jesus Christ prophesies that the dead will 'come forth; they that have done good, unto the resurrection of life; and they that have done evil, unto the resurrection of damnation.' They reported that when they pondered this verse they together beheld a vision of what awaited humankind after death" (Joseph Smith Papers, Historical Introduction to "Vision, 16 February 1832 [D&C 76]").

"The highlight of the section is a vision of the Father and the Son, the premortal life, and Lucifer's fall. The vision of the two supreme members of the Godhead was rich and glorious. . . . So powerful was the vision of what they both saw and heard, they chose to bear testimony of the Savior, a testimony declaring 'that he lives! For we saw him, even on the right hand of God; and we heard the voice bearing record that he is the Only Begotten of the Father' (D&C 76:22–23)" (Baugh, "Parting the Veil," 281).

President Wilford Woodruff taught, "I will refer to the 'Vision' [in section 76] alone, as a revelation which gives more light, more truth and more principle than any revelation contained in any other book we ever read. It makes plain to our understanding our present condition, where we came from, why we are here, and where we are going to. Any man may know through that revelation what his part and condition will be. For all men know what laws they keep, and the laws that men keep here will determine their position hereafter; they will be preserved by those laws and receive the blessings that belong to them" (*Wilford Woodruff* [manual], 120–21).

SECTION 76

A vision given to Joseph Smith the Prophet and Sidney Rigdon, at Hiram, Ohio, February 16, 1832. Prefacing the record of this vision, Joseph Smith's history states: "Upon my return from Amherst conference, I resumed the translation of the Scriptures. From sundry revelations which had been received, it was apparent that many important points touching the salvation of man had been taken from the Bible, or lost before it was compiled. It appeared self-evident from what truths were left, that if God rewarded every one according to the deeds done in the body the term 'Heaven,' as intended for the Saints' eternal home, must include more kingdoms than one. Accordingly, . . . while translating St. John's Gospel, myself and Elder Rigdon saw the following vision." At the time this vision was given, the Prophet was translating John 5:29.

Doctrine and Covenants 76:1–4. The Lord Is God

Why would this revelation address the heavens and the earth? (76:1) "The vision of the degrees of glory begins by saying, 'Hear, O ye heavens, and give ear, O earth' (D&C 76:1). In other words, in that revelation the Lord was announcing truth to heaven and to earth because those principles of salvation operate on both sides of the veil; and salvation is administered to an extent here to men, and it is administered to another extent in the spirit world. We correlate and combine our activities and do certain things for the salvation of men while we are in mortality, and then certain things are done for the salvation of men while they are in the spirit world awaiting the day of the Resurrection" (Bruce R. McConkie, "All Are Alike unto God," 4). ☉

What assurance do we have that the Lord's purposes will not fail? (76:3) President Boyd K. Packer testified: "The Church of Jesus Christ of Latter-day Saints will go forward 'until it has filled the whole earth' (D&C 65:2) and the great Jehovah announces that His work is done (see [Joseph Smith Papers, 'History, 1838–1856, volume C-1,' 1285]). The Church is a safe harbor. We will be protected by justice and comforted by mercy (see Alma 34:15–16). No unhallowed hand can stay the progress of this work (see D&C 76:3)" ("Do Not Fear," *Ensign*, May 2004, 80).

President Russell M. Nelson also stated: "We will see miraculous indications that God the Father and His Son, Jesus Christ, preside over this Church in majesty and glory" ("Revelation for the Church, Revelation for Our Lives," *Ensign*, May 2018, 96).

1 Hear, O ye heavens, and give ear, O earth, and rejoice ye inhabitants thereof, for the Lord is God, and beside him there is no Savior.

2 Great is his wisdom, marvelous are his ways, and the extent of his doings none can find out.

3 His purposes fail not, neither are there any who can stay his hand.

4 From eternity to eternity he is the same, and his years never fail.

What does the phrase "from eternity to eternity" mean? (76:4) "In both Hebrew and Greek the words for 'eternity' (*'olam* and *aion*, respectively) denote neither an endless linear time nor a state outside of time, but rather 'an age,' an 'epoch,' 'a long time,' 'world,' or some other such term—even 'a lifetime,' or 'a generation'—always a measurable *period* of time rather than *endless* time or timelessness" (Robinson, "Eternities That Come and Go," 1).

"From eternity to eternity means from the spirit existence through the probation which we are in, and then back again to the eternal existence which will follow" (Joseph Fielding Smith, *Doctrines of Salvation*, 1:12; styling altered).

Doctrine and Covenants 76:5–10. The Mysteries of the Kingdom Will Be Revealed to All the Faithful

5 For thus saith the Lord—I, the Lord, am merciful and gracious unto those who fear me, and delight to honor those who serve me in righteousness and in truth unto the end.

6 Great shall be their reward and eternal shall be their glory.

In what ways will the Lord be merciful and gracious to those who serve Him? (76:5) "Upon receiving eternal life, whatever the deprivations [shortcomings] of the faithful will have been in mortality, fulness will follow. Mortal deprivations will give way to God's celestial benefactions [blessings]. And He does not give grudgingly. Being a perfect Father, He delights to honor those who serve Him (see D&C 76:5)" (Maxwell, *Wonderful Flood of Light*, 58). ⊕

7 And to them will I reveal all mysteries, yea, all the hidden mysteries of my kingdom from days of old, and for ages to come, will I make known unto them the good pleasure of my will concerning all things pertaining to my kingdom.

8 Yea, even the wonders of eternity shall they know, and things to come will I show them, even the things of many generations.

9 And their wisdom shall be great, and their understanding reach to heaven; and before them the wisdom of the wise shall perish, and the understanding of the prudent shall come to naught.

How are the mysteries of God revealed? (76:7) "Mysteries of God are spiritual truths known only by revelation. God reveals His mysteries to those who are obedient to the gospel. Some of God's mysteries are yet to be revealed" (Guide to the Scriptures, "Mysteries of God").

The Book of Mormon prophet, Alma, taught that those who seek to know God's mysteries and harden not their hearts, it will be "given unto [them] to know the mysteries of God until [they] know them in full" (Alma 12:10).

Similarly, Ammon reasoned with his brethren, "Yea, he that repenteth and exerciseth faith, and bringeth forth good works, and prayeth continually without ceasing—unto such it is given to know the mysteries of God; yea, unto such it shall be given to reveal all things which never have been revealed" (Alma 26:22). See also commentary in this volume on Doctrine and Covenants 101:32–34; 121:27–28; and 121:28–32.

How can the Lord's Spirit enlighten a person? (76:10) "Remember the Lord's promise: 'I will impart unto you of my Spirit, which shall enlighten your mind, which shall fill your soul with joy' [D&C 11:13]. . . . Joy that fills our souls brings with it an eternal perspective in contrast to day-to-day living. That joy comes as peace amidst hardship or heartache. It provides comfort and courage, unfolds the truths of the gospel, and expands our love for the Lord and all God's children. Although the need for such blessings is so great, in many ways the world has forgotten and forsaken them" (Rasband, "Let the Holy Spirit Guide," *Ensign*, May 2017, 93).

Doctrine and Covenants 76:11–17. All Will Come Forth in the Resurrection of the Just or the Unjust

How does the Spirit open our eyes of understanding? (76:12) "When the power of the Holy Ghost descends directly upon an individual, the mortal veil that normally covers sight and understanding can be temporarily drawn aside, allowing them to see and participate in things beyond this natural world. It is only in this way—through the personal and protective indwelling of the Spirit—that human beings can see God and survive the experience (see vv. 116–18; D&C 67:11; Moses 1:11)" (Robinson and Garrett, *Commentary of the Doctrine and Covenants*, 2:290). ❂

10 For by my Spirit will I enlighten them, and by my power will I make known unto them the secrets of my will—yea, even those things which eye has not seen, nor ear heard, nor yet entered into the heart of man.

11 We, Joseph Smith, Jun., and Sidney Rigdon, being in the Spirit on the sixteenth day of February, in the year of our Lord one thousand eight hundred and thirty-two—

12 By the power of the Spirit our eyes were opened and our understandings were enlightened, so as to see and understand the things of God—

Eyewitness Testimony of the Vision (Doctrine and Covenants 76:11)

Joseph and Sidney were not alone when they received Doctrine and Covenants 76. One of those present was Philo Dibble. Sixty years later, he recalled:

"During the time that Joseph and Sidney were in the spirit and saw the heavens open, there were other men in the room, perhaps twelve, among whom I was one during a part of the time—probably two-thirds of the time,—I saw the glory and felt the power, but did not see the vision.

"The events and conversation, while they were seeing what is written (and many things were seen and related that are not written), I will relate as minutely as is necessary.

"Joseph would, at intervals, say: 'What do I see?' as one might say while looking out the window and beholding that all in the room could not see. Then he would relate what he had seen or what he was looking at. Then Sidney replied, 'I see the same.' Presently Sidney would say 'what do I see?' and would repeat what he had seen or was seeing, and Joseph would reply, 'I see the same.'

"'This manner of conversation was repeated at short intervals to the end of the vision, and during the whole time not a word was spoken by any other person. Not a sound nor motion made by anyone but Joseph and Sidney, and it seemed to me that they never moved a joint or limb during the time I was there, which I think was over an hour, and to the end of the vision.

"'Joseph sat firmly and calmly all the time in the midst of a magnificent glory, but Sidney sat limp and pale, apparently as limber as a rag, observing which, Joseph remarked, smilingly, 'Sidney is not used to it as I am'" (in *Juvenile Instructor*, Vol. 27, No. 10:303–4).

13 Even those things which were from the beginning before the world was, which were ordained of the Father, through his Only Begotten Son, who was in the bosom of the Father, even from the beginning;

14 Of whom we bear record; and the record which we bear is the fulness of the gospel of Jesus Christ, who is the Son, whom we saw and with whom we conversed in the heavenly vision.

15 For while we were doing the work of translation, which the Lord had appointed unto us, we came to the twenty-ninth verse of the fifth chapter of John, which was given unto us as follows—

16 Speaking of the resurrection of the dead, concerning those who shall hear the voice of the Son of Man:

17 And shall come forth; they who have done good, in the resurrection of the just; and they who have done evil, in the resurrection of the unjust.

18 Now this caused us to marvel, for it was given unto us of the Spirit.

19 And while we meditated upon these things, the Lord touched the eyes of our understandings and they were opened, and the glory of the Lord shone round about.

What do we learn from Joseph Smith's testimony of Jesus Christ? (76:13–14) "The fulness of Joseph Smith's testimony of Christ embraces all that the Prophet revealed, all that he taught, and all that he understood about the Only Begotten of the Father. Thus Joseph Smith becomes the great revelator, testator, and teacher of Christ for this dispensation. No man of whom we have record has revealed and taught more truth about Christ than Joseph Smith. The composite of all that he taught constitutes his testimony of Christ. This revelation (D&C 76) adds substantially to that testimony" (McConkie and Ostler, *Revelations of the Restoration*, 519).

What is noteworthy about the word *unjust* in these verses? (76:15–17) "The vision of the three degrees of glory, the lowest of which 'surpasses all understanding' [D&C 76:89], is a direct refutation of the then strong but erroneous doctrine that the majority would be doomed to hell and damnation.

"When you realize Joseph Smith was only 26 years old, had a limited education, and had little or no exposure to the classical languages from which the Bible was translated, he was truly an instrument in the Lord's hands. In the 17th verse of section 76, he was inspired to use the word *unjust* instead of *damnation* that was used in the Gospel of John [see John 5:29]" (Quentin L. Cook, "Conversion to the Will of God," *Liahona,* May 2022, 55). ☉

Doctrine and Covenants 76:18–24. The Inhabitants of Many Worlds Are Begotten Sons and Daughters unto God through the Atonement of Jesus Christ

What influence did meditating have on Joseph's ability to receive revelation? (76:18–19) "The vision came as a prophet and his scribe were *marveling* and *meditating* upon a gospel truth, which in this case they had just learned through the spirit of revelation. This seems to be a pattern. It is interesting to note how many of the great recorded visions through the ages came while prophets were engaged in 'pondering,' 'reflecting,' or 'meditating' upon some principle brought to their attention by the scriptures and the Spirit" (Dahl, "Vision of the Glories," 283).

President David O. McKay taught: "Meditation is the language of the soul. It is defined as 'a form of private devotion or spiritual exercise, consisting in deep, continued reflection on some religious theme.' . . .

"Meditation is one of the most secret, most sacred doors through which we pass into the presence of the Lord" (*David O. McKay* [manual], 31–32). ●

What did the Lord teach in the various visions that followed? (76:19) "The revelation contained in the 76th section provides a glorious vision of the degrees of glory where the vast majority of Heavenly Father's children who were valiant in their premortal estate are profoundly blessed following the ultimate judgment" (Quentin L. Cook, "Conversion to the Will of God," *Liahona*, May 2022, 55).

"First Vision—the Throne of God [D&C 76:19–24]. . . .

"Second Vision—the Fall of Satan [D&C 76:25–29]. . . .

"Third Vision—the Sons of Perdition [D&C 76:30–49]. . . .

"Fourth Vision—the Celestial Kingdom [D&C 76:50–70, 92–96]. . . .

"Fifth Vision—the Terrestrial Kingdom [D&C 76:71–80, 91, 97]. . . .

"Sixth Vision—the Telestial Kingdom [D&C 76:81–90, 98–113]" (Nyman, *Doctrine and Covenants Commentary*, 2:42, 44, 46, 50, 54, 56).

20 And we beheld the glory of the Son, on the right hand of the Father, and received of his fulness;

21 And saw the holy angels, and them who are sanctified before his throne, worshiping God, and the Lamb, who worship him forever and ever.

How Was Joseph and Sidney's Vision Similar to Visions of Other Prophets? (D&C 76:20–21)

"John's vision of God and the Lamb fits the ancient pattern of how God called his prophets. His vision in chapters 4 and 5 of the book of Revelation is consistent with the test of prophetic authenticity. Joseph Smith's own story parallels the prophetic motif. John and Joseph Smith experienced similar visions. John received a sealed book and Joseph received the gold plates, a part of which were sealed. They each saw Heavenly Father and his Son Jesus Christ sitting on the throne surrounded by sanctified beings giving them honor and glory forever and ever, in preparation for their prophetic service to the world" (Fowles, "John's Prophetic Vision," 81). See also Doctrine and Covenants 109:79 and 137:1–3.

Joseph Fielding McConkie explained: "The three clearest illustrations of prophetic experience with the [heavenly] council of the Lord are Micaiah, Isaiah, and Ezekiel. . . .

"Micaiah stated the authority for his message: 'I saw the Lord sitting on his throne, and all the host of heaven standing by him on his right hand and on his left' [1 Kings 22:19]. . . .

"The second clear prophetic experience with the Lord and his [Heavenly] council is found in Isaiah 6. This is the account of Isaiah's call to the ministry. As the account opens, Isaiah sees the Lord sitting upon his throne, surrounded by seraphim who are rendering expressions of praise to the Lord. . . .

"The third prophet who experienced and recorded a vision of the type experienced by Micaiah and Isaiah was Ezekiel . . . Ezekiel saw the Lord sitting upon a throne surrounded by heavenly beings. . . .

"And finally, what of the Prophet Joseph Smith? . . . We cite but one illustration, Doctrine and Covenants 76. Joseph Smith and Sidney Rigdon, being in the Spirit on the sixteenth day of February 1832, declared that by the power of the Spirit their eyes were opened to see the things of God—'Even those things which were from the beginning before the world was, which were ordained of the Father.' The glory of the Lord shone upon them and they saw 'the Son, on the right hand of the Father, . . . and saw the holy angels, and them who are sanctified before his throne, worshiping God, and the Lamb' [D&C 76:13, 20–21]" ("Premortal Existence, Foreordinations, and Heavenly Councils," 187, 188, 190, 194).

22 And now, after the many testimonies which have been given of him, this is the testimony, last of all, which we give of him: That he lives!

23 For we saw him, even on the right hand of God; and we heard the voice bearing record that he is the Only Begotten of the Father—

24 That by him, and through him, and of him, the worlds are and were created, and the inhabitants thereof are begotten sons and daughters unto God.

25 And this we saw also, and bear record, that an angel of God who was in authority in the presence of God, who rebelled against the Only Begotten Son whom the Father loved and who was in the bosom of the Father, was thrust down from the presence of God and the Son,

26 And was called Perdition, for the heavens wept over him—he was Lucifer, a son of the morning.

27 And we beheld, and lo, he is fallen! is fallen, even a son of the morning!

28 And while we were yet in the Spirit, the Lord commanded us that we should write the vision; for we beheld Satan, that old serpent, even the devil, who rebelled against God, and sought to take the kingdom of our God and his Christ—

What does this phrase "last of all" mean? (76:22–23) "'Last of all' . . . does not mean there will be no future testimonies born of him, rather that these brethren could now add their personal witness to all former testimonies that had been born to that time" (Dahl, "Vision of the Glories," 283).

For example, President Spencer W. Kimball added his testimony: "'I know that God lives. I know that Jesus Christ lives,' said John Taylor, my predecessor, 'for I have seen him.' I bear this testimony to you brethren in the name of Jesus Christ. Amen" ("Strengthening the Family," *Ensign*, May 1978, 48). ⊕

What do we know about the inhabitants on other worlds created by Jesus Christ? (76:24) President Russell M. Nelson declared: "This earth is but one of many creations over which God presides. 'Worlds without number have I created,' He said. 'And I also created them for mine own purpose; and by the Son I created them, which is mine Only Begotten.' Grand as it is, planet Earth is part of something even grander— that great plan of God. . . .

"Though our understanding of the Creation is limited, we know enough to appreciate its supernal significance. And that store of knowledge will be augmented in the future. Scripture declares: 'In that day when the Lord shall come [again], he shall reveal all things'" ("Creation," *Ensign*, May 2000, 85). ⊕

Doctrine and Covenants 76:25–29. An Angel of God Fell and Became the Devil

What do the various names used for Satan reveal about him? (76:25–27) "The titles given [Satan] in section 76 are revealing. That he was called 'Perdition' explains why the heavens wept over him. According to the dictionary, the word means to destroy, utter destruction, ruin, loss, eternal damnation, hell. . . . Lucifer means a torch bearer. As Isaiah also said, 'he was Lucifer, a son of the morning' (Isaiah 14:12). A 'son of the morning' is usually interpreted to mean he was one of the early born of the spirit children of Elohim. Thus, as one of the older of the children of God and being in a position of authority, the title of Lucifer implies he was not only rebelling against God but was leading others to do likewise; therefore, he is designated a torch bearer or crusader against God" (Nyman, *Doctrine and Covenants Commentary*, 2:45). ⊕

How does Satan make war with the saints of God? (76:29) "There are forces at play today designed to deliberately lead us away from absolute truth. These deceptions and lies go far beyond innocent mistaken identity and often have dire, not minor, consequences.

"Satan, the father of lies and the great deceiver, would have us question things as they really are and either ignore eternal truths or replace them with something that appears more pleasing. 'He maketh war with the saints of God' [D&C 76:29] and has spent millennia calculating and practicing the ability to persuade God's children to believe that *good is evil* and *evil is good*" (Stevenson, "Deceive Me Not," *Ensign*, Nov. 2019, 94). ⊕

Doctrine and Covenants 76:30–49. Sons of Perdition Suffer Eternal Damnation; All Others Gain Some Degree of Salvation

What leads a person to become a "son of perdition"? (76:31–36) The Prophet Joseph Smith explained in his King Follet discourse: "All sins shall be forgiven except the sin against the Holy Ghost: after a man has sinned against the Holy Ghost there is no repentance for him, he has got to say that the sun does not shine, while he sees it, he has got to deny Jesus Christ when the heavens were open to him, and from that time they begin to be enemies, . . . [They have] the same spirit that they had who crucified the Lord of Life: the same spirit that sins against the Holy Ghost. You cannot bring them to repentance" (Joseph Smith Papers, "Discourse, 7 April 1844, as Published in *Times and Seasons*," 616).

Why are the sons of perdition doomed? (76:32–33) "Peter said, 'It had been better for them not to have known the way of righteousness, than, after they have known it to turn from the holy commandment delivered unto them' [2 Pet. 2:20–21], and John called it a sin unto death [see 1 John 5:16]. It is a sin unto death, for it brings a spiritual banishment—the second death—by which those who partake of it are denied the presence of God and are consigned to dwell with the devil and his angels throughout eternity.

"All who partake of this, the greatest of sins . . . learn to hate the truth with an eternal hatred, and they learn to love wickedness. They reach a condition where they will not and cannot repent" (Joseph Fielding Smith, *Doctrines of Salvation*, 1:48–49).

29 Wherefore, he maketh war with the saints of God, and encompasseth them round about.

30 And we saw a vision of the sufferings of those with whom he made war and overcame, for thus came the voice of the Lord unto us:

31 Thus saith the Lord concerning all those who know my power, and have been made partakers thereof, and suffered themselves through the power of the devil to be overcome, and to deny the truth and defy my power—

32 They are they who are the sons of perdition, of whom I say that it had been better for them never to have been born;

33 For they are vessels of wrath, doomed to suffer the wrath of God, with the devil and his angels in eternity;

34 Concerning whom I have said there is no forgiveness in this world nor in the world to come—

35 Having denied the Holy Spirit after having received it, and having denied the Only Begotten Son of the Father, having crucified him unto themselves and put him to an open shame.

36 These are they who shall go away into the lake of fire and brimstone, with the devil and his angels—

37 And the only ones on whom the second death shall have any power;

38 Yea, verily, the only ones who shall not be redeemed in the due time of the Lord, after the sufferings of his wrath.

39 For all the rest shall be brought forth by the resurrection of the dead, through the triumph and the glory of the Lamb, who was slain, who was in the bosom of the Father before the worlds were made.

40 And this is the gospel, the glad tidings, which the voice out of the heavens bore record unto us—

41 That he came into the world, even Jesus, to be crucified for the world, and to bear the sins of the world, and to sanctify the world, and to cleanse it from all unrighteousness;

42 That through him all might be saved whom the Father had put into his power and made by him;

43 Who glorifies the Father, and saves all the works of his hands, except those sons of perdition who deny the Son after the Father has revealed him.

What is the second death and who suffers it? (76:37–39) "Those who have willfully rebelled against the light and truth of the gospel will suffer spiritual death. This death is often called the second death" (Guide to the Scriptures, "Death, Spiritual").

"The followers of Satan [sons of Perdition] who will suffer with him in eternity . . . include (1) those who followed Satan and were cast out of heaven for rebellion during premortality and (2) those who were permitted to be born to this world with physical bodies but then served Satan and turned utterly against God. Those in this second group will be resurrected from the dead but will not be redeemed from the second (spiritual) death and cannot dwell in a kingdom of glory (D&C 88:32, 35)" (Guide to the Scriptures, "Sons of Perdition").

What is the essence of the gospel? (76:40–41) The Prophet Joseph Smith affirmed: "The fundamental principles of our religion is the testimony of the apostles and prophets concerning Jesus Christ, 'that he died, was buried, and rose again the third day, and ascended up into heaven;' and all other things are only appendages to these, which pertain to our religion" (Joseph Smith Papers, "Questions and Answers, 8 May 1838," 44). ⊕

Who will be saved through the atonement of Jesus Christ? (76:42) "[Jesus Christ's] atonement is infinite—without an end. It was also infinite in that all humankind would be saved from never-ending death. . . . It was infinite in scope—it was to be done once for all [see Heb. 10:10]. And the mercy of the Atonement extends not only to an infinite number of people, but also to an infinite number or worlds created by Him [see D&C 76:24; Moses 1:33]. It was infinite beyond any human scale of measurement or mortal comprehension.

"Jesus was the only one who could offer such an infinite atonement, since He was born of a mortal mother and immortal Father. Because of the unique birthright, Jesus was an infinite Being" (Nelson, "Atonement," *Ensign*, Nov. 1996, 35). ⊕

How does the Lord save "all the works of his hands"? (76:43) "Modern revelation teaches that God has provided a plan for a mortal experience in which all can choose obedience to seek His highest blessings or make choices that lead to one of the less glorious kingdoms [see D&C 76:71–113]. Because of God's great love for all of His children, those lesser kingdoms are still more wonderful than mortals can comprehend [see D&C 76:89]. The Atonement of

Jesus Christ makes all of this possible, as He 'glorifies the Father, and *saves all the works of his hands*' [D&C 76:43; emphasis added]" (Oaks, "*Two* Great Commandments," *Ensign*, Nov. 2019, 75).

Why is it called an "eternal punishment"? (76:44)
The Lord revealed previously why His punishment is eternal, "For, behold, the mystery of godliness, how great is it! For, behold, I am endless, and the punishment which is given from my hand is endless punishment, for Endless is my name. Wherefore—Eternal punishment is God's punishment. Endless punishment is God's punishment" (D&C 19:10–12).

"We learn from the *Doctrine and Covenants* that eternal punishment, or everlasting punishment, does not mean that a man condemned will endure this punishment forever, but it is everlasting and eternal because it is God's punishment, and he is Everlasting and Eternal [D&C 19:4–12]" (Joseph Fielding Smith, *Doctrines of Salvation*, 2:160). See also commentary in this volume on Doctrine and Covenants 19:10.

What has the Lord revealed regarding the fate of the sons of perdition? (76:44–49) In a response to a letter from W. W. Phelps, Joseph Smith answered a question regarding sons of perdition and had a clerk record it: "God will bring every transgressor into Judgment. . . . [The] Lord never authorized [any

44 Wherefore, he saves all except them—they shall go away into everlasting punishment, which is endless punishment, which is eternal punishment, to reign with the devil and his angels in eternity, where their worm dieth not, and the fire is not quenched, which is their torment—

45 And the end thereof, neither the place thereof, nor their torment, no man knows;

46 Neither was it revealed, neither is, neither will be revealed unto man, except to them who are made partakers thereof;

47 Nevertheless, I, the Lord, show it by vision unto many, but straightway shut it up again;

"Through Him All Might Be Saved Whom the Father Had Put into His Power" (D&C 76:42)

President Boyd K. Packer related: "Some years ago I was in Washington, D.C., with President Harold B. Lee. Early one morning he called me to come into his hotel room. He was sitting in his robe reading *Gospel Doctrine*, by President Joseph F. Smith, and he said, 'Listen to this!

"'"Jesus had not finished his work when his body was slain, neither did he finish it after his resurrection from the dead; although he had accomplished the purpose for which he then came to the earth, he had not fulfilled all his work. And when will he? Not until he has redeemed and saved every son and daughter of our father Adam that have been or ever will be born upon this earth to the end of time, except the sons of perdition. That is his mission. We will not finish *our* work until we have saved ourselves, and then not until we shall have saved all depending upon us; for we are to become saviors upon Mount Zion, as well as Christ. We are called to this mission" [*Gospel Doctrine*, 442; emphasis added].'

"'There is never a time,' the Prophet Joseph Smith taught, 'when the spirit is too old to approach God. *All are within the reach of pardoning mercy, who have not committed the unpardonable sin* [*Joseph Smith* (manual), 76; emphasis added].'

"And so we pray, and we fast, and we plead, and we implore. We love those who wander, and we never give up hope.

"I bear witness of Christ and of the power of His atonement" ("Brilliant Morning of Forgiveness," *Ensign*, Nov. 1995, 20–21).

President Boyd K. Packer said earlier in this same address, "I repeat, save for the exception of the very few who defect to perdition, there is no habit, no addiction, no rebellion, no transgression, no apostasy, no crime exempted from the promise of complete forgiveness. That is the promise of the atonement of Christ" ("Brilliant Morning of Forgiveness," *Ensign*, Nov. 1995, 20).

48 Wherefore, the end, the width, the height, the depth, and the misery thereof, they understand not, neither any man except those who are ordained unto this condemnation.

49 And we heard the voice, saying: Write the vision, for lo, this is the end of the vision of the sufferings of the ungodly.

50 And again we bear record—for we saw and heard, and this is the testimony of the gospel of Christ concerning them who shall come forth in the resurrection of the just—

51 They are they who received the testimony of Jesus, and believed on his name and were baptized after the manner of his burial, being buried in the water in his name, and this according to the commandment which he has given—

52 That by keeping the commandments they might be washed and cleansed from all their sins, and receive the Holy Spirit by the laying on of the hands of him who is ordained and sealed unto this power;

person] to say that the Devil nor his Angels nor the sons of perdition should ever be restored[,] for their state of destiny was not revealed to man, [and] is not revealed nor ever shall be revealed save to those who are made partakers thereof[. Consequently] those who teach this doctrine have not received it of the spirit of the Lord" (Joseph Smith Papers, "Letterbook 1," 48; spelling modernized).

Doctrine and Covenants 76:50–70. The Glory and Reward of Exalted Beings in the Celestial Kingdom Is Described

---

Vision of the Celestial Kingdom (Doctrine and Covenants 76:50–70, 92–96)

"The Lord compared celestial glory to that of the sun, 'even the glory of God, the highest of all' (D&C 76:70; see also v. 96). Those who inherit this kingdom . . . :

- Receive a testimony of Jesus and believe on His name (see v. 51).
- Be baptized by immersion (see v. 51).
- Receive the Holy Ghost by the laying on of hands (see v. 52).
- Obey the commandments and be washed and cleansed of all sins (see v. 52).
- Overcome by faith (see v. 53).
- Be sealed by the Holy Spirit of Promise (see v. 53).

"Those who qualify for the celestial kingdom will receive, among other blessings:

- Be of a company of angels, of the general assembly and church of Enoch and of the Firstborn (see vv. 54, 67).
- Receive the fulness, glory, and grace of the Father (see vv. 55, 56, 94).
- Be priests and kings of the Most High God (see vv. 56–59).
- Overcome all things (see v. 60).
- Dwell forever in the presence of Heavenly Father and Jesus Christ (see v. 62).
- Be with Christ at the time of His Second Coming (see v. 63).
- Come forth in the First Resurrection (see vv. 64–65).
- Go up unto Mount Zion and unto the heavenly city of God (see v. 66).
- Minister to terrestrial and telestial beings (see vv. 87–88).
- Be able to have offspring, or in other words, gain the right to become eternal parents (see D&C 131:4)"
  (Maldonado, "Messages from the Doctrine and Covenants," *Ensign*, Apr. 2005, 63–64).

What is the "Holy Spirit of promise"? (76:53)
"The Holy Spirit of Promise is the ratifying power of
the Holy Ghost. When sealed by the Holy Spirit of
Promise, an ordinance, vow, or covenant is binding on
earth and in heaven. (See D&C 132:7.) Receiving this
'stamp of approval' from the Holy Ghost is the result
of faithfulness, integrity, and steadfastness in honoring gospel covenants 'in [the] process of time' (Moses
7:21). However, this sealing can be forfeited through
unrighteousness and transgression.

"Purifying and sealing by the Holy Spirit of
Promise constitute the culminating steps in the pro-
cess of being born again" (Bednar, "Ye Must Be Born
Again," *Ensign*, May 2007, 22). ⊕

**What does it mean to be part of the church of the
Firstborn? (76:54–55)** The Church of the Firstborn
"has reference to those who inherit the fulness of
salvation and exaltation. They belong not only to the
Church of Jesus Christ (who himself is the Firstborn),
but they constitute a church, the membership of
which consists only of those who are exalted and thus
have the *inheritance* of the firstborn. They are joint
heirs with Jesus in all that the Father has and are thus
the Church consisting of the firstborn. This is what the
gospel does for those who obey it fully; it causes them
to be born again and gives them an adoption in the
eternal patriarchal family so that they have an inheritance as the firstborn even though they are younger in
actual chronology (see also Gal. 3:26–27)" (Matthews,
"Olive Leaf," 342). See also commentary in this volume
on Doctrine and Covenants 78:21 and 93:21–22.

**What is the priesthood "after the order of Enoch"?
(76:57)** "Joseph Smith's translation of Genesis 14
indicates how Melchizedek was 'after the order of
Enoch.' Verse 34 indicates that Melchizedek followed
Enoch's example, leading a Zion-like community
that obtained a place in heaven. The Lord further explained that both Melchizedek and Enoch were 'after
the order of the Only Begotten Son' (D&C 76:57). This
relationship was reflected in the original name of the
higher priesthood (see D&C 107:3)" (Cowan, *Answers
to Your Questions*, 89).

Elder Bruce R. McConkie taught: "The holy priesthood did more to perfect men in the days of Enoch
than at any other time. Known then as the order of
Enoch (see D&C 76:57), it was the power by which he
and his people were translated. And they were translated because they had faith and exercised the power
of the priesthood" ("Doctrine of the Priesthood,"
Ensign, May 1982, 32). See also commentary in this
volume on Doctrine and Covenants 107:2–4.

53 And who overcome by faith, and are
sealed by the Holy Spirit of promise, which
the Father sheds forth upon all those who are
just and true.

54 They are they who are the church of the
Firstborn.

55 They are they into whose hands the Father
has given all things—

56 They are they who are priests and kings,
who have received of his fulness, and of his
glory;

57 And are priests of the Most High, after
the order of Melchizedek, which was after the
order of Enoch, which was after the order of
the Only Begotten Son.

58 Wherefore, as it is written, they are gods, even the sons of God—

59 Wherefore, all things are theirs, whether life or death, or things present, or things to come, all are theirs and they are Christ's, and Christ is God's.

60 And they shall overcome all things.

61 Wherefore, let no man glory in man, but rather let him glory in God, who shall subdue all enemies under his feet.

62 These shall dwell in the presence of God and his Christ forever and ever.

63 These are they whom he shall bring with him, when he shall come in the clouds of heaven to reign on the earth over his people.

64 These are they who shall have part in the first resurrection.

65 These are they who shall come forth in the resurrection of the just.

66 These are they who are come unto Mount Zion, and unto the city of the living God, the heavenly place, the holiest of all.

67 These are they who have come to an innumerable company of angels, to the general assembly and church of Enoch, and of the Firstborn.

68 These are they whose names are written in heaven, where God and Christ are the judge of all.

69 These are they who are just men made perfect through Jesus the mediator of the new covenant, who wrought out this perfect atonement through the shedding of his own blood.

What are the ultimate rewards for faithfulness? (76:58–59) In a doctrinal exposition by the First Presidency and the Twelve dated June 30, 1916, we learn: "Those who have been born unto God through obedience to the Gospel may by valiant devotion to righteousness obtain exaltation and even reach the status of Godhood" (*Messages of the First Presidency*, 5:31).

President Gordon B. Hinckley testified: "These are not, I submit, the words of Joseph Smith the man [see D&C 76:50–51, 55–56, 70]. They are words of divine revelation that speak of the glorious opportunity, the promised blessings made possible by the Son of God through His divine atonement in behalf of all who will listen and obey. These words are the promise of the Redeemer of the world, who rules and reigns in that celestial kingdom and who invites us to qualify ourselves to come into His presence" ("My Testimony," *Ensign*, Nov. 1993, 52).

Who will dwell in the presence of God forever? (76:62) "In the 'celestial' glory [1 Cor. 15:40] there are three levels [D&C 131:1], of which the highest is exaltation in the celestial kingdom. This is the dwelling of those 'who have received of his fulness, and of his glory,' wherefore, 'they are gods, even the sons [and daughters] of God' [D&C 76:56, 58] and 'dwell in the presence of God and his Christ forever and ever' [D&C 76:62]. Through revelation, God has revealed the eternal laws, ordinances, and covenants that must be observed to develop the godly attributes necessary to realize this divine potential. The Church of Jesus Christ of Latter-day Saints focuses on these because the purpose of this restored Church is to prepare God's children for salvation in the celestial glory and, more particularly, for exaltation in its highest degree" (Oaks, "Kingdoms of Glory," *Liahona*, Nov. 2023, 27). See also commentary in this volume on Doctrine and Covenants 137:7–9.

70 These are they whose bodies are celestial, whose glory is that of the sun, even the glory of God, the highest of all, whose glory the sun of the firmament is written of as being typical.

71 And again, we saw the terrestrial world, and behold and lo, these are they who are of the terrestrial, whose glory differs from that of the church of the Firstborn who have received the fulness of the Father, even as that of the moon differs from the sun in the firmament.

72 Behold, these are they who died without law;

73 And also they who are the spirits of men kept in prison, whom the Son visited, and preached the gospel unto them, that they might be judged according to men in the flesh;

74 Who received not the testimony of Jesus in the flesh, but afterwards received it.

Doctrine and Covenants 76:71–80. Those Who Will Inherit the Terrestrial Kingdom Are Described

What law is the Lord referring to in this verse? (76:72) "The law referred to here is the law of the gospel. Another four years would pass before Joseph Smith learned that the gospel will be taught to those who die without the opportunity to hear it in mortality. Among their number will be many who accept and live it. They, of course, will inherit the celestial kingdom. This phrase describes those who died without hearing the gospel and who did not accept it when it was taught to them in the spirit world, yet who lived worthy of a terrestrial glory. Every person will be rewarded according to the law he or she chooses to live" (McConkie and Ostler, *Revelations of the Restoration*, 534).

What do we know about the Savior's visit to the spirit world? (76:73) The Lord prepared the way that all the dead might hear the gospel message: "If we acknowledge they had not the opportunity of receiving it in the flesh, they must have it in the spirit world; for in the great judgment day all men are to be judged by the same Gospel, and consequently, in order to judge them, it was necessary that they should hear the same Gospel that was preached upon the earth, that they might have the privilege of entering into the presence of the Lord their God, or, if they rejected it, be justly condemned" (Orson Pratt, in *Journal of Discourses*, 2:372).

Who will be among those who will inherit the terrestrial kingdom? (76:74) "Those destined to inherit the terrestrial kingdom are: (1) those who died 'without law'—those . . . people who do not hear the gospel in this life, and who would not accept it with all their hearts should they hear it; (2) those who hear and reject the gospel in this life and then accept it in the spirit world; (3) those 'who are honorable men of the earth, who [are] blinded by the craftiness of men';

75 These are they who are honorable men of the earth, who were blinded by the craftiness of men.

76 These are they who receive of his glory, but not of his fulness.

77 These are they who receive of the presence of the Son, but not of the fulness of the Father.

78 Wherefore, they are bodies terrestrial, and not bodies celestial, and differ in glory as the moon differs from the sun.

79 These are they who are not valiant in the testimony of Jesus; wherefore, they obtain not the crown over the kingdom of our God.

80 And now this is the end of the vision which we saw of the terrestrial, that the Lord commanded us to write while we were yet in the Spirit.

81 And again, we saw the glory of the telestial, which glory is that of the lesser, even as the glory of the stars differs from that of the glory of the moon in the firmament.

and (4) those who are lukewarm members of the true church and who have testimonies, but who are not true and faithful in all things (see D&C 76:71–80)" (Bruce R. McConkie, *New Witness*, 146).

Who is the Lord referring to as "honorable" people? (76:75) "The terrestrial kingdom is inhabited by good people, people who were good neighbors and who lived according to the light they had. At some point, whether in this life or in the spirit world, these people accept the testimony of Jesus, and as a result they will rise in the first resurrection. They are worthy of enjoying the presence of Jesus in eternity. These terrestrial beings, basically good though they may be, would not either in this life or in the spirit world accept the fulness of the gospel, having allowed themselves to be misled by human arguments and reasoning. For this reason they will not receive celestial glory" (Robinson and Garrett, *Commentary on the Doctrine and Covenants*, 2:317). ☉

What is being "valiant in the testimony of Jesus"? (76:79) "The 76th section of the Doctrine and Covenants makes it clear that being 'valiant in the testimony of Jesus' [D&C 76:79] is the simple, essential test between those who will inherit the blessings of the celestial kingdom and those in the lesser terrestrial kingdom. To be valiant, we need to focus on the power of Jesus Christ and His atoning sacrifice to overcome death and, through our repentance, to cleanse us from sin, and we need to follow the doctrine of Christ [2 Ne. 31:17–21]. We also need the light and knowledge of the Savior's life and teachings to guide us on the covenant pathway, including the sacred ordinances of the temple. We must be steadfast in Christ, feast upon His word, and endure to the end [2 Ne. 31:20–21]" (Quentin L. Cook, "Valiant in the Testimony of Jesus," *Ensign*, Nov. 2016, 43).

Doctrine and Covenants 76:81–113. The Status of Those in the Telestial, Terrestrial, and Celestial Glories Is Explained

What does the word "telestial" mean? (76:81) "In contrast to *celestial* and *terrestrial*, which have meanings commonly used in our language, *telestial* is found uniquely in writings relating to latter-day revelation. This name appears to be related to the Greek *telos*, meaning 'end' or 'completion.' Paul explained that there will be an orderly sequence in resurrections, beginning with that of Christ and continuing until the *telos,* or 'end' (see 1 Corinthians 15:21–24). Those individuals who have earned the right to live in the telestial kingdom will be the last going to a kingdom of glory to be resurrected.

"The name *telestial* may also be related to the prefix *tele-,* meaning 'far off' or 'distant.' The telestial kingdom will be the kingdom of glory most removed from the presence and glory of God" (Cowan, *Answers to Your Questions*, 91).

What is the difference between the testimony of Jesus and the gospel of Christ? (76:82) "By speaking of 'the gospel of Christ' and 'the testimony of Jesus' as two factors, it appears that a person could have one, or both, or neither. In the context of this revelation, such an idea harmonizes with the concept that terrestrial-type souls receive a testimony of Jesus but are not valiant enough in that testimony to receive the fulness of the gospel; celestial personalities receive a testimony of Jesus *and* baptism and the Holy Ghost and a cleansing from all sin (i.e., the fulness of the gospel); telestial people do not receive either a testimony of Jesus or the gospel" (Dahl, "Vision of the Glories," 292–93). ⊕

How will the Lord minister to those in the terrestrial and telestial kingdoms? (76:86–88) President Joseph Fielding Smith taught: "Through his abundant mercy, the Lord will do for all the best that can be done, and therefore he will give to all a place somewhere—if not within the gates of the Holy City, then it must be on the outside—where those who are not entitled to the fulness of blessings may be ministered to by those who have greater glory. For we read also here in this vision, where the glories are spoken of, that those who dwell in the celestial kingdom shall minister unto those of the terrestrial kingdom; those in the terrestrial kingdom shall minister to those of the telestial kingdom" (*Doctrines of Salvation*, 2:5).

Why does even the telestial kingdom surpass all understanding? (76:89) "God thus takes into merciful account not only our desires and our performance, but also the degree of difficulty which our varied circumstances impose upon us. No wonder we will not complain at the final judgment, especially since even the telestial kingdom's glory 'surpasses all understanding' (D&C 76:89). God delights in blessing us, especially when we realize 'joy in that which [we] have desired' (D&C 7:8)" (Maxwell, "According to the Desire of [Our] Hearts," *Ensign*, Nov. 1996, 21).

82 These are they who received not the gospel of Christ, neither the testimony of Jesus.

83 These are they who deny not the Holy Spirit.

84 These are they who are thrust down to hell.

85 These are they who shall not be redeemed from the devil until the last resurrection, until the Lord, even Christ the Lamb, shall have finished his work.

86 These are they who receive not of his fulness in the eternal world, but of the Holy Spirit through the ministration of the terrestrial;

87 And the terrestrial through the ministration of the celestial.

88 And also the telestial receive it of the administering of angels who are appointed to minister for them, or who are appointed to be ministering spirits for them; for they shall be heirs of salvation.

89 And thus we saw, in the heavenly vision, the glory of the telestial, which surpasses all understanding;

90 And no man knows it except him to whom God has revealed it.

91 And thus we saw the glory of the terrestrial which excels in all things the glory of the telestial, even in glory, and in power, and in might, and in dominion.

92 And thus we saw the glory of the celestial, which excels in all things—where God, even the Father, reigns upon his throne forever and ever;

93 Before whose throne all things bow in humble reverence, and give him glory forever and ever.

94 They who dwell in his presence are the church of the Firstborn; and they see as they are seen, and know as they are known, having received of his fulness and of his grace;

95 And he makes them equal in power, and in might, and in dominion.

96 And the glory of the celestial is one, even as the glory of the sun is one.

97 And the glory of the terrestrial is one, even as the glory of the moon is one.

98 And the glory of the telestial is one, even as the glory of the stars is one; for as one star differs from another star in glory, even so differs one from another in glory in the telestial world;

99 For these are they who are of Paul, and of Apollos, and of Cephas.

100 These are they who say they are some of one and some of another—some of Christ and some of John, and some of Moses, and some of Elias, and some of Esaias, and some of Isaiah, and some of Enoch;

101 But received not the gospel, neither the testimony of Jesus, neither the prophets, neither the everlasting covenant.

102 Last of all, these all are they who will not be gathered with the saints, to be caught up unto the church of the Firstborn, and received into the cloud.

103 These are they who are liars, and sorcerers, and adulterers, and whoremongers, and whosoever loves and makes a lie.

What does it mean to inherit God's fulness? (76:94–95) The Prophet Joseph Smith addressed the Saints following the death of King Follett: "I want you to know that God in the last days, . . . is not trifling with you or me; it is the first principles of consolation. . . . they shall be heirs of God and joint heirs with Jesus Christ. What is it? to inherit the same glory, the same power and the same exaltation, until you ascend the throne of eternal power the same as those who are gone before" (Joseph Smith Papers, "Discourse, 7 Apr. 1844, as Published in *Times and Seasons*," 614).

104 These are they who suffer the wrath of God on earth.

105 These are they who suffer the vengeance of eternal fire.

106 These are they who are cast down to hell and suffer the wrath of Almighty God, until the fulness of times, when Christ shall have subdued all enemies under his feet, and shall have perfected his work;

107 When he shall deliver up the kingdom, and present it unto the Father, spotless, saying: I have overcome and have trodden the wine-press alone, even the wine-press of the fierceness of the wrath of Almighty God.

108 Then shall he be crowned with the crown of his glory, to sit on the throne of his power to reign forever and ever.

109 But behold, and lo, we saw the glory and the inhabitants of the telestial world, that they were as innumerable as the stars in the firmament of heaven, or as the sand upon the seashore;

110 And heard the voice of the Lord saying: These all shall bow the knee, and every tongue shall confess to him who sits upon the throne forever and ever;

111 For they shall be judged according to their works, and every man shall receive according to his own works, his own dominion, in the mansions which are prepared;

What does the wine-press represent? (76:107)

"The winepress represents the Savior *himself* being pressed therein until his blood is shed in the Garden of Gethsemane. *Gath* in Hebrew means 'winepress,' and *semane* means 'oil.' . . .

"Jesus is described as having 'trodden the wine-press *alone*' because on the one hand he *alone* conquers all things as victor, and because on the other hand he *alone* suffered all things as victim. Beyond this, we must remember that the Savior endured his infinite agony in the garden alone. When the worst came, there was no one to help him or comfort him—the Spirit left him, and even his Father withdrew from him, to leave him utterly and horribly alone in his infinite agony (see Matthew 27:46)" (Robinson and Garrett, *Commentary on the Doctrine and Covenants*, 2:327).

Why do our works matter in this life? (76:111)

"Each of you will be judged according to your individual works and the desires of your hearts. . . . Your eventual placement in the celestial, terrestrial, or telestial kingdom will not be determined by chance. The Lord has prescribed unchanging requirements for each. You can know what the scriptures teach, and pattern your lives accordingly" (Nelson, "Constancy amid Change," *Ensign*, Nov. 1993, 35).

Elder D. Todd Christofferson surmised: "Our repentance and obedience, our service and sacrifices do matter. We want to be among those described by Ether as 'always abounding in good works' [Ether 12:4]. But it is not so much because of some tally kept in celestial account books. These things matter because they engage us in God's work and are the means by which we collaborate with Him in our own transformation from natural man to saint" ("Our Relationship with God," *Liahona*, May 2022, 79).

112 And they shall be servants of the Most High; but where God and Christ dwell they cannot come, worlds without end.

113 This is the end of the vision which we saw, which we were commanded to write while we were yet in the Spirit.

Why won't everyone live eternally with Heavenly Father and Jesus Christ? (76:112) President Russell M. Nelson taught, "Mortal lifetime is hardly a nanosecond compared with eternity. But my dear brothers and sisters, what a crucial nanosecond it is! During this life we get to choose which laws we are willing to obey—those of the celestial kingdom, or the terrestrial, or the telestial [D&C 88:22–24]—and therefore in which kingdom of glory we will live forever" ("Choices for Eternity").

We receive these blessings as we follow Jesus Christ, who is the law (3 Nephi 15:9). A thoughtful study of the scriptures, including Doctrine and Covenants 76:112; 88:20–24; 131:4; and 132:17, provides valuable insight to the importance of mortal life.

Doctrine and Covenants 76:114–19. The Faithful May See and Understand the Mysteries of God's Kingdom by the Power of the Holy Spirit

114 But great and marvelous are the works of the Lord, and the mysteries of his kingdom which he showed unto us, which surpass all understanding in glory, and in might, and in dominion;

How great and marvelous was this revelation when it was received? (76:114) The Prophet Joseph Smith recorded: "Nothing could be more pleasing to the Saint, upon the order of the kingdom of the Lord, than the light which burst upon the world, through the foregoing vision. . . . The sublimity of the ideas; the purity of the language; the scope for action; the continued duration for completion, in order that the heirs of salvation, may confess the Lord and bow the knee; The rewards for faithfulness & the punishments for sins, are so much beyond the narrow mindedness of men, that every honest man is constrained to exclaim; *It came from God*" (Joseph Smith Papers, "History, 1838–1856, volume A-1," 192; spelling modernized).

A Profound View of the Afterlife (Doctrine and Covenants 76:114)

"The view of the afterlife laid out in 'the Vision' contrasted starkly with the beliefs of most Christians at the time. A majority believed in a strict heaven-and-hell theology of the world to come: those obedient to the gospel of Jesus Christ would be saved, but the wicked would be consigned to eternal punishment. However, there were a growing number who felt that this view was inconsistent with other biblical teachings about God's mercy, justice, and power to save. . . .

"Simply put, Universalists believed that God would not eternally punish sinners but that all would eventually be saved in God's kingdom. Joseph Smith's father and his grandfather Asael Smith held Universalist views. . . .

"Perhaps in a knee-jerk reaction to what seemed to be hints of Universalism, some early members overlooked the subtle beauty of 'the Vision.' Avoiding the extremes of Universalism and the orthodox view of heaven and hell, it suggested that the sufferings of the disobedient would indeed ultimately end but that the Lord also held out the promise of unimaginable rewards for those who are 'valiant in the testimony of Jesus'" (McBride, "Vision," 149, 150–51).

How much of the vision was written? (76:115) "It should be noted that Joseph and Sidney actually wrote very little of what they actually saw and heard. Over eleven years later, May 1843, the Prophet is reported to have said: 'I could explain a hundred fold more than I ever have of the glories of the kingdom manifested to me in the vision, were I permitted, and were the people prepared to receive them' ([Joseph Smith Papers, "History, 1838–1856, volume D-1," 1556]). Importantly, some parts of the vision were recorded while yet in the Spirit (see vv. 28, 80, and 113) and under the command of the Lord (v. 15), while other parts were not recorded, again by direction of the Lord's command (v. 115)" (Nyman, *Doctrine and Covenants Commentary*, 2:41–42).

How can we come to know the things of God for ourselves? (76:117) Joseph Smith wrote: "'To the honorable searchers for truth, we say, in the spirit of candor and meekness, search the revelations which we publish, and ask your Heavenly Father, in the name of his Son Jesus Christ, to manifest the truth unto you, and if you do it with an eye single to his glory, he will answer you by the power of his Holy Spirit; you will then know for yourselves, and not for another; you will not then be dependent on man for the knowledge of God; nor will there be any room for speculation. No; for when men receive their instruction from him that made them, they know how he will save them'" (Joseph Smith Papers, "History, 1838–1856, volume A-1," 227; orthography modernized).

How does the Lord prepare us for His glory? (76:118) Sister Jean B. Bingham related: "In preparation for my first trip to the temple, my mother and experienced Relief Society sisters helped me select the items I would need, including beautiful ceremonial clothing. But the most important preparation came even before knowing what to wear. After interviewing me to determine if I was worthy, my bishop explained the covenants I would make. His careful explanation gave me the chance to think about and be prepared to make those covenants.

"When the day came, I participated with a feeling of gratitude and peace. Even though I did not understand the full significance of the covenants I made, I did know that I was bound to God through those covenants and was promised blessings I could scarcely comprehend if I kept them. Since that first experience, I have been continually assured that keeping the covenants we make with God allows us to draw upon the Savior's power, which strengthens

115 Which he commanded us we should not write while we were yet in the Spirit, and are not lawful for man to utter;

116 Neither is man capable to make them known, for they are only to be seen and understood by the power of the Holy Spirit, which God bestows on those who love him, and purify themselves before him;

117 To whom he grants this privilege of seeing and knowing for themselves;

118 That through the power and manifestation of the Spirit, while in the flesh, they may be able to bear his presence in the world of glory.

119 And to God and the Lamb be glory, and honor, and dominion forever and ever. Amen.

us in our inevitable trials, provides protection from the adversary's influence, and prepares us for eternal glory" ("Covenants with God Strengthen, Protect, and Prepare Us," *Liahona*, May 2022, 66–67).

Introduction to Doctrine and Covenants 77

As Joseph Smith "continued his revision of the New Testament in February and March 1832, he reached the book of Revelation with its abundance of symbolic language. 'About the first of March, in connection with the translation of the scriptures,' a later [Joseph Smith] history explains, 'I received the following explanation of the Revelations of Saint John.' Given that [Joseph] was in Kirtland, Ohio, and was not working on the New Testament revisions between 29 February and 4 March 1832, this document was likely written sometime between 4 March and 20 March" (Joseph Smith Papers, Historical Introduction to "Answers to Questions, between circa 4 and circa 20 March 1832 [D&C 77]").

While studying this section regarding the Book of Revelation, it is important to remember what the Prophet Joseph Smith said: "I make this broad declaration, that whenever God gives a vision of an image, or beast, or figure of any kind, he always holds himself responsible to give a revelation or interpretation of the meaning thereof, otherwise we are not responsible or accountable for our belief in it. Don't be afraid of being damned for not knowing the meaning of a vision or figure if God has not given a revelation or interpretation of the subject" (Joseph Smith Papers, "History, 1838–1856, volume D-1," 1523).

"But this Revelation is not a complete interpretation of the book. It is a *key*. A key is a very small part of the house. It unlocks the door through which an entrance may be gained, but after the key has been turned, the searcher for treasure must find it for himself. It is like entering a museum in which the students must find out for themselves what they desire to know. The sources of information are there" (Smith and Sjodahl, *Doctrine and Covenants Commentary*, 478).

SECTION 77

Revelation given to Joseph Smith the Prophet, at Hiram, Ohio, about March 1832. Joseph Smith's history states, "In connection with the translation of the Scriptures, I received the following explanation of the Revelation of St. John."

1 Q. What is the sea of glass spoken of by John, 4th chapter, and 6th verse of the Revelation?

A. It is the earth, in its sanctified, immortal, and eternal state.

Doctrine and Covenants 77:1–4. Beasts Have Spirits and Will Dwell in Eternal Felicity

What did the Lord reveal to Joseph Smith about the "sea of glass spoken of by John" the Revelator? (77:1) The Prophet Joseph Smith said "'that when the earth was sanctified and became like a sea of glass, it would be one great urim and thummim, and the Saints could look in it and see as they are seen' [Joseph Smith Papers, 'History, 1838–1856, volume D-1,' 1472].

"President Brigham Young gave the following insight: 'This Earth will become a celestial body—be like a sea of glass, or like a Urim and Thummim; and when you wish to know anything, you can look in this Earth and see all the eternities of God' (in *Journal of Discourses*, 8:200; see also D&C 88:17–20, 25–26; 130:6–9)" (*Doctrine and Covenants Student Manual* [2001], 168). See also commentary in this volume on Doctrine and Covenants 130:8–9.

How does the spirit of man (our spirit bodies) relate to our physical bodies? (77:2) The First Presidency, in November 1909, taught that our spirits and bodies are in the likeness of Heavenly Parents: "The brother of Jared, was . . . favored by the Lord. He was even permitted to behold the spirit body of the foreordained Savior, prior to His incarnation; and so like the body of a man was gazing upon a being of flesh and blood. He first saw the finger and then the entire body of the Lord. . . .

"'Seest thou that ye are created after mine own image? Yea, even all men were created in the beginning after mine own image.

"'Behold, this body, which ye now behold, is the body of my spirit; and man have I created after the body of my spirit; and even as I appear unto thee to be in the spirit will I appear unto my people in the flesh' (Ether 3:6–16).

"What more is needed to convince us that man, both in spirit and in body, is the image and likeness of God and that God Himself is in the form of a man?" ("Origin of Man," *Ensign*, Feb. 2002, 29).

What can we learn regarding the four beasts that John saw and heard? (77:2–4) Joseph Smith said: "John heard the words of the beasts giving glory to God, and understood them. . . . The four beasts were four of the most noble animals that had filled the measure of their creation. . . . They were seen and heard by John praising and glorifying God" (Joseph Smith Papers, "History, 1838–1856, volume D-1," 1523). ☉

How can these beasts be both individual and also representative of "classes of beings"? (77:3) "John was shown several figurative beasts in order to represent the several different glories of different types or classes of creatures in eternity. Even the many eyes and wings of these figurative images are symbols, representing respectively the abstract concepts of knowledge and power or mobility. . . .

"The four 'images' of beasts that John describes, however, do symbolize both the multitude and the eternal nature of the many animals God has created. According to Joseph Smith, what John saw was intended to *symbolize* the many beasts that *actually* do exist in heaven" (Robinson and Garrett, *Commentary on the Doctrine and Covenants*, 2:339).

2 Q. What are we to understand by the four beasts, spoken of in the same verse?

A. They are figurative expressions, used by the Revelator, John, in describing heaven, the paradise of God, the happiness of man, and of beasts, and of creeping things, and of the fowls of the air; that which is spiritual being in the likeness of that which is temporal; and that which is temporal in the likeness of that which is spiritual; the spirit of man in the likeness of his person, as also the spirit of the beast, and every other creature which God has created.

3 Q. Are the four beasts limited to individual beasts, or do they represent classes or orders?

A. They are limited to four individual beasts, which were shown to John, to represent the glory of the classes of beings in their destined order or sphere of creation, in the enjoyment of their eternal felicity.

4 Q. What are we to understand by the eyes and wings, which the beasts had?

A. Their eyes are a representation of light and knowledge, that is, they are full of knowledge; and their wings are a representation of power, to move, to act, etc.

5 Q. What are we to understand by the four and twenty elders, spoken of by John?

A. We are to understand that these elders whom John saw, were elders who had been faithful in the work of the ministry and were dead; who belonged to the seven churches, and were then in the paradise of God.

6 Q. What are we to understand by the book which John saw, which was sealed on the back with seven seals?

A. We are to understand that it contains the revealed will, mysteries, and the works of God; the hidden things of his economy concerning this earth during the seven thousand years of its continuance, or its temporal existence.

7 Q. What are we to understand by the seven seals with which it was sealed?

A. We are to understand that the first seal

Doctrine and Covenants 77:5–7. This Earth Has a Temporal Existence of 7,000 Years

What might the twenty-four elders that John saw in his vision represent? (77:5) "John writes about twenty-four elders. Who are they? They were early Christian missionaries who belonged to branches of the Church in Asia. Having served faithfully, they are now in the spirit world" (Harper, *Making Sense of the Doctrine & Covenants*, 273–74).

Elder Bruce R. McConkie expanded on this idea: "Thus John is seeing what is to be in the future; he is seeing certain elders in celestial splendor who at that time were in their disembodied state in paradise awaiting the day of their resurrection and the receipt of eternal life. In principle it is the same as when Joseph Smith, on January 21, 1836, saw his father and mother—who were then still living in mortality—in the celestial kingdom of heaven ([see *Joseph Smith* (manual), 403])" (*Doctrinal New Testament Commentary*, 3:465).

What office in the Melchizedek Priesthood is essential for exaltation in the kingdom of God? (77:5) "It is worthy of note that these exalted persons who are sitting with God on his throne are elders: not seventies, not high priests, not patriarchs, not apostles, but elders—than which there is no more important priesthood in God's earthly kingdom. Indeed, every elder who magnifies his calling as an elder has the immutable promise of the Father, guaranteed by his personal oath, that he shall gain all that the Father hath, which is eternal life, which is godhood, which is to sit with him on his throne (D&C 84:33–41)" (Bruce R. McConkie, *Doctrinal New Testament Commentary*, 3:465).

What do we learn about the works of God from these verses? (77:6–7) "Understanding what is symbolized by the book in the right hand of God becomes critical to understanding the book of Revelation, because the remainder of the vision is what John sees as the Lamb opens the seals one at a time. Section 77 explains what the book symbolizes. We are told that it symbolizes the history of the earth, which was to last for seven thousand years (D&C 77:6), and that each seal represents one of the thousand-year periods (D&C 77:7). The book is shown in God's hand because it is under his control and management. Only the Lamb of God is worthy to open it because only through the atonement of Jesus Christ does the history and destiny of the world unfold" (Lund, "Things Which Must Shortly Come to Pass," 269–70).

Doctrine and Covenants 77:8–10. Various Angels Restore the Gospel and Minister on Earth

What is the mission of these four angels? (77:8) "These angels seem to fit the description of the angels spoken of in the parable of the wheat and the tares (Matt. 13:24–43 and D&C 86:17), who pled with the Lord that they might go forth to reap down the field. They were told to let the wheat and the tares grow together to the time of the end of the harvest, which is the end of the world (Matt. 13:38–39). . . .

"These angels have been given power over the four parts of the earth and they have the power of committing the everlasting Gospel to the peoples of the earth . . . [They] are now at work in the earth on their sacred mission" (Joseph Fielding Smith, *Church History and Modern Revelation*, 1:300, 301). ✪

Who is the Elias being spoken of in this verse? (77:9) "Referring to our day, Jesus said: 'Elias truly shall first come, and restore all things, as the prophets have written' (JST, Matthew 17:10). No single ancient prophet, standing alone, returned to restore all things. Angelic ministrants came from all of the great dispensations of the past. This promised Elias is, in effect, all of the angelic ministrants who have come in the latter days to restore truths and powers and keys, all of the things that, taken together, compose 'all things.' It was in this way that our dispensation became the dispensation of the fulness of times, meaning the dispensation of the fulness of all dispensations past. Someone came from each of these ancient dispensations to bring to us what was had among mortals in his day" (Bruce R. McConkie, *New Witness*, 629).

When are these things mentioned in the first few verses of Revelation 7 going to be accomplished? (77:10) "The work of spreading the gospel throughout the world to every nation, kindred, tongue, and people is the work of the latter-day Church. We now live in the sixth time period, or day, or thousand years—the period of time immediately before the glorious Millennium, which is the seventh time period or the sabbath day of the earth's temporal existence" (Robinson and Garrett, *Commentary on the Doctrine and Covenants*, 2:344).

contains the things of the first thousand years, and the second also of the second thousand years, and so on until the seventh.

8 Q. What are we to understand by the four angels, spoken of in the 7th chapter and 1st verse of Revelation?

A. We are to understand that they are four angels sent forth from God, to whom is given power over the four parts of the earth, to save life and to destroy; these are they who have the everlasting gospel to commit to every nation, kindred, tongue, and people; having power to shut up the heavens, to seal up unto life, or to cast down to the regions of darkness.

9 Q. What are we to understand by the angel ascending from the east, Revelation 7th chapter and 2nd verse?

A. We are to understand that the angel ascending from the east is he to whom is given the seal of the living God over the twelve tribes of Israel; wherefore, he crieth unto the four angels having the everlasting gospel, saying: Hurt not the earth, neither the sea, nor the trees, till we have sealed the servants of our God in their foreheads. And, if you will receive it, this is Elias which was to come to gather together the tribes of Israel and restore all things.

10 Q. What time are the things spoken of in this chapter to be accomplished?

A. They are to be accomplished in the sixth thousand years, or the opening of the sixth seal.

11 Q. What are we to understand by sealing the one hundred and forty-four thousand, out of all the tribes of Israel—twelve thousand out of every tribe?

A. We are to understand that those who are sealed are high priests, ordained unto the holy order of God, to administer the everlasting gospel; for they are they who are ordained out of every nation, kindred, tongue, and people, by the angels to whom is given power over the nations of the earth, to bring as many as will come to the church of the Firstborn.

12 Q. What are we to understand by the sounding of the trumpets, mentioned in the 8th chapter of Revelation?

A. We are to understand that as God made the world in six days, and on the seventh day he finished his work, and sanctified it, and also formed man out of the dust of the earth, even so, in the beginning of the seventh thousand years will the Lord God sanctify the earth, and complete the salvation of man, and judge all things, and shall redeem all things, except that which he hath not put into his power, when he shall have sealed all things, unto the end of all things; and the sounding of the trumpets of the seven angels are the preparing and finishing of his work, in the beginning of the seventh thousand years—the preparing of the way before the time of his coming.

Doctrine and Covenants 77:11. The Sealing of the 144,000

What could the sealing in these high priests' foreheads represent? (77:11) "The Prophet Joseph, in February 1844, 'made some remarks respecting the hundred and forty-four thousand mentioned by John the Revelator, showing that the selection of persons to form that number had already commenced' ([Joseph Smith Papers, "History Draft [1 January–21 June 1844]," 8). . . . 'There will be 144,000 saviors on Mount Zion, and with them an innumerable host that no man can number. Oh! I beseech you to go forward, go forward and make your calling and your election sure' ([Joseph Smith Papers, "History, 1838–1856, volume F-1," 19]). This suggests that the sealing in their foreheads (Revelation 7:3) is their calling and election made sure which will give them membership in the Church of the Firstborn, the eternal church (see also D&C 131:5–6)" (Nyman, *Doctrine and Covenants Commentary*, 2:31). See also commentary in this volume on Doctrine and Covenants 133:18.

Doctrine and Covenants 77:12–14. Christ Will Come in the Beginning of the Seventh Thousand Years

What do these verses suggest about the time of the Second Coming? (77:12–13) "Some have supposed that there is to be exactly six thousand years from the Fall to the Second Advent, but a careful reading of these verses suggests otherwise. Doctrine and Covenants 77:12 declares that 'in [not at] the beginning of the seventh thousand years,' Christ will complete his work, preparing the way 'before the time of his coming.' Verse 13 explains that events described in Revelation 9 are to occur after the seventh period of a thousand years begins but before Christ appears. Thus estimates of the time of his advent based on these verses must be more tentative and probably later than some have supposed" (Cowan, *Answers to Your Questions*, 95).

13 Q. When are the things to be accomplished, which are written in the 9th chapter of Revelation?

A. They are to be accomplished after the opening of the seventh seal, before the coming of Christ.

How might eating the little book symbolize John's mission? (77:14) "A 'mighty angel' delivered 'a little book' to John, and he 'ate it up' (Revelation 10:1–2, 10), symbolizing his mission to help 'gather the tribes of Israel' as part of the Restoration (D&C 77:14; see also D&C 7:1–3). Eating the book may suggest that John accepted his mission: it became a part of his being. That the book was 'sweet as honey' in John's mouth but 'bitter' in his belly (Revelation 10:10) may suggest that his mission would involve many sweet and joyous experiences but also rejection and painful experiences" (*New Testament Student Manual* [2018], 548). ●

14 Q. What are we to understand by the little book which was eaten by John, as mentioned in the 10th chapter of Revelation?

A. We are to understand that it was a mission, and an ordinance, for him to gather the tribes of Israel; behold, this is Elias, who, as it is written, must come and restore all things.

Doctrine and Covenants 77:15. Two Prophets Will Be Raised up to the Jewish Nation

What do we know about the identity of the two prophets? (77:15) Elder Bruce R. McConkie identified the two prophets as "followers of that humble man Joseph Smith, through whom the Lord of Heaven restored the fulness of his everlasting gospel in this final dispensation of grace. No doubt they will be members of the Council of the Twelve or of the First Presidency of the Church" (*Doctrinal New Testament Commentary*, 3:509). ●

15 Q. What is to be understood by the two witnesses, in the eleventh chapter of Revelation?

A. They are two prophets that are to be raised up to the Jewish nation in the last days, at the time of the restoration, and to prophesy to the Jews after they are gathered and have built the city of Jerusalem in the land of their fathers.

"On March 1, 1832, the Prophet Joseph Smith met with a group of high priests in Kirtland, Ohio, possibly to discuss the Church's mercantile and publication efforts. During the meeting, the Prophet dictated the revelation recorded in Doctrine and Covenants 78. Subsequently, the United Firm was created to better manage the Church's property and financial endeavors, such as the storehouses. The part of the United Firm that managed the Church's publishing efforts was called the Literary Firm.

"In an effort to protect this Church-operated entity from enemies of the Church, some of the language of this and other revelations was changed when they were first published in the 1835 edition of the Doctrine and Covenants (see D&C 82; 92; 96; 104). In this early edition, pseudonyms, or substitute names, were used to refer to individuals, places, and activities. This may have been done to prevent Church enemies from obtaining information that could potentially undermine the Church's objective to build Zion. In later editions of the Doctrine and Covenants, those substitute names were replaced with the actual names....

"The terms *firm* and *United Firm* were later changed to *order* and *United Order* in the Doctrine and Covenants (see D&C 78:4, 8; 82:20; 92:1; 104:1, 5, 10, 47–48, 53). The term *United Order* as used in the Doctrine and Covenants refers to the United Firm and should not be confused with the various systems of communal or cooperative sharing established years later when the Saints settled in the western United States. The United Firm was a business partnership based on the law of consecration between the Prophet Joseph Smith and a limited number of other Church leaders in Kirtland, Ohio, and Independence, Missouri (see D&C 82:11–12; 92:1–2; 96:8). From April 1832 until April 1834, when the Lord commanded Joseph Smith to dissolve the partnership, the United Firm played a vital role in Church administration" (*Doctrine and Covenants Student Manual* [2018], 415–17). See also commentary in this volume on the Introduction to Doctrine and Covenants 70; 70:1–3; 72:20–21; and 82:11–13, 15–18.

SECTION 78

Revelation given through Joseph Smith the Prophet, at Kirtland, Ohio, March 1, 1832. On that day, the Prophet and other leaders had assembled to discuss Church business. This revelation originally instructed the Prophet, Sidney Rigdon, and Newel K. Whitney to travel to Missouri and organize the Church's mercantile and publishing endeavors by creating a "firm" that would oversee these efforts, generating funds for the establishment of Zion and for the benefit of the poor. This firm, known as the United Firm, was organized in April 1832 and disbanded in 1834 (see section 82). Sometime after its dissolution, under the direction of Joseph Smith, the phrase "the affairs of the storehouse for the poor" replaced "mercantile and publishing establishments" in the revelation, and the word "order" replaced the word "firm."

1 The Lord spake unto Joseph Smith, Jun., saying: Hearken unto me, saith the Lord your God, who are ordained unto the high

Doctrine and Covenants 78:1–4. The Saints Should Organize and Establish a Storehouse

priesthood of my church, who have assembled yourselves together;

2 And listen to the counsel of him who has ordained you from on high, who shall speak in your ears the words of wisdom, that salvation may be unto you in that thing which you have presented before me, saith the Lord God.

What was the organization described in this passage? (78:3) "Verse 3 vaguely speaks about 'an organization of my people,' the manuscript versions more specifically refer to 'an organization of the literary and mercantile establishments of my church.' Joseph kept the issues behind section 78 as confidential as possible to avoid giving the Church's enemies information they could use to cripple it financially and thus undermine Zion. Essentially, the revelation tells how the Church could use its profitable mercantile assets (like Bishop Whitney's store) to finance its revealed priorities (buying land in Missouri and publishing the scriptures)" (Harper, "Historical Context and Background for D&C 78"). ⊕

3 For verily I say unto you, the time has come, and is now at hand; and behold, and lo, it must needs be that there be an organization of my people, in regulating and establishing the affairs of the storehouse for the poor of my people, both in this place and in the land of Zion—

What does it mean that the principles of the Lord's organization of His people are "permanent and everlasting"? (78:4) "What was to be permanent and everlasting was the establishment and regulation of a storehouse for the poor. The specific means of creating and funding the storehouse, in this case the united firm, was not necessarily permanent. Today bishops' storehouses are administered through the Presiding Bishopric" (Robinson and Garrett, *Commentary on the Doctrine and Covenants*, 353).

4 For a permanent and everlasting establishment and order unto my church, to advance the cause, which ye have espoused, to the salvation of man, and to the glory of your Father who is in heaven;

Doctrine and Covenants 78:5–12. Wise Use of the Saints' Properties Will Lead to Salvation

Why does the Lord consistently command us to be equal in earthly things? (78:5–6) "Throughout history, the Lord has measured societies and individuals by how well they cared for the poor. He has said:

"'For the earth is full, and there is enough and to spare; yea, I prepared all things, and have given unto the children of men to be agents unto themselves.

"'Therefore, if any man shall take of the abundance which I have made, and impart not his portion, according to the law of my gospel, unto the poor and the needy, he shall, with the wicked, lift up his eyes in

5 That you may be equal in the bonds of heavenly things, yea, and earthly things also, for the obtaining of heavenly things.

6 For if ye are not equal in earthly things ye cannot be equal in obtaining heavenly things;

hell, being in torment' (D&C 104:17–18; see also D&C 56:16–17).

"Furthermore, He declares, 'In your temporal things you shall be equal, and this not grudgingly, otherwise the abundance of the manifestations of the Spirit shall be withheld' (D&C 70:14; see also D&C 49:20; 78:5–7)" (Christofferson, "Come to Zion," *Ensign*, Nov. 2008, 39).

7 For if you will that I give unto you a place in the celestial world, you must prepare yourselves by doing the things which I have commanded you and required of you.

8 And now, verily thus saith the Lord, it is expedient that all things be done unto my glory, by you who are joined together in this order;

9 Or, in other words, let my servant Newel K. Whitney and my servant Joseph Smith, Jun., and my servant Sidney Rigdon sit in council with the saints which are in Zion;

How can we better prepare ourselves for the celestial world? (78:7) President Dallin H. Oaks warned about a "subtle form of deception—the idea that it is enough to hear and believe without acting on that belief. Many prophets have taught against that deception.... [e.g., James 1:22 and Mosiah 4:10]. And in modern revelation the Lord declares, 'If you will that I give unto you a place in the celestial world, you must prepare yourselves by doing the things which I have commanded you and required of you' (D&C 78:7).

"It is not enough to know that God lives, that Jesus Christ is our Savior, and that the gospel is true. We must take the high road by acting upon that knowledge" ("Be Not Deceived," *Ensign*, Nov. 2004, 46).

10 Otherwise Satan seeketh to turn their hearts away from the truth, that they become blinded and understand not the things which are prepared for them.

How does Satan seek to turn our hearts from the truth? (78:10) "One of Satan's clever tactics is to tempt us to concentrate on the present and ignore the future.... 'Satan seeketh to turn their hearts away from the truth, that they become blinded ...' (D&C 78:10). The 'things which are prepared for them' are the promised rewards of eternal life, which come as a result of obedience.... President Heber J. Grant said ... 'He throws dust, so to speak, in their eyes, and they are blinded with the things of this world.' ... He tempts us with the transitory pleasures of the world so that we will not focus our minds and efforts on the things that bring eternal joy. The devil is a dirty fighter, and we must be aware of his tactics" (Ballard, "Purity Precedes Power," *Ensign*, Nov. 1990, 36).

11 Wherefore, a commandment I give unto you, to prepare and organize yourselves by a bond or everlasting covenant that cannot be broken.

12 And he who breaketh it shall lose his office and standing in the church, and shall be delivered over to the buffetings of Satan until the day of redemption.

What is the meaning of organizing ourselves "by a bond or everlasting covenant"? (78:11–12) "The Prophet Joseph Smith, Newel K. Whitney, Sidney Rigdon, and others traveled to Missouri in April 1832 to meet with other Church leaders and formally organize the United Firm, with storehouses in Independence, Missouri, and Kirtland, Ohio. William W. Phelps and Sidney Gilbert were assigned to prepare 'a bond [written agreement] or everlasting covenant' for the firm (D&C 78:11). By entering into this covenant, these Church leaders agreed to consecrate their property to the United Firm and that together they would be responsible for the firm's debts. The Lord warned that if any of these men broke this covenant they would lose their calling in the Church and would be left vulnerable to Satan's influence (see D&C 78:12)" (*Doctrine and Covenants Student Manual* [2018], 419).

What does it mean to "be delivered over to the buffetings of Satan"? (78:12) "An individual who receives extensive spiritual knowledge, enters into sacred covenants, and then turns away from those promises to the Lord may be left to the buffetings of Satan until complete repentance has occurred. This sin differs in nature and category from one committed in ignorance. Paul alluded to such in 1 Corinthians 5:1–5" (Dennis D. Flake, "Buffetings of Satan," 1:236). See also commentary in this volume on Doctrine and Covenants 104:9–10.

Doctrine and Covenants 78:13–14.
The Church Should Be Independent of Earthly Powers

In what way is the Church to stand independent? (78:14) "The Lord gave instruction to leaders of His restored church to establish and maintain institutional integrity—'that the church may stand independent' [D&C 78:14]" (Nelson, "Teach Us Tolerance and Love," *Ensign*, May 1994, 70).

Years earlier Elder Bruce R. McConkie stated: "The Church, which administers the gospel, and the Saints who have received the gospel, must be independent of all the powers of earth, as they work out their salvation—temporally and spiritually. . . .

"It is the aim of the Church to help the Saints to care for themselves and . . . the Church must operate . . . in such a way as to be independent of the powers of evil in the world" ("Stand Independent above All Other Creatures," *Ensign*, May 1979, 94).

Doctrine and Covenants 78:15–16.
Michael (Adam) Serves under the Direction of the Holy One (Christ)

What was known of Adam-ondi-Ahman at the time this revelation was received? (78:15) "The original revelation given in March 1832 did not include the information regarding Adam-ondi-Ahman and Michael. These inspired additions were made in the summer of 1835 as the Doctrine and Covenants

13 Behold, this is the preparation wherewith I prepare you, and the foundation, and the ensample which I give unto you, whereby you may accomplish the commandments which are given you;

14 That through my providence, notwithstanding the tribulation which shall descend upon you, that the church may stand independent above all other creatures beneath the celestial world;

15 That you may come up unto the crown prepared for you, and be made rulers over many kingdoms, saith the Lord God, the Holy One of Zion, who hath established the foundations of Adam-ondi-Ahman;

was being prepared for publication. The changes to the revelation recorded in Doctrine and Covenants 78 included the addition of the phrase 'who hath established the foundations of Adam-ondi-Ahman' in verse 15, all of verse 16, and the title 'Son Ahman' in verse 20" (*Doctrine and Covenants Student Manual* [2018], 420). This is the first place "Adam-ondi-Ahman" is mentioned in the Doctrine and Covenants. See also commentary in this volume on Doctrine and Covenants 107:53–57 and Doctrine and Covenants 116:1.

16 Who hath appointed Michael your prince, and established his feet, and set him upon high, and given unto him the keys of salvation under the counsel and direction of the Holy One, who is without beginning of days or end of life.

What is Adam's role regarding the whole human family? (78:16) "Adam [Michael] has the responsibility to supervise and direct the work of God on earth through all generations. 'The Priesthood was first given to Adam,' explained the Prophet Joseph Smith; 'he obtained the First Presidency, and held the keys of it from generation to generation.' . . . 'The Priesthood is an everlasting principle, and existed with God from eternity, and will to eternity, without beginning of days or end of years. The keys have to be brought from heaven whenever the Gospel is sent. When they are revealed from heaven, it is by Adam's authority.' . . .

"Adam presides over the entire human family on this earth under the direction of the Savior. Jesus Christ presides over all the Father's children on many earths" (McConkie and Ostler, *Revelations of the Restoration*, 567). ◉

Doctrine and Covenants 78:17–22. Blessed Are the Faithful, for They Will Inherit All Things

17 Verily, verily, I say unto you, ye are little children, and ye have not as yet understood how great blessings the Father hath in his own hands and prepared for you;

18 And ye cannot bear all things now; nevertheless, be of good cheer, for I will lead you along. The kingdom is yours and the blessings thereof are yours, and the riches of eternity are yours.

Why should a person be grateful even during tribulations? (78:17–19) Sister Bonnie D. Parkin said: "Tribulations are frightening. And yet the Lord said . . . 'he who receiveth *all* things with thankfulness shall be made glorious' [D&C 78:18–19; emphasis added].

"The kind of gratitude that receives even tribulations with thanksgiving requires a broken heart and a contrite spirit, humility to accept that which we cannot change, willingness to turn everything over to the Lord—even when we do not understand, thankfulness for hidden opportunities yet to be revealed. Then comes a sense of peace.

"When was the last time you thanked the Lord for a trial or tribulation? Adversity compels us to go to our knees; does gratitude for adversity do that as well?" ("Gratitude," *Ensign*, May 2007, 35–36).

What blessings are promised to those who receive all things with thankfulness? (78:19) "The scriptural references do not speak of gratitude *for* things but rather suggest an overall spirit or attitude of gratitude.

"It is easy to be grateful *for* things when life seems to be going our way. . . .

"Could I suggest that we see gratitude as a disposition, a way of life that stands independent of our current situation? In other words, I'm suggesting that instead of being thankful *for* things, we focus on being thankful *in* our circumstances—whatever they may be. . . .

"This type of gratitude transcends whatever is happening around us. It surpasses disappointment, discouragement, and despair. It blooms just as beautifully in the icy landscape of winter as it does in the pleasant warmth of summer" (Uchtdorf, "Grateful in Any Circumstances," *Ensign*, May 2014, 70, 75).

What does *Son Ahman* mean? (78:20) According to the Prophet Joseph Smith, the word Ahman [sometimes spelled awmen] is the name of God in the pure language of Adam, and 'Son Ahman' is the name of the Son of God, Jesus Christ (see Joseph Smith Papers, "Sample of Pure Language, between circa 4 and circa 20 March 1832," 144). See also commentary in this volume on Doctrine and Covenants 95:17.

What is the Church of the Firstborn? (78:21) "Paul spoke of [Jesus Christ] as 'the firstborn among many brethren' (Rom. 8:29) and as 'the firstborn of every creature' (Col. 1:15). And as *The Church of Jesus Christ* is his earthly church, so *The Church of the Firstborn* is his heavenly church, albeit its members are limited to exalted beings, for whom the family unit continues and who gain an inheritance in the highest heaven of the celestial world (Heb. 12:22–23; D&C 93:22)" (Bruce R. McConkie, *Promised Messiah*, 47). See also commentary in this volume on Doctrine and Covenants 76:54–55 and 93:21–22.

19 And he who receiveth all things with thankfulness shall be made glorious; and the things of this earth shall be added unto him, even an hundred fold, yea, more.

20 Wherefore, do the things which I have commanded you, saith your Redeemer, even the Son Ahman, who prepareth all things before he taketh you;

21 For ye are the church of the Firstborn, and he will take you up in a cloud, and appoint every man his portion.

22 And he that is a faithful and wise steward shall inherit all things. Amen.

Introduction to Doctrine and Covenants 79

"Jared Carter was baptized in Colesville, New York, and moved to Ohio with the Colesville Saints. In the fall of 1831, he left on a mission to the East, preaching the gospel in Ohio, Pennsylvania, New York, and Vermont. After five months of proclaiming the gospel, he returned to his home in Ohio. A few weeks later he visited the Prophet Joseph Smith to inquire about his next mission. On March 12, 1832, Joseph Smith dictated the revelation recorded in Doctrine and Covenants 79" (*Doctrine and Covenants Student Manual* [2018], 421).

SECTION 79

Revelation given through Joseph Smith the Prophet, at Hiram, Ohio, March 12, 1832.

1 Verily I say unto you, that it is my will that my servant Jared Carter should go again into the eastern countries, from place to place, and from city to city, in the power of the ordination wherewith he has been ordained, proclaiming glad tidings of great joy, even the everlasting gospel.

2 And I will send upon him the Comforter, which shall teach him the truth and the way whither he shall go;

3 And inasmuch as he is faithful, I will crown him again with sheaves.

4 Wherefore, let your heart be glad, my servant Jared Carter, and fear not, saith your Lord, even Jesus Christ. Amen.

Doctrine and Covenants 79:1–4. Jared Carter Is Called to Preach the Gospel by the Comforter

What was the "power of the ordination" that Jared Carter received? (79:1) "Jared Carter . . . received the Melchizedek Priesthood and was ordained an elder prior to leaving on his first mission. After having received this revelation, he recorded: 'The word of the Lord came forth that showed that it was his will that I should go forth to the Eastern country as in the power of ordinance where with I had been ordained, which was to the high privilege of administering in the name of Jesus Christ even to seal on earth, to build up the Church of Christ and to work miracles in the name of Christ' (*Journal of Jared Carter*; spelling modernized). It appears from Jared Carter's entry that he was ordained a high priest at this time" (McConkie and Ostler, *Revelations of the Restoration*, 570–71).

In what way does the Comforter teach the truth? (79:2) "One . . . thing is indelibly clear from what the scriptures teach us about the Holy Spirit: *He is a Teacher*. In so many ways, that is what He does. He teaches. He does this by revealing truth, testifying of truth, confirming truth, enlightening the mind. He enhances faith, pricks us with guilt and shame when we do things that displease the Father and the Son, softens the heart so we can repent, strengthens our courage as we carry out Their will, and comforts us when the burdens of life weigh in upon us. All of those work to teach us of the love of God and the perfect saving grace of the Godhead" (Lund, *In Tune*, 17–18).

What were the "sheaves" promised to Jared Carter? (79:3–4) Jared Carter's journal describes the sheaves he was blessed with: "Since I left home and was ordained to preach the gospel and was preaching from place to place now I thought that I had great

---

Missionary Success of Jared Carter (Doctrine and Covenants 79:1)

Following his baptism in Colesville, Jared Carter returned to his home in Chenango, New York, "and shared his enthusiasm for sacred truths, 'some of my best friends, as I had formerly supposed became now my worst enemies.' They mocked his faith and promised him land if he would renounce Mormonism. His reaction: 'Not for fifteen of the best farms in the place would I stay in Chenango one year. . . . I commenced immediately to see my things and to make preparation to go on to the West' [Jared Carter Journal, Typescript, 1]. . . .

"Jared is most remembered for his missions to the eastern states. From 1831 to 1834 his missionary labors were exemplary. . . .

"His missionary labors in New York, Ohio, Pennsylvania, and Vermont led to the baptism of seventy-nine people" (Black, *Who's Who*, 51, 52). See also commentary in this volume on Doctrine and Covenants 94:14.

reason to thank and praise the Lord for what he had done me and my brothers and sisters of my father's family. For the whole family had now come into the glorious work of God, with their companions, except one sister. My three brothers were preachers in this glorious gospel. . . . I can say that God has blessed me according to the prophecy of brother [Joseph], before I went from Ohio. He has blessed me with sheaves and with health and blessed be his name" (Jared Carter Journal, Typescript, 8–9). See also commentary in this volume on Doctrine and Covenants 33:9 and 75:5.

Introduction to Doctrine and Covenants 80

"On March 7, 1832, the Prophet [Joseph Smith] received the revelation recorded as Doctrine and Covenants 80, calling Stephen Burnett to preach the gospel with Eden Smith" (*Doctrine and Covenants Student Manual* [2018], 421).

"At age seventeen, [Stephen] Burnett was ordained to the high priesthood at the October 1831 conference held in Orange, Cuyahoga County, Ohio. Three months later, at the 25 January 1832 conference in Amherst, Ohio, [Joseph Smith] dictated a revelation appointing Burnett to travel and preach with Ruggles Eames, though it is not known if Burnett and Eames fulfilled that assignment. This 7 March revelation appointed Burnett to travel and preach again, this time with Eden Smith. However, the two did not preach together until August 1832 because Eden Smith became sick on 7 March and remained ill 'for sometime.' Instead, two weeks after this revelation was dictated, Burnett began his mission with John Smith, Eden's father" (Joseph Smith Papers, Historical Introduction to "Revelation, 7 March 1832 [D&C 80]").

Doctrine and Covenants 80:1–5. Stephen Burnett and Eden Smith Are Called to Preach in Whatever Place They Choose

Why do so many revelations in the Doctrine and Covenants emphasize the need to preach the gospel? (80:1) President Russell M. Nelson taught that "the gospel of Jesus Christ has never been needed more than it is today. . . .

"[There is an] urgent need for us to follow the Lord's instruction to His disciples to 'go . . . into *all* the world, and preach the gospel to *every* creature' [Mark 16:15; Matthew 28:19]. We have the sacred responsibility to share the power and peace of Jesus Christ with all who will listen and who will let God prevail in their lives.

"Every person who has made covenants with God has promised to care about others and serve those in need. . . . Each of us has a role to play in the gathering of Israel" ("Preaching the Gospel of Peace," *Liahona,* May 2022, 6).

SECTION 80

Revelation given through Joseph Smith the Prophet to Stephen Burnett, at Hiram, Ohio, March 7, 1832.

1 Verily, thus saith the Lord unto you my servant Stephen Burnett: Go ye, go ye into the world and preach the gospel to every creature that cometh under the sound of your voice.

2 And inasmuch as you desire a companion, I will give unto you my servant Eden Smith.

3 Wherefore, go ye and preach my gospel, whether to the north or to the south, to the east or to the west, it mattereth not, for ye cannot go amiss.

4 Therefore, declare the things which ye have heard, and verily believe, and know to be true.

5 Behold, this is the will of him who hath called you, your Redeemer, even Jesus Christ. Amen.

What does the phrase "it mattereth not" mean in this context? (80:3) Elder David A. Bednar stated: "I do not believe that the phrase 'it mattereth not' as used by the Lord in this scripture suggests that He does not care where His servants labor. In fact, He cares deeply. But because the work of preaching the gospel is the Lord's work, He inspires, guides, and directs His authorized servants. As missionaries strive to be ever more worthy and capable instruments in His hands and do their best to fulfill faithfully their duties, then with His help they 'cannot go amiss'—wherever they serve. Perhaps one of the lessons the Savior is teaching us in this revelation is that an assignment to labor in a specific place is essential and important but secondary to a call to the work" ("Called to the Work," *Ensign*, May 2017, 68). See also commentary in this volume on Doctrine and Covenants 62:5. ☉

What are the Lord's servants admonished to declare? (80:4–5) Elder Neil L. Andersen observed, "'I know you talk to everyone who will listen to you,' he said. 'Wherever you are—in a bus, on the street, in a teaching situation, or in a home with a member, if you are ever unsure of what to say, speak of the Savior. Testify of Him. Speak of His doctrine, of faith in Him and His Atonement, repentance, baptism, the Gift of the Holy Ghost and enduring to the end. This is your purpose. This is your charge'" (Swensen, "Elder Neil L. Andersen Speaks").

Introduction to Doctrine and Covenants 81

"The Kirtland Revelation Book records that Doctrine and Covenants 81 was received in Hyrum Ohio, on 15 March 1832.

"Originally, Doctrine and Covenants 81 was directed to a man named Jesse Gause, who had been selected and ordained a counselor in the Presidency of the High Priesthood on 8 March 1832. Brother Gause left the Church before the end of the year, however, and was excommunicated December 1832. He was replaced as a counselor to Joseph Smith by Frederick G. Williams after a revelation was received by the Prophet on 5 January 1833; that revelation is not included in the Doctrine and Covenants" (Robinson and Garrett, *Commentary on the Doctrine and Covenants*, 3:1).

The Joseph Smith Papers indicate: "At a later point—sometime after the appointment of Williams as a counselor to [Joseph Smith] in January 1833—Oliver Cowdery replaced Gause's name with Williams's in the Revelation Book.... The published versions of this revelation in the 1835 edition of the Doctrine and Covenants, the 1844 edition of the Doctrine and Covenants, and the 15 August 1844 issue of the *Times and Seasons* all have Williams's name instead of Gause's. This indicates that [Joseph Smith] and others regarded this revelation as containing general information about the duties of a counselor, rather than instructions specific to Gause" (Joseph Smith Papers, Historical Introduction to "Revelation, 15 March 1832 [D&C 81]").

Doctrine and Covenants 81:1–2. The Keys of the Kingdom Are Always Held by the First Presidency

What are the "keys of the kingdom" given to Joseph Smith? (81:1–2) Elder Gary E. Stevenson taught regarding priesthood keys: "First, an understanding of these terms may be helpful. The priesthood, or priesthood authority, has been defined as 'the power and authority of God' and 'the consummate power on this earth.' Priesthood keys are defined for our understanding as well: 'Priesthood keys are the authority God has given to priesthood leaders to direct, control, and govern the use of His priesthood on earth.' Priesthood keys control the exercise of priesthood authority. Ordinances that create a record in the Church require keys and cannot be done without authorization. President Dallin H. Oaks taught that 'ultimately, all keys of the priesthood are held by the Lord Jesus Christ, whose priesthood it is. He is the one who determines what keys are delegated to mortals and how those keys will be used'" (Stevenson, "Where Are the Keys and Authority of the Priesthood?" *Ensign*, May 2016, 30). ⊕

SECTION 81

Revelation given through Joseph Smith the Prophet, at Hiram, Ohio, March 15, 1832. Frederick G. Williams is called to be a high priest and a counselor in the Presidency of the High Priesthood. The historical records show that when this revelation was received in March 1832, it called Jesse Gause to the office of counselor to Joseph Smith in the Presidency. However, when he failed to continue in a manner consistent with this appointment, the call was subsequently transferred to Frederick G. Williams. The revelation (dated March 1832) should be regarded as a step toward the formal organization of the First Presidency, specifically calling for the office of counselor in that body and explaining the dignity of the appointment. Brother Gause served for a time but was excommunicated from the Church in December 1832. Brother Williams was ordained to the specified office on March 18, 1833.

1 Verily, verily, I say unto you my servant Frederick G. Williams: Listen to the voice of him who speaketh, to the word of the Lord your God, and hearken to the calling wherewith you are called, even to be a high priest in my church, and a counselor unto my servant Joseph Smith, Jun.;

2 Unto whom I have given the keys of the kingdom, which belong always unto the Presidency of the High Priesthood:

3 Therefore, verily I acknowledge him and will bless him, and also thee, inasmuch as thou art faithful in counsel, in the office which I have appointed unto you, in prayer always, vocally and in thy heart, in public and in private, also in thy ministry in proclaiming the gospel in the land of the living, and among thy brethren.

What is the office of "the Presidency of the High Priesthood"? (81:2) "In November 1831, a revelation directed the appointment of a president of the high priesthood. The individual holding this office would serve as 'the Presiding high Priest over the high Priesthood of the Church' and would 'preside over the whole church.' He would also serve as 'a Seer, a revelator, a translator, & a prophet, having all the gifts of God, which he bestoweth upon the head of the church.' After [Joseph Smith's] ordination as president of the high priesthood on 25 January 1832, his position was sometimes referred to as 'the office of the presidency of the high Priesthood'" (Joseph Smith Papers Glossary, s.v. "Presidency of the high priesthood"). ⊕

Doctrine and Covenants 81:3–7. If Frederick G. Williams Is Faithful in His Ministry, He Will Have Eternal Life

What did it mean for Frederick G. Williams to be "faithful in counsel" in his appointed office? (81:3) "Counselors are called to do just that—to provide counsel—as well as to assist, strengthen, and support. Their role is to participate—actively and candidly—in the decision-making process, to support and sustain

"My Servant Frederick G. Williams" (Doctrine and Covenants 81:1)

"When Oliver Cowdery, Parley P. Pratt, Ziba Peterson, and Peter Whitmer Jr. came through northern Ohio in the fall of 1830 on the first extended missionary journey of this dispensation, they baptized the prominent physician Frederick G. Williams and his wife. . . . Immediately after his baptism, Brother Williams was ordained an elder and was invited to travel west with the missionaries who had converted him. Although he intended to return after three weeks, he became so involved in the work that he did not return for ten months.

Frederick G. Williams

"Dedicating all he had to the restored Church, Brother Williams soon became a man of influence in the Church and in the city of Kirtland. He was called by revelation to serve as second counselor to Joseph Smith. The love the Prophet had for Frederick is evidenced by the fact that he named his second son Frederick Granger Williams Smith. Of his counselor the Prophet wrote, 'Brother Frederick G. Williams is one of those men in whom I place the greatest confidence and trust, for I have found him ever full of love and brotherly kindness. He is not a man of many words, but is ever winning, because of his constant mind. He shall ever have place in my heart.'

"In addition to his duties in the First Presidency, Brother Williams was one of the scribes of the Joseph Smith Translation of the Bible, and he became a justice of the peace, proprietor of the Church's printing operation, trustee of the School of the Prophets, and president of the Kirtland Safety Society Bank. When the society failed in 1837, President Williams became involved in the disunity that afflicted many members and leaders of the Church. In November 1837, he was rejected by a vote of the membership of the Church and removed from the First Presidency. Over a year later he was excommunicated for having left the Saints 'in the time of . . . perils, persecutions and dangers, and . . . acting against the interests of the Church.' At the April conference in 1840 held in Nauvoo, Dr. Williams 'humbly asked forgiveness for his former wrongdoing. He expressed a determination to do the will of God.' He was received into full fellowship and died a faithful Latter-day Saint two years later" (Lawrence R. Flake, *Prophets and Apostles*, 239–40).

all council decisions, and to execute their implementation through their respective organizations" (Ballard, *Counseling with Our Councils*, rev. ed., 75).

How do each of us "stand in the office" the Lord has appointed us? (81:5) President Gordon B. Hinckley explained: "Your obligation is as serious in your sphere of responsibility as is my obligation in my sphere. No calling in this church is small or of little consequence. All of us in the pursuit of our duty touch the lives of others. To each of us in our respective responsibilities the Lord has said: 'Wherefore, be faithful; stand in the office which I have appointed unto you; succor the weak, lift up the hands which hang down, and strengthen the feeble knees' (D&C 81:5). . . .

"Whatever your calling, it is as fraught with the same kind of opportunity to accomplish good as is mine" ("This Is the Work of the Master," *Ensign*, May 1995, 71).

What should we remember as we "succor the weak"? (81:5) President Thomas S. Monson observed: "As I ponder his words [D&C 81:5–6], I can almost hear the shuffle of sandaled feet. . . .

"Not only by precept did Jesus teach, but also by example. He was faithful to his divine mission. He stretched forth his hand that others might be lifted toward God. . . .

"He lived not so to be ministered unto, but to minister; not to receive, but to give; not to save his life, but to pour it out for others.

"If [you] would see the star that should at once direct [your] feet and influence [your] destiny, [you] must look for it, not in the changing skies or outward circumstance, but each in the depth of his own heart and after the pattern provided by the Master" ("With Hand and Heart," *Ensign*, Dec. 1971, 131).

What do we know about the faithfulness of Frederick G. Williams? (81:5–6) "During the apostasy in Kirtland in 1837, Frederick G. Williams became estranged from the Church. A conference of elders in Far West refused to sustain him as a member of the First Presidency, and at a conference in March 1839 he was excommunicated from the Church. Happily, about a year later he appeared during a general conference of the Church and 'humbly asked forgiveness for his conduct [while in Missouri], and expressed his determination to do the will of God in the future' ([Joseph Smith Papers, "History, 1838–1856, volume C-1," 1046]). His petition was accepted, and he was rebaptized

4 And in doing these things thou wilt do the greatest good unto thy fellow beings, and wilt promote the glory of him who is your Lord.

5 Wherefore, be faithful; stand in the office which I have appointed unto you; succor the weak, lift up the hands which hang down, and strengthen the feeble knees.

6 And if thou art faithful unto the end thou shalt have a crown of immortality, and eternal life in the mansions which I have prepared in the house of my Father.

7 Behold, and lo, these are the words of Alpha and Omega, even Jesus Christ. Amen.

soon afterwards. He died in Nauvoo in 1842" (*Doctrine and Covenants Student Manual* [2001], 177).

What is the promise for those who receive eternal life"? (81:6) Sister Amy A. Wright declared: "Eternal life is eternal joy. Joy in this life, *right now*—not despite the challenges of our day but because of the Lord's help to learn from and ultimately overcome them—*and* immeasurable joy in the life to come. Tears will dry up, broken hearts will be mended, what is lost shall be found, concerns shall be resolved, families will be restored, and all that the Father hath will be ours" ("Abide the Day in Christ," *Liahona*, Nov. 2023, 11).

Introduction to Doctrine and Covenants 82

Doctrine and Covenants 82 was received by the Prophet Joseph Smith on April 26, 1832, when he was visiting Independence, Missouri. "[The Prophet] 'started for Missouri in company with Newel K. Whitney, Peter Whitmer, and Jesse Gause to fulfill the revelation' they had been given in Doctrine and Covenants 78 to visit Church leaders in Missouri and with them unify the Church's economic organization. . . .

"Joseph noted with relief that the Missouri Saints were glad to see them and sustained him as President of the High Priesthood and that Bishop Edward Partridge extended 'the right hand of fellowship' in a scene the Prophet called 'solemn, impressive, and delightful.' This was the desired but uncertain outcome of their arrival. Hard feelings had existed between the leaders in Missouri and Kirtland. Some in Missouri felt Joseph was power-hungry. And Sidney Rigdon was upset with Bishop Partridge for some reason. Joseph's history says that between meetings the 'difficulty or hardness which had existed between Bishop Partridge and Elder Rigdon was amicably settled, and when we came together in the afternoon all hearts seemed to rejoice, and I received the following Revelation given April, 1832, [showing] the order given to Enoch and the church in his day' [Jessee, *Papers of Joseph Smith*, 1:379–81]" (Harper, *Making Sense of the Doctrine & Covenants*, 288–89).

Part of this "revelation reiterated the need to organize a governing firm for the church's business and publishing interests and named the individuals who were to participate in this organization. They included five men living in Missouri ([Edward] Partridge, Sidney Gilbert, Oliver Cowdery, John Whitmer, and William W. Phelps) and four living in Ohio ([Joseph Smith], [Sidney] Rigdon, Newel K. Whitney, and Martin Harris). The revelation indicated that each of these individuals had a stewardship over some aspect of church business and that uniting them in the firm would allow them to draw on each other's resources to manage these endeavors, thereby producing more 'talents,' or surplus, for the church's storehouses" (Joseph Smith Papers, Historical Introduction to "Revelation, 26 April 1832 [D&C 82]"; spelling modernized).

SECTION 82

Revelation given to Joseph Smith the Prophet, in Independence, Jackson County, Missouri, April 26, 1832. The occasion was a council of high priests and elders of the Church. At the council, Joseph Smith was sustained as the President of the High Priesthood, to which office he had previously been ordained at a conference of high priests, elders, and members, at Amherst,

Doctrine and Covenants 82:1–4. Where Much Is Given, Much Is Required

How does the Lord bless the Saints for forgiving each other? (82:1) "The Lord requires us to forgive for our own good. But He does not ask us to do it without His help, His love, His understanding. Through our covenants with the Lord, we can each receive the strengthening power, guidance, and the help we need to both forgive and to be forgiven.

"Please know that forgiving someone does not mean that you put yourself in a position where you will continue to be hurt. 'We can work toward forgiving someone and still feel prompted by the Spirit to stay away from them'" (Yee, "Beauty for Ashes," *Liahona*, Nov. 2022, 37). ✪

Why does the Lord require so much from His followers? (82:3) Sheri Dew testified: "At times the demands of discipleship are heavy. But shouldn't we expect the journey towards eternal glory to stretch us? We sometimes rationalize our preoccupation with this world and our casual attempts to grow spiritually by trying to console each other with the notion that living the gospel really shouldn't require all that much of us. The Lord's standard of behavior will always be more demanding than the world's, but then the Lord's rewards are infinitely more glorious—including true joy, peace, and salvation" ("We Are Women of God," *Ensign*, Nov. 1999, 98). ✪

Doctrine and Covenants 82:5–7. Darkness Reigns in the World

What is the darkness spoken of here? (82:5) "'Darkness' here, as in John 1:5, means the condition of the world outside divine revelation. It refers to both spiritual and moral error. Revelation from God gives light, but when divine revelation is rejected, the adversary spreads his dominion among the children of men" (Smith and Sjodahl, *Doctrine and Covenants Commentary*, 490).

Ohio, January 25, 1832 (see the heading to section 75). This revelation reiterates instructions given in an earlier revelation (section 78) to establish a firm—known as the United Firm (under Joseph Smith's direction, the term "order" later replaced "firm")—to govern the Church's mercantile and publishing endeavors.

1 Verily, verily, I say unto you, my servants, that inasmuch as you have forgiven one another your trespasses, even so I, the Lord, forgive you.

2 Nevertheless, there are those among you who have sinned exceedingly; yea, even all of you have sinned; but verily I say unto you, beware from henceforth, and refrain from sin, lest sore judgments fall upon your heads.

3 For of him unto whom much is given much is required; and he who sins against the greater light shall receive the greater condemnation.

4 Ye call upon my name for revelations, and I give them unto you; and inasmuch as ye keep not my sayings, which I give unto you, ye become transgressors; and justice and judgment are the penalty which is affixed unto my law.

5 Therefore, what I say unto one I say unto all: Watch, for the adversary spreadeth his dominions, and darkness reigneth;

6 And the anger of God kindleth against the inhabitants of the earth; and none doeth good, for all have gone out of the way.

7 And now, verily I say unto you, I, the Lord, will not lay any sin to your charge; go your ways and sin no more; but unto that soul who sinneth shall the former sins return, saith the Lord your God.

8 And again, I say unto you, I give unto you a new commandment, that you may understand my will concerning you;

9 Or, in other words, I give unto you directions how you may act before me, that it may turn to you for your salvation.

10 I, the Lord, am bound when ye do what I say; but when ye do not what I say, ye have no promise.

How is it true that "none doeth good, for all have gone out of the way"? (82:6) "We know that the effects of [Adam's] fall passed upon all his posterity; all inherited a fallen state. . . . In this state all men sin. All are lost. All are fallen. All are cut off from the presence of God. All have become carnal, sensual, and devilish by nature. . . .

"Carnal man has been in this state of opposition to God since the fall of Adam; such is his present state, and he will so remain forever, unless provision is made whereby he can escape from the grasp of justice. . . .

"Men are commanded to repent lest they be smitten by the Lord's wrath and their sufferings be both sore and exquisite" (Bruce R. McConkie, *Promised Messiah*, 244–45, 247). ◉

How can we come to the point when we "sin no more"? (82:7) "Our progress in embracing the attributes of Jesus Christ in our own lives will not come in one experience of confessing and forsaking. It will come as we evaluate our actions daily and plead for our Savior's mercy as we seek to become better. Unfortunately, we may slip back at times, but let us quickly and humbly return to our knees and move again in the right direction.

"The Lord desires that we constantly strengthen ourselves and become better, trying not to repeat even the small sins of the past. . . .

"Once we have truly left the sin behind, we do not dwell on it, relish in it, or talk about it widely with others" (Andersen, *Divine Gift of Forgiveness*, 208, 209). ◉

Doctrine and Covenants 82:8–13. The Lord Is Bound When We Do What He Says

What does it mean that the Lord is "bound" when we obey Him? (82:10) "In this section, binding is mentioned three times, in this verse, in verse 11, and in verse 15. In the second two cases, it clearly means 'sealed by covenant.' It seems reasonable to assume that's what it means here too, especially given the explicit connection of *bound* and *promise* in this verse. We sometimes hear people using this verse to discuss 'binding God,' in other words, putting ourselves in a position where we force him to do what we want, but that seems fairly clearly to be a misunderstanding of the verse. The point is that he binds himself to us by covenant when we obey him, not that when we obey him we have power over him" (Faulconer, *Doctrine & Covenants Made Harder*, 92). See also commentary in this volume on Doctrine and Covenants 130:21. ◉

For what purpose were these men being "bound together"? (82:11–13) Soon after the Prophet Joseph Smith and his companions arrived in Jackson County, Missouri, they met "to establish a branch of the United Firm in Missouri according to the Lord's command (see D&C 78:3–4). The Lord revealed that members of the Literary Firm, previously called by the Lord, were to also be included in the organization of the United Firm. In addition, the eight members were to be joined by Bishop Edward Partridge (see D&C 82:11). The next day the council of brethren reconvened and determined that the names of the branches of the United Firm in Ohio and Missouri would be 'Gilbert, Whitney & Company in Zion. And Newel K. Whitney & Company in Kirtland Geauga Co. Ohio'" (Ostler, "Laws of Consecration, Stewardship, and Tithing," 164). See commentary in this volume on Doctrine and Covenants 70: introduction and verses 1–3; 72:20–21; 78: introduction and verses 1–4. ⊙

What is a *stake*? (82:13) "The clarion call to 'enlarge' and 'strengthen' the stakes of Zion was given anciently to Isaiah (Isa. 54:2), repeated to the Nephites (3 Ne. 22:2), and reiterated in our day (D&C 109:59; 133:9). A stake is an ecclesiastical unit of The Church of Jesus Christ of Latter-day Saints and covers a specific geographical area. According to the Lord, stakes are 'curtains or the strength of Zion' (D&C 101:21). They are places where the Saints of God may be instructed more perfectly in the doctrines of salvation" (Brewster, *Doctrine & Covenants Encyclopedia* [2012], 558).

A stake comprises a group of local Church congregations. "Creating a stake . . . requires 2,000 total members" ("First Presidency Announces Uniform, Worldwide Standards"). ⊙

Doctrine and Covenants 82:14–18. Zion Must Increase in Beauty and Holiness

How will Zion increase in beauty and holiness? (82:14) President Harold B. Lee explained that, "The pure in heart is the beginning of the growth of Zion. When the Lord therefore said: 'Zion must increase in beauty, and in holiness' (D&C 82:14), he was saying in effect, every individual member of the Church must strive to improve himself therein, within his own station, becoming greater in order to strengthen the place where he lives. . . .

"The borders of Zion, where the righteous and pure in heart may dwell, must now begin to be enlarged; the stakes of Zion must be strengthened—all this so that Zion may arise and shine by becoming

11 Therefore, verily I say unto you, that it is expedient for my servants Edward Partridge and Newel K. Whitney, A. Sidney Gilbert and Sidney Rigdon, and my servant Joseph Smith, and John Whitmer and Oliver Cowdery, and W. W. Phelps and Martin Harris to be bound together by a bond and covenant that cannot be broken by transgression, except judgment shall immediately follow, in your several stewardships—

12 To manage the affairs of the poor, and all things pertaining to the bishopric both in the land of Zion and in the land of Kirtland;

13 For I have consecrated the land of Kirtland in mine own due time for the benefit of the saints of the Most High, and for a stake to Zion.

14 For Zion must increase in beauty, and in holiness; her borders must be enlarged; her stakes must be strengthened; yea, verily I say unto you, Zion must arise and put on her beautiful garments.

15 Therefore, I give unto you this commandment, that ye bind yourselves by this covenant, and it shall be done according to the laws of the Lord.

16 Behold, here is wisdom also in me for your good.

17 And you are to be equal, or in other words, you are to have equal claims on the properties, for the benefit of managing the concerns of your stewardships, every man according to his wants and his needs, inasmuch as his wants are just—

18 And all this for the benefit of the church of the living God, that every man may improve upon his talent, that every man may gain other talents, yea, even an hundred fold, to be cast into the Lord's storehouse, to become the common property of the whole church—

increasingly diligent in carrying out the plan of salvation throughout the world" (*Teachings*, 409). ●

What did it mean for these men to bind themselves "by this covenant"? (82:15–18) "Essentially, this revelation stated that those members of the firm would receive sustenance for themselves and their families out of the mercantile and publishing establishments that they were commanded to manage and that they were to enter into a legal bond that would join them together in terms of their obligations for the firm's debts.

"The council met again the next day and . . . appointed Phelps and Gilbert to draft the bond that the members of the firm needed to enter as instructed by the revelation" (Godfrey, "Newel K. Whitney and the United Firm," 144).

What is the meaning of "talent" in this verse? (82:18) "In a beautiful statement about the law of consecration, the Lord declares the reason he has consecrated Zion and its stake in Kirtland to the Saints and why he commands them to covenant with him to consecrate [see verse 18]. *Talent* in these verses refers to the parable of the talents in Matthew 25, in which a *talent* is a Hebrew coin. This revelation is about economics. But by Joseph Smith's time the word talent has taken on the metaphorical meaning of a natural gift or endowment, which gives the Lord's usage of it here an enriched meaning" (Harper, *Making Sense of the Doctrine & Covenants*, 289).

How can we make best use of our God-given talents? (82:18) One early Latter-day Saint sister observed: "Having a knowledge that God is our Father, and that He holds us accountable for the use we make of the talents He has given us, how necessary it is that we should cultivate and improve those God-given germs and apply them to usefulness in his kingdom. We are living in the day when the Priesthood of God is on earth, and through the great mercy of God man partakes of its blessings; we are not left in darkness and ignorance like those who have not received the fullness of the Gospel. We have many advantages which others do not possess; we have means for acquiring a higher development of mind and of obtaining knowledge which is of the greatest worth" (Johnson and Reeder, *Witness of Women*, 88–89).

Doctrine and Covenants 82:19–24. Every Man Should Seek the Interest of His Neighbor

How can we seek the interest of our neighbor? (82:19) President M. Russell Ballard explained, "It is only when we love God and Christ with all of our hearts, souls, and minds that we are able to share this love with our neighbors through acts of kindness and service" ("Finding Joy through Loving Service," *Ensign*, May 2011, 47; see also Alma 37:36).

Sister Joy D. Jones summarized, "I testify that when Jesus Christ, through the power of His Atonement, works *on* us and *in* us, He begins to work *through* us to bless others. We serve them, but we do so by loving and serving Him" ("For Him," *Ensign*, Nov. 2018, 52).

Why would the Lord instruct the Saints to make "friends with the mammon of unrighteousness"? (82:22) S. Kent Brown explained the phrase "make unto yourselves friends of the mammon of

19 Every man seeking the interest of his neighbor, and doing all things with an eye single to the glory of God.

20 This order I have appointed to be an everlasting order unto you, and unto your successors, inasmuch as you sin not.

21 And the soul that sins against this covenant, and hardeneth his heart against it, shall be dealt with according to the laws of my church, and shall be delivered over to the buffetings of Satan until the day of redemption.

22 And now, verily I say unto you, and this is wisdom, make unto yourselves friends with the mammon of unrighteousness, and they will not destroy you.

Offerings for the Benefit of the Whole Church (Doctrine and Covenants 82:18)

"Sarah Granger Kimball (1818–1898) dedicated her life to the Lord but did not have her own material assets to offer. Like most nineteenth-century women, Sarah was dependent on her husband for resources. In a clever and progressive move for her time, she asked her husband to monetarily value her work in the home and with their son, enabling her own contribution to the Church.

"'My eldest son was born in Nauvoo. . . . When the babe was three days old[,] . . . the walls of the Nauvoo Temple were about three feet above the foundation. The Church was in need of help to assist in raising the Temple walls. I belonged to The Church of Jesus Christ of Latter-day Saints; my husband did not belong to the Church at that time. I wished to help on the Temple, but did not like to ask my husband (who owned considerable property) to help for my sake.

Sarah Granger Kimball

"'My husband came to my bedside, and as he was admiring our three days old darling, I said, "What is the boy worth?" He replied, "Oh, I don't know; he is worth a great deal." I said, "Is he worth a thousand dollars?" The reply was, "Yes, more than that if he lives and does well." I said, "Half of him is mine, is it not?" "Yes, I suppose so." "Then I have something to help on the Temple." (Pleasantly) "You have?" "Yes, and I am thinking of turning my share right in as tithing." "Well, I'll think about that."

"'Soon after the above conversation, Mr. Kimball met the Prophet . . . and said, "Sarah has got a little the advantage of me this time. She proposes to turn out the boy as church property." President Smith seemed pleased with the joke, and said. "I accept all such donations, and from this day the boy shall stand recorded, church property." Then turning to Willard Richards, his secretary, he said. "Make a record of this; and you are my witness." Joseph Smith then said, "Major (Mr. Kimball was major in the Nauvoo Legion), you now have the privilege of paying $500 and retaining possession, or receiving $500 and giving possession." Mr. Kimball asked if city property was good currency. President Smith replied that it was. "Then," said Mr. Kimball, "how will that block north of the Temple suit?" President Smith replied, "It is just what we want." The deed was soon made out and transferred in due form.

"'President Smith said to me, "You have consecrated your first born son. For this you are blessed of the Lord. I bless you in the name of the Lord God of Abraham, of Isaac and of Jacob. And I seal upon you all the blessings that pertain to the faithful"'" (Johnson and Reeder, *Witness of Women*, 87–88).

23 Leave judgment alone with me, for it is mine and I will repay. Peace be with you; my blessings continue with you.

24 For even yet the kingdom is yours, and shall be forever, if you fall not from your steadfastness. Even so. Amen.

unrighteousness" in connection with Luke 16:9, which has implications for the Lord's words in modern revelation: "Jesus' command offers a proper orientation to the modern world. We are to become friends with it, accepting what it brings, but not to embrace it and allow it to overpower our commitment to the world of righteousness. For how disciples deal with the world shapes to a large extent how and whether God 'will commit to [our] trust true riches' (16:11). This principle seeps into how we use possessions in the service of the kingdom: are we as careful and scrupulous as givers and stewards of donated funds, such as alms and tithes, as people are about their material goals? In a different vein, modern scripture renders this expression with a slightly different focus: 'make unto yourselves friends *with* the mammon of unrighteousness,' placing emphasis on making proper use of this world's goods (D&C 82:22; emphasis added)" (Brown, *Testimony of Luke*, 751). ⊕

Introduction to Doctrine and Covenants 83

"According to a later [Joseph Smith] history, [the Prophet] 'sat in council with the brethren' on 30 April 1832 in Independence, Jackson County, Missouri, and dictated a revelation clarifying the rights of women and children who had lost their husbands or fathers. Although there were civil laws outlining specific property rights for women upon the death of their husbands, it was not clear what would happen if a husband had consecrated property to the church. The 30 April revelation helped clarify the church's position in such instances. . . .

"[Joseph] apparently became concerned about such questions while in Missouri in April 1832. Perhaps one reason was his short trip from 28–29 April to visit the Saints from Colesville, New York, who had settled about twelve miles west of Independence in Kaw Township, Missouri. . . . Among those living in Kaw Township were at least two widows: Phebe Crosby Peck, who had four children, and Anna Slade Rogers, who had a daughter. These women's husbands died in 1829 before the revelation on the 'Laws of the Church of Christ' was dictated, but [Joseph's] association with them may have prompted him to wonder about a widow's claim to consecrated property, which may in turn have led to this 30 April revelation" (Joseph Smith Papers, Historical Introduction to "Revelation, 30 April 1832 [D&C 83]").

SECTION 83

Revelation given through Joseph Smith the Prophet, at Independence, Missouri, April 30, 1832. This revelation was received as the Prophet sat in council with his brethren.

1 Verily, thus saith the Lord, in addition to the laws of the church concerning women and children, those who belong to the church, who have lost their husbands or fathers:

Doctrine and Covenants 83:1–4. Women and Children Have Claim upon Their Husbands and Fathers for Their Support

What are the laws of the Church concerning women and children who lack temporal support? (83:1) President Gordon B. Hinckley stated, "Included among the women of the Church are those who have lost their husbands through abandonment, divorce, and death. Great is our obligation to you. . . .

"I hope that every woman who finds herself in [these kinds of circumstances is] blessed with an understanding and helpful bishop, with a Relief Society president who knows how to assist her, with [ministering brothers and sisters] who know where their duty lies and how to fulfill it, and with a host of ward members who are helpful without being intrusive" ("Women of the Church," *Ensign,* Nov. 1996, 68, 69).

What claim do women have on their husbands? (83:2) "The Family: A Proclamation to the World," declares the following: "By divine design, fathers are to preside over their families in love and righteousness and are responsible to provide the necessities of life and protection for their families. Mothers are primarily responsible for the nurture of their children. In these sacred responsibilities, fathers and mothers are obligated to help one another as equal partners. Disability, death, or other circumstances may necessitate individual adaptation. Extended families should lend support when needed" (*Ensign*, Nov. 1995, 102; see also *Ensign*, May 2017, 145).

What claim do children have on their parents? (83:4) "Husband and wife have a solemn responsibility to love and care for each other and for their children. . . . Parents have a sacred duty to rear their children in love and righteousness, to provide for their physical and spiritual needs. . . . Husbands and wives—mothers and fathers—will be held accountable before God for the discharge of these obligations" ("Family: A Proclamation," *Ensign*, Nov. 1995, 102; see also *Ensign*, May 2017, 145).

Doctrine and Covenants 83:5–6. Widows and Orphans Have Claim upon the Church for Their Support

What was the status of children in Independence, Missouri, at that time? (83:5) "These instructions have particular application within the laws of consecration as practiced at that time. Children were expected to provide for their own temporal welfare when sufficiently mature to do so. If their parents had means to provide an inheritance for them, they were to receive property from them. Those that entered into adulthood without any means of providing for themselves had claim upon the properties of the Church to receive an inheritance within the law of consecration" (McConkie and Ostler, *Revelations of the Restoration*, 584–85).

How is the Lord's storehouse used today? (83:6) "The Savior taught, 'Impart of your substance unto the poor, . . . and [it] shall be laid before the bishop . . . [and] shall be kept in my storehouse, to administer

2 Women have claim on their husbands for their maintenance, until their husbands are taken; and if they are not found transgressors they shall have fellowship in the church.

3 And if they are not faithful they shall not have fellowship in the church; yet they may remain upon their inheritances according to the laws of the land.

4 All children have claim upon their parents for their maintenance until they are of age.

5 And after that, they have claim upon the church, or in other words upon the Lord's storehouse, if their parents have not wherewith to give them inheritances.

6 And the storehouse shall be kept by the consecrations of the church; and widows and orphans shall be provided for, as also the poor. Amen.

to the poor and the needy' (Doctrine and Covenants 42:31, 34). All the resources available to the Church to help those with temporal needs are called the Lord's storehouse (see Doctrine and Covenants 82:18–19). These include members' offerings of time, talents, compassion, materials, and financial resources to help those in need.

"The Lord's storehouse exists in each ward and stake. Leaders can often help individuals and families find solutions to their needs by drawing on the knowledge, skills, and service offered by ward and stake members" (*General Handbook*, 22.2.1).

Introduction to Doctrine and Covenants 84

"During a conference of priesthood holders held in Amherst, Ohio, on January 25, 1832, a number of elders were called to preach the gospel in various locations in the United States (see D&C 75). In September 1832, some of these elders returned from their missions in the eastern states. Joseph and Emma Smith had just moved from the John and Alice (Elsa) Johnson home in Hiram, Ohio, to the living quarters in the Newel K. Whitney store in Kirtland, Ohio. When the missionaries returned to Kirtland, they reported their experiences, and the Prophet Joseph Smith rejoiced in their success. While the Prophet was with these elders on September 22, he inquired of the Lord and received revelation about the priesthood. The Prophet continued to receive instruction from the Lord the following day, September 23. This revelation, received over two days, is recorded in Doctrine and Covenants 84. Several individuals witnessed the Prophet Joseph Smith dictate the revelation. Doctrine and Covenants 84:1 suggests that six elders were present as the dictation began, but a note in an original handwritten copy of the revelation indicates that 10 high priests were present during the latter part of the revelation (see [*Joseph Smith Papers: Documents, Volume 2*, 289–90])" (*Doctrine and Covenants Student Manual* [2018], 436). For a map of Kirtland, Ohio 1830–1838, see Map 7 in the Appendix.

"It is clear that [during this period] Joseph had the temple on his mind. The Lord had already revealed to him the site for a temple in Independence, Missouri. Joseph had dedicated the ground. This revelation tells the Saints to build the temple and forges the gospel links between their missionary work, the gathering of scattered Israel, the fulfillment of ancient prophecies, and the building of New Jerusalem, crowned with its holy temple.

"Section 84 is a landmark revelation with a breathtaking scope. Joseph's history designates it a 'Revelation . . . On Priesthood.' It is certainly that and can just as accurately be described as a revelation on temple ordinances, covenants, the gathering of Israel, missionary work, the law of consecration, and the imminent coming of the Savior to 'reign with my people,' in Zion, as he says in closing (v. 119)" (Harper, *Making Sense of the Doctrine & Covenants*, 295).

In the October 2019 Women's session of general conference, President Russell M. Nelson counseled the sisters of the Church: "I entreat you to study prayerfully *all* the truths you can find about priesthood power. You might begin with Doctrine and Covenants sections 84 and 107. Those sections will lead you to other passages. The scriptures and teachings by modern prophets, seers, and revelators are filled with these truths. As your understanding increases and as you exercise faith in the Lord and His priesthood power, your ability to draw upon this spiritual treasure that the Lord has made available will increase. As you do so, you will find yourselves better able to help create eternal families that are united, sealed in the temple of the Lord, and full of love for our Heavenly Father and for Jesus Christ" ("Spiritual Treasures," *Ensign*, Nov. 2019, 79).

SECTION 84

Revelation given through Joseph Smith the Prophet, at Kirtland, Ohio, September 22 and 23, 1832. During the month of September, elders had begun to return from their missions in

Doctrine and Covenants 84:1–5. The New Jerusalem and the Temple Will Be Built in Missouri

Where will Mount Zion be located? (84:2–3) "All of the references to Mount Zion which talk of the Second Coming and related latter-day events appear to have in mind the new Mount Zion in Jackson County, Missouri. . . .

"It seems clear that the Lord and his exalted associates shall stand in glory upon the American Mount Zion, although it may well be that in his numerous other appearances, including that on the Mount of Olivet, which is itself but a few stones' throw from old Mount Zion, he shall also be accompanied by the 144,000 high priests, 'for they follow the Lamb whithersoever he goeth'" (Bruce R. McConkie, *Doctrinal New Testament Commentary*, 3:525–26).

Why is it so vital for the Saints to be gathered? (84:4) President Russell M. Nelson answered this question: "Why is this promise of gathering so crucial? Because the gathering of Israel is necessary to prepare the world for the Second Coming! And the Book of Mormon is God's instrument needed to accomplish both of these divine objectives. . . .

"Regarding the Second Coming, we know it is 'now nigh at hand, and in a time [yet] to come' (D&C 63:53). And when the Savior comes again, it will not be in secret. Meanwhile, much work must be done to gather Israel and prepare the world for the glorious Second Coming" ("Book of Mormon, the Gathering of Israel, and the Second Coming," *Ensign*, Jul. 2014, 29).

What does it mean that the temple will be built "in this generation"? (84:4) "The word *generation* may have different meanings. Often it refers to the time between the birth of parents and that of their children, but it sometimes refers to those born during a given period of time. . . .

"President Joseph Fielding Smith cited the Savior's allusion to 'an evil and adulterous generation' (Matthew 12:39) and concluded that 'this did not

the eastern states and to make reports of their labors. It was while they were together in this season of joy that the following communication was received. The Prophet designated it a revelation on priesthood.

1 A revelation of Jesus Christ unto his servant Joseph Smith, Jun., and six elders, as they united their hearts and lifted their voices on high.

2 Yea, the word of the Lord concerning his church, established in the last days for the restoration of his people, as he has spoken by the mouth of his prophets, and for the gathering of his saints to stand upon Mount Zion, which shall be the city of New Jerusalem.

3 Which city shall be built, beginning at the temple lot, which is appointed by the finger of the Lord, in the western boundaries of the State of Missouri, and dedicated by the hand of Joseph Smith, Jun., and others with whom the Lord was well pleased.

4 Verily this is the word of the Lord, that the city New Jerusalem shall be built by the gathering of the saints, beginning at this place, even the place of the temple, which temple shall be reared in this generation.

5 For verily this generation shall not all pass away until an house shall be built unto the Lord, and a cloud shall rest upon it, which cloud shall be even the glory of the Lord, which shall fill the house.

6 And the sons of Moses, according to the Holy Priesthood which he received under the hand of his father-in-law, Jethro;

7 And Jethro received it under the hand of Caleb;

8 And Caleb received it under the hand of Elihu;

9 And Elihu under the hand of Jeremy;

10 And Jeremy under the hand of Gad;

11 And Gad under the hand of Esaias;

12 And Esaias received it under the hand of God.

have reference to a period of years, but to a period of wickedness.' He therefore reasoned, 'A generation may mean the time of this present dispensation' (*Church History and Modern Revelation*, 1:337). If that definition is correct, it would mean the temple must be built during 'this generation,' that is, the dispensation of the fulness of times" (Cowan, *Answers to Your Questions*, 96).

What does the cloud resting upon the temple represent? (84:5) "The Lord manifested Himself in ancient Israel in a cloud, shaped as a pillar, which became luminous at night. It guided the people on the journey to Canaan. It stood at the entrance to the Sanctuary, and in it God spoke to Moses. It rested on the Sanctuary and filled it, when that sacred tent was set up. It was the visible sign of God's guiding and protecting care over His people" (Smith and Sjodahl, *Doctrine and Covenants Commentary*, 497).

Doctrine and Covenants 84:6–17. The Line of Priesthood from Moses to Adam Is Given

How did Moses's father-in-law have claim to the priesthood? (84:6) "The descent of this authority . . . from Adam to Moses is here given in the Lord's own words to Joseph Smith. Moses received it from Jethro, a priest of the house of Midian. The Midianites were descendants of Abraham, through the children of Keturah, wife of Abraham, therefore the Midianites, who were neighbors to the Israelites in Palestine, were related to the Israelites, and were Hebrews. As descendants of Abraham they were entitled through their faithfulness to his blessings (see Abraham 2:9–11), and in the days of Moses and preceding them, in Midian the Priesthood was found" (Smith, *Church History and Modern Revelation*, 1:338). ☉

Why does this revelation contain a detailed description of a priesthood line of authority? (84:7–17) "The Lord revealed in this section that Moses did not assume his authority. The authority of the priesthood was given him by one having that authority. . . .

"As it was in ancient times, so it is today. Priesthood holders in the Lord's church can identify the source of their authority. The Lord sent messengers from heaven in this dispensation to confer priesthood authority upon the Lord's designated representatives. These men, in turn, bestowed that authority upon other righteous men according to the Lord's pattern, and this process continues in the church today. Every official and authorized act or ordinance performed by a priesthood holder has the same efficacy as if the Lord performed it" (Otten and Caldwell, *Sacred Truths*, 2:70). ☉

What do we know about the Jeremy mentioned in this verse? (84:10) "This delineation of the priesthood line is not found in the Bible, nor are these individuals (except for Jethro) identified in the Bible. 'Jeremy' is used in the New Testament to refer to the prophet Jeremiah, but the Jeremy in this revelation appears to be a different person (see Matthew 27:9)" (Joseph Smith Papers, "Revelation, 22–23 September 1832 [D&C 84]," [1]fn8).

What could be meant by Esaias receiving the priesthood "under the hand of God"? (84:12) "Esaias, who received the priesthood 'under the hand of God' (D&C 84:12) seems to designate an apostasy prior to his lifetime. However, since he lived in the time of Abraham (v. 13), perhaps he was given the priesthood after Abraham had left 'the land of the Chaldeans' (Abraham 2:3–4), or it was given him in another part of the ancient lands. The Doctrine and Covenants text merely says that he lived in the day of Abraham, but does not tell us where" (Nyman, *Doctrine and Covenants Commentary*, 2:100–101).

On the other hand, it may be that, "Esaias received the holy priesthood from God (or one who had authority), then, at a subsequent time, received the fulness of the blessings of the priesthood under the hand of Abraham" (McConkie and Ostler, *Revelations of the Restoration*, 590).

What priesthood comes through the lineage of the fathers? (84:14) President Ezra Taft Benson shared: "The order of priesthood spoken of in the scriptures is sometimes referred to as the patriarchal order because it came down from father to son.

"But this order is otherwise described in modern revelation as an order of family government where a man and woman enter into a covenant with God— just as did Adam and Eve—to be sealed for eternity, to have posterity, and to do the will and work of God throughout their mortality" ("What I Hope You Will Teach Your Children," *Ensign*, Aug. 1985, 9).

When did Adam receive the priesthood? (84:16–17) Joseph Smith taught: "The Priesthood was first given to Adam, he obtained the first Presidency and held the Keys of it from generation to generation; he obtained it in the creation before the world

13 Esaias also lived in the days of Abraham, and was blessed of him—

14 Which Abraham received the priesthood from Melchizedek, who received it through the lineage of his fathers, even till Noah;

15 And from Noah till Enoch, through the lineage of their fathers;

16 And from Enoch to Abel, who was slain by the conspiracy of his brother, who received the priesthood by the commandments of God, by the hand of his father Adam, who was the first man—

17 Which priesthood continueth in the church of God in all generations, and is without beginning of days or end of years.

was formed as in Gen: 1. 26, 28. He had Dominion given him over every living creature. He is Michael the Archangel spoken of in the scriptures.... The Priesthood is an everlasting principle and existed with God from Eternity and will to Eternity, without beginning of days or end of years. The Keys have to be brought from Heaven whenever the Gospel is sent. When they are revealed from Heaven it is by Adam's Authority" (Joseph Smith Papers, "History, 1838–1856, volume C-1," 11 [addenda]). ⊕

What role do women have in the work of the priesthood in the church? (84:17) Sister Bonnie L. Oscarson stated: "All women need to see themselves as essential participants in the work of the priesthood. Women in this Church are presidents, counselors, teachers, members of councils, sisters, and mothers, and the kingdom of God cannot function unless we rise up and fulfill our duties with faith." ("Rise Up in Strength," *Ensign,* Nov. 2016, 14). ⊕

Doctrine and Covenants 84:18–25. The Greater Priesthood Holds the Key of the Knowledge of God

What is the holiest order of God? (84:18) President Ezra Taft Benson carefully taught: "When our Heavenly Father placed Adam and Eve on this earth, He did so with the purpose in mind of teaching them how to regain his presence.... Adam and his posterity were commanded by God to be baptized, to receive the Holy Ghost and to enter into the Order of the Son of God.

"To enter into the Order of the Son of God is the equivalent today of entering in to the fullness of the Melchizedek Priesthood, which is only received in the House of the Lord.

"Because Adam and Eve had complied with these requirements [to be baptized, to receive the Holy Ghost to enter into the Order of the Son of God], God said to each of them, 'Thou art after the Order of Him who was without beginning of days or end of years, from all eternity to all eternity' (Moses 6:67)" ("What I Hope You Will Teach Your Children," *Ensign*, Aug. 1985, 8).

18 And the Lord confirmed a priesthood also upon Aaron and his seed, throughout all their generations, which priesthood also continueth and abideth forever with the priesthood which is after the holiest order of God.

19 And this greater priesthood administereth the gospel and holdeth the key of the mysteries of the kingdom, even the key of the knowledge of God.

What does it mean that the greater priesthood holds "the key of the mysteries"? (84:19) The Prophet Joseph Smith said the Melchizedek Priesthood "is the channel through which all knowledge, doctrine, the plan of salvation, and every important matter is revealed from heaven.... It is the channel through which the Almighty commenced revealing His glory at the beginning of the creation of this earth, and through which He has continued to reveal Himself to the children of men to the present time, and through which He will make known His purposes to the end of time" (*Joseph Smith* [manual], 108–9).

How are ordinances and the power of godliness interwoven? (84:20–21) Elder David A. Bednar clarified: "Entering into sacred covenants and worthily receiving priesthood ordinances yoke us with and bind us to the Lord Jesus Christ and Heavenly Father. This simply means that we trust in the Savior as our Advocate and Mediator and rely on His merits, mercy, and grace during the journey of life. As we are steadfast in coming unto Christ and are yoked with Him, we receive the cleansing, healing, and strengthening blessings of His infinite and eternal Atonement.

"Living and loving covenant commitments creates a connection with the Lord that is deeply personal and spiritually powerful. As we honor the conditions of sacred covenants and ordinances, we gradually and incrementally are drawn closer to Him and experience the impact of His divinity and living reality in our lives" ("But We Heeded Them Not," *Liahona*, May 2022, 15). See also commentary in this volume on Doctrine and Covenants 128:4–5. ●

What is the antecedent of *this* as found in this passage? (84:22) It is the power of godliness. "Without the power of godliness, no man or woman can endure the presence of God. Moses saw God and spoke with Him face to face, and he said he would have 'withered and died' had he not been 'transfigured before [God]' (Moses 1:11). As recorded in Doctrine and Covenants 67, the Lord taught that only those 'quickened by the Spirit of God' can see God's face and abide His presence (see D&C 67:11–12). These accounts refer to transfiguration, a temporary change that has allowed righteous people in various dispensations to see God and live" (*Doctrine and Covenants Student Manual* [2018], 441). ●

Why were the children of Israel unable to endure the Lord's presence? (84:23–24) "Moses knew full well the transcendent powers of the Holy Priesthood. He had tasted of the joys associated with standing in the presence of Jehovah, and sought to make such unspeakable privileges available to the children of Israel. He desired to prepare his people for consummate blessings—to receive the fulness of the powers

20 Therefore, in the ordinances thereof, the power of godliness is manifest.

21 And without the ordinances thereof, and the authority of the priesthood, the power of godliness is not manifest unto men in the flesh;

22 For without this no man can see the face of God, even the Father, and live.

23 Now this Moses plainly taught to the children of Israel in the wilderness, and sought diligently to sanctify his people that they might behold the face of God;

24 But they hardened their hearts and could not endure his presence; therefore, the Lord in his wrath, for his anger was kindled against them, swore that they should not enter into his rest while in the wilderness, which rest is the fulness of his glory.

25 Therefore, he took Moses out of their midst, and the Holy Priesthood also;

26 And the lesser priesthood continued, which priesthood holdeth the key of the ministering of angels and the preparatory gospel;

27 Which gospel is the gospel of repentance and of baptism, and the remission of sins, and the law of carnal commandments, which the Lord in his wrath caused to continue

of the everlasting gospel, and thus become unto God 'a kingdom of priests, and an holy nation' (Exod. 19:6). A combination of fear and moral lethargy, however, seemed to preclude an intimate association between Israel and her God. Joseph Smith's inspired revision of Exodus teaches us of the lost opportunities of the people of the house of Israel. Moses returned from speaking with the Lord on Sinai, only to find his people wrapped in idolatry and immorality" (Millet, "Revelation on Priesthood," 312–13). ☉

What is the Lord's rest? (84:24) President Joseph F. Smith testified: "What does it mean to enter into the rest of the Lord? Speaking for myself, it means that through the love of God I have been won over to Him, so that I can feel at rest in Christ, that I may no more be disturbed by every wind of doctrine, by the cunning and craftiness of men. . . . I am established in the knowledge and testimony of Jesus Christ, so that no power can turn me aside from the straight and narrow path that leads back into the presence of God, to enjoy exaltation in His glorious kingdom; that from this time henceforth I shall enjoy that rest until I shall *rest* with Him in the heavens" (*Joseph F. Smith* [manual], 426). See also commentary in this volume on Doctrine and Covenants 19:9.

What priesthood did the Lord remove from the children of Israel? (84:25) Joseph Smith declared: "All Priesthood is Melchizedek; but there are different portions or degrees of it. That portion which brought Moses to speak with God face to face was taken away; but that which brought the ministry of angels remained. All the prophets had the Melchizedek Priesthood and were ordained by God himself" (Joseph Smith Papers, "Discourse, 5 January 1841, as Reported by William Clayton," 5; spelling modernized). ☉

Doctrine and Covenants 84:26–32. The Lesser Priesthood Holds the Key of the Ministering of Angels and of the Preparatory Gospel

What does it mean that the Aaronic Priesthood holds the key of "the preparatory gospel"? (84:26–27) "The preparatory gospel was defined as 'the gospel of repentance and of baptism, and the remission of sins, and the law of carnal commandments' (D&C 84:27). It is probably called the preparatory gospel because it is to prepare a person to receive the Melchizedek Priesthood. This priesthood also has the authority to administer the ordinances that will bring a remission of sins. While the ordinance of water baptism does not in itself bring a remission of sins, it prepares a person to receive the cleansing power of the Holy Ghost.... The preparatory gospel was given to Aaron and continued with his house 'among the children of Israel until John, whom God raised up, being filled with the Holy Ghost from his mother's womb' (D&C 84:27, compare Luke 1:39–41)" (Nyman, *Doctrine and Covenants Commentary*, 2:105–6).

Why was John ordained by an angel of God? (84:27–28) "It is certainly unusual to ordain an infant eight days old to the priesthood, but whether this was actually a priesthood ordination or a setting apart to his special calling is not entirely clear. Although the word 'ordain' is used, the nature of the event very much resembles what we today call a 'setting apart.' Zacharias was a priest after the order of Aaron and held true priesthood, and it would seem plausible that he would be the proper one to ordain his son. However, since John's particular calling was greater than that of any of his predecessors in the Aaronic order, it may be that no one then on earth (not even Zacharias) had the necessary keys to properly ordain and/or set him apart" (Matthews, *Burning Light*, 21–22). ◉

Doctrine and Covenants 84:33–44. Men Gain Eternal Life through the Oath and Covenant of the Priesthood

What are "these two priesthoods" and why is faithfulness the key to obtaining them? (84:33) "The two priesthoods are the Aaronic and Melchizedek, and *obtaining* means 'to be ordained to.' The key word that precedes *obtaining* is *faithful*. One must live so as to be judged worthy of receiving each of these priesthoods. President Joseph Fielding Smith explained that 'the Aaronic Priesthood is a preparatory priesthood to qualify us to make the covenant and receive the oath that attends this higher priesthood'" (Farley, "Oath and Covenant of the Priesthood," 42).

with the house of Aaron among the children of Israel until John, whom God raised up, being filled with the Holy Ghost from his mother's womb.

28 For he was baptized while he was yet in his childhood, and was ordained by the angel of God at the time he was eight days old unto this power, to overthrow the kingdom of the Jews, and to make straight the way of the Lord before the face of his people, to prepare them for the coming of the Lord, in whose hand is given all power.

29 And again, the offices of elder and bishop are necessary appendages belonging unto the high priesthood.

30 And again, the offices of teacher and deacon are necessary appendages belonging to the lesser priesthood, which priesthood was confirmed upon Aaron and his sons.

31 Therefore, as I said concerning the sons of Moses—for the sons of Moses and also the sons of Aaron shall offer an acceptable offering and sacrifice in the house of the Lord, which house shall be built unto the Lord in this generation, upon the consecrated spot as I have appointed—

32 And the sons of Moses and of Aaron shall be filled with the glory of the Lord, upon Mount Zion in the Lord's house, whose sons are ye; and also many whom I have called and sent forth to build up my church.

33 For whoso is faithful unto the obtaining these two priesthoods of which I have spoken, and the magnifying their calling, are sanctified by the Spirit unto the renewing of their bodies.

34 They become the sons of Moses and of Aaron and the seed of Abraham, and the church and kingdom, and the elect of God.

Being faithful and operating under priesthood authority applies to both men and women. President Dallin H. Oaks noted: "When a woman, young or old, is set apart to preach the gospel as a full-time missionary, she is given priesthood authority to perform a priesthood function. The same is true when a woman is set apart to function as an officer or teacher in a Church organization under the direction of one who holds the keys of the priesthood. Whoever functions in an office or calling received from one who holds priesthood keys exercises priesthood authority in performing her or his assigned duties" ("Keys and Authority of the Priesthood," *Ensign*, May 2014, 51).

What does magnifying our callings mean? (84:33) "It means to build it up in dignity and importance, to make it honorable and commendable in the eyes of all men, to enlarge and strengthen it, to let the light of heaven shine through it to the view of other men. And how does one magnify a calling? Simply by performing the service that pertains to it" (Thomas S. Monson, *Teachings*, 54–55).

In what way is the body renewed? (84:33) "*Renew* is defined as something that restores to a good state, rebuilds, repairs, confirms, revives, makes fresh and vigorous, transforms, implants holy affections, etc. It is not necessarily that the body is visibly transformed (though this could be the case at times), but the positive effects of the Spirit support and invigorate physical and mental well-being. In connection with the oath and covenant of the priesthood, the renewal of the body refers to an eternal effect as well as a mortal one. Ultimately, the one who is faithful to the oath and covenant will have the body renewed in celestial glory in the resurrection (see D&C 88:28–29)" (Farley, "Oath and Covenant of the Priesthood," 44).

The Oath and Covenant of the Priesthood (Doctrine and Covenants 84:34)

"While an oath may be defined in various ways, in this context, it is a solemn witness or declaration that God sincerely intends to do what He says. He makes a solemn attestation of the inviolability of His promises.

"The terms *oath* and *covenant* are sometimes used interchangeably, but they are not interchangeable when viewed in the context of the oath and covenant of the priesthood. The word *covenant* is of Latin origin, *con venire*, and literally means a 'coming together.' In the context of the priesthood, a 'covenant' is a coming together or an agreement between God and man. It presupposes that God and man come together to make a contract, to agree on promises, stipulations, privileges, and responsibilities. . . .

"A covenant made in this manner is immutable and unchangeable. It anchors the soul; it creates a steadfast and sure foundation for future expectations. . . .

"[Heavenly Father] actually makes an oath to cement the relationship between Him and man" (Renlund and Renlund, *Melchizedek Priesthood*, 60, 61).

What does the word *receive* depict? (84:35) Elder Neil L. Andersen taught: "To receive the blessings, power, and promises of the priesthood in this life and the next is one of the great opportunities and responsibilities of mortality. As we are worthy, the ordinances of the priesthood enrich our lives on earth and prepare us for the magnificent promises of the world ahead. . . .

"All of the ordinances invite us to increase our faith in Jesus Christ and to make and keep covenants with God. As we keep these sacred covenants, we receive priesthood power and blessings" ("Power in the Priesthood," *Ensign*, Nov. 2013, 92).

In what way does this promise to those ordained to the priesthood apply to all of God's children? (84:36) Sister Jean B. Bingham stated: "Although the oath and covenant of the priesthood as found in Doctrine and Covenants 84 speaks directly to men ordained to priesthood office, many of the promises and blessings given there also apply to covenant-keeping women. . . .

"It is important that women understand that we, too, will be blessed to receive 'all that [our] Father hath' when we receive, or heed and hearken to, the Lord's servants (Doctrine and Covenants 84:38)" ("Oath and Covenant of the Priesthood Is Relevant to Women").

How do we qualify for all that the Father has? (84:38) "The pure doctrine of Christ is powerful. It changes the life of everyone who understands it and seeks to implement it in his or her life. The doctrine of Christ helps us find and stay on the covenant path. Staying on the narrow but well-defined path will ultimately qualify us to receive all that God has [D&C 84:38]. Nothing could be worth more than *all* our Father has!" (Nelson, "Pure Truth, Pure Doctrine, and Pure Revelation," *Liahona*, Nov. 2021, 6).

President Lorenzo Snow taught: "They are to become like Him; they will see Him as He is; . . . becoming like unto Him in every particular" (*Lorenzo Snow* [manual], 86).

What are the consequences of altogether turning away from this covenant after having received it? (84:40–41) "Severe consequences result from breaking priesthood covenants and altogether turning from them. Being casual or apathetic in a priesthood calling is like introducing material fatigue into a rocket component. It jeopardizes the priesthood covenant because it can lead to mission failure. Disobedience to God's commandments breaks the

35 And also all they who receive this priesthood receive me, saith the Lord;

36 For he that receiveth my servants receiveth me;

37 And he that receiveth me receiveth my Father;

38 And he that receiveth my Father receiveth my Father's kingdom; therefore all that my Father hath shall be given unto him.

39 And this is according to the oath and covenant which belongeth to the priesthood.

40 Therefore, all those who receive the priesthood, receive this oath and covenant of my Father, which he cannot break, neither can it be moved.

41 But whoso breaketh this covenant after he hath received it, and altogether turneth therefrom, shall not have forgiveness of sins in this world nor in the world to come.

42 And wo unto all those who come not unto this priesthood which ye have received, which I now confirm upon you who are present this day, by mine own voice out of the heavens; and even I have given the heavenly hosts and mine angels charge concerning you.

43 And I now give unto you a commandment to beware concerning yourselves, to give diligent heed to the words of eternal life.

44 For you shall live by every word that proceedeth forth from the mouth of God.

45 For the word of the Lord is truth, and whatsoever is truth is light, and whatsoever is light is Spirit, even the Spirit of Jesus Christ.

46 And the Spirit giveth light to every man that cometh into the world; and the Spirit enlighteneth every man through the world, that hearkeneth to the voice of the Spirit.

47 And every one that hearkeneth to the voice of the Spirit cometh unto God, even the Father.

48 And the Father teacheth him of the covenant which he has renewed and confirmed upon you, which is confirmed upon you for your sakes, and not for your sakes only, but for the sake of the whole world.

49 And the whole world lieth in sin, and groaneth under darkness and under the bondage of sin.

50 And by this you may know they are under the bondage of sin, because they come not unto me.

51 For whoso cometh not unto me is under the bondage of sin.

52 And whoso receiveth not my voice is not acquainted with my voice, and is not of me.

53 And by this you may know the righteous from the wicked, and that the whole world groaneth under sin and darkness even now.

covenant. For a perpetual, unrepentant covenant-breaker, the promised blessings are withdrawn" (Renlund, "Priesthood and the Savior's Atoning Power," *Ensign*, Nov. 2017, 66). ⊕

Doctrine and Covenants 84:45–53. The Spirit of Christ Enlightens Men, and the World Lies in Sin

What is the Spirit that "giveth light to every man"? (84:46–48) "The Light of Christ, which is sometimes called the Spirit of Christ or the Spirit of God, 'giveth light to every man that cometh into the world' (D&C 84:46). This is the light 'which is in all things, which giveth life to all things' (D&C 88:13). The prophet Mormon taught that 'the Spirit of Christ is given to every man, that he may know good from evil' (Moroni 7:16; Moroni 7:19; 2 Nephi 2:5; Helaman 14:31). . . . The Light of Christ enlightens and gives understanding to all men (D&C 88:11)" (Oaks, *With Full Purpose of Heart*, 97–98).

Who is under the bondage of sin? (84:49–53) "Everyone in the whole world who has not received the gospel is in bondage to sin. This sin brings misery to their lives, and they groan under its influence. But some people see this bondage for what it is and seek to be freed from sin; others have no desire to be set free. Those who seek deliverance from bondage follow the influence of the light of Christ in their lives and seek ever greater light until they hear the gospel and recognize in it the voice they have heard faintly and followed before" (Robinson and Garrett, *Commentary on the Doctrine and Covenants*, 3:50–51). ⊕

How does one become acquainted with the Lord's voice? (84:52) "As we seek to be disciples of Jesus Christ, our efforts to *hear Him* need to be ever more intentional. It takes conscious and consistent effort to fill our daily lives with His words, His teachings, His truths....

"In a marketing-saturated world constantly infiltrated by noisy, nefarious efforts of the adversary, where *can* we go to hear Him?

"We can go to the scriptures....

"We can also *hear Him* in the temple....

"We also *hear Him* more clearly as we refine our ability to recognize the whisperings of the Holy Ghost....

"I renew my plea for you to do *whatever* it takes to increase your spiritual capacity to receive personal revelation" (Nelson, "Hear Him," *Ensign*, May 2020, 89, 90).

Doctrine and Covenants 84:54–61. The Saints Must Testify of Those Things They Have Received

What did the Church treat lightly to bring it under condemnation? (84:54–58) "As a member of the Quorum of the Twelve, President Benson had repeatedly preached about the importance of the Book of Mormon. As President of the Church, he gave the subject even greater attention. He declared that 'the whole Church [was] under condemnation' because Latter-day Saints were not studying the Book of Mormon enough or giving enough heed to its teachings. He said: 'The Book of Mormon has not been, nor is it yet, the center of our personal study, family teaching, preaching, and missionary work. Of this we must repent'" (*Ezra Taft Benson* [manual], 30). ⊕

54 And your minds in times past have been darkened because of unbelief, and because you have treated lightly the things you have received—

55 Which vanity and unbelief have brought the whole church under condemnation.

56 And this condemnation resteth upon the children of Zion, even all.

57 And they shall remain under this condemnation until they repent and remember the new covenant, even the Book of Mormon and the former commandments which I have given them, not only to say, but to do according to that which I have written—

58 That they may bring forth fruit meet for their Father's kingdom; otherwise there remaineth a scourge and judgment to be poured out upon the children of Zion.

59 For shall the children of the kingdom pollute my holy land? Verily, I say unto you, Nay.

60 Verily, verily, I say unto you who now hear my words, which are my voice, blessed are ye inasmuch as you receive these things;

61 For I will forgive you of your sins with this commandment—that you remain steadfast in your minds in solemnity and the spirit of prayer, in bearing testimony to all the world of those things which are communicated unto you.

62 Therefore, go ye into all the world; and unto whatsoever place ye cannot go ye shall send, that the testimony may go from you into all the world unto every creature.

63 And as I said unto mine apostles, even so I say unto you, for you are mine apostles, even God's high priests; ye are they whom my Father hath given me; ye are my friends;

64 Therefore, as I said unto mine apostles I say unto you again, that every soul who believeth on your words, and is baptized by water for the remission of sins, shall receive the Holy Ghost.

65 And these signs shall follow them that believe—

66 In my name they shall do many wonderful works;

Why are we forgiven as we testify of the gospel? (84:61) "The relationship between the bearing of testimony by the power of the Holy Ghost and the forgiveness of sins illustrates a glorious gospel truth. It is that whenever faithful saints gain the companionship of the Holy Spirit, they are clean and pure before the Lord, for the Spirit will not dwell in an unclean tabernacle. Hence, they thereby receive a remission of those sins committed after baptism" (Bruce R. McConkie, *Mortal Messiah*, 3:40–41n1).

Doctrine and Covenants 84:62–76. Latter-Day Saints Are to Preach the Gospel, and Signs Will Follow

Who are those the Savior sends where the Twelve Apostles cannot go? (84:62) "Before His final Ascension, [the Savior] commissioned [the Apostles] to 'go . . . and teach all nations, baptizing them in the name of the Father, and of the Son, and of the Holy Ghost' [Matthew 28:19]. The Apostles heeded that instruction. They also called upon others to help them fulfill the Lord's command.

"Today, under the direction of modern apostles and prophets, that same charge has been extended to missionaries of The Church of Jesus Christ of Latter-day Saints. . . . As representatives of the Lord Jesus Christ, they strive to fulfill that divine command— renewed in our day by the Lord Himself—to take the fulness of the gospel abroad and bless the lives of people everywhere" (Nelson, "Ask the Missionaries!" *Ensign*, Nov. 2012, 18–19).

Why were these early members called apostles? (84:63) "The office of an apostle had not yet been restored. It would be another two and half years before this would take place (D&C 107). An apostle is a messenger or an emissary for someone else. In the context of the gospel, he is a special witness of the Lord and his gospel. Those to whom reference is made in this verse were high priests who had proven faithful in both delivering the message of the restored gospel and in testifying of its verity; thus, the Lord refers to them as both his friends and as apostles" (McConkie and Ostler, *Revelations of the Restoration*, 608–9). ⊙

Who may call upon these spiritual signs or gifts? (84:65–73) "The signs listed here are apostolic privileges. Perhaps 'them that believe' [verse 65] refers to those who have been converted, called, commissioned, and in turn sent out as the Lord's special witnesses. In any case, the apostolic blessings and keys listed here *may* be passed to or enjoyed by others, but we should not assume that they are *always* available to every missionary or to every member" (Robinson and Garrett, *Commentary on the Doctrine and Covenants*, 3:56).

How was this promise that "poison . . . shall not hurt them" fulfilled? (84:71) One example was in 1832 when Newel K. Whitney broke his leg while returning from Missouri. Joseph Smith stayed with him in Greenville, Indiana, while he recovered. Joseph recalled, "I frequently walked out in the woods, where I saw several fresh graves; and one day when I rose from the dinner-table, I walked directly to the door and commenced vomiting most profusely; I raised large quantities of blood and poisonous matter, and so great were the muscular contortions of my system that my jaw was dislocated in a few moments; this I succeeded in replacing with my own hands, and made my way to Brother Whitney . . . [and] he laid his hands on me and administered in the name of the Lord, and I was healed in an instant" (Joseph Smith Papers, "History, 1838–1856, volume A-1," 215).

Why are we commanded not to speak publicly about priesthood healings? (84:73) "The message was clear: yes, the Saints would experience miraculous infusions of God's power, but such were for their own benefit and were not intended to convince the unbelieving (see D&C 63:9–12)" (Fluhman, "Joseph Smith Revelations," 79).

President Dallin H. Oaks pointed out: "Although we know of many cases where persons blessed by priesthood authority have been healed, we rarely refer to these healings in public meetings because modern revelation cautions us not to 'boast [ourselves] of these things, neither speak them before the world; for these things are given unto you for your profit and for salvation' (D&C 84:73)" ("Healing the Sick," *Ensign*, May 2010, 48).

What does it mean to upbraid, and who needed upbraiding? (84:76) "The word 'upbraid' seems to be used here in the same sense as 'reprove' in John 16:8. There it means 'convict.' It is the office of the Holy Spirit to convict the world of sin, of righteousness, and of judgment, in order to bring men and women

67 In my name they shall cast out devils;

68 In my name they shall heal the sick;

69 In my name they shall open the eyes of the blind, and unstop the ears of the deaf;

70 And the tongue of the dumb shall speak;

71 And if any man shall administer poison unto them it shall not hurt them;

72 And the poison of a serpent shall not have power to harm them.

73 But a commandment I give unto them, that they shall not boast themselves of these things, neither speak them before the world; for these things are given unto you for your profit and for salvation.

74 Verily, verily, I say unto you, they who believe not on your words, and are not baptized in water in my name, for the remission of their sins, that they may receive the Holy Ghost, shall be damned, and shall not come into my Father's kingdom where my Father and I am.

75 And this revelation unto you, and commandment, is in force from this very hour upon all the world, and the gospel is unto all who have not received it.

76 But, verily I say unto all those to whom the kingdom has been given—from you it must be preached unto them, that they shall repent of their former evil works; for they are to be upbraided for their evil hearts of

unbelief, and your brethren in Zion for their rebellion against you at the time I sent you.

to repentance. If those who are sent to the world with the gospel message are filled with the Holy Spirit, the result will be the conviction of sinners, and conviction will be followed by either condemnation or salvation—salvation, if the gospel is accepted; condemnation, if it is rejected" (Smith and Sjodahl, *Doctrine and Covenants Commentary*, 516–17). Those needing upbraiding were "your brethren in Zion . . . for their rebellion against [the Prophet Joseph]" (McConkie and Ostler, *Revelations of the Restoration*, 610).

Doctrine and Covenants 84:77–91. Elders Are to Go Forth without Purse or Scrip, and the Lord Will Care for Their Needs

77 And again I say unto you, my friends, for from henceforth I shall call you friends, it is expedient that I give unto you this commandment, that ye become even as my friends in days when I was with them, traveling to preach the gospel in my power;

How can we qualify to be called friends with God? **(84:77)** "'Ye are my friends, if ye do whatsoever I command you' (John 15:14). The Lord has declared that those who serve him and keep his commandments are called his servants. After they have been tested and tried and are found faithful and true in all things, they are called no longer servants, but friends. His friends are the ones he will take into his kingdom and with whom he will associate in an eternal inheritance (see D&C 93:45–46)" (Ashton, "What Is a Friend?" *Ensign*, Jan. 1973, 41–42).

78 For I suffered them not to have purse or scrip, neither two coats.

79 Behold, I send you out to prove the world, and the laborer is worthy of his hire.

Why would missionaries serve without "purse or scrip"? (84:78) "Modern dictionaries indicate that the word *scrip* is archaic, meaning 'a small bag or wallet.' Modern usage lists another definition as 'paper currency.' Thus, when a missionary is instructed to go forth without purse or scrip, he is not to be burdened by taking excessive money with him, but is to rely upon the Lord and those whom he teaches to supply him with the necessities of life. The custom of traveling without purse or scrip was followed in New Testament times and in the early part of this dispensation" (Daniel H. Ludlow, *Companion to Your Study*, 2:222).

80 And any man that shall go and preach this gospel of the kingdom, and fail not to continue faithful in all things, shall not be weary in mind, neither darkened, neither in body, limb, nor joint; and a hair of his head shall not fall to the ground unnoticed. And they shall not go hungry, neither athirst.

What is "weary in mind"? (84:80) "To be weary is to be tired or fatigued, usually because of an exertion of physical, mental, or spiritual energy. To be weary in mind is to be mentally fatigued. Among the promises the Lord gave to those who go forth in his work and 'fail not to continue faithful in all things' was that they 'shall not be weary in mind' (D&C 84:80)" (Brewster, *Doctrine & Covenants Encyclopedia* [2012], 628). ●

How do we "treasure up" God's word? (84:85)
"We treasure the word of God not only by reading the words of the scriptures but by studying them. We may be nourished more by pondering a few words, allowing the Holy Ghost to make them treasures to us, than by passing quickly and superficially over whole chapters of scripture" (Eyring, "Feed My Lambs," *Ensign*, Nov. 1997, 84). ◆

How do we qualify for the companionship of the Lord and His angels? (84:88) "May we recommit to seek after this Jesus of whom the prophets have testified. May we yoke ourselves to Him, draw liberally upon the matchless power of His Atonement, and rise up as sons and daughters of God and shake off the world. To 'those who will have him to be their God' (1 Nephi 17:40), the Lord has extended a magnificent promise: 'I will go before your face. I will be on your right hand and on your left, and my Spirit shall be in your hearts, and mine angels round about you, to bear you up' (D&C 84:88). Jesus Christ is our only chance. He will show us the way because He *is* the way" (Dew, "Our Only Chance," *Ensign*, May 1999, 67). ◆

81 Therefore, take ye no thought for the morrow, for what ye shall eat, or what ye shall drink, or wherewithal ye shall be clothed.

82 For, consider the lilies of the field, how they grow, they toil not, neither do they spin; and the kingdoms of the world, in all their glory, are not arrayed like one of these.

83 For your Father, who is in heaven, knoweth that you have need of all these things.

84 Therefore, let the morrow take thought for the things of itself.

85 Neither take ye thought beforehand what ye shall say; but treasure up in your minds continually the words of life, and it shall be given you in the very hour that portion that shall be meted unto every man.

86 Therefore, let no man among you, for this commandment is unto all the faithful who are called of God in the church unto the ministry, from this hour take purse or scrip, that goeth forth to proclaim this gospel of the kingdom.

87 Behold, I send you out to reprove the world of all their unrighteous deeds, and to teach them of a judgment which is to come.

88 And whoso receiveth you, there I will be also, for I will go before your face. I will be on your right hand and on your left, and my Spirit shall be in your hearts, and mine angels round about you, to bear you up.

89 Whoso receiveth you receiveth me; and the same will feed you, and clothe you, and give you money.

90 And he who feeds you, or clothes you, or gives you money, shall in nowise lose his reward.

91 And he that doeth not these things is not my disciple; by this you may know my disciples.

92 He that receiveth you not, go away from him alone by yourselves, and cleanse your feet even with water, pure water, whether in heat or in cold, and bear testimony of it unto your Father which is in heaven, and return not again unto that man.

93 And in whatsoever village or city ye enter, do likewise.

94 Nevertheless, search diligently and spare not; and wo unto that house, or that village or city that rejecteth you, or your words, or your testimony concerning me.

95 Wo, I say again, unto that house, or that village or city that rejecteth you, or your words, or your testimony of me;

96 For I, the Almighty, have laid my hands upon the nations, to scourge them for their wickedness.

97 And plagues shall go forth, and they shall not be taken from the earth until I have completed my work, which shall be cut short in righteousness—

Doctrine and Covenants 84:92–97. Plagues and Cursings Await Those Who Reject the Gospel

What does the practice of cleansing one's feet represent? (84:92) See commentary in this volume on Doctrine and Covenants 24:15 and 99:4.

What does it mean that the "Almighty" will send plagues to scourge the earth? (84:96) "The Lord uses the word 'scourge' as a general term for something that brings great suffering.

"In Webster's 1828 dictionary, 'scourge' is both a noun and a verb. The noun defined as 'whip, or lash, and instrument of punishment.' Therefore, a scourge is a person or a thing 'that greatly afflicts, harasses or destroys.'

"Though Webster does not include this concept in his definition, in the scriptures the idea of a scourge suggests conditions that last for a prolonged period of time [see D&C 84:96]" (Lund, *Second Coming of the Lord*, 165–66).

How long will there be plagues on earth? (84:97) "Despite . . . medical breakthroughs, the signs of the times spoken of in modern scripture almost reluctantly give place to a return of ancient Egypt's 'angel of death' and on a scale so terrifying as to stun the world [see Doctrine and Covenants 45:31; 97:23]. . . . Whether or not current diseases figure into this prophetic picture, the message remains: 'Plagues shall go forth, and they shall not be taken from the earth until I have completed my work' (D&C 84:97)" (Bennett, "Calamity That Should Come," 169).

Doctrine and Covenants 84:98–102. The New Song of the Redemption of Zion Is Given

When will this new song be sung? (84:98) "This is a hymn of great rejoicing. For century after century the scattered remnants of Israel have wandered the earth longing for that promised day when they would be gathered home again. . . .

"In that great day, Satan will be bound, for righteousness and truth will have swept the earth as a flood to gather out the elect from its four quarters into the New Jerusalem. The city of Enoch will return. Its inhabitants will fall upon their necks in rejoicing, and they will kiss each other. 'And there shall be mine abode,' the Lord said, 'and it shall be Zion' (Moses 7:64)" (McConkie and Ostler, *Revelations of the Restoration*, 611; see also Isaiah 52:7–8).

"The singing of this new song was foretold by the prophet Isaiah (see Isaiah 52:7–8)" (Nyman, *Doctrine and Covenants Commentary*, 2:121). See also commentary in this volume on Doctrine and Covenants 133:56.

What is the "election of grace"? (84:99) "An 'election of grace' spoken of in D&C 84:98–102 and Rom. 11:1–5 has reference to one's situation in mortality; that is, being born at a time, at a place, and in circumstances where one will come in favorable contact with the gospel. This election took place in the premortal existence. Those who are faithful and diligent in the gospel in mortality receive an even more desirable election in this life and become the elect of God. These receive the promise of a fulness of God's glory in eternity (D&C 84:33–41)" (Bible Dictionary, s.v. "Election," 634).

What significant change occurs when Satan is bound? (84:100) "During the Millennium, Satan will be bound. This means he will not have power to tempt those who are living at that time (see D&C 101:28). The 'children shall grow up without sin unto salvation' (D&C 45:58). 'Because of the righteousness of [the Lord's] people, Satan has no power; wherefore, he cannot be loosed for the space of many years; for he hath no power over the hearts of the people, for they dwell in righteousness, and the Holy One of Israel reigneth' (1 Nephi 22:26)" (*Gospel Principles*, 265–66).

98 Until all shall know me, who remain, even from the least unto the greatest, and shall be filled with the knowledge of the Lord, and shall see eye to eye, and shall lift up their voice, and with the voice together sing this new song, saying:

99 The Lord hath brought again Zion;
  The Lord hath redeemed his people, Israel,
  According to the election of grace,
  Which was brought to pass by the faith
  And covenant of their fathers.

100 The Lord hath redeemed his people;
  And Satan is bound and time is no longer.
  The Lord hath gathered all things in one.
  The Lord hath brought down Zion from above.
  The Lord hath brought up Zion from beneath.

101 The earth hath travailed and brought forth her strength;
  And truth is established in her bowels;
  And the heavens have smiled upon her;
  And she is clothed with the glory of her God;
  For he stands in the midst of his people.

102 Glory, and honor, and power, and might,
  Be ascribed to our God; for he is full of mercy,
  Justice, grace and truth, and peace,
  Forever and ever, Amen.

103 And again, verily, verily, I say unto you, it is expedient that every man who goes forth to proclaim mine everlasting gospel, that inasmuch as they have families, and receive money by gift, that they should send it unto them or make use of it for their benefit, as the Lord shall direct them, for thus it seemeth me good.

104 And let all those who have not families, who receive money, send it up unto the bishop in Zion, or unto the bishop in Ohio, that it may be consecrated for the bringing forth of the revelations and the printing thereof, and for establishing Zion.

105 And if any man shall give unto any of you a coat, or a suit, take the old and cast it unto the poor, and go on your way rejoicing.

106 And if any man among you be strong in the Spirit, let him take with him him that is weak, that he may be edified in all meekness, that he may become strong also.

107 Therefore, take with you those who are ordained unto the lesser priesthood, and send them before you to make appointments, and to prepare the way, and to fill appointments that you yourselves are not able to fill.

108 Behold, this is the way that mine apostles, in ancient days, built up my church unto me.

109 Therefore, let every man stand in his own office, and labor in his own calling; and let not the head say unto the feet it hath no need of the feet; for without the feet how shall the body be able to stand?

110 Also the body hath need of every member, that all may be edified together, that the system may be kept perfect.

Doctrine and Covenants 84:103–10. Let Every Man Stand in His Own Office and Labor in His Own Calling

Who were the bishops in Zion and in Ohio? (84:104) The bishop in Zion was Edward Partridge (see D&C 51:1; 58:24) and the bishop in Ohio was Newel K. Whitney (see D&C 72:7–8).

What do we learn in this passage about those who are strong and weak in the Spirit? (84:106–8) "And because we love God and have covenanted to serve Him, we can partner with the Savior to help provide temporal and spiritual relief for those in need—and in the process find our own relief in Jesus Christ. . . .

"[As Elder D. Todd Christofferson taught:] 'Our love of God elevates our ability to love others more fully and perfectly because we in essence *partner* with God in the care of His children'" (Camille N. Johnson, "Jesus Christ Is Relief," *Liahona*, May 2023, 81, 83n5).

What safeguards exist to keep the church's system [organization] perfect? (84:109–10) "Near the end of this great revelation on priesthood the Lord gave timely and timeless counsel which provides a formula for successful priesthood labors and overall effective Church government. The direction is priceless: [quotes D&C 84:109–10]. . . . At the October 1961 General Conference of the Church, Elder Harold B. Lee addressed the assembled body of priesthood. He quoted D&C 84:108–10 and introduced the Priesthood Correlation Program" (Millett, "Revelation on Priesthood," 322–23).

Doctrine and Covenants 84:111–20. The Lord's Servants Are to Proclaim the Abomination of Desolation of the Last Days

How are the poor blessed by the rich being humbled? (84:112) "The gospel message would make the rich humble enough to place sufficient means in the hands of the Bishop to enable him to administer to the wants of the poor. No true Latter-day Saint can hoard his means and neglect the poor. The words of our Lord, 'Ye have the poor always with you,' are frequently repeated as an excuse for the condition of destitution in which even the Christian world has left so great a portion of God's children. But He does not say, 'The poor ye *must* always have with you.' Poverty is one of the problems which the gospel undertakes to solve . . . ; for if it saves from sin, it saves from the consequences of sin, among which are poverty and destitution, sickness, and death" (Smith and Sjodahl, *Doctrine and Covenants Commentary*, 523).

Why were New York, Albany, and Boston singled out for destruction? (84:114) "In 1866, Elder Orson Pratt predicted impending destruction on this triad of Albany, New York, and Boston ([*Millennial Star*], 28:633–34). It may be that these 'great and magnificent cities,' as Elder Pratt described them, are merely symbolic of the wicked cities of the world that will be destroyed and left desolate unless the inhabitants thereof repent" (Brewster, *Doctrine & Covenants Encyclopedia* [2012], 11).

What will trigger the "desolation of abomination"? (84:117) "The servants of the Lord are called upon to warn the world and to set forth, clearly and understandingly, the 'desolation of abomination' in the last days. This expression is found in Daniel (11:31), where it refers to the pollution of the Temple and the destruction of Jerusalem by the Romans. . . . It is, in other words, sin and transgression, and especially the profanation of sacred things, for in the wake of sin follows destruction, sooner or later. When the Roman standards were planted on the battlements of the sacred precincts, desolation was near, but those pagan insignia were but symbolical

111 And behold, the high priests should travel, and also the elders, and also the lesser priests; but the deacons and teachers should be appointed to watch over the church, to be standing ministers unto the church.

112 And the bishop, Newel K. Whitney, also should travel round about and among all the churches, searching after the poor to administer to their wants by humbling the rich and the proud.

113 He should also employ an agent to take charge and to do his secular business as he shall direct.

114 Nevertheless, let the bishop go unto the city of New York, also to the city of Albany, and also to the city of Boston, and warn the people of those cities with the sound of the gospel, with a loud voice, of the desolation and utter abolishment which await them if they do reject these things.

115 For if they do reject these things the hour of their judgment is nigh, and their house shall be left unto them desolate.

116 Let him trust in me and he shall not be confounded; and a hair of his head shall not fall to the ground unnoticed.

117 And verily I say unto you, the rest of my servants, go ye forth as your circumstances shall permit, in your several callings, unto the great and notable cities and villages, reproving the world in righteousness of all their unrighteous and ungodly deeds, setting forth clearly and understandingly the desolation of abomination in the last days.

118 For, with you saith the Lord Almighty, I will rend their kingdoms; I will not only shake the earth, but the starry heavens shall tremble.

119 For I, the Lord, have put forth my hand to exert the powers of heaven; ye cannot see it now, yet a little while and ye shall see it, and know that I am, and that I will come and reign with my people.

120 I am Alpha and Omega, the beginning and the end. Amen.

of the apostasy that had taken place, which was the abomination which caused desolation" (Smith and Sjodahl, *Doctrine and Covenants Commentary,* 524). See also commentary in this volume on Doctrine and Covenants 88:85.

When will the Lord come to reign with His people? (84:119) President Joseph Fielding Smith taught: "*The Lord is not going to wait for us to get righteous.* When he gets ready to come, he is going to come—*when the cup of iniquity is full*—and if we are not righteous then, it will be just too bad for us, for we will be classed among the ungodly, and we will be as stubble, to be swept off the face of the earth, for the Lord says wickedness shall not stand.

"Do not think the Lord delays his coming, for *he will come at the appointed time*, not the time which I have heard some preach when the earth becomes righteous enough to receive him" (*Doctrines of Salvation,* 3:3). See also commentary in this volume on Doctrine and Covenants 39:21 and 49:7.

Introduction to Doctrine and Covenants 85

This revelation is an extract from a letter written by Joseph Smith [in Kirtland, Ohio] to William W. Phelps [in Independence, Missouri], November 27, 1832. "Matters pertaining to the establishing and building up of Zion weighed heavily on the mind of the Prophet Joseph Smith. His anxiety was very great because of the grave responsibilities which had been placed upon his shoulders and the shoulders of his brethren to see that the covenants pertaining to consecration were faithfully kept. Especially was he concerned over the duties and responsibilities of the bishop in Zion, for they were very great. It was the duty of the bishop [Edward Partridge], assisted by his brethren, to see that justice was done, as the Lord pointed out in the revelations, in the matter of deciding and allotting inheritances in Zion" (Otten and Caldwell, *Sacred Truths,* 2:80). For a map showing Independence, Missouri, see Map 8 in the Appendix.

"[Joseph Smith] began the letter anticipating a question on the part of [W. W.] Phelps. [Joseph] imagined Phelps wondering what was to be the fate of those church members who came to Zion but did not 'receive an inheritance by consecration' from the bishop. Why such individuals may not have received an inheritance is unclear from [Joseph's] letter, but Phelps discussed this subject in the November 1832 issue of *The Evening and the Morning Star.* After noting that a total of 810 individuals had migrated to Zion 'since the gathering commenced' in 1831, Phelps posed several questions, including, 'Have you all fulfilled the law of the church, which saith: Behold thou shalt consecrate all thy properties, that which thou hast, unto me, with a covenant and deed that cannot be broken?' Apparently, at least some individuals had not followed the commandment to consecrate their properties and had consequently not received an inheritance" (Joseph Smith Papers, Historical Introduction to "Letter to William W. Phelps, 27 November 1832," 1).

SECTION 85

Revelation given through Joseph Smith the Prophet, at Kirtland, Ohio, November 27, 1832. This section is an extract from a letter of the Prophet to William W. Phelps, who was

Doctrine and Covenants 85:1–5. Inheritances in Zion Are to Be Received through Consecration

Who was "the Lord's clerk" in 1832 and why was he charged to maintain these records? (85:1) The clerk designated at this time in Church history was John Whitmer. "Important instructions were given to the Lord's clerk in Zion (Missouri) regarding the keeping of a faithful record. . . . An accurate record of acts is maintained in the heavens comparable with recordings made in the 'book of the law of God' (D&C 85:1–5) kept by the Lord's clerk on the earth. In a later revelation, the Lord emphasized the necessity for keeping accurate records that there might be agreement with the 'book of life' which is kept in heaven (D&C 128:7)" (Roy W. Doxey, *Doctrine and Covenants Speaks*, 2:74, 75). See also commentary in this volume on Doctrine and Covenants 47:1, 4.

What happened to those who didn't receive their inheritance by consecration? (85:3) "The Lord directs that those who do not receive their inheritance by consecration, according to his law, are not to have their names enrolled with those who are to be known as his people. Neither they nor their fathers nor their children are to be acknowledged as having place among the children of the covenant" (McConkie and Ostler, *Revelations of the Restoration*, 616). See commentary in this volume on Doctrine and Covenants 42:31–33 and 51:4–6.

living in Independence, Missouri. It answers questions about those Saints who had moved to Zion but who had not followed the commandment to consecrate their properties and had thus not received their inheritances according to the established order in the Church.

1 It is the duty of the Lord's clerk, whom he has appointed, to keep a history, and a general church record of all things that transpire in Zion, and of all those who consecrate properties, and receive inheritances legally from the bishop;

2 And also their manner of life, their faith, and works; and also of the apostates who apostatize after receiving their inheritances.

3 It is contrary to the will and commandment of God that those who receive not their inheritance by consecration, agreeable to his law, which he has given, that he may tithe his people, to prepare them against the day of vengeance and burning, should have their names enrolled with the people of God.

The "One Mighty and Strong" (Doctrine and Covenants 85:7–8)

"Verses 7–8 of [D&C 85] have confused many readers. . . . Perhaps because their meaning is not explicit, they have been misinterpreted by deceivers intent on leading the faithful astray as well as by sincere believers. . . .

"By 1905, speculation had surged through the Church as to who would fulfill the prophecy of the 'one mighty and strong'—a role some assumed for themselves. An official explanation of verses 7 and 8 seemed necessary. Accordingly, the First Presidency published a letter in the *Deseret Evening News* on November 11, 1905, undersigned by Presidents Joseph F. Smith, John R. Winder, and Anthon H. Lund. . . .

"The Presidency clarified that verse 7 referred specifically to the office of bishop, since in 1832 it was the bishop's duty to 'arrange by lot the inheritances of the saints' in Zion (D&C 85:7). At the time of the revelation, Edward Partridge shouldered this responsibility of dividing the inheritances among the faithful in Jackson County, Missouri. Partridge became a key figure in the First Presidency's analysis of section 85, in which their treatment of verse 7 yielded two alternative interpretations. The first interpretation made verse 7 contingent upon Bishop Partridge's faithfulness; in other words, *if* Edward Partridge failed in his duties and fell into transgression, *then* the Lord would call 'one mighty and strong' to replace him (see D&C 42:10). The second interpretation held that the prophecy may yet be fulfilled in the future. The Presidency seemed to prefer the former but allowed for the

4 Neither is their genealogy to be kept, or to be had where it may be found on any of the records or history of the church.

5 Their names shall not be found, neither the names of the fathers, nor the names of the children written in the book of the law of God, saith the Lord of Hosts.

6 Yea, thus saith the still small voice, which whispereth through and pierceth all things, and often times it maketh my bones to quake while it maketh manifest, saying:

7 And it shall come to pass that I, the Lord God, will send one mighty and strong, holding the scepter of power in his hand, clothed with light for a covering, whose mouth shall utter words, eternal words; while his bowels shall be a fountain of truth, to set in order the house of God, and to arrange by lot the inheritances of the saints whose names are found, and the names of their fathers, and of their children, enrolled in the book of the law of God;

What is the genealogy to be kept in the "book of the law of God"? (85:4–5) "This reference is not to genealogical records in the modern sense but rather to family membership records. . . . In Joshua 24:26, we are told that Joshua wrote in 'the book of the law of God' an account of the covenant by which Israel entered the promised land. That same term is used here in a similar fashion to indicate a physical record of those who received inheritances in Missouri by covenant according to the law of God, that is, Doctrine and Covenants 42. Apparently, the terms 'book of the law of God' (vv. 5, 7), 'book of remembrance' (v. 9), and 'book of the law' (v. 11) all refer to the same record of those who have entered the covenant of consecration and are to receive inheritances in Zion" (Robinson and Garrett, *Commentary on the Doctrine and Covenants*, 3:73).

Doctrine and Covenants 85:6–12. One Mighty and Strong Will Give the Saints Their Inheritance in Zion

possibility of the latter interpretation. 'If . . . there are those who will still insist that the prophecy concerning the coming of one mighty and strong is still to be regarded as to the future, let the Latter-day Saints know that he will be a future bishop of the church who will be with the Saints in Zion. . . . This future bishop will also be called and appointed of God as Aaron of old, and as Edward Partridge was. He will be designated by the inspiration of the Lord, and will be accepted and sustained by the whole Church.' . . .

"It is interesting to note that the last paragraph of the Presidency letter is usually not included in the commentaries, which is surprising since introductions and conclusions are often the most carefully crafted. The Presidency stated that 'men of exceptional talents and abilities . . . will be called of the Lord through the appointed agencies of the Priesthood . . . just as Edward Partridge was called and accepted, and just as the "one mighty and strong" will be called and accepted when the time comes for his services.' This, together with the First Presidency's declaration that there is yet 'more light respecting the things which God reveals,' should keep teachers of modern revelation from waxing too dogmatic when interpreting Doctrine and Covenants 85:7–8" (Merrill and Harper, "It Maketh My Bones to Quake," 85–86, 91–92, 93).

What does the phrase "steady the ark of God" mean? (85:8) "The phrase *steady the ark of God*. . . . originated in the Old Testament story of a man named Uzza, who 'put forth his hand to hold the ark' and was struck dead because of his unauthorized encroachment on the sanctity of this sacred symbol (1 Chr. 13:9–10).

"Although Uzza's intentions to steady the ark were noble, he had no authority to do so. His death serves as a warning that the Lord will not tolerate forays into fields of labor in which we are unauthorized to serve.

"'And thou shalt not command him who is at thy head,' declared the Lord (D&C 28:6). Each is to stand firm within his designated stewardship, for therein lies accountability" (Brewster, *Doctrine & Covenants Encyclopedia* [2012], 24). ⊕

How are we to understand this "inheritance among the Saints" in our day? (85:9–11) "If a person's Church records show faithful obedience to the financial laws of God, then that individual will have a claim upon the Lord for an inheritance in his kingdom. Those Saints who have not kept their financial covenants will have no valid claim and will receive no inheritance in Zion or in the celestial kingdom. President Joseph F. Smith indicated that for contemporary Saints this referred particularly to the law of tithing [in Conference Report, Oct. 1899, 42]" (Robinson and Garrett, *Commentary on the Doctrine and Covenant*, 3:76).

What happened to the children of the priest described in Ezra 2:61–62? (85:12) "About 537 B.C. Cyrus, the Persian king, liberated the Jews from captivity and sent them back to Jerusalem to build a temple. Ezra identified the families that returned to help in the building process. He also noted that there existed certain descendants of priests who could no longer trace their genealogy (their priesthood lineage); they therefore were denied the priesthood. . . . In other words, if they could not trace their priesthood lineage, they were deemed not to hold it. One power line may look like all others, but if it does not extend back to the power plant, it has no power. It matters not if a man claims to hold the priesthood of God; if his priesthood lineage does not trace back to the Savior, he has no priesthood power" (Callister, *Inevitable Apostasy*, 302).

8 While that man, who was called of God and appointed, that putteth forth his hand to steady the ark of God, shall fall by the shaft of death, like as a tree that is smitten by the vivid shaft of lightning.

9 And all they who are not found written in the book of remembrance shall find none inheritance in that day, but they shall be cut asunder, and their portion shall be appointed them among unbelievers, where are wailing and gnashing of teeth.

10 These things I say not of myself; therefore, as the Lord speaketh, he will also fulfil.

11 And they who are of the High Priesthood, whose names are not found written in the book of the law, or that are found to have apostatized, or to have been cut off from the church, as well as the lesser priesthood, or the members, in that day shall not find an inheritance among the saints of the Most High;

12 Therefore, it shall be done unto them as unto the children of the priest, as will be found recorded in the second chapter and sixty-first and second verses of Ezra.

In Kirtland, Ohio, "On December 6, 1832, Joseph Smith received the revelation recorded in Doctrine and Covenants 86 as he was working on the inspired translation of the Bible. This revelation provided further explanation of the parable of the wheat and the tares and the role of the priesthood in helping the Lord gather the righteous in the last days" (*Doctrine and Covenants Student Manual* [2018], 453).

"So important is the lesson embodied in this parable, and so assured is the literal fulfilment of its contained predictions, that the Lord has given a further explication through revelation in the current dispensation, a period in which the application is direct and immediate" (Talmage, *Jesus the Christ*, 268).

SECTION 86

Revelation given through Joseph Smith the Prophet, at Kirtland, Ohio, December 6, 1832. This revelation was received while the Prophet was reviewing and editing the manuscript of the translation of the Bible.

1 Verily, thus saith the Lord unto you my servants, concerning the parable of the wheat and of the tares:

2 Behold, verily I say, the field was the world, and the apostles were the sowers of the seed;

3 And after they have fallen asleep the great persecutor of the church, the apostate, the whore, even Babylon, that maketh all nations to drink of her cup, in whose hearts the enemy, even Satan, sitteth to reign—behold he soweth the tares; wherefore, the tares choke the wheat and drive the church into the wilderness.

4 But behold, in the last days, even now while the Lord is beginning to bring forth the word, and the blade is springing up and is yet tender—

5 Behold, verily I say unto you, the angels are crying unto the Lord day and night, who

Doctrine and Covenants 86:1–7. The Lord Gives the Meaning of the Parable of the Wheat and Tares

What does this revelation teach about the parable of the wheat and the tares? (86:1–2) "In giving the parable of the wheat and the tares, Jesus was actually summarizing the doctrines of the apostasy, the restoration of the gospel in the latter-days, the growth and development of the latter-day kingdom, the millennial cleansing of the earth, the glorious advent of the Son of Man, and the ultimate celestial exaltation of the faithful" (Bruce R. McConkie, *Doctrinal New Testament Commentary*, 1:297).

What does the parable mean that the church was driven into the wilderness? (86:3) "Driving the Church into the Wilderness (D&C 86:3) had reference to the apostasy, while the Restoration has been described as calling forth the Church out of the wilderness (D&C 33:5)" (Cowan, *Doctrine and Covenants: Our Modern Scripture*, 129).

"To this, we must add the information given in Doctrine and Covenants 86:1–3, which states that the great and abominable church did its work after the Apostles had 'fallen asleep,' that is, after the end of the first century A.D." (Robinson, "Warring against the Saints of God," *Ensign*, Jan. 1988, 36).

How are the wheat and the tares distinguished from each other in the latter-days? (86:4–6) "The Lord explained that in this final time prior to His return, the 'wheat,' whom He describes as 'the children of the kingdom' [Matthew 13:38], would grow side by side with the 'tares,' or those who do not love God and do not keep His commandments. They would 'both grow together' [Matthew 13:30], side by side.

"This will be our world until the Savior returns, with much that is good and much that is evil on every side.

"You may at times not feel like a strong, mature strand of wheat. Be patient with yourself! The Lord said that the wheat would include tender blades springing up. We are all His Latter-day Saints, and although not yet all we want to be, we are serious in our desire to be His true disciples" (Andersen, "Drawing Closer to the Savior," *Liahona*, Nov. 2022, 73). ●

When will the angels begin to reap down the fields? (86:5–6) Elder Neal A. Maxwell taught: "Years ago, I wondered over the scriptural imagery of angels waiting 'day and night' for 'the great command' to come down and reap the tares in a wicked and suffering world; it seemed rather eager to me. (See D&C 38:12; 86:5.) Given such massive, needless human suffering, I don't wonder anymore!

"Even so, the final reaping will occur only when the Father determines that the world is 'fully ripe' (D&C 86:7). Meanwhile, brothers and sisters, the challenge is surviving spiritually in a deteriorating 'wheat and tares' world (see D&C 86:7)" ("Behold, the Enemy Is Combined," *Ensign*, May 1993, 76).

Why are the wheat and the tares allowed to grow together? (86:7) "Church members will live in this wheat-and-tares situation until the Millennium. Some real tares even masquerade as wheat, including the few eager individuals who lecture the rest of us about Church doctrines in which they no longer believe. They criticize the use of Church resources to which they no longer contribute. They condescendingly seek to counsel the Brethren whom they no longer sustain. Confrontive, except of themselves, of course, they leave the Church, but they cannot leave the Church alone (*Ensign*, Nov. 1980, 14). Like the throng on the ramparts of the 'great and spacious building,' they are intensely and busily preoccupied, pointing fingers of scorn at the steadfast iron-rodders (1 Ne. 8:26–28, 33)" (Maxwell, "'Becometh As A Child,'" *Ensign*, May 1996, 68). ●

Doctrine and Covenants 86:8–11. The Lord Explains Priesthood Blessings to Those Who Are Lawful Heirs according to the Flesh

How does the priesthood continue through the lineage of the fathers? (86:8–9) "The latter-day harvest of wheat, meaning the gathering of the righteous, is organized and carried out by the Lord's authorized servants. This was promised anciently to

are ready and waiting to be sent forth to reap down the fields;

6 But the Lord saith unto them, pluck not up the tares while the blade is yet tender (for verily your faith is weak), lest you destroy the wheat also.

7 Therefore, let the wheat and the tares grow together until the harvest is fully ripe; then ye shall first gather out the wheat from among the tares, and after the gathering of the wheat, behold and lo, the tares are bound in bundles, and the field remaineth to be burned.

8 Therefore, thus saith the Lord unto you, with whom the priesthood hath continued through the lineage of your fathers—

Abraham when Jehovah declared that Abraham's seed, or posterity, would 'bear this ministry and Priesthood unto all nations' and that through this priesthood 'shall all the families of the earth be blessed, even with the blessings of the Gospel, which are the blessings of salvation, even of life eternal' (Abraham 2:9, 11). Although we cannot identify descendants of Abraham by their outward appearance, the Lord knows who and where they are. The Prophet Joseph Smith learned that the Latter-day Saints are literal descendants of Abraham and 'heirs, according to the flesh,' qualifying them to receive the blessings of the priesthood" (*Doctrine and Covenants Student Manual* (2018), 461).

9 For ye are lawful heirs, according to the flesh, and have been hid from the world with Christ in God—

10 Therefore your life and the priesthood have remained, and must needs remain through you and your lineage until the restoration of all things spoken by the mouths of all the holy prophets since the world began.

What is meant by the expression "hid from the world with Christ in God"? (86:9–10) "An 1832 revelation spoke of the faithful as being 'hid from the world with Christ in God' (D&C 86:9). The Apostle Paul used this same phrase in writing to the early Saints in Colosse (Col. 3:3). The Prophet Joseph Smith gave an interpretation to this phrase. Placing his hands upon one of the faithful members of the Church, he said: 'Your life is hid with Christ in God, and so are many others. Nothing but the unpardonable sin can prevent you from inheriting eternal life for you are sealed up by the power of the priesthood unto eternal life, having taken the step necessary for that purpose' (Joseph Smith Papers, "History, 1838–1856, volume D-1," 1551). Thus, to be hid from the world is to be assured of eternal life or to have one's calling and election made sure" (Brewster, *Doctrine & Covenants Encyclopedia* [2012], 249).

11 Therefore, blessed are ye if ye continue in my goodness, a light unto the Gentiles, and through this priesthood, a savior unto my people Israel. The Lord hath said it. Amen.

How will one be a "light unto the Gentiles" and "a savior" unto the Lord's "people Israel"? (86:11) "In this final verse the Lord reminds us of two things. First, he reminds us of our responsibility to do missionary work here on the earth. Second, he informs us that we are not only to be messengers of salvation to the living, but saviors for our ancestors who went before us and who, though now dead, have paved the way whereby we might receive our present blessings. It is through them we received our priesthood. The promise was made that, even if they were born at a time and place where they could not hear the gospel preached in life, God would provide saviors for them from among their descendants. We are those saviors God promised through whom they can have every priesthood blessing" (Theodore M. Burton, "Salvation for the Dead," *Ensign*, May 1975, 71). ☉

Introduction to Doctrine and Covenants 87

"On December 25, 1832, [in Kirtland, Ohio,] Joseph Smith received the revelation now recorded in Doctrine and Covenants 87, which includes prophecies about the wars and judgments that would be poured out upon all nations in the last days. . . .

"Joseph Smith had learned about a political conflict between the state of South Carolina and the federal government of the United States over tariffs. (A tariff is a tax on imports.) Because residents of South Carolina relied more on imported manufactured products than did people in the northern states, they felt that federal tariffs were unfair and that they had been purposely levied at the expense of the South [to subvert their slave-based economy]. Government leaders in South Carolina adopted an ordinance invalidating, or nullifying, the federal laws, and many South Carolinians began to prepare for military action against the federal government. The president of the United States asserted that he would maintain the laws of the United States by force. In December 1832, newspapers throughout the United States were reporting on this conflict. It was at this time that Joseph Smith received the revelation in Doctrine and Covenants 87 prophesying that 'wars . . . will shortly come to pass, beginning at the rebellion of South Carolina' (D&C 87:1). In early 1833, not long after this prophecy was given, the United States government peacefully settled the issue with the state of South Carolina. Some may have believed the crisis had passed, but it had been only temporarily halted and South Carolina would still rebel" (*Doctrine and Covenants and Church History Seminary Teacher Manual*, 305, 306). For a map showing South Carolina, see Map 2 in the Appendix.

"In his wisdom, the Lord foresees the calamities which men and nations bring upon themselves and which will surely happen if they heed not the warning voice and repent. God not only foresees these calamities, but also through his prophets he seeks to prevent their occurrences. Thus the Lord forewarned Joseph Smith as early as 1832 of the imminence of Civil War in the United States, and Joseph Smith under the Lord's direction sought to turn people from the way of calamity and avert the impending bloodshed" (Berrett, *Teachings of the Doctrine and Covenants*, 249).

Doctrine and Covenants 87:1–4. War Is Foretold between the Northern States and the Southern States

What is significant about Joseph Smith's prophecy regarding war? (87:1–2) "Most Latter-day Saints are familiar with Joseph Smith's prophecy of the American Civil War, but all may not have noticed that Joseph Smith gave the Civil War as a sign that marks the beginning of the latter-day wars. . . .

"Elsewhere Joseph Smith gave the prophecy in a slightly different way but with the same meaning: 'I prophesy, in the name of the Lord God, that the commencement of the difficulties which will cause much bloodshed previous to the coming of the Son of Man will be in South Carolina (D&C 130:12–13)" (Parry and Parry, *Understanding the Signs of the Times*, 245). ☉

SECTION 87

Revelation and prophecy on war, given through Joseph Smith the Prophet, at or near Kirtland, Ohio, December 25, 1832. At this time disputes in the United States over slavery and South Carolina's nullification of federal tariffs were prevalent. Joseph Smith's history states that "appearances of troubles among the nations" were becoming "more visible" to the Prophet "than they had previously been since the Church began her journey out of the wilderness."

1 Verily, thus saith the Lord concerning the wars that will shortly come to pass, beginning at the rebellion of South Carolina, which will eventually terminate in the death and misery of many souls;

2 And the time will come that war will be poured out upon all nations, beginning at this place.

3 For behold, the Southern States shall be divided against the Northern States, and the Southern States will call on other nations, even the nation of Great Britain, as it is called, and they shall also call upon other nations, in order to defend themselves against other nations; and then war shall be poured out upon all nations.

When did other nations become involved in the American Civil War? (87:3) "Two separate historical periods are described in this verse. The first of these is the Civil War, during which the Southern States would enlist the aid of other nations, including Great Britain, against the Northern States. History shows that the South did seek aid and alliances from Great Britain and also from France, Holland, and Belgium. These nations offered passive support to the South but would not enter into official political and military alliances unless the Confederacy could demonstrate some likelihood of ultimate victory.

"A second historical period is described in the last half of this verse, when 'they shall also call upon other nations' to defend themselves from still 'other nations.' When the events described in this verse take place, war will become worldwide" (Robinson and Garrett, *Commentary on the Doctrine and Covenants*, 3:88).

4 And it shall come to pass, after many days, slaves shall rise up against their masters, who shall be marshaled and disciplined for war.

Was this uprising of slaves limited to the context of the Civil War? (87:4) "There are more slaves in the world than the African-American ones that were a dominant factor in the Civil War. Most wars were and are over the lack of freedom for one group or another. To 'destroy the agency of man' is the plan of Satan (Moses 4:3). Many of the Nephite wars were fought for 'their liberty, yea, their freedom from bondage' (Alma 43: 28–29; 51:6; 58:40; 61:21; Helaman 1:8; 3 Nephi 2:12). The wars against terrorism today are fighting for the same freedoms. The principle of freedom 'belongs to all mankind' (D&C 98:5). Those who attempt to take away the freedom of others are 'marshaled and disciplined for war' (D&C 87:4)" (Nyman, *Doctrine and Covenants Commentary*, 2:142–43).

"The Test of a True Prophet" (Doctrine and Covenants 87:1)

President Ezra Taft Benson testified: "The ultimate test of a true prophet is that when he speaks in the name of the Lord his words come to pass. . . .

"In 1832, [Joseph Smith] prophesied that the southern states and northern states would shortly be divided in civil war, that this war would be the beginning of world wars which would eventually involve all nations and result in the death and misery of many souls. Specifically, he said that the great Civil War would begin with a rebellion in South Carolina (see D&C 87). This prophecy was published to the world in 1851.

"As every schoolboy knows, the Civil War began with the secession of South Carolina from the Union, and other states followed. When Lincoln sent provisions to the Union forces at Fort Sumter, South Carolina, the Confederate forces opened fire on the fort. Since that fateful day in 1861, the world has seen as a result of warfare the death and misery of many souls.

"The desire of the Prophet Joseph Smith was to save the Union from that bloody conflict. He recognized the iniquity of slavery and urged Congress to abolish it and to pay the slaveholders from the sale of public lands. The message went unheeded, and nearly one-half million souls died in the Civil War" ("Joseph Smith: Prophet to Our Generation," *Ensign*, Nov. 1981, 62).

Doctrine and Covenants 87:5–8.
Great Calamities Will Fall upon All the Inhabitants of the Earth

What might be the "consumption decreed" noted in this revelation? (87:6) "The prophecy on war indicates that the inhabitants of the earth will be sorely vexed 'until the *consumption decreed* hath made a full end of all nations' (D&C 87:6; [emphasis] added). This 'consumption' is also spoken of in Isaiah's writings (Isa. 10:22, 23; 28:22; 2 Ne. 20:22, 23). It is the destruction declared for the wicked, or 'the calamity which should come upon the inhabitants of the earth' prior to the Second Coming (D&C 1:7–17). The footnote references to 'consumption decreed' refer to the numerous citations throughout the Doctrine and Covenants that touch upon premillennial upheavals of man's society and his physical environment" (Brewster, *Doctrine & Covenants Encyclopedia* [2012], 100).

What does "Lord of Sabaoth" mean? (D&C 87:7) "The title 'Lord of Sabaoth' was divinely defined to the Prophet Joseph in 1833: 'The creator of the first day, the beginning and the end' (D&C 95:7). . . . 'Sabaoth' is a Hebrew word meaning 'hosts.' It sometimes refers to the armies of Israel and other nations; sometimes to the priests officiating in the Sanctuary; sometimes to the people of God generally, and sometimes to the stars and planets in the sky. 'Lord of Hosts' is equivalent to the 'all-sovereign,' or 'omnipotent' Lord [Smith and Sjodahl, *Doctrine and Covenants Commentary*, 540].

"Thus, the Lord of Sabaoth is He who is Lord over the hosts or armies of Israel, as well as the creator of heaven and earth (Hel. 14:12; Mosiah 3:8). It is to Him that the people of God should look for leadership, hope, encouragement, and direction" (Brewster, *Doctrine & Covenants Encyclopedia* [2012], 335).

Where are the holy places in which we are to stand? (87:8) "Often when the Lord warns us about the perils of the last days, He counsels thus: 'Stand ye in holy places, and be not moved.' These 'holy places' certainly include the Lord's temples and meetinghouses. But as our ability to gather in these places has been restricted in varying degrees, we have learned that one of the holiest of places on earth is the home—yes, even *your* home" (Nelson, "What We Are Learning and Will Never Forget," *Liahona*, May 2021, 79). See also commentary in this volume on Doctrine and Covenants 45:32 and 115:7–8. ◆

5 And it shall come to pass also that the remnants who are left of the land will marshal themselves, and shall become exceedingly angry, and shall vex the Gentiles with a sore vexation.

6 And thus, with the sword and by bloodshed the inhabitants of the earth shall mourn; and with famine, and plague, and earthquake, and the thunder of heaven, and the fierce and vivid lightning also, shall the inhabitants of the earth be made to feel the wrath, and indignation, and chastening hand of an Almighty God, until the consumption decreed hath made a full end of all nations;

7 That the cry of the saints, and of the blood of the saints, shall cease to come up into the ears of the Lord of Sabaoth, from the earth, to be avenged of their enemies.

8 Wherefore, stand ye in holy places, and be not moved, until the day of the Lord come; for behold, it cometh quickly, saith the Lord. Amen.

"On December 27, 1832, the Prophet Joseph Smith met with several Church leaders and other members in the 'translating room,' located upstairs in Newel K. Whitney's store in Kirtland, Ohio. He desired further divine instruction about the elders' duties and about how to build up Zion. As this meeting, or conference, began, the Prophet explained that in order for revelation to be received, each person in the assembled group should exercise faith in God and be of one heart and mind. He proceeded to invite each person to take a turn praying aloud to know the Lord's will. The ensuing revelation [vv. 1–116] was then dictated by Joseph Smith until 9:00 p.m. that evening, at which time they stopped for the night. The next morning the group reassembled and prayed, and the remainder of the revelation was received [vv. 117–26]. Later, on January 3, 1833, the Prophet received additional revelation that was later added to the revelation he had received in December (see D&C 88:127–37). Beginning with the 1835 edition of the Doctrine and Covenants, the revelation that was given on January 3, 1833, was added to the one received on December 27–28, 1832, along with four more verses that were added at the end (see D&C 88:138–41)" (*Doctrine and Covenants Student Manual* [2018], 468–69).

Joseph Smith "called this revelation 'the Olive leaf which we have plucked from the tree of Paradise' and 'the Lord's message of peace to us' [Joseph Smith Papers, "Letter to William W. Phelps, 11 January 1833," 18; spelling modernized]. Perhaps [he] described the revelation in this way because it offset the stark apocalyptic imagery of the 25 December revelation [D&C 87] or perhaps because he saw its messages regarding the conduct of church members and the need for unity as a way to heal ongoing difficulties with Missouri church leaders. . . .

"These instructions came in response to specific prayers that God show 'his will . . . concerning the upbuilding of Zion,' which suggests that the revelation would apply only to church members in Missouri. Saints in Kirtland, Ohio, however, took the direction as a call to action. Just two weeks after [the Prophet] dictated this revelation, he informed church leaders in Missouri that the revelation provided a commandment from God 'to build an house of God, & establish a school for the Prophets' in Kirtland" (Joseph Smith Papers, Historical Introduction to "Revelation, 27–28 December 1832 [D&C 88:1–126]").

"It cannot be emphasized too greatly that section 88 is one of the most glorious documents given to man for his spiritual progress and attainment. It speaks of things in a simple, straightforward manner yet deals with concepts so profound and far-reaching that it takes extensive study and contemplation just to appreciate its grandeur. The careful reader is literally bathed in light as a consequence of the experience" (Matthews, "Olive Leaf," 356).

SECTION 88

Revelation given through Joseph Smith the Prophet at Kirtland, Ohio, December 27 and 28, 1832, and January 3, 1833. The Prophet designated it as the "'olive leaf' . . . plucked from the Tree of Paradise, the Lord's message of peace to us." The revelation was given after high priests at a conference prayed "separately and vocally to the Lord to reveal his will unto us concerning the upbuilding of Zion."

1 Verily, thus saith the Lord unto you who have assembled yourselves together to receive his will concerning you:

2 Behold, this is pleasing unto your Lord, and the angels rejoice over you; the alms of your prayers have come up into the ears of

Doctrine and Covenants 88:1–5. Faithful Saints Receive That Comforter, Which Is the Promise of Eternal Life

Who were the elders assembled when this revelation was received? (88:1) "Those present . . . were Joseph Smith, Sr., Sidney Rigdon, Orson Hyde, Joseph Smith, Jr., Hyrum Smith, Samuel H. Smith, Newel K. Whitney, Frederick G. Williams, Ezra Thayer, and John Murdock. Brother Williams served as scribe" (Matthews, "Olive Leaf," 340).

What could the phrase "alms of your prayers" mean? (88:2) The word *alms* "comes from the Greek word meaning righteousness, or acts of religious devotion" (Brewster, *Doctrine & Covenants Encyclopedia* [2012], 12).

This is "an unusual expression, but it conveys the idea that their prayers for a Revelation had been offered up freely, and that God would reward them, as He rewards alms-giving" (Smith and Sjodahl, *Doctrine and Covenants Commentary*, 540).

What do we understand about the "book of the names of the sanctified"? (88:2) This book is also known in scripture as the Lamb's book of life (see Bible Dictionary, s.v. "Book of life," 609). President Joseph Fielding Smith taught: "We are not going to be saved in the kingdom of God just because our names are on the records of the Church. It will require more than that. We will have to have our names written in the Lamb's Book of Life, and if they are written in the Lamb's book of Life then it is an evidence we have kept the commandments. Every soul who will not keep those commandments shall have his name blotted out of that book" (Smith, in Conference Report, Sep./Oct. 1950, 10).

What was the Holy Spirit of promise sent upon those who were assembled? (88:3–4) Elder David A. Bednar taught: "The Holy Spirit of Promise is the ratifying power of the Holy Ghost. When sealed by the Holy Spirit of Promise, an ordinance, vow, or covenant is binding on earth and in heaven (see D&C 132:7). Receiving this 'stamp of approval' from the Holy Ghost is the result of faithfulness, integrity, and steadfastness in honoring gospel covenants 'in [the] process of time' (Moses 7:21). However, this sealing can be forfeited through unrighteousness and transgression.

"Purifying and sealing by the Holy Spirit of Promise constitute the culminating steps in the process of being born again" ("Ye Must Be Born Again," *Ensign*, May 2007, 22).

Who will be the members of the Church of the Firstborn? (88:5) "The Savior revealed to Joseph Smith that in due time, if we keep the commandments of God, we can receive the 'fulness' of the Father (D&C 93:19–20). Here the Savior bears record that 'all those who are begotten through me are partakers of the glory of the [Father], and are the church of the Firstborn' (D&C 93:22). 'They are they into whose hands the Father has given all things. . . . Wherefore, as it is written, they are gods' who 'shall dwell in the presence of God and his Christ forever and ever' (D&C 76:55, 58, 62). . . . This is the ultimate significance

the Lord of Sabaoth, and are recorded in the book of the names of the sanctified, even them of the celestial world.

3 Wherefore, I now send upon you another Comforter, even upon you my friends, that it may abide in your hearts, even the Holy Spirit of promise; which other Comforter is the same that I promised unto my disciples, as is recorded in the testimony of John.

4 This Comforter is the promise which I give unto you of eternal life, even the glory of the celestial kingdom;

5 Which glory is that of the church of the Firstborn, even of God, the holiest of all, through Jesus Christ his Son—

6 He that ascended up on high, as also he descended below all things, in that he comprehended all things, that he might be in all and through all things, the light of truth;

7 Which truth shineth. This is the light of Christ. As also he is in the sun, and the light of the sun, and the power thereof by which it was made.

8 As also he is in the moon, and is the light of the moon, and the power thereof by which it was made;

9 As also the light of the stars, and the power thereof by which they were made;

10 And the earth also, and the power thereof, even the earth upon which you stand.

11 And the light which shineth, which giveth you light, is through him who enlighteneth your eyes, which is the same light that quickeneth your understandings;

12 Which light proceedeth forth from the presence of God to fill the immensity of space—

of taking upon us the name of Jesus Christ" (Oaks, "Taking upon Us the Name of Jesus Christ," *Ensign*, May 1985, 82). See also commentary in this volume on Doctrine and Covenants 76:54–55 and 93:21–22.

Doctrine and Covenants 88:6–13. All Things Are Controlled and Governed by the Light of Christ

What is the light of Christ? (88:7) "The Light of Christ is the divine energy, power, or influence that proceeds from God through Christ and gives life and light to all things. The Light of Christ influences people for good and prepares them to receive the Holy Ghost....

"In the scriptures, the Light of Christ is sometimes called the Spirit of the Lord, the Spirit of God, the Spirit of Christ, or the Light of Life.

"The Light of Christ should not be confused with the Holy Ghost. It is not a personage, as the Holy Ghost is. Its influence leads people to find the true gospel, be baptized, and receive the gift of the Holy Ghost (see John 12:46; Alma 26:14–15)" (Topics and Questions, s.v. "Light of Christ").

In what way can Jesus Christ be in the sun, moon, stars, and the earth? (88:7–10) "Since all energy is some form of the light of Christ, and since all living things require energy, then this light of Christ is also the source of life, breath, warmth, and so forth, for all living things. What we normally think of as the physical laws of the universe, the laws by which particles, bodies, and elements are governed and which give stability to existence and make life possible—these are also manifestations of the light of Christ and of his power displayed throughout the universe" (Robinson and Garrett, *Commentary on the Doctrine and Covenants*, 3:103).

How can the light of Christ quicken our understanding? (88:11) "The Light of Christ ... prompts all rational individuals throughout the earth to distinguish truth from error, right from wrong. It activates your conscience [see Moroni 7:16]. Its influence can be weakened through transgression and addiction and restored through proper repentance. The Light of Christ is not a person. It is a power and influence that comes from God and when followed can lead a person to qualify for the guidance and inspiration of the Holy Ghost [see John 1:9; D&C 84:46–47]" (Scott,

"Peace of Conscience and Peace of Mind," *Ensign*, Nov. 2004, 15). ⊕

How does the light of Christ govern all things? (88:13) "This glorious revelation of truth gives us an inkling of how the universe and all intelligence in it is governed and illuminated by the power of God in the form of divine light, even the light of Christ. This light sustains the physical operation of the universe and the vitality of all living forms therein; it also empowers our reasoning and understanding and underlies and informs the process of spiritual unfolding for all of God's children" (Pinegar and Allen, *Unlocking the Doctrine and Covenants*, 165). See also commentary in this volume on Doctrine and Covenants 93:2. ⊕

Doctrine and Covenants 88:14–16. The Resurrection Comes through the Redemption

Why is it important to understand that the soul is composed of both body and spirit? (88:15) "The gift of our physical bodies is a transcendent miracle. A unique body is given to each of us by our loving Heavenly Father. He created it as a tabernacle for our spirits, to assist each of us in our quest to fulfill the full measure of our creation....

"Each soul is composed of body and spirit, both of which emanate from God. A firm understanding of body and spirit will shape our thoughts and deeds for the good....

"The spirit is eternal; it existed in innocence in the premortal realm and will exist after the body dies. The spirit provides the body with animation and personality....

"Spirit and body, when joined together, become a living soul of supernal worth" (Nelson, "Your Body," *New Era*, Aug. 2019, 2, 4). ⊕

How is the resurrection from the dead the redemption of the soul? (88:16) "When the spirit and the body come together at mortal birth, the soul is created. Then, when they are parted by physical death, the soul is temporarily dissolved. The resurrection eventually reunites the spirit and the body, which never again will be separated (see Alma 11:45; 40:23). The resurrection is literally 'the redemption of the soul'" (Cowan, *Answers to Your Questions*, 105).

13 The light which is in all things, which giveth life to all things, which is the law by which all things are governed, even the power of God who sitteth upon his throne, who is in the bosom of eternity, who is in the midst of all things.

14 Now, verily I say unto you, that through the redemption which is made for you is brought to pass the resurrection from the dead.

15 And the spirit and the body are the soul of man.

16 And the resurrection from the dead is the redemption of the soul.

17 And the redemption of the soul is through him that quickeneth all things, in whose bosom it is decreed that the poor and the meek of the earth shall inherit it.

18 Therefore, it must needs be sanctified from all unrighteousness, that it may be prepared for the celestial glory;

19 For after it hath filled the measure of its creation, it shall be crowned with glory, even with the presence of God the Father;

20 That bodies who are of the celestial kingdom may possess it forever and ever; for, for this intent was it made and created, and for this intent are they sanctified.

21 And they who are not sanctified through the law which I have given unto you, even the law of Christ, must inherit another kingdom, even that of a terrestrial kingdom, or that of a telestial kingdom.

22 For he who is not able to abide the law of a celestial kingdom cannot abide a celestial glory.

23 And he who cannot abide the law of a terrestrial kingdom cannot abide a terrestrial glory.

24 And he who cannot abide the law of a telestial kingdom cannot abide a telestial glory; therefore he is not meet for a kingdom of glory. Therefore he must abide a kingdom which is not a kingdom of glory.

Doctrine and Covenants 88:17–31. Obedience to Celestial, Terrestrial, or Telestial Law Prepares Men for Those Respective Kingdoms and Glories

Why must the earth be sanctified? (88:18–20) "This earth is destined to be a celestial sphere. . . . All shall come forth from death and live in a resurrected state forever; the resurrection applies to men and animals and fowls and fishes and creeping things—all shall rise in immortality and live forever. . . .

"It is common among us to say that the Lord's plan is to make of this earth a heaven and of man a God. Earth and man, both sanctified by obedience to gospel law, shall go forward everlastingly together. And whereas Christ the Son will grace the millennial earth with his presence, even God the Father will take up his abode, from time to time, on this earth in its celestial day" (Bruce R. McConkie, *Millennial Messiah*, 694, 696, 699).

How can we become sanctified through the law? (88:21) "The law which sanctifies those who are to receive celestial glory, and thus inherit the earth, is the 'law of Christ.' This law includes provision for repentance and forgiveness through the atonement of Christ by our faith in him. It is important not to become too legalistic here and forget that the law which sanctifies us includes provision for our human sins and weaknesses, if we will only repent and come unto Christ. The law of Christ (faith, repentance, baptism, receiving the Holy Ghost, and enduring to the end) will sanctify or *make* holy those who cannot make themselves holy (and no one can; see Alma 22:14; Romans 3:23), but who have come to Christ in faith (anyone can, but not everyone does; see 3 Nephi 27:16)" (Robinson and Garrett, *Commentary on the Doctrine and Covenants*, 3:106).

What laws must we live in order to abide a celestial glory? (88:22–24) "Different kingdoms of glory have different requirements, with those for the celestial kingdom being the most rigorous. Each kingdom also has different privileges, with those of the celestial kingdom being the most grand and all-encompassing. Ironically, the Lord has not revealed very much about the telestial or terrestrial kingdoms. He has, however, told us a lot about the celestial kingdom, which is described in both the New Testament and the Doctrine and Covenants as having the 'glory of the sun.'

"Because of the glorious principle of agency, we each get to choose the kind of life we want to live eternally. Our eventual assignment to a kingdom of glory will be based largely on what we are willing to do in this life, the desires of our hearts, and what we 'are willing to receive' from God. For 'he who is not able to abide the law of a celestial kingdom cannot abide a celestial glory'" (Nelson, *Heart of the Matter*, 46). ⊕

What do we understand about the nature of the earth? (88:25–26) "The earth is spoken of as a living organism which does its work well and has earned the right of a celestial glory.... There will be a spiritual change which will transform the earth as well as human beings" (Widtsoe, *Message of the Doctrine and Covenants*, 165).

"Our present physical earth is a fallen, telestial planet. The earth will die, but it will be quickened again; it will become a glorified abode for celestial beings. In order to become celestial the earth will have to be sanctified.

"The earth has already experienced the Creation and the Fall and was baptized by water. At the Second Coming, it will be baptized by fire and the Holy Ghost; anything or anyone that cannot abide a terrestrial glory will be burned" (Woodger, *Essential Doctrine and Covenants Companion*, 172; paragraphing altered).

What is meant by a "spiritual body" in this verse? (88:27) President Joseph Fielding Smith taught: "In the resurrection from the dead, the bodies which were laid down *natural bodies* shall come forth *spiritual bodies*. That is to say, in *mortality* the life of the body is in the blood, but the body when raised to *immortality* shall be *quickened by the spirit* and not the blood. Hence, *it becomes spiritual*, but it will be *composed of flesh and bones*, just as the body of Jesus was, who is the prototype" (*Doctrines of Salvation*, 2:284–85).

What happens to those quickened by celestial glory? (88:28–31) "To be 'quickened by a portion of the celestial glory' appears to mean that if the major thrust of one's life has been in harmony with a celestial standard, that person will come forth in a celestial resurrection and thereafter be able to grow up into a fulness of that glory. The same principle would apply to those who come forth in the terrestrial and telestial resurrections" (McConkie and Ostler, *Revelations of the Restoration*, 632).

25 And again, verily I say unto you, the earth abideth the law of a celestial kingdom, for it filleth the measure of its creation, and transgresseth not the law—

26 Wherefore, it shall be sanctified; yea, notwithstanding it shall die, it shall be quickened again, and shall abide the power by which it is quickened, and the righteous shall inherit it.

27 For notwithstanding they die, they also shall rise again, a spiritual body.

28 They who are of a celestial spirit shall receive the same body which was a natural body; even ye shall receive your bodies, and your glory shall be that glory by which your bodies are quickened.

29 Ye who are quickened by a portion of the celestial glory shall then receive of the same, even a fulness.

30 And they who are quickened by a portion of the terrestrial glory shall then receive of the same, even a fulness.

31 And also they who are quickened by a portion of the telestial glory shall then receive of the same, even a fulness.

32 And they who remain shall also be quickened; nevertheless, they shall return again to their own place, to enjoy that which they are willing to receive, because they were not willing to enjoy that which they might have received.

33 For what doth it profit a man if a gift is bestowed upon him, and he receive not the gift? Behold, he rejoices not in that which is given unto him, neither rejoices in him who is the giver of the gift.

34 And again, verily I say unto you, that which is governed by law is also preserved by law and perfected and sanctified by the same.

35 That which breaketh a law, and abideth not by law, but seeketh to become a law unto itself, and willeth to abide in sin, and altogether abideth in sin, cannot be sanctified by law, neither by mercy, justice, nor judgment. Therefore, they must remain filthy still.

Doctrine and Covenants 88:32–35. Those Who Will to Abide in Sin Remain Filthy Still

Who are "they who remain" in this verse? (88:32) These are the sons of perdition, who will be resurrected but unworthy to receive a degree of glory. "These beings are men who come forth in the resurrection of the unjust, the worst of all men, men who had the requisite knowledge of God sufficient to exalt them had they continued obedient to the law of Christ they had once received. Instead, they suffer themselves through the power of the devil to be overcome and to deny the truth and to defy the Lord's power. . . . They are the only ones, finally, on whom the second death shall have any power" (Sperry, *Doctrine and Covenants Compendium*, 426–27).

What spiritual dangers can we face by choosing to abide in sin? (88:35) "When we discover that we are off the path, we can stay off, or because of the Atonement of Jesus Christ, we can choose to reverse our steps and get back on. In the scriptures, the process of deciding to change and return to the path is referred to as repentance. Failure to repent means that we choose to disqualify ourselves from the blessings God desires to give. If we are 'not willing to enjoy that which [we] might have received,' we will 'return . . . to [our] own place, to enjoy that which [we] are willing to receive' (D&C 88:32)—our choice, not God's" (Renlund, "Choose You This Day," *Ensign*, Nov. 2018, 106). ☉

Why can't those who abide in sin be sanctified by law, mercy, justice, or judgment? (88:35) "Since perdition refuses to abide any law, there are no conditions under which they can be saved, for all things that are preserved in eternity are preserved by obedience to law. Obedience *enables;* disobedience *disables.* There is no other way. Further, since perdition seeks to abide totally in sin and refuses to abide any law, there can be no atonement made in their behalf to rescue them from spiritual death. Thus, at the resurrection, those who inherit perdition are raised up with all others who have lived upon the earth, but unlike those who inherit some degree of glory, these are raised up 'filthy still' (2 Nephi 9:16), having refused all cleansing, mercy, and atonement" (Robinson and Garrett, *Commentary on the Doctrine and Covenants*, 3:109–10).

Doctrine and Covenants 88:36–41. All Kingdoms Are Governed by Law

Why is it important to understand that every kingdom is governed by law? (88:36–41) "We know from modern revelation that 'all kingdoms have a law given' and that the kingdom of glory we receive in the Final Judgment is determined by the laws we choose to follow in our mortal journey. Under that loving plan, there are multiple kingdoms—many mansions—so that all of God's children will inherit a kingdom of glory whose laws they can comfortably 'abide'" (Oaks, "Kingdoms of Glory," *Liahona*, Nov. 2023, 26–27). ⊕

How do our thoughts and actions prepare us to abide in a kingdom of glory? (88:38–39) "In the realm of the good, as elsewhere, light is the 'bound and condition' of all preferred ways of life [see D&C 88:28–31]. And these bounds and conditions are inexorable and exceptionless, not because they tell us what our choices must be but because they tell us what the *results* of our choices will be.... Every minute of every day we are increasing or decreasing in our receptivity to light, and there is no way to escape the inevitability of that consequence in our thoughts, our acts, our very breath. One can look upon the law of light either as the enemy of freedom or as freedom's guarantee.... One can abide the law only as one can abide the light, and vice versa" (Madsen, *Five Classics*, 313, 314).

What can these verses teach us about God and law? (88:40–41) "The announcement here is not simply that God knows all things but that he constitutes the source of their existence. All things are an expression of the existence of God. Every truth, every law, every form of existence—all evidence the hand of God. He created them all; there is nothing relative to them that he does not know. Thus he is above all things, he is the source of life to all things, and governs all things. Again, to suppose that there is place or knowledge that is presently beyond God is to suppose that in some place or in some matter God is other than, indeed less than, God. God himself testifies that this is not the case" (McConkie and Ostler, *Revelations of the Restoration*, 634).

36 All kingdoms have a law given;

37 And there are many kingdoms; for there is no space in the which there is no kingdom; and there is no kingdom in which there is no space, either a greater or a lesser kingdom.

38 And unto every kingdom is given a law; and unto every law there are certain bounds also and conditions.

39 All beings who abide not in those conditions are not justified.

40 For intelligence cleaveth unto intelligence; wisdom receiveth wisdom; truth embraceth truth; virtue loveth virtue; light cleaveth unto light; mercy hath compassion on mercy and claimeth her own; justice continueth its course and claimeth its own; judgment goeth before the face of him who sitteth upon the throne and governeth and executeth all things.

41 He comprehendeth all things, and all things are before him, and all things are round about him; and he is above all things, and in all things, and is through all things, and is round about all things; and all things are by him, and of him, even God, forever and ever.

42 And again, verily I say unto you, he hath given a law unto all things, by which they move in their times and their seasons;

43 And their courses are fixed, even the courses of the heavens and the earth, which comprehend the earth and all the planets.

44 And they give light to each other in their times and in their seasons, in their minutes, in their hours, in their days, in their weeks, in their months, in their years—all these are one year with God, but not with man.

45 The earth rolls upon her wings, and the sun giveth his light by day, and the moon giveth her light by night, and the stars also give their light, as they roll upon their wings in their glory, in the midst of the power of God.

46 Unto what shall I liken these kingdoms, that ye may understand?

47 Behold, all these are kingdoms, and any man who hath seen any or the least of these hath seen God moving in his majesty and power.

48 I say unto you, he hath seen him; nevertheless, he who came unto his own was not comprehended.

49 The light shineth in darkness, and the darkness comprehendeth it not; nevertheless, the day shall come when you shall comprehend even God, being quickened in him and by him.

Doctrine and Covenants 88:42–45. God Has Given a Law unto All Things

What can we learn about God from the heavens and the planets? (88:42–43) "In truth, the miraculous operation of the universe in accordance with divine law is another testament of Jesus Christ. . . . To see the evidence of universal laws in operation is a confirmation of our faith in the orderly process of spiritual development. We have faith that the Lord can redeem us through the Atonement, for we discern, line upon line and precept upon precept, the operation of divine principles of perfection at work in our own lives—just as in the physical universe around us. It is all from the same eternal hand; it is all a unified blending of eternal principles. We are not adrift on a sea of chaos. We are in the hands of the Master of order and purpose, glory and eternal joy" (Pinegar and Allen, *Unlocking the Doctrine and Covenants*, 168).

What could "the earth rolls upon her wings" represent? (88:45) "Wings, in these instances, 'are a representation of power,' having the ability 'to move, to act, etc.' (D&C 77:4)" (McConkie and Parry, *Guide to Scriptural Symbols*, 108).

"To say the earth and the stars roll upon their wings (D&C 88:45) is to indicate that these bodies move through the heavens as if they had wings" (Brewster, *Doctrine & Covenants Encyclopedia* [2012], 147).

Doctrine and Covenants 88:46–50. Man Will Comprehend Even God

How have you seen God moving among His creations in majesty and power? (88:47) Elder Neal A. Maxwell joyfully declared: "Whatever the scale of things, the Lord is there! Whether in speaking of how sun, moon, and stars show 'God moving in his majesty and power' (D&C 88:47) or in describing the lilies of the field as being better arrayed than Solomon in all his finery, who is better qualified than the Creator to make such descriptions of the heaven and such comparisons between raiment and flowers (see Matt. 6:28–29)?" ("Yet Thou Art There," *Ensign*, Nov. 1987, 31). ☉

How will it become possible to comprehend God? (88:49–50) "These passages speak of man seeing the face of God and even comprehending him (which means understanding him), and of man himself knowing all things. Such accomplishments are not by intellectual learning or by research alone, great as those are as aids to arriving at the truth. . . .

Secular learning is an aid, but is separate and distinct from the kind of learning that leads [humankind] to a full knowledge and acquaintance with God. . . . The things of God are such that they can be learned only by revelation; therefore, a study of the revelations which make known the character of God and what he requires of man are absolutely essential for salvation. Man will not comprehend God unless he becomes like him" (Matthews, "Olive Leaf," 346). ⊕

Doctrine and Covenants 88:51–61. The Parable of the Man Sending His Servants into the Field and Visiting Them in Turn

50 Then shall ye know that ye have seen me, that I am, and that I am the true light that is in you, and that you are in me; otherwise ye could not abound.

51 Behold, I will liken these kingdoms unto a man having a field, and he sent forth his servants into the field to dig in the field.

52 And he said unto the first: Go ye and labor in the field, and in the first hour I will come unto you, and ye shall behold the joy of my countenance.

53 And he said unto the second: Go ye also into the field, and in the second hour I will visit you with the joy of my countenance.

54 And also unto the third, saying: I will visit you;

55 And unto the fourth, and so on unto the twelfth.

56 And the lord of the field went unto the first in the first hour, and tarried with him all that hour, and he was made glad with the light of the countenance of his lord.

57 And then he withdrew from the first that he might visit the second also, and the third, and the fourth, and so on unto the twelfth.

The Parable of the Lord's Visits to His Children (Doctrine and Covenants 88:51–61)

Tad R. Callister wrote: "Doctrine and Covenants 88 speaks of 'the earth and all the planets' (D&C 88:43). It then refers to these creations collectively as 'kingdoms' (D&C 88:46). These kingdoms are likened unto a man with a field who sends his servants to dig and prepare the soil. The lord of the field visits each kingdom (i.e., planet) in its due time, one in the first hour, another in the second hour and finally the last in the twelfth hour, that each might behold the joy of his countenance. A portion of the parable reads as follows:

"'And *thus they all received the light of the countenance of their lord*, every man in his hour, and in his time, and in his season—beginning at the first, and so on unto the last; every man in his own order, . . . that his lord might be glorified in him, and he in his lord, *that they all might be glorified. Therefore, unto this parable I will liken all these kingdoms [i.e. planets], and the inhabitants thereof*' (D&C 88:58–61; emphasis added).

"Who is this Lord who visits these planets and their inhabitants, that they might be glorified? Orson Pratt gives the answer. He speaks of the Savior's millennial reign and the pure in heart who will be made glad by his countenance for a thousand years. Then, Orson Pratt says:

58 And thus they all received the light of the countenance of their lord, every man in his hour, and in his time, and in his season—

59 Beginning at the first, and so on unto the last, and from the last unto the first, and from the first unto the last;

60 Every man in his own order, until his hour was finished, even according as his lord had commanded him, that his lord might be glorified in him, and he in his lord, that they all might be glorified.

61 Therefore, unto this parable I will liken all these kingdoms, and the inhabitants thereof—every kingdom in its hour, and in its time, and in its season, even according to the decree which God hath made.

62 And again, verily I say unto you, my friends, I leave these sayings with you to ponder in your hearts, with this commandment which I give unto you, that ye shall call upon me while I am near—

63 Draw near unto me and I will draw near unto you; seek me diligently and ye shall find me; ask, and ye shall receive; knock, and it shall be opened unto you.

Doctrine and Covenants 88:62–73. Draw Near unto the Lord, and Ye Will See His Face

In what sense was the Lord near to the elders at this time? (88:62) The Prophet Joseph Smith had invited the gathered elders to unite in prayer as they petitioned the Lord for His will. Their actions had pleased the Lord (see verse 2). "Addressing the ten high priests as His friends (v. 62), undoubtedly because they had done 'whatsoever I command you' (John 15:13), the Savior commanded them to ponder His message of peace to them. . . . The Lord was certainly near to them at that time, and was inviting them to continue to seek revelation" (Nyman, *Doctrine and Covenants Commentary*, 2:177).

What is required for us to draw near to the Lord? (88:63) President Russell M. Nelson taught: "When you reach up for the Lord's power in your life with the same

"'He withdraws. What for? To fulfill other purposes; for he has other worlds or creations and other sons and daughters, perhaps just as good as those dwelling on this planet, and they, as well as we, will be visited, and they will be made glad with the countenance of their Lord. Thus he will go, in the time and in the season thereof, from kingdom to kingdom or from world to world, causing the pure in heart, the Zion that is taken from these creations, to rejoice in his presence' [in *Journal of Discourses*, 17:332].

"Why should these other inhabitants be glorified in the presence of our Savior (D&C 88:60)? Because he was also their Savior. Since Christ also created them, he loved them and he redeemed them. He is the Savior of all the works of his hands. He is not only the Creator, but also the Redeemer and Lord of the entire universe" (*Infinite Atonement*, 89–90).

intensity that a drowning person has when grasping and gasping for air, power from Jesus Christ will be yours. When the Savior knows you truly want to reach up to Him—when He can feel that the greatest desire of your heart is to draw His power into your life—you will be led by the Holy Ghost to know exactly what you should do (see [D&C] 88:63)" (*Teachings*, 104). ●

How do we learn what is expedient for us? (88:64)
"The Savior taught:

"'Remember that without faith you can do nothing; therefore *ask in faith. Trifle not* with these things; do not ask for that which you ought not' (D&C 8:10; [emphasis] added).

"'And whatsoever ye shall ask the Father in my name, *which is right,* believing that ye shall receive, behold it shall be given unto you' (3 Ne. 18:20; [emphasis] added).

"'Whatsoever ye ask the Father in my name it shall be given unto you, *that is expedient for you*' (D&C 88:64; [emphasis] added). . . .

"These teachings of Jesus Christ emphasize that it matters very much *what* we ask for and *how* we ask for it. I testify that when we seek His will and do it, we will obtain the greatest blessings in life" (Scott, "Obtaining Help from the Lord," *Ensign*, Nov. 1991, 84). ●

What can happen when we ask for things that are not expedient for us? (88:65) Gerald N. Lund cautioned: "When we ask for something that is counter to God's commandments, or when we seek His approval for a path that He has already clearly forbidden, we not only will not be edified, but we open the way for the darkening of our minds, and this makes us vulnerable to Satan's whisperings" (*Hearing the Voice of the Lord*, 221).

What might be meant by the reference to "the voice of one crying in the wilderness"? (88:66) "The Lord continues [his counsel to the elders] by expounding upon another prophecy of Isaiah (40:3) that is usually associated with the mission of John the Baptist. Its inclusion here shows it was His voice that was directing John, and it was also applicable to others. The wilderness for John was in Judea, but to others it is a wilderness in that they 'cannot see him.' His voice was the spirit of truth and would abound, or be abundant to them, not just occasional. It was the still small voice of revelation (v. 66; see also D&C 85:6, 1 Kings 19:12). Thus another principle for obtaining peace, the spirit of truth, was expanded upon" (Nyman, *Doctrine and Covenants Commentary*, 2:178).

64 Whatsoever ye ask the Father in my name it shall be given unto you, that is expedient for you;

65 And if ye ask anything that is not expedient for you, it shall turn unto your condemnation.

66 Behold, that which you hear is as the voice of one crying in the wilderness—in the wilderness, because you cannot see him—my voice, because my voice is Spirit; my Spirit is truth; truth abideth and hath no end; and if it be in you it shall abound.

67 And if your eye be single to my glory, your whole bodies shall be filled with light, and there shall be no darkness in you; and that body which is filled with light comprehendeth all things.

68 Therefore, sanctify yourselves that your minds become single to God, and the days will come that you shall see him; for he will unveil his face unto you, and it shall be in his own time, and in his own way, and according to his own will.

69 Remember the great and last promise which I have made unto you; cast away your idle thoughts and your excess of laughter far from you.

70 Tarry ye, tarry ye in this place, and call a solemn assembly, even of those who are the first laborers in this last kingdom.

71 And let those whom they have warned in their traveling call on the Lord, and ponder the warning in their hearts which they have received, for a little season.

72 Behold, and lo, I will take care of your flocks, and will raise up elders and send unto them.

What could it mean to have an eye single to the glory of God? (88:67) "Imagine, if you will, a pair of powerful binoculars. Two separate optical systems are joined together with a gear to focus two independent images into one three-dimensional view. To apply this analogy, let the scene on the left side of your binoculars represent *your perception* of your task. Let the picture on the right side represent the *Lord's* perspective of your task—the portion of His plan He has entrusted to you. Now, connect your system to His. By mental adjustment, fuse your focus. Something wonderful happens. Your vision and His are now the same. You have developed an 'eye single to the glory of God' (D&C 4:5; see also Morm. 8:15). With that perspective, look upward, above and beyond mundane things about you" (Nelson, "With God Nothing Shall Be Impossible," *Ensign*, May 1988, 34). See also commentary in this volume on Doctrine and Covenants 55:1. ☉

What was the fulfillment of the promise that some of the Saints would see the face of God? (88:68–69) "The 1830s were a season of unparalleled revelations and visions to Joseph Smith and the Saints of Kirtland, Ohio. The most significant visions were those of Deity. . . . In this revelatory period, Joseph was repeatedly in the presence of the Lord—seeing Him, listening to Him, and attesting to His specific guidance and instruction. . . .

"Picture the Saints' exhilaration and joy as they became aware that the heavens were actually opening to them and their prophet. They heard the Savior speak. They saw visions of Him. They received a divine witness of Him through heavenly manifestations. They powerfully felt His presence in meetings. . . . The Savior literally was directing the Church in the last and final dispensation of His gospel" (Karl Ricks Anderson, *Savior in Kirtland*, 127, 129).

Why were the Saints instructed to gather in solemn assembly? (88:70) "Anciently, solemn assemblies were a prominent part of worship among the Israelites and were a time for fasting and praying to the Lord (see Leviticus 23:36; Deuteronomy 16:8; Joel 1:14; 2:15–17). The Lord commanded the members of His restored Church to continue these sacred meetings as an important part of their worship (see D&C 124:39; 133:6). In the revelation recorded in Doctrine and Covenants 88, the Saints were commanded to prepare themselves to hold a solemn assembly where the Lord would fulfill 'the great and last promise' of unveiling His face to them (see D&C 88:68–70, 75) and, as He had previously promised, endowing them with 'power from on high' (D&C 38:32; see also D&C 95:8–9)" (*Doctrine and Covenants Student Manual* [2018], 482). See also commentary in this volume on Doctrine and Covenants 95:7.

What are some ways the Lord continues to hasten His work in His time? (88:73) Elder David A. Bednar noted: "The Lord is hastening His work, and it is no coincidence that . . . powerful communication innovations and inventions are occurring in the dispensation of the fulness of times. Social media channels are global tools that can personally and positively impact large numbers of individuals and families. And I believe the time has come for us as disciples of Christ to use these inspired tools appropriately and more effectively to testify of God the Eternal Father, His plan of happiness for His children, and His Son, Jesus Christ, as the Savior of the world; to proclaim the reality of the Restoration of the gospel in the latter days; and to accomplish the Lord's work" ("Flood the Earth through Social Media," *Liahona*, Aug. 2015, 50).

Doctrine and Covenants 88:74–80. Sanctify Yourselves and Teach One Another the Doctrines of the Kingdom

How were the "first laborers in this last kingdom" to prepare? (88:74–75) "The Lord instructed the Prophet to call a solemn assembly [see v. 70] of the 'first laborers in this last kingdom.' This was to be held in Kirtland and was to include a spiritual manifestation to those who were worthy. Much needed to be done in anticipation. . . . Those expecting to be invited to attend were to organize themselves and sanctify their lives, purify their hearts and cleanse their hands and feet, in order that they would be 'clean from the blood of this wicked generation' (vv. 69, 74–75)" (Matthews, *Selected Writings*, 419).

What was the "great and last promise"? (88:75) "The leaders of the Church are here commanded to prepare themselves for the blessings of the temple, which will in turn prepare them to receive the fulness of his 'great and last promise' (v. 75), that they will be clean and worthy of his personal appearance to them" (Robinson and Garrett, *Commentary on the Doctrine and Covenants*, 3:117–18).

How can the "doctrine of the kingdom" best be taught? (88:77) "Teachers who are commanded to teach 'the principles of [the] gospel' and 'the doctrine of the kingdom' (D&C 88:77) should generally forgo

73 Behold, I will hasten my work in its time.

74 And I give unto you, who are the first laborers in this last kingdom, a commandment that you assemble yourselves together, and organize yourselves, and prepare yourselves, and sanctify yourselves; yea, purify your hearts, and cleanse your hands and your feet before me, that I may make you clean;

75 That I may testify unto your Father, and your God, and my God, that you are clean from the blood of this wicked generation; that I may fulfil this promise, this great and last promise, which I have made unto you, when I will.

76 Also, I give unto you a commandment that ye shall continue in prayer and fasting from this time forth.

77 And I give unto you a commandment that you shall teach one another the doctrine of the kingdom.

teaching specific rules or applications. For example, they would not teach any rules. . . . Once a teacher has taught the doctrine and the associated principles from the scriptures and the living prophets, such specific applications or rules are generally the responsibility of individuals and families. Well-taught doctrines and principles have a more powerful influence on behavior than rules. When we teach gospel doctrine and principles, we can qualify for the witness and guidance of the Spirit to reinforce our teaching, and we enlist the faith of our students in seeking the guidance of that same Spirit in applying those teachings in their personal lives" (Oaks, "Gospel Teaching," *Ensign*, Nov. 1999, 79–80).

What can the Lord's servants learn to better fulfill their mission? (88:78–80) "Theology is not the only subject in which [members] should be interested. They should study:

"Things both in heaven—Astronomy.

"And in the earth—Everything pertaining to the cultivation of the soil.

"And under the earth—Mineralogy, geology, etc.

"Things which have been—History, in all its branches.

"Things which must shortly come to pass—Prophecies.

"Things which are at home and abroad—Domestic and foreign politics.

"Wars—perplexities—judgment—The signs of the times, by which the observer may know that the day of the Lord is at hand.

"A knowledge of countries and kingdoms—physical and political geography, languages, etc.

"[God] expects [members] to know enough of these things to be able to magnify their callings as His ambassadors to the world" (Widtsoe, *Priesthood and Church Government*, 55, 56).

Doctrine and Covenants 88:81–85. Every Man Who Has Been Warned Should Warn His Neighbor

What is one bold way we can warn our neighbors? (88:81–82) An early Latter-day Saint sister, Sarah Leavitt, noted: "I wanted very much to get the good will of my neighbors, for I knew that I could have no success in preaching Mormonism unless I did and I was so full of that spirit it was hard to hold my peace. Consequently, I mingled in the society of all, was cheerful and sociable . . . , but kept on the side of truth and right. . . .

78 Teach ye diligently and my grace shall attend you, that you may be instructed more perfectly in theory, in principle, in doctrine, in the law of the gospel, in all things that pertain unto the kingdom of God, that are expedient for you to understand;

79 Of things both in heaven and in the earth, and under the earth; things which have been, things which are, things which must shortly come to pass; things which are at home, things which are abroad; the wars and the perplexities of the nations, and the judgments which are on the land; and a knowledge also of countries and of kingdoms—

80 That ye may be prepared in all things when I shall send you again to magnify the calling whereunto I have called you, and the mission with which I have commissioned you.

81 Behold, I sent you out to testify and warn the people, and it becometh every man who hath been warned to warn his neighbor.

82 Therefore, they are left without excuse, and their sins are upon their own heads.

83 He that seeketh me early shall find me, and shall not be forsaken.

"I knelt down in the midst of all that Gentile throng and the Lord gave me great liberty of speech. I prayed with the spirit and understanding, also to Him be the glory. The people were astonished and began to think there was some truth in Mormonism notwithstanding the bad reports about them" (Johnson and Reeder, *Witness of Women*, 76, 77).

What might it mean to "bind up the law and seal up the testimony" for the last time? (88:84) "After the Lord's servants have testified to and warned the nations, they will figuratively 'bind,' 'tie up,' 'shut up,' or close their testimonies and 'affix [a] seal' to the law of God (the prophetic word)" (Parry and Parry, *Understanding the Signs of the Times*, 354–55).

"The phrases *bind up the law* or *testimony* and *seal up the law* or *testimony* are found in three volumes of scripture (D&C 88:84; 109:46; 133:72; Isa. 8:16; 2 Nephi 18:16). The law represents teachings, and the testimony represents the inspired utterances of God's messengers. . . . Binding and sealing of the law is the process of actually tying up a parchment roll whereon the teachings of the prophets are recorded as a witness against those to whom the message was delivered ([see *One Volume Bible Commentary*], 420)" (Brewster, *Doctrine & Covenants Encyclopedia* [2012], 45).

How can people escape God's wrath during the "desolation of abomination"? (88:85) "The only way for men to escape the abomination of desolation (JS—H 1:12–20; D&C 84:114, 117; 88:84–85) to be poured out upon the wicked in the last days is for them to repent and live the gospel. The gospel is the message of peace and salvation for all men. And we have been commanded to proclaim its saving truths to all men everywhere (Mark 16:15–15; D&C 88:81)" (Bruce R. McConkie, *Sermons and Writings*, 16). See also commentary in this volume on Doctrine and Covenants 84:117. ✪

What might the phrase "their garments are not clean from the blood of this generation" mean? (88:85) "The phrase 'clean from the blood of this wicked generation' refers to the 'watchman' principle described by Ezekiel (3:17–21; 33:7–9), and alluded to by Jacob (2 Nephi 9:44; Jacob 1:19, 2:2); Paul (Acts 20:26–27); King Benjamin (Mosiah 2:27–28); Mormon (Mormon 9:35); and Moroni (Ether 12:37–38). This means that God will, on one hand, hold us responsible for the sins of those whom we failed to warn when we had the knowledge, the commission, and the opportunity, and on the other hand, hold us guiltless for the sins of those who reject our warnings.

84 Therefore, tarry ye, and labor diligently, that you may be perfected in your ministry to go forth among the Gentiles for the last time, as many as the mouth of the Lord shall name, to bind up the law and seal up the testimony, and to prepare the saints for the hour of judgment which is to come;

85 That their souls may escape the wrath of God, the desolation of abomination which awaits the wicked, both in this world and in the world to come. Verily, I say unto you, let those who are not the first elders continue in the vineyard until the mouth of the Lord shall call them, for their time is not yet come; their garments are not clean from the blood of this generation.

"The same principle was established by the Lord in our dispensation. A few verses after the Lord commands the first laborers to sanctify themselves (D&C 88:74–75, 85), [the Lord revealed D&C 88:81–82]" (Rawlins, "Endowed with Power," 129; see also D&C 61:33–34; 88:74–75; 112:28, 33). ●

Doctrine and Covenants 88:86–94. Signs, Upheavals of the Elements, and Angels Prepare the Way for the Coming of the Lord

86 Abide ye in the liberty wherewith ye are made free; entangle not yourselves in sin, but let your hands be clean, until the Lord comes.

What is the liberty that makes us free? (88:86) "In terms of a person's purpose in life, true freedom is to be free from those practices which hinder one from advancing on to the goal of eternal perfection. When the Prophet Joseph Smith defined salvation, he said: 'Salvation is nothing more nor less than to triumph over all our enemies and put them under our feet' ([Joseph Smith Papers, "History, 1838–1856, volume D-1," 1549). . . . Members of the Church have found a new life in Jesus Christ through the benefits of release from the bondage of sin into freedom, a freedom which must be continually maintained through prayer, activity in the Church, and obedience to the other commandments. Habits and practices that bring one into bondage are contrary to the freedom which the gospel teaches one should seek" (Roy W. Doxey, *Doctrine and Covenants Speaks*, 2:127). ●

87 For not many days hence and the earth shall tremble and reel to and fro as a drunken man; and the sun shall hide his face, and shall refuse to give light; and the moon shall be bathed in blood; and the stars shall become exceedingly angry, and shall cast themselves down as a fig that falleth from off a fig tree.

How can we withstand the calamities of the last days? (88:87–91) "Our Savior and Redeemer, Jesus Christ, will perform some of His mightiest works between now and when He comes again. We will see miraculous indications that God the Father and His Son, Jesus Christ, preside over this Church in majesty and glory. But in coming days, it will not be possible to survive spiritually without the guiding, directing, comforting, and constant influence of the Holy Ghost" (Nelson, "Revelation for the Church, Revelation for Our Lives," *Ensign*, May 2018, 96). See also commentary in this volume on Doctrine and Covenants 43:25.

88 And after your testimony cometh wrath and indignation upon the people.

89 For after your testimony cometh the testimony of earthquakes, that shall cause groanings in the midst of her, and men shall fall upon the ground and shall not be able to stand.

90 And also cometh the testimony of the voice of thunderings, and the voice of lightnings, and the voice of tempests, and the voice of the waves of the sea heaving themselves beyond their bounds.

91 And all things shall be in commotion; and surely, men's hearts shall fail them; for fear shall come upon all people.

How can we remain strong when others around us fear and fail? (88:91) "The reward for keeping covenants with God is heavenly power—power that strengthens us to withstand our trials, temptations, and heartaches better. This power eases our way. Those who live the higher laws of Jesus Christ have access to His higher power. Thus, covenant keepers are entitled to a special kind of *rest* that comes to them through their covenantal relationship with God. . . .

"You can overcome the spiritually and emotionally exhausting plagues of the world, including arrogance, pride, anger, immorality, hatred, greed, jealousy, and fear. Despite the distractions and distortions that swirl around us, you can find true *rest*—meaning relief and peace—even amid your most vexing problems" (Nelson, "Overcome the World and Find Rest," *Liahona*, Nov. 2022, 96). ⊕

Who might be the angels that will fly through the heavens in the last days sounding the trumps of God? (88:92) "The angels that fly through the midst of heaven are mighty men of God who call upon the inhabitants of the earth to prepare for the Second Coming. . . .

"God's trumpets will announce the return of the resurrected Jesus Christ and the beginning of His judgment [see D&C 88:94–107]. Each of the seven blasts addresses a different category of people. The first trump will be answered by the celestial, then the terrestrial, then the telestial, then perdition, and then Zion will be established; Babylon will fall and the Saints will receive their inheritance. The second series of trumpet blasts will herald the review of the earth's

92 And angels shall fly through the midst of heaven, crying with a loud voice, sounding the trump of God, saying: Prepare ye, prepare ye, O inhabitants of the earth; for the judgment of our God is come. Behold, and lo, the Bridegroom cometh; go ye out to meet him.

How Does Doctrine and Covenants 88:87–116 Help Us Understand Revelation 7–22?

Brother Robert J. Matthews provided this significant insight for Doctrine and Covenants 88:87–116: "This large segment of section 88 [verses 87–116] bears a striking similarity to chapters 7–22 in the book of Revelation. It is a prophecy of destruction and calamity but also a message of hope. It is, as with all revealed scripture, an assurance that in the end righteousness will triumph over evil, Christ over the devil, and the Saints over their oppressors. Ultimate victory will come through the Lord Jesus Christ.

"The Prophet had been involved for many months with making an initial draft of an inspired translation of the New Testament, concluding with the book of Revelation in March 1832. In the process of making the translation, many important things were revealed to him about the gospel and in this case about the future events to take place on the earth (see D&C 45:60–62). This history of the earth, the ministry of seven angels who play a prominent part in the final judgment scenes, and the opening of the seven seals are significant aspects of the Revelation of John. These are reiterated and partially explained in D&C 77 as a consequence of the translation and were enlarged upon in these verses from section 88 [verses 87–116]. Thus we regard this part of section 88 as a further clarification and explanation of the Revelation of John" (*Selected Writings*, 422).

93 And immediately there shall appear a great sign in heaven, and all people shall see it together.

94 And another angel shall sound his trump, saying: That great church, the mother of abominations, that made all nations drink of the wine of the wrath of her fornication, that persecuteth the saints of God, that shed their blood—she who sitteth upon many waters, and upon the islands of the sea—behold, she is the tares of the earth; she is bound in bundles; her bands are made strong, no man can loose them; therefore, she is ready to be burned. And he shall sound his trump both long and loud, and all nations shall hear it.

95 And there shall be silence in heaven for the space of half an hour; and immediately after shall the curtain of heaven be unfolded, as a scroll is unfolded after it is rolled up, and the face of the Lord shall be unveiled;

history and announce the finishing of God's mortal work [see D&C 88:108–116]" (Woodger, *Essential Doctrine and Covenants Companion*, 173, 174).

What great sign will all people see in the last days? (88:93) Speaking of the signs that shall come in the last days, the Prophet Joseph taught: "There will be wars and rumors of wars, signs in the heavens above and on the earth beneath, the sun turned into darkness and the moon to blood, earthquakes in divers places, the seas heaving beyond their bounds [D&C 88:87]; *then will appear one grand sign of the Son of Man in Heaven.* But what will the world do? They will say it is a planet, a comet, etc. But the Son of Man will come as the sign of the coming of the Son of Man, which will be as the light of the morning cometh out of the east" (*Joseph Smith* [manual], 252–53; emphasis added).

What could "the mother of abominations" represent? (88:94) The "great church" or "mother of abominations" is "the great and abominable church, which is the whore of all the earth, . . . cast down by devouring fire" (D&C 29:21). As the righteous are gathered in the last days, "The wicked will also be 'gathered.' They will be 'bound in bundles' (D&C 86:7; 88:94; 101:66) of their own choosing, ripening in preparation for the final harvest. Neither the Spirit of God, nor the testimony of his servants, nor the terrible natural calamities, famines, plagues, or other events, will turn their hearts to God (D&C 43:23–25; 45:33)" (Dahl, "Second Coming of Jesus Christ," 101).

Doctrine and Covenants 88:95–102. Angelic Trumps Call Forth the Dead in Their Order

What could be the meaning of a half hour of silence in heaven? (88:95) "Several scriptural passages equate silence with God's withholding his judgments. . . . God breaks his silence by sending his judgments" (Parry and Parry, *Understanding the Book of Revelation*, 103). Elder Bruce R. McConkie suggested: "And when the Lamb 'had opened the seventh seal, there was silence in heaven about the space of half an hour' [Revelation 8:1]. If the time here mentioned is 'the Lord's time' in which one day is a thousand years, the half hour would be some twenty-one of our years (Abr. 3:4; 2 Pet. 3:8). Could this be interpreted to mean that such a period will elapse after the commencement of the seventh thousand-year period and before the outpouring of the woes about to be named?" (*Millennial Messiah*, 382).

When the Savior comes again, who will be "caught up" to meet Him? (88:96–98) "Our faith grows as we anticipate the glorious day of the Savior's return to the earth. The thought of His coming stirs my soul. It will be breathtaking! The scope and grandeur, the vastness and magnificence, will exceed anything mortal eyes have ever seen or experienced....

"You and I, or those who follow us, 'the saints... from [every quarter] of the earth' [D&C 45:46], 'shall be quickened and ... caught up to meet him' [D&C 88:96], and those who have died in righteousness, they too will 'be caught up to meet him in the midst ... of heaven' [D&C 88:97]" (Andersen, "Thy Kingdom Come," *Ensign*, May 2015, 122). ☉

Who are those redeemed or resurrected at the second trump? (88:99) President Joseph Fielding Smith explained: "After the Lord and the righteous who are caught up to meet him have descended upon the earth, there will come to pass another resurrection. This will be considered as a part of the first, although it comes later. In this resurrection will come forth those of the *terrestrial order*, who are not worthy to be caught up to meet him, but who are worthy to come forth to enjoy the millennial reign" (*Doctrines of Salvation*, 2:296).

What is to become of the dead identified by the third trump? (88:100–101) "At the sounding of the third trump, those who will inherit the telestial kingdom will be resurrected. This will take place at the end of the Millennium" (McConkie and Ostler, *Revelations of the Restoration*, 645–46).

At the sound of the fourth trump, who are those to be resurrected? (88:102) Those who remain until the end are the sons of perdition who are "the only ones who shall not be redeemed in the due time of the Lord" (D&C 76:38; see also verses 32–37). Robert L. Millet explained: "Those who have been righteous on earth shall receive a righteous body and inherit the reward of the righteous. Those, on the other hand, who have sowed seeds of wickedness on earth shall reap condemnation and never know or partake of the fruit of the tree of life. The devil and his angels, those who are filthy—including the sons of perdition (see D&C

96 And the saints that are upon the earth, who are alive, shall be quickened and be caught up to meet him.

97 And they who have slept in their graves shall come forth, for their graves shall be opened; and they also shall be caught up to meet him in the midst of the pillar of heaven—

98 They are Christ's, the first fruits, they who shall descend with him first, and they who are on the earth and in their graves, who are first caught up to meet him; and all this by the voice of the sounding of the trump of the angel of God.

99 And after this another angel shall sound, which is the second trump; and then cometh the redemption of those who are Christ's at his coming; who have received their part in that prison which is prepared for them, that they might receive the gospel, and be judged according to men in the flesh.

100 And again, another trump shall sound, which is the third trump; and then come the spirits of men who are to be judged, and are found under condemnation;

101 And these are the rest of the dead; and they live not again until the thousand years are ended, neither again, until the end of the earth.

102 And another trump shall sound, which is the fourth trump, saying: There are found among those who are to remain until that great and last day, even the end, who shall remain filthy still.

88:35, 102)—'shall be filthy still' after the Resurrection. These 'shall go away into everlasting fire, prepared for them; and their torment is as a lake of fire and brimstone, whose flame ascendeth up forever and ever and has no end' (2 Nephi 9:16)" (*Power of the Word*, 92).

103 And another trump shall sound, which is the fifth trump, which is the fifth angel who committeth the everlasting gospel—flying through the midst of heaven, unto all nations, kindreds, tongues, and people;

104 And this shall be the sound of his trump, saying to all people, both in heaven and in earth, and that are under the earth—for every ear shall hear it, and every knee shall bow, and every tongue shall confess, while they hear the sound of the trump, saying: Fear God, and give glory to him who sitteth upon the throne, forever and ever; for the hour of his judgment is come.

105 And again, another angel shall sound his trump, which is the sixth angel, saying: She is fallen who made all nations drink of the wine of the wrath of her fornication; she is fallen, is fallen!

106 And again, another angel shall sound his trump, which is the seventh angel, saying: It is finished; it is finished! The Lamb of God hath overcome and trodden the wine-press alone, even the wine-press of the fierceness of the wrath of Almighty God.

107 And then shall the angels be crowned with the glory of his might, and the saints shall be filled with his glory, and receive their inheritance and be made equal with him.

Doctrine and Covenants 88:103–16. Angelic Trumps Proclaim the Restoration of the Gospel, the Fall of Babylon, and the Battle of the Great God

What is the significance of the message delivered by the fifth angel? (88:104) Elder Neal A. Maxwell warned: "Yes, we are free to choose the mortal perks with their short shelf life. However, ahead lies that great moment when every knee shall bow and every tongue confess that Jesus is the Christ! (see Mosiah 27:31; D&C 88:104). Then the galleries and the mortal thrones will be empty. Even the great and spacious building will fall—and resoundingly! (see 1 Ne. 8:26–28). Then, too, those who have lived without God in the world will confess that God is God! (see Mosiah 27:31). Meanwhile, His character and attributes should evoke adoration and emulation from us" ("Tugs and Pulls of the World," *Ensign*, Nov. 2000, 37).

What truth is emphasized in the final angel's message? (88:106) "I speak of the loneliest journey ever made and the unending blessings it brought to all in the human family. I speak of the Savior's solitary task of shouldering alone the burden of our salvation. Rightly He would say: 'I have trodden the winepress alone; and of the people there was none with me. . . . I looked, and there was none to help; and I wondered that there was none to uphold [me]' (Isaiah 63:3, 5; see also D&C 88:106; 133:50). . . .

"With none to help or uphold Him, Jesus of Nazareth, the living Son of the living God, restored physical life where death had held sway and brought joyful, spiritual redemption out of sin, hellish darkness, and despair" (Holland, "None Were with Him," *Ensign*, May 2009, 86, 88).

How are we to understand being made equal with the Lord? (88:107) "One core belief of Latter-day Saints is 'that through the Atonement of Christ, all mankind may be saved, by obedience to the laws and ordinances of the Gospel' ([Articles of Faith] 1:3). To this end, the work and glory of the Father *and* the Son are centered in providing all of God's children with an equal opportunity to become as They—the Father and the Son—are. . . . Eternal life, . . . to live forever in the *presence* of the Father and Son—to fulfill the divine destiny to become as They are—is reserved for those who prove faithful to Them. The Lord declared that these 'shall be filled with his glory, and receive their inheritance and *be made equal with him*' (D&C 88:107; [emphasis] added)" (Brewster, *Doctrine & Covenants Encyclopedia* [2012], 162–63).

What will be revealed by the declarations of these seven angels? (88:108–10) "The Lord has revealed that for each of the seven thousand years of the earth's temporal existence since Adam's fall, men's acts have been recorded. The revealing of the secret acts of men and 'the thoughts and intents of their hearts' and the mighty works of God in each of these seven periods, will occur during the millennial period of peace and brotherhood upon the earth [D&C 88:108–110; 77:6–7, 12]" (Roy W. Doxey, *Doctrine and Covenants Speaks*, 2:130).

What might be meant by the phrase "time no longer"? (88:110) "In this setting, 'time no longer' may refer to the beginning of the Millennium, when time as we understand it with our calendar, seasons, hours, minutes, and seconds no longer exists. This seems to be the manner in which two revelations (Rev. 10:6, D&C 88:110) use the phrase 'time no longer': 'The Lord hath redeemed his people; and Satan is bound and time is no longer. The Lord hath gathered all things in one. The Lord hath brought down Zion from above. The Lord hath brought up Zion from beneath' (D&C 84:100)" (Parry and Parry, *Understanding the Book of Revelation*, 129).

What happens during this time when Satan is loosed "for a little season"? (88:111–16) "Satan will be 'loosed a little season' to work his wickedness in one last effort to gather souls to his evil cause (see Revelation 20:1–3; D&C 43:30–31; 88:110–111)" (Brewster, *Behold, I Come Quickly*, 222).

"It may be hard to comprehend why some who have experienced the blessings of the Millennium will begin to deny God. Nevertheless, there will be those who, having been partakers of God's power, will still deny the truth and knowingly and 'wilfully rebel against God' (3 Nephi 6:18; see also 4 Nephi 1:38; D&C 29:44–45; 76:31)" (*Doctrine and Covenants Student Manual* [2018], 172). ☉

108 And then shall the first angel again sound his trump in the ears of all living, and reveal the secret acts of men, and the mighty works of God in the first thousand years.

109 And then shall the second angel sound his trump, and reveal the secret acts of men, and the thoughts and intents of their hearts, and the mighty works of God in the second thousand years—

110 And so on, until the seventh angel shall sound his trump; and he shall stand forth upon the land and upon the sea, and swear in the name of him who sitteth upon the throne, that there shall be time no longer; and Satan shall be bound, that old serpent, who is called the devil, and shall not be loosed for the space of a thousand years.

111 And then he shall be loosed for a little season, that he may gather together his armies.

112 And Michael, the seventh angel, even the archangel, shall gather together his armies, even the hosts of heaven.

113 And the devil shall gather together his armies; even the hosts of hell, and shall come up to battle against Michael and his armies.

114 And then cometh the battle of the great God; and the devil and his armies shall be cast away into their own place, that they shall not have power over the saints any more at all.

115 For Michael shall fight their battles, and shall overcome him who seeketh the throne of him who sitteth upon the throne, even the Lamb.

116 This is the glory of God, and the sanctified; and they shall not any more see death.

117 Therefore, verily I say unto you, my friends, call your solemn assembly, as I have commanded you.

118 And as all have not faith, seek ye diligently and teach one another words of wisdom; yea, seek ye out of the best books words of wisdom; seek learning, even by study and also by faith.

119 Organize yourselves; prepare every needful thing; and establish a house, even a house of prayer, a house of fasting, a house of faith, a house of learning, a house of glory, a house of order, a house of God;

120 That your incomings may be in the name of the Lord; that your outgoings may be in the name of the Lord; that all your

Who is Michael the archangel, and what role will he play at the end of the Millennium? (88:112–15) The scriptures teach about "Adam's mortal role as the first man, . . . [but also] concerning his premortal and postmortal missions. Before the world was created, Adam was known as 'Michael, the prince, the archangel' (D&C 107:54). . . .

"At the end of the earth—meaning at the end of the Millennium (D&C 88:101; JS—M 1:55)—the final great battle between good and evil, known as the 'battle of the great God' (D&C 88:114) or the battle of Gog and Magog (Revelation 20:8), will take place. And once again, the mighty Michael, the eternal captain of Jehovah's army, will come face to face with his foe, Satan. . . .

"Michael's final victory is in preparation for the earth to be made celestial" (Top, "Adam," 20–21, 22).

Doctrine and Covenants 88:117–26. Seek Learning, Establish a House of God (a Temple), and Clothe Yourselves with the Bond of Charity

Why is it important to seek learning both by study and by faith? (88:118) "When we seek the truth about religion, we should use spiritual methods appropriate for that search: prayer, the witness of the Holy Ghost, and study of the scriptures and the words of modern prophets. I am always sad when I hear of one who reports a loss of religious faith because of secular teachings. Those who once had spiritual vision can suffer from self-inflicted spiritual blindness. . . .

"The methods of science lead us to what we call scientific truth. But 'scientific truth' is not the whole of life. Those who do not learn 'by study and also by faith' (Doctrine and Covenants 88:118) limit their understanding of truth to what they can verify by scientific means. That puts artificial limits on their pursuit of truth" (Oaks, "Truth and the Plan," *Ensign*, Nov. 2018, 25). ◉

Which "house" is being referred to in this passage? (88:119) Boyd K. Packer wrote: "Kirtland's most significant contribution . . . [was] the house of the Lord the Saints built out of their poverty and sacrifice—the Kirtland Temple. This was the first temple of the present dispensation. The command to build it came at the end of 1832: [see D&C 88:119; 95:11]. . . .

"It appears that serious construction work on the temple began on June 5, 1833, when 'George A. Smith [hauled] the first load of stone for the Temple, and Hyrum Smith and Reynolds Cahoon commenced digging the trench for the walls of the Lord's house, and finished the same with their own hands' ([Joseph Smith Papers, 'History, 1838–1856, Volume A-1,' 302])" (*Holy Temple*, 142).

Why must the Saints be careful of light speeches, laughter, and light-mindedness? (88:121) The Prophet Joseph warned: "The things of God are of deep import, and time and experience, and careful and ponderous and solemn thoughts can only find them out, thy mind O Man, if thou wilt lead a soul into Salvation[, thou] must stretch as High as the utmost Heavens, and search into and contemplate the darkest abyss, and expanse of eternity. Thou must commune with God. . . . How vain and trifling have been our Spirits, our conferences, our councils, our meetings, our private as well as public conversations, too low, too mean, too vulgar, too condescending, for the dignified Characters of the called and chosen of God, according to the purposes of his will from before the foundation of the world" (Joseph Smith Papers, "History, 1838–1856, volume C-1," 904[b]). ⊕

Why were the elders to appoint a teacher? (88:122) "This is one of the Lord's powerful patterns for learning and teaching. May I suggest another way of looking at this verse: 'Appoint among yourselves a teacher.' Who is the teacher? The Holy Ghost. Could it be that if you want the Holy Ghost to be the teacher, then 'let not all [speak] at once, but let one speak at a time and let all listen unto his sayings, that when all have spoken, that all may be edified of all'? The only one that can produce that edification is the Holy Ghost" (Bednar, "Learning in the Lord's Way," *Liahona*, Oct. 2018, 53).

How can ceasing to sleep longer than needed bless our lives? (88:124) As a new General Authority, Marion G. Romney sought counsel from then-Elder Harold B. Lee about how to succeed in his new calling. Elder Lee advised him: "'Go to bed early and get up early. If you do, your body and mind will become rested, and then in the quiet of those early-morning hours, you will receive more flashes of insight and inspiration than at any other time of the day.'

"President Romney said: 'From that day on, I put that counsel into practice, and I know it works. Whenever I have a serious problem, or some assignment of a creative nature with which I hope to receive the influence of the Spirit, I always receive more assistance in the early-morning hours than at any

salutations may be in the name of the Lord, with uplifted hands unto the Most High.

121 Therefore, cease from all your light speeches, from all laughter, from all your lustful desires, from all your pride and light-mindedness, and from all your wicked doings.

122 Appoint among yourselves a teacher, and let not all be spokesmen at once; but let one speak at a time and let all listen unto his sayings, that when all have spoken that all may be edified of all, and that every man may have an equal privilege.

123 See that ye love one another; cease to be covetous; learn to impart one to another as the gospel requires.

124 Cease to be idle; cease to be unclean; cease to find fault one with another; cease to sleep longer than is needful; retire to thy bed early, that ye may not be weary; arise early, that your bodies and your minds may be invigorated.

125 And above all things, clothe yourselves with the bond of charity, as with a mantle, which is the bond of perfectness and peace.

126 Pray always, that ye may not faint, until I come. Behold, and lo, I will come quickly, and receive you unto myself. Amen.

127 And again, the order of the house prepared for the presidency of the school of the prophets, established for their instruction in all things that are expedient for them, even for all the officers of the church, or in other words, those who are called to the ministry in the church, beginning at the high priests, even down to the deacons—

128 And this shall be the order of the house of the presidency of the school: He that is appointed to be president, or teacher, shall be found standing in his place, in the house which shall be prepared for him.

other time of the day'" (in Christensen, "Ten Ideas to Increase Your Spirituality," *Ensign*, Mar. 1999, 59).

How might others be blessed if the Lord's servants were clothed with charity? (88:125) Sister Sharon Eubank stated: "Brothers and sisters, through your ministry, donations, time, and love, you have been the answer to so many prayers. And yet there is so much more to do. As baptized members of the Church, we are under covenant to care for those in need. Our individual efforts don't necessarily require money or faraway locations; they do require the guidance of the Holy Spirit and a willing heart to say to the Lord, 'Here am I; send me'" ("I Pray He'll Use Us," *Liahona*, Nov. 2021, 55).

Why are the Lord's servants instructed to "pray always"? (88:126) "There is one admonition of our Savior that all the Saints of God should observe, but which I fear, we do not as we should, and that is, to pray always and faint not [see Luke 18:1; D&C 88:126]. I fear, as a people, we do not pray enough in faith. We should call upon the Lord in mighty prayer, and make all our wants known unto Him. For if He does not protect and deliver us, and save us, no other power will. Therefore our trust is entirely in Him. Therefore, our prayers should ascend into the ears of our Heavenly Father day and night" (*Wilford Woodruff* [manual], 110). ◉

Doctrine and Covenants 88:127–141. The Order of the School of the Prophets Is Set Forth, Including the Ordinance of Washing of Feet

What was the revealed order of the School of the Prophets? (88:127–29) "The school was established by revelation 'for their instruction in all things that are expedient for them, even for all the officers of the church, or in other words, those who are called to the ministry in the church' (D&C 88:127). In this revelation the curriculum, textbooks, and operation of the school are outlined by the Lord. The curriculum was very broad as those involved were instructed to seek wisdom 'out of the best books' and to seek learning not only by study but also by faith (D&C 88:118)" (Perkins, "School of the Prophets," 1077–78).

How were the elders in the School of the Prophets blessed by their participation? (88:130–37) "The teacher was instructed to kneel in prayer prior to entering the classroom (see verse 131). The bond of fellowship was given emphasis and ritualized by instructing the teacher to greet the students by standing with uplifted hands [see verse 133]. . . .

"The dual role of teacher and student to co-operate, respect each other's views, and edify each other was not ritualized, but specific instruction on that role was given—all should have an opportunity to speak (see verse 122). By inviting teacher-student interaction, students were given an opportunity to contribute insights that further enriched the subject matter and instruction.

"This approach to teaching brought about awe-inspiring results. During the process many present commented on the spirit felt. Some prophesied, and yet others saw the heavens opened" (James W. McConkie, *Looking at the Doctrine and Covenants Again*, 344–45).

129 Therefore, he shall be first in the house of God, in a place that the congregation in the house may hear his words carefully and distinctly, not with loud speech.

130 And when he cometh into the house of God, for he should be first in the house—behold, this is beautiful, that he may be an example—

131 Let him offer himself in prayer upon his knees before God, in token or remembrance of the everlasting covenant.

132 And when any shall come in after him, let the teacher arise, and, with uplifted hands to heaven, yea, even directly, salute his brother or brethren with these words:

133 Art thou a brother or brethren? I salute you in the name of the Lord Jesus Christ, in token or remembrance of the everlasting covenant, in which covenant I receive you to fellowship, in a determination that is fixed, immovable, and unchangeable, to be your friend and brother through the grace of God in the bonds of love, to walk in all the

The School of the Prophets (Doctrine and Covenants 88:127)

Doctrine and Covenants 88:119 "directed the Saints to 'organize [themselves]' and establish 'an house of prayer, an house of fasting, an house of faith, an house of learning, an house of glory, an house of order, an house of God.'

"Taken together with instructions to 'teach one another' and 'seek learning by study and also by faith' [D&C 88:118], Joseph Smith and the elders in Kirtland understood this revelation to deliver a twofold mandate. They were to 'build a house of God, & establish a school for the Prophets.' Joseph Smith and the Saints in Kirtland began acting on this instruction almost immediately. . . .

"Within weeks of the . . . revelation, the School of the Prophets was well under way, with as many as 25 men meeting in a small room above the Newel K. Whitney store" (Tait and Rogers, "House for Our God," 165, 166).

"The School of the Prophets was organized, according to the instructions in [D&C 88:127–141]" (Smith and Sjodahl, *Doctrine & Covenants Commentary*, 567).

"Held each winter from 1833 to 1836, the School of the Prophets in Kirtland offered participants spiritual as well as secular education. It helped prepare them for missionary service and for a promised 'endowment of power' when the Kirtland Temple was completed. The first session of the school opened on January 22, 1833, in an upper room of Newel K. Whitney's store. While the school was intended primarily to prepare men for missions, women also attended the first meeting and participated in the spiritual outpouring, which included powerful manifestations of the Holy Ghost and speaking in tongues. As commanded by revelation, participants began meetings with a formal greeting, and new members were welcomed to the school by the ordinance of the washing of feet" (Church History Topics, "School of the Prophets").

commandments of God blameless, in thanksgiving, forever and ever. Amen.

134 And he that is found unworthy of this salutation shall not have place among you; for ye shall not suffer that mine house shall be polluted by him.

135 And he that cometh in and is faithful before me, and is a brother, or if they be brethren, they shall salute the president or teacher with uplifted hands to heaven, with this same prayer and covenant, or by saying Amen, in token of the same.

136 Behold, verily, I say unto you, this is an ensample unto you for a salutation to one another in the house of God, in the school of the prophets.

137 And ye are called to do this by prayer and thanksgiving, as the Spirit shall give utterance in all your doings in the house of the Lord, in the school of the prophets, that it may become a sanctuary, a tabernacle of the Holy Spirit to your edification.

138 And ye shall not receive any among you into this school save he is clean from the blood of this generation;

139 And he shall be received by the ordinance of the washing of feet, for unto this end was the ordinance of the washing of feet instituted.

140 And again, the ordinance of washing feet is to be administered by the president, or presiding elder of the church.

141 It is to be commenced with prayer; and after partaking of bread and wine, he is to gird himself according to the pattern given in the thirteenth chapter of John's testimony concerning me. Amen.

What do we know about the ordinance of the washing of feet? (88:138–41) "During the Last Supper, Jesus took a towel and a basin of water and washed the feet of the disciples. Some Christian groups followed this New Testament precedent, washing feet as a token of humility or brotherhood. A revelation to Joseph Smith in December 1832 required participants in the School of the Prophets to participate in the washing of feet. The Lord commanded the elders to 'clean your hands, and your feet, before me' as witness that they were 'clean, from the blood of this, wicked generation.' . . . Accordingly, on March 29 and 30, 1836, about 300 priesthood holders from the Kirtland area, including Joseph Smith and other Church leaders, met to wash one another's feet" (Church History Topics, "Washing of Feet").

Introduction to Doctrine and Covenants 89

"On the 27th day of February, 1833, [at Kirtland, Ohio,] the Prophet received the revelation known as the Word of Wisdom, warning the people to abstain from impurities and grossness in their food and drink, and promising them rich blessings of physical strength and protection from the power of the adversary as a reward for their obedience. . . . Its delivery to Joseph marks another step in the divine plan for man's eventual elevation to divine acceptability" (George Q. Cannon, *Life of Joseph Smith the Prophet*, 130).

"While no contemporaneous sources describing the circumstances under which [Joseph Smith] dictated this 27 February 1833 revelation have been located, later accounts indicate that it was recorded in connection with the activities of the School of the Prophets. According to Brigham Young, heavy tobacco use—in the form of both smoking and chewing—among members of the school, combined with Emma Smith's and others' complaints about cleaning tobacco juice from the floor, led [Joseph] 'to inquire of the Lord with regard to use of tobacco' and 'to the conduct of the elders with this particular practice.' This revelation—composed largely of warnings and counsel regarding not only the use of tobacco, but also the consumption of various foods, 'hot drinks,' wine, and 'Strong drinks'—was the result of his inquiries. Known among church members as the 'Word of Wisdom,' referring to the opening phrase of the text, the revelation was evidently recorded in [Joseph's] translating room in Newel K. Whitney's store. Zebedee Coltrin, who was present, recalled [Joseph Smith] coming out of his translation room and reading the revelation to over twenty members of the school then in attendance. Joel Johnson added that the revelation was given in the evening" (Joseph Smith Papers, Historical Introduction to "Revelation, 27 February 1833 [D&C 89]").

SECTION 89

Revelation given through Joseph Smith the Prophet, at Kirtland, Ohio, February 27, 1833. As a consequence of the early brethren using tobacco in their meetings, the Prophet was led to ponder upon the matter; consequently, he inquired of the Lord concerning it. This revelation, known as the Word of Wisdom, was the result.

The Word of Wisdom—Context and Observance (Doctrine and Covenants 89)

"The Word of Wisdom appeared at a time of intense public debate about bodily health in general and alcohol abuse in particular. In the United States, many adults in the 1830s had been raised in families where alcoholic beverages were consumed at breakfast, lunch, and dinner. Many became concerned about the social and health-related consequences of increased alcohol consumption. Beginning in the 1810s, reformers called for abstinence from hard liquor; many of their hearers went further, taking a pledge against all alcoholic beverages, including beer. At the same time, some reformers spoke out against tobacco chewing and recommended coffee as a substitute for alcohol, given that clean water was not always available.

"Within the context of this debate, Emma Smith approached her husband, concerned about the environment in the School of the Prophets. The same space Joseph used to record revelations and work on his inspired Bible translation was also used as the schoolroom, in which attendees often smoked, chewed, and spat tobacco. Joseph inquired of the Lord and received the Word of Wisdom. The revelation helped Saints navigate many of the issues debated by reformers and also addressed Emma's specific concerns. 'Strong drinks' and 'hot drinks,' the revelation said, were 'not for the belly.' Neither was tobacco, which was better used as an herb for sick cattle. Sources make clear that many early Latter-day Saints understood 'hot drinks' to refer to coffee and tea. Some groups, like the

1 A WORD OF WISDOM, for the benefit of the council of high priests, assembled in Kirtland, and the church, and also the saints in Zion—

2 To be sent greeting; not by commandment or constraint, but by revelation and the word of wisdom, showing forth the order and will of God in the temporal salvation of all saints in the last days—

Doctrine and Covenants 89:1–9. The Use of Wine, Strong Drinks, Tobacco, and Hot Drinks Is Proscribed

What was the council of high priests referred to in this verse? (89:1) "In June 1831, at a conference in Kirtland, nineteen men were the first to be ordained to the office of high priest in modern times ([*Essentials in Church History*], 106). This office of the Melchizedek Priesthood had been mentioned in a revelation received several months earlier (D&C 42:31, 71)" (Brewster, *Doctrine & Covenants Encyclopedia* [2012], 252).

Since the high priests were not organized into quorums until 1836 (see "High Priests," *Encyclopedia of Mormonism*, 587), it is apparent that this group of high priests belonged to a different council. "The reference in this revelation to the 'council of high priests, assembled in Kirtland' is to those involved in the School of the Prophets, which met in the upper room of the Whitney store" (McConkie and Ostler, *Revelations of the Restoration*, 652).

Why was the Word of Wisdom not given as a commandment when first revealed? (89:2) "The reason undoubtedly why the Word of Wisdom was given—as not by 'commandment or restraint' was that at that time, at least, if it had been given as a commandment it would have brought every man, addicted to the use of these noxious things, under condemnation; so the Lord was merciful and gave them a chance to overcome, before He brought them under the law. Later on, it was announced from this stand, by President Brigham Young [in *Journal of Discourses*, 12:118] that the Word of Wisdom was a revelation and a command of the Lord" (Joseph F. Smith, in Conference Report, Oct. 1913, 14). ●

Shakers, advised against eating meat, while others advocated no restriction. The Word of Wisdom took an independent position, saying that the Lord ordained the use of meat, on condition that it be eaten 'sparingly.' The Word of Wisdom also advocated the use of grain and fruit.

"For the next two generations, Church leaders taught the Word of Wisdom as a command from God, but they tolerated a variety of viewpoints on how strictly this commandment should be observed. Many Saints continued to drink coffee and tea, and some chewed tobacco. In territorial Utah, Church leaders denounced public intoxication and whiskey drinking but were often silent on the moderate use of milder alcoholic drinks. This tolerance gave the Saints time to develop their own tradition of abstinence from habit-forming substances.

"Even so, Church leaders looked forward to the time when a higher standard would be observed. In the 1860s and 1870s, Brigham Young called on the Saints to reject all use of tea, coffee, tobacco, and liquor. . . .

"In the early 1900s, the Saints replaced wine with water for sacramental use. . . . In 1921, the Lord inspired President Heber J. Grant to require all Saints to abstain from alcohol, tobacco, coffee, and tea in order to obtain a temple recommend" (Church History Topics, "Word of Wisdom [D&C 89]").

How can all people live the Word of Wisdom? (89:3)
"The standards are set, known, and easily available to each of us.

"The Savior has said that all of us are capable of meeting the standards. The Word of Wisdom is evidence of this, indicating that it is 'given for a principle with promise, adapted to the capacity of the weak and the weakest of *all* saints, who are or can be called saints' (D&C 89:3; emphasis added).

"The Savior also teaches that we will 'not be tempted above that which [we are] able to bear' (D&C 64:20), but we must 'watch and pray continually' (Alma 13:28)" (Packer, "Heavenly Father's Fixed Standards," *Ensign*, Aug. 2015, 71).

What are examples of "evils and designs" in the world today that we can avoid by following the Word of Wisdom? (89:4) "The Lord foresaw the situation of today when motives for money would cause men to conspire to entice others to take noxious substances into their bodies. Advertisements which promote beer, wine, liquors, coffee, tobacco, and other harmful substances are examples of what the Lord foresaw. But the most pernicious example of an evil conspiracy in our time is those who induce young people into the use of drugs. . . .

"We give you warning that Satan and his emissaries will strive to entice you to use harmful substances, because they well know if you partake, your spiritual powers will be inhibited and you will be in their evil power. . . . Keep the commandments of God and you will have the wisdom to know and discern that which is evil" (Benson, "Principle with a Promise," *Ensign*, May 1983, 54–55).

What are some reasons the Lord counsels His Saints to avoid strong drinks? (89:5) At the October 1942 general conference, the First Presidency made a statement regarding the Word of Wisdom: "Over the earth, . . . the demon drink is in control. Drunken with strong drink, men have lost their reason; their counsel has been destroyed; their judgment and vision are fled; they reel forward to destruction.

"Drink brings cruelty into the home; it walks arm in arm with poverty; its companions are disease and plague; it puts chastity to flight; and it knows neither honesty nor fair dealing; it is a total stranger to truth; it drowns conscience; it is the bodyguard of evil; it curses all who touch it.

"Drink has brought more woe and misery, broken more hearts, wrecked more homes, committed more crimes, filled more coffins, than all the wars the world has suffered" (*Messages of the First Presidency*, 6:171). ⊕

3 Given for a principle with promise, adapted to the capacity of the weak and the weakest of all saints, who are or can be called saints.

4 Behold, verily, thus saith the Lord unto you: In consequence of evils and designs which do and will exist in the hearts of conspiring men in the last days, I have warned you, and forewarn you, by giving unto you this word of wisdom by revelation—

5 That inasmuch as any man drinketh wine or strong drink among you, behold it is not good, neither meet in the sight of your Father, only in assembling yourselves together to offer up your sacraments before him.

6 And, behold, this should be wine, yea, pure wine of the grape of the vine, of your own make.

7 And, again, strong drinks are not for the belly, but for the washing of your bodies.

8 And again, tobacco is not for the body, neither for the belly, and is not good for man, but is an herb for bruises and all sick cattle, to be used with judgment and skill.

9 And again, hot drinks are not for the body or belly.

10 And again, verily I say unto you, all wholesome herbs God hath ordained for the constitution, nature, and use of man—

11 Every herb in the season thereof, and every fruit in the season thereof; all these to be used with prudence and thanksgiving.

What was considered the "pure wine of the grape"? (89:6) "This has reference to Joseph making sure the wine was pure and not tampered with by the enemies of the Church. Some have interpreted this as a commandment to use only grape juice rather than fermented wine for the sacrament, but this cannot be correct, because the Church continued to use fermented sacramental wine both in Kirtland and in Nauvoo" (Robinson and Garrett, *Commentary on the Doctrine and Covenants*, 1:179). See also commentary in this volume on Doctrine and Covenants 20:75 and 27:3.

How did alcohol use change among members over the years? (89:7) "When the Word of Wisdom was first made known to the Saints, some Church members immediately stopped drinking alcohol, while others saw occasional or moderate use to be acceptable. Others viewed it as appropriate to drink alcohol for medical needs (see [*Joseph Smith Papers: Documents, Volume 3*], 15–17). At the time this revelation was given, medicines were rare and alcohol was a valuable cleansing agent and disinfectant for wounds. Over time, the Word of Wisdom was understood by Church leaders and members to prohibit the drinking of any alcohol (see [Woodworth, "Word of Wisdom," 186])" (*Doctrine and Covenants Student Manual* [2018], 499–500).

What constitutes "hot drinks"? (89:9) "The Word of Wisdom is a commandment of God. He revealed it for the physical and spiritual benefit of His children. Prophets have clarified that the teachings in Doctrine and Covenants 89 include abstinence from tobacco, strong drinks (alcohol), and hot drinks (tea and coffee).

"There are other harmful substances and practices that are not specified in the Word of Wisdom or by Church leaders. Members should use wisdom and prayerful judgment in making choices to promote their physical, spiritual, and emotional health" (*General Handbook*, 38.7.14). ⊕

Doctrine and Covenants 89:10–17. Herbs, Fruits, Flesh, and Grain Are Ordained for the Use of Man and of Animals

How does a person decide which herbs, drinks, flesh, etc. are appropriate for consumption? (89:10–12) In October 2022, Elder Dieter F. Uchtdorf introduced the revised pamphlet *For the Strength of Youth: A Guide for Making Choices*. All Church members can benefit from living the following truths regarding the Word of Wisdom:

"Your soul is made up of your body and your spirit. For this reason, physical health and spiritual health are closely connected. The Savior revealed the Word of Wisdom to teach principles of caring for your body—and to promise physical and spiritual blessings. . . .

"Do things that will strengthen your body—nothing that will hurt or damage it. Enjoy with gratitude the many good things God has provided. But remember that alcohol, tobacco, coffee, tea, and other harmful drugs and substances are not for your body or your spirit. Even helpful substances, like prescription drugs, can be destructive if not used correctly. . . .

"The Lord has promised great treasures of knowledge to those who keep the Word of Wisdom. A healthy body, free from addiction, also increases your ability to receive personal revelation, think clearly, and serve the Lord" (*For the Strength of Youth*, 23, 25, 26).

What is the Lord's counsel concerning the use of meat? (89:12–13) "Previous revelations had already addressed issues relative to the use of meat by the Saints. They first announced that anyone who forbade the use of meat did so without the authority of God [see D&C 49:19]. . . . In the second revelation on the matter, the Lord told the Saints that 'the fulness of the earth is yours, the beasts of the field and the fowls of the air' [D&C 59:16]. . . . As with all things that the Lord has given us, these are to be used 'with judgment, not to excess' [D&C 59:20]. 'Wo be unto man that sheddeth blood or that wasteth flesh and hath no need,' the Lord warned (D&C 49:21)" (McConkie and Ostler, *Revelations of the Restoration*, 655). See also commentary in this volume on Doctrine and Covenants 49:18–19.

Doctrine and Covenants 89:12–13 reveal that the Lord has "ordained [meat] for the use of man." It should be used with gratitude, frugality, and moderation (see Webster, *American Dictionary* [1828], s.v. "sparingly"). ✛

Why might the Saints have been told to eat meat "only in times of winter, or of cold, or famine"? (89:13) "When this revelation was first printed in the Doctrine and Covenants (1835), there was no comma after this phrase ["they should not be used"]. The addition of the comma [after used, in the 1921 edition] clarifies the meaning of the text, thus dramatizing the importance of proper punctuation. The addition of the comma is in harmony with the context of the revelation, which is that meat should be used sparingly" (McConkie and Ostler, *Revelations of the Restoration*, 655–56).

12 Yea, flesh also of beasts and of the fowls of the air, I, the Lord, have ordained for the use of man with thanksgiving; nevertheless they are to be used sparingly;

13 And it is pleasing unto me that they should not be used, only in times of winter, or of cold, or famine.

14 All grain is ordained for the use of man and of beasts, to be the staff of life, not only for man but for the beasts of the field, and the fowls of heaven, and all wild animals that run or creep on the earth;

15 And these hath God made for the use of man only in times of famine and excess of hunger.

16 All grain is good for the food of man; as also the fruit of the vine; that which yieldeth fruit, whether in the ground or above the ground—

17 Nevertheless, wheat for man, and corn for the ox, and oats for the horse, and rye for the fowls and for swine, and for all beasts of the field, and barley for all useful animals, and for mild drinks, as also other grain.

18 And all saints who remember to keep and do these sayings, walking in obedience to the commandments, shall receive health in their navel and marrow to their bones;

19 And shall find wisdom and great treasures of knowledge, even hidden treasures;

What has the passage of time taught us about the diet revealed in these verses? (89:14–17) "Certainly all kinds of diets are being recommended by one seeming authority or another. The diets in fashion change from year to year. Consistently over the years, however, the evidence favors a diet in keeping with the recommendations contained in the Word of Wisdom. The medical community widely accepts that a low-fat diet consisting mostly of complex carbohydrates found in whole grains, fruits, and vegetables, along with limited amounts of nuts and high-protein foods like low-fat meats, is associated with lower incidences of disease and a longer life" (Stephenson, "Cancer, Nutrition, and the Word of Wisdom," *Ensign*, Jul. 2008, 45).

Doctrine and Covenants 89:18–21. Obedience to Gospel Law, Including the Word of Wisdom, Brings Temporal and Spiritual Blessings

How can living the Word of Wisdom bring health to both your body and spirit? (89:18–19) President Russell M. Nelson taught: "Remarkable as your body is, its prime purpose is even of greater importance—to serve as tenement for your spirit. . . .

"Your spirit acquired a body at birth and became a soul to live in mortality through periods of trial and testing. Part of each test is to determine if your body can become mastered by the spirit that dwells within it. . . .

"If you yield to anything that can addict, and thus defy the Word of Wisdom, your spirit surrenders to the body. The *flesh* then enslaves the *spirit*. This is contrary to the purpose of your mortal existence. And in the process of such addiction, your life span is likely to be shortened, thereby reducing the time available for repentance by which your spirit might attain self-mastery over your body" ("Self-Mastery," *Ensign*, Nov. 1985, 30, 31).

What hidden treasures can be found by those who faithfully keep the Word of Wisdom? (89:19) "The physical blessings of health and strength that are promised through obedience to the Word of Wisdom are now well-known and well documented. In addition, the spiritual blessings of 'wisdom and great treasures of knowledge, even hidden treasures,' come to those who keep their bodies free from addictive substances. When we obey the Word of Wisdom, windows of personal revelation are opened to us and our souls are filled with divine light and truth. If we keep our bodies undefiled, the Holy Ghost 'shall come upon [us] and . . . dwell in [our] heart[s]' and teach us 'the peaceable things of immortal glory' (Wirthlin, "Windows of Light and Truth," *Ensign*, Nov. 1995, 76). ◉

What are ways the phrase "run and not be weary, and walk and not faint" can be fulfilled? (89:20) "To run and not be weary (v. 20) appears to be another physical blessing—may we suggest that it is speaking of a social blessing. [Consider how] those who are actively involved in the Church, are usually involved in the community, their children's school activities, their business and professional obligations, and other social events. They are on the run in a different sense. The Lord is promising that they will be blessed with the ability to keep up their responsibilities as a citizen of the community, a family person, and be successful in their occupation" (Nyman, *Doctrine and Covenants Commentary*, 2:199).

What could it mean that the "destroying angel shall pass by" those who keep the Word of Wisdom? (89:21) The destroying angel refers to the miracle of the Passover, recorded in Exodus 12:1–30. Regarding the Lord's promise in D&C 89:21, President Boyd K. Packer explained: "It is not from [the destroying angel of] mortal death that we shall be spared in such a passover if we walk in obedience to these commandments, for each of us in time shall die. But there is spiritual death which you need not suffer. If you are obedient, that spiritual death will pass over you, for 'Christ our passover is sacrificed for us,' the revelation teaches (1 Cor. 5:7).

"While the Word of Wisdom requires strict obedience, in return it promises health, great treasures of knowledge, and that redemption bought for us by the Lamb of God, who was slain that we might be redeemed" ("Word of Wisdom," *Ensign*, May 1996, 19).

20 And shall run and not be weary, and shall walk and not faint.

21 And I, the Lord, give unto them a promise, that the destroying angel shall pass by them, as the children of Israel, and not slay them. Amen.

This revelation was given to the Prophet Joseph Smith on March 8, 1833, at Kirtland, Ohio.

"Marking a significant development in the church's chief governing body, this revelation announced that the counselors in the presidency of the high priesthood were equal with [Joseph Smith] 'in holding the keys of this Last Kingdom.' The presidency of the high priesthood had its beginnings sixteen months earlier, on 11 November 1831, when a revelation established the office of the president of the high priesthood. . . .

"In addition to giving instructions regarding the presidency of the high priesthood, this revelation expressed displeasure with some church members in Missouri. [Joseph Smith's] interactions with Missouri leaders in spring 1832, his series of letters with William W. Phelps and Sidney Gilbert from June 1832 to January 1833, and a revelation dated 22 and 23 September 1832 emphasized that Missouri church leaders needed to repent of ongoing disputes and perceived backbiting against [Joseph Smith]. . . .

"This revelation also directed members of the presidency of the high priesthood to set their houses in order, gave instructions concerning the residences of Joseph Smith Sr. and Sidney Rigdon, and emphasized the need to continue the ongoing translation of the Old Testament" (Joseph Smith Papers, Historical Introduction to "Revelation, 8 March 1833 [D&C 90]").

SECTION 90

Revelation to Joseph Smith the Prophet, given at Kirtland, Ohio, March 8, 1833. This revelation is a continuing step in the establishment of the First Presidency (see the heading to section 81); as a consequence thereof, the counselors mentioned were ordained on March 18, 1833.

1 Thus saith the Lord, verily, verily I say unto you my son, thy sins are forgiven thee, according to thy petition, for thy prayers and the prayers of thy brethren have come up into my ears.

2 Therefore, thou art blessed from henceforth that bear the keys of the kingdom given unto you; which kingdom is coming forth for the last time.

3 Verily I say unto you, the keys of this kingdom shall never be taken from you, while thou art in the world, neither in the world to come;

Doctrine and Covenants 90:1–5. The Keys of the Kingdom Are Committed to Joseph Smith and through Him to the Church

Why might forgiveness have been extended by the Lord on this occasion? (90:1) "Neither the Prophet Joseph, nor his brethren, had any great transgressions, as measured by worldly standards, on their consciences, but no mortal is entirely free from sin. The fact is that, the nearer a man draws to the presence of God, the more keenly he feels his imperfections and shortcomings, and the more natural it is to exclaim with Peter, 'Depart from me; for I am a sinful man, O Lord!' (Luke 5:8). It is not surprising, therefore, to learn that the Prophet and his brethren, coming, as it were, from the very presence of the Lord, engaged in prayers for the forgiveness of their sins and received the assurance quoted" (Smith and Sjodahl, *Doctrine and Covenants Commentary*, 576–77).

Why will the Prophet Joseph Smith always retain the keys of the kingdom? (90:3) "The Prophet [Joseph Smith] holds the keys of this dispensation through all time and eternity . . .

"The Prophet does not stand at the head of former dispensations, but of the dispensation of the fulness of times. President Brigham Young and succeeding presidents of the Church held the keys and authorities while living, but the keys held by the Prophet, as holding the keys of the dispensation for time and eternity, were never transferred and are still held by him" (Joseph Fielding Smith, *Doctrines of Salvation*, 3:128). See also commentary in this volume on Doctrine and Covenants 112:30–31. ●

What are oracles and how did Joseph give them to others? (90:4) "The 'oracles,' as the term is used here, mean the divine revelations (as in v. 5). The process of how Joseph's revelations will be disseminated through his counselors and others is further clarified in verses 6–11 (especially v. 9). The Prophet Joseph will receive the word of God and will then share it with his counselors in the Presidency. Through the First Presidency, the word will then be delivered to the Church (see v. 40 and through the Church to the world (see v. 9)" (Robinson and Garrett, *Commentary on the Doctrine and Covenants*, 3:157–58).

Doctrine and Covenants 90:6–7. Sidney Rigdon and Frederick G. Williams Are to Serve in the First Presidency

What power is held by the counselors in the First Presidency? (90:6–7) Elder John A. Widtsoe wrote, "The question as to whether the Counselors held the same power as the President was soon debated among the people. What could the Counselors do without direct appointment from the President? These questions were answered in a meeting on

4 Nevertheless, through you shall the oracles be given to another, yea, even unto the church.

5 And all they who receive the oracles of God, let them beware how they hold them lest they are accounted as a light thing, and are brought under condemnation thereby, and stumble and fall when the storms descend, and the winds blow, and the rains descend, and beat upon their house.

6 And again, verily I say unto thy brethren, Sidney Rigdon and Frederick G. Williams, their sins are forgiven them also, and they are accounted as equal with thee in holding the keys of this last kingdom;

The First Presidency—Oracles of God (Doctrine and Covenants 90:1–5)

"When Joseph Smith organized the Church in April 1830, a revelation designated him 'a seer, and Translator, and Prophet, an Apostle of Jesus Christ, an Elder of the Church' [D&C 21:1]. Accordingly, Church members sustained Joseph as first elder and Oliver Cowdery as second elder, the earliest titles for leaders of the Church. In November 1831, another revelation to Joseph Smith established the office of the 'president of the high priesthood.' This president would 'be like unto Moses' and would 'be a Seer, a revelator, a translator, and a prophet, having all the gifts of God which he bestoweth upon the head of the church.' At a conference on January 25, 1832, Joseph Smith was appointed president of the high priesthood.

"About six weeks after Joseph Smith's appointment, he selected two men—Jesse Gause and Sidney Rigdon—as his counselors in 'the ministry of the presidency of the high Priesthood.' Gause continued as a counselor until December 1832, when he was excommunicated from the Church for unspecified reasons. In January 1833, Frederick G. Williams replaced Gause in the presidency.

"Two months after Williams's appointment, Joseph Smith received a revelation stating that Rigdon and Williams were 'equal' with him 'in holding the keys of this Last Kingdom.' Accordingly, at a council of high priests in Kirtland, Ohio, on March 18, 1833, Joseph ordained Rigdon and Williams 'to be equal with him in holding the Keys of the Kingdom and also to the Presidency of the high Priest hood.' The three men were referred to as the presidency of the high priesthood and acted under Joseph Smith's direction. Another revelation instructed that, as a presidency, they had the 'authority to preside . . . over all the Concerns of the church.'

7 As also through your administration the keys of the school of the prophets, which I have commanded to be organized;

8 That thereby they may be perfected in their ministry for the salvation of Zion, and of the nations of Israel, and of the Gentiles, as many as will believe;

9 That through your administration they may receive the word, and through their administration the word may go forth unto the ends of the earth, unto the Gentiles first, and then, behold, and lo, they shall turn unto the Jews.

January 16, 1836. The Prophet there said, 'The Twelve are not subject to any other than the First Presidency ... and where I am not, there is no First Presidency over the Twelve.' In other words were the President taken, the Counselors would have no authority. The Counselors do not possess the power of the President and cannot act in Church matters without direction and consent of the President. All this defined clearly the position and authority of the President of the Church" (*Joseph Smith*, 303).

Doctrine and Covenants 90:8–11. The Gospel Is to Be Preached to the Nations of Israel, to the Gentiles, and to the Jews, Every Man Hearing in His Own Tongue

What is the order of gospel preaching in this dispensation? (90: 8–9) "The Gospel was ... taken first to the Jews in the Meridian Dispensation, and when the Jews rejected it, then it was taken to the Gentiles [Acts 11:18; 13:46]. The Lord promised that the first should be last and last first in the final dispensation. Therefore the Gospel was revealed and declared to the Gentiles in this dispensation and then it must go to the Jews" (Joseph Fielding Smith, *Church History and Modern Revelation*, 1:390). ⊕

"When Joseph Smith set up high councils in Kirtland, Ohio, and Clay County, Missouri, in 1834, each high council had a presidency. The presidency in Kirtland consisted of Joseph Smith, Sidney Rigdon, and Frederick G. Williams, the same members as the presidency of the high priesthood. The presidency in Missouri consisted of David Whitmer, William W. Phelps, and John Whitmer. To differentiate between these two high council presidencies, Church leaders and members began referring to the presidency of the high priesthood as the 'First Presidency.' The first written reference to the body as the First Presidency came in a revelation published in the 1835 Doctrine and Covenants [see D&C 68]. . . .

"After Joseph Smith's martyrdom in June 1844, the First Presidency was dissolved and leadership of the Church fell to the Quorum of the Twelve Apostles, with Brigham Young as President. On December 27, 1847, more than three years after the death of Joseph Smith, Brigham Young reorganized the First Presidency, with Heber C. Kimball and Willard Richards as his counselors. Similarly, John Taylor waited more than three years after the death of his predecessor to reorganize the First Presidency, and Wilford Woodruff waited almost two years. Both men led the Church in the interim as President of the Quorum of the Twelve. Beginning with Lorenzo Snow in 1898, new Church Presidents have generally reorganized the First Presidency quickly after the death of the previous prophet" (Church History Topics, "First Presidency").

What is occurring in our day to help fulfill this prophecy? (90:11) In 2020, Elder Gerrit W. Gong stated: "Today, members of The Church of Jesus Christ of Latter-day Saints live in 196 nations and territories, with 3,446 Church stakes in 90 of them. . . .

"Today, general conference is available in 100 languages. President Nelson has testified of Jesus Christ and His restored gospel in 138 nations and counting. . . .

"Some 192 million copies of all or part of the Book of Mormon have been published in 112 languages. Book of Mormon translations are also widely available digitally. Current Book of Mormon translations include most of the 23 world languages spoken by 50 million people or more, collectively the native tongues of some 4.1 billion people" ("All Nations, Kindreds, and Tongues," *Liahona*, Nov. 2020, 39).

Doctrine and Covenants 90:12–18. Joseph Smith and His Counselors Are to Set the Church in Order

What is a major responsibility of the President of the Church? (90:13) "At an earlier date the Prophet and Sidney Rigdon were engaged in the 'translation' (revision) of the Bible. The Prophet's present responsibility was to work on this revision and then to attend to his other duties.

"Only some of the responsibilities of the Prophet are mentioned in this revelation to indicate ways in which he was to preside over the affairs of the Church. The president of the Church is to receive revelation and thus to make known the mysteries of the kingdom (D&C 90:13–14). Here again is repeated the important principle that the Prophet is to receive revelation for the Church and to 'set in order all the affairs of this church and kingdom' ([v.] 16)" (Roy W. Doxey, *Doctrine and Covenants Speaks*, 2:164). ✚

What have Church members been counseled relative to secular learning? (90:15) "Furthering education need not challenge, but should increase your faith. In fact, we have a religious responsibility to educate our minds. 'The glory of God is intelligence' (D&C 93:36). We have a divine command to 'obtain a

10 And then cometh the day when the arm of the Lord shall be revealed in power in convincing the nations, the heathen nations, the house of Joseph, of the gospel of their salvation.

11 For it shall come to pass in that day, that every man shall hear the fulness of the gospel in his own tongue, and in his own language, through those who are ordained unto this power, by the administration of the Comforter, shed forth upon them for the revelation of Jesus Christ.

12 And now, verily I say unto you, I give unto you a commandment that you continue in the ministry and presidency.

13 And when you have finished the translation of the prophets, you shall from thenceforth preside over the affairs of the church and the school;

14 And from time to time, as shall be manifested by the Comforter, receive revelations to unfold the mysteries of the kingdom;

15 And set in order the churches, and study and learn, and become acquainted with all good books, and with languages, tongues, and people.

knowledge of history, and of countries, and of kingdoms, of laws of God and man' (D&C 93:53). Similarly, the Lord exhorted us to 'study and learn, and become acquainted with all good books, and with languages, tongues, and people' (D&C 90:15).

"The scriptures further admonish, 'Learn wisdom in thy youth' (Alma 37:35, see also Proverbs 29:3). 'Teach one another the doctrine of the kingdom. Teach ye diligently and my grace shall attend you' (D&C 88:77–78)" (Nelson, "Begin with the End in Mind," 4).

What are some of the duties and responsibilities of the counselors in the First Presidency? (90:16–18) "While the counselors were to assist the President as they were directed by him, they were to be equal as they sat as a quorum, 'to preside in Council, and set in order all the affairs of this church and kingdom' (v. 16). ... This heavy responsibility could not be carried out if they were shy [ashamed], not confident [confounded], not willing to be admonished by each other, or arrogant [high-minded] or prideful, which would be a snare to them individually as well as collectively as a Council (v. 17). They must also be an example to the Church through their own families [houses], habits [slothfulness], and personal living [uncleanness] (v. 18)" (Nyman, *Doctrine and Covenants Commentary*, 2:211–12).

16 And this shall be your business and mission in all your lives, to preside in council, and set in order all the affairs of this church and kingdom.

17 Be not ashamed, neither confounded; but be admonished in all your high-mindedness and pride, for it bringeth a snare upon your souls.

18 Set in order your houses; keep slothfulness and uncleanness far from you.

Doctrine and Covenants 90:19–37. Various Individuals Are Counseled by the Lord to Walk Uprightly and Serve in His Kingdom

What instructions in verses 19–33 show us of the Lord's involvement in people's lives? (90:19–33) "In this section the Lord gives instruction on many subjects, most of them of a temporal character. The Saints were to provide a place of residence for Frederick G. Williams (v. 19). Sidney Rigdon was to remain where he resided, as was the Prophet's father (vv. 20–21). Bishop Whitney was to find a brother who could act as his agent (vv. 22–23. See also Sects. 51:8, 58:49; 84:113). They were to keep down the expense of their households (vv. 25–27); Vienna Jaques was to go to Zion (28–31); and they were to advise the Saints in Zion that the jurisdiction of the First Presidency extended over Jackson County and the West as well as over Kirtland and the East (v. 32). Thus the First Presidency was to be a means of preservation of the unity of the Church" (Smith and Sjodahl, *Doctrine and Covenants Commentary*, 582). ✦

19 Now, verily I say unto you, let there be a place provided, as soon as it is possible, for the family of thy counselor and scribe, even Frederick G. Williams.

20 And let mine aged servant, Joseph Smith, Sen., continue with his family upon the place where he now lives; and let it not be sold until the mouth of the Lord shall name.

21 And let my counselor, even Sidney Rigdon, remain where he now resides until the mouth of the Lord shall name.

22 And let the bishop search diligently to obtain an agent, and let him be a man who has got riches in store—a man of God, and of strong faith—

knowledge, "History and foundations and laws of the kingdom of God (D&C 90:15). Similarly, the Lord exhorted us to study and learn and become acquainted with all good books and with languages, tongues and people (D&C 90:15).

What covenants are being referred to in this verse? (90:24) "The expression 'the covenant wherewith ye have covenanted one with another' has at least two meanings. First, when one enters the Church by baptism he covenants to keep the commandments of the Lord. The member of the Church who does not continue in this agreement no longer represents the Lord and, thus, his actions cast reflection upon all members who are endeavoring to demonstrate their true citizenship in the kingdom. Secondly, the agreement to work for the salvation of the living and the dead was also made in the pre-earth life. [President Joseph Fielding Smith stated:] 'Joseph Smith, by revelation, instructed the Saints and said that the Lord "ordained and prepared" the means, "before the foundation of the world, for the salvation of the dead who should die without a knowledge of the Gospel"' [*Way to Perfection*, 176]" (Roy W. Doxey, *Doctrine and Covenants Speaks*, 2:165–66).

What is meant by the counsel in this verse for families to be small? (90:25) "In 1833, because many of the Saints were in temporal need, Church leaders, including the Prophet Joseph Smith's father, had opened their homes to assist them. This circumstance had the potential of hindering Church leaders' efforts to accomplish the Lord's work. The counsel to 'let your families be small' (D&C 90:25) did not refer to the number of children the Saints might choose to have in their families but rather was a caution to Joseph Smith Sr. and other Church leaders to exercise wisdom and judgment in giving of their temporal resources to those outside their own families and to not include more in their household than they could adequately care for" (*Doctrine and Covenants Student Manual* [2018], 506–7).

What do we know about Vienna Jaques? (90:28–31) "Emma Smith and Vienna Jaques are the only women who are mentioned by name in the Doctrine and Covenants (see D&C 25; 90:28). Vienna Jaques is an example of the faithfulness of many early Latter-day Saints. She was born June 10, 1787. After she met the missionaries in Boston, Massachusetts, she traveled to Kirtland, Ohio, in 1831. She stayed there six weeks and was baptized. Upon returning to Boston, Vienna was active in missionary work, helping to

23 That thereby he may be enabled to discharge every debt; that the storehouse of the Lord may not be brought into disrepute before the eyes of the people.

24 Search diligently, pray always, and be believing, and all things shall work together for your good, if ye walk uprightly and remember the covenant wherewith ye have covenanted one with another.

25 Let your families be small, especially mine aged servant Joseph Smith's, Sen., as pertaining to those who do not belong to your families;

26 That those things that are provided for you, to bring to pass my work, be not taken from you and given to those that are not worthy—

27 And thereby you be hindered in accomplishing those things which I have commanded you.

28 And again, verily I say unto you, it is my will that my handmaid Vienna Jaques should receive money to bear her expenses, and go up unto the land of Zion;

29 And the residue of the money may be consecrated unto me, and she be rewarded in mine own due time.

30 Verily I say unto you, that it is meet in mine eyes that she should go up unto the land of Zion, and receive an inheritance from the hand of the bishop;

31 That she may settle down in peace inasmuch as she is faithful, and not be idle in her days from thenceforth.

32 And behold, verily I say unto you, that ye shall write this commandment, and say unto your brethren in Zion, in love greeting, that I have called you also to preside over Zion in mine own due time.

33 Therefore, let them cease wearying me concerning this matter.

34 Behold, I say unto you that your brethren in Zion begin to repent, and the angels rejoice over them.

35 Nevertheless, I am not well pleased with many things; and I am not well pleased with my servant William E. McLellin, neither with my servant Sidney Gilbert; and the bishop also, and others have many things to repent of.

36 But verily I say unto you, that I, the Lord, will contend with Zion, and plead with her strong ones, and chasten her until she overcomes and is clean before me.

37 For she shall not be removed out of her place. I, the Lord, have spoken it. Amen.

bring several members of her family into the Church, and helped the missionaries establish a small branch of the Church there. She then 'settled up her business, and went back to Kirtland to unite her interests forever with the Church' (['Home Affairs,' *Woman's Exponent*, Jul. 1, 1878, 21])" (*Doctrine and Covenants Student Manual* [2018], 507). ✦

How were the Saints to understand the Lord's chastening? (90:36–37) "The Revelation closes with a warning and a promise regarding Zion. All the brethren in Zion were not keeping the commandments of God faithfully. Some of them were jealous of the position and influence of the Prophet Joseph, and denied his authority to direct the temporal affairs of the Church. . . . Furthermore, the Saints in Zion failed to keep the laws of God concerning consecration. Hence the warning: The Lord would contend with Zion, plead with her strong ones, and chasten her 'until she overcomes and is clean before me.' That is the warning. The promise is: 'She shall not be removed out of her place'" (Smith and Sjodahl, *Doctrine and Covenants Commentary*, 583).

Introduction to Doctrine and Covenants 91

"On 8 March 1833, Joseph Smith received a revelation (D&C 90) concerning the First Presidency of the Church and its role in taking the gospel to the world. In that revelation, it was also indicated to Joseph that he was to continue his work on the Joseph Smith Translation by completing his inspired revision 'of the prophets' (D&C 90:13), that is, the Old Testament books. Accordingly, on the very next day, 9 March 1833, Joseph resumed work on the Joseph Smith Translation in his quarters above Newel Whitney's store. It appears, however, that a question soon arose concerning the exact definition of 'the prophets.' The Roman Catholic and Eastern Orthodox churches include in their Old Testament a dozen or so books known as 'the Apocrypha,' which they consider to be inspired scripture and the word of God. Unfortunately, ancient Hebrew manuscripts of the Bible do not include these books, so Protestants, following the example of Martin Luther, have generally excluded the Apocrypha from their Bibles. However, the copy of the King James Bible that Joseph Smith used in his work on the Joseph Smith Translation did contain the Apocrypha at the end of the Old Testament, so naturally the question arose: Exactly which books belong in the Old Testament? Were the Apocrypha part of 'the prophets' and therefore part of Joseph's translation obligation according to the instructions in Doctrine and Covenants 90:13, or were they later additions to the Bible and therefore beyond the scope of his translation of the biblical scriptures?" (Robinson and Garrett, *Commentary on the Doctrine and Covenants*, 3:165–66).

On 9 March 1833, the Lord revealed that "there are many things contained [in the Apocrypha] that are true" (D&C 91:1). "Nevertheless, this revelation instructed [Joseph] that he need not translate the Apocrypha along with the other, canonical books of the Bible, and he apparently never did. He repeated the teachings of the revelation in a letter to the Missouri members a few months later, telling them that 'respecting the Apochraphy the Lord Said to us that there were many things in it which were true and there were many things in it which were not true and to those who desired, it should be given by the spirit to know true from the false'" (Joseph Smith Papers, Historical Introduction to "Revelation, 9 March 1833 [D&C 91]").

Doctrine and Covenants 91:1–3. The Apocrypha Is Mostly Translated Correctly but Contains Many Interpolations by the Hands of Men That Are Not True

What is the Apocrypha? (91:1–3) The word *Apocrypha* means "secret" or "hidden." "By this word is generally meant those sacred books of the Jewish people that were not included in the Hebrew Bible. . . . They are valuable as forming a link connecting the Old and New Testaments and are regarded in the Church as useful reading, although not all the books are of equal value. They are the subject of a revelation recorded in D&C 91, in which it is stated that the contents are mostly correct but with many interpolations by man" (Bible Dictionary, s.v. "Apocrypha," 593).

SECTION 91

Revelation given through Joseph Smith the Prophet, at Kirtland, Ohio, March 9, 1833. The Prophet was at this time engaged in the translation of the Old Testament. Having come to that portion of the ancient writings called the Apocrypha, he inquired of the Lord and received this instruction.

1 Verily, thus saith the Lord unto you concerning the Apocrypha—There are many things contained therein that are true, and it is mostly translated correctly;

2 There are many things contained therein that are not true, which are interpolations by the hands of men.

3 Verily, I say unto you, that it is not needful that the Apocrypha should be translated.

Doctrine and Covenants 91:4–6. The Apocrypha Benefits Those Enlightened by the Spirit

4 Therefore, whoso readeth it, let him understand, for the Spirit manifesteth truth;

5 And whoso is enlightened by the Spirit shall obtain benefit therefrom;

6 And whoso receiveth not by the Spirit, cannot be benefited. Therefore it is not needful that it should be translated. Amen.

What are appropriate ways to understand the Apocrypha? (91:4–6) "The key to understanding the Apocrypha, as given in the revelation, is *not* either total rejection or uncritical acceptance of the texts, but reading them with the aid of the Spirit of the Lord (D&C 91:4–6). That has always been the real test in reading . . . , for one cannot unravel the secrets and treasures of the heavens except through revelation. The same key to understanding is also valid for the many additions to the body of apocryphal writings recovered in recent decades, with the result that 'whoso is enlightened by the Spirit shall obtain benefit therefrom; and whoso receiveth not by the Spirit, cannot be benefited' (D&C 91:5–6)" (Griggs, "Origin and Formation of the Corpus of Apocryphal Literature," 51–52). ⊕

The Apocrypha (Doctrine and Covenants 91:1)

"This March 1833 revelation [D&C 91] provided a guide to members of the Church in Joseph Smith's day for their study of this section found in their Bibles. Since then, however, most Protestant Bibles, including the King James Version adopted by The Church of Jesus Christ of Latter-day Saints today, no longer include the Apocrypha. The general inaccessibility of the Apocrypha since it was removed from the Bible during the nineteenth century has made it difficult for Latter-day Saints to study the 'many things contained therein that are true,' unlike members of the Church living during Joseph Smith's ministry. . . .

"The books of the Apocrypha found in early Protestant versions of the Bible are described briefly in the Bible Dictionary published in the Latter-day Saint Edition of the King James Version of the Bible" (Brown and Holzapfel, *Between the Testaments*, 128–29).

Among other writings, the Apocrypha includes the following: the First and Second Books of Esdras; the Book of Tobit; the Book of Judith; the rest of the chapters of the Book of Esther; the Book of the Wisdom of Solomon; Wisdom of Jesus the Son of Sirach, or Ecclesiasticus; the Book of Baruch; the Song of the Three Children; the History of Susanna; Bel and the Dragon; the Prayer of Manasses; and the First and Second Books of Maccabees (see Bible Dictionary, s.v. "Apocrypha," 593–94).

Introduction to Doctrine and Covenants 92

"On 8 March 1833, a revelation [D&C 90:6] declared Frederick G. Williams equal 'in holding the keys of this Last Kingdom' with [Joseph Smith] and Sidney Rigdon in the presidency of the high priesthood. A week later, the following revelation [D&C 92], dated 15 March, elevated Williams within the United Firm [or also known as United Order] from assistant scribe to a member in full partnership with [Joseph Smith], Rigdon, and other founding members of the firm. In addition to becoming equal with [Joseph Smith] and Rigdon in holding the keys, Williams now became similarly responsible for overseeing the financial and temporal matters of the church under [Joseph Smith's] direction. . . .

"As a governing financial council, the firm was responsible for printing church publications, holding church properties in trust, assisting the poor, and operating general stores in Independence, Missouri, and Kirtland, Ohio, to generate funds for the church. Among other duties, members of the United Firm oversaw city planning for Independence and Kirtland, including the construction of a house of the Lord and other buildings. The firm was also directed to manage land, including allotting portions of Williams's farmland to members of the church" (Joseph Smith Papers, Historical Introduction to "Revelation, 15 March 1833 [D&C 92]").

SECTION 92

Revelation given to Joseph Smith the Prophet, at Kirtland, Ohio, March 15, 1833. The revelation instructs Frederick G. Williams, who had recently been appointed a counselor to Joseph Smith, on his duties in the United Firm (see the headings to sections 78 and 82).

Doctrine and Covenants 92:1–2. The Lord Gives a Commandment Relative to Admission to the United Order

What is the difference between the law of consecration and the united order? (92:1) "The law of consecration is a divine principle whereby men and women voluntarily dedicate their time, talents, and material wealth to the establishment and building up of God's kingdom" (Guide to the Scriptures, "Consecrate, Law of Consecration").

The United Order was an "organization through which the Saints in the early days of the restored Church sought to live the law of consecration. Individuals shared property, goods, and profits, receiving these things according to their wants and needs (D&C 51:3; 78:1–15; 104)" (Guide to the Scriptures, "United Order").

1 Verily, thus saith the Lord, I give unto the united order, organized agreeable to the commandment previously given, a revelation and commandment concerning my servant Frederick G. Williams, that ye shall receive him into the order. What I say unto one I say unto all.

What is "a lively member of the church"? (92:2) "A lively member is one who works diligently for the advancement of the goals and principles of the group or movement to which he belongs. A major purpose of the order of Enoch was to help the Church become 'independent above all other creatures beneath the celestial world' (D&C 78:14)" (*Doctrine and Covenants Student Manual* [2001], 216). ☉

2 And again, I say unto you my servant Frederick G. Williams, you shall be a lively member in this order; and inasmuch as you are faithful in keeping all former commandments you shall be blessed forever. Amen.

"On May 6, 1833, [in Kirtland, Ohio,] the Prophet Joseph Smith received a significant revelation about the nature of God and man and the eternal destiny of God's children. While it is unknown why the Lord revealed the revelation recorded in Doctrine and Covenants 93 at that specific time, it is interesting to note that just as the Saints were preparing to build a temple in which to worship the Lord and a building in which the School of the Prophets could be instructed, the Lord gave a revelation comparing the human body to 'the tabernacle of God' or a 'temple' (D&C 93:35) and emphasized the need for God's children to receive truth and light (see D&C 93:28, 31–32, 42, 53). The revelation also contains specific instructions for Joseph Smith, Sidney Rigdon, and Frederick G. Williams, who were members of the First Presidency, and for Bishop Newel K. Whitney" (*Doctrine and Covenants Student Manual* [2018], 511).

"The revelation . . . directly challenged several prevailing Christian beliefs of the time, including doctrines regarding the nature of Jesus Christ, especially his humanity and divinity, that most Christians believed had been settled by the Council of Chalcedon in A.D. 451. That council held that Jesus Christ was both fully human and fully divine, 'that in Christ two distinct natures were united in one person, without any change, mixture, or confusion.' This revelation instead describes Jesus as having 'received not of the fulness at the first but received grace for grace and he received not of the fulness but continued from grace to grace until he received a fulness' [D&C 93:12–13]" (Joseph Smith Papers, Historical Introduction, to "Revelation, 6 May 1833 [D&C 93]," [1]).

"Section 93 of the Doctrine and Covenants is . . . critical to understanding the Latter-day Saint conception of Jesus and his nature. Section 93, in fact, is one of the most theologically rich and provocative revelations Joseph Smith received. Beginning with a short discussion on the nature of the Savior and his relationship with the Father, the revelation quickly transitions into what seems to be an excerpt of a record written by John [the Baptist] that describes several key events relating to Jesus, such as his baptism and his reception of power. The revelation then transitions again, this time into a discussion of the origins of humanity and an elaboration of the principles of truth and intelligence. Then, perhaps most surprisingly of all, beginning in verse 40 the revelation abruptly transitions from these theologically complex topics toward more practical, mundane affairs as the Lord mentions several members of the Church by name and chastens them for, among other things, their lack of attention to their families" (Frederick, "Incarnation, Exaltation, and Christological Tension," 12).

"Joseph Smith spent the rest of his life pondering the implications of these stunning revelatory teachings [in Doctrine and Covenants 93]. Years later in Nauvoo, he gave these truths their most complete expression in his last conference sermon. Echoing the words of the revelation, he taught that men and women were co-eternal with God and could become like Him by 'going from a small capacity to a great capacity,' until eventually they dwell 'in everlasting burnings.' Speaking with revealed assurance, he taught: 'The soul, the mind of man, where did it come from? The learned says God made it in the beginning, but it is not so. I know better. God has told me so'" (McBride, "Man Was Also in the Beginning with God," 194; spelling modernized).

SECTION 93

Revelation given through Joseph Smith the Prophet, at Kirtland, Ohio, May 6, 1833.

1 Verily, thus saith the Lord: It shall come to pass that every soul who forsaketh his sins and cometh unto me, and calleth on my name, and obeyeth my voice, and keepeth my commandments, shall see my face and know that I am;

2 And that I am the true light that lighteth every man that cometh into the world;

Doctrine and Covenants 93:1–5. All Who Are Faithful Will See the Lord

How can we prepare to see the face of the Lord? (93:1) "I promise that if you accept this invitation and pattern your life after His example, His redemptive influence will come into your life. Through the power of the Holy Ghost, the Savior will transform you day after day 'until the perfect day' when you will, as He declared, 'see my face and know that I am'" (Caussé, "Living Witness of a Living Christ," *Ensign*, May 2020, 40). ⊕

In what way is Jesus Christ the "true light" given to each of God's children? (93:2) "Before you ever received the gift of the Holy Ghost, you had the Light of Christ planted in your soul [see John 1:9; D&C 93:2], that 'light which is in all things, . . . giveth life to all things' [D&C 88:13], and is the influence for good in the hearts of all people who have ever lived or ever will live. That light was given to protect you and teach you. One of its central messages is that life is the most precious of all gifts, a gift which is obtained eternally only through the Atonement of the Lord Jesus Christ. As the Light and Life of the World, the Only Begotten Son of God came to give us life by conquering death" (Holland, "Fear Not," *Liahona*, May 2022, 35–36). See also commentary in this volume on Doctrine and Covenants 88:7–11, 13.

How are God the Father and His Son Jesus Christ considered to be one? (93:3–5) President Joseph F. Smith wrote: "Jesus and his Father are . . . one in knowledge, in truth, in wisdom, in understanding, and in purpose; just as the Lord Jesus himself admonished his disciples to be one with him, and to be in him, that he might be in them [see John 17:11, 20–23]. It is in this sense that I understand this language, and not as it is construed by some people, that Christ and his Father are one person. I declare to you that they are not one person, but that they are two persons, two bodies, separate and apart, and as distinct as are any father and son within the sound of my voice. Yet, Jesus is the Father of this world, because it was by him that the world was made" (*Gospel Doctrine*, 68).

How is Jesus both the Father and the Son? (93:4) The First Presidency and Quorum of the Twelve Apostles in 1916 declared: A "reason for applying the title 'Father' to Jesus Christ is found in the fact that in all His dealings with the human family Jesus the Son has represented and yet represents Elohim His Father in power and authority. This is true of Christ in His preexistent, antemortal, or unembodied state, in the which He was known as Jehovah; also during His embodiment in the flesh; and during His labors as a disembodied spirit in the realm of the dead; and since that period in His resurrected state. . . . Thus the Father placed His name upon the Son; and Jesus Christ spoke and ministered in and through the Father's name" ("Father and the Son," *Ensign*, Apr. 2002, 17). ⊕

How were the works of the Father manifested through Jesus Christ? (93:5) "One great aspect of [the mission of Jesus Christ] often goes uncelebrated. His followers did not understand it fully at the time, and many in modern Christianity do not grasp it now, but the Savior Himself spoke of it repeatedly

3 And that I am in the Father, and the Father in me, and the Father and I are one—

4 The Father because he gave me of his fulness, and the Son because I was in the world and made flesh my tabernacle, and dwelt among the sons of men.

5 I was in the world and received of my Father, and the works of him were plainly manifest.

and emphatically. It is the grand truth that in all that Jesus came to say and do, including and especially in His atoning suffering and sacrifice, He was showing us who and what God our Eternal Father is like, how completely devoted He is to His children in every age and nation. In word and in deed Jesus was trying to reveal and make personal to us the true nature of His Father, our Father in Heaven" (Holland, "Grandeur of God," *Ensign*, Nov. 2003, 70). ●

Doctrine and Covenants 93:6–18. John Bore Record That the Son of God Went from Grace to Grace until He Received a Fulness of the Glory of the Father

Was it John the Baptist or John the Apostle who saw the Lord's glory and made a record? (93:6)
"From latter-day revelation we learn that the material in the forepart of the gospel of John (the Apostle, Revelator, and Beloved Disciple) was written originally by John the Baptist. By revelation the Lord restored to Joseph Smith part of what John the Baptist had written and promised to reveal the balance when men became sufficiently faithful to warrant receiving it (D&C 93:6–18). Verse 15 of this passage is the key to the identity of the particular John spoken of. . . .

"There is little doubt but that the Beloved Disciple had before him the Baptist's account when he wrote his gospel. The latter John either copied or paraphrased what the earlier prophet of the same name had written" (Bruce R. McConkie, *Doctrinal New Testament Commentary*, 1:70–71).

Why do we refer to Jesus Christ as "the Word"? (93:7–10) "John the Beloved begins his Gospel by saying: 'In the beginning was the Word, and the Word was with God, and the Word was God . . .' (John 1:1, 3). Later in the same chapter, John identifies the Word of God as Christ, the One who 'was made flesh and dwelt among us, (and we beheld his glory, the glory as of the only begotten of the Father,) full of grace and truth' (John 1:14) The Joseph Smith Translation more directly identifies the Word as Jesus Christ, the Son of God (JST, John 1:16). . . . [Jesus Christ] is the Word of God. He is the means and end of our salvation. He is the embodiment of God's word and will" (Top, "Word of God," 665, 666).

6 And John saw and bore record of the fulness of my glory, and the fulness of John's record is hereafter to be revealed.

7 And he bore record, saying: I saw his glory, that he was in the beginning, before the world was;

8 Therefore, in the beginning the Word was, for he was the Word, even the messenger of salvation—

9 The light and the Redeemer of the world; the Spirit of truth, who came into the world, because the world was made by him, and in him was the life of men and the light of men.

10 The worlds were made by him; men were made by him; all things were made by him, and through him, and of him.

In what way was the experience of Jesus in mortal life like our own? (93:12–14) While Jesus was always sinless in mortal life, "[He] was not perfect at first; he received not a fulness at first, but he received grace for grace, and he continued to receive more and more until he received a fulness. . . . If Jesus, the Son of God, and the Father of the heavens and the earth in which we dwell, received not a fulness at the first, but increased in faith, knowledge, understanding and grace until he received a fulness, is it not possible for all men who are born of women to receive little by little, line upon line, precept upon precept, until they shall receive a fulness, as he has received a fulness, and be exalted with him in the presence of the Father?" (Joseph F. Smith, *Gospel Doctrine*, 68). ⊕

How did Jesus receive a fulness of the glory of the Father? (93:15–17) "Though Christ is the true light, a member of the Godhead, and the Creator, he still needed to come to this earth and gain a body and experience earth life. . . .

"In spite of all that Christ was before he came to this earth . . . he still needed to work out his exaltation [see D&C 93:12–14]. . . .

"Christ worked out his salvation by making covenants with the Father and remaining faithful to those covenants. He was thus able to receive the fulness of the Father. This is the type of being that we worship: one who has worked out his salvation grace by grace and fulfilled all that the Father has commanded him to do" (Garrett, *Great Teachings*, 106, 107, 108).

What do we know about the record of John? (93:18) "John the Baptist . . . [was] destined to write of the gospel of that Lord whose witness he is, but his account, perhaps because it contains truths and concepts that the saints and the world are not yet prepared to receive, has so far not been given to men. On May 6, 1833, however, the Lord did reveal to Joseph Smith eleven verses of the Baptist's writings, and promised that 'the fulness of the record of John' would be revealed when the faith of men entitled them to receive it (D&C 93:6–18)" (Bruce R. McConkie, *Mortal Messiah*, 1:426).

11 And I, John, bear record that I beheld his glory, as the glory of the Only Begotten of the Father, full of grace and truth, even the Spirit of truth, which came and dwelt in the flesh, and dwelt among us.

12 And I, John, saw that he received not of the fulness at the first, but received grace for grace;

13 And he received not of the fulness at first, but continued from grace to grace, until he received a fulness;

14 And thus he was called the Son of God, because he received not of the fulness at the first.

15 And I, John, bear record, and lo, the heavens were opened, and the Holy Ghost descended upon him in the form of a dove, and sat upon him, and there came a voice out of heaven saying: This is my beloved Son.

16 And I, John, bear record that he received a fulness of the glory of the Father;

17 And he received all power, both in heaven and on earth, and the glory of the Father was with him, for he dwelt in him.

18 And it shall come to pass, that if you are faithful you shall receive the fulness of the record of John.

19 I give unto you these sayings that you may understand and know how to worship, and know what you worship, that you may come unto the Father in my name, and in due time receive of his fulness.

20 For if you keep my commandments you shall receive of his fulness, and be glorified in me as I am in the Father; therefore, I say unto you, you shall receive grace for grace.

Doctrine and Covenants 93:19–20. Faithful Men, Going from Grace to Grace, Will Also Receive of the Lord's Fulness

How does this revelation teach us how to worship as well as identifying what we worship and why? (93:19) Elder Bruce R. McConkie taught: "Perfect worship is emulation. We honor those whom we imitate. The most perfect way of worship is to be holy as Jehovah is holy. It is to be pure as Christ is pure. It is to do the things that enable us to become like the Father. The course is one of obedience, of living by every word that proceedeth from the mouth of God, of keeping the commandments.

"How do we worship the Lord? We do it by going from grace to grace, until we receive the fulness of the Father and are glorified in light and truth as is the case with our Pattern and Prototype, the Promised Messiah" (*Promised Messiah*, 568–69).

What does it mean to receive of His fulness? (93:20) Sister Reyna I. Aburto stated: "We have been promised that if we keep the Lord's commandments, we will receive of the fulness of the Father. What does that fulness consist of?

"We know that His fulness includes the greatest of all of the gifts of God: eternal life. With that comes Godly qualities and attributes. God's capacity to feel love and to show love is one of His divine, eternal attributes. His perfect love is part of His fulness—part of that fulness we may receive in due time" ("Love Thy God and Thy Neighbor," 1). ◉

How can we prepare to be "glorified" in Jesus Christ? (93:20) "We worship God our Father as did our Master, namely by serving our fellowmen and growing line upon line . . . Thus perfect worship is emulation; imitation. It might thus be said that the Christian quest consists of a life devoted to the imitation of Christ. To strive with all our might to become more like him 'marks the difference between the mere admiration of Him and the greater adoration of Him, between verbal veneration and genuine emulation' [Maxwell, *Even as I Am*, 35–36]" (Millet, *Christ-Centered Living*, 136).

Doctrine and Covenants 93:21–22. Those Who Are Begotten through Christ Are the Church of the Firstborn

How do we partake of the glory of the "Firstborn"? (93:21–22) "The Savior revealed to Joseph Smith that in due time, if we keep the commandments of God, we can receive the 'fulness' of the Father (D&C 93:19–20). Here the Savior bears record that 'all those who are begotten through me are partakers of the glory of the [Father], and are the church of the Firstborn' (D&C 93:22). 'They are they into whose hands the Father has given all things. . . . Wherefore, as it is written, they are gods' who 'shall dwell in the presence of God and his Christ forever and ever' (D&C 76:55, 58, 62). 'And this is life eternal, that they might know thee the only true God, and Jesus Christ, whom thou hast sent' (John 17:3; see also D&C 88:4–5)" (Oaks, "Taking upon Us the Name of Jesus Christ," *Ensign*, May 1985, 82). See also commentary in this volume on Doctrine and Covenants 76:54–55 and 107:19. ⊕

Doctrine and Covenants 93:23–28. Christ Received a Fulness of All Truth, and Man by Obedience May Do Likewise

What do we know about our existence "in the beginning with the Father"? (93:23) In November 1909, the First Presidency wrote: "The doctrine of the [premortal life]—revealed so plainly, particularly in latter days, pours a wonderful flood of light upon the otherwise mysterious problem of man's origin. It shows that man, as a spirit, was begotten and born of heavenly parents, and reared to maturity in the eternal mansions of the Father, prior to coming upon the earth in a temporal body to undergo an experience in mortality. It teaches that all men existed in the spirit before any man existed in the flesh, and that all who have inhabited the earth since Adam have taken bodies and become souls in like manner" (*Messages of the First Presidency*, 4:205). ⊕

How can we know what truth is? (93:24–25) "Some things are simply true. The arbiter of truth is God—not your favorite social media news feed, not Google, and certainly not those who are disaffected from the Church.

"President Spencer W. Kimball taught that absolute truth cannot be 'altered by the opinions of men.

21 And now, verily I say unto you, I was in the beginning with the Father, and am the Firstborn;

22 And all those who are begotten through me are partakers of the glory of the same, and are the church of the Firstborn.

23 Ye were also in the beginning with the Father; that which is Spirit, even the Spirit of truth;

24 And truth is knowledge of things as they are, and as they were, and as they are to come;

25 And whatsoever is more or less than this is the spirit of that wicked one who was a liar from the beginning.

... If men are really humble, they will realize that they *discover*, but do not *create*, truth' ["Absolute Truth"].

"Many now claim that truth is relative and that there is no such thing as divine law or a divine plan. ... Truth is based upon the laws God has established for the dependability, protection, and nurturing of His children. Eternal laws operate in and affect each of our lives, whether we believe them or not" (Nelson, "Love and Laws of God," 1–2). ⊕

26 The Spirit of truth is of God. I am the Spirit of truth, and John bore record of me, saying: He received a fulness of truth, yea, even of all truth;

How can Jesus Christ be described as "the Spirit of truth"? (93:26) "Referring to an embodied being as a spirit is not common in the scriptures. However, because the body and the spirit constitute the 'soul of man' (Doctrine and Covenants 88:15) and because in the Godhead the Father, Son, and Holy Ghost are, except for their physical distinctiveness, completely united, it is certainly appropriate to interchange descriptive appellations given to divine Beings. This is especially true in this instance, inasmuch as it was Jesus Himself who said, 'I am the Spirit of truth' (Doctrine and Covenants 93:9, 26)" (Holland, *Witness for His Names*, 144).

27 And no man receiveth a fulness unless he keepeth his commandments.

28 He that keepeth his commandments receiveth truth and light, until he is glorified in truth and knoweth all things.

What is the connection between obedience and receiving truth and light? (93:27–28) "To know the truth, we need to live the gospel and 'experiment' on the word. We are cautioned to not resist the Spirit of the Lord. Repentance, coupled with a determination to keep the commandments, is an important part of each individual's search for truth. In fact, we may need to be willing to 'give away all' our sins in order to know the truth. . . .

"Patiently keeping our covenants while we 'do [what] is necessary' to receive answers from the Lord is part of God's pattern for learning truth. . . . Patient covenant keeping increases our humility, deepens our desire to know truth, and allows the Holy Ghost to 'guide [us] in wisdom's paths that [we] may be blessed, prospered, and preserved' [Mosiah 2:36]" (Evans, "Truth of All Things," *Ensign*, Nov. 2017, 69). ⊕

Doctrine and Covenants 93:29–32. Man Was in the Beginning with God

29 Man was also in the beginning with God. Intelligence, or the light of truth, was not created or made, neither indeed can be.

30 All truth is independent in that sphere in which God has placed it, to act for itself, as all intelligence also; otherwise there is no existence.

What do we understand about the meaning of "intelligence"? (93:29–30) "An element of every human being is divine and eternal. Joseph Smith used several different terms to refer to that eternal essence—*spirit, soul, mind,* and *intelligence*. He received the knowledge that 'man was also in the beginning with God. Intelligence, or the light of truth, was not created or made, neither indeed can be' (D&C 93:29). He taught that 'the mind of man is as immortal as God himself' and that 'the Spirit of Man [meaning intelligence] is not a created being.'

"He did not define, however, this element's form and substance, nor did he identify its attributes, other than its eternal nature. This eternal element of intelligence or light of truth is something other than the spirit bodies God created later; these later entities were 'the intelligences that were organized' and were the spirits that Abraham saw. . . .

"In our own primeval births, the eternal intelligence part of us was 'organized' and provided opportunity to become part of God's plan of salvation—with the potential to become like him. This doctrine is ennobling and intriguing" (Cannon, Dahl, and Welch, "Restoration of Major Doctrines," *Ensign*, Jan. 1989, 30, 31).

What is the connection between agency and condemnation? (93:31–32) "Here [in Doctrine and Covenants 93:29–32] the nature of man and truth is given as nowhere else. . . . Truth is eternal certainly if man is eternal. Truth has no real existence except as intelligence operates upon it. It does not become alive. It does not function. It has no connection with us except as we use it. Indeed there is no existence unless truth is in action. Truth and action imply existence. Herein is found the doctrine of the agency of man. Man is a free agent, just as truth is independent. Truth becomes known to man only through his will. The use of truth through the will determines whether man shall receive blessings or condemnation" (Widtsoe, *Message of the Doctrine and Covenants*, 69). ⊕

31 Behold, here is the agency of man, and here is the condemnation of man; because that which was from the beginning is plainly manifest unto them, and they receive not the light.

32 And every man whose spirit receiveth not the light is under condemnation.

The Eternal Nature of Man (Doctrine and Covenants 93:29–30)

"Since the fifth century, Christian orthodoxy had imposed an almost impassable gulf between the Creator and His creations. Humankind, Christians came to believe, was created from nothing. God was not a craftsman who refashioned existing materials but wholly different and apart from His creation—mysterious and unknowable. The Bible's parent-child description of God's relationship to us was understood largely as a metaphor instead of a literal kinship. To suggest otherwise, in the estimation of most Christian thinkers, blasphemously lessened God or dangerously elevated humankind.

"The May 6 revelation [D&C 93] was bold and new, yet also ancient and familiar. As with so many of Joseph Smith's revelations, it recovered lost truths that were apparently known to biblical figures, in this case the Apostle John. It declared that as Christ 'was in the [beginning] with the father,' so 'man was also in the [beginning] with God.' It dismissed the long-held belief in creation out of nothing: '[Intelligence] or the Light of truth was not created or made neither indeed can be.' In other words, the spirits of mortal men and women were as eternal as God Himself" (McBride, "Man Was Also in the Beginning with God," 193).

**Doctrine and Covenants 93:33–35.
The Elements Are Eternal, and Man
May Receive a Fulness of Joy in the
Resurrection**

33 For man is spirit. The elements are eternal, and spirit and element, inseparably connected, receive a fulness of joy;

34 And when separated, man cannot receive a fulness of joy.

How does the connection of body and spirit constitute a fulness of joy? (93:33–34) "When we come to this earth life, our spirit is united with our body. We experience all the joys and challenges associated with mortal life. When a person dies, their spirit is separated from their body. Resurrection makes it possible for a person's spirit and body to be united again. . . .

"After resurrection, the spirit will never again be separated from the body because the Savior's Resurrection brought total victory over death. In order to obtain our eternal destiny, we need to have this immortal soul—a spirit and body—united forever. With spirit and immortal body inseparably connected, we can 'receive a fulness of joy.' In fact, without the Resurrection we could never receive a fulness of joy but would be miserable forever" (Paul V. Johnson, "And There Shall Be No More Death," *Ensign*, May 2016, 121, 122).

35 The elements are the tabernacle of God; yea, man is the tabernacle of God, even temples; and whatsoever temple is defiled, God shall destroy that temple.

What does it mean that God will destroy a temple if it is defiled? (93:35) The Apostle Paul taught the Corinthians that members of the Church are like the tabernacle or temple of God. "Evidently [1 Corinthians 3:16–17] has reference to those who have become members of the Church with the gift of the Holy Ghost. It is a serious thing to receive the gift of the Holy Ghost, and then defile the body, and those who do so shall be destroyed. Destruction here spoken of does not mean that the individual will be annihilated and cease to exist. Destruction means that the individual shall be banished from the presence of God which is destruction. The body cannot be destroyed permanently because through the atonement of Jesus Christ every spirit and body shall receive the resurrection that they can die no more" (Smith and Sjodahl, *Doctrine and Covenants Commentary*, 596).

Doctrine and Covenants 93:36–37. The Glory of God Is Intelligence

36 The glory of God is intelligence, or, in other words, light and truth.

How can a person gain more intelligence? (93:36) "It is evident that this passage has a broader meaning than just supporting education. However, applying this verse to gaining an education is appropriate because 'truth,' one of the attributes characterizing God's glory, is defined in this same revelation as a 'knowledge of things as they are, and as they were, and as they are to come' (v. 24). Elder John A. Widtsoe distinguished between intelligence and mere learning: 'It often happens that a person of limited knowledge but who earnestly and prayerfully obeys the law, rises to a higher intelligence or wisdom, than one of vast Gospel learning who does not comply in his daily life with the requirements of the Gospel. Obedience to law is a mark of intelligence' ([in Conference Report], Apr. 1938, 50)" (Cowan and Manscill, *A to Z of the Doctrine and Covenants*, 137). ✛

How do we gain light and truth to forsake Satan? (93:37) President Henry B. Eyring explained, "It is by obedience to commandments that we qualify for further revelation of truth and light. . . . God not only loves the obedient, He enlightens them. . . .

"Whatever invites the Holy Ghost as your companion will bring you the greater wisdom and the greater ability to obey God. For instance, you are promised that if you always remember the Savior you will have His Spirit to be with you. You are commanded to pray that you may have the Holy Ghost. You are commanded to pray that you might not be overcome by temptation and so be clean and worthy of the Holy Spirit. You are commanded to study the word of God that you may have His Spirit" ("Life Founded in Light and Truth," *Ensign*, Jul. 2001, 13).

37 Light and truth forsake that evil one.

"The Glory of God Is Intelligence" (Doctrine and Covenants 93:36)

"A son in a poor family, Joseph Smith had limited learning opportunities outside the home. Along with his own divine tutoring from heaven came instruction to all the Saints about the importance of education in eternity. As the Saints gathered for the first time in Kirtland, Ohio, Joseph received several revelations on education—both spiritual and temporal. These revelations offered the Saints new knowledge as well as a charge to make education central in their lives. Learning the things of God was essential, as was studying the history of the world 'out of the best books.' They learned that 'the glory of God is intelligence,' and the Lord petitioned them to 'bring up [their] children in light and truth.'

"As the Saints worked to apply these teachings, Kirtland became home to a broad spectrum of opportunities to learn about things of God and things of the world. Classes were offered for the young and the old, male and female, including both general and specialized classes: a School of the Prophets, a School for the Elders, Hebrew School, geography classes, and more. Though many of these were usually reserved for elders, Sarah M. Kimball attended the School of the Prophets as well as Hebrew School. Eliza R. Snow started a school for girls in Kirtland in 1836 and in Nauvoo in 1842. . . .

"As the Saints moved from place to place they would continue to focus on education, even when in extreme conditions. As Elizabeth Barlow related, 'The understanding and knowledge we have of the scriptures makes friends and everything appear in a very different light to me.' Learning had the ability to change their entire view of the world and eternity" (Johnson and Reeder, *Witness of Women*, 131, 132).

Doctrine and Covenants 93:38–40. Children Are Innocent before God Because of the Redemption of Christ

38 Every spirit of man was innocent in the beginning; and God having redeemed man from the fall, men became again, in their infant state, innocent before God.

Why are God's children considered innocent at birth? (93:38) "We know that one of the unconditional benefits and blessings deriving from the matchless atonement of Christ is that little children will live; that they are redeemed from the foundation of the world; that they are freed from what the Christian world has come to know as the 'original sin'; that those who die before the age of accountability are saved in the celestial kingdom. In short, 'little children are whole, for they are not capable of committing sin; wherefore the curse of Adam is taken from them in me; that it hath no power over them' (Moroni 8:8; see also Mosiah 3:16; 15:25; D&C 29:46; 74:7; 137:10; Moses 6:53–54; JST, Matthew 19:13)" (Millet, *Precept upon Precept*, 207). ⊕

39 And that wicked one cometh and taketh away light and truth, through disobedience, from the children of men, and because of the tradition of their fathers.

How does the wicked one take away light and truth from God's children? (93:39) "The two greatest enemies of light and truth are disobedience and false traditions. Disobedience causes the light to withdraw; and, thus, what truths are left become distorted by dark shadows. 'He that repents not,' the Lord said, 'from him shall be taken even the light which he has received; for my Spirit shall not always strive with man, saith the Lord of Hosts' (D&C 1:33). False traditions are also antithetical to truth, providing a convenient place to hide from the responsibility to listen, see, and know, thus ostensibly freeing the spiritually lethargic from the responsibility that inevitably follows knowledge of the truth" (McConkie and Ostler, *Revelations of the Restoration*, 682).

40 But I have commanded you to bring up your children in light and truth.

How do we go about raising children in light and truth? (93:40) "Children are indeed 'an heritage of the Lord,' and we have been commanded to raise them in light and truth. However, no parent is perfect at this. Parenting is arguably the toughest—and most important—job on earth. As parents, we get tired, lose our patience, struggle to understand what our children need, and get worn down by dealing with the same problems again and again. However, we can try our best, and then try again. To weary parents, I say, just keep going, and pray for strength and wisdom to shepherd your children with love. The eventual rewards will be immeasurable" (Nelson, *Heart of the Matter*, 74). ⊕

Doctrine and Covenants 93:41–53. The Leading Brethren Are Commanded to Set Their Families in Order

What emphasis does the Lord place on fulfilling family responsibilities? (93:41–50) "The Lord singles out and names all the members of the First Presidency and Bishop Newel K. Whitney for failures in their most important responsibilities—their family responsibilities. This part of the revelation is not disconnected from the lofty verses preceding it. All of them tell how to raise children and why. God organizes life and provides his children a setting in which they can act freely. He endows them with light, truth, or knowledge to act upon independently, leaving them free to choose to obey or disobey when 'that wicked one cometh and taketh away light and truth, through disobedience, from the children of men, and because of the tradition of their fathers' (v. 39)" (Harper, *Making Sense of the Doctrine & Covenants*, 347). ◐

What do we learn from the Lord's willingness to call these Church leaders His friends? (93:45–46) "It should be obvious to each of us that our ultimate friendship should be with our Heavenly Father and His Son, Jesus Christ. The Savior has affectionately said to us, 'I will call you friends, for you are my friends' (D&C 93:45). His greatest desire for us, His brothers and sisters, is to bring us back to our Father. And the way for us is clear: develop in our lives, to the degree that we can, the qualities and attributes of Christ. Obey His commandments and do His work and His will" (Hughes, "What Greater Goodness Can We Know," *Ensign*, May 2005, 76).

Why was Joseph Smith rebuked by the Lord? (93:47–48) "President Boyd K. Packer explained that the only time the Lord used the word *rebuke* to chasten Joseph Smith was when he failed to teach his children (*Ensign*, Nov. 1998, 22). Even with all his weighty responsibilities as the head of the dispensation of the fulness of times, the Prophet was still expected to teach his children the gospel, to bring them up 'in light and truth' (D&C 93:40). We are to do the same. Whatever our stewardship in the kingdom may be, our family should not suffer or fall into disbelief because of our busyness—even if that busyness is for worthwhile purposes. . . . Our marriages and family relationships . . . are worthy of our best and most diligent efforts" (Millet and Newell, *Draw Near unto Me*, 263).

41 But verily I say unto you, my servant Frederick G. Williams, you have continued under this condemnation;

42 You have not taught your children light and truth, according to the commandments; and that wicked one hath power, as yet, over you, and this is the cause of your affliction.

43 And now a commandment I give unto you—if you will be delivered you shall set in order your own house, for there are many things that are not right in your house.

44 Verily, I say unto my servant Sidney Rigdon, that in some things he hath not kept the commandments concerning his children; therefore, first set in order thy house.

45 Verily, I say unto my servant Joseph Smith, Jun., or in other words, I will call you friends, for you are my friends, and ye shall have an inheritance with me—

46 I called you servants for the world's sake, and ye are their servants for my sake—

47 And now, verily I say unto Joseph Smith, Jun.—You have not kept the commandments, and must needs stand rebuked before the Lord;

48 Your family must needs repent and forsake some things, and give more earnest heed unto your sayings, or be removed out of their place.

49 What I say unto one I say unto all; pray always lest that wicked one have power in you, and remove you out of your place.

50 My servant Newel K. Whitney also, a bishop of my church, hath need to be chastened, and set in order his family, and see that they are more diligent and concerned at home, and pray always, or they shall be removed out of their place.

What are some ways that we might be "more diligent and concerned at home"? (93:50) "We can begin to become more diligent and concerned at home by telling the people we love that we love them. . . .

"We also can become more diligent and concerned at home by bearing testimony to those whom we love about the things we know to be true by the witness of the Holy Ghost. . . .

"Our consistency in doing seemingly small things can lead to significant spiritual results. . . . We need to be and become more consistent. . . .

"As we seek the Lord's help and in His strength, we can gradually reduce the disparity between what we say and what we do, between expressing love and consistently showing it, and between bearing testimony and steadfastly living it" (Bednar, "More Diligent and Concerned at Home," *Ensign*, Nov. 2009, 17, 18, 20).

51 Now, I say unto you, my friends, let my servant Sidney Rigdon go on his journey, and make haste, and also proclaim the acceptable year of the Lord, and the gospel of salvation, as I shall give him utterance; and by your prayer of faith with one consent I will uphold him.

52 And let my servants Joseph Smith, Jun., and Frederick G. Williams make haste also, and it shall be given them even according to the prayer of faith; and inasmuch as you keep my sayings you shall not be confounded in this world, nor in the world to come.

What does it mean to "proclaim the acceptable year of the Lord"? (93:51) "The term *acceptable year of the Lord* appears once in the Doctrine and Covenants (D&C 93:51), once in the Old Testament (Isa. 61:2), and once in the New Testament (Luke 4:19). . . . 'The acceptable year of the Lord,' according to Elder Bruce R. McConkie, is '*the proper designated, approved, appointed, or accepted time, in the divine order of things, for a particular work to be done*' [*Doctrinal New Testament Commentary*, 1:161; (emphasis) added]. Thus, its use in the Doctrine and Covenants denotes the imminence of Christ's coming; this is the time in which to receive His gospel of salvation, to prepare for His arrival" (Brewster, *Doctrine & Covenants Encyclopedia* [2012], 4–5).

53 And, verily I say unto you, that it is my will that you should hasten to translate my scriptures, and to obtain a knowledge of history, and of countries, and of kingdoms, of laws of God and man, and all this for the salvation of Zion. Amen.

What do we know about Joseph Smith's efforts to hasten the translation of the Bible? (93:53) "[In Doctrine and Covenants 93:53] Joseph Smith was instructed to hasten the translation. . . .

"Hasten they did, completing the work on 2 July 1833. A letter 'To the Brethren in Zion,' written by Sidney Rigdon and signed by the First Presidency, dated 2 July 1833, contains the following statements about the [Joseph Smith Translation]: 'We are exceedingly fatigued, owing to a great press of business. We this day finished the translating of the scriptures, for which we returned gratitude to our Heavenly Father. . . . Having finished the translation of the Bible, a few hours since. . . .' [Joseph Smith Papers, 'Revelation, 6 May 1833 (D&C 93),' 6]" (Dahl, "Joseph Smith Translation and the Doctrine and Covenants," 118).

Introduction to Doctrine and Covenants 94

"In early publications of the Doctrine and Covenants, the revelation recorded in Doctrine and Covenants 94 was incorrectly dated as May 6, 1833. The corrected date of the revelation, August 2, 1833, is included in the 2013 edition of the scriptures, though the order in which the sections appear has not changed" (*Doctrine and Covenants Student Manual* [2018], 525).

"*Three Sacred Buildings* were to be at the heart of the city of Kirtland—the temple and two others. On the first lot south of the temple, a house for the presidency was to be built, and on the second lot a house for the publication of God's word was to stand (see D&C 94:3, 10). All three of these buildings were to have the same dimensions (compare v. 4 and 11 with D&C 95:15). All were to be regarded as sacred (v. 8–9, 12). These latter two structures were not to be built until the Lord gave further instruction (see D&C 94:16). This direction was not given before the Saints were forced to flee from Kirtland, so these structures were never built. On the other hand, less than a month after Doctrine and Covenants 94 had been received, the Lord gave further instruction concerning the design and building of His temple (see D&C 95:8–17). Within a few weeks of receiving these revelations, the Prophet drew up his plan for the city of Zion, in which he called for not three but twenty-four sacred structures to serve as 'houses of worship, schools, etc.' at the city's center ([Joseph Smith Papers, 'History, 1838–1856, volume A-1,' 306])" (Cowan and Manscill, *A to Z of the Doctrine and Covenants*, 137–38).

SECTION 94

Revelation given through Joseph Smith the Prophet, at Kirtland, Ohio, August 2, 1833. Hyrum Smith, Reynolds Cahoon, and Jared Carter are appointed as a Church building committee.

Doctrine and Covenants 94:1–9. The Lord Gives a Commandment Relative to the Erection of a House for the Work of the Presidency

What was "the foundation of the city of the stake of Zion"? (94:1) "On March 23, 1833, a committee was appointed to purchase acreage for the purpose of building a stake of Zion in Kirtland. After the requisite acreage had been purchased, it was surveyed beginning at the site where the Kirtland Temple would one day be built. This site was to be the center of Zion" (Black, *400 Questions and Answers*, 164).

"The city [Kirtland] was to be laid out with the temple as the starting point, and the rest of the city being built in relation to it. This pattern was followed by Brigham Young in laying out Salt Lake City. He first identified the spot upon which the temple would be built and paralleled all the streets out from what is called Temple Square" (McConkie and Ostler, *Revelations of the Restoration*, 685).

What was the Lord's pattern referred to in this verse? (94:2) The Lord instructed the Saints to lay out the city of Kirtland "according to the pattern" which He had given to the Prophet Joseph Smith (D&C 94:2). This pattern likely refers to the plan for the city of Zion in Missouri. Frederick G. Williams drew a plan, or plat, for the city of Kirtland similar to the one for the

1 And again, verily I say unto you, my friends, a commandment I give unto you, that ye shall commence a work of laying out and preparing a beginning and foundation of the city of the stake of Zion, here in the land of Kirtland, beginning at my house.

2 And behold, it must be done according to the pattern which I have given unto you.

city of Zion. The Kirtland plat reflected the Lord's instructions that the city be laid out with the temple as the starting point and that the rest of the city be built in relation to it (see *Joseph Smith Papers: Documents, Volume 3*, 208–11).

What happened to this house for the First Presidency? (94:3) "Unfortunately, the Kirtland Temple consumed the funds of the Saints, making it difficult to begin construction on a house for the presidency. On October 10, 1833, however, Church leaders decided to build a single building that would accommodate a printing press and a space for the School of the Prophets. This model of having a building for multiple uses set the standard for the next several decades. The First Presidency used locations such as the Kirtland Temple, schoolhouses, Joseph's home, and the Red Brick Store in Nauvoo for their administration meetings" (Richardson, "House for the Presidency," 232).

What is the order of the priesthood for laying foundations? (94:6) The Prophet Joseph Smith taught, "If the strict order of the Priesthood, were carried out in the building of Temples, the first stone will be laid at the South East Corner by the First Presidency of the Church; the South West Corner should be laid next, the Third or N.W. Corner next, and the fourth or N.E. corner the last. The first presidency should lay the S.E. Corner stone, and dictate who are the proper persons to lay the other Corner Stones" (Joseph Smith Papers, "History, 1838–1856, volume C-1," 1186; orthography modernized).

Why would the Lord instruct the Saints to not suffer any unclean thing to enter this dedicated building? (94:8–9) "This is the first reference in the Restoration that entrance to sacred buildings is to be restricted to worthy individuals. The leaders of the Church have taken this responsibility seriously. One purpose of temple recommends is to meet the obligations the Lord has placed on the Saints to see that the unworthy do not inhibit the Spirit of God from being poured out on those in the Lord's house" (McConkie and Ostler, *Revelations of the Restoration*, 686).

---

3 And let the first lot on the south be consecrated unto me for the building of a house for the presidency, for the work of the presidency, in obtaining revelations; and for the work of the ministry of the presidency, in all things pertaining to the church and kingdom.

4 Verily I say unto you, that it shall be built fifty-five by sixty-five feet in the width thereof and in the length thereof, in the inner court.

5 And there shall be a lower court and a higher court, according to the pattern which shall be given unto you hereafter.

6 And it shall be dedicated unto the Lord from the foundation thereof, according to the order of the priesthood, according to the pattern which shall be given unto you hereafter.

7 And it shall be wholly dedicated unto the Lord for the work of the presidency.

8 And ye shall not suffer any unclean thing to come in unto it; and my glory shall be there, and my presence shall be there.

9 But if there shall come into it any unclean thing, my glory shall not be there; and my presence shall not come into it.

Doctrine and Covenants 94:10–12.
A Printing House Is to Be Built

Why were the Saints commanded to build a printing office? (94:10) "The importance of the Joseph Smith Translation to the Lord, and other materials to be printed, i.e., the Doctrine and Covenants, is again shown by His commandment to build a house for printing" (Nyman, *Doctrine and Covenants Commentary*, 2:239). ⊕

Doctrine and Covenants 94:13–17.
Certain Inheritances Are Assigned

Who was Jared Carter? (94:14) "Jared is most remembered for his missions to the eastern states. From 1831 to 1834 his missionary labors were exemplary.... [Unfortunately] seeds of apostasy became apparent in the life of Jared Carter. He also noted the change, reporting that 'the spirit of God in a measure has left me,' but he failed to completely rectify the problem. While struggling to regain his testimony he was assigned an inheritance in Kirtland and appointed to a Church building committee (see D&C 94:14–15). Heber C. Kimball wrote that the committee members

10 And again, verily I say unto you, the second lot on the south shall be dedicated unto me for the building of a house unto me, for the work of the printing of the translation of my scriptures, and all things whatsoever I shall command you.

11 And it shall be fifty-five by sixty-five feet in the width thereof and the length thereof, in the inner court; and there shall be a lower and a higher court.

12 And this house shall be wholly dedicated unto the Lord from the foundation thereof, for the work of the printing, in all things whatsoever I shall command you, to be holy, undefiled, according to the pattern in all things as it shall be given unto you.

13 And on the third lot shall my servant Hyrum Smith receive his inheritance.

14 And on the first and second lots on the north shall my servants Reynolds Cahoon and Jared Carter receive their inheritances—

Reynolds Cahoon (Doctrine and Covenants 94:14)

Reynolds Cahoon is one of "the prominent names in early Church history, and he is mentioned four times in the Doctrine and Covenants (D&C 52:30; D&C 61:35; D&C 75:32; D&C 94:14). In 1831, the Lord indicated His pleasure with the labors of Cahoon and Samuel Smith (D&C 61:35). He later received an inheritance in Kirtland from the Lord (D&C 94:14) and served as a member of the three-man building committee for the temple. He was a member of the Montrose, Iowa, high council ([Joseph Smith Papers, "Church Officers in Iowa Territory, September 1839–January 1841"]) and a counselor in the stake at Adam-ondi-Ahman, Missouri ([Joseph Smith Papers, "Journal, March–September 1838," fn127]).

Reynolds Cahoon

"Unfortunately, he was one of those who persuaded the Prophet Joseph to place his life in the hands of the authorities at Carthage, where his blood was shed ([Joseph Smith Papers, "History, 1838–1856, volume F-1," 148]). Cahoon served as a member of the bodyguard that accompanied the Prophet's body back to Nauvoo in what must have been a particularly painful journey for him ([Joseph Smith Papers, 'History, 1838–1856, volume F-1']). Brigham Young appointed him captain of the sixth

'used every exertion in their power to forward the work' on the Kirtland Temple. Jared assisted in laying the foundation stones of the temple on 23 July 1834. . . . Unfortunately, by 1838 Jared had again become disaffected" (Black, *Who's Who*, 52–53). See also commentary in this volume on Doctrine and Covenants 79:1.

15 That they may do the work which I have appointed unto them, to be a committee to build mine houses, according to the commandment, which I, the Lord God, have given unto you.

How would a committee help in building the Lord's houses? (94:15) "In this revelation the Lord called men to serve as a committee to build His houses (see D&C 94:13–15). The need for such a committee has not diminished since the time of this revelation. As the church has grown, its need for buildings and various physical facilities has dramatically increased. Now, even more than in 1833, there is a need for someone to be responsible for the planning, approving, constructing and maintaining of buildings erected and dedicated to the Lord for His purposes. Hence, the church still has need of a building committee which functions under the directions of the First Presidency" (Otten and Caldwell, *Sacred Truths*, 2:147–48).

16 These two houses are not to be built until I give unto you a commandment concerning them.

17 And now I give unto you no more at this time. Amen.

Why did the Saints not complete these two buildings? (94:16) "The administration building and the printing office were not to be built either in Kirtland or in Missouri until the Lord gave further instructions concerning them. Since building the Kirtland Temple exhausted both the Saints and their resources in Ohio and mob action drove the Saints from Jackson County in Missouri, these two auxiliary 'houses' were never constructed in either location, although a smaller structure was built for Church offices, the printing office, and the Elders' School in Kirtland" (Robinson and Garrett, *Commentary on the Doctrine and Covenants*, 3:202).

company of one hundred Saints that left Nauvoo in October 1845. . . . He was later chosen as a counselor in the presidency of one of the emigrating camps" (Brewster, *Doctrine & Covenants Encyclopedia* [2012], 67).

When he died in Salt Lake Valley in 1861, "a *Deseret News* obituary [stated] that Reynolds was 'a true friend to the prophet of God while he was living; full of integrity and love for the truth and always acted cheerfully the part assigned him in the great work of the last Days'" (Black, *Who's Who*, 48).

Reynolds Cahoon had an interesting connection to the Book of Mormon's brother of Jared. "While residing in Kirtland Elder Reynolds Cahoon had a son born to him. One day when President Joseph Smith was passing his door he called the Prophet in and asked him to bless and name the baby. Joseph did so and gave the boy the name of Mahonri Moriancumer. When he had finished the blessing he laid the child on the bed, and turning to Elder Cahoon he said, 'The name I have given your son is the name of the brother of Jared; the Lord has just shown (or revealed) it to me.' Elder William F. Cahoon, who was standing near, heard the Prophet make this statement to his father; and this was the first time the name of the brother of Jared was known in the Church in this dispensation" (George Reynolds, in *Juvenile Instructor*, Vol. 27, No. 9 [1 May 1982] 282, fn).

Introduction to Doctrine and Covenants 95

The Prophet Joseph Smith received the revelation of what is now Doctrine and Covenants 95 on June 1, 1833. "Although the Prophet had been commanded by the Lord to build the temple [in Kirtland, Ohio], overwhelming problems and other priorities delayed construction. On June 1, 1833, the Lord chastised the Church for not having made greater progress on the sacred edifice (see D&C 95:1–6). Needless to say, activity started immediately. The ground was broken on June 5. Lucy Mack Smith wrote: 'Joseph took the brethren with him, for the purpose of selecting a spot for the building to stand upon. The place which they made choice of was situated in the north-west corner of a field of wheat, which was sown by my sons the fall previous, on the farm upon which we were then living. In a few minutes the fence was removed, and the standing grain was levelled, in order to prepare a place for the building and Hyrum commenced digging a trench for the wall, he having declared that he would strike the first blow upon the house'" (Karl Ricks Anderson, *Joseph Smith's Kirtland*, 158).

In obedience to this revelation, "Construction of the temple began in early June. Joseph Smith, Hyrum Smith, Brigham Young and his brother Lorenzo D. Young, and Reynolds Cahoon rode south in search of a quarry where stone suitable for the temple walls might be secured. They located one about two miles from the temple site and filled Lorenzo Young's wagon with stones to transport back to the temple lot" (Backman, *Heavens Resound*, 147).

SECTION 95

Revelation given through Joseph Smith the Prophet, at Kirtland, Ohio, June 1, 1833. This revelation is a continuation of divine directions to build a house for worship and instruction, the house of the Lord (see section 88:119–36).

1 Verily, thus saith the Lord unto you whom I love, and whom I love I also chasten that their sins may be forgiven, for with the chastisement I prepare a way for their deliverance in all things out of temptation, and I have loved you—

2 Wherefore, ye must needs be chastened and stand rebuked before my face;

3 For ye have sinned against me a very grievous sin, in that ye have not considered the great commandment in all things, that I have given unto you concerning the building of mine house;

Doctrine and Covenants 95:1–6. The Saints Are Chastened for Their Failure to Build the House of the Lord

Why does the Lord chasten those He loves? (95:1–2) "Divine chastening has at least three purposes: (1) to persuade us to repent, (2) to refine and sanctify us, and (3) at times to redirect our course in life to what God knows is a better path" (Christofferson, "As Many as I Love, I Rebuke and Chasten," *Ensign*, May 2011, 98). ☉

Why did the Lord call the delay of building a temple a grievous sin? (95:3) "The Lord chastened and rebuked the Saints for neglecting to obey His 'great commandment . . . concerning the building of [His] house' in Kirtland, and He called their neglect 'a very grievous sin' (D&C 95:3). The Lord reminded them that He chastened them because He loved them. . . . The Lord's chastening was not meant to punish but rather to correct and bring His people to repentance, 'that their sins may be forgiven' (D&C 95:1). Other scripture passages attest to the Lord's loving purposes for chastening His people, including to help them 'remember him' (Helaman 12:3), to help them 'learn obedience' (D&C 105:6), and to refine them 'as gold' (Job 23:10)" (*Doctrine and Covenants Student Manual* [2018], 528).

4 For the preparation wherewith I design to prepare mine apostles to prune my vineyard for the last time, that I may bring to pass my strange act, that I may pour out my Spirit upon all flesh—

5 But behold, verily I say unto you, that there are many who have been ordained among you, whom I have called but few of them are chosen.

6 They who are not chosen have sinned a very grievous sin, in that they are walking in darkness at noon-day.

7 And for this cause I gave unto you a commandment that you should call your solemn assembly, that your fastings and your mourning might come up into the ears of the Lord of Sabaoth, which is by interpretation, the creator of the first day, the beginning and the end.

What is the Lord's "strange act"? (95:4) It is the Lord's work. "Spread over many centuries, running like a golden thread in the happenings of the peoples and governments of this earth, the Lord has been bringing to pass his strange act to accomplish his divine purposes in the earth, both here and hereafter" (Reeve, "Lord's Strange Act," 2). See also commentary in this volume on Doctrine and Covenants 101:95.

How might one end up walking in darkness at noonday? (95:6) "A solar eclipse is indeed a remarkable phenomenon of nature during which the beauty, warmth, and light of the sun can be completely covered by a comparatively insignificant object, causing darkness and chill.

"A similar phenomenon can be replicated in a spiritual sense, when otherwise small and insignificant matters are drawn too close and block the beauty, warmth, and heavenly light of the gospel of Jesus Christ, replacing it with cold darkness. . . .

"If you discover anything that seems to be blocking the light and joy of the gospel in *your* life, I invite you to place it in a gospel perspective. . . . In short, don't let life's distractions eclipse heaven's light" (Stevenson, "Spiritual Eclipse," *Ensign*, Nov. 2017, 47).

Doctrine and Covenants 95:7–10. The Lord Desires to Use His House to Endow His People with Power from on High

What is a solemn assembly and what is its purpose? (95:7) "Special, sacred meetings of the Church are designated as 'solemn assemblies.' These meetings were mentioned in revelation as early as November 1831, and appear eight times in the Doctrine and Covenants (D&C 88:70, 117; 95:7; 108:4; 109:6, 10; 124:39; 133:6). . . . [In April 1974 general conference, President Spencer W. Kimball noted:] 'Joseph Smith led the first solemn assembly, and after closing his discourse, he called upon the several quorums, commencing with the presidency, to manifest by rising, their willingness to acknowledge him as the prophet and seer and uphold him as such by their prayers and faith. All the quorums in turn cheerfully complied with this request. He then called upon all the congregation of Saints also to give their assent by rising to their feet' (in Conference Report, Apr. 1974, 64–65)" (Brewster, *Doctrine & Covenants Encyclopedia* [2012], 540). See also commentary in this volume on Doctrine and Covenants 88:70.

What might the inspired definition of the title "Lord of Sabaoth" help us understand about the Savior? (95:7) While "hosts" is one definition of the term *Sabaoth*, "the creation of the divine 'hosts' involved more than simply bringing spirits into existence (the Father's unique role), but 'bringing to pass' or 'making' every stage of their development 'happen,' including their mortality and resurrection from the dead. This was (and is) the responsibility of the one designated '*Yhwh*' [Lord, or Jesus Christ] from 'the beginning' all the way to the 'end.' . . .

"That 'the creator of the first day, the beginning and the end' is the one who 'causes to happen'— creating worlds and causing them to pass away 'by the word of his power' (Moses 1:35)—is key to understanding Christ's role in 'bring[ing] to pass the resurrection of the dead' [2 Nephi 2:8]" (Bowen, "Creator of the First Day," 72, 73). ✦

How were the Saints endowed with divine power from on high? (95:8) "The promised endowment encompassed several events in early 1836, including a Pentecost-like season surrounding the dedication of the House of the Lord in Kirtland, Ohio. Although Joseph Smith later introduced a temple ordinance he also called an endowment, the phrase 'endowment of power' is often associated with the outpouring of spiritual gifts and the restoration of priesthood keys in Kirtland" (Church History Topics, "Endowment of Power").

"Virtually all references to the endowment in the scriptures are in the context of missionary work, which suggests a more immediate purpose for the endowment. There is ample scriptural and apostolic authority for the proposition that the endowment is intended for the here and now, as preparation for our ministry in fulfilling the mission of the Church— on both sides of the veil. This is a very practical and direct purpose for the endowment" (Rawlins, "Endowed with Power," 125–26).

Doctrine and Covenants 95:11–17. The House Is to Be Dedicated as a Place of Worship and for the School of the Apostles

What does it mean that the Father's love will not continue with the disobedient? (95:11–12) "Beginning in verse 11, the Lord promises the Saints power to build the temple *if* they keep his commandments. 'If you keep not my commandments,' he

8 Yea, verily I say unto you, I gave unto you a commandment that you should build a house, in the which house I design to endow those whom I have chosen with power from on high;

9 For this is the promise of the Father unto you; therefore I command you to tarry, even as mine apostles at Jerusalem.

10 Nevertheless, my servants sinned a very grievous sin; and contentions arose in the school of the prophets; which was very grievous unto me, saith your Lord; therefore I sent them forth to be chastened.

11 Verily I say unto you, it is my will that you should build a house. If you keep my commandments you shall have power to build it.

12 If you keep not my commandments, the love of the Father shall not continue with you, therefore you shall walk in darkness.

13 Now here is wisdom, and the mind of the Lord—let the house be built, not after the manner of the world, for I give not unto you that ye shall live after the manner of the world;

14 Therefore, let it be built after the manner which I shall show unto three of you, whom ye shall appoint and ordain unto this power.

15 And the size thereof shall be fifty and five feet in width, and let it be sixty-five feet in length, in the inner court thereof.

16 And let the lower part of the inner court be dedicated unto me for your sacrament offering, and for your preaching, and your fasting, and your praying, and the offering up of your most holy desires unto me, saith your Lord.

17 And let the higher part of the inner court be dedicated unto me for the school of mine apostles, saith Son Ahman; or, in other words, Alphus; or, in other words, Omegus; even Jesus Christ your Lord. Amen.

emphasized, 'the love of the Father shall not continue with you, therefore you shall walk in darkness' (D&C 95:12). The revelation does not say that the love of God will not continue, only that it will not continue with those who choose to reject it, who 'love darkness rather than light' (D&C 29:45). By juxtaposing his love with darkness, the Lord equates his love with light and the synonyms for it described in sections 88 and 93, including truth, glory, intelligence, power, and life" (Harper, "Historical Context and Background of D&C 95"). ⊕

What do we know about the Kirtland Temple's floor plan and the purposes of its organization? (95:16–17) "The chapel on the main floor was to be used 'for your sacrament offering, and for your preaching, and your fasting, and your praying.' A similar hall on the second floor was to house 'the school of mine apostles' (D&C 95:16–17). Five small rooms in the attic were used as offices or classrooms.

"Thus, 'the design and construction of the Kirtland Temple,' [President] Boyd K. Packer explained, 'was different from that of all other latter-day temples because its purpose was different. While

"If You Keep My Commandments You Shall Have Power to Build It" (D&C 95:11)

Eliza R. Snow, who lived in Kirtland while the temple was being built, recalled: "The Saints were few in number, and most of them very poor; and, had it not been for the assurance that God had spoken, and had commanded that a house should be built to His name, . . . an attempt towards building that Temple, under the then existing circumstances, would have been, by all concerned, pronounced preposterous. . . .

"With very little capital except brain, bone and sinew, combined with unwavering trust in God, men, women, and even children, worked with their might" [in *Eliza R. Snow: An Immortal* (1957), 54, 57]" (*Latter-day Saint History: 1815–1846* [manual], 103).

Here is one way the Lord helped the Saints build a temple in their poverty: "[John Tanner] 'received an impression by dream or vision of the night, that he . . . must go immediately to the Church' in Kirtland. He disposed of his property—several flourishing farms, a hotel, and orchards—loaded his numerous family and several neighbors into wagons on Christmas morning, and traversed the five hundred mile distance to arrive in Kirtland on a Sunday, January 1835.

"He had indeed been needed. A mortgage on the temple site was falling due and, according to some accounts, the impoverished Prophet Joseph and some of the brethren had been praying for assistance.

"John Tanner did not hesitate. He loaned the Prophet two thousand dollars and took his note, loaned the temple committee thirteen thousand dollars, signed a note for thirty thousand dollars with the Prophet and others for goods purchased in New York, and made 'liberal donations' toward the building of the temple" (Arrington, "John Tanner Family," *Ensign*, Mar. 1979, 46).

already in 1836 certain ordinances had been introduced in a limited way which later would form part of the regular temple ordinances, the sacred ordinances and ceremonies performed in today's temples were not done in this first temple' [*Holy Temple*, 129]" (Cowan, "Doctrine and Covenants on Temples," 18).

What does "Son Ahman" mean? (95:17) "Elder Bruce R. McConkie points out that, according to Orson Pratt, the Prophet Joseph Smith received a revelation in which he was informed that the name of God the Father in the language of Adam is *Ahman*.

The Lord Revealed His Design for the Kirtland Temple (Doctrine and Covenants 95:13–17)

"'A council was called and Joseph requested the brethren, each one, to rise and give his views, and after they were through he would give his opinion. . . . Some thought that it would be better to build a frame [house]. Others said that a frame [house] was too costly . . . , and the majority concluded upon the putting up [of] a log house and made their calculations about what they could do towards building it. Joseph rose and reminded them that they were not making a house for themselves or any other man but a house for God: "And shall we, brethren, build a house for our God of logs? No, brethren. I have a better plan than that. I have the plan of the house of the Lord given by Himself. You will see by this the difference between our calculations and His ideas." The Prophet then provided the "plan in full of the house of the Lord at Kirtland," which "highly delighted" the

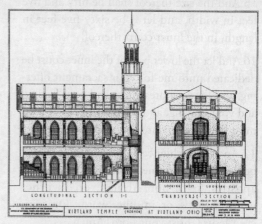

Architectural Rendering of the Kirtland Temple

brethren. After the meeting, they walked to the building site and began to work—removing a fence, clearing the ground, and digging a trench for the wall' ([Joseph Smith Papers, 'Lucy Mack Smith, History,' book 14, pages 1–2]; spelling, punctuation, and capitalization modernized)" (*Doctrine and Covenants Student Manual* [2018], 530–31).

This plan for the Lord's temple was revealed to the First Presidency: Joseph Smith, Sidney Rigdon, and Frederick G. Williams. Frederick recalled speaking with the temple builders: "Carpenter Rolph said, 'Doctor [Williams], what do you think of the house?' [Williams] answered, 'It looks to me like the pattern precisely.' He then related the following: 'Joseph [Smith] received the word of the Lord for him to take his two counselors, Williams and Rigdon, and come before the Lord, and He would show them the plan or model of the house to be built. We went upon our knees, called on the Lord, and the building appeared within viewing distance, I being the first to discover it. Then we all viewed it together. After we had taken a good look at the exterior, the building seemed to come right over us, and the makeup of the Hall seemed to coincide with that I there saw to a minutiae'" (Robison, *First Mormon Temple*, 8).

"In a letter to John Taylor in 1885, Truman O. Angell confirmed the fact that the temple had been seen in vision: 'F. G. Williams came into the Temple about the time the main hall 1st floor was ready for dedication. He was asked, how does the house look to you. He answered that it looked to him like the model he had seen. He said President Joseph Smith, Sidney Rigdon and himself were called to come before the Lord and the model was shown them. He said the vision of the Temple was thus shown them and he could not see the difference between it and the House as built.' He further stated in his journal that 'the leading mechanic' recommended to Joseph Smith that the seats in the building be rearranged. The Prophet responded by saying he had seen them in vision and insisted that the original plans be carried out" (Karl Ricks Anderson, *Joseph Smith's Kirtland*, 157).

From Moses 6:57 we learn that the name of God in the language of Adam is *Man of Holiness*. Elder McConkie teaches that *Ahman* essentially means *Man of Holiness*, and that 'God revealed himself to Adam by this name to signify that he is a *Holy Man*.' . . . Jesus is the *Son of Man of Holiness*, or *Son of Man* (see D&C 49:5–6; D&C 130:14–17)" (Woodford, "Remarkable Doctrine and Covenants," *Ensign*, Jan. 1997, 48n7). See also commentary in this volume on Doctrine and Covenants 78:20.

Introduction to Doctrine and Covenants 96

This revelation was received on June 4, 1833, in Kirtland, Ohio. "In the spring of 1833, high priests in Kirtland met to plan how to acquire several farms in the area, particularly a farm and tavern owned by an early settler named Peter French. The Saints hoped to build a stake of Zion surrounding the house of the Lord, which they intended to build on French's farm. They sent a committee to ask the farm owners the terms on which they would be willing to sell. The committee returned with news that the farms could be bought for around eleven thousand dollars. . . . The funds were raised, and the farms purchased, leading to another council on June 4. This council disagreed about who should be the steward of the French farm, 'but all agreed to inquire of the Lord.' Doctrine and Covenants 96 was the result" (Harper, *Making Sense of the Doctrine & Covenants*, 355).

SECTION 96

Revelation given to Joseph Smith the Prophet, showing the order of the city or stake of Zion at Kirtland, Ohio, June 4, 1833, as an example to the Saints in Kirtland. The occasion was a conference of high priests, and the chief subject of consideration was the disposal of certain lands, known as the French farm, possessed by the Church near Kirtland. Since the conference could not agree who should take charge of the farm, all agreed to inquire of the Lord concerning the matter.

1 Behold, I say unto you, here is wisdom, whereby ye may know how to act concerning this matter, for it is expedient in me that this stake that I have set for the strength of Zion should be made strong.

Doctrine and Covenants 96:1. The Kirtland Stake of Zion Is to Be Made Strong

When was the Kirtland Stake organized? (96:1) On April 26, 1832, "Kirtland was designated as one of the locations where a stake of Zion would be established [see D&C 82:13], and in the summer of 1833, the Saints were commanded 'to commence a work of laying out and preparing' a 'stake of Zion' there, in harmony with the pattern that had previously been revealed to the Prophet [see D&C 94:1].

"Less than a year later, a more formal organization of the first stake of the Church occurred with the creation of the first high council. On February 17, 1834, approximately sixty members of the Church gathered at the home of Joseph Smith to attend a special meeting. Following the invocation, the Prophet announced that the purpose of the meeting was to select twelve high priests to serve as members of a high council" (Backman, *Heavens Resound*, 244–45).

Doctrine and Covenants 96:2–5. The Bishop Is to Divide the Inheritances for the Saints

Over what place was Newel K. Whitney tasked to take charge? (96:2–3) "In answer to their prayer of inquiry, the Lord informed the brethren that the person with responsibility for the Lord's properties in Kirtland was the bishop in Kirtland, Newel K. Whitney. The building committee was to oversee construction, but control of Church-owned properties and the structures built upon them would remain with the bishop" (Robinson and Garrett, *Commentary on the Doctrine and Covenants*, 3:213).

What is the "order" which will bring forth God's word to His children? (96:4–5) "United orders or firms were partnerships set up to accomplish a specific economic objective, as was the case in this instance—to manage and supervise Church properties. . . . The united order instituted to oversee the French farm properties [see verses 2–3] was different from the 'order' referred to in verse 4. This reference alluded to the Literary Firm" (James W. McConkie, *Looking at the Doctrine and Covenants Again*, 382).

The Literary Firm "was composed of Church leaders given stewardship over the revelations and their publication. The needs of those who labored for the Literary Firm were to be provided for so that their labors could continue expeditiously" (McConkie and Ostler, *Revelations of the Restoration*, 698).

Doctrine and Covenants 96:6–9. John Johnson Is to Be a Member of the United Order

What was John Johnson's offering? (96:6–8) "Brother Johnson was a member of the Church living in Hiram, Ohio. The Smith and Rigdon families had lived at the Johnson farm while Joseph, with Sidney as scribe, translated much of the Joseph Smith Translation. Joseph and Emma occupied part of the Johnson home, and Joseph received several revelations there, including Doctrine and Covenants 76. The Johnson home was also the location of several Church conferences. Here also Joseph and Sidney were tarred and feathered by a mob [John Johnson's collar bone was broken during the attack]. . . . Unavoidably, all of these things had put additional burdens upon the Johnson family. . . . Members of this order consecrated their possessions to the Church,

2 Therefore, let my servant Newel K. Whitney take charge of the place which is named among you, upon which I design to build mine holy house.

3 And again, let it be divided into lots, according to wisdom, for the benefit of those who seek inheritances, as it shall be determined in council among you.

4 Therefore, take heed that ye see to this matter, and that portion that is necessary to benefit mine order, for the purpose of bringing forth my word to the children of men.

5 For behold, verily I say unto you, this is the most expedient in me, that my word should go forth unto the children of men, for the purpose of subduing the hearts of the children of men for your good. Even so. Amen.

6 And again, verily I say unto you, it is wisdom and expedient in me, that my servant John Johnson whose offering I have accepted, and whose prayers I have heard, unto whom I give a promise of eternal life inasmuch as he keepeth my commandments from henceforth—

7 For he is a descendant of Joseph and a partaker of the blessings of the promise made unto his fathers—

and Brother Johnson was to put up the security to pay off the Peter French property for the firm (see v. 9)" (Robinson and Garrett, *Commentary on the Doctrine and Covenants*, 3:214).

8 Verily I say unto you, it is expedient in me that he should become a member of the order, that he may assist in bringing forth my word unto the children of men.

What was the "order" that John Johnson was to become a member of? (96:8) "The order of which he was to become a member was a business firm composed of some of the leading elders of the Church and was referred to as the United Order or United Firm. Members of this order covenanted to consecrate their surplus property and business profits for the poor and needy of the Church. At this time, as indicated in section 96, the order had negotiated the purchase of a farm from Peter French that included a house, or inn. As a member of the order, John was instructed by the Lord that he was to 'seek diligently to take away incumbrances that are upon the house named among you' (D&C 96:9)" (Ostler, "Real Covenants and Real People," 125–26).

9 Therefore ye shall ordain him unto this blessing, and he shall seek diligently to take away incumbrances that are upon the house named among you, that he may dwell therein. Even so. Amen.

What were the incumbrances? (96:9) "The revelation specifically directed John Johnson to 'seek diligently to take away the encumbrances that are upon the house named among you, that ye may dwell therein' (D&C 96:9). This statement may have referred to a contractual arrangement that Peter French made with Thomas Knight to operate a store in the building. Joseph C. Kingsbury continued to clerk in the Knight store for an unspecified period of time after the property was transferred to N. K. Whitney & Company. In the fall of 1833, Thomas Knight sold the eight and a half acres he owned in Kirtland and apparently moved away, suggesting that John Johnson was able to remove the 'incumbrances' fairly quickly" (Staker, *Hearken O Ye People*, 415).

Introduction to Doctrine and Covenants 97

This revelation was received on August 2, 1833. Joseph Smith [previously] received a letter from Oliver Cowdery on July 9 and a letter from members of the school in Zion. The Prophet Joseph wrote, "We now answer them both in one letter as relates to the school in Zion according to your request we inquired of the Lord and send in this letter the communication which we received from the Lord concerning the school in Zion" (Joseph Smith Papers, "Letter to Church Leaders in Jackson County, Missouri, 6 August 1833," [1]).

"In the month of July the persecution of the Saints in Jackson County, Missouri, commenced. At the beginning of the following month, the Prophet Joseph Smith received a revelation that concerned primarily the saints in Missouri (D&C 97). He did not know what had happened to the saints in Jackson County, although he knew that trouble was possible" (Roy W. Doxey, *Doctrine and Covenants Speaks*, 2:216).

On July 20, 1833, about two weeks before the revelation recorded in section 97 was received, "an armed mob, approved by the state Lieutenant Governor Lilburn W. Boggs, demanded that all Mormons remove from Jackson County, Missouri. They ransacked the home of William W. Phelps and destroyed the unbound sheets of the Book of Commandments that were in the printing office above his home. The printing press was destroyed, and Brother Phelps's personal belongings were plundered. Bishop Edward Partridge and another member, Charles Allen, were taken into the county courthouse square where they were stripped of their clothing, tarred, and feathered. Sidney Gilbert was forced to agree to close his mercantile store. Three days later, leaders among the Saints signed a treaty with the mob that they would leave the county" (McConkie and Ostler, *Revelations of the Restoration*, 697).

"Joseph Smith did not receive detailed news of these events until August 9, 1833. . . . The 900 miles that separated Independence from Kirtland ensured that written accounts sent through the mail or published in newspapers did not reach Ohio until mid-August. In the meantime, Joseph Smith had received two revelations (Doctrine and Covenants 97 and 98) in early August that, although they did not address the specific difficulties experienced by Church members in Jackson County on July 20, nevertheless offered words of divine consolation and guidance that Phelps and the other Missouri Saints could later use to help them make sense of their experiences and sufferings" (Grua, "Waiting for the Word of the Lord," 197–98).

SECTION 97

Revelation given through Joseph Smith the Prophet, at Kirtland, Ohio, August 2, 1833. This revelation deals particularly with the affairs of the Saints in Zion, Jackson County, Missouri, in response to the Prophet's inquiry of the Lord for information. Members of the Church in Missouri were at this time subjected to severe persecution and, on July 23, 1833, had been forced to sign an agreement to leave Jackson County.

Doctrine and Covenants 97:1–2. Many of the Saints in Zion (Jackson County, Missouri) Are Blessed for Their Faithfulness

Why was it essential for the Saints in Missouri to be "truly humble"? (97:1) "The Lord expressed his approval for those in Zion who were 'truly humble and . . . seeking diligently to learn wisdom and to find truth' (D&C 97:1). Humility is a basic requirement for a proper relationship with the Lord. It is listed first among the requirements for baptism (D&C 20:37). It must accompany confession and repentance (D&C 20:6; 61:2). It is a key to receiving the blessings of prayer (D&C 112:10; 136:32), even to the rending of the veil (D&C 67:10). And humility is essential for those who would be gathered in the last days (D&C 29:1–2)" (Cloward, "Counsel to the Exiles," 384).

1 Verily I say unto you my friends, I speak unto you with my voice, even the voice of my Spirit, that I may show unto you my will concerning your brethren in the land of Zion, many of whom are truly humble and are seeking diligently to learn wisdom and to find truth.

2 Verily, verily I say unto you, blessed are such, for they shall obtain; for I, the Lord, show mercy unto all the meek, and upon all whomsoever I will, that I may be justified when I shall bring them unto judgment.

3 Behold, I say unto you, concerning the school in Zion, I, the Lord, am well pleased that there should be a school in Zion, and also with my servant Parley P. Pratt, for he abideth in me.

4 And inasmuch as he continueth to abide in me he shall continue to preside over the school in the land of Zion until I shall give unto him other commandments.

5 And I will bless him with a multiplicity of blessings, in expounding all scriptures and mysteries to the edification of the school, and of the church in Zion.

6 And to the residue of the school, I, the Lord, am willing to show mercy; nevertheless, there are those that must needs be chastened, and their works shall be made known.

7 The ax is laid at the root of the trees; and every tree that bringeth not forth good fruit shall be hewn down and cast into the fire. I, the Lord, have spoken it.

What blessings come from meekness? (97:2)
"Meekness is an essential aspect of the divine nature and can be received and developed in our lives because of and through the Savior's Atonement.... I promise that He will guide, protect, and strengthen us as we walk in the meekness of His Spirit" (Bednar, "Meek and Lowly of Heart," *Ensign*, May 2018, 33).

Doctrine and Covenants 97:3–5. Parley P. Pratt Is Commended for His Labors in the School in Zion

Doctrine and Covenants 97:6–9. Those Who Observe Their Covenants Are Accepted by the Lord

What is the Lord warning His people about by stating that the axe is at the root of the trees? (97:7) "The quotation here corresponds most closely with the language of Alma from the Book of Mormon (see Alma 5:52) but also closely parallels Matthew 3:10 and Luke 3:9. In the Book of Mormon, this warning is given to the people of Alma who were about to experience the great Lamanite wars. In the New

Parley P. Pratt Describes His Experience in the School of the Elders (D&C 97:3–5)

Parley P. Pratt described his experience in ministering and the school of the elders: "In the latter part of summer and in the autumn, I devoted almost my entire time in ministering among the churches; holding meetings; visiting the sick; comforting the afflicted, and giving counsel. A school of Elders was also organized, over which I was called to preside. This class, to the number of about sixty, met for instruction once a week. The place of meeting was in the open air, under some tall trees, in a retired place in the wilderness, where we prayed, preached and prophesied, and exercised ourselves in the gifts of the Holy Spirit. Here great blessings were poured out, and many great and marvelous things were manifested and taught. The Lord gave me great wisdom, and enabled me to teach and edify the Elders, and comfort and encourage them in their preparations for the great work which lay before us. I was also much edified and strengthened. To attend this school I had to travel on foot, and sometimes with bare feet at that, about six miles. This I did once a week, besides visiting and preaching in five or six branches a week" (*Autobiography of Parley P. Pratt*, 93–94).

Testament, it was delivered to the Jews who would soon be devastated by their failed First Revolt against Rome. The same warning is now addressed here specifically to the faltering Saints in Missouri, for whom persecutions had already begun but for whom deliverance was still possible if they would only repent" (Robinson and Garrett, *Commentary on the Doctrine and Covenants*, 3:220–21).

Why is willingness important in observing our covenants? (97:8) "In this dispensation, the Lord reaffirmed that commandment [of a broken heart and contrite spirit] in 1831 (see D&C 59:8) and then two years later added a very meaningful and most significant word to the commandment: 'Verily I say unto you, all among them who know their hearts are honest, and are broken, and their spirits contrite, and are *willing* to observe their covenants by sacrifice—yea, every sacrifice which I, the Lord, shall command—they are *accepted* of me' (D&C 97:8; emphasis added). Whatever sacrifice we may be asked to make, the Lord has emphasized that we are to make it with a *willingness* to do so. A sacrifice made unwillingly is not a fulfillment of the Lord's expectation" (Caldwell, "Acceptance of the Lord," 11–12).

Who shall receive the Lord's blessing of "a very fruitful tree . . . by a pure stream"? (97:8–9) "A consecrated life is a beautiful thing. Its strength and serenity are 'as a very fruitful tree which is planted in a goodly land, by a pure stream, that yieldeth much precious fruit' (D&C 97:9). Of particular significance is the influence of a consecrated man or woman upon others, especially those closest and dearest. The consecration of many who have gone before us and others who live among us has helped lay the foundation for our happiness. In like manner future generations will take courage from your consecrated life, acknowledging their debt to you for the possession of all that truly matters" (Christofferson, "Reflections on a Consecrated Life," *Ensign*, Nov. 2010, 19).

Doctrine and Covenants 97:10–17. A House Is to Be Built in Zion in Which the Pure in Heart Will See God

How was tithing understood in 1833? (97:11) "Prior to 8 July 1838 [when the revelation on tithing was received (see Doctrine and Covenants 119)] the term *tithing* included not only one-tenth, but all donations made (D&C 64:23; 85:3; 97:11)" (Clark V. Johnson, "Law of Consecration," 111).

8 Verily I say unto you, all among them who know their hearts are honest, and are broken, and their spirits contrite, and are willing to observe their covenants by sacrifice—yea, every sacrifice which I, the Lord, shall command—they are accepted of me.

9 For I, the Lord, will cause them to bring forth as a very fruitful tree which is planted in a goodly land, by a pure stream, that yieldeth much precious fruit.

10 Verily I say unto you, that it is my will that a house should be built unto me in the land of Zion, like unto the pattern which I have given you.

11 Yea, let it be built speedily, by the tithing of my people.

12 Behold, this is the tithing and the sacrifice which I, the Lord, require at their hands, that there may be a house built unto me for the salvation of Zion—

What was the "house" to be built unto the Lord? (97:12) The house was a temple. "The three uses of *house*, all in section 97, deal specifically with the structure the Saints were commanded to erect [in Zion] at that time" (Cowan, "Doctrine and Covenants on Temples," 26–27).

"When the Lord first revealed the location for the city of Zion, He identified the place for the location of a temple (see D&C 57:1–3). Later, in June 1833, the First Presidency instructed the brethren in Missouri (Zion) to begin immediately to build the first portion of the temple complex (see [Joseph Smith Papers, 'Letter to Church Leaders in Jackson County, Missouri, 25 June 1833,' (1)]). Then, in August of 1833, the Lord reminded the saints that they were to build the temple and that it should be done speedily (see D&C 97:10–11)" (Otten and Caldwell, *Sacred Truths*, 2:160).

13 For a place of thanksgiving for all saints, and for a place of instruction for all those who are called to the work of the ministry in all their several callings and offices;

14 That they may be perfected in the understanding of their ministry, in theory, in principle, and in doctrine, in all things pertaining to the kingdom of God on the earth, the keys of which kingdom have been conferred upon you.

How can the temple become a place of thanksgiving for the Saints? (97:13) "The Lord said that the temple in Missouri was to be "a place of thanksgiving for all saints, and for a place of instruction for all those who are called to the work of the ministry" (D&C 97:13). It was to serve as a meeting place for the school of the elders, where they could be instructed in principles and doctrines pertaining to God's kingdom. This instruction would help prepare those who had been called to do the work of the Lord. Temples today continue to serve as places of thanksgiving, or worship, and instruction for Latter-day Saints" (*Doctrine and Covenants Student Manual* [2018], 537).

15 And inasmuch as my people build a house unto me in the name of the Lord, and do not suffer any unclean thing to come into it, that it be not defiled, my glory shall rest upon it;

16 Yea, and my presence shall be there, for I will come into it, and all the pure in heart that shall come into it shall see God.

What does it mean to be pure in heart? (97:15–16) The Lord counseled His people to be pure in heart as they prepared to build a temple. "It is significant that the Lord, with great emphasis, said, 'for this is Zion—the pure in heart' (D&C 97:21). The phrase *pure in heart* is used several times in the Doctrine and Covenants (D&C 56:18; 97:16, 21; 101:18; 122:2; 124:54; 136:11) and is reminiscent of the famous phrase employed in sermons on two continents, 'Blessed are the pure in heart: for they shall see God' (Matt. 5:8; 3 Ne. 12:8). . . .

"In commenting on Psalm 24:3–4 and Alma 5:19, President Dallin H. Oaks said: 'If we refrain from evil acts, we have clean hands. If we refrain from forbidden thoughts we have pure hearts. Those who would ascend and stand in the ultimate holy place must have both' ["Desires of Our Hearts," 29]" (Brewster, *Doctrine & Covenants Encyclopedia* [2012], 452). ☉

What does it mean to defile? (97:17) As part of their temple preparation, the Lord warned the Missouri Saints that He would not come into a defiled space. To *defile* is "to make unclean; to render foul or dirty; . . . to make impure; . . . to soil or sully; to tarnish; as reputation, etc.; . . . to pollute; to make ceremonially unclean" (Webster, *American Dictionary* [1828], s.v. "defile").

"Until 1891 the President of the Church signed each temple recommend to protect the sanctity of the temple. That responsibility was then delegated to bishops and stake presidents" (Quentin L. Cook, "See Yourself in the Temple," *Ensign*, May 2016, 98).

Doctrine and Covenants 97:18–21. Zion Is the Pure in Heart

In what way will Zion be terrible? (97:18–19) The word *terrible* can also mean "formidable" and to inspire "solemn awe" (Webster, *American Dictionary* [1828], s.v. "terrible"). In a revelation the Prophet received on March 7, 1831, the Lord revealed that in the last days, the wicked would say: "Let us not go up to battle against Zion, for the inhabitants of Zion are terrible, wherefore we cannot stand" (D&C 45:70; see also D&C 115:5–6).

What does the Lord require for His people to become Zion? (97:21) The Lord reminds the Saints in Missouri that Zion "is The Church of Jesus Christ of Latter-day Saints and its members throughout the world, who endeavor to become 'of one heart and one mind, and [dwell] in righteousness' (Moses 7:18)" (Jackson, "Prophecies of the Last Days," 166).

"Zion is a people as much as a place. This principle had recently been reinforced in section 97 . . . where the Lord clearly explained: 'This is Zion—THE PURE IN HEART' (v. 21). We are in bondage to our sins and weaknesses until we allow the Lord to redeem us through our faith, repentance, and covenant faithfulness. In Christ's atoning sacrifice . . . [as] we choose redemption, His sanctifying power brings us out of bondage to the natural man and makes us Zion, the pure in heart" (Lane, "Redemption's Grand Design," 193). ◉

Doctrine and Covenants 97:22–28. Zion Will Escape the Lord's Scourge If She Is Faithful

17 But if it be defiled I will not come into it, and my glory shall not be there; for I will not come into unholy temples.

18 And, now, behold, if Zion do these things she shall prosper, and spread herself and become very glorious, very great, and very terrible.

19 And the nations of the earth shall honor her, and shall say: Surely Zion is the city of our God, and surely Zion cannot fall, neither be moved out of her place, for God is there, and the hand of the Lord is there;

20 And he hath sworn by the power of his might to be her salvation and her high tower.

21 Therefore, verily, thus saith the Lord, let Zion rejoice, for this is Zion—THE PURE IN HEART; therefore, let Zion rejoice, while all the wicked shall mourn.

22 For behold, and lo, vengeance cometh speedily upon the ungodly as the whirlwind; and who shall escape it?

23 The Lord's scourge shall pass over by night and by day, and the report thereof shall vex all people; yea, it shall not be stayed until the Lord come;

24 For the indignation of the Lord is kindled against their abominations and all their wicked works.

25 Nevertheless, Zion shall escape if she observe to do all things whatsoever I have commanded her.

26 But if she observe not to do whatsoever I have commanded her, I will visit her according to all her works, with sore affliction, with pestilence, with plague, with sword, with vengeance, with devouring fire.

27 Nevertheless, let it be read this once to her ears, that I, the Lord, have accepted of her offering; and if she sin no more none of these things shall come upon her;

28 And I will bless her with blessings, and multiply a multiplicity of blessings upon her, and upon her generations forever and ever, saith the Lord your God. Amen.

What is the Lord's scourge? (97:23) The Lord promised Zion that He had the power to scourge her enemies. "One definition of a *scourge* is a whip used to flog and inflict great pain upon individuals. From time to time the Lord uses a scourge (meaning, the Lord punishes or afflicts) to whip earth's inhabitants on account of their wickedness. . . .

"The Lord has decreed one or more great scourges for the last days, scourges that will cleanse the world. Four separate passages from the Doctrine and Covenants speak of such latter-day scourges (D&C 5:19; 45:30; 84:96; 97:23), named 'a desolating scourge' or 'an overflowing scourge' (D&C 5:19; 45:31). These passages inform us that the scourge will come because of wicked works" (Parry and Parry, *Understanding the Signs of the Times*, 347).

What were the Saints promised for being obedient? (97:25) "Obedience is the basis upon which all blessings are received. The saints in Missouri were promised that they would prosper, become great, and not be moved out of their place if they would be obedient unto that which the Lord required of them in this revelation. . . . The principle of obedience is stressed by the Lord in this revelation. The key to Zion's future, salvation, and prosperity was and is this first law of heaven. When saints are obedient in erecting and properly using temples of the Lord, they have the assurance of having the power of the Lord in their midst" (Otten and Caldwell, *Sacred Truths*, 2:161).

What lesson can we learn from these prophetic warnings? (97:26) The Prophet Joseph Smith taught: "If Zion, will not purify herself so as to be approved of in all things in his sight he will seek—another people for his work will go on until Israel is gathered & they who will not hear his voice must expect to feel his wrath, Let me say to you, seek to purify yourselves, & also all the inhabitants of Zion lest the Lords anger be kindled to fierceness, repent, repent, is the voice of God, to Zion, & yet strange as it may appear, yet it is true mankind will persist in self-justification until all their iniquity is exposed & their character past being redeemed, & that which is treasured up in their hearts be exposed to the gaze of mankind, I say to you—(& what I say to you, I say to all) hear the warning voice of God lest Zion fall, & the Lord swear in his wrath the inhabitants of Zion shall not enter into my rest" (Joseph Smith Papers, "Letter to William W. Phelps, 11 January 1833," 19; spelling modernized).

Introduction to Doctrine and Covenants 98

Joseph Smith received Doctrine and Covenants 98, August 6, 1833, as he became more aware of the persecution inflicted upon the Missouri Saints.

"By the summer of 1833, it is estimated that more than 1,200 Church members had settled in Missouri.... This growing population of Latter-day Saints, or Mormons, became a great concern to the original settlers of Jackson County because of the significant cultural, political, and religious differences between the two groups, which led to misunderstanding and conflict" (*Doctrine and Covenants Student Manual* [2018], 542).

"In particular, the Mormons were accused of encouraging insubordination among Missouri slaves. William W. Phelps, editor of the church's newspaper, *The Evening and the Morning Star,* published an article in July 1833 that opponents trumpeted as proof that Mormons intended to encourage free people of color to move to Missouri. The idea that Mormons were undermining delicate master-slave relations in Missouri, on top of the general irritation over the growing Mormon political and economic presence, brought matters to a decisive head" (*Joseph Smith Papers,* Introduction to *Documents, Volume 3*).

The editorial noted above, by William W. Phelps, "created significant tension, and days later, approximately 300 citizens signed a document calling for all Mormons to leave Jackson County. On July 20, 1833, a committee representing these citizens presented Church leaders in Jackson County with their list of demands and ordered that they respond within 15 minutes. When Church leaders refused to comply with the group's demands, a hostile crowd in the city of Independence proceeded to destroy the Church's print shop where the Book of Commandments was being produced....

"Three days later, on July 23, 1833, a mob of about 500 residents threatened further violence against Church members living in Jackson County. Six Church leaders '"offered themselves as a ransom [to the mob] for the church, willing to be scourged or die, if that [would] appease their anger toward the church"' ... but the mob declared that all church members must leave or die' ([*Joseph Smith Papers: Documents, Volume 3,* 187]). Under this threat of violence, Church leaders signed an agreement pledging that Church leaders and half of the members of the Church would leave Jackson County by January 1, 1834, with the rest leaving by April 1, 1834" (*Doctrine and Covenants Student Manual* [2018], 542).

Joseph Smith "dictated this 6 August 1833 revelation, which encouraged peace amid escalating violence, approximately two weeks after a church leader [Bishop Edward Partridge] and another member [Charles Allen] were tarred and feathered and the church printing office was destroyed in Jackson County, Missouri. Though he may have known about increasing tensions in Missouri, at this time [the Prophet] had no knowledge of these specific events" (Joseph Smith Papers, Historical Introduction to "Revelation, 6 August 1833 [D&C 98]").

SECTION 98

Revelation given through Joseph Smith the Prophet, at Kirtland, Ohio, August 6, 1833. This revelation came in consequence of the persecution upon the Saints in Missouri. Increased settlement of Church members in Missouri troubled some other settlers, who felt threatened by the Saints' numbers, political and economic influence, and cultural and religious differences. In July 1833, a mob destroyed Church property, tarred and feathered two Church members, and demanded that the Saints leave Jackson County. Although some news of the problems in Missouri had no doubt reached the Prophet in Kirtland (nine hundred miles away), the seriousness of the situation could have been known to him at this date only by revelation.

1 Verily I say unto you my friends, fear not, let your hearts be comforted; yea, rejoice evermore, and in everything give thanks;

2 Waiting patiently on the Lord, for your prayers have entered into the ears of the Lord of Sabaoth, and are recorded with this seal and testament—the Lord hath sworn and decreed that they shall be granted.

3 Therefore, he giveth this promise unto you, with an immutable covenant that they shall be fulfilled; and all things wherewith you have been afflicted shall work together for your good, and to my name's glory, saith the Lord.

Doctrine and Covenants 98:1–3. The Afflictions of the Saints Will Be for Their Good

Why are we charged to give thanks in times of affliction? (98:1–3) "When we give thanks in all things, we see hardships and adversities in the context of the purpose of life. We are sent here to be tested. There must be opposition in *all* things. We are meant to learn and grow through that opposition, through meeting our challenges, and through teaching others to do the same. Our beloved colleague Elder Neal A. Maxwell has given us a noble example of this. His courage, his submissive attitude in accepting his affliction with cancer, and his stalwart continued service have ministered comfort to thousands and taught eternal principles to millions. His example shows that the Lord will not only consecrate our afflictions for our gain, but He will use them to bless the lives of countless others" (Oaks, "Give Thanks in All Things," *Ensign*, May 2003, 97–98).

Why does this revelation caution the Saints in Missouri to wait patiently on the Lord? (98:2) "Bishop Edward Partridge had been tarred and feathered, the Church's press destroyed, and the Saints given an ultimatum to leave Jackson County or face continued oppression....

"Foreseeing the Saints' emotional reactions to the violence, in Doctrine and Covenants 98 the Lord

Why Did Missourians Persecute the Saints in Jackson County? (Doctrine and Covenants 98:1)

"In July 1833 the tension manifested itself in public meetings, accusations, and then violence toward the Saints. The consensus of the old settlers was stated in five areas which they envisioned as the cause of conflict:

"(1) The Mormon people had a peculiar religion, which made them stand aloof from all other people in the county, as they did not participate in the contemporary community life....

"(2) The Saints were accused of interfering with the settlers' black slaves, making them discontented by preaching a strange gospel to them.

"(3) The cultural mores of the Saints were not in harmony with those of the earlier inhabitants of the county, which were essentially Yankee in origin. The old settlers were mostly of southern backgrounds, with their roots in the slave culture.

"(4) The Mormons presented a political threat to the old settlers. Already 1200 of the 3500 inhabitants of the county were adherents of the new religion. More continued to arrive each month and it was openly boasted that thousands more were coming to settle in the county....

"(5) Economically the Mormons were a detriment to the city and county. They did not purchase goods from the local merchants, as they had no money, but traded among themselves at the Church storehouse....

"In July a meeting at Independence, attended by about five hundred Missourians, drew up these demands: (1) No additional Mormons were to settle in Jackson County. (2) Those then resident in the county were to sell their property as soon as they could and leave the vicinity. (3) The periodical, *The Evening and the Morning Star*, must cease publication. (4) All Mormon shops and the storehouse were to close as soon as possible" (Lyon, "Independence, Missouri, and the Mormons," 17, 18; paragraphing altered).

prescribes 'be comforted,' 'rejoice,' 'give thanks' and wait [for the Lord] to answer their prayers, for he has sworn to do so (vv. 1–2). This is his covenant with them. He promises that 'all things wherewith you have been afflicted shall work together for your good, and to my name's glory' (v. 3)" (Harper, *Making Sense of the Doctrine & Covenants*, 360). ⊕

How do afflictions work for the good of the individual? (98:3) Sister Susan W. Tanner stated: "The Lord has promised us that He will not forget us because He has 'graven [us] upon the palms of [His] hands' (Isa. 49:16). And our promise to Him is that we will not forget Him, for we have engraven Him in our hearts.

"The early Saints were taught this in their sufferings in Missouri. The Lord counseled them to wait 'patiently on the Lord, for your prayers have entered into the ears of the Lord. . . .

"'Therefore, he giveth this promise unto you, with an immutable covenant that they shall be fulfilled; and all things wherewith you have been afflicted shall work together for your good' (D&C 98:2–3). This promise didn't remove their trials, but it did comfort them, giving them hope for the future" ("Steadfast in our Covenants," *Ensign*, May 2003, 101). ⊕

Doctrine and Covenants 98:4–8. The Saints Are to Befriend the Constitutional Law of the Land

How did Joseph Smith feel about the Constitution of the United States? (98:4–6) The Prophet Joseph Smith said: "I am the greatest advocate of the Constitution of the United States there is on the earth. In my feelings I am always ready to die for the protection of the weak and oppressed in their just rights" (Joseph Smith Papers, "History, 1838–1856, volume E-1," 1754).

Why are the Saints commanded to befriend the law even if others ignored the law? (98:4–8) Joseph Smith "counseled the Saints to be patient, rebuild the printing office and store, and seek legal ways to recover their losses. . . .

"Although mob leaders had threatened to harm the Saints if they tried to seek compensation for their losses, [Bishop Edward Partridge] collected accounts of the abuses the Saints had endured that summer and sent them to Missouri's governor, Daniel Dunklin. . . .

"'Ours is a government of laws,' [Dunklin] told them. If the court system in Jackson County failed to execute the law peacefully, the Saints could notify him and he would step in to help. . . .

4 And now, verily I say unto you concerning the laws of the land, it is my will that my people should observe to do all things whatsoever I command them.

5 And that law of the land which is constitutional, supporting that principle of freedom in maintaining rights and privileges, belongs to all mankind, and is justifiable before me.

6 Therefore, I, the Lord, justify you, and your brethren of my church, in befriending that law which is the constitutional law of the land;

7 And as pertaining to law of man, whatsoever is more or less than this, cometh of evil.

8 I, the Lord God, make you free, therefore ye are free indeed; and the law also maketh you free.

"The governor's letter gave . . . the Saints hope. They began to rebuild their community, and Edward and other church leaders in Zion hired lawyers from a neighboring county to take their case" (*Saints*, 1:185, 186).

How and why are Latter-day Saints to uphold the constitutional law of the land? (98:6–8) President Dallin H. Oaks stated: "Our belief in divine inspiration gives Latter-day Saints a unique responsibility to uphold and defend the United States Constitution and principles of constitutionalism wherever we live. We should trust in the Lord and be positive about this nation's future.

"What else are faithful Latter-day Saints to do? We must pray for the Lord to guide and bless all nations and their leaders. This is part of our article of faith. Being subject to presidents or rulers of course poses no obstacle to our opposing individual laws or policies. It does require that we exercise our influence civilly and peacefully within the framework of our constitutions and applicable laws. On contested issues, we should seek to moderate and unify" ("Defending Our Divinely Inspired Constitution," *Liahona*, May 2021, 107). See also commentary in this volume on Doctrine and Covenants 101:80. ❂

How are the Saints to respond to laws of men that are not in accordance with the Constitution? (98:7) "Pending the overruling by Providence in favor of religious liberty, it is the duty of the saints to submit themselves to the laws of their country. Nevertheless, they should use every proper method, as citizens or subjects of their several governments, to secure for themselves and for all men the boon of freedom in religious service. It is not required of them to suffer without protest imposition by lawless persecutors, or through the operation of unjust laws; but their protests should be offered in legal and proper order" (Talmage, *Articles of Faith*, 383).

How does freedom come from God and the law? (98:8) "Without freedom there can be no salvation. To compel choice is to deny choice. Agency, which is the power to act on choices that have been freely made, was the gift of God to each of his spirit children at the time of their spirit birth (Moses 4:3) and is the God-given right of every soul born into this world (2 Nephi 2:26–27). It can be set down as an eternal principle that that which enhances the freedom of choice comes from God. . . .

"Every law that has come from God and every wise and just law found in the governments of men has been established to preserve and protect the freedom of those for whom it was given" (McConkie and Ostler, *Revelations of the Restoration*, 709–10).

Doctrine and Covenants 98:9–10. Honest, Wise, and Good Men Should Be Supported for Secular Government

How can we keep wicked people from ruling? (98:9) President Ezra Taft Benson explained: "Righteousness is an indispensable ingredient to liberty. Virtuous people elect wise and good representatives. Good representatives make good laws and then wisely administer them. This tends to preserve righteousness. An unvirtuous citizenry tend to elect representatives who will pander to their covetous lustings. The burden of self-government is a great responsibility. It calls for restraint, righteousness, responsibility, and reliance upon God. It is a truism from the Lord that 'when the wicked rule the people mourn' (D&C 98:9)" ("Constitution," *Ensign*, May 1976, 93).

What are some considerations when seeking to elect wise men and women? (98:10) "There are many political issues, and no party, platform, or individual candidate can satisfy all personal preferences. Each citizen must therefore decide which issues are most important to him or her at any particular time. Then members should seek inspiration on how to exercise their influence according to their individual priorities. This process will not be easy. It may require changing party support or candidate choices, even from election to election.

"Such independent actions will sometimes require voters to support candidates or political parties or platforms whose other positions they cannot approve.... We teach correct principles and leave our members to choose how to prioritize and apply those principles on the issues presented from time to time. We also insist, and we ask our local leaders to insist, that political choices and affiliations not be the subject of teachings or advocacy in any of our Church meetings" (Oaks, "Defending Our Divinely Inspired Constitution," *Liahona*, May 2021, 108).

9 Nevertheless, when the wicked rule the people mourn.

10 Wherefore, honest men and wise men should be sought for diligently, and good men and wise men ye should observe to uphold; otherwise whatsoever is less than these cometh of evil.

11 And I give unto you a commandment, that ye shall forsake all evil and cleave unto all good, that ye shall live by every word which proceedeth forth out of the mouth of God.

12 For he will give unto the faithful line upon line, precept upon precept; and I will try you and prove you herewith.

13 And whoso layeth down his life in my cause, for my name's sake, shall find it again, even life eternal.

14 Therefore, be not afraid of your enemies, for I have decreed in my heart, saith the Lord, that I will prove you in all things, whether you will abide in my covenant, even unto death, that you may be found worthy.

15 For if ye will not abide in my covenant ye are not worthy of me.

Doctrine and Covenants 98:11–15. Those Who Lay down Their Lives in the Lord's Cause Will Have Eternal Life

What does it mean to "forsake all evil and cleave unto all good"? (98:11–15) "*All* evil includes everything that is contrary to the will of God and detrimental to the advancement of His children in holiness before Him. The Saints must forsake not only the sins and crimes common in the world, but a great many evils which are not recognized by the world as evils. Evil companionship, evil amusements, evil aspirations for worldly power and honor, evil conversation, evil thoughts, and evil sentiments are all included. *All* good includes all that is in harmony with the will of God, no matter whence it comes. Saints cannot be clannish or partisan. They must be cosmopolitans, for there is some good everywhere for them to recognize and to cleave to" (Smith and Sjodahl, *Doctrine and Covenants Commentary*, 619).

What are some reasons the Lord tests or "proves" us? (98:12) "The test a loving God has set before us is not to see if we can endure difficulty. It is to see if we can endure it well. We pass the test by showing that we remembered Him and the commandments He gave us. And to endure well is to keep those commandments whatever the opposition, whatever the temptation, and whatever the tumult around us" (Eyring, "In the Strength of the Lord," *Ensign*, May 2004, 17).

What blessings do faithful martyrs for the gospel receive? (98:13–14) "Man is that he might have joy (2 Ne. 2:25), but that fulness of joy is not to be found in this world (D&C 101:35–38), for we sometimes have to suffer as Christ did (Rom. 8:16–18; 1 Pet. 1:6–7 . . .). Eventually, however, we will receive eternal joy for our suffering (D&C 109:76). Those who resist temptation, and endure trials and sufferings while remaining faithful stewards, shall eventually inherit eternal life and 'shall enter into the joy of the Lord' (D&C 51:19). Joseph Smith summarized this by saying that 'those who have died in Jesus Christ may expect to enter into all the fruitions of joy when they come forth, which they possessed or anticipated here' ([Joseph Smith Papers, 'History, 1838–1856, volume D-1,' 1534])" (Garrard, "Origin and Destiny of Man," 376n21).

What might it mean to be proven by the Lord? (98:14) "Tests in the school of mortality are a vital element of our eternal progression. Interestingly, however, the word *test* is not found even one time in the scriptural text of the standard works in English. Rather, words such as *prove, examine,* and *try* are used to describe various patterns of demonstrating appropriately our spiritual knowledge about, understanding of, and devotion to our Heavenly Father's eternal plan of happiness and our capacity to seek for the blessings of the Savior's Atonement.

"He who authored the plan of salvation described the very purpose of our mortal probation using the words *prove, examine,* and *try* in ancient and modern scripture" (Bednar, "We Will Prove Them Herewith," *Ensign,* Nov. 2020, 8).

Doctrine and Covenants 98:16–18. Renounce War and Proclaim Peace

Why are Latter-day Saints to renounce war and proclaim peace? (98:16–18) "Now, as members of The Church of Jesus Christ of Latter-day Saints, what does the Lord expect of us? As a Church, we must 'renounce war and proclaim peace' [D&C 98:16]. As individuals, we should 'follow after the things which make for peace' [Rom. 14:19]. We should be personal peacemakers. We should live peacefully—as couples, families, and neighbors. We should live by the Golden Rule. We have writings of the descendants of Judah as now merged with writings of the descendants of Ephraim. We should employ them and expand our circle of love to embrace the whole human family. We should bring divine love and revealed doctrines of restored religion to our neighbors and friends. We should serve them according to our abilities and opportunities. We should keep our principles on a high level and stand for the right. We should continue

16 Therefore, renounce war and proclaim peace, and seek diligently to turn the hearts of the children to their fathers, and the hearts of the fathers to the children;

17 And again, the hearts of the Jews unto the prophets, and the prophets unto the Jews; lest I come and smite the whole earth with a curse, and all flesh be consumed before me.

18 Let not your hearts be troubled; for in my Father's house are many mansions, and I have prepared a place for you; and where my Father and I am, there ye shall be also.

The Lord's Instructions Regarding Entering War (Doctrine and Covenants 98:16)

"Christ's Church should not make war, for the Lord is a Lord of peace. He has said to us in this dispensation, 'therefore, renounce war and proclaim peace' (D&C 98:16). Thus the Church is and must be against war. The Church itself cannot wage war, unless and until the Lord shall issue new commands. It cannot regard war as a righteous means of settling international disputes; these should and could be settled—the nations agreeing—by peaceful negotiation and adjustment" (*Messages of the First Presidency,* 6:158).

"There are, however, two conditions which may justify a truly Christian man to enter—mind you, I say *enter, not begin*—a war: (1) An attempt to dominate and to deprive another of his free agency, and, (2) Loyalty to his country. Possibly there is a third, viz., defense of a weak nation that is being unjustly crushed by a strong, ruthless one. . . .

"Paramount among these reasons, of course, is the defense of man's freedom. An attempt to rob man of his free agency caused dissension even in Heaven. . . .

"The greatest responsibility of the state is to guard the lives, and to protect the property and rights of its citizens; and if the state is obligated to protect them from lawlessness within its boundaries, it is equally obligated to protect them from lawless encroachments from without—whether the attacking criminals be individuals or nations" (McKay, in Conference Report, Apr. 1942, 72, 73).

to gather scattered Israel from the four corners of the earth and offer the ordinances and covenants that seal families together forever. These blessings we are to bring to people of all nations" (Nelson, "'Blessed Are the Peacemakers,'" *Ensign*, Nov. 2002, 41). See also commentary in this volume on Doctrine and Covenants 105:38–40. ⊕

What did the Lord mean when He spoke of "many mansions"? (98:18) "Joseph Smith said the meaning of Jesus' statement is: 'In my Father's kingdom are many kingdoms'" (Joseph Smith Papers, "Discourse, 12 May 1844, as Reported by Thomas Bullock," [2]).

"From modern revelation we know that the ultimate destiny of all who live on the earth is not the inadequate idea of heaven for the righteous and the eternal sufferings of hell for the rest. God's loving plan for His children includes this reality taught by our Savior, Jesus Christ: 'In my Father's house are many mansions' [John 14:2].

"The revealed doctrine of the restored Church of Jesus Christ of Latter-day Saints teaches that *all the children of God*—with exceptions too limited to consider here—will ultimately inherit one of three kingdoms of glory, even the least of which 'surpasses all understanding' [D&C 76:89]. After a period in which the disobedient suffer for their sins, which suffering prepares them for what is to follow, all will be resurrected and proceed to the Final Judgment of the Lord Jesus Christ. There, our loving Savior, who, we are taught, 'glorifies the Father, and saves all the works of his hands' [D&C 76:43], will send all the children of God to one of these kingdoms of glory according to the desires manifested through their choices" (Oaks, "Kingdoms of Glory," *Liahona*, Nov. 2023, 26).

Doctrine and Covenants 98:19–22. The Saints in Kirtland Are Reproved and Commanded to Repent

Why was the Lord displeased with many in Kirtland at this time? (98:19–22) "The saints [in Jackson County] desired to live in peace. They had not harmed their neighbors. They had possessed their homes legally by purchase, but their God-given and constitutional rights were denied them. While this persecution was going on, and it came upon them in part by the disobedience of some members of the Church, the Lord felt the need of administering a severe rebuke to some of the inhabitants of Kirtland. They were reminded that they had among them some who were guilty of evil ways, pride of heart,

19 Behold, I, the Lord, am not well pleased with many who are in the church at Kirtland;

20 For they do not forsake their sins, and their wicked ways, the pride of their hearts, and their covetousness, and all their detestable things, and observe the words of wisdom and eternal life which I have given unto them.

21 Verily I say unto you, that I, the Lord, will chasten them and will do whatsoever

and covetousness, and that there also awaited them a chastening if they did not repent" (Joseph Fielding Smith, *Church History and Modern Revelation*, 1:434).

In what ways does obedience to God protect us from the gates of hell? (98:22) "Our safety lies in repentance. Our strength comes of obedience to the commandments of God.

"Let us be prayerful. Let us pray for righteousness. Let us pray for the forces of good. Let us reach out to help men and women of goodwill, whatever their religious persuasion and wherever they live. Let us stand firm against evil, both at home and abroad. Let us live worthy of the blessings of heaven, reforming our lives where necessary and looking to Him, the Father of us all. He has said, 'Be still, and know that I am God' (Ps. 46:10)" (Hinckley, "Times in Which We Live," *Ensign*, Nov. 2001, 74).

Doctrine and Covenants 98:23–32. The Lord Reveals His Laws Governing the Persecutions and Afflictions Imposed on His People

What is the Lord's law on retaliation? (98:23–30) "The Missouri exiles needed answers for their normal and human questions about whether or not to retaliate against their enemies. The Lord's answers included principles that could refine them into a celestial people. At one point, he bluntly taught them that if they and their families did not bear their smitings patiently, their impatience itself would render their smitings just (D&C 98:24)! The Lord's laws of retaliation, war, and revenge in section 98 were ultimately laws of mercy, peace, and reconciliation. While allowing for justice, they encouraged forebearance, kindness, and love" (Cloward, "Counsel to the Exiles," 383).

I list, if they do not repent and observe all things whatsoever I have said unto them.

22 And again I say unto you, if ye observe to do whatsoever I command you, I, the Lord, will turn away all wrath and indignation from you, and the gates of hell shall not prevail against you.

23 Now, I speak unto you concerning your families—if men will smite you, or your families, once, and ye bear it patiently and revile not against them, neither seek revenge, ye shall be rewarded;

24 But if ye bear it not patiently, it shall be accounted unto you as being meted out as a just measure unto you.

25 And again, if your enemy shall smite you the second time, and you revile not against your enemy, and bear it patiently, your reward shall be an hundred-fold.

26 And again, if he shall smite you the third time, and ye bear it patiently, your reward shall be doubled unto you four-fold;

27 And these three testimonies shall stand against your enemy if he repent not, and shall not be blotted out.

28 And now, verily I say unto you, if that enemy shall escape my vengeance, that he be not brought into judgment before me, then ye shall see to it that ye warn him in my name,

that he come no more upon you, neither upon your family, even your children's children unto the third and fourth generation.

29 And then, if he shall come upon you or your children, or your children's children unto the third and fourth generation, I have delivered thine enemy into thine hands;

30 And then if thou wilt spare him, thou shalt be rewarded for thy righteousness; and also thy children and thy children's children unto the third and fourth generation.

31 Nevertheless, thine enemy is in thine hands; and if thou rewardest him according to his works thou art justified; if he has sought thy life, and thy life is endangered by him, thine enemy is in thine hands and thou art justified.

32 Behold, this is the law I gave unto my servant Nephi, and thy fathers, Joseph, and Jacob, and Isaac, and Abraham, and all mine ancient prophets and apostles.

33 And again, this is the law that I gave unto mine ancients, that they should not go out unto battle against any nation, kindred, tongue, or people, save I, the Lord, commanded them.

34 And if any nation, tongue, or people should proclaim war against them, they should first lift a standard of peace unto that people, nation, or tongue;

35 And if that people did not accept the offering of peace, neither the second nor the third time, they should bring these testimonies before the Lord;

How does the Book of Mormon align with the Lord's direction in this dispensation? (98:32) "The Book of Mormon provides us with a concept of war that is consistent with the counsel given in Section 98. [Captain] Moroni, who lived in the first century before Christ, is described as a man of perfect understanding, a true believer in liberty, and one who did not delight in bloodshed. The Nephites at that time followed this instruction: [see Alma 48:14–16]" (Roy W. Doxey, *Doctrine and Covenants Speaks*, 2:224).

Doctrine and Covenants 98:33–38. War Is Justified Only When the Lord Commands It

What might justify acts of war? (98:33–38) "The Lord's law of just war includes the commandment that his people 'should not go out unto battle against any nation, kindred, tongue, or people, save I, the Lord, commanded them' (v. 33). When an enemy declares war, the Saints 'should first lift a standard of peace' (v. 34). If that gesture is rejected three times, the Saints should testify to the Lord of their good faith efforts. 'Then I, the Lord, would give unto them a commandment, and justify them in going out to battle against that nation,' and then the Lord would be on the Saints' side (v. 36)" (Harper, *Making Sense of the Doctrine & Covenants*, 361).

36 Then I, the Lord, would give unto them a commandment, and justify them in going out to battle against that nation, tongue, or people.

37 And I, the Lord, would fight their battles, and their children's battles, and their children's children's, until they had avenged themselves on all their enemies, to the third and fourth generation.

38 Behold, this is an ensample unto all people, saith the Lord your God, for justification before me.

For whom is the Lord willing to fight battles? (98:37) "Now, how does the Lord *feel* about people who will let God prevail? Nephi summed it up well: '[The Lord] *loveth* those who will have him to be their God. Behold, he loved our fathers, and he covenanted with them, yea, even Abraham, Isaac, and Jacob; and he remember[s] the covenants which he [has] made' [1 Nephi 17:40; emphasis added].

"And what is the Lord willing to *do* for Israel? The Lord has pledged that He will 'fight [our] battles, and [our] children's battles, and our children's children's [battles] . . . to the third and fourth generation' [D&C 98:37; see also Psalm 31:23; Isaiah 49:25; D&C 105:14]" (Nelson, "Let God Prevail," *Ensign*, Nov. 2020, 95).

Doctrine and Covenants 98:39–48. The Saints Are to Forgive Their Enemies, Who, If They Repent, Will Also Escape the Lord's Vengeance

What insights do these verses add to the doctrine of forgiveness? (98:39–48) "Verses 39–48 deal with matters of individual forgiveness. Many people are confused by what they consider to be conflicting instructions in scripture on the topic of forgiveness. On the one hand, the Savior says to forgive 'seventy times seven' (Matthew 18:22) and 'of you it is required to forgive all men' (D&C 64:10). On the other hand, verses 39–48 seem to limit forgiveness to 'three strikes and you're out.'

"The crucial distinction that allows us to resolve the apparent conflict is whether the offender in a given instance is repentant or not. If he or she is repentant and asks for our forgiveness, then we, as true children of a merciful Father in Heaven, must grant mercy and forgiveness even as we hope to be forgiven" (Robinson and Garrett, *Commentary on the Doctrine and Covenants*, 3:245). ⊙

39 And again, verily I say unto you, if after thine enemy has come upon thee the first time, he repent and come unto thee praying thy forgiveness, thou shalt forgive him, and shalt hold it no more as a testimony against thine enemy—

40 And so on unto the second and third time; and as oft as thine enemy repenteth of the trespass wherewith he has trespassed against thee, thou shalt forgive him, until seventy times seven.

41 And if he trespass against thee and repent not the first time, nevertheless thou shalt forgive him.

42 And if he trespass against thee the second time, and repent not, nevertheless thou shalt forgive him.

43 And if he trespass against thee the third time, and repent not, thou shalt also forgive him.

44 But if he trespass against thee the fourth time thou shalt not forgive him, but shalt bring these testimonies before the Lord; and they shall not be blotted out until he repent and reward thee four-fold in all things wherewith he has trespassed against thee.

45 And if he do this, thou shalt forgive him with all thine heart; and if he do not this, I, the Lord, will avenge thee of thine enemy an hundred-fold;

46 And upon his children, and upon his children's children of all them that hate me, unto the third and fourth generation.

47 But if the children shall repent, or the children's children, and turn to the Lord their God, with all their hearts and with all their might, mind, and strength, and restore four-fold for all their trespasses wherewith they have trespassed, or wherewith their fathers have trespassed, or their fathers' fathers, then thine indignation shall be turned away;

48 And vengeance shall no more come upon them, saith the Lord thy God, and their trespasses shall never be brought any more as a testimony before the Lord against them. Amen.

Introduction to Doctrine and Covenants 99

On August 29, 1832, at Hiram, Ohio, the Prophet Joseph Smith "dictated this revelation calling John Murdock on a preaching mission to the 'eastern countries.' Following his conversion and baptism in Kirtland, Ohio, on 30 November 1830, Murdock spent much time as a traveling missionary, baptizing around seventy people in four months.... In June 1831, a revelation instructed him to go to Missouri, 'preaching the word by the way' [D&C 52:8–9]. Murdock followed this instruction and departed for Missouri, despite the recent death of his wife, Julia Clapp Murdock, during childbirth, which left him with five children under the age of seven, including newborn twins. Before leaving, he arranged for several individuals to watch over his older children; Joseph Smith and Emma Smith adopted the twins....

"[Section 99 instructed John Murdock] to resume his preaching, this time in the eastern United States.... This revelation's call for Murdock to continue as a missionary until his death, notwithstanding his family responsibilities, was an unusual sacrifice apparently not expected of other early church members and may have resulted from his earlier determination to devote himself 'full time to the ministry.' ... Murdock then left on his mission on 24 September 1832" (Joseph Smith Papers, Historical Introduction to "Revelation, 29 August 1832 [D&C 99]").

SECTION 99

Revelation given through Joseph Smith the Prophet to John Murdock, August 29, 1832, at Hiram, Ohio. For over a year, John Murdock had been preaching the gospel while his children—motherless after the death of his wife, Julia Clapp, in April 1831—resided with other families in Ohio.

Doctrine and Covenants 99:1–8. John Murdock Is Called to Proclaim the Gospel, and Those Who Receive Him Receive the Lord and Will Obtain Mercy

1 Behold, thus saith the Lord unto my servant John Murdock—thou art called to go into the eastern countries from house to house, from village to village, and from city to city, to proclaim mine everlasting gospel unto the inhabitants thereof, in the midst of persecution and wickedness.

2 And who receiveth you receiveth me; and you shall have power to declare my word in the demonstration of my Holy Spirit.

3 And who receiveth you as a little child, receiveth my kingdom; and blessed are they, for they shall obtain mercy.

Why are we to receive missionaries as servants of the Lord? (99:2) "Missionaries are sent forth to proclaim the new and everlasting gospel 'from house to house ... and from city to city' (D&C 99:1). They are called to serve as the Lord's representatives and function as his agents in the work of the kingdom. The Lord has always worked through his authorized representatives, stating 'whether by mine own voice or by the voice of my servant, it is the same' (D&C 1:38). We, too, are called to share the gospel truth with others, by example and precept. When the humble and honest in heart embrace the message of the Restoration, as presented by representatives of the Lord, and enter into a covenant relationship with Christ, they are blessed beyond measure" (Millet and Newell, *Draw Near unto Me*, 279).

How do we declare the Lord's words "in the demonstration of [His] Holy Spirit"? (99:2–3) "When the Twelve or any other witnesses stand before the Congregations of the earth and they preach in the power and demonstration of the Spirit of God and the people are astonished and confounded at the Doctrine and say that man has preached a powerful discourse, a great sermon, then let that man or those men take care that they do not ascribe the glory unto themselves, but be careful that they are humble and ascribe the praise and glory to God and the Lamb for it is by the Power of the Holy Priesthood and Holy Ghost they have power thus to speak. What art thou O man but dust and from whom dost thou receive thy power and Blessings but from God" (Joseph Smith Papers, "History, 1838–1856, volume C-1," 10 [addenda]). ➌

4 And whoso rejecteth you shall be rejected of my Father and his house; and you shall cleanse your feet in the secret places by the way for a testimony against them.

What is the act of "cleansing the feet"? (99:4) "The act of cleansing the feet as a testimony against those who reject the servants of the Lord is an ordinance of cursing and is not just a demonstration that a witness of the truth has been given and has been rejected. Through this cleansing ordinance, those who rejected the truth are on their own, and those who preached the gospel to them are no longer responsible for them before the Lord (see D&C 88:81–82). It is apparent in this and other scriptures . . . that this ordinance

John Murdock's Life and His Vision of Jesus Christ (Doctrine and Covenants 99:1)

"The name of John Murdock surfaces in two revelations, once in section 52 when he is called to accompany Hyrum Smith to Missouri by way of Detroit (D&C 52:8), and again in section 99, which is given in total to Murdock. This latter revelation called him on a mission to the east.

"Murdock's name is intertwined with that of Joseph Smith, for it was his two motherless twins who were adopted by the Prophet and his wife Emma. The twins, Joseph S. and Julia, were born the same day that Emma gave birth to twins who lived but three hours, dying the same day that Sister Murdock passed away. The infant Joseph S. died some eleven months later as a result of the exposure he suffered the night his adopted father—the Prophet—was dragged from his home and brutally beaten, tarred, and feathered. As a result of this death

John Murdock

in March 1832, the *Millennial Star* of March 18, 1889, referred to the toddler as 'the first martyr of this dispensation'" (Brewster, *Doctrine & Covenants Encyclopedia* [2012], 378).

"During the winter of 1832–33 John received a glorious vision of the Savior: 'I saw the form of a man, most lovely, the visage of his face was sound and fair as the sun. His hair a bright silver grey, curled in most majestic form, His eyes a keen penetrating blue, and the skin of his neck a most beautiful white and he was covered from the neck to the feet with a loose garment, pure white, whiter than any garment I have ever before seen. His countenance was most penetrating, and yet most lovely'" (Black, *Who's Who*, 202).

"He traveled to Missouri as a member of Zion's Camp in 1834. John served in the Church on high councils in Far West and Salt Lake City and presided as bishop both in Nauvoo and in the Salt Lake Fourteenth Ward. He also presided over a mission in Australia in 1851. Upon returning home to Lehi, Utah, he was ordained a patriarch. He died 23 December 1871 in Beaver, Utah, having been a faithful member of the Church since his baptism" (Ostler, "Murdock, John," 804).

is to be performed only when the Lord expressly commands it (see also D&C 75:20–22)" (*Doctrine and Covenants Student Manual* [2001], 50). See also commentary in this volume on Doctrine and Covenants 24:15 and 75:20.

What might be "the volume of the book" that recorded the ungodly deeds referred to in this verse? (99:5) "'The book' referred to here could be the book of Enoch, which is the source of the quotation cited, the New Testament book of Jude, in which the quotation appears (1:14–15), or the Bible itself, which contains the book of Jude" (Robinson and Garrett, *Commentary on the Doctrine and Covenants*, 3:250).

How was the Lord's counsel to John Murdock later fulfilled? (99:6–7) John Murdock "was permitted to postpone his departure for the mission, until his motherless children had been sent to Zion [where Bishop Edward Partridge arranged for their care with other families]. . . .

"John Murdock was a member of Zion's camp, and made the journey to Zion in that choice company of men. In 1834, he was appointed a member of the High Council in Clay County, and in 1837, of the High Council in Far West. In 1838, he and George M. Hinckle, as trustees for the Church, purchased a townsite at De Witt, on the Missouri River, and in 1842, he was appointed Bishop of the Nauvoo Fifth Ward" (Smith and Sjodahl, *Doctrine and Covenants Commentary*, 629).

5 And behold, and lo, I come quickly to judgment, to convince all of their ungodly deeds which they have committed against me, as it is written of me in the volume of the book.

6 And now, verily I say unto you, that it is not expedient that you should go until your children are provided for, and sent up kindly unto the bishop of Zion.

7 And after a few years, if thou desirest of me, thou mayest go up also unto the goodly land, to possess thine inheritance;

8 Otherwise thou shalt continue proclaiming my gospel until thou be taken. Amen.

Introduction to Doctrine and Covenants 100

This revelation was given at Perrysburg, New York, October 12, 1833, to Joseph Smith and Sidney Rigdon. "While on a mission to Canada and other places in the eastern United States, Joseph Smith became concerned about his family and their well-being. He made the following entry in his journal, dated October 11, 1833: 'I feel very well in mind. The Lord is with us, but have much anxiety about my family' ([Joseph Smith Papers, "Journal, 1832–1834," 7]). In this revelation . . . the Lord assured Joseph and Sidney Rigdon that their families were well and were in the care of the Lord (see D&C 100:1).

"The Lord also gave assurance to Joseph as to the eventual redemption and status of Zion (see D&C 100:13–17). At that time, the saints in Missouri were suffering at the hands of mobocrats. But the Lord made it clear that His work would not be thwarted and He would still raise up a pure people and establish Zion upon the earth.

"Having given these brethren peace of mind concerning their families and the future status of Zion, the Lord instructed them concerning the way He desired them to carry out their responsibilities as teachers and ministers of the gospel. He directed them as to how and what they were to teach and gave them certain promises if they would be obedient to His direction" (Otten and Caldwell, *Sacred Truths*, 2:178).

SECTION 100

Revelation given to Joseph Smith the Prophet and Sidney Rigdon, at Perrysburg, New York, October 12, 1833. The two brethren, having been absent from their families for several days, felt some concern about them.

1 Verily, thus saith the Lord unto you, my friends Sidney and Joseph, your families are well; they are in mine hands, and I will do with them as seemeth me good; for in me there is all power.

2 Therefore, follow me, and listen to the counsel which I shall give unto you.

3 Behold, and lo, I have much people in this place, in the regions round about; and an effectual door shall be opened in the regions round about in this eastern land.

Doctrine and Covenants 100:1–4. Joseph and Sidney to Preach the Gospel for the Salvation of Souls

Why might Joseph Smith have been concerned about his family? (100:1) "At least two concerns were occupying the Prophet's attentions at this time that could have made it difficult for him to leave his home and family for an extended period. On August 9, 1833, he learned that the Church's efforts to build the city of Zion in Independence, Jackson County, Missouri, had been dealt a severe blow....

"Meanwhile, Joseph was also dealing with a threat closer to home. A former Church member named Doctor Philastus Hurlbut, after being excommunicated in June 1833 for immoral conduct, began an aggressive campaign to discredit Joseph and the Church. His approach included stirring up persecution locally, traveling broadly to gather statements critical of Joseph, and threatening Joseph's life" (Eric Smith, "Mission to Canada," 202, 203). ⊕

Why was it important that the Lord assured His missionaries regarding their families? (100:1–2) "The Lord is mindful of His servants. Knowing that they would be unable to put their best efforts into missionary work if they were full of anxiety for their families, He gave them the assurance that their loved ones at home were well, and that He would take care of them during the temporary separation" (Smith and Sjodahl, *Doctrine and Covenants Commentary*, 630–31).

President Dallin H. Oaks reminds us that, "[The Lord] will do more than what is best for us. He will do what is best for us and for all of our Heavenly Father's children. The conviction that the Lord knows more than we do and that he will answer our prayers in the way that is best for us and for all of his other children is a vital ingredient of faith in the Lord Jesus Christ" ("Faith in the Lord Jesus Christ," *Ensign*, May 1994, 99).

What was the "effectual door" the Lord opened for Joseph and Sidney? (100:3) "Joseph and Sidney spent only one month on this particular mission, ... and they baptized at least eighteen individuals. However, the real fruits of their labors would come two years later when Parley P. Pratt would return to the same area in Canada through the 'effectual door' that had been opened by Joseph and Sidney. What they had sowed,

Brother Pratt harvested, preaching to thousands and baptizing hundreds. Among those converts were John Taylor, . . . and Mary Fielding, mother of President Joseph F. Smith and grandmother of President Joseph Fielding Smith. The month-long mission of Joseph Smith and Sidney Rigdon to New York and Canada indeed opened an 'effectual door' through which passed hundreds of Saints and three future Church presidents" (Robinson and Garrett, *Commentary on the Doctrine and Covenants*, 3:253–54). ●

Doctrine and Covenants 100:5–8. It Will Be Given Joseph and Sidney in the Very Hour What They Should Say

What is meant by receiving spiritual understanding in their hearts? (100:5) President Boyd K. Packer taught: "That sweet, quiet voice of inspiration comes more as a feeling than it does as a sound. Pure intelligence can be spoken into the mind. The Holy Ghost communicates with our spirits through the mind more than through the physical senses. This guidance comes as thoughts, as feelings through promptings and impressions [see D&C 11:13]. We may feel the words of spiritual communication more than *hear* them and *see* with spiritual rather than with mortal eyes [see 1 Nephi 17:45]" ("Prayer and Promptings," *Ensign*, Nov. 2009, 44).

How does the Lord fulfill the promise to give utterance in the very moment? (100:5–6) "You don't have to be an outgoing person or an eloquent, persuasive teacher. If you have an abiding love and hope within you, the Lord has promised if you 'lift up your voices unto this people [and] speak the thoughts that [He] shall put into your hearts, . . . you shall not be confounded before men; '[And] it shall be given you . . . in the very moment, what ye shall say' (D&C 100:5–6)" (Ballard, "Put Your Trust in the Lord," *Ensign*, Nov. 2013, 44).

"This may [also] consist of inspiration giving a person the words to speak on a particular occasion, such as in the blessings pronounced by a patriarch or in sermons or other words spoken under the influence of the Holy Ghost" (Oaks, "Revelation," 13).

How might the Holy Ghost bear record of what is taught? (100:7–8) "It is the Holy Ghost that bears witness of your words when you teach and testify. It is the Holy Ghost that, as you speak in hostile venues, puts into your heart what you should say and fulfills the Lord's promise that 'you shall not be confounded

4 Therefore, I, the Lord, have suffered you to come unto this place; for thus it was expedient in me for the salvation of souls.

5 Therefore, verily I say unto you, lift up your voices unto this people; speak the thoughts that I shall put into your hearts, and you shall not be confounded before men;

6 For it shall be given you in the very hour, yea, in the very moment, what ye shall say.

7 But a commandment I give unto you, that ye shall declare whatsoever thing ye declare in my name, in solemnity of heart, in the spirit of meekness, in all things.

8 And I give unto you this promise, that inasmuch as ye do this the Holy Ghost shall be shed forth in bearing record unto all things whatsoever ye shall say.

9 And it is expedient in me that you, my servant Sidney, should be a spokesman unto this people; yea, verily, I will ordain you unto this calling, even to be a spokesman unto my servant Joseph.

10 And I will give unto him power to be mighty in testimony.

11 And I will give unto thee power to be mighty in expounding all scriptures, that thou mayest be a spokesman unto him, and he shall be a revelator unto thee, that thou mayest know the certainty of all things pertaining to the things of my kingdom on the earth.

12 Therefore, continue your journey and let your hearts rejoice; for behold, and lo, I am with you even unto the end.

13 And now I give unto you a word concerning Zion. Zion shall be redeemed, although she is chastened for a little season.

before men' (D&C 100:5). It is the Holy Ghost that reveals how you may clear the next seemingly insurmountable hurdle. It is by the Holy Ghost in you that others may feel the pure love of Christ and receive strength to press forward. It is also the Holy Ghost, in His character as the Holy Spirit of Promise, that confirms the validity and efficacy of your covenants and seals God's promises upon you" (Christofferson, "Power of Covenants," *Ensign*, May 2009, 22).

Doctrine and Covenants 100:9–12. Sidney Is to Be a Spokesman and Joseph Is to Be a Revelator and Mighty in Testimony

In what ways did Sidney serve as a spokesman? (100:9–10) President George Q. Cannon said: "Those who knew Sidney Rigdon, know how wonderfully God inspired him, and with what wonderful eloquence he declared the word of God to the people. He was a mighty man in the hands of God, as a spokesman, as long as the prophet lived, or up to a short time before his death. Thus you see that even this which many might look upon as a small matter, was predicted about 1,700 years before the birth of the Savior [see 2 Nephi 3:18], and was quoted by Lehi 600 years before the same event, and about 2,400 years before its fulfillment, and was translated by the power of God, through his servant Joseph, as was predicted should be the case" (in *Journal of Discourses*, 25:126).

What was Sidney to understand about the role the Lord gave Joseph? (100:11) "While Sidney was to be 'a spokesman' for the Prophet, Joseph Smith was to be 'a revelator' unto Sidney, and in this way Sidney Rigdon was to 'know the certainty of all things pertaining to the things of [the Lord's] kingdom on the earth' (D&C 100:11). Sadly, it was this calling as 'spokesman' that Sidney Rigdon used to falsely claim the right to be 'a guardian to the people,' or the person who should lead the Church, in the weeks following the death of the Prophet Joseph Smith" (*Doctrine and Covenants Student Manual* [2018], 555).

Doctrine and Covenants 100:13–17. The Lord Will Raise up a Pure People, and the Obedient Will Be Saved

What did the Prophet know regarding when Zion would be redeemed? (100:13) During the uncertain and troubling times in Jackson County, Missouri, the Prophet Joseph Smith declared: "I know that Zion, in the due time of the Lord, will be redeemed; but how many will be the days of her purification, tribulation, and affliction, the Lord has kept hid from my eyes; and when I inquire concerning this subject, the voice of the Lord is: Be still, and know that I am God! All those who suffer for my name shall reign with me, and he that layeth down his life for my sake shall find it again" (*Joseph Smith* [manual], 186).

How can we become the pure and righteous people the Lord desires? (100:15–16) President Russell M. Nelson has declared: "The reward for keeping covenants with God is heavenly power—power that strengthens us to withstand our trials, temptations, and heartaches better. This power eases our way. Those who live the higher laws of Jesus Christ have access to His higher power....

"One crucial element of this gathering is preparing a people who are able, ready, and worthy to receive the Lord when He comes again, a people who have already chosen Jesus Christ over this fallen world, a people who rejoice in their agency to live the higher, holier laws of Jesus Christ.

"I call upon you, my dear brothers and sisters, to become this righteous people. Cherish and honor your covenants above all other commitments" ("Overcome the World and Find Rest," *Liahona*, Nov. 2022, 96, 98).

14 Thy brethren, my servants Orson Hyde and John Gould, are in my hands; and inasmuch as they keep my commandments they shall be saved.

15 Therefore, let your hearts be comforted; for all things shall work together for good to them that walk uprightly, and to the sanctification of the church.

16 For I will raise up unto myself a pure people, that will serve me in righteousness;

17 And all that call upon the name of the Lord, and keep his commandments, shall be saved. Even so. Amen.

Introduction to Doctrine and Covenants 101

On December 16 and 17, 1833, Joseph Smith received the revelation now known as Doctrine and Covenants 101 at Kirtland, Ohio. The revelation addressed some of the persecutions and the expulsion of the Saints from Jackson County, Missouri, that occurred between July and November 1833. In this difficult time more than 1,000 Saints were ultimately driven from Jackson County, and more than 200 of their homes were burned. "The Prophet Joseph Smith learned of the Saints' grave situation from Elders Orson Hyde and John Gould when they returned to Kirtland from Missouri and from letters by Church leaders in Missouri. Joseph repeatedly petitioned the Lord for answers concerning the reasons for the Saints' sufferings. Earlier he wrote: 'Now, there are two things of which I am ignorant; and the Lord will not show them unto me, perhaps for a wise purpose in Himself—I mean in some respects—and they are these: Why God has suffered so great a calamity to come upon Zion, and what the great moving cause of this great affliction is; and again, by what means He will return her back to her inheritance, with songs of everlasting joy upon her head' [Joseph Smith Papers, "Letter to Edward Partridge and Others, 10 December 1833," 71]" (McConkie and Ostler, *Revelations of the Restoration*, 729–30).

"The revelation gave clear reasons for the ejection of Missouri church members from Jackson County, stating that they were expelled because of their transgressions. Yet the revelation also provided hope that the Lord would be merciful to the Missouri church members and that Zion would not be moved out of her place. It reiterated that church members were not to sell their lands in Jackson County and that they were to seek redress through the judicial system, the governor of Missouri, and the president of the United States" (Joseph Smith Papers, Historical Introduction to "Revelation, 16–17 December 1833 [D&C 101]").

SECTION 101

Revelation given to Joseph Smith the Prophet, at Kirtland, Ohio, December 16 and 17, 1833. At this time the Saints who had gathered in Missouri were suffering great persecution. Mobs had driven them from their homes in Jackson County; and some of the Saints had tried to establish themselves in Van Buren, Lafayette, and Ray Counties, but persecution followed them. The main body of the Saints was at that time in Clay County, Missouri. Threats of death against individuals of the Church were many. The Saints in Jackson County had lost household furniture, clothing, livestock, and other personal property; and many of their crops had been destroyed.

1 Verily I say unto you, concerning your brethren who have been afflicted, and persecuted, and cast out from the land of their inheritance—

2 I, the Lord, have suffered the affliction to come upon them, wherewith they have been afflicted, in consequence of their transgressions;

Doctrine and Covenants 101:1–8. The Saints Are Chastened and Afflicted Because of Their Transgressions

What did the Saints experience as they were cast out from Jackson County? (101:1) "Much of Jackson county was now mobilizing for battle. Messengers canvased the countryside, enlisting armed men to help drive the Saints from the area. . . .

"On November 6, William Phelps wrote to the church leaders in Kirtland. 'It is a horrid time,' he told them. 'Men, women, and children are fleeing, or preparing to, in all directions.' Most of the Saints trudged north, ferrying across the frigid Missouri River into neighboring Clay County, where scattered family members found each other. Wind and rain beat against them, and soon snow began to fall. Once the Saints cross the river, Edward and other leaders set up tents and built rough log shelters to shield them from the elements" (*Saints*, 1:191, 192). ◉

Why does God chasten His people when they transgress? (101:2) "Sometimes God manifests His love by chastening us. It is a way of reminding us that He loves us and that He knows who we are. His promised blessing of peace is open to all those who courageously walk the covenant path and are willing to receive correction.

"When we recognize the chastening and are willing recipients, it becomes a spiritual surgery. Who

Timeline and Context for Doctrine and Covenants 101 (Doctrine and Covenants 101:1)

"In late 1833, mobs attacked Church members in Jackson County, Missouri, and forced them from their homes. When news of the violence reached the Prophet Joseph Smith in Kirtland, Ohio, he grieved for the Missouri Saints and pled with the Lord to return them to their lands and homes. On December 16–17, 1833, the Lord revealed to the Prophet why He had allowed His Saints to suffer. This revelation, which is recorded in Doctrine and Covenants 101, also included counsel and words of comfort regarding 'the redemption of Zion' (D&C 101:43).

"July 23, 1833—Under threat of mob violence, Church leaders in Missouri signed an agreement that all Mormons would leave Jackson County by April 1, 1834.

"October 20, 1833—Church leaders in Missouri announced that the Saints intended to remain in Jackson County and defend their property rights.

"October 31–November 8, 1833—Mobs attacked Mormon settlements in Jackson County, burning homes and forcing the Saints to leave the county.

"November 25, 1833—The Prophet Joseph Smith learned that mob violence had expelled the Saints from Jackson County.

"December 16–17, 1833—Doctrine and Covenants 101 was received" (*Doctrine and Covenants Student Manual* [2018], 557; paragraphing altered).

likes surgery, by the way? But to those who need it and are willing to receive it, it can be lifesaving. The Lord chastens whom He loves. . . . That chastening, or spiritual surgery, will bring about needed change in our lives. We will realize, brothers and sisters, that it refines and purifies our inner vessels" (Wakolo, "God Loves His Children," *Liahona*, May 2021, 96). See also commentary in this volume on Doctrine and Covenants 103:4 and 105:6.

Who qualifies to become the Lord's jewels? (101:3) "Despite the Saints' transgressions, the Lord said He would still 'own them,' promising they would be His when He comes again to 'make up [His] jewels' (D&C 101:3; see also Malachi 3:17). The Lord's 'jewels' refer to His faithful Saints, who are precious to Him and will be set apart as His treasure when He returns. To be prepared to become His jewels, the Saints needed to be 'chastened and tried, even as Abraham' (D&C 101:4). Abraham's faith was severely tested when the Lord commanded him to sacrifice his son Isaac (see Genesis 22:1–13).

"Similarly, in order to prove their faith and help them understand their need for repentance, the Lord allowed the Saints in Missouri to be afflicted and chastened" (*Doctrine and Covenants Student Manual* [2018], 562).

3 Yet I will own them, and they shall be mine in that day when I shall come to make up my jewels.

An Example of Offering Up an Only Son (Doctrine and Covenants 101:4–5)

"When Drusilla Dorris Hendricks (1810–1881) spoke at the Smithfield Relief Society in August 1871, she talked about trusting the Lord when faced with significant challenges. . . . As new converts to the Church of Jesus Christ of Latter-day Saints, she and her husband, James Hendricks, joined other members in Clay County, Missouri, in May 1836. James was injured at the Battle of Crooked River, a skirmish between Latter-day Saint and Missouri militia forces on October 25, 1838. He remained paralyzed for the rest of his life, and his wife both nursed him and provided for the family. . . .

James and Drusilla Hendricks

"After her husband was shot down in Missouri and then dragged about by the merciless mob when unable to help himself, and they were driven from their home, when a call was made for volunteers to go in the Battalion she was so indignant at the way in which the Mormons had been treated she said her boy could not go, and kept him from making any preparations until the morning the company was to start. . . .

"Then came a peculiar sensation and it was as though a voice said to her, 'Do you not want the highest glory?' She answered naturally, 'Yes,' and the voice continued, 'How do you think to gain it save by making the greatest sacrifices?' She questioned—'Lord, what lack I yet?' 'Let the son go in the Battalion,' was the answer . . .

"Her prayer was, 'Lord, if you want my son, take him, only let him be restored to me again as was the son of Abraham,' and the answer came in spirit—'So shall it be, even as thou hast said.' She arose and with the help of some of her neighbors quickly prepared her boy and sent him from her with the firm conviction that God would be as good as his word and restore her son to her again. During his absence it was her constant labor to pray for him, and he was restored to her as a recompense for her faithfulness" ("Prayer of Faith," 51, 52, 54).

4 Therefore, they must needs be chastened and tried, even as Abraham, who was commanded to offer up his only son.

5 For all those who will not endure chastening, but deny me, cannot be sanctified.

6 Behold, I say unto you, there were jarrings, and contentions, and envyings, and strifes, and lustful and covetous desires among them; therefore by these things they polluted their inheritances.

7 They were slow to hearken unto the voice of the Lord their God; therefore, the Lord their God is slow to hearken unto their prayers, to answer them in the day of their trouble.

8 In the day of their peace they esteemed lightly my counsel; but, in the day of their trouble, of necessity they feel after me.

What does it mean to be chastened and tried even as Abraham? (101:4–5) Joseph Smith observed: "that the ancients, though persecuted and afflicted . . . obtained from God promises of such weight and glory, that our hearts are often filled with gratitude, that we are even permitted to look upon them . . . that those who have kept the faith will be crowned with a crown of righteousness" (Joseph Smith Papers, "Letter to the Church, circa March 1834," 144).

"God hath said that He would have a tried people, that He would purge them as gold, . . . [that] it will be a trial of our faith equal to that of Abraham, and that the ancients will not have whereof to boast over us in the day of judgment, as being called to pass through heavier afflictions; that we may hold an even weight in the balance with them" (Joseph Smith Papers, "History, 1838–1856, volume C-1," 904[a]; spelling modernized).

What were some reasons for the Saints' difficulties in Missouri? (101:6) "Historians have pointed out that there were various sources of tension between the Mormons and other Missourians. . . .

"There may be truth in such explanations, but the Lord pinpointed quite a different reason for the difficulties: the Saints themselves were guilty of transgressions, disunity, lustfulness, greed; and they were slow to hearken to the Lord (see D&C 101:2–6; 103:4; 105:3–4). These deficiencies were in marked contrast to the qualities required of those who would build Zion: they must be 'of one heart and one mind' and dwell 'in righteousness' (Moses 7:18), and they must also be pure in heart (see D&C 97:21). Hence, the Saints needed to be chastened to help them become worthy" (Cowan, *Answers to Your Questions*, 120). ❏

What are the consequences of being slow to hearken to the Lord's voice? (101:7–8) "[The Lord] wants us to be happy. This happiness comes by our faith in Jesus Christ, by our sincere and true repentance, by our obedience to His commandments, and by our endurance to the end.

"Sometimes we might think that the Lord does not hear or answer our prayers. At such times, we need to stop and ponder what we have done throughout our lives. If necessary, we must put our lives in harmony with the gospel of Jesus Christ. Through the Prophet Joseph Smith, the Lord revealed [D&C 101:2, 7–8].

"When we have the sincere desire to put our lives in harmony with the will of the Lord, He will always be ready to help ease our burdens" (Damiani, "Be of Good Cheer and Faithful in Adversity," *Ensign*, May 2005, 95).

Doctrine and Covenants 101:9–15. The Lord's Indignation Will Fall upon the Nations, but His People Will Be Gathered and Comforted

What does it mean that the Lord will not "cast them off" but "will remember mercy"? (101:9) "Though Zion has been chastened and the immediate plans of the Saints have been frustrated, the Saints have not been rejected as God's people, and God has not canceled his long-term plans for the physical Zion.... In the short term, this statement could refer to the plight of the Missouri Saints, who were suffering a day of wrath ... but whom the Lord would bless in times to come. More likely, however, this is a reference to the Lord's day of wrath before his second coming (see D&C 87:5–8; 97:22–25), when the Saints as a body will be shown mercy and be spared the fate of the nations through their establishment of Zion" (Robinson and Garrett, *Commentary on the Doctrine and Covenants*, 3:265–66).

When will the Lord's indignation "be poured out without measure"? (101:10–11) President Joseph Fielding Smith observed: "The sword of indignation commenced to fall upon the enemies of the saints shortly after the saints were driven from Missouri, and from time to time it has fallen, both in this land, and in foreign lands, and we may truly say that it fell upon the nations during the World [Wars]. However, it has not fallen 'without measure,' but this is shortly to come for the nations are filling the cup of their iniquity which must be full before Christ comes. The leaven is at work, and the Lord is preparing to make an end of all nations because of their sins, and the time for Christ to come and reign is drawing nigh" (*Church History and Modern Revelation*, 1:460).

What characterizes Israel as being on the "watch-tower"? (101:12) "The people upon the watch-tower is a figurative reference to those who watch and guard against evil [see D&C 101:57], and they are equated with 'all Mine Israel' by the Lord. It will be remembered that anciently Paul the Apostle wrote 'that blindness in part is happened to Israel, until the fullness of the Gentiles be come in' ... (Rom. 11:25–27). The fulness of the Gentiles has now come in [see D&C 14:10; 45:9, 25–30], and the Lord is ready to keep his word to Israel. Scattered Israel is to be gathered from his long dispersion [see D&C 45:24, 43; 29:7–8], and ... [those] who will have given their lives for the sake of

9 Verily I say unto you, notwithstanding their sins, my bowels are filled with compassion towards them. I will not utterly cast them off; and in the day of wrath I will remember mercy.

10 I have sworn, and the decree hath gone forth by a former commandment which I have given unto you, that I would let fall the sword of mine indignation in behalf of my people; and even as I have said, it shall come to pass.

11 Mine indignation is soon to be poured out without measure upon all nations; and this will I do when the cup of their iniquity is full.

12 And in that day all who are found upon the watch-tower, or in other words, all mine Israel, shall be saved.

13 And they that have been scattered shall be gathered.

14 And all they who have mourned shall be comforted.

15 And all they who have given their lives for my name shall be crowned.

the Lord's cause shall be crowned" (Sperry, *Doctrine and Covenants Compendium*, 514–15).

Doctrine and Covenants 101:16–21. Zion and Her Stakes Will Be Established

Why may we be comforted concerning Zion and its future? (101:16) President Gordon B. Hinckley observed: "God is weaving his tapestry according to his own grand design. All flesh is in his hands. It is not our prerogative to counsel him. It is our responsibility and our opportunity to be at peace in our minds and in our hearts, and to know that he is God, that this is his work, and that he will not permit it to fail" ("He Slumbers Not, nor Sleeps," *Ensign*, May 1983, 6).

President Russell M. Nelson noted: "So many wonderful things are ahead. In coming days, we will see the *greatest* manifestations of the Savior's power that the world has *ever* seen. Between now and the time He returns 'with power and great glory' [JS—M 1:36], He will bestow countless privileges, blessings, and miracles upon the faithful" ("Overcome the World and Find Rest," *Liahona*, Nov. 2022, 95).

16 Therefore, let your hearts be comforted concerning Zion; for all flesh is in mine hands; be still and know that I am God.

17 Zion shall not be moved out of her place, notwithstanding her children are scattered.

18 They that remain, and are pure in heart, shall return, and come to their inheritances, they and their children, with songs of everlasting joy, to build up the waste places of Zion—

19 And all these things that the prophets might be fulfilled.

20 And, behold, there is none other place appointed than that which I have appointed; neither shall there be any other place appointed than that which I have appointed, for the work of the gathering of my saints—

21 Until the day cometh when there is found no more room for them; and then I have other places which I will appoint unto them, and they shall be called stakes, for the curtains or the strength of Zion.

What did the Lord reveal about Zion being "moved out of her place"? (101:17–20) "The 16–17 December 1833 revelation featured here provided the direction that [Joseph Smith] and other church leaders sought. The revelation gave clear reasons for the ejection of Missouri church members from Jackson County, stating that they were expelled because of their transgressions. Yet the revelation also provided hope that the Lord would be merciful to the Missouri church members and that Zion would not be moved out of her place" (Joseph Smith Papers, Historical Introduction to "Revelation, 16–17 December 1833 [D&C 101]").

"Despite the Saints' expulsion from Jackson County, Missouri, the Lord reaffirmed that 'Zion shall not be moved out of her place, notwithstanding her children are scattered' (D&C 101:17). Although the stakes of Zion have spread over the face of the earth, 'the center place,' Jackson County, continues to be designated by the Lord as the location for the city of New Jerusalem (see D&C 57:1–3; 101:17, 20–21)" (*Doctrine and Covenants Student Manual* [2018], 564).

How can stakes contribute to the building of Zion? (101:21) "With the creation of stakes and the construction of temples in most nations with sizeable populations of the faithful, the current commandment is not to gather to one place but to gather in stakes in our own homelands. There the faithful can enjoy the full blessings of eternity in a house of the Lord. There, in their own homelands, they can obey the Lord's command to enlarge the borders of His people and strengthen her stakes (see D&C 101:21; D&C 133:9, 14). In this way, the stakes of Zion are 'for a defense, and for a refuge from the storm, and from wrath when it shall be poured out without mixture upon the whole earth' (D&C 115:6)" (Oaks, "Preparation for the Second Coming," *Ensign*, May 2004, 8).

Doctrine and Covenants 101:22–31. The Nature of Life during the Millennium Is Set Forth

What could the removal of the veil of the temple symbolize? (101:22–23) "Anciently, a veil hung between the two holy chambers of the tabernacle (Exodus 26:31–33). Its presence in Herod's temple is supported by the statement in each of the synoptic gospels that at the time of Christ's death the veil of the temple was rent from top to bottom (Matthew 27:51; Mark 15:38; Luke 23:45). Christ, by his sacrificial death, opened a way for the faithful to enter the holiest place, meaning the celestial kingdom, 'through the veil, that is to say, his flesh' (Hebrews 10:20). The present text, drawing on this imagery, suggests that the veil separating us from the presence of the Lord will be rent, and all will be able to see what otherwise would remain hidden to them" (McConkie and Ostler, *Revelations of the Restoration*, 733). ✷

What is meant by the elements melting with fervent heat? (101:24–25) "We know that elsewhere in the scriptures, fire and burning are used as a metaphor for the shame that the guilty will experience when they come before God's presence for judgment. It is compared to a lake of fire (see, for example, 2 Nephi 9:16, 26; Jacob 3:11; D&C 63:17; Revelation 19:20). . . ."

But Gerald N. Lund noted that the scriptures "talk about a burning of the wicked at His Second Coming, using metaphors like the 'stubble' left after grain is harvested or 'the tares' that are bound into bundles and burned (see D&C 38:12; 86:7; 88:94). Obviously some of that burning will come with the consciousness of guilt and shame as noted above. And some may actually die in the fires and other natural disasters sent by the Lord as warning voices to the wicked. . . .

"The scriptures are quite explicit that there will be a burning and cleansing process connected directly with the Second Coming. And this seems to be directly connected to the actual presence of Jesus Christ. We're not given specifics on how this might

22 Behold, it is my will, that all they who call on my name, and worship me according to mine everlasting gospel, should gather together, and stand in holy places;

23 And prepare for the revelation which is to come, when the veil of the covering of my temple, in my tabernacle, which hideth the earth, shall be taken off, and all flesh shall see me together.

24 And every corruptible thing, both of man, or of the beasts of the field, or of the fowls of the heavens, or of the fish of the sea, that dwells upon all the face of the earth, shall be consumed;

25 And also that of element shall melt with fervent heat; and all things shall become new, that my knowledge and glory may dwell upon all the earth.

work, but it seems to be tied to a Being whose glory is celestial and who is likened unto the sun itself. This sounds quite literal and not like symbolic fire" (*Second Coming of the Lord*, 349, 350).

What is the enmity that shall end? (101:26) "This is something that is frequently mentioned, and usually with specific examples, such as children leading a lion or playing around the den of poisonous serpents. Even beasts of prey will start eating grass. Perhaps some of that is also metaphorical imagery, but . . . it is mentioned again and again, with very specific details. . . .

"The animal kingdom may experience peace and harmony. No one will hurt or destroy in the Lord's holy mountain. It is hard for us to see how this could be, if this is literal and not just symbolic. But remember that Christ has promised us that [the paradisiacal earth in the Millennium] will be a new world" (Lund, *Second Coming of the Lord*, 373–74, 377). ❂

26 And in that day the enmity of man, and the enmity of beasts, yea, the enmity of all flesh, shall cease from before my face.

How might prayer change during the Millennium? (101:27) In the Millennial day, "the Saints shall have been cleansed of sin, and their motives will have been purified; they will no longer ask amiss for that which they ought not. Thus, 'in that day whatsoever any man shall ask, it shall be given unto him' (D&C 101:27). 'And it shall come to pass, that before they call, I will answer; and while they are yet speaking, I will hear' (Isaiah 65:24). During the thousand years the covenant people from Christ's church on earth will have internalized the principles of his gospel and incorporated the law of the Lord into their very being. They will then see 'eye to eye' with one another and with their Lord and Master (D&C 84:98)" (Millet, "Life in the Millennium," 183–84).

27 And in that day whatsoever any man shall ask, it shall be given unto him.

What does it mean to bind Satan? (101:28) "Our revelation says: 'And in that day Satan shall not have power to tempt any man' (D&C 101:28). Does this mean that power is withdrawn from Satan so that he can no longer entice men to do evil? Or does it mean that men no longer succumb to his enticements because their hearts are so set on righteousness that they refuse to forsake that which is good to follow him who is evil? Clearly it means the latter. . . .

"How, then, will Satan be bound during the Millennium? It will be by the righteousness of the people" (Bruce R. McConkie, *Millennial Messiah*, 668). ❂

28 And in that day Satan shall not have power to tempt any man.

What is the nature of death during the Millennium? (101:29–31) "No graves will be dug during the Millennium. Death and suffering as we now know them

29 And there shall be no sorrow because there is no death.

will not exist. The body and the spirit will no longer separate for a long period of time. For now the body returns to the dust while the spirit awaits in a world of spirits for the day of its reunion with a perfected body, but in that day the body will not see corruption, and the spirit will not go to a spirit world. The separation of body and spirit will be virtually instantaneous and their reunion inseparable. 'Children shall grow up until they become old; old men shall die; but they shall not sleep in the dust, but they shall be changed in the twinkling of an eye' (D&C 63:51). The Lord told the Three Nephites: 'Ye shall never endure the pains of death; but when I shall come in my glory ye shall be changed in the twinkling of an eye from mortality to immortality; and then shall ye be blessed in the kingdom of my Father' (3 Nephi 28:8)" (McConkie and Ostler, *Revelations of the Restoration*, 735).

Doctrine and Covenants 101:32–42. The Saints Will Be Blessed and Rewarded in the Millennium

What will we learn about the earth when the Lord comes? (101:32–34) "Though our understanding of the Creation is limited, we know enough to appreciate its supernal significance. And that store of knowledge will be augmented in the future. Scripture declares: 'In that day when the Lord shall come [again], he shall reveal all things—' [D&C 101:32–34]....

"Yes, further light and knowledge will come. The Lord said, 'If there be bounds set to the heavens or to the seas, or to the dry land, or to the sun, moon, or stars—

"'All the times of their revolutions, all the appointed days, months, and years, . . . and all their glories, laws, and set times, shall be revealed in the days of the dispensation of the fulness of times' [D&C 121:30–31]" (Nelson, "Creation," *Ensign*, May 2000, 85). ◉

What counsel did the Lord give the Saints who were suffering persecution? (101:35–36) "In the stark face of persecution, loss of property, and even the threat of death, the Lord counseled the Saints to have hope: 'Fear not even unto death; for in this world your joy is not full, but in me your joy is full' (D&C 101:36). What godly perspective, compared to the reactions of the natural man! Neither anger nor self-pity were acceptable responses to the Lord's chastening. He was teaching his people to center their focus on him, not on their difficulties" (Cloward, "Counsel to the Exiles," 384). ◉

30 In that day an infant shall not die until he is old; and his life shall be as the age of a tree;

31 And when he dies he shall not sleep, that is to say in the earth, but shall be changed in the twinkling of an eye, and shall be caught up, and his rest shall be glorious.

32 Yea, verily I say unto you, in that day when the Lord shall come, he shall reveal all things—

33 Things which have passed, and hidden things which no man knew, things of the earth, by which it was made, and the purpose and the end thereof—

34 Things most precious, things that are above, and things that are beneath, things that are in the earth, and upon the earth, and in heaven.

35 And all they who suffer persecution for my name, and endure in faith, though they are called to lay down their lives for my sake yet shall they partake of all this glory.

36 Wherefore, fear not even unto death; for in this world your joy is not full, but in me your joy is full.

37 Therefore, care not for the body, neither the life of the body; but care for the soul, and for the life of the soul.

38 And seek the face of the Lord always, that in patience ye may possess your souls, and ye shall have eternal life.

39 When men are called unto mine everlasting gospel, and covenant with an everlasting covenant, they are accounted as the salt of the earth and the savor of men;

40 They are called to be the savor of men; therefore, if that salt of the earth lose its savor, behold, it is thenceforth good for nothing only to be cast out and trodden under the feet of men.

41 Behold, here is wisdom concerning the children of Zion, even many, but not all; they were found transgressors, therefore they must needs be chastened—

What could it mean to "care not for the . . . life of the body"? (101:37–38) Elder Neal A. Maxwell taught: "Within the swirling global events—events from which we are not totally immune—is humanity's real and continuing struggle: whether or not, amid the cares of the world, we will really choose, in the words of the Lord, to 'care . . . for the life of the soul' (D&C 101:37). Whatever our anxious involvements with outward events, this inner struggle proceeds in both tranquil and turbulent times. Whether understood or recognized, this is the unchanging mortal agendum from generation to generation. . . .

"Uncertainty as to world conditions does not justify moral uncertainty. . . . Likewise, the obscuring mists of the moment cannot change the reality that Christ is the Light of the World!" ("Care for the Life of the Soul," *Ensign*, May 2003, 68, 69).

Who can qualify for eternal life? (101:38) "President M. Russell Ballard taught, 'Scriptures and latter-day prophets confirm that everyone who is faithful in keeping gospel covenants will have the opportunity for exaltation.' Citing President Nelson and President Oaks, President Ballard continued, 'The precise time and manner in which the blessings of exaltation are bestowed have not all been revealed, but they are nonetheless assured.' I see such hope and power in their teachings. They enable all the faithful, regardless of whether you have a sealed spouse with you or not, to look forward with an eye of faith and see yourselves exalted in the presence of our Heavenly Father and our Savior. These glorious promises transport many of us back to the highest rooms of the holy temple but will be fulfilled for all the faithful in the highest degree of the celestial kingdom" (Corbitt, "Graduating Your Faith to the Next Level," 10).

Why might those who keep covenants be called "the salt of the earth and the savor of men"? (101:39–40) "To perform our covenant duty as the salt of the earth, we must be different from those around us. . . .

"This requires us to make some changes from our family culture, our ethnic culture, or our national culture. We must change all elements of our behavior that are in conflict with gospel commandments, covenants, and culture. . . .

"The changes we must make to become part of the gospel culture require prolonged and sometimes painful effort, and our differences must be visible. As the 'salt of the earth,' we are also the 'light of the world,' and our light must not be hidden (see Matt.

5:13–16)" (Oaks, "Repentance and Change," *Ensign*, Nov. 2003, 39, 40). See also commentary in this volume on Doctrine and Covenants 103:10.

Why might the Saints be cautioned about exalting themselves? (101:42) "Disciples of Jesus Christ understand that compared to eternity, our existence in this mortal sphere is only 'a small moment' in space and time. They know that a person's true value has little to do with what the world holds in high esteem. They know you could pile up the accumulated currency of the entire world and it could not buy a loaf of bread in the economy of heaven.

"Those who will 'inherit the kingdom of God' [3 Nephi 11:38] are those who become 'as a child, submissive, meek, humble, patient, full of love' [Mosiah 3:19]. 'For every one that exalteth himself shall be abased; and he that humbleth himself shall be exalted' [Luke 18:14]" (Uchtdorf, "You Matter to Him," *Ensign*, Nov. 2011, 20).

Doctrine and Covenants 101:43–62. The Parable of the Nobleman and the Olive Trees Signifies the Troubles and Eventual Redemption of Zion

Why might the Lord have used a parable in this revelation? (101:43) Elder David A. Bednar explained: "Parables are a defining feature of the Lord Jesus Christ's masterful approach to teaching. Simply defined, the Savior's parables are stories used to compare spiritual truths with material things and mortal experiences. . . .

42 He that exalteth himself shall be abased, and he that abaseth himself shall be exalted.

43 And now, I will show unto you a parable, that you may know my will concerning the redemption of Zion.

44 A certain nobleman had a spot of land, very choice; and he said unto his servants: Go ye unto my vineyard, even upon this very

---

The Prophet's Letter to the Missouri Saints During Their Suffering (D&C 101:41–42)

On 10 December 1833, the Prophet Joseph Smith wrote an important letter to Edward Partridge and others emphasizing the need for humility during adversity. "When I contemplate upon all things that have been manifested, I am sensible that I ought not to murmur and do not murmur only in this, but that those who are innocent are compelled to suffer for the iniquities of the guilty; and I cannot account for this, only on this wise, that the saying of the Savior has not been strictly observed: If thy right eye offend thee pluck it out and cast it from thee or if thy right arm offend thee pluck it off and cast it from thee. Now the fact is, if any of the members of our body are disordered, the rest of our body will be affected with them and then all is brought into bondage together. And yet notwithstanding all this, it is with difficulty that I can restrain my feelings; when I know that you my brethren with whom I have had so many happy hours, sitting as it were in heavenly places in Christ Jesus and also having the witness which I feel, and even have felt, of the purity of your motives—are cast out, and are as strangers and pilgrims on the earth, exposed to hunger, cold, nakedness, peril, sword &c. I say when I contemplate this, it is with difficulty that I can keep from complaining and murmurings against this dispensation; but I am sensible that this is not right and may God grant that notwithstanding your great afflictions and sufferings there may not any thing separate us from the Love of Christ" (Joseph Smith Papers, "Letter to Edward Partridge and Others," 10 December 1833, 71–72; spelling modernized).

choice piece of land, and plant twelve olive trees;

45 And set watchmen round about them, and build a tower, that one may overlook the land round about, to be a watchman upon the tower, that mine olive trees may not be broken down when the enemy shall come to spoil and take upon themselves the fruit of my vineyard.

46 Now, the servants of the nobleman went and did as their lord commanded them, and planted the olive trees, and built a hedge round about, and set watchmen, and began to build a tower.

47 And while they were yet laying the foundation thereof, they began to say among themselves: And what need hath my lord of this tower?

48 And consulted for a long time, saying among themselves: What need hath my lord of this tower, seeing this is a time of peace?

49 Might not this money be given to the exchangers? For there is no need of these things.

50 And while they were at variance one with another they became very slothful, and they hearkened not unto the commandments of their lord.

51 And the enemy came by night, and broke down the hedge; and the servants of the nobleman arose and were affrighted, and fled; and the enemy destroyed their works, and broke down the olive trees.

52 Now, behold, the nobleman, the lord of the vineyard, called upon his servants, and said unto them, Why! what is the cause of this great evil?

"The intended meaning or message of a parable typically is not expressed explicitly. Rather, the story only conveys divine truth to a receiver in proportion to his or her faith in God, personal spiritual preparation, and willingness to learn. Thus, an individual must exercise moral agency and actively 'ask, seek, and knock' to discover the truths embedded in a parable" ("Put On Thy Strength, O Zion," *Liahona*, Nov. 2022, 92).

What might the tower in the parable have symbolized? (101:45) "The interpretation of the tower in the parable is not clear. It may represent the temple that the Lord commanded the Saints to build in Jackson County (see D&C 57:2–3; 84:1–5; 97:10–12). More broadly, the tower may represent Zion, which the Saints could build up only by obeying the Lord's commandments (see D&C 101:11–12; 105:3–6)" (*Doctrine and Covenants Student Manual* [2018], 569).

How were the actions of the Missouri Saints similar to those of the servants in the parable? (101:53) "When the Missouri Saints [the servants in the parable] inquired of the Prophet Joseph Smith to know why such great persecution had come upon them, the Lord said, 'They have been afflicted in consequence of their transgression' (D&C 101:2). He reproached them for the 'jarrings, and contentions, and envyings, and strifes, and lustful and covetous desires among them' (D&C 101:6). The Lord also said that 'many, but not all, . . . were found transgressors, therefore they must needs be chastened' (D&C 101:41). They further learned from this revelation that their failure to promptly build a temple in Jackson County, as had been commanded by the Lord (see D&C 57:3; 58:57; 84:3–5), was an additional cause for receiving the Lord's chastisement (see also D&C 101:75; 105:9–13)" (Max H Parkin, "Lessons from the Experience," *Ensign*, Jul. 2001, 52). ⊕

What was the meaning of gathering the strength of the Lord's house to "redeem [His] vineyard"? (101:55–58) "This part of the parable refers to Zion's Camp, which the Lord would explain to the Prophet Joseph more fully in Doctrine and Covenants 103 and 105. Zion's Camp was an attempt by Joseph Smith and about two hundred brethren from the eastern churches to redeem Zion by force of arms. . . . [That] attempt did not achieve its stated goal of regaining possession of the Jackson County properties" (Robinson and Garrett, *Commentary on the Doctrine and Covenants*, 3:277–78). See also commentary in this volume on Doctrine and Covenants 103:21, 29–30, 37–40 and 105:17–19.

What can this parable help us understand about the future establishment of Zion? (101:59–62) "After many days, a designated period in which we still live, those who are called, chosen, selected, appointed, and sent forth by the voice of the Spirit, as it speaks to the President of the Church, shall build the New Jerusalem and the holy temple to which the Lord Jesus Christ shall come in power and glory as the great Millennium

53 Ought ye not to have done even as I commanded you, and—after ye had planted the vineyard, and built the hedge round about, and set watchmen upon the walls thereof—built the tower also, and set a watchman upon the tower, and watched for my vineyard, and not have fallen asleep, lest the enemy should come upon you?

54 And behold, the watchman upon the tower would have seen the enemy while he was yet afar off; and then ye could have made ready and kept the enemy from breaking down the hedge thereof, and saved my vineyard from the hands of the destroyer.

55 And the lord of the vineyard said unto one of his servants: Go and gather together the residue of my servants, and take all the strength of mine house, which are my warriors, my young men, and they that are of middle age also among all my servants, who are the strength of mine house, save those only whom I have appointed to tarry;

56 And go ye straightway unto the land of my vineyard, and redeem my vineyard; for it is mine; I have bought it with money.

57 Therefore, get ye straightway unto my land; break down the walls of mine enemies; throw down their tower, and scatter their watchmen.

58 And inasmuch as they gather together against you, avenge me of mine enemies, that by and by I may come with the residue of mine house and possess the land.

59 And the servant said unto his lord: When shall these things be?

60 And he said unto his servant: When I will; go ye straightway, and do all things whatsoever I have commanded you;

61 And this shall be my seal and blessing

upon you—a faithful and wise steward in the midst of mine house, a ruler in my kingdom.

62 And his servant went straightway, and did all things whatsoever his lord commanded him; and after many days all things were fulfilled.

63 Again, verily I say unto you, I will show unto you wisdom in me concerning all the churches, inasmuch as they are willing to be guided in a right and proper way for their salvation—

64 That the work of the gathering together of my saints may continue, that I may build them up unto my name upon holy places; for the time of harvest is come, and my word must needs be fulfilled.

65 Therefore, I must gather together my people, according to the parable of the wheat and the tares, that the wheat may be secured in the garners to possess eternal life, and be crowned with celestial glory, when I shall come in the kingdom of my Father to reward every man according as his work shall be;

66 While the tares shall be bound in bundles, and their bands made strong, that they may be burned with unquenchable fire.

67 Therefore, a commandment I give unto all the churches, that they shall continue to gather together unto the places which I have appointed.

68 Nevertheless, as I have said unto you in a former commandment, let not your gathering be in haste, nor by flight; but let all things be prepared before you.

is ushered in. In the meantime, our work as a people is to keep the commandments and sanctify ourselves so that if the call comes in our day, we shall be worthy to respond" (Bruce R. McConkie, *New Witness*, 619). ◑

Doctrine and Covenants 101:63–75. The Saints Are to Continue Gathering Together

How is the Lord establishing holy places as He gathers His Saints? (101:64) "This doctrine of the gathering is one of the important teachings of The Church of Jesus Christ of Latter-day Saints. The Lord has declared: 'I give unto you a sign . . . that I shall gather in, from their long dispersion, my people, O house of Israel, and shall establish again among them my Zion' [3 Nephi 21:1]. The coming forth of the Book of Mormon is a sign to the entire world that the Lord has commenced to gather Israel and fulfill covenants He made to Abraham, Isaac, and Jacob. We not only teach this doctrine, but we participate in it. We do so as we help to gather the elect of the Lord on both sides of the veil" (Nelson, "Gathering of Scattered Israel," *Ensign*, Nov. 2006, 80). ◑

What are the wheat and the garners in this parable? (101:65–66) "The Lord likened the gathering of His people to the gathering of wheat into 'garners' (D&C 101:65). Anciently, wheat was gathered into garners, or granaries, to safely store and protect it. While speaking about Alma 26:5, in which Ammon refers to 'sheaves,' or bundles of grain, being 'gathered into the garners,' Elder David A. Bednar of the Quorum of the Twelve Apostles taught, 'The garners are the holy temples' (["Honorably Hold a Name and Standing," *Ensign*, May 2009, 97]). Members of the Church receive protective blessings and are prepared for celestial glory and eternal life as they gather to the Lord's holy temples to receive saving ordinances and enter into covenants for themselves and on behalf of their ancestors" (*Doctrine and Covenants Student Manual* [2018], 570). ◑

How might the command to purchase lands in Jackson County increase the Saints' faith that Zion would still be established? (101:70–74) President Lorenzo Snow declared, "I remember one time hearing President [Orson] Hyde . . . speaking in regard to our going back to Jackson County, and he said that inasmuch as they had abused the Saints and wrested from them some of their possessions, when we went back we would follow the same course toward them. And after he had got through, President [Brigham] Young spoke upon this, and he said the Latter-day Saints never would get possession of that land by fighting and destroying life; but we would purchase the land, as the Lord had commanded in the first place. And I will tell you that that land never will be purchased, except it is purchased by the tithing of the Latter-day Saints and their consecrations; never, worlds without end. But the Latter-day Saints never will be in that condition of disobedience as were the people that colonized Jackson County" (in Conference Report, Oct. 1899, 26–27). See also commentary in this volume on Doctrine and Covenants 103:23.

Doctrine and Covenants 101:76–80. The Lord Established the Constitution of the United States

How were the Saints directed to seek redress from government officials? (101:76) "The Lord instructed the Missouri Saints to 'importune,' or appeal to, the government 'for redress, and redemption' (D&C 101:76), meaning they should continue to seek justice and help in returning to their lands in Jackson County" (*Doctrine and Covenants Student Manual* [2018], 571).

How does the Constitution influence our desire to exercise our agency? (101:77–78) "The Lord has told us in modern revelation that he established the Constitution of the United States to assure 'that every

69 And in order that all things be prepared before you, observe the commandment which I have given concerning these things—

70 Which saith, or teacheth, to purchase all the lands with money, which can be purchased for money, in the region round about the land which I have appointed to be the land of Zion, for the beginning of the gathering of my saints;

71 All the land which can be purchased in Jackson county, and the counties round about, and leave the residue in mine hand.

72 Now, verily I say unto you, let all the churches gather together all their moneys; let these things be done in their time, but not in haste; and observe to have all things prepared before you.

73 And let honorable men be appointed, even wise men, and send them to purchase these lands.

74 And the churches in the eastern countries, when they are built up, if they will hearken unto this counsel they may buy lands and gather together upon them; and in this way they may establish Zion.

75 There is even now already in store sufficient, yea, even an abundance, to redeem Zion, and establish her waste places, no more to be thrown down, were the churches, who call themselves after my name, willing to hearken to my voice.

76 And again I say unto you, those who have been scattered by their enemies, it is my will that they should continue to importune for redress, and redemption, by the hands of those who are placed as rulers and are in authority over you—

77 According to the laws and constitution of the people, which I have suffered to be established, and should be maintained for the

rights and protection of all flesh, according to just and holy principles;

78 That every man may act in doctrine and principle pertaining to futurity, according to the moral agency which I have given unto him, that every man may be accountable for his own sins in the day of judgment.

79 Therefore, it is not right that any man should be in bondage one to another.

80 And for this purpose have I established the Constitution of this land, by the hands of wise men whom I raised up unto this very purpose, and redeemed the land by the shedding of blood.

81 Now, unto what shall I liken the children of Zion? I will liken them unto the parable of the woman and the unjust judge, for men ought always to pray and not to faint, which saith—

82 There was in a city a judge which feared not God, neither regarded man.

man may act . . . according to the moral agency which I have given unto him' (D&C 101:78). In other words, God established our Constitution to give us the vital political freedom necessary for us to act upon our personal choices in civil government. This revelation shows the distinction between *agency* (the power of choice), which is God-given, and *freedom*, the right to act upon our choices, which is protected by the Constitution and laws of the land" (Oaks, "Free Agency and Freedom," 12). ☉

How should members of the Church view the Constitution of the United States? (101:80) "The United States Constitution is unique because God revealed that He 'established' it 'for the rights and protection of all flesh' [no man should be in bondage one to another] (Doctrine and Covenants 101:77; see also [verses 79]–80). That is why this constitution is of special concern for The Church of Jesus Christ of Latter-day Saints throughout the world. Whether or how its principles should be applied in other nations of the world is for them to decide" (Oaks, "Defending Our Divinely Inspired Constitution," *Liahona*, May 2021, 105–6). See also commentary in this volume on Doctrine and Covenants 98:6–8 and 109:54.

Doctrine and Covenants 101:81–101. The Saints Are to Importune for the Redress of Grievances, according to the Parable of the Woman and the Unjust Judge

How was the parable of the unjust judge similar to the circumstances of the Saints? (101:81–89) "The Lord indicated that he would liken 'the children of Zion' unto this parable. The widow in the parable

---

The Divine Establishment of the United States Constitution (D&C 101:77–80)

    "What was God's purpose in establishing the United States Constitution? We see it in the doctrine of moral agency. In the first decade of the restored Church, its members on the western frontier were suffering private and public persecution. Partly this was because of their opposition to the human slavery then existing in the United States. In these unfortunate circumstances, God revealed through the Prophet Joseph Smith eternal truths about His doctrine.

    "God has given His children moral agency—the power to decide and to act. The most desirable condition for the exercise of that agency is maximum freedom for men and women to act according to their individual choices. Then, the revelation explains, 'every man may be accountable for his own sins in the day of judgment' (Doctrine and Covenants 101:78). 'Therefore,' the Lord revealed, 'it is not right that any man should be in bondage one to another' (Doctrine and Covenants 101:79). This obviously means that human slavery is wrong. And according to the same principle, it is wrong for citizens to have no voice in the selection of their rulers or the making of their laws" (Oaks, "Defending Our Divinely Inspired Constitution," *Liahona*, May 2021, 105–6).

is evidently representative of the children of Zion (members of the Church), while the unjust judge is representative of the various state and national leaders who had it in their power to redress the wrongs of the Saints (children of Zion), but refused to do so" (Daniel H. Ludlow, *Companion to Your Study*, 1:527). ◑

What possible consequences befell the Missourians for their persecution and banishment of the Saints? (101:89–91) While the Civil War is likely not the only fulfillment of the Lord's fury vexing the nation, Missouri experienced more than its share of violence and hardship during the Civil War. "Partisan warfare along the Kansas-Missouri border continued the violence that had begun in 1854. The vicious conflicts between Border Ruffians and Jayhawkers expanded a hundredfold after 1861 as they gained sanction from Confederate and Union governments. The guerrilla fighting in Missouri produced a form of terrorism that exceeded anything else in the war" (McPherson, *Battle Cry of Freedom*, 784).

Under what is referred to as "General Order No. 11," issued in August 1863, the United States Army forced all residents of rural areas, especially Jackson County, to leave their property. Animals and other property were stolen or destroyed and houses, barns and outbuildings burnt to the ground, leaving only charred chimneys and burnt stubble remaining where once-fertile farms had stood (see Castel, "Order No. 11 and the Civil War on the Border," 357–68).

What is the Lord's "strange act" and "strange work"? (101:95) "The Lord has said by the mouth of the prophet Isaiah, that he would proceed to do a marvelous work and a wonder (Isaiah 29:14); and when I look at the rise in progress of this church, when I behold the great work the Lord has performed, it was a marvelous work and a wonder indeed. . . . It

83 And there was a widow in that city, and she came unto him, saying: Avenge me of mine adversary.

84 And he would not for a while, but afterward he said within himself: Though I fear not God, nor regard man, yet because this widow troubleth me I will avenge her, lest by her continual coming she weary me.

85 Thus will I liken the children of Zion.

86 Let them importune at the feet of the judge;

87 And if he heed them not, let them importune at the feet of the governor;

88 And if the governor heed them not, let them importune at the feet of the president;

89 And if the president heed them not, then will the Lord arise and come forth out of his hiding place, and in his fury vex the nation;

90 And in his hot displeasure, and in his fierce anger, in his time, will cut off those wicked, unfaithful, and unjust stewards, and appoint them their portion among hypocrites, and unbelievers;

91 Even in outer darkness, where there is weeping, and wailing, and gnashing of teeth.

92 Pray ye, therefore, that their ears may be opened unto your cries, that I may be merciful unto them, that these things may not come upon them.

93 What I have said unto you must needs be, that all men may be left without excuse;

94 That wise men and rulers may hear and know that which they have never considered;

95 That I may proceed to bring to pass my act, my strange act, and perform my work, my strange work, that men may discern between the righteous and the wicked, saith your God.

96 And again, I say unto you, it is contrary to my commandment and my will that my servant Sidney Gilbert should sell my storehouse, which I have appointed unto my people, into the hands of mine enemies.

97 Let not that which I have appointed be polluted by mine enemies, by the consent of those who call themselves after my name;

98 For this is a very sore and grievous sin against me, and against my people, in consequence of those things which I have decreed and which are soon to befall the nations.

99 Therefore, it is my will that my people should claim, and hold claim upon that which I have appointed unto them, though they should not be permitted to dwell thereon.

100 Nevertheless, I do not say they shall not dwell thereon; for inasmuch as they bring forth fruit and works meet for my kingdom they shall dwell thereon.

101 They shall build, and another shall not inherit it; they shall plant vineyards, and they shall eat the fruit thereof. Even so. Amen.

is the only true church upon the face of the whole earth. Its history is before the world. It has continued to grow and increase from the day it was organized until the present time. This is the Zion of God. . . . This is certainly a strange work and a wonder. There has been every exertion made to stay it. Armies have been sent forth to destroy this people; But we have been upheld and sustained by the hand of the Lord until today" (Woodruff, in *Journal of Discourses*, 21:124, 125). See also commentary in this volume on D&C 95:4.

What did the Lord mean that the Saints should "hold claim upon that which [He had] appointed unto them"? (101:99) In August 1833, Joseph wrote to the Saints in Missouri: "[Let] your sufferings be what they may; it is better, in the eyes of God, that you should die, than that you should give up the land of Zion; the inheritances which you have purchased with your moneys; for every man that giveth not up his inheritances, though he should die, yet when the Lord shall come, he shall stand upon it, and, with Job, in his flesh he shall see God. Therefore this is my counsel that you retain your land; even unto the uttermost, and seek every lawful means to seek redress of your enemies, [etc.], and pray to God, day and night, to return you in peace and in safety to the Lands of your inheritance" (Joseph Smith Papers, "History, 1838–1856, volume A-1," 394–95).

Introduction to Doctrine and Covenants 102

Doctrine and Covenants 102 comprises the minutes of the organization of the first stake high council in Kirtland, Ohio. "On 17 February 1834 at a meeting that included priesthood holders and other members of the church, [Joseph Smith] oversaw the initial organization of a standing 'Presidents Church Council' in Kirtland, Ohio. [It later became known as the 'high council of the Church of Christ,' or the Kirtland high council.] Orson Hyde, the clerk of the meeting, noted in the minutes of that meeting that 'many questions have been asked during the time of the organization of this Council and doubtless some errors have been committed, it was, therefore, voted by all present that Bro Joseph should make all necessary corrections by the spirit of inspiration hereafter.' [The Prophet] worked on amending the minutes the following day 'with all the strength and wisdom that he had' and presented the revised minutes . . . to a council of sixty-two priesthood holders and church members on 19 February. . . . The council unanimously voted to accept the revised minutes as 'a form, and constitution of the high Council of the Church of Christ hereafter. . . .' After giving several blessings and items of instruction to members of the new council . . . 'the Council was organized according to the ancient order, and also according to the mind of the Lord'" (Joseph Smith Papers, Historical Introduction to "Revised Minutes, 18–19 February 1834 [D&C 102]").

Of all the sections in the Doctrine and Covenants, 102 "is unique in that it consists of an extract from the minutes of the meeting in which the first high council in the Church was organized. This event marks the formal beginning of the Kirtland Stake, the first stake in the Church" (Cowan, *Doctrine and Covenants: Our Modern Scripture*, 156).

This section of the Doctrine and Covenants unfolds insights about councils. "Bro. Joseph . . . said he would show the order of councils in ancient days . . . as shown to him by vision. The law by which to govern the council in the Church of Christ. Jerusalem was the seat of the Church Council in ancient days. The apostle, Peter, was the president of the Council and held the keys of the Kingdom of God on the earth [and] was appointed to this office by the voice of the Savior and acknowledged in it by the voice of the Church. . . . It was not the order of heaven in ancient councils to plead for and against the guilty as in our judicial Courts (so called) but that every counselor when he arose to speak, should speak precisely according to evidence and according to the teaching of the Spirit of the Lord" (Joseph Smith Papers, "Minute Book 1," 29–30).

Doctrine and Covenants 102:1–8. A High Council Is Appointed to Settle Important Difficulties That Arise in the Church

What was the difference between the twenty-four high priests and the twelve high priests? (102:1)

"To avoid confusion, it must be remembered that a general council of high priests, priests, and members (see v. 5) had met on this occasion to nominate and sustain twelve high priests and a presidency as a high council. The two bodies should not be confused"

SECTION 102

Minutes of the organization of the first high council of the Church, at Kirtland, Ohio, February 17, 1834. The original minutes were recorded by Elders Oliver Cowdery and Orson Hyde. The Prophet revised the minutes the following day, and the next day the corrected minutes were unanimously accepted by the high council as "a form and constitution of the high council" of the Church. Verses 30 through 32, having to do with the Council of the Twelve Apostles, were added in 1835 under Joseph Smith's direction when this section was prepared for publication in the Doctrine and Covenants.

1 This day a general council of twenty-four high priests assembled at the house of Joseph Smith, Jun., by revelation, and proceeded to organize the high council of the church of Christ, which was to consist of twelve high priests, and one or three presidents as the case might require.

2 The high council was appointed by revelation for the purpose of settling important difficulties which might arise in the church, which could not be settled by the church or the bishop's council to the satisfaction of the parties.

3 Joseph Smith, Jun., Sidney Rigdon and Frederick G. Williams were acknowledged presidents by the voice of the council; and Joseph Smith, Sen., John Smith, Joseph Coe, John Johnson, Martin Harris, John S. Carter, Jared Carter, Oliver Cowdery, Samuel H. Smith, Orson Hyde, Sylvester Smith, and Luke Johnson, high priests, were chosen to be a standing council for the church, by the unanimous voice of the council.

4 The above-named councilors were then asked whether they accepted their appointments, and whether they would act in that office according to the law of heaven, to which they all answered that they accepted their appointments, and would fill their offices according to the grace of God bestowed upon them.

5 The number composing the council, who voted in the name and for the church in appointing the above-named councilors were forty-three, as follows: nine high priests, seventeen elders, four priests, and thirteen members.

6 Voted: that the high council cannot have power to act without seven of the above-named councilors, or their regularly appointed successors are present.

(Robinson and Garrett, *Commentary on the Doctrine and Covenants*, 3:284–85).

What kind of difficulties did the early high council of the Church confront? (102:2) The high council, appointed by revelation, "became necessary very early for the following reasons: (1) There was need for doctrinal and ecclesiastical clarification in the Church. Definitions of acceptable orthodoxy and ecclesiastical function often came from actual cases handled by early Church [councils]. . . . (2) There was need for dealing with both internal and external apostasy in the early days of the Church, when many succumbed to the trials of persecution or temptation. . . . (3) There was need for a full restoration of correct principles . . . as a part of the restoration of all things in this dispensation. . . . Procedures outlined in section 102 met all of these needs" (Moss, "Church Judicial System," 395–96).

In what way was the Kirtland high council a "standing council"? (102:3) In this verse the word *standing* meant "that the council was not to be adjourned after handling pressing issues but would continue 'standing' as a council for future needs" (*Doctrine and Covenants Student Manual* [2018], 577).

Then-Elder George A. Smith stated: "I remember very well the organization of the High Council at Kirtland as a permanent institution. There had been several Councils of twelve High Priests called for special cases, but they organized it permanently on 17th Feb. 1834" (in *Journal of Discourses*, 11:7). See also commentary in this volume on Doctrine and Covenants 107:36–37.

What was the role of these forty-three individuals? (102:5) "These forty-three people, chosen from the sixty who attended the meeting held at the home of the Prophet on 17 February, in turn nominated the twelve men who were called to serve as the first high council in the Church" (McConkie and Ostler, *Revelations of the Restoration*, 745).

7 These seven shall have power to appoint other high priests, whom they may consider worthy and capable to act in the place of absent councilors.

8 Voted: that whenever any vacancy shall occur by the death, removal from office for transgression, or removal from the bounds of this church government, of any one of the above-named councilors, it shall be filled by the nomination of the president or presidents, and sanctioned by the voice of a general council of high priests, convened for that purpose, to act in the name of the church.

Doctrine and Covenants 102:9–18. Procedures Are Given for Hearing Cases

How did the Prophet's position as president of the Kirtland high council set a precedent for later councils? (102:9–10) "On 17 February 1834, a general council was held at the Prophet Joseph Smith's home. From this council of 24 high priests, 12 brethren were selected to become the first high council in the first stake of the Church. It was known as the Kirtland Stake, over which the First Presidency of the Church became the stake presidency. The purpose of the high council was to settle difficulties that arose in the stake and to assist the presidency in organizing and regulating Church affairs.

"Through the years, the First Presidency has addressed the duties and responsibilities of the high council and, among other things, has encouraged the high council and the stake presidency to become one. The high council is to advise and counsel the stake presidency" (Stanley A. Johnson, "High Council," 479).

9 The president of the church, who is also the president of the council, is appointed by revelation, and acknowledged in his administration by the voice of the church.

10 And it is according to the dignity of his office that he should preside over the council of the church; and it is his privilege to be assisted by two other presidents, appointed after the same manner that he himself was appointed.

11 And in case of the absence of one or both of those who are appointed to assist him, he has power to preside over the council without an assistant; and in case he himself is absent,

The Development of Church Membership Councils (Doctrine and Covenants 102:12–18)

Doctrine and Covenants 102 contains minutes describing what the Lord instructed the Church in 1834 pertaining to the Kirtland High Council. Principles continue to apply today, but policies and procedures can be modified by the President of the Church. President Russell M. Nelson explained, "Though we of the First Presidency and Quorum of the Twelve Apostles cannot change the laws of God, we do have the charge 'to build up the church, and regulate all the affairs of the same in all nations' [D&C 107:33]. Thus we can adjust policy when the Lord directs us to do so. You have recently seen such examples. Because the Restoration is ongoing, policy changes will surely continue [see Articles of Faith 1:9]" ("Love and Laws of God," 4).

Today, additional adjustments to the General Handbook refer to "membership councils," not "disciplinary councils," as the setting for helping members guilty of serious offenses to repent (see General Handbook, 32.5).

"Most repentance takes place between an individual, a loving God, and those who have been affected by a person's sins. However, if a Church member commits a serious sin, the bishop or stake president may need to assist him or her in repentance (see Mosiah 26:29).

"As part of his or her repentance for a serious sin, a member may lose some Church membership privileges for a time. Decisions about membership and membership privileges are sometimes made in a membership council.

the other presidents have power to preside in his stead, both or either of them.

12 Whenever a high council of the church of Christ is regularly organized, according to the foregoing pattern, it shall be the duty of the twelve councilors to cast lots by numbers, and thereby ascertain who of the twelve shall speak first, commencing with number one and so in succession to number twelve.

13 Whenever this council convenes to act upon any case, the twelve councilors shall consider whether it is a difficult one or not; if it is not, two only of the councilors shall speak upon it, according to the form above written.

14 But if it is thought to be difficult, four shall be appointed; and if more difficult, six; but in no case shall more than six be appointed to speak.

15 The accused, in all cases, has a right to one-half of the council, to prevent insult or injustice.

16 And the councilors appointed to speak before the council are to present the case, after the evidence is examined, in its true light before the council; and every man is to speak according to equity and justice.

How might these instructions apply to the Church president and his counselors today? (102:10–11)
"When the President [of the Church] is ill or not able to function fully in all of the duties of his office, his two Counselors together comprise a Quorum of the First Presidency. They carry on with the day-to-day work of the Presidency. In exceptional circumstances, when only one may be able to function, he may act in the authority of the office of the Presidency as set forth in [D&C 102:10–11]" (*Gordon B. Hinckley* [manual], 265).

The purposes of Church membership councils are to help protect others, help a person access the redeeming power of Jesus Christ through repentance (see Alma 26:13), and protect the integrity of the Church.

"In a membership council, the bishop or stake president determines through counsel and a spirit of love and inspiration from the Lord if the person remains in good standing or if a person's Church membership should be restricted or withdrawn" (Topics and Questions, s.v. "Membership Councils").

Elder Neil L. Andersen emphasized the gospel principles upon which membership councils are based: "The stake president and bishop have been given the authority, when necessary, to convene a council on worthiness matters. These councils are not tribunals of persecution or punishment. Absolutely the opposite. Their purpose is to lovingly help someone return to God. The highest priority of the priesthood leaders in these councils is to protect others who could be harmed. They also have the sacred responsibility to help the person desiring to repent to access the redeeming power of Jesus Christ. Finally, they are to help safeguard the integrity and good name of the Savior's Church by not allowing the conduct of a member of the Church to impair the moral influence of Jesus Christ and of His Church" (*Divine Gift of Forgiveness*, 242–43).

17 Those councilors who draw even numbers, that is, 2, 4, 6, 8, 10, and 12, are the individuals who are to stand up in behalf of the accused, and prevent insult and injustice.

Doctrine and Covenants 102:19–23. The President of the Council Renders the Decision

How does the president of the council make final decisions over difficult issues? (102:19–23) "The three brethren of the bishopric, or the three brethren of the stake presidency, or the three brethren of the presidency of the Church, sit together, discuss matters together, pray together, in the process of reaching a decision. I wish to assure you . . . that I think there is never a judgment rendered until after prayer has been had. Action [regarding] a member is too serious a matter to result from the judgment of men alone, and particularly of one man alone. There must be the guidance of the Spirit, earnestly sought for and then followed, if there is to be justice" (Hinckley, "In . . . Counsellors There Is Safety," *Ensign*, Nov. 1990, 50).

Doctrine and Covenants 102:24–34. Appellate Procedure Is Set Forth

18 In all cases the accuser and the accused shall have a privilege of speaking for themselves before the council, after the evidences are heard and the councilors who are appointed to speak on the case have finished their remarks.

19 After the evidences are heard, the councilors, accuser and accused have spoken, the president shall give a decision according to the understanding which he shall have of the case, and call upon the twelve councilors to sanction the same by their vote.

20 But should the remaining councilors, who have not spoken, or any one of them, after hearing the evidences and pleadings impartially, discover an error in the decision of the president, they can manifest it, and the case shall have a re-hearing.

21 And if, after a careful re-hearing, any additional light is shown upon the case, the decision shall be altered accordingly.

22 But in case no additional light is given, the first decision shall stand, the majority of the council having power to determine the same.

23 In case of difficulty respecting doctrine or principle, if there is not a sufficiency written to make the case clear to the minds of the council, the president may inquire and obtain the mind of the Lord by revelation.

24 The high priests, when abroad, have power to call and organize a council after the manner of the foregoing, to settle difficulties, when the parties or either of them shall request it.

25 And the said council of high priests shall have power to appoint one of their own number to preside over such council for the time being.

26 It shall be the duty of said council to transmit, immediately, a copy of their proceedings, with a full statement of the testimony accompanying their decision, to the high council of the seat of the First Presidency of the Church.

27 Should the parties or either of them be dissatisfied with the decision of said council, they may appeal to the high council of the seat of the First Presidency of the Church, and have a re-hearing, which case shall there be conducted, according to the former pattern written, as though no such decision had been made.

28 This council of high priests abroad is only to be called on the most difficult cases of church matters; and no common or ordinary case is to be sufficient to call such council.

29 The traveling or located high priests abroad have power to say whether it is necessary to call such a council or not.

30 There is a distinction between the high council or traveling high priests abroad, and the traveling high council composed of the twelve apostles, in their decisions.

31 From the decision of the former there can be an appeal; but from the decision of the latter there cannot.

32 The latter can only be called in question by the general authorities of the church in case of transgression.

33 Resolved: that the president or presidents of the seat of the First Presidency of the Church shall have power to determine whether any such case, as may be appealed, is justly entitled to a re-hearing, after examining the appeal and the evidences and statements accompanying it.

How may a Church member appeal a decision of a membership council? (102:26–27) "A member may appeal the decision of a ward membership council to the stake president.... The stake president holds a stake membership council to consider the appeal. He may also ask a bishop to reconvene a council and reconsider a decision, particularly if there is new information.

"A member may appeal the decision of a stake membership council by writing a letter to the First Presidency....

"A person who appeals a decision specifies in writing the alleged errors or unfairness in the procedure or decision....

"First Presidency decisions are final and cannot be appealed again" (*General Handbook* [2022], 32.13).

How do these verses clarify the distinction between the various councils? (102:30–32) "It should be noted that vv. 30–32 were not part of the minutes of the 17 February 1834 meeting, but were added by Joseph Smith in 1835 when the Doctrine and Covenants was being prepared for publication. These verses deal with the twelve apostles, which were not called until [February] 1835" (Moss, "Church Judicial System," 396).

In other words, the "high council or traveling high priests abroad" (see verses 24, 30) represent what we call today the stake high council. The "traveling high council" (see verse 30) is the Quorum of the Twelve Apostles.

34 The twelve councilors then proceeded to cast lots or ballot, to ascertain who should speak first, and the following was the result, namely: 1, Oliver Cowdery; 2, Joseph Coe; 3, Samuel H. Smith; 4, Luke Johnson; 5, John S. Carter; 6, Sylvester Smith; 7, John Johnson; 8, Orson Hyde; 9, Jared Carter; 10, Joseph Smith, Sen.; 11, John Smith; 12, Martin Harris.

After prayer the conference adjourned.

OLIVER COWDERY,
ORSON HYDE,
Clerks

Introduction to Doctrine and Covenants 103

"On 24 February 1834, [at Kirtland, Ohio,] the Prophet Joseph Smith received a revelation [D&C 103] concerning the organization of Zion's camp to help the Saints regain possession of their inheritance [in Jackson County, Missouri]" (Fowles, "Missouri and the Redemption of Zion," 167).

The Saints living in Missouri had been driven from their homes amidst bitter violence and persecution in Jackson County. Parley P. Pratt and Lyman Wight came from Missouri to report the condition of the Saints to Joseph Smith, who was residing in Kirtland, Ohio, at the time.

"[Brothers Parley] Pratt and [Lyman] Wight, messengers from Zion, arose and laid their business before the council and delivered their message. The substance of which was an inquiry when, how, and by what means Zion was to be redeemed from our enemies. They said that our brethren who had been driven away from their lands and scattered abroad had found so much favor in the eyes of the people that they could obtain food and raiment of them for their labor insomuch that they were comfortable. But the idea of being driven away from the land of Zion pained their very souls and they desired of God, by earnest prayer, to return. . . .

"Bro. Joseph then arose and said that he was going to Zion to assist in redeeming it. He then called for the voice of the council to sanction his going, which was given without a dissenting voice. He then called for volunteers to go with him, when some thirty or forty volunteered to go who were then present at the council. . . . Joseph Smith Jun. was nominated and seconded to be the Commander in Chief of the Armies of Israel and the leader of those who volunteered to go and assist in the redemption of Zion" (Joseph Smith Papers, "Minutes, 24 February 1834," 41; spelling modernized).

After the report of these brethren, Joseph Smith received the revelation (D&C 103) to organize a group to help the Saints in Missouri. "This expedition, known today as Zion's Camp, was initially called the Camp of Israel. . . . The revelation instructed Church leaders to recruit at least 100, and preferably 500, men to travel to Missouri. In March, Joseph Smith and others traveled through New York to obtain volunteers and funding for the expedition" (Church History Topics, "Zion's Camp [Camp of Israel]").

The goal of Zion's Camp was "to join forces in Jackson County, Missouri, with the state militia to restore lands to the 1,200 Latter-day Saints who had been driven from the area by local residents. . . . For Joseph Smith, Zion's Camp would test his leadership skills at an early stage in his prophetic ministry" (Baugh, "Joseph Smith and Zion's Camp," *Ensign*, Jun. 2005, 43).

SECTION 103

Revelation given through Joseph Smith the Prophet, at Kirtland, Ohio, February 24, 1834. This revelation was received after the arrival in Kirtland, Ohio, of Parley P. Pratt and Lyman Wight, who had come from Missouri to counsel with the Prophet as to the relief and restoration of the Saints to their lands in Jackson County.

1 Verily I say unto you, my friends, behold, I will give unto you a revelation and commandment, that you may know how to act in the discharge of your duties concerning the salvation and redemption of your brethren, who have been scattered on the land of Zion;

2 Being driven and smitten by the hands of mine enemies, on whom I will pour out my wrath without measure in mine own time.

3 For I have suffered them thus far, that they might fill up the measure of their iniquities, that their cup might be full;

4 And that those who call themselves after my name might be chastened for a little season with a sore and grievous chastisement, because they did not hearken altogether unto the precepts and commandments which I gave unto them.

Doctrine and Covenants 103:1–4. Why the Lord Permitted the Saints in Jackson County to Be Persecuted

How was Joseph Smith to discharge his duties concerning the redemption of those who were driven from their homes in Jackson County? (103:1–2) "Joseph received a revelation, now Doctrine and Covenants 103, which instructed him to recruit as many as 500 'of the strength of [the Lord's] house'—young and middle-aged members of the Church—to go to Zion, where they would reclaim the Lord's vineyard. A few months earlier, in December 1833, the Lord had hinted at this effort to redeem Zion in the revelation that is now Doctrine and Covenants 101. The revelation contained a parable of a nobleman whose vineyard was overrun by his enemies and who instructed his servant to raise an army to retake his land. In the February 1834 revelation, the Lord designated Joseph Smith as the servant in the parable and appointed him to lead an expedition to Zion" (Godfrey, "Acceptable Offering of Zion's Camp," 214).

Why did the Lord permit the wicked to persecute the Saints? (103:3) "We learn by revelation that the Lord allows atrocities on the part of wicked people that they might merit the judgment he has in store for them. When the wicked inhabitants of Ammonihah destroyed faithful women and children by fire,. . . . [Alma taught] 'for behold the Lord receiveth them up unto himself, in glory; and he doth suffer that they may do this thing, or that the people may do this thing unto them, according to the hardness of their hearts, that the judgments which he shall exercise upon them in his wrath may be just; and the blood of the innocent shall stand as a witness against them, yea, and cry mightily against them at the last day' [see Alma 14:11; 60:13]" (McConkie and Ostler, *Revelations of the Restoration*, 749–50).

Why did the Saints' failure to hearken to the Lord result in such severe chastening? (103:4) "Joseph was one of those prophets whose souls were fired by the vision of Zion. . . .

"This grand end, however, was never realized during the Prophet's lifetime. Joseph Smith and the Lord were willing, but the Saints were unprepared. . . .

"Though the Lord had something to say about those who abused and drove out the Saints, he did not allow the Saints to forget that the greater responsibility for failure was theirs. He said, 'They were found transgressors, therefore they must needs be chastened' (D&C 101:41). This would be 'a sore and grievous chastisement, because they did not hearken altogether unto the precepts and commandments which I gave unto them' (D&C 103:4)" (Draper, "Maturing toward the Millennium," 389–90). See also commentary in this volume on Doctrine and Covenants 101:2 and 105:6.

Doctrine and Covenants 103:5–10. The Saints Will Prevail If They Keep the Commandments

Why is it essential to strive to observe all the Lord's words? (103:5–8) M. Joseph Brough taught, "In our family, we have a saying that became an important part of our mission. President Russell M. Nelson has been teaching the concept for a while. He said it this way: 'Obedience brings success; exact obedience brings miracles.'

"Our family and mission version is 'Obedience brings blessings, but exact obedience brings miracles.'

"I do not completely understand what exact obedience means, but here is what I have come to understand. It does not mean that we are perfectly obedient right now in all things, although we can be perfect in obeying many of the Lord's commandments. Hence, repentance must be a key part of exact obedience. Exact obedience requires a commitment to all the warnings and promptings and commandments Heavenly Father gives us" ("Still, Small Voice among Big Decisions," *Ensign*, Dec. 2018, 40).

How can the Saints be "a light unto the world"? (103:8–9) "As Church members, blessed with the truths of the gospel, the Lord expects us to be honest, morally clean, chaste, free from profanity and vulgarity, trustworthy, and exemplary in all our conduct. The Lord said to Church members of this dispensation:

"'But inasmuch as they keep not my commandments, and hearken not to observe all my words, the kingdoms of the world shall prevail against them.

"'For they were set to be a light unto the world, and to be the saviors of men . . .' [D&C 103:8–10].

"One of our best missionary tools is the sterling examples of members who live the gospel" (Benson, "Our Responsibility to Share the Gospel," *Ensign*, May 1985, 7).

5 But verily I say unto you, that I have decreed a decree which my people shall realize, inasmuch as they hearken from this very hour unto the counsel which I, the Lord their God, shall give unto them.

6 Behold they shall, for I have decreed it, begin to prevail against mine enemies from this very hour.

7 And by hearkening to observe all the words which I, the Lord their God, shall speak unto them, they shall never cease to prevail until the kingdoms of the world are subdued under my feet, and the earth is given unto the saints, to possess it forever and ever.

8 But inasmuch as they keep not my commandments, and hearken not to observe all my words, the kingdoms of the world shall prevail against them.

9 For they were set to be a light unto the world, and to be the saviors of men;

How can the Saints become "saviors"? (103:9)
"Jesus Christ is the Savior of all.... However, the Savior in his mercy often allows his Saints the opportunity and joy—and therefore the responsibility and obligation—of sharing in his redemptive work and becoming with him 'saviours . . . upon mount Zion' (Obadiah 1:21). Although this phrase includes our obligation to perform temple work, nothing in scripture limits it to this application alone. Missionaries who preach the gospel to the living, parents who lovingly raise and teach their children, Saints who serve in the Church, members who light the path and ease the burdens of their neighbors—all these in some degree serve their Lord and are, therefore, his agents as saviors on mount Zion" (Robinson and Garrett, *Commentary on the Doctrine and Covenants*, 3:291). ⊕

What is the Lord teaching us in this verse? (103:10)
"Those who are baptized in the Church of Jesus Christ make covenants. In modern revelation the Lord declared, 'When men are called unto mine everlasting gospel, and covenant with an everlasting covenant, they are accounted as the salt of the earth and the savor of men' (D&C 101:39). To perform our covenant duty as the salt of the earth, we must be different from those around us. As Jesus taught: 'I give unto you to be the salt of the earth; but if the salt shall lose its savor wherewith shall the earth be salted? The salt shall be thenceforth good for nothing, but to be cast out and to be trodden under foot of men' (3 Ne. 12:13; see also Matt. 5:13; D&C 101:40)" (Oaks, "Repentance and Change," *Ensign*, Nov. 2003, 39). See also commentary in this volume on Doctrine and Covenants 101:39–40.

10 And inasmuch as they are not the saviors of men, they are as salt that has lost its savor, and is thenceforth good for nothing but to be cast out and trodden under foot of men.

Doctrine and Covenants 103:11–20. The Redemption of Zion Will Come by Power, and the Lord Will Go before His People

What are some of the blessings that come when we endure tribulation? (103:12–14) "The greatest blessing that will come when we prove ourselves faithful to our covenants during our trials will be a change in our natures. By our choosing to keep our covenants, the power of Jesus Christ and the blessings of His Atonement can work in us. Our hearts can be softened to love, to forgive, and to invite others to come unto the Savior. Our confidence in the Lord increases. Our fears decrease.

"Now, even with such blessings promised through tribulation, we do not seek tribulation. In the mortal experience, we will have ample opportunity to prove ourselves, to pass tests hard enough to become

11 But verily I say unto you, I have decreed that your brethren which have been scattered shall return to the lands of their inheritances, and shall build up the waste places of Zion.

12 For after much tribulation, as I have said unto you in a former commandment, cometh the blessing.

13 Behold, this is the blessing which I have promised after your tribulations, and the tribulations of your brethren—your redemption, and the redemption of your brethren, even their restoration to the land of Zion, to be established, no more to be thrown down.

ever more like the Savior and our Heavenly Father" (Eyring, "Tested, Proved, and Polished," *Ensign*, Nov. 2020, 98). See also commentary in this volume on Doctrine and Covenants 58:2.

How and when will the Saints return to Jackson County, Missouri, to rebuild Zion? (103:13) "We shall go back to Jackson County. Not that all this people will leave these mountains, or all be gathered together in a camp, but when we go back there will be a very large organization consisting of thousands, and tens of thousands, and they will march forward, the glory of God overshadowing their camp by day in the form of a cloud, and a pillar of flaming fire by night, the Lord's voice being uttered forth before his army. Such a period will come in the history of this people. . . . And his people will go forth and build up Zion according to celestial law" (Orson Pratt, in *Journal of Discourses*, 15:364).

What can we learn from the Lord's use of language referring to the exodus of ancient Israel? (103:15–20) "In likening the events of our day to those of Moses' day, we as a people still appear unwilling and unready to redeem Zion. We have not yet sanctified ourselves that we might stand in the presence of God, and we have not obtained the discipline and faith necessary to live the law of consecration. When a sanctified generation comes, the Lord will call a modern Moses who will lead the armies of Israel with the same power in his priesthood as that known to his ancient counterpart from whom we received the keys of the gathering of Israel" (McConkie and Ostler, *Revelations of the Restoration*, 752). ✪

What type of power is needed to redeem Zion? (103:15) Elder Bruce R. McConkie taught that a spiritual power, "a perfection born of full obedience" is what will establish Zion. "By obedience, the saints have power to redeem Zion, to prevail in all things against their enemies, and to stand triumphant over earth and hell, even down to the Millennial day when the kingdoms of this world cease and only the kingdom of God remains. . . .

"It would have taken power in that day, and it will take power in the day when it is destined to be" (*New Witness*, 612, 613).

Who will be the man like unto Moses? (103:16) "Joseph Smith was such a man for his day, and another like him shall wear his mantle when the future hour of our redemption arrives" (Bruce R. McConkie, *New Witness*, 613).

14 Nevertheless, if they pollute their inheritances they shall be thrown down; for I will not spare them if they pollute their inheritances.

15 Behold, I say unto you, the redemption of Zion must needs come by power;

16 Therefore, I will raise up unto my people a man, who shall lead them like as Moses led the children of Israel.

"The Lord explained in an earlier revelation that not only was the Prophet Joseph Smith like a latter-day Moses, but that each President of the Church would 'be like unto Moses' as well (D&C 107:91; see also D&C 28:2)" (*Doctrine and Covenants Student Manual* [2018], 595).

17 For ye are the children of Israel, and of the seed of Abraham, and ye must needs be led out of bondage by power, and with a stretched-out arm.

18 And as your fathers were led at the first, even so shall the redemption of Zion be.

How did Joseph Smith refer to this expedition? (103:17) "Most Church members and scholars today use the name 'Zion's Camp' to refer to the Camp of Israel. However, records indicate that 'Zion's Camp' was not a contemporary name; instead, the 'Camp of Israel' was generally used. This name stemmed from the February 1834 revelation instructing Joseph Smith to form the camp. That revelation declared that Smith was to lead the expedition 'like as Moses led the children of Israel.' When Joseph Smith announced his intentions of forming the expedition, the Kirtland high council nominated him as the 'Commander in Chief of the Armies of Israel.' Accordingly, when Smith wrote a letter to his wife Emma while on the expedition, he stated that he was in the 'Camp of Israel in Indiana State town of Richmond'" (Godfrey, "Redemption of Zion Must Needs Come by Power," 130). See also other references to the analogy of this journey of modern-day Israel to the journey of ancient Israel in Doctrine and Covenants 103:16; 105:27; 107:91.

19 Therefore, let not your hearts faint, for I say not unto you as I said unto your fathers: Mine angel shall go up before you, but not my presence.

20 But I say unto you: Mine angels shall go up before you, and also my presence, and in time ye shall possess the goodly land.

How was the Lord's promise to Zion's Camp fulfilled? (103:19–20) Elder B. H. Roberts recorded, "The brethren of Zion's Camp knew the object of the expedition to be a noble one. They were conscious of God's approval, and of the presence in their midst of his angels; and strengthened by this knowledge, they fearlessly marched on to accomplish the work of redeeming Zion" (*Missouri Persecutions*, 131).

George A. Smith remembered men entering the camp swearing they would never reach Jackson County alive. "Joseph told the camp not to worry about harm from such enemies because he had seen 'the angels of God' watching over the expedition [Reuben McBride, journal, 3]" (Godfrey, "Camp of Israel's March to Missouri," 55).

When will the Saints possess the "goodly land" designated as Zion? (103:20) "It appears from this declaration that the redemption of Zion was not to come immediately, but was to be postponed to some future day [see D&C 58:3–4]. Moreover, that day would not come until the members of the Church were willing to keep their covenants and walk unitedly, for until the members of the Church learn to walk in full accord and in obedience with all of the commandments, this day cannot come. It may be necessary in order to bring this to pass for the Lord to use drastic measures and cleanse the Church from everything that offends. This he has promised to do when he is ready to redeem Zion (see Matt. 13:41)" (Smith, *Church History and Modern Revelation*, 1:484).

Doctrine and Covenants 103:21–28. The Saints Are to Gather in Zion, and Those Who Lay down Their Lives Will Find Them Again

What was the parable referred to in this verse? (103:21) "From these words we learned that the Lord's parable of the watchtower and the vineyard given in Section 101 was in prophetic anticipation of the formation of Zion's Camp under the direction of Joseph Smith (see 101:45, 55). As such, Joseph Smith would prefigure the man—'like as Moses' (D&C 103:16)—who would rise up in the last days to reclaim and redeem Zion. In all of this, the Lord gives the promise that His presence would be with the faithful Saints, and that individuals who would lay down their lives for the cause would 'find it again' as His true disciples" (Pinegar and Allen, *Unlocking the Doctrine and Covenants*, 205). See also commentary in this volume on Doctrine and Covenants 101:43, 45, 53, 55–62. ⊕

What instructions did Joseph Smith receive from the Lord to rescue the Saints in Missouri? (103:22) "The Prophet Joseph . . . asked the Lord what he should do. The Lord told him to go to and gather up the strength of the Lord's house, the young men and middle aged, and go up and redeem Zion. . . . It was the will of God that they should gather up 500 men, but they were not to go with less than 100 [see D&C 103]. The Saints of the Lord gathered up 205 men, most of whom assembled in Kirtland in the spring of 1834. . . . We were organized into companies of tens with a captain over each, and the Prophet of God led this company of 205 men of Zion's Camp 1,000 miles" (*Wilford Woodruff* [manual], 135). ⊕

How was the land of Zion to be obtained? (103:23) "It was never intended that the land could be obtained by any method other than purchase. The Lord said: 'The Land of Zion shall not be obtained but by purchase . . .' [D&C 63:29].

"Two years later [1833] the Lord instructed the Saints 'to purchase all the lands with money . . . in the

21 Verily, verily I say unto you, that my servant Joseph Smith, Jun., is the man to whom I likened the servant to whom the Lord of the vineyard spake in the parable which I have given unto you.

22 Therefore let my servant Joseph Smith, Jun., say unto the strength of my house, my young men and the middle aged—Gather yourselves together unto the land of Zion, upon the land which I have bought with money that has been consecrated unto me.

23 And let all the churches send up wise men with their moneys, and purchase lands even as I have commanded them.

24 And inasmuch as mine enemies come against you to drive you from my goodly land, which I have consecrated to be the land of Zion, even from your own lands after these testimonies, which ye have brought before me against them, ye shall curse them;

25 And whomsoever ye curse, I will curse, and ye shall avenge me of mine enemies.

26 And my presence shall be with you even in avenging me of mine enemies, unto the third and fourth generation of them that hate me.

27 Let no man be afraid to lay down his life for my sake; for whoso layeth down his life for my sake shall find it again.

28 And whoso is not willing to lay down his life for my sake is not my disciple.

region round about the land which I have appointed . . .' [D&C 101:70].

"The following year, the Prophet was directed to send 'wise men, to fulfil that which I have commanded concerning the purchasing of all the lands in Jackson county that can be purchased' [D&C 105:28]" (Alma P. Burton, *Toward the New Jerusalem*, 121). See also commentary in this volume on Doctrine and Covenants 101:70–74.

Would the Saints have been justified in taking revenge? (103:25–26) "The mobs in Missouri had not merely fought against the Saints, they had fought directly against the establishment of Zion and against properties and possessions consecrated to the Lord for the holiest of purposes. In addition, it should be noted that by this time the enemies of the Saints in Missouri had come against them more than three times. Assuming that the approach of Zion's Camp would constitute a warning to the mobs in Missouri, any further attack upon the Saints in that state would, according to Doctrine and Covenants 98:28, justify retaliation according to the principles given the Saints by the Lord" (Robinson and Garrett, *Commentary on the Doctrine and Covenants*, 3:293–94).

How did this promise apply to members of Zion's camp who died in Missouri? (103:27–28) "George A. Smith reported that the Prophet said 'our murmuring and fault-finding and want of humility had kindled the anger of the Lord against us; and that a severe scourge would come upon the Camp and many would die like sheep with the rot. . . .'

"[Weeks later] cholera struck the camp. . . . For several days the disease ravaged the camp in fulfillment of the foretold 'scourge'" (Baugh, "Joseph Smith and Zion's Camp," *Ensign*, Jun. 2005, 45, 46–47).

"Regarding those who gave their lives in the experience, Elder Joseph Young related that the Prophet Joseph Smith explained, 'Brethren, I have seen those men who died of cholera in our camp; and the Lord knows, if I get a mansion as bright as theirs, I ask no more.' At this relation he wept, and for some time could not speak' [Turley, 'Calling of the Twelve Apostles,' 369–70]" (Ostler, "Zion's Camp," 228).

Doctrine and Covenants 103:29–40. Various Brethren Are Called to Organize Zion's Camp and Go to Zion; They Are Promised Victory If They Are Faithful

What did the Lord require of the eastern congregations? (103:29) "The 24 February 1834 revelation also instructed several individuals, including Joseph Smith, Parley P. Pratt, and Lyman Wight, to depart Kirtland and begin recruiting the people and obtaining the funds necessary for the redemption of Zion. Joseph and the others quickly acted on the revelation's directions. On February 26, he and Parley P. Pratt 'started from home to obtain volunteers for Zion,' and Orson Pratt and Orson Hyde did the same. Lyman Wight, Sidney Rigdon, Hyrum Smith, and Frederick G. Williams, also appointed in the revelation as recruiters, left shortly thereafter....

"These men held meetings in which they preached, recruited volunteers, and raised funds to aid in the effort to restore the Mormon refugees to their homes in Jackson County" (Rogers, "Prelude to the March," 26).

How were the camps of Zion assembled? (103:30) "Zion's Camp was comprised of two divisions, one under the leadership of Joseph Smith and a smaller contingent under the leadership of Hyrum Smith and Lyman Wight. The divisions were divided into companies of twelve men. Each company elected its own captain who, in turn, arranged each man in his company according to his 'post and duty.' Some were assigned to be cooks, firemen, watermen, waggoners, horsemen, and commissaries, while others were appointed captains over fifties and hundreds according to the ancient order of Israel" (Black, *400 Questions and Answers*, 176).

29 It is my will that my servant Sidney Rigdon shall lift up his voice in the congregations in the eastern countries, in preparing the churches to keep the commandments which I have given unto them concerning the restoration and redemption of Zion.

30 It is my will that my servant Parley P. Pratt and my servant Lyman Wight should not return to the land of their brethren, until they have obtained companies to go up unto the land of Zion, by tens, or by twenties, or by fifties, or by an hundred, until they have obtained to the number of five hundred of the strength of my house.

31 Behold this is my will; ask and ye shall receive; but men do not always do my will.

32 Therefore, if you cannot obtain five hundred, seek diligently that peradventure you may obtain three hundred.

33 And if ye cannot obtain three hundred, seek diligently that peradventure ye may obtain one hundred.

34 But verily I say unto you, a commandment I give unto you, that ye shall not go up unto the land of Zion until you have obtained a hundred of the strength of my house, to go up with you unto the land of Zion.

35 Therefore, as I said unto you, ask and ye shall receive; pray earnestly that peradventure my servant Joseph Smith, Jun., may go with you, and preside in the midst of my people, and organize my kingdom upon the consecrated land, and establish the children of Zion upon the laws and commandments which have been and which shall be given unto you.

36 All victory and glory is brought to pass unto you through your diligence, faithfulness, and prayers of faith.

37 Let my servant Parley P. Pratt journey with my servant Joseph Smith, Jun.

38 Let my servant Lyman Wight journey with my servant Sidney Rigdon.

39 Let my servant Hyrum Smith journey with my servant Frederick G. Williams.

40 Let my servant Orson Hyde journey with my servant Orson Pratt, whithersoever my servant Joseph Smith, Jun., shall counsel them, in obtaining the fulfilment of these commandments which I have given unto you, and leave the residue in my hands. Even so. Amen.

What principles of the gospel can we learn from this verse? (103:36) Francisco J. Viñas applied this verse to enduring adversity. "How can we endure well the suffering that can come from adversity? During the hours that my wife lay in the hospital, and at other times when adversity has knocked at our door, our family has learned three basic principles that help us endure and overcome. They are found in a revelation given to Joseph Smith: 'All victory and glory is brought to pass unto you through your diligence, faithfulness, and prayers of faith' (D&C 103:36)" ("If Thou Endure It Well," *Ensign*, Jul. 2009, 11).

How should we respond to the Lord's call or assignments? (103:37–40) "The revelation ends with the Lord's assigning certain brethren their companions for travel in behalf of Zion's redemption. Elder Parley P. Pratt . . . is to travel with the Prophet, Elder Lyman Wight . . . with Sidney Rigdon . . . , Hyrum Smith with Frederick G. Williams, and Elder Orson Hyde with Orson Pratt, withersoever the Prophet counseled them, for the purpose of bringing about the fulfillment of the commandments given the brethren. . . .

"It should be noted, as the matter of history, that the brethren left almost immediately to fulfill their assignments in Zion's behalf" (Sperry, *Doctrine and Covenants Compendium*, 536–37).

Introduction to Doctrine and Covenants 104

Joseph Smith received the revelation recorded in Doctrine and Covenants 104 on April 23, 1834, at or near Kirtland, Ohio. Section 104 "contains instructions for the reorganization of the United Firm, which was formed in April 1832 to manage the church's mercantile and publishing endeavors and had served as an important administrative structure since that time. . . .

"By 1834, the firm faced several significant issues. Because of the violence that drove church members from Jackson County in summer and fall 1833, William W. Phelps's printing office and Gilbert's store were no longer in operation. Yet the firm was still responsible for debts incurred to supply these establishments. In Ohio, firm members became increasingly indebted to N. K. Whitney & Co., which was in turn indebted to New York companies for store goods. . . . According to [D&C 104], such covetous attitudes effectively broke the covenant and bond that members were required to take upon joining the firm. . . .

"Facing such problems, members of the Kirtland branch of the United Firm met on 10 April 1834 and decided 'that the firm should be [dissolved] and each one' receive a stewardship, or property, to manage. This 23 April revelation provided firm members in Kirtland with these stewardships and declared that all things were God's and that the members of the firm needed to manage their stewardships wisely" (Joseph Smith Papers, Historical Introduction to "Revelation, 23 April 1834 [D&C 104]"). See also commentary in this volume on Doctrine and Covenants 70, introduction and 1–3; 72:20–21; 78, introduction and 3–4; and 82:11–13, 15–18.

SECTION 104

Revelation given to Joseph Smith the Prophet, at or near Kirtland, Ohio, April 23, 1834, concerning the United Firm (see the headings to sections 78 and 82). The occasion was likely that of a council meeting of members of the United Firm, which discussed the pressing temporal needs of the Church. An earlier meeting of the firm on April 10 had resolved that the organization be dissolved. This revelation directs that the firm instead be reorganized; its properties were to be divided among members of the firm as their stewardships. Under Joseph Smith's direction, the phrase "United Firm" was later replaced with "United Order" in the revelation.

Doctrine and Covenants 104:1–10. Saints Who Transgress against the United Order Will Be Cursed

What was another name for the "united order" referred to in this revelation? (104:1) "In later editions [1835–1981] of the Doctrine and Covenants, the United Firm was called the 'United Order,' and code names were inserted in place of the participants' names. In addition, language about the firm's purpose was changed so that it referred more vaguely to meeting the needs of the poor. This was done to protect the identity of those involved in the firm and to keep its purposes confidential. The names of the individuals were restored to the revelations in the 1980s, but the firm is still referred to as the United Order in the 2013 edition of the Doctrine and Covenants" (Godfrey, "Newel K. Whitney and the United Firm," 146).

1 Verily I say unto you, my friends, I give unto you counsel, and a commandment, concerning all the properties which belong to the order which I commanded to be organized and established, to be a united order, and an everlasting order for the benefit of my church, and for the salvation of men until I come—

2 With promise immutable and unchangeable, that inasmuch as those whom I commanded were faithful they should be blessed with a multiplicity of blessings;

3 But inasmuch as they were not faithful they were nigh unto cursing.

4 Therefore, inasmuch as some of my servants have not kept the commandment, but have broken the covenant through covetousness, and with feigned words, I have cursed them with a very sore and grievous curse.

5 For I, the Lord, have decreed in my heart, that inasmuch as any man belonging to the order shall be found a transgressor, or, in other words, shall break the covenant with which ye are bound, he shall be cursed in his life, and shall be trodden down by whom I will;

6 For I, the Lord, am not to be mocked in these things—

7 And all this that the innocent among you may not be condemned with the unjust; and that the guilty among you may not escape; because I, the Lord, have promised unto you a crown of glory at my right hand.

What were those who were "not faithful" required to do to avoid being cursed? (104:3) "The revelation begins with the Lord calling them 'my friends,' but He soon rebukes unspecified members of the firm for breaking their covenant, the covenant found in section 82 (D&C 104:2–10). The Lord's unchangeable promise is that those who are faithful to the covenant will be blessed and those who are not will be cursed, or at least 'they [are] nigh unto cursing' (D&C 104:3). He promises covenant keepers a crown at His right hand but promises covenant breakers His wrath and the buffetings of Satan. The Lord reviews, in stronger terms than ever before in His revelations to Joseph, the doctrines of stewardship and accountability. Those doctrines, along with agency, underlie the law of consecration" (Harper, *Let's Talk about the Law of Consecration*, 59).

What are "feigned words" and how can they impact making covenants with God? (104:4) "Although this refers specifically to those who broke their covenants in the United Order [or Firm] at Kirtland, the principle applies to any who pronounce their agreement and loyalty to covenants and promises with feigned (pretended, insincere, or false) words. Such will bring down a cursing upon their heads [see vv. 5–8].

"In this respect it would be well to consider the words of Jesus Christ in an 1831 revelation: 'Wherefore, let all men beware how they take my name in their lips—For behold, verily I say, that many there be who are under this condemnation, who use the name of the Lord, and use it in vain, having not authority' (D&C 63:61–62)" (Brewster, *Doctrine & Covenants Encyclopedia* [2012], 184–85).

How are we affected by failing to keep our covenants? (104:5–8) "As the keeping of covenants brings the blessings of heaven, so the breaking of covenants brings sorrows of all kinds. And as affirmed by a host of scriptures, the curses that flow from disobedience are both temporal and spiritual.... Those who disobey God hardly need wait for the world to come to reap as they have sown" (McConkie and Ostler, *Revelations of the Restoration*, 759).

What are the "buffetings of Satan"? (104:9–10)
"When one is guilty of serious transgression and loses
the right to the Spirit and the protective blessings of
the priesthood, he is essentially 'delivered unto the
buffetings of Satan' (D&C 132:26), such that 'Lucifer is
free to torment, persecute, and afflict such a person
without let or hindrance. When the bars are down,
the cuffs and curses of Satan, both in this world and
in the world to come, bring indescribable anguish
typified by burning fire and brimstone' (cf. D&C 78:12;
82:20–21; 104:9–10; 1 Cor. 5:1–5)" (Millet, "New and
Everlasting Covenant," 520). See also commentary in
this volume on Doctrine and Covenants 78:12.

Doctrine and Covenants 104:11–16. The Lord Provides for His Saints in His Own Way

What were the stewardships given to the members of the United Firm? (104:11) Bishop Gérald
Caussé explained, "The word *stewardship* designates
a sacred spiritual or temporal responsibility to take
care of something that belongs to God for which we
are accountable" ("Our Earthly Stewardship," *Liahona*,
Nov. 2022, 57).

In section 104, the Lord assigned "stewardships
to the different members of the [united] firm. The
stewardships were specific pieces of property that individual members of the firm became responsible for.
For example, Newel K. Whitney was given his houses
and store, the lots on which they were located, and
the lot on which his ashery was located. Others were
given land and buildings resting on properties owned
by Frederick G. Williams and John Johnson" (Godfrey,
"Newel K. Whitney and the United Firm," 145–46).

**How is accountability related to stewardship?
(104:13)** "The law of consecration and stewardship
makes free agents of stewards by appointing them
their 'own property' without giving a false sense of
ownership (D&C 42:32). The underlying doctrines
here are agency and accountability....

"The Lord is adamant about the connections
between agency, stewardship, and accountability.
Because He has empowered us to act independently
with His property, we will be held accountable. He
repeats this point clearly throughout the Doctrine
and Covenants" (Harper, "All Things Are the Lord's,"
219, 220). ✛

8 Therefore, inasmuch as you are found
transgressors, you cannot escape my wrath in
your lives.

9 Inasmuch as ye are cut off for transgression,
ye cannot escape the buffetings of Satan until
the day of redemption.

10 And I now give unto you power from this
very hour, that if any man among you, of the
order, is found a transgressor and repenteth
not of the evil, that ye shall deliver him over
unto the buffetings of Satan; and he shall not
have power to bring evil upon you.

11 It is wisdom in me; therefore, a commandment I give unto you, that ye shall organize yourselves and appoint every man his
stewardship;

12 That every man may give an account unto
me of the stewardship which is appointed
unto him.

13 For it is expedient that I, the Lord, should
make every man accountable, as a steward
over earthly blessings, which I have made and
prepared for my creatures.

14 I, the Lord, stretched out the heavens, and built the earth, my very handiwork; and all things therein are mine.

15 And it is my purpose to provide for my saints, for all things are mine.

16 But it must needs be done in mine own way; and behold this is the way that I, the Lord, have decreed to provide for my saints, that the poor shall be exalted, in that the rich are made low.

17 For the earth is full, and there is enough and to spare; yea, I prepared all things, and have given unto the children of men to be agents unto themselves.

18 Therefore, if any man shall take of the abundance which I have made, and impart not his portion, according to the law of my gospel, unto the poor and the needy, he shall, with the wicked, lift up his eyes in hell, being in torment.

Why might the Lord emphasize His ownership of the earth? (104:14) "Our culture ignores God's ultimate ownership of everything, but the law of consecration is founded on that fundamental truth . . . This truth has important implications for the law of consecration. According to the scriptures, God owns everything, including us (see 1 Cor. 6:19–20). . . . [Consecration] requires covenant keepers to acknowledge that the Lord owns everything—all of it—and that each of us is to be a hardworking 'steward' who is accountable to the Lord, who requires us to freely consecrate all He has given us to relieve poverty and build Zion" (Harper, *Let's Talk about the Law of Consecration*, 13, 15).

What is the Lord's way to "provide for [His] saints" today? (104:15–16) "Church leaders have often encouraged Latter-day Saints 'to prepare for adversity in life by having a basic supply of food and water and some money in savings' [*All Is Safely Gathered In* (pamphlet, 2007), 1]. At the same time, we are encouraged to 'be wise' and 'not go to extremes' [*All Is Safely Gathered In*, 1] in our efforts to establish a home storage supply and a financial reserve. A resource entitled *Personal Finances for Self-Reliance*, published in 2017 and currently available on the Church website in 36 languages, begins with a message from the First Presidency, which states:

"'The Lord has declared, "It is my purpose to provide for my saints" [D&C 104:15]. This revelation is a promise from the Lord that He will provide temporal blessings and open the door of self-reliance'" (Waddell, "There Was Bread," *Ensign*, Nov. 2020, 43). ◉

Doctrine and Covenants 104:17–18.
Gospel Law Governs the Care of the Poor

Doctrine and Covenants 104:19–46.
The Stewardships and Blessings
of Various Brethren Are Designated

Why were properties and stewardships managed by the United Order (or United Firm) reassigned to the individuals listed in these verses? (104:19–46) "By such a plan the property of the Church managed by the United Firm could be protected. [Those who had loaned the Church money] would not have claim on property owned by individuals, but only on the property held by the United Firm. This was not to escape responsibility for paying their debts, but rather to give more time to gather the funds needed ['to pay all (their) debts' (Doctrine and Covenants 104:78)]" (Ostler, "Laws of Consecration, Stewardship, and Tithing," 168–69).

What can these verses teach you about the Lord? (104:19–46) Multiple times the Lord teaches when and how He will bless His servants. For example, in verse 23, He declares he will bless Sidney Rigdon "inasmuch as he will be humble before me." Additionally, in verses 25, 31, 33, 35, 38, 42, and 46, He promises blessings for faithfulness.

19 And now, verily I say unto you, concerning the properties of the order—

20 Let my servant Sidney Rigdon have appointed unto him the place where he now resides, and the lot of the tannery for his stewardship, for his support while he is laboring in my vineyard, even as I will, when I shall command him.

21 And let all things be done according to the counsel of the order, and united consent or voice of the order, which dwell in the land of Kirtland.

22 And this stewardship and blessing, I, the Lord, confer upon my servant Sidney Rigdon for a blessing upon him, and his seed after him;

23 And I will multiply blessings upon him, inasmuch as he will be humble before me.

24 And again, let my servant Martin Harris have appointed unto him, for his stewardship, the lot of land which my servant John Johnson obtained in exchange for his former inheritance, for him and his seed after him;

Punishments Await Those Who Do Not Share the Lord's Abundance (D&C 104:18)

Steven C. Harper shared: "This potent passage [in Doctrine and Covenants 104:18] evokes the New Testament story of Lazarus and the rich man in Luke 16:19–31, especially verse 23. In the Savior's story, the rich man had 'fared sumptuously' in life while a 'beggar named Lazarus' waited in vain for some of his table scraps. When the two men died, angels carried Lazarus into Abraham's bosom while the rich man went to hell. 'And in hell he lift up his eyes, being in torments,' and he begs Lazarus to relieve his suffering. The revelation in Doctrine and Covenants 104 evokes this story and applies it to Latter-day Saints....

"Withholding from the poor leads to deep, perhaps eternal, regret. Abundance is not the problem. The problem is choosing to keep the Lord's abundance from those who need it" (Let's Talk about the Law of Consecration, 60–61).

Elder Joseph B. Wirthlin taught: "There are those among us who have been blessed abundantly with enough and to spare. Our Heavenly Father expects that we do more with our riches than build larger barns to hold them. Will you consider what more you can do to build the kingdom of God? Will you consider what more you can do to bless the lives of others and bring light and hope into their lives?" ("Earthly Debts, Heavenly Debts," Ensign, May 2004, 43).

25 And inasmuch as he is faithful, I will multiply blessings upon him and his seed after him.

26 And let my servant Martin Harris devote his moneys for the proclaiming of my words, according as my servant Joseph Smith, Jun., shall direct.

27 And again, let my servant Frederick G. Williams have the place upon which he now dwells.

28 And let my servant Oliver Cowdery have the lot which is set off joining the house, which is to be for the printing office, which is lot number one, and also the lot upon which his father resides.

29 And let my servants Frederick G. Williams and Oliver Cowdery have the printing office and all things that pertain unto it.

30 And this shall be their stewardship which shall be appointed unto them.

31 And inasmuch as they are faithful, behold I will bless, and multiply blessings upon them.

32 And this is the beginning of the stewardship which I have appointed them, for them and their seed after them.

33 And, inasmuch as they are faithful, I will multiply blessings upon them and their seed after them, even a multiplicity of blessings.

34 And again, let my servant John Johnson have the house in which he lives, and the inheritance, all save the ground which has been reserved for the building of my houses, which pertains to that inheritance, and those lots which have been named for my servant Oliver Cowdery.

35 And inasmuch as he is faithful, I will multiply blessings upon him.

36 And it is my will that he should sell the lots that are laid off for the building up of the city of my saints, inasmuch as it shall be made known to him by the voice of the Spirit, and according to the counsel of the order, and by the voice of the order.

37 And this is the beginning of the stewardship which I have appointed unto him, for a blessing unto him and his seed after him.

38 And inasmuch as he is faithful, I will multiply a multiplicity of blessings upon him.

39 And again, let my servant Newel K. Whitney have appointed unto him the houses and lot where he now resides, and the lot and building on which the mercantile establishment stands, and also the lot which is on the corner south of the mercantile establishment, and also the lot on which the ashery is situated.

40 And all this I have appointed unto my servant Newel K. Whitney for his stewardship, for a blessing upon him and his seed after him, for the benefit of the mercantile establishment of my order which I have established for my stake in the land of Kirtland.

41 Yea, verily, this is the stewardship which I have appointed unto my servant N. K. Whitney, even this whole mercantile establishment, him and his agent, and his seed after him.

42 And inasmuch as he is faithful in keeping my commandments, which I have given unto him, I will multiply blessings upon him and his seed after him, even a multiplicity of blessings.

43 And again, let my servant Joseph Smith, Jun., have appointed unto him the lot which is laid off for the building of my house, which is forty rods long and twelve wide, and also the inheritance upon which his father now resides;

What do we know about Newel K. Whitney's faithfulness to fulfill his stewardship and the Lord's commandments? (104:39–42) "In April 1834, Newel K. Whitney, the bishop of the Church in Kirtland, Ohio, and a prominent businessman, forgave over $3,600 in debts owed to him by several individuals, including Joseph Smith, Sidney Rigdon, and Oliver Cowdery. The debts had accumulated over two years as these men worked together [in the United Firm] . . .

"Newel K. Whitney's participation in the United Firm left him with increased indebtedness, but he never showed any bitterness towards Joseph Smith or the Lord because of this. Whitney did not record his feelings about forgiving the large sum of $3,600, but his forgiveness of the debts showed his willingness to follow the Prophet even in temporal matters" (Godfrey, "Newel K. Whitney and the United Firm," 142, 146). ✚

44 And this is the beginning of the stewardship which I have appointed unto him, for a blessing upon him, and upon his father.

45 For behold, I have reserved an inheritance for his father, for his support; therefore he shall be reckoned in the house of my servant Joseph Smith, Jun.

46 And I will multiply blessings upon the house of my servant Joseph Smith, Jun., inasmuch as he is faithful, even a multiplicity of blessings.

47 And now, a commandment I give unto you concerning Zion, that you shall no longer be bound as a united order to your brethren of Zion, only on this wise—

48 After you are organized, you shall be called the United Order of the Stake of Zion, the City of Kirtland. And your brethren, after they are organized, shall be called the United Order of the City of Zion.

49 And they shall be organized in their own names, and in their own name; and they shall do their business in their own name, and in their own names;

50 And you shall do your business in your own name, and in your own names.

51 And this I have commanded to be done for your salvation, and also for their salvation, in consequence of their being driven out and that which is to come.

52 The covenants being broken through transgression, by covetousness and feigned words—

53 Therefore, you are dissolved as a united order with your brethren, that you are not bound only up to this hour unto them, only on this wise, as I said, by loan as shall be agreed by this order in council, as your circumstances will admit and the voice of the council direct.

Doctrine and Covenants 104:47–53. The United Order in Kirtland and the Order in Zion Are to Operate Separately

Why was it necessary to divide the economic operations of Zion in Missouri and Kirtland? (104:47–53) "[The Lord] commanded that there should be a separation of the United Order [or Firm] in Zion from the Order [or Firm] in Kirtland. Each was to act henceforth independently of the other. Distance was too great between these places for unity of purpose in all things. Each order was to be organized in the names of the brethren residing in each place, and to do business in their own names. This separation and dissolving of the former order came about also because of transgression and covetousness on the part of some. They were to understand that all the properties were the Lord's, otherwise their faith was vain, and therefore they were stewards before the Lord" (Joseph Fielding Smith, *Church History and Modern Revelation*, 1:489).

Doctrine and Covenants 104:54–66. The Sacred Treasury of the Lord Is Set Up for the Printing of the Scriptures

Why does the Lord underscore that all the properties are His? (104:55–56) "All things belong to God. He created them and he sustains and upholds them. A vital realization on the part of the man or woman who commits to follow the Redeemer is that he or she owns nothing, that we are stewards over God's properties" (Millet, *Christ-Centered Living*, 94).

What was "the fulness of my scriptures" the Lord commanded to be printed? (104:58) "The Lord's mention of 'the fulness of my scriptures' refers to the Prophet Joseph Smith's inspired translation of the Bible [see D&C 104:58, footnote *a*]. At the time the Prophet received this revelation, the work of translation was already completed. On 2 July 1833 the First Presidency wrote from Kirtland to the brethren in Zion: 'We are exceedingly fatigued, owing to a great press of business. We this day finished the translating of the Scriptures, for which we returned gratitude to our Heavenly Father' [Joseph Smith Papers, "History, 1838–1856, volume A-1," 316]. . . . Lack of financial support from the Saints, persecution, and pressing temporal concerns prevented the new translation of the Bible from being printed during the Prophet's lifetime" (McConkie and Ostler, *Revelations of the Restoration*, 764). See commentary in this volume on Doctrine and Covenants 35:20.

What were the "avails of the sacred things" that were to be kept in this treasury? (104:60–66) The word *avails* refers to "profits, or proceeds" (D&C 104:64*a*). "When the Lord dissolved the United Firm, he commanded Church leaders to create two treasuries. The first was designated as 'exclusive of the sacred things, for the purpose of printing these sacred things,' a reference to the scriptures (D&C 104:60–66). At the same time the Lord set up 'another treasury' for the purpose of 'improving upon the properties which I have appointed unto you' (D&C 104:67–68)" (Griffiths, "Covenant and a Deed," 126–27).

54 And again, a commandment I give unto you concerning your stewardship which I have appointed unto you.

55 Behold, all these properties are mine, or else your faith is vain, and ye are found hypocrites, and the covenants which ye have made unto me are broken;

56 And if the properties are mine, then ye are stewards; otherwise ye are no stewards.

57 But, verily I say unto you, I have appointed unto you to be stewards over mine house, even stewards indeed.

58 And for this purpose I have commanded you to organize yourselves, even to print my words, the fulness of my scriptures, the revelations which I have given unto you, and which I shall, hereafter, from time to time give unto you—

59 For the purpose of building up my church and kingdom on the earth, and to prepare my people for the time when I shall dwell with them, which is nigh at hand.

60 And ye shall prepare for yourselves a place for a treasury, and consecrate it unto my name.

61 And ye shall appoint one among you to keep the treasury, and he shall be ordained unto this blessing.

62 And there shall be a seal upon the treasury, and all the sacred things shall be delivered into the treasury; and no man among you shall call it his own, or any part of it, for it shall belong to you all with one accord.

63 And I give it unto you from this very hour; and now see to it, that ye go to and make use of the stewardship which I have appointed unto you, exclusive of the sacred things, for the purpose of printing these sacred things as I have said.

64 And the avails of the sacred things shall be had in the treasury, and a seal shall be upon it; and it shall not be used or taken out of the treasury by any one, neither shall the seal be loosed which shall be placed upon it, only by the voice of the order, or by commandment.

65 And thus shall ye preserve the avails of the sacred things in the treasury, for sacred and holy purposes.

66 And this shall be called the sacred treasury of the Lord; and a seal shall be kept upon it that it may be holy and consecrated unto the Lord.

67 And again, there shall be another treasury prepared, and a treasurer appointed to keep the treasury, and a seal shall be placed upon it;

68 And all moneys that you receive in your stewardships, by improving upon the properties which I have appointed unto you, in houses, or in lands, or in cattle, or in all things save it be the holy and sacred writings, which I have reserved unto myself for holy and sacred purposes, shall be cast into the treasury as fast as you receive moneys, by hundreds, or by fifties, or by twenties, or by tens, or by fives.

69 Or in other words, if any man among you obtain five dollars let him cast them into the treasury; or if he obtain ten, or twenty, or fifty, or an hundred, let him do likewise;

70 And let not any among you say that it is his own; for it shall not be called his, nor any part of it.

Doctrine and Covenants 104:67–77. The General Treasury of the United Order Is to Operate on the Basis of Common Consent

What was the purpose of the second treasury? (104:67–75) The second treasury "worked in harmony with the storehouse and was used to take care of the poor, to purchase lands, to build buildings, and to satisfy the needs of the Saints. All monies received from stewardship improvements were placed in this treasury as fast as they were received" (Clark V. Johnson, "Law of Consecration," 105).

What role did common consent play? (104:71–75)
"Having 'all things in common' meant two things to the Latter-day Saints: a *common storehouse* upon which to draw, and *common consent* as to how the moneys were to be expended in the community (D&C 104:71–75)" (Millet, *Precept upon Precept*, 174).

"[When] items were placed in the treasury they no longer were a part of an individual's stewardship but belonged to the Order; none could be removed without the approval of those in the Order (vv. 70–71). If an individual in the United Order needed anything in this 'other treasury' to assist him in his stewardship, with the approval and the common consent of the Order, the treasurer could give him what was required" (Backman and Perkins, "United under the Laws," 183).

71 And there shall not any part of it be used, or taken out of the treasury, only by the voice and common consent of the order.

72 And this shall be the voice and common consent of the order—that any man among you say to the treasurer: I have need of this to help me in my stewardship—

73 If it be five dollars, or if it be ten dollars, or twenty, or fifty, or a hundred, the treasurer shall give unto him the sum which he requires to help him in his stewardship—

74 Until he be found a transgressor, and it is manifest before the council of the order plainly that he is an unfaithful and an unwise steward.

75 But so long as he is in full fellowship, and is faithful and wise in his stewardship, this shall be his token unto the treasurer that the treasurer shall not withhold.

76 But in case of transgression, the treasurer shall be subject unto the council and voice of the order.

77 And in case the treasurer is found an unfaithful and an unwise steward, he shall be subject to the council and voice of the order, and shall be removed out of his place, and another shall be appointed in his stead.

Debt Can Be a Bondage (Doctrine and Covenants 104:83–84)

The Lord counseled Martin Harris: "Pay the debt thou hast contracted," and called debt "bondage" (D&C 19:35; see also D&C 104:83–84). President Gordon B. Hinckley once testified: "I urge you . . . to look to the condition of your finances. I urge you to be modest in your expenditures; discipline yourselves in your purchases to avoid debt to the extent possible. Pay off debt as quickly as you can, and free yourselves from bondage" (*Gordon B. Hinckley* [manual], 198).

President Henry B. Eyring testified how following a prophet blessed his family: "Years ago I heard President Ezra Taft Benson speak in a conference. . . . He counseled us to do all we could to get out of debt and stay out. He mentioned mortgages on houses. He said that it might not be possible, but it would be best if we could pay off all our mortgage debt.

"I turned to my wife after the meeting and asked, 'Do you think there is any way we could do that?' At first we couldn't. And then by evening I thought of a property we had acquired in another state. For years we had tried to sell it without success.

78 And again, verily I say unto you, concerning your debts—behold it is my will that you shall pay all your debts.

79 And it is my will that you shall humble yourselves before me, and obtain this blessing by your diligence and humility and the prayer of faith.

80 And inasmuch as you are diligent and humble, and exercise the prayer of faith, behold, I will soften the hearts of those to whom you are in debt, until I shall send means unto you for your deliverance.

81 Therefore write speedily to New York and write according to that which shall be dictated by my Spirit; and I will soften the hearts of those to whom you are in debt, that it shall be taken away out of their minds to bring affliction upon you.

82 And inasmuch as ye are humble and faithful and call upon my name, behold, I will give you the victory.

83 I give unto you a promise, that you shall be delivered this once out of your bondage.

84 Inasmuch as you obtain a chance to loan money by hundreds, or thousands, even until you shall loan enough to deliver yourself from bondage, it is your privilege.

Doctrine and Covenants 104:78–86. Those in the United Order Are to Pay All Their Debts, and the Lord Will Deliver Them from Financial Bondage

How can we apply the Lord's counsel to our own financial situations? (104:78–86) "The Lord wants His Saints free from debt (D&C 104:78). . . . The formula for getting the Lord's help in removing debt is diligence, humility, and the prayer of faith (vv. 79–80). . . . That the Lord had advised them previously against debt is implied by His offer to deliver them 'this once out of your bondage' (v. 83), and to pledge their properties as security to loan [borrow] money as a 'privilege this once' (vv. 85–86)" (Nyman, *Doctrine and Covenants Commentary*, 2:364).

"But because we trusted God and a few words from the midst of His servant's message, we placed a phone call Monday morning to the man . . . who had our property listed to sell. I had called him a few weeks before, and he had said then, 'We haven't had anyone show interest in your property for years.'

"But on the Monday after conference, I heard an answer that to this day strengthens my trust in God and His servants.

"The man on the phone said, 'I am surprised by your call. A man came in today inquiring whether he could buy your property.' In amazement I asked, 'How much did he offer to pay?' It was a few dollars more than the amount of our mortgage.

"A person might say that was only a coincidence. But our mortgage was paid off. And our family still listens for any word in a prophet's message that might be sent to tell what we should do to find the security and peace God wants for us" ("Trust in God, Then Go and Do," *Ensign*, Nov. 2010, 72–73).

85 And pledge the properties which I have put into your hands, this once, by giving your names by common consent or otherwise, as it shall seem good unto you.

86 I give unto you this privilege, this once; and behold, if you proceed to do the things which I have laid before you, according to my commandments, all these things are mine, and ye are my stewards, and the master will not suffer his house to be broken up. Even so. Amen.

Introduction to Doctrine and Covenants 105

The Prophet Joseph Smith received this revelation on June 22, 1834, during a council held near Fishing River in Clay County, Missouri, while discussing how Zion's Camp should proceed. Just a few days earlier, "after receiving news that they would not receive assistance from Governor Dunklin, the members of Zion's Camp proceeded toward the displaced Saints who were sheltered in Clay County, Missouri, and then camped approximately 10 miles northeast of Liberty, Missouri, between two forks of the Fishing River. On June 19, five armed men approached the camp and threatened that approximately 400 men were planning to attack the camp that night. However, the members of Zion's Camp were protected when a thunderstorm dropped large hailstones and caused the Fishing River to rise nearly 40 feet, preventing the mob from attacking. (See [*Joseph Smith Papers: Documents, Volume 4*], 63.) Members of Zion's camp viewed the storm as evidence that God was protecting them. One member of the camp, Nathan Baldwin, stated, 'The Lord had previously said He would fight the battles of His saints . . . and it seemed as though the mandate had gone forth from His presence, to ply the artillery of Heaven in defense of His servants' [in Godfrey, "Acceptable Offering of Zion's Camp"]" (*Doctrine and Covenants Student Manual* [2018], 598).

    "Because it had never been Joseph's intention to go to war contrary to the laws of the state and of the nation, the governor's change of policy effectively changed the mission of Zion's Camp. Joseph used the donated funds and supplies to aid the Missouri Saints in Clay County. He reorganized the leadership of the Missouri Saints and disbanded the volunteers of Zion's Camp" (Robinson and Garrett, *Commentary on the Doctrine and Covenants*, 3:305).

    "The revelation powerfully refocused Joseph Smith and the Church. Zion remained the ultimate goal, but the revelation declared that Zion would not be redeemed until the Saints were endowed with power. . . . The brethren were to return to the house of the Lord in Kirtland, to be endowed with power on conditions of humility and faithfulness (v. 12), and then spread out over the globe to gather Israel. Then, when the army became very great both numerically and in obedience to the law of consecration, they would regain Zion" (Harper, *Making Sense of the Doctrine & Covenants*, 391).

SECTION 105

Revelation given through Joseph Smith the Prophet, on Fishing River, Missouri, June 22, 1834. Under the leadership of the Prophet, Saints from Ohio and other areas marched to Missouri in an expedition later known as Zion's Camp. Their purpose was to escort the expelled Missouri Saints back to their lands in Jackson County. Missourians who had previously persecuted the Saints feared retaliation from Zion's Camp and preemptively attacked some Saints living in Clay County, Missouri. After the Missouri governor withdrew his promise to support the Saints, Joseph Smith received this revelation.

1 Verily I say unto you who have assembled yourselves together that you may learn my will concerning the redemption of mine afflicted people—

2 Behold, I say unto you, were it not for the transgressions of my people, speaking concerning the church and not individuals, they might have been redeemed even now.

3 But behold, they have not learned to be obedient to the things which I required at their hands, but are full of all manner of evil, and do not impart of their substance, as becometh saints, to the poor and afflicted among them;

4 And are not united according to the union required by the law of the celestial kingdom;

Doctrine and Covenants 105:1–5. Zion Will Be Built Up by Conformity to Celestial Law

Who is the Lord referring to when He mentions "mine afflicted people" and the "transgressions of my people"? (105:1–2) "The redemption of mine afflicted people" (verse 1) refers to the Saints in Missouri. "The transgressions of my people" (verse 2) "should not be limited to the Missouri Saints alone. The Lord had originally requested five hundred volunteers from Kirtland and the East, and Joseph had set out originally with barely one hundred. There had been complaining and contentions among members of Zion's Camp along the way, leading eventually to the scourge of cholera as punishment. Both the Missouri and the Kirtland churches had been warned in previous revelations about their sins (see D&C 95:2–6; 98:19–21; 101:2, 6–8, 50)" (Robinson and Garrett, *Commentary on the Doctrine and Covenants*, 3:306).

What things did the Lord require of the Saints? (105:3) "At the end of this expedition, the Lord again revealed that the Saints had transgressed the laws necessary to redeem Zion [see D&C 101:2, 6–7]. They had not learned to be obedient to the Law of Consecration (D&C 105:3–5). The Saints were counseled at that time, which evidently remains in force in the Church today, to give freely of their money to the cause, to be taught more perfectly, to have experience, and to purchase lands in Jackson County" (Fowles, "Missouri and the Redemption of Zion," 167). ☉

How can we become more united as a people so that we can inherit the celestial kingdom? (105:4) "As we consider the unity required for Zion to flourish, we should ask ourselves if we have overcome jarrings, contentions, envyings, and strifes (see D&C 101:6). Are we individually and as a people free from strife and contention and united 'according to the union required by the law of the celestial kingdom'? (D&C 105:4). Forgiveness of one another is essential to this unity. Jesus said, 'I, the Lord, will forgive whom I will forgive, but of you it is required to forgive all men' (D&C 64:10).

"We will become of one heart and one mind as we individually place the Savior at the center of our lives and follow those He has commissioned to lead us" (Christofferson, "Come to Zion," *Ensign*, Nov. 2008, 38).

How must Zion be built up? (105:5) "Zion is Zion because of the character, attributes, and faithfulness of her citizens. . . . If we would establish Zion in our homes, branches, wards, and stakes, we must rise to this standard. It will be necessary (1) to become unified in one heart and one mind; (2) to become, individually and collectively, a holy people; and (3) to care for the poor and needy with such effectiveness that we eliminate poverty among us. We cannot wait until Zion comes for these things to happen—Zion will come only as they happen" (Christofferson, "Come to Zion," *Ensign*, Nov. 2008, 38).

Doctrine and Covenants 105:6–13. The Redemption of Zion Is Deferred for a Little Season

Why does the Lord chasten His people? (105:6) "Consider first of all repentance, the necessary condition for forgiveness and cleansing. The Lord declared, 'As many as I love, I rebuke and chasten: be zealous therefore, and repent' (Revelation 3:19). Again He said, 'And my people must needs be chastened until they learn obedience, if it must needs be, by the things which they suffer' (D&C 105:6; see also D&C 1:27)" (Christofferson, "As Many as I Love, I Rebuke and Chasten," *Ensign*, May 2011, 98). See also commentary in this volume on Doctrine and Covenants 101:2 and 103:4.

How does the Lord respond to those who want God to show His power before they will exercise faith? (105:8) "The Lord addresses the skepticism of those Latter-day Saints who are waiting to see whether or not God will redeem Zion *before* they will commit their money to Zion's Camp or to the larger interests of establishing Zion at all. This, of course, is backwards. While it might make good sense in the logic of Babylon, in the Lord's economy the blessings only come *after* the trial of one's faith or after much tribulation (see D&C 58:4)" (Robinson and Garrett, *Commentary on the Doctrine and Covenants*, 3:306–7).

How long is "a little season"? (105:9) "A little season—how long will it last? Will it be two hundred years? or three hundred? Though the day of the Second Coming is fixed, the day for the redemption of Zion depends upon us. After we as a people live the law of the celestial kingdom; after we gain the needed experience and learn our duties; after we become by faith and obedience as were our fellow saints in the days of Enoch; after we are worthy to be translated, if

5 And Zion cannot be built up unless it is by the principles of the law of the celestial kingdom; otherwise I cannot receive her unto myself.

6 And my people must needs be chastened until they learn obedience, if it must needs be, by the things which they suffer.

7 I speak not concerning those who are appointed to lead my people, who are the first elders of my church, for they are not all under this condemnation;

8 But I speak concerning my churches abroad—there are many who will say: Where is their God? Behold, he will deliver them in time of trouble, otherwise we will not go up unto Zion, and will keep our moneys.

9 Therefore, in consequence of the transgressions of my people, it is expedient in me that mine elders should wait for a little season for the redemption of Zion—

10 That they themselves may be prepared, and that my people may be taught more perfectly, and have experience, and know more perfectly concerning their duty, and the things which I require at their hands.

11 And this cannot be brought to pass until mine elders are endowed with power from on high.

the purposes of the Lord should call for such a course in this day—then Zion will be redeemed, and not before" (Bruce R. McConkie, *New Witness*, 616). ◉

How are the Saints to be perfected? (105:10) "The redemption of Zion involves more than a location, more than a city or a temple. It requires the purging of one's heart and soul by the Holy Ghost of all un-Christlike motives; it means overcoming selfishness, covetousness, greediness, and idleness—problems specifically condemned by the Lord in these early revelations; it means overcoming tendencies to complain, criticize, and backbite; it means serving God with all one's heart, might, mind, and strength; it means self-mastery; it means being endowed with the power of God through keeping covenants; it means willingly sacrificing all that one has for the sake of the kingdom of God; it means taking on the divine nature; it requires becoming a holy person. Zion's redemption must await a generation of Saints equal to this standard" (William O. Nelson, "To Prepare a People," *Ensign*, Jan. 1979, 21). ◉

How would the elders receive an endowment of power from the Lord? (105:11–12) "The men of Zion's Camp, as it came to be known, walked in faith, the considerable faith required to kiss their families good-bye and march with a small, poorly-equipped

Lessons from Zion's Camp (Doctrine and Covenants 105:10)

"Because of the failure to reestablish the Saints on their lands in Jackson County, Zion's Camp was considered by some an unsuccessful and unprofitable endeavor. A brother in Kirtland . . . met Brigham Young on his return from Missouri and asked, 'Well, what did you gain on this useless journey to Missouri with Joseph Smith?' 'All we went for,' promptly replied Brigham Young. 'I would not exchange the experience I gained in that expedition for all the wealth of Geauga County,' the county in which Kirtland was then located. . . .

"I believe at least two overarching lessons are to be found in Brother Brigham's answer to that taunting question: (1) the lesson of testing, sifting, and preparing, and (2) the lesson of observing, learning from, and following the Brethren" (Bednar, "On the Lord's Side," *Ensign*, Jul. 2017, 29).

President Wilford Woodruff related: "'I was in Zion's Camp with the Prophet of God. I saw the dealings of God with him. I saw the power of God with him. I saw that he was a Prophet. What was manifest to him by the power of God upon that mission was of great value to me and to all who received his instructions'" (*Wilford Woodruff* [manual], 135).

"Truly, Zion's Camp was a refiner's fire for all of the volunteers in general and for many future leaders of the Lord's church in particular.

"The experiences gained by the volunteers in the army of the Lord also were a preparation for larger, future migrations of Church members. More than 20 of the Zion's Camp participants became captains and lieutenants in two great exoduses—the first but four years in the future, involving the removal of 8,000 to 10,000 people from Missouri to Illinois; and the second, 12 years in the future, the great western movement of approximately 15,000 Latter-day Saints from Illinois to the Salt Lake and other Rocky Mountain valleys. As a preparatory training, Zion's Camp was of immense value to the Church. The year 1834 was the time to show—and to prepare for 1838 and for 1846" (Bednar, "On the Lord's Side," *Ensign*, Jul. 2017, 30).

band to an unknown encounter for the cause of Zion. As a result of section 103, the Lord let many, though not as many as he asked for, pledge their allegiance to him and his cause. Their lives were his. He let them march all the way there before explaining that the power to redeem Zion would come not from a confrontation in Missouri but from an endowment in the house of the Lord back in Kirtland" (Harper, *Making Sense of the Doctrine & Covenants*, 381). ⊕

What great endowment did the elders receive in the Kirtland Temple? (105:12) "The endowment referred to is administered in temples. The ordinances associated with the endowment were received in this dispensation in the Kirtland Temple. These included washings and anointings, as well as a pouring out of the Lord's Spirit as on the day of Pentecost in Acts 2. The fulness of the endowment as administered in temples today was not available until the Nauvoo Temple was built" (McConkie and Ostler, *Revelations of the Restoration*, 770–71).

Why is it important for the Saints to trust in the Lord's timing for the redemption of Zion? (105:13) "There is no occasion for uncertainty or anxiety about the building up of Zion—meaning the New Jerusalem—in the last days. The Lord once offered his people the chance to build that Zion from which the law shall go forth to all the world. They failed. Why? Because they were unprepared and unworthy, as is yet the case with those of us who now comprise the kingdom. When we as a people are prepared and worthy, the Lord will again command us and work will go forward—on schedule, before the Second Coming, and at the direction of the President of the Church. Until then, none of us need take any personal steps toward gathering to Missouri or preparing for a landed-inheritance there" (Bruce R. McConkie, *New Witness*, 586).

Doctrine and Covenants 105:14–19. The Lord Will Fight the Battles of Zion

What was the Lord's promise to the faithful in Zion's Camp? (105:14) "The Lord had promised the Saints ten months earlier in Doctrine and Covenants 98:37 that he would fight their battles. Most of Zion's Camp were grateful that the Lord had accepted their offering, but a few, caught up in the spirit of war and bloodshed, were disappointed, and some even apostatized when the Camp was disbanded without fighting" (Robinson and Garrett, *Commentary on the Doctrine and Covenants*, 3:307).

12 For behold, I have prepared a great endowment and blessing to be poured out upon them, inasmuch as they are faithful and continue in humility before me.

13 Therefore it is expedient in me that mine elders should wait for a little season, for the redemption of Zion.

14 For behold, I do not require at their hands to fight the battles of Zion; for, as I said in a former commandment, even so will I fulfil—I will fight your battles.

15 Behold, the destroyer I have sent forth to destroy and lay waste mine enemies; and not many years hence they shall not be left to pollute mine heritage, and to blaspheme my name upon the lands which I have conse-crated for the gathering together of my saints.

16 Behold, I have commanded my servant Joseph Smith, Jun., to say unto the strength of my house, even my warriors, my young men, and middle-aged, to gather together for the redemption of my people, and throw down the towers of mine enemies, and scatter their watchmen;

17 But the strength of mine house have not hearkened unto my words.

18 But inasmuch as there are those who have hearkened unto my words, I have prepared a blessing and an endowment for them, if they continue faithful.

19 I have heard their prayers, and will accept their offering; and it is expedient in me that they should be brought thus far for a trial of their faith.

20 And now, verily I say unto you, a commandment I give unto you, that as many as have come up hither, that can stay in the region round about, let them stay;

What were some of the trials faced by those in Zion's Camp? (105:17–19) "Throughout the journey, participants occasionally suffered from a lack of food and water. Since the group marched as much as 40 miles a day, some also experienced blistered and bloody feet" (Church History Topics, "Zion's Camp [Camp of Israel]").

"Quarreling and contention within the camp became its most vexing problem. Several men feared possible dangers, some complained about changes in their life-style, and a few questioned the decisions of their leaders. For forty-five days they marched together, and the inevitable personality clashes were exacerbated by the harsh conditions they encountered. Grumblers often blamed Joseph Smith for their discomfort" (*Church History in the Fulness of Times* [manual], 145).

Doctrine and Covenants 105:20–26. The Saints Are to Be Wise and Not Boast of Mighty Works as They Gather

Cholera Strikes the Camp of Israel (Doctrine and Covenants 105:19)

"Heber C. Kimball, a member of Zion's Camp who later served in the First Presidency, recorded that before the members of Zion's Camp entered Missouri, the Prophet Joseph Smith had warned them of a scourge: 'Brother Joseph got up in a wagon and said he would deliver a prophecy. After giving the brethren much good advice, he exhorted them to faithfulness and humility, and said the Lord had told him that there would be scourge come upon the camp in consequence of the fractious and unruly spirits that appeared among them, and they would die like sheep with the rot; still if they would repent and humble themselves before the Lord, the scourge in great measure might be turned away; 'but, as the Lord lives, this camp will suffer for giving way to their unruly temper'; which afterwards actually did take place to the sorrow of the brethren' [Whitney, *Life of Heber C. Kimball*, 47–48].

"Two days after the revelation recorded in Doctrine and Covenants 105 was received, the camp experienced the beginnings of an outbreak of cholera, causing vomiting and severe diarrhea. As a result, 68 people, including the Prophet Joseph Smith, suffered from the sickness, and 13 members of the camp and 2 other Latter-day Saints who were living in Clay County died (see [*Joseph Smith Papers: Documents, Volume 4*, 72n334])" (*Doctrine and Covenants Student Manual* [2018], 598–99).

What are the dangers of sharing too much sacred knowledge? (105:23) The Prophet Joseph Smith explained that "the reason we do not have the secrets of the Lord revealed unto us, is because we do not keep them but reveal them; we do not keep our own secrets, but reveal our difficulties to the world, even to our enemies, then how would we keep the secrets of the Lord?" (Joseph Smith Papers, "Discourse, 19 December 1841, as Reported by Wilford Woodruff," [116]).

Why did the Lord warn the Saints not to boast of faith and mighty works? (105:23–24) "To understand the Lord's instructions not to disclose or boast of the revelation concerning Zion (D&C 105:23–24), we must know the background of what had taken place there. In 1831, the Saints arrived in Independence in the midst of a rough group of settlers. There, they boasted of building up Zion and implied that they were going to drive out all of the inhabitants. This attitude undoubtedly contributed to their being driven out. The Lord chastised the Saints for their behavior and admonished them to go about their future building up of stakes quietly, without conceit, living the gospel and preparing for the Second Coming" (Nyman, *Doctrine and Covenants Commentary*, 2:342–4).

Where did many of the exiled saints gather? (105:24) "Most of the exiled Mormons traveled north across the Missouri River into Clay County. . . .

"Clay County citizens treated the exiles well, hiring them to cut wood, construct buildings, teach school, and work on their farms. One employer, Joseph Thorp, had no sympathy with their religion but praised the Mormons for their general character: 'The Mormons, in the main were industrious, good workers, and gave general satisfaction to their employers, and could live on less than any people I ever knew' [Joseph Thorp, *Liberty Tribune*, Oct. 12, 1883, 1]. . . .

"[However,] later that same summer, trouble erupted in Clay County as well. . . .

"Church leaders in Clay County were willing to move elsewhere and had already looked . . . in nearby

21 And those that cannot stay, who have families in the east, let them tarry for a little season, inasmuch as my servant Joseph shall appoint unto them;

22 For I will counsel him concerning this matter, and all things whatsoever he shall appoint unto them shall be fulfilled.

23 And let all my people who dwell in the regions round about be very faithful, and prayerful, and humble before me, and reveal not the things which I have revealed unto them, until it is wisdom in me that they should be revealed.

24 Talk not of judgments, neither boast of faith nor of mighty works, but carefully gather together, as much in one region as can be, consistently with the feelings of the people;

25 And behold, I will give unto you favor and grace in their eyes, that you may rest in peace and safety, while you are saying unto the people: Execute judgment and justice for us according to law, and redress us of our wrongs.

26 Now, behold, I say unto you, my friends, in this way you may find favor in the eyes of the people, until the army of Israel becomes very great.

northern Ray County" (Max H Parkin, "Missouri's Impact on the Church," *Ensign*, Apr. 1979, 60, 61). ⊕

What was the counsel to the Saints living in Clay County and the surrounding areas? (105:24–26) "These instructions offered the Saints another opportunity to regain their lands in Zion after a little season. In addition to the personal purification required of the Saints, they were to make friends of the nonmembers in Clay County and surrounding regions. If they did so, the Lord promised them success in being reinstated to their inheritances in Zion. The endowment of power required before the Saints would be fully prepared to redeem Zion was administered in the Kirtland Temple in early 1836" (McConkie and Ostler, *Revelations of the Restoration*, 776).

Doctrine and Covenants 105:27–30. Lands in Jackson and Adjoining Counties Should Be Purchased

27 And I will soften the hearts of the people, as I did the heart of Pharaoh, from time to time, until my servant Joseph Smith, Jun., and mine elders, whom I have appointed, shall have time to gather up the strength of my house,

28 And to have sent wise men, to fulfil that which I have commanded concerning the purchasing of all the lands in Jackson county that can be purchased, and in the adjoining counties round about.

29 For it is my will that these lands should be purchased; and after they are purchased that my saints should possess them according to the laws of consecration which I have given.

30 And after these lands are purchased, I will hold the armies of Israel guiltless in taking possession of their own lands, which they have previously purchased with their moneys, and of throwing down the towers of mine enemies that may be upon them, and scattering their watchmen, and avenging me of mine enemies unto the third and fourth generation of them that hate me.

Why did the Lord command the Saints to continue purchasing lands in Missouri? (105:28–29) The redemption of Zion requires "the purchase, not conquest, of the land of New Jerusalem" (Nyman, *Doctrine and Covenants Commentary*, 2:344).

"The Lord instructed the Saints in other areas to send money to the land of Zion to make purchases. . . . Just as David was forbidden to build the temple because he was a man of war (1 Chronicles 28:2–3), it seems that we, as a people, will also be forbidden to enter Zion if we attempt to obtain the land by force. The land in Missouri will be purchased, not conquered (D&C 105:28–29)" (Nyman, "When Will Zion Be Redeemed?" 151).

Doctrine and Covenants 105:31–34. The Elders Are to Receive an Endowment in the House of the Lord in Kirtland

What does the phrase "fair as the sun, and clear as the moon" mean? (105:31) See commentary in this volume on Doctrine and Covenants 5:14.

What great blessing awaited these first elders? (105:33) "The June 1834 Fishing River revelation ending Zion's Camp redirected Joseph's attention. The revelation explained that Zion's future success depended on completion of the Kirtland Temple and the need for the elders to purify their lives to be able to commune with God in the House of the Lord where they would receive an endowment of his power in anticipation of impending eschatological events and the millennial reign of Christ (see Doctrine and Covenants 105:9–13). Pursuant to these objectives, upon returning from Zion's Camp, Joseph Smith's primary goal was to move forward with the construction of the temple and to prepare selected men to receive a spiritual endowment. Construction on the Kirtland Temple, which had begun in June 1833, resumed in September 1834 under the direction of Artemus Millet, a Mormon convert from Canada" (Baugh, "Joseph Smith and the Redemption of Zion," 179).

What is this verse suggesting regarding the law of consecration? (105:34) "Some commentators have suggested that D&C 105:34 rescinds, postpones, or suspends the law of consecration, but that is not what the revelation says. It says that the specific commands for the bishop to give the Saints inheritances in the land of Zion and to establish a storehouse and print the scriptures there will need to wait until the Saints reclaim the land (see D&C 57). That will never happen unless enough Saints voluntarily keep their covenant to live the law of consecration first" (Harper, *Let's Talk about the Law of Consecration*, 69).

31 But first let my army become very great, and let it be sanctified before me, that it may become fair as the sun, and clear as the moon, and that her banners may be terrible unto all nations;

32 That the kingdoms of this world may be constrained to acknowledge that the kingdom of Zion is in very deed the kingdom of our God and his Christ; therefore, let us become subject unto her laws.

33 Verily I say unto you, it is expedient in me that the first elders of my church should receive their endowment from on high in my house, which I have commanded to be built unto my name in the land of Kirtland.

34 And let those commandments which I have given concerning Zion and her law be executed and fulfilled, after her redemption.

Doctrine and Covenants 105:35–37. Saints Who Are Both Called and Chosen Will Be Sanctified

35 There has been a day of calling, but the time has come for a day of choosing; and let those be chosen that are worthy.

How did the Lord choose His leaders? (105:35) "In February 1835, when the Prophet organized the Twelve Apostles and the Quorum of the Seventy, nine of the Twelve Apostles and all of the Seventy had served in Zion's Camp. As recalled by Joseph Young, one of the original members of the Seventy, the Prophet explained to a group of these brethren: 'God did not want you to fight. He could not organize His kingdom with twelve men to open the Gospel door to the nations of the earth, and with seventy men under their direction to follow in their tracks, unless He took them from a body of men who had offered their lives, and who had made as great a sacrifice as did Abraham'" (*Joseph Smith* [manual], 283). ❂

36 And it shall be manifest unto my servant, by the voice of the Spirit, those that are chosen; and they shall be sanctified;

Who were those that were called and chosen by Joseph Smith to receive an endowment of power? (105:36) The Prophet Joseph Smith later recorded that "a council of High Priests assembled in fulfillment of the revelation given the day previous [D&C 105], and the following individuals were called and chosen as they were made manifest unto me by the voice of the Spirit, and Revelation, to receive their endowment."

The Prophet then identified Edward Partridge, William W. Phelps, Isaac Morley, John Corrill, John Whitmer, David Whitmer, Sidney Gilbert, Peter Whitmer, Jr., Simeon Carter, Newel Knight, Parley P. Pratt, Christian Whitmer, Solomon Hancock, Thomas B. Marsh, and Lyman Wight. He wrote that each of these brethren were "called and chosen" and that each was appointed to "receive his endowment [in Kirtland] with power from on high" (Joseph Smith Papers, "History, 1838–1856, volume A-1," 503).

37 And inasmuch as they follow the counsel which they receive, they shall have power after many days to accomplish all things pertaining to Zion.

What is the Lord's counsel regarding the redemption of Zion? (105:37) "The building of the New Jerusalem lies in the future, at a time yet to be designated by revelation. There is no present call for the saints to purchase lands or to live in Jackson County or in any place connected therewith. The revealed word relative to the gathering to Independence and its environs will come through the prophet of God on earth. When it does come—with the consequent return of the saints to that Zion which shall not be moved out of its place—that call will not be for the saints in general to assemble there. The return to Jackson County will be by delegates, as it were. Those whose services are needed there will assemble as appointed. The rest of Israel will remain in their appointed places" (Bruce R. McConkie, *Millennial Messiah*, 294). ●

Doctrine and Covenants 105:38–41. The Saints Are to Lift an Ensign of Peace to the World

What should be our relationship to all people? (105:38) "As disciples of Jesus Christ, we are to be examples of how to interact with others—*especially* when we have differences of opinion. One of the easiest ways to identify a *true follower* of Jesus Christ is how compassionately that person treats other people.

"The Savior made this clear in His sermons to followers in both hemispheres. 'Blessed are the peacemakers,' He said [Matt. 5:9]. 'Whosoever shall smite thee on thy right cheek, turn to him the other also' [Matt. 5:39]. And then, of course, He gave the admonition that challenges each of us: 'Love your enemies, bless them that curse you, do good to them that hate you, and pray for them which despitefully use you, and persecute you' [Matt. 5:44]" (Nelson, "Peacemakers Needed," *Liahona*, May 2023, 98–99). ●

Why does the Lord require the Saints to promote peace? (105:38–40) "Prophets have foreseen our day, when there would be wars and rumors of wars and when the whole earth would be in commotion. As followers of Jesus Christ, we plead with leaders of nations to find peaceful resolutions to their differences. . . .

"The gospel of Jesus Christ has never been needed more than it is today. Contention violates everything the Savior stood for and taught. I love the Lord Jesus Christ and testify that His gospel is the *only* enduring solution for peace. His gospel is a gospel of peace. . . .

"We have the sacred responsibility to share the power and peace of Jesus Christ with all who will listen and who will let God prevail in their lives" (Nelson, "Preaching the Gospel of Peace," *Liahona*, May 2022, 6). See also commentary in this volume on Doctrine and Covenants 98:16–17.

What can we do to invite the Lord to be with us? (105:41) "We can trust that [the Lord] will help us, not necessarily in the way we want but in the way that will best help us to grow. Submitting our will to His may be difficult, but it is essential to becoming like Him and finding the peace He offers us. . . .

"'If you trust in the Lord, truly you can overcome any of life's challenges.' . . .

38 And again I say unto you, sue for peace, not only to the people that have smitten you, but also to all people;

39 And lift up an ensign of peace, and make a proclamation of peace unto the ends of the earth;

40 And make proposals for peace unto those who have smitten you, according to the voice of the Spirit which is in you, and all things shall work together for your good.

41 Therefore, be faithful; and behold, and lo, I am with you even unto the end. Even so. Amen.

"Speaking to each of us, the Lord says, 'Fear . . . not; . . . I am with thee: be not dismayed; for I am thy God: I will strengthen thee; . . . I will help thee; yea, I will uphold thee with the right hand of my righteousness' [Isaiah 41:10]" (Stevens, "Fear Not; I Am with Thee," *Ensign*, May 2014, 82, 83).

Introduction to Doctrine and Covenants 106

"On 25 November 1834, [the Prophet Joseph Smith] dictated this revelation [in Kirtland, Ohio,] explaining God's will for Warren Cowdery, the older brother of Oliver Cowdery. Warren Cowdery, who lived in Freedom, New York, had been baptized into the church sometime between May and September 1834. Before his baptism, he . . . opened his home to [Joseph Smith] when [he] and others came to Freedom in March 1834 to recruit members for the Camp of Israel. Shortly after [the Prophet's] visit, a branch of the church was established in Freedom; . . . Sometime after his own baptism, Warren Cowdery noted that the members of the church in Freedom were in need of 'a preacher of our order' who could 'do us good, by strengthening and building us up in the most holy faith.' Although he seemed to be calling for an elder to be sent to the branch, he may have meant that the branch needed a presiding authority, the position to which he was called in this revelation. In an October 1834 letter, he told Oliver that he 'had thoughts of requesting you to enquire what is the will of the Lord concerning me,' stating that he sometimes thought he could be 'useful in the vineyard of the Lord.' This revelation was apparently dictated after Oliver received Warren's letter. In addition to designating Warren as a presiding high priest in Freedom, the revelation gave admonitions and promises to him and provided instruction concerning the second advent of Jesus Christ" (Joseph Smith Papers, Historical Introduction to "Revelation, 25 November 1834 [D&C 106]").

Around the time Joseph Smith received this revelation, his history records: "No month ever found me more busily engaged than November [1834]; but as, my life consisted of activity and unyielding exertion, I made this my rule, when the Lord commands, *do it*" (Joseph Smith Papers, "History, 1838–1856, volume B-1," 558).

SECTION 106

Revelation given through Joseph Smith the Prophet, at Kirtland, Ohio, November 25, 1834. This revelation is directed to Warren A. Cowdery, an older brother of Oliver Cowdery.

1 It is my will that my servant Warren A. Cowdery should be appointed and ordained a presiding high priest over my church, in the land of Freedom and the regions round about;

Doctrine and Covenants 106:1–3. Warren A. Cowdery Is Called as a Local Presiding Officer

Who was Warren A. Cowdery? (106:1) "Warren Cowdery was born in October 1788. He learned about the Church from his younger brother Oliver, and was baptized in late 1831. . . . From time to time, Brother Cowdery allowed his pride to get the best of him. For example, while serving as branch president in Freedom, he 'preferred charges against the Twelve Apostles for their alleged failure to teach the Saints while in Freedom.' . . . Although on this occasion Warren made an apology, he eventually lost confidence in the Church and its leaders and left it about the same time as his brother, Oliver, in 1838. He never returned and died in Ohio in 1851" (Leavitt and Christensen, *Scripture Study for Latter-day Saint Families: Doctrine and Covenants*, 235). ☉

What was Warren Cowdery's calling and how was his family to be supported at this time? (106:2–3) "Warren A. Cowdery's calling was to preside over the branch in Freedom and to declare the gospel full time there and in the adjoining counties. His calling was similar to that of a mission president today. Having no time to provide for his family, he was directed by the Lord to receive his support from the Church" (McConkie and Ostler, *Revelations of the Restoration*, 782–83).

Doctrine and Covenants 106:4–5. The Second Coming Will Not Overtake the Children of Light as a Thief

How will the righteous prepare and be ready for the Lord's Second Coming? (106:4–5) After quoting verses 4 and 5, Robert L. Millet writes: "The faithful shall not be surprised. The children of light, those who honor their covenants and are true to their trusts, who seek for and cultivate the spirit of revelation, these shall be in a position to read the signs of the times and be prepared for the great and terrible day of the Lord. They shall abide the day, be caught up to meet their Master, and feel peace and confidence in his presence. In harmony with the soul-cry of the beloved Revelator (Revelation 22:20), they exclaim: 'Even so, come, Lord Jesus'" (Millet, "Life in the Millennium," 189–90).

Who are the "children of light"? (106:5) "To become children of light means to reject the power of the adversary and to choose daily to follow the Light of Christ.

"The phrase 'children of light' describes a people in whom the light of the gospel shines brightly. It describes a people who seek the light and are drawn to that which is virtuous, clean, and pure. There is an expectation that children of light are alert and watchful—not sleeping, in a spiritual sense, when they should be awake (see 2 Nephi 1:13; 1 Thessalonians 5:5–8). Children of light do not sit passively in darkness; they have the courage to stand up and stand out" (Craig C. Christensen, "Becoming Children of Light," *Ensign*, Aug. 2014, 67). ☉

2 And should preach my everlasting gospel, and lift up his voice and warn the people, not only in his own place, but in the adjoining counties;

3 And devote his whole time to this high and holy calling, which I now give unto him, seeking diligently the kingdom of heaven and its righteousness, and all things necessary shall be added thereunto; for the laborer is worthy of his hire.

4 And again, verily I say unto you, the coming of the Lord draweth nigh, and it overtaketh the world as a thief in the night—

5 Therefore, gird up your loins, that you may be the children of light, and that day shall not overtake you as a thief.

6 And again, verily I say unto you, there was joy in heaven when my servant Warren bowed to my scepter, and separated himself from the crafts of men;

7 Therefore, blessed is my servant Warren, for I will have mercy on him; and, notwithstanding the vanity of his heart, I will lift him up inasmuch as he will humble himself before me.

8 And I will give him grace and assurance wherewith he may stand; and if he continue to be a faithful witness and a light unto the church I have prepared a crown for him in the mansions of my Father. Even so. Amen.

Doctrine and Covenants 106:6–8. Great Blessings Follow Faithful Service in the Church

What might the heavens know about our actions? (106:6) "As the heavens wept when Satan and his legions were lost, so they rejoice when children of our Eternal Father choose the course that will enable them to return to his presence. The text suggests that angels are aware of what their earthly counterparts are doing (D&C 62:3)" (McConkie and Ostler, *Revelations of the Restoration*, 784).

What constitutes the "crafts of men"? (106:6) "The Lord expressed joy when Warren A. Cowdery 'separated himself from the crafts of men' (D&C 106:6). Beyond its use as a synonym for a vessel that travels on water (D&C 60:5), the word *craft* generally refers to a skilled occupation. However, in the sense in which it is used with Cowdery it refers to something derogatory, an unrighteous activity" (Brewster, *Doctrine & Covenants Encyclopedia*, 112).

Why must humility precede repentance? (106:7) "Spiritual humility—the recognition of one's dependence upon God for all things temporal and spiritual, coupled with a willingness to accept his law—is a precondition for true repentance. Some achieve this humility only after they have been 'compelled to be humble.' . . . Some do so only after they have been brought face-to-face with the stark truth about themselves and the God they defied, or never knew.

"Some will never learn humility and, therefore, never repent even when they stand before God with a 'perfect knowledge' of their guilt and uncleanness" (Turner, "Faith unto Salvation," 19–20).

Introduction to Doctrine and Covenants 107

"The first Quorum of the Twelve Apostles in this dispensation was called on February 14, 1835, and its members were ordained between February and April of that year. They met frequently [in Kirtland] to receive instructions from Joseph [Smith]. In their March 12 council meeting, Joseph proposed that the apostles spend the summer traveling 'through the Eastern States, to the Atlantic Ocean, and hold conferences in the vicinity of the several branches of the Church for the purpose of regulating all things necessary for their welfare.' As the time for their departure neared [which was May 4, 1835], the apostles made a written request asking Joseph 'to inquire of God for us, and obtain a revelation' to help them fulfill their callings. . . .

"The Lord answered with the first 58 verses of Doctrine and Covenants 107. . . . Joseph had received most of [verses 60–100] earlier in November 1831. When he was editing the revelation for publication in the 1835 Doctrine and Covenants, Joseph joined these two texts on priesthood organization and function into a single document. . . . Verse 58 transitions between the two major segments of Section 107 and gives the apostles responsibility for implementing the November 1831 revelation by ordaining priesthood holders and setting the Church in order under their direction" (Harper, *Making Sense of the Doctrine & Covenants*, 395, 397).

"As He did with many truths of the restored gospel, the Lord revealed the pattern of priesthood organization and Church governance 'line upon line' (D&C 98:12). Originally titled 'On Priesthood,' the revelation recorded in Doctrine and Covenants 107 adds to and clarifies earlier revelations on priesthood offices, responsibilities, and organization (see [*Joseph Smith Papers: Documents, Volume* 4], 308–9; see also D&C 20; 84)" (*Doctrine and Covenants Student Manual* [2018], 607).

"This revelation established the organization of Church government and distinguishes between the Aaronic and Melchizedek priesthoods. The Lord is clear that the right of the presidency belongs to the Melchizedek Priesthood, whereas the bishop is designated as the president of the Aaronic Priesthood. Presiding bishops are to be chosen from the high priesthood unless there is a literal descendent of Aaron. The Twelve constitute the traveling presiding high council. The duties of various offices in the priesthood are defined" (Woodger, *Essential Doctrine and Covenants Companion*, 212–3).

Doctrine and Covenants 107:1–6. There Are Two Priesthoods: The Melchizedek and the Aaronic

What do we know about the two priesthoods in the Church? (107:1) "'All priesthood is Melchizedek,' the Prophet Joseph Smith taught, 'but there are different portions or degrees of it' ([*Joseph Smith* (manual),] 109). The different 'portions or degrees' of the priesthood are enumerated in modern revelation: 'There are, in the church, two priesthoods, namely,

SECTION 107

Revelation on the priesthood, given through Joseph Smith the Prophet, at Kirtland, Ohio, about April 1835. Although this section was recorded in 1835, the historical records affirm that most of verses 60 through 100 incorporate a revelation given through Joseph Smith on November 11, 1831. This section was associated with the organization of the Quorum of the Twelve in February and March 1835. The Prophet likely delivered it in the presence of those who were preparing to depart May 3, 1835, on their first quorum mission.

1 There are, in the church, two priesthoods, namely, the Melchizedek and Aaronic, including the Levitical Priesthood.

the Melchizedek and Aaronic, including the Levitical Priesthood' (D&C 107:1). Each of these have unique roles, responsibilities, and powers—all working together to bring the power of God into the lives of His children and by that power to lead them back into his presence" (Top, "Priesthood," 503). ⊕

2 Why the first is called the Melchizedek Priesthood is because Melchizedek was such a great high priest.

3 Before his day it was called *the Holy Priesthood, after the Order of the Son of God.*

4 But out of respect or reverence to the name of the Supreme Being, to avoid the too frequent repetition of his name, they, the church, in ancient days, called that priesthood after Melchizedek, or the Melchizedek Priesthood.

Who was the high priest called Melchizedek? (107:2–4) "Melchizedek was a believer in Jesus Christ and was a preacher of the gospel of Christ. For example, Melchizedek was a high priest after the order of the holy priesthood. Alma also explains that such a high priest is ordained 'after the order of the Son, the Only Begotten of the Father' ([Alma 13:9]). The same declaration is made of Melchizedek in [JST, Genesis 14:25–40]. Because of latter-day revelation we know that Melchizedek had faith in Christ and was baptized, received the gift of the Holy Ghost, was ordained, and was endowed with the same ordinances in the same gospel we know in the Church today" (Matthews, *Selected Writings*, 140).

Why do we avoid calling the priesthood after the name that was used anciently? (107:3–4) "The Melchizedek Priesthood is . . . spoken of in the scriptures as the 'greater priesthood' or the priesthood 'which is after the holiest order of God' (D&C 84:18–19) and the priesthood 'after the order of mine Only Begotten Son' (D&C 124:123; see also D&C 76:57). . . .

The Development of Priesthood Quorums, Relations, and Duties (D&C 107)

During general conference in April 1935, Elder John A. Widtsoe made the following observations regarding the coming forth of Doctrine and Covenants 107:

"[D&C 107] is one of the most remarkable documents in the possession of man. It stands absolutely unique; there is none like it. . . . It sets forth, in plainness and simplicity, the organization of the quorums of the priesthood; the mutual relations of the quorums to one another; the judicial system of the Church is foreshadowed and outlined; and there is a wonderful picture of the early history of the priesthood. . . .

"This revelation, now known as Section 107, together with two or three other revelations [D&C 20, 84, 121], forms, as it were, the constitution of the Church of Jesus Christ of Latter-day Saints, upon which we are building today, and upon which we will build until the Lord comes. It is so comprehensive in its brevity, so magnificent in its simplicity, that we have found no occasion, up to the present, to wish that it might have been more complete. . . .

"After the organization of the Church a series of great revelations came to the Prophet. . . . As I read human history I know of no other period of five years [1830–1835], save the years of the Savior's ministry, that is so rich in the presentation of new, eternal truth, as these first five years in the history of the restored Church of Christ. Elders were provided for in 1830. High priests were ordained in 1831. A year or two later the first presidency was organized. In the spring of 1835 apostles and seventies were called. Then all at once, as it were, God summed up all that he had given the Prophet and the people, and gave a simple revelation, Section 107 in the book of [Doctrine and Covenants], to serve as another foundation stone for the building of the Church of Christ.

"That is God's way; that is the natural way. We men and women, when we build nations often attempt to write their constitutions in full at the beginning. The natural way is God's way, to receive here a little and there a little, wuntil the time of ripening comes and completion is attained" (in Conference Report, Apr. 1935, 80, 81).

"We can understand why it should be. The name of the priesthood is frequently talked about in meetings and lessons and is printed in handbooks and manuals. It would be irreverent to use informally the sacred title which includes the name of Deity" (Packer, "What Every Elder Should Know," *Ensign*, Feb. 1993, 7).

In what way are Church "authorities" and "offices" appendages to the priesthood? (107:5) "The priesthood is greater than any of its offices. . . . All offices derive their authority from the priesthood.

"The priesthood is not divisible. An elder holds as much priesthood as an Apostle (see D&C 20:38). When a man receives the priesthood, he receives all of it. However, there are offices within the priesthood—divisions of authority and responsibility. A man may exercise his priesthood according to the rights of the office to which he is ordained or set apart" (Packer, "Honor and Order of the Priesthood," *Ensign*, Jun. 2012, 22).

What are the two divisions or grand heads of the Melchizedek Priesthood? (107:6) "As the higher priesthood was named after Melchizedek, so the lesser priesthood was named after Aaron, the brother [of] Moses. Aaron was the high priest, meaning presiding priest, over the Aaronic order, in which capacity he served for nearly forty years. This priesthood is also called the Levitical Priesthood because Aaron was a descendant of Levi, the third son of Jacob and Leah, whose descendants were given the birthright to this priesthood. They properly performed its functions from the time of Moses and Aaron to the coming of Christ.

5 All other authorities or offices in the church are appendages to this priesthood.

6 But there are two divisions or grand heads— one is the Melchizedek Priesthood, and the other is the Aaronic or Levitical Priesthood.

How Does Priesthood Apply to Women in the Church? (Doctrine and Covenants 107:5)

In an important address by President Dallin H. Oaks, he explained: "I come now to the subject of priesthood authority. I begin with the three principles just discussed: (1) priesthood is the power of God delegated to man to act for the salvation of the human family, (2) priesthood authority is governed by priesthood holders who hold priesthood keys, and (3) since the scriptures state that 'all other authorities [and] offices in the church are appendages to this [Melchizedek] priesthood' (D&C 107:5), all that is done under the direction of those priesthood keys is done with priesthood authority.

"How does this apply to women? In an address to the Relief Society, President Joseph Fielding Smith, then President of the Quorum of the Twelve Apostles, said this: 'While the sisters have not been given the Priesthood, it has not been conferred upon them, that does not mean that the Lord has not given unto them authority. . . . A person may have authority given to him, or a sister to her, to do certain things in the Church that are binding and absolutely necessary for our salvation, such as the work that our sisters do in the House of the Lord. They have authority given unto them to do some great and wonderful things, sacred unto the Lord, and binding just as thoroughly as are the blessings that are given by the men who hold the Priesthood' ["Relief Society," 4].

"In that notable address, President Smith said again and again that women have been given authority. To the women he said, 'You can speak with authority, because the Lord has placed authority upon you.' He also said that

7 The office of an elder comes under the priesthood of Melchizedek.

8 The Melchizedek Priesthood holds the right of presidency, and has power and authority over all the offices in the church in all ages of the world, to administer in spiritual things.

9 The Presidency of the High Priesthood, after the order of Melchizedek, have a right to officiate in all the offices in the church.

10 High priests after the order of the Melchizedek Priesthood have a right to officiate in their own standing, under the direction of the presidency, in administering spiritual things, and also in the office of an elder, priest (of the Levitical order), teacher, deacon, and member.

11 An elder has a right to officiate in his stead when the high priest is not present.

12 The high priest and elder are to administer in spiritual things, agreeable to the covenants

"Some argue that the Aaronic and Levitical Priesthoods are different priesthoods. This revelation, however, does not support such a distinction" (McConkie and Ostler, *Revelations of the Restoration*, 787).

Doctrine and Covenants 107:7–12. Those Who Hold the Melchizedek Priesthood Have Power to Officiate in All Offices in the Church

What is the right of presidency in the Melchizedek Priesthood? (107:8–12) "The Melchizedek Priesthood is 'the Holy Priesthood, after the Order of the Son of God' (Doctrine and Covenants 107:3). It is the power by which the sons and daughters of God can become like Him (see Doctrine and Covenants 84:19–21; 132:19–20).

"'The Melchizedek Priesthood holds the right of presidency.' It has 'power and authority over all the offices in the church in all ages of the world, to administer in spiritual things' (Doctrine and Covenants 107:8). Through this authority, Church leaders direct and administer all the spiritual work of the Church (see Doctrine and Covenants 107:18).

"The President of the Church is the presiding high priest over the Melchizedek Priesthood (see Doctrine and Covenants 107:65–67). The stake president is the presiding high priest in the stake (see Doctrine and Covenants 107:8, 10 . . .). The bishop is the presiding high priest in the ward (see Doctrine and Covenants 107:17 . . .)" (*General Handbook* [2022], 3.3.1). See also commentary in this volume on Doctrine and Covenants 107:64–67.

the Relief Society '[has] been given power and authority to do a great many things. The work which they do is done by divine authority.' And, of course, the Church work done by women or men, whether in the temple or in the wards or branches, is done under the direction of those who hold priesthood keys. Thus, speaking of the Relief Society, President Smith explained, '[The Lord] has given to them this great organization where they have authority to serve under the directions of the bishops of the wards . . . , looking after the interest of our people both spiritually and temporally' ["Relief Society," 4–5].

"Thus, it is truly said that Relief Society is not just a class for women but something they belong to—a divinely established appendage to the priesthood [see Packer, "Relief Society," *Ensign*, May 1998, 72].

"We are not accustomed to speaking of women having the authority of the priesthood in their Church callings, but what other authority can it be? When a woman—young or old—is set apart to preach the gospel as a full-time missionary, she is given priesthood authority to perform a priesthood function. The same is true when a woman is set apart to function as an officer or teacher in a Church organization under the direction of one who holds the keys of the priesthood. Whoever functions in an office or calling received from one who holds priesthood keys exercises priesthood authority in performing her or his assigned duties" ("Keys and Authority of the Priesthood," *Ensign*, May 2014, 50–51).

Doctrine and Covenants 107:13–17. The Bishopric Presides over the Aaronic Priesthood, Which Administers in Outward Ordinances

Which bishopric is being described here? (107:13–15) "The statement 'the bishopric is the presidency of this priesthood' (D&C 107:15) refers to the responsibility of bishops and their counselors to preside over those who hold the Aaronic Priesthood. 'The Presiding Bishopric is the presidency of the Aaronic Priesthood throughout the Church. The Presiding Bishop and his two counselors also serve under the direction of the First Presidency to administer the temporal affairs of the Church'" (*Doctrine and Covenants Student Manual* [2018], 611). See also commentary in this volume on Doctrine and Covenants 68:16–21.

What does it mean that the Aaronic priesthood is an appendage to the Melchizedek? (107:14) "The word *appendage* means the two [priesthoods, Aaronic and Melchizedek,] are connected. This connection is important to the priesthood becoming the force and the blessing it can be, in this world and forever, for it 'is without beginning of days or end of years' [D&C 84:17].

"The connection is a simple one. The Aaronic Priesthood prepares young men for an even more sacred trust.

"'The power and authority of the higher, or Melchizedek Priesthood, is to hold the keys of all the spiritual blessings of the church' [D&C 107:18]" (Eyring, "That He May Become Strong Also," *Ensign,* Nov. 2016, 75). ⊕

What are "outward ordinances"? (107:14) "A great revelation on priesthood revealed that the lesser or Aaronic Priesthood 'has power in administering outward ordinances' (D&C 107:14, 20). The nature of these ordinances was discussed by Elder Orson Pratt, who said: 'The Priesthood of Aaron, being an appendage to the higher Priesthood, has power to administer in *temporal* [or outward] *ordinances,* such as that of baptism for remission of sins, the administration of the Lord's Supper, and in attending to temporal things for the benefit of the people of God' ([in *Journal of Discourses*], 18:363–64; [emphasis] added). . . .

"Less tangible ordinances, such as the laying on of hands—whereby the gift of the Holy Ghost is received—and the sealing blessings of the temple, pertain to the higher priesthood, which is Melchizedek" (Brewster, *Doctrine & Covenants Encyclopedia*, 410).

and commandments of the church; and they have a right to officiate in all these offices of the church when there are no higher authorities present.

13 The second priesthood is called the Priesthood of Aaron, because it was conferred upon Aaron and his seed, throughout all their generations.

14 Why it is called the lesser priesthood is because it is an appendage to the greater, or the Melchizedek Priesthood, and has power in administering outward ordinances.

15 The bishopric is the presidency of this priesthood, and holds the keys or authority of the same.

16 No man has a legal right to this office, to hold the keys of this priesthood, except he be a literal descendant of Aaron.

17 But as a high priest of the Melchizedek Priesthood has authority to officiate in all the lesser offices, he may officiate in the office of bishop when no literal descendant of Aaron can be found, provided he is called and set apart and ordained unto this power by the hands of the Presidency of the Melchizedek Priesthood.

18 The power and authority of the higher, or Melchizedek Priesthood, is to hold the keys of all the spiritual blessings of the church—

19 To have the privilege of receiving the mysteries of the kingdom of heaven, to have the

Why does a literal descendant of Aaron have a legal right to the office of Presiding Bishop? (107:16–17) "By virtue of his birth he is entitled to hold 'the keys of authority of the same.' This has reference only to the one who *presides over the Aaronic Priesthood. It has no reference whatever to bishops of wards.* Further, such a one must be designated by the First Presidency of the Church and receive his anointing and ordination under their hands. The revelation comes from the Presidency, not from the patriarch, to establish a claim to the right to preside in this office. In the absence of knowledge concerning such a descendant, any high priest, chosen by the Presidency, may hold the office of Presiding Bishop and serve with counselors" (Joseph Fielding Smith, *Doctrines of Salvation*, 3:92–93). See also commentary in this volume on Doctrine and Covenants 68:18–22 and 107:69–70.

What is the distinction between being "set apart" and "ordained"? (107:17) "The difference between being ordained and being set apart is that to be ordained is to receive an office that one holds forever even though additional offices or calls may come. For example, though he stood as the senior Apostle in the Church, President Spencer W. Kimball once declared to an assembled priesthood body, 'I am a deacon. . . . and a teacher, and a priest' ([in Conference Report], Apr. 1975, 117). In being 'set apart,' one receives no permanent office or title. Nevertheless, whether one is ordained or set apart to an office, his stewardship extends only to the day of his release. Thus, for example, if a man is released from presiding over a ward as a bishop, he retains his ordination but not his *office*. If, at any future date, he were once again called to serve as an active bishop, he would merely be *set apart* to his office for he had previously received his ordination" (Brewster, *Doctrine & Covenants Encyclopedia* [revised edition], 405).

Doctrine and Covenants 107:18–20. The Melchizedek Priesthood Holds the Keys of All Spiritual Blessings; the Aaronic Priesthood Holds the Keys of the Ministering of Angels

What are we to understand about the keys of the priesthood? (107:18–20) "The term *priesthood keys* is used in two different ways. The first refers to a specific right or privilege conferred upon all who receive the Aaronic or Melchizedek Priesthood. . . . Aaronic Priesthood holders receive the keys of the ministering of angels and the keys of the preparatory gospel. . . . Melchizedek Priesthood holders receive the key of the mysteries of the kingdom, . . . and the keys of all the spiritual blessings of the Church. . . .

"The second way the term *priesthood keys* is used refers to leadership. Priesthood leaders receive additional keys, the right to preside over an organizational division of the Church or a quorum. In this regard, priesthood keys are the authority and power to direct, lead, and govern the Church" (Renlund and Renlund, *Melchizedek Priesthood*, 26). ⊙

What are the spiritual blessings of the Church? (107:18–19) "Because the Melchizedek Priesthood has been restored, both covenant-keeping women and men have access to '*all* the spiritual blessings of the church' (D&C 107:18) or, we might say, to all the spiritual treasures the Lord has for His children.

"Every woman and every man who makes covenants with God and keeps those covenants, and who participates worthily in priesthood ordinances, has direct access to the power of God. Those who are endowed in the house of the Lord receive a gift of God's priesthood power by virtue of their covenant, along with a gift of knowledge to know how to draw

heavens opened unto them, to commune with the general assembly and church of the Firstborn, and to enjoy the communion and presence of God the Father, and Jesus the mediator of the new covenant.

20 The power and authority of the lesser, or Aaronic Priesthood, is to hold the keys of the ministering of angels, and to administer in outward ordinances, the letter of the gospel, the baptism of repentance for the remission of sins, agreeable to the covenants and commandments.

What Access to the Priesthood Does God Grant to Women? (D&C 107:18–19)

The Prophet Joseph Smith once taught the early Relief Society sisters that "'the Society should move according to the ancient Priesthood' . . . explaining that the women of Relief Society must become a 'select Society separate from all the evils of the world, choice, virtuous, and holy.'

"The 'ancient Priesthood' to which the Prophet referred is the higher or Melchizedek Priesthood, which provides all of us—men and women—with access to God's greatest blessings. These include the supernal privileges of having the 'heavens opened unto [us]' and 'receiving the mysteries of the kingdom of heaven,' which the Lord defined as 'the key of the knowledge of God.' So when Joseph Smith instructed the women to 'move according to the ancient Priesthood,' he was not only indicating the power and authority under which the Relief Society would operate but inviting the sisters to prepare for sacred temple ordinances, which ordinances would bless them with an endowment of knowledge and power that would open the heavens to them" (Dew, *Women and the Priesthood*, rev. ed., 87–88).

Former Relief Society General President Jean B. Bingham explained: "From the Prophet Joseph Smith's day to ours, the ongoing restoration of all things has brought enlightenment on the necessity of the authority and power of the priesthood in helping both men and women accomplish their divinely appointed responsibilities. Recently we have been taught that women who are set apart under the direction of one holding priesthood keys operate with *priesthood authority* in their callings [see Oaks, "Keys and the Authority of the Priesthood," *Ensign*, May 2014, 49–52].

" . . . President Russell M. Nelson [has] taught that women who are endowed in the temple have *priesthood power* in their lives and in their homes as they keep those sacred covenants they made with God [see Nelson, "Spiritual Treasures," *Ensign*, Nov. 2019, 78, 79]" (Bingham, "United in Accomplishing God's Work," *Ensign*, May 2020, 61).

President Russell M. Nelson also declared: "The heavens are just as open to *women* who are endowed with God's power flowing from their priesthood covenants as they are to men who bear the priesthood. I pray that truth will register upon each of your hearts because I believe it will change your life. Sisters, you have the right to draw liberally upon the Savior's power to help your family and others you love" ("Spiritual Treasures," *Ensign*, Nov. 2019, 77).

upon that power" (Nelson, "Spiritual Treasures," *Ensign*, Nov. 2019, 77).

Who are the "general assembly and church of the Firstborn"? (107:19) "The phrase *general assembly and church of the Firstborn* appears three times in scripture (D&C 76:67; 107:19; Heb. 12:23). The 'general assembly' appears to be the congregation of exalted beings who will inherit a celestial sphere and will comprise the church of the Firstborn" (Brewster, *Doctrine & Covenants Encyclopedia* [2012], 210). See also commentary in this volume on Doctrine and Covenants 76:54–55 and 93:21–22.

Who are ministering angels? (107:20) "From the beginning of time, God has 'sent angels to minister unto the children of men, to make manifest . . . the coming of Christ.' Angels are heavenly beings bearing God's message. In both Hebrew and Greek, the root word of *angel* is 'messenger.'

"In much the same way that angels are authorized messengers sent by God to declare His word and thereby build faith, we who hold the Aaronic Priesthood have been ordained to 'teach, and invite all to come unto Christ.' . . .

"Young men, you are authorized messengers. Through your words and actions, you can bring faith in Christ to the hearts of God's children. As President Russell M. Nelson said, 'To them you will be as a ministering angel'" (Holmes, "What Every Aaronic Priesthood Holder Needs to Understand," *Ensign*, May 2018, 51). See also commentary in this volume on Doctrine and Covenants 13:1.

Doctrine and Covenants 107:21–38. The First Presidency, the Twelve, and the Seventy Constitute the Presiding Quorums, Whose Decisions Are to Be Made in Unity and Righteousness

What quorum is constituted from these "three Presiding High Priests"? (107:22) These three leaders make up the First Presidency of the Church. "All members of the First Presidency and the Twelve are regularly sustained as 'prophets, seers, and revelators.' . . . This means that any one of the Apostles, so chosen and ordained, could preside over the Church. . . .

"Three things are required of those who are called to this position [First Presidency]. They must be ordained, they must be chosen by the Twelve, and third, to me one of the most significant things, is to

21 Of necessity there are presidents, or presiding officers growing out of, or appointed of or from among those who are ordained to the several offices in these two priesthoods.

22 Of the Melchizedek Priesthood, three Presiding High Priests, chosen by the body, appointed and ordained to that office, and upheld by the confidence, faith, and prayer of the church, form a quorum of the Presidency of the Church.

be upheld by the confidence, faith, and prayers of the Church (see D&C 107:22). That means by the faith of the total individual membership of the Church" (Lee, *Teachings*, 535, 538). See also commentary in this volume on Doctrine and Covenants 107:64–67.

How are the Apostles "special witnesses" of the name of Christ? (107:23) President Russell M. Nelson explained: "The title 'Apostle' is sacred. It has been given of God and belongs only to those who have been called and ordained as 'special witnesses of the name of Christ in all the world' (D&C 107:23). An Apostle speaks in the name of Him whose special witness he is. This hallowed title is not used in ordinary forms of address. The preferred title for one of the Twelve is 'Elder' or 'Brother'" ("Honoring the Priesthood," *Ensign*, May 1993, 38). ✪

In what sense is the Quorum of the Twelve equal in authority with the First Presidency? (107:23–24) "As a council, [the Twelve] 'form a quorum, equal in authority and power to the three presidents [First Presidency] previously mentioned' (D&C 107:24). As explained by the Prophet Joseph, this principle has reference to succession, and this council's authority is not fully exercised until the First Presidency is dissolved upon the death of the President. The Twelve as a council then have authority to reorganize the First Presidency. This doctrine has been followed precisely since the death of Joseph Smith for every succeeding president of the Church" (Nyman, "Priesthood, Keys, Councils, and Covenants," 120). ✪

Why must decisions by the presiding quorums of the Church be unanimous? (107:27–31) President James E. Faust testified: "This requirement of unanimity provides a check on bias and personal idiosyncrasies. It ensures that God rules through the Spirit, not man through majority or compromise. It ensures that the best wisdom and experience is focused on an issue before the deep, unassailable impressions of revealed direction are received. It guards against the foibles of man" ("Continuous Revelation," *Ensign*, Nov. 1989, 10). ✪

23 The twelve traveling councilors are called to be the Twelve Apostles, or special witnesses of the name of Christ in all the world—thus differing from other officers in the church in the duties of their calling.

24 And they form a quorum, equal in authority and power to the three presidents previously mentioned.

25 The Seventy are also called to preach the gospel, and to be especial witnesses unto the Gentiles and in all the world—thus differing from other officers in the church in the duties of their calling.

26 And they form a quorum, equal in authority to that of the Twelve special witnesses or Apostles just named.

27 And every decision made by either of these quorums must be by the unanimous voice of the same; that is, every member in each quorum must be agreed to its decisions, in order to make their decisions of the same power or validity one with the other—

28 A majority may form a quorum when circumstances render it impossible to be otherwise—

29 Unless this is the case, their decisions are not entitled to the same blessings which the decisions of a quorum of three presidents were anciently, who were ordained after the order of Melchizedek, and were righteous and holy men.

30 The decisions of these quorums, or either of them, are to be made in all righteousness, in holiness, and lowliness of heart, meekness and long-suffering, and in faith, and virtue, and knowledge, temperance, patience, godliness, brotherly kindness and charity;

31 Because the promise is, if these things abound in them they shall not be unfruitful in the knowledge of the Lord.

32 And in case that any decision of these quorums is made in unrighteousness, it may be brought before a general assembly of the several quorums, which constitute the spiritual authorities of the church; otherwise there can be no appeal from their decision.

33 The Twelve are a Traveling Presiding High Council, to officiate in the name of the Lord, under the direction of the Presidency of the Church, agreeable to the institution of heaven; to build up the church, and regulate all the affairs of the same in all nations, first unto the Gentiles and secondly unto the Jews.

34 The Seventy are to act in the name of the Lord, under the direction of the Twelve

What is distinctive in the Lord's direction that His latter-day servants go first to the Gentiles and later to the Jews? (107:33–35) "Though the Twelve are commissioned to travel throughout the world to build up the Church and regulate its affairs, they do so under the direction of the First Presidency. The Seventy, in like manner, act under the direction of the Twelve. In declaring the gospel to the world, the charge given to those of both quorums is that they go first to the Gentiles and then to the Jews. This is a reversal of the charge given by Christ to the Twelve and

Decisions Must Be Made by the Unanimous Voice of the Quorum (D&C 107:27–31)

"In terms of organizational structure, the Lord governs His Church through a unique pattern of presidencies, councils, and quorums. In the order of the Lord, although there is always a senior Apostle who presides over the others ordained as prophets, seers, and revelators, no one leader—even the senior Apostle—acts alone. Modern-day revelation is clear about how the First Presidency and Quorum of the Twelve Apostles are to operate: 'Every decision made by either of these quorums must be by the unanimous voice of the same.' [D&C 107:27]. . . .

"Then-Elder Russell M. Nelson elaborated on the significance of unanimity: 'The calling of 15 men to the holy apostleship provides great protection for us as members of the Church. Why? Because decisions of these leaders must be unanimous. Can you imagine how the Spirit needs to move upon 15 men to bring about unanimity?' ["Sustaining the Prophets," *Ensign*, Nov. 2014].

"On another occasion, this time after he had become President of the Church, President Nelson added further clarification: 'In our meetings, the majority never rules! We listen prayerfully to one another and talk with each other until we are united. Then when we have reached complete accord, the unifying influence of the Holy Ghost is spine-tingling! . . . No member of the First Presidency or Quorum of the Twelve would ever leave decisions for the Lord's Church to his own best judgment!' ["Revelation for the Church," *Ensign*, May 2018]. . . .

"And here is why: Because even the senior Apostle, the prophet, is not the head of The Church of Jesus Christ of Latter-day Saints. Jesus Christ is, and He *is* perfect. Jesus Christ *is* infallible. Prophets take their instructions from Him who knows all, sees all, has all power, understands all things, and sees the end from the beginning—and has from the beginning of time [see 1 Nephi 9:6]" (Dew, *Prophets See around Corners*, 35–36, 37–38).

Seventy in the meridian of time. In that day the gospel was taken first to the Jews and then to the Gentiles (see Acts 13:46–48; Romans 11:7–26)" (McConkie and Ostler, *Revelations of the Restoration*, 794).

What were the "standing high councils" referred to in this passage? (107:36–37) "At the time this Revelation was given, there were two standing High Councils in the Church: One in Kirtland, organized February 17th, 1834, and one in Clay County, Mo., organized July 3rd, the same year" (Smith and Sjodahl, *Doctrine and Covenants Commentary*, 702). "Today, there is a 'standing high council' in every stake of the Church, presided over by a stake presidency, and jurisdictionally confined to the areas in which they are located" (Brewster, *Doctrine & Covenants Encyclopedia*, 560). See also commentary in this volume on Doctrine and Covenants 102:3.

How do the Twelve "call upon the Seventy" today? (107:38) "The Seventy do not receive additional priesthood keys, but with each assignment they receive from the First Presidency or the Quorum of the Twelve Apostles, they are delegated authority to accomplish the assignment given. . . .

"Following the pattern established in the time of the Prophet Joseph Smith, the modern-day Quorums of the Seventy are 'instituted for traveling elders to bear record of my name in all the world, wherever . . . mine apostles, shall send them to prepare a way before my face' (D&C 124:139).

"The Seventy consider it a great privilege to serve under the direction of the First Presidency and the Quorum of the Twelve Apostles" (Tingey, "Quorums of the Seventy," *Ensign*, Aug. 2005, 48–49, 50).

Doctrine and Covenants 107:39–52. The Patriarchal Order Is Established from Adam to Noah

Who are the "evangelical ministers"? (107:39) "One of the responsibilities of the Council of the Twelve [was] to 'ordain evangelical ministers, as they shall be designated unto them by revelation' (D&C 107:39). Joseph Smith said that evangelical ministers are patriarchs ([see Joseph Smith Papers, 'Instruction

or the traveling high council, in building up the church and regulating all the affairs of the same in all nations, first unto the Gentiles and then to the Jews—

35 The Twelve being sent out, holding the keys, to open the door by the proclamation of the gospel of Jesus Christ, and first unto the Gentiles and then unto the Jews.

36 The standing high councils, at the stakes of Zion, form a quorum equal in authority in the affairs of the church, in all their decisions, to the quorum of the presidency, or to the traveling high council.

37 The high council in Zion form a quorum equal in authority in the affairs of the church, in all their decisions, to the councils of the Twelve at the stakes of Zion.

38 It is the duty of the traveling high council to call upon the Seventy, when they need assistance, to fill the several calls for preaching and administering the gospel, instead of any others.

39 It is the duty of the Twelve, in all large branches of the church, to ordain evangelical ministers, as they shall be designated unto them by revelation—

on Priesthood, between ca. 1 March and ca. 4 May 1835']}" (Roy W. Doxey, *Doctrine and Covenants Speaks*, 2:307). "A patriarch . . . holds an ordained office in the Melchizedek Priesthood. . . . Every stake in the Church usually has one or two ordained patriarchs" (*Encyclopedia of Latter-day Saint History*, 898). ⊕

40 The order of this priesthood was confirmed to be handed down from father to son, and rightly belongs to the literal descendants of the chosen seed, to whom the promises were made.

41 This order was instituted in the days of Adam, and came down by lineage in the following manner:

42 From Adam to Seth, who was ordained by Adam at the age of sixty-nine years, and was blessed by him three years previous to his (Adam's) death, and received the promise of God by his father, that his posterity should be the chosen of the Lord, and that they should be preserved unto the end of the earth;

43 Because he (Seth) was a perfect man, and his likeness was the express likeness of his father, insomuch that he seemed to be like unto his father in all things, and could be distinguished from him only by his age.

44 Enos was ordained at the age of one hundred and thirty-four years and four months, by the hand of Adam.

45 God called upon Cainan in the wilderness in the fortieth year of his age; and he met Adam in journeying to the place Shedolamak. He was eighty-seven years old when he received his ordination.

46 Mahalaleel was four hundred and ninety-six years and seven days old when he was ordained by the hand of Adam, who also blessed him.

47 Jared was two hundred years old when he was ordained under the hand of Adam, who also blessed him.

What do we understand about the "order of the priesthood" revealed in this passage? (107:40–52) "Joseph Smith taught, 'All Priesthood is Melchizedek; but there are different portions or degrees of it' ([*Joseph Smith* (manual),] 109). One of the degrees or orders of the Melchizedek Priesthood is the patriarchal order, a family-centered system of government that operated from the days of Adam until the time of Moses" (Millet, "Patriarchal Order," 483).

"We refer to [the] great prophets and spiritual leaders that preceded Moses . . . as 'the patriarchs.' Their age is referred to as the patriarchal period because they not only presided as natural patriarchs over their families but they also held the keys of the priesthood and administered the principles and ordinances of the gospel for their respective generations (D&C 107:40–53)" (Top, "Patriarch," 480).

In what way was Adam's son, Seth, a perfect man? (107:43) The "scriptures have described Noah, Seth, and Job as *perfect* men (see Genesis 6:9; Doctrine and Covenants 107:43; Job 1:1). No doubt the same term might apply to a large number of faithful disciples in various dispensations. . . .

"This does not mean that these people never made mistakes or never had need of correction. . . .

"Mortal perfection can be achieved as we try to perform every duty, keep every law, and strive to be as perfect in our sphere as our Heavenly Father is in His. If we do the best we can, the Lord will bless us according to our deeds and the desires of our hearts (see Doctrine and Covenants 137:9)" (Nelson, *Teachings*, 250).

What are a few things we know about Enoch from latter-day revelation? (107:48–49) "In a revelation to the Church given in March of 1831, the 'God of Enoch' spoke of the ancient Zion as having been 'separated from the earth, and . . . received unto myself—a city reserved until a day of righteousness shall come' (D&C 45:11–12). We know . . . that Enoch, the seventh from Adam, was true to his charge and preached the gospel with unusual spiritual power, being the means of preparing a people (over a period of 365 years; D&C 107:49) to become Zion, the City of Holiness, a holy commonwealth in which the people 'were of one heart and one mind, and dwelt in righteousness; and there was no poor among them' (Moses 7:18)" (Millet, *Precept upon Precept*, 372).

Doctrine and Covenants 107:53–57. Ancient Saints Assembled at Adam-Ondi-Ahman, and the Lord Appeared to Them

What do we learn from this gathering of ancient patriarchs? (107:53–56) "These verses detail the great, ancient meeting at Adam-ondi-Ahman, in which Adam's righteous posterity gathered and received great blessings. . . .

"Joseph Smith testified: 'I saw Adam in the valley of Adam-ondi-Ahman. He called together his children and blessed them with a patriarchal blessing. The Lord appeared in their midst, and he (Adam) blessed them all, and foretold what should befall them to the latest generation. This is why Adam blessed his posterity; he wanted to bring them into the presence of God' [Joseph Smith Papers, "Discourse, between circa 26 June and circa 4 August. 1839–A, as Reported by Unidentified Scribe," 3].

48 Enoch was twenty-five years old when he was ordained under the hand of Adam; and he was sixty-five and Adam blessed him.

49 And he saw the Lord, and he walked with him, and was before his face continually; and he walked with God three hundred and sixty-five years, making him four hundred and thirty years old when he was translated.

50 Methuselah was one hundred years old when he was ordained under the hand of Adam.

51 Lamech was thirty-two years old when he was ordained under the hand of Seth.

52 Noah was ten years old when he was ordained under the hand of Methuselah.

53 Three years previous to the death of Adam, he called Seth, Enos, Cainan, Mahalaleel, Jared, Enoch, and Methuselah, who were all high priests, with the residue of his posterity who were righteous, into the valley of Adam-ondi-Ahman, and there bestowed upon them his last blessing.

54 And the Lord appeared unto them, and they rose up and blessed Adam, and called him Michael, the prince, the archangel.

55 And the Lord administered comfort unto Adam, and said unto him: I have set thee to

Adam Meets with Ancient Patriarchs at Adam-ondi-Ahman (D&C 107:53–57)

"Three years before Adam's death, a great event occurred. He took his son Seth, his grandson Enos, and other high priests who were his direct-line descendants, with others of his righteous posterity, into a valley called Adam-ondi-Ahman. There Adam gave to these righteous descendants his last blessing.

"The Lord then appeared to them.

"The vast congregation rose up and blessed Adam and called him Michael, the prince and archangel. The Lord himself declared Adam to be a prince forever over his own posterity.

"Then Adam in his aged condition rose up and, being filled with the spirit of prophecy, predicted 'whatsoever should befall his posterity unto the latest generation.' All this is recorded in section 107 of the Doctrine and Covenants (vv. 53–56).

"The Prophet Joseph Smith said that Adam blessed his posterity because 'he wanted to bring them into the presence of God' [Joseph Smith Papers, "Discourse, between circa 26 June and circa 4 August 1839–A, as Reported by William Clayton," 15].

be at the head; a multitude of nations shall come of thee, and thou art a prince over them forever.

56 And Adam stood up in the midst of the congregation; and, notwithstanding he was bowed down with age, being full of the Holy Ghost, predicted whatsoever should befall his posterity unto the latest generation.

57 These things were all written in the book of Enoch, and are to be testified of in due time.

58 It is the duty of the Twelve, also, to ordain and set in order all the other officers of the church, agreeable to the revelation which says:

59 To the church of Christ in the land of Zion, in addition to the church laws respecting church business—

"In the last days, before Christ's second coming, another great gathering will take place at Adam-ondi-Ahman. This second great gathering will parallel, in many respects, the earlier one" (Parry and Parry, *Understanding the Signs of the Times*, 442). See also commentary in this volume on Doctrine and Covenants 116:1.

Doctrine and Covenants 107:58–67. The Twelve Are to Set the Officers of the Church in Order

According to this verse, what is the duty of the Twelve pertaining to all other officers in the Church? (107:58) "Verses 41–57 constitute an explanation of the patriarchal order. In verse 58, the topic of the revelation returns to the government of the Church. . . .

"[Verse 58] is an important passage, and one that is sometimes overlooked, relative to the succession in Church leadership. It is the duty of the Twelve to set in order all other offices of the Church, including the First Presidency (vv. 66, 82, 91). Verse 58 clarifies that this includes offices which had been previously revealed and explained to the Church" (Robinson and Garrett, *Commentary on the Doctrine and Covenants*, 4:26–27).

What is the other revelation referenced in this verse? (107:58) "A manuscript copy of a revelation dated November 1831 corresponds to [D&C 107:59–100], which seems to be the earlier revelation to which the Lord refers in verse 58. The references between verses 61 and 88 to literal descendants of Aaron and the bishopric and the material in verses

"Here is an illuminating passage from Section 107 of the Doctrine and Covenants which tells us how Adam was able to bring himself and his righteous posterity into God's presence:

"'The order of this priesthood was confirmed to be handed down from father to son, and rightly belongs to the literal descendants of the chosen seed, to whom the promises were made.

"'This order was instituted in the days of Adam, and came down by lineage in [order] . . . that his posterity should be the *chosen of the Lord,* and that *they should be preserved unto the end of the earth*' (D&C 107:40–42; [emphasis] added).

"How did Adam bring his descendants into the presence of the Lord?

"The answer: Adam and his descendants entered into the priesthood order of God. Today we would say they went to the House of the Lord and received their blessings" (Benson, *Sermons and Writings* [2003], 225–27).

93 through 98 on the Seventy were added when this earlier revelation was merged into section 107 [see Woodford, *Historical Development of the Doctrine and Covenants*, 1403]. This means that the material on the duties of quorum presidencies was known as early as 1831, rather than 1835" (Cowan, *Answers to Your Questions*, 126). ⊕

What is the role of presiding officers? (107:60–63)
"If we are to exercise priesthood—a power which is not our own, but sent from God—then we must certainly learn to receive his direction. One of the great priesthood lessons is to learn that much of his direction comes through his agents who are appointed principals over us in his priesthood. So much of the Lord's direction, and a prime means of testing the faith and obedience of his children, is not direct but through presiding intermediaries. President Joseph F. Smith summarized the idea in these words: 'Every man should be willing to be presided over, and he is not fit to preside over others until he can submit sufficiently to the presidency of *his brethren*' [*Improvement Era*, 21 (Dec. 1917): 105; (emphasis) added]" (Wilson K. Andersen, "Revelations on Priesthood, Keys, and Quorums," 409). ⊕

Who is the "President of the High Priesthood of the Church"? (107:64–67) "The offices of the Melchizedek Priesthood are Apostle, Seventy, patriarch, high priest, and elder. The President of the High Priesthood is the President of the Church (see Doctrine and Covenants 107:64–66)" (Gospel Topics, "Melchizedek Priesthood").

"The President of the Church holds the keys over all the Church. . . . In him is concentrated the power of the Priesthood. He holds all the keys of every nature, pertaining to the dispensation of the Fulness of Times. All the keys of former dispensations which have been revealed, are vested in him" (*Joseph Fielding Smith* [manual], 157). See also commentary in this volume on Doctrine and Covenants 41:8–12.

Doctrine and Covenants 107:68–76. Bishops Serve as Common Judges in Israel

What bishop is being described and what are his responsibilities? (107:68–76) "From the time of Aaron to John the Baptist, the high priest in Israel (according to the Aaronic order) presided over the priesthood and the temple. It is not surprising, therefore, that with the restoration of that office in

60 Verily, I say unto you, saith the Lord of Hosts, there must needs be presiding elders to preside over those who are of the office of an elder;

61 And also priests to preside over those who are of the office of a priest;

62 And also teachers to preside over those who are of the office of a teacher, in like manner, and also the deacons—

63 Wherefore, from deacon to teacher, and from teacher to priest, and from priest to elder, severally as they are appointed, according to the covenants and commandments of the church.

64 Then comes the High Priesthood, which is the greatest of all.

65 Wherefore, it must needs be that one be appointed of the High Priesthood to preside over the priesthood, and he shall be called President of the High Priesthood of the Church;

66 Or, in other words, the Presiding High Priest over the High Priesthood of the Church.

67 From the same comes the administering of ordinances and blessings upon the church, by the laying on of the hands.

68 Wherefore, the office of a bishop is not equal unto it; for the office of a bishop is in administering all temporal things;

69 Nevertheless a bishop must be chosen from the High Priesthood, unless he is a literal descendant of Aaron;

70 For unless he is a literal descendant of Aaron he cannot hold the keys of that priesthood.

71 Nevertheless, a high priest, that is, after the order of Melchizedek, may be set apart unto the ministering of temporal things, having a knowledge of them by the Spirit of truth;

72 And also to be a judge in Israel, to do the business of the church, to sit in judgment upon transgressors upon testimony as it shall be laid before him according to the laws, by the assistance of his counselors, whom he has chosen or will choose among the elders of the church.

73 This is the duty of a bishop who is not a literal descendant of Aaron, but has been ordained to the High Priesthood after the order of Melchizedek.

this dispensation there would be some confusion as to just what authority was appended to this position. We are told that this office—known to us today as the presiding bishop—is not equal to that of the president of the high priesthood but rather is to preside over temporal things. To hold the keys of this office one must be either a high priest or a literal descendant of Aaron. This office of bishop also carries with it the responsibility to be a judge in Israel. 'Other bishops' are also spoken of who are to function in their designated area of authority after the pattern of the presiding bishop" (McConkie and Ostler, *Revelations of the Restoration*, 801–2).

When may a "literal descendant of Aaron" serve as the Presiding Bishop? (107:69–70) A literal descendant of Aaron may hold the "office of a bishop known as the Presiding Bishop of the Church. . . . This is the office that Aaron held in Old Testament times. . . .

"The Presiding Bishop is called of God through the mouth of his prophet, the President of the Church. . . . He holds the keys of presidency over the Aaronic Priesthood of the entire church.

"In the absence of a revelation to the President of the Church revealing the lineage of a man to hold this Levitical presidency, the First Presidency is empowered to choose 'a high priest of the Melchizedek Priesthood' to hold the office (D&C 107:17). All of those chosen thus far in this dispensation have been such high priests" (Oscar W. McConkie, *Aaronic Priesthood*, 60). See also commentary in this volume on Doctrine and Covenants 68:16–22. ☉

What duties of bishops are noted in these verses? (107:71–75) "These verses detail two main duties of a bishop. These are to minister in the temporal affairs of the Church and to be a judge in Israel. He therefore maintains and distributes the physical resources of the Church and also determines individual worthiness for participation in the ordinances and activities of the Church. Verses 74 and 75 clarify that these duties apply not only to Presiding Bishops but to all other bishops in the Church" (Robinson and Garrett, *Commentary on the Doctrine and Covenants*, 4:28–29). ☉

How does a bishop serve as a "common judge" for Church members? (107:74) "Repentance and forgiveness come by and through the Lord Jesus Christ. The Lord, however, has called and designated certain Church leaders as judges in Israel. They have a sacred responsibility in protecting the ordinances and ministering to members relative to their worthiness to participate [see 3 Nephi 18:28–29, 32]. . . .

"If a member of The Church of Jesus Christ of Latter-day Saints sets aside holy ordinances and covenants he or she has made with the Lord and willfully disobeys God's commandments, the bishop [acts as a servant] of the Lord in helping the member to repent. . . . The help from a priesthood leader normally begins with private discussions between the person wanting to repent and the bishop" (Neil L. Andersen, *Divine Gift of Forgiveness*, 240–41). ●

Doctrine and Covenants 107:77–84. The First Presidency and the Twelve Constitute the Highest Court in the Church

When might the First Presidency review decisions about a person's membership? (107:78–81) "The judiciary system of the Lord allows for appeals to, or reviews by, the higher councils of the Church. . . . Once it has reached the highest council [the First Presidency] it is the 'final decision,' and 'an end to controversy' (vv. 80, 83). We learn from this revelation that no person belonging to the Church is exempt from a trial for his worthiness (vv. 81, 84)" (Nyman, *Doctrine and Covenants Commentary*, 2:393–94).

What is the "highest council of the church of God"? (107:80–81) The First Presidency "'is the highest council of the church of God, and a final decision upon controversies in spiritual matters' (D&C 107:80). These three men jointly hold the 'keys of the kingdom, which belong always unto the Presidency of the High Priesthood' (D&C 81:2)" (Nyman, "Priesthood, Keys, Councils, and Covenants," 118–19).

74 Thus shall he be a judge, even a common judge among the inhabitants of Zion, or in a stake of Zion, or in any branch of the church where he shall be set apart unto this ministry, until the borders of Zion are enlarged and it becomes necessary to have other bishops or judges in Zion or elsewhere.

75 And inasmuch as there are other bishops appointed they shall act in the same office.

76 But a literal descendant of Aaron has a legal right to the presidency of this priesthood, to the keys of this ministry, to act in the office of bishop independently, without counselors, except in a case where a President of the High Priesthood, after the order of Melchizedek, is tried, to sit as a judge in Israel.

77 And the decision of either of these councils, agreeable to the commandment which says:

78 Again, verily, I say unto you, the most important business of the church, and the most difficult cases of the church, inasmuch as there is not satisfaction upon the decision of the bishop or judges, it shall be handed over and carried up unto the council of the church, before the Presidency of the High Priesthood.

79 And the Presidency of the council of the High Priesthood shall have power to call other high priests, even twelve, to assist as counselors; and thus the Presidency of the High Priesthood and its counselors shall have power to decide upon testimony according to the laws of the church.

80 And after this decision it shall be had in remembrance no more before the Lord; for this is the highest council of the church of God, and a final decision upon controversies in spiritual matters.

81 There is not any person belonging to the church who is exempt from this council of the church.

82 And inasmuch as a President of the High Priesthood shall transgress, he shall be had in remembrance before the common council of the church, who shall be assisted by twelve counselors of the High Priesthood;

83 And their decision upon his head shall be an end of controversy concerning him.

84 Thus, none shall be exempted from the justice and the laws of God, that all things may be done in order and in solemnity before him, according to truth and righteousness.

What is to be done if a member of the First Presidency must be tried for committing a serious sin? (107:82–84) "Section 107 sets out [Church membership council procedures] for all leaders in the Church, including members of the First Presidency. 'There is not any person belonging to the church who is exempt from this council of the church' ([v. 81]). Therefore, if a member of the First Presidency 'transgress, he shall be had in remembrance before the common council of the church . . . ; and their decision upon his head shall be an end of controversy concerning him' ([vv. 82–83]). For that reason, no one is 'exempted from the justice and laws of God, that all things may be done in order and in solemnity' ([v. 84]). In other words, all members of the Church are under the same obligation to live the commandments, for God is not partial" (James W. McConkie, *Looking at the Doctrine and Covenants Again*, 425).

Doctrine and Covenants 107:85–100. Priesthood Presidents Govern Their Respective Quorums

What are primary duties of a quorum president? (107:85–90) "The duty of a quorum president is to sit in counsel with members of the quorum and teach them their specific quorum and priesthood duties. This obligation applies as much to the president of a deacons quorum as to an elders quorum president. The Lord also here limits the size of each of the local quorums as they were constituted in 1831. Verse 90 clarifies that these presidencies are local, in contrast to the Quorums of the Twelve and of the Seventy, which have the obligation to travel into all the world (see also v. 98)" (Robinson and Garrett, *Commentary on the Doctrine and Covenants*, 4:30). ●

85 And again, verily I say unto you, the duty of a president over the office of a deacon is to preside over twelve deacons, to sit in council with them, and to teach them their duty, edifying one another, as it is given according to the covenants.

86 And also the duty of the president over the office of the teachers is to preside over twenty-four of the teachers, and to sit in council with them, teaching them the duties of their office, as given in the covenants.

87 Also the duty of the president over the Priesthood of Aaron is to preside over forty-eight priests, and sit in council with them, to teach them the duties of their office, as is given in the covenants—

88 This president is to be a bishop; for this is one of the duties of this priesthood.

89 Again, the duty of the president over the office of elders is to preside over ninety-six elders, and to sit in council with them, and to teach them according to the covenants.

In what ways is the living prophet to be like unto Moses? (107:91–92) "The living prophet is as Moses for our day. He leads modern Israel out of the bondage of sin and into the promised land of righteousness; he receives revelation to guide the Church today; he holds and exercises the keys of the priesthood to bless the Saints. The president of the Church presides over all of its members and over all of the gifts given the faithful Saints of God to aid in the building of his earthly kingdom (D&C 46:26). . . . As in ancient days, the living prophet's sacred stewardship is to testify boldly as a special witness of the Lord and build up the Church in faith and testimony. Moses is the example and pattern followed by the man who stands as the earthly head of the Church" (Millet and Newell, *Draw Near unto Me*, 305).

Why is it so important to have living prophets, seers, and revelators? (107:92) "There is a crucial difference between prophets, seers, and revelators and the rest of us: They have priesthood keys that allow them to see things we do not yet see and understand things we do not yet understand. . . . A seer has the capacity to see the future and reveal truth, because the Lord does 'nothing, but he revealeth his secret unto his servants the prophets' [Amos 3:7].

"This is why prophets have the ability to make us smarter than any other leaders or influencers on earth can. Prophets help us see dangers we cannot yet see and opportunities we cannot yet imagine" (Dew, *Prophets See around Corners*, 23).

What is the "vision showing the order of the Seventy" referred to in this verse? (107:93) "The precise content of this vision is not known, but it may have been alluded to in a history of the Seventy written by Joseph Young, the first senior president of that quorum. On Sunday, 8 February 1835, the Prophet Joseph Smith invited Brigham and Joseph Young to meet with him privately. After describing a vision 'of the state and condition of those men who died in Zion's Camp, in Missouri,' . . . [he turned] to Elder Joseph Young with quite an earnestness, as though the vision of his mind was extended still further, and addressing him, said: 'Brother Joseph, the Lord has made you President of the Seventies'" (Young, *History of the Organization of the Seventies*, 1–2)" (Cowan, *Answers to Your Questions*, 126–27; see also Joseph

90 This presidency is a distinct one from that of the seventy, and is designed for those who do not travel into all the world.

91 And again, the duty of the President of the office of the High Priesthood is to preside over the whole church, and to be like unto Moses—

92 Behold, here is wisdom; yea, to be a seer, a revelator, a translator, and a prophet, having all the gifts of God which he bestows upon the head of the church.

93 And it is according to the vision showing the order of the Seventy, that they should have seven presidents to preside over them, chosen out of the number of the seventy;

94 And the seventh president of these presidents is to preside over the six;

Smith Papers, Historical Introduction to "Minutes and Blessings, 28 February–1 March 1835").

95 And these seven presidents are to choose other seventy besides the first seventy to whom they belong, and are to preside over them;

96 And also other seventy, until seven times seventy, if the labor in the vineyard of necessity requires it.

97 And these seventy are to be traveling ministers, unto the Gentiles first and also unto the Jews.

98 Whereas other officers of the church, who belong not unto the Twelve, neither to the Seventy, are not under the responsibility to travel among all nations, but are to travel as their circumstances shall allow, notwithstanding they may hold as high and responsible offices in the church.

99 Wherefore, now let every man learn his duty, and to act in the office in which he is appointed, in all diligence.

100 He that is slothful shall not be counted worthy to stand, and he that learns not his duty and shows himself not approved shall not be counted worthy to stand. Even so. Amen.

How do the "seventy" serve in the Church today? (107:95–97) "The Seventies are to constitute traveling quorums, to go into all the earth, whithersoever the Twelve Apostles shall call them.

"The Seventies are not called to serve tables [see Acts 6:1–2], . . . but are to preach the Gospel and build [churches] up, and set others, who do not belong to these quorums, to preside over [the churches], who are High Priests. The Twelve also are . . . to bear the keys of the Kingdom to all nations, and unlock the door of the Gospel to them, and call upon the Seventies to follow after them, and assist them" (*Joseph Smith* [manual], 142).

What does it mean to "act in the office" appointed? (107:99–100) "Intrinsic to the doctrine of the priesthood is a requirement that a priesthood holder learn and fulfill his duty. . . .

"Learning his duty may be the easiest part of a priesthood holder's responsibility. Handbooks, training meetings, and scriptures all provide sources for learning our duty. Fulfilling that duty, however, is more difficult. President Thomas S. Monson admonished: 'Brethren, it is in doing—not just dreaming—that lives are blessed. Others are guided, souls are saved. "Be ye doers of the word, and not hearers only, deceiving your own selves" (James 1:22)' ["Do Your Duty—That Is Best," *Ensign*, Nov. 2005, 59]" (Renlund and Renlund, *Melchizedek Priesthood*, 131–32). ⊕

What Is the Order of the Quorum of the Seventy? (Doctrine and Covenants 107:93–97)

In addition to Section 107's earlier descriptions of the Seventy (see commentary in this volume on Doctrine and Covenants 107:33–35), the following can be learned from verses 93–97: "This quorum consists of seventy men who are to be presided over by seven presidents chosen from among the seventy, with one of the seven presidents presiding over the other six (D&C 107:93–94). . . .

"President Gordon B. Hinckley . . . spoke of the office of seventy as 'an office that carries with it the responsibility of bearing apostolic witness of the name of Christ' ["Special Witnesses for Christ," *Ensign*, May 1984, 50]. They 'are to be traveling ministers, unto the Gentiles first and also unto the Jews' (v. 97; see also 124:139). As the kingdom grows and 'the labor in the vineyard' requires more traveling ministers, the seven presidents are to call other seventy, even seven times seventy (D&C 107:95–96). . . .

"The flexibility of this quorum, or eventually quorums, to meet the needs of a growing church has been demonstrated through the history of the Church and particularly in recent years" (Nyman, "Priesthood, Keys, Councils, and Covenants," 122).

Introduction to Doctrine and Covenants 108

"On the morning after Christmas Day in 1835, Lyman Sherman, one of the presidents of the Seventy, asked [Joseph Smith] to petition God for a revelation that 'should make known [his] duty.' In response, [the Prophet] dictated this revelation [at Kirtland, Ohio].

"Sherman, then thirty-one years old, had distinguished himself as a faithful Latter-day Saint prior to his request. He joined the church in western New York in January 1832 and relocated his family 120 miles west to Kirtland, Ohio, sometime around June 1833. Sherman marched to Missouri in May 1834 with about two hundred others as part of the Camp of Israel expedition. In February 1835, he was called as one of seven presidents over the Seventy, a newly established priesthood office. In his ordination blessing, Sherman was told, 'Your ministry shall be great and you shall proclaim to various nations. Your faith shall be unshaken and you shall be delivered from great afflictions.' At a May 1835 conference, church leaders voted that Sherman, along with the other presidents of the Seventy, should 'hold himself in readiness to go at the call of the Twelve, when the Lord opens the way.' Sherman likely left Kirtland during summer 1835 to preach in local communities, though he may have remained in Kirtland and prepared himself to preach as he had been instructed" (Joseph Smith Papers, Historical Introduction to "Revelation, 26 December 1835 [D&C 108]").

Doctrine and Covenants 108:1–3. Lyman Sherman Forgiven of His Sins

Why was Lyman Sherman asked to meet with Joseph Smith? (108:1) "When Lyman Sherman was a high priest serving as one of the presidents of the Seventy, there arose some contention whether he or the Seventies had the most authority in the presidency. The Prophet decided to release him from his assignment in the seventies quorum and asked him to come see him. Brother Sherman felt disappointed and hurt but responded to the Prophet's call and went to his office. The Lord then gave him this blessing: 'Verily thus saith the Lord unto you, my servant Lyman: Your sins are forgiven you, because you have obeyed my voice in coming up hither this morning to receive counsel of him whom I have appointed' (D&C 108:1)" (Melchin, "Thy Sins Are Forgiven," *Ensign,* Jan. 1995, 20).

Why was Lyman Sherman concerned about his "spiritual standing"? (108:2) "Lyman Sherman had passed through one of those mental struggles in which faith is tried to the utmost. It had been a question with him whether to go forward, or to turn back. It is evident, also, that he had conquered doubt and had determined to continue in the faith. At this stage

SECTION 108

Revelation given through Joseph Smith the Prophet, at Kirtland, Ohio, December 26, 1835. This section was received at the request of Lyman Sherman, who had previously been ordained a seventy and who had come to the Prophet with a request for a revelation to make known his duty.

1 Verily thus saith the Lord unto you, my servant Lyman: Your sins are forgiven you, because you have obeyed my voice in coming up hither this morning to receive counsel of him whom I have appointed.

2 Therefore, let your soul be at rest concerning your spiritual standing, and resist no more my voice.

of the trial, it occurred to him that he had sinned by resisting the voice of the Lord, and that perhaps he had lost his standing among the brethren. Tortured by this thought, he heard the voice of the Spirit whispering in his soul and prompting him to visit the Prophet and ask for the Word of God through His servant" (Smith and Sjodahl, *Doctrine and Covenants Commentary*, 713).

3 And arise up and be more careful henceforth in observing your vows, which you have made and do make, and you shall be blessed with exceeding great blessings.

In what context is the word *vow* being used in this verse? (108:3) "A vow is a solemn promise or pledge, especially one made to God in which the person dedicates himself to service or a way of life. The word is used in association with words having similar meanings, such as covenants, contracts, bonds, obligations, oaths, and performances. It can be rightly said that every person who has accepted membership into the Church has made vows whereby he will abide by the laws of that kingdom" (Roy W. Doxey, *Doctrine and Covenants Speaks*, 2:310).

Doctrine and Covenants 108:4–5. Lyman Sherman Is to Be Numbered with the Leading Elders of the Church

What was the solemn assembly? (108:4) "On 22 January 1836, Brother Sherman attended a special meeting in the temple with the leading councils and general authorities of the Church to receive initiatory ordinances of washing and anointing. It is likely, however, that the solemn assembly meant here—if only one is meant—was the twenty-four-hour meeting held on Wednesday, 30 March 1836, three days after the dedication of the Kirtland Temple. On that occasion, most of the priesthood holders in Kirtland received initiatory ordinances in the temple. Lyman Sherman had by then been presented and sustained by the Church as one of the presidents of the Seventy and on March 29 had, with other general authorities, also received the ordinance of washing of the feet in the temple" (Robinson and Garrett, *Commentary on the Doctrine and Covenants*, 4:36–37).

4 Wait patiently until the solemn assembly shall be called of my servants, then you shall be remembered with the first of mine elders, and receive right by ordination with the rest of mine elders whom I have chosen.

5 Behold, this is the promise of the Father unto you if you continue faithful.

What ordination was Lyman Sherman promised to receive if he continued faithful? (108:4–5) "This revelation informed Lyman Sherman that he was to be numbered among the first to receive the endowment. These were those who had proven themselves worthy of such an honor in Zion's Camp. Preparation for the endowment occupied much of the Church leaders' time during the early months of 1836. Those selected to participate in this sacred ritual met regularly in the Kirtland Temple during January and February of 1836.

"Of these preparations Joseph Smith said: 'We must have all things prepared, and call our solemn assembly as the Lord has commanded us, that we may be able to accomplish His great work, and it must be done in God's own way' [Joseph Smith Papers, 'History, 1834–1836,' 127]" (McConkie and Ostler, *Revelations of the Restoration*, 862).

Doctrine and Covenants 108:6–8. Lyman Sherman Is Called to Preach the Gospel and Strengthen His Brethren

What does it mean to "strengthen your brethren in all your conversation"? (108:7) "Let love be the Polar Star of our lives in reaching out to those who need our strength. There are many among us who lie alone in pain. Medicine helps, but kind words can bring to pass miracles. Many there are who walk in frightening circumstances, fearful and unable to cope. There are good bishops and Relief Society officers who are available to help, but these cannot do it all. Each of us can and must be anxiously engaged. It was said of the Savior, 'He went about doing good' (Acts 10:38)" (Hinckley, "Let Love Be the Lodestar of Your Life," *Ensign*, May 1989, 66–67). ⊕

6 And it shall be fulfilled upon you in that day that you shall have right to preach my gospel wheresoever I shall send you, from henceforth from that time.

7 Therefore, strengthen your brethren in all your conversation, in all your prayers, in all your exhortations, and in all your doings.

8 And behold, and lo, I am with you to bless you and deliver you forever. Amen.

Introduction to Doctrine and Covenants 109

The time for the dedication of the Kirtland Temple was at hand. On Sunday, March 27, 1836, Joseph Smith recorded: "The congregation began to assemble at the Temple at about [7 a.m.], an hour earlier than the doors were to be opened. Many brethren had come in from the regions round about to witness the dedication of the Lord's House, and share in his blessings, and such was the anxiety on this occasion, that some hundreds (probably five or six) assembled before the doors were opened. . . . [We] dedicated the pulpits and consecrated them to the Lord. The doors were then opened. President [Sidney] Rigdon, President [Oliver] Cowdery and myself seated the congregation as they came in, and according to the best calculation we could make, we received between nine and ten hundred, which were as many as could be comfortably situated" (Joseph Smith Papers, "History, 1838–1856, volume B-1]," 713).

The most important part of the dedication services was the dedicatory prayer. Joseph noted that early in the morning the previous day, 26 March 1836, he "met with the Presidency to make arrangements for the Solemn Assembly, which occupied the remainder of the day" (Joseph Smith Papers, "History, 1838–1856, volume B-1," 713). Oliver Cowdery added: "This day our school did not keep, we prepared for the dedication of the Lord's house. I met in the president's room, pres. [Joseph] Smith, jr. [Sidney] Rigdon, my brother [Warren] A. Cowdery & Elder [Warren] Parrish, and assisted in writing a prayer for the dedication of the house" (Arrington, "Oliver Cowdery's Kirtland," 426).

"The Lord inspired the prophet to pray for the fulfillment of earlier instructions and promises concerning the temple (compare [D&C 109:]6–9, 19–20 with D&C 88:117–20; 132–34). The Prophet asked the Lord to sanctify the temple with His presence, that all who entered might feel His power and holiness, and that those who would go forth from it would do so armed with testimony (vv. 12–13, 22–23). This prayer petitions blessings not only for the Church, but also for many other worthy purposes, such as the gathering of the Jews, the Lamanites, and other scattered remnants of Israel (vv. 61–67). There was even a prayer for members of 'the wicked mob,' that they might repent (v. 50). The Lord was also asked to bless the leaders of the Church and their 'immediate connections' or relatives (vv. 68–72)" (Cowan and Manscill, *A to Z of the Doctrine and Covenants*, 158–59).

SECTION 109

Prayer offered at the dedication of the temple at Kirtland, Ohio, March 27, 1836. According to the Prophet's written statement, this prayer was given to him by revelation.

1 Thanks be to thy name, O Lord God of Israel, who keepest covenant and showest mercy unto thy servants who walk uprightly before thee, with all their hearts—

2 Thou who hast commanded thy servants to build a house to thy name in this place [Kirtland].

3 And now thou beholdest, O Lord, that thy servants have done according to thy commandment.

4 And now we ask thee, Holy Father, in the name of Jesus Christ, the Son of thy bosom, in whose name alone salvation can be administered to the children of men, we ask thee, O Lord, to accept of this house, the workmanship of the hands of us, thy servants, which thou didst command us to build.

Doctrine and Covenants 109:1–5. The Kirtland Temple Was Built as a Place for the Son of Man to Visit

What is significant about the opening line of Joseph's dedicatory prayer? (109:1) "This prayer at the dedication of the Kirtland Temple begins almost exactly as Solomon's prayer did when he dedicated the first Jerusalem temple (see 1 Kings 8:23), with an expression of gratitude to God for His faithfulness and mercy. The Prophet then asked God to accept the house that had been built in obedience to His commandments and sought blessings for the servants of the Lord, the Saints generally, himself, and the structure itself" (Woodger, *Essential Doctrine and Covenants Companion*, 217).

When had the Saints previously been commanded to build the temple? (109:2) See commentary in this volume on Doctrine and Covenants 57:3; 88:119; 95:3, 8, 11; 97:12, 13.

Why Are the Temple Dedicatory Prayers So Important? (Doctrine and Covenants 109)

"President Joseph Fielding Smith taught: '. . . When we dedicate a house to the Lord, what we really do is dedicate ourselves to the Lord's service, with a covenant that we shall use the house in the way He intends that it shall be used. . . . Dedicatory prayers for temples, however, are formal and long and cover many matters of doctrine and petition. This pattern was set by the Prophet Joseph Smith in the dedication of the Kirtland Temple. The prayer given on that occasion was revealed to him by the Lord; all prayers used since then have been written by the spirit of inspiration and have been read by such of the Brethren as have been appointed to do so' (*Church News*, Feb. 12, 1972)" (Otten and Caldwell, *Sacred Truths*, 2:240).

The Kirtland Temple

How did the building of the Kirtland Temple exemplify the principle of sacrifice? (109:5) Heber C. Kimball remembered: "At this time the brethren were laboring night and day building the house of the Lord. Our women were engaged in spinning and knitting in order to clothe those who were laboring at the building, and the Lord only knows the scenes of poverty, tribulation, and distress which we passed through in order to accomplish this thing. . . . Elder [Sidney] Rigdon . . . frequently used to go upon the walls of the building both by night and day and frequently wetting the walls with his tears, crying aloud to the Almighty to send means whereby we might accomplish the building" ("Extracts from H. C. Kimball's Journal," 867). 🔵

Doctrine and Covenants 109:6–21. The Kirtland Temple Is to Be a House of Prayer, Fasting, Faith, Learning, Glory, and Order, and a House of God

Why did the Lord command the Saints to call a "solemn assembly"? (109:6–10) "Anciently, solemn assemblies were a prominent part of worship among the Israelites and were a time for fasting and praying to the Lord (see Leviticus 23:36; Deuteronomy 16:8; Joel 1:14; 2:15–17). The Lord commanded the members of His restored Church to continue these sacred meetings as an important part of their worship (see D&C 124:39; 133:6). In the revelation recorded in Doctrine and Covenants 88, the Saints were commanded to prepare themselves to hold a solemn assembly where the Lord would fulfill 'the great and last promise' of unveiling His face to them (see D&C 88:68–70, 75) and, as He had previously promised, endowing them with 'power from on high' (D&C 38:32; see also D&C 95:8–9). They were directed to prepare for this solemn assembly by sanctifying and purifying themselves (see D&C 88:68, 74)" (*Doctrine and Covenants Student Manual* [2018], 482). 🔵

How can we apply the Lord's pattern for organizing a house of God? (109:8) As the Lord revealed truths about the temple in Kirtland, He provided steps for sanctifying His house and His people. Sister Susan W. Tanner observed how this process of preparation applied not only to the temple, but to our homes as well: "Did I tell you . . . how to make your home a haven of peace and a fortress of strength? You should follow the pattern you witnessed as you entered the Lord's house, to 'establish a house . . . of prayer, a house of fasting, a house of faith, a house

5 For thou knowest that we have done this work through great tribulation; and out of our poverty we have given of our substance to build a house to thy name, that the Son of Man might have a place to manifest himself to his people.

6 And as thou hast said in a revelation, given to us, calling us thy friends, saying—Call your solemn assembly, as I have commanded you;

7 And as all have not faith, seek ye diligently and teach one another words of wisdom; yea, seek ye out of the best books words of wisdom, seek learning even by study and also by faith;

8 Organize yourselves; prepare every needful thing, and establish a house, even a house of prayer, a house of fasting, a house of faith, a house of learning, a house of glory, a house of order, a house of God;

9 That your incomings may be in the name of the Lord, that your outgoings may be in the name of the Lord, that all your salutations may be in the name of the Lord, with uplifted hands unto the Most High—

10 And now, Holy Father, we ask thee to assist us, thy people, with thy grace, in calling our solemn assembly, that it may be done to thine honor and to thy divine acceptance;

11 And in a manner that we may be found worthy, in thy sight, to secure a fulfilment of the promises which thou hast made unto us, thy people, in the revelations given unto us;

12 That thy glory may rest down upon thy people, and upon this thy house, which we now dedicate to thee, that it may be sanctified and consecrated to be holy, and that thy holy presence may be continually in this house;

13 And that all people who shall enter upon the threshold of the Lord's house may feel thy power, and feel constrained to acknowledge that thou hast sanctified it, and that it is thy house, a place of thy holiness.

14 And do thou grant, Holy Father, that all those who shall worship in this house may be taught words of wisdom out of the best books, and that they may seek learning even by study, and also by faith, as thou hast said;

of learning, . . . a house of order' (D&C 109:8). As we follow this pattern, great peace will dwell within our homes in a world of increasing turmoil" ("Did I Tell You . . . ?" *Ensign*, May 2003, 73).

What were the promises previously made to the Saints in Kirtland? (109:11) The fulfillment of the prophet Joseph Smith's prayer included: "And if your eye be single to my glory, your whole bodies shall be filled with light, and there shall be no darkness in you; and that body which is filled with light comprehendeth all things.

"Therefore, sanctify yourselves that your minds become single to God, and the days will come that you shall see him; for he will unveil his face unto you, and it shall be in his own time, and in his own way, and according to his own will" ([D&C 88:67–69).

Joseph wrote William W. Phelps that "We will obey, as on conditions of our obedience, he has promised us great things, yea even a visit from the heavens to honor us with his own presence" (Joseph Smith Papers, "Letter to William W. Phelps, 11 January 1833," 19). See also commentary in this volume on Doctrine and Covenants 93:20; 97:15–16 and 110:7–8.

What does it mean that the Lord's house is sanctified and consecrated to be holy? (109:12–13) "The basic meaning of 'sanctified' and 'consecrated'— *hagios, kadosh, sanctus,* holy, etc.,—is 'fenced off from the world.' That is the permanent condition of the temple: 'that the holy presence may be *continually* in this house.' Many holy places are open to secular use throughout the year except during the formal set times of assembly and celebration. Not so with the temple; there everything that happens is removed from the everyday world" (Nibley, "House of Glory," 35).

How did the Kirtland Temple fulfill the Lord's counsel to seek learning and wisdom out of the best books? (109:14) A variety of classes for the elders' instruction took place in the Kirtland Temple. "The 1835–36 school term commenced on November 2, 1835, and on January 18, 1836, the School of the Prophets moved into the temple. One of the subjects that year was Hebrew, taught by Joshua Seixas, an instructor at a seminary in Hudson, Ohio. He was hired for seven weeks at a salary of $320.00 and was given an office in the building. Forty-five students initially enrolled for the series of one-hour lectures. By February 4, additional classes were created. Joseph Smith was elated with the course" (Karl Ricks Anderson, *Joseph Smith's Kirtland,* 118).

How do we "grow up" in the Lord and receive a fullness of the Holy Ghost? (109:15) Elder Dale G. Renlund instructed: "We live as perpetual children if we are ignorant of the eternal perspective gained in temples. There we grow up in the Lord, 'receive a fullness of the Holy Ghost' [D&C 109:15], and become more fully committed as disciples of the Savior. As we keep our covenants, we receive God's power in our lives" ("Your Divine Nature and Eternal Destiny," *Liahona*, May 2022, 76). ⊕

Why are only the worthy and clean permitted entrance into the temple? (109:17–20) "Our Redeemer requires that His temples be protected from desecration. No unclean thing may enter His hallowed house. Yet anyone is welcome who prepares well. Each person applying for a recommend will be interviewed by a judge in Israel—the bishop—and by a stake president. They hold keys of priesthood authority and the responsibility to help us know when our preparation and timing are appropriate to enter the temple. . . .

"Because the temple is the house of the Lord, standards for admission are set by Him. One enters as His guest. To hold a temple recommend is a priceless privilege and a tangible sign of obedience to God and His prophets" (Nelson, "Personal Preparation for Temple Blessings," *Ensign*, May 2001, 33). See also commentary in this volume on Doctrine and Covenants 110:7–8. ⊕

What are some of the blessings ordained to be poured out upon the Saints for worthy temple attendance? (109:21) "In the temple, the precious plan of God is taught. It is in the temple that eternal covenants are made. The temple lifts us, exalts us, stands as a beacon for all to see, and points us toward celestial glory. It is the house of God. All that occurs within the walls of the temple is uplifting and ennobling. . . .

"As we touch the temple and love the temple, our lives will reflect our faith. As we go to the holy house, as we remember the covenants we make therein, we will be able to bear every trial and overcome each temptation. The temple provides purpose for our lives. It brings peace to our souls—not the peace provided by men but the peace promised by the Son of God when He said, 'Peace I leave with you, my peace I give unto you: not as the world giveth, give I unto you. Let not your heart be troubled, neither let it be afraid'" (Thomas S. Monson, "Blessings of the Temple," *Ensign*, Oct. 2010, 13, 15). ⊕

15 And that they may grow up in thee, and receive a fulness of the Holy Ghost, and be organized according to thy laws, and be prepared to obtain every needful thing;

16 And that this house may be a house of prayer, a house of fasting, a house of faith, a house of glory and of God, even thy house;

17 That all the incomings of thy people, into this house, may be in the name of the Lord;

18 That all their outgoings from this house may be in the name of the Lord;

19 And that all their salutations may be in the name of the Lord, with holy hands, uplifted to the Most High;

20 And that no unclean thing shall be permitted to come into thy house to pollute it;

21 And when thy people transgress, any of them, they may speedily repent and return unto thee, and find favor in thy sight, and be restored to the blessings which thou hast ordained to be poured out upon those who shall reverence thee in thy house.

22 And we ask thee, Holy Father, that thy servants may go forth from this house armed with thy power, and that thy name may be upon them, and thy glory be round about them, and thine angels have charge over them;

23 And from this place they may bear exceedingly great and glorious tidings, in truth, unto the ends of the earth, that they may know that this is thy work, and that thou hast put forth thy hand, to fulfil that which thou hast spoken by the mouths of the prophets, concerning the last days.

Doctrine and Covenants 109:22–33. May the Unrepentant Who Oppose the Lord's People Be Confounded

What part can angels play in an individual's life? (109:22) President Jeffrey R. Holland testified: "From the beginning down through the dispensations, God has used angels as His emissaries in conveying love and concern for His children. . . .

"Usually such beings are *not* seen. Sometimes they are. But seen or unseen they are *always* near. Sometimes their assignments are very grand and have significance for the whole world. Sometimes the messages are more private. Occasionally the angelic purpose is to warn. But most often it is to comfort, to provide some form of merciful attention, guidance in difficult times. . . .

"I testify of angels, both the heavenly and the mortal kind. In doing so I am testifying that God never leaves us alone, never leaves us unaided in the challenges that we face" ("Ministry of Angels," *Ensign*, Nov. 2008, 29, 31). ☉

What does it mean to go forth from the temple "armed with thy power"? (109:22–23) Sister Bonnie L. Oscarson stated: "The temple holds a place at the very center of our most sacred beliefs, and the Lord asks that we attend, ponder, study, and find personal meaning and application individually. We will come to understand that through the ordinances of the temple, the power of godliness is manifest in our lives (see D&C 84:20) and that because of temple ordinances, we can be armed with God's power, and His name will be upon us, His glory round about us, and His angels have charge over us (see D&C 109:22). I wonder if we are fully drawing upon the power of those promises" ("Rise Up in Strength," *Ensign*, Nov. 2016, 13).

President Russell M. Nelson Speaks of the Temple as the Center of Our Strength (D&C 109:21)

"The temple lies at the center of strengthening our faith and spiritual fortitude because the Savior and His doctrine are the very heart of the temple. Everything taught in the temple, through instruction and through the Spirit, increases our understanding of Jesus Christ. His essential ordinances bind us to Him through sacred priesthood covenants. Then, as we keep our covenants, He endows us with *His* healing, strengthening power [see D&C 109:15, 22]. And oh, how we will need His power in the days ahead.

"We have been promised that 'if [we] are prepared [we] shall not fear' [D&C 38:30]. This assurance has profound implications today. The Lord has declared that despite today's unprecedented challenges, those who build their foundations upon Jesus Christ, and have learned how to draw upon His power, need not succumb to the unique anxieties of this era" (Nelson, "Temple and Your Spiritual Foundation," *Liahona*, Nov. 2021, 93–94).

What does it mean to be established as a people with a name and a standing in the Lord's house? (109:24) "Those who receive the ordinances and blessings of the temple have a power for righteousness that comes from the Lord. They can better withstand evil and can better propagate truth as an influence for good to all of Father's children. Those who are armed with this power of the Lord shall be established by the Lord with an honorable name in His house to be remembered throughout generations to come" (Otten and Caldwell, *Sacred Truths*, 2:242). ●

What is the Lord's promise of deliverance for those who take His name upon them in the Holy Temple? (109:24–28) After referring to Doctrine and Covenants 109:24–28, and specifically quoting verse 28, Elder David A. Bednar promises the following: "Please consider these verses in light of the current raging of the adversary and . . . about our willingness to take upon us the name of Jesus Christ and the blessing of protection promised to those who honorably hold a name and standing in the holy temple. Significantly, these covenant blessings are to all generations and for all eternity. I invite you to study repeatedly and ponder prayerfully the implications of these scriptures in your life and for your family.

"We should not be surprised by Satan's efforts to thwart or discredit temple worship and work. The devil despises the purity in and the power of the Lord's house. And the protection available to each of us in and through temple ordinances and covenants stands as a great obstacle to the evil designs of Lucifer" ("Honorably Hold a Name and a Standing," *Ensign*, May 2009, 99–100).

What is the Lord's promise regarding the adversary's opposition to the building of His house? (109:25–26) Elder David A. Bednar remarked: "We live in a great day of temple building around the world. And the adversary surely is mindful of the increasing number of temples that now dot the earth. As always, the building and dedicating of these sacred structures are accompanied by opposition from enemies of the Church as well as by ill-advised criticism from some within the Church. . . .

"We as faithful Saints have been strengthened by adversity and are the recipients of the Lord's tender mercies. We have moved forward under the promise of the Lord: 'I will not suffer that [mine enemies] shall destroy my work; yea, I will show unto them that my wisdom is greater than the cunning of the devil' (D&C 10:43)" ("Honorably Hold a Name and a Standing," *Ensign*, May 2009, 98, 99). ●

24 We ask thee, Holy Father, to establish the people that shall worship, and honorably hold a name and standing in this thy house, to all generations and for eternity;

25 That no weapon formed against them shall prosper; that he who diggeth a pit for them shall fall into the same himself;

26 That no combination of wickedness shall have power to rise up and prevail over thy people upon whom thy name shall be put in this house;

27 And if any people shall rise against this people, that thine anger be kindled against them;

28 And if they shall smite this people thou wilt smite them; thou wilt fight for thy people as thou didst in the day of battle, that they may be delivered from the hands of all their enemies.

What does it mean to put the Lord's name upon us? (109:26) "Time after time in succeeding revelations, the Lord and his servants referred to the future temple as a house for 'the name' of the Lord God of Israel. . . . After the temple was dedicated, the Lord appeared to Solomon and told him that He had hallowed the temple 'to put my name there forever' (1 Kgs. 9:3; 2 Chr. 7:16).

"Similarly, in modern revelations the Lord refers to temples as houses built 'unto my holy name' (D&C 124:39; 105:33; 109:2–5). In the inspired dedicatory prayer of the Kirtland Temple, the Prophet Joseph Smith asked the Lord for a blessing upon 'thy people upon whom thy name shall be put in this house' (D&C 109:26)" (Oaks, "Taking upon Us the Name of Jesus Christ," *Ensign*, May 1985, 81). ●

29 We ask thee, Holy Father, to confound, and astonish, and to bring to shame and confusion, all those who have spread lying reports abroad, over the world, against thy servant or servants, if they will not repent, when the everlasting gospel shall be proclaimed in their ears;

30 And that all their works may be brought to naught, and be swept away by the hail, and by the judgments which thou wilt send upon them in thine anger, that there may be an end to lyings and slanders against thy people.

Why were "lying reports" spread over the world against the Lord's servants? (109:29–30) "Satan, who has been 'a liar from the beginning' (D&C 93:25), must . . . misrepresent the truth about the Church to create the kind of universal hatred that brings persecution. Jesus explained to his New Testament followers that 'whosoever killeth you will think that he doeth God service' (John 16:2). They will be wrong, of course, but they will *think* that in opposing the Church, they are fighting a great evil. Because of those who 'spread lying reports,' Jesus, the one sinless human being who ever lived, was crucified as a vile criminal. Because of lying reports, the early Christians were persecuted and martyred in the Roman world. And because of lying reports, the modern Church has suffered unjust opposition from the Restoration until the present time" (Robinson and Garrett, *Commentary on the Doctrine and Covenants*, 4:47). ●

31 For thou knowest, O Lord, that thy servants have been innocent before thee in bearing record of thy name, for which they have suffered these things.

32 Therefore we plead before thee for a full and complete deliverance from under this yoke;

33 Break it off, O Lord; break it off from the necks of thy servants, by thy power, that we may rise up in the midst of this generation and do thy work.

What is the yoke spoken of in these verses? (109:31–33) In Joseph's day a yoke was defined as "a piece of timber . . . fitted with bows for receiving the necks of oxen." It was "a mark of servitude; slavery; bondage" (Webster, *American Dictionary* [1828], s.v. "yoke"). The yoke described here was forged from persecution and the spread of lying reports over the world (see D&C 109:28–29). "'To have evil spoken of is the heritage of the Saints of God in all ages. Such will not end until that great day in which Satan is bound and his tongue silenced. Nevertheless, we have the assurance that truth will prevail and the promise of Moroni that the Church will increase the more it is opposed' (*Messenger and Advocate*, 2:199)" (McConkie and Ostler, *Revelations of the Restoration*, 872).

Doctrine and Covenants 109:34–42. May the Saints Go Forth in Power to Gather the Righteous to Zion

What does the sealing of the anointing of the Lord's ministers mean? (109:35) "The endowment of the Kirtland Temple was an endowment of preparatory, or initiatory, temple ordinances. Beginning in January 1836, members of the leading quorums and then, eventually, other members of the Church received washings and anointings (first in the printing office and later in the upper stories of the temple), which were also sealed by ordinance at the time. The prayer here is that those who had received, or who soon would receive, these ordinances will enjoy a direct outpouring of power from the heavens through the Spirit as a consequence of the holy ordinances they had received in the temple" (Robinson and Garrett, *Commentary on the Doctrine and Covenants*, 4:49).

What is the significance of the Prophet's prayer for an outpouring of the Spirit like the Day of Pentecost? (109:36–37) The Prophet's dedicatory prayer for a Pentecostal experience was fulfilled. According to the First Presidency: "We read that Jesus, after his resurrection, breathed upon his disciples and said, 'Receive ye the Holy Ghost.' But we also read that he said, 'Behold, I send the promise of my father upon you: but tarry ye in the city of Jerusalem, until ye be endued [endowed] with power from on high' (John 20:22; Luke 24:49). . . . Thus the promise was made, but the fulfilment came after, so

34 O Jehovah, have mercy upon this people, and as all men sin, forgive the transgressions of thy people, and let them be blotted out forever.

35 Let the anointing of thy ministers be sealed upon them with power from on high.

36 Let it be fulfilled upon them, as upon those on the day of Pentecost; let the gift of tongues be poured out upon thy people, even cloven tongues as of fire, and the interpretation thereof.

37 And let thy house be filled, as with a rushing mighty wind, with thy glory.

The Pentecostal Season in Kirtland, Ohio (Doctrine and Covenants 109:36–37)

January to April 1836 was, perhaps, the greatest Pentecostal season this earth has experienced. The heavens were opened and men, women, and children participated in the outpouring of the Spirit and the bestowal of spiritual gifts. Concerning the Kirtland Temple dedication, Joseph Smith remarked: "Brother George A. Smith arose and began to prophesy when a voice was heard like the sound of a rushing mighty wind which filled the Temple, and all the congregation simultaneously arose being moved upon by an invisible power. Many began to speak in Tongues and prophesy; others saw glorious visions, and I beheld the Temple was filled with angels, which fact I declared to the congregation. The people in the neighborhood came running together (hearing an unusual sound within and seeing a bright light like a pillar of Fire resting upon the Temple) and were astonished at what was transpiring" (Joseph Smith Papers, "History, 1838–1856, volume B-1," 3–4 [addenda]; spelling and punctuation modernized).

Eliza R. Snow summed the overwhelming events of the Temple dedication: "There we had the gift of prophecy—the gift of tongues—the interpretation of tongues—visions and marvelous dreams were related—the singing of heavenly choirs was heard, and wonderful manifestations of the healing power, through the administrations of the Elders, were witnessed. The sick were healed—the deaf made to hear—the blind to see and the lame to walk, in very many instances. It was plainly manifest that a sacred and divine influence—a spiritual atmosphere pervaded that holy edifice" (*Biography and Family Record of Lorenzo Snow*, 11).

that the Holy Ghost sent by Jesus from the Father did not come in person until the day of Pentecost, and the cloven tongues of fire were the sign of his coming. This manifestation was repeated in this dispensation at the endowment in the Kirtland Temple, in the month of [January], 1836" (First Presidency [1916], "'Receiving' the Holy Ghost," 460–61).

38 Put upon thy servants the testimony of the covenant, that when they go out and proclaim thy word they may seal up the law, and prepare the hearts of thy saints for all those judgments thou art about to send, in thy wrath, upon the inhabitants of the earth, because of their transgressions, that thy people may not faint in the day of trouble.

Why did Joseph plead that the "testimony of the covenant" be placed upon the hearts of the Lord's servants? (109:38) "Before the judgments of the end can befall the world, authorized witnesses must be sent to testify of the truth of the gospel covenant and to raise a voice of warning to all people (v. 40; D&C 1:2–16). That testimony of the truth and the authority to bear it to the nations, and, thus, to seal up the law (see v. 46), are part of the endowment of power prayed for and received in the Kirtland Temple" (Robinson and Garrett, *Commentary on the Doctrine and Covenants*, 4:49–50). ⊕

39 And whatsoever city thy servants shall enter, and the people of that city receive their testimony, let thy peace and thy salvation be upon that city; that they may gather out of that city the righteous, that they may come forth to Zion, or to her stakes, the places of thine appointment, with songs of everlasting joy;

40 And until this be accomplished, let not thy judgments fall upon that city.

Where are the places the righteous are to be gathered in the last days? (109:39) "In the revealed prayer dedicating the Kirtland Temple (1836), the Prophet importuned for the righteous, 'that they may come forth to Zion, or to her stakes. . . .'

"We now have stakes of Zion in many nations, in Europe and Asia and South America and upon the islands of the sea. Before the Lord comes, there will be stakes in all lands and among all peoples. Any portion of the surface of the earth that is organized into a stake of Zion—a City of Holiness, as it were—becomes a part of Zion. A stake of Zion is a part of Zion—it is just that simple. And every stake becomes the place of gathering for the saints who live in the area involved" (Bruce R. McConkie, *Millennial Messiah*, 295).

41 And whatsoever city thy servants shall enter, and the people of that city receive not the testimony of thy servants, and thy servants warn them to save themselves from this untoward generation, let it be upon that city according to that which thou hast spoken by the mouths of thy prophets.

42 But deliver thou, O Jehovah, we beseech thee, thy servants from their hands, and cleanse them from their blood.

What is an "untoward generation"? (109:41) "Webster defines *untoward* as 'difficult to manage, stubborn, or troublesome.' Thus, when the Lord cries, 'Save yourselves from this untoward generation,' He is admonishing all to step away from any leanings toward rebelliousness against His holy laws (D&C 36:6; 109:41). An 'untoward generation' is a 'rebellious generation which refuses to change its ungodly course' ([*Doctrinal New Testament Commentary*], 2:42)" (Brewster, *Doctrine & Covenants Encyclopedia* [2012], 611).

Doctrine and Covenants 109:43–53. May the Saints Be Delivered from the Terrible Things to Be Poured out upon the Wicked in the Last Days

What is the "day of burning"? (109:45–46) "The scriptures are quite explicit, that there will be a burning and cleansing process, connected directly with the Second Coming. And this seems to be directly connected to the actual presence of Jesus Christ. We are not given specifics on how this might work, but it seems to be tied to a being whose glory is celestial, and who is likened into the sun itself.... *'Every corruptible thing, both of man, or of beasts of the field, or a fouls of the heavens, or of the fish of the sea, that dwells upon the face of the Earth shall be consumed*; and also that of *element shall melt with fervent* heat; and all things shall become new'* [D&C 101:23–25; emphasis added]" (Lund, *Second Coming of the Lord*, 350–51). ◉

What was Joseph's plea on behalf of the Saints in Missouri and its inhabitants? (109:47–51) "As part of the dedicatory prayer, the Prophet Joseph Smith pleaded with the Lord to remember the Saints in Missouri in their afflictions. He beseeched the Lord to have mercy on the mobs so that they might repent (see D&C 109:50). But the Prophet asked the Lord to show forth His power on behalf of His people, letting His anger and indignation fall upon those guilty of causing the sufferings, if they did not repent" (*Doctrine and Covenants Student Manual* [1981], 272). See also commentary in this volume on Doctrine and Covenants 101:1.

43 O Lord, we delight not in the destruction of our fellow men; their souls are precious before thee;

44 But thy word must be fulfilled. Help thy servants to say, with thy grace assisting them: Thy will be done, O Lord, and not ours.

45 We know that thou hast spoken by the mouth of thy prophets terrible things concerning the wicked, in the last days—that thou wilt pour out thy judgments, without measure;

46 Therefore, O Lord, deliver thy people from the calamity of the wicked; enable thy servants to seal up the law, and bind up the testimony, that they may be prepared against the day of burning.

47 We ask thee, Holy Father, to remember those who have been driven by the inhabitants of Jackson county, Missouri, from the lands of their inheritance, and break off, O Lord, this yoke of affliction that has been put upon them.

48 Thou knowest, O Lord, that they have been greatly oppressed and afflicted by wicked men; and our hearts flow out with sorrow because of their grievous burdens.

49 O Lord, how long wilt thou suffer this people to bear this affliction, and the cries of their innocent ones to ascend up in thine ears, and their blood come up in testimony before thee, and not make a display of thy testimony in their behalf?

50 Have mercy, O Lord, upon the wicked mob, who have driven thy people, that they may cease to spoil, that they may repent of their sins if repentance is to be found;

51 But if they will not, make bare thine arm, O Lord, and redeem that which thou didst appoint a Zion unto thy people.

52 And if it cannot be otherwise, that the cause of thy people may not fail before thee may thine anger be kindled, and thine indignation fall upon them, that they may be wasted away, both root and branch, from under heaven;

53 But inasmuch as they will repent, thou art gracious and merciful, and wilt turn away thy wrath when thou lookest upon the face of thine Anointed.

54 Have mercy, O Lord, upon all the nations of the earth; have mercy upon the rulers of our land; may those principles, which were so honorably and nobly defended, namely, the Constitution of our land, by our fathers, be established forever.

55 Remember the kings, the princes, the nobles, and the great ones of the earth, and all people, and the churches, all the poor, the needy, and afflicted ones of the earth;

56 That their hearts may be softened when thy servants shall go out from thy house, O Jehovah, to bear testimony of thy name; that their prejudices may give way before the truth, and thy people may obtain favor in the sight of all;

Doctrine and Covenants 109:54–58. May Nations and Peoples and Churches Be Prepared for the Gospel

How have prophets and apostles spoken about the US constitution and other nations' constitutions? (109:54) "A constitution is the foundation of government. It provides structure and limits for the exercise of government powers. The United States Constitution is the oldest written constitution still in force today. Though originally adopted by only a small number of colonies, it soon became a model worldwide. Today, every nation except three have adopted written constitutions" (Oaks, "Defending Our Divinely Inspired Constitution," *Liahona*, May 2021, 105). See also commentary in this volume on Doctrine and Covenants 101:77–80.

For what principles did the Prophet pray that would prepare the nations of the earth for the Lord's coming? (109:54–58) The Prophet "then pled for mercy upon all nations of the earth, and for the principles of the United States Constitution to be extended to all (D&C 109:54–55). This was the law to come forth out of Zion (Isaiah 2:3), and belonged to all [humankind] (D&C 98:5). He prayed that the truth

The Prophet Joseph Prays for Blessings upon All People (Doctrine and Covenants 109:54–55)

"The Lord inspired the Prophet Joseph Smith to pray for various groups of people in the earth:

"1. The enemies of the church (see D&C 109:50–53)

"2. The nations of the earth (see D&C 109:54)

"3. The leaders of America (see D&C 109:54)

"4. The rulers and leaders of other nations (see D&C 109:55)

"5. The peoples of the earth (see D&C 109:55)

"6. The churches in the world (see D&C 109:55)

"7. The poor, needy, and afflicted (see D&C 109:55)

"Why might the Lord give counsel to pray for these people of the earth? Perhaps there are many reasons, but one is given by the Lord in this revelation. Hearts of the people of the world need to be softened. They can then more readily accept and respond favorably to the Lord's servants who leave His temple endowed with power to proclaim the message of the gospel for all [people] (see D&C 109:56–57).

"Members of the church have been encouraged and requested to pray for the leaders of nations for this very purpose" (Otten and Caldwell, *Sacred Truths*, 2:242).

may spread—or the gospel of Jesus Christ—and gather the people to build up stakes of Zion and a holy city unto the Lord (D&C 109:54–59). The holy city was the New Jerusalem (see Moses 7:62, 3 Nephi 21:23). The establishing of Zion and her stakes would cut short the work of the destruction of the wicked at the Second Coming of Christ (see D&C 84:96–97)" (Nyman, *Doctrine and Covenants Commentary*, 2:412).

Doctrine and Covenants 109:59–67. May the Jews, the Lamanites, and All Israel Be Redeemed

In what way will the Lord's work be "cut short in righteousness"? (109:59) "The Saints of latter days are commanded to preach repentance to the world and to invite them to come unto Christ. Those who hearken to the message of the Restoration are commanded to gather to the stakes of Zion before the wicked are destroyed.... As the prophesied destruction of the last days gets closer, the Lord will prosper the preaching of the gospel to all nations. Doors now locked to our missionaries will be opened. The Lord's work will be hastened by the blessings that he bestows upon the earth that all might know the truth. The Lord's work being cut short in righteousness will happen according to a divinely predetermined timetable" (McConkie and Ostler, *Revelations of the Restoration*, 879).

Why are those among the House of Israel identified with the Gentiles in these verses? (109:60–61) "The gathering is on a number of fronts. Though we 'are identified with the Gentiles,' there are many 'children of Jacob, who have been scattered upon the mountains.' The gathering is a complex operation entailing the cooperation of the Gentiles, Israel, [and] the Jews.... This refers us to Doctrine and Covenants 49:24–26: 'But before the great day of the Lord shall come, Jacob shall flourish in the wilderness, and the Lamanites shall blossom as the rose. Zion shall flourish upon the hills and rejoice upon the mountains, and shall be assembled together unto the place which I have appointed.... Go forth as I have commanded you.' And so we have come full circle" (Nibley, "House of Glory," 45).

What was the relationship between the dedication of the Kirtland Temple and the gathering of the "children of Jacob"? (109:62–64) Eight days following the temple dedication, "a singular event occurred.... Moses appeared in the Kirtland Temple

57 That all the ends of the earth may know that we, thy servants, have heard thy voice, and that thou hast sent us;

58 That from among all these, thy servants, the sons of Jacob, may gather out the righteous to build a holy city to thy name, as thou hast commanded them.

59 We ask thee to appoint unto Zion other stakes besides this one which thou hast appointed, that the gathering of thy people may roll on in great power and majesty, that thy work may be cut short in righteousness.

60 Now these words, O Lord, we have spoken before thee, concerning the revelations and commandments which thou hast given unto us, who are identified with the Gentiles.

61 But thou knowest that thou hast a great love for the children of Jacob, who have been scattered upon the mountains for a long time, in a cloudy and dark day.

62 We therefore ask thee to have mercy upon the children of Jacob, that Jerusalem, from this hour, may begin to be redeemed;

63 And the yoke of bondage may begin to be broken off from the house of David;

64 And the children of Judah may begin to return to the lands which thou didst give to Abraham, their father.

65 And cause that the remnants of Jacob, who have been cursed and smitten because of their transgression, be converted from their wild and savage condition to the fulness of the everlasting gospel;

66 That they may lay down their weapons of bloodshed, and cease their rebellions.

67 And may all the scattered remnants of Israel, who have been driven to the ends of the earth, come to a knowledge of the truth, believe in the Messiah, and be redeemed from oppression, and rejoice before thee.

and delivered to the Prophet Joseph 'the keys of the gathering of Israel from the four parts of the earth' (D&C 110:11)....

"[Subsequently], during April conference 1840, the Prophet commissioned Elder [Orson] Hyde to go to Palestine and there dedicate that land for the return of the Jewish people....

"[Elder Hyde's prayer] focused on three themes: (1) the gathering of Judah, (2) the building up of Jerusalem, and (3) the rearing of a temple. The balance of the prayer, for the most part, is a supplication that these three objectives be accomplished" (Galbraith, "Orson Hyde's 1841 Mission," *Ensign*, Oct. 1991, 16, 18).

Who are the "remnants of Jacob"? (109:65–66)
"The term *remnant of Jacob* is synonymous with *remnant of Israel*, referring to all the scattered people of the twelve tribes. However, a particular passage of scripture may refer to a specific branch of Jacob's posterity. For example, the footnote references associated with its use in Doctrine and Covenants 52:2 refer to the Lamanites (D&C 19:27; 49:24; 109:65; see also 2 Ne. 30:3; Alma 46:23). Moroni, on the title page of the Book of Mormon, calls the Lamanites 'a remnant of the house of Israel.' And the Lord himself identifies the Lamanites—the seed of father Lehi—as the 'remnant' of whom he spoke in Nephi's writings (1 Ne. 13:34). During his visit among the people of the American continent, the resurrected Savior specifically spoke of that people being a 'remnant of the house of Jacob' and of their posterity participating in the building of the New Jerusalem (3 Ne. 21:2, 22–23)" (Brewster, *Doctrine & Covenants Encyclopedia* [2012], 462).

What is the hope for all scattered Israel? (109:67)
Joseph Smith put forth: "The land of America is a promised land ... and unto it, all the tribes of Israel will come with as many of the Gentiles as shall comply with the requisitions of the new covenant. But the tribe of Judah will return to old Jerusalem. The city of Zion, spoken of by David ... will be built upon the land of America, 'and the ransomed of the Lord shall return and come to it.' ... But Judah shall obtain deliverance at Jerusalem.... The good shepherd will put forth his own sheep, and lead them out from all nations where they have been scattered in a cloudy and dark day, to Zion, and to Jerusalem" (Joseph Smith Papers, "History, 1838–1856, volume A-1," 261–62).

Doctrine and Covenants 109:68–80. May the Saints Be Crowned with Glory and Honor and Gain Eternal Salvation

In what ways did Joseph sincerely strive to do the Lord's will? (109:68) "Joseph Smith was an obedient man. . . . His life was an example of obedience. He was shown the Book of Mormon plates; he knew where they were; despite his natural eagerness to possess them, he obediently saw them for four years only once a year, as commanded. Obediently, as the Lord directed, he went from place to place, built temples in the midst of his people's poverty, subjected himself to trials and toils, accepted plural marriage in the face of his training for monogamy—and in every manner throughout his life showed obedience to the Lord's will. As did Abraham of old, his all could be laid on the altar of the Lord. By these tests, as by many others, Joseph Smith was a great man" (Widtsoe, *Joseph Smith*, 333).

Why did the Prophet pray that "prejudices" be "broken up"? (109:70) "The Lord drew boundary lines to define acceptable limits of tolerance. Danger rises when those divine limits are disobeyed. . . . Though He loved the sinner, the Lord said that He 'cannot look upon sin with the least degree of allowance.' His Apostle Paul specified some of those sins [Galatians 5:19–21].

"To Paul's list I might add the regrettable attitudes of bigotry, hypocrisy, and prejudice. These were also decried in 1834 by early Church leaders who foresaw the eventual rise of this church 'amid the frowns of bigots and the calumny of hypocrites.' The Prophet Joseph Smith prayed that 'prejudices may give way before the truth.' Hatred stirs up strife and digs beneath the dignity of mature men and women in our enlightened era" (Nelson, "Teach Us Tolerance and Love," *Ensign*, May 1994, 71).

How might this prophecy of the Church coming forth "out of the wilderness" be fulfilled? (109:72–74) "We must stand firm. We must hold back the world. . . . Others may not agree with us, but I am confident that they will respect us. We will not be left alone. There are many not of our faith but who feel as we do. They will support us. They will sustain us in our efforts.

"Let us glory in this wonderful season of the work of the Lord. Let us not be proud or arrogant. Let us be humbly grateful. And let us, each one, resolve within himself or herself that we will add to the luster

68 O Lord, remember thy servant, Joseph Smith, Jun., and all his afflictions and persecutions—how he has covenanted with Jehovah, and vowed to thee, O Mighty God of Jacob—and the commandments which thou hast given unto him, and that he hath sincerely striven to do thy will.

69 Have mercy, O Lord, upon his wife and children, that they may be exalted in thy presence, and preserved by thy fostering hand.

70 Have mercy upon all their immediate connections, that their prejudices may be broken up and swept away as with a flood; that they may be converted and redeemed with Israel, and know that thou art God.

71 Remember, O Lord, the presidents, even all the presidents of thy church, that thy right hand may exalt them, with all their families, and their immediate connections, that their names may be perpetuated and had in everlasting remembrance from generation to generation.

72 Remember all thy church, O Lord, with all their families, and all their immediate connections, with all their sick and afflicted ones, with all the poor and meek of the earth; that the kingdom, which thou hast set up without hands, may become a great mountain and fill the whole earth;

73 That thy church may come forth out of the wilderness of darkness, and shine forth fair as the moon, clear as the sun, and terrible as an army with banners;

74 And be adorned as a bride for that day when thou shalt unveil the heavens, and cause the mountains to flow down at thy presence, and the valleys to be exalted, the rough places made smooth; that thy glory may fill the earth;

75 That when the trump shall sound for the dead, we shall be caught up in the cloud to meet thee, that we may ever be with the Lord;

76 That our garments may be pure, that we may be clothed upon with robes of righteousness, with palms in our hands, and crowns of glory upon our heads, and reap eternal joy for all our sufferings.

77 O Lord God Almighty, hear us in these our petitions, and answer us from heaven, thy holy habitation, where thou sittest enthroned, with glory, honor, power, majesty, might, dominion, truth, justice, judgment, mercy, and an infinity of fulness, from everlasting to everlasting.

78 O hear, O hear, O hear us, O Lord! And answer these petitions, and accept the dedication of this house unto thee, the work of our hands, which we have built unto thy name;

79 And also this church, to put upon it thy name. And help us by the power of thy Spirit, that we may mingle our voices with those bright, shining seraphs around thy throne, with acclamations of praise, singing Hosanna to God and the Lamb!

of this magnificent work of the Almighty, that it may shine across the earth as a beacon of strength and goodness for all the world to look upon" (*Gordon B. Hinckley* [manual], 64–65).

What can we expect when the trump of the Lord calls forth the dead? (109:75–76) Joseph anticipated this day: "The expectation of seeing my friends in the morning of the resurrection, cheers my soul, and makes me bear up against the evils of life.... God has revealed his Son from the heavens and the doctrine of the resurrection also, and we have a knowledge that those we bring here, God will bring them up again, clothed upon, and quickened by the Spirit of the Great God, and what mattereth it, whether we lay them down, or we lay down with them.... Let these truths sink down in our hearts, that we may even here begin to enjoy that which shall be in full hereafter. Hosanna, Hosanna, Hosanna to Almighty God, that rays of light begin to burst forth upon us, even now" (Joseph Smith Papers, "History, 1838–1856, volume D-1," 1535).

Why did the Prophet repeat "O hear" three times? (109:77–78) "These two verses actually mark the climax of the prayer, in which God is asked to accept the dedication of the Kirtland Temple. This part of the prayer was answered on 3 April 1836, when the Savior appeared to Joseph Smith and Oliver Cowdery in the Kirtland Temple and accepted its dedication (D&C 110:7). The threefold 'O hear, O hear, O hear,' is reminiscent of the threefold 'Holy, holy, holy,' called the *trishagion*, with which the seraphim and other heavenly beings praise God (Isaiah 6:3; Revelation 4:8). This connection is likely intended because the Saints are associated with the praise of the seraphim in the following verse (v. 79). The threefold address may be linked symbolically to the threefold nature of the Godhead" (Robinson and Garrett, *Commentary on the Doctrine and Covenants*, 4:53–54).

What are seraphs or seraphim? (109:79) "The terms *Seraphic hosts of heaven* and *Seraphs* each appear once in the Doctrine and Covenants (D&C 38:1; 109:79). The prophet Isaiah spoke of having seen 'seraphim' in the presence of the Lord (Isa. 6:2; 2 Ne. 16:2).

"According to Smith and Sjodahl, seraphim are the 'attendants of Jehovah, reflecting His glory and majesty' ([*Doctrine and Covenants Commentary*], 198)....

"It is clear that seraphs include the unembodied spirits of preexistence, for our Lord 'looked upon the wide expanse of eternity, and *all the seraphic hosts of heaven, before the world was made*' (D&C 38:1). Whether the name seraphs also applies to perfected and resurrected angels is not clear" (Brewster, *Doctrine & Covenants Encyclopedia* [2012], 510).

What does it mean to mingle our voices with the seraphs around God's throne? (109:79–80) "The veil is very thin in the temples, especially when we join in worshipping through music. At temple dedications I have seen more tears of joy elicited by music than by the spoken word. I have read accounts of angelic choirs joining in these hymns of praise, and I think I have experienced this on several occasions. In dedicatory sessions featuring beautiful and well-trained choirs of about thirty voices, there are times when I have heard what seemed to be ten times thirty voices praising God with a quality and intensity of feeling that can be experienced but not explained. Some who are listening today will know what I mean" (Oaks, "Worship through Music," *Ensign*, Nov. 1994, 10).

80 And let these, thine anointed ones, be clothed with salvation, and thy saints shout aloud for joy. Amen, and Amen.

Introduction to Doctrine and Covenants 110

"A few days following the temple dedication in Kirtland, Ohio, and the solemn assembly that empowered church elders for the ministry, [Joseph Smith]'s journal records that [he] and Oliver Cowdery had a vision of heavenly messengers in the House of the Lord. On the afternoon of Easter Sunday, 3 April 1836, [the Prophet] helped other members of the church presidency distribute the sacrament of the Lord's Supper to the congregation that had assembled in the lower court of the House of the Lord. After the sacrament, the curtains were dropped, dividing the court into four quarters. . . . At some point during the meeting, more veils were lowered, enclosing the west pulpits and dividing them into their four levels. [Joseph and Oliver] 'retired to the pulpit'—apparently the top tier, which was reserved for the presidency—where they bowed 'in solemn, but silent prayer to the Most High.'

"According to the journal, after [Joseph] and Cowdery prayed, secluded in the curtains and pulpits of the temple, they had a miraculous vision of Jesus Christ, who accepted the House of the Lord as [the Prophet] had prayed for at the dedication [see D&C 109:4, 78]. . . . Following the appearance of Christ, the journal records, [Joseph and Oliver] also received visitations from the biblical prophets Moses, Elias, and Elijah, who bestowed upon the two church leaders 'the Keys of this dispensation.' These keys authorized [Joseph Smith] and [Oliver] Cowdery to exercise in new ways the priesthood they had received from the apostles Peter, James, and John in 1829. The bestowal of 'the Keys of this dispensation,' particularly those concerning the gathering of Israel and turning 'the hearts of the Fathers to the children,' marked a vital moment for Latter-day Saint missionary work and temple ordinances. Just over a year after receiving these keys, [the Prophet] sent preachers to England to begin the gathering of Israel from abroad. Later, in Nauvoo, Illinois, he would teach and administer new temple ordinances that offered salvation to the deceased and bound them to the living, including baptisms for the dead, endowments, and sealings. The Latter-day Saints had shown their willingness to build the Lord a house, and these visitations on 3 April 1836 were not only a continuation of great spiritual outpouring; they were also a beginning for Latter-day Saint understanding of the purpose and power of temples" (Joseph Smith Papers, Historical Introduction to "Visions, 3 April 1836 [D&C 110]").

SECTION 110

Visions manifested to Joseph Smith the Prophet and Oliver Cowdery in the temple at Kirtland, Ohio, April 3, 1836. The occasion was that of a Sabbath day meeting. Joseph Smith's history states: "In the afternoon, I assisted the other Presidents in distributing the Lord's Supper to the Church, receiving it from the Twelve, whose privilege it was to officiate at the sacred desk this day. After having performed this service to my brethren, I retired to the pulpit, the veils being dropped, and bowed myself, with Oliver Cowdery, in solemn and silent prayer. After rising from prayer, the following vision was opened to both of us."

1 The veil was taken from our minds, and the eyes of our understanding were opened.

2 We saw the Lord standing upon the breastwork of the pulpit, before us; and under his feet was a paved work of pure gold, in color like amber.

3 His eyes were as a flame of fire; the hair of his head was white like the pure snow; his countenance shone above the brightness of

Doctrine and Covenants 110:1–10. The Lord Jehovah Appears in Glory and Accepts the Kirtland Temple as His House

What is "the breastwork of the pulpit"? (110:2) "In the Kirtland Temple there are two stands or pulpit structures on the main floor—one at the west side for leading officers of the Melchizedek Priesthood and the other at the east side for leading officers of the Aaronic Priesthood. Each of these pulpit structures had a *breastwork*, which literally means 'a temporary fortification.' In this case it was a railing about four feet high" (Black, *400 Questions and Answers*, 188).

What are we to understand from this description of the Savior? (110:3) "It would be difficult for a mortal being to describe a celestial personage and do so within the communicative limitations of mortal

The Pulpits of the Kirtland Temple (Doctrine and Covenants 110:2)

"In each of [the main] rooms were built two pulpits, one in each end. Each pulpit consisted of four different apartments: the fourth standing on a platform raised a suitable height above the floor; the third stood directly behind and elevated a little above the fourth; the second in rear of and elevated above the third; and in like manner the first above the second. Each of these apartments was just large enough and rightly calculated to seat three persons, and the breastwork in front of each of these three last mentioned was constituted of three semi-circles joining each other, and finished in good style. The fourth or lower one, was straight in front, and had an elegant table leaf attached to it, that could be raised at pleasure for the convenience of administering the sacrament" (Whitney, *Life of Heber C. Kimball*, 88–89).

Melchizedek Priesthood Pulpit, Kirtland Temple

language. When Joseph described the Savior, he used descriptive language which conveyed illustrations that are familiar to mortal man....

"A flame of fire has an intensity about it that demands one's attention.... Joseph also noted that the Lord's entire countenance had a brilliance.... There is a brilliance associated with the glory that accompanies the members of the Godhead.

"The voice of the Lord was described.... Anyone who has heard the rushing of great quantities of water knows there is a penetrating power associated with that experience" (Otten and Caldwell, *Sacred Truths*, 2:247). Compare with Daniel 10:5–6; Revelation 1:13–15.

Why is the phrase "I am" repeated in this verse? (110:4) "Four times, in a voice like rushing water [the Lord] declares, 'I am,' evoking Old Testament revelations in which he repeatedly identified himself, saying, 'I am the Lord thy God' (Exodus 20:2; Leviticus 19:3). This is a play on the related words of the Hebrew verb meaning 'to be' and the name transliterated in English as *Jehovah*. It is the Lord Jesus Christ declaring that he is the God who told Moses to tell the Israelites that 'I AM hath sent me unto you' (Exodus 3:14). It is Christ testifying that he is the God of Israel, the promised Messiah.

"In a powerful juxtaposition of present and past, [in D&C 110:4,] the risen Savior declares himself the crucified Christ who conquered death" (Harper, *Making Sense of the Doctrine & Covenants*, 407).

When did the Lord manifest Himself to other Saints in the Kirtland Temple? (110:7–8) "The Savior appeared in five different meetings held in the temple. Visions, including a vision of the Father and the Son, were beheld at eight meetings, and the congregation saw heavenly beings or angels in nine meetings. In other sessions many Saints reported that they experienced such manifestations as the gift of tongues, the sounds of a mighty wind, a pillar of fire resting down upon the temple roof, prophesying, and the voices of angels. Over one thousand people attended these meetings, many of whom testified to having had sacred experiences....

"Many journals of the Saints testify that the year 1836 was indeed the 'year of jubilee,' a 'time of rejoicing,' when communication with the heavens was constant and real" (Karl Ricks Anderson, *Joseph Smith's Kirtland*, 170, 173, 175).

the sun; and his voice was as the sound of the rushing of great waters, even the voice of Jehovah, saying:

4 I am the first and the last; I am he who liveth, I am he who was slain; I am your advocate with the Father.

5 Behold, your sins are forgiven you; you are clean before me; therefore, lift up your heads and rejoice.

6 Let the hearts of your brethren rejoice, and let the hearts of all my people rejoice, who have, with their might, built this house to my name.

7 For behold, I have accepted this house, and my name shall be here; and I will manifest myself to my people in mercy in this house.

8 Yea, I will appear unto my servants, and speak unto them with mine own voice, if my people will keep my commandments, and do not pollute this holy house.

9 Yea the hearts of thousands and tens of thousands shall greatly rejoice in consequence of the blessings which shall be poured out, and the endowment with which my servants have been endowed in this house.

10 And the fame of this house shall spread to foreign lands; and this is the beginning of the blessing which shall be poured out upon the heads of my people. Even so. Amen.

11 After this vision closed, the heavens were again opened unto us; and Moses appeared before us, and committed unto us the keys of the gathering of Israel from the four parts of the earth, and the leading of the ten tribes from the land of the north.

12 After this, Elias appeared, and committed the dispensation of the gospel of Abraham, saying that in us and our seed all generations after us should be blessed.

Why would so many people rejoice because of the Kirtland Temple? (110:9–10) "Please note the phrases *the hearts of thousands and tens of thousands shall greatly rejoice* and *the fame of this house shall spread to foreign lands*. These were stunning declarations in April of 1836, when the Church had only a relative handful of members and one temple. . . .

"Houses of the Lord are being constructed on the 'isles of the sea' [2 Nephi 29:7] and in countries and locations previously considered by many unlikely to warrant a temple.

"The endowment ceremony . . . will become available in many additional languages as temples are built to bless more of God's children. . . .

"As members of the Lord's restored Church, we stand all amazed at the ever-accelerating pace of His work in the latter days. And more temples are coming" (Bednar, "Let This House Be Built unto My Name," *Ensign*, May 2020, 86, 87).

Doctrine and Covenants 110:11–12. Moses and Elias Each Appear and Commit Their Keys and Dispensations

Why is the location of the ten tribes often referred to as being "from the land of the north"? (110:11) "One [reason] may simply be that the tribes are scattered predominantly, . . . throughout the northern hemisphere. Another reason is the geography of Israel itself. . . . Historically [enemy] armies approached Palestine from the north to the south and departed from the south to the north. This meant that their captives were always carried away 'into the north.' . . .

"The northernmost city of Israel, Dan, later became particularly associated with idolatry and apostasy (1 Kings 12:28–30). . . . So, anciently, the north was associated symbolically with idolatry, apostasy, and political defeat. . . . The gathering of Israel will bring the ten tribes back from this symbolic north land—even though they are actually scattered in all four directions" (Robinson and Garrett, *Commentary on the Doctrine and Covenants*, 4:63–64).

Who was Elias? (110:12) "A man called Elias apparently lived in mortality in the days of Abraham, who committed the dispensation of the gospel of Abraham to Joseph Smith and Oliver Cowdery in the Kirtland (Ohio) Temple on April 3, 1836 (D&C 110:12). We have no specific information as to the details of his mortal life or ministry" (Bible Dictionary, s.v. "Elias," 635).

"At the dedication of the Kirtland Temple in 1836 . . . Elias also appeared. His purpose? To commit to

Joseph Smith and Oliver Cowdery the keys of 'the dispensation of the gospel of Abraham, saying that in us and our seed all generations after us should be blessed.' Thus, 'the Master conferred upon Joseph [and Oliver] priesthood authority and the right to convey [the unique] blessings of the Abrahamic covenant to others.'

"In the Church, we travel the covenant path both individually and collectively. Just as marriages and families share a unique *lateral* bond that creates a special love, so does the new relationship formed when we bind ourselves by covenant *vertically* to our God!" (Nelson, *Heart of the Matter*, 41–42). ✛

Doctrine and Covenants 110:13–16. Elijah Returns and Commits the Keys of His Dispensation as Promised by Malachi

What do we know about the timing of Elijah's return? (110:13–14) Historians note that April 3, 1836, corresponded with the Jewish celebration of Passover. "At one point during the *Seder,* the traditional Hebrew name for the Passover ritual, a child is sent to the door to see if Elijah may be standing outside and to invite him in...."

13 After this vision had closed, another great and glorious vision burst upon us; for Elijah the prophet, who was taken to heaven without tasting death, stood before us, and said:

What Was Restored by Moses, Elias, and Elijah in the Kirtland Temple? (D&C 110:11–16)

On April 3, 1836, Moses, Elias, and Elijah appeared to Joseph Smith and committed to him the priesthood authority necessary to accomplish the work of salvation and exaltation in the latter-days (see *General Handbook* [2022], 3.1).

Elder Bruce R. McConkie taught: "Moses, who in the majesty of the Melchizedek Priesthood led enslaved Israel out of Egyptian bondage into their promised Palestine, brings back those very keys. These keys empower mortals to gather the lost sheep of Israel from the Egypt of the world, and bring them to their promised Zion, where the scales of enslaving darkness will drop from their eyes.

"These keys empower those who hold them to lead all Israel, the ten tribes included, from all the nations of the earth, coming as the prophetic word affirms, one by one and two by two, to the mountains of the Lord's houses, there to be endowed with power from on high.

"The man Elias brings back 'the gospel of Abraham,' the great Abrahamic covenant whereby the faithful receive promises of eternal increase, promises that through celestial marriage their eternal posterity shall be as numerous as the sands upon the seashore or as the stars in heaven for multitude. Elias gives the promise—received of old by Abraham, Isaac, and Jacob—that in modern men and in their seed all generations shall be blessed. And we are now offering the blessings of Abraham, Isaac, and Jacob to all who will receive them" ("Keys of the Kingdom," *Ensign*, May 1983, 22).

"Elijah was sent to restore keys—directing powers—of the patriarchal order of the priesthood, rights which had not been fully operational in this dispensation. Elijah restored the keys whereby families (organized in the patriarchal order through the keys delivered by Elias) could be bound and sealed for eternity....

"Because Elijah came, all other ordinances for the living and the dead (e.g. baptisms, confirmations, ordinations, etc.) have real meaning and are thus of efficacy, virtue, and force in eternity. The ordinances associated with the ministry of Elijah (centering in the temples) are the 'capstone blessings' of the gospel and the consummation of the work of the Church; they provide purpose and perspective for all other sacred activities" (Backman and Millet, "Heavenly Manifestations in the Kirtland Temple," 427, 428).

14 Behold, the time has fully come, which was spoken of by the mouth of Malachi—testifying that he [Elijah] should be sent, before the great and dreadful day of the Lord come—

15 To turn the hearts of the fathers to the children, and the children to the fathers, lest the whole earth be smitten with a curse—

16 Therefore, the keys of this dispensation are committed into your hands; and by this ye may know that the great and dreadful day of the Lord is near, even at the doors.

"The appearance of Elijah and Moses at Passover season to Joseph Smith and Oliver Cowdery thus represents a fulfillment and a promise. Elijah did come at Passover time—as pious Jews had long hoped he would" (Ricks, "Appearance of Elijah and Moses," 484, 486). See also commentary in this volume on Doctrine and Covenants 2:1. ❂

What are we to understand about turning "the hearts of the fathers to the children, and the children to the fathers"? (110:15) Joseph Smith taught that "the word *turn* . . . should be translated *bind* or *seal*" (Joseph Smith Papers, "History, 1838–1856, volume E-1," 1866).

"Elijah's mission was not only to help families love one another but also to create eternal families through covenants and ordinances that bind individuals as families throughout eternity. That the responsibility of doing this work is laid on the children of this generation is again evidenced as we read in D&C 98:16, 'Seek diligently to turn the hearts of the children to their fathers.' The teachings of the Prophet and the revelations he received from the Lord greatly enhance our understanding of what it means to turn our hearts. The priesthood keys Joseph received from Elijah make it possible for Latter-day Saints to fulfill our obligation to bind our families together in eternity" (Cynthia Doxey, "Elijah's Mission, Message, and Milestones," 160). ❂

Introduction to Doctrine and Covenants 111

Doctrine and Covenants 111 is a revelation given through the Prophet Joseph Smith on August 6, 1836, at Salem, Massachusetts.

"In late July 1836, Joseph Smith Jr., Sidney Rigdon, Oliver Cowdery, and Hyrum Smith started traveling from Kirtland, Ohio, to the eastern United States. In the weeks before their departure, worries about the temporal affairs of the Church weighed heavily on Joseph's mind. In Missouri, the Saints held on to the titles to lands they had been driven from in Jackson County as a sign of their commitment to building Zion, but they had no foreseeable way to return. At the same time, the Church was weighed down with debts after the construction of the Kirtland Temple. What could be done?

"These concerns likely continued to occupy Joseph Smith's thoughts as his small group traveled to New York City and Boston. According to a later account, Joseph and other leaders had been told about a hidden treasure in Salem, Massachusetts, and hoped to find it. Both the hope for financial relief and worry over Zion were key parts of the context for a revelation the Prophet received in Salem on August 6, 1836" (Kuehn, "More Treasures Than One," 229).

SECTION 111

Revelation given through Joseph Smith the Prophet, at Salem, Massachusetts, August 6, 1836. At this time the leaders of the Church were heavily in debt due to their labors in the ministry.

Doctrine and Covenants 111:1–5. The Lord Looks to the Temporal Needs of His Servants

Why might this journey to Salem have been considered a folly? (111:1) "It appears that one of the purposes for the Prophet Joseph Smith and his companions to travel to Salem, Massachusetts, was to try to improve the Church's financial situation. They may have viewed Brother Burgess's claim about money hidden in a house as a possible fulfillment of the Lord's promise to 'send means unto [them] for [their] deliverance' (D&C 104:80) from their debts....

"A *folly* is a mistake or error in judgment. It may have been a 'folly' for these brethren to rely on Brother Burgess's claim and their own efforts to solve the Church's financial difficulties. However, throughout the rest of the revelation recorded in Doctrine and Covenants 111 the Lord mercifully promised them ongoing help and guidance" (*Doctrine and Covenants Student Manual* [2018], 644). ⊕

How did the gathering of Saints in the Salem area begin? (111:2) "Five years later, at a [Philadelphia, Pennsylvania,] Church conference in July 1841, Hyrum Smith and William Law of the First Presidency left instructions for Elders Erastus Snow and Benjamin Winchester about Salem. These instructions included a copy of [the Salem revelation] and expressed the First Presidency's belief that 'the due time of the Lord had come' for the revelation to be fulfilled and the people of Salem to be gathered into His kingdom....

"Erastus Snow organized the Salem branch on March 5, 1842, with 53 members. By June 1842 the branch had increased to about 90 members.... They helped build up the Church in the Salem-Boston area, which served as a vibrant and historically significant Church area in the 1840s" (Kuehn, "More Treasures Than One," 230, 232).

Hearing that a large amount of money would be available to them in Salem, the Prophet, Sidney Rigdon, Hyrum Smith, and Oliver Cowdery traveled there from Kirtland, Ohio, to investigate this claim, along with preaching the gospel. The brethren transacted several items of Church business and did some preaching. When it became apparent that no money was to be forthcoming, they returned to Kirtland. Several of the factors prominent in the background are reflected in the wording of this revelation.

1 I, the Lord your God, am not displeased with your coming this journey, notwithstanding your follies.

2 I have much treasure in this city for you, for the benefit of Zion, and many people in this city, whom I will gather out in due time for the benefit of Zion, through your instrumentality.

3 Therefore, it is expedient that you should form acquaintance with men in this city, as you shall be led, and as it shall be given you.

4 And it shall come to pass in due time that I will give this city into your hands, that you shall have power over it, insomuch that they shall not discover your secret parts; and its wealth pertaining to gold and silver shall be yours.

What could be meant by the phrase "not discover your secret parts"? (111:4) "In the Old Testament, this statement is a Hebrew idiom for being thoroughly and publicly humiliated. The Hebrew could be translated more literally 'uncover your private parts,' and carries the connotation of being publicly stripped and humiliated (1 Samuel 5:9; Isaiah 3:17). In the context here, it is a promise that the brethren will not be publicly embarrassed or shamed" (Robinson and Garrett, *Commentary on the Doctrine and Covenants*, 4:76).

5 Concern not yourselves about your debts, for I will give you power to pay them.

Why were Church leaders concerned about financial debt? (111:5) "Heavy debt weighed upon the leaders of the Church due to loans secured to purchase land, to acquire goods for the mercantile establishments of the Church, and to build the Kirtland Temple. In addition, in 1833, when mobs expelled the Saints from Jackson County, Missouri, they also took control of the Church-owned printing press and goods from the Church-owned store. Earlier, leaders in Ohio and in Missouri formed a joint business to manage the Church's assets. . . . Joseph counted on both of the Missouri enterprises—the printing press and the store—to raise funds to help repay creditors in New York City. With the loss of the income-producing printing press and store commodities, the Church was unable to pay for the goods that members of the United Firm had purchased on credit" (Ostler, "Treasures, Witches, and Ancient Inhabitants," 222).

6 Concern not yourselves about Zion, for I will deal mercifully with her.

Doctrine and Covenants 111:6–11. The Lord Will Deal Mercifully with Zion and Arrange All Things for the Good of His Servants

7 Tarry in this place, and in the regions round about;

8 And the place where it is my will that you should tarry, for the main, shall be signalized unto you by the peace and power of my Spirit, that shall flow unto you.

What lessons can we learn from the Prophet's time in Salem? (111:7–8) Joseph and his companions followed the Lord's instructions to "tarry in this place" (verse 7) for several weeks. "Righteous servants of the Lord who seek His help in their decisions can know that He approves their actions through the peace and confidence that comes to their souls. By being sensitive to the Spirit, the Lord's people can be continually led by Him in their lives (see Alma 58:11; D&C 6:22–23; 8:2–3). This verse [D&C 111:8] is also a reminder that when we follow the Spirit, [we] know where the Lord wants [us] to be" (*Doctrine and Covenants Student Manual* [2001], 278).

What might the Church leaders learn about the settlers and founders of the Salem area? (111:9) "During their stay in Salem, Massachusetts, the Prophet Joseph Smith and his companions traveled throughout Salem and its surrounding areas visiting museums, historical sites, and libraries (see [*Joseph Smith Papers: Documents, Volume 5*, 278n248]). They learned more about the city's founding by the Puritan pilgrims in the early 1600s and about the American Revolutionary War and the establishment of the United States (see [Joseph Smith Papers, "Manuscript History of the Church, vol. B-1,"] 749).

"Some of the brethren spent time learning about the Salem witch trials (see [Oliver Cowdery, "Prospectus," *Messenger and Advocate*], 388–91). In addition, the Prophet Joseph Smith and his companions visited the remains of the Charlestown Ursuline Convent, which had been destroyed by an anti-Catholic mob motivated by religious intolerance" (*Doctrine and Covenants Student Manual* [2018], 647).

In what way was Salem, Massachusetts, a source of treasure for Joseph Smith? (111:10) "Many of Joseph's direct ancestry, i.e., the Smiths, had lived for generations in Massachusetts at least as far back as Robert Smith who settled there in the 1600s [in nearby Topsfield]. Others of Joseph Smith's ancestry also lived in the New England area. . . . While there seems to be no evidence that Joseph Smith collected any written genealogical information while in Salem, it is probable that his thoughts turned to his ancestry" (Godfrey, "More Treasures Than One," 195–96).

What could it mean to be "as wise as serpents"? (111:11) "When the Savior sent His disciples out to preach the gospel, He told them to be 'wise as serpents, and harmless as doves' (Matthew 10:16). In modern times, the Savior gave similar counsel to His disciples, declaring, 'Be ye as wise as serpents and yet without sin' (D&C 111:11). Both accounts teach that the Savior's disciples should combine wisdom with innocence and purity. The Joseph Smith Translation emphasizes the importance of being a wise servant of the Master: 'Be ye therefore wise *servants*, and as harmless as doves' ([JST], Matthew 10:14; compare Matthew 10:16)" (*New Testament Student Manual* [2018], 36–37).

9 This place you may obtain by hire. And inquire diligently concerning the more ancient inhabitants and founders of this city;

10 For there are more treasures than one for you in this city.

11 Therefore, be ye as wise as serpents and yet without sin; and I will order all things for your good, as fast as ye are able to receive them. Amen.

Introduction to Doctrine and Covenants 112

The Prophet Joseph Smith received this revelation during troubled times in Kirtland, Ohio on July 23, 1837. He "wrote that during the year 1837 a spirit of speculation in lands and property of all kinds, which was prevalent throughout the country, took hold of the members of the Church. Out of this practice other evils developed, such as faultfinding, evil-surmising, dissension, and apostasy. He said that no quorum of the Church was entirely exempt from the influence of these evil powers, and that even some of the twelve apostles were overcome with this spirit. Amidst this unrest and apostasy, the Lord revealed to him that 'something new must be done for the salvation of His Church' ([*Joseph Smith* (manual), 327]). As a result, the first foreign mission of the Church was organized under the leadership of Elder Heber C. Kimball of the Quorum of the Twelve. Consequently, in June 1837, he was set apart to preside over the missionary work in England. The same day the gospel of Jesus Christ was first preached in England, the Lord gave Section 112 for the special benefit of Elder Thomas B. Marsh, President of the Quorum of the Twelve, and also for the other members of that quorum. ([Joseph Smith Papers, 'History, 1838–1856, volume B-1,' 761])" (Roy W. Doxey, *Doctrine and Covenants Speaks*, 2:335).

In the early months of 1837, Thomas B. Marsh noticed that "relationships among the Twelve Apostles had deteriorated significantly. It was a time of intensifying conflicts and dissatisfaction within the Church in Kirtland. Among the Twelve, youth and inexperience, a lack of precedence, and disagreements about their role and purpose and the bounds of their authority caused disharmony. These difficulties were compounded by distance and communication struggles, as some resided in Kirtland and some in Missouri, and quorum members from both places were often called to serve missions elsewhere.

"Hoping to bolster quorum unity, Marsh returned to Kirtland in July, only to find that some Apostles had left for a mission to Great Britain and several others had apostatized. Seeking counsel, Marsh visited Joseph Smith [on July 23, 1837], who dictated a revelation for him (now Doctrine and Covenants 112). The revelation was a source of great guidance and comfort to Marsh, as well as stern admonition" (Kay Darowski, "Faith and Fall of Thomas Marsh," 56–57).

"Doctrine and Covenants 112 is notable for the penetrating way it addresses Thomas Marsh and the other apostles. Aspiring and full of potential, Marsh and some of the apostles found themselves divided and unfulfilled. The revelation acknowledges the apostles' receipt of priesthood keys handed down from prior dispensations and the greatness of their calling, but it simultaneously implies pride, even blasphemy and apostasy, among some, and it points out the need for Marsh and other Quorum members to repent and then preach repentance and baptism, in anticipation of apocalyptic punishments, beginning with the Latter-day Saints (vv. 23–26)" (Harper, *Making Sense of the Doctrine & Covenants*, 414).

SECTION 112

Revelation given through Joseph Smith the Prophet to Thomas B. Marsh, at Kirtland, Ohio, July 23, 1837, concerning the Twelve Apostles of the Lamb. This revelation was received on the day Elders Heber C. Kimball and Orson Hyde first preached the gospel in England. Thomas B. Marsh was at this time President of the Quorum of the Twelve Apostles.

1 Verily thus saith the Lord unto you my servant Thomas: I have heard thy prayers; and thine alms have come up as a memorial before me, in behalf of those, thy brethren, who were chosen to bear testimony of my name

Doctrine and Covenants 112:1–10. The Twelve Are to Send the Gospel and Raise the Warning Voice to All Nations and People

Why was the Lord not pleased with some of the actions of Thomas B. Marsh? (112:1–2) "Although the Lord commended Thomas B. Marsh for praying and working to help his fellow members of the Quorum of the Twelve Apostles, He also acknowledged, 'There have been some few things in thine heart and with thee with which I, the Lord, was not well pleased' (D&C 112:2). While we do not know exactly why the Lord was not 'well pleased,' it may be that Thomas B. Marsh was still upset that the Prophet Joseph Smith had called Elders Kimball and Hyde to serve in England without consulting him" (*Doctrine and Covenants Student Manual* [2018], 651). See also commentary in this volume on Doctrine and Covenants 31:1, 3, and 9–13.

What are "alms"? (112:1) "The word *alms* is mentioned in three of the standard works (see Matt. 6:1–4; 3 Ne. 13:1–4; D&C 88:2; 112:1). *Alms* comes from the Greek word meaning righteousness, or acts of religious devotion" (Brewster, *Doctrine & Covenants Encyclopedia*, 12).

Why are Apostles commanded to bear record of the Lord's name? (112:4–6) "The word [*Apostle*] means 'one sent forth.' It was the title Jesus gave (Luke 6:13) to the Twelve whom He chose and ordained (John 15:16) to be His closest disciples during His ministry on earth and whom He sent forth to represent Him after His Ascension into heaven. The calling of an Apostle is to be a special witness of the name of Jesus Christ in all the world, particularly of His divinity and of His bodily resurrection from the dead (Acts 1:22; D&C 107:23)" (Bible Dictionary, s.v. "Apostle," 595). ◉

and to send it abroad among all nations, kindreds, tongues, and people, and ordained through the instrumentality of my servants.

2 Verily I say unto you, there have been some few things in thine heart and with thee with which I, the Lord, was not well pleased.

3 Nevertheless, inasmuch as thou hast abased thyself thou shalt be exalted; therefore, all thy sins are forgiven thee.

4 Let thy heart be of good cheer before my face; and thou shalt bear record of my name, not only unto the Gentiles, but also unto the Jews; and thou shalt send forth my word unto the ends of the earth.

5 Contend thou, therefore, morning by morning; and day after day let thy warning voice go forth; and when the night cometh let not the inhabitants of the earth slumber, because of thy speech.

The Kirtland Safety Society and Apostasy among the Saints

"In October 1836, as part of their plans to develop the city of Kirtland, Ohio, and to alleviate Church debt, the Prophet Joseph Smith and other Church leaders bought property in and around Kirtland and prepared to open a bank in Kirtland, to be named the Kirtland Safety Society Bank (see [*Joseph Smith Papers: Documents, Volume 5*], 285).

"After failing to receive a bank charter, or the authority to enact banking transactions, from the State of Ohio, the Prophet Joseph Smith and other Church leaders reorganized the Kirtland Safety Society as a joint-stock company on January 2, 1837. This meant that Church members could become part owners in the Kirtland Safety Society by buying stock, or shares in the company, thus helping fund the company's operations. (See [*Joseph Smith Papers: Documents, Volume 5*], 286–89.) In the January 1837 edition of the *Latter Day Saints' Messenger and Advocate*, the Prophet called upon Church members to buy stock in the new institution (see [*Joseph Smith Papers: Documents, Volume 5*], 325).

"The Kirtland Safety Society faced opposition almost immediately after it opened. Local newspapers ran stories claiming the Safety Society's banknotes were worthless and warned readers not to accept them. Individuals in and around Kirtland also 'actively campaigned against the Kirtland Safety Society' by spreading rumors that the Safety Society had stopped doing business and would not allow customers to trade in their banknotes for regular currency (in [*Joseph Smith Papers: Documents, Volume 5*], 287–88). Several lawsuits were also filed against the Safety Society's leaders for performing bank-like operations without a bank charter. In addition, the Safety Society encountered problems with underfunding by its stockholders. (See [*Joseph Smith Papers: Documents, Volume 5*], 291–93.) Adding to these challenges, a national economic crisis, later known as the Panic of 1837, began in the spring of 1837 and forced hundreds of banks to close throughout the United States (see [*Joseph Smith Papers: Documents, Volume 5*], 363).

What could the word *contend* mean in this context? (112:5) In Webster's 1828 *American Dictionary*, the phrase "contend thou" had the following meanings: "to strive; to use earnest efforts to obtain, or to defend and preserve" (Webster, *American Dictionary* [1828], s.v. "contend").

President Dallin H. Oaks used the word *contend* in this context when he said: "Eternal doctrine also provides a distinctive perspective on children. Through this perspective we see the bearing and nurturing of children as part of the divine plan. It is a joyful and sacred duty of those given the power to participate in it. Therefore, we are commanded to teach and *contend* for principles and practices that provide the best conditions for the development and happiness of children under God's plan" ("Divine Love in the Father's Plan," *Liahona*, May 2022, 102; emphasis added).

6 Let thy habitation be known in Zion, and remove not thy house; for I, the Lord, have a great work for thee to do, in publishing my name among the children of men.

Why was Thomas B. Marsh counseled not to move his residence? (112:6) "Since 1832 Thomas Marsh had moved his residence at least four times, not counting extended visits to Kirtland. As president of the Quorum of the Twelve, it was important for him to maintain a more or less permanent address from which he could always be reached. It was natural that Elder Marsh might be tempted at this time to move yet again, from Missouri to Kirtland, to give greater support to the Prophet and be closer to quorum members. Yet, the Church was soon going to move to

"The Prophet Joseph Smith and his family had made significant investments in the Kirtland Safety Society and may have had the most to lose if it did not continue. However, as the Safety Society faced ongoing challenges, Joseph and other members of the Smith family, based on his recommendation, chose not to redeem their shares as others had. Instead, they turned their stock over to Oliver Granger and Jared Carter to ensure that all debts were fully settled. (See Mark Lyman Staker, [*Hearken, O Ye People*], 528.) By July of that year, the Prophet Joseph Smith had transferred the operation of the Kirtland Safety Society to others (see [*Joseph Smith Papers: Documents, Volume 5*], 418). Near the end of the summer of 1837, the Kirtland Safety Society ended (see [*Joseph Smith Papers: Documents, Volume 5*], 366)" (*Doctrine and Covenants Student Manual*, [2018], 647–49).

On June 1, 1837, the Prophet Joseph Smith wrote: "At this time a spirit of Speculation, in lands and property of all kinds, which was so prevalent throughout the whole nation, was taking deep root in the church, as the fruits of this spirit, evil surmisings, fault finding, disunion, dissention and apostasy followed in quick succession, and it seemed as though all the powers of earth and hell were combining their influence in an especial manner to overthrow the church at once, and make a final end. Other banking institutions refused the Kirtland Safety Society's Notes; the enemy abroad and apostates in our midst united in their schemes; flour and provisions were turned toward other markets; and many became disaffected toward me as though I were the sole cause of those very evils I was most strenuously striving against; and which were actually brought upon us, by the brethren not giving heed to my counsel. No quorum in the church was entirely exempt from the influence of those false spirits, who were striving against me, for the Mastery; even some of the Twelve were so far lost to their high and responsible calling, as to begin to take sides, secretly with the enemy" (Joseph Smith Papers, "History, 1838–1856, volume B-1," 761; spelling modernized).

Missouri, and Elder Marsh's home in Far West would be at its center" (Robinson and Garrett, *Commentary on the Doctrine and Covenants*, 4:83).

What is the meaning of the phrase "let thy feet be shod"? (112:7) "To have one's feet *shod* meant to have one's shoes on and to be ready to travel. To show that they were ready for their journey, the Israelites were commanded to eat the Passover with their shoes on (Exodus 12:11). Similarly, Christ commanded his disciples to be 'shod with sandals' (Mark 6:9) that they might be ready to go and publish the gospel. The Lord here directs Thomas B. Marsh to stand ready to travel in the duty of his office" (McConkie and Ostler, *Revelations of the Restoration*, 899).

Who were those to be rebuked by Thomas B. Marsh? (112:8–9) "Verses 8 and 9 indicate that [Thomas] Marsh's word will bring down the exalted and exalt the lowly and that he will rebuke the transgressor. Priesthood leaders generally share this responsibility to rebuke when so inspired. Given the history of his quorum, one might conclude that these two verses apply to counseling his brethren, but because a reminder about that specific responsibility begins with verse 12, this reference appears to be more general" (Ronald K. Esplin, "Exalt Not Yourselves," 120).

What can the Lord's instructions to Thomas B. Marsh teach us about the importance of humility? (112:10) President Gordon B. Hinckley stated: "There is no place for arrogance in our lives. There is no place for conceit. There is no place for egotism. We have a great work to do. We have things to accomplish. We need direction in the pursuit of our education. We need help in choosing an eternal companion."

President Hinckley then quoted Doctrine and Covenants 112:10 and declared: "What a tremendous

7 Therefore, gird up thy loins for the work. Let thy feet be shod also, for thou art chosen, and thy path lieth among the mountains, and among many nations.

8 And by thy word many high ones shall be brought low, and by thy word many low ones shall be exalted.

9 Thy voice shall be a rebuke unto the transgressor; and at thy rebuke let the tongue of the slanderer cease its perverseness.

10 Be thou humble; and the Lord thy God shall lead thee by the hand, and give thee answer to thy prayers.

What Lessons Can Be Learned from the Life of Thomas B. Marsh? (D&C 112)

President Gordon B. Hinckley spoke about lessons learned from Thomas B. Marsh's life: "Brother Marsh rose to the pulpit. This man, who was named the first President of the Council of the Twelve Apostles and to whom the Lord had spoken in so marvelous a manner, as recorded in [D&C 112:16]. . . . said to the people: . . .

"'Many have said to me . . . "How is it that a man like you, who understood so much of the revelations of God as recorded in the Book of Doctrine and Covenants, should fall away?" I told them not to feel too secure, but to take heed lest they also should fall; for I had no scruples in my mind as to the possibility of men falling away.' . . .

"'[Thomas B. Marsh] went before a magistrate and swore that the "Mormons" were hostile towards the state of Missouri.

"'That affidavit brought from the government of Missouri an exterminating order, which drove some 15,000 Saints from their homes and habitations, and some thousands perished through suffering the exposure consequent on this state of affairs' (in *Journal of Discourses*, 3:283–84). Such is George A. Smith's account.

promise is given in this statement. If we are without conceit and pride and arrogance, if we are humble and obedient, then the Lord will lead us by the hand and answer our prayers. What greater thing could we ask for? . . .

"I believe the meek and the humble are those who are teachable. They are willing to learn. They are willing to listen to the whisperings of the still, small voice for guidance in their lives. They place the wisdom of the Lord above their own wisdom" ("Prophet's Counsel and Prayer for Youth," *Ensign*, Jan. 2001, 10). ☉

Doctrine and Covenants 112:11–15. The Twelve Are to Take up Their Cross, Follow Jesus, and Feed His Sheep

11 I know thy heart, and have heard thy prayers concerning thy brethren. Be not partial towards them in love above many others, but let thy love be for them as for thyself; and let thy love abound unto all men, and unto all who love my name.

12 And pray for thy brethren of the Twelve. Admonish them sharply for my name's sake, and let them be admonished for all their sins, and be ye faithful before me unto my name.

13 And after their temptations, and much tribulation, behold, I, the Lord, will feel after them, and if they harden not their hearts,

What charge was President Marsh given in these verses concerning those in the Quorum of the Twelve Apostles? (112:11–12) "Our Lord instructs the President of the Council to continue to pray for the members, and also to admonish them 'sharply.' Admonition without prayer is barren of results. He promised to feel after them, when they had passed through the tribulations awaiting them because they had yielded to temptations. And then, if they would not harden their hearts, they would be converted and healed" (Smith and Sjodahl, *Doctrine and Covenants Commentary*, 734).

How can we apply the principles given to Thomas B. Marsh in these verses? (112:12–13) "I believe the principles expressed in these verses apply to all of us. The temptations and tribulations we experience, plus any testing that the Lord sees fit to impose, can lead to our full conversion and healing. But this happens if, and only if, we do not harden our hearts or stiffen our necks against Him. If we remain

"What a very small and trivial thing—a little cream over which two women quarreled. But it led to, or at least was a factor in, Governor Boggs' cruel exterminating order which drove the Saints from the state of Missouri, with all of the terrible suffering and consequent death that followed. The man who should have settled this little quarrel, but who, rather, pursued it, troubling the officers of the Church, right up to the Presidency, literally went through hell for it. He lost his standing in the Church. He lost his testimony of the gospel. For nineteen years he walked in poverty and darkness and bitterness, experiencing illness, and loneliness. He grew old before his time. Finally, like the prodigal son in the parable of the Savior (see Luke 15:11–32), he recognized his foolishness and painfully made his way to this valley, and asked Brigham Young to forgive him and permit his rebaptism into the Church. He had been the first President of the Council of the Twelve, loved, respected, and honored in the days of Kirtland, and the early days of Far West. Now he asked only that he might be ordained a deacon and become a doorkeeper in the house of the Lord" ("Small Acts Lead to Great Consequences," *Ensign*, May 1984, 83).

firm and steadfast, come what may, we achieve the conversion the Savior intended when He said to Peter, 'When thou art converted, strengthen thy brethren' [Luke 22:32], a conversion so complete that it cannot be undone. The promised healing is the cleansing and sanctification of our sin-wounded souls, making us holy" (Christofferson, "Firm and Steadfast in the Faith of Christ," *Ensign*, Nov. 2018, 33).

What was the meaning of the phrases "gird up your loins" and "take up your cross"? (112:14) "To 'gird up your loins' is a New Testament term meaning to prepare for battle. The Twelve must battle Satan and his evil ways that come against the Saints. To 'take up your cross' is for a man 'to deny himself all ungodliness, and every worldly lust, and keep my commandments' (JST, Matthew 16:26). To 'follow me' is to go where the Lord directs, and to 'feed my sheep' is to teach the principles and doctrines of the kingdom to the members of the Church (D&C 112:14). Such is the role of every member of the Quorum of the Twelve" (Nyman, *Doctrine and Covenants Commentary*, 2:427).

Why were some of the Twelve warned to not exalt themselves or rebel against the Prophet Joseph? (112:15) "During the tumultuous times of 1837, some members of the Quorum of the Twelve Apostles living in Kirtland, Ohio, were guilty of exalting themselves, or believing they were better or more intelligent than others, and of rebelling against the Prophet Joseph Smith (see D&C 112:15). For example, because many Church members experienced economic difficulties in 1837, several members of the Quorum of the

and stiffen not their necks against me, they shall be converted, and I will heal them.

14 Now, I say unto you, and what I say unto you, I say unto all the Twelve: Arise and gird up your loins, take up your cross, follow me, and feed my sheep.

15 Exalt not yourselves; rebel not against my servant Joseph; for verily I say unto you, I am with him, and my hand shall be over him; and the keys which I have given unto him, and also to youward, shall not be taken from him till I come.

The Mission of the Twelve in the British Isles Opens "An Effectual Door" (D&C 112:19)

During a time of speculation and apostasy in Kirtland, the Prophet Joseph Smith extended a mission call to Heber C. Kimball: "In this state of things, and but a few weeks before the Twelve were expecting to meet in full quorum, (some of them having been absent for some time,) God revealed to me that something new must be done for the salvation of his church, and on or about the first of June 1837, Heber C. Kimball, one of the Twelve, was set apart by the spirit of prophecy and Revelation, Prayer and the laying on of the hands of the First Presidency, to preside over a mission to England" (Joseph Smith Papers, "History, 1838–1856, volume B-1," 761).

Heber C. Kimball

Heber C. Kimball described his missionary call to England: "'On Sunday, the 4th day of June, 1837 … the Prophet Joseph came to me, while I was seated in front of the stand, above the sacrament table, on the Melchizedek side of the Temple, in Kirtland, and whispering to me, said, "Brother Heber, the Spirit of the Lord has whispered to me: 'Let my servant Heber go to England and proclaim my Gospel, and open the door of salvation to that nation'"'" (Whitney, *Life of Heber C. Kimball*, 103–4).

"Accompanied by fellow Apostle Orson Hyde and five other missionaries, Heber landed in Liverpool, England, in mid-July. After seeking the Lord's guidance, the missionaries felt inspired to travel to Preston, England, where

Twelve Apostles and other Church members publicly criticized the Prophet Joseph Smith for his handling of the Church's business dealings. President Brigham Young recalled that some felt that the Prophet should not involve himself in temporal affairs (see [*Discourses of Brigham Young*], 461)" (*Doctrine and Covenants Student Manual* [2018], 652).

Doctrine and Covenants 112:16–20. Those Who Receive the First Presidency Receive the Lord

16 Verily I say unto you, my servant Thomas, thou art the man whom I have chosen to hold the keys of my kingdom, as pertaining to the Twelve, abroad among all nations—

17 That thou mayest be my servant to unlock the door of the kingdom in all places where my servant Joseph, and my servant Sidney, and my servant Hyrum, cannot come;

18 For on them have I laid the burden of all the churches for a little season.

19 Wherefore, whithersoever they shall send you, go ye, and I will be with you; and in whatsoever place ye shall proclaim my name an effectual door shall be opened unto you, that they may receive my word.

What "keys" are referred to by the Lord in these verses? (112:16–18) "Each member of the Quorum of the Twelve holds all the keys of the kingdom, which they receive at the time of their ordination to that quorum. Nevertheless, they use those keys—which constitute the right of presidency—only under the direction of the First Presidency and their own quorum president. Such discipline is essential if the Lord's house is to remain a house of order" (McConkie and Ostler, *Revelations of the Restoration*, 904).

What is the role of the Twelve in this dispensation? (112:16–19) "Jesus said to the Jerusalem Twelve: 'Go ye into all the world, and preach the gospel to every creature' (Mark 16:15). The same mission is given the Twelve in this last dispensation (D&C 112:16). They are to represent the First Presidency wherever they are unable to go (v. 17). Hyrum was now serving as an assistant counselor in place of Frederick G. Williams, who had been excommunicated. The First Presidency's first priority at this

they found great success in preaching the gospel. Shortly before their first baptisms in England, the missionaries experienced a confrontation with the forces of the adversary. They also faced opposition from leaders of other churches. However, through the assistance and power of the Spirit, the missionaries converted between fifteen hundred and two thousand people and established branches of the Church in Preston and in the surrounding towns and villages.

"**Early June 1837** Through revelation to Joseph Smith, the Lord called Heber C. Kimball to serve a mission to England.

"**July 19 or 20, 1837** Heber C. Kimball and Orson Hyde, accompanied by five other missionaries, arrived in Liverpool, England.

"**July 30, 1837** The first converts in England were baptized.

"**August 6, 1837** The first branch of the Church in England was organized in Preston.

"**May 22, 1838** Heber C. Kimball returned to Kirtland, Ohio, from his mission to England" (*Latter-day Saint History: 1815–1846 Teacher Material* [2018]).

time was the Church in Kirtland, where much work was needed (v. 18)" (Nyman, *Doctrine and Covenants Commentary*, 2:428).

What might be the context in which Joseph, Sidney, and Hyrum "cannot come"? (112:17) The First Presidency was to stay while the Twelve were sent abroad; thus Joseph, Sidney, and Hyrum were to remain. "Doctrine and Covenants 112:17 and 20 makes it clear that Hyrum Smith was already functioning in the First Presidency by 23 July 1837, and Joseph referred to Hyrum as 'President Smith' as early as 12 June 1837. . . .

"Although the formal release of Frederick G. Williams as second counselor in the First Presidency and the formal sustaining of Hyrum Smith in his stead did not take place until 7 November 1837, it is clear that in the eyes of the Lord, Brother Williams was no longer functioning in that capacity by the time of this revelation (23 July 1837)" (Robinson and Garrett, *Commentary on the Doctrine and Covenants*, 4:87–88).

In what ways were effectual doors opened for the preaching of the gospel? (112:19) Elder Heber C. Kimball prophesied of Elder Parley P. Pratt's mission in 1836 to Canada: "From the things growing out of this mission, shall the fulness of the gospel spread into England, and cause a great work to be done in that land" (Parley P. Pratt, *Autobiography of Parley P. Pratt*, 110).

"The Fieldings of Canada wrote to their reverend brother in Preston an account of the rise in progress of the latter-day work, and thus prepared him for the advent of the Elders upon British shores. He, in turn, told his congregation and [they began] . . . praying for the coming of the Elders from America. Their faith shook the heavens, and in dreams, and visions many were shown the very men whom the Lord was about to send into their midst. Heber C. Kimball, especially, on his arrival in Preston, was recognized by persons, who had never until then beheld him in the flesh" (Whitney, *Life of Heber C. Kimball*, 124).

What does it mean that the Lord has sent the First Presidency? (112:20) "May I say that there is no chance in the call of these brethren [the First Presidency] to direct the Lord's work on earth. His hand is in it. He knows the end from the beginning. He ordained and established the plan of salvation and decreed that his everlasting gospel should be revealed to man in a series of dispensations commencing with Adam and continuing to Joseph Smith. And he—the Almighty—chooses the prophets and apostles who

20 Whosoever receiveth my word receiveth me, and whosoever receiveth me, receiveth those, the First Presidency, whom I have sent, whom I have made counselors for my name's sake unto you.

minister in his name and present his message to the world in every age and dispensation. He selects and foreordains his ministers; he sends them to earth at the times before appointed; he guides and directs their continuing mortal preparations; and he then calls them to those positions they were foreordained to receive from before the foundations of the earth" (Bruce R. McConkie, "God Foreordains His Prophets and His People," *Ensign*, May 1974, 72).

Doctrine and Covenants 112:21–29. Darkness Covers the Earth, and Only Those Who Believe and Are Baptized Will Be Saved

When will nations open their doors to the gospel? (112:21–22) "Brothers and sisters, as surely as the Lord has inspired more missionaries to serve, He is also awakening the minds and opening the hearts of more good and honest people to receive His missionaries. You already know them or will know them. They are in your family and live in your neighborhood. They walk past you on the street, sit by you in school, and connect with you online. You too are an important part of this unfolding miracle....

"Our desire to share the gospel takes all of us to our knees, and it should, because we need the Lord's help....

"As we earnestly and unitedly petition our Father in Heaven, the Lord will continue to open important doors for us" (Neil L. Andersen, "It's a Miracle," *Ensign*, May 2013, 78).

What can we do to remain at peace despite such warnings from the Lord? (112:23–24) Sister Lisa L. Harkness taught: "Certainly, the Savior of the world understands our mortal limitations, for He teaches us how to feel peace and calm even when the winds blow fiercely around us and billowing waves threaten to sink our hopes.

"To those with proven faith, childlike faith, or even the smallest particle of faith, Jesus invites, saying: 'Come unto me' [Matt. 11:28]. 'Believe on my name' [Ether 3:14]. 'Learn of me, and listen to my words' [D&C 19:23]. He tenderly commands, 'Repent and [be] baptized in my name' [3 Nephi 18:11], 'Love one another; as I have loved you' [John 13:34], and 'Always remember me' [3 Nephi 18:7]. Jesus reassures, explaining: 'These things I have spoken unto you, that in me ye might have peace. In the world ye shall have tribulation: but be of good cheer; I have overcome

21 And again, I say unto you, that whosoever ye shall send in my name, by the voice of your brethren, the Twelve, duly recommended and authorized by you, shall have power to open the door of my kingdom unto any nation whithersoever ye shall send them—

22 Inasmuch as they shall humble themselves before me, and abide in my word, and hearken to the voice of my Spirit.

23 Verily, verily, I say unto you, darkness covereth the earth, and gross darkness the minds of the people, and all flesh has become corrupt before my face.

24 Behold, vengeance cometh speedily upon the inhabitants of the earth, a day of wrath, a day of burning, a day of desolation, of weeping, of mourning, and of lamentation; and as a whirlwind it shall come upon all the face of the earth, saith the Lord.

25 And upon my house shall it begin, and from my house shall it go forth, saith the Lord;

26 First among those among you, saith the Lord, who have professed to know my name

the world' [John 16:33]" (Harkness, "Peace, Be Still," *Ensign*, Nov. 2020, 81). See commentary in this volume on Doctrine and Covenants 63:34.

What is the Lord's warning to the members of the Church in the last days? (112:24–26) "In light of all the wonderful promises, those words [D&C 112:24–26] are almost shocking. Upon His house? But, knowing of all our imperfections, should we really be surprised? The Lord has also reminded us that He cannot look upon sin 'with the least degree of allowance' (Alma 45:16; D&C 1:31; 19:20). Sin and transgression are two of the great separating influences of life. Therefore, the Lord warns us sternly of their consequences. He also states very clearly that those who have made solemn and sacred covenants with Him are held to a higher level of accountability than those who have not. This is because they were given the gift of the Holy Ghost after baptism, which gives them more light and knowledge than others. Thus, the Lord makes it emphatically clear that His elect are held to a higher standard" (Lund, *Second Coming of the Lord*, 389). ⊕

Why is it important to purify our hearts before the Lord? (112:28) "Seek help from the Lord, the source of spiritual power. If you 'call on his holy name, and watch and pray continually,' you will 'not be tempted above that which ye can bear' (Alma 13:28). Your daily prayers must include a heartfelt request for help in keeping your commitment to remain morally clean. When you do this, the Lord will bless you with the strength to remain morally clean.

"Remember . . . that purity precedes power. The Lord said, 'But purify your hearts before me; and then go ye into all the world, and preach my gospel unto every creature who has not received it' (D&C 112:28). Missionaries discover this very early in their missions and make every effort to be worthy so they can serve with power" (Ballard, "Purity Precedes Power," *Ensign*, Nov. 1990, 37–38).

Doctrine and Covenants 112:30–34. The First Presidency and the Twelve Hold the Keys of the Dispensation of the Fulness of Times

What is a dispensation? (112:30–31) "[Dispensations] are . . . time periods in which the Lord placed on the earth the necessary knowledge, priesthood, and keys of authority to implement his plan of salvation for his children. This plan, along with priesthood, was first given to Adam . . . , but as a consequence of later

and have not known me, and have blasphemed against me in the midst of my house, saith the Lord.

27 Therefore, see to it that ye trouble not yourselves concerning the affairs of my church in this place, saith the Lord.

28 But purify your hearts before me; and then go ye into all the world, and preach my gospel unto every creature who has not received it;

29 And he that believeth and is baptized shall be saved, and he that believeth not, and is not baptized, shall be damned.

30 For unto you, the Twelve, and those, the First Presidency, who are appointed with you to be your counselors and your leaders, is the power of this priesthood given, for the last days and for the last time, in the which is the dispensation of the fulness of times,

31 Which power you hold, in connection with all those who have received a dispensation at any time from the beginning of the creation;

32 For verily I say unto you, the keys of the dispensation, which ye have received, have come down from the fathers, and last of all, being sent down from heaven unto you.

33 Verily I say unto you, behold how great is your calling. Cleanse your hearts and your garments, lest the blood of this generation be required at your hands.

34 Be faithful until I come, for I come quickly; and my reward is with me to recompense every man according as his work shall be. I am Alpha and Omega. Amen.

apostasy and fragmentation among his descendants, it did not remain constantly upon the earth. Hence, from time to time the Lord called new prophets and again revealed the plan and bestowed the necessary priesthood authority, creating a new dispensation.

"Each new dispensation, or period of restored truth, presents men and women with a divine stewardship in performing the Lord's work on earth. The recipients become custodians and coworkers with God in bringing to pass his purposes" (Lassetter, "Dispensations of the Gospel," 1:388–89). See also commentary in this volume on Doctrine and Covenants 90:3.

What are the keys of the dispensation? (112:30–32) "The priesthood, or priesthood authority, has been defined as 'the power and authority of God' and 'the consummate power on this earth.' Priesthood keys are defined for our understanding as well: 'Priesthood keys are the authority God has given to priesthood leaders to direct, control, and govern the use of His priesthood on earth.' Priesthood keys control the exercise of priesthood authority. Ordinances that create a record in the Church require keys and cannot be done without authorization. President Dallin H. Oaks taught that 'ultimately, all keys of the priesthood are held by the Lord Jesus Christ, whose priesthood it is. He is the one who determines what keys are delegated to mortals and how those keys will be used'" (Stevenson, "Where Are the Keys and Authority of the Priesthood?" *Ensign*, May 2016, 30). See also commentary in this volume on Doctrine and Covenants 90:3. ⊕

How might the blood of this generation be required at one's hands? (112:33) "Given the powers and keys described in Doctrine and Covenants 112, the task of taking the gospel to the world in this generation falls upon those who are blessed to hold its keys and powers in any degree. Should those who hold the powers and keys of the priesthood do their duty and warn their neighbors and build Zion, then they will be held guiltless when those who have been so warned refuse to be cleansed by the atonement of Christ or to gather to safety in Zion. On the other hand, should we fail in our duty to preach the gospel and to build Zion, then the blood of those we should have warned, but didn't, will come upon our garments because of our negligence" (Robinson and Garrett, *Commentary on the Doctrine and Covenants*, 4:93).

What is the definition of Alpha and Omega? (112:34) See also commentary in this volume on Doctrine and Covenants 19:1, 35:1, and 38:1.

This revelation, received around March 1838 in Far West, Missouri, contains inspired questions and answers regarding passages written by the Prophet Isaiah in chapters 11 and 52. It should be remembered that during Moroni's first visit to the Joseph Smith on the night of September 21, 1823, he quoted "the eleventh chapter of Isaiah, saying that it was about to be fulfilled" (JS—H 1:40).

"Sometime after [Joseph Smith] arrived in Far West, Missouri, he apparently answered two sets of questions, one regarding Isaiah chapter 11 and the other, labeled 'Questions by Elias [Higbee],' relating to Isaiah chapter 52. The dating of these two sets of questions and answers is uncertain, but they were probably produced sometime between 16 and 29 March 1838.... The answers to the first set of questions, regarding Isaiah 11, begin with 'thus saith the Lord.' The revealed answers may have provoked Higbee to ask the questions about Isaiah 52:1–2, though the answers given to Higbee's questions do not include the same revelatory language. These verses regard the redemption of Zion and introduce Isaiah's suffering servant [prophecies], including the material in chapter 53, which is one of traditional Christianity's most important texts for [seeing Messianic prophecies of Christ in] the Old Testament. Isaiah 52:1–2 is quoted twice in the Book of Mormon, and other passages in chapter 52 also appear in the book. [Joseph Smith's] revelations also repeat or allude to verses in this chapter, using them to explain the gathering and reestablishment of the house of Israel in the latter days" (Joseph Smith Papers, Historical Introduction to "Questions and Answers, between circa 16 and circa 29 March 1838–B [D&C 113:7–10]").

Doctrine and Covenants 113:1–6. The Stem of Jesse, the Rod Coming Therefrom, and the Root of Jesse Are Identified

Why is "the Stem of Jesse" used to describe Jesus Christ? (113:1–2) "Doctrine and Covenants 113 clearly identifies 'the Stem of Jesse' not as the family of David generally but specifically as Christ, out of whom would come *both* a 'rod' *and* a 'branch' ...

"The key lies in understanding the word *stump*, translated 'stem' in the King James Version. In contemporary English, *stem* implies life, but it is likely that Isaiah meant to convey the opposite sense and that the Hebrew should here be understood as 'stump.' ... [Isaiah] is describing the lineage of

SECTION 113

Answers to certain questions on the writings of Isaiah, given by Joseph Smith the Prophet, at or near Far West, Missouri, March 1838.

1 Who is the Stem of Jesse spoken of in the 1st, 2d, 3d, 4th, and 5th verses of the 11th chapter of Isaiah?

2 Verily thus saith the Lord: It is Christ.

"One of the most important passages in all of Isaiah is rich with nuances of the Restoration and is a favorite of Latter-day Saints [Isaiah 11:1–5]....

"The discussion of the tree in Isaiah 11:1 is a natural continuation of the prophecy through that portion of Isaiah in which the Lord is cutting down boughs, hewing the particularly lofty and arrogant ones, leveling thickets of the forest in every direction (see Isaiah 10). Israel's history, as is so often the case, is compared to a tree. At this point in Isaiah 11, all that remains of it is a stump. Heaven's forester carefully trims his trees—Latter-day Saints think instantly of Jacob 5 in the Book of Mormon—and in this manner, he clears out the evil trees of his forest and prepares the way for flourishing new shoots to come out of the stump of Jesse. (Donald Parry [says] that 'shoot' is a better translation from the Hebrew 'rod' and 'stump' is better than 'stem.')

"So it is with the restoration of the gospel. It is like the new shoot out of the old stump, and we see the fruits of those labors in—and with—Zion" (Holland, "More Fully Persuaded," 12–13).

David apparently ended and the kingship of David finished—a thing cut down, dead, and lifeless. Thus, the Stem, or Stump, of Jesse represents the crucified Christ, or son of David, rejected by his own and cut down in his prime" (Robinson and Garrett, *Commentary on the Doctrine and Covenants*, 4:98).

3 What is the rod spoken of in the first verse of the 11th chapter of Isaiah, that should come of the Stem of Jesse?

4 Behold, thus saith the Lord: It is a servant in the hands of Christ, who is partly a descendant of Jesse as well as of Ephraim, or of the house of Joseph, on whom there is laid much power.

What is the rod that grows out of the Stem of Jesse? (113:3–4) Sidney B. Sperry reasoned, "[D&C 113:4] tells us that 'it is a servant in the hands of Christ,' but an express name is not given. . . . The 'servant' or 'rod' referred to is none other than the Prophet Joseph Smith himself. . . .

Brother Sperry then identified "the individual of verse 4 [a servant in the hands of Christ] with the one in verse 6 [a descendant of Jesse]. Who holds the keys of the gathering in this dispensation? Joseph Smith. Therefore the 'rod' of Isaiah 11:1 is Joseph Smith. That is one of the reasons why Moroni quoted the chapter to the modern prophet, and doubtless explained to him that Isaiah saw his coming" (*Voice of Israel's Prophets*, 35).

Who is the descendant of Jesse and Ephraim? (113:4) "With respect to Joseph's lineage, Brigham Young declared he was 'a pure Ephraimite' ([in *Journal of Discourses*], 2:269). However, as President Joseph Fielding Smith pointed out, 'No one can lay claim to a perfect descent from father to son through just one lineage' [*Answers to Gospel Questions*, 3:61]. Therefore, though Joseph's lineage may be traceable directly back to Ephraim through a given line, of necessity there were intermarriages that took place, making it possible for his descent to have also come from Jesse through his forefather, Judah" (Brewster, *Doctrine & Covenants Encyclopedia* [2012], 482).

"Isaiah 11:2–5 must be understood within the context established in verse 1, including the 'rod' (servant) mentioned there, and verses 2 through 4 especially may refer to Joseph Smith. 'The spirit of the Lord shall rest upon him.' As Doctrine and Covenants 5:6–10 clearly points out, Joseph Smith was chosen to give the Lord's word to this generation. These verses may have a double reference to both Christ and Joseph Smith. (Isaiah uses double references in other passages as well. . . .) After all, the servant was to be an instrument in the hands of Christ to carry out his work. As the Spirit of the Lord came upon Joseph Smith, he did attain wisdom, understanding, and knowledge; further, Joseph did judge in righteousness through the Spirit of the Lord" (Nyman, *"Great Are the Words of Isaiah,"* 72).

See also commentary on 2 Nephi 21:1–5 in *Book of Mormon Study Guide: Start to Finish*, rev. ed., as well as commentary on Isaiah 11:1–5 in *Old Testament Study Guide: Start to Finish*.

What is the "root of Jesse"? (113:5–6) Joseph Fielding McConkie put forth, "There can be no question that [the 'root'] is describing the Prophet Joseph Smith. By way of revelation he was told that he held the right to the priesthood (see D&C 86:8–9). That the keys of the kingdom had been given to him is a matter of record; that his labors were to stand as an 'ensign' to which the nations of the earth will gather is also a matter of scriptural promise (D&C 29:4, 7–8; 35:25; 38:33; 39:11; 45:9, 28)" ("Joseph Smith as Found in Ancient Manuscripts," 18). ✦

Doctrine and Covenants 113:7–10. The Scattered Remnants of Zion Have a Right to the Priesthood and Are Called to Return to the Lord

What is meant by "Put on thy strength, O Zion"? (113:7–8) President Boyd K. Packer taught that the strength of the church lies in the power of the priesthood: "Priesthood is the authority and the power which God has granted to men on earth to act for Him. . . .

"We have done very well at distributing the *authority* of the priesthood. . . . We have quorums of elders and high priests worldwide. But distributing the *authority* of the priesthood has raced, I think, ahead of distributing the *power* of the priesthood. The priesthood does not have the strength that it should have and will not have until the *power* of the priesthood is firmly fixed in the families as it should be" ("Power of the Priesthood," *Ensign*, May 2010, 7). ✦

What does it mean that members in Zion have a right to priesthood authority by lineage? (113:8) "The covenant that the Lord first made with Abraham and reaffirmed with Isaac and Jacob is of transcendent significance. It contained several promises [including] Abraham's posterity would be numerous, entitled to eternal increase and to bear the priesthood. . . .

"We are also children of the covenant. We have received, as did they of old, the holy priesthood and the everlasting gospel. Abraham, Isaac, and Jacob are our ancestors. *We are of Israel. We have the right to receive the gospel, blessings of the priesthood, and eternal life.* Nations of the earth will be blessed by our efforts and by the labors of our posterity. The literal seed of Abraham and those who are gathered into his family by adoption receive these promised blessings—predicated upon acceptance of the Lord and obedience to his commandments" (Nelson, "Children of the Covenant," *Ensign*, May 1995, 33; emphasis added). ✦

5 What is the root of Jesse spoken of in the 10th verse of the 11th chapter?

6 Behold, thus saith the Lord, it is a descendant of Jesse, as well as of Joseph, unto whom rightly belongs the priesthood, and the keys of the kingdom, for an ensign, and for the gathering of my people in the last days.

7 Questions by Elias Higbee: What is meant by the command in Isaiah, 52d chapter, 1st verse, which saith: Put on thy strength, O Zion—and what people had Isaiah reference to?

8 He had reference to those whom God should call in the last days, who should hold the power of priesthood to bring again Zion, and the redemption of Israel; and to put on her strength is to put on the authority of the priesthood, which she, Zion, has a right to by lineage; also to return to that power which she had lost.

9 What are we to understand by Zion loosing herself from the bands of her neck; 2d verse?

10 We are to understand that the scattered remnants are exhorted to return to the Lord from whence they have fallen; which if they do, the promise of the Lord is that he will speak to them, or give them revelation. See the 6th, 7th, and 8th verses. The bands of her neck are the curses of God upon her, or the remnants of Israel in their scattered condition among the Gentiles.

What does Zion "loosing herself from the bands of her neck" mean? (113:9–10) "Isaiah promised that the bands upon the neck of Zion would be loosed, or the curses of God removed, when the Lord spoke again from the heavens to descendants of ancient Israel in the last days. The restoration of the gospel through the Prophet Joseph Smith fulfills this promise. The word of the Lord through Isaiah, as referred to in this verse, was that when such took place: 'My people shall know my name: therefore they shall know in that day that I am he that doth speak: behold, it is I. How beautiful upon the mountains are the feet of him that bringeth good tidings, that publisheth peace; that bringeth good tidings of good, that publisheth salvation; that saith unto Zion, Thy God Reigneth!' (Isaiah 52:6–8)" (McConkie and Ostler, *Revelations of the Restoration*, 913).

Introduction to Doctrine and Covenants 114

"On 11 April 1838, [Joseph Smith] dictated a revelation for David W. Patten, directing him to settle his business affairs and prepare for a mission. At the time, Patten and fellow apostle Brigham Young were serving as assistants to Thomas B. Marsh in the [temporary stake] presidency over the church in Missouri. This appointment was apparently temporary because, as members of the Quorum of the Twelve Apostles, Marsh, Patten, and Young were eventually expected to travel, proselytize, and supervise the church conferences and branches outside of Zion and its stakes—that is, outside of the main church congregation in Missouri and any other places designated for gathering. . . .

"The 11 April 1838 revelation . . . stated that Patten would be sent on a mission the following spring and implied that he would go with the other apostles. Another revelation, received about three months later, specified that in 1839 the twelve apostles would 'depart to go over the great waters and there promulge my gospel,' suggesting they would serve a mission in Europe to follow up on the success of [Heber C.] Kimball and [Orson] Hyde's mission ['Revelation, 8 July 1838–A' (D&C 118:4)]. [Elder] Patten, however, was killed in October 1838 in the conflict between the Latter-day Saints and other Missourians" (Joseph Smith Papers, Historical Introduction to "Revelation, 11 April 1838 [D&C 114]").

"Elder David W. Patten, a member of the Quorum of the Twelve Apostles, obeyed the Lord's counsel recorded in Doctrine and Covenants 114 and put his affairs in order in preparation for serving a mission the following spring (see D&C 114:1). His death, which occurred not long after the Prophet Joseph Smith received this revelation, demonstrates the wisdom of the Lord's counsel to Elder Patten to 'settle up all his business as soon as he possibly can' (D&C 114:1). Elder Patten's decision to obey the Lord later became a blessing after receiving a wound in battle that would soon take his life. He was able to depart this life confident that he had kept the faith and that his life was in order" (*Doctrine and Covenants Student Manual* [2018], 658).

SECTION 114

Revelation given through Joseph Smith the Prophet, at Far West, Missouri, April 11, 1838.

1 Verily thus saith the Lord: It is wisdom in my servant David W. Patten, that he settle up all his business as soon as he possibly can,

Doctrine and Covenants 114:1–2. Church Positions Held by Those Who Are Not Faithful Will Be Given to Others

and make a disposition of his merchandise, that he may perform a mission unto me next spring, in company with others, even twelve including himself, to testify of my name and bear glad tidings unto all the world.

2 For verily thus saith the Lord, that inasmuch as there are those among you who deny my name, others shall be planted in their stead and receive their bishopric. Amen.

What does "bishopric" mean in this passage?
(114:2) "To partake of the spirit of apostasy is to deny the name of Christ. Specific reference is made in this instance to those men who lost the spirit of their calling and thus their place as 'Apostles, or special witnesses of the name of Christ' (D&C 107:23). . . .

"The Greek word for bishopric is *episkope,* meaning 'overseership,' or 'office.' It was not originally used in reference to religious callings and can properly be used to describe any of a variety of duties. Peter referred to the place of Judas among the Twelve Apostles as a 'bishoprick' (Acts 1:20). Here it is used in reference to the office of an apostle" (McConkie and Ostler, *Revelations of the Restoration,* 915). ●

David W. Patten: A Faithful Witness for Jesus Christ (Doctrine and Covenants 114:1)

When David W. Patten was ordained to be an apostle on February 15, 1835, his blessing included, "O God, give this, thy servant a knowledge of thy will; May he be like one of old who bore testimony of Jesus. May he be a new man from this day forth. He shall be equal with his brethren, the twelve, and have all the qualifications of the Prophets before him" (Joseph Smith Papers, "Minutes, Discourse, and Blessings, 14–15 February 1835," 152).

"David joined other members of the Quorum of the Twelve Apostles to serve a mission to the eastern states before serving a mission to the southern states. While preaching in Tennessee, he and his companion were arrested for promising the Holy Ghost to anyone who would accept baptism" (Black, "David W. Patten").

"Until his death in 1838, Patten served almost continuously as a missionary for the Church. He established numerous branches of the Church on each of his proselytizing journeys and was renowned for his spiritual gift of healing. . . .

"During the latter part of 1836, Elder Patten settled in Far West, Missouri. . . .

"In April 1838, Joseph Smith received a revelation instructing Patten to prepare for a mission with the Twelve the following spring (D&C 114); however, Patten did not live to fulfill the assignment. He died on October 25, 1838, from a wound suffered in a battle at Crooked River when a contingent of Caldwell County militia (all Mormons), under his leadership, attempted to rescue three Latter-day Saints who had been taken prisoners by a company of Missourians from Ray County. He was buried in Far West, Missouri, two days later. In January 1841 a revelation was given to Joseph Smith in which the Lord indicated that David W. Patten 'is with me at this time' (D&C 124:19, 130)" (Baugh, "David W. Patten," 3:1068).

This revelation was received on April 26, 1838, at Far West, Missouri. "The revelation was addressed to [Joseph Smith], other church leaders, and all other members of the 'Church of Jesus Christ of Latter Day Saints'—which the revelation specified was the new official name of the church. The revelation enjoined the church's leaders and members to continue gathering to Far West, to sanctify the city through consecrated living, and to build the temple. The Saints were instructed to begin work on the temple on 4 July and to build it according to a pattern that would be revealed to the First Presidency....

"The Latter-day Saints followed the direction of the revelation by laying the cornerstones of the temple on 4 July 1838" (Joseph Smith Papers, Historical Introduction to "Revelation, 26 Apr. 1838 [D&C 115]").

SECTION 115

Revelation given through Joseph Smith the Prophet, at Far West, Missouri, April 26, 1838, making known the will of God concerning the building up of that place and of the Lord's house. This revelation is addressed to the presiding officers and the members of the Church.

1 Verily thus saith the Lord unto you, my servant Joseph Smith, Jun., and also my servant Sidney Rigdon, and also my servant Hyrum Smith, and your counselors who are and shall be appointed hereafter;

2 And also unto you, my servant Edward Partridge, and his counselors;

3 And also unto my faithful servants who are of the high council of my church in Zion, for thus it shall be called, and unto all the elders and people of my Church of Jesus Christ of Latter-day Saints, scattered abroad in all the world;

4 For thus shall my church be called in the last days, even The Church of Jesus Christ of Latter-day Saints.

5 Verily I say unto you all: Arise and shine forth, that thy light may be a standard for the nations;

Doctrine and Covenants 115:1–4. The Lord Names His Church The Church of Jesus Christ of Latter-day Saints

What was the Church called before the Lord made His declaration? (115:3–4) "Even before the Church was organized, Oliver Cowdery followed Book of Mormon precedent in proposing 'the Church of Christ' as a name for the Church. On the day the Church was organized, Joseph Smith was called by revelation as an 'Elder unto this Church of Christ.' Thereafter, the early revelations repeatedly referred to the Church as 'the Church of Christ' and to its members as 'saints'" (Church History Topics, "Name of the Church"). ◉

Doctrine and Covenants 115:5–6. Zion and Her Stakes Are Places of Defense and Refuge for the Saints

How does the call to "arise and shine forth, that thy light may be a standard for the nations" apply to the members of the Church today? (115:5) Sister Elaine S. Dalton taught, "By the way you live the gospel, you reflect [the Savior's] light. Your example will have a powerful effect for good on the earth.

'Arise and shine forth, that thy light may be a standard for the nations' [D&C 115:5] is a call to each of you. It is a call to move to higher ground. It is a call to leadership—to lead out in decency, purity, modesty, and holiness. It is a call to share this light with others. It is time to 'arise and shine forth'" ("It Shows in Your Face," *Ensign*, May 2006, 109).

What is the purpose of stakes in Zion? (115:6)

"With the creation of stakes and the construction of temples in most nations with sizable populations of the faithful, the current commandment is not to gather to one place but to gather in stakes in our own homelands. There the faithful can enjoy the full blessings of eternity in a house of the Lord. There, in their own homelands, they can obey the Lord's command to enlarge the borders of His people and strengthen her stakes (see D&C 101:21; 133:9, 14). In this way the stakes of Zion are 'for a defense, and for a refuge from the storm, and from wrath when it shall be poured out without mixture upon the whole earth' (D&C 115:6)" (Oaks, "Preparation for the Second Coming," *Ensign*, May 2004, 8). ☉

Doctrine and Covenants 115:7–16. The Saints Are Commanded to Build a House of the Lord at Far West

What will make this land, or any land of Zion, holy? (115:7–8) "The holy word . . . affirms that Israel gathers to Zion to escape the abomination of desolation that shall be poured out upon a wicked world in the last days. In Zion there will be safety. . . .

6 And that the gathering together upon the land of Zion, and upon her stakes, may be for a defense, and for a refuge from the storm, and from wrath when it shall be poured out without mixture upon the whole earth.

7 Let the city, Far West, be a holy and consecrated land unto me; and it shall be called most holy, for the ground upon which thou standest is holy.

The Correct Name of the Church (Doctrine and Covenants 115:4)

President Russell M. Nelson declared: "Today I feel compelled to discuss with you a matter of great importance. Some weeks ago, I released a statement regarding a course correction for the name of the Church [official statement, Aug. 16, 2018]. I did this because the Lord impressed upon my mind the importance of the name He decreed for His Church, even The Church of Jesus Christ of Latter-day Saints. . . .

"It *is* a correction. It *is* the command of the Lord. Joseph Smith did not name the Church restored through him; neither did Mormon. It was the Savior Himself who said, 'For thus shall my church be called in the last days, even The Church of Jesus Christ of Latter-day Saints' [D&C 115:4]. . . .

"Thus, the name of the Church is not negotiable. When the Savior clearly states what the name of His Church should be and even precedes His declaration with, 'Thus shall my church be called,' He is serious. And if we allow nicknames to be used or adopt or even sponsor those nicknames ourselves, He is offended.

"What's in a name or, in this case, a nickname? When it comes to nicknames of the Church, such as the 'LDS Church,' the 'Mormon Church,' or the 'Church of the Latter-day Saints,' the most important thing *in* those names is the *absence* of the Savior's name. To remove the Lord's name from the Lord's Church is a major victory for Satan. When we *discard* the Savior's name, we are subtly *disregarding* all that Jesus Christ did for us—even His Atonement" ("Correct Name of the Church," *Ensign*, Nov. 2018, 87–88).

8 Therefore, I command you to build a house unto me, for the gathering together of my saints, that they may worship me.

9 And let there be a beginning of this work, and a foundation, and a preparatory work, this following summer;

10 And let the beginning be made on the fourth day of July next; and from that time forth let my people labor diligently to build a house unto my name;

11 And in one year from this day let them re-commence laying the foundation of my house.

12 Thus let them from that time forth labor diligently until it shall be finished, from the cornerstone thereof unto the top thereof, until there shall not anything remain that is not finished.

13 Verily I say unto you, let not my servant Joseph, neither my servant Sidney, neither my servant Hyrum, get in debt any more for the building of a house unto my name;

14 But let a house be built unto my name according to the pattern which I will show unto them.

15 And if my people build it not according to the pattern which I shall show unto their presidency, I will not accept it at their hands.

"But let us . . . recite the crowning reason for gathering to Zion or to her stakes. It is to receive the blessings found in the temples of the Lord. . . . All of the places appointed for the gathering of the saints are holy places, and the center and crown of each place is that sacred sanctuary, the holy temple, wherein the fulness of the blessings of heaven may be received" (Bruce R. McConkie, *New Witness*, 574, 575). See also commentary in this volume on Doctrine and Covenants 45:32 and 87:8.

How did the Saints follow the instructions given in these verses? (115:9–10) "Independence [Day,] July 4th [, 1838] was spent in celebrating the declaration of the Independence of the United States of America, and . . . also in laying the corner stones of the house of the Lord, agreeably to the commandment of the Lord unto us given April 26th, 1838" (Joseph Smith Papers, "History, 1838–1856, volume B-1," 800; orthography modernized). ◐

What do we know about laying the Far West temple foundation one year later? (115:11) See commentary in this volume on Doctrine and Covenants 118:4–5.

How much debt did the church incur when building the Kirtland Temple? (115:13) "This command came on the heels of debt shackling the Church incurred from building the Kirtland Temple. Elder Heber C. Kimball explained, 'This building [Kirtland Temple] the Saints commenced in 1833, in poverty, and without means to do it. In 1834 they completed the walls, and in 1835–6 they nearly finished it. The cost was between sixty and seventy thousand dollars. A committee was appointed to gather donations; they traveled among the churches and collected a considerable amount, but not sufficient, so that in the end they found themselves between thirteen and fourteen thousand dollars in debt' (Whitney, *Life of Heber C. Kimball*, 88)" (McConkie and Ostler, *Revelations of the Restoration*, 920–21).

What pattern of building temples did the Lord provide His servant Joseph Smith? (115:15–16) Brigham Young described how, with the Kirtland Temple, the Prophet Joseph Smith had previously received guidance according to the Lord's pattern: "Joseph not only received revelation and commandment to build a Temple, but he received a *pattern* also, as did Moses for the Tabernacle, and Solomon for his Temple; for without a pattern, he could not know what was wanting, having never seen [a temple prior to the one built in Kirtland], and not having experienced its use" (in *Journal of Discourses*, 2:31).

"According to John W. Rigdon, son of Sidney Rigdon, Far West temple was to have been similar to Kirtland temple in function, including lower floor auditorium and upper floor to be used for school" (Joseph Smith Papers, "House of the Lord (planned site), Far West, Missouri").

Doctrine and Covenants 115:17–19. Joseph Smith Holds the Keys of the Kingdom of God on Earth

What do we know about the saints gathering speedily to build up Far West? (115:17) "Far West grew to become the principal Latter-day Saint settlement in Missouri following the Saints' displacement from Clay and Ray Counties beginning in mid-1836. At the time of Joseph's arrival in 1838, Far West had a population of 4,900 with '150 homes, four dry goods stores, three family groceries, several blacksmith shops, two hotels, a printing shop, and a large schoolhouse that doubled as a church and a courthouse.' Finding affordable settlement lands for the anticipated arrival of a large influx of impoverished Kirtland Saints to Missouri became an immediate priority" (Olmstead, "Far West and Adam-ondi-Ahman," 236).

Why were stakes of Zion needed in various regions round about? (115:17–18) This was a direction for Church leaders to gather to Far West and establish other stakes nearby such as the one at Diahman. "The concept of the stake was revealed gradually, beginning in 1831, as the Church began dividing geographically between Zion, in Missouri, and Kirtland, Ohio. There would be a center place, and other organized areas would be the stakes of the tent of Zion (D&C 82:13–14; 101:21; 115:17–18). . . . The term *stake* was not applied to these geographical areas until a few years later" (Jackson, *From Apostasy to Restoration*, 176, 177). ⊕

What keys were given to Joseph Smith? (115:19) "With the priesthood, the Prophet also received certain keys. First, he received the office of an apostle under the hands of Peter, James, and John, who held the keys of 'the kingdom of heaven' (see Matt. 16:19;

16 But if my people do build it according to the pattern which I shall show unto their presidency, even my servant Joseph and his counselors, then I will accept it at the hands of my people.

17 And again, verily I say unto you, it is my will that the city of Far West should be built up speedily by the gathering of my saints;

18 And also that other places should be appointed for stakes in the regions round about, as they shall be manifested unto my servant Joseph, from time to time.

19 For behold, I will be with him, and I will sanctify him before the people; for unto him have I given the keys of this kingdom and ministry. Even so. Amen.

D&C 27:12–13). Later, through Moses, Elias, and Elijah, he received the keys necessary for this dispensation and was told that thus the world would know that the 'great and dreadful day of the Lord' was near at hand (D&C 110:11–16). With these keys for the gathering of Israel, missionary work, the sealing powers of the temple, and other powers, Joseph Smith had the authority to usher in the dispensation of the fullness of times (D&C 65:2; 107:8; 115:18–19; 128:10–14, 20–21)" (Victor L. Ludlow, *Isaiah: Prophet, Seer, and Poet*, 172–73).

Introduction to Doctrine and Covenants 116

"On 18 May [1838], Joseph Smith and a small company of men set out from Far West on an exploratory mission to Daviess County to locate other areas for possible future Mormon settlement. The following day, 19 May, the company arrived at the homesite of Lyman Wight, who lived near the base of a gentle slopping hill, called 'Spring Hill' by the Latter-day Saints who had settled in the region. On this occasion, George W. Robinson, Smith's clerk, recorded a significant entry in the Prophet's journal regarding the area: 'Spring Hill a name appropriated by the bretheren [*sic*] present, But afterwards named by the mouth of [the] Lord and was called Adam Ondi Awmen [Adam-ondi-Ahman], because said he it is the place where Adam shall come to visit his people, or the Ancient of days shall sit as spoken of by Daniel the Prophet.' The entry is significant for two reasons. First, it marks the first time that Joseph Smith identified the location where Adam-ondi-Ahman was actually located; and second, it specified that the 'Ancient of days' spoken of by Daniel was none other than Father Adam, who, at a future day, would appear at Adam-ondi-Ahman to a gathering of faithful Saints in fulfillment of Daniel's prophecy (see Daniel 7:9–10, 13–14). After identifying the region, the Prophet spent a few more days surveying the area, then returned to Far West, where he arrived on 24 May" (Baugh, "History and Doctrine of the Adam-ondi-Ahman Revelation," 172–74).

"Although the 'temple block' was dedicated, apparently no corner stones were laid, and no temple was built. Persecution soon forced the Saints to flee to Illinois, and thus the settlement had a short existence lasting only a few months, because by November 1838 the Saints were leaving their homes and abandoning Adam-ondi-Ahman" (Matthews, "Adam-ondi-Ahman," 34).

"Located in northern Missouri, the place called Adam-ondi-Ahman has been important during three distinct periods. First, just before his death, Adam gathered his righteous posterity together, blessed them, and gave them inspired instructions; the Lord also appeared and honored Adam as patriarch of the human family (see D&C 107:53–56). Next, during the later 1830s, Adam-ondi-Ahman was one of the Saints' larger settlements in northern Missouri. Finally, just before the Second Coming, another great council will be held at Adam-ondi-Ahman" (Cowan, *Answers to Your Questions*, 133).

SECTION 116

Revelation given to Joseph Smith the Prophet, near Wight's Ferry, at a place called Spring Hill, Daviess County, Missouri, May 19, 1838.

1 Spring Hill is named by the Lord Adam-ondi-Ahman, because, said he, it is the place where Adam shall come to visit his people, or the Ancient of Days shall sit, as spoken of by Daniel the prophet.

Doctrine and Covenants 116:1. Adam Shall Come to Adam-ondi-Ahman

What does the name "Adam-ondi-Ahman" mean? (116:1) "The term *Adam-ondi-Ahman* was introduced into Latter-day Saint vocabulary by a revelation that stated that God had 'established the foundations of Adam-ondi-Ahman.' A revelation of ca. April 1835 explicitly applied the term to a place, 'the valley of Adam-ondi-Ahman,' where Adam gave his posterity his 'last blessing.' [Joseph Smith's] journal indicated that a site in Daviess County, Missouri, which was selected on 19 May 1838 for a settlement of the Saints, was 'after wards named by the mouth of [the] Lord and was called Adam Ondi Awmen, because said he it is the place where Adam shall come to visit his people, or the Ancient of days shall sit as spoken of by Daniel the Prophet'" (Joseph Smith Papers Glossary, "Adam-ondi-Ahman").

"The Prophet Joseph Smith . . . said of Adam: 'I saw Adam in the valley of Adam-ondi-Ahman. He called together his children and blessed them with a patriarchal blessing. *The Lord appeared in their midst,* and he [Adam] blessed them all, and foretold what should befall them to the latest generation'" (Matthews, *Selected Writings*, 134, emphasis added). See also commentary in this volume on Doctrine and Covenants 107:53–56 and 78:15. ◐

What does the prophet Daniel say regarding the Ancient of Days? (116:1) "Daniel in his seventh chapter speaks of the Ancient of Days; he means the oldest man, our Father Adam, Michael; he will call his children together and hold a council with them to prepare them for the coming of the Son of Man [see Daniel 7:9–14]. He (Adam) is the father of the human family, and presides over the spirits of all men, and all that have had the keys must stand before him in this grand council. . . . The Son of Man stands before him, and there is given him glory and dominion. Adam delivers up his stewardship to Christ, that which was

The Grand Council at Adam-ondi-Ahman (Doctrine and Covenants 116:1)

"All that happened at Adam-ondi-Ahman in those early days was but a type and a shadow—a similitude, if you will—of what shall happen at the same blessed place in the last days when Adam and Christ and the residue of men who are righteous assemble again in solemn worship" (Bruce R. McConkie, *Millennial Messiah*, 580).

"This council in the valley of Adam-ondi-Ahman is to be of the greatest importance to this world. At that time there will be a transfer of authority from the usurper and impostor, Lucifer, to the rightful King, Jesus Christ. Judgment will be set and all who have held keys will make their reports and deliver their

The area surrounding Spring Hill, Missouri. The Lord designated this area as Adam-ondi-Ahman.

stewardships, as they shall be required. Adam will direct this judgment, and then he will make his report, as the one holding the keys for this earth, to his Superior Officer, Jesus Christ. Our Lord will then assume the reins of government; directions will be given to the Priesthood; and He, whose right it is to rule, will be installed officially by the voice of the priesthood there assembled. This grand council of Priesthood will be composed, not only of those who are faithful who now dwell on the earth, but also of the prophets and apostles of old, who have had directing authority. Others may also be there, but if so they will be there by appointment, for this is to be an official council called to attend to the most momentous matters concerning the destiny of this earth" (Joseph Fielding Smith, *Way to Perfection*, 291).

delivered to him as holding the keys of the universe, but retains his standing as head of the human family" (*Joseph Smith* [manual], 104).

Introduction to Doctrine and Covenants 117

Doctrine and Covenants 117 was received on July 8, 1838, in Far West, Missouri. "At a three-day conference of the Church on July 6–8, 1838, in Far West, Missouri, the Prophet received five revelations. This revelation was given to William Marks, Newel K. Whitney, and Oliver Granger.

"The Lord had commanded the Saints to gather and build up Far West. A company of 513 Saints known as the 'Kirtland Camp' left Ohio on July 6, 1838, headed for Far West. The camp arrived in Adam-ondi-Ahman on October 4. William Marks, Newel K. Whitney, and Oliver Granger were not a part of this company. At Far West at the time, Joseph Smith had no way of knowing who had and had not left Kirtland—but this revelation commanding William Marks and Newell K. Whitney to leave Kirtland shows that the Lord did have that knowledge" (Woodger, *Essential Doctrine and Covenants Companion*, 232).

"The First Presidency expected that William Marks, a bookseller who had remained in Kirtland to preside over the Saints there, and Newel K. Whitney, the bishop in Kirtland, would obey the revelations to leave Kirtland and come to Far West. Yet these men dragged their feet. Whitney was Kirtland's most prosperous merchant. He owned a store and a profitable ashery situated near the main intersection through town. He was torn between his material prosperity and the revelations" (Harper, *Making Sense of the Doctrine & Covenants*, 431).

"Although the decision of these two leaders to remain in Kirtland would have been unknown to the Prophet Joseph Smith, who was a thousand miles away, yet the Lord was aware of their actions. Two days after the exodus of the Kirtland Camp, the Lord expressed his displeasure with these two men in this revelation and appointed Oliver Granger as an agent to transact business of Church-owned properties" (McConkie and Ostler, *Revelations of the Restoration*, 927).

SECTION 117

Revelation given through Joseph Smith the Prophet, at Far West, Missouri, July 8, 1838, concerning the immediate duties of William Marks, Newel K. Whitney, and Oliver Granger.

1 Verily thus saith the Lord unto my servant William Marks, and also unto my servant Newel K. Whitney, let them settle up their business speedily and journey from the land of Kirtland, before I, the Lord, send again the snows upon the earth.

2 Let them awake, and arise, and come forth, and not tarry, for I, the Lord, command it.

3 Therefore, if they tarry it shall not be well with them.

4 Let them repent of all their sins, and of all their covetous desires, before me, saith the Lord; for what is property unto me? saith the Lord.

Doctrine and Covenants 117:1–9. The Lord's Servants Should Not Covet Temporal Things, for "What Is Property unto the Lord?"

How did William Marks and Newell K. Whitney respond to this revelation? (117:1–4) "Oliver Granger was designated to settle all the Church's accounts in Kirtland, and he delivered a letter to Marks and Whitney containing the revelation. In the letter, the First Presidency expressed confidence in the pair's willingness to obey the revelation and to 'act accordingly.' Obedient to the instruction, both Marks and Whitney forsook their possessions in Kirtland. Eventually they joined with the main body of the Saints to attend to the 'more weighty matters' of administering to the needs of the Saints" (Olmstead, "Far West and Adam-ondi-Ahman," 239–40).

How has the Lord blessed His children by making places "to bud and to blossom" for them? (117:7) In past dispensations, the Lord blessed His covenant people with places that provided abundantly for their needs (see Deuteronomy 7:13–15; Isaiah 27:6). In our dispensation, consider the movement and settlements of the Latter-day Saints. "In each instance the Lord caused the unwanted, solitary places . . . , ranging from swamps to deserts, 'to bud and . . . to bring forth in abundance'" (McConkie and Ostler, *Revelations of the Restoration*, 928).

What are the plains of Olaha Shinehah? (117:8) This name is "associated with Adam-ondi-Ahman. *Shinehah* defined as 'sun' and *Olea* as 'moon' in [Joseph Smith's] translated Book of Abraham" (Joseph Smith Papers, Places, "Olah Shinehah"). See also Abraham 3:11–14.

How can our own possessions distract us from things of greater importance? (117:8) "The Lord commanded William Marks and Newel K. Whitney to 'repent of all their covetous desires' that may have prevented them from obeying Him (see D&C 117:4). 'As used in the scriptures, to covet is to envy someone or to have an excessive desire for something' ([Guide to the Scriptures, "Covet"]). After telling these men to 'repent of all their sins, and of all their covetous desires,' the Lord asked, 'For what is property unto me?' (D&C 117:4), emphasizing that their property and other material possessions were 'that which is but the drop' compared to what He had prepared for them (D&C 117:8; see also D&C 117:6–7; Moses 1:27–33)" (*Doctrine and Covenants Student Manual* [2018], 669).

Where is the Lord asking them to come when He says "even Zion"? (117:9) "Shortly after this revelation was received, Brother Marks and Bishop Whitney responded with faith to the Lord's chastening counsel and left Kirtland, Ohio, for [Far West,] Missouri" (*Doctrine and Covenants Student Manual* [2018], 668). See also commentary in this volume on Doctrine and Covenants 63:24–25.

5 Let the properties of Kirtland be turned out for debts, saith the Lord. Let them go, saith the Lord, and whatsoever remaineth, let it remain in your hands, saith the Lord.

6 For have I not the fowls of heaven, and also the fish of the sea, and the beasts of the mountains? Have I not made the earth? Do I not hold the destinies of all the armies of the nations of the earth?

7 Therefore, will I not make solitary places to bud and to blossom, and to bring forth in abundance? saith the Lord.

8 Is there not room enough on the mountains of Adam-ondi-Ahman, and on the plains of Olaha Shinehah, or the land where Adam dwelt, that you should covet that which is but the drop, and neglect the more weighty matters?

9 Therefore, come up hither unto the land of my people, even Zion.

Doctrine and Covenants 117:10–16. The Lord's Servants Are to Forsake Littleness of Soul, and Their Sacrifices Will Be Sacred unto the Lord

10 Let my servant William Marks be faithful over a few things, and he shall be a ruler over many. Let him preside in the midst of my people in the city of Far West, and let him be blessed with the blessings of my people.

11 Let my servant Newel K. Whitney be ashamed of the Nicolaitane band and of all their secret abominations, and of all his littleness of soul before me, saith the Lord, and come up to the land of Adam-ondi-Ahman, and be a bishop unto my people, saith the Lord, not in name but in deed, saith the Lord.

12 And again, I say unto you, I remember my servant Oliver Granger; behold, verily I say unto him that his name shall be had in sacred remembrance from generation to generation, forever and ever, saith the Lord.

13 Therefore, let him contend earnestly for the redemption of the First Presidency of my

When did William Marks fulfill his calling to preside over the Saints? (117:10) "Before he could obey the directive the Saints were driven by mobocracy from Missouri. William joined the exiles in Quincy, Illinois.

"At the conference on 5 October 1839 at Commerce (later Nauvoo), William was appointed to preside over the stake there" (Black, *Who's Who*, 184). ●

What was the Nicolaitane band? (117:11) "The name appears in the book of Revelation (Rev. 2:6, 15) and has been defined as 'members of the Church who were trying to maintain their church standing while continuing to live after the manner of the world' [*Doctrinal New Testament Commentary*, 3:446]" (Brewster, *Doctrine & Covenants Encyclopedia* [2012], 386).

"Whoever the Nicolaitans at Kirtland were, Bishop Whitney doubtless understood whom the Lord meant, and he is here commanded to cease his associations with them. George A. Smith later expressed his opinion that the Nicolaitans at Kirtland consisted of those who professed to be Saints but who secretly sought personal gain from the destruction of the Kirtland Anti-Banking Society" (Robinson and Garrett, *Commentary on the Doctrine and Covenants*, 4:126–27).

Why was Oliver Granger to be held in sacred remembrance? (117:12–13) In a May 13, 1839, letter of introduction, the First Presidency described Oliver Granger as "a man of the most strict integrity, and moral virtue, and in fine to be a man of God. We have had long experience and acquaintance with Br. Granger, we have entrusted vast business concerns to him, which have been managed skillfully to the

The Lord Compliments and Trusts Oliver Granger (Doctrine and Covenants 117:12–15)

Oliver Granger "was born 7 February 1794 in Phelps, Ontario County, New York. . . . A few months after the publication of the Book of Mormon, Oliver obtained a copy and was converted following a heavenly visitation from Moroni. This angel commanded Oliver to bear testimony that the Book of Mormon is true, and prophesied that he would 'hereafter be ordained to preach the everlasting Gospel to the children of men.' . . .

"Granger was baptized and ordained an elder in Wayne County, New York, in the early 1830s and moved to Kirtland in 1833 to be with the Saints. There he was appointed a member of the high council, served missions to the East, and helped with the building of the temple" (*Encyclopedia of Latter-day Saint History*, 435–36).

"On July 8, 1838, Oliver was called by revelation to help settle the financial affairs of the Church [in Kirtland, Ohio]—a mission he performed with distinction earning him the respect and appreciation of the Prophet and the eternal commendation of the Savior [see Doctrine and Covenants 117:12–15]" (Pinegar and Allen, *Doctrine and Covenants Who's Who*, 37–38).

support of our Characters and interest, as well as that of the Church, and he is now authorized by a general Conference to go forth and engage in vast and important concerns as an Agent for the Church, that he may fill a station of usefulness in obedience to the commandments of God" (Joseph Smith Papers, "History, 1838–1856, volume C-1," 937).

"Oliver Granger is an example of one who reaps the blessings of faithfulness. . . . Oliver Granger lived and died as a faithful Latter-day Saint. His name was placed upon the records of the Lord's church and will so remain there forever among those who are true and faithful" (Otten and Caldwell, *Sacred Truths*, 2:283–84). ⊕

How was Oliver Granger able to help with the debt incurred by the First Presidency? (117:13) "Much of the church's debt [mostly from the Kirtland Temple] was still unpaid, and many Saints had been left destitute by ongoing persecution, the national economic problems, the financial collapse in Kirtland, and the costly move to Missouri. Furthermore, the Lord had forbidden the First Presidency to borrow more money. The church needed funds but still had no reliable system for collecting them. . . .

"Joseph and other church leaders prayed about these problems and received a flood of revelation. The Lord appointed [Oliver Granger] to represent the First Presidency in paying off the church's debts. The properties the Saints had given up in Kirtland were to be sold and applied toward the debt" (*Saints*, 1:319, 320).

How did the remaining Saints in Kirtland with stewardship over the temple "keep and preserve it holy"? (117:16) "Faithful Saints were still living in Kirtland in the summer of 1838, and the stake was not disorganized there until 1841. Nevertheless, there were factions among those who professed to be Saints, and it was difficult to know who really was on the Lord's side. Many different parties struggled for control of the Kirtland Temple, and there were deep differences of opinion concerning its proper uses and function. Many Kirtland members thought of the temple as a financial resource and thus became 'moneychangers.' Note, for example, the disagreement over public 'exhibitions' in the temple and Oliver Granger's correct refusal to hand over the temple keys to some Church leaders in Ohio who favored using the building for profane purposes" (Robinson and Garrett, *Commentary on the Doctrine and Covenants*, 4:128).

Church, saith the Lord; and when he falls he shall rise again, for his sacrifice shall be more sacred unto me than his increase, saith the Lord.

14 Therefore, let him come up hither speedily, unto the land of Zion; and in the due time he shall be made a merchant unto my name, saith the Lord, for the benefit of my people.

15 Therefore let no man despise my servant Oliver Granger, but let the blessings of my people be on him forever and ever.

16 And again, verily I say unto you, let all my servants in the land of Kirtland remember the Lord their God, and mine house also, to keep and preserve it holy, and to overthrow the moneychangers in mine own due time, saith the Lord. Even so. Amen.

"Four of the original members of the Quorum of the Twelve Apostles had been excommunicated or otherwise removed from office by July 1838 for transgression or apostasy: John F. Boynton, Luke Johnson, Lyman Johnson, and William E. McLellin. This caused great sorrow among Church members. On Sunday, July 8, 1838, during a leadership meeting [held at Far West, Missouri], the Prophet Joseph Smith received the revelation recorded in Doctrine and Covenants 118 in response to the plea to 'show unto us thy will O, Lord concerning the Twelve' (see [*Joseph Smith Papers: Documents, Volume 6*], 176–78). John Taylor, John E. Page, Wilford Woodruff, and Willard Richards were appointed to fill the vacancies in the Quorum of the Twelve Apostles" (*Doctrine and Covenants Student Manual* [2018], 671).

SECTION 118

Revelation given through Joseph Smith the Prophet, at Far West, Missouri, July 8, 1838, in response to the supplication, "Show us thy will, O Lord, concerning the Twelve."

1 Verily, thus saith the Lord: Let a conference be held immediately; let the Twelve be organized; and let men be appointed to supply the place of those who are fallen.

2 Let my servant Thomas remain for a season in the land of Zion, to publish my word.

3 Let the residue continue to preach from that hour, and if they will do this in all lowliness of heart, in meekness and humility, and long-suffering, I, the Lord, give unto them a promise that I will provide for their families; and an effectual door shall be opened for them, from henceforth.

4 And next spring let them depart to go over the great waters, and there promulgate my gospel, the fulness thereof, and bear record of my name.

5 Let them take leave of my saints in the city of Far West, on the twenty-sixth day of April next, on the building-spot of my house, saith the Lord.

Doctrine and Covenants 118:1–3. The Lord Will Provide for the Families of the Twelve

Why did the Twelve need to be reorganized? (118:1–2) By the summer of 1838, "the Apostles had yet to demonstrate much unity or power as a quorum, and worse, Joseph Smith had removed four of the Apostles in the aftermath of the Kirtland difficulties. At the conference on 7 April, David Patten had reviewed the status of each of the Twelve, including his concerns about William Smith and [Elder Patten's] unwillingness to recommend to the Saints Elders [William] McLellin, [John] Boynton, [Luke] Johnson, and [Lyman] Johnson. Later that month the latter four Apostles, along with Oliver Cowdery and David Whitmer, were each formally tried and cut off. After months of concern and labor with his quorum, Thomas Marsh's twelve now numbered only eight—and one of those could not be relied upon" (Ronald K. Esplin, "Brigham Young and the Transformation," 65). ⊕

Doctrine and Covenants 118:4–6. Vacancies in the Twelve Are Filled

How did the Twelve fulfill this commandment to start their missions from Far West? (118:4–5) "When the revelation was given [in 1838], all was peace and quietude in Far West, Missouri, the city where most of the Latter-day Saints dwelt; but before the time came for its fulfillment, the Saints of God had been driven out of the State of Missouri into the State of Illinois. . . . The mobocrats of Missouri had declared that they would see that [this prophecy] should not be fulfilled. . . .

"[However], on the morning of the 26th of April, 1839, notwithstanding the threats of our enemies . . .

we moved on to the temple ground in the city of Far West, and held a council, and fulfilled the revelation and commandment given unto us" (*Wilford Woodruff* [manual], 139). ●

Who called these four new members of the Quorum of the Twelve Apostles? (118:6) "Though Joseph was the presiding priesthood authority and the Lord's mouthpiece upon the earth, he did not choose or select men to occupy these positions. The reason is simple and clear. Such men were not to be representatives of Joseph Smith. They were to be special witnesses of the name of Jesus Christ (see D&C 107:23). Only the Lord could give a man the special witness needed to adequately perform his role in such a high and sacred calling. Such a call would have to come by revelation from the Lord.

"In this revelation, the Lord gave Joseph Smith the names of the men who should be called (see D&C 118:1, 6)" (Otten and Caldwell, *Sacred Truths*, 286).

6 Let my servant John Taylor, and also my servant John E. Page, and also my servant Wilford Woodruff, and also my servant Willard Richards, be appointed to fill the places of those who have fallen, and be officially notified of their appointment.

Introduction to Doctrine and Covenants 119

On July 8, 1838, at Far West, Missouri, the Lord revealed His will concerning tithing, "a standing law" unto His Church forever (D&C 119:4).

"In late 1837, Bishop Newel K. Whitney in Ohio and Bishop Edward Partridge in Missouri began asking Church members to pay tithing. At that time Church members believed that tithing meant any offering willingly donated to the Church (see [Harper, 'Tithing of My People,' 251]). In Kirtland, Ohio, the bishopric began 'calling on church members everywhere to "bring their tithes into the store house" to relieve church debts and to help establish the community of Saints in Missouri. While this general request did not include recommended donation amounts, in December 1837 a committee [of Church leaders in Missouri] proposed that every head of household be asked to annually donate a certain percentage of net worth, with the percentage based on church needs for the year. To cover anticipated church expenses for 1838, the committee proposed a "tithing" of 2 percent. The committee believed that such a program would "be in some degree fulfilling the law of consecration"' (in [*Joseph Smith Papers: Documents, Volume 6*], 184–85; spelling modernized)" (*Doctrine and Covenants Student Manual* [2018], 673).

Like many revelations, this revelation was given in response to a direct question the Prophet and others asked: "O Lord show unto thy servants how much thou requirest of the properties of thy people for a tithing?" (Joseph Smith Papers, "Revelation, 8 July 1838–C [D&C 119]," [1]).

In answer to this prayer, the language and instruction of Doctrine and Covenants 119 was received through the Prophet Joseph Smith.

SECTION 119

Revelation given through Joseph Smith the Prophet, at Far West, Missouri, July 8, 1838, in answer to his supplication: "O Lord! Show unto thy servants how much thou requirest of the properties of thy people for a tithing." The law of tithing, as understood today, had not been given to the Church previous to this revelation. The term tithing in the prayer just quoted and in previous revelations (64:23; 85:3; 97:11) had meant not just one-tenth, but all free-will offerings, or contributions, to the Church funds. The Lord had previously given to the Church the law of consecration and stewardship of property, which members (chiefly the leading elders) entered into by a covenant that was to be everlasting. Because of failure on the part of many to abide by this covenant, the Lord withdrew it for a time and gave instead the law of tithing to the whole Church. The Prophet asked the Lord how much of their property He required for sacred purposes. The answer was this revelation.

1 Verily, thus saith the Lord, I require all their surplus property to be put into the hands of the bishop of my church in Zion,

2 For the building of mine house, and for the laying of the foundation of Zion and for the priesthood, and for the debts of the Presidency of my Church.

Doctrine and Covenants 119:1–5. The Saints Are to Pay Their Surplus Property and Then Give, as Tithing, One-Tenth of Their Interest Annually

How was surplus or excess property identified? (119:1) Joseph Smith asked Brigham Young and others to find out what surplus property there was for consecration. "Brigham asked Joseph, 'Who shall be the judge of what is surplus property?' Joseph answered, 'Let them be the judges themselves.'

"As they were taught the will of the Lord, the Saints became accountable stewards who could choose whether or not to offer their tithes of their own free will. 'Saints have come up day after day to consecrate,' the Prophet's journal says, 'and to bring their offerings into the store house of the Lord.' But not all Saints exercised their agency to be wise stewards. Brigham lamented that some Saints were stingy with their offerings" (Harper, *Let's Talk about the Law of Consecration*, 77).

What are tithing contributions used for today? (119:2) "These sacred funds are used in a rapidly growing church to spiritually bless individuals and families by constructing and maintaining temples and houses of worship, supporting missionary work, translating and publishing scriptures, fostering family history research, funding schools and religious education, and accomplishing many other Church purposes as directed by the Lord's ordained servants. . . .

"How can the temporal affairs of an organization as large as the restored Church of Jesus Christ possibly operate throughout the entire world using such succinct instructions [D&C 119–120]? To me the answer is quite straightforward: this is the Lord's work. . . . The Savior inspires and directs His servants as they apply His directions and labor in His cause" (Bednar, "Windows of Heaven," *Ensign*, Nov. 2013, 19).

How is tithing a standing law? (119:3–4) "'This,' the revelation says, 'shall be the beginning of the tithing of my people.' That instance of the word *tithing* is the first of three (*tithing* or *tithed*) in section 119. All of them refer to the Saints' voluntary offering of surplus property. 'And after that,' the revelation says, 'those who have thus been tithed shall pay one-tenth of all their interest annually.' The revelation does not call it a lesser law to be replaced someday, but 'a standing Law unto them forever' and applicable to all Saints everywhere" (Harper, "Tithing of My People," 252).

Why is it so vital that we live the law of tithing? (119:5) "To develop enduring faith, an enduring commitment to be a full-tithe payer is essential. Initially it takes faith to tithe. Then the tithe payer develops more faith to the point that tithing becomes a precious privilege. Tithing is an ancient law from God. He made a promise to His children that He would open 'the windows of heaven, and pour . . . out a blessing, that there shall not be room enough to receive it' (Malachi 3:10). Not only that, tithing will keep your name enrolled among the people of God and protect you in 'the day of vengeance and burning' [D&C 85:3]" (Nelson, "Face the Future with Faith," *Ensign*, May 2011, 35).

Doctrine and Covenants 119:6–7. Such a Course Will Sanctify the Land of Zion

How does living the law of tithing sanctify the land and the people of Zion? (119:6–7) Elder Neil L. Andersen taught: "The spiritual power of the divine law of tithing is not measured by the amount of money contributed, for both the prosperous and the poor are commanded by the Lord to contribute 10 percent of their income. The power comes from placing our trust in the Lord.

3 And this shall be the beginning of the tithing of my people.

4 And after that, those who have thus been tithed shall pay one-tenth of all their interest annually; and this shall be a standing law unto them forever, for my holy priesthood, saith the Lord.

5 Verily I say unto you, it shall come to pass that all those who gather unto the land of Zion shall be tithed of their surplus properties, and shall observe this law, or they shall not be found worthy to abide among you.

6 And I say unto you, if my people observe not this law, to keep it holy, and by this law sanctify the land of Zion unto me, that my statutes and my judgments may be kept thereon, that it may be most holy, behold, verily I say unto you, it shall not be a land of Zion unto you.

7 And this shall be an ensample unto all the stakes of Zion. Even so. Amen.

"This Shall Be a Standing Law" (Doctrine and Covenants 119:4)

Joseph F. Smith noted: "I recollect very vividly a circumstance that occurred in the days of my childhood. My mother [Mary Fielding Smith] was a widow, with a large family to provide for. One spring when we opened our potato pits she had her boys get a load of the best potatoes, and she took them to the tithing office; potatoes were scarce that season. I was a little boy at the time, and drove the team. When we drove up to the steps of the tithing office ready to unload the potatoes, one of the clerks came out and said to my mother: 'Widow Smith, it's a shame that you should have to pay tithing.' He said a number of other things that I remember well, but they are not necessary for me to repeat here. The first two letters of the name of that tithing clerk was W[illiam] T[hompson], and he chided my mother for paying her tithing, called her anything but wise and prudent; and said there were others able to work that were supported from the tithing office. My mother turned upon him and said: 'William, you ought to be ashamed of yourself. Would you deny me a blessing? If I did not pay my tithing I should expect the Lord to withhold His blessings from me; I pay my tithing, not only because it is a law of God but because I expect a blessing by doing it. By keeping this and other laws, I expect to prosper and to be able to provide for my family'" (Johnson and Reeder, *Witness of Women*, 109–10).

"The added abundance of the Lord conveyed through your generous tithes has strengthened the reserves of the Church, providing opportunities to advance the Lord's work beyond anything we have yet experienced. All is known by the Lord, and in time, we will see His sacred purposes fulfilled" ("Tithing," *Liahona*, Nov. 2023, 34).

Introduction to Doctrine and Covenants 120

"At the time Joseph Smith arrived in Far West, the Saints were flocking to this new headquarters from branches of the Church in the United States and Canada. They settled throughout the region, necessitating the formation of a new stake. By July of 1838, the prospects of establishing an enduring stronghold in northern Missouri appeared promising. But the daunting task of building a temple loomed. The Church needed to raise the means to build the Lord's house [in Far West] in spite of other pressing needs [such as debts from Kirtland].

"With this challenge in mind, Joseph gathered several leaders on Sunday morning, July 8, 1838. It was apparently in this meeting that he received both the revelation on tithing (now canonized as Doctrine and Covenants 119) and the revelation on the disposition of tithes (now Doctrine and Covenants 120)" (Harper, "Tithing of My People," 251–52).

Doctrine and Covenants 120 "is a promise that the Lord will guide His servants by His Spirit in the expenditure of the offerings of the Saints—a promise that, as the results prove, has been fulfilled" (Smith and Sjodahl, *Doctrine and Covenants Commentary*, 750).

SECTION 120

Revelation given through Joseph Smith the Prophet, at Far West, Missouri, July 8, 1838, making known the disposition of the properties tithed as named in the preceding revelation, section 119.

1 Verily, thus saith the Lord, the time is now come, that it shall be disposed of by a council, composed of the First Presidency of my Church, and of the bishop and his council, and by my high council; and by mine own voice unto them, saith the Lord. Even so. Amen.

Doctrine and Covenants 120:1. The Lord Establishes His Council for the Disposition of Tithes

Who determines how tithing is disposed of or spent? (120:1) The Lord "directed that the use of these sacred tithes would be prayerfully considered by a council of the First Presidency, the Quorum of the Twelve Apostles, the Presiding Bishopric, 'and by mine own voice unto them, saith the Lord.'

"These sacred funds do not belong to the leaders of the Church. They belong to the Lord. His servants are painstakingly aware of the sacred nature of their stewardship.

"President Gordon B. Hinckley recounted this childhood experience: 'When I was a boy I raised a question with my father . . . concerning the expenditure of Church funds. He reminded me that mine is the God-given obligation to pay my tithes and offerings. When I do so, [my father said,] that which I give is no longer mine. It belongs to the Lord to whom I consecrate it.' His father added: 'What the authorities of the Church do with it need not concern [you, Gordon]. They are answerable to the Lord, who will require an accounting at their hands'" (Neil L. Andersen, "Tithing," *Liahona*, Nov. 2023, 33).

Introduction to Doctrine and Covenants 121

After nearly five months of being imprisoned, Joseph Smith wrote a letter from Liberty Jail, dated March 20, 1839. The letter was addressed to: "Bishop Edward Partridge; church members in Quincy, Illinois; and the Saints 'scattered abroad.' . . .

"The epistle contains an extended meditation on the Latter-day Saints' recent sufferings and the prisoners' frustrations in jail. This part of the [letter] includes a prayer in which [the Prophet] pleads with God to deliver the Saints from their oppressors. . . . The voice of the letter transitions from that of the prisoners to that of the Lord providing an answer to the letter's earlier prayer, explaining the deeper significance of the Saints' persecutions and pronouncing judgments against the church's enemies" (Joseph Smith Papers, Historical Introduction to "Letter to the Church and Edward Partridge, 20 March 1839"). To see the location of Liberty, Missouri, see Map 8 in the Appendix.

"Historians Dean Jessee and John Welch noted that Joseph Smith's lengthy [letter] is a Pauline-like epistle. For example, Joseph called himself 'a prisoner for the Lord Jesus Christ's sake' and wrote that 'nothing therefore can separate us from the love of God,' language similar to the Apostle Paul's writings to the Ephesians and Romans. Joseph then detailed the sufferings of the 'poor and much injured saints,' including the families wandering helplessly and hopelessly between Missouri and Illinois, as well as the dismal experience he and his companions were having in Liberty Jail" (Bray, "Within the Walls of Liberty Jail," 260).

"In 1874, Orson Pratt became Church Historian and General Church Recorder, placing him in a position to oversee the Church's historical collections, including early manuscripts of revelations. Under the direction of Brigham Young, who was in the last years of his life, Elder Pratt made the most significant changes to the Doctrine and Covenants since the days of Joseph Smith. . . .

"Most significant of all, Elder Pratt, under Brigham Young's direction, added twenty-six new sections to the Doctrine and Covenants, dramatically expanding the volume. . . .

"Elder Pratt drew sections 121, 122, and 123 from a letter in two parts that Joseph Smith and his fellow prisoners wrote from jail in Liberty, Missouri, on March 20, 1839. . . . The extracts selected by Elder Pratt illustrate how Joseph Smith received some of his most memorable spiritual impressions while languishing in this 'prison-temple'" (Turley and Slaughter, *How We Got the Doctrine and Covenants*, 81, 85).

Doctrine and Covenants 121:1–6. The Prophet Pleads with the Lord for the Suffering Saints

Why does it sometimes feel as though God does not respond to our pleas for help and relief? (121:1–4) "In the depths of his anguish in Liberty Jail, the Prophet Joseph Smith cried out. . . . Many of us, in moments of personal anguish, feel that God is far from us. The pavilion that seems to intercept divine aid does not cover God but occasionally covers us. God is never hidden, yet sometimes we are, covered by a pavilion of motivations that draw us away from

SECTION 121

Prayer and prophecies written by Joseph Smith the Prophet in an epistle to the Church while he was a prisoner in the jail at Liberty, Missouri, dated March 20, 1839. The Prophet and several companions had been months in prison. Their petitions and appeals directed to the executive officers and the judiciary had failed to bring them relief.

1 O God, where art thou? And where is the pavilion that covereth thy hiding place?

2 How long shall thy hand be stayed, and thine eye, yea thy pure eye, behold from the eternal heavens the wrongs of thy people and of thy servants, and thine ear be penetrated with their cries?

3 Yea, O Lord, how long shall they suffer these wrongs and unlawful oppressions, before thine heart shall be softened toward them, and thy bowels be moved with compassion toward them?

4 O Lord God Almighty, maker of heaven, earth, and seas, and of all things that in them are, and who controllest and subjectest the devil, and the dark and benighted dominion of Sheol—stretch forth thy hand; let thine eye pierce; let thy pavilion be taken up; let thy hiding place no longer be covered; let thine ear be inclined; let thine heart be softened; and thy bowels moved with compassion toward us.

5 Let thine anger be kindled against our enemies; and, in the fury of thine heart, with thy sword avenge us of our wrongs.

6 Remember thy suffering saints, O our God; and thy servants will rejoice in thy name forever.

God and make Him seem distant and inaccessible. . . . God is not unable to see us or communicate with us, but we may be unwilling to listen or submit to His will and His time" (Eyring, "Where Is the Pavilion?" *Ensign*, Nov. 2012, 72). ✚

What is meant by the "dark and benighted dominion of Sheol"? (121:4) "[Sheol is] the Hebrew name for the abode of departed spirits (corresponding to the Greek Hades), translated in the KJV 'grave,' 'pit,' and 'hell,' depending on the context (see Gen. 37:35; Job 17:16; Ps. 16:10)" (Bible Dictionary, s.v. "Sheol," 727).

The Missouri War (Doctrine and Covenants 121)

"The Mormon-Missouri War (also called the Mormon War or the Missouri War) was an armed conflict between the Latter-day Saints and other citizens of northern Missouri in the fall of 1838. The conflict expanded to involve state officials, including the governor, and resulted in the incarceration of Joseph Smith and the forced expulsion of the Saints from Missouri. . . .

"The Saints appealed to the government for protection, and some troops came to keep the peace. But a diplomatic resolution was interrupted when a mob destroyed a Mormon settlement at De Witt, Carroll County, forcing the Saints there to flee for their lives. The governor of Missouri, Lilburn W. Boggs, responded to a plea for help by saying the Saints and the Missourians must fight their own battles. As reports of mobs burning Mormon homes in other counties mounted, the Saints decided to fight back.

"Armed fighting lasted two weeks. In mid-October, Mormons raided and burned homes and stores in Gallatin and Millport. At Crooked River, Mormon and Missouri militiamen skirmished, resulting in the deaths of one Missourian and two Mormons, including Apostle David W. Patten. In the wake of these outbursts, Governor Boggs, who had previously supported anti-Mormon activities in Jackson County, issued what came to be known as the 'extermination order,' which authorized the state militia to drive the Mormons from the state or exterminate them if necessary. The most horrific event of the war came a few days later on October 30, when a group of armed Missourians opened fire on Saints at Hawn's Mill, killing and brutally dismembering 17 men and boys.

"The militia, under the command of Major General Samuel D. Lucas, laid siege to Far West on October 31. Lucas arrested Joseph Smith and a few other Mormon leaders and ordered their execution for the next day. Another general named Alexander Doniphan challenged the order, and Joseph and several others were incarcerated and ordered to stand trial on charges of treason and murder. Meanwhile, the main body of Latter-day Saints sought refuge in the neighboring state of Illinois" (Church History Topics, "Mormon-Missouri War of 1838").

Doctrine and Covenants 121:7–10. The Lord Speaks Peace to the Prophet

What good resulted from the adversity and affliction of Liberty Jail? (121:7) "Elder Brigham H. Roberts (1857–1933) of the First Council of the Seventy, in recording the history of the Church, spoke of [Liberty Jail] as a temple, or, more accurately, a 'prison-temple.' . . .

"In what sense could Liberty Jail be called a 'temple' . . . ? In precisely this sense: that you can have sacred, revelatory, profoundly instructive experiences with the Lord in *any* situation you are in. Indeed, you can have sacred, revelatory, profoundly instructive experiences with the Lord *in the most miserable experiences of your life*—in the worst settings, while enduring the most painful injustices, when facing the most insurmountable odds and opposition you have ever faced" (Holland, "Lessons from Liberty Jail," *Ensign*, Sep. 2009, 28). ◐

What is gained by enduring through adversity? (121:8) "The Lord taught the Prophet Joseph Smith in Liberty Jail that the reward for enduring his trials well would help qualify him for eternal life [see D&C 121:7–8]. . . .

"A loving God has not set such tests before us simply to see if we can endure difficulty but rather to see if we can endure them well and so become polished. . . .

"Our trials and our difficulties give us the opportunity to learn and grow, and they may even change our very nature. If we can turn to the Savior in our extremity, our souls can be polished as we endure" (Eyring, "Reward for Enduring Well," *Ensign*, Jul. 2017, 4). ◐

7 My son, peace be unto thy soul; thine adversity and thine afflictions shall be but a small moment;

8 And then, if thou endure it well, God shall exalt thee on high; thou shalt triumph over all thy foes.

9 Thy friends do stand by thee, and they shall hail thee again with warm hearts and friendly hands.

Joseph Smith's Imprisonment and the Suffering of the Saints (D&C 121:5–6)

"On December 1, 1838, the Prophet Joseph Smith, his brother Hyrum, and other brethren were taken from Richmond, Missouri, where they had been incarcerated in a log home, to the jail in Liberty, Missouri. There they would remain for more than four months, awaiting trial on false charges arising from the persecution of the Saints in Missouri. During this time, Church members were being driven from their homes in Missouri by their persecutors, causing tremendous suffering. The trials of the Saints were a source of great anxiety to the Prophet and his companions during their long imprisonment.

"Liberty Jail was divided into an upper room and a 14-foot-square lower dungeon, where the prisoners were kept. The Prophet described their situation: 'We are kept under a strong guard, night and day, in a prison of double walls and doors, proscribed in our liberty of conscience. Our food is scant, uniform, and coarse; we have not the privilege of cooking for ourselves; we have been compelled to sleep on the floor with straw, and not blankets sufficient to keep us warm; and when we have a fire, we are obliged to have almost a constant smoke. The Judges have gravely told us from time to time that they knew we were innocent, and ought to be liberated, but they dare not administer the law unto us, for fear of the mob' [Letter from Joseph Smith to Isaac Galland, Mar. 22, 1839].

10 Thou art not yet as Job; thy friends do not contend against thee, neither charge thee with transgression, as they did Job.

How might the story of Job in the Old Testament be of comfort to Joseph Smith during this time of great suffering? (121:10) "Although he was innocent of wrongdoing, Job was accused of sin by his wife and his closest friends. All of them accused him of having secretly caused his own misfortunes by some hidden iniquity, and they all urged him to confess his guilt (see Job 4:7–8, 17; 8:6, 20; 22:5, 23). The friends and family of Joseph Smith, however, stood by him in misfortune and continued to believe in his innocence and his good character" (Robinson and Garrett, *Commentary on the Doctrine and Covenants*, 4:153).

Doctrine and Covenants 121:11–17. Cursed Are All Those Who Raise False Cries of Transgression against the Lord's People

11 And they who do charge thee with transgression, their hope shall be blasted, and their prospects shall melt away as the hoar frost melteth before the burning rays of the rising sun;

Who charged Joseph Smith with transgression? (121:11) "By mid-December [1838], Joseph had already had enough of his dreary cell.... He openly named and condemned his accusers, particularly his former friends and associates, most notably George M. Hinckle, Reed Peck, John Corrill, William W. Phelps, Sampson Avard, and John Clemenson, who, during the Mormon surrender and military occupation, cooperated with the Missouri militia officers and later testified as witnesses in behalf of the state during the Richmond hearing. In addition to these men, the Prophet mentioned Martin Harris, David Whitmer, John Whitmer, Oliver Cowdery, William E. McLellin, Thomas B. Marsh, and Orson Hyde, each of whom had apostatized from the Church during the past year and who [the Prophet] also characterized as traitors to the cause" (Baugh, "1838, Joseph Smith in Northern Missouri," 329).

"The room was not tall enough to allow the men to stand upright, and Alexander McRae, one of the prisoners, said the food was 'very coarse, and so filthy that we could not eat it until we were driven to it by hunger.'...

"During the Prophet's imprisonment, his wife, Emma, was able to visit him only three times. Their only other communication was through letters. On April 4, 1839, the Prophet wrote: 'Dear and affectionate wife. Thursday night, I sit down just as the sun is going down, as we peek through the grates of this lonesome prison, to write to you, that I may make known to you my situation. It is, I believe, now about five months and six days since I have been under the grimace of a guard night and day, and within the walls, grates, and screeching iron doors of a lonesome, dark, dirty prison. With emotions known only to God do I write this letter. The contemplations of the mind under these circumstances defy the pen or tongue or angels to describe or paint to the human being who never experienced what we experience.... We lean on the arm of Jehovah and none else for our deliverance' [Letter from Joseph Smith to Emma Smith, Apr. 4, 1839]" (*Joseph Smith* [manual], 359–60).

What leads some apostates to persecute the Lord, His prophets, and the Saints? (121:12–13) "From apostates the faithful have received the severest persecutions. Judas was rebuked and immediately betrayed his Lord into the hands of His enemies, because Satan entered into him.

"There is a superior intelligence bestowed upon such as obey the Gospel with full purpose of heart, which, if sinned against, the apostate is left naked and destitute of the Spirit of God, and he is, in truth, nigh unto cursing, and his end is to be burned. When once that light which was in them is taken from them they become as much darkened as they were previously enlightened, and then, no marvel, if all their power should be enlisted against the truth, and they, Judas-like, seek the destruction of those who were their greatest benefactors" (*Joseph Smith* [manual], 321).

What does it mean to "lift up the heel against mine anointed"? (121:16–17) "During the Last Supper, Jesus Christ announced that one of His disciples would betray Him. He quoted [Psalm 41:9]. . . . The phrase 'hath lifted up his heel against me' describes a person who has decided to openly oppose or fight against the Lord and His work or to turn his or her back and walk away from it. The use of this phrase in John 13:18 referred to the treachery of Judas, who betrayed Jesus Christ into the hands of His enemies. As recorded in Doctrine and Covenants 121, the Lord used the same phrase when referring to the apostates who had turned against the Prophet Joseph Smith and were seeking his destruction (see D&C 121:16)" (*Doctrine and Covenants Student Manual* [2018], 694–95).

Why do some people cry transgression against church leaders and others? (121:17) Glen L. Pace spoke of critics today: "Some former members speak evil of the Brethren. Joseph Smith received his share of this criticism from the dissidents of his day. The Lord's revelation to him is applicable to us today [see D&C 121:16–17]. . . .

"It seems that history continues to teach us: You can leave the Church, but you can't leave it alone. The basic reason for this is simple. Once someone has received a witness of the Spirit and accepted it, he leaves neutral ground. One loses his testimony only by listening to the promptings of the evil one, and Satan's goal is not complete when a person leaves the Church, but when he comes out in open rebellion against it" (Pace, "Follow the Prophet," *Ensign*, May 1989, 26).

12 And also that God hath set his hand and seal to change the times and seasons, and to blind their minds, that they may not understand his marvelous workings; that he may prove them also and take them in their own craftiness;

13 Also because their hearts are corrupted, and the things which they are willing to bring upon others, and love to have others suffer, may come upon themselves to the very uttermost;

14 That they may be disappointed also, and their hopes may be cut off;

15 And not many years hence, that they and their posterity shall be swept from under heaven, saith God, that not one of them is left to stand by the wall.

16 Cursed are all those that shall lift up the heel against mine anointed, saith the Lord, and cry they have sinned when they have not sinned before me, saith the Lord, but have done that which was meet in mine eyes, and which I commanded them.

17 But those who cry transgression do it because they are the servants of sin, and are the children of disobedience themselves.

18 And those who swear falsely against my servants, that they might bring them into bondage and death—

19 Wo unto them; because they have offended my little ones they shall be severed from the ordinances of mine house.

20 Their basket shall not be full, their houses and their barns shall perish, and they themselves shall be despised by those that flattered them.

21 They shall not have right to the priesthood, nor their posterity after them from generation to generation.

22 It had been better for them that a millstone had been hanged about their necks, and they drowned in the depth of the sea.

23 Wo unto all those that discomfort my people, and drive, and murder, and testify against them, saith the Lord of Hosts; a generation of vipers shall not escape the damnation of hell.

24 Behold, mine eyes see and know all their works, and I have in reserve a swift judgment in the season thereof, for them all;

25 For there is a time appointed for every man, according as his works shall be.

26 God shall give unto you knowledge by his Holy Spirit, yea, by the unspeakable gift of the Holy Ghost, that has not been revealed since the world was until now;

Doctrine and Covenants 121:18–25. False Accusers Will Not Have Right to the Priesthood and Will Be Damned

At whom might these verses be directed? (121:18–22) "These verses seem to be directed specifically at apostates who turned against the Prophet and the Saints in Missouri and who sought to protect themselves from the mobs by swearing to false charges against their former friends. Without repentance, individuals such as these would be severed from the blessings of the temple (see v. 19), the bounties of the earth (see v. 20), and from any right to or blessing of the priesthood for themselves and their posterity (see v. 21). . . . Although [some] individuals eventually repented of their treachery, were forgiven by the Saints, and returned to the Church, they could never undo the hardships they had earlier caused their friends by their betrayal in Missouri. Many others who turned traitor to the Saints to save themselves never did repent and return, including, for example, Sampson Avard and William McLellin" (Robinson and Garrett, *Commentary on the Doctrine and Covenants*, 4:154–55).

Doctrine and Covenants 121:26–32. Glorious Revelations Promised Those Who Endure Valiantly

Why is the Holy Ghost described as an "unspeakable gift"? (121:26) "[The Holy Ghost] is the source of testimony and spiritual gifts. It enlightens minds, fills our souls with joy, teaches us all things, and brings forgotten knowledge to our remembrance. The Holy Ghost also 'will show unto [us] all things what [we] should do.' [2 Nephi 32:5] . . .

"President Gordon B. Hinckley taught, 'How great a blessing it is to have the ministering influence of a member of the Godhead' [*Teachings*, 259]. Think of what this means, the ability and the right to receive the ministrations of a member of the Godhead, to commune with infinite wisdom, infinite knowledge, and infinite power!" (Wirthlin, "Unspeakable Gift," *Ensign*, May 2003, 26–27).

When is the time when "nothing shall be with-held"? (121:27–28) "We live in the day that 'our forefathers have awaited with anxious expectation' [D&C 121:27]. We have front-row seats to *witness live* what the prophet Nephi saw *only in vision* [see 1 Nephi 14:14]. . . .

"*You*, my brothers and sisters, are among those men, women, and children whom Nephi saw. Think of that!

"Regardless of where you live or what your circumstances are, the Lord Jesus Christ is *your* Savior, and God's prophet Joseph Smith is *your* prophet. He was foreordained before the foundation of the earth to be the prophet of this last dispensation, when 'nothing shall be withheld' [D&C 121:28] from the Saints. Revelation continues to flow from the Lord during this ongoing process of restoration" (Nelson, "Hear Him," *Ensign*, May 2020, 88). ✪

Why were several promised blessings included in this revelation? (121:29) "[D&C 121:26–33] are the promised blessings of a covenant, the terms and con-ditions of which precede the promises but were not included in the canonized part of Joseph's letter. 'Let honesty and sobriety, and candor and solemnity, and virtue, and pureness, and meekness, and simplicity, crown our heads in every place, and in fine become as little children without malice, guile, or hypocrisy: and now, Brethren, after your tribulations *if* you do these things, and exercise fervent prayer, and faith in the sight of God,' *then* God will grant the exalting bless-ings promised in verses 26–33" (Harper, *Making Sense of the Doctrine & Covenants*, 449).

What do we know about the Lord's promised outpouring of knowledge? (121:30–32) "According to what was revealed in Liberty Jail, the Restoration was not—and is not—fully finished yet! There is much more to come, as we see in [D&C 121:26–32]. . . .

"Will the faithful then know what ancient Abraham earlier knew? Yes, but also more! Some promised knowledge concerns the astro-physical order of the cosmos, its appointed days and years, the set times, glories, and laws that pertain to the sun, the moon, the stars, and the heavens. Perhaps even more important, we will then learn about matters 'accord-ing to that which was ordained in the midst of the Council of the Eternal God of all other gods before the world was'" (Maxwell, *But for a Small Moment*, 112–13).

27 Which our forefathers have awaited with anxious expectation to be revealed in the last times, which their minds were pointed to by the angels, as held in reserve for the fulness of their glory;

28 A time to come in the which nothing shall be withheld, whether there be one God or many gods, they shall be manifest.

29 All thrones and dominions, principalities and powers, shall be revealed and set forth upon all who have endured valiantly for the gospel of Jesus Christ.

30 And also, if there be bounds set to the heavens or to the seas, or to the dry land, or to the sun, moon, or stars—

31 All the times of their revolutions, all the appointed days, months, and years, and all the days of their days, months, and years, and all their glories, laws, and set times, shall be revealed in the days of the dispensation of the fulness of times—

32 According to that which was ordained in the midst of the Council of the Eternal God of all other gods before this world was, that should be reserved unto the finishing and the end thereof, when every man shall enter into his eternal presence and into his immortal rest.

33 How long can rolling waters remain impure? What power shall stay the heavens? As well might man stretch forth his puny arm to stop the Missouri river in its decreed course, or to turn it up stream, as to hinder the Almighty from pouring down knowledge from heaven upon the heads of the Latter-day Saints.

34 Behold, there are many called, but few are chosen. And why are they not chosen?

35 Because their hearts are set so much upon the things of this world, and aspire to the honors of men, that they do not learn this one lesson—

36 That the rights of the priesthood are inseparably connected with the powers of heaven, and that the powers of heaven cannot be controlled nor handled only upon the principles of righteousness.

Doctrine and Covenants 121:33–40. Why Many Are Called and Few Are Chosen

What is the meaning of "rolling waters"? (121:33)
"[In the non-canonized portion of the letter] the Prophet Joseph first spoke of the filthiness caused by newly rolling water. It was at first full of all kinds of debris and impurities. . . . The Prophet knew that . . . opposition and trial would 'bring to [the Saints] the fountain as clear as crystal, and as pure as snow.' He understood that opposition has a purpose in purifying the moving water.

"In our time, this principle is still true. As a newly converted individual begins to implement the laws of the gospel in his or her life, opposition is often stirred up. However, as the individual continues in righteousness, that opposition has a purifying effect" (Wessel, "Textual Context of Doctrine and Covenants 121–123," 107–8).

What does it mean to be "called" and "chosen"? (121:34–35) Elder David A. Bednar explained what it means to be called and chosen when he referred to the parable of the wedding feast. "*The invitation to* the wedding feast and the *choice to partake in* the feast are related but different. The invitation is to all men and women. An individual may even accept the invitation and sit down at the feast—yet not be chosen to partake because he or she does not have the appropriate wedding garment of converting faith in the Lord Jesus and His divine grace. Thus, we have both God's call and our individual response to that call, and many may be called but few chosen.

"To be or to become chosen is not an exclusive status conferred upon us. Rather, you and I ultimately can choose to be chosen through the righteous exercise of our moral agency" ("Put On Thy Strength, O Zion," *Liahona*, Nov. 2022, 94).

How can we qualify for priesthood power? (121:36) President Russell M. Nelson declared: "Every woman and every man who makes covenants with God and keeps those covenants, and who participates worthily in priesthood ordinances, has direct access to the power of God. Those who are endowed in the house of the Lord receive a gift of God's priesthood power by virtue of their covenant, along with a gift of knowledge to know how to draw upon that power.

"The heavens are just as open to women who are endowed with God's power flowing from their priesthood covenants as they are to men who bear the priesthood. I pray that truth will register upon each of your hearts because I believe it will change your life. Sisters, you have the right to draw liberally upon the Savior's power to help your family and others you love.

"Now, you might be saying to yourself, 'This sounds wonderful, but how do I do it? How do I draw the Savior's power into my life?'

"You won't find this process spelled out in any manual. The Holy Ghost will be your personal tutor as you seek to understand what the Lord would have you know and do. This process is neither quick nor easy, but it is spiritually invigorating. What could possibly be more exciting than to labor with the Spirit to understand God's power—priesthood power?" ("Spiritual Treasures," *Ensign*, Nov. 2019, 77). ⊕

What impact does unrighteous behavior have on a priesthood holder? (121:37) Speaking to a priesthood session of general conference but teaching principles that apply to all, President Gordon B. Hinckley stated: "We who hold the priesthood of God must stand above the ways of the world....

"Our behavior in public must be above reproach. Our behavior in private is even more important. It must clear the standard set by the Lord. We cannot indulge in sin, let alone try to cover our sins....

"If we do any of these things, the powers of heaven are withdrawn. The Spirit of the Lord is grieved. The very virtue of our priesthood is nullified. Its authority is lost.

"The manner of our living, the words we speak, and our everyday behavior have a bearing upon our effectiveness as men and boys holding the priesthood" ("Personal Worthiness to Exercise the Priesthood," *Ensign*, May 2002, 52).

What is the meaning of "kick against the pricks"? (121:38) "A 'prick' refers to a goad, which is a sharp spear or stick used to poke animals to make them move ahead. Rather than move forward, stubborn animals sometimes kick back to retaliate, literally kicking 'against the pricks.' Such a reaction only adds distress as the animal incurs more painful prompting

37 That they may be conferred upon us, it is true; but when we undertake to cover our sins, or to gratify our pride, our vain ambition, or to exercise control or dominion or compulsion upon the souls of the children of men, in any degree of unrighteousness, behold, the heavens withdraw themselves; the Spirit of the Lord is grieved; and when it is withdrawn, Amen to the priesthood or the authority of that man.

38 Behold, ere he is aware, he is left unto himself, to kick against the pricks, to persecute the saints, and to fight against God.

What Is Priesthood Power? (Doctrine and Covenants 121:36)

"Priesthood power is God's power, which He uses to bless His children. God's priesthood power flows to all members of the Church—female and male—as they keep the covenants they have made with Him. Members make these covenants as they receive priesthood ordinances (see Doctrine and Covenants 84:19–20).

"The blessings of priesthood power that members can receive include:

"• Guidance for their lives.

"• Revelation to know how to fulfill the work they are ordained, set apart, or assigned to do.

"• Help and strength to become more like Jesus Christ and Heavenly Father" (*General Handbook* [2023], 3.5).

from its master. The Savior is making clear that if Saul continues to fight against Him, he will only bring distress upon himself. In Greek literature, 'kicking against the pricks' was a well-known metaphor for opposing deity" (*New Testament Student Manual* [2018], 295).

How do we recognize when "unrighteous dominion" is being used? (121:39) "Anytime we try to compel someone to righteousness who *can* and *should* be exercising his or her own moral agency, we are acting unrighteously. . . .

"We simply cannot force others to do the right thing. The scriptures make it clear that this is not God's way. Compulsion builds resentment. It conveys mistrust, and it makes people feel incompetent. Learning opportunities are lost when controlling persons pridefully assume they have all the right answers for others. . . .

"Unrighteous dominion is often accompanied by constant criticism and the withholding of approval or love. Those on the receiving end feel they can never please such leaders or parents and that they always fall short" (Wilson, "Only upon the Principles of Righteousness," *Ensign*, May 2012, 103–4).

39 We have learned by sad experience that it is the nature and disposition of almost all men, as soon as they get a little authority, as they suppose, they will immediately begin to exercise unrighteous dominion.

40 Hence many are called, but few are chosen.

Doctrine and Covenants 121:41–46. The Priesthood Should Be Used Only in Righteousness

Why are the attributes in this passage essential for the proper exercise of the priesthood? (121:41–45) "[God's Spirit] is ever ready to guide and instruct those who tune in by upright living and who sincerely seek him. . . .

"To hold the priesthood of God by divine authority is one of the greatest gifts that can come to a man, and worthiness is of first importance. The very essence of priesthood is eternal. He is greatly blessed who feels the responsibility of representing Deity. He should feel it to such an extent that he would be conscious of his actions and words under all conditions. No man who holds the Holy Priesthood should treat his wife disrespectfully. No man who holds that priesthood should fail to . . . kneel with his wife and children and ask for God's guidance. A home is transformed because a man holds and honors the priesthood" (*David O. McKay* [manual], 118). ●

41 No power or influence can or ought to be maintained by virtue of the priesthood, only by persuasion, by long-suffering, by gentleness and meekness, and by love unfeigned;

42 By kindness, and pure knowledge, which shall greatly enlarge the soul without hypocrisy, and without guile—

How can we act in kindness? (121:42) Sister Elaine L. Jack taught: "We owe each other kindness. Kindness can be shown in so many small ways. The scriptures don't say that we should go on a date with someone we don't choose to be with. They only say we must be kind in saying no to the offer. The scriptures don't say we have to loan money to a brother or sister, or to a roommate. They don't tell us we have to write a paper for a boyfriend, girlfriend, or spouse. They do say clearly that we must be kind about our dealings with one another. Kindness does require that we measure our own responses against a righteous standard. Sometimes kindness means we should keep quiet or leave a situation. Sometimes kindness requires us to remain and try to make things right. Ask yourself before you act or speak, 'Is what I am about to do or say kind?' If it is, proceed confidently. If it isn't, frame another response" ("Get a Life," 251).

What is the meaning of "reproving betimes with sharpness"? (121:43) "Only the Holy Ghost should prompt and authorize a priesthood holder to reprove or chasten another, and then only with clarity and focus. Thereafter, the priesthood holder must clearly demonstrate that the main reason for the correction is love of the individual. . . .

"In this verse, 'reproving' simply means correcting. 'Betimes' means early on, right away, or soon. 'Sharpness' means clarity. The Holy Ghost must be present for 'sharpness' not to be offensive" (Renlund and Renlund, *Melchizedek Priesthood*, 4, 159). ⊕

How does virtue change our perception of others? (121:45) Sister Gladys N. Sitati testified from her life's experiences: "I wish to add here that most things that we fret about—what someone has said about us or done to us—do not contribute to their salvation or to ours. They are things of no consequence compared to what God has for all of us in his glorious realm. Our human exteriors may be different, but inside of us, we are the same. We feel bad when we are treated unfairly by others or when we are dismissed, not respected, or discriminated against. If thinking well of other people does not come easily to us, let us pray for this valuable gift. 'Let virtue garnish thy thoughts unceasingly; then shall thy confidence wax strong in the presence of God'" ("Resolving Conflicts," 338).

How can the "doctrine of the priesthood" distil upon our souls? (121:45) "What, then, is the doctrine of the priesthood? . . .

"It is that we have power, by faith, to govern and control all things, both temporal and spiritual; to work miracles and perfect lives; to stand in the presence of God and be like him because we have gained his faith, his perfections, and his power, or in other words the

43 Reproving betimes with sharpness, when moved upon by the Holy Ghost; and then showing forth afterwards an increase of love toward him whom thou hast reproved, lest he esteem thee to be his enemy;

44 That he may know that thy faithfulness is stronger than the cords of death.

45 Let thy bowels also be full of charity towards all men, and to the household of faith, and let virtue garnish thy thoughts unceasingly; then shall thy confidence wax strong in the presence of God; and the doctrine of the priesthood shall distil upon thy soul as the dews from heaven.

46 The Holy Ghost shall be thy constant companion, and thy scepter an unchanging scepter of righteousness and truth; and thy dominion shall be an everlasting dominion, and without compulsory means it shall flow unto thee forever and ever.

fullness of his priesthood" (Bruce R. McConkie, "Doctrine of the Priesthood," *Ensign*, May 1982, 33, 34).

What is the "unchanging scepter of righteousness and truth"? (121:46) "References to a scepter [in the Doctrine and Covenants], unless specifically identified as an actual rod or staff, are metaphorical expressions of supreme power. The scepter of Jesus Christ is one of righteousness (Heb. 1:8), and those who take the Holy Ghost as their constant companion are promised 'an unchanging scepter of righteousness and truth' (D&C 121:46). In other words, such faithful ones are filled with great spiritual power and understanding.

"Just as kings often have tangible scepters to demonstrate their earthly authority, those who hold keys of authority from the King of kings symbolically hold scepters of spiritual power (see D&C 85:7)" (Brewster, *Doctrine & Covenants Encyclopedia* [2012], 495).

Introduction to Doctrine and Covenants 122

"Through the winter of 1838–39, the Prophet Joseph Smith and his companions suffered in the unheated and filthy environment of Liberty Jail. Added to their misery was the fact that they could not help their families and other Church members who were being driven from Missouri without adequate provisions in the middle of a bitter winter. . . . It was under these extremely difficult conditions that the Prophet Joseph Smith sought for and eventually received comfort and spiritual understanding from the Lord. On March 20, 1839, the Prophet dictated a letter to Bishop Edward Partridge and Church members in Quincy, Illinois, and in other locations. It was followed approximately two days later by another letter to Bishop Partridge and the Saints, in which the Prophet offered comfort and provided counsel. . . . Portions of these letters are recorded in Doctrine and Covenants 121–23" (*Doctrine and Covenants Student Manual* [2018], 679).

"Section 122 takes up where 121 ends, and though directed to the Saints, it is given as an individual experience—most likely a burst of insight or comprehension which came as [the Prophet Joseph Smith] dictated the letter, all the while pondering past events that made it necessary and the circumstances from which it was emerging. It is, nevertheless, stated in a manner that each member upon reading it or hearing it read could identify with its message in a personal way. Though included here [as section 122], it is closely identified with those parts of the letter which now appear as vv. 1–25 of section 121" (Christianson, "Ray of Light in an Hour of Darkness," 472).

SECTION 122

The word of the Lord to Joseph Smith the Prophet, while a prisoner in the jail at Liberty, Missouri. This section is an excerpt from an epistle to the Church dated March 20, 1839 (see the heading to section 121).

1 The ends of the earth shall inquire after thy name, and fools shall have thee in derision, and hell shall rage against thee;

Doctrine and Covenants 122:1–4. The Ends of the Earth Will Inquire after the Name of Joseph Smith

Why has there always been opposition to the Prophet Joseph Smith? (122:1–2) "Opposition, criticism, and antagonism are companions to the truth. Whenever the truth with regard to the purpose and destiny of man is revealed, there will always be a force to oppose it. . . . [There] has always been and will ever be an effort to deceive, derail, oppose, and frustrate the plan of life. . . .

"Look for one who brought forth another testament of Jesus Christ and other scripture, look for one who was the instrument by which the fulness of the gospel and the Church of Jesus Christ were restored to the earth, look for him and expect to find the dirt flying....

"Why? Because he taught the truth, and the truth will always be opposed" (Corbridge, "Prophet Joseph Smith," *Ensign*, May 2014, 104).

Doctrine and Covenants 122:5–7. All the Prophet's Perils and Travails Will Give Him Experience and Be for His Good

What was the significance of the trials the Lord listed in this passage? (122:5–7) "The events described in these verses had already happened to Joseph. He had been abandoned by his brethren and accused falsely.... [The Prophet later recorded,] 'Who can realize the feelings which I experienced at that time, to be thus torn from my companion, and leave her surrounded with monsters in the shape of men, and my children, too, not knowing how their wants would be supplied.... My partner wept, my children clung to me, until they were thrust from me by the swords of the guards' [Joseph Smith Papers, "History,

2 While the pure in heart, and the wise, and the noble, and the virtuous, shall seek counsel, and authority, and blessings constantly from under thy hand.

3 And thy people shall never be turned against thee by the testimony of traitors.

4 And although their influence shall cast thee into trouble, and into bars and walls, thou shalt be had in honor; and but for a small moment and thy voice shall be more terrible in the midst of thine enemies than the fierce lion, because of thy righteousness; and thy God shall stand by thee forever and ever.

5 If thou art called to pass through tribulation; if thou art in perils among false brethren; if thou art in perils among robbers; if thou art in perils by land or by sea;

6 If thou art accused with all manner of false accusations; if thine enemies fall upon thee; if they tear thee from the society of thy father and mother and brethren and sisters; and if with a drawn sword thine enemies tear thee from the bosom of thy wife, and of thine

"Thy Voice Shall Be More Terrible . . . Than the Fierce Lion" (Doctrine and Covenants 122:4)

Elder Parley P. Pratt was with Joseph Smith in early November 1838 when he was imprisoned in Richmond, Missouri, prior to being taken to the Clay County jail in Liberty, Missouri. Elder Pratt witnessed the Prophet confront his enemies in remarkable power:

"In one of those tedious nights we had lain as if in sleep till the hour of midnight had passed, and our ears and hearts had been pained, while we had listened for hours to the obscene jests, the horrid oaths, the dreadful blasphemies and filthy language of our guards....

"I had listened till I became so disgusted, shocked, horrified, and so filled with the spirit of indignant justice that I could scarcely refrain from rising upon my feet and rebuking the guards; but had said nothing to Joseph,... although I lay next to him and knew he was awake. On a sudden he arose to his feet, and spoke in a voice of thunder, or as the roaring lion, uttering, as near as I can recollect, the following words:

"'SILENCE, ye fiends of the infernal pit. In the name of Jesus Christ I rebuke you, and command you to be still; I will not live another minute and hear such language. Cease such talk, or you or I die THIS INSTANT!'

"He ceased to speak. He stood erect in terrible majesty. Chained, and without a weapon; calm, unruffled and dignified as an angel, he looked upon the quailing guards, whose knees smote together, and who, shrinking into a corner, or crouching at his feet, begged his pardon, and remained quiet till a change of guards.

"I have seen the ministers of justice, clothed in magisterial robes, ... while life was suspended on a breath, in the Courts of England; I have witnessed a Congress in solemn session to give laws to nations; I have tried to conceive of kings, of royal courts, of thrones and crowns; and of emperors assembled to decide the fate of kingdoms; but dignity and majesty have I seen but *once*, as it stood in chains, at midnight, in a dungeon in an obscure village of Missouri" (*Autobiography of Parley P. Pratt*, 210–11).

offspring, and thine elder son, although but six years of age, shall cling to thy garments, and shall say, My father, my father, why can't you stay with us? O, my father, what are the men going to do with you? and if then he shall be thrust from thee by the sword, and thou be dragged to prison, and thine enemies prowl around thee like wolves for the blood of the lamb;

7 And if thou shouldst be cast into the pit, or into the hands of murderers, and the sentence of death passed upon thee; if thou be cast into the deep; if the billowing surge conspire against thee; if fierce winds become thine enemy; if the heavens gather blackness, and all the elements combine to hedge up the way; and above all, if the very jaws of hell shall gape open the mouth wide after thee, know thou, my son, that all these things shall give thee experience, and shall be for thy good.

1838–1856, volume B-1," 849]. Literally in 'the hands of murderers,' Joseph and his companions were 'dragged to prison' and eventually 'cast into the pit' at Liberty Jail" (Robinson and Garrett, *Commentary on the Doctrine and Covenants*, 4:171–72).

How was Joseph Smith able to endure the tribulation described in this passage? (122:7) "The Prophet Joseph Smith provided a model in handling personal tragedy and opposition....

"[After his experience in Liberty Jail,] Joseph Smith continued to righteously endure a life full of adversity. He offered this faith-filled perspective: 'And as for the perils which I am called to pass through, they seem but a small thing to me.... Deep water is what I am wont to swim in.... I... glory in tribulation; for ... God ... [has] delivered me out of them all, and will deliver me from henceforth' (D&C 127:2). Joseph's confidence in overcoming constant opposition was based on his ability to continually turn to the Lord" (Hallstrom, "Turn to the Lord," *Ensign*, May 2010, 80). ⊕

How can we manage living through difficult experiences? (122:7) Isaac K. Morrison stated: "Reflecting on my own experiences, I realize I have learned some of my best lessons during the hardest times in my life, times that took me out of my comfort zone. Difficulties I encountered as a youth, while learning about the Church through seminary, as a recent convert, and as a full-time missionary and challenges I faced in my education, in striving to magnify my callings, and in raising a family have prepared me for the future. The more I cheerfully respond to difficult circumstances with faith in the Lord, the more I grow in my discipleship.

"The hard things in our lives should come as no surprise once we have entered the strait and narrow path. Jesus Christ learned 'obedience by the things which he suffered.' As we follow Him, especially in our difficult times, we can grow to become more like Him" ("We Can Do Hard Things through Him," *Liahona*, Nov. 2022, 116). See also commentary in this volume on Doctrine and Covenants 127:2. ⊕

Doctrine and Covenants 122:8–9. The Son of Man Has Descended below Them All

8 The Son of Man hath descended below them all. Art thou greater than he?

How did Jesus Christ descend below all things? (122:8) "Uniquely, atoning Jesus ... 'descended below all things, in that he comprehended all things' (D&C 88:6; see also D&C 122:8). How deep that descent into despair and abysmal agony must have been! He did it to rescue us and in order to comprehend human suffering. Therefore, let us not resent those tutoring experiences which can develop our own empathy further (see Alma 7:11–12). A slothful heart will not do, and neither will a resentful heart. So being admitted fully to 'the fellowship of his sufferings' requires the full dues of discipleship (Philip. 3:10; see also 1 Cor. 1:9)" (Maxwell, "Plow in Hope," *Ensign*, May 2001, 60).

How can we "hold on [our] way" when we experience adversity? (122:9) Sister Tamara W. Runia taught: "As humans, we have an earthbound point of view, but God sees the grand overview of the universe. He sees all creation, all of us, and is filled with hope.

"Is it possible to begin to see as God sees even while living on the surface of this planet—to feel this *overview* feeling? I believe we can, through the eye of faith, zoom out and view ourselves and our families with hope and joy.

"The scriptures agree. Moroni speaks about those whose faith was so 'exceedingly strong' that they 'truly saw . . . with an eye of faith, *and they were glad*' [Ether 12:19; emphasis added].

"With an eye focused on the Savior, they felt joy and knew this truth: because of Christ, it all works out. Everything *you* and *you* and *you* are worried about— it's all going to be OK! And those who look with an eye of faith can *feel* that it's going to be OK *now*" ("Seeing God's Family," *Liahona*, Nov. 2023, 62).

9 Therefore, hold on thy way, and the priesthood shall remain with thee; for their bounds are set, they cannot pass. Thy days are known, and thy years shall not be numbered less; therefore, fear not what man can do, for God shall be with you forever and ever.

Introduction to Doctrine and Covenants 123

"While Joseph Smith was incarcerated in Liberty Jail from December 1, 1838, to April 6, 1839, he wrote eight surviving letters in his own hand. Four were addressed to Emma, his wife, and all of them display the sterling character of the Prophet Joseph under trials of the most extreme conditions imaginable. His letter of March 20, 1839, directed to 'the church of Latter-day saints at Quincy, Illinois and scattered abroad and to Bishop Partridge in particular,' is one of the most revealing and most significant letters ever written by a prophet of God in the dispensation of the fullness of times. Embedded in this lengthy letter, which was written in two parts on twenty-nine sheets of paper, are the words now contained in sections 121–23 of the Doctrine and Covenants" (Jessee and Welch, "Revelations in Context," 125).

"The saints were counseled to gather information pertaining to the abuses that were inflicted upon them by their enemies in Missouri (see D&C 123:1–5). The purposes for gathering such information were revealed by the Lord as follows: (see D&C 123:6–13)

"a. That they might publish such information to the heads of government and to all the world.

"b. That the nation might be left without excuse.

"c. That the saints might be justified in calling upon the Lord to send forth His power in their behalf.

"d. That the saints might fulfill their duty before the Lord, angels, wives, children, and the rising generation.

"Whatever total use the Lord may make of this information in the future, we do not know. We do know it was essential to the Lord's plans" (Otten and Caldwell, *Sacred Truths*, 2:306–7).

SECTION 123

Duty of the Saints in relation to their persecutors, as written by Joseph Smith the Prophet while a prisoner in the jail at Liberty, Missouri. This section is an excerpt from an epistle to the Church dated March 20, 1839 (see the heading to section 121).

1 And again, we would suggest for your consideration the propriety of all the saints gathering up a knowledge of all the facts, and sufferings and abuses put upon them by the people of this State;

2 And also of all the property and amount of damages which they have sustained, both of character and personal injuries, as well as real property;

3 And also the names of all persons that have had a hand in their oppressions, as far as they can get hold of them and find them out.

4 And perhaps a committee can be appointed to find out these things, and to take statements and affidavits; and also to gather up the libelous publications that are afloat;

5 And all that are in the magazines, and in the encyclopedias, and all the libelous histories that are published, and are writing, and by whom, and present the whole concatenation of diabolical rascality and nefarious and murderous impositions that have been practiced upon this people—

6 That we may not only publish to all the world, but present them to the heads of government in all their dark and hellish hue, as the last effort which is enjoined on us by our Heavenly Father, before we can fully and completely claim that promise which shall call him forth from his hiding place; and also that the whole nation may be left without excuse before he can send forth the power of his mighty arm.

Doctrine and Covenants 123:1–6. The Saints Should Collect and Publish an Account of Their Sufferings and Persecutions

Why were the Saints told to gather accounts of their suffering and persecution? (123:1–4) "[Joseph Smith] instructed the Saints to assemble all their grievances against Missouri, to organize a committee, and to present the information to the U.S. government (D&C 123:1–6). Joseph sent word to the Saints to prepare affidavits of their recent experiences with the design of securing redress from the federal government for the losses they had suffered in Missouri at the hands of mobocrats. In 1839, Church members commenced writing affidavits of their Missouri experiences and swearing to their authenticity before civil authorities, including justices of the peace, clerks of the court, clerks of the circuit court, clerks of county commissioner's courts, and notary publics in two counties in Iowa and ten counties in Illinois" (Clark V. Johnson, *Mormon Redress Petitions*, xix).

What is the meaning of "concatenation of diabolical rascality"? (123:5) "In this instance, *concatenation* was referred to as connections (like links in a chain) to describe the suffering of the Latter-day Saints at the hands of wicked men. Although such rascality was unbecoming of even the vilest of men, the First Presidency of the Church in April 1911 wrote of a positive outcome from the evil intent: 'It is impossible to take up all the misrepresentations given to the world by anti–"Mormon" preachers and writers. They have one merit. They stir up interest in what is called the "Mormon" question. People are led thus to investigate and many of them find out the truth, and unite with the people who are so greatly maligned' [in Conference Report, Apr. 1911, 130]" (Black, *400 Questions and Answers*, 208).

Doctrine and Covenants 123:7–10. The Same Spirit That Established the False Creeds Also Leads to Persecution of the Saints

What is the "spirit" that has brought so much persecution to the Saints? (123:7–10) "Opposition to God and His Christ, opposition to light and truth has existed since the beginning to the present day. This is the warfare that commenced in heaven, that has existed through all time, and that will continue until the winding up scene, until He reigns whose right it is to reign, when He shall come in clouds of glory to reward every man according to the deeds done in the body.

"The spirit of warfare that is manifested in these days has existed in all ages when the priesthood was upon the earth. There was always a war between light and darkness, God and the devil, saint and sinner, correct principles and false doctrines" (*Wilford Woodruff* [manual], 219–20). ⊕

Doctrine and Covenants 123:11–17. Many among All Sects Will Yet Receive the Truth

How can we help those who are kept from the truth to find it? (123:11–13) "My dear friends, why is shining our light so important? The Lord has told us that 'there are many yet on the earth . . . who are only kept from the truth because they know not where to find it' (D&C 123:12). We can help. We can intentionally shine our light so others may see. We can extend an invitation. We can walk the journey with those who are taking a step toward the Savior, no matter how halting. We can gather Israel" (Cordon, "That They May See," *Ensign*, May 2020, 80). ⊕

7 It is an imperative duty that we owe to God, to angels, with whom we shall be brought to stand, and also to ourselves, to our wives and children, who have been made to bow down with grief, sorrow, and care, under the most damning hand of murder, tyranny, and oppression, supported and urged on and upheld by the influence of that spirit which hath so strongly riveted the creeds of the fathers, who have inherited lies, upon the hearts of the children, and filled the world with confusion, and has been growing stronger and stronger, and is now the very mainspring of all corruption, and the whole earth groans under the weight of its iniquity.

8 It is an iron yoke, it is a strong band; they are the very handcuffs, and chains, and shackles, and fetters of hell.

9 Therefore it is an imperative duty that we owe, not only to our own wives and children, but to the widows and fatherless, whose husbands and fathers have been murdered under its iron hand;

10 Which dark and blackening deeds are enough to make hell itself shudder, and to stand aghast and pale, and the hands of the very devil to tremble and palsy.

11 And also it is an imperative duty that we owe to all the rising generation, and to all the pure in heart—

12 For there are many yet on the earth among all sects, parties, and denominations, who are blinded by the subtle craftiness of men, whereby they lie in wait to deceive, and who are only kept from the truth because they know not where to find it—

13 Therefore, that we should waste and wear out our lives in bringing to light all the hidden things of darkness, wherein we know them; and they are truly manifest from heaven—

14 These should then be attended to with great earnestness.

15 Let no man count them as small things; for there is much which lieth in futurity, pertaining to the saints, which depends upon these things.

16 You know, brethren, that a very large ship is benefited very much by a very small helm in the time of a storm, by being kept workways with the wind and the waves.

17 Therefore, dearly beloved brethren, let us cheerfully do all things that lie in our power; and then may we stand still, with the utmost assurance, to see the salvation of God, and for his arm to be revealed.

What is a helm and how might it benefit us? (123:16) "A 'helm' is a wheel or tiller and the associated equipment used to steer a ship or boat. And 'workways with the wind and the waves' denotes turning a ship so that it maintains its balance and does not capsize during a storm.

"Gospel principles are for me and you what a helm is to a ship. Correct principles enable us to find our way and to stand firm, steadfast, and immovable so we do not lose our balance and fall in the raging latter-day storms of darkness and confusion" (Bednar, "Principles of My Gospel," *Liahona*, May 2021, 126).

Why can we be cheerful during adversity? (123:16–17) "Sometimes [the Lord] removes the affliction, sometimes He strengthens us to endure, and sometimes He gives us an eternal perspective to better understand their temporary nature. . . .

"[After suffering and pleading with the Lord in Liberty Jail,] Joseph . . . understood that this bitter experience was but a dot on the eternal spectrum. With this enhanced vision, he wrote the Saints from that same prison cell, 'Dearly beloved brethren, let us cheerfully do all things that lie in our power; and then may we stand still, with the utmost assurance, to see the salvation of God.' Because of the Savior's Atonement, we can have an eternal perspective that gives meaning to our trials and hope for our relief" (Callister, "Atonement of Jesus Christ," *Ensign*, May 2019, 86, 87). ◉

Introduction to Doctrine and Covenants 124

"On 19 January 1841, [the Prophet Joseph Smith] dictated a revelation in Nauvoo, Illinois [D&C 124], designating the city as the new gathering place for the Latter-day Saints. The revelation initially addressed [Joseph Smith] personally before instructing other individuals and the Saints generally. Over the coming years, the lengthy revelation would function as a sort of sacred charter for the Saints in Nauvoo. . . .

"Since their expulsion from northern Missouri in winter 1838–1839, the Saints had devoted much of their time to resettling in the area of Commerce, Illinois, where they cleared the heavily forested peninsula, drained the swampy flats along the Mississippi River, planted crops, and built homes for the rapid influx of church members. Consequently, winter 1840–1841 provided church leaders the first real opportunity after the disruptive expulsion from Missouri to formally organize the new community and to restructure the church. The timing and content of the January revelation came after a series of efforts over the preceding months to seek incorporation of both the city and church from the Illinois legislature. . . .

"This revelation assured church members that relocating to Illinois did not entail abandoning their efforts to establish Zion in Missouri. The revelation stated that Nauvoo was to be 'a corner stone of Zion' (or a 'stake') of Zion) but not Zion itself. . . .

"In order to have somewhere to host the anticipated distinguished visitors, the 'weary traveler,' or anyone coming to Nauvoo to 'contemplate the word of the Lord,' the revelation directed that a boardinghouse be built. The revelation devoted more space to the subject of building this 'Nauvoo House' than to any other topic. . . .

"In some cases, rather than giving new instruction, the revelation provided formal approval and authority to earlier decisions and actions. The commandment to build a temple in Nauvoo, for instance, gave divine mandate to an instruction that [Joseph Smith] had been voicing publicly for over half a year. The revelation underscored the importance of building a temple in Nauvoo by declaring that certain ordinances—like baptisms for the dead—were appropriately performed only in the temple. . . .

"One of the few revelations from the Illinois period to be later canonized by the church, the 19 January revelation served as divine direction for the Saints for the duration of their time in Nauvoo" (Joseph Smith Papers, Historical Introduction to "Revelation, 19 January 1841 [D&C 124]").

Doctrine and Covenants 124:1–14. Joseph Smith Is Commanded to Make a Solemn Proclamation of the Gospel to the President of the United States, the Governors, and the Rulers of All Nations

Why does the Lord call upon the weak of the earth to "show forth [His] wisdom"? (124:1) "It may seem counterintuitive that the Lord would call upon the weak to accomplish a mighty work. Yet those who recognize their weakness can be moved by that very weakness to seek the Lord's strength. Those who thus humble themselves in faith will be strengthened by Him who has all power in heaven and earth (see Matthew 28:18; Mosiah 4:9). . . .

"In a literal sense it is *out of weakness* that Joseph was made strong. Motivated in part by his weakness, he sought the help of God in faith, determined to act according to His will. . . .

"So do not be discouraged; the process of being made strong is gradual and requires patience with

SECTION 124

Revelation given to Joseph Smith the Prophet, at Nauvoo, Illinois, January 19, 1841. Because of increasing persecutions and illegal procedures against them by public officers, the Saints had been compelled to leave Missouri. The exterminating order issued by Lilburn W. Boggs, governor of Missouri, dated October 27, 1838, had left them no alternative. In 1841, when this revelation was given, the city of Nauvoo, occupying the site of the former village of Commerce, Illinois, had been built up by the Saints, and here the headquarters of the Church had been established.

1 Verily, thus saith the Lord unto you, my servant Joseph Smith, I am well pleased with your offering and acknowledgments, which you have made; for unto this end have I raised you up, that I might show forth my wisdom through the weak things of the earth.

2 Your prayers are acceptable before me; and in answer to them I say unto you, that you are now called immediately to make a solemn proclamation of my gospel, and of this stake which I have planted to be a cornerstone of Zion, which shall be polished with the refinement which is after the similitude of a palace.

3 This proclamation shall be made to all the kings of the world, to the four corners thereof, to the honorable president-elect, and the high-minded governors of the nation in which you live, and to all the nations of the earth scattered abroad.

4 Let it be written in the spirit of meekness and by the power of the Holy Ghost, which shall be in you at the time of the writing of the same;

5 For it shall be given you by the Holy Ghost to know my will concerning those kings and authorities, even what shall befall them in a time to come.

6 For, behold, I am about to call upon them to give heed to the light and glory of Zion, for the set time has come to favor her.

7 Call ye, therefore, upon them with loud proclamation, and with your testimony, fearing them not, for they are as grass, and all their glory as the flower thereof which soon falleth, that they may be left also without excuse—

8 And that I may visit them in the day of visitation, when I shall unveil the face of my covering, to appoint the portion of the oppressor among hypocrites, where there is gnashing of teeth, if they reject my servants and my testimony which I have revealed unto them.

a steadfast determination to follow the Savior and abide by His will, come what may" (Marcus B. Nash, "Joseph Smith," *Ensign*, Dec. 2017, 55, 60).

In what ways was Nauvoo a "cornerstone" of Zion? (124:2) "Nauvoo can be considered a cornerstone stake because it had community ideal, a revealed civic plan, ecclesiastical structure even more so than before, and most importantly it had a temple that offered the full endowment where individuals could receive every blessing pertaining to exaltation. This pattern seems to be acceptable to the Lord. Therefore, the Nauvoo stake could be called a cornerstone of Zion. It was a model or prototype. A pattern for future city-stakes yet to be created" (Jenkins, *New Jerusalem*, 72).

Why is it imperative we continue to call upon nations and their leaders in our day? (124:7) "The Lord has chosen a royal Priesthood and a holy people from among the weak things of the world, in fulfillment of his revelations; and we have been commanded to go forth and bear record of these things, and we have done it. We should have been condemned and the curse of God would have rested upon us if we had not, because the full set time has come to build up and favor Zion, to build up the kingdom of God, to warn the world and prepare them for the judgments of the Almighty. The Millennium is dawning upon the world, we are at the end of the sixth thousand years, and the great day of rest, the Millennium of which the Lord has spoken, will soon dawn and the Savior will come in the clouds of heaven to reign over his people on the earth one thousand years" (Woodruff, in *Journal of Discourses*, 18:113).

Why would civic leaders be referenced as grass? (124:7–8) "It is natural to common mortals to 'look up' to kings and potentates with a feeling of timidity and awe.... [However,] the servants of the Lord are encouraged to proclaim the Gospel to kings and rulers without fear, for 'they are as grass.' Their power and glory are transient. The gospel is the only permanent factor in human history. The Priesthood is eternal" (Smith and Sjodahl, *Doctrine and Covenants Commentary*, 769).

Who was Robert B. Thompson? (124:12–14) "Robert [B. Thompson] was born on October 1, 1811, at Great Driffield, Yorkshire, England. He was a Methodist preacher before immigrating to Canada in 1834. Through the missionary work of Parley P. Pratt, Robert joined the Church in May 1836 and then journeyed to Kirtland the following year before returning to Canada on a mission.... [He] served as a scribe for the Prophet Joseph Smith. Robert also served as general clerk for the Church....

"[He] assisted Don Carlos Smith as associate editor of the *Times and Seasons*. He was suddenly overcome with a serious illness (the same that had taken the life of Don Carlos Smith) and passed away on August 27, 1841, at the age of twenty-nine" (Pinegar and Allen, *Doctrine and Covenants Who's Who*, 160).

9 And again, I will visit and soften their hearts, many of them for your good, that ye may find grace in their eyes, that they may come to the light of truth, and the Gentiles to the exaltation or lifting up of Zion.

10 For the day of my visitation cometh speedily, in an hour when ye think not of; and where shall be the safety of my people, and refuge for those who shall be left of them?

11 Awake, O kings of the earth! Come ye, O, come ye, with your gold and your silver, to the help of my people, to the house of the daughters of Zion.

12 And again, verily I say unto you, let my servant Robert B. Thompson help you to write this proclamation, for I am well pleased with him, and that he should be with you;

13 Let him, therefore, hearken to your counsel, and I will bless him with a multiplicity of blessings; let him be faithful and true in all things from henceforth, and he shall be great in mine eyes;

14 But let him remember that his stewardship will I require at his hands.

"A Solemn Proclamation of My Gospel" (Doctrine and Covenants 124:2–12)

When and how was this proclamation sent to the civic leaders of the world?

"The Lord commanded the Prophet Joseph Smith to 'make a solemn proclamation of [His] gospel' to the leaders of 'all the nations of the earth' (D&C 124:2–3). He said that He would 'visit and soften their hearts, ... that they may come to the light of truth, and the Gentiles to the exaltation or lifting up of Zion' (D&C 124:9). In writing the proclamation, the Prophet was to follow the inspiration he would receive 'by power of the Holy Ghost' (D&C 124:4) and boldly proclaim the truth, 'fearing them not' (D&C 124:7)....

"Although the Prophet Joseph Smith worked on writing this proclamation, other concerns and challenges took precedence, including the construction of the Nauvoo Temple. Also, Robert B. Thompson, whom the Lord had commanded to assist the Prophet in writing the proclamation, died unexpectedly in August 1841. As a result, the proclamation was not written until after the Prophet Joseph Smith's death....

"In the October 1975 general conference, President Ezra Taft Benson ... quoted from this proclamation and then reaffirmed its central message: 'To the rulers and peoples of all nations, we solemnly declare again that the God of heaven has established his latter-day kingdom upon the earth in fulfillment of prophecies. Holy angels have

15 And again, verily I say unto you, blessed is my servant Hyrum Smith; for I, the Lord, love him because of the integrity of his heart, and because he loveth that which is right before me, saith the Lord.

16 Again, let my servant John C. Bennett help you in your labor in sending my word to the kings and people of the earth, and stand by you, even you my servant Joseph Smith, in the hour of affliction; and his reward shall not fail if he receive counsel.

17 And for his love he shall be great, for he shall be mine if he do this, saith the Lord. I have seen the work which he hath done, which I accept if he continue, and will crown him with blessings and great glory.

Doctrine and Covenants 124:15–21. Hyrum Smith, David W. Patten, Joseph Smith Sr., and Others among the Living and the Dead Are Blessed for Their Integrity and Virtues

What do we know of Hyrum Smith's character? (124:15) Joseph Smith said of his older brother Hyrum: "I could pray in my heart that all my brethren were like unto my beloved brother Hyrum, who possesses the mildness of a lamb and the integrity of a Job, and in short the meekness and humility of Christ, and I love him with that love that is stronger than death" (Joseph Smith Papers, "Journal, 1835–1836," 76).

John Taylor, who was an eyewitness to the character and martyrdom of Hyrum, said: "If ever there was an exemplary, honest, and virtuous man, an embodiment of all that is noble in human form, Hyrum Smith was its representative" (Joseph Smith Papers, "John Taylor, Martyrdom Account," 53). See also commentary in this volume on Doctrine and Covenants 11:10–14, 22. ⊕

What counsel was given to John C. Bennett? (124:16–17) "John C. Bennett, Nauvoo's first mayor and later a member of the First Presidency, was promised that his 'reward shall not fail if he receive counsel.' But he apostatized only a year and a half later and became a bitter opponent of the Church" (Alex D. Smith, "Organizing the Church in Nauvoo," 269). ⊕

again communed with men on the earth. God has again revealed himself from heaven and restored to the earth his holy priesthood with power to administer in all the sacred ordinances necessary for the exaltation of his children. His church has been reestablished among men with all the spiritual gifts enjoyed anciently. All this is done in preparation for Christ's second coming. The great and dreadful day of the Lord is near at hand. In preparation for this great event and as a means of escaping the impending judgments, inspired messengers have gone, and are now going, forth to the nations of the earth carrying this testimony and warning. . . .

"'. . . As humble servants of the Lord, we call upon the leaders of nations to humble themselves before God, to seek his inspiration and guidance. We call upon rulers and people alike to repent of their evil ways. Turn unto the Lord, seek his forgiveness, and unite yourselves in humility with his kingdom. There is no other way. If you will do this, your sins will be blotted out, peace will come and remain, and you will become a part of the kingdom of God in preparation for Christ's second coming' ([*"*Message to the World," *Ensign*, Nov. 1975, 33–34])" (*Doctrine and Covenants Student Manual* [2018], 710).

18 And again, I say unto you that it is my will that my servant Lyman Wight should continue in preaching for Zion, in the spirit of meekness, confessing me before the world; and I will bear him up as on eagles' wings; and he shall beget glory and honor to himself and unto my name.

19 That when he shall finish his work I may receive him unto myself, even as I did my servant David Patten, who is with me at this time, and also my servant Edward Partridge, and also my aged servant Joseph Smith, Sen., who sitteth with Abraham at his right hand, and blessed and holy is he, for he is mine.

What might it mean that these three men had been received by the Lord? (124:19) "David Patten, Edward Partridge, and Joseph Smith Sr., named in this verse, had all died. David Patten died on 25 October 1838, at Crooked River, Missouri (see D&C 116), Bishop Edward Partridge died in Nauvoo on 27 December 1840, and Father Smith died in Nauvoo on 14 September 1840. This verse was undoubtedly reassuring to the families of these men and the Saints generally, as it indicated that these brethren were accepted before God and enjoying his presence" (Robinson and Garrett, *Commentary on the Doctrine and Covenants*, 4:185).

Who was George Miller and what became of him? (124:20–21) "George [Miller] was born on November 25, 1794, in Orange County, Virginia. Having heard the Prophet Joseph Smith preach, he became converted and was baptized on August 10, 1839. . . .

"In [D&C 124:20–23, 62, 70] George, a carpenter by trade, was called to assist in the construction of the Nauvoo House. . . . His association with the Prophet Joseph Smith was always very close. However, he later had differences with Brigham Young over administrative issues associated with the exodus and thus resigned from the Church in March 1847" (Pinegar and Allen, *Doctrine and Covenants Who's Who*, 99, 100).

Doctrine and Covenants 124:22–28. The Saints Are Commanded to Build Both a House for the Entertainment of Strangers and a Temple in Nauvoo

What is this "house for boarding" for strangers? (124:22–24) "The Spirit of Revelation direct[ed] the Saints to build a fine hotel for the entertainment of strangers. There is no greater inducement for travelers to visit a place than good hotel accommodations. This Revelation proves that the Lord wanted the tourists of the world to visit and become acquainted with the Saints. These were not to be surrounded by a wall of isolation. They had nothing to hide from the world" (Smith and Sjodahl, *Doctrine and Covenants Commentary*, 772–73). ◐

20 And again, verily I say unto you, my servant George Miller is without guile; he may be trusted because of the integrity of his heart; and for the love which he has to my testimony I, the Lord, love him.

21 I therefore say unto you, I seal upon his head the office of a bishopric, like unto my servant Edward Partridge, that he may receive the consecrations of mine house, that he may administer blessings upon the heads of the poor of my people, saith the Lord. Let no man despise my servant George, for he shall honor me.

22 Let my servant George, and my servant Lyman, and my servant John Snider, and others, build a house unto my name, such a one as my servant Joseph shall show unto them, upon the place which he shall show unto them also.

23 And it shall be for a house for boarding, a house that strangers may come from afar to lodge therein; therefore let it be a good house, worthy of all acceptation, that the weary traveler may find health and safety while he shall contemplate the word of the Lord; and the cornerstone I have appointed for Zion.

24 This house shall be a healthful habitation if it be built unto my name, and if the governor which shall be appointed unto it shall not suffer any pollution to come upon it. It shall be holy, or the Lord your God will not dwell therein.

25 And again, verily I say unto you, let all my saints come from afar.

26 And send ye swift messengers, yea, chosen messengers, and say unto them: Come ye, with all your gold, and your silver, and your precious stones, and with all your antiquities; and with all who have knowledge of antiquities, that will come, may come, and bring the box tree, and the fir tree, and the pine tree, together with all the precious trees of the earth;

27 And with iron, with copper, and with brass, and with zinc, and with all your precious things of the earth; and build a house to my name, for the Most High to dwell therein.

28 For there is not a place found on earth that he may come to and restore again that which was lost unto you, or which he hath taken away, even the fulness of the priesthood.

29 For a baptismal font there is not upon the earth, that they, my saints, may be baptized for those who are dead—

30 For this ordinance belongeth to my house, and cannot be acceptable to me, only in the days of your poverty, wherein ye are not able to build a house unto me.

What did the Lord intend to restore in the Nauvoo Temple? (124:27–28) "Temple ordinances and covenants are ancient. The Lord instructed Adam and Eve to pray, make covenants, and offer sacrifices. . . . The standard works are replete with references to temple teachings, clothing, language, and more. *Everything* we believe and *every* promise God has made to His covenant people come together in the temple. In *every* age, the temple has underscored the precious truth that those who make covenants with God and keep them are children of the covenant.

"Thus, in the house of the Lord, we can make the same covenants with God that Abraham, Isaac, and Jacob made. And we can receive the same blessings!" (Nelson, "Temple and Your Spiritual Foundation," *Liahona*, Nov. 2021, 94).

Doctrine and Covenants 124:29–36. Baptisms for the Dead Are to Be Performed in Temples

What is unique about the baptismal font mentioned in verses 29–30? (124:29–30) "Until the time of the building [of] the Nauvoo Temple, there was no baptismal font any place on the earth where baptisms for the dead could be performed. . . . The Lord gave the commandment that one be placed in the Nauvoo Temple. There was no font in the Kirtland Temple, because the work of salvation for the dead had not been revealed when that Temple was built. For a short time, while a place in the Nauvoo Temple was being prepared, the Lord granted the saints the privilege of being baptized for their dead in the Mississippi River" (Smith and Sjodahl, *Doctrine and Covenants Commentary*, 776). See also commentary in this volume on Doctrine and Covenants 128:12–13.

What can we learn from the Lord's emphasis on His house in these verses? (124:31–36) "Among the thousands of verses of scripture in the standard works of the Church, few are more important to Latter-day Saints than those found in three sections of the Doctrine and Covenants and in a single verse of Paul's writings (D&C 124:28–42; D&C 127:6; D&C 128:11–18; 1 Cor. 15:29). Each of these deals with the topic of baptism for the dead and, by extension, all vicarious ordinance work for our deceased ancestors. . . .

"Because there are billions who have passed from this earth without that saving ordinance, God has set in place the means whereby the living may perform this ordinance in behalf of the dead. It is a

31 But I command you, all ye my saints, to build a house unto me; and I grant unto you a sufficient time to build a house unto me; and during this time your baptisms shall be acceptable unto me.

32 But behold, at the end of this appointment your baptisms for your dead shall not be acceptable unto me; and if you do not these things at the end of the appointment ye shall be rejected as a church, with your dead, saith the Lord your God.

The Fulness of the Priesthood Restored in the Nauvoo Temple (D&C 124:27–28)

"In January 1841, however, the Lord revealed that the 'fulness of the priesthood' was not held by the Prophet, for there was no place yet on the earth where the Lord could 'restore' such a blessing (D&C 124:28). Thus, the need for a temple at Nauvoo was revealed" (Brewster, *Doctrine & Covenants Encyclopedia*, 204–5).

Joseph Smith stated: "If a man gets a fulness of the priesthood of God, he has to get it in the same way that Jesus Christ obtained it, and that was by keeping all the commandments and obeying all the ordinances of the house of the Lord. . . .

"All men who become heirs of God and joint-heirs with Jesus Christ will have to receive the fulness of the ordinances of his kingdom; and those who will not receive all the ordinances will come short of the fulness of that glory" (*Joseph Smith* [manual], 419).

President Joseph Fielding Smith taught: "You cannot receive the fullness of the priesthood . . . unless you receive the ordinances of the house of the Lord; and when you receive these ordinances, the door is then open so you can obtain all the blessings which any man can gain" (in Conference Report, Apr. 1970, 58).

President Gordon B. Hinckley testified regarding the fulness of the priesthood: "The blessings of the temple represent that fulness of the priesthood of which the Lord spoke when He revealed His will unto the Prophet Joseph Smith. With the location of temples much nearer to the homes of our people, there is made more available to them all of the ordinances to be had in the Lord's house for both the living and the dead" ("Work Goes On," *Ensign*, May 2001, 5).

Daguerreotype of the Nauvoo Temple, circa 1850.

33 For verily I say unto you, that after you have had sufficient time to build a house to me, wherein the ordinance of baptizing for the dead belongeth, and for which the same was instituted from before the foundation of the world, your baptisms for your dead cannot be acceptable unto me;

34 For therein are the keys of the holy priesthood ordained, that you may receive honor and glory.

35 And after this time, your baptisms for the dead, by those who are scattered abroad, are not acceptable unto me, saith the Lord.

36 For it is ordained that in Zion, and in her stakes, and in Jerusalem, those places which I have appointed for refuge, shall be the places for your baptisms for your dead.

37 And again, verily I say unto you, how shall your washings be acceptable unto me, except ye perform them in a house which you have built to my name?

38 For, for this cause I commanded Moses that he should build a tabernacle, that they should bear it with them in the wilderness, and to build a house in the land of promise, that those ordinances might be revealed which had been hid from before the world was.

labor of love performed within the House of Him who authorizes such saving service" (Brewster, *Doctrine & Covenants Encyclopedia*, 35). See also commentary in this volume on Doctrine and Covenants 128:15–17.

Doctrine and Covenants 124:37–44. The Lord's People Always Build Temples for the Performance of Holy Ordinances

What can receiving temple ordinances indicate? (124:37–38) "God surely knows our inner thoughts and feelings, our hearts, minds, and intentions, and can judge us perfectly. So why not judge us without reference to any outward ordinances? . . .

"Ordinances show our visible, outward obedience to the Lord and His plan of salvation. . . .

"Hence ordinances are required not because God lacks the omniscience needed to know our true spiritual status, but because we need to make visible, outward compliance for our own sakes. One day, when the Book of Life is opened, it will be incontestably shown, along with our other defining deeds, that we actually participated in certain ordinances, and also what our subsequent pattern of living was in connection with each ordinance and its associated covenants" (Maxwell, *Lord, Increase Our Faith*, 74, 75).

The First Baptism for the Dead in This Dispensation (Doctrine and Covenants 124:29–30)

"Jane Harper Neyman (1792–1880) was baptized in 1838 and moved to Nauvoo in 1840 with her family. Her son, Cyrus, died before they learned about the Church. Their son's early death had been a constant concern for Jane and her husband. When she heard about the doctrine of baptism for the dead in August 1840 from Joseph Smith, she eagerly requested to perform the ordinance for her son that same day. [She then went and was baptized for her son Cyrus Livingston Neyman by Harvey Olmstead]. She is considered to be the first person in this dispensation to be baptized for the dead, as noted in this statement. Similarly, Emma Smith and Emmeline B. Wells, among others, were baptized for deceased male family members before the gendered regulation became official" (Johnson and Reeder, *Witness of Women*, 180).

What ordinances were performed in the tabernacle during Moses's day? (124:38) "We do not fully understand the extent of the ordinances practiced by the Israelites during the time of Moses. Moses initially taught the children of Israel what was needed to prepare them to behold the face of God, which would have included the higher ordinances of the Melchizedek Priesthood and the temple. Nevertheless, the Israelites 'hardened their hearts.... Therefore, [the Lord] took Moses out of their midst, and the Holy Priesthood also; and the lesser priesthood continued' (D&C 84:24–26). Thus, the ordinances generally available to the Israelites in the tabernacle in the wilderness would have been those pertaining to the lesser, or Aaronic, Priesthood" (Robinson and Garrett, *Commentary on the Doctrine and Covenants*, 4:189–90).

What can we learn from the symbolism of being washed and anointed? (124:39) "The ordinances of washing and anointing are referred to often in the temple as initiatory ordinances. It will be sufficient for our purposes to say . . . [they are] mostly symbolic in nature, but promising definite, immediate blessings as well as future blessings. . . .

"In connection with these ordinances, in the temple you will be officially clothed in the garment and promised marvelous blessings in connection with it. It is important that you listen carefully as these ordinances are administered and that you try to remember the blessings promised and the conditions upon which they will be realized" (Packer, "Come to the Temple," *Ensign*, Oct. 2007, 20). ●

39 Therefore, verily I say unto you, that your anointings, and your washings, and your baptisms for the dead, and your solemn assemblies, and your memorials for your sacrifices by the sons of Levi, and for your oracles in your most holy places wherein you receive conversations, and your statutes and judgments, for the beginning of the revelations and foundation of Zion, and for the glory, honor, and endowment of all her municipals, are ordained by the ordinance of my holy house, which my people are always commanded to build unto my holy name.

When Was the Endowment First Administered in This Dispensation? (D&C 124:41–42)

"On May 4, 1842 . . . Joseph Smith administered the endowment to a small group of faithful brethren.

"The group met in the large upper room of the Prophet's Red Brick Store, which had been 'arranged representing the interior of a temple as much as the circumstances would permit.' . . .

"The Prophet's history records: 'I spent the day in the upper part of the store, . . . in council with General James Adams, of Springfield, Patriarch Hyrum Smith, Bishops Newel K. Whitney and George Miller, and President Brigham Young and Elders Heber C. Kimball and Willard Richards, instructing them in the principles and order of the Priesthood, attending to washings, anointings, endowments and the communication of keys pertaining to the Aaronic Priesthood, and so on to the highest order of the Melchizedek Priesthood, setting forth the order pertaining to the Ancient of Days, and all those plans and principles by which anyone is enabled to secure the fullness of those blessings which have been prepared for the Church of the First Born, and come up and abide in the presence of the Eloheim in the eternal worlds. In this council was instituted the ancient order of things for the first time in these last days.

"'And the communications I made to this council were of things spiritual, and to be received only by the spiritually minded: and there was nothing made known to these men but what will be made known to all the Saints of the last days, so soon as they are prepared to receive, and a proper place is prepared to communicate them, even

40 And verily I say unto you, let this house be built unto my name, that I may reveal mine ordinances therein unto my people;

41 For I deign to reveal unto my church things which have been kept hid from before the foundation of the world, things that pertain to the dispensation of the fulness of times.

42 And I will show unto my servant Joseph all things pertaining to this house, and the priesthood thereof, and the place whereon it shall be built.

43 And ye shall build it on the place where you have contemplated building it, for that is the spot which I have chosen for you to build it.

44 If ye labor with all your might, I will consecrate that spot that it shall be made holy.

How did Joseph describe receiving the temple plans to the architect? (124:42) Joseph Smith said that "Elder William Weeks (whom I had employed as architect of the Temple), came in for instruction. I instructed him in relation to the circular windows designed to light the offices in the dead work on the arch between stories. He said that round windows in the broad side of a building were a violation of all known rules of architecture, and contended that they should be semi-circular—the building was too low for round windows. I told him I would have the circles, if he had to make the Temple ten feet higher than it was originally calculated. . . . I wish you to carry out my designs. I have seen in vision the splendid appearance of that building illuminated, and will have it built according to the pattern shown me" (Lundwall, *Temples of the Most High*, 409).

to the weakest of the Saints; therefore let the Saints be diligent in building the Temple, and all houses which they have been, or shall hereafter be, commanded of God to build'" (*Joseph Smith* [manual], 413, 414).

"Until his martyrdom, Joseph Smith continued to receive revelations that furthered the restoration of the endowment and sealing ordinances. He recognized, however, that further refinement was needed. After administering the endowment to Brigham Young in May 1842, Joseph told Brigham, 'This is not arranged right, but we have done the best we could under the circumstances in which we are placed, and I wish you to take this matter in hand and organize and systematize all these ceremonies'" (Nelson, "Temple and Your Spiritual Foundation," *Liahona*, Nov. 2021, 94).

In 2021, President Russell M. Nelson further stated: "Under the Lord's direction and in answer to our prayers, recent procedural adjustments have been made. *He* is the One who wants you to understand with great clarity exactly what you are making covenants to do. *He* is the One who wants you to experience fully *His* sacred ordinances. *He* wants you to comprehend your privileges, promises, and responsibilities. *He* wants you to have spiritual insights and awakenings you've never had before. This He desires for *all* temple patrons, no matter where they live" ("Temple and Your Spiritual Foundation," *Liahona*, Nov. 2021, 94–95).

Doctrine and Covenants 124:45–55. The Saints Are Excused from Building the Temple in Jackson County Because of the Oppression of Their Enemies

How can we better hearken unto the Lord and His appointed servants? (124:45–48) "I am convinced that salvation in this world and the world to come is contingent upon how well we accept the Lord's servants—not give lip service, but genuinely accept their counsel and teachings. . . . When a member of the Church refuses to accept the counsel of the prophets, seers, and revelators, he lays the foundation for insecurity. . . . In refusing to receive the teachings of the Brethren, we're expressing contrary ideas, or, in my opinion, false teachings" (Roy W. Doxey, "Accept Divine Counsel," 4, 5).

Concerning hearing the Lord, President Russell M. Nelson stated: "As we seek to be disciples of Jesus Christ, our efforts to *hear Him* need to be ever more intentional. It takes conscious and consistent effort to fill our daily lives with His words, His teachings, His truths" ("Hear Him," *Ensign*, May 2020, 89).

Why did the Saints delay their efforts to build Zion and a temple in Missouri? (124:49–51) "The Lord gave a command to build a temple in Zion (see D&C 97:10–15), but the members of the Church were driven out of Jackson County before they were able to fulfill that command. The Saints were commanded to build a temple in Far West but were driven out of the state by servants of the evil one before they could carry out that command. The Lord informed them in these verses that he accepted their sacrifice and would not hold them accountable for the unfulfilled commandments. Instead, the iniquity and transgression of those commands would be placed upon those who prevented the work from being performed. We gain from these verses the assurance that the Lord expects us to do the best we can. Our best is what he expects of us. If we do all we can to fulfill his commandments, he will accept our sacrifice. If others interfere and prevent us from performing, he will hold our enemies

45 And if my people will hearken unto my voice, and unto the voice of my servants whom I have appointed to lead my people, behold, verily I say unto you, they shall not be moved out of their place.

46 But if they will not hearken to my voice, nor unto the voice of these men whom I have appointed, they shall not be blest, because they pollute mine holy grounds, and mine holy ordinances, and charters, and my holy words which I give unto them.

47 And it shall come to pass that if you build a house unto my name, and do not do the things that I say, I will not perform the oath which I make unto you, neither fulfil the promises which ye expect at my hands, saith the Lord.

48 For instead of blessings, ye, by your own works, bring cursings, wrath, indignation, and judgments upon your own heads, by your follies, and by all your abominations, which you practice before me, saith the Lord.

49 Verily, verily, I say unto you, that when I give a commandment to any of the sons of men to do a work unto my name, and those sons of men go with all their might and with all they have to perform that work, and cease not their diligence, and their enemies come upon them and hinder them from performing that work, behold, it behooveth me to require that work no more at the hands of those sons of men, but to accept of their offerings.

50 And the iniquity and transgression of my holy laws and commandments I will visit upon the heads of those who hindered my work, unto the third and fourth generation, so long as they repent not, and hate me, saith the Lord God.

51 Therefore, for this cause have I accepted the offerings of those whom I commanded to build up a city and a house unto my name, in Jackson county, Missouri, and were hindered by their enemies, saith the Lord your God.

52 And I will answer judgment, wrath, and indignation, wailing, and anguish, and gnashing of teeth upon their heads, unto the third and fourth generation, so long as they repent not, and hate me, saith the Lord your God.

53 And this I make an example unto you, for your consolation concerning all those who have been commanded to do a work and have been hindered by the hands of their enemies, and by oppression, saith the Lord your God.

54 For I am the Lord your God, and will save all those of your brethren who have been pure in heart, and have been slain in the land of Missouri, saith the Lord.

55 And again, verily I say unto you, I command you again to build a house to my name, even in this place, that you may prove yourselves unto me that ye are faithful in all things whatsoever I command you, that I may bless you, and crown you with honor, immortality, and eternal life.

guilty unto the third and fourth generations, unless they repent. God will not hold us accountable for that which is beyond our control" (Robinson and Garrett, *Commentary on the Doctrine and Covenants*, 4:192).

How did knowing the Lord accepted their offerings in Missouri change the Saints' perspective and efforts? (124:49–54) "For all there was to do in Illinois, Joseph Smith's trip to Washington DC in 1839–1840 demonstrates his continued preoccupation with Missouri. A revelation dated 19 January 1841 [D&C 124], however, marked a turning point in his history. In effect, the revelation released Smith and the church from their obligation—for the time being, at least—to build a city and temple in Missouri and refocused their attention on Illinois. . . . Freed from the immediate responsibility to build a temple and the city of Zion in Missouri, Joseph Smith and the church turned their attention to Nauvoo.

"The same revelation identified several priorities for the Saints in Illinois, including the need to construct two buildings in Nauvoo—neither one of which Joseph Smith would live to see completed" (Joseph Smith Papers, Introduction to Journals: Volume 2, "Nauvoo Journals, December 1841–April 1843").

When will the building of New Jerusalem and its temple [in Jackson County] be accomplished? (124:51–54) "The command to purchase lands, to build the New Jerusalem, to build the chief temple of this dispensation in the appointed generation—all these were revoked by the same power that gave the commands in the first instance. The Lord's people were to retreat, regroup, and prepare themselves for the great battles of the future. . . .

"Though the city and the temple were not built within the appointed generation, and though the early saints were excused from that labor, yet the ultimate triumph of the cause of Zion remains unchanged. . . . Zion remains where she has ever been; the New Jerusalem shall yet be built in the appointed place, and the Latter-day Saints will build the decreed temple in that day which the mouth of the Lord shall name" (Bruce R. McConkie, *New Witness*, 603–4). ⊕

Why didn't persecution and poverty excuse the Saints from building additional temples? (124:55) The Prophet Joseph Smith said: "The church is not fully organized, in its Proper order, and cannot be, until the temple is completed, where places will be provided for the Administration of the ordinances of the Priesthood" (Joseph Smith Papers, "History, 1838–1856, volume C-1 Addenda," 26).

"Whenever the Lord has had a people on the earth who will obey His word, they have been commanded to build temples in which the ordinances of the gospel and other spiritual manifestations that pertain to exaltation and eternal life may be administered.... Building and properly using a temple is one of the marks of the true Church in any dispensation and is especially so in the present day" (Bible Dictionary, s.v. "Temple," 734–35).

Doctrine and Covenants 124:56–83. Directions Are Given for the Building of the Nauvoo House

Who was to stay and care for the Nauvoo House? (124:56–59) "In this section special instructions are given concerning the Nauvoo House. It was to be dedicated to the Lord. The Prophet Joseph, or one of his descendants after him from generation to generation [v. 56] was to live there. This does not imply that the Presidency of the Church should be transmitted as an inheritance from father to son. It refers only to the shares of stock in the Nauvoo House Association. The Prophet Joseph owned a portion of that stock that was transferable property, and it was perfectly proper that he and any of his descendants who owned the stock should have their residence in the House as part of the dividend on the money invested, when that condition was understood and agreed on from the beginning" (Smith and Sjodahl, *Doctrine and Covenants Commentary*, 783). ●

In what ways are the blessings pronounced to Abraham and Joseph and their posterity still being fulfilled? (124:57–58) "A careful reading of the covenant made to Abraham reveals that it was never fully fulfilled [in the flesh] (see Abraham 2:9–11). For example, the land promised to Abraham, 'from the river of Egypt unto the great river, the river Euphrates' (Genesis 15:18) has never been fully occupied by his seed as a covenant people of the Lord.... Joseph Smith is designated as the man who will begin the fulfillment of this covenant in these latter days.... The building of the Nauvoo House was to be a part of the covenant fulfillment, Nauvoo being a cornerstone of the glory of Zion (v. 60).... The commencement of that corner-stone of Zion being laid is again underway" (Nyman, *Doctrine and Covenants Commentary*, 2:488–89).

56 And now I say unto you, as pertaining to my boarding house which I have commanded you to build for the boarding of strangers, let it be built unto my name, and let my name be named upon it, and let my servant Joseph and his house have place therein, from generation to generation.

57 For this anointing have I put upon his head, that his blessing shall also be put upon the head of his posterity after him.

58 And as I said unto Abraham concerning the kindreds of the earth, even so I say unto my servant Joseph: In thee and in thy seed shall the kindred of the earth be blessed.

59 Therefore, let my servant Joseph and his seed after him have place in that house, from generation to generation, forever and ever, saith the Lord.

60 And let the name of that house be called Nauvoo House; and let it be a delightful habitation for man, and a resting-place for the weary traveler, that he may contemplate the glory of Zion, and the glory of this, the cornerstone thereof;

61 That he may receive also the counsel from those whom I have set to be as plants of renown, and as watchmen upon her walls.

62 Behold, verily I say unto you, let my servant George Miller, and my servant Lyman Wight, and my servant John Snider, and my servant Peter Haws, organize themselves, and appoint one of them to be a president over their quorum for the purpose of building that house.

63 And they shall form a constitution, whereby they may receive stock for the building of that house.

64 And they shall not receive less than fifty dollars for a share of stock in that house, and they shall be permitted to receive fifteen thousand dollars from any one man for stock in that house.

65 But they shall not be permitted to receive over fifteen thousand dollars stock from any one man.

66 And they shall not be permitted to receive under fifty dollars for a share of stock from any one man in that house.

67 And they shall not be permitted to receive any man, as a stockholder in this house, except the same shall pay his stock into their hands at the time he receives stock;

What are "plants of renown" and watchmen in this context? (124:61) "Those the Lord has chosen to lead his people are here referred to in the imagery of the Bible as 'plant[s] of renown' (Ezekiel 34:29), and as 'watchmen upon [her] walls' (Isaiah 62:6)" (McConkie and Ostler, *Revelations of the Restoration*, 978).

How were the funding and building of the Nauvoo House organized? (124:62–83) "A corporation [was] established in February 1841 to oversee the building of the Nauvoo House. . . . The association's charter named four men—George Miller, Lyman Wight, John Snider, and Peter Haws—as trustees of the association. William Allred, Henry Miller, the Quorum of the Twelve, and others later assisted the trustees as stock agents. The Nauvoo House Association was responsible for managing construction of the Nauvoo House, selling stock to fund its construction, and employing laborers on the project. . . . In March 1844, [Joseph Smith] directed that construction of the Nauvoo House be suspended to concentrate resources on completing the temple. Construction on the Nauvoo House resumed in April 1845 but ceased permanently that September. . . . The building was never completed" (Joseph Smith Papers, Glossary, "Nauvoo House Association").

What happened to the Nauvoo House and its property after the Saints left Nauvoo? (124:63) "When the Saints left Nauvoo in 1846, the Nauvoo House walls were up above the windows of the second story. The large unfinished building on the south end of Main Street facing the Mississippi River became the property of Joseph Smith's widow, Emma Smith. Subsequently, Emma's second husband, Lewis C. Bidamon, tore down the extremities of the L-shaped structure and used their bricks to complete the central portion as a smaller hotel, variously known as the Bidamon House and the Riverside Mansion. He and Emma lived there from 1871 until they died. After Bidamon's death, the Reorganized Church of Jesus Christ of Latter-day Saints [now known as the Community of Christ] purchased the Nauvoo House" (Holt, "Nauvoo House," 3:997). In 2024, the Nauvoo House was sold to The Church of Jesus Christ of Latter-day Saints.

68 And in proportion to the amount of stock he pays into their hands he shall receive stock in that house; but if he pays nothing into their hands he shall not receive any stock in that house.

69 And if any pay stock into their hands it shall be for stock in that house, for himself, and for his generation after him, from generation to generation, so long as he and his heirs shall hold that stock, and do not sell or convey the stock away out of their hands by their own free will and act, if you will do my will, saith the Lord your God.

70 And again, verily I say unto you, if my servant George Miller, and my servant Lyman Wight, and my servant John Snider, and my servant Peter Haws, receive any stock into their hands, in moneys, or in properties wherein they receive the real value of moneys, they shall not appropriate any portion of that stock to any other purpose, only in that house.

71 And if they do appropriate any portion of that stock anywhere else, only in that house, without the consent of the stockholder, and do not repay four-fold for the stock which they appropriate anywhere else, only in that house, they shall be accursed, and shall be moved out of their place, saith the Lord God; for I, the Lord, am God, and cannot be mocked in any of these things.

72 Verily I say unto you, let my servant Joseph pay stock into their hands for the building of that house, as seemeth him good; but my servant Joseph cannot pay over fifteen thousand dollars stock in that house, nor under fifty dollars; neither can any other man, saith the Lord.

73 And there are others also who wish to know my will concerning them, for they have asked it at my hands.

74 Therefore, I say unto you concerning my servant Vinson Knight, if he will do my will let him put stock into that house for himself, and for his generation after him, from generation to generation.

75 And let him lift up his voice long and loud, in the midst of the people, to plead the cause of the poor and the needy; and let him not fail, neither let his heart faint; and I will accept of his offerings, for they shall not be unto me as the offerings of Cain, for he shall be mine, saith the Lord.

76 Let his family rejoice and turn away their hearts from affliction; for I have chosen him and anointed him, and he shall be honored in the midst of his house, for I will forgive all his sins, saith the Lord. Amen.

77 Verily I say unto you, let my servant Hyrum put stock into that house as seemeth him good, for himself and his generation after him, from generation to generation.

78 Let my servant Isaac Galland put stock into that house; for I, the Lord, love him for the work he hath done, and will forgive all his sins; therefore, let him be remembered for an interest in that house from generation to generation.

79 Let my servant Isaac Galland be appointed among you, and be ordained by my servant William Marks, and be blessed of him, to go with my servant Hyrum to accomplish the work that my servant Joseph shall point out to them, and they shall be greatly blessed.

80 Let my servant William Marks pay stock into that house, as seemeth him good, for himself and his generation, from generation to generation.

81 Let my servant Henry G. Sherwood pay stock into that house, as seemeth him good,

How can an individual or family "rejoice and turn away their hearts from affliction"? (124:76) "When the focus of our lives is on . . . Jesus Christ and His gospel, we can feel joy regardless of what is happening—or not happening—in our lives. . . .

"We can start by 'looking unto Jesus the author and finisher of our faith' [Hebrews 12:2] 'in every thought' [D&C 6:36]. . . . As our Savior becomes more and more real to us and as we plead for His joy to be given to us, our joy will increase. . . .

"Jesus Christ is our ultimate exemplar, 'who for the joy that was set before him endured the cross.' Think of that! In order for Him to endure the most excruciating experience ever endured on earth, our Savior focused on *joy!*" (Nelson, "Joy and Spiritual Survival," *Ensign*, Nov. 2016, 82–83). ◉

for himself and his seed after him, from generation to generation.

82 Let my servant William Law pay stock into that house, for himself and his seed after him, from generation to generation.

83 If he will do my will let him not take his family unto the eastern lands, even unto Kirtland; nevertheless, I, the Lord, will build up Kirtland, but I, the Lord, have a scourge prepared for the inhabitants thereof.

What might be meant by the Lord preparing a scourge for Kirtland? (124:83) "It is difficult to tell exactly what the scourge was, but when the body of the Saints fled from Kirtland, the gospel, along with the prophets, priesthood keys, and their attendant blessings went with them. . . . Kirtland declined in population and wealth until by 1890 only 909 individuals lived there. In 1979, Ezra Taft Benson, president of the Quorum of the Twelve, presided over the groundbreaking for a new chapel in Kirtland. During his address, he removed the scourge that had been placed on Kirtland. Since that time a stake has been organized, and the Church has returned to the area in greater force" (Robinson and Garrett, *Commentary on the Doctrine and Covenants*, 4:193).

What Was the Scourge on Kirtland? (Doctrine and Covenants 124:83)

"There are three possibilities.

"1. The scourge came when the body of the Saints left Kirtland, with the gospel and its blessings withdrawn from the community. In past gospel dispensations, the Lord placed scourges upon a land by withdrawing the prophets. It seems reasonable to conclude that one aspect of the scourge was that the Prophet Joseph Smith had left from Kirtland. Some of those who remained in Kirtland eventually joined other churches or religious movements.

"2. A second possibility might be Kirtland's continual decline in population. At the time the Saints were there in the 1830s, it was one of the largest towns in northern Ohio, with an estimated population of 3,230. Kirtland and a neighboring town, Cleveland, had about equal populations. But by 1890 Kirtland's population dwindled to 909 while Cleveland's mushroomed to 261,000.

"3. Not only did the population of Kirtland dwindle, but commerce and industry also declined after the Saints left, while other areas in northeastern Ohio, such as Cleveland, Youngstown, and Akron, became major industrial centers. . . .

"While in Kirtland, President Benson declared, 'The scourge that was placed upon the people in that prophecy [D&C 124:83] is being lifted today.' He then added, 'Our prophecy said that yet your children may possess the Kirtland lands, but not until many years shall pass away. Those many years have, I feel, passed away, and now is the time. Now is the time to arise and shine and look forward to great progress in this part of the Lord's vineyard.'

"Those who heard President Benson will never forget this day. Stake President Gordon Watts, a descendent of early Kirtland pioneer Israel Barlow, described his feelings as the scourge was lifted, saying, 'It was as if a light broke through the heavens. Kirtland would never be the same'" (Karl Ricks Anderson, *Joseph Smith's Kirtland*, 244, 247).

84 And with my servant Almon Babbitt, there are many things with which I am not pleased; behold, he aspireth to establish his counsel instead of the counsel which I have ordained, even that of the Presidency of my Church; and he setteth up a golden calf for the worship of my people.

85 Let no man go from this place who has come here essaying to keep my commandments.

86 If they live here let them live unto me; and if they die let them die unto me; for they shall rest from all their labors here, and shall continue their works.

87 Therefore, let my servant William put his trust in me, and cease to fear concerning his family, because of the sickness of the land. If ye love me, keep my commandments; and the sickness of the land shall redound to your glory.

88 Let my servant William go and proclaim my everlasting gospel with a loud voice, and with great joy, as he shall be moved upon by my Spirit, unto the inhabitants of Warsaw, and also unto the inhabitants of Carthage, and also unto the inhabitants of Burlington, and also unto the inhabitants of Madison, and await patiently and diligently for further instructions at my general conference, saith the Lord.

Doctrine and Covenants 124:84–96. Hyrum Smith Is Called to Be a Patriarch, to Receive the Keys, and to Stand in the Place of Oliver Cowdery

How was Almon Babbitt guilty of setting up a "golden calf"? (124:84) "Some of Joseph Smith's followers had tried to maintain Kirtland as a spiritual center after he left. . . . Joseph Smith called [Almon] Babbitt to serve as Kirtland's stake president October 3, 1840, and announced the call to Kirtland's members in a letter: 'It has been deemed prudent to advise the eastern brethren who desire to locate in Kirtland, to do so.' In Kirtland, Babbitt embraced those instructions so energetically that he not only encouraged members in the East to gather to Kirtland, but tried to persuade English Saints . . . to jettison their plans to reach Nauvoo and stay in Kirtland. . . . Babbitt even recruited members already in Nauvoo to gather in Kirtland" (Staker, *Hearken, O Ye People*, 552).

What type of work continues in the spirit world after we die? (124:86) "We know from the scriptures that after our bodies die we continue to live as spirits in the spirit world. . . . [The scriptures] describe how some faithful spirits teach the gospel to those who have been wicked or rebellious (see 1 Peter 3:19; Doctrine and Covenants 138:19–20, 29, 32, 37). Most important, modern revelation reveals that the work of salvation goes forward in the spirit world (see Doctrine and Covenants 138:30–34, 58), and although we are urged not to procrastinate our repentance during mortality (see Alma 13:27), we are taught that some repentance is possible there (see Doctrine and Covenants 138:58)" (Oaks, "Trust in the Lord," *Ensign*, Nov. 2019, 26).

What was the sickness of the land? (124:87) "'Ague and fever,' [was] commonly referred to as the 'shakes.' The humid, wet climate of riverside Nauvoo was the perfect breeding ground for the mosquitos that carried this disease, now known as malaria, which was the most common affliction not only in Nauvoo, but also throughout the Mississippi Valley. The 'sickly season,' as it was called, stretched from midsummer until the first frosts of fall, but the 'shakes' could recur anytime" (Knight, "Introduction to the 1845–1846 Journal of Thomas Bullock," 11). The Lord promised William Law that He would redound (drive back) the sickness.

What constituted the "new translation" referred to in verse 89? (124:89) "[From] July 1833 on, Joseph Smith spoke no longer of translating the Bible but of publishing it, which he wanted and intended to accomplish 'as soon as possible.' He sought to find the means to print it as a book, and he repeatedly encouraged Church members to donate money for the publication. But because of lack of funds and the other priorities of the Saints, it was not printed in his lifetime. Excerpts were published in the Church's newspapers and elsewhere, so some sections were available for early Church members. Still, when Joseph Smith was martyred in 1844, he had not seen the realization of his desire to have the entire New Translation appear in print" (*Joseph Smith's New Translation*, 7). ☉

How did William Law respond to these promised blessings? (124:90) "Wonderful opportunities were offered to Wm. Law, which he neglected to embrace. If he had done faithfully what God here gave him to do, he would have received the blessings promised, but when he failed to obey the Lord, even his appointment in the First Presidency could not save him from falling. When he lost the Spirit of God he became one of the most bitter enemies of the Church. Apostates and persecutors rallied around him, and he tried to form a church of his own of such material" (Smith and Sjodahl, *Doctrine and Covenants Commentary*, 785). ☉

What is meant by Hyrum taking the "office of Priesthood" and "Patriarch"? (124:91–95) "Hyrum [was] also called to replace Oliver Cowdery as Assistant President, or second elder of the Church (vv. 94–95). The office of Assistant President is not understood by many members of the Church. It was an office that was no longer needed after the martyrdom, but needed until that time as a second witness of the Restoration.... Note that [Hyrum Smith] was

89 If he will do my will let him from henceforth hearken to the counsel of my servant Joseph, and with his interest support the cause of the poor, and publish the new translation of my holy word unto the inhabitants of the earth.

90 And if he will do this I will bless him with a multiplicity of blessings, that he shall not be forsaken, nor his seed be found begging bread.

91 And again, verily I say unto you, let my servant William be appointed, ordained, and anointed, as counselor unto my servant Joseph, in the room of my servant Hyrum, that my servant Hyrum may take the office of Priesthood and Patriarch, which was appointed unto him by his father, by blessing and also by right;

Hyrum Smith Is Appointed as a Prophet, Seer, and Revelator (D&C 124:94–95)

"The Lord conferred upon Hyrum Smith, [an] important and special honor, in making him as well as Joseph Smith a holder of the *keys of authority* in this dispensation of the fulness of times. These are the words of that appointment: 'And from this time forth I appoint unto him that he may be a prophet, and a seer, and a revelator unto my church, as well as my servant Joseph' [D&C 124:94].

"This was a *special* blessing given to Hyrum Smith, and in accepting it he took the place of Oliver Cowdery, upon whom these keys had previously been bestowed....

"'That he [Hyrum Smith] may act in concert also with my servant Joseph; and that he shall receive counsel from my servant Joseph, who shall show unto him the keys whereby he may ask and receive, and be crowned with *the same blessing, and glory, and honor, and priesthood, and gifts of the priesthood, that once were put upon him that was my servant Oliver Cowdery;* That my servant Hyrum may *bear record of the things which I shall show unto him,* that his name may be had in honorable remembrance from generation to generation, forever and ever' [D&C 124:95–96].

92 That from henceforth he shall hold the keys of the patriarchal blessings upon the heads of all my people,

93 That whoever he blesses shall be blessed, and whoever he curses shall be cursed; that whatsoever he shall bind on earth shall be bound in heaven; and whatsoever he shall loose on earth shall be loosed in heaven.

94 And from this time forth I appoint unto him that he may be a prophet, and a seer, and a revelator unto my church, as well as my servant Joseph;

95 That he may act in concert also with my servant Joseph; and that he shall receive counsel from my servant Joseph, who shall show unto him the keys whereby he may ask and receive, and be crowned with the same blessing, and glory, and honor, and priesthood, and gifts of the priesthood, that once were put upon him that was my servant Oliver Cowdery;

96 That my servant Hyrum may bear record of the things which I shall show unto him, that his name may be had in honorable remembrance from generation to generation, forever and ever.

97 Let my servant William Law also receive the keys by which he may ask and receive blessings; let him be humble before me, and be without guile, and he shall receive of my

to be 'a prophet, and a seer, and a revelator unto my church, as well as my servant Joseph' (D&C 124:94), and 'that he may bear record of the things which I shall show unto him' (v. 95)" (Nyman, *Doctrine and Covenants Commentary*, 2:494–95).

Doctrine and Covenants 124:97–122. William Law and Others Are Counseled in Their Labors

What does it mean to be "without guile"? (124:97)
"To be without guile is to be free of deceit, cunning, hypocrisy, and dishonesty in thought or action.... A person without guile is a person of innocence,

"And thus, according to promise, the Lord opened the vision of Hyrum Smith and showed to him those things which were necessary to qualify him for this exalted position, and upon him were conferred by Joseph Smith all the keys and authorities by which he, Hyrum Smith, was able to act in concert with his younger brother as a prophet, seer, and revelator, and president of the Church, 'as well as my servant Joseph.'

"The Prophet Joseph blessed Hyrum as follows: 'Blessed of the Lord is my brother Hyrum, for the integrity of his heart.... He shall stand in the tracks of his father and be numbered among those who hold the *right of Patriarchal Priesthood, even the Evangelical Priesthood, and power shall be upon him*'" (Joseph Fielding Smith, *Doctrines of Salvation*, 3:165, 166).

honest intent, and pure motives, whose life reflects the simple practice of conforming his [or her] daily actions to principles of integrity....

"If we are without guile, we are honest, true, and righteous. All of these are attributes of Deity and are required of the Saints. Those who are honest are fair and truthful in their speech, straightforward in their dealings, free of deceit, and above stealing, misrepresentation, or any other fraudulent action. Honesty is of God and dishonesty of the devil" (Wirthlin, "Without Guile," *Ensign*, May 1988, 80–81).

What mission did the Lord assign to William Law and Hyrum Smith? (124:102) "William Law and Hyrum Smith were appointed to travel to the eastern states. They left Nauvoo, 4 September 1842, to counter false statements of John C. Bennett and to attend a conference of the Church in Philadelphia.... They returned on 4 November" (McConkie and Ostler, *Revelations of the Restoration*, 983).

What did it mean that Sidney Rigdon was a spokesman for the Prophet Joseph? (124:103–4) See commentary in this volume on Doctrine and Covenants 100:9–11.

Spirit, even the Comforter, which shall manifest unto him the truth of all things, and shall give him, in the very hour, what he shall say.

98 And these signs shall follow him—he shall heal the sick, he shall cast out devils, and shall be delivered from those who would administer unto him deadly poison;

99 And he shall be led in paths where the poisonous serpent cannot lay hold upon his heel, and he shall mount up in the imagination of his thoughts as upon eagles' wings.

100 And what if I will that he should raise the dead, let him not withhold his voice.

101 Therefore, let my servant William cry aloud and spare not, with joy and rejoicing, and with hosannas to him that sitteth upon the throne forever and ever, saith the Lord your God.

102 Behold, I say unto you, I have a mission in store for my servant William, and my servant Hyrum, and for them alone; and let my servant Joseph tarry at home, for he is needed. The remainder I will show unto you hereafter. Even so. Amen.

103 And again, verily I say unto you, if my servant Sidney will serve me and be counselor unto my servant Joseph, let him arise and come up and stand in the office of his calling, and humble himself before me.

104 And if he will offer unto me an acceptable offering, and acknowledgments, and remain with my people, behold, I, the Lord your God, will heal him that he shall be healed; and he shall lift up his voice again on the mountains, and be a spokesman before my face.

105 Let him come and locate his family in the neighborhood in which my servant Joseph resides.

106 And in all his journeyings let him lift up his voice as with the sound of a trump, and warn the inhabitants of the earth to flee the wrath to come.

107 Let him assist my servant Joseph, and also let my servant William Law assist my servant Joseph, in making a solemn proclamation unto the kings of the earth, even as I have before said unto you.

108 If my servant Sidney will do my will, let him not remove his family unto the eastern lands, but let him change their habitation, even as I have said.

109 Behold, it is not my will that he shall seek to find safety and refuge out of the city which I have appointed unto you, even the city of Nauvoo.

110 Verily I say unto you, even now, if he will hearken unto my voice, it shall be well with him. Even so. Amen.

111 And again, verily I say unto you, let my servant Amos Davies pay stock into the hands of those whom I have appointed to build a house for boarding, even the Nauvoo House.

112 This let him do if he will have an interest; and let him hearken unto the counsel of my servant Joseph, and labor with his own hands that he may obtain the confidence of men.

113 And when he shall prove himself faithful in all things that shall be entrusted unto his care, yea, even a few things, he shall be made ruler over many;

114 Let him therefore abase himself that he may be exalted. Even so. Amen.

115 And again, verily I say unto you, if my servant Robert D. Foster will obey my voice, let him build a house for my servant Joseph,

What was the "solemn proclamation"? (124:107) See commentary in this volume on Doctrine and Covenants 124:2–12.

What did the Lord require of Sidney so he could be blessed? (124:108–110) "Sidney Rigdon, according to a generally prevailing impression, was more or less, under the influence of a spirit of apostasy. It is related that, in Liberty jail, he declared to his fellow-prisoners that the sufferings of the Lord were nothing compared with his, and while the faithful Saints were straining every nerve to complete the Nauvoo Temple, he had no word of encouragement to them. As a consequence of his disposition, he did not have good health. Like the Corinthians who partook unworthily of the Sacrament (1 Cor. 11:30), he was 'weak and sickly.' The Lord, therefore, points out to him the cause of his ailments and promises to heal him, if he will do his duty and stand by the Prophet as a true counselor" (Smith and Sjodahl, *Doctrine and Covenants Commentary*, 788). ❂

Who was Amos Davies and what were his challenges? (124:111–114) "From this Revelation it is evident that Amos Davies, notwithstanding his prominence, had some weaknesses. He was slow to obey counsel, and he shunned work. He is, therefore, commanded to 'labor with his own hands' and prove himself faithful in all things. It is to be feared that he heeded this commandment only in part, for on the 9th of March, 1842, he indulged in abusive language concerning the Prophet, whereupon the court bound him over, to keep the peace" (Smith and Sjodahl, *Doctrine and Covenants Commentary*, 789).

Who was Robert Foster and what were his challenges? (124:115–18) Robert Foster was a physician who joined the church. "There are about three dozen references to him in Joseph Smith's history, with the majority of them mentioning his misdeeds" (Brewster, *Doctrine & Covenants Encyclopedia* [2012], 198).

He eventually participated in the conspiracy causing the death of the Prophet Joseph Smith. Later he would say, "If I could recall eighteen months of my life I would be willing to sacrifice everything I have upon earth, my wife and child not excepted. I did love Joseph Smith more than any man that ever lived, if I had been present, I would have stood between him and death" (Black, *Who's Who*, 92).

according to the contract which he has made with him, as the door shall be open to him from time to time.

116 And let him repent of all his folly, and clothe himself with charity; and cease to do evil, and lay aside all his hard speeches;

117 And pay stock also into the hands of the quorum of the Nauvoo House, for himself and for his generation after him, from generation to generation;

118 And hearken unto the counsel of my servants Joseph, and Hyrum, and William Law, and unto the authorities which I have called to lay the foundation of Zion; and it shall be well with him forever and ever. Even so. Amen.

119 And again, verily I say unto you, let no man pay stock to the quorum of the Nauvoo House unless he shall be a believer in the Book of Mormon, and the revelations I have given unto you, saith the Lord your God;

120 For that which is more or less than this cometh of evil, and shall be attended with cursings and not blessings, saith the Lord your God. Even so. Amen.

The Nauvoo House and the Book of Mormon (Doctrine and Covenants 124:119)

"In Doctrine and Covenants 124:111–22, the Lord calls on other Church members to purchase stock in the Nauvoo House. Consistent with other revelations in the Doctrine and Covenants, a line is not drawn between temporal and spiritual things (D&C 29:34–35). Building a hotel for guests might be considered a strictly temporal affair, but the Lord asks that anyone who purchases stock in the venture to 'be a believer in the Book of Mormon, and the revelations I have given unto you, saith the Lord your God' (D&C 124:119). Given this connection between the builders of the Nauvoo House and a belief in the Book of Mormon, it is fitting that the building itself played a unique role in the history of the book.

The Nauvoo House

"The original manuscript of the Book of Mormon was kept by Joseph Smith. It remained in his care until he placed it in the cornerstone of the Nauvoo House during the building's cornerstone ceremony held on October 2, 1841. Warren Foote, a Church member present at the ceremony, recorded, 'I was standing very near the cornerstone when Joseph Smith came up with the manuscript of the Book

121 And again, verily I say unto you, let the quorum of the Nauvoo House have a just recompense of wages for all their labors which they do in building the Nauvoo House; and let their wages be as shall be agreed among themselves, as pertaining to the price thereof.

122 And let every man who pays stock bear his proportion of their wages, if it must needs be, for their support, saith the Lord; otherwise, their labors shall be accounted unto them for stock in that house. Even so. Amen.

123 Verily I say unto you, I now give unto you the officers belonging to my Priesthood, that ye may hold the keys thereof, even the Priesthood which is after the order of Melchizedek, which is after the order of mine Only Begotten Son.

124 First, I give unto you Hyrum Smith to be a patriarch unto you, to hold the sealing blessings of my church, even the Holy Spirit of promise, whereby ye are sealed up unto the day of redemption, that ye may not fall notwithstanding the hour of temptation that may come upon you.

125 I give unto you my servant Joseph to be a presiding elder over all my church, to be a translator, a revelator, a seer, and prophet.

Doctrine and Covenants 124:123–45. General and Local Officers Are Named, along with Their Duties and Quorum Affiliations

In what sense does a patriarch hold sealing blessings in the Church? (124:124) "A patriarch has sealing power only so far as can be pronounced in patriarchal blessings. He does not have authority as a patriarch to administer ordinances of salvation and exaltation. He is under the direction of those who preside over him. In the case of the patriarch to the Church, the First Presidency and the Quorum of the Twelve preside over him. In the case of a patriarch in a stake of Zion, the stake president presides over him as the president of the high priests quorum. Hyrum Smith was unique among those who have been

of Mormon, and said he wanted to put that in there as he had had trouble enough with it. It appeared to be written on foolscap paper and was about three inches in thickness . . . a close-fitting stone cover was laid in cement, and the wall built over it.'

"In 1882, over forty years later, the original manuscript was removed from the cornerstone by the second husband of Emma Smith, Lewis Bidamon. When the manuscript was in the cornerstone, water seeped in and destroyed most of it. Only portions of the beginning of the book (1 Nephi) and its middle (Alma 22 into the early parts of the book of Helaman) remained intact. In the following six years, Bidamon gave away most of the better-preserved portions to several individuals, mostly Latter-day Saints from Utah, among them Church historians Andrew Jenson, Edward Stephenson, and Joseph W. Summerhays. Bidamon kept a few fragments of the manuscript for himself, and they remained with his son, Charles, until 1937, when Wilford Wood, an avid collector of Latter-day Saint memorabilia, purchased the fragments. Today, only about 28 percent of the original manuscript of the Book of Mormon is extant. Nearly all of it (roughly 25 percent of the current text) is held by the historical department of The Church of Jesus Christ of Latter-day Saints" (Griffiths, "Commentary on Doctrine and Covenants 124"). See also commentary in this volume on Doctrine and Covenants 124:56–83.

ordained patriarchs because he was also set apart as the Assistant President of the Church and had been given keys to preside over the entire Church under the direction of the Prophet Joseph Smith" (McConkie and Ostler, *Revelations of the Restoration*, 984–85).

What keys are held by President Brigham Young and the Quorum of the Twelve Apostles? (124:127–128) "Brigham Young, as the President of the Twelve traveling high council, or the Twelve Apostles (v. 127; see 107:23), held the keys to open the doors of the nations unto the four corners of the earth, to take unto them the kingdom of God, or the restored gospel (D&C 124:128; see 112:21). The Twelve Apostles named here are not the original Twelve, as many had apostatized, and David Patten had been killed. Others had been appointed in their stead (v. 130; see 118:6)" (Nyman, *Doctrine and Covenants Commentary*, 2:499).

Who was David Patten? (124:130) See commentary in this volume on Doctrine and Covenants 114:1; 124:19.

126 I give unto him for counselors my servant Sidney Rigdon and my servant William Law, that these may constitute a quorum and First Presidency, to receive the oracles for the whole church.

127 I give unto you my servant Brigham Young to be a president over the Twelve traveling council;

128 Which Twelve hold the keys to open up the authority of my kingdom upon the four corners of the earth, and after that to send my word to every creature.

129 They are Heber C. Kimball, Parley P. Pratt, Orson Pratt, Orson Hyde, William Smith, John Taylor, John E. Page, Wilford Woodruff, Willard Richards, George A. Smith;

130 David Patten I have taken unto myself; behold, his priesthood no man taketh from him; but, verily I say unto you, another may be appointed unto the same calling.

131 And again, I say unto you, I give unto you a high council, for the cornerstone of Zion—

132 Namely, Samuel Bent, Henry G. Sherwood, George W. Harris, Charles C. Rich, Thomas Grover, Newel Knight, David Dort, Dunbar Wilson—Seymour Brunson I have

Brigham Young—Lion of the Lord (Doctrine and Covenants 124:127)

"The great colonizer and prophet Brigham Young, a modern-day Moses, was born on June 1, 1801, in Whittingham, Windham County, Vermont, to John Young and Abigail Howe. Perhaps in the same sense that Joseph Smith's name was to be 'had for good and evil' (JS—H 1:33), the name of Brigham Young evokes similar responses. . . .

"Of his conversion to the Church, to which he gave his all, the following has been said: 'Never a credulous man, nor one to be hurried in his judgments, Brigham subjected the new religion over a period of two years to the test of careful study, scriptural comparison, and critical analysis. On April 14, 1832, he was baptized and became a member of the church at the age of thirty-one. From that day until the day of his death he trod a thorny path mid scenes of turbulence and violence of which for over thirty years he was the central figure' [*Acceptance of the Statue of Brigham Young*, 13]. . . . In his own words, he embraced the gospel 'for all day long.' Whatever Brigham Young did was done with full commitment, for, said he, 'I have believed all my life that that which was worth doing was worth doing well' ([*New Era*], Sep. 1977, 17).

Brigham Young

taken unto myself; no man taketh his priesthood, but another may be appointed unto the same priesthood in his stead; and verily I say unto you, let my servant Aaron Johnson be ordained unto this calling in his stead—David Fullmer, Alpheus Cutler, William Huntington.

133 And again, I give unto you Don C. Smith to be a president over a quorum of high priests;

134 Which ordinance is instituted for the purpose of qualifying those who shall be appointed standing presidents or servants over different stakes scattered abroad;

135 And they may travel also if they choose, but rather be ordained for standing presidents; this is the office of their calling, saith the Lord your God.

136 I give unto him Amasa Lyman and Noah Packard for counselors, that they may preside over the quorum of high priests of my church, saith the Lord.

137 And again, I say unto you, I give unto you John A. Hicks, Samuel Williams, and Jesse Baker, which priesthood is to preside over the quorum of elders, which quorum is instituted for standing ministers; nevertheless they may travel, yet they are ordained to be

What is the difference between "standing" and "traveling" ministers? (124:133–140) "As used in the revelations, the word *standing* seems to refer to functions within the Church while *traveling* denotes external responsibilities. For example, the Quorum of the Twelve is identified as a 'traveling presiding high council' (D&C 107:33), whereas 'standing high councils' function within stakes (v. 36). Similarly, high priests are called 'standing presidents' (D&C 124:33–34), and elders are designated 'standing ministers' (v.137). On the other hand, the seventy, who are to be 'especial witnesses unto the Gentiles and in all the world' (D&C 107:25), are designated 'traveling ministers' (v. 97) or 'traveling elders' (D&C 124:138–39)" (Cowan, *Answers to Your Questions*, 141).

"Two years after his baptism, he was ordained one of the original members of the Quorum of the Twelve Apostles in this dispensation. It is as a member of this august body that he is first mentioned in the Doctrine and Covenants (124:127). His loyalty to the Prophet Joseph knew no bounds. 'I have lain upon the floor scores and scores of nights,' he said, 'ready to receive the mobs who sought his [Joseph's] life' ([in *Journal of Discourses*], 18:361).

"Brigham was noted for 'his *strict obedience* to the Prophet. Brother Joseph never made any requirements of him that he did not strictly comply with,' said George Q. Cannon ([*Juvenile Instructor*], 20:222). The Lord's feelings for this faithful man are expressed in this revelatory salutation: '*Dear and well-beloved brother*, Brigham Young' (D&C 126:1).

"Joseph and Brigham's relationship was strong from the beginning. It was from Brigham's mouth that the Prophet first heard the Adamic tongue, which Joseph declared was from God; 'the time will come,' he said, 'when brother Brigham Young will preside over this Church' (*Millennial Star*, 25:439)" (Brewster, *Doctrine & Covenants Encyclopedia* [2012], 654–55).

standing ministers to my church, saith the Lord.

138 And again, I give unto you Joseph Young, Josiah Butterfield, Daniel Miles, Henry Herriman, Zera Pulsipher, Levi Hancock, James Foster, to preside over the quorum of seventies;

139 Which quorum is instituted for traveling elders to bear record of my name in all the world, wherever the traveling high council, mine apostles, shall send them to prepare a way before my face.

140 The difference between this quorum and the quorum of elders is that one is to travel continually, and the other is to preside over the churches from time to time; the one has the responsibility of presiding from time to time, and the other has no responsibility of presiding, saith the Lord your God.

141 And again, I say unto you, I give unto you Vinson Knight, Samuel H. Smith, and Shadrach Roundy, if he will receive it, to preside over the bishopric; a knowledge of said bishopric is given unto you in the book of Doctrine and Covenants.

142 And again, I say unto you, Samuel Rolfe and his counselors for priests, and the president of the teachers and his counselors, and also the president of the deacons and his counselors, and also the president of the stake and his counselors.

143 The above offices I have given unto you, and the keys thereof, for helps and for governments, for the work of the ministry and the perfecting of my saints.

What are the responsibilities of the priesthood office of the Seventy? (124:138–140) "In these passages the special calling and duties of the Seventies are so clearly set forth that neither comment nor amplification is necessary, since these foregoing quotations are the word of the Lord, and evidence the fact that the Twelve, with the Seventy, constitute the foreign ministry of the Church. They are special witnesses of God and Christ to the truth of the gospel, and that is their special and peculiar calling in the Church. Not that the whole responsibility of preaching the gospel rests upon the Twelve and the Seventy alone. That responsibility rests upon the whole body of the Church. These quorums, the Twelve and Seventy, are merely the instrumentality through which the Church discharges its obligations to the people of the world in making known to them the truth" (Roberts, *Seventy's Course in Theology*, 1:14–15). See also commentary in this volume on Doctrine and Covenants 107:93–97.

In what way does the church organization help perfect the members? (124:143) "The purpose of the Church is 'for the perfecting of the saints ... till we all come in the unity of the faith ... unto a perfect man, unto the measure of the stature of the fulness of Christ' (Ephesians 4:12–13). The Lord's primary purpose is to perfect His Saints. The Church serves to support that objective.

"Thus, we will be thrilled by what we find in our history if we expect it to demonstrate how the process of the Restoration not only established the Lord's true Church on earth but also provided the experiences by which its leaders and members could grow toward perfection as they learned from their triumphs and their mistakes" (Cornish, "True Church," *Liahona*, Sep. 2018, 24).

144 And a commandment I give unto you, that you should fill all these offices and approve of those names which I have mentioned, or else disapprove of them at my general conference;

145 And that ye should prepare rooms for all these offices in my house when you build it unto my name, saith the Lord your God. Even so. Amen.

What are the purposes of general conference in the Church? (124:144) "Reference to the Doctrine and Covenants will disclose the fact that there are four principal purposes of holding conferences of the Church: First, to transact current Church business [D&C 20:62]. Second, to hear reports and general Church statistics [D&C 73:2]. Third, to 'approve those names which I (the Lord) have appointed, or to disapprove of them' [D&C 124:144]. Fourth, to worship the Lord in sincerity and reverence, and to give and to receive encouragement, exhortation, and instruction [D&C 58:56; 72:7]" (McKay, in Conference Report, Oct. 1938, 130–31).

Introduction to Doctrine and Covenants 125

This revelation was given at Nauvoo, Illinois, in March 1841. "After Governor Lilburn W. Boggs issued the executive order to remove all Mormons from the state of Missouri in October 1838, thousands of Church members fled to Iowa Territory and Illinois. The Prophet Joseph Smith and other Church leaders arranged to buy 700 acres of land in Commerce (later named Nauvoo), Illinois, and nearly 18,000 acres in Lee County, Iowa Territory. Branches of the Church were eventually established in Iowa Territory in Zarahemla and Nashville and in other small settlements near the existing community of Montrose. During a Church conference held on October 5, 1839, the Iowa Stake was created. In March 1841 the Prophet Joseph Smith received the revelation recorded in Doctrine and Covenants 125, in which the Lord named Zarahemla and Nashville as principal gathering places for Church members in Iowa Territory. In August 1841 the name of the Iowa Stake was changed to the Zarahemla Stake. However, because all available Church members were needed to help build the Nauvoo Temple and complete other construction projects in Nauvoo, Illinois, the Zarahemla Stake was dissolved in January 1842 after numerous Church members moved from Iowa Territory to Nauvoo" (*Doctrine and Covenants Student Manual* [2018], 726).

SECTION 125

Revelation given through Joseph Smith the Prophet, at Nauvoo, Illinois, March 1841, concerning the Saints in the territory of Iowa.

1 What is the will of the Lord concerning the saints in the Territory of Iowa?

2 Verily, thus saith the Lord, I say unto you, if those who call themselves by my name and are essaying to be my saints, if they will do my will and keep my commandments concerning them, let them gather themselves together unto the places which I shall appoint

Doctrine and Covenants 125:1–4. The Saints Are to Build Cities and Gather to the Stakes of Zion

How does the important work of the gathering of Israel continue today? (125:2) "Several of the revelations recorded in the Doctrine and Covenants taught that Church members were to gather to places designated by the Lord through His prophet (see D&C 37:3; 57:1–2; 101:20–21; 115:6–8). By gathering together, these Church members received spiritual strength, gospel instruction, and other benefits of associating with each other and with Church leaders. In the revelation the Prophet Joseph Smith received in March 1841, the Lord explained that Church members in Iowa Territory were to 'build up cities unto my name' (D&C 125:2). . . . Today, Church members are not commanded to gather to one particular place; rather, each member is assigned to a local ward or branch within a stake or mission in the area in which he or she lives" (*Doctrine and Covenants Study Manual* [2018], 728). ⊕

Why did the Lord designate the name *Zarahemla* for one of the branches in Iowa? (125:3) "One of [the] branches [in Iowa] was named Zarahemla, [and] organized to serve a townsite chosen by Joseph Smith in 1839. . . . A revelation in March 1841 designated Zarahemla and Nashville, three miles south of Montrose, as Iowa's central gathering places. . . . In August, under the direction of two members of the Twelve, the Iowa stake was renamed the Zarahemla stake. This name had meaning for the exiled Missouri Saints in Iowa. Zarahemla was an ancient American land of refuge for a Book of Mormon people who fled Babylonia's conquest of Jerusalem in 587 to 586 B.C. Later on in the Book of Mormon narrative, the city of Zarahemla became the center of political, military, and religious life for the Nephite people" (Leonard, *Nauvoo*, 96–97).

unto them by my servant Joseph, and build up cities unto my name, that they may be prepared for that which is in store for a time to come.

3 Let them build up a city unto my name upon the land opposite the city of Nauvoo, and let the name of Zarahemla be named upon it.

4 And let all those who come from the east, and the west, and the north, and the south, that have desires to dwell therein, take up their inheritance in the same, as well as in the city of Nashville, or in the city of Nauvoo, and in all the stakes which I have appointed, saith the Lord.

Introduction to Doctrine and Covenants 126

"On 9 July 1841, [the Prophet Joseph Smith] dictated a revelation for Brigham Young, releasing him from extended travel and admonishing him to remain with and care for his family. From the time Young joined the church in 1832, missionary travels marked his life. Young had departed Nauvoo, Illinois, almost two years earlier for a mission to Europe with other apostles and church members, leaving his family behind. . . . During Young's sojourn in England, his wife, Mary Ann Angell Young, and their children struggled with poverty, lacked essential goods, and suffered from illness" (Joseph Smith Papers, Historical Introduction to "Revelation, 9 July 1841 [D&C 126]").

"Upon returning to Nauvoo [after his British Mission] on July 1, 1841, after a 22-month absence, Brigham learned just how impoverished Mary Ann and the children had been. He set to work immediately to improve their situation. When not 'at the call of bro. Joseph, in the service of the church,' Brigham said, 'I spent [my time] in draining, fencing and cultivating my lot, building a temporary shed for my cow, chinking and otherwise finishing my house.' At the same time, he began work on the red brick home that still stands in Nauvoo, although he was not able to move his family into it until May 1843.

"A week after Brigham's return, on July 9, 1841, Joseph Smith visited him at his home. Mary Ann was likely there. No account survives of the conversation or circumstances of the day, but no doubt Joseph saw firsthand the evidence of the Young family's sacrifice and continuing need. He dictated a revelation on the spot, now found in Doctrine and Covenants 126. 'Dear & well beloved Brother, Brigham Young,' it read, 'it is no more required at your hand to leave your family as in times past, for your offering is acceptable to me.' He was instructed to 'take special care of your family from this time henceforth and forever.' Though the revelation was addressed to Brigham, it was an unmistakable affirmation of Mary Ann's sacrifice and faithful support. 'This evening I am with my wife a lone by my fire Side for the first time for years,' Brigham recorded in his journal six months after returning from England, reflecting the welcome relief his presence at home brought to them both. 'We enjoy it and feel to praise the Lord.'

"The revelation changed where Brigham Young served, but not how much. He was absent from home for only three short missions in the ensuing years, but his time was still dedicated to serving the Lord. Mary Ann continued to support him and to make sacrifices for her faith, including accepting the principle of plural marriage and welcoming new wives into the family. And there were more hardships to come. In the midst of the Saints' forced exodus from Nauvoo, Mary Ann was said to be 'benevolent and hospitable in the extreme,' administering generous 'advice and assistance' to those in need. Throughout her life, she served family, friends, and fellow Saints and helped build up the kingdom of God" (Tait and Orton, "Take Special Care of Your Family," 247–48).

SECTION 126

Revelation given through Joseph Smith the Prophet, in the house of Brigham Young, at Nauvoo, Illinois, July 9, 1841. At this time Brigham Young was President of the Quorum of the Twelve Apostles.

1 Dear and well-beloved brother, Brigham Young, verily thus saith the Lord unto you: My servant Brigham, it is no more required at your hand to leave your family as in times past, for your offering is acceptable to me.

2 I have seen your labor and toil in journeyings for my name.

Doctrine and Covenants 126:1–3. Brigham Young Is Commended for His Labors and Is Relieved of Future Travel Abroad

What was Brigham Young's offering to the Lord?
(126:1) President Brigham Young said: "I came into this Church in the spring of 1832. Previous to my being baptized, I took a mission to Canada at my own expense; and from the time that I was baptized until the day of our sorrow and affliction, at the martyrdom of Joseph and Hyrum, no summer passed over my head but what I was traveling and preaching, and the only thing I ever received from the Church, during over twelve years, and the only means that were ever given me by the Prophet, that I now recollect, was in 1842, when brother Joseph sent me the half of a small pig that the brethren had brought to him. I did not ask him for it" (in *Journal of Discourses*, 4:34). ☉

Why did the Lord give Brigham Young the authority to "send my word abroad"? (126:3) "The revelation's direction that [Brigham]Young no longer leave his family for extended periods was likely also connected to Young's increasing responsibilities in Nauvoo. A month after dictating this revelation, [Joseph Smith] declared in a public discourse that 'the time had come when the twelve should be called upon to stand in their place next to the first presidency, and attend to the settling of [immigrants] and the business of the church at the stakes.' [The Prophet Joseph] further stated that the Twelve Apostles had earned the right to stay with their families, where they would have better opportunity to provide for them" (Joseph Smith Papers, Historical Introduction to "Revelation, 9 July 1841 [D&C 126]"). ⊕

3 I therefore command you to send my word abroad, and take especial care of your family from this time, henceforth and forever. Amen.

Mary Ann Angell Young: An Abiding Trust in the Lord (Doctrine and Covenants 126:3)

Mary Ann Angell
Young

A beloved wife of Brigham Young, Mary Ann Angell Young also sacrificed for the building of the Lord's kingdom. "Fortunate to grow up in a home that prioritized scripture reading, Mary Ann Angell (1803–82) gained a fondness for reading the Bible, especially the teachings of the Savior, at an early age. She developed a firm foundation in religious principles through her scripture study and teachings from her mother, Phebe Morton Angell. . . . Through her mother's example, Mary Ann learned that she could hear the Lord's voice through the scriptures and find solace in His teachings.

"Mary Ann's biblical foundation prepared her for new religious messages. She heard the restored gospel of Jesus Christ preached in Rhode Island, USA, in 1831. After obtaining and reading the Book of Mormon, Mary Ann gained a testimony of the restored gospel and remained steadfast in her faith thereafter. She later testified of her sure knowledge 'that this is the everlasting Gospel, revealed by the power of God's inspiration' ["Biography of Mrs. Mary Ann Young," *Woman's Exponent*, Sep. 15, 1887, 59].

"Around 1833, Mary Ann moved to Kirtland, Ohio, USA, to gather with Church members. There she met Brigham Young. They were married in early 1834, beginning a long life of relocations, trials, and afflictions—but of happiness and joy as well. . . .

"Brigham departed for a mission to Great Britain in 1839 just 10 days after Mary Ann gave birth to their daughter Alice. For the 20 months that followed, Mary Ann and their six children struggled with illness and poverty. They survived primarily on corn bread, milk, and a few garden vegetables. Mary Ann managed to find a little work to support her family. . . .

"While Brigham spread the gospel message on many missions away from home, Mary Ann furthered the work of the Lord at home, raising her children, running the household alone, and caring for her neighbors. Though it was challenging, she maintained her trust that Brigham was where he was supposed to be. . . .

"She rejoiced in Brigham's efforts: 'I am glad to hear the work of the Lord is prospering in England; it gives me much joy' [Mary Ann Angell Young letter to Brigham Young, Apr. 15, 1841]. Like Alma in the Book of Mormon, she found a fuller joy in the successful work of others—a work to which she contributed (see Alma 29:14). . . .

"Her 1882 obituary states: 'Her trials and sufferings here were severe but she bore all with meekness and resignation and her reward will be sure. Her life was a labor of love, rich in good deeds that can never die' [Wells, "In Memoriam," *Woman's Exponent,* Jul. 15, 1882, 28–29]. Mary Ann was remembered as 'one of the kindest and most benevolent of women,' always providing relief, care, or comfort to those in sorrow or in need" (Rogers, "Mary Ann Angell Young," *Liahona*, Jul. 2021).

"On 1 September 1842, [Joseph Smith] dictated to William Clayton a letter addressed to church members in Nauvoo, Illinois, informing them that he was planning to leave the city in order to evade arrest and extradition to Missouri. [Joseph] had been eluding officers seeking his arrest for most of August, primarily by concealing himself in private residences of friends in and near Nauvoo and just across the Mississippi River in Iowa Territory" (Joseph Smith Papers, Historical Introduction to "Letter to 'All the Saints in Nauvoo,' 1 September 1842 [D&C 127]").

"Before this revelation [D&C 127] was communicated to the Saints, an attempt had been made on the life of Lilburn Boggs, former governor of Missouri. With no evidence other than their own bitterness, enemies of the Prophet in Missouri accused Orrin Porter Rockwell, bodyguard and faithful friend of the Prophet's, as being the hapless would-be assassin, with Joseph Smith as his accessory. They hoped to extradite Joseph to Missouri to answer the charge so that they could get him back into the hands of the Missouri mobbers" (McConkie and Ostler, *Revelations of the Restoration*, 1021).

"In this 1 September letter, [Joseph Smith] urged church members in Nauvoo to remain faithful during periods of tribulation, assured them that his business affairs would be attended to by authorized representatives, and advised them that he would return when the attempts to arrest him had ended. [Joseph] also included in the letter the text of a revelation on baptisms for the dead. He had first taught the doctrine of baptizing individuals on behalf of their deceased relatives in August 1840. Latter-day Saints performed the first of such baptisms in the Mississippi River until the font in the basement of the unfinished Nauvoo temple was dedicated on 8 November 1841, after which the ordinance was performed almost exclusively in the font. The Saints recorded many, but not all, of these early baptisms for deceased individuals. In this letter, [the Prophet] emphasized the importance of having a recorder witness each baptism. [Joseph] also informed the Saints that a number of additional revelations concerning the ordinance and other topics were forthcoming and promised that he would send additional instruction in future correspondence [see D&C 128]" (Joseph Smith Papers, Historical Introduction to "Letter to 'All the Saints in Nauvoo,' 1 September 1842 [D&C 127]").

SECTION 127

An epistle from Joseph Smith the Prophet to the Latter-day Saints at Nauvoo, Illinois, containing directions on baptism for the dead, dated at Nauvoo, September 1, 1842.

1 Forasmuch as the Lord has revealed unto me that my enemies, both in Missouri and this State, were again in the pursuit of me; and inasmuch as they pursue me without a cause, and have not the least shadow or coloring of justice or right on their side in the getting up of their prosecutions against me; and inasmuch as their pretensions are all founded in falsehood of the blackest dye, I have thought it expedient and wisdom in me to leave the place for a short season, for my own safety and the safety of this people. I would say to all those with whom I have business, that I have left my affairs with agents and clerks who will transact all

Doctrine and Covenants 127:1–4. Joseph Smith Glories in Persecution and Tribulation

Why were Joseph Smith's enemies constantly pursuing him? (127:1) The Prophet Joseph Smith proclaimed: "I will from time to time reveal to you the subjects that are revealed by the Holy Ghost to me. All the lies that are now hatched up against me are of the devil, and the influence of the devil and his servants will be used against the kingdom of God. The servants of God teach nothing but principles of eternal life, by their works ye shall know them. A good man will speak good things and holy principles, and an evil man evil things. I feel, in the name of the Lord, to rebuke all such bad principles, liars, etc., and I warn all of you to look out whom you are going after" (*Joseph Smith* [manual], 521). ●

What did Joseph Smith teach about his fore-ordained calling? (127:2) The Prophet Joseph Smith declared, "In relation to the Kingdom of God, the devil always sets up his Kingdom at the very same time in opposition to God. Every man who has a calling to minister to the inhabitants of the world, was ordained to that very purpose in the grand [Council] of Heaven before this world was. I suppose that I was ordained to this very office in that grand council. It is the testimony that I want that I am God's servant, and this people his people" (Joseph Smith Papers, "History, 1838–1856, volume F-1," 18).

How can we, like Joseph Smith, be so calm during tribulations? (127:2) "When [Joseph] asked for peace of soul in moments of great anguish, like us he did not always receive the Lord's full explanation.... If we are close enough to the Lord and if we have the assurance that we are filling our missions as appointed, it should not come as any great shock or surprise that we sometimes walk in affliction....

"Joseph was simply given assurance, the whisper of peace, the 'Be still, Joseph, and know that I am God' [see D&C 101:16; see also vv. 9–18]" (Truman G. Madsen, *Joseph Smith the Prophet*, 63). See also commentary in this volume on Doctrine and Covenants 122:7. ⊕

Why is it important for temple work to continue and not cease? (127:4) Just as in the days of Nauvoo, temple building continues today. "Jesus Christ is the reason we build temples. Each is His holy house. Making covenants and receiving essential ordinances in the temple, as well as seeking to draw closer to Him there, will bless your life in ways no other kind of worship can. For this reason, we are doing all within our power to make the blessings of the temple more accessible to our members around the world" (Nelson, "Answer Is Always Jesus Christ," *Liahona*, May 2023, 127–28).

business in a prompt and proper manner, and will see that all my debts are canceled in due time, by turning out property, or otherwise, as the case may require, or as the circumstances may admit of. When I learn that the storm is fully blown over, then I will return to you again.

2 And as for the perils which I am called to pass through, they seem but a small thing to me, as the envy and wrath of man have been my common lot all the days of my life; and for what cause it seems mysterious, unless I was ordained from before the foundation of the world for some good end, or bad, as you may choose to call it. Judge ye for yourselves. God knoweth all these things, whether it be good or bad. But nevertheless, deep water is what I am wont to swim in. It all has become a second nature to me; and I feel, like Paul, to glory in tribulation; for to this day has the God of my fathers delivered me out of them all, and will deliver me from henceforth; for behold, and lo, I shall triumph over all my enemies, for the Lord God hath spoken it.

3 Let all the saints rejoice, therefore, and be exceedingly glad; for Israel's God is their God, and he will mete out a just recompense of reward upon the heads of all their oppressors.

4 And again, verily thus saith the Lord: Let the work of my temple, and all the works which I have appointed unto you, be continued on and not cease; and let your diligence, and your perseverance, and patience, and your works be redoubled, and you shall in nowise lose your reward, saith the Lord of Hosts. And if they persecute you, so persecuted they the prophets and righteous men that were before you. For all this there is a reward in heaven.

5 And again, I give unto you a word in relation to the baptism for your dead.

6 Verily, thus saith the Lord unto you concerning your dead: When any of you are baptized for your dead, let there be a recorder, and let him be eye-witness of your baptisms; let him hear with his ears, that he may testify of a truth, saith the Lord;

7 That in all your recordings it may be recorded in heaven; whatsoever you bind on earth, may be bound in heaven; whatsoever you loose on earth, may be loosed in heaven;

8 For I am about to restore many things to the earth, pertaining to the priesthood, saith the Lord of Hosts.

Doctrine and Covenants 127:5–12. Records Must Be Kept Relative to Baptisms for the Dead

How important is temple work for our own ancestors? (127:5) "The Lord in initial revelatory instructions referred to 'baptism for *your* dead' [D&C 127:5; emphasis added]. Our doctrinal obligation is to our own ancestors. This is because the celestial organization of heaven is based on families. The First Presidency has encouraged members, especially youth and young single adults, to emphasize family history work and ordinances for their own family names or the names of ancestors of their ward and stake members. We need to be connected to both our roots and branches. The thought of being associated in the eternal realm is indeed glorious" (Quentin L. Cook, "Roots and Branches," *Ensign*, May 2014, 45).

What doctrine of the gospel did the Saints need to learn? (127:6–7) "As Wilford Woodruff observed, the Saints did not understand that a record needed to be kept of all ordinances performed and that there had to be witnesses to the performing of the ordinances. Here the Prophet instructed the Saints that in order for things to be recorded in heaven, they must be recorded on earth. The record should be kept in the temple for generations thereafter to have access to" (Robinson and Garrett, *Commentary on the Doctrine and Covenants*, 4:206). See also commentary in this volume on Doctrine and Covenants 128:2–3.

What things pertaining to the priesthood were about to be restored? (127:8) George Q. Cannon remembered: "'Previous to his death, the Prophet Joseph manifested great anxiety to see the [Nauvoo] temple completed, . . . 'Hurry up the work, brethren,' he used to say,—'let us finish the temple; the Lord has a great endowment in store for you, and I am anxious that the brethren should have their endowments and receive the fullness of the priesthood.' He urged the Saints forward continually, preaching unto them the importance of completing that building, so that therein the ordinances of life and salvation might be administered to the whole people, but especially to the quorums of the holy priesthood; 'then,' said he, 'the Kingdom will be established, and I do not care what shall become of me' [George Q. Cannon, *Deseret News*, 2]" (*Joseph Smith* [manual], 507).

How does the Church value and preserve its records today? (127:9) "Since the 1840s, official records of the Church have been created all over the world and the single office of Church Historian and Recorder has borne the general responsibility to care for the Church's records and histories....

"Today, the records of the Church are organized, managed, and preserved according to the highest standards....

"We keep the records because of the Lord's commandments, and we use them to support the Church's work of salvation and to help the Saints remember. Records help us see and understand the hand of God and His dealings in our lives" (Steven E. Snow, "Sacred Duty of Record Keeping," *Ensign*, Apr. 2019).

Who is the "prince of this world"? (127:11) "The prince of this world (v. 11) is Satan. This verse is a quote from John 14:30. The Joseph Smith Translation makes the verse much clearer: 'Hereafter I will not talk much with you; for the prince of *darkness, who* is of this world, cometh, *but* hath *no power over me, but he hath power over you*' (italics show changes)" (Nyman, *Doctrine and Covenants Commentary*, 2:511).

9 And again, let all the records be had in order, that they may be put in the archives of my holy temple, to be held in remembrance from generation to generation, saith the Lord of Hosts.

10 I will say to all the saints, that I desired, with exceedingly great desire, to have addressed them from the stand on the subject of baptism for the dead, on the following Sabbath. But inasmuch as it is out of my power to do so, I will write the word of the Lord from time to time, on that subject, and send it to you by mail, as well as many other things.

11 I now close my letter for the present, for the want of more time; for the enemy is on the alert, and as the Savior said, the prince of this world cometh, but he hath nothing in me.

12 Behold, my prayer to God is that you all may be saved. And I subscribe myself your servant in the Lord, prophet and seer of The Church of Jesus Christ of Latter-day Saints.

JOSEPH SMITH.

Introduction to Doctrine and Covenants 128

The prophet Joseph Smith wrote a previous letter [D&C 127] to the Saints urging them to be faithful during perse-cution and included instructions regarding the doctrine of baptism for the dead. On September 6, 1842, in Nauvoo, Illinois, "Joseph Smith dictated a second letter on the same subject [the doctrine of baptism for the dead], 'which he ordered to be read next Sabbath,' September 11. This second letter is now found in Doctrine and Covenants 128. In it, the Prophet gave a more detailed record-keeping proposal, calling for witnesses, a recorder in each of Nauvoo's 10 wards, and a general recorder who would compile all the ward records into a 'general Church Book'" (McBride, "Letters on Baptism for the Dead," 274).

Several years earlier, "in January 1836, Joseph Smith saw a vision of the celestial kingdom in which he learned that those who did not receive the fulness of the gospel in this life but would have if given the chance, such as his brother Alvin, would not be denied the highest rewards in the life to come. With this vision, the Lord began to gradually reveal the doctrines and practices surrounding baptism for the dead to Joseph Smith and his successors over the course of several years. . . .

"At the funeral of Seymour Brunson on August 15, 1840, Joseph Smith taught the principle that men and women on earth could act for their deceased kin and fulfill the requirement of baptism on their behalf. The Saints joyfully embraced this opportunity and began almost immediately to be baptized for departed loved ones in rivers and streams near Nauvoo" (McBride, "Letters on Baptism for the Dead," 272, 273).

Sometime in December 1840, Joseph wrote a letter to the Quorum of the Twelve Apostles stating, "I first men-tioned the doctrine in public, when preaching the funeral sermon of brother Seymour Brunson, and have since then given general instructions to the Church on the subject. The Saints have the privilege of being baptized for those of their relatives who are dead. . . . Without enlarging on the subject, you will undoubtedly see its consis-tency and reasonableness and it presents the Gospel of Christ in probably a more enlarged scale than some have imagined it" (Joseph Smith Papers, "History, 1838–1856, volume C-1," 1118).

SECTION 128

An epistle from Joseph Smith the Prophet to The Church of Jesus Christ of Latter-day Saints, containing further directions on baptism for the dead, dated at Nauvoo, Illinois, September 6, 1842.

1 As I stated to you in my letter before I left my place, that I would write to you from time to time and give you information in relation to many subjects, I now resume the subject of the baptism for the dead, as that subject seems to occupy my mind, and press itself upon my feelings the strongest, since I have been pursued by my enemies.

2 I wrote a few words of revelation to you concerning a recorder. I have had a few addi-tional views in relation to this matter, which I now certify. That is, it was declared in my former letter that there should be a recorder, who should be eye-witness, and also to hear

Doctrine and Covenants 128:1–5. Local and General Recorders Must Certify to the Fact of Baptisms for the Dead

What can we learn about receiving revelation from the Prophet's experience? (128:1) *"A subject may occupy the mind or weigh continually upon you.* This truth from Joseph Smith's epistle on baptism for the dead is another way that the Spirit speaks: 'That subject seems to occupy my mind, and press itself upon my feelings the strongest' (D&C 128:1). Having impressions that persist until we act are real and sacred" (Jay E. Jensen, "Unspeakable Gift of the Holy Ghost," 7).

What happens if ordinances are not properly recorded? (128:2–3) "In the early days of the Church, some baptisms for the dead that were not properly witnessed and recorded, were rejected of the Lord, and the work had to be done over again. We know that great care and attention is given to this matter today in our Temples, and that efficient help must be secured to do this. . . . Truly it is a great and marvelous work, and not the least important thing about it is that these ordinances are all carefully recorded in the books. . . . Nothing that is done in that Temple will be accepted of the Lord, except it is properly witnessed and recorded" (Clawson, in Conference Report, Apr. 1900, 43, 44). See also commentary in this volume on Doctrine and Covenants 127:6–7.

What is an ordinance? (128:4–5) "The word *ordinance* means, 'a religious or ceremonial observance'; 'an established rite.' . . .

"The word *ordinance* comes from the word *order*, which means, 'a rank, a row, a series.' The word *order* appears frequently in the scriptures. Some examples are: ' . . . established the *order* of the Church' (Alma 8:1); ' . . . all things should be restored to their proper *order*' (Alma 41:2); ' . . . all things may be done in order' (D&C 20:68); 'mine house is a house of *order*' (D&C 132:8). . . .

"*Ordinance* [is] the ceremony by which things are put in proper order" (Packer, *Holy Temple*, 144, 145).

"To worthily receive [ordinances and covenants] is the quest of a lifetime; to keep them thereafter is the challenge of mortality" (Packer, "Covenants," *Ensign*, May 1987, 24). See also commentary in this volume on Doctrine and Covenants 84:20–21.

What can we do to provide an opportunity for those who have died without a knowledge of the gospel? (128:5) "Surely we on this side of the veil have a great work to do. . . . We can see that the building of temples has deep significance for ourselves and mankind, and our responsibilities become clear. We must accomplish the priesthood temple ordinance work necessary for our own exaltation; then we must do the necessary work for those who did not have the opportunity to accept the gospel in life. Doing work for others is accomplished in two

with his ears, that he might make a record of a truth before the Lord.

3 Now, in relation to this matter, it would be very difficult for one recorder to be present at all times, and to do all the business. To obviate this difficulty, there can be a recorder appointed in each ward of the city, who is well qualified for taking accurate minutes; and let him be very particular and precise in taking the whole proceedings, certifying in his record that he saw with his eyes, and heard with his ears, giving the date, and names, and so forth, and the history of the whole transaction; naming also some three individuals that are present, if there be any present, who can at any time when called upon certify to the same, that in the mouth of two or three witnesses every word may be established.

4 Then, let there be a general recorder, to whom these other records can be handed, being attended with certificates over their own signatures, certifying that the record they have made is true. Then the general church recorder can enter the record on the general church book, with the certificates and all the attending witnesses, with his own statement that he verily believes the above statement and records to be true, from his knowledge of the general character and appointment of those men by the church. And when this is done on the general church book, the record shall be just as holy, and shall answer the ordinance just the same as if he had seen with his eyes and heard with his ears, and made a record of the same on the general church book.

5 You may think this order of things to be very particular; but let me tell you that it is only to answer the will of God, by conforming to the ordinance and preparation that the Lord ordained and prepared before the foundation of the world, for the salvation of the dead who should die without a knowledge of the gospel.

steps: first, by family history research to ascertain our progenitors, and second, by performing the temple ordinances to give them the same opportunities afforded to the living" (Hunter, "Temple-Motivated People," *Ensign*, Feb. 1995, 4). ⊙

Doctrine and Covenants 128:6–9. Their Records Are Binding and Recorded on Earth and in Heaven

Which books are being referred to? (128:6–7) "The book of life is the heavenly record that contains the names of the sanctified who will inherit eternal life (see D&C 132:19). The other books are the complementary records kept by proper authority on earth that show that the necessary ordinances have been performed for the sanctified (D&C 132:6–8; compare Dan. 7:10)" (Draper and Rhodes, *Revelation of John the Apostle*, 777).

The "other books" include "the records of the Church wherein are recorded the faith and good works of the saints—the records of their baptism, celestial marriage, tithe paying, missionary service, and their acts of devotion and worship" (Bruce R. McConkie, *Doctrinal New Testament Commentary*, 3:578).

6 And further, I want you to remember that John the Revelator was contemplating this very subject in relation to the dead, when he declared, as you will find recorded in Revelation 20:12—*And I saw the dead, small and great, stand before God; and the books were opened; and another book was opened, which is the book of life; and the dead were judged out of those things which were written in the books, according to their works.*

7 You will discover in this quotation that the books were opened; and another book was opened, which was the book of life; but the dead were judged out of those things which were written in the books, according to their works; consequently, the books spoken of must be the books which contained the record of their works, and refer to the records which are kept on the earth. And the book which was the book of life is the record which is kept in heaven; the principle agreeing precisely with the doctrine which is commanded you in the revelation contained in the letter which I wrote to you previous to my leaving my place—that in all your recordings it may be recorded in heaven.

8 Now, the nature of this ordinance consists in the power of the priesthood, by the revelation of Jesus Christ, wherein it is granted that whatsoever you bind on earth shall be bound in heaven, and whatsoever you loose on earth shall be loosed in heaven. Or, in other words, taking a different view of the translation, whatsoever you record on earth

What is the power to bind? (128:9) "The Prophet Joseph Smith said, 'It may seem to some to be a very bold doctrine that we talk of—a power which records or binds on earth and binds in heaven' [D&C 128:9]. The sociality we create here can exist with eternal glory there [D&C 130:2]. Indeed, 'we without [our family members] cannot be made perfect; neither can they without us be made perfect,' that is, in 'a whole and complete and perfect union' [D&C 128:18]" (Gong, "We Each Have a Story," *Liahona*, May 2022, 45).

Doctrine and Covenants 128:10–14. The Baptismal Font Is a Similitude of the Grave

What might the "rock" represent in this context? (128:10) "As the Savior taught Peter about revelation, He used a wordplay on Peter's name, declaring to Simon, 'Thou art Peter *[Petros],* and upon this rock *[petra]* I will build my church' (Matthew 16:18). The Greek word *petros* means an isolated small rock or stone. The Greek word *petra* can also mean 'a stone,' but in addition it can refer to stony soil, bedrock, or a large mass of rock. From these words we learn that it was not upon Peter as a man that the Church would be built, but upon the bedrock of revelation" (*New Testament Student Manual* [2018], 53). Christ also told Simon Peter he would be called "Cephas, which is, by interpretation, *a seer, or* a stone" (JST, John 1:42; italics mark changes).

What are "the gates of hell"? (128:10) "As used in scripture, hell has reference to the place of departed spirits ([see Bible Dictionary, s.v. "Hell," 656–57]). In some passages, though certainly not all, it refers to

shall be recorded in heaven, and whatsoever you do not record on earth shall not be recorded in heaven; for out of the books shall your dead be judged, according to their own works, whether they themselves have attended to the ordinances in their own *propria persona,* or by the means of their own agents, according to the ordinance which God has prepared for their salvation from before the foundation of the world, according to the records which they have kept concerning their dead.

9 It may seem to some to be a very bold doctrine that we talk of—a power which records or binds on earth and binds in heaven. Nevertheless, in all ages of the world, whenever the Lord has given a dispensation of the priesthood to any man by actual revelation, or any set of men, this power has always been given. Hence, whatsoever those men did in authority, in the name of the Lord, and did it truly and faithfully, and kept a proper and faithful record of the same, it became a law on earth and in heaven, and could not be annulled, according to the decrees of the great Jehovah. This is a faithful saying. Who can hear it?

10 And again, for the precedent, Matthew 16:18, 19: *And I say also unto thee, That thou art Peter, and upon this rock I will build my church; and the gates of hell shall not prevail against it. And I will give unto thee the keys of the kingdom of heaven: and whatsoever thou shalt bind on earth shall be bound in heaven; and whatsoever thou shalt loose on earth shall be loosed in heaven.*

the place of torment or the abiding place of wicked spirits. The point of this passage of scripture is that the keys being promised to Peter will have power to open such gates. A gate prevails when it keeps something in or out of a particular place. For keys to prevail is for them to either lock or unlock such a gate so that people can enter or leave the gated area" (McConkie and Ostler, *Revelations of the Restoration*, 1029). ⊕

What do the words *summum bonum* mean? (128:11) The phrase *summum bonum* is defined as: "'The supreme or highest good, . . . in which all other goods are included or from which they are derived' [*Webster's Third New International Dictionary*, s.v. 'summum bonum']. In other words, through the power of the priesthood and the one who holds the keys to the priesthood will come all the knowledge needed for salvation" (Robinson and Garrett, *Commentary on the Doctrine and Covenants*, 4:210–11).

How are baptismal fonts in temples symbolic of work for the dead? (128:12–13) "According to the plan of heaven—even before the creation of the earth—all gospel ordinances were instituted as types to testify of Christ and the principles of his gospel. Relative to baptism, Paul testified to the Saints in Rome, saying, 'Know ye not, that so many of us as were baptized into Jesus Christ were baptized into his death? Therefore we are buried with him by baptism into death: that like as Christ was raised up from the dead by the glory of the Father, even so we also should walk in newness of life. . . .'

"In harmony with this symbolism, the baptismal font in which baptisms are performed for the dead in our temples is always to be placed below the surface of the earth. Thus, those for whom we are baptized are symbolically invited to come forth from their grave into the kingdom of God" (McConkie and Ostler, *Revelations of the Restoration*, 1030–31). See also commentary in this volume on Doctrine and Covenants 124:29–30.

11 Now the great and grand secret of the whole matter, and the *summum bonum* of the whole subject that is lying before us, consists in obtaining the powers of the Holy Priesthood. For him to whom these keys are given there is no difficulty in obtaining a knowledge of facts in relation to the salvation of the children of men, both as well for the dead as for the living.

12 Herein is glory and honor, and immortality and eternal life—The ordinance of baptism by water, to be immersed therein in order to answer to the likeness of the dead, that one principle might accord with the other; to be immersed in the water and come forth out of the water is in the likeness of the resurrection of the dead in coming forth out of their graves; hence, this ordinance was instituted to form a relationship with the ordinance of baptism for the dead, being in likeness of the dead.

13 Consequently, the baptismal font was instituted as a similitude of the grave, and was commanded to be in a place underneath where the living are wont to assemble, to show forth the living and the dead, and that all things may have their likeness, and that they may accord one with another—that which is earthly conforming to that which is heavenly, as Paul hath declared, 1 Corinthians 15:46, 47, and 48:

14 *Howbeit that was not first which is spiritual, but that which is natural; and afterward that which is spiritual. The first man is of the earth, earthy; the second man is the Lord from*

Doctrine and Covenants 128:15–17. Elijah Restored Power Relative to Baptism for the Dead

What responsibility do we have to our deceased ancestors? (128:15) The Prophet Joseph Smith taught this about baptism for the dead: "This doctrine, . . . presented in a clear light, the wisdom and mercy of God, in preparing an ordinance for the salvation of the dead, being baptized by proxy, their names recorded in heaven, and they judged according to the deeds done in the body. This doctrine was the burden of the scriptures. Those saints who neglect it, in behalf of their deceased relatives, do it at the peril of their own salvation" (Joseph Smith Papers, "Discourse, 3 October 1841, as Published in *Times and Seasons*," 578). See also commentary in this volume on Doctrine and Covenants 124:31–36. ●

How could one understand the word "turn" in this verse? (128:17) Joseph Smith taught, "Now, the word *turn* here should be translated *bind*, or seal. But what is the object of this important mission? or how is it to be fulfilled? The keys are to be delivered, the spirit

heaven. *As is the earthy, such are they also that are earthy; and as is the heavenly, such are they also that are heavenly.* And as are the records on the earth in relation to your dead, which are truly made out, so also are the records in heaven. This, therefore, is the sealing and binding power, and, in one sense of the word, the keys of the kingdom, which consist in the key of knowledge.

15 And now, my dearly beloved brethren and sisters, let me assure you that these are principles in relation to the dead and the living that cannot be lightly passed over, as pertaining to our salvation. For their salvation is necessary and essential to our salvation, as Paul says concerning the fathers—that they without us cannot be made perfect—neither can we without our dead be made perfect.

16 And now, in relation to the baptism for the dead, I will give you another quotation of Paul, 1 Corinthians 15:29: *Else what shall they do which are baptized for the dead, if the dead rise not at all? Why are they then baptized for the dead?*

17 And again, in connection with this quotation I will give you a quotation from one of the prophets, who had his eye fixed on the restoration of the priesthood, the glories to

Christ's Vicarious Sacrifice for Us (Doctrine and Covenants 128:16)

President Howard W. Hunter explained: "As we study ecclesiastical history, we find that baptism for the dead was practiced by the early Christians. There was vicarious work for the dead at that time, and there is today. Indeed, vicarious work is not something new or strange to us. We remember that the Savior himself in a vicarious manner atoned for the sins of all mankind. Today, baptisms are again performed by the living in behalf of individuals who have died, as is also the laying on of hands for the bestowal of the gift of the Holy Ghost for these same deceased people. These ordinances for the deceased, however, are performed only in the house of the Lord" ("Temple-Motivated People," *Ensign*, Feb. 1995, 2).

In speaking about the Greek construction for 1 Corinthians 15:29, Richard Lloyd Anderson explained, "The preposition behind the King James 'for' is *huper*, followed by the noun in a possessive form. The meaning can be physically 'over' or 'beyond,' but it is regularly the concept of representation of one person for another. . . . This same construction appears over a hundred times to describe Christ's vicarious sacrifice 'for us' (1 Cor 5:7; 11:24:15:3). Since baptism for the dead is mentioned in the same wording as the Atonement, it is hard to argue that the latter is vicarious but not the former. Just as Christ in suffering represented others, the Saints [in Corinth] were empowered to be agents for their loved ones in baptism" (*Understanding Paul*, 405).

be revealed in the last days, and in an especial manner this most glorious of all subjects belonging to the everlasting gospel, namely, the baptism for the dead; for Malachi says, last chapter, verses 5th and 6th: *Behold, I will send you Elijah the prophet before the coming of the great and dreadful day of the Lord: And he shall turn the heart of the fathers to the children, and the heart of the children to their fathers, lest I come and smite the earth with a curse.*

18 I might have rendered a plainer translation to this, but it is sufficiently plain to suit my purpose as it stands. It is sufficient to know, in this case, that the earth will be smitten with a curse unless there is a welding link of some kind or other between the fathers and the children, upon some subject or other—and behold what is that subject? It is the baptism for the dead. For we without them cannot be made perfect; neither can they without us be made perfect. Neither can they nor we be made perfect without those who have died in the gospel also; for it is necessary in the ushering in of the dispensation of the fulness of times, which dispensation is now beginning to usher in, that a whole and complete and perfect union, and welding together of dispensations, and keys, and powers, and glories should take place, and be revealed from the days of Adam even to the present time. And not only this, but those things which never have been revealed from the foundation of the world, but have been kept hid from the wise and prudent, shall be revealed unto babes and sucklings in this, the dispensation of the fulness of times.

19 Now, what do we hear in the gospel which we have received? A voice of gladness! A voice of mercy from heaven; and a voice of truth out of the earth; glad tidings for the dead; a voice of gladness for the living and the dead; glad tidings of great joy. How beautiful upon the mountains are the feet of those that bring

of Elijah is to come, the Gospel to be established, the Saints of God gathered, Zion built up, and the Saints to come up as saviors on Mount Zion [see Obadiah 1:21]" (*Joseph Smith* [manual], 472–73). ⊙

Doctrine and Covenants 128:18–21. All of the Keys, Powers, and Authorities of Past Dispensations Have Been Restored

How does the welding link of vicarious ordinances safeguard the earth from being smitten with a curse? (128:18) President Jeffrey R. Holland taught that without the sealing power to weld parents to children, "no family ties would exist in the eternities, and indeed the family of man would have been left in eternity with 'neither root [ancestors] nor branch [descendants].'

"Inasmuch as . . . a sealed, united, celestially saved family of God is the ultimate purpose of mortality, any failure here would have been a curse indeed, rendering the entire plan of salvation 'utterly wasted'" (*Christ and the New Covenant*, 297–98).

How could Joseph know about the "dews of Carmel"? (128:19) Danel Bachman wrote: "Though Mt. Carmel is mentioned in the Bible, the 'dews of Carmel' *are not.* . . .

"'Dewfall provides a limited amount of moisture even during the dry summer. . . . In general, the Coastal Plain has more dew than inland regions; richest is Mount Carmel, which has an average 250 nights of dew per year' [Efraim Orni and Elisha Efrat, *Geography of Israel*, 147].

"How did Joseph Smith know that? . . . I bet some have tried to find a source available in America in 1842, when Section 128 was written. . . . For me, the answer is simple. He did not know that information, but the Lord God, the Creator of heaven and earth did. And he was Joseph Smith's source" ("Why I Believe").

What do we know about the restoration of the Melchizedek Priesthood? (128:20) Although we do not have the precise date of the restoration of the Melchizedek Priesthood, the "Doctrine and Covenants attests in several places that the higher priesthood *was* subsequently restored. In Section 27 (August 1830), the Lord refers to the restoration of the Melchizedek Priesthood as something which had already taken place" (Larry C. Porter, "Dating the Restoration of the Melchizedek Priesthood," *Ensign*, Jun. 1979, 6).

"The Prophet wrote of 'the voice of Peter, James, and John in the wilderness between Harmony, Susquehanna county, and Colesville, Broome county, on the Susquehanna river, declaring themselves as possessing the keys of the kingdom, and of the dispensation of the fulness of times!' (D&C 128:20)" (Larry C. Porter, "Restoration of the Aaronic and Melchizedek Priesthoods," *Ensign*, Dec. 1996, 42). ☉

How was Joseph Smith so conversant regarding these ancient prophets and apostles? (128:21) President John Taylor related, "'The principles which [Joseph Smith] had, placed him in communication with the Lord, and not only with the Lord, but with the ancient apostles and prophets; such men, for instance, as Abraham, Isaac, Jacob, Noah, Adam, Seth, Enoch, and Jesus and the Father, and the apostles that lived on this continent. . . . He seemed to be as familiar with these people as we are with one another' [in *Journal of Discourses*, 21:94]. Joseph B. Noble, an early Latter-day Saint convert, reported that Joseph Smith told him that he knew the angels so well that he could recognize them by the sound of their voices even before he saw their faces [*Remembering Joseph*, 24]" (Brian L. Smith, "Taught from on High," 336).

glad tidings of good things, and that say unto Zion: Behold, thy God reigneth! As the dews of Carmel, so shall the knowledge of God descend upon them!

20 And again, what do we hear? Glad tidings from Cumorah! Moroni, an angel from heaven, declaring the fulfilment of the prophets—the book to be revealed. A voice of the Lord in the wilderness of Fayette, Seneca county, declaring the three witnesses to bear record of the book! The voice of Michael on the banks of the Susquehanna, detecting the devil when he appeared as an angel of light! The voice of Peter, James, and John in the wilderness between Harmony, Susquehanna county, and Colesville, Broome county, on the Susquehanna river, declaring themselves as possessing the keys of the kingdom, and of the dispensation of the fulness of times!

21 And again, the voice of God in the chamber of old Father Whitmer, in Fayette, Seneca county, and at sundry times, and in divers places through all the travels and tribulations of this Church of Jesus Christ of Latter-day Saints! And the voice of Michael, the archangel; the voice of Gabriel, and of Raphael, and of divers angels, from Michael or Adam down to the present time, all declaring their dispensation, their rights, their keys, their honors, their majesty and glory, and the power of their priesthood; giving line upon line, precept upon precept; here a little, and there a little; giving us consolation by holding forth that which is to come, confirming our hope!

22 Brethren, shall we not go on in so great a cause? Go forward and not backward. Courage, brethren; and on, on to the victory! Let your hearts rejoice, and be exceedingly glad. Let the earth break forth into singing. Let the dead speak forth anthems of eternal praise to the King Immanuel, who hath ordained, before the world was, that which would enable us to redeem them out of their prison; for the prisoners shall go free.

23 Let the mountains shout for joy, and all ye valleys cry aloud; and all ye seas and dry lands tell the wonders of your Eternal King! And ye rivers, and brooks, and rills, flow down with gladness. Let the woods and all the trees of the field praise the Lord; and ye solid rocks weep for joy! And let the sun, moon, and the morning stars sing together, and let all the sons of God shout for joy! And let the eternal creations declare his

Doctrine and Covenants 128:22–25. Glad and Glorious Tidings Are Acclaimed for the Living and the Dead

How will those in spirit prison go free? (128:22) "Temple and family history work is not just about us. Think of those on the other side of the veil waiting for the saving ordinances that would free them from the bondage of spirit prison. *Prison* is defined as 'a state of confinement or captivity.' . . .

"One faithful sister shared a special spiritual experience in the Salt Lake Temple. While in the confirmation room, after a vicarious confirmation ordinance was pronounced, she heard, 'And the prisoner shall go free!' She felt a great sense of urgency for those who were waiting for their baptismal and confirmation work. Upon returning home, she searched the scriptures for the phrase she had heard. She found Joseph Smith's declaration in section 128 of the Doctrine and Covenants [D&C 128:22; see also D&C 138:42]" (Quentin L. Cook, "Roots and Branches," *Ensign*, May 2014, 46).

How do all things, even the earth itself, bear testimony of Jesus Christ? (128:23) The Lord instructed Adam, "Behold, all things have their likeness, and all things are created and made to bear record of me, both things which are temporal, and things which are spiritual; things which are in the heavens above, and things which are on the earth, and things which are in the earth, and things which are under the earth . . . all things bear record of me" [Moses 6:63]. . . .

"If we had sufficient insight, we would see . . . in all things Deity gives his people, something that typifies the eternal ministry of the Eternal Christ. . . .

"Shall We Not Go on in So Great a Cause?" (Doctrine and Covenants 128:22)

President Spencer W. Kimball provided insight into the meaning of this verse in its context: "We have asked the members of the Church to further the work of turning the hearts of the children to the fathers by getting their sacred family records in order. These records, including especially the 'book containing the records of our dead' (D&C 128:24), are a portion of the 'offering in righteousness' referred to by Malachi (Mal. 3:3), which we are to present in His holy temple, and without which we shall not abide the day of His coming.

"We also have asked that the families of the Church organize themselves to perform more efficiently their sacred missionary, welfare, home education, temple, and genealogical responsibilities and to set the pattern for things to come. I recall it was said that the last public words of my grandfather, Heber C. Kimball, were to the effect that the time had come for all men to set their houses in order.

"The Prophet Joseph Smith said: 'Brethren, shall we not go on in so great a cause? Go forward and not backward. Courage, brethren; and on, on to the victory! Let your hearts rejoice, and be exceedingly glad' (D&C 128:22).

"My prayer for all of us who are members of the Church in this great dispensation of the fulness of times is that we might indeed go forward in this great work so that we will not stand in jeopardy of our eternal reward" ("Things of Eternity," *Ensign*, Jan. 1977, 7).

"It is wholesome and proper to look for similitudes of Christ everywhere and to use them repeatedly in keeping him and his laws uppermost in our minds" (Bruce R. McConkie, *Promised Messiah*, 378, 453).

What is the offering the sons of Levi will offer unto the Lord in righteousness? (128:24) "Moroni ... promised that the priesthood would be revealed. John the Baptist next came to begin its revelation and added that the priesthood would remain on the earth until the sons of Levi made an offering in righteousness to the Lord. In section 84, the sons of Levi were identified as all priesthood holders, and it was revealed that the offering would be made in the temple. . . . Doctrine and Covenants 128 invited all the Saints to participate in the offering, and the offering was identified. It would be a book containing all the records of ordinance work for the dead" (Wilcox, *House of Glory*, 116). ◉

name forever and ever! And again I say, how glorious is the voice we hear from heaven, proclaiming in our ears, glory, and salvation, and honor, and immortality, and eternal life; kingdoms, principalities, and powers!

24 Behold, the great day of the Lord is at hand; and who can abide the day of his coming, and who can stand when he appeareth? For he is like a refiner's fire, and like fuller's soap; and he shall sit as a refiner and purifier of silver, and he shall purify the sons of Levi, and purge them as gold and silver, that they may offer unto the Lord an offering in righteousness. Let us, therefore, as a church and a people, and as Latter-day Saints, offer unto the Lord an offering in righteousness; and let us present in his holy temple, when it is finished, a book containing the records of our dead, which shall be worthy of all acceptation.

25 Brethren, I have many things to say to you on the subject; but shall now close for the present, and continue the subject another time. I am, as ever, your humble servant and never deviating friend,

JOSEPH SMITH.

"On 9 February 1843, [Joseph Smith] delivered an instruction to guests he was entertaining at his home in Nauvoo, Illinois. [The Prophet] apparently gave the remarks during a casual conversation with apostles Orson Pratt and Parley P. Pratt and others who had called on him in the afternoon. Though they were not delivered as a formal discourse, his teachings were significant enough that William Clayton and Willard Richards, who were both present on this occasion, wrote them down. Prefacing his remarks, [Joseph] 'related some of his history' and then instructed those in attendance how they 'might know whether any administration was from God' [Clayton, Journal, 9 Feb. 1843]. . . .

"[The Prophet]'s remarks in February 1843 centered on an explanation of the ways to distinguish between various types of heavenly messengers and the devil. Among eighteenth- and nineteenth-century Protestants, there were several competing ideas about the identification of angels, most of them based on a passage in the epistle to the Hebrews that mentions 'an innumerable company of angels' and the 'spirits of just men made perfect' [Hebrews 12:22–23]. . . .

"[Joseph] suggested a new idea, which classified heavenly messengers as either resurrected corporeal beings or disembodied spirits awaiting resurrection. These distinctions may have appeared in Latter-day Saint theology as early as 1829, when the Book of Mormon suggested a difference between 'angels and ministering spirits.' In [the Prophet]'s 'new translation' of the Bible, however, Hebrews 1:7 explained that 'angels are ministering spirits.' . . .

"[Joseph Smith] used this occasion in February 1843 to refine that explanation by distinguishing between 'resurrected personages' and 'the spirits of just men made perfect' who were still awaiting resurrection" (Joseph Smith Papers, Historical Introduction to "Instruction, 9 February 1843 [D&C 129], as Reported by Willard Richards").

SECTION 129

Instructions given by Joseph Smith the Prophet, at Nauvoo, Illinois, February 9, 1843, making known three grand keys by which the correct nature of ministering angels and spirits may be distinguished.

1 There are two kinds of beings in heaven, namely: Angels, who are resurrected personages, having bodies of flesh and bones—

2 For instance, Jesus said: *Handle me and see, for a spirit hath not flesh and bones, as ye see me have.*

3 Secondly: the spirits of just men made perfect, they who are not resurrected, but inherit the same glory.

Doctrine and Covenants 129:1–3. There Are Both Resurrected and Spirit Bodies in Heaven

What do we understand about the nature of angels? (129:1–3) "[Angels] are messengers of the Lord and are spoken of in the epistle to the Hebrews as 'ministering spirits' (Heb. 1:14). We learn from latter-day revelation that there are two classes of heavenly beings who minister for the Lord: those who are spirits and those who have bodies of flesh and bone. Spirits are those beings who either have not yet obtained a body of flesh and bone (unembodied) or who have once had a mortal body and have died and are awaiting the Resurrection (disembodied). Ordinarily the word *angel* means those ministering persons who have a body of flesh and bone, being either resurrected from the dead (reembodied), or else translated, as were Enoch, Elijah, etc. (D&C 129)" (Bible Dictionary, s.v. "Angels," 591). ●

What does the phrase "spirits of just men made perfect" mean? (129:3) "No mortal person lives a perfect life. Some, however, live the gospel so well that they become, before their life is over, what the scriptures describe as 'just men.' But being just is not enough. The Savior commanded, 'Be ye therefore perfect' (Matthew 5:48), and we cannot do that without His help. So the scriptures speak of 'just men *made* perfect through Jesus the mediator of the new covenant' (D&C 76:69; [emphasis] added)" (*Doctrine and Covenants Student Manual* [2001], 320). "Just men" refers to faithful "spirits who have once had a mortal body and are awaiting resurrection" (Guide to the Scriptures, "Angels").

Doctrine and Covenants 129:4–9. Keys Are Given Whereby Messengers from beyond the Veil May Be Identified

What does shaking an angelic messenger's hand reveal? (129:4–9) "Doctrine and Covenants 129 contains esoteric knowledge. That is, it says much more to those who have been taught than to those who have not. It is a temple-related text. It gives those who understand it power to discern true from false messengers (see v. 8; see also D&C 128:20), for if Satan could appear in the guise of an angel without our having any ability to know better, 'we could not be free agents' [Joseph Smith Papers, "Account of Meeting and Discourse, circa 16 March 1841," (16)]" (Harper, *Making Sense of the Doctrine & Covenants*, 473).

Where else in the scriptures do we find this manner of confirming true heavenly messengers? (129:4–5) "There is a recorded instance of mortals who had a need to test a personage. Joseph Smith referred to Jesus's visitation to his eleven apostles in Jerusalem the day that he was resurrected; the apostles 'were terrified and affrighted, and supposed that they had seen a spirit. . . .' [see Luke 24:37–39]. On this occasion, Jesus was offering one of the keys—'to prove spirits.' Joseph Smith taught, '[Jesus' disciples] were afraid and thought they had seen a spirit but he convinces them of their mistake by telling them to handle him for, says he, a spirit has not flesh and bones as ye see me have' [Joseph Smith Papers, "Discourse, 9 October 1943, as Reported by James Burgess, (18–19); punctuation modernized]" (Parry, *Angels*, 194).

Why can a spirit of a just man only appear in glory? (129:6) "Without a physical tabernacle of flesh and bones, such as a resurrected angel possesses, a perfected spirit cannot hide his glory from the one to whom he appears. It seems that hiding one's glory is a prerogative of resurrected beings (Luke 24:15–16, 31; John 20:14–15; 21:4)" (Robinson and Garrett, *Commentary on the Doctrine and Covenants*, 4:218).

4 When a messenger comes saying he has a message from God, offer him your hand and request him to shake hands with you.

5 If he be an angel he will do so, and you will feel his hand.

6 If he be the spirit of a just man made perfect he will come in his glory; for that is the only way he can appear—

7 Ask him to shake hands with you, but he will not move, because it is contrary to the order of heaven for a just man to deceive; but he will still deliver his message.

8 If it be the devil as an angel of light, when you ask him to shake hands he will offer you his hand, and you will not feel anything; you may therefore detect him.

9 These are three grand keys whereby you may know whether any administration is from God.

Why wouldn't an evil spirit simply refuse to extend his hand when deceiving? (129:8) "God, who governs all things, has placed limits and bounds on the adversary as to what he can and cannot do. In the instance here cited, Satan, or those acting in his name, must either extend his hand or withdraw, and in either case he will be detected. William Clayton recorded the Prophet as saying in 1840 that 'if an angel or spirit appears, offer him your hand; if he is a spirit from God, he will stand still and not offer you his hand. If from the Devil, he will either shrink back from you or offer his hand, which if he does you will feel nothing, but be deceived' [Joseph Smith Papers, "Discourse, December 1840, as Reported by William Clayton," 3]" (McConkie and Ostler, *Revelations of the Restoration*, 1042). ⊕

What did Joseph Smith teach about keys for discerning true messengers? (129:9) "When an angel of God appears unto man face to face in personage & reaches out his hand unto the man & he takes hold of the angels hand & feels a substance the Same as one man would in shaking hands with another he may then know that it is an angel of God, & he should place all Confidence in him Such personages or angels are Saints with their resurrected Bodies, but if a personage appears unto man & offers him his hand & the man takes hold of it & he feels nothing or does not sense any substance he may know it is the devil, for when a Saint whose body is not resurrected appears unto man in the flesh he will not offer him his hand for this is against the law given him & in keeping in mind these things we may detect the devil that he deceived us not" (Joseph Smith Papers, "Wilford Woodruff, Journal, Discourse, 27 June 1839, as Reported by Wilford Woodruff–B," 85; spelling modernized). ⊕

Introduction to Doctrine and Covenants 130

"On 2 April 1843 the Prophet went to a meeting in Ramus, Illinois, in which Orson Hyde spoke of Christ appearing at the time of His second coming as a warrior riding on a horse and how each of us can have the Father and the Son dwelling in our hearts. 'We dined with my sister Sophronia McCleary,' the Prophet said, 'when I told Elder Hyde that I was going to offer some corrections to his sermon this morning. He replied, "They shall be thankfully received."' Joseph then delivered what we now have as the first seventeen verses of Doctrine and Covenants 130. He explained, among other things, that when the Savior appears he will appear as a man and that the idea of the Father and Son dwelling in our hearts is an old sectarian notion and is false. Later that day instructions that constitute verses 18–23 of section 130 were given" (Millet, *Precept upon Precept*, 311).

Doctrine and Covenants 130:1–3. The Father and the Son May Appear Personally to Men

What are we to understand about Jesus Christ being "a man like ourselves"? (130:1) "When the resurrected Christ ascended into heaven, two angels stood by testifying to the Twelve who were with him, 'Ye men of Galilee, why stand ye gazing up into heaven? This same Jesus, which is taken up from you into heaven, shall so come in like manner as ye have seen him go into heaven' (Acts 1:11). It was a man with 'flesh and bones' who ascended from their sight that day, one whom they had embraced and felt the warmth of his body, one with whom they had taken meat, walked, talked, and shared the sociality known to them before his death upon the cross" (McConkie and Ostler, *Revelations of the Restoration*, 1044–45).

What is the "sociality" that will exist among us in eternity? (130:2) "The promise to the faithful in The Church of Jesus Christ of Latter-day Saints is that we may have associations and an expansion of families in the eternities. That assurance changes forever and for the better all of our associations in families. . . .

"Because of the restoration of the knowledge of eternal families, we are more hopeful and more kindly in all our family relations. The greatest joys in this life center in families, as they will in the worlds to come. I am so grateful for the assurance . . . that if we are faithful, the same sociality which we enjoy here in this life will be forever with us in the world to come, in eternal glory" (Eyring, "True and Living Church," *Ensign*, May 2008, 22). ⊕

What is the meaning of John 14:23? (130:3) "The passage in question quotes Jesus as saying: 'If a man love me, he will keep my words: and my Father will love him, and we will come unto him, and make our abode

SECTION 130

Items of instruction given by Joseph Smith the Prophet, at Ramus, Illinois, April 2, 1843.

1 When the Savior shall appear we shall see him as he is. We shall see that he is a man like ourselves.

2 And that same sociality which exists among us here will exist among us there, only it will be coupled with eternal glory, which glory we do not now enjoy.

3 John 14:23—The appearing of the Father and the Son, in that verse, is a personal appearance; and the idea that the Father and the Son dwell in a man's heart is an old sectarian notion, and is false.

4 In answer to the question—Is not the reckoning of God's time, angel's time, prophet's time, and man's time, according to the planet on which they reside?

5 I answer, Yes. But there are no angels who minister to this earth but those who do belong or have belonged to it.

with him.' The Prophet Joseph explained that this statement is literal, not a figure of speech. It is a promise that the Father and the Son will appear to a person" (*Doctrine and Covenants Student Manual* [2001], 321). ⊕

Doctrine and Covenants 130:4–7. Angels Reside in a Celestial Sphere

How does God measure time? (130:4) Elder Neal A. Maxwell taught, "God does not live in the dimension of time as do we. Moreover, since 'all things are present with' God [Moses 1:6], his is not simply a predicting based solely upon the past. In ways which are not clear to us, he actually *sees*, rather than *foresees*, the future—because all things are, at once, present, before him! . . .

"He is the living God who is, at once, in all the dimensions of time—the past and present and future—while we labor constrained by the limitations of time itself" ("Meeting the Challenges of Today," 7). ⊕

What do we know about angels and their relationship to this earth? (130:4–5) "When messengers are sent to minister to the inhabitants of this earth, they are not strangers, but from the ranks of our kindred, friends, and fellow-beings and fellow-servants. The ancient prophets who died were those who came to visit their fellow creatures upon the earth. They came to Abraham, to Isaac, and to Jacob; it was such beings—holy beings if you please—who waited upon the Savior and administered to him on the Mount. The angel that visited John, when an exile and unfolded to his vision future events in the history of man upon the earth, was one who had been here, who had toiled and suffered in common with the people of God" (Joseph F. Smith, *Gospel Doctrine*, 435–36).

"The Appearing of the Father and the Son" (Doctrine and Covenants 130:3)

Addressing the passage in John 14:12–27, the Prophet Joseph Smith explained: "After a person hath faith in Christ, repents of his sins, and is baptized for the remission of his sins, and receives the Holy Ghost (by the laying on of hands) which is the first Comforter, then let him continue to humble himself before God, hungering and thirsting after Righteousness, and living by every word of God, and the Lord will soon say unto him, Son thou shalt be exalted &c. When the Lord has [thoroughly] proved him, and finds that the man is determined to serve him at all hazard, then the man will find his calling and Election made sure, then it will be his privilege to receive the *other Comforter*. . . . Now what is this other *Comforter*? It is no more or less than the *Lord Jesus Christ* himself, and this is the sum and substance of the whole matter, that when any man obtains this last Comforter he will have the personage of Jesus Christ to attend him or appear unto him from time to time, and even he will manifest the Father unto him, and they will take up their abode with him, and the visions of the heavens will be opened unto him and the Lord will teach him face to face, and he may have a perfect knowledge of the mysteries of the kingdom of God" (Joseph Smith Papers, "History, 1838–1856, volume C-1," 8–9 [addenda]).

Where do the angels of God live and what is it like there? (130:6–7) "Angels live 'in the presence of God' (D&C 130:7). As messengers of the Most High, they minister among His children. The scripture states that the place where God and the angels live is one vast 'Urim and Thummim' (v. 8). All things necessary for the angels' glory is manifest to them there: the past, the present, and the future" (*Doctrine and Covenants Student Manual* [1981, 2001], 322).

How can God see all things continually? (130:7) "In the presence of God all things are manifest (which means 'made clear'), including what is *past*, *present*, and *future*, and are continually before the Lord. . . . In this life, time comes to us in a linear fashion. We can remember the past and imagine the future, but we can only experience the present. And that moment we call 'the present' is always, inexorably moving forward. But what Joseph taught seems to suggest that God is *above* the timeline, not *on* it. Thus He can look 'down' on us and see our past, our present, and our future simultaneously. This would explain one of His divine attributes, that He is an all-knowing Being" (Lund, *Second Coming of the Lord*, 64).

Doctrine and Covenants 130:8–9. The Celestial Earth Will Be a Great Urim and Thummim

How might we better understand the earth becoming a Urim and Thummim? (130:8–9) "On February 18, 1843, Joseph Smith [first] taught that the earth would eventually be sanctified and become a Urim and Thummim (see [*Joseph Smith Papers: Journals, Volume 2*], 266). . . . This is a symbolic expression. Isaiah spoke of a future day when 'the earth shall be full of the knowledge of the Lord, as the waters cover the sea' (Isaiah 11:9). . . . Just as the Urim and Thummim revealed light and truth to God's servants, the celestialized earth will be a place where the glory, power, and knowledge of God will be manifested" (*Doctrine and Covenants Student Manual* [2018], 754–55). See also commentary in this volume on Doctrine and Covenants 77:1.

6 The angels do not reside on a planet like this earth;

7 But they reside in the presence of God, on a globe like a sea of glass and fire, where all things for their glory are manifest, past, present, and future, and are continually before the Lord.

8 The place where God resides is a great Urim and Thummim.

9 This earth, in its sanctified and immortal state, will be made like unto crystal and will be a Urim and Thummim to the inhabitants who dwell thereon, whereby all things pertaining to an inferior kingdom, or all kingdoms of a lower order, will be manifest to those who dwell on it; and this earth will be Christ's.

Doctrine and Covenants 130:10–11. A White Stone Is Given to All Who Enter the Celestial World

10 Then the white stone mentioned in Revelation 2:17, will become a Urim and Thummim to each individual who receives one, whereby things pertaining to a higher order of kingdoms will be made known;

11 And a white stone is given to each of those who come into the celestial kingdom, whereon is a new name written, which no man knoweth save he that receiveth it. The new name is the key word.

What will be a purpose of the white stone? (130:10–11) "Everyone who inherits the celestial kingdom will receive 'a white stone,' which will be for them a personal or private Urim and Thummim, just as the earth itself will become a public Urim and Thummim common to all who dwell upon it. In this way, information concerning lower kingdoms will be available to all (through the sea of glass and fire), while information concerning higher kingdoms will be revealed privately (through the white stone) according to each individual's readiness for further light and knowledge" (Robinson and Garrett, *Commentary on the Doctrine and Covenants*, 4:226–27).

What is the importance of receiving a new name? (130:11) "Ours is the day and dispensation of restoration. It seems appropriate that if names and their meanings were of such importance to the ancient Saints, they ought to carry that same richness of meaning for us. Our theology ought to embrace the idea, as did that of the ancients, that there are occasions, very sacred in nature, when in the context of making sacred covenants and receiving blessings we too would be found receiving new names" (Joseph Fielding McConkie, *Gospel Symbolism*, 192–93).

Doctrine and Covenants 130:12–17. The Time of the Second Coming Is Withheld from the Prophet

12 I prophesy, in the name of the Lord God, that the commencement of the difficulties which will cause much bloodshed previous to the coming of the Son of Man will be in South Carolina.

13 It may probably arise through the slave question. This a voice declared to me, while I was praying earnestly on the subject, December 25th, 1832.

14 I was once praying very earnestly to know the time of the coming of the Son of Man, when I heard a voice repeat the following:

15 Joseph, my son, if thou livest until thou art eighty-five years old, thou shalt see the face of the Son of Man; therefore let this suffice, and trouble me no more on this matter.

What did the Prophet Joseph Smith prophesy regarding the Civil War? (130:12–13) See commentary in this volume on Doctrine and Covenants 87.

What does this passage teach us regarding the timing of the Second Coming? (130:14–17) On March 10, 1844, almost a year after the instructions of section 130 were given, the Prophet taught: "Jesus Christ never did reveal to any man the precise time that he would come [see Matthew 24:36; D&C 49:7]. Go and read the Scriptures, and you cannot find anything that specifies the exact hour He would come; and all that say so are false teachers" (*Joseph Smith* [manual], 253). ●

Doctrine and Covenants 130:18–19. Intelligence Gained in This Life Rises with Us in the Resurrection

What is the eternal advantage of obtaining knowledge? (130:18–19) "Knowledge is revelation. Hear, all ye brethren, this grand key: knowledge is the power of God unto salvation. . . .

"Knowledge does away with darkness, suspense and doubt; for these cannot exist where knowledge is. . . . In knowledge there is power. . . .

"A man is saved no faster than he gets knowledge, for if he does not get knowledge, he will be brought into captivity by some evil power in the other world, as evil spirits will have more knowledge, and consequently more power than many men who are on the earth. Hence it needs revelation to assist us, and give us knowledge of the things of God" (*Joseph Smith* [manual], 265, 266). ◉

Doctrine and Covenants 130:20–21. All Blessings Come by Obedience to Law

What must we do to be blessed by God's laws? (130:20) "Divine law . . . is unchanging and incontrovertible. Cling to it as a firm bulwark of security. It will provide stability through the storms of life. It will provide intelligence to guide each of you, whether your career be that of farmer, mother, surgeon, or teacher. It will provide reassurance that a desired result can be reached—by strict obedience to the law that pertains to a desired objective (see Doctrine and Covenants 130:21). To comprehend divine law requires careful searching and prayerful study. To be blessed by divine law requires meticulous compliance, with no requests for personal exceptions or shortcuts" (Nelson, *Teachings*, 179). ◉

How is obedience related to the Lord's blessings? (130:20–21) Elder Dale G. Renlund stated: "The principle of activating blessings that flow from God is eternal. . . . [We] must act on our faith in Jesus Christ to be blessed. . . . That being said, you do not earn a blessing—that notion is false—but you do have to qualify for it. Our salvation comes only through the merits and grace of Jesus Christ [see 2 Nephi 10:24; 25:23]. . . .

16 I was left thus, without being able to decide whether this coming referred to the beginning of the millennium or to some previous appearing, or whether I should die and thus see his face.

17 I believe the coming of the Son of Man will not be any sooner than that time.

18 Whatever principle of intelligence we attain unto in this life, it will rise with us in the resurrection.

19 And if a person gains more knowledge and intelligence in this life through his diligence and obedience than another, he will have so much the advantage in the world to come.

20 There is a law, irrevocably decreed in heaven before the foundations of this world, upon which all blessings are predicated—

21 And when we obtain any blessing from God, it is by obedience to that law upon which it is predicated.

"When you receive any blessing from God, you can conclude that you have complied with an eternal law governing reception of that blessing [see D&C 130:20–21]. But remember that the 'irrevocably decreed' law is time insensitive, meaning blessings come on God's timetable" ("Abound with Blessings," *Ensign*, May 2019, 71, 72). See also commentary in this volume on Doctrine and Covenants 82:10. ●

Doctrine and Covenants 130:22–23. The Father and the Son Have Bodies of Flesh and Bones

What does it mean for the Holy Ghost to "dwell in us"? (130:22) "The Holy Ghost as a personage does not inhabit the bodies of mortal men, but that member of the Godhead dwells in a man in the sense that his promptings, the whisperings of the Spirit, find lodgment in the human soul. When the Holy Spirit speaks to the spirit in man, the Holy Ghost is thereby dwelling in man, for the truths that man then gives forth are those which have come from the Holy Ghost" (Bruce R. McConkie, *Doctrinal New Testament Commentary*, 1:738). ●

22 The Father has a body of flesh and bones as tangible as man's; the Son also; but the Holy Ghost has not a body of flesh and bones, but is a personage of Spirit. Were it not so, the Holy Ghost could not dwell in us.

23 A man may receive the Holy Ghost, and it may descend upon him and not tarry with him.

What can we learn from knowing that the Holy Ghost may "not tarry" with us? (130:23) "The presentation or 'gift' of the Holy Ghost simply confers

What Is the Godhead? (Doctrine and Covenants 130:22–23)

"There are three separate persons in the Godhead: God, the Eternal Father; His Son, Jesus Christ; and the Holy Ghost. We believe in each of Them ([Articles of Faith] 1:1). From latter-day revelation we learn that the Father and the Son have tangible bodies of flesh and bone and that the Holy Ghost is a personage of spirit, without flesh and bone (D&C 130:22–23). These three persons are one in perfect unity and harmony of purpose and doctrine (John 17:21–23; 2 Ne. 31:21; 3 Ne. 11:27, 36).

"*God the Father:* It is generally the Father, or Elohim, who is referred to by the title God. He is called the Father because He is the father of our spirits.... God the Father is the supreme ruler of the universe. He is all powerful ..., all knowing ..., and everywhere present through his Spirit.... [Humankind] has a special relationship to God that sets man apart from all other created things: men and women are God's spirit children....

"*God the Son:* The God known as Jehovah is the Son, Jesus Christ.... Jesus works under the direction of the Father and is in complete harmony with him. All [people] are His brothers and sisters, for He is the eldest of the spirit children of Elohim. Some scripture references refer to Him by the word *God*. For example, the scripture says that 'God created the heaven and the earth' (Gen. 1:1), but it was actually Jesus who was the Creator under the direction of God the Father....

"*God the Holy Ghost:* The Holy Ghost is also a God and is called the Holy Spirit, the Spirit, and the Spirit of God, among other similar names and titles" (Guide to the Scriptures, "God, Godhead"; paragraphing altered).

"[The Holy Ghost] 'witnesses of the Father and the Son' (2 Nephi 31:18) and reveals and teaches 'the truth of all things' (Moroni 10:5). We can receive a sure testimony of Heavenly Father and Jesus Christ only by the power of the Holy Ghost. His communication to our spirit carries far more certainty than any communication we can receive through our natural senses" (Topics and Questions, s.v. "Holy Ghost").

upon a man the right to receive at any time, when he is worthy of it and desires it, the power and light of truth of the Holy Ghost, although he may often be left to his own spirit and judgment. . . .

"[The Holy Ghost] may be conferred upon men, and he may dwell with them for a while, or he may continue to dwell with them in accordance with their worthiness, and he may depart from them at his will" (Joseph F. Smith, *Gospel Doctrine*, 60–61, 466). ⊕

Introduction to Doctrine and Covenants 131

The truths in Doctrine and Covenants 131 were taught by the Prophet Joseph Smith in Ramus, Illinois, on May 16 and 17, 1843. "Ramus . . . was a settlement situated about 22 miles southeast of Nauvoo. The Prophet often visited this place and preached some powerful discourses there.

"On the 16th of May, 1843, a little company, consisting of Joseph Smith, George Miller, William Clayton, Eliza and Lydia Partridge, and [Julia Murdock Smith], went to Ramus. The Prophet and William Clayton stayed at Benjamin F. Johnson's over night. Before retiring, the little party of friends engaged in conversation on spiritual topics" (Smith and Sjodahl, *Doctrine and Covenants Commentary*, 818).

"Doctrine and Covenants 131 is composed largely of several short journal entries kept by William [Clayton] during May 1843. Among these were teachings regarding eternal marriage . . . [The Prophet] taught that men and women needed to enter into the new and everlasting covenant of marriage in order to obtain God's highest blessings. He then sealed Benjamin and Melissa for eternity.

"For William [Clayton], recording these prophetic utterances was more than a duty; it was one of the great privileges of his life. He thrilled at the way Joseph Smith collapsed the distance between this world and the next and made the things of eternity feel tangible and real" (McBride, "Our Hearts Rejoiced to Hear Him Speak," 279–80).

"This section is a compilation of inspired statements made by the Prophet Joseph Smith on three separate occasions: . . . 1. Three degrees in the celestial glory 2. The more sure word of prophecy 3. A man cannot be saved in ignorance 4. Spirit is matter" (Otten and Caldwell, *Sacred Truths*, 2:348; paragraphing altered).

Doctrine and Covenants 131:1–4. Celestial Marriage Is Essential to Exaltation in the Highest Heaven

What do these verses teach about those who receive the highest degree of the Celestial Kingdom? (131:1–3) "While salvation is an individual matter, exaltation is a family matter. Only those who are married in the temple and whose marriage is sealed by the Holy Spirit of Promise will continue as spouses after death [See D&C 76:53; 132:7] and receive the highest degree of celestial glory, or exaltation. A temple marriage is also called a celestial marriage. Within the celestial glory are three levels. To obtain the highest, a husband and wife must be sealed for time and all eternity and keep their covenants made in a holy temple [see D&C 131:1–3]" (Nelson, "Celestial Marriage," *Ensign,* Nov. 2008, 92).

SECTION 131

Instructions by Joseph Smith the Prophet, given at Ramus, Illinois, May 16 and 17, 1843.

1 In the celestial glory there are three heavens or degrees;

2 And in order to obtain the highest, a man must enter into this order of the priesthood [meaning the new and everlasting covenant of marriage];

3 And if he does not, he cannot obtain it.

In what ways do both men and women "enter into this order of the priesthood"? (131:2) President Russell M. Nelson stated: "Men and women receive the highest ordinance in the house of the Lord together and equally, or not at all (see D&C 131:1–3)" ("Woman—Of Infinite Worth," *Ensign*, Nov. 1989, 20).

"We can enter an order of the priesthood named the new and everlasting covenant of marriage (see D&C 131:2), named also the patriarchal order, because of which order we can create for ourselves eternal family units of our own, patterned after the family of God our Heavenly Father" (Bruce R. McConkie, "Doctrine of the Priesthood," *Ensign*, May 1982, 34). ⊕

What is "the new and everlasting covenant of marriage"? (131:2) "The new and everlasting covenant of marriage is a portion of *the* new and everlasting covenant, which is the fulness of the gospel. It is a sacred marriage, solemnized between husband and wife in one of the holy temples of the Lord and performed by one authorized of the Lord through His earthly prophet. It is an everlasting marriage which transcends time and endures throughout eternity....

"Only those who enter into this order of marriage, and through their life-long righteousness have this relationship ratified, will receive the blessings of exaltation and eternal increase, as husband and wife together, throughout the eternities (D&C 131:1–4; 132:4, 7, 18–20)" (Brewster, *Doctrine & Covenants Encyclopedia*, 386–87).

Why is celestial marriage between a man and a woman essential for exaltation? (131:2–4) Elder David A. Bednar declared in answer to the question why marriage is essential: "In 'The Family: A Proclamation to the World,' the First Presidency and Council of the Twelve Apostles proclaim 'that marriage between a man and a woman is ordained of God and that the family is central to the Creator's plan for the eternal destiny of His children.' This keynote sentence of the proclamation teaches us much about the doctrinal significance of marriage and emphasizes the primacy of marriage and family in the Father's plan. Righteous marriage is a commandment and an essential step in the process of creating a loving family relationship that can be perpetuated beyond the grave" ("Marriage Is Essential to His Eternal Plan," 82–83). ⊕

4 He may enter into the other, but that is the end of his kingdom; he cannot have an increase.

What is the increase referred to in this verse? (131:4) "On May 16, 1843, William Clayton reported that the Prophet Joseph Smith 'put his hand on my knee and [said that] ... except a man and his wife enter into an everlasting covenant and be married for eternity while in this probation by the power and authority of the Holy priesthood they will cease to increase when they die [meaning] they will not have any children in the resurrection, but those who are married by the power & authority of the priesthood in this life & continue without committing the sin against the Holy Ghost will continue to increase & have children in the celestial glory'" (Joseph Smith Papers, "Instruction, 16 May 1843, as Reported by William Clayton," [13–15]). ⊕

Doctrine and Covenants 131:5–6. How Men Are Sealed up unto Eternal Life Is Explained

What is the "more sure word of prophecy"? (131:5) There are those "in this life who conduct themselves with fidelity and devotion to God and his gospel . . . who have lived by every word of God and are willing to serve the Lord at all hazards. They have, according to Joseph Smith, made their calling and election sure. For them the day of judgment has been advanced, and the blessings associated with the glories of the celestial kingdom are assured. They receive what the prophets have called the 'more sure word of prophecy' (2 Peter 1:19). . . .

"[Elder Bruce R. McConkie taught that] 'if we die in the faith, that is the same thing as saying that our calling and election has been made sure'" (Millet, *Precept upon Precept*, 104, 105). ⊕

5 (May 17th, 1843.) The more sure word of prophecy means a man's knowing that he is sealed up unto eternal life, by revelation and the spirit of prophecy, through the power of the Holy Priesthood.

What kind of knowledge leads to salvation? (131:6) President Russell M. Nelson said: "I would like to speak about *how* we can draw into our lives the power of our Lord and Master, Jesus Christ.

"We begin by learning about Him. 'It is impossible for [us] to be saved in ignorance.' The more we know about the Savior's ministry and mission—the more we understand His doctrine and what He did for us— the more we know that He can provide the power that we need for our lives" ("Drawing the Power of Jesus Christ into Our Lives," *Ensign*, May 2017, 39). ⊕

6 It is impossible for a man to be saved in ignorance.

Doctrine and Covenants 131:7–8. All Spirit Is Matter

Why is it important to recognize that "spirit is matter"? (131:7–8) "For thousands of years . . . religious teachers have divided the universe into two parts—the material world and the spiritual world. Many of these teachers have taught that the physical

7 There is no such thing as immaterial matter. All spirit is matter, but it is more fine or pure, and can only be discerned by purer eyes;

8 We cannot see it; but when our bodies are purified we shall see that it is all matter.

world was a trap in which spiritual elements had become mired. Others taught that the physical or material world was only illusory and actually had no real existence. . . .

"Joseph Smith was one of the first religious leaders to deny the great gap between spirit and matter. Here he states the grand unifying principle that heals the great divide in the universe that had been created and taught by men for thousands of years: all things, including spirits, are made of matter" (Robinson and Garrett, *Commentary on the Doctrine and Covenants*, 4:239). ⊕

Introduction to Doctrine and Covenants 132

The revelation now known as Doctrine and Covenants 132 was dictated by the Prophet Joseph Smith on July 12, 1843.

"In February and March 1831, the Prophet Joseph Smith was working in the book of Genesis as part of the inspired translation of the Old Testament. As he [later] worked on the translation [of the New Testament], the Prophet inquired of the Lord about the plural marriages of ancient patriarchs such as Abraham, Isaac, Jacob, and others. In response, the Lord revealed principles about plural marriage. Joseph Smith was eventually commanded to live that principle (see Gospel Topics Essays, 'Plural Marriage')" (*Doctrine and Covenants Student Manual* [2018], 770).

"Joseph Smith gradually introduced the doctrine of eternal marriage to select associates. In the winter of 1840, Joseph Smith taught Apostle Parley P. Pratt that he could remain with his wife 'for time and all eternity' and that their posterity could increase even after death. Parley rejoiced; his view of heaven transformed from a place 'weaned' of family affection to a paradise filled with loved ones. The promise that family relationships could have divine permanence brought great happiness and peace to the small number of Saints to whom Joseph taught this early doctrine. Parley later reflected, though, that Joseph 'had merely lifted a corner of the veil and given me a single glance into eternity.' Parley had learned of marriage's eternity, but not yet of its potential plurality. Eventually, Joseph Smith's revelations about marriage would place the sealing ordinance at the core of exaltation, eternally uniting the Saints together with generations untold, making family the foundation of heavenly life" (Brittany Chapman Nash, *Let's Talk about Polygamy*, 10).

"The importance of the new and everlasting covenant of marriage in God's plan was [also] emphasized in the Prophet's May 1843 revelation received in Ramus, Illinois (see D&C 131:1–4)" (*Doctrine and Covenants Student Manual* [2018], 770).

"Initially, Hyrum was staunchly opposed to the practice of polygamy, which he had heard of through rumors, but in May 1843 he became both intellectually and spiritually convinced that the doctrine was inspired. Believing that Emma could be convinced of the doctrine, Hyrum told [Joseph] he could persuade her with the aid of a written revelation. 'If you will write the revelation,' Hyrum reportedly told [the Prophet], 'I will take, and read it to Emma, and I believe I can convince her of its truth, and you will hereafter have peace.' [Joseph] expressed his doubts, to which Hyrum replied, 'The doctrine is so plain I can convince any reasonable man or woman of its truth, purity and heavenly origin.'

"Assenting to Hyrum's urging, [Joseph] dictated the revelation that morning to Clayton in [his] office. Clayton recalled that [Joseph] dictated the 'Revelation on Celestial marriage' over the course of three hours, speaking slowly, 'sentence by sentence,' as Clayton wrote. Following the initial creation of the document, he remembered, 'Joseph requested me to read it slowly and carefully which I did, and he then pronounced it correct.' . . . The revelation framed both eternal and plural marriages as contracts ratified by priesthood authority. Unlike civil marriages, sealings performed by priesthood authority did not have to end with the death of either party but could persist into eternity. In addition, the revelation outlined regulations for plural marriages and the rights of first wives. The revelation did not distinguish between types of plural marriages; nevertheless, reminiscent statements of some individuals who were sealed to [Joseph] or who otherwise participated in plural marriage in this era suggest that early Latter-day Saints distinguished between sealings for time and eternity—involving relationships in this life and in the next life—and sealings for eternity alone—involving commitments only in the next life" (Joseph Smith Papers, Historical Introduction to "Revelation, 12 July 1843 [D&C 132]").

Understandably, Emma had a difficult time with the revelation. "Regardless of Emma's opposition to the plural marriage revelation, it was read confidentially to other Saints and considered the word of God by those who accepted it. It remained a private document for almost a decade, even as the number of polygamous Church members increased. It was not until 1852 that the revelation was read from the pulpit to reinforce that the principle had been revealed to Joseph Smith. The revelation was published as scripture in the 1876 edition of the Doctrine and Covenants and is now known as Doctrine and Covenants 132" (Brittany Chapman Nash, *Let's Talk about Polygamy*, 21).

Doctrine and Covenants 132 "is divided into two parts. The first, comprising vv. 3–33, deals mainly with the principle of celestial marriage, or marriage for time and all eternity; the second, comprising the remaining verses, deals with plural marriage. The doctrine of celestial marriage remains in force; the practice of plural marriage was abandoned by the acceptancy by the Church, in Conference assembled October 6th, 1890, of the *Manifesto* of President Woodruff" (Smith and Sjodahl, *Doctrine and Covenants Commentary*, 821).

SECTION 132

Revelation given through Joseph Smith the Prophet, at Nauvoo, Illinois, recorded July 12, 1843, relating to the new and everlasting covenant, including the eternity of the marriage covenant and the principle of plural marriage. Although the revelation was recorded in 1843, evidence indicates that some of the principles involved in this revelation were known by the Prophet as early as 1831. See Official Declaration 1.

Doctrine and Covenants 132:1–6.
Exaltation Is Gained through the New and Everlasting Covenant

What prompted Joseph Smith to ask the Lord why He justified the ancient prophets and patriarchs in having many wives and concubines? (132:1)
"While working on the inspired translation of the Old Testament, the Prophet Joseph Smith read about ancient patriarchs such as Abraham, Isaac, and Jacob 'having many wives and concubines' (D&C 132:1; see also Genesis 16:1–3; 25:6; 30:1–13; 2 Samuel 5:13; 1 Kings 11:1–6). This prompted the Prophet to [later] ask the Lord about this practice. Such marriages were not only contrary to the cultural . . . standards of Joseph Smith's day but also to the Lord's standard of marriage. . . . The Lord expressly forbade plural marriage unless He commanded His people otherwise (see Jacob 2:30; D&C 132:34–35).

"In response to the Prophet's question, the Lord first provided an explanation of the principle of eternal marriage, known as 'the new and everlasting covenant of marriage' (D&C 131:2; see D&C 132:3–33). Then, as recorded in Doctrine and Covenants 132:34,

1 Verily, thus saith the Lord unto you my servant Joseph, that inasmuch as you have inquired of my hand to know and understand wherein I, the Lord, justified my servants Abraham, Isaac, and Jacob, as also Moses, David and Solomon, my servants, as touching the principle and doctrine of their having many wives and concubines—

2 Behold, and lo, I am the Lord thy God, and will answer thee as touching this matter.

the Lord returned to Joseph Smith's question about the ancient practice of plural marriage" (*Doctrine and Covenants Student Manual* [2018], 772).

What is a concubine? (132:1) "A concubine was a wife who came from a position of lower social standing, and who thus did not enjoy the same status as one of higher birth. Under ancient practice, where caste systems were much more common than at present, a man could take a slave or non-citizen as a legal wife, but it was understood that she was of a lower status. This was the case with Sarah (the first wife) and Hagar (the servant who became a concubine)" (Millet, "New and Everlasting Covenant," 525n12).

3 Therefore, prepare thy heart to receive and obey the instructions which I am about to give unto you; for all those who have this law revealed unto them must obey the same.

What is a crucial step in preparing to receive direction from the Lord? (132:3) Sister Leone Jacobs explained: "In the Old Testament we read this: 'For Ezra had prepared his heart to seek the law of the Lord and to do it.' . . .

"What a lovely ideal for us to work to.

"And in the Doctrine and Covenants the Lord said to the Prophet Joseph Smith: 'Therefore, prepare thine heart to receive and obey the instructions which I am about to give unto you.'

"I believe preparing one's heart is perhaps the most decisive point in progress toward any goal. True, the carrying out of our plans is important too, but once our hearts are fully and staunchly prepared, the action is comparatively easy" ("Prepare Thy Heart," 147). ❍

Plural Marriage and The Church of Jesus Christ of Latter-day Saints (D&C 132:1)

"Latter-day Saints believe that the marriage of one man and one woman is the Lord's standing law of marriage. In biblical times, the Lord commanded some to practice plural marriage—the marriage of one man and more than one woman. By revelation, the Lord commanded Joseph Smith to institute the practice of plural marriage among Church members in the early 1840s. For more than half a century, plural marriage was practiced by some Latter-day Saints under the direction of the Church President.

"Latter-day Saints do not understand all of God's purposes in instituting, through His prophets, the practice of plural marriage. The Book of Mormon identifies one reason for God to command it: to increase the number of children born in the gospel covenant in order to 'raise up seed unto [the Lord]' [Jacob 2:30]" (Gospel Topic Essays, "Plural Marriage in The Church of Jesus Christ of Latter-day Saints").

"This principle [of plural marriage] was among the most challenging aspects of the Restoration—for Joseph personally and for other Church members. Plural marriage tested faith and provoked controversy and opposition. Few Latter-day Saints initially welcomed the restoration of a biblical practice entirely foreign to their sensibilities. But many later testified of powerful spiritual experiences that helped them overcome their hesitation and gave them courage to accept this practice.

"Many details about the early practice of plural marriage are unknown because participants were asked to keep their actions confidential. The historical record of early plural marriage is therefore thin: few records of the time provide details, and later reminiscences are not always reliable" (Church History Topics, "Joseph Smith and Plural Marriage").

Is plural marriage a required part of the new and everlasting covenant? (132:4) "Some people, including some Church members, inaccurately read Doctrine and Covenants 132:4 to mean that plural marriage is necessary for exaltation, leading them to believe that plural marriage is a necessary prerequisite for exaltation in the eternal realm. This, however, is not supported in the revelations. As recorded in Doctrine and Covenants 131 and 132, the Lord introduced the law of eternal marriage by expressly referring to the sealing of one man and one woman (see Doctrine and Covenants 132:4–7, 15–25). By setting forth the law of eternal marriage in the context of a monogamous marriage, the Lord makes plain that the blessings of exaltation, extended to each man and each woman who worthily enters into the covenant of eternal marriage performed by proper priesthood authority, are independent of whether that marriage is plural or monogamous [see D&C 132:15–25]" (Marcus B. Nash, "New and Everlasting Covenant," *Ensign*, Dec. 2015, 44). ✚

What was the "law" that was "instituted from before the foundation of the world"? (132:5) "Marriage between a man and a woman is fundamental to the Lord's doctrine and crucial to God's eternal plan. Marriage between a man and a woman is God's pattern for a fulness of life on earth and in heaven. God's marriage pattern cannot be abused, misunderstood, or misconstrued. Not if you want true joy....

"In our day civil governments have a vested interest in protecting marriage because strong families constitute the best way of providing for the health, education, welfare, and prosperity of rising generations. But civil governments are heavily influenced by

4 For behold, I reveal unto you a new and an everlasting covenant; and if ye abide not that covenant, then are ye damned; for no one can reject this covenant and be permitted to enter into my glory.

5 For all who will have a blessing at my hands shall abide the law which was appointed for that blessing, and the conditions thereof, as were instituted from before the foundation of the world.

6 And as pertaining to the new and everlasting covenant, it was instituted for the fulness of my glory; and he that receiveth a fulness thereof must and shall abide the law, or he shall be damned, saith the Lord God.

"The" New and Everlasting Covenant vs. "A" New and Everlasting Covenant

Marcus B. Nash wrote: "The new and everlasting covenant 'is the sum total of all gospel covenants and obligations' given anciently and again restored to the earth in these latter days. This is explained in Doctrine and Covenants 66:2: 'Verily I say unto you, blessed are you for receiving *mine everlasting covenant, even the fulness of my gospel,* sent forth unto the children of men, that they might have life and be made partakers of the glories which are to be revealed in the last days, as it was written by the prophets and apostles in days of old.' Because the covenant has been restored in the last dispensation of time, it is 'new,' and because it spans all eternity, it is 'everlasting.'

"In the scriptures the Lord speaks of both 'the' new and everlasting covenant and 'a' new and everlasting covenant. For example, in Doctrine and Covenants 22:1, He refers to baptism as '*a* new and an everlasting covenant, even that which was from the beginning.' In Doctrine and Covenants 132:4, He likewise refers to eternal marriage as '*a* new and an everlasting covenant.' When He speaks of 'a' new and everlasting covenant, He is speaking of one of the many covenants encompassed by His gospel.

"When the Lord speaks generally of 'the' new and everlasting covenant, He is speaking of the fulness of the gospel of Jesus Christ, which embraces all ordinances and covenants necessary for the salvation and exaltation of [humankind]. Neither baptism nor eternal marriage is 'the' new and everlasting covenant; rather, they are each parts of the whole" ("New and Everlasting Covenant," *Ensign*, Dec. 2015, 42–43).

social trends and secular philosophies as they write, rewrite, and enforce laws. Regardless of what civil legislation may be enacted, the doctrine of the Lord regarding marriage and morality *cannot be changed*" (Nelson, "Decisions for Eternity," *Ensign*, Nov. 2013, 108).

Doctrine and Covenants 132:7–14. The Terms and Conditions of the New and Everlasting Covenant Are Set Forth

Who will be together in the eternities? (132:7) "The Lord has clearly taught that only men and women who are sealed as husband and wife in the temple, and who keep their covenants, will be together throughout the eternities. He said, 'All covenants, contracts, bonds, obligations, oaths, vows, performances, connections, associations, or expectations, that are not made and entered into and sealed by the Holy Spirit of promise . . . have an end when men are dead.'

"Thus, if we *unwisely* choose to live *telestial* laws now, we are choosing to be resurrected with a *telestial* body. We are choosing *not* to live with our families forever.

"So, my dear brothers and sisters, *how* and *where* and with *whom* do *you* want to live forever? You get to choose" (Nelson, "Think Celestial," *Liahona*, Nov. 2023, 118).

What does it mean to be "sealed by the Holy Spirit of promise"? (132:7) "The Savior's promise of the Holy Ghost to the Apostles is of supreme importance in recognizing the preeminent role of the Holy Ghost, the third member of the Godhead. The Holy Ghost is a personage of spirit, the Comforter, who bears witness of the Father and the Son, reveals the truth of all things, and sanctifies those who have repented and been baptized. He is referred to as the Holy Spirit of Promise and as such confirms as acceptable to God the righteous acts, ordinances, and covenants of each of us. They who are sealed by the Holy Spirit of Promise receive all that the Father has" (Quentin L. Cook, "We Follow Jesus Christ," *Ensign*, May 2010, 85). ◉

How do these verses support that God's house is a house of order? (132:8–11) "God's course is straight and narrow. He does not wander nor vary from that course (Alma 7:20). If he commands, it must be done. If he gives a law, it must be obeyed. No deviations, no exceptions, no looking the other way. In order to appease the demands of justice, he extends his mercy, through the atonement of Jesus Christ, to help overcome the fallen nature of [people] and the sins

7 And verily I say unto you, that the conditions of this law are these: All covenants, contracts, bonds, obligations, oaths, vows, performances, connections, associations, or expectations, that are not made and entered into and sealed by the Holy Spirit of promise, of him who is anointed, both as well for time and for all eternity, and that too most holy, by revelation and commandment through the medium of mine anointed, whom I have appointed on the earth to hold this power (and I have appointed unto my servant Joseph to hold this power in the last days, and there is never but one on the earth at a time on whom this power and the keys of this priesthood are conferred), are of no efficacy, virtue, or force in and after the resurrection from the dead; for all contracts that are not made unto this end have an end when men are dead.

8 Behold, mine house is a house of order, saith the Lord God, and not a house of confusion.

9 Will I accept of an offering, saith the Lord, that is not made in my name?

10 Or will I receive at your hands that which I have not appointed?

of [humankind], but he will not remove the demands of justice and judgment (see Alma 42:9–11). In these verses the Lord asked three 'Will I' questions. Will he accept an offering not done in his name, or one which is not appointed, or anything that is not by his law? Of course not" (Robinson and Garrett, *Commentary on the Doctrine and Covenants*, 4:246–47).

How do we come unto the Father through the Son? (132:12) "Our Savior, Jesus Christ, is the ultimate pioneer in preparing the way. Indeed, He *is* 'the way' [John 14:6] for the plan of salvation to be accomplished so that we can repent and, through faith in Him, return to our Heavenly Father" (Ballard, "Follow Jesus Christ with Footsteps of Faith," *Liahona*, Nov. 2022, 35).

What things are destroyed and what things remain? (132:13–14) "The important truth is here taught that all institutions in this world, not founded on divine law but erected by human ingenuity, cease to exist on this side of the veil. Man-made governments are obliterated, as are the sand castles children build on the tide-swept beach. Man-made religions and churches are swallowed up in death. Not a trace of them will be seen on the shores of eternity. Social customs and habits not sanctioned by God, will not continue. On the other hand, all institutions founded on the Word of God will remain throughout all eternity. The Church will remain. The family will remain. All the organizations of which God is the author are eternal (v. 14)" (Smith and Sjodahl, *Doctrine and Covenants Commentary*, 824).

Doctrine and Covenants 132:15–20. Celestial Marriage and a Continuation of the Family Unit Enable Men to Become Gods

Why is the Lord's approval of marriage essential? (132:15–18) "Marriage can endure for eternity when we comply with the conditions the Lord has set. All the wishful thinking in the world will not bind us together as an eternal couple without the sealing keys of priesthood power, without the ratifying seal of approval from the Holy Ghost, without worthiness on the part of the couple as they both wholeheartedly strive to live the gospel. . . . The glory of everlasting life together as a couple is reserved for those who live the law of celestial marriage" (Millet and Newell, *Draw Near unto Me*, 374). ⊕

11 And will I appoint unto you, saith the Lord, except it be by law, even as I and my Father ordained unto you, before the world was?

12 I am the Lord thy God; and I give unto you this commandment—that no man shall come unto the Father but by me or by my word, which is my law, saith the Lord.

13 And everything that is in the world, whether it be ordained of men, by thrones, or principalities, or powers, or things of name, whatsoever they may be, that are not by me or by my word, saith the Lord, shall be thrown down, and shall not remain after men are dead, neither in nor after the resurrection, saith the Lord your God.

14 For whatsoever things remain are by me; and whatsoever things are not by me shall be shaken and destroyed.

15 Therefore, if a man marry him a wife in the world, and he marry her not by me nor by my word, and he covenant with her so long as he is in the world and she with him, their covenant and marriage are not of force when they are dead, and when they are out of the world; therefore, they are not bound by any law when they are out of the world.

16 Therefore, when they are out of the world they neither marry nor are given in marriage; but are appointed angels in heaven, which angels are ministering servants, to minister for those who are worthy of a far more, and an exceeding, and an eternal weight of glory.

17 For these angels did not abide my law; therefore, they cannot be enlarged, but remain separately and singly, without exaltation, in their saved condition, to all eternity; and from henceforth are not gods, but are angels of God forever and ever.

18 And again, verily I say unto you, if a man marry a wife, and make a covenant with her for time and for all eternity, if that covenant is not by me or by my word, which is my law, and is not sealed by the Holy Spirit of promise, through him whom I have anointed and appointed unto this power, then it is not valid neither of force when they are out of the world, because they are not joined by me, saith the Lord, neither by my word; when they are out of the world it cannot be received there, because the angels and the gods are appointed there, by whom they cannot pass; they cannot, therefore, inherit my glory; for my house is a house of order, saith the Lord God.

19 And again, verily I say unto you, if a man marry a wife by my word, which is my law, and by the new and everlasting covenant, and it is sealed unto them by the Holy Spirit of promise, by him who is anointed, unto whom I have appointed this power and the keys of this priesthood; and it shall be said unto them—Ye shall come forth in the first resurrection; and if it be after the first resurrection, in the next resurrection; and shall inherit thrones, kingdoms, principalities, and powers, dominions, all heights and depths—then shall it be written in the Lamb's Book of Life, that he shall commit no murder

Why is it vital to be married by proper authority in mortality? (132:16) Elder James E. Talmage taught: "In the resurrection there will be no marrying nor giving in marriage; for all questions of marital status must be settled before that time, under the authority of the Holy Priesthood, which holds the power to seal in marriage for both time and eternity" (*Jesus the Christ*, 548).

What does separate and single without exaltation mean? (132:17) *"There will be no marrying, neither giving in marriage among those who reject the truth of the everlasting gospel. That privilege is confined to those who keep the commandments of the Lord in their fulness and who are obedient to the laws of God.*

"Restrictions will be placed upon those who enter the terrestrial and telestial kingdoms, and even those in the celestial kingdom who do not get the exaltation; *changes will be made in their bodies to suit their condition*; and there will be no marrying or giving in marriage, nor living together of men and women, because of these restrictions" (Joseph Fielding Smith, *Doctrines of Salvation*, 2:73). See commentary in this volume on Doctrine and Covenants 131:4.

What is the Lamb's Book of Life? (132:19) "The 'Book of Life' or 'Lamb's Book of Life' is a record of the 'names of the faithful and an account of their righteous covenants and deeds' (D&C 128:6–7; Ps. 69:28; Rev. 3:5; 21:27). It is a record of those who will inherit eternal life—the greatest gift of God, for they will be sanctified for all eternity (see Dan. 12:1–4; Heb. 12:23)" (Black, *400 Questions and Answers*, 222).

How does marriage by God's authority prepare us for exaltation? (132:19–20) "To qualify for eternal life, we must make an eternal and everlasting covenant with our Heavenly Father [see D&C 132:19]. This means that a temple marriage is not only between husband and wife; it embraces a partnership with God [see Matthew 19:6]. . . .

"When a family is sealed in the temple, that family may become as eternal as the kingdom of God itself [see D&C 132:19–20]. . . .

"Celestial marriage is a pivotal part of preparation for eternal life. It requires one to be married to the right person, in the right place, by the right authority, and to obey that sacred covenant faithfully. Then one may be assured of exaltation in the celestial kingdom of God" (Nelson, "Celestial Marriage," *Ensign*, Nov. 2008, 93, 94). ☉

Doctrine and Covenants 132:21–25. The Strait and Narrow Way Leads to Eternal Lives

What is the "continuation of the lives"? (132:22) "To obtain eternal life is also to obtain eternal '*lives*,' that is, the continuation of seed throughout eternity. Similar terms are 'increase' (D&C 131:4), 'enlarged' (v. 17), and 'a continuation of the seeds' (v. 19)" (McConkie and Ostler, *Revelations of the Restoration*, 1064).

According to these verses, what must we do to be exalted? (132:22–25) "The promised blessings of God to the faithful are glorious and inspiring. Among them are 'thrones, kingdoms, principalities, and powers, dominions, all heights and depths' [D&C 132:19]. And it takes more than a spiritual birth certificate or a 'Child of God Membership Card' to qualify for these incomprehensible blessings.

"But how do we attain them?

"The Savior has answered this question in our time:

"'Except ye abide my law ye cannot attain to this glory.

"'For strait is the gate, and narrow the way that leadeth unto the exaltation. . . .

"' . . . Receive ye, therefore, my law' [D&C 132:21–22, 24].

"For this reason, we speak of walking the path of discipleship.

whereby to shed innocent blood, and if ye abide in my covenant, and commit no murder whereby to shed innocent blood, it shall be done unto them in all things whatsoever my servant hath put upon them, in time, and through all eternity; and shall be of full force when they are out of the world; and they shall pass by the angels, and the gods, which are set there, to their exaltation and glory in all things, as hath been sealed upon their heads, which glory shall be a fulness and a continuation of the seeds forever and ever.

20 Then shall they be gods, because they have no end; therefore shall they be from everlasting to everlasting, because they continue; then shall they be above all, because all things are subject unto them. Then shall they be gods, because they have all power, and the angels are subject unto them.

21 Verily, verily, I say unto you, except ye abide my law ye cannot attain to this glory.

22 For strait is the gate, and narrow the way that leadeth unto the exaltation and continuation of the lives, and few there be that find it, because ye receive me not in the world neither do ye know me.

23 But if ye receive me in the world, then shall ye know me, and shall receive your exaltation; that where I am ye shall be also.

24 This is eternal lives—to know the only wise and true God, and Jesus Christ, whom he hath sent. I am he. Receive ye, therefore, my law.

25 Broad is the gate, and wide the way that leadeth to the deaths; and many there are that go in thereat, because they receive me not, neither do they abide in my law.

26 Verily, verily, I say unto you, if a man marry a wife according to my word, and they are sealed by the Holy Spirit of promise, according to mine appointment, and he or she shall commit any sin or transgression of the new and everlasting covenant whatever, and all manner of blasphemies, and if they commit no murder wherein they shed innocent blood, yet they shall come forth in the first resurrection, and enter into their exaltation; but they shall be destroyed in the flesh, and shall be delivered unto the buffetings of Satan unto the day of redemption, saith the Lord God.

27 The blasphemy against the Holy Ghost, which shall not be forgiven in the world nor out of the world, is in that ye commit murder wherein ye shed innocent blood, and assent unto my death, after ye have received my new and everlasting covenant, saith the Lord God; and he that abideth not this law can in nowise enter into my glory, but shall be damned, saith the Lord.

28 I am the Lord thy God, and will give unto thee the law of my Holy Priesthood, as was ordained by me and my Father before the world was.

29 Abraham received all things, whatsoever he received, by revelation and commandment, by my word, saith the Lord, and hath entered into his exaltation and sitteth upon his throne.

30 Abraham received promises concerning his seed, and of the fruit of his loins—from whose loins ye are, namely, my servant

"We speak of obedience to God's commandments.

"We speak of living the gospel joyfully, with all our heart, might, mind, and soul" (Uchtdorf, "Living the Gospel Joyful," *Ensign*, Nov. 2014, 121).

Doctrine and Covenants 132:26–27. The Law Is Given Relative to Blasphemy against the Holy Ghost

What is meant by being sealed by the Holy Spirit of Promise? (132:26) "The Holy Spirit of Promise is the ratifying power of the Holy Ghost. When sealed by the Holy Spirit of Promise, an ordinance, vow, or covenant is binding on earth and in heaven (see D&C 132:7). Receiving this 'stamp of approval' from the Holy Ghost is the result of faithfulness, integrity, and steadfastness in honoring gospel covenants 'in [the] process of time' (Moses 7:21). However, this sealing can be forfeited through unrighteousness and transgression" (Bednar, "Ye Must Be Born Again," *Ensign*, May 2007, 22). See also commentary in this volume on Doctrine and Covenants 132:7.

What constitutes blasphemy against the Holy Ghost? (132:27) "The innocent blood is that of Christ; and those who commit blasphemy against the Holy Ghost, which is the unpardonable sin (Matt. 12:31–32), thereby 'crucify to themselves the Son of God afresh, and put him to an open shame' (Heb. 6:6). They are, in other words, people who would have crucified Christ, having the while a perfect knowledge that he was the Son of God" (Bruce R. McConkie, *Doctrinal New Testament Commentary*, 3:345).

Doctrine and Covenants 132:28–39. Promises of Eternal Increase and Exaltation Are Made to Prophets and Saints in All Ages

How can we receive the blessings of Abraham, including exaltation? (132:29–32) "You know of the historic declaration the Lord gave to the Prophet Joseph Smith. It came by revelation. The Lord said to Joseph, 'This promise is yours also, because ye are of Abraham, and the promise was made unto Abraham' ([D&C] 132:31).

"Thereby, this everlasting covenant was restored as part of the great Restoration of the gospel in its fulness. Think of it! A marriage covenant made in the temple is tied directly to that Abrahamic covenant. In the temple a couple is introduced to *all* the blessings reserved for the faithful posterity of Abraham, Isaac, and Jacob. . . .

"You and I personally entered the covenant path at baptism. Then we enter it more completely in the temple. The blessings of the Abrahamic covenant are conferred in holy temples. These blessings allow us, upon being resurrected, to 'inherit thrones, kingdoms, powers, principalities, and dominions, to our "exaltation and glory in all things" (D&C 132:19)' [Nelson, in 'Special Witnesses of Christ,' *Ensign*, April 2001, 7]" (Nelson, "Everlasting Covenant," *Liahona*, Oct. 2022, 6). ⊕

What are the "works of Abraham"? (132:32–33)
"To obtain the promises given to Abraham, we must do what he did: enter into the law of the new and everlasting covenant of marriage and live so that the Holy Spirit of promise can seal it for eternity. Abraham followed the Savior, sought diligently the blessings of the priesthood, gave prompt obedience to the commands of God, paid a full tithe, presided over his family in righteousness, kept the covenants he had made with God at all costs, and was full of faith and integrity. These are the works of Abraham" (Robinson and Garrett, *Commentary on the Doctrine and Covenants*, 4:254). ⊕

Why wasn't Abraham condemned for taking a second wife? (132:34–35) "The Patriarch Abraham was instructed to take Hagar, the servant of Sarah, as a second wife, as a part of fulfilling the promises made earlier to the Father of the Faithful that his posterity would be as numerous as the stars in the heavens or the sands upon the seashore (Genesis 22:17; Abraham 3:14). This modern revelation [D&C 132] helps to clarify the Old Testament story considerably (see Genesis 16) and shows that the decision to take an additional wife was a God-inspired directive, and not simply a desperate move by Sarah to ensure mortal posterity for her grieving husband. Joseph Smith was told that because of Abraham's perfect obedience he was granted the privilege of eternal increase" (Millet, "New and Everlasting Covenant," 175–76).

What can we learn about Abraham from his response to this difficult commandment? (132:36)
"The sacrifice God was requiring was astonishing to the Saints, but not without precedent. To help them understand, God compared His command to marry

Joseph—which were to continue so long as they were in the world; and as touching Abraham and his seed, out of the world they should continue; both in the world and out of the world should they continue as innumerable as the stars; or, if ye were to count the sand upon the seashore ye could not number them.

31 This promise is yours also, because ye are of Abraham, and the promise was made unto Abraham; and by this law is the continuation of the works of my Father, wherein he glorifieth himself.

32 Go ye, therefore, and do the works of Abraham; enter ye into my law and ye shall be saved.

33 But if ye enter not into my law ye cannot receive the promise of my Father, which he made unto Abraham.

34 God commanded Abraham, and Sarah gave Hagar to Abraham to wife. And why did she do it? Because this was the law; and from Hagar sprang many people. This, therefore, was fulfilling, among other things, the promises.

35 Was Abraham, therefore, under condemnation? Verily I say unto you, Nay; for I, the Lord, commanded it.

36 Abraham was commanded to offer his son Isaac; nevertheless, it was written: Thou shalt not kill. Abraham, however, did not refuse, and it was accounted unto him for righteousness.

more than one wife to His command for Abraham to kill his son Isaac. Abraham's willingness to sacrifice Isaac was in direct defiance of God's universal law not to kill, yet it was 'accounted unto him for righteousness.' Similarly, God's command to Joseph Smith and the ancient prophets to marry more than one wife conflicted with another of His commandments: 'Thou shalt love thy wife with all thy heart, and shall cleave unto her and none else.' Nevertheless, God, the lawgiver and ultimate judge, can make exceptions to His own laws and promise blessings rather than condemnation to those who obey Him" (Mackley, *Wilford Woodruff's Witness*, 76).

Under what circumstances were plural marriages in biblical times acceptable to God? (132:37–39) "Plural marriages cannot be adultery because the husband receives his wives by recognized authority [see D&C 132:61–62]. The Lord therefore justified the ancient patriarchs in their plural marriage relationships. For example, He had given David and Solomon many wives and concubines and they sinned only when they took that which was not given them by the Lord (v. 38). A concubine was not a mistress, but rather a wife of lower social status, such as the 'handmaids' who became wives of Abraham and Jacob (see Gen. 16:3; 30:4, 9)" (Cowan and Manscill, *A to Z of the Doctrine and Covenants*, 192).

What does it mean that Abraham, Isaac, and Jacob are now "gods"? (132:37) The Prophet Joseph Smith taught: "Every man who reigns in celestial glory is a God to his dominions. . . . They who obtain a glorious resurrection from the dead are exalted far above principalities, powers, thrones, dominions, and angels; and are expressly declared to be heirs of God, and joint heirs with Jesus Christ, all having eternal power" (Joseph Smith Papers, "History, 1838–1856, volume F-1," 104).

37 Abraham received concubines, and they bore him children; and it was accounted unto him for righteousness, because they were given unto him, and he abode in my law; as Isaac also and Jacob did none other things than that which they were commanded; and because they did none other things than that which they were commanded, they have entered into their exaltation, according to the promises, and sit upon thrones, and are not angels but are gods.

Tried Even as Abraham (Doctrine and Covenants 132:36)

Regarding the extreme test concerning Abraham and his son Isaac, Truman Madsen wrote, "Now we are back to the statement, the *wise* statement, of Elder [Hugh B.] Brown: 'Abraham needed to learn something about Abraham.' What did he learn? He learned that he did love God unconditionally, that God could now bless him unconditionally. Do you think his prayers had a different temper and tone after that? Do you think he could pray in faith saying, 'Lord, you know my heart,' and the echo would say, 'And *I* know it'? John Taylor said that the prophet taught that if God could have found a deeper way to test Abraham he would have used that (see [*Journal of Discourses*,] 24:264). As Paul looked back and wondered how Abraham could have his willingness account for righteousness, his conviction was that Abraham believed Jehovah could raise his son from the dead if necessary in order to fulfill the promise, which that sacrifice scene contradicts. That is what God did ultimately with his own Son (see Hebrews 11:19)" ("Power from Abrahamic Tests," 4–5).

What were "those things" in which David and others sinned? (132:38–39) "[This] is a modern prophetic commentary on the condemnation sounded in the Book of Mormon against David and Solomon's practice of plural marriage (Jacob 2:23–24). The problem was not plural marriage per se, for others of the ancients had been commanded to have more than one wife. The problem was with the *unauthorized* practice. David's adultery with Bathsheba (2 Samuel 11–12) and Solomon's taking of foreign wives who turned his heart away from the worship of Jehovah (1 Kings 11) were not sanctioned by those who held the keys of the priesthood and certainly not sanctioned by the Lord himself. Joseph Smith taught that *'no man shall have but one wife at a time, unless the Lord directs otherwise'* [Joseph Smith Papers, "History, 1838–1856, volume E-1," 1746]" (Millet and Newell, *Draw Near unto Me*, 381).

Doctrine and Covenants 132:40–47. Joseph Smith Is Given the Power to Bind and Seal on Earth and in Heaven

In verse 40, what are the "things" that the Lord will restore through the Prophet Joseph Smith? (132:40) "All the ordinances and duties that ever have been required by the Priesthood, under the directions and commandments of the Almighty in any of the dispensations, shall all be had in the last dispensation, therefore all things had under the authority of the Priesthood at any former period, shall be had again, bringing to pass the restoration spoken of by the mouth of all the Holy Prophets" (*Joseph Smith* [manual], 511). ☉

Why did Joseph Smith ask the Lord about adultery? (132:41–44) "In essence, the question of the Prophet was: 'Why were not such polygamous relationships violations of the law of chastity? Why was this not considered adultery?' The Lord's answer was

38 David also received many wives and concubines, and also Solomon and Moses my servants, as also many others of my servants, from the beginning of creation until this time; and in nothing did they sin save in those things which they received not of me.

39 David's wives and concubines were given unto him of me, by the hand of Nathan, my servant, and others of the prophets who had the keys of this power; and in none of these things did he sin against me save in the case of Uriah and his wife; and, therefore he hath fallen from his exaltation, and received his portion; and he shall not inherit them out of the world, for I gave them unto another, saith the Lord.

40 I am the Lord thy God, and I gave unto thee, my servant Joseph, an appointment, and restore all things. Ask what ye will, and it shall be given unto you according to my word.

41 And as ye have asked concerning adultery, verily, verily, I say unto you, if a man receiveth a wife in the new and everlasting covenant, and if she be with another man,

---

Joseph Smith's Practice of Plural Marriage (Doctrine and Covenants 132:40)

"After receiving a revelation commanding him to practice plural marriage, Joseph Smith married multiple wives and introduced the practice to close associates. This principle was among the most challenging aspects of the Restoration—for Joseph personally and for other Church members. . . .

"Joseph told associates that an angel appeared to him three times between 1834 and 1842 and commanded him to proceed with plural marriage when he hesitated to move forward. During the third and final appearance, the angel came with a drawn sword, threatening Joseph with destruction unless he went forward and obeyed the commandment fully. . . .

"The first plural marriage in Nauvoo took place when Louisa Beaman and Joseph Smith were sealed in April 1841. Joseph married many additional wives and authorized other Latter-day Saints to practice plural marriage. . . .

and I have not appointed unto her by the holy anointing, she hath committed adultery and shall be destroyed.

42 If she be not in the new and everlasting covenant, and she be with another man, she has committed adultery.

43 And if her husband be with another woman, and he was under a vow, he hath broken his vow and hath committed adultery.

44 And if she hath not committed adultery, but is innocent and hath not broken her vow, and she knoweth it, and I reveal it unto you, my servant Joseph, then shall you have power, by the power of my Holy Priesthood, to take her and give her unto him that hath not committed adultery but hath been faithful; for he shall be made ruler over many.

45 For I have conferred upon you the keys and power of the priesthood, wherein I restore all things, and make known unto you all things in due time.

simple and forthright, although considerable space was devoted to the issue in the revelation: any action inspired, authorized, or commanded of God is moral and good. More specifically, marriages approved of the Almighty are recognized and acknowledged as sacred institutions, despite the values or opinions of earth or hell. Joseph wrote in 1839: 'How much more dignified and noble are the thoughts of God, than the vain imaginations of the human heart!' [Joseph Smith Papers, "History, 1838–1856, volume C-1," 904(b)]. Verse 36 of this section sheds light on this principle, the idea that whatever God requires is right" (Millet, "New and Everlasting Covenant," 177).

What are the keys and power that God conferred upon Joseph Smith? (132:45) "The Prophet Joseph Smith was called of God to restore . . . great blessings to earth and to stand at the head of the dispensation of the fulness of times. During the Prophet's ministry, all things were restored that were necessary to lay the foundation of the greatest dispensation of all time. The priesthood, with its essential keys, was restored; the Book of Mormon was translated; the Church was organized; and doctrines, ordinances, and covenants were revealed, including the ordinances and covenants of the endowment and the marriage sealing. The Lord declared that He had committed unto Joseph Smith 'the keys of my kingdom, and a dispensation of the gospel for the last times' . . . (D&C 27:13)" (*Joseph Smith* [manual], 509). ⊕

"During the era in which plural marriage was practiced, Latter-day Saints distinguished between sealings for time and eternity and sealings for eternity only. Sealings for time and eternity included commitments and relationships during this life, generally including the possibility of sexual relations. Eternity-only sealings indicated relationships in the next life alone.

"Evidence indicates that Joseph Smith participated in both types of sealings. The exact number of women to whom he was sealed in his lifetime is unknown because the evidence is fragmentary. Some of the women who were sealed to Joseph Smith later testified that their marriages were for time and eternity, while others indicated that their relationships were for eternity alone" (Gospel Topics Essays, "Plural Marriage in Kirtland and Nauvoo").

Why did the Lord bless Joseph Smith with this sacred sealing power? (132:46–47) "The tremendous powers accorded to the Prophet are obvious in these verses; hence the powers held by the Presidents of the Church since his time. Notice that the blessing and cursing powers of verse 47 come as a result of the promises made by the Lord to Abraham (Abr. 2:11) and seem to have been confirmed later through the keys held by Elias ([see D&C] 110:12; 124:93). . . .

"The Lord had unlimited confidence in the Prophet, and not without reason. By means of His mighty power, He could foresee the Prophet's faithfulness to the end" (Sperry, *Doctrine and Covenants Compendium*, 734).

Doctrine and Covenants 132:48–50. The Lord Seals upon Joseph Smith His Exaltation

What promise does the Lord give to Joseph Smith in these verses? (132:49–50) "The Prophet of the Restoration received the consummate promise of eternal life and exaltation through the voice of the Lord. That is, he passed the tests of mortality and advanced, as it were, the day of judgment. His salvation was secure. Why? Because he was perfect? No, only the Lord Jesus has attained perfection. . . . The promise of eternal life came to Brother Joseph for the same reason it will come [to all the faithful]; because they

46 And verily, verily, I say unto you, that whatsoever you seal on earth shall be sealed in heaven; and whatsoever you bind on earth, in my name and by my word, saith the Lord, it shall be eternally bound in the heavens; and whosoever sins you remit on earth shall be remitted eternally in the heavens; and whosoever sins you retain on earth shall be retained in heaven.

47 And again, verily I say, whomsoever you bless I will bless, and whomsoever you curse I will curse, saith the Lord; for I, the Lord, am thy God.

48 And again, verily I say unto you, my servant Joseph, that whatsoever you give on earth, and to whomsoever you give any one on earth, by my word and according to my law, it shall be visited with blessings and not cursings, and with my power, saith the Lord, and shall be without condemnation on earth and in heaven.

49 For I am the Lord thy God, and will be with thee even unto the end of the world, and through all eternity; for verily I seal upon you your exaltation, and prepare a throne for you in the kingdom of my Father, with Abraham your father.

50 Behold, I have seen your sacrifices, and will forgive all your sins; I have seen your

Emma Smith and Plural Marriage (Doctrine & Covenants 132:51–66)

"Despite the difficulties of poverty, displacement, and persecution, Emma and Joseph maintained a deep love for and bond with each other. Their marriage faced unusual challenges due to the hardships of founding and leading the Church. Together they weathered the financial collapse and threats against Joseph's life in Kirtland, Ohio; the persecution of Church members in Missouri; and the separation imposed by Joseph's imprisonment in Liberty Jail. Their correspondence reveals not only their difficult circumstances but their commitment to each other. 'My heart is entwined around yours forever and ever,' Joseph wrote to Emma in 1838. Emma wrote to him in Liberty Jail in 1839: 'I still live and am yet willing to suffer more if it is the will of kind Heaven, that I should for your sake.'

"Emma struggled deeply with the principle of plural marriage. Joseph introduced the practice carefully and incrementally, marrying many additional wives, each of whom vowed to keep their participation confidential. Little is known about Emma's knowledge and feelings about these marriages, some of which entailed commitments in this life while others involved commitments for the next life only. Nevertheless, it is apparent that Joseph withheld knowledge of some of these relationships from Emma. When he did share limited information with her, she

sacrifices in obedience to that which I have told you. Go, therefore, and I make a way for your escape, as I accepted the offering of Abraham of his son Isaac.

51 Verily, I say unto you: A commandment I give unto mine handmaid, Emma Smith, your wife, whom I have given unto you, that she stay herself and partake not of that which I commanded you to offer unto her; for I did it, saith the Lord, to prove you all, as I did Abraham, and that I might require an offering at your hand, by covenant and sacrifice.

52 And let mine handmaid, Emma Smith, receive all those that have been given unto my servant Joseph, and who are virtuous and pure before me; and those who are not pure, and have said they were pure, shall be destroyed, saith the Lord God.

53 For I am the Lord thy God, and ye shall obey my voice; and I give unto my servant Joseph that he shall be made ruler over many things; for he hath been faithful over a few things, and from henceforth I will strengthen him.

have given themselves, without let or hindrance, at all hazards, to the Savior and sought to maintain an eye single to his glory. They have obtained the promise of the highest heaven because they have been willing to sacrifice all for the truth's sake (D&C 97:8)" (Millet and Newell, *Draw Near unto Me,* 382).

Doctrine and Covenants 132:51–57. Emma Smith Is Counseled to Be Faithful and True

What commandments did the Lord give to Emma Smith? (132:51–57) "The first commandment to Emma was actually a cancellation of a commandment that had been given to Joseph as a test for both of them. It is not known what that commandment was, but both of them had apparently passed the test (v. 51).

"The second commandment was for Emma to receive all the plural wives 'that have been given unto my servant Joseph . . . ' (v. 52) . . .

"The third commandment was an extension of the second commandment. Emma was 'to abide and cleave unto [Christ's] servant Joseph, and to none else' (D&C 132:54). . . .

"The fourth commandment to Emma was for her to forgive her husband of his trespasses . . . (D&C 132:56)" (Nyman, *Doctrine and Covenants Commentary,* 2:552, 553).

struggled, shifting her perspective and support over time. In early 1843, Emma appears to have accepted plural marriage and personally consented to and witnessed Joseph's marriages to four women. But by July, her attitude toward the practice had shifted again, and she burned a manuscript copy of the revelation on plural marriage now found in Doctrine and Covenants 132. There is no record Joseph entered into any additional marriages after the fall of 1843.

"Emma rarely spoke about the practice after Joseph's death. After her death in 1879, her sons published a transcript of an interview in which she purportedly denied Joseph had ever sanctioned plural marriage. Notwithstanding the religious and emotional turmoil over this practice, Emma maintained a deep love for Joseph. In June 1844, immediately preceding her husband's death, Emma wrote, 'I desire with all my heart to honor and respect my husband as my head, ever to live in his confidence and by acting in unison with him retain the place which God has given me by his side'" (Church History Topics, "Emma Hale Smith").

What does it mean that Emma will be destroyed if she didn't abide the Lord's law? (132:54–55)

"There is no threat here of physical harm. The intent of the word 'destroyed' is the same as that found in the prophecy of Moses relative to those who would reject Christ [see Deuteronomy 18:15–19]. ' . . . And it shall come to pass, that every soul, which will not hear that prophet, shall be *destroyed* from among the people' (Acts 3:22–23; emphasis added). This same prophecy as translated in the Book of Mormon was rendered 'cut off from among the people' (1 Nephi 22:20), or perhaps most correctly, 'cut off from among my people who are of the covenant' (3 Nephi 21:11; see also Alma 30:46)" (McConkie and Ostler, *Revelations of the Restoration*, 1075–76).

Doctrine and Covenants 132:58–66. Laws Governing Plural Marriage Are Set Forth

54 And I command mine handmaid, Emma Smith, to abide and cleave unto my servant Joseph, and to none else. But if she will not abide this commandment she shall be destroyed, saith the Lord; for I am the Lord thy God, and will destroy her if she abide not in my law.

55 But if she will not abide this commandment, then shall my servant Joseph do all things for her, even as he hath said; and I will bless him and multiply him and give unto him an hundred-fold in this world, of fathers and mothers, brothers and sisters, houses and lands, wives and children, and crowns of eternal lives in the eternal worlds.

56 And again, verily I say, let mine handmaid forgive my servant Joseph his trespasses; and then shall she be forgiven her trespasses, wherein she has trespassed against me; and I, the Lord thy God, will bless her, and multiply her, and make her heart to rejoice.

57 And again, I say, let not my servant Joseph put his property out of his hands, lest an enemy come and destroy him; for Satan seeketh to destroy; for I am the Lord thy God, and he is my servant; and behold, and lo, I am with him, as I was with Abraham, thy father, even unto his exaltation and glory.

58 Now, as touching the law of the priesthood, there are many things pertaining thereunto.

59 Verily, if a man be called of my Father, as was Aaron, by mine own voice, and by the voice of him that sent me, and I have endowed him with the keys of the power of this priesthood, if he do anything in my name, and according to my law and by my word, he will not commit sin, and I will justify him.

60 Let no one, therefore, set on my servant Joseph; for I will justify him; for he shall do the sacrifice which I require at his hands for his transgressions, saith the Lord your God.

61 And again, as pertaining to the law of the priesthood—if any man espouse a virgin, and desire to espouse another, and the first give her consent, and if he espouse the second, and they are virgins, and have vowed to no other man, then is he justified; he cannot commit adultery for they are given unto him; for he cannot commit adultery with that that belongeth unto him and to no one else.

62 And if he have ten virgins given unto him by this law, he cannot commit adultery, for they belong to him, and they are given unto him; therefore is he justified.

63 But if one or either of the ten virgins, after she is espoused, shall be with another man, she has committed adultery, and shall be destroyed; for they are given unto him to multiply and replenish the earth, according to my commandment, and to fulfil the promise which was given by my Father before the foundation of the world, and for their exaltation in the eternal worlds, that they may bear the souls of men; for herein is the work of my Father continued, that he may be glorified.

64 And again, verily, verily, I say unto you, if any man have a wife, who holds the keys of this power, and he teaches unto her the law of my priesthood, as pertaining to these things, then shall she believe and administer unto him, or she shall be destroyed, saith the Lord your God; for I will destroy her; for I will magnify my name upon all those who receive and abide in my law.

65 Therefore, it shall be lawful in me, if she receive not this law, for him to receive all things whatsoever I, the Lord his God, will give unto him, because she did not believe

Why might the Lord use the word "virgins" to describe plural marriage wives? (132:61–63) "The word *virgin* can refer to any unmarried woman who is chaste. This definition corresponds with what President John Taylor . . . taught when he said that 'none but the more pure, virtuous, honorable and upright' were to practice plural marriage ("Discourse," *Deseret News*, Apr. 26, 1882, 212). Though it is not clear why or how the word *virgin* is being used in Doctrine and Covenants 132:61–63, plural marriage as practiced by the Prophet Joseph Smith and the early Saints did not exclude widows or women who had previously been married. The passage seems to illustrate that plural marriages performed according to God's law and by His authority and direction were acceptable to Him" (*Doctrine and Covenants Student Manual* [2018], 794). ⊕

What was a main purpose given by the Lord for the practice of plural marriage? (132:63) "The Prophet Joseph Smith learned that one of the purposes of plural marriage is 'to multiply and replenish the earth' (D&C 132:63; see also Genesis 1:28). The Book of Mormon prophet Jacob explained that the Lord sometimes commands His people to practice plural marriage so that they can 'raise up seed unto [Him]' (Jacob 2:30). To 'raise up seed unto [the Lord]' means to 'bring up . . . children in [the] light and truth' of the gospel (see D&C 93:40). Thus, the Lord has at times established the practice of plural marriage to provide His people with further opportunities to raise children in the gospel covenant. The practice of plural marriage in the Church in the 19th century 'did result in the birth of large numbers of children within faithful Latter-day Saint homes' ([Gospel Topics, "Plural Marriage"])" (*Doctrine and Covenants Student Manual* [2018], 794–95).

What is the "law of Sarah"? (132:64–66) "The instructions recorded in Doctrine and Covenants 132:64–66 apparently related to Joseph and Emma Smith's specific circumstances. The Lord refers to a man 'who holds the keys of this power' and the man's wife (D&C 132:64; see also D&C 132:7). The Lord explained that after the Prophet Joseph Smith had taught Emma 'the law of my priesthood' regarding plural marriage, she had an obligation to 'believe' and support Joseph as he obeyed the Lord's commandment to marry additional women (D&C 132:64). In so doing, Emma would follow the example of Sarah, 'who administered unto Abraham according to the law when [the Lord] commanded Abraham to take Hagar to wife' (D&C 132:65; see also D&C 132:34)" (*Doctrine and Covenants Student Manual* [2018], 795–96).

and administer unto him according to my word; and she then becomes the transgressor; and he is exempt from the law of Sarah, who administered unto Abraham according to the law when I commanded Abraham to take Hagar to wife.

66 And now, as pertaining to this law, verily, verily, I say unto you, I will reveal more unto you, hereafter; therefore, let this suffice for the present. Behold, I am Alpha and Omega. Amen.

Introduction to Doctrine and Covenants 133

"On 1 November 1831, Joseph Smith and the leading elders of the Church began a series of conference meetings at the home of John Johnson in Hiram, Ohio, to organize the revelations and decide details of their publication. Between the morning and afternoon sessions of the conference on 1 November, the Lord revealed Doctrine and Covenants 1 to Joseph Smith as 'the Lord's Preface' to the proposed Book of Commandments. Two days later, on 3 November 1831, Joseph received Doctrine and Covenants 133, which he called 'the Appendix' to the Book of Commandments" (Robinson and Garrett, *Doctrine and Covenants Commentary*, 4:261). "Like Doctrine and Covenants 1, it warned the inhabitants of the earth of Christ's imminent return and the need to repent and accept God's direction as provided in the revelations He had given to Joseph" (Godfrey, "William McLellin's Five Questions," 140).

The Prophet Joseph Smith noted: "At this time there were many things which the elders desired to know relative to preaching the gospel to the inhabitants of the earth, and concerning the gathering: and, in order to walk by the true light, and be instructed from on high. . . . I enquired of the Lord and received the following Revelation, which from its importance, and for distinction has Since been added to the Book of Doctrine and Covenants, and called the Appendix" (Joseph Smith Papers, "History, 1838–1856, volume A-1," 166).

"Doctrine and Covenants 133 continues and even escalates the apocalyptic tone of section 1. Echoing themes of the Apocalypse, the Revelation of John, which concludes the Bible by prophesying a tumultuous future of merciful triumph for the repentant sealed believers and unavoidable justice for the unrepentant damned, section 133 tells readers what they should have learned from the Doctrine and Covenants. It announces that Christ will come soon, dramatically. He will come to judge all that forget God, including the ungodly Latter-day Saints. So the Saints should prepare for his coming by sanctifying their lives and becoming Zion" (Harper, *Making Sense of the Doctrine & Covenants*, 490–91).

SECTION 133

Revelation given through Joseph Smith the Prophet, at Hiram, Ohio, November 3, 1831. Prefacing this revelation, Joseph Smith's history states, "At this time there were many things which the Elders desired to know relative to preaching the Gospel to the inhabitants of the earth, and concerning the gathering; and in order to walk by the true light, and be instructed from on high, on the 3rd of November,

1831, I inquired of the Lord and received the following important revelation." This section was first added to the book of Doctrine and Covenants as an appendix and was subsequently assigned a section number.

1 Hearken, O ye people of my church, saith the Lord your God, and hear the word of the Lord concerning you—

2 The Lord who shall suddenly come to his temple; the Lord who shall come down upon the world with a curse to judgment; yea, upon all the nations that forget God, and upon all the ungodly among you.

3 For he shall make bare his holy arm in the eyes of all the nations, and all the ends of the earth shall see the salvation of their God.

4 Wherefore, prepare ye, prepare ye, O my people; sanctify yourselves; gather ye together, O ye people of my church, upon the land of Zion, all you that have not been commanded to tarry.

Doctrine and Covenants 133:1–6. The Saints Are Commanded to Prepare for the Second Coming

When did this prophecy begin to be fulfilled? (133:1–2) "The subject is the Second Coming of the Lord Jesus Christ. He was yet to come to His temple when this revelation was given (v. 2), but in the sequence of the published revelations, the appendix being placed at the end, he has now suddenly appeared, on April 3, 1836, in the Kirtland Temple (D&C 110:1–10). When He comes down upon the world, He will curse the nations that had forgotten God, and all the ungodly individuals among those who profess Him (v. 2)" (Nyman, *Doctrine and Covenants Commentary*, 2:564).

What does it mean to "make bare his holy arm"? (133:3) "In ancient times, men prepared for battle by throwing their cloak away from the shoulder of their fighting arm (Ps. 74:11). At the second coming of Christ, God will 'make bare' his arm when he shows forth his power for all to see (D&C 133:2–3). This phrase and the remainder of the verse is a quotation from Isa. 52:10" (Parry and Parry, *Understanding the Signs of the Times*, 298).

Where are the Saints to gather? (133:4) "Another sign of the times is the gathering of the faithful (see D&C 133:4). In the early years of this last dispensation, a gathering to Zion involved various locations in the United States. . . . Always these were gatherings to prospective temples. With the creation of stakes and the construction of temples in most nations with sizable populations of the faithful, the current commandment is not to gather to one place but to gather in stakes in our own homelands. There the faithful can enjoy the full blessings of eternity in a house of the Lord" (Oaks, "Preparation for the Second Coming," *Ensign*, May 2004, 8).

Once gathered, the Saints can receive an "endowment that is received in the house of the Lord. The endowment is a ritual cleansing and is requisite to being sanctified" (McConkie and Ostler, *Revelations of the Restoration*, 1108).

What are the vessels of the Lord? (133:5) "Anciently [vessels of the Lord] had at least two meanings, both related to the work of the priesthood.

"The first refers to the recovery and return to Jerusalem of various temple [vessels] that had been carried into Babylon by King Nebuchadnezzar. . . .

"The second meaning is related to the first. Similar bowls and implements were used for ritual purification in the home. . . .

"In both of these biblical accounts the message is that as priesthood bearers not only are we to *handle* sacred vessels and emblems of God's power—think of preparing, blessing, and passing the sacrament, for example—but we are also to *be* a sanctified instrument as well" (Holland, "Sanctify Yourselves," *Ensign*, Nov. 2000, 39).

What is the reason for calling together these "solemn assemblies"? (133:6) See commentary in this volume on Doctrine and Covenants 88:70 and 95:7.

Doctrine and Covenants 133:7–16. All Men Are Commanded to Flee from Babylon, Come to Zion, and Prepare for the Great Day of the Lord

What is Babylon and why should we flee it? (133:7) "The antithesis and antagonist of Zion is Babylon. The city of Babylon was originally Babel, of Tower of Babel fame, and later became the capital of the Babylonian empire. . . . Its worldliness, its worship of evil, and the captivity of Judah there following the conquest of 587 B.C. all combine to make Babylon the symbol of decadent societies and spiritual bondage.

"It is with this backdrop that the Lord said to the members of His Church, 'Go ye out of Babylon; gather ye out from among the nations. . . . (D&C 133:7). He called for the elders of His Church to be sent forth across the world to accomplish this gathering, commencing an effort that continues in full vigor today" (Christofferson, "Come to Zion," *Ensign*, Nov. 2008, 37). See also commentary in this volume on Doctrine and Covenants 1:16. ⊙

Why is it important to send missionaries throughout the world? (133:8) Elder Neil L. Andersen testified:

"The priesthood of God has been restored to the earth, and the Lord has set His hand to prepare the world for His glorious return. These are days of great opportunity and important responsibilities. These are your days. . . .

5 Go ye out from Babylon. Be ye clean that bear the vessels of the Lord.

6 Call your solemn assemblies, and speak often one to another. And let every man call upon the name of the Lord.

7 Yea, verily I say unto you again, the time has come when the voice of the Lord is unto you: Go ye out of Babylon; gather ye out from among the nations, from the four winds, from one end of heaven to the other.

8 Send forth the elders of my church unto the nations which are afar off; unto the islands of the sea; send forth unto foreign lands; call upon all nations, first upon the Gentiles, and then upon the Jews.

"Your mission will be a sacred opportunity to bring others to Christ and help prepare for the Second Coming of the Savior. . . .

"The world is being prepared for the Second Coming of the Savior in large measure because of the Lord's work through His missionaries" ("Preparing the World for the Second Coming," *Ensign*, May 2011, 49, 50, 51).

Why is it so important to gather to Zion and her stakes? (133:9) "This, then, is the message of gathering: Come unto Christ; repent and be baptized; receive the gift of the Holy Ghost and become pure, as pure and untainted from the sins of the world as is a newly born babe. Then assemble with the saints that the sanctifying processes may work in your life and you become a fit subject to stand before the King of Zion when he comes to reign in his glory" (Bruce R. McConkie, *Millennial Messiah*, 292–93).

What does the coming of the Bridegroom represent? (133:10) "The marriage of the Lamb, who is Christ (D&C 33:17–18) to his bride, who is the Church (D&C 109:73–74) as well as the New Jerusalem (21:2, 9–10), is a metaphor for the union between the Lord and his people, made possible through the atonement of Christ. In fact, the very name of Christ's sacrifice (*at-one-ment*) suggests the purpose of that sacrifice: to make us one with both the Father and the Son (John 17:11, 19–23). To underscore the sweetness and blessing of that union, the Lord uses marriage as a symbol. There is no sweeter or more meaningful relationship on earth than that between a holy husband and a holy wife" (Parry and Parry, *Understanding the Book of Revelation*, 251–52).

When will the Lord return? (133:11) President M. Russell Ballard explained: "I am called as one of the apostles to be a special witness of Christ in these exciting, trying times, and I do not know when He is going to come again.

"As far as I know, none of my brethren in the Council of the Twelve or even in the First Presidency know [when the Lord's Second Coming will be]. And I would humbly suggest to you, my young brothers and sisters, that if we do not know, then nobody knows, no matter how compelling their arguments or how reasonable their calculations. The Savior said that 'of that day and hour knoweth no man, no, not the angels of heaven, but my Father only' (Matthew 24:36)" ("When Shall These Things Be?" 2). ☉

9 And behold, and lo, this shall be their cry, and the voice of the Lord unto all people: Go ye forth unto the land of Zion, that the borders of my people may be enlarged, and that her stakes may be strengthened, and that Zion may go forth unto the regions round about.

10 Yea, let the cry go forth among all people: Awake and arise and go forth to meet the Bridegroom; behold and lo, the Bridegroom cometh; go ye out to meet him. Prepare yourselves for the great day of the Lord.

11 Watch, therefore, for ye know neither the day nor the hour.

Why does the Lord urge all to go out from Babylon and flee to Zion? (133:12–14) The Prophet Joseph Smith stated: "The time is soon coming when no man will have any peace but in Zion and her Stakes" (Joseph Smith Papers, "History, 1838–1856, volume C-1," 13 [addenda]).

What does it mean to look back? (133:15) "So, if history is this important—and it surely is—what did Lot's wife do that was so wrong? As something of a student of history, I have thought about that and offer this as a partial answer. Apparently what was wrong with Lot's wife was that she wasn't just *looking* back; in her heart she wanted to *go* back. It would appear that even before they were past the city limits, she was already missing what Sodom and Gomorrah had offered her. As Elder Maxwell once said, such people know they should have their primary residence in Zion, but they still hope to keep a summer cottage in Babylon" (Holland, "Remember Lot's Wife," 2).

Doctrine and Covenants 133:17–35. The Lord Will Stand on Mount Zion, the Continents Will Become One Land, and the Lost Tribes of Israel Will Return

What does it mean to "make his paths straight"? (133:17) "This phrase means 'prepare the way of the Lord,' or prepare for the Second Coming by making the Saints' path back to God's presence level

12 Let them, therefore, who are among the Gentiles flee unto Zion.

13 And let them who be of Judah flee unto Jerusalem, unto the mountains of the Lord's house.

14 Go ye out from among the nations, even from Babylon, from the midst of wickedness, which is spiritual Babylon.

15 But verily, thus saith the Lord, let not your flight be in haste, but let all things be prepared before you; and he that goeth, let him not look back lest sudden destruction shall come upon him.

16 Hearken and hear, O ye inhabitants of the earth. Listen, ye elders of my church together, and hear the voice of the Lord; for he calleth upon all men, and he commandeth all men everywhere to repent.

17 For behold, the Lord God hath sent forth the angel crying through the midst of heaven, saying: Prepare ye the way of the Lord, and make his paths straight, for the hour of his coming is nigh—

Christ's Appearances During His Second Coming (Doctrine and Covenants 133:17–22)

Christ's Appearances to All People

"When the Lord returns He will make some appearances to specific groups and then culminate His return by His appearance in great power, majesty, and glory, in such a manner that all the world will see Him (see D&C 133:17–22 and 101:22–23). Four appearances of the Lord have had particular mention by the prophets: two of these appearances will be to the Saints; one appearance will be to the Jews; and the fourth will be His final coming to the world.

"*The appearance at the city of New Jerusalem.*

"The Lord 'shall suddenly come to his temple' (D&C 133:2), a temple yet to be built in Jackson County, Missouri (see D&C 84:1–5; 97:10, 15–16). . . .

"*The appearance at At Adam-ondi-Ahman.*

"The Lord will appear to the Saints at a great sacrament meeting at Adam-ondi-Ahman in Daviess County, Missouri, attended by those who have held the keys of the priesthood during all the gospel dispensations and by faithful Saints from all ages. The Prophet Joseph Smith said that 'Daniel in his seventh chapter speaks of the Ancient of Days; he means the oldest man, our father Adam, Michael, he will call his children together and hold

18 When the Lamb shall stand upon Mount Zion, and with him a hundred and forty-four thousand, having his Father's name written on their foreheads.

19 Wherefore, prepare ye for the coming of the Bridegroom; go ye, go ye out to meet him.

or smooth (that is, remove all obstacles out of the way so that others can be obedient to the laws and ordinances of the gospel)" (Parry, Parry, and Peterson, *Understanding Isaiah*, 341). See also commentary in this volume on Doctrine and Covenants 65:1.

Who are these 144,000 who come with Christ? (133:18) "The opening verses of Revelation 14 describe a group who have the 'Father's name written in their foreheads' (verse 1); they are clean and chaste, 'follow the Lamb whithersoever he goeth,' and are redeemed from among men (verse 4); and they are honest and 'without fault' before God (verse 5).

"Through the Prophet Joseph Smith, the Lord revealed that the 144,000 'are high priests, ordained unto the holy order of God, to administer the everlasting gospel; for they are they who are ordained out of every nation, kindred, tongue, and people'" (*New Testament Student Manual* [2018], 555). See also commentary in this volume on Doctrine and Covenants 77:11.

What does the Lord invite His people to do, regardless of where they live? (133:19) "There is a specific invitation extended to His covenant people. . . . This invitation suggests that His Saints will be found everywhere in the world in the last days, and that no matter where they may be, they are to go out to meet Him. This will be part of the actual Second Coming of Christ, for this is the 'wedding supper,' which symbolizes our joining into a covenant contract with Him, which is likened to the eternal commitment a husband and wife make with each other (see Matthew 22:1–14; Matthew 25:1–13)" (Lund, *Second Coming of the Lord*, 315).

a council with them to prepare them for the coming of the Son of Man' [Joseph Smith Papers, 'History Draft (1 March–31 December 1843),' 14]. . . .

"*The appearance at the Mount of Olives.*

"The Savior's appearance to the Jews will occur when Jerusalem and its environs are besieged by many nations. At the close of a long and costly war, known as the battle of Armageddon, the Jews will flee for safety to the Mount of Olives. There the Savior will make His appearance (see D&C 45:48–53; 77:15; 133:35; Revelation 11:1–13; Zechariah 14:1–9). . . .

"*The Second Coming: the appearance to the whole world.*

"As the Lord's Second Coming approaches, signs will mark this epochal event. One of the last of these signs is the sign of the Son of Man (see D&C 88:93; JS—M 1:36). The Prophet Joseph Smith said: 'Then will appear one grand sign of the Son of Man in heaven. But what will the world do? They will say it is a planet, a comet, etc. But the Son of Man will come as the sign of the coming of the Son of Man, which will be as the light of the morning cometh out of the east' [Joseph Smith Papers, "History, 1838–1856, volume D-1," 1520]" (adapted from *Doctrine and Covenants Student Manual* [2001], 404–5; paragraphing altered).

President Russell M. Nelson directed: "May we go forward together to fulfill our divine mandate—that of preparing ourselves and the world for the Second Coming of the Lord" ("New Normal," *Liahona*, Nov. 2020, 119). ⊕

What is noteworthy about the Bridegroom standing on Mount Olivet? (133:20) "The Millennial era will not be ushered in by the righteousness of the people. Christ will come in the midst of war such as has never been known before in the whole history of the world. All the nations of the earth will be engaged. Those who oppose freedom and liberty and Christianity and the Jews will attack Jerusalem. The focal point will be the ancient battlegrounds of Megiddo and Armageddon. In the midst of this war, 'this same Jesus' who ascended from Olivet 'shall so come in like manner' as he went up into heaven (Acts 1:11). His feet shall once again stand upon the Mount of Olives. And in the Valley of Jehoshaphat, which is between Jerusalem and Olivet, he shall sit to judge the heathen nations" (Bruce R. McConkie, *New Witness*, 637).

Why is the Lord's voice described as the voice of many waters and great thunder? (133:22) "The voice of the Lord is as 'many waters' (see also Ezek. 43:2), 'as the sound of the rushing of great waters' (D&C 110:3), 'like the noise of great waters' (Ezek. 1:24), 'as the voice of many waters, and as the voice of a great thunder' (D&C 133:22), and 'like the voice of a multitude' (Dan. 10:6). These expressions seem to describe the power, authority, uniqueness, and intensity that exists in the Lord's voice" (Parry and Parry, *Understanding the Book of Revelation*, 23).

What will happen to the earth as part of the Second Coming? (133:23–24) "The earth is to be renewed and receive again its paradisiacal glory. It is to rise from the fallen celestial state to the terrestrial state it once enjoyed. . . . When the change comes, it will be so dramatic and the earth will be altered in so many respects that it will have a new aerial heaven and become, in fact, a new earth" (Bruce R. McConkie, *New Witness*, 649). ⊕

Who are "they who are in the north countries"? (133:26) "The phrase 'they who are in the north countries' (D&C 133:26) has reference to the ten lost tribes of Israel. Anciently, these 'ten tribes . . . made up the northern kingdom of Israel and were carried away captive into Assyria in 721 B.C. At that time, they

20 For behold, he shall stand upon the mount of Olivet, and upon the mighty ocean, even the great deep, and upon the islands of the sea, and upon the land of Zion.

21 And he shall utter his voice out of Zion, and he shall speak from Jerusalem, and his voice shall be heard among all people;

22 And it shall be a voice as the voice of many waters, and as the voice of a great thunder, which shall break down the mountains, and the valleys shall not be found.

23 He shall command the great deep, and it shall be driven back into the north countries, and the islands shall become one land;

24 And the land of Jerusalem and the land of Zion shall be turned back into their own place, and the earth shall be like as it was in the days before it was divided.

25 And the Lord, even the Savior, shall stand in the midst of his people, and shall reign over all flesh.

26 And they who are in the north countries shall come in remembrance before the Lord; and their prophets shall hear his voice, and shall no longer stay themselves; and they

shall smite the rocks, and the ice shall flow down at their presence.

27 And an highway shall be cast up in the midst of the great deep.

went to the "north countries" and became lost to the knowledge of others' ([Guide to the Scriptures, 'Israel']). The Book of Mormon prophet Nephi explained: 'There are many who are . . . lost from the knowledge of those who are at Jerusalem. Yea, the more part of all the tribes [of Israel] have been led away; . . . and whither they are none of us knoweth . . .' (1 Nephi 22:4). Thus, the ten lost tribes of Israel have been scattered throughout the earth" (*Doctrine and Covenants Student Manual,* [2018], 815–16). ⊕

In what ways will the rocks be smitten, the ice flow, and a highway be cast up? (133:26–27) "Perhaps an appeal to apocalyptic or symbolic interpretation may be helpful here. . . . Are the 'ice' and 'rocks' physical ice and rocks, or a representation of communication barriers which must be broken down to facilitate the understanding and acceptance of the gospel? Is the highway a literal road, or a highway designated by the prophet Isaiah as 'the way of holiness,' a path the 'unclean shall not pass over' but on which 'the ransomed of the Lord shall return, and come to Zion with songs of everlasting joy'? (Isaiah 35:8–10; 51:10–11)" (Robinson and Garrett, *Commentary on the Doctrine and Covenants,* 269–70).

28 Their enemies shall become a prey unto them,

29 And in the barren deserts there shall come forth pools of living water; and the parched ground shall no longer be a thirsty land.

What will happen to those who oppose God's people? (133:28) "The promise granted to the returning tribes is that 'their enemies shall become a prey unto them' (D&C 133:28). This is a reference to the destruction of the wicked (the enemies of God) at the time of the Second Coming. . . . Nephi prophesied that the mother of abominations would gather great multitudes 'upon the face of all the earth, among all the nations of the Gentiles, to fight against the Lamb of God' (1 Nephi 14:13–15) and that the wrath of God would be poured our upon the great 'whore of all the earth,' who would then 'war among themselves, and the sword of their own hands'. . . (1 Nephi 22:13–14). How fitting that those thirsting for the blood of the Saints will eventually turn upon their own in that same spirit of vengeance!" (Millet and McConkie, *Doctrinal Commentary on the Book of Mormon,* 1:167–68).

30 And they shall bring forth their rich treasures unto the children of Ephraim, my servants.

31 And the boundaries of the everlasting hills shall tremble at their presence.

What are the rich treasures? (133:30) "Although these separated children of Israel will undoubtedly bring with them tangible treasures of a temporal nature, such as were brought out of Egypt centuries earlier (see Ex. 12:35–36), they will also bring with them treasures of a spiritual nature, such as their own scriptures (2 Ne. 29:13)" (Brewster, *Doctrine & Covenants Encyclopedia* [2012], 603).

What role does the tribe of Ephraim play in the gathering of Israel? (133:32) "Ephraim was given the birthright in Israel (1 Chr. 5:1–2; Jer. 31:9). In the last days their privilege and responsibility is to bear the priesthood, take the message of the restored gospel to the world, and raise an ensign to gather scattered Israel (Isa. 11:12–13; 2 Ne. 21:12–13). The children of Ephraim will crown with glory those from the north countries who return in the last days (D&C 133:26–34)" (Guide to the Scriptures, "Ephraim").

What needs to happen before Judah is sanctified? (133:35) "In the dedicatory prayer of the Kirtland Temple, the Prophet Joseph Smith pleaded with the Lord 'to have mercy upon the children of Jacob, that Jerusalem, from this hour, may begin to be redeemed; . . . and the children of Judah may begin to return to the lands which thou didst give to Abraham, their father' (D&C 109:62–64). Little by little this prophetic prayer is being fulfilled. The fulness of the gospel will be taught to the descendants of Judah and, in time, many Jews 'shall be persuaded to believe in Christ, the Son of God' ([2 Nephi 25:16]). As they accept the Savior and His gospel, 'they also of the tribe of Judah, after their pain, shall be sanctified in holiness before the Lord, to dwell in his presence day and night, forever and ever' ([D&C 133:35])" (*Doctrine and Covenants Student Manual* [2018], 817–18).

Doctrine and Covenants 133:36–40. The Gospel Was Restored through Joseph Smith to Be Preached in All the World

Who is the angel that was sent forth? (133:36) This angel may represent the many angelic messengers who were sent to restore the gospel. "Paul makes the apt statement that the gospel consists of two parts: the word and the power (1 Thess. 1:5). Thus Moroni brought the word, or at least that portion found in the Book of Mormon, for that record summarizes and teaches, in large part, what men must do to be saved. It records the terms and conditions of the plan of salvation. Also, before November 3, 1831, John the Baptist, and Peter, James, and John, as angelic ministrants, had brought keys and powers. But other angels were yet to come—Moses, Elias, Elijah, Gabriel, Raphael, and 'divers angels'" (Bruce R. McConkie, *Doctrinal New Testament Commentary*, 3:530).

32 And there shall they fall down and be crowned with glory, even in Zion, by the hands of the servants of the Lord, even the children of Ephraim.

33 And they shall be filled with songs of everlasting joy.

34 Behold, this is the blessing of the everlasting God upon the tribes of Israel, and the richer blessing upon the head of Ephraim and his fellows.

35 And they also of the tribe of Judah, after their pain, shall be sanctified in holiness before the Lord, to dwell in his presence day and night, forever and ever.

36 And now, verily saith the Lord, that these things might be known among you, O inhabitants of the earth, I have sent forth mine angel flying through the midst of heaven, having the everlasting gospel, who hath appeared unto some and hath committed it unto man, who shall appear unto many that dwell on the earth.

37 And this gospel shall be preached unto every nation, and kindred, and tongue, and people.

38 And the servants of God shall go forth, saying with a loud voice: Fear God and give glory to him, for the hour of his judgment is come;

39 And worship him that made heaven, and earth, and the sea, and the fountains of waters—

40 Calling upon the name of the Lord day and night, saying: O that thou wouldst rend the heavens, that thou wouldst come down, that the mountains might flow down at thy presence.

41 And it shall be answered upon their heads; for the presence of the Lord shall be as the melting fire that burneth, and as the fire which causeth the waters to boil.

42 O Lord, thou shalt come down to make thy name known to thine adversaries, and all nations shall tremble at thy presence—

43 When thou doest terrible things, things they look not for;

44 Yea, when thou comest down, and the mountains flow down at thy presence, thou shalt meet him who rejoiceth and worketh righteousness, who remembereth thee in thy ways.

45 For since the beginning of the world have not men heard nor perceived by the ear, neither hath any eye seen, O God, besides thee, how great things thou hast prepared for him that waiteth for thee.

46 And it shall be said: Who is this that cometh down from God in heaven with dyed garments; yea, from the regions which are not

How literal is taking the gospel to every nation? (133:37) "President Spencer W. Kimball challenged the Latter-day Saints to take literally the divinely received commission to deliver the gospel to all the earth: 'It seems to me that the Lord chose his words when he said "every nation," "every land," "uttermost bounds of the earth," "every tongue," "every people," "every soul," "all the world," "many lands." Surely there is significance in these words! . . . I feel that when we have done all in our power that the Lord will find a way to open doors. . . . Is anything too hard for the Lord? . . . If he commands: certainly he can fulfill. . . . I believe the Lord can do anything he sets his mind to do'" (quoted in Jackson, "Signs of the Times," 189).

What does it mean to "rend the heavens"? (133:40) "To rend the heavens is to tear open the veil, so that God can be seen" (Parry, Parry, and Peterson, *Understanding Isaiah*, 564).

Doctrine and Covenants 133:41–51. The Lord Will Come Down in Vengeance upon the Wicked

How will the Lord be as a "melting fire"? (133:41–44) "In section 133 of the Doctrine and Covenants, the Lord . . . adds that the very presence of Christ, a celestial being whose glory is like that of the sun, is likened unto fire [quotes D&C 133:40–44]. . . .

"The scriptures are quite explicit that there will be a burning and cleansing process connected directly with the Second Coming. And this seems to be directly connected to the actual presence of Jesus Christ. We're not given specifics on how this might work, but it seems to be tied to a Being whose glory is celestial and who is likened unto the sun itself. This sounds quite literal and not like symbolic fire" (Lund, *Second Coming of the Lord*, 349–50).

What blessings come to those who wait on the Lord? (133:45) "The personal growth one can achieve now while waiting upon the Lord and His promises is an invaluable, sacred element of His plan for each one of us. The contributions one can make now to help build up the Church on earth and to gather Israel are much needed. Marital status has nothing to do with one's capacity to serve. The Lord honors those who serve and wait upon Him in patience and faith" (Ballard, "Hope in Christ," *Liahona*, May 2021, 55). ✪

known, clothed in his glorious apparel, traveling in the greatness of his strength?

47 And he shall say: I am he who spake in righteousness, mighty to save.

How is the Lord mighty to save? (133:47) "Miracles, signs, and wonders abound among followers of Jesus Christ today, in your lives and in mine. Miracles are divine acts, manifestations and expressions of God's limitless power....

"Miracles are wrought by divine power by Him who is 'mighty to save.' Miracles are extensions of God's eternal plan; miracles are a lifeline from heaven to earth" (Rasband, "Behold, I Am a God of Miracles," *Liahona*, May 2021, 109–10).

Why will the Savior appear in red apparel? (133:48) "The Lord will return to the land that He made holy by His mission there in mortality. In triumph, He will come again to Jerusalem. In royal robes of red to symbolize His blood, which oozed from every pore, He shall return to the Holy City" (Nelson, "Future of the Church," *Liahona*, Apr. 2020, 10).

"Red is symbolic of victory—victory over the devil, death, hell, and endless torment. It is the symbol of salvation, of being placed beyond the power of all one's enemies. Christ's red apparel will also symbolize both aspects of His ministry to fallen humanity—His mercy and His justice.... He has descended below all things and mercifully taken upon Him our stains, our blood, [and] our sins" (Millet, "Second Coming of Christ," 209–10).

48 And the Lord shall be red in his apparel, and his garments like him that treadeth in the wine-vat.

49 And so great shall be the glory of his presence that the sun shall hide his face in shame, and the moon shall withhold its light, and the stars shall be hurled from their places.

What is noteworthy about Christ treading the wine press alone? (133:50) "The Atonement was a selfless act of infinite, eternal consequence, arduously earned alone, by the Son of God" (Scott, "The Atonement Can Secure Your Peace and Happiness," *Ensign*, Nov. 2006, 42).

President Jeffrey R. Holland observed: "I speak of the loneliest journey ever made and the unending blessings it brought to all in the human family. I speak of the Savior's solitary task of shouldering alone the burden of our salvation. Rightly He would say: 'I have trodden the winepress alone; and of the people there was none with me.... I looked, and there was none to help; and I wondered that there was none to uphold [me]'" ("None Were with Him," *Ensign*, May 2009, 86).

50 And his voice shall be heard: I have trodden the wine-press alone, and have brought judgment upon all people; and none were with me;

How will the Savior tread in anger upon the wicked? (133:51) "This is grim imagery—people being thrown into a winepress or onto a pressing floor. The Savior trampling them under His feet. Blood splattering on His clothing.... This is not a literal

51 And I have trampled them in my fury, and I did tread upon them in mine anger, and their blood have I sprinkled upon my garments, and stained all my raiment; for

this was the day of vengeance which was in my heart.

52 And now the year of my redeemed is come; and they shall mention the loving kindness of their Lord, and all that he has bestowed upon them according to his goodness, and according to his loving kindness, forever and ever.

53 In all their afflictions he was afflicted. And the angel of his presence saved them; and in his love, and in his pity, he redeemed them, and bore them, and carried them all the days of old;

54 Yea, and Enoch also, and they who were with him; the prophets who were before him; and Noah also, and they who were before him; and Moses also, and they who were before him;

55 And from Moses to Elijah, and from Elijah to John, who were with Christ in his resurrection, and the holy apostles, with Abraham, Isaac, and Jacob, shall be in the presence of the Lamb.

56 And the graves of the saints shall be opened; and they shall come forth and stand on the right hand of the Lamb, when he shall stand upon Mount Zion, and upon the holy city, the New Jerusalem; and they shall sing

future event where human beings are going to be bound and thrown onto some great pressing floor to be trampled and crushed. . . . We learn that the process of pressing symbolizes a time of judgment upon the wicked, a time when the Savior and Redeemer comes down in a spirit of judgment and vengeance. . . . It is not Christ that is crushing them under His feet; it is the weight of their own guilt, which comes when they realize with perfect remembrance just what they have done" (Lund, *Second Coming of the Lord*, 341, 342, 343).

Doctrine and Covenants 133:52–56. It Will Be the Year of the Lord's Redeemed

What is the "year of my redeemed"? (133:52) "The Lord, through Isaiah, spoke of 'the day of vengeance' and the 'year of my redeemed' (Isa. 63:4). This latter phrase is also used within the context of the Second Coming in the Doctrine and Covenants (133:52). . . . Inasmuch as the 'day of redemption' has specific reference to the day of resurrection, it appears that the 'year of my redeemed' is that special time when 'they who are Christ's at His Coming' will be redeemed from the bondage of death through the resurrection (D&C 88:16; [*Doctrines of Salvation*], 2:97)" (Brewster, *Doctrine & Covenants Encyclopedia* [2012], 653). ⊕

Who is "the angel of his presence"? (133:53) "Jacob referred to Christ as 'the Angel which redeemed me from all evil' (Gen. 48:16), and Abraham was spared death at the hands of the priests of Pharaoh by 'the angel of his [the Almighty's] presence' (Abr. 1:15). In a revelation given to Joseph Smith, the 'angel of his presence' is identified as the Savior (D&C 133:52–56). Christ is chief among all the messengers of his Father; he is the Messenger of Salvation, the 'messenger of the covenant' (Mal. 3:1)" (McConkie and Parry, *Guide to Scriptural Symbols*, 115).

What is "the song of the Lamb"? (133:56) "'The song of the Lamb' as recorded in Doctrine and Covenants 133:56 is unique among latter-day scripture, although in ancient writ reference is made to this song in the Apostle John's writings (Rev. 14:1–3; 15:2–4). The Lamb, of course, is Christ (D&C 76:85;

John 1:29, 36). The song—to be sung by the celestial Saints, who will inhabit the celestialized sphere which is as 'a sea of glass mingled with fire'—is at least partially identified by the Revelator ([see] Rev. 15:2–4)" (Brewster, *Doctrine & Covenants Encyclopedia* [2012], 544). See also commentary in this volume on Doctrine and Covenants 84:98.

Doctrine and Covenants 133:57–74. The Gospel Is to Be Sent Forth to Save the Saints and for the Destruction of the Wicked

How does the Lord prepare the weak? (133:58) Sister Julie B. Beck spoke of her ministry among Relief Society sisters: "With the Lord's Spirit, weak and simple women can know what to do. I have been to places in the world where women aren't able to read. They haven't had the opportunity or have not been taught, but because of the Lord's power that is placed upon them, the covenants they have made in the temple, and His Spirit that is poured out upon them, they are powerful women. They can discern His will, solve major problems, and feel peace, comfort, and guidance in their lives. Education is wonderful, but being able to feel the Lord's power and Spirit upon us is the highest education we can achieve. With that, we have power and influence" ("Choose Ye This Day to Serve the Lord," 3).

How will the Lord use the weak things of the earth to thresh the nations? (133:59) "The weak and simple who come unto Christ will break down the strong and mighty. By proclaiming the commandments of God and thrusting in their sickle with all their might, they will confound the wise, thrash the nations by the power of God's Spirit, and lay up for themselves treasures in heaven and salvation to their souls (see D&C 1:18–23; 4:4; 133:59; 1 Corinthians 1:27).

"Such power and salvation will come not because their weaknesses have been wrapped up, shelved, and forgotten, but rather because Christ has promised that the light of the gospel will reveal their weaknesses (see Ether 12:27–37; 2 Corinthians 12:9–10)" (Thomas, "Weak Things of the World," 302).

What can we do to receive eternal life? (133:62) Elder Neil L. Andersen compared eternal life with literally living with God. "Our residency in the 'City Eternal' cannot be earned by our own efforts, for

the song of the Lamb, day and night forever and ever.

57 And for this cause, that men might be made partakers of the glories which were to be revealed, the Lord sent forth the fulness of his gospel, his everlasting covenant, reasoning in plainness and simplicity—

58 To prepare the weak for those things which are coming on the earth, and for the Lord's errand in the day when the weak shall confound the wise, and the little one become a strong nation, and two shall put their tens of thousands to flight.

59 And by the weak things of the earth the Lord shall thresh the nations by the power of his Spirit.

60 And for this cause these commandments were given; they were commanded to be kept from the world in the day that they were given, but now are to go forth unto all flesh—

61 And this according to the mind and will of the Lord, who ruleth over all flesh.

62 And unto him that repenteth and sanctifieth himself before the Lord shall be given eternal life.

63 And upon them that hearken not to the voice of the Lord shall be fulfilled that which was written by the prophet Moses, that they should be cut off from among the people.

64 And also that which was written by the prophet Malachi: For, behold, the day cometh that shall burn as an oven, and all the proud, yea, and all that do wickedly, shall be stubble; and the day that cometh shall burn them up, saith the Lord of hosts, that it shall leave them neither root nor branch.

65 Wherefore, this shall be the answer of the Lord unto them:

66 In that day when I came unto mine own, no man among you received me, and you were driven out.

67 When I called again there was none of you to answer; yet my arm was not shortened at all that I could not redeem, neither my power to deliver.

68 Behold, at my rebuke I dry up the sea. I make the rivers a wilderness; their fish stink, and die for thirst.

69 I clothe the heavens with blackness, and make sackcloth their covering.

70 And this shall ye have of my hand—ye shall lie down in sorrow.

71 Behold, and lo, there are none to deliver you; for ye obeyed not my voice when I called to you out of the heavens; ye believed not my servants, and when they were sent unto you ye received them not.

the gift is both free and priceless. We can, however, prepare ourselves and sanctify our lives so that we may continually receive the divine gift of forgiveness. Overcoming the world through true and constant repentance throughout our mortal life allows us to experience the joy of receiving this heavenly gift" (*Divine Gift of Forgiveness*, 275–76).

What does it mean to have neither root nor branch? (133:64) "This expression simply means that wicked and indifferent persons who reject the gospel of Jesus Christ will have no family inheritance or patriarchal lineage—neither root (ancestors or progenitors) nor branch (children or posterity). Such persons cannot be received into the celestial kingdom of glory of resurrected beings, but must be content with a lesser blessing" (Theodore M. Burton, in Conference Report Oct. 1967, 81).

How can we trust in the Lord's power to deliver? (133:67) "I am not saying that the days ahead will be easy, but I promise you that the future will be glorious for those who are prepared and who continue to prepare to be instruments in the Lord's hands. . . .

"Let us not just *endure* this current season. Let us *embrace the future with faith*! Turbulent times are opportunities for us to thrive spiritually. They are times when our influence can be much more penetrating than in calmer times.

"I promise that as we create places of security, prepare our minds to be faithful to God, and never stop preparing, God will bless us" (Nelson, "Embrace the Future with Faith," *Ensign*, Nov. 2020, 76).

What do these images of the sea and fish represent? (133:68–69) Isaiah uses these same images (Isa. 50:2–3). "The Lord uses these as examples of his power. These phrases may refer to drought and to the smoke of war (which, although perpetrated by man, can also be a judgment of God) that obscures the sky, and they remind us of the miracles of Moses in Egypt (Ex. 7:18–21; 10:21; 14:26). They may also refer not only to events of the past but also to the Second Coming, an event of the future (Rev. 6:12; 8:12; D&C 45:42; 133:66). The Lord gave the same prophecy through Jeremiah (Jer. 51:36). Just as the Lord has great power over the elements, so also does he have power to redeem and deliver" (Parry, Parry, and Peterson, *Understanding Isaiah*, 440).

What is sealing up the testimony and binding up the law? (133:72) "According to this passage of scripture, these actions of binding and sealing the testimony and the law fit into a divine sequence: the Saints must first receive their temple endowments, then they warn the world's inhabitants of God's coming judgments; this is followed by the binding up of the testimony and the sealing of the law; finally the judgments of God will come (D&C 88:84; 109:38, 46; 133:72). After the Lord's servants have testified to and warned the nations, they will figuratively 'bind,' 'tie up,' 'shut up' or close their testimonies and 'affix [a] seal' to the law of God (the prophetic word)" (Parry and Parry, *Understanding the Signs of the Times*, 354–55).

Why might it be referred to as "outer darkness"? (133:73) "The subject of these verses is the servants of God (see vv. 71 and 38). These servants had been given the power to seal up the unbelieving and the rebellious unto the day when the wrath of God would be poured out upon the wicked. The appendix [D&C 133], placed at the end of the Doctrine and Covenants, is describing the day when that power had been exercised (vv. 72–73). The darkness may refer to the spirit world during the Millennium where the telestial beings would be for a thousand years awaiting the resurrection, or it may be referring to the sons of perdition who were to be cast into outer darkness for eternity. It is applicable to both, but the difference is the length of time" (Nyman, *Doctrine and Covenants Commentary*, 2:580).

72 Wherefore, they sealed up the testimony and bound up the law, and ye were delivered over unto darkness.

73 These shall go away into outer darkness, where there is weeping, and wailing, and gnashing of teeth.

74 Behold the Lord your God hath spoken it. Amen.

Introduction to Doctrine and Covenants 134

"A general assembly of priesthood leaders convened in Kirtland, Ohio, on August 17, 1835, to listen to Oliver Cowdery and Sidney Rigdon present the Doctrine and Covenants for their approval. Oliver introduced the book and its contents to the assembled councils, after which the priesthood leaders unanimously testified of their satisfaction with the work. Then Oliver Cowdery read a statement entitled 'Of Governments and Laws in General,' which is probably primarily if not exclusively the product of his mind and pen. The assembly 'accepted and adopted,' it for inclusion also, and thus section 134, though not a revelation, became canonized as part of the Doctrine and Covenants. . . .

"Joseph was in Michigan when the general assembly made these decisions. He did not write Doctrine and Covenants 134, but he endorsed it in April 1836 [*Messenger and Advocate* (Apr. 1836): 239–41]. The principles in section 134 continue to guide the Church's actions regarding political questions and controversies. The principles in verses 4–6 are more concisely expressed in Articles of Faith 1:11–12" (Harper, *Making Sense of the Doctrine & Covenants*, 493, 494).

This "declaration on government and law outlined the church's beliefs regarding the proper role of government in society. The most apparent motive for the declaration was the expulsion of church members from Jackson County, Missouri, in 1833. The first eleven of the declaration's twelve articles [or verses] address the role and duty of government in protecting and ensuring the free exercise of religion and could be read as an indictment of local, state, and national governments for failing to fulfill their duties in protecting the church from persecution" (Joseph Smith Papers, Historical Introduction to "Appendix 4: Declaration on Government and Law, circa August 1835 [D&C 134]").

SECTION 134

A declaration of belief regarding governments and laws in general, adopted by unanimous vote at a general assembly of the Church held at Kirtland, Ohio, August 17, 1835. Many Saints gathered together to consider the proposed contents of the first edition of the Doctrine and Covenants. At that time, this declaration was given the following preamble: "That our belief with regard to earthly governments and laws in general may not be misinterpreted nor misunderstood, we have thought proper to present, at the close of this volume, our opinion concerning the same."

1 We believe that governments were instituted of God for the benefit of man; and that he holds men accountable for their acts in relation to them, both in making laws and administering them, for the good and safety of society.

2 We believe that no government can exist in peace, except such laws are framed and held inviolate as will secure to each individual the free exercise of conscience, the right and control of property, and the protection of life.

3 We believe that all governments necessarily require civil officers and magistrates to enforce the laws of the same; and that such as will administer the law in equity and justice should be sought for and upheld by the voice of the people if a republic, or the will of the sovereign.

Doctrine and Covenants 134:1–4. Governments Should Preserve Freedom of Conscience and Worship

What does the phrase mean that "governments were instituted of God"? (134:1) "The concept of government comes from God. It is a divine principle....

"All secular governments, to one degree or another, are imperfect. Only the government of God is perfect. As noted by Hyrum M. Smith and Janne M. Sjodahl: 'The Lord in the very beginning revealed to Adam a perfect form of government, and this was "instituted of God for the benefit of man"; but we do not hold that all governments, or any man-made government, was inspired of God although the Lord holds a controlling hand over them.'...

"That being said, however, it should be noted that LDS Church leaders have taught that even poor governments are preferable to no government at all" (Skinner, "Government," 286).

What are the basic individual rights that government must protect? (134:2) At a time the Latter-day Saints [as well as many others across the country and world] were being denied these rights, the Prophet Joseph Smith declared that the Constitution of the United States "guarantees to every citizen, even the humblest, the enjoyment of life, liberty, and property. It promises to all, religious freedom, the right to all to worship God beneath their own vine and fig tree, according to the dictates of their conscience. It guarantees to all the citizens of the several states the right to become citizens of any one of the states, and to enjoy all the rights and immunities of the citizens of the state of his adoption" (Joseph Smith Papers, "History, 1838–1856, volume C-1," 986).

How should religious liberty function? (134:4)
President Dallin H. Oaks offered important counsel: "Even though the First Amendment obviously guarantees the right to *exercise* or practice religious beliefs and affiliations, that right is not absolute. As advocates for religious freedom, we must yield to the fact that in a nation with citizens of many different religious beliefs or disbeliefs, the government must sometimes limit the right of some to *act* upon their beliefs when it is necessary to protect the health, safety, and welfare of all" ("Going Forward with Religious Freedom and Nondiscrimination," 120). ⊕

What is government's responsibility regarding religious freedom? (134:4) "The First Amendment in the Bill of Rights singles out the 'free exercise' of religion for specific protection, along with the related freedoms of speech, press, and assembly. These rights enjoy singular status because of their paramount significance to the foundations of our constitutional republic. They are rights on which all other rights depend. Protecting them is essential to safeguarding and perpetuating all constitutional freedoms. That is why religious exercise and religious expression enjoy special constitutional protection" (Oaks, "Going Forward with Religious Freedom and Nondiscrimination," 120).

Doctrine and Covenants 134:5–8. All Men Should Uphold Their Governments and Owe Respect and Deference to the Law

What are Latter-day Saints' responsibilities regarding governments and law in their own land? (134:5) "The three significant words used in the 12th Article of Faith express the proper attitude of the membership of the Church toward law. These words are—obey, honor, and sustain.

"The Article does not say we believe in submission to the law. Obedience implies a higher attitude than mere submission, for obedience has its root in good intent; submission may spring from selfishness or meanness of spirit. Though obedience of submission both imply restraint on one's own will, we are obedient only from a sense of right; submissive from a sense of necessity. . . .

"We obey law from a sense of right.

"We honor law, because of its necessity and strength to society.

"We sustain law by keeping it in good repute" (McKay, in Conference Report, Apr. 1937, 28).

4 We believe that religion is instituted of God; and that men are amenable to him, and to him only, for the exercise of it, unless their religious opinions prompt them to infringe upon the rights and liberties of others; but we do not believe that human law has a right to interfere in prescribing rules of worship to bind the consciences of men, nor dictate forms for public or private devotion; that the civil magistrate should restrain crime, but never control conscience; should punish guilt, but never suppress the freedom of the soul.

5 We believe that all men are bound to sustain and uphold the respective governments in which they reside, while protected in their inherent and inalienable rights by the laws of such governments; and that sedition and rebellion are unbecoming every citizen thus protected, and should be punished accordingly; and that all governments have a right to enact such laws as in their own judgments are best calculated to secure the public interest; at the same time, however, holding sacred the freedom of conscience.

6 We believe that every man should be honored in his station, rulers and magistrates as such, being placed for the protection of the innocent and the punishment of the guilty; and that to the laws all men owe respect and deference, as without them peace and harmony would be supplanted by anarchy and terror; human laws being instituted for the express purpose of regulating our interests as individuals and nations, between man and man; and divine laws given of heaven, prescribing rules on spiritual concerns, for faith and worship, both to be answered by man to his Maker.

7 We believe that rulers, states, and governments have a right, and are bound to enact laws for the protection of all citizens in the free exercise of their religious belief; but we do not believe that they have a right in justice to deprive citizens of this privilege, or proscribe them in their opinions, so long as a regard and reverence are shown to the laws and such religious opinions do not justify sedition nor conspiracy.

8 We believe that the commission of crime should be punished according to the nature of the offense; that murder, treason, robbery, theft, and the breach of the general peace, in all respects, should be punished according to their criminality and their tendency to evil among men, by the laws of that government in which the offense is committed; and for the public peace and tranquility all men

Why should Latter-day Saints understand this warning about "sedition and rebellion"? (134:5) "A saint is an honorable citizen, knowing that the very country which provides opportunity and protection deserves support, including prompt payment of taxes and personal participation in its legal political process" (Nelson, "Thus Shall My Church Be Called," *Ensign*, May 1990, 16–17).

Why did God give divine laws "prescribing rules on spiritual concerns"? (134:6) Joseph Smith declared: "God has given certain laws to the human family, which, if observed, are sufficient to prepare them to inherit this [celestial] rest. This, then, we conclude, was the purpose of God in giving his laws to us: if not, why, or for what were they given? . . . All the commandments contained in the law of the Lord, have the sure promise annexed of a reward to all who obey; predicated upon the fact, that they are really the promises of a Being who cannot lie, and who is abundantly able to fulfil every tittle of his word" (Joseph Smith Papers, "Letter to the Church, circa February 1834," 136).

Why is freedom of speech vital to religion? (134:7) "The right to exercise religion would be seriously diminished if we couldn't say what we believe. Fortunately, in common with all Americans, religious believers and organizations are entitled to the freedom of speech. Their right to speak on matters of public concern is beyond dispute. The Supreme Court has taught 'that private religious speech, far from being a First Amendment orphan, is as fully protected under the Free Speech Clause as secular private expression.' Religious speech cannot be singled out for government suppression. Nor is there any question that churches and other religious organizations—not just individuals—hold the right of free speech too" (Christofferson, "Religious Freedom," 4).

What is our duty when we know of illegal activity? (134:8) "Now, the Lord has provided that those in his church shall live according to the law, and he makes a distinction between the law pertaining to the church, and what we call the secular law, or the law of the land, but he requires obedience to each. My love for my brother in this church does not mean that I am to stand between him and righteous judgment. This church is no organization like that as the secret combinations of old, which the Lord has said he hates, the members of which were pledged, and bound by oath that they would . . . cover up one another's crimes, that they would justify one another in theft and murder, and in all things that were unclean" (Talmage, in Conference Report, Oct. 1920, 63).

Doctrine and Covenants 134:9–10. Religious Societies Should Not Exercise Civil Powers

What is the Church's position on the separation of church and state? (134:9) President Dallin H. Oaks reflected: "60 years ago, the popular metaphor of the relationship between church and state was that of a 'wall of separation.' Introduced into Supreme Court jurisprudence in the 1879 case Reynolds v. United States and brought into mainstream vernacular in its 1947 Everson case in April 1907[, the] unfortunate connotations of the 'wall of separation' metaphor persist to the present day. . . .

"I reject the idea of a wall between church and state. The more appropriate metaphor to express that relation—reinforced by various decisions of the United States Supreme Court—is a *curtain* that defines boundaries but is not a barrier to the passage of light and love and mutual support from one side to another" ("Boundary between Church and State").

should step forward and use their ability in bringing offenders against good laws to punishment.

9 We do not believe it just to mingle religious influence with civil government, whereby one religious society is fostered and another proscribed in its spiritual privileges, and the individual rights of its members, as citizens, denied.

10 We believe that all religious societies have a right to deal with their members for disorderly conduct, according to the rules and regulations of such societies; provided that such dealings be for fellowship and good standing; but we do not believe that any religious society has authority to try men on the right of property or life, to take from them this world's goods, or to put them in jeopardy of either life or limb, or to inflict any physical punishment upon them. They can only excommunicate them from their society, and withdraw from them their fellowship.

Church Membership Status (Doctrine and Covenants 134:10)

"Most repentance takes place between an individual, God, and those who have been affected by a person's sins. However, sometimes a bishop or stake president needs to help Church members in their efforts to repent.

"When assisting members with repentance, bishops and stake presidents are loving and caring. They follow the example of the Savior, who lifted individuals and helped them turn away from sin and turn toward God (see Matthew 9:10–13; John 8:3–11). . . .

"If a member commits a serious sin, the bishop or stake president helps him or her repent. As part of this process, he may need to restrict some Church membership privileges for a time. In some situations, he may need to withdraw a person's membership for a time.

"Restricting or withdrawing a person's membership is not intended to punish. Rather, these actions are sometimes necessary to help a person repent and experience a change of heart. They also give a person time to prepare spiritually to renew and keep his or her covenants again.

"The bishop or stake president oversees membership restrictions or withdrawal. . . . These actions are accompanied by conditions of repentance. As a person sincerely repents, he or she may have the privileges of Church membership restored. . . .

"Church membership restrictions are ecclesiastical, not civil or criminal. They affect only a person's standing in the Church (see Doctrine and Covenants 134:10)" (*General Handbook* [2022], 32.0, 32.2).

Doctrine and Covenants 134:11–12. Men Are Justified in Defending Themselves and Their Property

11 We believe that men should appeal to the civil law for redress of all wrongs and grievances, where personal abuse is inflicted or the right of property or character infringed, where such laws exist as will protect the same; but we believe that all men are justified in defending themselves, their friends, and property, and the government, from the unlawful assaults and encroachments of all persons in times of exigency, where immediate appeal cannot be made to the laws, and relief afforded.

12 We believe it just to preach the gospel to the nations of the earth, and warn the righteous to save themselves from the corruption of the world; but we do not believe it right to interfere with bond-servants, neither preach the gospel to, nor baptize them contrary to the will and wish of their masters, nor to meddle with or influence them in the least to cause them to be dissatisfied with their situations in this life, thereby jeopardizing the lives of men; such interference we believe to be unlawful and unjust, and dangerous to the peace of every government allowing human beings to be held in servitude.

How should we feel about defending our own and others' lawful rights? (134:11) The Prophet Joseph Smith declared: "I am bold to declare before Heaven that I am just as ready to die in defending the rights of a Presbyterian, a Baptist, or a good man of any other denomination; for the same principle which would trample upon the rights of the Latter-day Saints would trample upon the rights of the Roman Catholics, or of any other denomination who may be unpopular and too weak to defend themselves.

"It is a love of liberty which inspires my soul—civil and religious liberty to the whole of the human race. Love of liberty was diffused into my soul by my grandfathers while they dandled me on their knees. . . .

"If I esteem mankind to be in error, shall I bear them down? No. I will lift them up, and in their own way too, if I cannot persuade them my way is better; and I will not seek to compel any man to believe as I do, only by the force of reasoning, for truth will cut its own way" (*Joseph Smith* [manual], 345).

Why was it not considered "right to interfere with bond-servants" during this period? (134:12) "This statement must be understood in the context of the 1830s, when the issues of slavery and states' rights in the United States were being debated and when slavery was legal in some states" (Robinson and Garrett, *Commentary on the Doctrine and Covenants*, 4:280).

"Violent opposition and a traumatic uprooting—felt collectively by church members from Missouri to Ohio—undoubtedly discouraged church leaders from actively engaging in issues of slavery and race from 1833 onward. In addition to their experiences in Missouri, successful missionary efforts in Tennessee and Kentucky from 1834 to 1836 likely made [Joseph Smith] and other leaders wary of openly supporting any antislavery movement that could potentially hinder proselytizing or ignite tensions between new converts and their Southern neighbors" (Joseph Smith Papers, Historical Introduction to "Letter to Oliver Cowdery, circa 9 April 1836," 289).

When Joseph Smith later ran for president of the United States, he urged Congress to abolish slavery and pay the slaveholders from the sale of public lands. The Prophet wrote: "Petition . . . ye goodly inhabitants of the slave states, your legislators to abolish slavery by the year 1850, or now. . . . Break off the shackles from the poor black man, and hire him to labor like other human beings; for 'an hour of virtuous liberty on earth, is worth a whole eternity of bondage!'" (Joseph Smith Papers, "General Smith's Views of the Powers and Policy of the Government of the United States, circa 26 January–7 February 1844," 9).

Introduction to Doctrine and Covenants 135

The Prophet Joseph Smith once declared: "I speak boldly and faithfully and with authority. . . . I know what I say; I understand my mission and business. God Almighty is my shield; and what can man do if God is my friend? I shall not be sacrificed until my time comes; then I shall be offered freely" (*Joseph Smith* [manual], 522–23). The Prophet's time came June 27, 1844, at Carthage, Illinois.

"Doctrine and Covenants 135 is a eulogy of the Prophet and an indictment of the state and nation that allowed him and his brother to be slain. As such, its tone is a rich mixture of reverence and disdain, praise and contempt. . . . It declares Joseph Smith's significance to [humankind], his translation of the Book of Mormon and spreading of the gospel, his receipt of revelations, gathering of Israel, founding of Nauvoo, and, with Hyrum, the sealing of his testimony with the ultimate sacrifice of his life" (Harper, *Making Sense of the Doctrine & Covenants*, 496).

"Since at least the early 20th century, commentators and Church leaders had assumed that [D&C 135] was written by John Taylor, an Apostle and the head of the printing office. The section was never attributed to Taylor during his lifetime, however, and it may have been the work of Taylor, Richards, Phelps, or another regular contributor in the Nauvoo printing office. Regardless of authorship, the statement drew heavily on the eyewitness testimonies of Taylor and Richards and quoted from earlier newspaper editorials and notices published by the Church that they had helped write. Like those earlier published accounts, this statement echoed themes of martyrdom, innocence, and divine judgment—themes that likewise appeared in the private writings of Latter-day Saints" (Mahas, "Remembering the Martyrdom," 304–5).

Doctrine and Covenants 135:1–2. Joseph and Hyrum Martyred in Carthage Jail

What impact did Joseph and Hyrum's martyrdom have on the Saints? (135:1) "Many women recorded the events leading up to and immediately following the martyrdom, providing a detailed record. Some knew him intimately; others revered him from a distance. The whole community of Saints mourned, both privately and publicly. Even nature itself expressed a depth of grief and despair at the time of the death and burial of Joseph and Hyrum Smith on June 27, 1844. Jane Manning James stated, 'I shall never forget that time of agony and sorrow.' . . .

"Sister Mary Horne wrote: 'May I never experience another day similar to that! I do not wish to recall the scene but for a moment. That terrible martyrdom deeply scarred the hearts and bewildered the senses of all our people. We could scarcely realize the awful event, except in the agony of our feelings; nor comprehend the dark hour, beyond the solemn loneliness which pervaded the city and made the void in

SECTION 135

Announcement of the martyrdom of Joseph Smith the Prophet and his brother, Hyrum Smith the Patriarch, at Carthage, Illinois, June 27, 1844. This document was included at the end of the 1844 edition of the Doctrine and Covenants, which was nearly ready for publication when Joseph and Hyrum Smith were murdered.

1 To seal the testimony of this book and the Book of Mormon, we announce the martyrdom of Joseph Smith the Prophet, and Hyrum Smith the Patriarch. They were shot in Carthage jail, on the 27th of June, 1844, about five o'clock p.m., by an armed mob—painted black—of from 150 to 200 persons. Hyrum was shot first and fell calmly, exclaiming: *I am a dead man!* Joseph leaped from the window, and was shot dead in the

attempt, exclaiming: *O Lord my God!* They were both shot after they were dead, in a brutal manner, and both received four balls.

2 John Taylor and Willard Richards, two of the Twelve, were the only persons in the room at the time; the former was wounded in a savage manner with four balls, but has since recovered; the latter, through the providence of God, escaped, without even a hole in his robe.

our stricken hearts still more terrible to bear. For the moment the sun of our life had set'" (Johnson and Reeder, *Witness of Women*, 199, 206). ●

Why was it important that both John Taylor and Willard Richards survive the Carthage Jail violence? (135:2) "In the providence of the Lord, as it was necessary for two men to seal their testimonies with their blood at Carthage, so it was necessary for two men to escape. Had Joseph and Hyrum been alone then, the only accounts that we would have of the events of that day would have been those written by men with the blood of the Lord's anointed on their hands. Had but one man survived, his testimony would have been refuted. So it was, in the wisdom of him who foreknows all things, that two men, whose reputation for truth was such that it could not be refuted, survived to tell the story" (McConkie and Ostler, *Revelations of the Restoration*, 1129).

A Timeline of the Martyrdom of Joseph and Hyrum Smith (Doctrine and Covenants 135:1)

"On Friday, June 7, 1844, dissenters from the Church published the one and only issue of an opposition newspaper they called the *Nauvoo Expositor*.... Using inflammatory language, they voiced their discontent with the practice of plural marriage, Joseph Smith's teachings on the nature of God ..., and his mixing of religious and civic authority in Nauvoo....

"With the sanction of the city council, Joseph Smith ordered a marshal, with the assistance of the Nauvoo Legion, to destroy the printing press. On Monday evening, June 10, the marshal and his posse of approximately 100 men removed the press, scattered the type, and burned the remaining copies of the newspaper....

"Trying to prevent a civil war, Illinois governor Thomas Ford reviewed the Nauvoo City Council's legal justifications for suppressing the newspaper and decided that Joseph Smith needed to stand trial in Carthage, the county seat, on the charge of 'riot' (Church History Topics, "Nauvoo Expositor").

"*Mon. 24.* [June 1844]—Joseph and Hyrum Smith, accompanied by seventeen friends, started for Carthage ... under pledge of protection from [Illinois governor Thomas] Ford....

"*Tue. 25.*—Joseph Smith and his brethren surrendered themselves to a constable at Carthage and submitted to a trial, after which they were, contrary to law, remanded to prison.

"*Wed. 26.*—Gov. Thos. Ford had a long interview with the prisoners in Carthage jail. He renewed his promises of protection and said, if he went to Nauvoo, he would take them with him.

"*Thur. 27.*—Gov. Thos. Ford went to Nauvoo, leaving the prisoners in jail to be guarded by their most bitter enemies, the 'Carthage Greys.' About 5:20 p. m. an armed mob with blackened faces surrounded and entered the jail, and murdered Joseph and Hyrum Smith in cold blood; Apostle John Taylor was severely wounded, while Apostle Willard Richards only received a slight wound on his ear.

"*Fri. 28.*—Apostle Willard Richards and Samuel H. Smith conveyed the bodies of the martyrs to Nauvoo, where they were met by the officers of the Nauvoo Legion and a very large number of Saints.

"*Sat. 29.*—About ten thousand persons visited and viewed the remains of the martyred Prophet and Patriarch at Nauvoo. The funeral took place in the evening" (Jenson, *Church Chronology*, 25–26).

Doctrine and Covenants 135:3. The Preeminent Position of the Prophet Is Acclaimed

What does it mean that Joseph Smith did more, "save Jesus only, for the salvation of man"? (135:3)
President Joseph F. Smith declared: "Where shall we go to find another man who has accomplished a one-thousandth part of the good that Joseph Smith accomplished? . . . No man in the nineteenth century, except Joseph Smith, has discovered to the world a ray of light upon the keys and power of the holy Priesthood, or the ordinances of the gospel, either for the living or the dead. Through Joseph Smith, God has revealed many things which were kept hidden from the foundation of the world in fulfilment of the prophets. . . . And this is strictly in keeping with the objects and character of this great latter-day work, destined to consummate the great purposes and designs of God concerning the dispensation of the fulness of times" (*Joseph F. Smith* [manual], 18). ●

What is a significant point about the deaths of Joseph and Hyrum Smith together? (135:3) "From the time of their deaths, Hyrum Smith has jointly held the keys of this dispensation with his brother Joseph. Not only was Hyrum the Patriarch of the Church, he was also a prophet, seer, and revelator. Hyrum Smith took the place of Oliver Cowdery as the second elder and second witness of the Restoration when Oliver apostatized. The sealing of testimonies with blood would not have been complete with the death of Joseph Smith alone" (Woodger, *Essential Doctrine and Covenants Companion*, 269).

3 Joseph Smith, the Prophet and Seer of the Lord, has done more, save Jesus only, for the salvation of men in this world, than any other man that ever lived in it. In the short space of twenty years, he has brought forth the Book of Mormon, which he translated by the gift and power of God, and has been the means of publishing it on two continents; has sent the fulness of the everlasting gospel, which it contained, to the four quarters of the earth; has brought forth the revelations and commandments which compose this book of Doctrine and Covenants, and many other wise documents and instructions for the benefit of the children of men; gathered many thousands of the Latter-day Saints, founded a great city, and left a fame and name that cannot be slain. He lived great, and he died great in the eyes of God and his people; and like most of the Lord's anointed in ancient times, has sealed his mission and his works with his own blood; and so has his brother Hyrum. In life they were not divided, and in death they were not separated!

Joseph and Hyrum Smith Were Faithful Witnesses before God (D&C 135:3)

President Jeffrey R. Holland reflected on the sacrifice of Joseph and Hyrum Smith: "In this their greatest—and last—hour of need, I ask you: would these men blaspheme before God by continuing to fix their lives, their honor, and their own search for eternal salvation on a book (and by implication a church and a ministry) they had fictitiously created out of whole cloth?

"Never mind that their wives are about to be widows and their children fatherless. Never mind that their little band of followers will yet be 'houseless, friendless and homeless' and that their children will leave footprints of blood across frozen rivers and an untamed prairie floor. Never mind that legions will die and other legions live declaring in the four quarters of this earth that they know the Book of Mormon and the Church which espouses it to be true. Disregard all of that, and tell me whether in this hour of death these two men would enter the presence of their Eternal Judge quoting from and finding solace in a book which, if *not* the very word of God, would brand them as imposters and charlatans until the end of time? *They would not do that!* They were willing to die rather than deny the divine origin and the eternal truthfulness of the Book of Mormon" ("Safety for the Soul," *Ensign*, Nov. 2009, 89).

Statue of Joseph and Hyrum Smith; Nauvoo, Illinois

4 When Joseph went to Carthage to deliver himself up to the pretended requirements of the law, two or three days previous to his assassination, he said: "I am going like a lamb to the slaughter; but I am calm as a summer's morning; I have a conscience void of offense towards God, and towards all men. I SHALL DIE INNOCENT, AND IT SHALL YET BE SAID OF ME—HE WAS MURDERED IN COLD BLOOD."—The same morning, after Hyrum had made ready to go—shall it be said to the slaughter? yes, for so it was—he read the following paragraph, near the close of the twelfth chapter of Ether, in the Book of Mormon, and turned down the leaf upon it:

5 *And it came to pass that I prayed unto the Lord that he would give unto the Gentiles grace, that they might have charity. And it came to pass that the Lord said unto me: If they have not charity it mattereth not unto thee, thou hast been faithful; wherefore thy garments shall be made clean. And because thou hast seen thy weakness, thou shalt be made strong, even unto the sitting down in the place which I have prepared in the mansions of my Father. And now I . . . bid farewell unto the Gentiles; yea, and also unto my brethren whom I love, until we shall meet before the judgment-seat of Christ, where all men shall know that my garments are not spotted with your blood.* The testators are now dead, and their testament is in force.

6 Hyrum Smith was forty-four years old in February, 1844, and Joseph Smith was thirty-eight in December, 1843; and henceforward

Doctrine and Covenants 135:4–7. Their Innocent Blood Testifies of the Truth and Divinity of the Work

What did Joseph Smith know about his impending death? (135:4) "[Joseph] told Stephen Markham that if [he] and Hyrum were ever taken again we should be massacred, or [he] was not a prophet of God" (Joseph Smith Papers, "History, 1838–1856, volume F-1," 147).

Joseph feared that his death would not appease his enemies. "It is thought by some that our enemies would be satisfied with my destruction; but I tell you that as soon as they have shed my blood they will thirst for the blood of every man in whose heart dwells a single spark of the spirit of the fullness of the Gospel. The opposition of these men is moved by the spirit of the adversary of all righteousness. It is not only to destroy me, but every man and woman who dares believe the doctrines that God hath inspired me to teach to this generation" (Joseph Smith Papers, "History, 1838–1856, volume F-1," 118). ☉

What is the significance of Hyrum reading from the end of the Book of Ether before leaving for Carthage? (135:4–5) "This quotation from the prophet Moroni [see Ether 12:37–38] deals with the rejection of the Book of Mormon by the Gentiles. It reminded Joseph and Hyrum, as it had Moroni, that they had done all they could, that the blood of the people was not upon them, the prophets, and that they would stand as judges of the people" (Robinson and Garrett, *Commentary on the Doctrine and Covenants*, 4:286).

What is a testator? (135:5) "A testator is one who leaves a will or testament. The will is valid only after the testator's death. While the testator lives, the will has no legal power. In the gospel context a testator is someone who provides to [humankind] a witness of God's covenants. The Prophet Joseph Smith's testament was that God had revealed through him the sealing power by which 'all covenants, contracts, bonds, obligations, oaths, vows, performances, connections, associations,' shall be in force and recognized as valid in the eternal worlds (D&C 132:7). The death of the testator places a seal of truth on the testament" (*Doctrine and Covenants Student Manual* [2001], 350).

In what way were Joseph and Hyrum Smith considered martyrs? (135:6) "Joseph and Hyrum Smith willingly gave their lives for the latter-day Kingdom of God. 'They lived for glory; they died for glory; and glory is their eternal reward. From age to age shall their names go down to posterity as gems for the sanctified' (D&C 135:6). They were guiltless of any crime, but they were persecuted and jailed by wicked men. Their innocent blood calls to the honest people among the nations as a beacon of righteousness (D&C 135:7). These two brothers, Prophet and Patriarch in the last and greatest gospel dispensation, united themselves in purpose and blood to usher in the return of the Lord Jesus Christ. Two greater brothers and martyrs never lived" (Millet and Newell, *Draw Near unto Me,* 388).

What does "escutcheon" mean? (135:7) "This is a reference to the state shield on which symbols or memorials are proudly displayed. [The] martyrs' blood is a stain upon the once-proud shield of Illinois. The blood of Joseph and Hyrum is further described . . . as 'a broad seal affixed to Mormonism,' meaning the blood of the martyrs is a conspicuous mark on the state shield" (Black, *400 Questions and Answers,* 226).

What is meant by this reference to the altar that John saw? (135:7) "[This reference] is to the vision seen by John the Revelator in the book of Revelation. He saw under the altar of the temple 'the souls of them that were slain for the word of God, and for the testimony which they held' [Revelation 6:9–11]. . . .

"John sees the blood of those who died for Christ as being—like the blood of the sacrificial lambs—Christ's blood, for these were his servants and acted in his name. As he was to be honored with crowns of glory, so will they be honored" (McConkie and Ostler, *Revelations of the Restoration,* 1130).

their names will be classed among the martyrs of religion; and the reader in every nation will be reminded that the Book of Mormon, and this book of Doctrine and Covenants of the church, cost the best blood of the nineteenth century to bring them forth for the salvation of a ruined world; and that if the fire can scathe a green tree for the glory of God, how easy it will burn up the dry trees to purify the vineyard of corruption. They lived for glory; they died for glory; and glory is their eternal reward. From age to age shall their names go down to posterity as gems for the sanctified.

7 They were innocent of any crime, as they had often been proved before, and were only confined in jail by the conspiracy of traitors and wicked men; and their *innocent blood* on the floor of Carthage jail is a broad seal affixed to "Mormonism" that cannot be rejected by any court on earth, and their *innocent blood* on the escutcheon of the State of Illinois, with the broken faith of the State as pledged by the governor, is a witness to the truth of the everlasting gospel that all the world cannot impeach; and their *innocent blood* on the banner of liberty, and on the *magna charta* of the United States, is an ambassador for the religion of Jesus Christ, that will touch the hearts of honest men among all nations; and their *innocent blood,* with the innocent blood of all the martyrs under the altar that John saw, will cry unto the Lord of Hosts till he avenges that blood on the earth. Amen.

"In February 1846, Brigham Young led a handpicked vanguard company of 300 men across the ice-filled Mississippi River. At the time, their plan was to reach a place of refuge in the Rocky Mountains that summer and plant crops to feed those who would follow that year. But the ensuing months did not go according to plan. Heavy rains caused streams and rivers to rise well above normal levels, turning Iowa's rolling plains into muddy quagmires. At the same time, over 1,000 Saints, many of them poorly prepared for the journey, insisted on joining the advance company, longing to be close to Church leaders in a time of uncertainty. . . .

"Besides this advance group of pioneers, thousands of other Latter-day Saints left Nauvoo, most according to a prearranged schedule. By the fall of 1846, more than 7,000 people were living at Winter Quarters in caves, wagons, makeshift hovels, and hastily built cabins. Another 3,000 wintered at various locations along the trail under similar conditions. Many were sick from malnutrition and exposure, and some were experiencing a crisis of faith. These trying circumstances made the winter of 1846–47 among the most difficult periods of Brigham Young's life" (Orton, "This Shall Be Our Covenant," 307–8).

"On 11 January 1847, [Brigham] Young told of [a] dream he had the night before of Joseph Smith and his mother, Lucy Mack Smith, and reported that he and Joseph 'conversed freely about the best manner of organizing companies for emigration.' Three days later, he presented his one and only canonized revelation to the church. Recorded today in the Doctrine and Covenants, and then received as 'the Word and Will of the Lord concerning the Camp of Israel in their journeyings to the West,' the document was a brilliant and well-timed statement not because of what it said regarding the organization of companies (since they had already had companies of hundreds, fifties, and tens all across Iowa) but for what it declared concerning the source of final authority. Above all, it was a lecture on apostolic supremacy.

"Given first to the Twelve on 14 January [1847], to the High Council two days later, to the general priesthood quorums on Sunday, 17 January, and finally to the general membership on 19 January, 'the Word and Will of the Lord' said many things, perhaps, but perhaps nothing more important than this—that their journey westward, its matter of organization, and its conduct all must be 'under the direction of the Twelve Apostles'" (Bennett, *Mormons at the Missouri*, 156–57).

SECTION 136

The word and will of the Lord, given through President Brigham Young at Winter Quarters, the camp of Israel, Omaha Nation, on the west bank of the Missouri River, near Council Bluffs, Iowa.

1 The Word and Will of the Lord concerning the Camp of Israel in their journeyings to the West:

Doctrine and Covenants 136:1–16. How the Camp of Israel Is to Be Organized for the Westward Journey Is Explained

What did this declaration of the will of the Lord mean to the Saints? (136:1) "For the first time since Joseph Smith, the faithful proclaimed, God had once again given direction, had not left his people alone in the wilderness, and had stated unequivocally who was in charge. Though it said nothing about their final destination or the feasibility of a way station, it did establish final authority. Not the Council of Fifty, not the High Council, nor any other group but the Twelve was in control. And those who participated in the meetings and procedures to ratify the revelation did not miss the issue" (Bennett, *Mormons at the Missouri*, 157). ◉

In what manner was the Camp of Israel to be organized? (136:2–4) "The key words in the early verses of section 136 are *organized* and *covenant*. The Saints were to be organized into companies 'under the direction of the Twelve Apostles' (v. 3). 'And this shall be our covenant—that we will walk in all the ordinances of the Lord' (v. 4). [Hundreds] of them had recently made sacred covenants as they received the ordinances of the temple in Nauvoo. They had covenanted to consecrate their lives to Zion. Section 136 tells them how to do so. It reiterates the principles of consecration that pervade so many of Joseph's revelations" (Harper, *Making Sense of the Doctrine & Covenants,* 500–501).

How did the Lord's organization help the Saints care for the poor and widowed? (136:8) "The pioneer legacy is a legacy of *inclusion*. When the

2 Let all the people of The Church of Jesus Christ of Latter-day Saints, and those who journey with them, be organized into companies, with a covenant and promise to keep all the commandments and statutes of the Lord our God.

3 Let the companies be organized with captains of hundreds, captains of fifties, and captains of tens, with a president and his two counselors at their head, under the direction of the Twelve Apostles.

4 And this shall be our covenant—that we will walk in all the ordinances of the Lord.

5 Let each company provide themselves with all the teams, wagons, provisions, clothing, and other necessaries for the journey, that they can.

6 When the companies are organized let them go to with their might, to prepare for those who are to tarry.

7 Let each company, with their captains and presidents, decide how many can go next spring; then choose out a sufficient number of able-bodied and expert men, to take teams, seeds, and farming utensils, to go as pioneers to prepare for putting in spring crops.

8 Let each company bear an equal proportion, according to the dividend of their property, in taking the poor, the widows,

The Lord's Promises to the Camp of Israel (Doctrine and Covenants 136:10–37)

"A covenant involves two parties. After describing His expectations of His people, the Lord declared His portion of the covenant in the form of certain promises that would be fulfilled in His own due time. Some of the promises the Lord made to the Camp of Israel were as follows:

"1. **Necessities of Life.** The saints were promised that obedience to the Lord's law would result in their having sufficient of the world's goods to provide for their needs. Wealth was not implied, but adequacy was assured. Food and clothing are essential to the well-being of a child of God (see D&C 136:10–11).

"2. **[Protection from] Enemies.** No mortal man can stop the work of the Lord. He told the saints there was no need to fear their enemies. The saints were promised that the work of the Lord will prevail (see D&C 136:17).

"3. **Redemption of Zion.** Since the beginning of the work of restoration in this dispensation, the Lord has spoken of the building and establishing of Zion. This revelation was directing the saints in a journey that would take them even further from the designated site of the city of Zion. Yet, the Lord reaffirmed His intention and promised the saints He would yet redeem Zion and fulfill His word pertaining to that anticipated work (see D&C 136:18).

the fatherless, and the families of those who have gone into the army, that the cries of the widow and the fatherless come not up into the ears of the Lord against this people.

Saints were driven out of Missouri, many were so poor that they lacked teams and wagons to move. Their Church leaders were adamant that none of the poor would be left behind. The response was the same in the exodus from Nauvoo. At a conference of the Church in October 1845, the membership entered into a covenant to take all the Saints with them. Thereafter, in the initial epic struggle across Iowa, the companies that arrived first at their stopping place on the Missouri River sent rescue wagons back toward Nauvoo to gather those who had been too poor to leave earlier. The revelation that guided their next exodus on the trip west directed each company to 'bear an equal proportion in taking . . . the poor, the widows, the fatherless, and the families of those who have gone into the army' (D&C 136:8). When the wagons and handcarts moved west, their movement was always one of inclusion, and no day's journey ended until every straggler was accounted for" (Oaks, "Following the Pioneers," *Ensign*, Nov. 1997, 73).

9 Let each company prepare houses, and fields for raising grain, for those who are to remain behind this season; and this is the will of the Lord concerning his people.

10 Let every man use all his influence and property to remove this people to the place where the Lord shall locate a stake of Zion.

11 And if ye do this with a pure heart, in all faithfulness, ye shall be blessed; you shall be blessed in your flocks, and in your herds, and in your fields, and in your houses, and in your families.

How did the pioneers prepare for those who would follow later? (136:9–10) "Not all members of the Church living in the Winter Quarters area traveled in the first company of Saints to the Great Salt Lake Valley. . . . An advance group of 148 members . . . would find and establish the place of settlement for the other Saints. In the meantime, the Saints still in the Midwest would build houses and plant crops so that others preparing for the trip to the Rocky Mountains would have places to stay and food to eat. . . . The Saints established settlements at Garden Grove and Mount Pisgah, Iowa, and at other locations between Nauvoo and Winter Quarters, where they built cabins and planted crops for the Saints to use as they made their way across Iowa" (Robinson and Garrett, *Commentary on the Doctrine and Covenants*, 4:289).

"4. *Glory of God.* People who keep their covenants with the Lord are pure in heart. Such people were promised that if they remained pure, they would yet behold the glory of God (see D&C 136:37).

"These promises were given when the saints were living in very trying circumstances. They were suffering from the lack of physical comforts in life. They had been driven from one place to another by their enemies. The establishment of Zion that had once appeared to be a glorious hope was deteriorating to the realm of a lost cause. There was reason why some may wonder if this suffering group of Latter-day Israelites would ever enjoy the blessed presence of the Lord in their midst.

"Under these very difficult conditions, the Lord delivered these specific promises to His covenant people while they wandered in the wilderness of discouragement and despair. Such promises loomed large as the basis for hope, both in their present trials, and in their anticipation of future fulfillment. The Lord has said that all of His promises will be fulfilled (see D&C 1:37)" (Otten and Caldwell, *Sacred Truths*, 2:386–87).

Where was this stake of Zion to be located?
(136:10) "Salt Lake City and its numerous satellite
communities—were observed as *stakes of Zion*. At
Winter Quarters, before the Saints pushed further
west, Brigham Young received and recorded a revelation. The Rocky Mountains were ahead of them.
The migrating Saints needed to establish a place
of gathering to the west of those mountains. It was
going to take everyone and their combined resources
to establish *a stake of Zion*. The revelation given to
President Young states: 'Let every man use all his
influence and property to remove this people to
the place *where the Lord shall locate a stake of Zion*'"
(Jenkins, *New Jerusalem*, 72). ✪

Doctrine and Covenants 136:17–27.
The Saints Are Commanded to Live by
Numerous Gospel Standards

**What did the Lord require of His people as they
prepared to journey west? (136:17–27)** To prepare
to build Zion, the Saints "were not to build themselves up (D&C 136:19), covet what was their brother's
(v. 20), or take the name of the Lord in vain (v. 21). . . .
They were not to contend, speak evil, but edify one
another in words. They were to cease drunkenness,
implying it was happening then (vv. 23–24). . . . They
were to not borrow without returning it, and help
search for what the neighbor had lost ([vv. 25–26]).
They were to be wise stewards, turn to the Lord in
praise and thanksgiving as well as in sorrow (D&C
136:27–29). Again He promises to take care of their
enemies (v. 30; see v. 17)" (Nyman, *Doctrine and Covenants Commentary*, 2:601).

**Why might the Lord invoke the memory of the
children of Israel leaving Egypt? (136:22)** "The title
for my message tonight is 'The Exodus Repeated.' I
have chosen this topic because of the many instructive parallels that exist between the exodus from
Egypt of the Israelites under Moses and the exodus
from the United States of the Latter-day Saint pioneers under Brigham Young. . . . [I] chose this topic
because we can learn much from these stalwarts of
ancient and modern Israel. . . .

"[The exodus from Egypt] was a type, and
shadow, for the exodus of the pioneers" (Nelson,
"Exodus Repeated").

12 Let my servants Ezra T. Benson and
Erastus Snow organize a company.

13 And let my servants Orson Pratt and
Wilford Woodruff organize a company.

14 Also, let my servants Amasa Lyman and
George A. Smith organize a company.

15 And appoint presidents, and captains of
hundreds, and of fifties, and of tens.

16 And let my servants that have been appointed go and teach this, my will, to the
saints, that they may be ready to go to a land
of peace.

17 Go thy way and do as I have told you,
and fear not thine enemies; for they shall not
have power to stop my work.

18 Zion shall be redeemed in mine own due
time.

19 And if any man shall seek to build up
himself, and seeketh not my counsel, he shall
have no power, and his folly shall be made
manifest.

20 Seek ye; and keep all your pledges one
with another; and covet not that which is thy
brother's.

21 Keep yourselves from evil to take the
name of the Lord in vain, for I am the Lord
your God, even the God of your fathers, the
God of Abraham and of Isaac and of Jacob.

22 I am he who led the children of Israel out
of the land of Egypt; and my arm is stretched
out in the last days, to save my people Israel.

23 Cease to contend one with another; cease
to speak evil one of another.

24 Cease drunkenness; and let your words
tend to edifying one another.

25 If thou borrowest of thy neighbor, thou
shalt restore that which thou hast borrowed;

and if thou canst not repay then go straightway and tell thy neighbor, lest he condemn thee.

26 If thou shalt find that which thy neighbor has lost, thou shalt make diligent search till thou shalt deliver it to him again.

27 Thou shalt be diligent in preserving what thou hast, that thou mayest be a wise steward; for it is the free gift of the Lord thy God, and thou art his steward.

28 If thou art merry, praise the Lord with singing, with music, with dancing, and with a prayer of praise and thanksgiving.

29 If thou art sorrowful, call on the Lord thy God with supplication, that your souls may be joyful.

30 Fear not thine enemies, for they are in mine hands and I will do my pleasure with them.

31 My people must be tried in all things, that they may be prepared to receive the glory that I have for them, even the glory of Zion; and he that will not bear chastisement is not worthy of my kingdom.

32 Let him that is ignorant learn wisdom by humbling himself and calling upon the Lord his God, that his eyes may be opened that he may see, and his ears opened that he may hear;

33 For my Spirit is sent forth into the world to enlighten the humble and contrite, and to the condemnation of the ungodly.

Doctrine and Covenants 136:28–33. The Saints Should Sing, Dance, Pray, and Learn Wisdom

What role did singing and music play as the Saints worshipped the Lord? (136:28) William Henry Jackson recorded a typical evening among the traveling Saints: "'From a little distance one of these encampments, at night, resembles an illuminated city in miniature, and as one approaches nearer there is usually the sound of revelry. In every Mormon train there are usually some musicians, for they seem to be very fond of song and dance, and as soon as the camp work is done the younger element gather in groups and "trip the light fantastic toe" with as much vim as if they had not had a twenty mile march that day' [*Diaries of William Henry Jackson: Frontier Photographer*, 64–65]" (Church History Topics, "Chimney Rock"). ◉

How could the Saints' trials prepare them for future glory? (136:31) While in Liberty Jail, Joseph Smith wrote to the Saints: "Inasmuch as God hath said that he would have a tried people, that he would purge them as gold, now we think that . . . if we get through with any degree of safety and shall have kept the faith that it will be a sign to this generation altogether sufficient to bear them without excuse, . . . it will be a trial of our faith equal to that of Abraham, and that the Ancients will not have, whereof, to boast over us in the day of Judgment, as being called to pass through heavier afflictions, that we may hold an even weight in the balances with them" (Joseph Smith Papers, "History, 1838–1856, volume C-1," 904[a]).

In what ways can humility enlighten us and help us gain the Lord's wisdom? (136:32–33) "In summary . . . how does one keep himself from falling, as some have, into teaching and living semi-truths? Is it not by maintaining his own spirituality? What is true spirituality? Is it knowledge, intellect, academic learning? Perhaps more than anything else it is an ongoing, purifying condition of the heart. It is an eye single to God. It is a broken heart and a contrite spirit" (Gene R. Cook, "Spiritual Guides," *Ensign*, May 1982, 27). ◉

Doctrine and Covenants 136:34–42. Prophets Are Slain So That They Might Be Honored and the Wicked Condemned

What causes the "day of their calamity"? (136:34–35) "In this last dispensation, a nation rejected the testimony of the Lord's servants, killed the Lord's prophets, and drove out the Lord's people. For these acts of wickedness, the Lord forewarned that calamity would befall that nation if they did not repent (see D&C 136:34–36). History provides the evidence of the fulfillment of the Lord's warning. The great civil war caused the death and misery of many thousands of citizens as a result of the rejection of the Lord's servants at that time" (Otten and Caldwell, *Sacred Truths*, 2:387).

Why should we not "marvel" at the death of the Prophet Joseph? (136:37) Joseph Smith testified: "My feelings at the present time are that, inasmuch as the Lord Almighty has preserved me until today, He will continue to preserve me, by the united faith and prayers of the Saints, until I have fully accomplished my mission in this life, and so firmly established the dispensation of the fulness of the priesthood in the last days, that all the powers of the earth and hell can never prevail against it" (*Joseph Smith* [manual], 531).

How did the Saints feel about the faithfulness and prophetic role of Joseph Smith? (136:38) Emmeline B. Wells described first meeting the Prophet: "[The Prophet Joseph Smith] came to me, and when he took my hand, I was simply electrified,—thrilled through and through to the tips of my fingers, and every part of my body. . . .

"The one thought that filled my soul was, I have seen the Prophet of God, he has taken me by the hand, and this testimony has never left me in all the 'perils by the way.' It is as vivid today as ever it was. For many years, I felt it too sacred an experience even to mention. . . .

"I heard him preach all his last sermons, and frequently met him and shook hands with him, and always felt in my inmost soul, he is indeed a man unlike all others" (in Johnson and Reeder, *Witness of Women*, 51–52). ◉

34 Thy brethren have rejected you and your testimony, even the nation that has driven you out;

35 And now cometh the day of their calamity, even the days of sorrow, like a woman that is taken in travail; and their sorrow shall be great unless they speedily repent, yea, very speedily.

36 For they killed the prophets, and them that were sent unto them; and they have shed innocent blood, which crieth from the ground against them.

37 Therefore, marvel not at these things, for ye are not yet pure; ye can not yet bear my glory; but ye shall behold it if ye are faithful in keeping all my words that I have given you, from the days of Adam to Abraham, from Abraham to Moses, from Moses to Jesus and his apostles, and from Jesus and his apostles to Joseph Smith, whom I did call upon by mine angels, my ministering servants, and by mine own voice out of the heavens, to bring forth my work;

38 Which foundation he did lay, and was faithful; and I took him to myself.

39 Many have marveled because of his death; but it was needful that he should seal his testimony with his blood, that he might be honored and the wicked might be condemned.

Why did the Lord say that He took Joseph to Himself? (136:38–39) Wilford Woodruff observed: "I used to have peculiar feelings about [Joseph Smith's] death and the way in which his life was taken. . . . But since then I have been fully reconciled to the fact that it was according to the programme, that it was required of him, as the head of this dispensation, that he should seal his testimony with his blood, and go hence to the spirit world, holding the keys of this dispensation, to open up the mission that is now being performed by way of preaching the Gospel to the 'spirits in prison' (1 Peter 3:19)" (quoted in *Joseph Smith* [manual], 537). ✪

40 Have I not delivered you from your enemies, only in that I have left a witness of my name?

In what way had the Lord delivered His people? (136:40) "From the Lord's vantage point, allowing Joseph to die as a testator left an enduring witness of His name even as it delivered the Saints, including Joseph, from their enemies (v. 40). . . . Section 136 would sustain the Saints who had covenanted to 'walk in all the ordinances of the Lord' up and over the Rocky Mountains as outcasts opposed by all kinds of influences. Joseph was gone, but the prophet Brigham Young would lead them onward according to the word and will of the Lord" (Harper, *Making Sense of the Doctrine & Covenants*, 502, 503).

41 Now, therefore, hearken, O ye people of my church; and ye elders listen together; you have received my kingdom.

42 Be diligent in keeping all my commandments, lest judgments come upon you, and your faith fail you, and your enemies triumph over you. So no more at present. Amen and Amen.

What might the Lord have meant by saying, "you have received my kingdom"? (136:41–42) "Knowing his mortal ministry would soon come to a close, the Prophet met frequently with members of the Quorum of the Twelve Apostles to instruct them and to give them the priesthood keys necessary to govern the Church. . . . In March 1844 . . . the Prophet charged the Twelve to govern the Church after his death, explaining that he had conferred upon them all the ordinances, authority, and keys necessary to do so. 'I roll the burden and responsibility of leading this church off from my shoulders on to yours,' he declared. 'Now, round up your shoulders and stand under it like men; for the Lord is going to let me rest awhile'" (*Joseph Smith* [manual], 529).

Introduction to Doctrine and Covenants 137

On January 21, 1836, the Prophet Joseph Smith "met on the top floor of the nearly finished house of the Lord [in Kirtland, Ohio,] with the other members of the First Presidency, his father, who was the patriarch to the church, Joseph's secretary, and the bishoprics from Missouri and Ohio. The brethren came to the meeting freshly bathed, symbolizing their efforts to repent and present themselves in the temple clean before the Lord. The First Presidency consecrated oil and then anointed and blessed Father Smith, who in turn anointed and blessed Joseph. Oliver Cowdery wrote that 'the glorious scene is too great to be described. . . . I only say, that the heavens were opened to many, and great and marvelous things were shown.' . . .

"Joseph was the only one present to describe in detail some of what he experienced. Doctrine and Covenants 137 is a passage from his journal entry for January 21, 1836" (Harper, *Making Sense of the Doctrine & Covenants*, 505).

"Though consisting of but ten verses this is one of the most significant revelations in the Doctrine and Covenants. It lays the doctrinal foundation upon which rests the whole concept of our labors in behalf of our kindred dead. It clearly separates this doctrine from any notion that the living can neglect their responsibilities in this life, believing that they can attend to them or have someone else attend to them when they have died" (McConkie and Ostler, *Revelations of the Restoration*, 1138).

"Though this vision was known and used by the Church, it was not canonized as a part of the standard works until April 3, 1976, when it was approved as an addition to the Pearl of Great Price. On June 22, 1979, this revelation was moved from the Pearl of Great Price to the Doctrine and Covenants and became section 137" (Woodger, *Essential Doctrine and Covenants Companion*, 272).

Doctrine and Covenants 137:1–6. The Prophet Sees His Brother Alvin in the Celestial Kingdom

Why might Joseph have said he was unsure about his physical state during this vision? (137:1) "When the Lord gives revelation to mortal men and women, He reveals truths by his Spirit to their spirits (see 1 Corinthians 2:9–14), and they become enveloped in the Spirit and filled with His glory to such an extent that they become oblivious to the things of the natural world" (*Doctrine and Covenants Student Manual* [2018], 846).

The Prophet Joseph later explained, "All things whatsoever God in his infinite wisdom has seen fit and proper to reveal to us, while we are dwelling in mortality, in regard to our mortal bodies, are revealed to us in the abstract, and independent of affinity of [or connection to] this mortal tabernacle, but are revealed to our spirits precisely as though we had no bodies at all" (*Joseph Smith* [manual], 475).

What could be meant by describing God and the celestial kingdom in terms of fire? (137:2–4) In the scriptures, fire is "a symbol for cleansing, purifying, or sanctifying. Fire can also serve as a symbol of God's presence" (Guide to the Scriptures, "Fire").

SECTION 137

A vision given to Joseph Smith the Prophet, in the temple at Kirtland, Ohio, January 21, 1836. The occasion was the administration of ordinances in preparation for the dedication of the temple.

1 The heavens were opened upon us, and I beheld the celestial kingdom of God, and the glory thereof, whether in the body or out I cannot tell.

2 I saw the transcendent beauty of the gate through which the heirs of that kingdom will enter, which was like unto circling flames of fire;

3 Also the blazing throne of God, whereon was seated the Father and the Son.

4 I saw the beautiful streets of that kingdom, which had the appearance of being paved with gold.

Joseph Fielding McConkie noted, "On the head of, or surrounding a person, fire represents divine power, glory, and holiness (Ezek. 8:2). . . . Fire is associated with spiritual power, illumination, inspiration, and enlightenment" (*Gospel Symbolism*, 259). See Isaiah 66:15–16; 1 Nephi 22:17; Doctrine and Covenants 133:41.

How often had Joseph Smith seen the Father and the Son in vision? (137:3) President Russell M. Nelson stated: "As we know, the Restoration began with the First Vision. In response to Joseph's prayer in 1820, Heavenly Father and His Son, Jesus Christ, appeared to the boy Joseph. They told him to join none of the current churches and '[promised] that the fulness of the gospel should at some future time be made known unto [him].'

"In addition to the First Vision, we know of at least *nine* other occasions when Joseph saw the Father *or* the Son. Four of these visions included both the Father *and* the Son, while the Savior appeared to the Prophet another five times by Himself.

"Two of these sublime manifestations of the Father and the Son are canonized in sections 76 and 137 of the Doctrine and Covenants. Four years later in the nearly completed Kirtland Temple, Joseph 'beheld the celestial kingdom of God' and the 'blazing throne of God, whereon was seated the Father and the Son.' The other appearances of the Father and the Son occurred at a conference in Kirtland in 1831 and at the School of the Prophets" (*Heart of the Matter*, 144–45).

5 I saw Father Adam and Abraham; and my father and my mother; my brother Alvin, that has long since slept;

6 And marveled how it was that he had obtained an inheritance in that kingdom, seeing that he had departed this life before the Lord had set his hand to gather Israel the second time, and had not been baptized for the remission of sins.

What is noteworthy about the individuals Joseph saw in the celestial kingdom? (137:5–6) "The Prophet names five people that he saw in the vision: Adam, Abraham, his own father and mother, and his brother Alvin who had passed away (D&C 137:5). It was appropriate for him to mention Adam since he was the father of 'the family of all the earth' (2 Nephi 2:20); and Abraham, since he was the father of the covenant people that Joseph was responsible for fulfilling the promises regarding his seed. The vision shown to Joseph was of the future since both his father and his mother were still alive. . . . Seeing [Alvin] in the celestial kingdom was amazing to Joseph since Alvin's death had occurred before he had heard the restored gospel and been baptized" (Nyman, *Doctrine and Covenants Commentary*, 2:611). ⊕

Doctrine and Covenants 137:7–9. The Doctrine of Salvation for the Dead Is Revealed

What does this glorious vision reveal about God's plan and His character? (137:7–9) "At the time Joseph Smith received revelations and organized the Church, the vast majority of churches taught that the Savior's Atonement would *not* bring about the salvation of most of mankind. The common precept was that a few would be saved and the overwhelming majority would be doomed to endless tortures of the most awful and unspeakable intensity. The marvelous doctrine revealed to the Prophet Joseph unveiled to us a plan of salvation that is applicable to all mankind, including those who do not hear of Christ in this life, children who die before the age of accountability, and those who have no understanding [see D&C 29:46–50; 137:7–10]" (Quentin L. Cook, "Our Father's Plan," *Ensign*, May 2009, 36–37). See also commentary in this volume on Doctrine and Covenants 76:62. ◉

How can those who die without receiving the gospel become heirs to the celestial kingdom? (137:7–8) "Those who do not have the opportunity

7 Thus came the voice of the Lord unto me, saying: All who have died without a knowledge of this gospel, who would have received it if they had been permitted to tarry, shall be heirs of the celestial kingdom of God;

8 Also all that shall die henceforth without a knowledge of it, who would have received it with all their hearts, shall be heirs of that kingdom;

9 For I, the Lord, will judge all men according to their works, according to the desire of their hearts.

Alvin Smith, Brother to the Prophet (Doctrine and Covenants 137:5–6)

"Alvin Smith was born on 11 February 1798 in Tunbridge, Vermont, the first-born of Joseph Sr. and Lucy Mack Smith. His was a pleasant and loving disposition, and he always sought out opportunities to aid the family in their continual financial struggles. Joseph Jr. later described his oldest brother as one in whom there was no guile. 'He was a very handsome man, surpassed by none but Adam and Seth' [Joseph Smith Papers, "History, 1838–1856, volume D-1," 1452].

"Lucy Mack writes that on the morning of 15 November in 1823, 'Alvin was taken very sick with the bilious colic' [*History of Joseph Smith*, 86–89]. One physician hurried to the Smith home and administered calomel to Alvin. The dose of calomel 'lodged in his stomach,' and on the third day of sickness, Alvin became aware of the fact that death was near" (Millet, "Salvation beyond the Grave," 551).

"Knowing he was dying, Alvin called his brothers and sisters to him and spoke to each of them. To Joseph, who was almost 18 years old and had not yet received the gold plates, Alvin said, 'I want you to be a good boy and do everything that lies in your power to obtain the records. Be faithful in receiving instruction and keeping every commandment that is given you. Your brother Alvin must now leave you, but remember the example which he has set for you, and set a good example for the children that are younger than you.'

"When Alvin died, the family asked a Presbyterian minister in Palmyra, New York, to officiate at his funeral. As Alvin had not been a member of the minister's congregation, the clergyman asserted in his sermon that Alvin could not be saved. William Smith, Joseph's younger brother, recalled: '[The minister, Reverend Benjamin Stockton,] . . . intimated very strongly that [Alvin] had gone to hell, for Alvin was not a church member, but he was a good boy and my father did not like it' (*Joseph Smith* [manual], 401, 403).

"Joseph later revealed the ordinance of baptism for the dead that enables all [people] to make and keep the gospel covenants. . . . In contrast to his reaction to Reverend Stockton's sermon, Father Smith 'was delighted to hear' the truth and asked Joseph to attend to the ordinance of baptism on Alvins' behalf. Joseph and Hyrum fulfilled their father's dying wish. 'I see Alvin,' Father Smith said just a few minutes before his own passing" (Harper, *Making Sense of the Doctrine & Covenants*, 506–7).

to embrace the gospel in this life will yet learn of its exalting power in the hereafter—and will be judged 'according to men in the flesh, but live according to God in the spirit' (1 Pet. 4:6). The Lord knows our hearts and dispositions. He will judge based on our character. All will have a chance to exercise their agency and come into the fold of Christ" (Pinegar and Allen, *Unlocking the Doctrine and Covenants*, 286).

While not specified in Doctrine and Covenants 137, later revelations received by the Prophet Joseph Smith clarified the need for the vicarious performance of essential saving ordinances for these individuals. See also commentary in this volume on Doctrine and Covenants 127, 128, and 138. ⊕

Why are both our works and the desires of our hearts the foundation for the Lord's judgment? (137:9) President Dallin H. Oaks observed: "Just as we will be accountable for our evil desires, we will also be rewarded for our righteous ones. Our Father in Heaven will receive a truly righteous desire as a substitute for actions that are genuinely impossible. . . .

"This principle means that when we have *done* all that we can, our *desires* will carry us the rest of the way. It also means that if our desires are right, we can be forgiven for the unintended errors or mistakes we will inevitably make as we try to carry those desires into effect. What a comfort for our feelings of inadequacy!" (*Pure in Heart*, 59). ⊕

"The Salvation of Little Children" (Doctrine and Covenants 137:10)

Elder Bruce R. McConkie proclaimed: "Among all the glorious gospel verities given of God to his people there is scarcely a doctrine so sweet, so soul satisfying, and so soul sanctifying, as the one which proclaims—*Little children shall be saved. They are alive in Christ and shall have eternal life. For them the family unit will continue, and the fulness of exaltation is theirs. No blessing shall be withheld. They shall rise in immortal glory, grow to full maturity, and live forever in the highest heaven of the celestial kingdom*—all through the merits and mercy and grace of the Holy Messiah, all because of the atoning sacrifice of Him who died that we might live. . . .

"There is no such thing as original sin as such is defined in the creeds of Christendom. Such a concept denies the efficacy of the atonement [of Jesus Christ]. Our revelation says: 'Every spirit of man was innocent in the beginning'—meaning that spirits started out in a state of purity and innocence in preexistence—'and God having redeemed man from the fall, men became again, in their infant state, innocent before God' (D&C 93:38)—meaning that all children start out their mortal probation in purity and innocence because of the atonement. . . .

"They are saved through the atonement [of Jesus Christ] and because they are free from sin. They come from God in purity; no sin or taint attaches to them in this life; and they return in purity to their Maker. Accountable persons must become pure through repentance and baptism and obedience. Those who are not accountable for sins never fall spiritually and need not be redeemed from a spiritual fall which they never experienced. Hence the expression that little children are alive in Christ" ("Salvation of Little Children," *Ensign*, Apr. 1977, 3, 4).

Doctrine and Covenants 137:10. All Children Are Saved in the Celestial Kingdom

How was this doctrine of the salvation of little children received in Joseph's day? (137:10) "The revelation ... no doubt brought comfort to many Church members, including Emma and Joseph Smith, who had lost infant children to death. By the time this revelation was received, Joseph and Emma Smith had already lost four of their first six children....

"At the time of this revelation, many churches taught that children who died before they were baptized were damned, meaning that they could not be saved by God. Several latter-day scriptures, including this revelation recorded in Doctrine and Covenants 137, reveal God's mercy to children who die before the age of accountability, which is eight years old (see Moroni 8:8–22; D&C 29:46–47; 68:25, 27)" (*Doctrine and Covenants Student Manual* [2018], 849). See also Mosiah 15:25. ⊕

10 And I also beheld that all children who die before they arrive at the years of accountability are saved in the celestial kingdom of heaven.

Introduction to Doctrine and Covenants 138

"The immediate context of Doctrine and Covenants 138 is given in the first eleven verses of the section by President Joseph F. Smith himself. President Smith received a vision on October 3, 1918, the day before general conference....

"A combination of declining health, worry over world events, and a series of personal tragedies combined to create one of the most difficult and trying times of President Smith's life. The revelation in Doctrine and Covenants 138 was received just thirty-eight days before the end of the most devastating war in history to that point.... But in the wake of the Great War, another threat was rising. The influenza epidemic of 1918 would eventually cause more than double the number of deaths as the war....

"In the midst of these worldwide challenges facing the Saints, President Smith suffered a heartbreaking series of personal tragedies in his own family. On January 23, 1918, President Smith's oldest son, Hyrum Mack, died of complications of a ruptured appendix.... Hyrum Mack's widow, Ida Bowman Smith, died of heart failure on September 24, just days after giving birth to a son, whom she named Hyrum after his departed father. Hyrum and Ida's passing left their five young children as orphans" (Griffiths, "Additional Context").

"These catastrophes formed a visible backdrop at the October [1918] general conference.... Mustering his failing strength, President Smith made a surprise appearance and presided at four sessions of the conference. 'I have been undergoing a siege of very serious illness for the last five months,' he said in his opening remarks. 'Although somewhat weakened in body,' he affirmed, 'my mind is clear with reference to my duty.' Then President Smith hinted at a message he was still struggling to find words to express. 'I will not, I dare not, attempt to enter upon many things that are resting upon my mind this morning,' he said, 'and I shall postpone until some future time, the Lord being willing, my attempt to tell you some of the things that are in my mind, and that dwell in my heart.' He continued: 'I have not lived alone these five months. I have dwelt in the spirit of prayer, of supplication, of faith and of determination; and I have had my communication with the Spirit of the Lord continuously' [Joseph F. Smith, in Conference Report, Oct. 1918, 2]....

"President Smith's desire to speak of these things to the Saints in person was not fulfilled. Ten days after general conference, he dictated the vision to his son Joseph Fielding Smith. Two weeks later, on October 31, Joseph Fielding Smith read the text to the First Presidency and Quorum of the Twelve Apostles at their regular council meeting in the temple" (Tait, "Susa Young Gates," 318, 319).

"At the April 1976 general conference, the vision was 'accepted as scripture and approved for publication in the Pearl of Great Price.' In June 1979 the First Presidency of the Church announced that the 'Vision of the Redemption of the Dead' would become section 138 of the Doctrine and Covenants" (Black, *400 Questions and Answers*, 229).

President Gordon B. Hinckley affirmed, "President Joseph F. Smith had an understanding of the eternal nature of man that few others have ever possessed. As a member of the Quorum of the Twelve, I participated in the [1979] motion to include in the Doctrine and Covenants section 138—the vision of President Smith in 1918. It is a document without parallel.... There is nothing quite like it in all of our sacred literature" ("Remarks at the Dedication of the Joseph F. Smith Building," 4).

SECTION 138

A vision given to President Joseph F. Smith in Salt Lake City, Utah, on October 3, 1918. In his opening address at the 89th Semiannual General Conference of the Church, on October 4, 1918, President Smith declared that he had received several divine communications during the previous months. One of these, concerning the Savior's visit to the spirits of the dead while

Doctrine and Covenants 138:1–10. President Joseph F. Smith Ponders upon the Writings of Peter and Our Lord's Visit to the Spirit World

How can President Smith's example lead us to better ponder and pray about the scriptures? (138:1–4) Elder D. Todd Christofferson observed, "You should care more about the amount of time you spend in the scriptures than about the amount you read in that time. I see you sometimes reading a few verses, stopping to ponder them, carefully reading the verses again, and as you think about what they mean, praying for understanding, asking questions in your mind, waiting for spiritual impressions, and writing down the impressions and insights that come so you can remember and learn more. Studying in this way, you may not read a lot of chapters or verses in a half hour, but you will be giving place in your heart for the word of God, and He will be speaking to you" ("When Thou Art Converted," *Ensign*, May 2004, 11). ●

In what way was the great and wonderful love of the Father and the Son to be illustrated in President Smith's vision? (138:2–4) "Jesus had not finished his work when his body was slain, neither did he finish it after his resurrection from the dead; although he had accomplished the purpose for which he then came to the earth, he had not fulfilled all his work. And when will he? Not until he has redeemed and saved every son and daughter of our father Adam that have been or ever will be born upon this earth to the end of time, except the sons of perdition. That is his mission" (*Joseph F. Smith* [manual], 410). See also commentary in this volume on Doctrine and Covenants 76:42.

How can this verse help us better understand the relationship between obedience and the Atonement of Jesus Christ? (138:4) "Some gifts coming from the Atonement [of Jesus Christ] are universal, infinite, and unconditional. These include His ransom for Adam's original transgression . . . [and] the Resurrection from the dead of every man, woman, and child who . . . will live on earth.

"Other aspects of Christ's atoning gift are conditional. They depend on one's diligence in keeping God's commandments. For example, while

His body was in the tomb, President Smith had received the previous day. It was written immediately following the close of the conference. On October 31, 1918, it was submitted to the counselors in the First Presidency, the Council of the Twelve, and the Patriarch, and it was unanimously accepted by them.

1 On the third of October, in the year nineteen hundred and eighteen, I sat in my room pondering over the scriptures;

2 And reflecting upon the great atoning sacrifice that was made by the Son of God, for the redemption of the world;

3 And the great and wonderful love made manifest by the Father and the Son in the coming of the Redeemer into the world;

4 That through his atonement, and by obedience to the principles of the gospel, mankind might be saved.

5 While I was thus engaged, my mind reverted to the writings of the apostle Peter, to the primitive saints scattered abroad throughout Pontus, Galatia, Cappadocia, and other parts of Asia, where the gospel had been preached after the crucifixion of the Lord.

all members of the human family are freely given a reprieve from Adam's sin through no effort of their own, they are not given a reprieve from their own sins unless they pledge faith in Christ, repent of those sins, are baptized in His name, receive the gift of the Holy Ghost and confirmation into Christ's Church, and press forward in faithful endurance the remainder of life's journey" (Holland, "Atonement of Jesus Christ," *Ensign*, Mar. 2008, 35). ⊙

6 I opened the Bible and read the third and fourth chapters of the first epistle of Peter, and as I read I was greatly impressed, more than I had ever been before, with the following passages:

How does Doctrine and Covenants 138 provide clarification for Peter's teachings on the redemption of the dead? (138:6–10) "Because of unrepented sins, [the wicked] are in what the Apostle Peter referred to as spirit 'prison' (1 Peter 3:19; see also Doctrine and Covenants 138:42). These spirits are described as 'bound' or as 'captives' (Doctrine and Covenants 138:31, 42) or as 'cast out into outer darkness' with 'weeping, and wailing, and gnashing of teeth' as they await resurrection and judgment (Alma 40:13–14). . . .

7 "For Christ also hath once suffered for sins, the just for the unjust, that he might bring us to God, being put to death in the flesh, but quickened by the Spirit:

"The gospel is preached [in spirit prison] to the ignorant, the unrepentant, and the rebellious so they can be freed from their bondage and go forward to the blessings a loving Heavenly Father has in store for them" (Oaks, "Trust in the Lord," *Ensign*, Nov. 2019, 27). ⊙

8 "By which also he went and preached unto the spirits in prison;

9 "Which sometime were disobedient, when once the longsuffering of God waited in the days of Noah, while the ark was a preparing, wherein few, that is, eight souls were saved by water." (1 Peter 3:18–20.)

10 "For for this cause was the gospel preached also to them that are dead, that they might be judged according to men in the flesh, but live according to God in the spirit." (1 Peter 4:6.)

How can the dead be judged "according to the flesh" if they have lived in the spirit world? (138:10) "There are those who suppose that death brings with it a restoration of pre-earth knowledge. The scriptures do not sustain such an idea. Were this the case, those in the spirit world who had not heard the gospel could hardly be judged according to men in the flesh, as revelation ancient and modern asserts (see 1 Pet. 4:6; D&C 138:10). Such faith would be supplanted by knowledge. Yet, without faith it is impossible to please God (see Heb. 11:6). The fruits of the tree of knowledge must be plucked individually; they do not just fall into our baskets" (Millet and McConkie, *Life Beyond*, 62).

Doctrine and Covenants 138:11–24. President Smith Sees the Righteous Dead Assembled in Paradise and Christ's Ministry among Them

Who were those included in this innumerable gathering? (138:11–12) "This vast multitude had died firm in their testimony of Jesus Christ and consequently were filled with joyful anticipation of the Savior's advent into the spirit world. They knew that His coming meant the end of the separation of their spirit from their body. They were to be resurrected in conjunction with the Savior's own resurrection never again to suffer death" (Otten and Caldwell, *Sacred Truths*, 2:395).

How are we blessed by suffering tribulation in the Savior's name? (138:13) "When we respond to our accusers as the Savior did, we not only become more Christlike, we invite others to feel His love and follow Him as well.

"To respond in a Christlike way cannot be scripted or based on a formula. The Savior responded differently in every situation. . . .

"As we respond to others, each circumstance will be different. Fortunately, the Lord knows the hearts of our accusers and how we can most effectively respond to them. *As true disciples seek guidance from the Spirit, they receive inspiration tailored to each encounter.* And in every encounter, *true disciples respond in ways that invite the Spirit of the Lord*" (Hales, "Christian Courage," *Ensign*, Nov. 2008, 72, 73).

In what sense were the righteous captive in the spirit world? (138:15–16, 18) "The work of salvation in the spirit world consists of freeing spirits from what the scriptures frequently describe as 'bondage.' All in the spirit world are under some form of bondage. . . .

"The spirit-world bondage that applies to righteous converted souls is their need to await—and perhaps even be allowed to prompt—the performance of their proxy ordinances on earth so they can be baptized and enjoy the blessings of the Holy Ghost (see Doctrine and Covenants 138:30–37, 57–58). These mortal proxy ordinances also empower them to go forward under priesthood authority to enlarge the hosts of the righteous who can preach the gospel to the spirits in prison" (Oaks, "Trust in the Lord," *Ensign*, Nov. 2019, 26, 27). See also commentary in this volume on Doctrine and Covenants 45:17. ◉

11 As I pondered over these things which are written, the eyes of my understanding were opened, and the Spirit of the Lord rested upon me, and I saw the hosts of the dead, both small and great.

12 And there were gathered together in one place an innumerable company of the spirits of the just, who had been faithful in the testimony of Jesus while they lived in mortality;

13 And who had offered sacrifice in the similitude of the great sacrifice of the Son of God, and had suffered tribulation in their Redeemer's name.

14 All these had departed the mortal life, firm in the hope of a glorious resurrection, through the grace of God the Father and his Only Begotten Son, Jesus Christ.

15 I beheld that they were filled with joy and gladness, and were rejoicing together because the day of their deliverance was at hand.

16 They were assembled awaiting the advent of the Son of God into the spirit world, to declare their redemption from the bands of death.

17 Their sleeping dust was to be restored unto its perfect frame, bone to his bone, and the sinews and the flesh upon them, the spirit and the body to be united never again to be divided, that they might receive a fulness of joy.

18 While this vast multitude waited and conversed, rejoicing in the hour of their deliverance from the chains of death, the Son of God appeared, declaring liberty to the captives who had been faithful;

19 And there he preached to them the everlasting gospel, the doctrine of the resurrection and the redemption of mankind from the fall, and from individual sins on conditions of repentance.

20 But unto the wicked he did not go, and among the ungodly and the unrepentant who had defiled themselves while in the flesh, his voice was not raised;

21 Neither did the rebellious who rejected the testimonies and the warnings of the ancient prophets behold his presence, nor look upon his face.

22 Where these were, darkness reigned, but among the righteous there was peace;

23 And the saints rejoiced in their redemption, and bowed the knee and acknowledged the Son of God as their Redeemer and Deliverer from death and the chains of hell.

24 Their countenances shone, and the radiance from the presence of the Lord rested upon them, and they sang praises unto his holy name.

Why will the Resurrection bring about a fulness of joy? (138:17) "After resurrection, the spirit will never again be separated from the body because the Savior's Resurrection brought total victory over death. In order to obtain our eternal destiny, we need to have this immortal soul—a spirit and body—united forever. With spirit and immortal body inseparably connected, we can 'receive a fulness of joy' [D&C 93:33; 138:17]. In fact, without the Resurrection we could never receive a fulness of joy but would be miserable forever [see 2 Nephi 9:8–9; D&C 93:34]. Even faithful, righteous people view the separation of their bodies from their spirits as captivity. We are released from this captivity through the Resurrection, which is redemption from the bands or chains of death. There is no salvation without both our spirit and our body" (Paul V. Johnson, "And There Shall Be No More Death," *Ensign*, May 2016, 122).

What was the response of faithful "captives" at the hour of their deliverance? (138:18–19, 23–24) "A multitude awaited the advent of the Son of God into the spirit world to declare their redemption from the bands of death. Their sleeping dust was to be restored unto its perfect frame. The spirit and the body were to be united, never again to be divided, that they might receive a fulness of joy. While the vast multitude waited and commenced rejoicing in the hour of their deliverance from the chains of death, the Son of God appeared. He preached to them the everlasting gospel, the doctrine of the resurrection and redemption of mankind from the Fall and from individual sins on conditions of repentance (see D&C 138:16–19)" (Hales, "Lessons from the Atonement," *Ensign*, Nov. 1985, 20).

Doctrine and Covenants 138:25–37. President Smith Sees How the Preaching of the Gospel Was Organized among the Spirits

What did the Savior accomplish during His brief ministry in the spirit world? (138:25–27) "It is while pondering the question of how the Savior could have taught the gospel to so many in the spirit world in so short a time (the time intervening between his death on Friday and his rise from the tomb on Sunday morning) that President Smith received what may well be the most significant doctrinal insight of the entire vision. The President came to understand 'that the Lord went not in person among the wicked and disobedient'—those in hell—but rather 'organized his forces and appointed messengers, clothed with power and authority,' that such representatives might carry the message of the gospel 'unto whom he [the Lord] could not go personally, because of their rebellion and transgression' (vv. 20–22, 25–30, 37)" (Millet, "Salvation beyond the Grave," 558–59). ☉

Why might there be an emphasis on preaching to those who lived in the days of Noah? (138:28, 32) "They had been guilty of gross offenses, and had wantonly rejected the teachings and admonitions of Noah, the earthly minister of Jehovah. For their flagrant sin they had been destroyed in the flesh, and their spirits had endured in a condition of imprisonment, without hope, from the time of their death to the advent of Christt. . . . We are not to assume from Peter's illustrative mention of the disobedient antediluvians that they alone were included in the blessed opportunities offered through Christ's ministry in the spirit realm; on the contrary, we conclude in reason and consistency that all whose wickedness in the flesh had brought their spirits into the prison house were sharers in the possibilities of expiation [payment of debt], repentance, and release" (Talmage, *Jesus the Christ*, 372–73).

Why did the Lord send messengers to preach to the spirits in darkness? (138:29–31) "All people—both living and dead—who desire entrance into Heavenly Father's kingdom must receive the principles and ordinances of the gospel. In our dispensation this was made possible for the dead beginning on August 15, 1840, when the Prophet Joseph Smith introduced the doctrine of vicarious baptism for the dead [see *Joseph Smith* [manual], 403].

25 I marveled, for I understood that the Savior spent about three years in his ministry among the Jews and those of the house of Israel, endeavoring to teach them the everlasting gospel and call them unto repentance;

26 And yet, notwithstanding his mighty works, and miracles, and proclamation of the truth, in great power and authority, there were but few who hearkened to his voice, and rejoiced in his presence, and received salvation at his hands.

27 But his ministry among those who were dead was limited to the brief time intervening between the crucifixion and his resurrection;

28 And I wondered at the words of Peter—wherein he said that the Son of God preached unto the spirits in prison, who sometime were disobedient, when once the long-suffering of God waited in the days of Noah—and how it was possible for him to preach to those spirits and perform the necessary labor among them in so short a time.

29 And as I wondered, my eyes were opened, and my understanding quickened, and I perceived that the Lord went not in person among the wicked and the disobedient who had rejected the truth, to teach them;

30 But behold, from among the righteous, he organized his forces and appointed messengers, clothed with power and authority, and

commissioned them to go forth and carry the light of the gospel to them that were in darkness, even to all the spirits of men; and thus was the gospel preached to the dead.

31 And the chosen messengers went forth to declare the acceptable day of the Lord and proclaim liberty to the captives who were bound, even unto all who would repent of their sins and receive the gospel.

32 Thus was the gospel preached to those who had died in their sins, without a knowledge of the truth, or in transgression, having rejected the prophets.

33 These were taught faith in God, repentance from sin, vicarious baptism for the remission of sins, the gift of the Holy Ghost by the laying on of hands,

34 And all other principles of the gospel that were necessary for them to know in order to qualify themselves that they might be judged according to men in the flesh, but live according to God in the spirit.

35 And so it was made known among the dead, both small and great, the unrighteous as well as the faithful, that redemption had been wrought through the sacrifice of the Son of God upon the cross.

36 Thus was it made known that our Redeemer spent his time during his sojourn in the world of spirits, instructing and preparing the faithful spirits of the prophets who had testified of him in the flesh;

37 That they might carry the message of redemption unto all the dead, unto whom he could not go personally, because of their rebellion and transgression, that they through the ministration of his servants might also hear his words.

Whether individuals hear the gospel in mortality or in the spirit world, Heavenly Father ensures that all will have the opportunity to accept or reject the gospel so that all of His children can be judged according to the same standard" (*Doctrine and Covenants Student Manual* [2018], 858).

When was vicarious baptism instituted among the children of men? (138:33–35) "Basic to all Christian understanding is the timeless statement made by Jesus: 'Except a man be born of water and of the Spirit, he cannot enter into the kingdom of God' [John 3:5].

"Following His crucifixion, Jesus ministered in the spirit world, setting in motion missionary work among those who had died without hearing the gospel [see 1 Pet. 4–6; D&C 138:10–37]. Baptism for these souls would logically be expected. . . .

"From the days of Adam to the meridian of time, temple ordinances were performed for the living only. Ordinances for the dead had to await the Atonement and postmortal ministry of the Savior" (Nelson, "Spirit of Elijah," *Ensign*, Nov. 1994, 84, 85).

The Prophet Joseph Smith introduced the doctrine of vicarious baptism for the dead in this dispensation on August 15, 1840 (see *Joseph Smith* [manual], 403). ⊕

Doctrine and Covenants 138:38–52. President Smith Sees Adam, Eve, and Many of the Holy Prophets in the Spirit World Who Considered Their Spirit State before Their Resurrection as a Bondage

Who are some of "the great and mighty ones" that President Smith saw in vision? (138:38–52) "By the power of the Holy Ghost President Smith perceived the identity of many of the noble and great from the beginning of time, including Adam, Seth, Noah, Abraham, Isaiah, the Nephite prophets before Christ, and many more. In addition, the President recognized Mother Eve and many of her faithful daughters" (Millet, "Salvation beyond the Grave," 559).

What can we learn from this vision about the role of righteous women in the spirit world? (138:39) President Joseph F. Smith taught: "Who is going to preach the gospel to the women? Who is going to carry the testimony of Jesus Christ to the hearts of the women who have passed away without a knowledge of the gospel? Well, to my mind, it is a simple thing. These good sisters who have been set apart, ordained to the work, called to it, authorized by the authority of the holy Priesthood to minister for their sex, in the House of God for the living and for the dead, will be fully authorized and empowered to preach the gospel and minister to the women" (*Gospel Doctrine*, 461). ⊕

38 Among the great and mighty ones who were assembled in this vast congregation of the righteous were Father Adam, the Ancient of Days and father of all,

39 And our glorious Mother Eve, with many of her faithful daughters who had lived through the ages and worshiped the true and living God.

40 Abel, the first martyr, was there, and his brother Seth, one of the mighty ones, who was in the express image of his father, Adam.

41 Noah, who gave warning of the flood; Shem, the great high priest; Abraham, the father of the faithful; Isaac, Jacob, and Moses, the great law-giver of Israel;

42 And Isaiah, who declared by prophecy that the Redeemer was anointed to bind up the broken-hearted, to proclaim liberty to the captives, and the opening of the prison to them that were bound, were also there.

43 Moreover, Ezekiel, who was shown in vision the great valley of dry bones, which were to be clothed upon with flesh, to come forth again in the resurrection of the dead, living souls;

44 Daniel, who foresaw and foretold the establishment of the kingdom of God in the latter days, never again to be destroyed nor given to other people;

45 Elias, who was with Moses on the Mount of Transfiguration;

46 And Malachi, the prophet who testified of the coming of Elijah—of whom also Moroni spake to the Prophet Joseph Smith, declaring that he should come before the ushering in of the great and dreadful day of the Lord—were also there.

47 The Prophet Elijah was to plant in the hearts of the children the promises made to their fathers,

48 Foreshadowing the great work to be done in the temples of the Lord in the dispensation of the fulness of times, for the redemption of the dead, and the sealing of the children to their parents, lest the whole earth be smitten with a curse and utterly wasted at his coming.

49 All these and many more, even the prophets who dwelt among the Nephites and testified of the coming of the Son of God, mingled in the vast assembly and waited for their deliverance,

50 For the dead had looked upon the long absence of their spirits from their bodies as a bondage.

51 These the Lord taught, and gave them power to come forth, after his resurrection from the dead, to enter into his Father's kingdom, there to be crowned with immortality and eternal life,

52 And continue thenceforth their labor as had been promised by the Lord, and be partakers of all blessings which were held in reserve for them that love him.

How are our efforts critical in helping to accomplish the Lord's glorious work of redemption? (138:48, 51–52) "Some of us have had occasion to wait for someone or something for a minute, an hour, a day, a week, or even a year. Can you imagine how our progenitors must feel, some of whom have perhaps been waiting for decades and even centuries for the temple work to be done for them? I have tried, in my mind's eye, to envision our progenitors who are anxiously waiting for those of us who are their descendants and are members of the Church on the earth to do our duty toward them. I have also thought what a dreadful feeling it would be for us to see them in the hereafter and have to acknowledge that we had not been as faithful as we should have been here on earth in performing these ordinances in their behalf" (Kimball, *Teachings*, 541). ☉

Doctrine and Covenants 138:53–60. The Righteous Dead of This Day Continue Their Labors in the World of Spirits

How have temple work and the gathering of Israel been affected by the restoration of these eternal truths about God's plan? (138:53–54) President Russell M. Nelson noted, "[The Lord] is making His temples more accessible. He is accelerating the pace at which we are building temples. He is increasing our ability to help gather Israel" ("Focus on the Temple," *Liahona*, Nov. 2022, 121).

Elder Quentin L. Cook observed, "What a great time to be alive. This is the last dispensation, and we can feel the hastening of the work of salvation in every area where a saving ordinance is involved. We now have temples across much of the world to provide these saving ordinances. . . .

"It is nothing short of miraculous to see the hastening of the work of salvation in our day" ("Roots and Branches," *Ensign*, May 2014, 46).

How were the "noble and great ones," including faithful Saints of our generation, prepared to assist in the work of salvation? (138:55–56) Speaking to young adults of the Church, President Russell M. Nelson taught: "A true millennial is one who taught and who was taught the gospel of Jesus Christ premortally and who made covenants there with our Heavenly Father about courageous things—even *morally* courageous things—that he or she would do while here on earth. . . .

"You were taught in the spirit world to prepare you for anything and everything you would encounter during this latter part of these latter days (see D&C 138:56). That teaching endures within you!

"You are living in the 'eleventh hour.' The Lord has declared that this is the last time He will call laborers into His vineyard to gather the elect from the four quarters of the earth. . . . This is part of your identity and your purpose as the seed of Abraham (see Galatians 3:26–29)!" ("Stand as True Millennials," *Ensign*, Oct. 2016, 24, 26; paragraphing altered). ◉

What is the continuing role of the righteous after death? (138:57) The Prophet Joseph Smith taught: "All those who die in the faith go to the prison of spirits to preach to the dead in body, but they are alive in the spirit; and those spirits preach to the spirits [who are in prison] that they may live according to God in the spirit, and men do minister for them in the flesh" (*Joseph Smith* [manual], 474). ◉

53 The Prophet Joseph Smith, and my father, Hyrum Smith, Brigham Young, John Taylor, Wilford Woodruff, and other choice spirits who were reserved to come forth in the fulness of times to take part in laying the foundations of the great latter-day work,

54 Including the building of the temples and the performance of ordinances therein for the redemption of the dead, were also in the spirit world.

55 I observed that they were also among the noble and great ones who were chosen in the beginning to be rulers in the Church of God.

56 Even before they were born, they, with many others, received their first lessons in the world of spirits and were prepared to come forth in the due time of the Lord to labor in his vineyard for the salvation of the souls of men.

57 I beheld that the faithful elders of this dispensation, when they depart from mortal life, continue their labors in the preaching of the gospel of repentance and redemption, through the sacrifice of the Only Begotten Son of God, among those who are in darkness and under the bondage of sin in the great world of the spirits of the dead.

58 The dead who repent will be redeemed, through obedience to the ordinances of the house of God,

59 And after they have paid the penalty of their transgressions, and are washed clean, shall receive a reward according to their works, for they are heirs of salvation.

60 Thus was the vision of the redemption of the dead revealed to me, and I bear record, and I know that this record is true, through the blessing of our Lord and Savior, Jesus Christ, even so. Amen.

When will repentant spirits receive the glory for which they qualify? (138:58–59) "Modern revelation reveals that the work of salvation goes forward in the spirit world (see D&C 138:30–34, 58), and . . . we are taught that some repentance is possible there (see D&C 138:58). . . .

"Our Savior initiated the work of declaring liberty to the captives . . . , and that work continues as worthy and qualified messengers continue to preach the gospel, including repentance, to those who still need its cleansing effect (see D&C 138:57)" (Oaks, "Trust in the Lord," *Ensign*, Nov. 2019, 26, 29).

President Harold B. Lee taught: "When they shall have . . . satisfied justice, then they shall be brought forth out of the grasp of Satan and shall be assigned to that place in our Father's celestial, terrestrial, or telestial world merited by their life here upon this earth" (*Teachings*, 59).

How can the truthfulness of this vision influence our testimonies of Heavenly Father's plan? (138:60) President M. Russell Ballard affirmed: "I testify that the vision President Joseph F. Smith received is true. I bear witness that every person can read it and come to know it is true. Those who do not receive this knowledge in this life will surely come to know its truthfulness when everyone will arrive in the spirit world. There, all will love and praise God and the Lord Jesus Christ for the great plan of salvation and the blessing of the promised Resurrection when body and spirit will once again be reunited, never to be separated again (see D&C 88:32–35)" ("Vision of the Redemption of the Dead," *Ensign*, Nov. 2018, 73). ●

OFFICIAL DECLARATIONS

"On September 25, 1890, President Woodruff wrote in his journal that he was 'under the necessity of acting for the Temporal Salvation of the Church.' He stated, 'After Praying to the Lord & feeling inspired by his spirit I have issued . . . [a] Proclamation.' This proclamation, now published in the Doctrine and Covenants as Official Declaration 1, was released to the public on September 25 and became known as the Manifesto" (Gospel Topics Essays, "Manifesto and the End of Plural Marriage").

"For much of the 19th century, a significant number of members of The Church of Jesus Christ of Latter-day Saints practiced plural marriage—the marriage of one man to more than one woman. The beginning and end of the practice were directed by revelation through God's prophets. The initial command to practice plural marriage came through Joseph Smith, the founding Prophet and President of the Church. In 1890 President Wilford Woodruff issued the Manifesto, which led to the end of plural marriage in the Church.

"The end of plural marriage required great faith and sometimes complicated, painful—and intensely personal—decisions on the part of individual members and leaders of the Church. Like the beginning of plural marriage in the Church, the end of the practice was a process rather than a single event" (Church History Topics, "Manifesto").

"Beginning in 1862, the U.S. government passed laws against the practice of plural marriage. Outside opponents mounted a campaign against the practice, stating that they hoped to protect Mormon women and American civilization. For their part, many Latter-day Saint women publicly defended the practice of plural marriage, arguing in statements that they were willing participants.

"After the U.S. Supreme Court found the anti-polygamy laws to be constitutional in 1879, federal officials began prosecuting polygamous husbands and wives during the 1880s. Believing these laws to be unjust, Latter-day Saints engaged in civil disobedience by continuing to practice plural marriage and by attempting to avoid arrest. When convicted, they paid fines and submitted to jail time. To help their husbands avoid prosecution, plural wives often separated into different households or went into hiding under assumed names, particularly when pregnant or after giving birth" (Gospel Topics Essays, "Plural Marriage and Families in Early Utah").

"Between 1885 and 1889, most Apostles, stake presidents, and other Church leaders were in hiding or in prison, and many aspects of Church government were severely curtailed. The Manifesto issued by Wilford Woodruff in 1890 effectively ended these challenges and eventually led to the end of plural marriage" (Church History Topics, "Antipolygamy Legislation").

"Wilford Woodruff's 1890 Manifesto regarding plural marriage . . . had been appended to Latter-day Saint editions of the Doctrine and Covenants since 1908, [and] was also included in the 1921 edition under the heading 'Official Declaration'" (Turley and Slaughter, *How We Got the Doctrine and Covenants*, 105, 140n10).

OFFICIAL DECLARATION 1

The Bible and the Book of Mormon teach that monogamy is God's standard for marriage unless He declares otherwise (see 2 Samuel 12:7–8 and Jacob 2:27, 30). Following a revelation to Joseph Smith, the practice of plural marriage was instituted among Church members in the early 1840s (see section 132). From the 1860s to the 1880s, the United States government passed laws to make this religious practice illegal. These laws were eventually upheld by the U.S. Supreme Court. After receiving revelation, President Wilford Woodruff issued the following Manifesto, which was accepted by the Church as authoritative and binding on October 6, 1890. This led to the end of the practice of plural marriage in the Church.

To Whom It May Concern:

Press dispatches having been sent for political purposes, from Salt Lake City, which have been widely published, to the effect that the Utah Commission, in their recent report to the Secretary of the Interior, allege that plural marriages are still being solemnized and that forty or more such marriages have been contracted in Utah since last June or during the past year, also that in public discourses the leaders of the Church have taught, encouraged and urged the continuance of the practice of polygamy—

I, therefore, as President of The Church of Jesus Christ of Latter-day Saints, do hereby, in the most solemn manner, declare that these charges are false. We are not teaching polygamy or plural marriage, nor permitting any person to enter into its practice, and I deny that either forty or any other number of plural marriages have during that period been solemnized in our Temples or in any other place in the Territory.

Official Declaration 1. "To Whom It May Concern"

What led President Woodruff to issue the Manifesto? (OD1, "To Whom," paragraphs 1–2) "In August 1890, Church leaders learned that the United States government intended to seize the Logan, Manti, and St. George Temples. . . . This led President Wilford Woodruff to counsel with other Church leaders and earnestly seek the Lord's will regarding the practice of plural marriage. On September 25, 1890, he recorded the following in his journal: ' . . . I am under the necessity of acting for the temporal salvation of the church. The United States government has taken a stand and passed laws to destroy the Latter-day Saints on the subject of polygamy . . . and after praying to the Lord and feeling inspired, I have issued the following proclamation which is sustained by my counselors and the twelve apostles'" (*Doctrine and Covenants Student Manual* [2018], 797).

What was the Utah commission? (OD1, "To Whom," paragraphs 1–2) "Wilford [Woodruff] and his counselors . . . [learned] that the Utah Commission, a group of federal officials who managed Utah's elections and monitored the Saints' compliance with antipolygamy laws, had just sent its annual report to the federal government. This year [1890], the report falsely claimed that Church leaders were still publicly encouraging and sanctioning plural marriage. . . .

"Although [President Woodruff] had issued no public statement about the status of plural marriage in the Church, he had already determined that no plural marriages should be performed in Utah or anywhere else in the United States. Furthermore, he had done much over the past year to discourage new plural marriages, despite the report's claim to the opposite" (*Saints*, 2:597–98).

What was the Endowment House? (OD1, "To Whom," paragraph 3) "The Endowment House, formerly located in the northwest corner of the Temple Block (known today as Temple Square) in Salt Lake City, served as a 'temporary temple' from 1855 until 1889. Designed by Truman O. Angell, it was dedicated on 5 May 1855 by Heber C. Kimball. The building was a two-story structure.... An addition was erected later to accommodate baptisms for the dead.... By 1889, temples at St. George, Logan, and Manti were in full operation, and construction of the Salt Lake Temple was moving forward. In a symbolic effort to eliminate non-Mormon opposition to plural marriage and statehood, Church leaders razed the Endowment House, where many plural marriages had been performed previously" (Holzapfel, "Endowment House," 336–37).

Official Declaration 1. "President Lorenzo Snow Offered the Following [Statement]"

How was the Manifesto presented to the Church? (OD1, "President Lorenzo Snow statement") Published in the Deseret News two weeks earlier, "the Manifesto was formally presented to the Church at the semiannual general conference held in the Salt Lake Tabernacle in October 1890. On Monday, October 6, Orson F. Whitney, a Salt Lake City bishop, stood at the pulpit and read the Articles of Faith, which included the line that Latter-day Saints believe in 'obeying, honoring, and sustaining the law.' These articles were sustained by uplifted hand. Whitney then read the Manifesto, and Lorenzo Snow, President

One case has been reported, in which the parties allege that the marriage was performed in the Endowment House, in Salt Lake City, in the Spring of 1889, but I have not been able to learn who performed the ceremony; whatever was done in this matter was without my knowledge. In consequence of this alleged occurrence the Endowment House was, by my instructions, taken down without delay.

Inasmuch as laws have been enacted by Congress forbidding plural marriages, which laws have been pronounced constitutional by the court of last resort, I hereby declare my intention to submit to those laws, and to use my influence with the members of the Church over which I preside to have them do likewise.

There is nothing in my teachings to the Church or in those of my associates, during the time specified, which can be reasonably construed to inculcate or encourage polygamy; and when any Elder of the Church has used language which appeared to convey any such teaching, he has been promptly reproved. And I now publicly declare that my advice to the Latter-day Saints is to refrain from contracting any marriage forbidden by the law of the land.

WILFORD WOODRUFF
President of The Church of Jesus Christ
of Latter-day Saints.

President Lorenzo Snow offered the following:

"I move that, recognizing Wilford Woodruff as the President of The Church of Jesus Christ of Latter-day Saints, and the only man on the earth at the present time who holds the keys of the sealing ordinances, we consider him fully authorized by virtue of his position to issue the Manifesto which has been read in our hearing, and which is dated

September 24th, 1890, and that as a Church in General Conference assembled, we accept his declaration concerning plural marriages as authoritative and binding."

Salt Lake City, Utah, October 6, 1890.

EXCERPTS FROM THREE ADDRESSES BY PRESIDENT WILFORD WOODRUFF REGARDING THE MANIFESTO

The Lord will never permit me or any other man who stands as President of this Church to lead you astray. It is not in the programme. It is not in the mind of God. If I were to attempt that, the Lord would remove me out of my place, and so He will any other man who attempts to lead the children of men astray from the oracles of God and from their duty. (Sixty-first Semiannual General Conference of the Church, Monday, October 6, 1890, Salt Lake City, Utah. Reported in *Deseret Evening News,* October 11, 1890, p. 2.)

It matters not who lives or who dies, or who is called to lead this Church, they have got to lead it by the inspiration of Almighty God. If they do not do it that way, they cannot do it at all. . . .

of the Quorum of the Twelve, moved that the document be accepted as 'authoritative and binding.' The assembly was then asked to vote on this motion. The *Deseret News* reported that the vote was 'unanimous'; most voted in favor, though some abstained from voting" (Gospel Topics Essays, "Manifesto and the End of Plural Marriage").

Why was a sustaining vote taken at general conference to approve the Manifesto? (OD1, "President Lorenzo Snow statement") "When we sustain prophets and other leaders, we invoke the law of common consent. . . .

"This gives us, as members of the Lord's Church, confidence and faith as we strive to keep the scriptural injunction to heed the Lord's voice as it comes through the voice of His servants the prophets. All leaders in the Lord's Church are called by proper authority. No prophet or any other leader in this Church, for that matter, has ever called himself or herself. . . .

"Our sustaining of prophets is a personal commitment that we will do our utmost to uphold their prophetic priorities. Our sustaining is an oath-like indication that we recognize their calling as a prophet to be legitimate and binding upon us" (Nelson, "Sustaining the Prophets," *Ensign,* Nov. 2014, 74–75).

Official Declaration—1. "Excerpts from Three Addresses by President Wilford Woodruff Regarding the Manifesto"

Why can we trust that the President of the Church is being led by God? (OD1, "Excerpts," paragraphs 1–2) "The Lord would permit no man to stand at the head of this Church unless he was governed and controlled by revelation. . . .

"The Lord will lead [the President of the Church] where [He] wants him to go. We know God is with him, and has led him all the time. . . . It requires [the prophet] to tell us what is right and what is wrong in many things, because that is his place and calling. . . . A perfect channel exists between the Lord and him, through which he obtains wisdom, which is diffused through other channels to the people. That we know. We have got to learn to bring this knowledge into practice" (*Wilford Woodruff* [manual], 198, 199). ☉

I have had some revelations of late, and very important ones to me, and I will tell you what the Lord has said to me. Let me bring your minds to what is termed the manifesto. . . .

The Lord has told me to ask the Latter-day Saints a question, and He also told me that if they would listen to what I said to them and answer the question put to them, by the Spirit and power of God, they would all answer alike, and they would all believe alike with regard to this matter.

The question is this: Which is the wisest course for the Latter-day Saints to pursue—to continue to attempt to practice plural marriage, with the laws of the nation against it and the opposition of sixty millions of people, and at the cost of the confiscation and loss of all the Temples, and the stopping of all the ordinances therein, both for the living and the dead, and the imprisonment of the First Presidency and Twelve and the heads of families in the Church, and the confiscation of personal property of the people (all of which of themselves would stop the practice); or, after doing and suffering what we have through our adherence to this principle to cease the practice and submit to the law, and through doing so leave the Prophets, Apostles and fathers at home, so that they can instruct the people and attend to the duties of the Church, and also leave the Temples in the hands of the Saints, so that they can attend to the ordinances of the Gospel, both for the living and the dead?

In what ways was the Church being affected by the antipolygamy laws? (OD1, "Excerpts," paragraphs 4–8) "The laws that were created to deter plural marriage denied men who practiced plural marriage the right to vote and hold political office; repealed, or canceled, the right of women to vote in the Utah Territory; dissolved the Church as a legal institution; and authorized the government to seize all Church properties valued at $50,000 or more. . . . The Church challenged this law as being unconstitutional, but it was eventually upheld by the United States Supreme Court (see *Encyclopedia of Mormonism*, "History of the Church: c. 1878–1898," 2:625–27).

"In August 1890, Church leaders learned that the United States government intended to seize the Logan, Manti, and St. George Temples" (*Doctrine and Covenants Student Manual* [2018], 796–97).

How Were Families Affected by the Antipolygamy Measures? (Official Declaration 1)

"This antipolygamy campaign created great disruption in Mormon communities. The departure of husbands left wives and children to tend farms and businesses, causing incomes to drop and economic recession to set in. The campaign also strained families. New plural wives had to live apart from their husbands, their confidential marriages known only to a few. Pregnant women often chose to go into hiding, at times in remote locales, rather than risk being subpoenaed to testify in court against their husbands. Children lived in fear that their families would be broken up or that they would be forced to testify against their parents. Some children went into hiding and lived under assumed names" (Gospel Topics Essays, "Manifesto and the End of Plural Marriage").

The Lord showed me by vision and revelation exactly what would take place if we did not stop this practice. If we had not stopped it, you would have had no use for . . . any of the men in this temple at Logan; for all ordinances would be stopped throughout the land of Zion. Confusion would reign throughout Israel, and many men would be made prisoners. This trouble would have come upon the whole Church, and we should have been compelled to stop the practice. Now, the question is, whether it should be stopped in this manner, or in the way the Lord has manifested to us, and leave our Prophets and Apostles and fathers free men, and the temples in the hands of the people, so that the dead may be redeemed. A large number has already been delivered from the prison house in the spirit world by this people, and shall the work go on or stop? This is the question I lay before the Latter-day Saints. You have to judge for yourselves. I want you to answer it for yourselves. I shall not answer it; but I say to you that that is exactly the condition we as a people would have been in had we not taken the course we have.

. . . I saw exactly what would come to pass if there was not something done. I have had this spirit upon me for a long time. But I want to say this: I should have let all the temples go out of our hands; I should have gone to prison myself, and let every other man go there, had not the God of heaven commanded me to do what I did do; and when the hour came that I was commanded to do that, it was all clear to me. I went before the Lord, and I wrote what the Lord told me to write. . . .

I leave this with you, for you to contemplate and consider. The Lord is at work with us. (Cache Stake Conference, Logan, Utah, Sunday, November 1, 1891. Reported in *Deseret Weekly,* November 14, 1891.)

"The Manifesto was not simply a political document. It represented many deep-rooted religious principles, some of which were more important to the Latter-day Saints even than the principle of plural marriage. One of these was their firm belief that through Joseph Smith the kingdom of God had been established in preparation for the second coming of Christ and the establishment of the Millennium. . . . To allow the spiritual kingdom, the Church, to be destroyed would be, in President Woodruff's opinion, the greatest failure possible. Above all else, even if it meant withdrawing approval for new plural marriages, the Church must be preserved to meet the Savior when he came" (Allen and Leonard, *Story of the Latter-day Saints*, 419).

Now I will tell you what was manifested to me and what the Son of God performed in this thing. . . . All these things would have come to pass, as God Almighty lives, had not that Manifesto been given. Therefore, the Son of God felt disposed to have that thing presented to the Church and to the world for purposes in his own mind. The Lord had decreed the establishment of Zion. He had decreed the finishing of this temple. He had decreed that the salvation of the living and the dead should be given in these valleys of the mountains. And Almighty God decreed that the Devil should not thwart it. If you can understand that, that is a key to it. (From a discourse at the sixth session of the dedication of the Salt Lake Temple, April 1893. Typescript of Dedicatory Services, Archives, Church Historical Department, Salt Lake City, Utah.)

What Was the Response to the Manifesto? (Official Declaration 1)

"During this transitional period [following the Manifesto], a small number of plural marriages continued to occur with special permission from specific Church authorities. The majority of these post-Manifesto marriage ceremonies took place in Canada and Mexico, although some were performed in the United States and even at sea. Most Latter-day Saints, however, accepted the Manifesto at face value and began assimilating into monogamous marriage culture. . . .

"With the law prohibiting plural marriages and Church leaders discouraging them, it was up to individual polygamous families to determine their own course. Some men abandoned their plural wives and children, an action that was roundly condemned. Other couples amicably separated. However, the majority of Latter-day Saints, including General Authorities, continued relations with their plural families, interpreting the Manifesto to mean that only no new plural marriages could occur. . . .

"To confirm to both members and nonmembers the Church's unequivocal stance to discontinue polygamy, President Joseph F. Smith issued a Second Manifesto in general conference in April 1904 and banned new plural marriages globally. In his official statement, he declared, 'all such marriages are prohibited, and if any officer or member of the Church shall assume to solemnize or enter into any such marriage he will be deemed in transgression against the Church . . . and excommunicated therefrom.'

"This prohibition did not apply to existing plural families, but after the Second Manifesto, again, some plural families chose to separate while others continued to quietly cohabit for the rest of their lives. For Latter-day Saints who continued to perform new polygamous marriages, the Second Manifesto marked a clear point of departure from the Church. They were excommunicated, and schismatic groups continue the practice of polygamy today" (Brittany Chapman Nash, *Let's Talk about Polygamy*, 44–45, 46–47).

Introduction to Official Declaration 2

"As missionary work spread across the world during the 20th century, Church leaders prayed for further guidance concerning restrictions that had existed on priesthood ordination and temple ordinances for Church members of black African descent. On June 1, 1978, the Lord revealed to President Spencer W. Kimball, his counselors in the First Presidency, and members of the Quorum of the Twelve Apostles that these restrictions should be removed. On June 8, 1978, the First Presidency announced this revelation in a letter to Church leaders. This letter is recorded in Official Declaration 2" (*Doctrine and Covenants Student Manual* [2018], 861).

President Russell M. Nelson clarified: "In the meridian of time and again in the latter days, the Lord has stressed His essential doctrine of equal opportunity for His children. . . . '[The Lord] denieth none that come unto him, black and white, bond and free, male and female; . . . all are alike unto God' (2 Nephi 26:33).

"On every continent and across the isles of the sea, faithful people are being gathered into The Church of Jesus Christ of Latter-day Saints. Differences in culture, language, gender, race, and nationality fade into insignificance as the faithful enter the covenant path and come unto our beloved Redeemer.

"Ultimately, we realize that only the comprehension of the true Fatherhood of God can bring full appreciation of the true brotherhood of men and the true sisterhood of women. That understanding inspires us with passionate desire to build bridges of cooperation instead of walls of segregation" ("Building Bridges," *New Era*, Aug. 2018, 6).

In general conference of October 2020, President Russell M. Nelson reiterated: "Each of us has a divine potential because each is a child of God. Each is equal in His eyes. The implications of this truth are profound. Brothers and sisters, please listen carefully to what I am about to say. God does not love one race more than another. His doctrine on this matter is clear. He invites *all* to come unto Him, 'black and white, bond and free, male and female.'

"I assure you that your standing before God is not determined by the color of your skin. Favor or disfavor with God is dependent upon your devotion to God and His commandments and not the color of your skin.

"I grieve that our Black brothers and sisters the world over are enduring the pains of racism and prejudice. Today I call upon our members everywhere to lead out in abandoning attitudes and actions of prejudice. I plead with you to promote respect for all of God's children" ("Let God Prevail," *Ensign*, Nov. 2020, 94).

OFFICIAL DECLARATION 2

The Book of Mormon teaches that "all are alike unto God," including "black and white, bond and free, male and female" (2 Nephi 26:33). Throughout the history of the Church, people of every race and ethnicity in many countries have been baptized and have lived as faithful members of the Church. During Joseph Smith's lifetime, a few black male members of the Church were ordained to the priesthood. Early in its history, Church leaders stopped conferring the priesthood on black males of African descent. Church records offer no clear insights into the origins of this practice. Church leaders believed that a revelation from God was needed to alter this practice and prayerfully sought guidance. The revelation came to Church President Spencer W. Kimball and was affirmed to other Church leaders in the Salt Lake Temple on

What was the Church's early practice regarding the priesthood ban? (OD2, Introduction)
"For much of its history—from the mid-1800s until 1978—the Church did not ordain men of black African descent to its priesthood or allow black men or women to participate in temple endowment or sealing ordinances.

"The Church was established in 1830, during an era of great racial division in the United States. At the time, many people of African descent lived in slavery, and racial distinctions and prejudice were not just common but customary among white Americans. . . . [However, from] the beginnings of the Church, people of every race and ethnicity could be baptized and received as members. . . . [and] during the first two decades of the Church's existence, a few black men were ordained to the priesthood. . . .

"In 1852, President Brigham Young publicly announced that men of black African descent could no longer be ordained to the priesthood, though thereafter blacks continued to join the Church through baptism and receiving the gift of the Holy Ghost. Following the death of Brigham Young, subsequent Church presidents restricted blacks from receiving the temple endowment or being married in the temple" (Gospel Topics Essays, "Race and the Priesthood"; for a more complete historical introduction, see the full essay).

Official Declaration 2. "To Whom It May Concern"

Why was President Kimball going to the temple to pray? (OD2, "To Whom It May Concern," paragraph 2) President Kimball shared his feelings about his personal preparation to receive the Lord's will: "I knew that something was before us that was extremely important to many of the children of God. . . . Day after day I went alone and with great solemnity and seriousness in the upper rooms of the temple, and there I offered my soul and offered my efforts to go forward with the program. I wanted to do what he wanted. I talked about it to him and said, 'Lord, I want only what is right. We are not making any plans to be

June 1, 1978. The revelation removed all restrictions with regard to race that once applied to the priesthood.

To Whom It May Concern:

On September 30, 1978, at the 148th Semiannual General Conference of The Church of Jesus Christ of Latter-day Saints, the following was presented by President N. Eldon Tanner, First Counselor in the First Presidency of the Church:

In early June of this year, the First Presidency announced that a revelation had been received by President Spencer W. Kimball extending priesthood and temple blessings to all worthy male members of the Church. President Kimball has asked that I advise the conference that after he had received this revelation, which came to him after extended meditation and prayer in the sacred rooms of the holy temple, he presented it to

Reflections on Priesthood and Temple Restrictions (Official Declaration 2)

Some people offered their personal opinions for why there were priesthood restrictions. President Dallin H. Oaks reflected on such opinions: "I observed the pain and frustration experienced by those who suffered these restrictions and those who criticized them and sought for reasons. I studied the reasons then being given and could not feel confirmation of the truth of any of them. As part of my prayerful study, I learned that, in general, the Lord rarely gives reasons for the commandments and directions He gives to His servants. I determined to be loyal to our prophetic leaders and to pray—as promised from the beginning of these restrictions—that the day would come when all would enjoy the blessings of priesthood and temple" ("Be One," [transcript]).

Over the years, a variety of theories were advanced to justify the restriction. President Jeffrey R. Holland emphasized: "The folklore must never be perpetuated. . . . I have to concede to my earlier colleagues[;] . . . they, I'm sure, in their own way, were doing the best they knew to give shape to [the policy], to give context for it, to give even history to it. All I can say is however well intended the explanations were, I think almost all of them were inadequate and/or wrong. . . .

It probably would have been advantageous to say nothing, to say we just don't know, and, [as] with many religious matters, whatever was being done was done on the basis of faith at that time. But some explanations were given and had been given for a lot of years. . . . At the very least, there should be no effort to perpetuate those efforts to explain why that doctrine existed. I think, to the extent that I know anything about it . . . we simply do not know why that practice, that policy, that doctrine was in place" (in "The Mormons").

Ahmad Corbitt wrote: "Although more than four decades have passed since the revelation on the priesthood, some continue to have questions about the priesthood ban. And while enemies of the Church will likely always try to leverage it for their own designs, in my experience, some who ask these questions sit in our seminary, institute,

his counselors, who accepted it and approved it. It was then presented to the Quorum of the Twelve Apostles, who unanimously approved it, and was subsequently presented to all other General Authorities, who likewise approved it unanimously.

President Kimball has asked that I now read this letter:

June 8, 1978
To all general and local priesthood officers of The Church of Jesus Christ of Latter-day Saints throughout the world:

Dear Brethren:

As we have witnessed the expansion of the work of the Lord over the earth, we have been grateful that people of many nations have responded to the message of the restored gospel, and have joined the Church in ever-increasing numbers. This, in turn, has inspired us with a desire to extend to every worthy member of the Church all of the privileges and blessings which the gospel affords.

spectacularly moving. We want only the thing that thou dost want, and we want it when you want it and not until'" (*Spencer W. Kimball* [manual], 238). ⊙

Official Declaration 2. "June 8, 1978" Letter

and Sunday classes and before our full-time missionaries. Their motivation in asking questions is usually sincere and heartfelt, born of spirit-deep feelings of justice, fairness, and love. They are not unlike some of Jesus Christ's ancient disciples who once asked questions about a man who suffered a disability from birth. 'Master, who did sin, this man, or his parents, that he was born blind?' Jesus's disciples queried. Recognizing God to be just, they thought the denial of such a basic blessing as sight must have been a punishment for someone's sinfulness— either the man's own, in the premortal world, or his parents', sometime before he was born. Jesus's answer taught a powerful lesson that I believe relates to the priesthood ban: 'Neither hath this man sinned, nor his parents: but that the works of God should be made manifest in him' (John 9:2–3).

"I hear the Savior's answer this way: *You're not asking the right question or thinking from a godly perspective. You're trying to make sense of a sad situation by assigning blame without knowing all the facts; but I see this man's condition as an opportunity for me to bless him and show forth the power of God through a miraculous work.*

"How does this story relate to the priesthood ban? I believe when we analyze the priesthood ban in a way that seeks to assign blame, either to early leaders of the Church or to people of African descent—and blame has been assigned to both groups—we become distracted. According to Jesus's teaching, we have a beam in our eye that blinds us from seeing clearly. We miss the Lord's grander, more eternal vision and opportunity. We essentially ask, 'Master, who did sin, Black people or the early Church leaders, that the priesthood ban was imposed?' I believe if the Savior stood beside us, His answer would be just as forward-looking and glorious as His response to His disciples' question about the blind man: *Neither have my Black children sinned, nor the prophets: but that the power of God should be made manifest through a miraculous work*" ("Revelation That Changed the World," 37–39).

What promises were made by Church presidents prior to the Official Declaration 2 pertaining to those who ultimately would receive the priesthood? (OD2, "Jun. 8, 1978" Letter, paragraph 2) In 1852, when announcing the policy restricting priesthood ordination, Brigham Young "said that at some future day, black Church members would 'have [all] the privilege and more' enjoyed by other members" (Gospel Topics Essays, "Race and the Priesthood").

President Harold B. Lee answered a news reporter's question regarding the end of the priesthood restriction: "'It's only a matter of time . . . we're just waiting for that time'" (Goates, *Harold B. Lee*, 506).

What faithfulness was demonstrated by those who were not permitted to hold the priesthood? (OD2, "Jun. 8, 1978" Letter, paragraph 2) "In 1964, Joseph William Billy Johnson of Cape Coast, Ghana, gained a testimony of the restored gospel after reading the Book of Mormon and other Church literature that had been given to him. Brother Johnson and others who joined the Church sent letters to President David O. McKay requesting that missionaries be sent to Africa to baptize him and others with whom he had shared the gospel. President McKay responded that missionaries would be sent 'in the Lord's own due time,' but until then, Brother Johnson should continue to study the gospel and help his fellow believers (in E. Dale LeBaron, "Steadfast African Pioneer," *Ensign,* Dec. 1999, 45–49).

"Although there was no opportunity for Brother Johnson to be baptized at that time, he and a few others diligently spread the message of the gospel in Ghana for many years. Brother Johnson organized a number of congregations of believers and led them in regular fasts in which they pled for missionaries to come to their land and establish the Church among them (see [Maki, "People Prepared"]).

Aware of the promises made by the prophets and presidents of the Church who have preceded us that at some time, in God's eternal plan, all of our brethren who are worthy may receive the priesthood, and witnessing the faithfulness of those from whom the priesthood has been withheld, we have pleaded long and earnestly in behalf of these, our faithful brethren, spending many hours in the Upper Room of the Temple supplicating the Lord for divine guidance.

Sister Tracy Y. Browning's Testimony

Sister Tracy Y. Browning of the General Primary Presidency testified: "God told me when I was sixteen years old that The Church of Jesus Christ of Latter-day Saints was His Church. That the Book of Mormon was His word. That prophets and apostles still lived and guided His work. That I was to gather myself with His people, in the water and in the temple, and make covenants with Him. He told me that I belonged; that I was His. That I was purchased with the blood of our Savior Jesus Christ. That my inheritance was eternal life with God the Father, and God the Son. And He told me that the melanin in my skin, or the skin of my children, or the skin of my ancestors, would never change these truths. Not even an uncomfortable part of the Church's history can change it. The gospel of Jesus Christ is not racist, and He stands at the head of His Church. And I know that whenever His children are in peril of being lost to the mist, the rod of iron is available to provide clarity and to keep us pressing forward toward the tree of life" ("Hope for a Better World," 97).

"Like the believers in Ghana, thousands of other people of black African descent gained testimonies of the restored gospel as missionary work spread throughout the earth during the 20th century. Leaders of the Church were inspired by the faith of these individuals and desired to extend the blessings of the priesthood and temple to them" (*Foundations of the Restoration Class Preparation Material* [manual], Lesson 27, Section 2).

What can we learn about Heavenly Father and Jesus Christ through this revelation? (OD2, "Jun. 8, 1978" Letter, paragraph 3) President Kimball taught: "We had the glorious experience of having the Lord indicate clearly that the time had come when all worthy men and women everywhere can be fellowheirs and partakers of the full blessings of the gospel. I want you to know, as a special witness of the Savior, how close I have felt to him and to our Heavenly Father as I have made numerous visits to the upper rooms in the temple, going on some days several times by myself. The Lord made it very clear to me what was to be done" (*Spencer W. Kimball* [manual], 239).

He has heard our prayers, and by revelation has confirmed that the long-promised day has come when every faithful, worthy man in the Church may receive the holy priesthood, with power to exercise its divine authority, and enjoy with his loved ones every blessing that flows therefrom, including the blessings of the temple. Accordingly, all worthy male members of the Church may be ordained to the priesthood without regard for race or color. Priesthood leaders are instructed to follow the policy of carefully interviewing all candidates for ordination to either the Aaronic or the Melchizedek Priesthood to insure that they meet the established standards for worthiness.

The Martins Family and the Revelation on the Priesthood

In June 1990, Helvécio Martins was the first Black man to be called as a General Authority of the Church. His family's story illustrates the steadfast faith of many who awaited the long-promised day.

"The [Rudá Tourinho de Assis and Helvécio Martins] family was baptized on 2 July 1972. According to Elder Martins, 'We had found the truth, and nothing would stop us from living it'—not even the fact that their family could not directly enjoy the blessings of the priesthood. But 'when the Spirit tells you the gospel is true,' says Helvécio, 'how can you deny it?' . . .

"In 1974, he was called to be public communications coordinator for the North Brazil Region. In 1975 President Spencer W. Kimball announced the construction of the São Paulo Temple.

"'Although we didn't expect to enter it, we worked for the construction of the temple just like other members,' remembers Elder Martins. 'It was the house of the Lord, after all.' Sister Martins sold her jewelry to help with fundraising, and Brother Martins served on the publicity committee.

"At the cornerstone-laying ceremony in March 1977, recalls Elder Martins, President Kimball 'took hold of my arm and privately told me, "Brother, what is necessary for you is faithfulness."' This counsel strengthened the Martinses' commitment—faith that had led them to set up a missionary fund for their son, Marcus, whose patriarchal blessing in 1973 said that he would preach the gospel. Elder Martins also recalls that one day as he and Rudá visited the future temple site 'we were overcome by the Spirit. We held each other and wept.'

"On 9 June 1978, they learned of the revelation that all worthy male members could hold the priesthood. Immediately, they knelt and thanked the Lord. The Martinses were sealed as a family when the São Paulo temple opened, and Marcus served a mission" ("Elder Helvécio Martins of the Seventy," *Ensign*, May 1990, 106).

How did the Lord make known His will to the First Presidency and Quorum of the Twelve Apostles? (OD2, "Jun. 8, 1978" Letter, paragraph 4) President Gordon B. Hinckley, who was with the First Presidency and the Council of the Twelve Apostles in the Salt Lake Temple on Thursday, June 1, 1978, testified: "We joined in prayer in the most sacred of circumstances. President Kimball himself was voice in that prayer.... It felt as if a conduit opened between the heavenly throne and the kneeling, pleading prophet of God who was joined by his Brethren. The Spirit of God was there. And by the power of the Holy Ghost there came to that prophet an assurance that the thing for which he prayed was right, that the time had come, and that now the wondrous blessings of the priesthood should be extended to worthy men everywhere regardless of lineage" (Hinckley, "Priesthood Restoration," *Ensign*, Oct. 1988, 70). ✪

What specific gospel blessings has the revelation on the priesthood provided for God's children? (OD2, "Jun. 8, 1978" Letter, paragraph 4) "As a result of the revelation ending the restriction, Church members around the world experience real and meaningful integration with their fellow Saints. Through [ministering], Church callings, service, and fellowship, members with different racial backgrounds often become deeply involved in each other's lives. Members learn from each other, take counsel from each other, and have opportunities to better understand each other's perspectives and experiences.

"Latter-day Saints still wrestle with the problems created by centuries of slavery, colonization, suspicion, and division. But Church fellowship offers [all Church members] the chance to become of one heart and one mind as they minister to each other in love. As they press forward in humility and faith, members of the Church find healing and strength through Jesus Christ, the Savior of us all" (Goldberg, "Witnessing the Faithfulness," 340).

As one example among many, "Sister Julia N. Mavimbela said that before she joined the Church and came to the word *Israel,* she would 'throw the book aside and say, "It is for the whites. It is not for us. We are not chosen." Today I know I belong to a royal family, if I live righteously. I am an Israelite, and when I was doing my ordinances in the temple, I captured the feeling that we are all on earth as one family' (in *"All Are Alike unto God,"* 151)" (quoted in Quentin L. Cook, "Safely Gathered Home," *Liahona*, May 2023, 24n25).

We declare with soberness that the Lord has now made known his will for the blessing of all his children throughout the earth who will hearken to the voice of his authorized servants, and prepare themselves to receive every blessing of the gospel.

Sincerely yours,

Spencer W. Kimball
N. Eldon Tanner
Marion G. Romney

The First Presidency

Recognizing Spencer W. Kimball as the prophet, seer, and revelator, and president of The Church of Jesus Christ of Latter-day Saints, it is proposed that we as a constituent assembly accept this revelation as the word and will of the Lord. All in favor please signify by raising your right hand. Any opposed by the same sign.

The vote to sustain the foregoing motion was unanimous in the affirmative.

Salt Lake City, Utah, September 30, 1978.

MAPS

GEOGRAPHIC LOCATIONS OF DOCTRINE AND COVENANTS SECTIONS

MAP 1

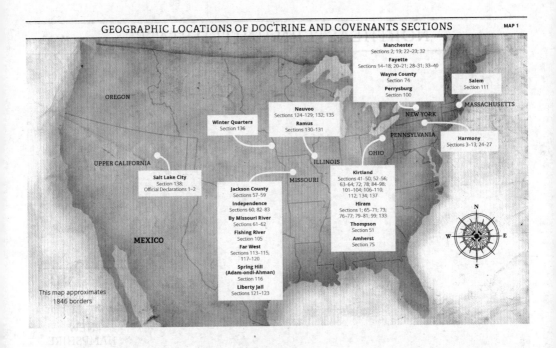

Manchester
Sections 2; 19; 22–23; 32

Fayette
Sections 14–18; 20–21; 28–31; 33–40

Wayne County
Section 74

Perrysburg
Section 100

Salem
Section 111

OREGON

NEW YORK

MASSACHUSETTS

Winter Quarters
Section 136

Nauvoo
Sections 124–129; 132; 135

Ramus
Sections 130–131

PENNSYLVANIA

OHIO

Harmony
Sections 3–13; 24–27

UPPER CALIFORNIA

ILLINOIS

Salt Lake City
Section 138;
Official Declarations 1–2

MISSOURI

Kirtland
Sections 41–50; 52–56;
63–64; 72; 78; 84–98;
101–104; 106–110;
112; 134; 137

Jackson County
Sections 57–59

Independence
Sections 60; 82–83

By Missouri River
Sections 61–62

Fishing River
Section 105

Far West
Sections 113–115;
117–120

Spring Hill
(Adam-ondi-Ahman)
Section 116

Liberty Jail
Sections 121–123

Hiram
Sections 1; 65–71; 73;
76–77; 79–81; 99; 133

Thompson
Section 51

Amherst
Section 75

MEXICO

This map approximates
1846 borders

SOME IMPORTANT LOCATIONS IN EARLY CHURCH HISTORY

MAP 2

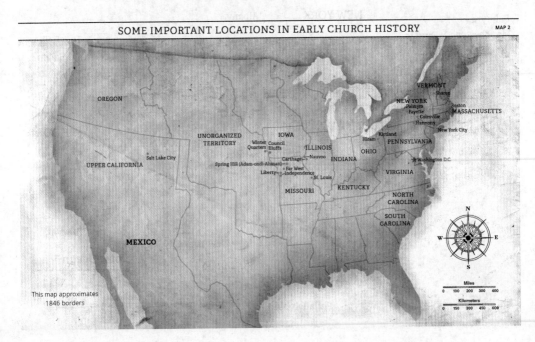

OREGON

VERMONT
Sharon

NEW YORK
Palmyra
Fayette
Colesville
Harmony

Boston
MASSACHUSETTS

New York City

UNORGANIZED
TERRITORY

IOWA

Winter
Quarters

Council
Bluffs

ILLINOIS

Kirtland
Hiram

PENNSYLVANIA

OHIO

INDIANA

Washington D.C.

UPPER CALIFORNIA

Salt Lake City

Spring Hill (Adam-ondi-Ahman)

Liberty

Carthage
Nauvoo

Far West
Independence
St. Louis

VIRGINIA

KENTUCKY

NORTH
CAROLINA

SOUTH
CAROLINA

MISSOURI

MEXICO

This map approximates
1846 borders

Miles
0   100   200   300   400

Kilometers
0   150   300   450   600

NORTHEASTERN UNITED STATES

MAP 3

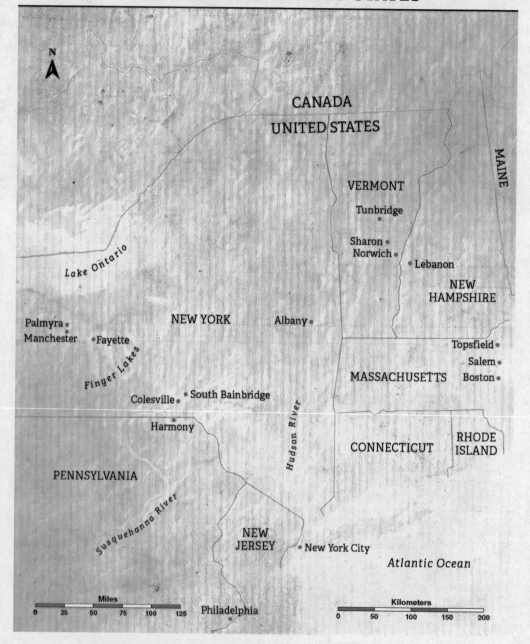

N

CANADA
UNITED STATES

VERMONT

Tunbridge

Sharon
Norwich

Lebanon

MAINE

NEW
HAMPSHIRE

Lake Ontario

Palmyra
Manchester   Fayette

NEW YORK   Albany

Topsfield

Salem
Boston

MASSACHUSETTS

Finger Lakes

Colesville   South Bainbridge

Harmony

Hudson River

CONNECTICUT

RHODE
ISLAND

PENNSYLVANIA

Susquehanna River

NEW
JERSEY   New York City

Atlantic Ocean

Miles
0   25   50   75   100   125

Kilometers
0   50   100   150   200

Philadelphia

PALMYRA-MANCHESTER, NEW YORK, 1820–1831

MAP 4

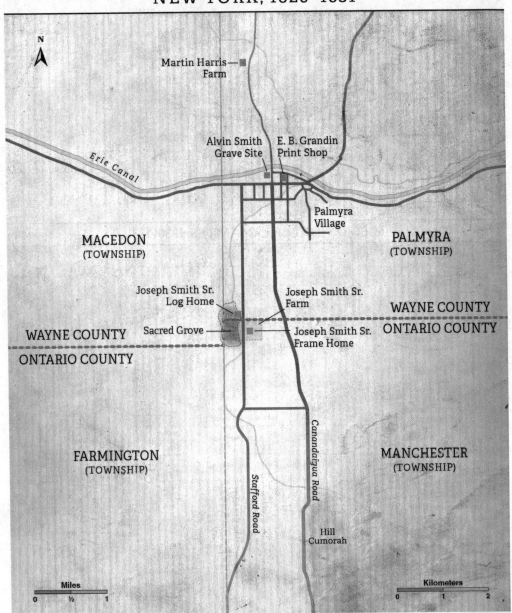

N

Martin Harris Farm

Erie Canal

Alvin Smith Grave Site

E. B. Grandin Print Shop

Palmyra Village

MACEDON (TOWNSHIP)

PALMYRA (TOWNSHIP)

Joseph Smith Sr. Log Home

Joseph Smith Sr. Farm

WAYNE COUNTY
ONTARIO COUNTY

Sacred Grove

Joseph Smith Sr. Frame Home

WAYNE COUNTY
ONTARIO COUNTY

FARMINGTON (TOWNSHIP)

MANCHESTER (TOWNSHIP)

Canandaigua Road

Stafford Road

Hill Cumorah

Miles
0   ½   1

Kilometers
0   1   2

THE NEW YORK, PENNSYLVANIA, AND OHIO AREA OF THE UNITED STATES

MAP 5

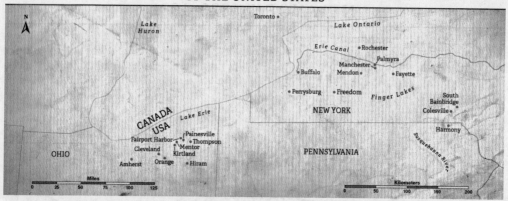

MISSION TO THE LAMANITES, 1830–1831

MAP 6

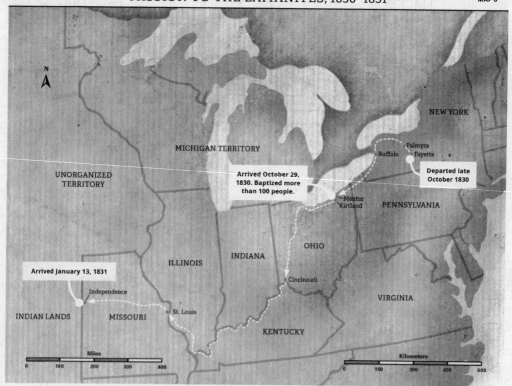

KIRTLAND, OHIO, 1830–1838

MAP 7

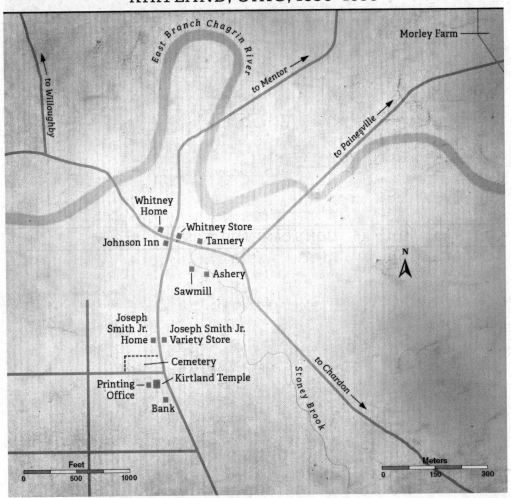

THE MISSOURI, ILLINOIS, AND IOWA AREA OF THE UNITED STATES

MAP 8

ZION'S CAMP ROUTE, 1834

MAP 9

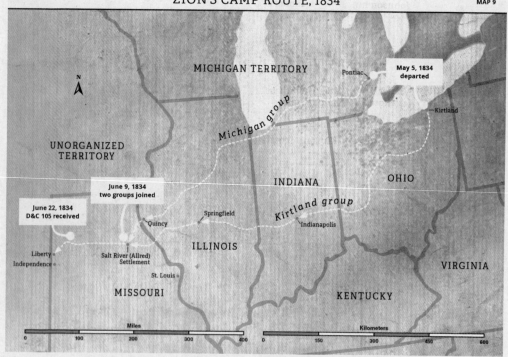

NAUVOO, ILLINOIS, 1839–1846

MAP 10

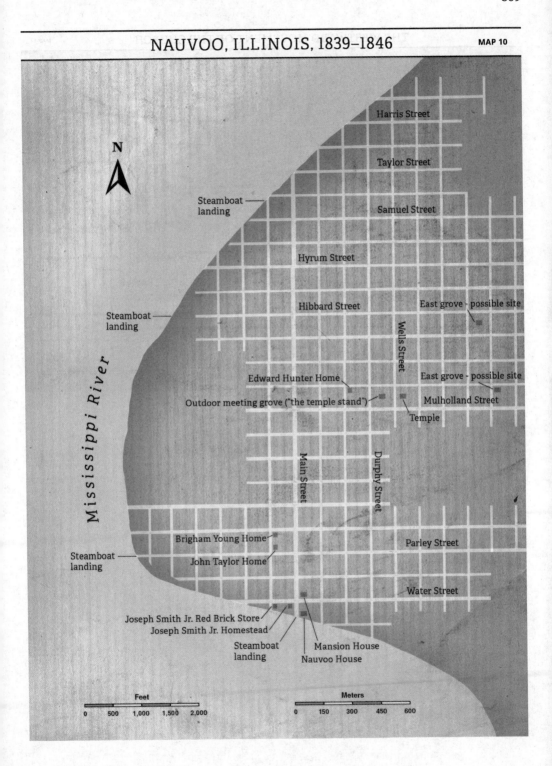

THE WESTWARD MOVEMENT OF THE CHURCH

MAP 11

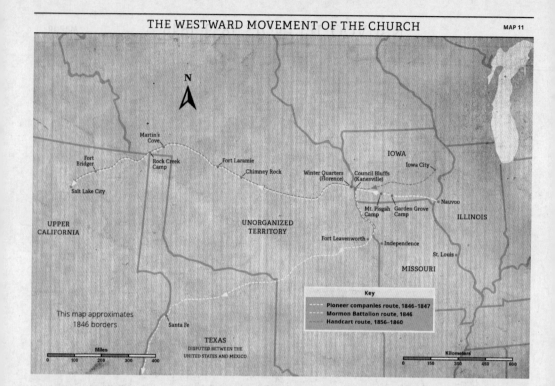

N

Martin's Cove
Fort Bridger
Rock Creek Camp
Fort Laramie
Chimney Rock
Winter Quarters (Florence)
Council Bluffs (Kanesville)
IOWA
Iowa City
Salt Lake City
Nauvoo
Mt. Pisgah Camp
Garden Grove Camp
ILLINOIS
UPPER CALIFORNIA
UNORGANIZED TERRITORY
Fort Leavenworth
Independence
St. Louis
MISSOURI

Key
- - - Pioneer companies route, 1846–1847
- - - Mormon Battalion route, 1846
- - - Handcart route, 1856–1860

This map approximates 1846 borders

Santa Fe

TEXAS
DISPUTED BETWEEN THE
UNITED STATES AND MEXICO

Miles
0   100   200   300   400

Kilometers
0   150   300   450   600

SOURCES

"Aaronic Priesthood Quorum and Young Women Class Presidency Orientation," 1–2.

Aburto, Reyna I. "Love Thy God and Thy Neighbor." BYU–I devotional, 4 Jun. 2019, 1–16.

———. "With One Accord." *Liahona*, Nov. 2018, 78–80.

Acceptance of the Statue of Brigham Young. United States Government Printing Office. 1950.

Acts to Revelation. Edited by Robert L. Millet and Kent P. Jackson. Vol. 6 of Studies in Scripture series. 1987.

"Age of Accountability." Book of Mormon Central. BookofMormonCentral.org.

Allen, James B., and Glen M. Leonard. *The Story of the Latter-day Saints.* 1992.

Alma: The Testimony of the Word. Edited by Monte S. Nyman and Charles D. Tate. 1992.

Alma 30–Moroni. Edited by Kent P. Jackson. Vol. 8 of Studies in Scripture series. 1988.

Andersen, Neil L. *The Divine Gift of Forgiveness.* 2019.

———. "Drawing Closer to the Savior." *Liahona*, Nov. 2022, 73–76.

———. "The Eye of Faith." *Ensign*, May 2019, 34–38.

———. "It's a Miracle." *Ensign*, May 2013, 77–80.

———. "Overcoming the World." *Ensign*, May 2017, 58–62.

———. "Power in the Priesthood." *Ensign*, Nov. 2013, 92–95.

———. "Preparing the World for the Second Coming." *Ensign*, May 2011, 49–52.

———. "The Prophet of God." *Ensign*, May 2018, 24–27.

———. "Thy Kingdom Come." *Ensign*, May 2015, 119–23.

———. "Tithing: Opening the Windows of Heaven." *Liahona*, Nov. 2023, 32–35.

———. "We Talk of Christ." *Ensign*, Nov. 2020, 88–91.

———. "Wounded." *Ensign*, Nov. 2018, 83–86.

Andersen, Wilson K. "Revelations on Priesthood, Keys, and Quorums." In *The Doctrine and Covenants*, edited by Robert L. Millet and Kent P. Jackson, 403–16. Vol. 1 of Studies in Scripture series. 1985.

Anderson, A. Gary. "Being Valiant by Following the Lord's Anointed." In *The Heavens Are Open*, edited by Byron R. Merrill, Brent L. Top, David R. Seely, and Vern D. Sommerfeldt, 34–47. Sperry Symposium series. 1993.

Anderson, Karl Ricks. *Joseph Smith's Kirtland: Eyewitness Accounts.* 1989.

———. *Joseph Smith's Kirtland.* 1996.

———. *The Savior in Kirtland: Personal Accounts of Divine Manifestations.* 2012.

Anderson, Richard Lloyd. "Cowdery, Oliver." In *Encyclopedia of Mormonism*, edited by Daniel H. Ludlow, 1:335–40. 1992.

———. *Investigating the Book of Mormon Witnesses.* 1981.

———. "The Organization Revelations (D&C 20, 21, and 22)." In *The Doctrine and Covenants*, edited by Robert L. Millet and Kent P. Jackson, 109–23. Vol. 1 of Studies in Scripture series. 1985.

———. *Understanding Paul.* 1983.

Apocryphal Writings and the Latter-day Saints. Edited by C. Wilford Griggs. 1986.

Ardern, Ian S. "A Time to Prepare." *Ensign*, Nov. 2011, 31–33.

Arrington, Leonard J. "The John Tanner Family," *Ensign*, Mar. 1979, 46–51.

———. "Oliver Cowdery's Kirtland, Ohio, 'Sketch Book.'" *BYU Studies* 12, no. 4 (1972): 410–26.

Arrington, Leonard J., Feramorz Y. Fox, and Dean L. May. *Building the City of God: Community and Cooperation among the Mormons.* 2nd edition. 1992.

"The Articles and Covenants of the Church: Museum Treasures." History.ChurchofJesusChrist.org.

Asay, Carlos E. "Salt of the Earth: Savor of Men and Saviors of Men." *Ensign*, May 1980, 42–44.

———. "The Temple Garment: An Outward Expression of an Inward Commitment." *Ensign*, Aug. 1997, 18–23.

Ashton, Marvin J. "The Measure of Our Hearts." *Ensign*, Nov. 1988, 15–17.

———. "What Is a Friend?" *Ensign*, Jan. 1973, 41–43.

At the Pulpit: 185 Years of Discourses by Latter-day Saint Women. Edited by Jennifer Reeder and Kate Holbrook. 2017.

Bachman, Danel. "Why I Believe: Evidence Thirty-Three: Joseph Smith and the 'Dews of Carmel.'" *Living Philosophies*, 24 Mar. 2015. LivingPhilosophies.blogspot.com.

Backman, Milton V. Jr. *The Heavens Resound: A History of the Latter-Day Saints in Ohio, 1830–1838.* 1983.

Backman, Milton V. Jr., and Richard O. Cowan. *Joseph Smith and the Doctrine and Covenants.* 1992.

Backman, Milton V. Jr., and Robert L. Millet. "Heavenly Manifestations in the Kirtland Temple." In *The Doctrine and Covenants*, edited by Robert L. Millet and Kent P. Jackson, 417–31. Vol. 1 Studies in Scripture series. 1985.

Backman, Milton V. Jr., and Keith W. Perkins. "United under the Laws of the Celestial Kingdom: Consecration, Stewardship, and the United Order, 1830–1838." In *The Doctrine and Covenants,* edited by Robert L. Millet and Kent P. Jackson, 170–85. Vol. 1 of Studies in Scripture series. 1985.

Ball, Terry B. "The Day of Judgment as Taught in the Doctrine and Covenants." In *The Doctrine and Covenants: A Book of Answers*, edited by Leon R. Hartshorn, Dennis A. Wright, and Craig J. Ostler, 189–204. Sperry Symposium series. 1996.

Ballard, M. Russell. "The Atonement and the Value of One Soul." *Ensign*, May 2004, 84–87.

———. "Be Strong in the Lord." *Ensign*, Jul. 2004, 8–14.

———. "Beware of False Prophets and False Teachers." *Ensign*, Nov. 1999, 62–64.

———. *Counseling with Our Councils: Learning to Minister Together in the Church and in the Family.* Revised edition. 2012.

———. "The Essential Role of Member Missionary Work." *Ensign*, May 2003, 37–40.

———. "Finding Joy through Loving Service." *Ensign*, May 2011, 46–49.

———. "Follow Jesus Christ with Footsteps of Faith." *Liahona*, Nov. 2022, 33–35.

———. "God Is at the Helm." *Ensign*, Nov. 2015, 24–27.

———. "The Greatest Generation of Young Adults." *Ensign*, May 2015, 67–70.

———. "Here Am I, Send Me." Brigham Young University devotional, 13 Mar. 2001. Speeches.BYU.edu.

———. "Hope in Christ." *Liahona*, May 2021, 53–56.

———. "Hyrum Smith: 'Firm as The Pillars of Heaven.'" In *The Prophet and His Work*, 75–83.

———. "The Importance of a Name." *Ensign*, Nov. 2011, 79–82.

———. "The Legacy of Hyrum." *Ensign*, Sep. 1994, 57–59.

———. "Like a Flame Unquenchable." *Ensign*, May 1999, 85–87.

———. "Men and Women in the Work of the Lord." *New Era*, Apr. 2014, 2–5.

———. "Missionary Service Blessed My Life Forever." *Liahona*, May 2022, 8–10.

———. "O That Cunning Plan of the Evil One." *Ensign*, Nov. 2010, 108–110.

———. "Purity Precedes Power." *Ensign*, Nov. 1990, 35–38.

———. "Put Your Trust in the Lord." *Ensign*, Nov. 2013, 43–45.

———. "The Truth of God Shall Go Forth." *Ensign*, Nov. 2008, 81–84.

———. "The Vision of the Redemption of the Dead." *Ensign*, Nov. 2018, 71–74.

———. "Watch Thee Therefore, and Pray Always." *Ensign*, Nov. 2020, 77–79.

———. "When Shall These Things Be?" BYU devotional, 12 Mar. 1996. Speeches.BYU.edu.

Ballard, Melvin J. In Conference Report, Apr. 1937, 87–95.

Barrett, Ivan J. *Joseph Smith and the Restoration*. 1973.

Baugh, Alexander L. "David W. Patten." In *Encyclopedia of Mormonism*, edited by Daniel H. Ludlow, 3:1068. 1992.

———. "1838, Joseph Smith in Northern Missouri." In *Joseph Smith: The Prophet and Seer*, edited by Richard Neitzel Holzapfel and Kent P. Jackson, 290–346. 2010.

———. "The History and Doctrine of the Adam-ondi-Ahman Revelation (D&C 116)." In *Foundations of the Restoration: Fulfillment of the Covenant Purposes*, edited by Barbara E. Morgan, Michael Hubbard MacKay, and Craig James Ostler, 157–88. Sperry Symposium series. 2016.

———. "Joseph Smith and the Redemption of Zion, 1834." In *Joseph Smith: The Prophet and Seer*, edited by Richard Neitzel Holzapfel and Kent P. Jackson, 151–94. 2010.

———. "Joseph Smith and Zion's Camp." *Ensign*, Jun. 2005, 42–47.

———. "Parting the Veil: Joseph Smith's Seventy-Six Documented Visionary Experiences." In *Opening the Heavens: Accounts of Divine Manifestations 1820–1844*, edited by John W. Welch and Erick B. Carlson, 265–306. 2005.

Beck, Julie B. "Choose Ye This Day to Serve the Lord." BYU Women's Conference, 29 Apr. 2010.

———. "Daughters in My Kingdom: The History and Work of Relief Society." *Ensign*, Nov. 2010, 113–15.

———. "A 'Mother Heart.'" *Ensign*, May 2004, 75–77.

———. "An Outpouring of Blessings." *Ensign*, May 2006, 11–13.

———. "Teaching the Doctrine of the Family." Seminaries and Institutes of Religion satellite broadcast, 4 Aug. 2009.

———. "What I Hope My Granddaughters (and Grandsons) Will Understand about Relief Society." *Ensign*, Nov. 2011, 109–13.

———. "What Latter-day Saint Women Do Best: Stand Strong and Immovable." *Ensign*, Nov. 2007, 109–12.

Bednar, David A. "But We Heeded Them Not." *Liahona*, May 2022, 14–17.

———. "Called to the Work." *Ensign*, May 2017, 67–70.

———. "Chosen to Bear Testimony of My Name." *Ensign*, Nov. 2015, 128–31.

———. "Converted unto the Lord." *Ensign*, Nov. 2012, 106–109.

———. "Flood the Earth through Social Media." *Liahona*, Aug. 2015, 48–53.

———. "The Hearts of the Children Shall Turn." *Ensign*, Nov. 2011, 24–27.

———. "Honorably Hold a Name and a Standing." *Ensign*, May 2009, 97–100.

———. "Learning in the Lord's Way." *Liahona*, Oct. 2018, 50–53.

———. "Let This House Be Built unto My Name." *Ensign*, May 2020, 84–87.

———. "Marriage Is Essential to His Eternal Plan." *Ensign*, Jun. 2006, 82–87.

———. "Meek and Lowly of Heart." *Ensign*, May 2018, 30–33.

————. "More Diligent and Concerned at Home." *Ensign*, Nov. 2009, 17–20.

————. "On The Lord's Side: Lessons from Zion's Camp." *Ensign*, Jul. 2017, 26–35.

————. "A Pattern in All Things." Inspiration, 1 Jun. 2021, digital version only. ChurchofJesusChrist.org.

————. "The Powers of Heaven." *Ensign*, May 2012, 48–51.

————. "Pray Always." *Ensign*, Nov. 2008, 41–44.

————. "The Principles of My Gospel." *Liahona*, May 2021, 123–26.

————. "Put On Thy Strength, O Zion." *Liahona*, Nov. 2022, 92–95.

————. "Quick to Observe." *Ensign*, Dec. 2006, 30–36.

————. "Receive the Holy Ghost." *Ensign*, Nov. 2010, 94–97.

————. "Reservoir of Living Water." Brigham Young University devotional, 4 Feb. 2007. Speeches.BYU.edu.

————. "The Spirit of Revelation." *Ensign*, May 2011, 87–90.

————. *The Spirit of Revelation.* 2021.

————. "The Tender Mercies of the Lord." *Ensign*, May 2005, 99–102.

————. "That Ye May Believe, Part 1." University of Utah Institute of Religion devotional, 28 Aug. 2022.

————. "Watchful unto Prayer Continually." *Ensign*, Nov. 2019, 31–35.

————. "Welcome to Seminary: The Doctrine and Covenants" [video]. Time code 3:25–4:25.

————. "We Will Prove Them Herewith." *Ensign*, Nov. 2020, 8–11.

————. "The Windows of Heaven." *Ensign*, Nov. 2013, 17–20.

————. "With the Power of God in Great Glory." *Liahona*, Nov. 2021, 28–30.

————. "Ye Must Be Born Again." *Ensign*, May 2007, 19–22.

Belnap, R. Kirk. "Wars, Rumors of Wars, and Wise and Faithful Servants." Brigham Young University devotional, 8 Jul. 2003. Speeches.BYU.edu.

Bennett, Richard E. "The Calamity That Should Come." In *The Religious Educator*, Vol. 18, No. 3 (2017): 158–73.

————. *Mormons at the Missouri, 1846–1852: "And Should We Die. . ."* 1987.

Benson, Ezra Taft. "Beware of Pride." *Ensign*, May 1989, 4–7.

————. "The Book of Mormon and the Doctrine and Covenants." *Ensign*, May 1987, 83–85.

————. In Conference Report, Apr. 1945, 105–10.

————. "The Constitution—A Glorious Standard." *Ensign*, May 1976, 91–93.

————. "Do Not Despair." *Ensign*, Nov. 1974, 65–67.

————. *Ezra Taft Benson.* Teachings of Presidents of the Church series. 2014.

————. "I Testify." *Ensign*, Nov. 1988, 86–88.

————. "Joseph Smith: Prophet to Our Generation." *Ensign*, Nov. 1981, 61–63.

————. "A Message to the World." *Ensign*, Nov. 1975, 32–34.

————. "Missionary Work: A Major Responsibility." *Ensign*, May 1974, 104–106.

————. "A New Witness for Christ." *Ensign*, Nov. 1984, 6–8.

————. "Our Responsibility to Share the Gospel." *Ensign*, May 1985, 6–8.

————. "A Principle with a Promise." *Ensign*, May 1983, 53–55.

————. *Sermons and Writings of President Ezra Taft Benson.* 2003.

————. "To the Elect Women of the Kingdom of God." In *Woman*, 69–76. 1980.

————. "What I Hope You Will Teach Your Children about the Temple." *Ensign*, Aug. 1985, 6–10.

Berrett, William E. *Teachings of the Doctrine and Covenants.* 1956. Bible Dictionary. The Church of Jesus Christ of Latter-day Saints. 2013.

Bingham, Jean B. "Covenants with God Strengthen, Protect, and Prepare Us for Eternal Glory." *Liahona*, May 2022, 66–69.

———. "Endowed with Power." Brigham Young University Women's Conference, 2 May 2019.

———. "Ministering as the Savior Does." *Liahona*, Nov. 2018, 104–7.

———. "The Oath and Covenant of the Priesthood Is Relevant to Women."

———. "United in Accomplishing God's Work." *Ensign*, May 2020, 61–63.

Black, Susan Easton. "David W. Patten." In Doctrine and Covenants Central. DoctrineandCovenants Central.org.

———. *400 Questions and Answers about the Doctrine and Covenants*. 2012.

———. "Gilbert, Sidney A." In *Encyclopedia of Latter-day Saint History*, edited by Arnold K. Garr, Donald Q. Cannon, and Richard O. Cowan, 429. 2000.

———. "Sidney Rigdon." In Book of Mormon Central. BookofMormonCentral.org.

———. *Who's Who in the Doctrine and Covenants*. 2001.

Book of Mormon Central. BookofMormonCentral.org.

The Book of Mormon: Second Nephi, The Doctrinal Structure. Edited by Monte S. Nyman and Charles D. Tate Jr. Book of Mormon Symposium series. 1989.

Book of Mormon: The Tenth Annual Church Educational System Religious Educators' Symposium Book. 1986.

"Book of Mormon Translation." In Gospel Topics Essays.

Boone, David F. "A Time for Commitment (D&C 117 and 118)." In *The Doctrine and Covenants*, edited by Robert L. Millet and Kent P. Jackson, 445–55. Vol. 1 of Studies in Scripture series. 1985.

Bowen, Matthew L. "'Creator of the First Day': The Glossing of Lord of Sabaoth in D&C 95:7." *Interpreter: A Journal of Latter-day Saint Faith and Scholarship*, Vol. 22 [2016]:51–77.

Bray, Justin R. "Within the Walls of Liberty Jail." In *Revelations in Context: The Stories behind the Sections of the Doctrine and Covenants*, edited by Matthew McBride and James Goldberg. 2016.

Brewerton, Ted E. "Profanity and Swearing." *Ensign*, May 1983, 72–74.

Brewster, Hoyt W. Jr. *Behold, I Come Quickly: The Last Days and Beyond*. 1994.

———. *Doctrine & Covenants Encyclopedia*. Revised edition. 2012.

———. *Isaiah Plain and Simple: The Message of Isaiah in the Book of Mormon*. 1995.

———. *Prophets, Priesthood Keys, and Succession*. 1991.

Brinley, Douglas E. "Strengthening Marriage and Family Relationships—The Lord's Way." In *The Heavens Are Open*, edited by Byron R. Merrill, Brent L. Top, David R. Seely, and Vern D. Sommerfeldt, 83–99. Sperry Symposium series. 1993.

Brooks, Juanita. *On the Mormon Frontier: The Diary of Hosea Stout, Volume One, 1844–1848*. 1982.

Brooks, Kent R. "Paul's Inspired Teachings on Marriage." In *Go Ye into All the World: Messages of the New Testament Apostles*, edited by Ray L. Huntington, Patty Smith, Thomas A. Wayment, and Jerome M. Perkins, 75–97. Sperry Symposium series. 2002.

Brough, M. Joseph. "A Still, Small Voice among Big Decisions." *Ensign*, Dec. 2018, 38–41.

Brown, S. Kent. *The Testimony of Luke*. Brigham Young University: New Testament Commentary. 2015.

Brown, S. Kent and Richard Neitzel Holzapfel. *Between the Testaments: From Malachi to Matthew*. 2002.

Browning, Tracy Y. "Hope for a Better World." In Lawrence-Costley, et al., *Stay Thou Nearby: Reflections on the 1978 Revelation on the Priesthood*, 75–98.

———. "Preserving Our Relationship with Heavenly Father and Jesus Christ." Brigham Young University devotional, 14 Feb. 2023. Speeches.BYU.edu.

———. "Seeing More of Jesus Christ in Our Lives." *Liahona*, Nov. 2022, 13–15.

Burnett, M. Dallas. "General Conference." In *Encyclopedia of Mormonism*, edited by Daniel H. Ludlow, 2:307–8. 1992.

Burton, Alma P. *Toward the New Jerusalem*. 1985.

Burton, Linda K. "Priesthood Power—Available to All." *Ensign*, Jun. 2014, 36–41.

Burton, Marshall T. "Meridian of Time." In *Encyclopedia of Mormonism*, edited by Daniel H. Ludlow, 2:891–92. 1992.

Burton, Theodore M. "A Born-Again Christian." Brigham Young University devotional, 26 Oct. 1982. Speeches.BYU.edu.

———. In Conference Report, Oct. 1967, 79–82.

———. In Conference Report, Oct. 1969, 33–35.

———. "Salvation for the Dead—A Missionary Activity." *Ensign*, May 1975, 69–71.

Bushman, Richard Lyman. *Joseph Smith: Rough Stone Rolling*. 2007.

By Our Rites of Worship: Latter-day Saint Views on Ritual in Scripture, History, and Practice. Edited by Daniel L. Belnap. 2013.

Caldwell, C. Max. "Acceptance of the Lord." In *The Doctrine and Covenants: Revelations in Context*, edited by Andrew H. Hedges, J. Spencer Fluhman, and Alonzo L. Gaskill, 1–22. Sperry Symposium series. 2008.

———. "A Quest for Zion." In *The Capstone of Our Religion: Insights into the Doctrine and Covenants*, edited by Robert L. Millet and Larry E. Dahl, 129–44. 1989.

Callister, Tad R. "The Atonement of Jesus Christ." *Ensign*, May 2019, 85–87.

———. *The Blueprint of Christ's Church*. 2015.

———. *The Inevitable Apostasy and the Promised Restoration*. 2006.

———. *The Infinite Atonement*. 2000.

———. "The Lord's Standard of Morality." *Ensign*, Mar. 2014, 45–49.

———. "Parents: The Prime Gospel Teachers of Their Children." *Ensign*, Nov. 2014, 32–34.

———. "Receiving and Recognizing Revelation." BYU–Hawaii devotional, 18 Aug. 2009. Speeches .BYUH.edu.

Camargo, Milton. "Ask, Seek, and Knock." *Ensign*, Nov. 2020, 106–108.

Cannon, Donald Q., Larry E. Dahl, and John W. Welch. "The Restoration of Major Doctrines through Joseph Smith: The Godhead, Mankind, and the Creation." *Ensign*, Jan. 1989, 27–33.

Cannon, George Q. "Beneficial Results of Continual Obedience." In *Millennial Star*, No. 40, Vol. 25 (3 Oct. 1863): 632–34.

———. In Conference Report, Oct. 1900, 63–69.

———. *Gospel Truth: Discourses and Writings of President George Q. Cannon* (two volumes in one). Selected, arranged, and edited by Jerreld L. Newquist. 1987.

———. In *Journal of Discourses*, 13:99.

———. In *Journal of Discourses*, 15:146–57.

———. In *Journal of Discourses*, 24:357–67.

———. In *Journal of Discourses*, 25:119–29.

———. *Life of Joseph Smith the Prophet*. 2005.

Cannon, Jeffrey G. "All Things Must Be Done in Order." In *Revelations in Context: The Stories behind the Sections of the Doctrine and Covenants*, edited by Matthew McBride and James Goldberg. 2016.

———. "Build Up My Church." In *Revelations in Context: The Stories behind the Sections of the Doctrine and Covenants*, edited by Matthew McBride and James Goldberg. 2016.

———. "Oliver Cowdery's Gift." In *Revelations in Context: The Stories behind the Sections of the Doctrine and Covenants*, edited by Matthew McBride and James Goldberg. 2016.

"Can nonmembers take the sacrament?" *Liahona*, Mar. 2012, 47.

The Capstone of Our Religion: Insights into the Doctrine and Covenants. Edited by Robert L. Millet and Larry E. Dahl. 1989.

Cardon, Craig A. "The Savior Wants to Forgive." *Ensign*, May 2013, 15–18.

Caring for the Needy: Study Guide. 1986.

Carlson, Bruce A. "When the Lord Commands." *Ensign*, May 2010, 38–40.

Castel, Albert. "Order No. 11 and the Civil War on the Border." In *Missouri Historical Review*, Vol. 57, no. 4 (Jul. 1963): 357–68.

Caussé, Gérald. "A Living Witness of a Living Christ." *Ensign*, May 2020, 38–40.

———. "Our Earthly Stewardship." *Liahona*, Nov. 2022, 57–59.

Christensen, Craig C. "Becoming Children of Light." *Ensign*, Aug. 2014, 64–69.

———. "An Unspeakable Gift from God." *Ensign*, Nov. 2012, 12–15.

Christensen, Joe J. "Ten Ideas to Increase Your Spirituality." *Ensign*, Mar. 1999, 58–61.

Christianson, James R. "And Now Come . . . Let Us Reason Together." In *The Doctrine and Covenants*, edited by Robert L. Millet and Kent P. Jackson, 201–10. Vol. 1 of Studies in Scripture series. 1985.

———. "A Ray of Light in an Hour of Darkness." In *The Doctrine and Covenants*, edited by Robert L. Millet and Kent P. Jackson, 463–75. Vol. 1 of Studies in Scripture series. 1985.

Christofferson, D. Todd. "As Many as I Love, I Rebuke and Chasten." *Ensign*, May 2011, 97–100.

———. "Born Again." *Ensign*, May 2008, 76–79.

———. "Come to Zion." *Ensign*, Nov. 2008, 37–40.

———. "The Divine Gift of Repentance." *Ensign*, Nov. 2011, 38–41.

———. "The Elders Quorum." *Ensign*, May 2018, 55–58.

———. "Firm and Steadfast in the Faith of Christ." *Ensign*, Nov. 2018, 30–33.

———. "Justification and Sanctification." *Ensign*, Jun. 2001, 18–25.

———. "Our Relationship with God." *Liahona*, May 2022, 78–81.

———. "The Power of Covenants." *Ensign*, May 2009, 19–23.

———. "Preparing for the Lord's Return." *Ensign*, May 2019, 81–84.

———. "Redemption." *Ensign*, May 2013, 109–12.

———. "The Redemption of the Dead and the Testimony of Jesus." *Ensign*, Nov. 2000, 9–12.

———. "Reflections on a Consecrated Life." *Ensign*, Nov. 2010, 16–19.

———. "Religious Freedom—A Cherished Heritage to Defend." Brigham Young University devotional, 26 Jun. 2016. Speeches.BYU.edu.

———. "The Sealing Power." *Liahona*, Nov. 2023, 19–22.

———. "A Sense of the Sacred." *New Era*, Jun. 2006, 28–31.

———. "Steps to Happiness." *Liahona*, Sep. 2013, 46–47.

———. "When Thou Art Converted." *Ensign*, May 2004, 11–13.

Church Historic Sites. The Church of Jesus Christ of Latter-day Saints.

Church History in the Fulness of Times Student Manual: Religion 341 through 343. 2003.

Church History Topics. "Chimney Rock." The Church of Jesus Christ of Latter-day Saints.

Church History Topics. The Church of Jesus Christ of Latter-day Saints.

Clark, J. Reuben Jr. In Conference Report, Apr. 1936, 61–65.

———. In Conference Report, Oct. 1953, 83–84.

———. "When Are the Writings or Sermons of Church Leaders Entitled to the Claim of Scripture?" Address delivered to seminary and institute of religion personnel, 7 Jul. 1954.

Clark, Kim B. "Look unto Jesus Christ." *Ensign*, May 2019, 54–57.

Clarke, J. Richard. "The Value of Work." *Ensign*, May 1982, 77–79.

Clawson, Rudger. In Conference Report, Apr. 1900, 42–46.

Cloward, Robert A. "Counsel to the Exiles." In *The Doctrine and Covenants*, edited by Robert L. Millet and Kent P. Jackson, 379–87. Vol. 1 of Studies in Scripture series. 1985.

———. "Revelations in Nauvoo." In *The Doctrine and Covenants*, edited by Robert L. Millet and Kent P. Jackson, 476–89. Vol. 1 in Studies in Scripture series. 1985.

Come Follow Me—For Individuals and Families: Book of Mormon 2020. 2019.

Cook, Gene R. "Inviting Others to 'Come unto Christ.'" *Ensign*, Nov. 1988, 37–39.

———. "Spiritual Guides for Teachers of Righteousness." *Ensign*, May 1982, 25–27.

Cook, Mary N. "Seek Learning: You Have a Work to Do." *Ensign*, May 2012, 120–22.

Cook, Quentin L. "Bishops—Shepherds over the Lord's Flock." *Liahona*, May 2021, 56–60.

———. "The Blessing of Continuing Revelation to Prophets and Personal Revelation to Guide Our Lives." *Ensign*, May 2020, 96–100.

———. "Conversion to the Will of God." *Liahona*, May 2022, 54–57.

———. "The Eternal Everyday." *Ensign*, Nov. 2017, 51–54.

———. "Our Father's Plan—Big Enough for All His Children." *Ensign*, May 2009, 34–38.

———. "Personal Peace: The Reward of Righteousness." *Ensign*, May 2013, 32–35.

———. "Prepare to Meet God." *Ensign*, May 2018, 114–17.

———. "Roots and Branches." *Ensign*, May 2014, 44–48.

———. "Safely Gathered Home." *Liahona*, May 2023, 20–23.

———. "See Yourself in the Temple." *Ensign*, May 2016, 97–101.

———. "The Songs They Could Not Sing." *Ensign*, Nov. 2011, 104–107.

———. "Valiant in the Testimony of Jesus." *Ensign*, Nov. 2016, 40–44.

———. "We Follow Jesus Christ." *Ensign*, May 2010, 83–86.

Corbitt, Ahmad S. "Graduating Your Faith to the Next Level." BYU–I Devotional, 21 Sep. 2021, 1–18.

———. "The Revelation That Changed the World." In Lawrence-Costley, et al., *Stay Thou Nearby: Reflections on the 1978 Revelation on the Priesthood*, 23–47.

Corbridge, Lawrence E. "The Prophet Joseph Smith." *Ensign*, May 2014, 103–105.

Cordon, Bonnie H. "Never Give Up an Opportunity to Testify of Christ." *Liahona*, May 2023, 10–12.

———. "150th Anniversary of the Young Women's Organization." *Liahona*, Jun. 2020, 54–57.

———. "That They May See." *Ensign*, May 2020, 78–80.

Cornish, J. Devn. "The True Church: 'For the Perfecting of the Saints.'" *Liahona*, Sep. 2018, 24–26.

Cowan, Richard O. *Answers to Your Questions about the Doctrine and Covenants.* 1996.

———. "Calls to Preach the Gospel." In *The Doctrine and Covenants,* edited by Robert L. Millet and Kent P. Jackson, 158–63. Vol. 1 of Studies in Scripture series. 1985.

———. "Church, Names of." In *Encyclopedia of Latter-day Saint History*, edited by Arnold K. Garr, Donald Q. Cannon, and Richard O. Cowan, 206. 2000.

———. "The Doctrine and Covenants on Temples and Their Functions." In *Doctrines for Exaltation*, edited by H. Dean Garrett and Rex C. Reeve Jr., 16–28. Sperry Symposium series. 1989.

———. *Doctrine & Covenants: Our Modern Scripture.* 1978.

———. "How Our Doctrine and Covenants Came to Be." In *The Capstone of Our Religion: Insights into the Doctrine and Covenants*, edited by Robert L. Millet and Larry E. Dahl, 1–16. 1989.

Cowan, Richard O., and Craig K. Manscill. *The A to Z of the Doctrine and Covenants and Church History*. 2008.

Craig, Michelle. "Spiritual Capacity." *Ensign*, Nov. 2019, 19–21.

Curtis, Lindsay R. "How does one live the Word of Wisdom?" *New Era*, Feb. 1971, 6.

Dahl, Larry E. "Doctrinal Teachings in Nauvoo: A Two-edged Sword." In *Regional Studies in Latter-day Saint Church History: Illinois*, edited by H. Dean Garrett, 125–38. 1995.

———. "The Doctrine and Covenants and the Second Coming of Christ." Handout at *CES Symposium on the Doctrine and Covenants/Church History*, 10–12 Aug. 1993.

———. "The Joseph Smith Translation and the Doctrine and Covenants." In *Plain and Precious Truths Restored: The Doctrinal and Historical Significance of the Joseph Smith Translation*, edited by Robert L. Millet and Robert J. Matthews, 104–33. 2001.

———. "The Second Coming of Jesus Christ." In *The Capstone of Our Religion: Insights into the Doctrine and Covenants*, edited by Robert L. Millet and Larry E. Dahl, 95–112. 1989.

———. "The Second Comings of the Lord." In *Watch and Be Ready: Preparing for the Second Coming of the Lord*, 134–66. 2003.

———. "The Vision of the Glories." In *The Doctrine and Covenants*, edited by Robert L. Millet and Kent P. Jackson, 279–308. Vol. 1 of Studies in Scripture series. 1985.

Dalton, Elaine S. "It Shows in Your Face." *Ensign*, May 2006, 109–111.

———. "A Return to Virtue." *Ensign*, Nov. 2008, 78–80.

Damiani, Adhemar. "Be of Good Cheer and Faithful in Adversity." *Ensign*, May 2005, 94–96.

Darowski, Joseph F. "The Journey of the Colesville Branch." In *Revelations in Context: The Stories behind the Sections of the Doctrine and Covenants*, edited by Matthew McBride and James Goldberg. 2016.

Darowski, Kay. "The Faith and Fall of Thomas Marsh." In *Revelations in Context: The Stories behind the Sections of the Doctrine and Covenants*, edited by Matthew McBride and James Goldberg. 2016.

Day, Laurel C. "What Are You Waiting For?" In *To Cheer and to Bless: Celebrating 20 Years of Time Out for Women*, 58–74. 2022.

Dennis, Ronald D. "The Martyrdom of Joseph Smith and His Brother Hyrum by Dan Jones." In *BYU Studies*, vol. 24, no. 1 [1984]:78–109.

Derrick, Royden G. "Valiance in the Drama of Life." *Ensign*, May 1983, 23–25.

Dew, Sheri. *Amazed by Grace*. 2015.

———. "Are You the Woman I Think You Are?" *Ensign*, Nov. 1997, 91–93.

———. *God Wants a Powerful People*. 2007.

———. "Knowing Who You Are—and Who You Have Always Been." In *At the Pulpit*, edited by Jennifer Reeder and Kate Holbrook, 265–75. 2017.

———. *No One Can Take Your Place*. 2004.

———. "Our Only Chance." *Ensign*, May 1999, 66–67.

———. *Prophets See around Corners*. 2023.

———. "We Are Women of God." *Ensign*, Nov. 1999, 97–99.

———. *Women and the Priesthood: What One Latter-day Saint Woman Believes*. Revised edition. 2021.

———. *Worth the Wrestle*. 2017.

Dibble, Philo. "Philo Dibble's Narrative." In *Early Scenes in Church History*, 8:74–96. 1882.

The Discourses of Wilford Woodruff. Edited by G. Homer Durham. 1946. Reprint 1990.

"Divining Rods." Church History Topics.

The Doctrine and Covenants. Edited by Robert L. Millet and Kent P. Jackson. Vol. 1 of Studies in Scripture series. 1985.

The Doctrine and Covenants: A Book of Answers. Edited by Leon R. Hartshorn, Dennis A. Wright, and Craig J. Ostler. Sperry Symposium series. 1996.

Doctrine and Covenants and Church History Seminary Teacher Manual. 2017.

Doctrine and Covenants and Church History Study Guide for Home-Study Seminary Students. 2017.

Doctrine and Covenants Central. DoctrineandCovenantsCentral.org.

Doctrine and Covenants Historical Resources. The Church of Jesus Christ of Latter-day Saints. 2020.

The Doctrine and Covenants: Revelations in Context. Edited by Andrew H. Hedges, J. Spencer Fluhman, and Alonzo L. Gaskill. Sperry Symposium series. 2008.

Doctrine and Covenants Student Manual Religion 324 and 325. 2001.

Doctrine and Covenants Student Manual Religion 324–325. 2018.

Doctrines for Exaltation: The 1989 Sperry Symposium on the Doctrine and Covenants. Edited by H. Dean Garrett and Rex C. Reeve Jr. Sperry Symposium series. 1989.

Documents, Volume 12: March–July 1843. Volume 12 of the Documents series of *The Joseph Smith Papers*, edited by Matthew C. Godfrey, R. Eric Smith, Matthew J. Grow, and Ronald K. Esplin. 2021.

"Do General Authorities Get Paid?" Learn More about The Church of Jesus Christ of Latter-day Saints. Frequently Asked Questions (FAQ).

Douglas, Sean. "Facing Our Spiritual Hurricanes by Believing in Christ." *Liahona*, Nov. 2021, 109–11.

Doxey, Cynthia. "Elijah's Mission, Message, and Milestones of Development in Family History and Temple Work." In *Joseph Smith and the Doctrinal Restoration*, edited by W. Jeffrey Marsh, 157–71. Sperry Symposium series. 2005.

Doxey, Roy W. "Accept Divine Counsel." Brigham Young University devotional, 30 Jul. 1974.

———. *The Doctrine and Covenants Speaks.* Volumes 1–2. 1964.

Draper, Richard D. "Maturing toward the Millennium." In *The Doctrine and Covenants*, edited by Robert L. Millet and Kent P. Jackson, 388–94. Vol. 1 of Studies in Scripture series. 1985.

———. "To Do the Will of the Lord." In *The Doctrine and Covenants*, edited by Robert L. Millet and Kent P. Jackson, 225–33. Vol. 1 of Studies in Scripture series. 1985.

Draper, Richard D., and Michael D. Rhodes. *Paul's First Epistle to the Corinthians.* In *Brigham Young University New Testament Commentary* series. 2017.

———. *The Revelation of John the Apostle.* In *Brigham Young University New Testament Commentary* series. 2016.

Dunn, Loren C. "The Spirit Giveth Life." *Ensign*, May 1979, 70–72.

———. "Testimony." *Ensign*, Nov. 2000, 13–14.

Early Scenes in Church History. Volume 8. Juvenile Instructor Office. 1882.

Easton-Flake, Amy. "Revealing Parables: A Call to Action within the Doctrine and Covenants." In *You Shall Have My Word: Exploring the Text of the Doctrine and Covenants*, edited by Scott C. Esplin, Richard O. Cowan, and Rachel Cope, 149–66. Sperry Symposium series. 2012.

Edwards, David A. "The Resurrection of Jesus Christ and Truths about the Body." *Ensign*, Apr. 2017, 27–31.

"1845 Proclamation of the Twelve Apostles of the Church of Jesus Christ of Latter-day Saints." In *Oracles of God*, Special Collections (digital), Brigham Young University—Idaho.

"Elder Helvécio Martins of the Seventy." *Ensign*, May 1990, 106.

Elieson, Kurt. *Historical Context of the Doctrine and Covenants and Other Modern Scriptures*. Vol. 1. 2011.

"Emer Harris Statement, 6 April 1856." In Utah Stake General Minutes, 1855–1860, 273. LR 9629, Series 11, Vol. 10, 273, LDS Church Archives.

Encyclopedia of Latter-day Saint History. Edited by Arnold K. Garr, Donald Q. Cannon, and Richard O. Cowan. 2000.

Encyclopedia of Mormonism. Edited by Daniel H. Ludlow, et al. 5 vols. 1992.

Esplin, Ronald K. "Brigham Young and the Transformation of the 'First' Quorum of the Twelve." In *Lion of the Lord: Essays on the Life and Service of Brigham Young*, edited by Susan Easton Black and Larry C. Porter, 54–84. 1995.

———. "'Exalt Not Yourselves': The Revelations and Thomas Marsh, an Object Lesson for Our Day." In *The Heavens Are Open*, edited by Byron R. Merrill, Brent L. Top, David R. Seely, and Vern D. Sommerfeldt, 112–29. Sperry Symposium series. 1993.

Esplin, Scott C. "'Let Zion in Her Beauty Rise': Building Zion by Becoming Zion." In *You Shall Have My Word: Exploring the Text of the Doctrine and Covenants*, edited by Scott C. Esplin, Richard O. Cowan, and Rachel Cope, 134–48. Sperry Symposium series. 2012.

Eubank, Sharon. "And the Lord Called His People Zion." *Liahona*, Mar. 2020, 26–29.

———. "Christ: The Light That Shines in Darkness." *Ensign*, May 2019, 73–76.

———. "I Pray He'll Use Us." *Liahona*, Nov. 2021, 53–55.

Evans, David F. "The Truth of All Things." *Ensign*, Nov. 2017, 68–70.

"Extending the Blessings of the Priesthood." *Ensign*, Jun. 2018, 30–33.

"Extracts from H. C. Kimball's Journal." *Times and Seasons*, Vol. 6, no. 7 (1845): 866–69.

Eyring, Henry B. "Always." *Ensign*, Oct. 1999, 6–12.

———. "Come unto Christ." *Ensign*, Mar. 2008, 49–52.

———. "Come unto Me." *Ensign*, May 2013, 22–25.

———. "Education for Real Life." *Ensign*, Oct. 2002, 14–21.

———. "Faith and the Oath and Covenant of the Priesthood." *Ensign*, May 2008, 61–64.

———. "Feed My Lambs." *Ensign*, Nov. 1997, 82–85.

———. "Finding Safety in Counsel." *Ensign*, May 1997, 24–26.

———. "Gratitude on the Sabbath Day." *Ensign*, 2016, 99–102.

———. "He Goes before Us." *Ensign*, May 2020, 66–69.

———. "His Spirit to Be with You." *Ensign*, May 2018, 86–89.

———. "In the Strength of the Lord." *Ensign*, May 2004, 16–19.

———. "A Life Founded in Light and Truth." Brigham Young University Education Week address, 15 Aug. 2000. Speeches.BYU.edu.

———. "A Life Founded in Light and Truth." *Ensign*, Jul. 2001, 6–13.

———. "Our Hearts Knit as One." *Ensign*, Nov. 2008, 68–71.

———. "The Preparatory Priesthood." *Ensign*, Nov. 2014, 59–62.

———. "The Reward for Enduring Well." *Ensign*, Jul. 2017, 4–5.

———. "Rise to Your Call." *Ensign*, Nov. 2002, 75–78.

———. "Tested, Proved, and Polished." *Ensign*, Nov. 2020, 96–99.

———. "That He May Become Strong Also." *Ensign*, Nov. 2016, 75–78.

———. "The True and Living Church." *Ensign*, May 2008, 20–24.

———. "Trust in God, Then Go and Do." *Ensign*, Nov. 2010, 70–73.

———. "A Voice of Warning." *Ensign*, Nov. 1998, 32–35.

———. "Where Is the Pavilion?" *Ensign*, Nov. 2012, 72–75.

———. "Where Two or Three Are Gathered." *Ensign*, May 2016, 19–22.

FAIR: Faithful Answers, Informed Response. FairLatterDaySaints.org.

Faith. 1983.

"The Family: A Proclamation to the World." *Ensign*, Nov. 1995, 102.

"The Family: A Proclamation to the World." *Ensign*, May 2017, 145.

Farley, Brent L. "The Oath and Covenant of the Priesthood." In *Doctrines for Exaltation*, edited by H. Dean Garrett and Rex C. Reeve Jr., 42–54. Sperry Symposium series. 1989.

Farnes, Sherilyn. "A Bishop unto the Church." In *Revelations in Context: The Stories behind the Sections of the Doctrine and Covenants*, edited by Matthew McBride and James Goldberg. 2016.

"The Father and the Son: A Doctrinal Exposition by the First Presidency and the Quorum of the Twelve Apostles." [Originally published in 1916.] *Ensign*, Apr. 2002, 13–18.

Faulconer, James E. *The Doctrine & Covenants Made Harder*. 2014.

Faust, James E. "The Blessings of Adversity." *Ensign*, Feb. 1998, 2–7.

———. "Continuous Revelation." *Ensign*, Nov. 1989, 8–11.

———. "Discipleship." *Ensign*, Nov. 2006, 20–23.

———. "Father, Come Home." *Ensign*, May 1993, 35–37.

———. "The Gift of the Holy Ghost: A Sure Compass." *Ensign*, Apr. 1996, 2–6.

———. "Gratitude as a Saving Principle." *Ensign*, May 1990, 85–87.

———. "The Great Imitator." *Ensign*, Nov. 1987, 33–36.

———. "The Prophetic Voice." *Ensign*, May 1996, 4–7.

———. "The Responsibility for Welfare Rests with Me and My Family." *Ensign*, May 1986, 20–23.

A Firm Foundation: Church Organization and Administration. Edited by Arnold K. Garr and David J. Whittaker. 2011.

"First Presidency Announces Uniform, Worldwide Standards for Ward and Stake Boundaries." Newsroom, 1 Dec. 2023.

The First Presidency. "Eleventh General Epistle of the Presidency of The Church of Jesus Christ of Latter-day Saints, to the Saints." In *Messages of the First Presidency*, edited by James R. Clark, 2:127–43. 1965.

———. "'Receiving' the Holy Ghost." *Improvement Era*, Mar. 1916, 460–61.

Flake, Dennis D. "Buffetings of Satan." In *Encyclopedia of Mormonism*, edited by Daniel H. Ludlow, 1:236. 1992.

Flake, Lawrence R. *Prophets and Apostles of the Last Dispensation*. 2001.

Fluhman, J. Spencer. "Joseph Smith Revelations." In *The Doctrine and Covenants: Revelations in Context*, edited by Andrew H. Hedges, J. Spencer Fluhman, and Alonzo L. Gaskill, 66–89. Sperry Symposium series. 2008.

For the Strength of Youth: A Guide for Making Choices. The Church of Jesus Christ of Latter-day Saints. 2022.

Foundations of the Restoration Class Preparation Material (Religion 225). 2019.

Foundations of the Restoration: Fulfillment of the Covenant Purposes. Edited by Craig James Ostler, Michael Hubbard MacKay, and Barbara Morgan Gardner. Sperry Symposium series. 2016.

Fowles, John L. "John's Prophetic Vision of God and the Lamb." In *The Testimony of John the Beloved*, edited by Daniel K Judd, Craig J. Ostler, and Richard D. Draper, 74–82. Sperry Symposium series. 1998.

———. "Missouri and the Redemption of Zion: A Setting for Conflict." In *Regional Studies in Latter-day Saint Church History: Missouri*, edited by Arnold K. Garr and Clark V. Johnson, 155–71. 1994.

———. "Zenos' Prophetic Allegory of Israel." In *Book of Mormon, The Tenth Annual Church Educational System Religious Educators' Symposium Book*, 29–36. 1986.

Franco, Cristina B. "Finding Joy in Sharing the Gospel." *Ensign*, Nov. 2019, 83–86.

Frankel, Ellen, and Betsy Platkin Teutsch. *The Encyclopedia of Jewish Symbols.* 1992.

Frederick, Nicholas J. "Incarnation, Exaltation, and Christological Tension in Doctrine and Covenants 93:1–20." In *How and What You Worship: Christology and Praxis in the Revelations of Joseph Smith*, edited by Rachel Cope, Carter Charles, and Jordan T. Watkins, 11–41. Sperry Symposium series. 2020.

Freeman, Emily Belle. "Walking in Covenant Relationship with Christ." *Liahona*, Nov. 2023, 76–79.

Fyans, J. Thomas. "Draw Near unto Me." *Ensign*, Nov. 1985, 90.

Galbraith, David B. "Orson Hyde's 1841 Mission to the Holy Land." *Ensign*, Oct. 1991, 16–19.

Gardiner, Annelise. "The Doctrine and Covenants: An Overview." *For the Strength of Youth*, Jan. 2021, 14–15.

Gardner, Barbara Morgan. "Connecting Daughters of God with His Priesthood Power." *Ensign*, Mar. 2019, 31–37.

Gardner, Norman W. "What We Know about Premortal Life." *New Era*, Feb. 2015, 12–13.

Gardner, R. Quinn. "Bishop's Storehouse." In *Encyclopedia of Mormonism*, edited by Daniel H. Ludlow, 1:123–25. 1992.

Garrard, Lamar E. "The Origin and Destiny of Man." In *The Doctrine and Covenants*, edited by Robert L. Millet and Kent P. Jackson, 365–78. Vol. 1 in Studies in Scripture series. 1985.

Garrett, H. Dean. "Doctrine and Covenants." In *Encyclopedia of Latter-day Saint History*, edited by Arnold K. Garr, Donald Q. Cannon, and Richard O. Cowan, 300–2. 2000.

———. *Great Teachings from the Doctrine and Covenants.* 1992.

———. "Missionary Work: A View from The Doctrine & Covenants." In *The Heavens Are Open*, edited by Byron R. Merrill, Brent L. Top, David R. Seely, and Vern D. Sommerfeldt, 130–40. Sperry Symposium series. 1993.

———. "The Three Most Abominable Sins." In *Alma: The Testimony of the Word*, edited by Monte S. Nyman and Charles D. Tate, 157–72. 1992.

Gaskill, Alonzo L. *Lost Language of Symbolism: An Essential Guide for Recognizing and Interpreting Symbols of the Gospel.* 2003.

General Handbook: Serving in The Church of Jesus Christ of Latter-day Saints. 2021–2023.

Gentry, Leland H. "The Design of God in Latter-day Saint Church History." In *A Sesquicentennial Look at Church History*, 123–33. Sperry Symposium series. 1980.

———. "God Will Fulfill His Covenants with the House of Israel." In *The Book of Mormon: Second Nephi, The Doctrinal Structure*, edited by Monte S. Nyman and Charles D. Tate, Jr., 159–76.

Goates, L. Brent. *Harold B. Lee: Prophet and Seer.* 1985.

Godfrey, Kenneth W. "More Treasures Than One: Section 111." In *Hearken O Ye People*, 191–204. Sperry Symposium series. 1984.

Godfrey, Matthew C. "The Acceptable Offering of Zion's Camp." In *Revelations in Context: The Stories behind the Sections of the Doctrine and Covenants*, edited by Matthew McBride and James Goldberg. 2016.

———. "The Camp of Israel's March to Missouri." In *Zion's Camp 1834: March of Faith*, edited by Matthew C. Godfrey et al., 33–66.

———. "Newel K. Whitney and the United Firm." In *Revelations in Context: The Stories behind the Sections of the Doctrine and Covenants*, edited by Matthew McBride and James Goldberg. 2016.

———. "'The Redemption of Zion Must Needs Come by Power': Insights into the Camp of Israel Expedition, 1834." *BYU Studies* 53, no. 4 (2014): 125–46.

———. "William McLellin's Five Questions." In *Revelations in Context: The Stories behind the Sections of the Doctrine and Covenants*, edited by Matthew McBride and James Goldberg. 2016.

Goldberg, James. "Witnessing the Faithfulness." In *Revelations in Context: The Stories behind the Sections of the Doctrine and Covenants,* edited by Matthew McBride and James Goldberg. 2016.

Gong, Gerrit W. "All Nations, Kindreds, and Tongues." *Liahona*, Nov. 2020, 38–42.

———. "Christ the Lord Is Risen Today." *Ensign*, May 2018, 97–98.

———. "Trust Again." *Liahona*, Nov. 2021, 97–99.

———. "We Each Have a Story." *Liahona*, May 2022, 43–46.

"Gospel Classics: The Origin of Man." *Ensign*, Feb. 2002, 26–30.

Gospel Principles. The Church of Jesus Christ of Latter-day Saints. 2011.

The Gospels. Edited by Kent P. Jackson and Robert L. Millet. Vol. 5 of Studies in Scripture series. 1986.

Gospel Topic Essays. The Church of Jesus Christ of Latter-day Saints.

Go Ye into All the World: Messages of the New Testament Apostles. Edited by Ray L. Huntington, Patty Smith, Thomas A. Wayment, and Jerome M. Perkins. Sperry Symposium series. 2002.

Grant, Heber J. In Conference Report, Oct. 1910, 116–20.

Grant, Jedediah M. In *Journal of Discourses*, 2:272–79.

Griffiths, Casey Paul. "Additional Context." In *Historical Context and Background of D&C 138*. Doctrine and Covenants Central. DoctrineandCovenantsCentral.org.

———. "Commentary on Doctrine & Covenants 124." Scripture Central. ScriptureCentral.org.

———. "'A Covenant and a Deed Which Cannot Be Broken': The Continuing Saga of Consecration." In *Foundations of the Restoration*, edited by Craig James Ostler, Michael Hubbard MacKay, and Barbara Morgan Gardner, 121–37. Sperry Symposium series. 2016.

———. "Historical Context and Background of D&C 69: Additional Context." Doctrine and Covenants Central. DoctrineandCovenantsCentral.org.

Griggs, C. Wilfred. "The Origin and Formation of the Corpus of Apocryphal Literature." In *Apocryphal Writings and the Latter-day Saints*, edited by C. Wilfred Griggs, 35–52. 1986.

Grist, Elicia A. "We Have Each a Mission to Perform." In *At the Pulpit*, edited by Jennifer Reeder and Kate Holbrook, 33–36. 2017.

Groberg, John H. "The Beauty and Importance of the Sacrament." *Ensign*, May 1989, 38–40.

Grow, Matthew J. "The Extraordinary Life of Parley P. Pratt." *Ensign*, Apr. 2007, 56–61.

———. "Thou Art an Elect Lady." In *Revelations in Context: The Stories behind the Sections of the Doctrine and Covenants*, edited by Matthew McBride and James Goldberg. 2016.

Grua, David W. "Waiting for the Word of the Lord." In *Revelations in Context: The Stories behind the Sections of the Doctrine and Covenants*, edited by Matthew McBride and James Goldberg. 2016.

Guide to the Scriptures. The Church of Jesus Christ of Latter-day Saints. 2013.

Hafen, Bruce C. "The Atonement: All for All." *Ensign*, May 2004, 97–99.

———. *The Broken Heart: Applying the Atonement to Life's Experiences.* 1989.

Haight, David B. "Remembering the Savior's Atonement." *Ensign*, Apr. 1988, 6–13.

———. "Solemn Assemblies." *Ensign*, Nov. 1994, 14–17.

Hales, Brian C., and Laura Harris Hales. "The Practice of Polygamy." In *A Reason for Faith: Navigating LDS Doctrine & Church History*, edited by Laura Harris Hales, 119–27. 2016.

Hales, Robert D. "Becoming A Disciple of Our Lord Jesus Christ." *Ensign*, May 2017, 46–48.

———. "Christian Courage: The Price of Discipleship." *Ensign*, Nov. 2008, 72–75.

———. "Eternal Life—to Know Our Heavenly Father and His Son, Jesus Christ." *Ensign*, Nov. 2014, 80–82.

———. "Fulfilling Our Duty to God." *Ensign*, Nov. 2001, 38–41.

———. "Gaining a Testimony of God the Father; His Son, Jesus Christ; and the Holy Ghost." *Ensign*, May 2008, 29–32.

———. "General Conference: Strengthening Faith and Testimony." *Ensign*, Nov. 2013, 6–8.

———. "Gifts of the Spirit." *Ensign*, Feb. 2002, 12–20.

———. "The Holy Ghost." *Ensign*, May 2016, 105–7.

———. "Holy Scriptures: The Power of God unto Our Salvation." *Ensign*, Nov. 2006, 24–27.

———. "Lessons from the Atonement That Help Us to Endure to the End." *Ensign*, Nov. 1985, 18–21.

———. "Preparing for a Heavenly Marriage." *Ensign*, Feb. 2006, 2–5.

———. "Tithing: A Test of Faith with Eternal Blessings." *Ensign*, Nov. 2002, 26–29.

———. "Waiting upon the Lord: Thy Will Be Done." *Ensign*, Nov. 2011, 71–74.

Hallstrom, Donald L. "The Heart and a Willing Mind." *Ensign*, Jun. 2011, 30–33.

———. "Turn to the Lord." *Ensign*, May 2010, 78–80.

Hanks, Marion D. "My Specialty Is Mercy." *Ensign*, Nov. 1981, 73–75.

Harkness, Lisa L. "Honoring His Name." *Ensign*, Nov. 2019, 60–62.

———. "Peace, Be Still." *Ensign*, Nov. 2020, 80–82.

Harper, Steven C. "'All Things Are the Lord's': The Law of Consecration in the Doctrine and Covenants." In *The Doctrine and Covenants: Revelations in Context*, edited by Andrew H. Hedges, J. Spencer Fluhman, and Alonzo L. Gaskill, 212–27. Sperry Symposium series. 2008.

———. "Endowed with Power." *The Religious Educator*, Vol. 5, No. 2 (2004): 83–99.

———. "Historical Context and Background of D&C 45." Doctrine and Covenants Central. DoctrineandCovenantsCentral.org.

———. "Historical Context and Background for D&C 78: Brief Synopsis by Steven C. Harper." Doctrine and Covenants Central. DoctrineandCovenantsCentral.org.

———. "Historical Context and Background of D&C 84." Doctrine and Covenants Central. DoctrineandCovenantsCentral.org.

———. "Historical Context and Background of D&C 95." Doctrine and Covenants Central. DoctrineandCovenantsCentral.org.

———. "The Law." In *Revelations in Context: Stories behind the Sections of the Doctrine and Covenants*, edited by Matthew McBride and James Goldberg. 2016.

———. *Let's Talk about the Law of Consecration.* 2022.

———. *Making Sense of the Doctrine & Covenants: A Guided Tour through Modern Revelations.* 2008.

———. "The Tithing of My People," in *Revelations in Context: The Stories behind the Sections of the Doctrine and Covenants*, edited by Matthew McBride and James Goldberg. 2016.

Hartshorn, Leon R. "Where I Am Ye Shall Be Also." In *The Doctrine and Covenants*, edited by Robert L. Millet and Kent P. Jackson, 124–31. 1985. Vol. 1 of Studies in Scripture series. 1985.

Haws, J. B. "Wrestling with Comparisons." Brigham Young University devotional, 7 May 2019. Speeches. BYU.edu.

Hearken, O Ye People: Discourses on the Doctrine and Covenants. Sperry Symposium. 1984.

The Heavens Are Open. Edited by Byron R. Merrill, Brent L. Top, David R. Seely, and Vern D. Sommerfeldt. Sperry Symposium series. 1993.

Hendricks, Drusilla D. "The Prayer of Faith." In *At the Pulpit*, edited by Jennifer Reeder and Kate Holbrook,
51–54. 2017.

Heroes of the Restoration. 1997.

Hill, Donna. *Joseph Smith: The First Mormon.* 1977.

Hinckley, Gordon B. "And the Greatest of These Is Love." *Ensign*, Mar. 1984, 3–5.

———. "The Continuing Pursuit of Truth." *Ensign*, Apr. 1986, 2–6.

———. "The Father, Son, and Holy Ghost." *Ensign*, Nov. 1986, 49–51.

———. "God Is at the Helm." *Ensign*, May 1994, 53–60.

———. *Gordon B. Hinckley.* Teachings of Presidents of the Church series. 2016.

———. "He Slumbers Not, nor Sleeps." *Ensign*, May 1983, 5–8.

———. "An Honest Man—God's Noblest Work." *Ensign*, May 1976, 60–62.

———. "In . . . Counsellors There Is Safety." *Ensign*, Nov. 1990, 48–51.

———. "Let Love Be the Lodestar of Your Life." *Ensign*, May 1987, 65–67.

———. "Living in the Fulness of Times." *Ensign*, Nov. 2001, 4–6.

———. "Magnify Your Calling." *Ensign*, May 1989, 46–49.

———. "The Marvelous Foundation of Our Faith." *Ensign*, Nov. 2002, 78–81.

———. "My Testimony." *Ensign*, Nov. 1993, 51–53.

———. "The Order and Will of God." *Ensign*, Jan. 1989, 2–5.

———. "Personal Worthiness to Exercise the Priesthood." *Ensign*, May 2002, 52–59.

———. "Priesthood Restoration." *Ensign*, Oct. 1988, 69–72.

———. "A Prophet's Counsel and Prayer for Youth." *Ensign*, Jan. 2001, 2–11.

———. "Remarks at the Dedication of the Joseph F. Smith Building at Brigham Young University." 20 Sep.
2005, 1–5. Speeches.BYU.edu.

———. "Small Acts Lead to Great Consequences." *Ensign*, May 1984, 81–83.

———. "The State of the Church." *Ensign*, Nov. 2003, 4–7.

———. "The Stone Cut Out of the Mountain." *Ensign*, Nov. 2007, 83–86.

———. *Teachings of Gordon B. Hinckley.* 1997.

———. "This Is the Work of the Master." *Ensign*, May 1995, 69–71.

———. "The Times in Which We Live." *Ensign*, Nov. 2001, 72–74.

———. "Upon You My Fellow Servants." *Liahona*, May 1989, 2–6.

———. "War and Peace." *Ensign*, May 2003, 78–81.

———. "We Need Not Fear His Coming." Brigham Young University fireside, 25 Mar. 1979. Speeches
.BYU.edu.

———. "The Women in Our Lives." *Ensign*, Nov. 2004, 82–85.

———. "Women of the Church." Nov. 1996, 67–70.

———. "The Work Goes On." *Ensign*, May 2001, 4–6.

"History of the Church: c. 1878–1898." In *Encyclopedia of Latter-day Saint History*, edited by Arnold K.
Garr, Donald Q. Cannon, and Richard O. Cowan, 2:625–27. 2000.

Holland, Jeffrey R. "Abide in Me." *Ensign*, May 2004, 30–32.

———. "The Atonement of Jesus Christ." *Ensign*, Mar. 2008, 32–38.

———. "Be With and Strengthen Them." *Ensign*, May 2018, 101–3.

———. *Broken Things to Mend.* 2008.

———. "Cast Not Away Therefore Your Confidence." Brigham Young University devotional, 2 Mar. 1999. Speeches.BYU.edu.

———. *Christ and the New Covenant: The Messianic Message of the Book of Mormon.* 1997.

———. "An Ensign to the Nations." *Ensign,* May 2011, 111–13.

———. "Fear Not: Believe Only!" *Liahona,* May 2022, 34–36.

———. "The First Great Commandment." *Liahona,* Nov. 2012, 83–85.

———. "For a Wise Purpose." *Ensign,* Jan. 1996, 12–19.

———. "A Future Filled with Hope." Worldwide Devotional for Young Adults, 8 Jan. 2023.

———. "The Grandeur of God." *Ensign,* Nov. 2003, 70–73.

———. "He Hath Filled the Hungry with Good Things." *Ensign,* Nov. 1997, 64–66.

———. "Lessons from Liberty Jail." *Ensign,* Sep. 2009, 26–33.

———. "The Lord's Preface (D&C 1)." In *Sperry Symposium Classics: The Doctrine and Covenants,* edited by Craig K. Manscill, 23–34. Sperry Symposium series. 2004.

———. "The Ministry of Angels." *Ensign,* Nov. 2008, 29–31.

———. "The Ministry of Reconciliation." *Ensign,* Nov. 2018, 77–79.

———. "'More Fully Persuaded': Isaiah's Witness of Christ's Ministry." In *Isaiah in the Book of Mormon,* edited by Donald W. Parry and John W. Welch, 1–18. 1998.

———. "My Words . . . Never Cease." *Ensign,* May 2008, 91–94.

———. "None Were with Him." *Ensign,* May 2009, 86–88.

———. "The Other Prodigal." *Ensign,* May 2002, 62–64.

———. *Our Day Star Rising: Exploring the New Testament with Jeffrey R. Holland.* 2022.

———. "A Prayer for the Children." *Ensign,* May 2003, 85–87.

———. "Prophets, Seers, and Revelators." *Ensign,* Nov. 2004, 6–9.

———. "Remember Lot's Wife." Brigham Young University devotional, 13 Jan. 2009. Speeches.BYU.edu.

———. "Safety for the Soul." *Ensign,* Nov. 2009, 88–90.

———. "Sanctify Yourselves." *Ensign,* Nov. 2000, 38–40.

———. "A Teacher Come from God." *Ensign,* May 1998, 25–27.

———. "Teaching, Preaching, Healing." *Ensign,* Jan. 2003, 32–42.

———. "Terror, Triumph, and a Wedding Feast." Church Educational System devotional, 12 Sep. 2004. Speeches.BYU.edu.

———. "This Do in Remembrance of Me." *Ensign,* Nov. 1995, 67–69.

———"Whom Say Ye That I Am?" *Ensign,* Sep. 1974, 6–11.

———. "Witnesses unto Me." *Ensign,* May 2001, 14–16.

———. *Witness for His Names.* 2019.

Holland, Matthew S. "The Exquisite Gift of the Son." *Ensign,* Nov. 2020, 45–47.

Holmes, Douglas D. "What Every Aaronic Priesthood Holder Needs to Understand." *Ensign,* May 2018, 50–53.

Holt, Helene. "Nauvoo House." In *Encyclopedia of Mormonism,* edited by Daniel H. Ludlow, 3:997. 1992.

Holzapfel, Richard Neitzel. "Endowment House." In *Encyclopedia of Latter-day Saint History,* edited by Arnold K. Garr, Donald Q. Cannon, and Richard O. Cowan, 336–37. 2000.

Holzapfel, Richard Neitzel, Dana M. Pike, and David Rolph Seely. *Jehovah and the World of the Old Testament.* 2009.

Hord, Seth. "Beings Divine or Devilish: Which Is the Destroyer Riding upon the Waters?" *The Religious Educator*, Vol. 21, No. 3 (2020): 99–115.

Horton, George A. Jr. "Knowing the Calamity." In *The Doctrine and Covenants*, edited by Robert L. Millet and Kent P. Jackson, 39–56. Vol. 1 of Studies in Scripture series. 1985.

"House of Revelation." *Ensign*, Jan. 1993, 31–37.

How and What You Worship: Christology and Praxis in the Revelations of Joseph Smith. Edited by Rachel Cope, Carter Charles, and Jordan T. Watkins. Sperry Symposium series. 2020.

Hughes, Kathleen H. "What Greater Goodness Can We Know: Christlike Friends." *Ensign*, May 2005, 74–76.

Hunter, Howard W. In Conference Report, Oct. 1964, 106–10.

———. *Howard W. Hunter*. Teachings of Presidents of the Church series. 2015.

———. *The Teachings of Howard W. Hunter*. Edited by Clyde J. Williams. 1997.

———. "A Temple-Motivated People." *Ensign*, Feb. 1995, 2–5.

Huntsman, Eric D. "John, the Disciple Whom Jesus Loved." *Ensign*, Jan. 2019, 18–23.

Hyde, Orson. "Night of the Martyrdom." In *Scrapbook of Mormon Literature*, edited by Ben E. Rich, 283–285. 2 vols. 1913.

Hyde, Paul Nolan. *A Comprehensive Commentary of the Doctrine and Covenants: Sections 1 through 72*. 2018.

———. *A Comprehensive Commentary of the Doctrine and Covenants: Section 73 through Official Declaration 2*. 2018.

Hymns of The Church of Jesus Christ of Latter-day Saints. 1985.

Isaiah and the Prophets: Inspired Voices from the Old Testament. Edited by Monte S. Nyman. 1984.

Isaiah in the Book of Mormon. Edited by Donald W. Parry and John W. Welch. 1998.

Jack, Elaine L. "Get a Life." In *At the Pulpit,* edited by Jennifer Reeder and Kate Holbrook, 242–52. 2017.

Jackson, Kent P. *From Apostasy to Restoration*. 1996.

———. "May the Kingdom of God Go Forth." In *The Doctrine and Covenants*, edited by Robert L. Millet and Kent P. Jackson, 251–57. Vol. 1 of Studies in Scripture series. 1985.

———. "New Discoveries in the Joseph Smith Translation of the Bible." In *The Religious Educator*, Vol. 6, No. 3 (2005): 149–60.

———. "Prophecies of the Last Days." In *The Heavens Are Open*, edited by Byron R. Merrill, Brent L. Top, David R. Seely, and Vern D. Sommerfeldt, 163–81. Sperry Symposium series. 1993.

———. "Revelations Concerning Isaiah." In *The Doctrine and Covenants*, edited by Robert L. Millet and Kent P. Jackson, 326–34. Vol. 1 of Studies in Scripture series. 1985.

———. "The Signs of the Times: 'Be Not Troubled.'" In *The Doctrine and Covenants*, edited by Robert L. Millet and Kent P. Jackson, 186–200. Vol. 1 of Studies in Scripture series. 1985.

Jacobs, Leone O. "Prepare Thy Heart." In *At the Pulpit*, 145–48.

Jared Carter Journal. Typescript, 8–9. Church History Catalog.

Jenkins, Ryan C. *The New Jerusalem: A Holy City Not Forsaken*. 2022.

Jensen, Jay E. "The Holy Ghost and Revelation." *Ensign*, Nov. 2010, 77–80.

———. "The Unspeakable Gift of the Holy Ghost." Brigham Young University devotional, 8 Jan. 2012. Speeches.BYU.edu.

Jensen, Marlin K. "An Eye Single to the Glory of God." *Ensign*, Nov. 1989, 27–28.

———. "The Power of a Good Life." *Ensign*, May 1994, 47–49.

———. "Remember and Perish Not." *Ensign*, May 2007, 36–38.

———. "To Walk Humbly with God." *Ensign*, May 2001, 9–11.

Jenson, Andrew. *Church Chronology: A Record of Important Events, Pertaining to the History of the Church of Jesus Christ of Latter-day Saints.* 2nd edition. 1914.

———. *The Historical Record.* 9 volumes. (1886–1890).

———. "Plural Marriage." *Historical Record*, Vol. 6, Nos. 3–5 (May 1887): 225–26.

Jessee, Dean. "Joseph Knight's Recollection of Early Mormon History." *BYU Studies* 17, no. 1 (1977): 29–39.

———. "Joseph Smith Jr.—in His Own Words, Part 1." *Ensign*, Dec. 1984, 22–31.

———. *The Papers of Joseph Smith.* 2 volumes. 1989–1992.

———. "'Steadfastness and Patient Endurance': The Legacy of Edward Partridge." *Ensign*, Jun. 1979, 41–47.

Jessee, Dean C., and John W. Welch. "Revelations in Context: Joseph Smith's Letter from Liberty Jail, March 20, 1839," *BYU Studies*, Vol. 39, No. 3 (2000): 125–45.

Johnson, Camille N. "Aligning with the Lord." BYU Women's Conference, 5 May 2023.

———. "Jesus Christ Is Relief." *Liahona*, May 2023, 81–84.

Johnson, Clark V. "The Law of Consecration: The Covenant That Requires All and Gives Everything." In *Doctrines for Exaltation*, edited by H. Dean Garrett and Rex C. Reeve Jr., 97–113. Sperry Symposium series. 1989.

———. *Mormon Redress Petitions: Documents of the 1833–1838 Missouri Conflict.* 1992.

Johnson, Janiece, and Jennifer Reeder. *The Witness of Women: Firsthand Experiences and Testimonies from the Restoration.* 2016.

Johnson, Paul V. "And There Shall Be No More Death." *Ensign*, May 2016, 121–23.

———. "The Blessings of General Conference." *Ensign*, Nov. 2005, 50–52.

Johnson, Stanley A. "High Council." In *Encyclopedia of Latter-day Saint History*, edited by Arnold K. Garr, Donald Q. Cannon, and Richard O. Cowan, 479. 2000.

Jones, Ellenor G. "The Power of Prayer." In *At the Pulpit*, edited by Jennifer Reeder and Kate Holbrook, 75–77. 2017.

Jones, Joy D. "An Especially Noble Calling." *Ensign*, May 2020, 15–18.

———. "Essential Conversations." *Liahona*, May 2021, 12–15.

———. "For Him." *Ensign*, Nov. 2018, 50–52.

———. "A Sin-Resistant Generation." *Ensign*, May 2017, 87–90.

Jorgensen, McKell A. "Shame versus Guilt: Help for Discerning God's Voice from Satan's Lies." *Ensign*, Jan. 2020.

Joseph: Exploring the Life and Ministry of the Prophet. Edited by Susan Easton Black and Andrew C. Skinner. 2005.

Joseph Smith and the Doctrinal Restoration. Edited by W. Jeffrey Marsh. Sperry Symposium series. 2005.

Joseph Smith's New Translation of the Bible: Original Manuscripts. Edited by Scott H. Faulring, Kent P. Jackson, and Robert J. Matthews. 2004.

Joseph Smith: The Prophet and Seer. Edited by Richard Neitzel Holzapfel and Kent P. Jackson. 2010.

Journal History: 1847, Jan.–Jun. Historical Department. 1830–2008.

Journal of Discourses. 26 vols. 1854–86.

The Journals of William E. McLellin. Edited by Jan Shipps and John W. Welch. 1994.

Judd, Frank F., and Terrence L. Szink. "John the Beloved in Latter-day Scripture (D&C 7)." In *The*

Doctrine and Covenants: Revelations in Context, edited by Andrew H. Hedges, J. Spencer Fluhman, and Alonzo L. Gaskill, 90–107. Sperry Symposium series. 2008.

The Juvenile Instructor. Edited by George Q. Cannon. 1866–1929.

The Juvenile Instructor. May 15, 1892, Vol. 27, No. 10.

Kapp, Ardeth G. "Drifting, Dreaming, Directing." In *At the Pulpit*, edited by Jennifer Reeder and Kate Holbrook, 193–203. 2017.

Kendrick, L. Lionel. "Personal Revelation," *Ensign*, Sep. 1999, 6–13.

———. "Strength During Struggles." *Ensign*, Oct. 2001, 24–31.

Kimball, Edward L. "Disciplinary Councils." In *Encyclopedia of Latter-day Saint History*, edited by Arnold K. Garr, Donald Q. Cannon, and Richard O. Cowan, 296. 2000.

Kimball, Spencer. "Absolute Truth." BYU devotional, 6 Sep. 1977. Speeches.BYU.edu.

———. In Conference Report, Oct. 1968, 127–31.

———. "The Example of Abraham." *Ensign*, Jun. 1975, 2–7.

———. *Faith Precedes the Miracle.* 1972.

———. "The False Gods We Worship." *Ensign*, Jun. 1976, 3–6.

———. "Give the Lord Your Loyalty." *Ensign*, Mar. 1980, 2–4.

———. "It Becometh Every Man." *Ensign*, Oct. 1977, 3–7.

———. *The Miracle of Forgiveness.* 1969.

———. "No Unhallowed Hand Can Stop the Work." *Ensign*, May 1980, 4–6.

———. "President Kimball Speaks Out on Personal Journals." *Ensign*, Dec. 1980, 60–61.

———. *Spencer W. Kimball.* Teachings of Presidents of the Church series. 2011.

———. "Strengthening the Family—the Basic Unit of the Church." *Ensign*, May 1978, 45–48.

———. *The Teachings of Spencer W. Kimball.* 1982.

———. "The Things of Eternity—Stand We in Jeopardy?" *Ensign*, Jan. 1977, 3–7.

———. "We Need a Listening Ear." *Ensign*, Nov. 1979, 4–6.

Knight, Gregory R. "Introduction to the 1845–1846 Journal of Thomas Bullock." In *BYU Studies*, Vol. 31, No. 1:5–14.

Knight, Newel. *Autobiography and Journal, circa 1846–1847.* Church History Library.

Knowles, Eleanor. *Howard W. Hunter.* 1994.

Kofford, Cree-L. "Marriage in the Lord's Way, Part Two." *Ensign*, Jul. 1998, 14–23.

Kuehn, Elizabeth. "More Treasures Than One: D&C 111." In *Revelations in Context,* edited by Matthew S. McBride and James Goldberg. 2016.

Kyungu, Alfred. "To Be a Follower of Christ." *Liahona*, Nov. 2021, 68–70.

Lane, Jennifer C. "Choosing Divinity, Choosing Christ." In *How and What You Worship: Christology and Praxis in the Revelations of Joseph Smith*, edited by Rachel Cope, Carter Charles, and Jordan T. Watkins, 43–73. Sperry Symposium series. 2020.

———. "Redemption's Grand Design." In *The Doctrine and Covenants: Revelations in Context*, edited by Andrew H. Hedges, J. Spencer Fluhman, and Alonzo L. Gaskill, 188–211. Sperry Symposium series. 2008.

Larsen, Sharon G. "Standing in Holy Places." *Ensign*, May 2002, 91–93.

Lassetter, Courtney J. "Dispensations of the Gospel." In *Encyclopedia of Mormonism*, edited by Daniel H. Ludlow, 1:388–90. 1992.

Latter-day Saint History: 1815–1846: Teacher Material. 2018.

Latter-day Saints' Millennial Star. Manchester, England, May 1840–Mar. 1842; Liverpool, Apr. 1842–Mar. 3, 1932; London, Mar. 10, 1932–Dec. 1970.

Lawrence-Costley, Carol. "Directed by His Light." In Lawrence-Costley, et al., *Stay Thou Nearby: Reflections on the 1978 Revelation on the Priesthood,* 5–21.

Lawrence–Costley, Carol, Ahmad S. Corbitt, Edward Dube, and Tracy Y. Browning. *Stay Thou Nearby: Reflections on the 1978 Revelation on the Priesthood.* 2023.

Lawrence, Larry R. "The War Goes On." *Ensign,* Apr. 2017, 33–39.

LDS Beliefs: A Doctrinal Reference. Edited by Robert L. Millet, Camille Fronk Olson, Andrew C. Skinner, and Brent L. Top. 2011.

Learn More about The Church of Jesus Christ of Latter-day Saints. Frequently Asked Questions (FAQ). Church ofJesusChrist.org.

Leavitt, Dennis H., and Richard O. Christensen. *Scripture Study for Latter-day Saint Families: The Doctrine and Covenants.* 2004.

The Lectures on Faith. 1985.

Lee, Harold B. "Admonitions for the Priesthood of God." *Ensign,* Jan. 1973, 104–8.

———. "Closing Remarks." *Ensign,* Jan. 1974, 125–29.

———. In Conference Report, Apr. 1943, 124–130.

———. *Decisions for Successful Living.* 1973.

———. *Harold B. Lee.* Teachings of Presidents of the Church series. 2000.

———. *Stand Ye in Holy Places: Selected Sermons and Writings of President Harold B. Lee.* 1974.

———. "Strengthen the Stakes of Zion." *Ensign,* Jul. 1973, 2–6.

———. *The Teachings of Harold B. Lee.* Edited by Clyde J. Williams. 2015.

———. "Understanding Who We Are Brings Self-Respect." *Ensign,* Jan. 1974, 2–6.

Leonard, Glen M. *Nauvoo: A Place of Peace, a People of Promise.* 2002.

"Letter from the First Presidency." *Liahona,* Dec. 1999, 1.

Lion of the Lord: Essays on the Life and Service of Brigham Young. Edited by Susan Easton Black and Larry C. Porter. 1995.

"The Living Christ: The Testimony of the Apostles." *Ensign,* Apr. 2000, 2–3.

Lewis, Barbara A. "Forgiving Others," *Ensign,* Feb. 2019, 36–39.

Lloyd, R. Scott. "Elder Christofferson Says Book of Mormon Is 'Tool of the Harvest.'" *Church News,* 7 Jul. 2017.

Ludlow, Daniel H. *A Companion to Your Study of the Doctrine and Covenants.* Vols. 1–2. 1978.

———. *Selected Writings of Daniel H. Ludlow.* 2000.

Ludlow, Victor L. *Isaiah: Prophet, Seer, and Poet.* 1982.

———. *Principles and Practices of the Restored Gospel.* 1992.

Lund, Gerald N. *Hearing the Voice of the Lord.* 2007.

———. *In Tune: The Role of the Spirit in Teaching and Learning.* 2013.

———. "Sanctification and Justification Are Just and True." In *Sperry Symposium Classics: The New Testament,* edited by Frank F. Judd Jr. and Gaye Strathearn, 46–58. 2006.

———. *The Second Coming of the Lord.* 2020.

———. "Things Which Must Shortly Come to Pass." In *Acts to Revelation,* edited by Robert L. Millet and Kent P. Jackson. Vol. 6 of Studies in Scripture series. 1987.

Lund, Robert E. "Teaching Old Testament Laws." *The Religious Educator,* Vol. 8, No. 3 (2007): 50–64. 2007.

Lundwall, N. B. *Temples of the Most High*. 1941.

Lybbert, Merlin R. "The Special Status of Children." *Ensign*, May 1994, 32–33.

Lyon, T. Edgar. "Independence, Missouri, and the Mormons, 1827–1833." *BYU Studies* 13, no. 1 (1972): 10–19.

Mackley, Jennifer Ann. *Wilford Woodruff's Witness: The Development of Temple Doctrine*. 2022.

Madsen, Ann M. "The Lord Requires Our Hearts." In *The Doctrine and Covenants*, edited by Robert L. Millet and Kent P. Jackson, 242–50. Vol. 1 of Studies in Scripture series. 1985.

Madsen, Carol Cornwall. "The 'Elect Lady' Revelation (D&C 25): Its Historical and Doctrinal Context." In *Sperry Symposium Classics: The Doctrine and Covenants*, edited by Craig K. Manscill, 117–33. 2004.

Madsen, Truman G. *Five Classics*. 2001.

———. "The Intimate Touch of Prayer." In *Prayer*. 2005.

———. "Joseph Smith Lecture 3: Joseph Smith and Spiritual Gifts," 1–12. Brigham Young University devotional. 23 Aug. 1978. Speeches.BYU.edu.

———. *Joseph Smith the Prophet*. 1989.

———. "Power from Abrahamic Tests." Brigham Young University devotional, 12 Oct. 1971. Speeches. BYU.edu.

———. *The Radiant Life*. 1994.

Mahas, Jeffrey. "Remembering the Martyrdom." In *Revelations in Context: The Stories behind the Sections of the Doctrine and Covenants*, edited by Matthew S. McBride and James Goldberg. 2016.

Maki, Elizabeth. "Go to the Ohio." In *Revelations in Context: The Stories behind the Sections of the Doctrine and Covenants*, edited by Matthew McBride and James Goldberg. 2016.

———. "A People Prepared." Church History. The Church of Jesus Christ of Latter-day Saints.

Malan, Jayne B. "The Summer of the Lambs." *Ensign*, Nov. 1989, 78–80.

Maldonado, B. Renato. "Messages from the Doctrine and Covenants: The Three Degrees of Glory." *Ensign*, Apr. 2005, 62–65.

Manscill, Craig K. "Rigdon, Sidney." In *Encyclopedia of Latter-day Saint History*, edited by Arnold K. Garr, Donald Q. Cannon, and Richard O. Cowan, 1030–33. 2000.

Marrott, Robert L. "Booth, Ezra." In *Encyclopedia of Latter-day Saint History*, edited by Arnold K. Garr, Donald Q. Cannon, and Richard O. Cowan, 123. 2000.

Mathews, Mark A. "The Salvation of Little Children Who Die: What We Do and Don't Know." *Liahona*, Jul. 2021, 12–15.

Matsumori, Vicki F. "Helping Others Recognize the Whisperings of the Spirit." *Ensign*, Nov. 2009, 10–12.

Matthews, Robert J. "Adam-ondi-Ahman." *BYU Studies* 13, no. 1 (1972): 27–35.

———. *A Bible! A Bible!* 1990.

———. *A Burning Light: The Life and Ministry of John the Baptist*. 1972.

———. "Doctrinal Connections with the Joseph Smith Translation." In *The Doctrine and Covenants: A Book of Answers*, edited by Leon R. Hartshorn, Dennis A. Wright, and Craig J. Ostler, 27–42. Sperry Symposium series. 1996.

———. "The Established Order of the Kingdom of God." In *Joseph Smith and the Doctrinal Restoration*. Sperry Symposium series. 2005. 272–86.

———. "The Olive Leaf." In *The Doctrine and Covenants*, edited by Robert L. Millet and Kent P. Jackson, 340–57. Vol. 1 of Studies in Scripture series. 1985.

———. "Plain and Precious Things Restored." *Ensign*, Jul. 1982, 14–20.

———. *"A Plainer Translation": Joseph Smith's Translation of the Bible, A History and Commentary*. 1985.

———. "The Restoration of All Things: What the Doctrine & Covenants Says." In *The Heavens Are Open*, edited by Byron R. Merrill, Brent L. Top, David R. Seely, and Vern D. Sommerfeldt, 222–42. Sperry Symposium series. 1993.

———. "Resurrection." *Ensign*, Apr. 1991, 6–11.

———. "Searching the Scriptures: How to Magnify Our Callings." *Ensign*, Mar. 1973, 54–55.

———. *Selected Writings of Robert J. Matthews*. Gospel Scholars Series. 1999.

———. "Using the 1981 Edition of the Doctrine and Covenants." In *The Doctrine and Covenants*, edited by Robert L. Millet and Kent P. Jackson, 23–38. Vol. 1 of Studies in Scripture series. 1985.

Maxwell, Neal A. "According to the Desire of [Our] Hearts." *Ensign*, Nov. 1996, 21–23.

———. "Becometh as a Child." *Ensign*, May 1996, 68–70.

———. "Behold, the Enemy Is Combined (D&C 38:12)." *Ensign*, May 1993, 76–79.

———. "Be of Good Cheer." *Ensign*, Nov. 1982, 66–68.

———. *But for a Small Moment*. 1986.

———. "Care for the Life of the Soul." *Ensign*, May 2003, 68–70.

———. "Deny Yourselves of All Ungodliness." *Ensign*, May 1995, 66–68.

———. "Endure It Well." *Ensign*, May 1990, 33–35.

———. *Even as I Am*. 1982.

———. "For I Will Lead You Along." *Ensign*, May 1988, 7–9.

———. "The Inexhaustible Gospel." *Ensign*, Apr. 1993, 68–73.

———. "Lest Ye Be Wearied and Faint in Your Minds." *Ensign*, May 1991, 88–91.

———. *Lord, Increase Our Faith*. 1994.

———. "Meeting the Challenges of Today." Brigham Young University devotional, 10 Oct. 1978. Speeches .BYU.edu.

———. *Men and Women of Christ*. 1991.

———. "Murmur Not." *Ensign*, Nov. 1989, 82–85.

———. "Notwithstanding My Weakness." *Ensign*, Nov. 1976, 12–14.

———. *Notwithstanding My Weakness*. 1981.

———. "Plow in Hope." *Ensign*, May 2001, 59–61.

———. "Put Off the Natural Man, and Come Off Conqueror." *Ensign*, Nov. 1990, 14–17.

———. "Settle This in Your Hearts." *Ensign*, Nov. 1992, 65–67.

———. "Swallowed Up in the Will of the Father." *Ensign*, Nov. 1995, 22–24.

———. "Take Especial Care of Your Family." *Ensign*, May 1994, 88–91.

———. "Those Seedling Saints Who Sit before You." An address given to CES Religious Educators, 19 Aug. 1983.

———. "The Tugs and Pulls of the World." *Ensign*, Nov. 2000, 35–37.

———. *A Wonderful Flood of Light*. 1990.

———. "Yet Thou Art There." *Ensign*, Nov. 1987, 30–33.

McBride, Matthew. "The Contributions of Martin Harris." In *Revelations in Context: The Stories behind the Sections of the Doctrine and Covenants*, edited by Matthew McBride and James Goldberg. 2016.

———. "Ezra Booth and Isaac Morley." In *Revelations in Context: The Stories behind the Sections of the Doctrine and Covenants*, edited by Matthew McBride and James Goldberg. 2016.

———. "Leman Copley and the Shakers." In *Revelations in Context: The Stories behind the Sections of the Doctrine and Covenants*, edited by Matthew McBride and James Goldberg. 2016.

———. "Letters on Baptism for the Dead." In *Revelations in Context: The Stories behind the Sections of the Doctrine and Covenants*, edited by Matthew McBride and James Goldberg. 2016.

———. "Man Was Also in the Beginning with God." In *Revelations in Context: The Stories behind the Sections of the Doctrine and Covenants*, edited by Matthew McBride and James Goldberg. 2016.

———. "Our Hearts Rejoiced to Hear Him Speak." In *Revelations in Context: The Stories behind the Revelations of the Doctrine and Covenants*, edited by Matthew McBride and James Goldberg. 2016.

———. "Religious Enthusiasm among Early Ohio Converts." In *Revelations in Context: The Stories behind the Sections of the Doctrine and Covenants*, edited by Matthew McBride and James Goldberg. 2016.

———. "The Vision." In *Revelations in Context: The Stories behind the Sections of the Doctrine and Covenants*, edited by Matthew McBride and James Goldberg. 2016.

McConkie, Bruce R. "Agency and Inspiration." *Liahona*, Jun. 2012, 16–19.

———. "All Are Alike unto God." In *CES Religious Educators' Symposium*. 1978.

———. "Be Valiant in the Fight of Faith." *Ensign*, Nov. 1974, 33–35.

———. "Come: Let Israel Build Zion." *Ensign*, May 1977, 115–18.

———. In Conference Report, Oct. 1950, 13–17.

———. *Doctrinal New Testament Commentary.* 3 vols. 1965–1973.

———. "The Doctrine of the Priesthood." *Ensign*, May 1982, 32–34.

———. *Doctrines of the Restoration: Sermons and Writings of Bruce R. McConkie.* Edited and arranged by Mark L. McConkie. 1989.

———. "God Foreordains His Prophets and His People." *Ensign*, May 1974, 71–73.

———. "The Keys of the Kingdom." *Ensign*, May 1983, 21–23.

———. "Let the Word Go Forth." *Ensign*, Feb. 1985, 72–74.

———. *The Millennial Messiah: The Second Coming of the Son of Man.* 1982.

———. *Mortal Messiah: From Bethlehem to Calvary.* 4 vols. 1979–1981.

———. "A New Commandment: Save Thyself and Thy Kindred!" *Ensign*, Aug. 1976, 7–11.

———. *A New Witness for the Articles of Faith.* 1985.

———. "Obedience, Consecration, and Sacrifice." *Ensign*, Apr. 1975, 50–52.

———. *The Promised Messiah: The First Coming of Christ.* 1978.

———. "The Purifying Power of Gethsemane." *Ensign*, May 1985, 9–11.

———. "The Salvation of Little Children." *Ensign*, Apr. 1977, 3–7.

———. "Stand Independent above All Other Creatures." *Ensign*, May 1979, 92–94.

———. "This Generation Shall Have My Word through You." In *Sperry Symposium Classics: The Doctrine and Covenants*, edited by Craig K. Manscill, 35–47. 2004.

———. "Thou Shalt Receive Revelation." *Ensign*, Nov. 1978. 60–61.

McConkie, Carol F. "Live according to the Words of the Prophets." *Ensign*, Nov. 2014, 77–79.

McConkie, James W. II. *Looking at the Doctrine and Covenants Again for the Very First Time: A Study Guide for Families Organized by Location.* 2010.

McConkie, Joseph Fielding. "From Father to Son: Joseph F. McConkie on Gospel Teaching." In *The Religious Educator*, Vol. 6, No. 1 (2005): 24–25.

———. *Gospel Symbolism.* 1985.

———. *Here We Stand.* 1995.

———. "Joseph Smith as Found in Ancient Manuscripts." In *Isaiah and the Prophets*, edited by Monte S. Nyman, 11–31.

———. "Premortal Existence, Foreordinations, and Heavenly Councils." In *Apocryphal Writings and the Latter-day Saints,* edited by C. Wilford Griggs, 173–98. 1986.

———. "The Principle of Revelation." In *The Doctrine and Covenants,* edited by Robert L. Millet and Kent P. Jackson, 80–85. Vol. 1 of Studies in Scripture series. 1985.

———. *Prophets and Prophecy.* 1988.

McConkie, Joseph Fielding, and Craig J. Ostler. *Revelations of the Restoration: A Commentary on the Doctrine and Covenants and Other Modern Revelations.* 2000.

McConkie, Joseph Fielding, and Donald W. Parry. *A Guide to Scriptural Symbols.* 1990.

McConkie, Joseph Fielding, and Robert L. Millet. *A Doctrinal Commentary on the Book of Mormon.* Vols. 1–3. 1987–1991.

———. *The Holy Ghost.* 1989.

McConkie, Joseph Fielding, Robert L. Millet, and Brent L. Top. *A Doctrinal Commentary on the Book of Mormon.* Vol. 4. 1992.

McConkie, Oscar W. *Aaronic Priesthood.* 1977.

———. *Angels.* 1975.

McKay, David. O. In Conference Report, Apr. 1937, 27–31.

———. In Conference Report, Oct. 1938, 130–35.

———. In Conference Report, Apr. 1942, 70–74.

———. In Conference Report, Apr. 1954, 22–26.

———. In Conference Report, Oct. 1962, 5–8.

———. *David O. McKay.* Teachings of Presidents of the Church series. 2011.

———. *Gospel Ideals.* 1976.

McMullin, Keith B. "Our Path of Duty." *Ensign,* May 2010, 13–15.

McPherson, James M. *Battle Cry of Freedom: The Civil War Era.* 1988.

Melchin, Gerald E. "Thy Sins Are Forgiven." *Ensign,* Jan. 1995, 18–21.

"Melchizedek Priesthood: Further Instructions on Duties of High Councilors and Special Items." *The Improvement Era,* Feb. 1955, 112–13, 120.

Merrill, Byron R. "Agency and Freedom in the Divine Plan." In *Window of Faith: Latter-day Saint Perspectives on World History,* edited by Roy A. Prete. 2005.

Merrill, Timothy G., and Steven C. Harper. "'It Maketh My Bones to Quake': Teaching Doctrine and Covenants 85." In *The Religious Educator,* Vol. 6, No. 2 (2005): 85–95.

Meservy, Keith H. "New Testament Items in the Doctrine and Covenants." In *The Doctrine and Covenants,* edited by Robert L. Millet and Kent P. Jackson, 266–78. Volume 1 of Studies in Scripture series. 1985.

Messages of the First Presidency of The Church of Jesus Christ of Latter-day Saints. Edited by James R. Clark. 6 Vols. 1965–1971.

Mickelson, Lynn A. "Eternal Laws of Happiness." *Ensign,* Nov. 1995, 78–81.

Millet, Robert L. "Angels." In *LDS Beliefs: A Doctrinal Reference,* edited by Robert L. Millet, et al., 36–37. 2011.

———. *The Atoning One.* 2018.

———. "Children of God." In *LDS Beliefs: A Doctrinal Reference,* edited by Robert L. Millet et al., 107–8. 2011.

———. *Christ-Centered Living.* 1994.

———. *An Eye Single to the Glory of God: Reflections on the Cost of Discipleship.* 1991.

———. "Gentiles, Times of." In *LDS Beliefs: A Doctrinal Reference*, edited by Robert L. Millet et al., 253–54. 2011.

———. "Gospel." In *LDS Beliefs: A Doctrinal Reference*, edited by Robert L. Millet et al., 280. 2011.

———. *The Holy Spirit: His Identity, Mission, and Ministry.* 2019.

———. "Latter-day Insights into the Life Beyond." In *The Capstone of Our Religion: Insights into the Doctrine and Covenants*, edited by Robert L. Millet and Larry E. Dahl, 197–215. 1989.

———. "Learning the Spirit of Revelation." In *The Capstone of Our Religion: Insights into the Doctrine and Covenants*, edited by Robert L. Millet and Larry E. Dahl, 41–62. 1989.

———. *Life in Christ: Discovering the Transforming Power of the Savior.* 1990.

———. "Life in the Millennium." In *Watch and Be Ready: Preparing for the Second Coming of the Lord*, edited by Robert L. Millet, 167–91. 2003.

———. *Living in the Eleventh Hour.* 2014.

———. "The Man Adam." *Ensign*, Jan. 1994, 8–15.

———. "Millennium." In *LDS Beliefs: A Doctrinal Reference*, edited by Robert L. Millet et al., 425–31. 2011.

———. "A New and Everlasting Covenant." In *The Doctrine and Covenants*, edited by Robert L. Millet and Kent P. Jackson, 512–26. Vol. 1 of Studies in Scripture series. 1985.

———. "A New and Everlasting Covenant of Marriage." In *The Capstone of Our Religion*, edited by Robert L. Millet and Larry E. Dahl, 163–82. 1989.

———. "Patriarchal Order." In *LDS Beliefs: A Doctrinal Reference*, edited by Robert L. Millet et al., 483–04. 2011.

———. *The Power of the Word: Saving Doctrines from the Book of Mormon.* 1994.

———. *Precept upon Precept: Joseph Smith and the Restoration of Doctrine.* 2016.

———. "A Revelation on Priesthood." In *The Doctrine and Covenants*, edited by Robert L. Millet and Kent P. Jackson, 309–25. Vol. 1 of Studies in Scripture series. 1985.

———. "Salvation beyond the Grave." In *The Doctrine and Covenants*, edited by Robert L. Millet and Kent P. Jackson, 549–63. Vol. 1 of Studies in Scripture series. 1985.

———. "The Second Coming of Christ: Questions and Answers." In *Sperry Symposium Classics: The Doctrine and Covenants,* edited by Craig K. Manscill, 202–20. 2004.

———. *Selected Writings of Robert L. Millet.* Gospel Scholars Series. 2000.

———. "The Vision of the Redemption of the Dead." In *Sperry Symposium Classics: The Doctrine and Covenants*, edited by Craig K. Manscill, 314–31. 2004.

Millet, Robert L., and Joseph Fielding McConkie. *In His Holy Name.* 1988.

———. *The Life Beyond.* 1986.

Millet, Robert L., and Lloyd D. Newell. *Draw Near unto Me: Daily Reflections on the Doctrine and Covenants.* 2004.

Monson, Earl M. "Establishing the Church." *Ensign*, Nov. 1998, 80–81.

Monson, Thomas S. "Blessings of the Temple." *Ensign*, Oct. 2010, 13–19.

———. "Called to the Work." *Ensign*, Jun. 2017, 4–5.

———. In Conference Report, Oct. 1969, 92–97.

———. "Guiding Principles of Personal and Family Welfare." *Ensign*, Sep. 1986, 2–5.

———. "Keep the Commandments." *Ensign*, Nov. 2015, 83–85.

———. *Teachings of Thomas S. Monson.* Compiled by Lynne F. Cannegieter. 2014.

———. "True to Our Priesthood Trust." *Ensign*, Nov. 2006, 56–59.

————. "With Hand and Heart." *Ensign*, Dec. 1971, 131–33.

"The Mormons." Interview with Jeffrey R. Holland. 4 Mar. 2006.

Morrison, Alexander B. *Visions of Zion*. 2010.

Morrison, Isaac K. "We Can Do Hard Things through Him," *Liahona*, Nov. 2022, 116–18.

Moss, James R. "The Church Judicial System." In *The Doctrine and Covenants*, edited by Robert L. Millet and Kent P. Jackson, 395–402. Vol. 1 of Studies in Scripture series. 1985.

Mutombo, Thierry K. "Ye Shall Be Free." *Liahona*, May 2021, 50–52.

Nadauld, Margaret D. "The Joy of Womanhood." *Ensign*, Nov. 2000, 14–16.

Nash, Brittany Chapman. *Let's Talk about Polygamy*. 2021.

Nash, Marcus B. "The Great Plan of Happiness." *Ensign*, Nov. 2006, 49–50.

————. "Hold Up Your Light." *Liahona*, Nov. 2021, 71–73.

————. "Joseph Smith: Strength Out of Weakness." *Ensign*, Dec. 2017, 55–61.

————. "The New and Everlasting Covenant." *Ensign*, Dec. 2015, 40–47.

Nelson, Russell M. "The Answer Is Always Jesus Christ." *Liahona*, May 2023, 127–28.

————. "Ask, Seek, Knock." *Ensign*, Nov. 2009, 81–84.

————. "Ask the Missionaries! They Can Help You!" *Ensign*, Nov. 2012, 18–21.

————. "The Atonement." *Ensign*, Nov. 1996, 33–36.

————. "Begin with the End in Mind." Brigham Young University devotional, 30 Sep. 1984. Speeches .BYU.edu.

————. "Blessed Are the Peacemakers." *Ensign*, Nov. 2002, 39–41.

————. "The Book of Mormon, the Gathering of Israel, and the Second Coming." *Ensign*, Jul. 2014, 26–31.

————. "The Book of Mormon: What Would Your Life Be Like without It?" *Ensign*, Nov. 2017, 60–63.

————. "Building Bridges." *New Era*, Aug. 2018, 6.

————. "Celestial Marriage." *Ensign*, Nov. 2008, 92–95.

————. "Children of the Covenant." *Ensign*, May 1995, 32–35.

————. "Choices." *Ensign*, Nov. 1990, 73–75.

————. "Choices for Eternity." Worldwide Devotional for Young Adults with President Nelson, 15 May 2022.

————. "Christ Is Risen; Faith in Him Will Move Mountains." *Liahona*, May 2021, 101–104.

————. "Constancy amid Change." *Ensign*, Nov. 1993, 33–36.

————. "The Correct Name of the Church." *Ensign*, Nov. 2018, 87–90.

————. "The Creation." *Ensign*, May 2000, 84–87.

————. "Decisions for Eternity." *Ensign*, Nov. 2013, 106–9.

————. "Doors of Death." *Ensign*, May 1992, 72–75.

————. "Drawing the Power of Jesus Christ into Our Lives." *Ensign*, May 2017, 39–42.

————. "Embrace the Future with Faith." *Ensign*, Nov. 2020, 73–76.

————. "The Everlasting Covenant." *Liahona*, Oct. 2022, 4–11.

————. "The Exodus Repeated." CES fireside for Young Adults, 7 Sep. 1997.

————. "Face the Future with Faith." *Ensign*, May 2011, 34–36.

————. "Focus on the Temple." *Liahona*, Nov. 2022, 121.

————. "The Future of the Church: Preparing the World for the Savior's Second Coming." *Ensign*, Apr. 2020, 13–17.

————. *The Gateway We Call Death*. 1995.

———. "The Gathering of Scattered Israel." *Ensign*, Nov. 2006, 79–82.

———. "Hear Him." *Liahona*, May 2020, 88–92.

———. *Heart of the Matter: What 100 Years of Living Have Taught Me.* 2023.

———. "Honoring the Priesthood," *Ensign*, May 1993, 38–41.

———. "Hope of Israel." Worldwide Youth devotional, 3 Jun. 2018.

———. "In the Lord's Own Way." *Ensign*, May 1986, 25–28.

———. "Joy and Spiritual Survival." *Ensign*, Nov. 2016, 81–84.

———. "Let God Prevail." *Ensign*, Nov. 2020, 92–95.

———. "Let Your Faith Show." *Ensign*, May 2014, 29–32.

———. "Living by Scriptural Guidance." *Ensign*, Nov. 2000, 16–18.

———. "The Love and Laws of God." Brigham Young University devotional, 17 Sep. 2019. Speeches .BYU.edu.

———. "A New Normal." *Liahona*, Oct. 2020, 118–19.

———. "Now Is the Time to Prepare." *Ensign*, May 2005, 16–18.

———. "Our Sacred Duty to Honor Women." *Ensign*, May 1999, 38–40.

———. "Overcome the World and Find Rest." *Liahona*, Nov. 2022, 95–98.

———. "Peacemakers Needed." *Liahona*, May 2023, 98–101.

———. "Personal Preparation for Temple Blessings." *Ensign*, May 2001, 32–35.

———. "The Power and Protection of Worthy Music." *Ensign*, Dec. 2009, 13–17.

———. "The Power of Spiritual Momentum." *Liahona*, May 2022, 97–100.

———. "Preaching the Gospel of Peace." *Liahona*, May 2022, 6–7.

———. "Prophets, Leadership, and Divine Law." Worldwide devotional for Young Adults, 8 Jan. 2017.

———. "Pure Truth, Pure Doctrine, and Pure Revelation." *Liahona*, Nov. 2021, 6–7.

———. "Repentance and Conversion." *Ensign*, May 2007, 102–5.

———. "Revelation for the Church, Revelation for Our Lives." *Ensign*, May 2018, 93–96.

———. "The Sabbath Is a Delight." *Ensign*, May 2015, 129–32.

———. "Self-Mastery." *Ensign*, Nov. 1985, 30–32.

———. In "Special Witnesses of Christ." *Ensign*, Apr. 2001, 2–21.

———. "The Spirit of Elijah." *Ensign*, Nov. 1994, 84–87.

———. "Spiritual Treasures." *Ensign*, Nov. 2019, 76–79.

———. "Stand as True Millennials." *Ensign*, Oct. 2016, 24–31.

———. "Sustaining the Prophets." *Ensign*, Nov. 2014, 74–76.

———. "Sweet Power of Prayer." *Ensign*, May 2003, 7–9.

———. *Teachings of Russell M. Nelson.* 2018.

———. "Teach Us Tolerance and Love." *Ensign*, May 1994, 69–71.

———. "The Temple and Your Spiritual Foundation." *Liahona*, Nov. 2021, 93–96.

———. "A Testimony of the Book of Mormon." *Ensign*, Nov. 1999, 69–71.

———. "Think Celestial." *Liahona*, Nov. 2023, 117–120.

———. "Thus Shall My Church Be Called." *Ensign*, May 1990, 16–18.

———. "We Can Do Better and Be Better." *Ensign*, May 2019, 67–69.

———. "Welcome Message." *Liahona*, May 2021, 6–7.

———. "What We Are Learning and Will Never Forget." *Liahona*, May 2021, 78–80.

———. "Where Is Wisdom?" *Ensign*, Nov. 1992, 6–8.

———. "With God Nothing Shall Be Impossible." *Ensign*, May 1988, 33–35.

———. "Woman—Of Infinite Worth." *Ensign*, Nov. 1989, 20–22.

———. "Worshiping at Sacrament Meeting." *Ensign*, Aug. 2004, 25–28.

———. "Your Body: A Magnificent Gift to Cherish." *New Era*, Aug. 2019, 2–7.

Nelson, William O. "To Prepare a People." *Ensign*, Jan. 1979, 18–22.

Neuenschwander, Dennis B. "Living Prophets, Seers, and Revelators." *Ensign*, Nov. 2000, 40–42.

Newel Knight's Journal, "Scraps of Biography: Tenth Book of the Faith Promoting Series." *Classic Experiences and Adventures: Laborers in the Vineyard; Eventful Narratives; Scraps of Biography; Helpful Visions.* 46–104. 1969.

Newsroom. The Church of Jesus Christ of Latter-day Saints.

New Testament Student Manual: Religion 211–212. 2018.

Nibley, Hugh. "A House of Glory." In *Temples of the Ancient World*, edited by Donald W. Parry, 29–47. 1994.

———. *Mormonism and Early Christianity.* 1987.

Nyman, Monte S. *Doctrine and Covenants Commentary, Volume 1: More Precious Than Gold.* 2008.

———. *Doctrine and Covenants Commentary, Volume 2: It Came from God.* 2009.

———. "A Great and Marvelous Work." In *The Doctrine and Covenants*, edited by Robert L. Millet and Kent P. Jackson, 73–79. Vol. 1 of the Studies in Scripture series. 1985.

———. *"Great Are the Words of Isaiah."* 1980.

———. "Priesthood, Keys, Councils, and Covenants." In *The Capstone of Our Religion: Insights into the Doctrine and Covenants.* Edited by Robert L. Millet and Larry E. Dahl. 1989.

———. "The Redemption of Zion (D&C 57–62)." In *The Doctrine and Covenants*, edited by Robert L. Millet and Kent P. Jackson, 234–41. Vol. 1 of the Studies in Scripture series. 1985.

———. "Six Visions of Eternity: Section 76." In *Hearken, O Ye People*, 105–18. Sperry Symposium series. 1984.

———. "The Stumbling Blocks of First Corinthians." In *Sperry Symposium Classics: The New Testament*, edited by Frank F. Judd Jr. and Gaye Strathearn, 284–95. Sperry Symposium series. 2006.

———. "When Will Zion Be Redeemed?" In *The Doctrine and Covenants: A Book of Answers*, edited by Leon R. Hartshorn, Dennis A. Wright, and Craig J. Ostler, 137–53. Sperry Symposium series. 1996.

———. "The Witnesses of the Book of Mormon." In *The Doctrine and Covenants*, edited by Robert L. Millet and Kent P. Jackson, 64–72. Vol. 1 of Studies in Scripture series. 1985.

Oaks, Dallin H. "The Aaronic Priesthood and the Sacrament." *Ensign*, Nov. 1998, 37–40.

———. Address given at the "Be One" celebration marking the 40th anniversary of the revelation on the priesthood. Conference Center, Salt Lake City, 1 Jun. 2018. Transcript.

———. "Alternate Voices." *Ensign*, May 1989, 27–31.

———. "Balancing Truth and Tolerance." *Ensign*, Feb. 2013, 24–31.

———. "Be Not Deceived." *Ensign*, Nov. 2004, 43–46.

———. "Be of Good Cheer." *Liahona*, Nov. 2022, 70–72.

———. "Bible Stories and Personal Protection." *Ensign*, Nov. 1992, 37–40.

———. "The Blessing of Commandments." Brigham Young University devotional, 10 Sep. 1974. Speeches.BYU.edu.

———. "The Boundary between Church and State." Second Annual Sacramento Court/Clergy Conference, Sacramento California, 20 Oct. 2015.

———. "Defending Our Divinely Inspired Constitution." *Liahona*, May 2021, 105–8.

———. "The Desires of Our Hearts." *Ensign*, Jun. 1986, 64–67.

———. "Divine Love in the Father's Plan." *Liahona*, May 2022, 101–4.

———. "Faith in the Lord Jesus Christ." *Ensign*, May 1994, 98–100.

———. "Following the Pioneers." *Ensign*, Nov. 1997, 72–74.

———. "Free Agency and Freedom." In *Second Nephi, The Doctrinal Structure*, edited by Monte S. Nyman and Charles D. Tate Jr., 3:1–17. Book of Mormon Symposium series. 1989.

———. "Give Thanks in All Things." *Ensign*, May 2003, 95–98.

———. "Going Forward with Religious Freedom and Nondiscrimination." *BYU Studies* no.1 (2022): 117–128.

———. "Gospel Teaching." *Ensign*, Nov. 1999, 78–81.

———. "Healing the Sick." *Ensign*, May 2010, 47–50.

———. "Joseph, the Man and the Prophet." *Ensign*, May 1996, 71–73.

———. "Judge Not and Judging." Brigham Young University devotional, 1 Mar. 1998. Speeches.BYU.edu.

———. "The Keys and Authority of the Priesthood," *Ensign*, May 2014, 49–52.

———. "Kingdoms of Glory." *Liahona*, Nov. 2023, 26–29.

———. "The Light and Life of the World." *Ensign*, Nov. 1987, 63–66.

———. "The Lord Leads His Church through Prophets and Apostles." *Ensign*, Mar. 2020, 14–19.

———. *The Lord's Way*. 1995.

———. "Love and Law." *Ensign*, Nov. 2009, 26–29.

———. "Love Your Enemies." *Ensign*, Nov. 2020, 26–29.

———. "The Only True and Living Church." *New Era*, Aug. 2011, 3–5.

———. "Opposition in All Things." *Ensign*, May 2016, 114–17.

———. "Preparation for the Second Coming." *Ensign*, May 2004, 7–10.

———. *Pure in Heart*. 1988.

———. "Recent Events Involving Church History and Forged Documents." *Ensign*, Oct. 1987, 63–69.

———. "Repentance and Change." *Ensign*, Nov. 2003, 37–40.

———. "Revelation." Brigham Young University devotional, 29 Sep. 1981. Speeches.BYU.edu.

———. "Revelation." In *Sperry Symposium Classics: The Doctrine and Covenants*, edited by Craig K. Manscill, 10–22. Sperry Symposium series. 2004.

———. "Reverent and Clean." *Ensign*, May 1986, 49–51.

———. "Sacrament Meeting and the Sacrament." *Ensign*, Nov. 2008, 17–20.

———. "Sins and Mistakes." Brigham Young University devotional, 16 Aug. 1994. Speeches.BYU.edu.

———. "Sins, Crimes, and Atonement." Address to CES Educators, 7 Feb. 1992.

———. "Spirituality." *Ensign*, Nov. 1985, 61–64.

———. "Taking upon Us the Name of Jesus Christ." *Ensign*, May 1985, 80–83.

———. "Teaching and Learning by the Spirit." *Ensign*, Mar. 1997, 6–14.

———. "Trust in the Lord." *Ensign*, Nov. 2019, 26–29.

———. "Truth and the Plan." *Ensign*, Nov. 2018, 25–28.

———. "*Two* Great Commandments." *Ensign*, Nov. 2019, 73–76.

———. "What Has Our Savior Done for Us?" *Liahona*, May 2021, 75–77.

———. "What Think Ye of Christ?" *Ensign*, Nov. 1988, 65–68.

———. "Why Do We Serve?" *Ensign*, Nov. 1984, 12–15.

———. *With Full Purpose of Heart*. 2002.

———. "Witnesses of Christ." *Ensign*, Nov. 1990, 29–32.

———. "The Witness: Martin Harris." *Ensign*, May 1999, 35–37.

————. "Worship through Music." *Ensign*, Nov. 1994, 9–12.

O'Driscoll, Jeffrey S. *Hyrum Smith: A Life of Integrity.* 2003.

Ojediran, Adeyinka A. "The Covenant Path: The Way to Eternal Life," *Liahona*, May 2022, 104–06.

Olmstead, Jacob W. "Far West and Adam–ondi–Ahman: D&C 115, 116, 117." In *Revelations in Context: The Stories behind the Sections of the Doctrine and Covenants,* edited by Matthew McBride and James Goldberg. 2016.

Olsen, Sheila. "Life, Death, the Known, and the Unknown." In *Women of Wisdom and Knowledge: Talks Selected from the BYU Women's Conferences,* edited by Marie Cornwall and Susan Howe, 45–50. 1990.

Olson, Camille Fronk. "Baptism." In *LDS Beliefs: A Doctrinal Reference,* edited by Robert L. Millet et al., 63–65. 2011.

Opening the Heavens: Accounts of Divine Manifestations 1820–1844. Edited by John W. Welch and Erick B. Carlson. 2005.

Oracles of God. Special Collections (digital), Brigham Young University—Idaho.

Orton, Chad M. "This Shall be Our Covenant." In *Revelations in Context: The Stories behind the Sections of the Doctrine and Covenants,* edited by Matthew McBride and James Goldberg. 2016.

Oscarson, Bonnie L. "Rise Up in Strength, Sisters in Zion." *Ensign*, Nov. 2016, 12–15.

Ostler, Craig J. "The Articles and Covenants: A Handbook for New Branches." In *A Firm Foundation: The History of Church Organization and Administration*, edited by Arnold K. Garr and David J. Whittaker, 82–95. 2011.

————. "The Laws of Consecration, Stewardship, and Tithing." In *Sperry Symposium Classics: The Doctrine and Covenants*, edited by Craig K. Manscill, 155–75. Sperry Symposium series. 2004.

————. "Murdock, John." In *Encyclopedia of Latter-day Saint History*, edited by Arnold K. Garr, Donald Q. Cannon, and Richard O. Cowan, 804–5. 2000.

————. "Real Covenants and Real People." In *The Doctrine and Covenants: A Book of Answers*, edited by Leon R. Hartshorn, Dennis A. Wright, and Craig J. Ostler, 123–37. Sperry Symposium series. 1996.

————. "Treasures, Witches, and Ancient Inhabitants (D&C 111)." In *You Shall Have My Word: Exploring the Text of the Doctrine and Covenants*, edited by Scott C. Esplin, Richard O. Cowan, and Rachel Cope, 222–33. Sperry Symposium series. 2012.

————. "Zion's Camp." In *Joseph: Exploring the Life and Ministry of the Prophet*, edited by Susan Easton Black and Andrew C. Skinner, 218–29. 2010.

Otten, Leaun G. "Heeding the Lord's Call (D&C 37–41)." In *The Doctrine and Covenants*, edited by Robert L. Millet and Kent P. Jackson, 164–69. Vol. 1 of Studies in Scripture series. 1985.

Otten, Leaun G., and C. Max Caldwell. *Sacred Truths of the Doctrine and Covenants.* 2 volumes. 1982–1983.

Otterson, Michael. "On The Record." From transcript of a presentation at FAIRMormon conference. Newsroom.ChurchofJesusChrist.org.

Pace, Glen L. "Follow the Prophet." *Ensign*, May 1989, 25–27.

Packer, Allan F. "Heavenly Father's Fixed Standards." *Ensign*, Aug. 2015, 69–71.

Packer, Boyd K. "The Bishop and His Counselors." *Ensign*, May 1999, 57–63.

————. "The Brilliant Morning of Forgiveness." *Ensign*, Nov. 1995, 18–21.

————. "The Cloven Tongues of Fire." *Ensign*, May 2000, 7–9.

————. "Come to the Temple." *Ensign*, Oct. 2007, 18–22.

————. "Covenants." *Ensign*, May 1987, 22–25.

————. "A Defense and a Refuge." *Ensign*, Nov. 2006, 85–88.

———. "Do Not Fear." *Ensign*, May 2004, 77–80.

———. "From Such Turn Away." *Ensign*, May 1985, 33–35.

———. "The Golden Years." *Ensign*, May 2003, 82–84.

———. *The Holy Temple*. 1980.

———. "The Honor and Order of the Priesthood." *Ensign*, Jun. 2012, 21–25.

———. "The Least of These." *Ensign*, Nov. 2004, 86–88.

———. "The Power of the Priesthood." *Ensign*, May 2010, 6–10.

———. "Prayer and Promptings." *Ensign*, Nov. 2009, 43–46.

———. "The Redemption of the Dead." *Ensign*, Nov. 1975, 97–99.

———. "Revelation in a Changing World." *Ensign*, Nov. 1989, 14–16.

———. *The Shield of Faith*. 1998.

———. "The Weak and the Simple of the Church." *Ensign*, Nov. 2007, 6–9.

———. "What Every Elder Should Know—and Every Sister as Well: A Primer on Principles of Priesthood Government." *Ensign*, Feb. 1993, 6–13.

———. "Word of Wisdom: The Principle and the Promises." *Ensign*, May 1996, 17–19.

Page, Hiram. "Letter to William E. McLellin, Ray Co., Missouri, 30 May 1847." In *Ensign of Liberty of the Church of Christ*, Vol. 1, No. 4 (Jan. 1848): 49–64.

Parkin, Bonnie D. "Eternally Encircled in His Love." *Ensign*, Nov. 2006, 108–10.

———. "Gratitude: A Path to Happiness." *Ensign*, May 2007, 34–36.

———. "With Holiness of Heart." In *At the Pulpit*, edited by Jennifer Reeder and Kate Holbrook, 276–82. 2017.

Parkin, Max H. "Lessons from the Experience." *Ensign*, Jul. 2001, 52–53.

———. "Missouri's Impact on the Church." *Ensign*, Apr. 1979, 57–63.

Parry, Donald W. *Angels: Agents of Light, Love, and Power*. 2013.

Parry, Donald W., and Jay A. Parry. *Understanding the Book of Revelation*. 1998.

———. *Understanding the Signs of the Times*. 1999.

Parry, Donald W., Jay A. Parry, and Tina M. Peterson. *Understanding Isaiah*. 1998.

Penrose, Charles W. In *Journal of Discourses*, 22:82–97.

Perkins, Keith W. "The Ministry to the Shakers." In *The Doctrine and Covenants*, edited by Robert L. Millet and Kent P. Jackson, 211–24. Vol. 1 of Studies in Scripture series. 1985.

———. "School of the Prophets." In *Encyclopedia of Latter-day Saint History*, edited by Arnold K. Garr, Donald Q. Cannon, and Richard O. Cowan, 1077–78. 2000.

———. "Trials and Tribulations in Our Spiritual Growth: Insights from Doctrine & Covenants 121 and 122." In *The Heavens Are Open*, edited by Byron R. Merrill, Brent L. Top, David R. Seely, and Vern D. Sommerfeldt, 278–289. Sperry Symposium series. 1993.

Perry, L. Tom. "The Gospel of Jesus Christ." *Ensign*, May 2008, 44–46.

———. "How to Endure to the End." *New Era*, Jun. 2012, 48.

———. "If Ye Are Prepared Ye Shall Not Fear." *Ensign*, Nov. 1995, 35–37.

Petersen, Mark E. In Conference Report, Oct. 1945, 88–92.

———. *Moses: Man of Miracles*. 1977.

———. "The Sabbath Day." *Ensign*, May 1975, 47–49.

Peterson, Melvin J. "Revelations Resulting from Important Church Conferences." In *The Doctrine and Covenants*, edited by Robert L. Millet and Kent P. Jackson, 258–65. Vol. 1 of Studies in Scripture series. 1985.

Pieper, Paul B. "All Must Take upon Them the Name Given of the Father." *Ensign*, Nov. 2018, 43–46.

———. "To Hold Sacred." *Ensign*, May 2012, 109–11.

Pinegar, Ed J., and Richard J. Allen. *Doctrine and Covenants Who's Who Illustrated Edition: A Comprehensive Guide to the People in the Doctrine and Covenants.* 2008.

———. *Unlocking the Doctrine and Covenants: A Side by Side Commentary.* 2008.

Plain and Precious Truths Restored: The Doctrinal and Historical Significance of the Joseph Smith Translation. Edited by Robert L. Millet and Robert J. Matthews. 1995.

Poelman, Ronald E. "Priesthood Councils: Key to Meeting Temporal and Spiritual Needs." *Ensign*, May 1980, 90–92.

Porter, Bruce D. "A Broken Heart and a Contrite Spirit." *Ensign*, Nov. 2007, 31–32.

Porter, Larry C. "Dating the Restoration of the Melchizedek Priesthood." *Ensign*, Jun. 1979, 4–10.

———. "Historical Background of the Fifteen Harmony Revelations." In *The Seventh Annual Sidney B. Sperry Symposium: The Doctrine and Covenants*, 164–84. Sperry Symposium series. 1979.

———. "The Restoration of the Aaronic and Melchizedek Priesthoods." *Ensign*, Dec. 1996, 30–47.

Porter, Susan. "Receiving the Gifts of God." Brigham Young University devotional, 1 Nov. 2022. Speeches .BYU.edu.

Pratt, Orson. In *Journal of Discourses*, 2:368–72.

———. In *Journal of Discourses*, 7:176–90.

———. In *Journal of Discourses*, 15:354–66.

———. In *Journal of Discourses*, 16:284–300.

———. In *Journal of Discourses*, 17:102–13.

———. In *Journal of Discourses*, 17:322–33.

———. In *Journal of Discourses*, 18:335–48.

———. In *Journal of Discourses*, 20:8–18.

———. In *Journal of Discourses*, 21:146–54.

———. In *Journal of Discourses*, 22:27–38.

———. "Keep a True and Faithful Record." In *Latter-day Saints' Millennial Star*, Vol. 11, No. 10 (15 May 1849): 151–53.

———. *Orson Pratt's Works on the Doctrines of the Gospel.* Vol. 1. 1945.

Pratt, Parley P. *Autobiography of Parley P. Pratt.* 1938.

Prayer. 2005.

Preach My Gospel: A Guide to Sharing the Gospel of Jesus Christ. Second edition. The Church of Jesus Christ of Latter-day Saints. 2023.

"Presiding Bishopric." The Church of Jesus Christ of Latter-day Saints. ChurchofJesusChrist.org.

The Prophet and His Work: Essays from General Authorities on Joseph Smith and the Restoration. 1996.

Quinn, Robert E. "Common Consent." In *Encyclopedia of Mormonism*, edited by Daniel H. Ludlow, 1:297–98. 1992.

Rasband, Ronald A. "Behold, I Am a God of Miracles." *Liahona*, May 2021, 109–12.

———. "Be Not Troubled." *Ensign*, Nov. 2018, 18–21.

———. "Build a Fortress of Spirituality and Protection." *Ensign*, May 2019, 107–10.

———. "The Divine Call of a Missionary." *Ensign*, May 2010, 51–53.

———. "Lest Thou Forget." *Ensign*, Nov. 2016, 113–15.

———. "Let the Holy Spirit Guide." *Ensign*, May 2017, 93–96.

Rawlins, Peter B. "Endowed with Power." In *The Religious Educator*, Vol. 13, No. 1 (2012): 125–39.

A Reason for Faith: Navigating LDS Doctrine & Church History. Edited by Laura Harris Hales. 2016.

"Recollections of the Prophet Joseph Smith." In *Juvenile Instructor*, Vol. 27, No. 10 (15 May 1892): 302–4.

Reeve, Rex C. Sr. "The Lord's Strange Act." Brigham Young University devotional, 25 Feb. 1986. Speeches .BYU.edu.

Reeves, Linda S. "Worthy of Our Promised Blessings." *Ensign*, Nov. 2015, 9–11.

Regional Studies in Latter-day Saint Church History: Illinois. Edited by H. Dean Garrett. 1995.

Regional Studies in Latter-day Saint Church History: Missouri. Edited by Arnold K. Garr and Clark V. Johnson. 1994.

Relief Society General Presidency. "Seeking the Best Gifts." *Ensign*, Jan. 1997, 55.

Religious Educators' Symposium: A Symposium on the Book of Mormon. 1978.

Remembering Joseph: Personal Recollections of Those Who Knew the Prophet Joseph Smith. Compiled by Mark L. McConkie. 2003.

Renlund, Dale G. "Abound with Blessings." *Ensign*, May 2019, 70–73.

———. "Choose You This Day." *Ensign*, Nov. 2018, 104–107.

———. "Consider the Goodness and Greatness of God." *Ensign*, May 2020, 41–44.

———. "Do Justly, Love Mercy, and Walk Humbly with God." *Ensign*, Nov. 2020, 109–12.

———. "Our Good Shepherd." *Ensign*, May 2017, 29–32.

———. "The Priesthood and the Savior's Atoning Power." *Ensign*, Nov. 2017, 64–67.

———. "Repentance: A Joyful Choice." *Ensign*, Nov. 2016, 121–24.

———. "Your Divine Nature and Eternal Destiny." *Liahona*, May 2022, 70, 75–77.

Renlund, Dale G., and Ruth Lybbert Renlund. *The Melchizedek Priesthood: Understanding the Doctrine, Living the Principles.* 2018.

Revelations in Context: The Stories behind the Sections of the Doctrine and Covenants. Edited by Matthew McBride and James Goldberg. 2016.

Reynolds, George. In *The Juvenile Instructor*, Vol. 27, No. 9 (1 May 1892): 282–85.

Reynolds, Noel B. "The Gospel according to Nephi" (2015). *Faculty Publications*, 1478.

———. "Gospel of Jesus Christ." In *Encyclopedia of Mormonism*, edited by Daniel H. Ludlow, 2:556–60. 1992.

Reynolds, Sydney S. "He Knows Us; He Loves Us." *Ensign*, Nov. 2003, 76–78.

Richards, George F. In Conference Report, Oct. 1940, 50–55.

Richards, LeGrand. In Conference Report, Apr. 1951, 39–45.

———. In Conference Report, Apr. 1961, 42–46.

Richardson, Matthew O. "A House for the Presidency: The History of the Church Administration Building." In *Salt Lake City: The Place Which God Prepared*, edited by Scott C. Esplin and Kenneth L. Alford, 231–57. 2011.

———. "Teachings after the Manner of the Spirit." *Ensign*, Nov. 2011, 94–96.

Ricks, Stephen D. "The Appearance of Elijah and Moses in the Kirtland Temple and the Jewish Passover." *BYU Studies* 23, no. 4 [1983]:483–86.

Robbins, Lynn G. "Oil in Our Lamps." *Ensign*, Jun. 2007, 44–48.

———. "Which Way Do you Face?" *Ensign*, Nov. 2014, 9–11.

Roberts, B. H. *A Comprehensive History of the Church of Jesus Christ of Latter-day Saints.* 6 vols. 1957.

———. *The Missouri Persecutions.* Revised edition. 2001.

———. *The Seventy's Course in Theology* [Salt Lake City: Deseret News, 1907–1912], Reprint Edition.

Robertson, Lori. "How can we feel the joy and rejoicing the scriptures equate with fasting?" *Ensign*, Oct. 1993, 61–62.

Robinson, Stephen E. "Eternities That Come and Go." *Religious Studies Center Newsletter*, Vol. 8, No. 3 (May 1994).

———. "Warring against the Saints of God." *Ensign*, Jan. 1988, 34–39.

Robinson, Stephen E., and H. Dean Garrett. *A Commentary on the Doctrine and Covenants*. Vols. 1–4. 2000–2005.

Robison, Elwin Clark. *The First Mormon Temple: Design, Construction, and Historic Context of the Kirtland Temple*. 1997.

Rogers, Brent M. "Mary Ann Angell Young: Trusting in the Lord." *Liahona*, Jul. 2021, digital only.

———. "Prelude to the March: The Expulsion from Zion and Plans for Redemption." In *Zion's Camp 1834: March of Faith*, edited by Matthew C. Godfrey et al. 5–30.

Romney, Marion G. "The Book of Mormon." *Ensign*, May 1980, 65–67.

———. "Church Welfare—Some Fundamentals." *Ensign*, Jan. 1974, 89–92.

———. In Conference Report, Oct. 1944, 53–58.

———. In Conference Report, Oct. 1945, 155–59.

———. In Conference Report, Oct. 1948, 72–77.

———. "A Disciple of Christ." *Ensign*, Nov. 1978, 38–40.

———. "Jesus Christ, Lord of the Universe." *Improvement Era*, Nov. 1968, 46–49.

———. "The Light Shineth," *Ensign*, Dec. 1971, 75–78.

———. "The Role of a Bishop in the Church Welfare Program." *Ensign*, Nov. 1979, 94–96.

———. "Satan—The Great Deceiver." *Ensign*, Jun. 1971, 35–37.

———. "Seek Not to Counsel the Lord." *Ensign*, Aug. 1985, 2–5.

———. "A Silver Lining." *Ensign*, May 1977, 51–53.

———. "Trust in the Lord." *Ensign*, May 1979, 40–43.

Runia, Tamara W. "Seeing God's Family through the Overview Lens." *Liahona*, Nov. 2023, 62–69.

Rust, Richard Dilworth. "A Mission to the Lamanites." In *Revelations in Context: The Stories behind the Sections of the Doctrine and Covenants*, edited by Matthew McBride and James Goldberg. 2016.

Saints: The Story of The Church of Jesus Christ in the Latter Days. Volume 1: The Standard of Truth, 1815–1846. 2018.

Saints: The Story of The Church of Jesus Christ in the Latter Days. Volume 2: No Unhallowed Hand 1846–1893. 2020.

Salt Lake City: The Place Which God Prepared. Edited by Scott C. Esplin and Kenneth L. Alford. 2011.

"School of the Prophets." Church History Topics.

Schmutz, Evan A. "God Shall Wipe Away All Tears." *Ensign*, Nov. 2016, 116–18.

Scott, Richard G. "The Atonement Can Secure Your Peace and Happiness." *Ensign*, Nov. 2006, 40–43.

———. "First Things First." *Ensign*, May 2001, 6–9.

———. "How to Obtain Revelation and Inspiration for Your Personal Life." *Ensign*, May 2012, 45–47.

———. "The Joy of Redeeming the Dead." *Ensign*, Nov. 2012, 93–95.

———. "Obtaining Help from the Lord." *Ensign*, Nov. 1991, 84–86.

———. "Peace of Conscience and Peace of Mind." *Ensign*, Nov. 2004, 15–18.

———. "The Power of Righteousness." *Ensign*, Nov. 1998, 68–70.

———. "The Power of Scripture." *Ensign*, Nov. 2011, 6–8.

———. "To Be Healed." *Ensign*, May 1994, 7–9.

Scrapbook of Mormon Literature. Edited by Ben E. Rich. 2 vols. 1913.

Seely, David Rolph. "The Joseph Smith Translation: 'Plain and Precious Things' Restored." *Ensign*, Aug. 1997, 8–16.

———. "The Olivet Discourse." In *The Gospels*, edited by Kent P. Jackson and Robert L. Millet, 391–404. Vol. 5 of Studies in Scripture series. 1986.

A Sesquicentennial Look at Church History. Sperry Symposium series. 1980.

The Seventh Annual Sidney B. Sperry Symposium: The Doctrine and Covenants. Sperry Symposium series. 1979.

The Seventy's Course in Theology: Outline History of the Seventy and a Survey of the Books of Holy Scripture. Edited by B. H. Roberts. Vol. 1. Reprint, 1976.

Sitati, Gladys N. "Resolving Conflicts Using Gospel Principles." In *At the Pulpit*, edited by Jennifer Reeder and Kate Holbrook, 331–42. 2017.

Skinner, Andrew C. "Government." In *LDS Beliefs: A Doctrinal Reference*, edited by Robert L. Millet et al., 235–38. 2011.

Smart, Donna Toland. *Exemplary Elder: Mission Diaries and History of Perrigrine Sessions, 1814–1893.* 2002.

Smith, Alex D. "Organizing the Church in Nauvoo." In *Revelations in Context: The Stories behind the Sections of the Doctrine and Covenants*, edited by Matthew S. McBride and James Goldberg. 2016.

Smith, Brian L. "'Taught from on High': The Ministry of Angelic Messengers to the Prophet Joseph Smith." In *Joseph Smith and the Doctrinal Restoration*, edited by W. Jeffrey Marsh, 332–45. Sperry Symposium series. 2005.

Smith, Eric. "A Mission to Canada." In *Revelations in Context: The Stories behind the Sections of the Doctrine and Covenants*, edited by Matthew McBride and James Goldberg. 2016.

Smith, George A. In *Journal of Discourses*, 2:323–34.

———. In *Journal of Discourses*, 11:1–12.

Smith, Hyrum M., and Janne M. Sjodahl. *Doctrine and Covenants Commentary.* Reprint, 1978.

Smith, Joseph. "The Answer." In *Times and Seasons*, Vol. 4, No. 6 (1 Feb. 1843): 82–85.

———. *History of the Church: An Introduction and Notes by B. H. Roberts.* 7 vols. 1948.

———. *Joseph Smith.* Teachings of Presidents of the Church series. 2011.

———. The Joseph Smith Papers. JosephSmithPapers.org.

———. The Joseph Smith Papers Glossary. JosephSmithPapers.org/reference/topics.

———. *Joseph Smith Papers: Histories, Volume 1: Joseph Smith Histories, 1832–1844.* Edited by Karen Lynn Davidson, David J. Whittaker, Mark Ashurst-McGee, and Richard L. Jensen. 2012.

Smith, Joseph F. In Conference Report, Oct. 1899, 39–46.

———. In Conference Report, Apr. 1904, 1–5.

———. In Conference Report, Oct. 1913, 14.

———. In *The Contributor*, Vol. 8, No. 4 (Feb. 1887): 157–60.

———. *Gospel Doctrine: Selections from the Sermons and Writings of Joseph F. Smith.* 1919.

———. *Joseph F. Smith.* Teachings of Presidents of the Church series. 2011.

Smith, Joseph Fielding. *Answers to Gospel Questions.* 5 vols. 1957–1966.

———. *Church History and Modern Revelation.* 2 vols. 1953.

———. In Conference Report, Oct. 1919, 141–46.

———. In Conference Report, Oct. 1928, 99–102.

———. In Conference Report, Oct. 1941, 91–95.

———. In Conference Report, Sep./Oct. 1950, 9–13.

———. In Conference Report, Apr. 1970, 58–60.

———. *Doctrines of Salvation: Sermons and Writings of Joseph Fielding Smith.* Edited by Bruce R. McConkie. 3 vols. 1954–1956. Reprint, 1999.

———. *Essentials in Church History.* 1979.

———. *Joseph Fielding Smith.* Teachings of Presidents of the Church series. 2013.

———. *The Life of Joseph F. Smith.* 1938.

———. *The Progress of Man.* 1944.

———. *Seek Ye Earnestly.* 1970.

———. *Signs of the Times.* 1952.

———. *The Way to Perfection.* 1953.

Snow, Eliza R. *Biography and Family Record of Lorenzo Snow.* 1884.

Snow, Lorenzo. In Conference Report, Oct. 1899, 23–29.

———. In *Journal of Discourses,* 20:361–72.

———. *Lorenzo Snow.* Teachings of Presidents of the Church series. 2012.

Snow, Steven E. "Be Thou Humble." *Ensign,* May 2016, 36–38.

———. "The Sacred Duty of Record Keeping." *Ensign,* Apr. 2019.

Soares, Ulisses. "Prophets Speak by the Power of the Holy Spirit." *Ensign,* May 2018, 98–99.

———. "Yes, We Can and Will Win!" *Ensign,* May 2015, 70, 75–77.

Sorensen, David E. "Forgiveness Will Change Bitterness to Love." *Ensign,* May 2003, 10–12.

"Special Witnesses of Christ." In *Ensign,* Apr. 2001, 2–21.

Spencer, Stan. "The Faith to See: Burning in the Bosom and Translating the Book of Mormon in Doctrine and Covenants 9." *Interpreter: A Journal of Mormon Scripture,* Vol. 18 (2016): 219–32.

Sperry Symposium Classics: The Doctrine and Covenants. Edited by Craig K. Manscill. 2004.

Sperry Symposium Classics: The New Testament. Edited by Frank F. Judd Jr. and Gaye Strathearn. 2006.

Sperry, Sidney B. *Doctrine and Covenants Compendium.* 1960.

———. *The Voice of Israel's Prophets.* 1961.

Staker, Mark Lyman. *Hearken O Ye People: The Historical Setting of Joseph Smith's Ohio Revelations.* 2009.

———. "Thou Art the Man." *Ensign,* Apr. 2005, 34–39.

Stapley, Delbert L. "The Blessings of Righteous Obedience." *Ensign,* Nov. 1977, 18–21.

———. "Reponsibility to the Lamanites." *Improvement Era,* Jun. 1956, 416–18.

Stephens, Calvin R. "Patriarch: Patriarch to the Church." In *Encyclopedia of Mormonism,* edited by Daniel H. Ludlow, 3:1065–66. 1992.

Stephens, Carole M. "Do We Know What We Have?" *Ensign,* Nov. 2013, 12–14.

Stephenson, William T. "Cancer, Nutrition, and the Word of Wisdom." *Ensign,* Jul. 2008, 42–47.

Stevens, Jean A. "Fear Not; I Am with Thee." *Ensign,* May 2014, 81–83.

Stevenson, Gary E. "Deceive Me Not." *Ensign,* Nov. 2019, 93–96.

———. "How to Avoid Deception." *New Era,* Aug. 2020, 48.

———. "Love, Share, Invite." *Liahona,* May 2022, 84–87.

———. "Spiritual Eclipse." *Ensign,* Nov. 2017, 44–47.

———. "Where Are the Keys and Authority of the Priesthood?" *Ensign,* May 2016, 29–32.

Stone, David R. "Zion in the Midst of Babylon." *Ensign,* May 2006, 90–93.

"Summary of Approved Adjustments for the 2013 Edition of the Scriptures." ChurchofJesusChrist.org.

Swensen, Jason. "Elder Neil L. Andersen speaks at Worldwide Missionary Broadcast on 'the doctrine of Christ.'" *Church News,* in *Deseret News,* 21 Jan 2016.

Swinton, Heidi S. *To the Rescue: The Biography of Thomas S. Monson.* 2010.

"Symposium Examines Apocryphal Literature." *Ensign,* Dec. 1983, 70–71.

Tait, Lisa Olsen. "Susa Young Gates and the Vision of the Redemption of the Dead." In *Revelations in Context: The Stories behind the Sections of the Doctrine and Covenants,* edited by Matthew McBride and James Goldberg. 2016.

———. "Warren Cowdery." In *Revelations in Context: The Stories behind the Sections of the Doctrine and Covenants,* edited by Matthew McBride and James Goldberg. 2016.

Tait, Lisa Olsen, and Chad M. Orton. "Take Special Care of Your Family." In *Revelations in Context: The Stories behind the Sections of the Doctrine and Covenants,* edited by Matthew McBride and James Goldberg. 2016.

Tait, Lisa Olsen, and Brent Rogers. "A House for Our God." In *Revelations in Context: The Stories behind the Sections of the Doctrine and Covenants,* edited by Matthew McBride and James Goldberg. 2016.

Talmage, James E. In Conference Report, Oct. 1913, 116–21.

———. In Conference Report, Apr. 1917, 65–69.

———. In Conference Report, Oct. 1920, 59–67.

———. In Conference Report, Apr. 1930, 94–98.

———. In Conference Report, Oct. 1931, 49–53.

———. *Jesus the Christ: A Study of the Messiah and His Mission according to Holy Scriptures Both Ancient and Modern.* 1915. Reprint, 1981.

———. *A Study of the Articles of Faith: Being a Consideration of the Principal Doctrines of The Church of Jesus Christ of Latter-day Saints.* 1984.

Tanner, John S. "Christ, Our Advocate and High Priest." In *The Religious Educator,* Vol. 8, No. 2 (2007): 27–34.

Tanner, N. Eldon. "Put on the Whole Armor of God." *Ensign,* May 1979, 43–46.

———. "Where Art Thou?" *Ensign,* Dec. 1971, 32–35.

Tanner, Susan W. "Did I Tell You . . . ?" *Ensign,* May 2003, 73–75.

———. "Steadfast in our Covenants," *Ensign,* May 2003, 100–102.

Taylor, John. *Gospel Kingdom: Selections from the Writings and Discourses of John Taylor,* compiled by G. Homer Durham. 1943.

———. *John Taylor.* Teachings of Presidents of the Church series. 2001.

Teaching in the Savior's Way: For All Who Teach in the Home and in the Church. The Church of Jesus Christ of Latter-day Saints. 2022.

Temples of the Ancient World: Ritual and Symbolism. Edited by Donald W. Parry. 1994.

The Testimony of John the Beloved. Edited by Daniel K Judd, Craig J. Ostler, Richard D. Draper. Sperry Symposium series. 1998.

Theological Dictionary of the New Testament. Edited by Gerhard Kittel. Vol. 1. 1964.

Thomas, Brent P. "The Weak Things of the World." In *The Heavens Are Open,* edited by Byron R. Merrill, Brent L. Top, David R. Seely, and Vern D. Sommerfeldt, 302–16. Sperry Symposium series. 1993.

Thompson, A. Keith. "Joseph Smith and the Doctrine of Sealing." In *Interpreter: A Journal of Latter-day Saint Faith and Scholarship,* 21 (2016), 1–21.

Thompson, Barbara. "And of Some Have Compassion, Making a Difference." *Ensign,* Nov. 2010, 119–21.

———. "Cleave unto the Covenants." *Ensign,* Nov. 2011, 117–19.

Thompson, Heber M. "What is the purpose and history of Church membership records?" *Ensign*, Jun. 1994, 59–60.

Times and Seasons. Edited by John Taylor, 6 vols. 1839–1846.

Tingey, Earl C. "The Quorums of the Seventy." *Ensign*, Aug. 2005, 48–50.

To Cheer and to Bless: Celebrating 20 Years of Time Out for Women. 2022.

Top, Brent L. "Forgiveness." In *LDS Beliefs: A Doctrinal Reference*, edited by Robert L. Millet et al., 235–38. 2011.

———. "Heathen Nations." In *LDS Beliefs: A Doctrinal Reference*, edited by Robert L. Millet et al., 299. 2011.

———. "Keys of the Kingdom." In *LDS Beliefs: A Doctrinal Reference*, edited by Robert L. Millet et al., 362–63. 2011.

———. "Patriarch." In *LDS Beliefs: A Doctrinal Reference*, edited by Robert L. Millet et al., 480–81. 2011.

———. "Priesthood." In *LDS Beliefs: A Doctrinal Reference*, edited by Robert L. Millet et al., 501–03. 2011.

———. "Sabbath." In *LDS Beliefs: A Doctrinal Reference*, edited by Robert L. Millet et al., 544–47. 2011.

———. "Second Coming of Christ, Signs of." In *LDS Beliefs: A Doctrinal Reference*, edited by Robert L. Millet et al., 570–76. 2011.

———. "Word of God." In *LDS Beliefs: A Doctrinal Reference*, edited by Robert L. Millet et al., 665–66. 2011.

Topics and Questions. The Church of Jesus Christ of Latter-day Saints.

Tullidge, Edward W. *The Women of Mormondom*. 1877.

Turley, Richard E. Jr. "The Calling of the Twelve Apostles and the Seventy in 1835." In *Joseph Smith and the Doctrinal Restoration*, edited by W. Jeffrey Marsh, 369–80. Sperry Symposium series. 2005.

Turley, Richard E. Jr., and William W. Slaughter. *How We Got the Doctrine and Covenants*. 2012.

Turner, Rodney. "A Faith unto Salvation." In *Alma 30 to Moroni*, edited by Kent P. Jackson, 16–26. Vol. 8 of Studies in Scripture series. 1988.

———. "Jesus Christ and the Command to Repent." In *The Doctrine and Covenants*, edited by Robert L. Millet and Kent P. Jackson, 100–108. Vol. 1 of Studies in Scripture series. 1985.

Tuttle, A. Theodore. "Developing Faith." *Ensign*, Nov. 1986, 72–73.

Uchtdorf, Dieter F. "Four Titles," *Ensign*, May 2013, 58–61.

———. "The Fruits of the First Vision." *Ensign*, May 2005, 36–38.

———. "God among Us." *Liahona*, May 2021, 8–11.

———. "Grateful in Any Circumstances." *Ensign*, May 2014, 70–77.

———. "The Greatest among You." *Ensign*, May 2017, 78–81.

———. "The Joy of the Priesthood." *Ensign*, Nov. 2012, 57–60.

———. "Living the Gospel Joyful." *Ensign*, Nov. 2014, 120–123.

———. "Missionary Work: Sharing What Is in Your Heart." *Ensign*, May 2019, 15–18.

———. "Of Things That Matter Most." *Ensign*, Nov. 2021, 19–22.

———. "On Being Genuine." *Ensign*, May 2015, 80–83.

———. "Point of Safe Return." *Ensign*, May 2007, 99–101.

———. "Pride and the Priesthood." *Ensign*, Nov. 2010, 55–58.

———. "We Are Doing a Great Work and Cannot Come Down." *Ensign*, May 2009, 59–62.

———. "A Yearning for Home." *Ensign*, Nov. 2017, 21–24.

———. "You Are My Hands." *Ensign*, May 2010, 68–75.

————. "You Matter to Him." *Ensign*, Nov. 2011, 19–22.

————. "Your Great Adventure." *Liahona*, Nov. 2019, 86–89.

Underwood, Grant. "1831—A Flood of Revelations." In *Joseph Smith: The Prophet and Seer*, edited by Richard Neitzel Holzapfel and Kent P. Jackson, 77–100. 2010.

————. "'The Laws of the Church of Christ' (D&C 42): A Textual and Historical Analysis." In *The Doctrine and Covenants: Revelations in Context*, edited by Andrew H. Hedges, J. Spencer Fluhman, and Alonzo L. Gaskill, 108–41. Sperry Symposium series. 2008.

Valentine, LaNae. "Discerning the Will of the Lord for Me." Brigham Young University devotional, 29 Jun. 2004. Speeches.BYU.edu.

Van Orden, Bruce A. "Important Items of Instruction." In *The Doctrine and Covenants*, edited by Robert L. Millet and Kent P. Jackson, 497–511. Vol. 1 of Studies in Scripture series. 1985.

————. "The Law of Consecration." In *The Capstone of Our Religion: Insights into the Doctrine and Covenants*. Edited by Robert L. Millet and Larry E. Dahl, 81–94. 1989.

Viñas, Francisco J. "If Thou Endure It Well." *Ensign*, Jul. 2009, 10–11.

Waddell, W. Christopher. "There Was Bread." *Ensign*, Nov. 2020, 42–45.

Wakolo, Taniela B. "God Loves His Children." *Liahona*, May 2021, 94–96.

"Washing of Feet." Church History Topics.

Watch and Be Ready: Preparing for the Second Coming of the Lord. Edited by Robert L. Millet. 1994.

Watson, Kent D. "Being Temperate in All Things." *Ensign*, Nov. 2009, 38–39.

Webster, Noah. *An American Dictionary of the English Language.* 1828. Reprint, 1995.

Webster's Third International Dictionary. Edited by Philip Babcock Gove, et al. 2002.

Wessel, Ryan J. "The Textual Context of Doctrine and Covenants 121–123." *Religious Educator* 13, no. 1 (2012): 102–15.

West, Aaron L. "Questions and Answers about the Temple Lot in Independence, Missouri." Church History Sites.

Whitney, Orson F. In Conference Report, Jun. 1919, 45–48.

————. *The Life of Heber C. Kimball.* 1945, reprint 1992.

"Why do we use water instead of wine for the sacrament?" *New Era*, Nov. 2008, 22.

Wickman, Lance B. "In a Holy Place." *New Era*, Apr. 2005, 42–45.

Widstoe, John A. In Conference Report, Apr. 1922, 94–98.

————. In Conference Report, Apr. 1935, 79–84.

————. *Evidences and Reconciliations.* 1960. Reprint, 1987.

————. *Joseph Smith—Seeker after Truth, Prophet of God.* 1951.

————. *The Message of the Doctrine and Covenants.* 1969.

————. *Priesthood and Church Government.* 1939.

————. *Program of the Church of Jesus Christ of Latter-day Saints.* 1941.

Wilcox, S. Michael. *House of Glory: Finding Personal Meaning in the Temple.* 1995.

Wilson, Larry Y. "Only upon the Principles of Righteousness." *Ensign*, May 2012, 103–5.

————. "Take the Holy Spirit as Your Guide." *Ensign*, May 2018, 75–77.

Window of Faith: Latter-day Saint Perspectives on World History. Edited by Roy A. Prete. 2005.

Wirthlin, Joseph B. "Deep Roots." *Ensign*, Nov. 1994, 75–77.

————. "Earthly Debts, Heavenly Debts." *Ensign*, May 2004, 40–43.

————. "Living Water to Quench Spiritual Thirst." *Ensign*, May 1995, 18–20.

———. "Newel K. Whitney: Faithful Steward, Steadfast Saint." In *Heroes of the Restoration*, 194–210. 1997.

———. "Press On." *Ensign*, Nov. 2004, 101–4.

———. "True to the Truth." *Ensign*, May 1997, 15–17.

———. "The Unspeakable Gift." *Ensign*, May 2003, 26–29.

———. "Windows of Light and Truth," *Ensign*, Nov. 1995, 75–78.

———. "Without Guile." *Ensign*, May 1988, 80–83.

Woman. 1980.

Women of Wisdom and Knowledge: Talks Selected from the BYU Women's Conferences. Edited by Marie Cornwall and Susan Howe. 1990.

Wood, Alison. "Seeing Commandments as Blessings." *Liahona*, Apr. 2022, digital only. ChurchofJesusChrist .org.

Woodford, Robert J. "Joseph Smith and 'The Vision,' 1832." In *Joseph Smith: The Prophet and Seer*, edited by Richard Neitzel Holzapfel and Kent P. Jackson, 101–26. 2010.

———. "The Remarkable Doctrine and Covenants." *Ensign*, Jan. 1997, 42–49.

Woodger, Mary Jane. *The Essential Doctrine and Covenants Companion: Key Insights to Your Gospel Study*. 2012.

Woodruff, Wilford. In Conference Report, Apr. 1880, 6–14.

———. "History of Joseph Smith." *The Latter-day Saints Millennial Star*, Vol. 5, No. 9 (Feb. 1845): 135–36.

———. In *Journal of Discourses*, 2:191–202.

———. In *Journal of Discourses*, 10:9–17.

———. In *Journal of Discourses*, 15:275–83.

———. In *Journal of Discourses*, 21:121–27.

———. *Wilford Woodruff*. Teachings of Presidents of the Church series. 2011.

———. Wilford Woodruff Papers.

Woodworth, Jed. "The Center Place." In *Revelations in Context: The Stories behind the Sections of the Doctrine and Covenants*, edited by Matthew McBride and James Goldberg. 2016.

———. "James Covel and the 'Cares of the World.'" In *Revelations in Context: The Stories behind the Sections of the Doctrine and Covenants*, edited by Matthew McBride and James Goldberg. 2016.

———. "The Word of Wisdom." In *Revelations in Context: The Stories behind the Sections of the Doctrine and Covenants*, edited by Matthew McBride and James Goldberg. 2016.

Woolley, Doreen. "I Have a Question." *Ensign*, Dec. 1987, 27–28.

Workman, H. Ross. "Beware of Murmuring." *Ensign*, Nov. 2001, 85–86.

Worthen, Kevin J. "Choose to Be Humble." Brigham Young University devotional, 4 Jan. 2022. Speeches .BYU.edu.

Wright, Amy A. "Abide the Day in Christ," *Liahona*, Nov. 2023, 9–12.

Yee, Kristin M. "Beauty for Ashes: The Healing Path of Forgiveness," *Liahona*, Nov. 2022, 36–38.

You Shall Have My Word: Exploring the Text of the Doctrine and Covenants. Edited by Scott C. Esplin, Richard O. Cowan, and Rachel Cope. Sperry Symposium series. 2012.

Young, Brigham. *Discourses of Brigham Young: Second President of The Church of Jesus Christ of Latter-day Saints*. Compiled by John A. Widtsoe. 1954.

———. In *Journal of Discourses*, 4:33–42.

———. In *Journal of Discourses*, 4:51–57.

———. In *Journal of Discourses*, 6:314–22.

———. In *Journal of Discourses*, 7:282–91.

———. In *Journal of Discourses*, 11:291–305.

———. In *Journal of Discourses*, 15:62–66.

———. In *Journal of Discourses,* 18:230–35.

Zion's Camp 1834: March of Faith. Edited by Matthew C. Godfrey et al. 2018.

Zivic, Claudio D. "He That Shall Endure unto the End, the Same Shall Be Saved." *Ensign*, May 2018, 83–85.

Zobell, Albert L. Jr. "A Modern Prophet at Ninety-Five." *Ensign*, Jul. 1971, 31–34.

IMAGE CREDITS

INDEX

Carthage Jail, 821. *See also* martyrdom of Joseph and Hyrum Smith

Caussé, Gérald, 606

Celestial kingdom: and salvation of children, 167–68; vision of, 411, 761, 832–36; exaltation in, 413; preparation for, 429; and sanctification of Earth, 481; "quickened by celestial glory," 482; inheriting, 617; white sone in, 777; degrees of, 780

Celestial marriage, 672, 780, 781, 783–84, 789–90

Celibacy, 267, 268, 270

Center place, Independence, Missouri, as, 303, 351

Certificates, for priesthood holders, 121–22

Chaff, 287

Chariton, Ohio, 336–38

Charity, 32; clothed with, 501

Chastening, 538, 570–71, 595–96, 618, 718

Cheerfulness, 725. *See also* joy

Chemical warfare, 163

Children: promises of fathers planted in hearts of, 23; salvation of, 167–68, 531, 835–36; accountability of, 168, 375–76; teaching, 168; during Millennium, 252, 781–82; Saints called "little," 280–81; parents as examples for, 374–75; raising, 374–75, 531–33, 679; baptism of, 375–76; support for, 445–46; innocence of, 531; turning of fathers' hearts to, 673

Children of God, 79, 138–39, 182, 206, 855

"Children of light," 628

Choices, 337–38. *See also* agency; freedom

Cholera, 332, 601, 617, 621

"Chosen," 715

Christofferson, D. Todd: on Book of Mormon, 73; on repentance, 74; on children of God, 79; on Christ as Redeemer, 98; on sanctification and justification through Christ, 118; on priesthood offices, 119; on counseling God, 130; on laborers in vineyard, 209; on sacred things, 214; on establishing Zion, 228; on hypocrisy, 276; on caring for poor, 300, 428–29; on commandments, 321; on new and everlasting covenant, 364–65; on consecration and stewardship, 383; on works, 418; on love for God and others, 465; on chastening, 538, 618; on consecrated life, 548; on Holy Ghost, 568–69;

on building up Zion, 618; on conversion and healing, 681–82; on Babylon, 802; on freedom of speech and religion, 817; on scripture study, 838

Church and state, separation of, 818

Church building committee, 536–37

Church discipline, 229–31, 355, 590–91, 646–47, 818

Church leaders: imperfection of, 37; financial support for, 228–29, 234, 382, 383; and discernment of spiritual gifts, 262–63; to reason together, 277; and discernment of false spirits, 280; criticizing, 297–98, 712; functioning of, 591–92; selection of, 625; and Melchizedek Priesthood, 633; unity among, 638, 639; debt of, 675; heeding counsel of, 736; and Church discipline, 818; sustaining, 851

Church meeting(s), 120, 255, 256, 259, 361

Church of Jesus Christ of Latter-day Saints, The: establishment of, 18–19; name of, 113, 693–97; organization of, 114–15, 125, 146, 240; confirmation as member of, 122; records of, 124–25, 126, 263–65, 378, 379, 468, 469, 760; women's roles in, 140; revelations for, 156; government of, 213, 233–34, 465; disaffiliation from, 272; criticizing, 297–98; to sit in judgment over nations in last days, 360; growth of, 362, 402, 514; as kingdom of God, 363; attacks against, 386; as presided over by God and Jesus Christ, 402; spreading gospel as work of, 424; independence of, 430; diversity in, 514; lively member of, 520; policy changes in, 590; members of, as "light unto the world," 596; financial situation of, 673–74; Lord's warning to members of, 686; abundance of settlements of, 700; and perfection of Saints, 752–53; and plural marriage, 785; position on separation of church and state, 818; federal seizure of properties of, 849; President of, as led by God, 851

Church of the devil, 99

Church of the Firstborn, 412, 432, 478–79, 526, 637

Church Welfare Services, 389. *See also* storehouse

Circumcision, 394

Civic leaders: calling upon, 727; solemn